LET US KNOW WHAT YOU THINK

In order to produce a directory that will serve you best, we ask that you take the time to fill out this short questionnaire. Thank you for your continued support and please feel free to photocopy this form or attach additional sheets.

Is this the first time you have purchased the ***Conservation Directory***? ❑ Yes ❑ No

If no, how long have you been purchasing the ***Conservation Directory***?__________________

How would you categorize yourself? (check one)

- ❑ Environmental Professional
- ❑ College or University Library
- ❑ Career Center
- ❑ Public Library
- ❑ Environmental Activist
- ❑ Business or Corporation
- ❑ Environmental Lawyer
- ❑ Conservation Organization
- ❑ Educator
- ❑ Student
- ❑ Scientist
- ❑ Other

What resources would you like to see added to the ***Conservation Directc***

____

What would you like to see removed from the ***Conservation Directory***?

____

Are you pleased with the format of the ***2003 Conservation Directory***? ❑ Yes ❑ No

If no, what suggestions do you have for the future organization of the ***Conservation Directory***?

____

____

Which index is most useful to you?

- ❑ Geographic Index
- ❑ Staff Name Index
- ❑ Keyword Index
- ❑ Organization Name Index
- ❑ I do not use the indices

If organization listings contained less information would the directory be as useful? ❑ Yes ❑ No

Please be sure to fill in the information on this page and to send both sides if faxing.

MAIL TO: NATIONAL WILDLIFE FEDERATION
ATTN: CONSERVATION DIRECTORY
11100 WILDLIFE CENTER DRIVE
RESTON, VA 20190-5362
FAX: 703-438-6061

******There are forms in the back of this book for information updates and to suggest new organizations******

You may also visit the *Conservation Directory* online at www.nwf.org to update or add information.

Prefix First Name/MI Last Name Suffix

Are you interested in any of the following?

❑ After school programs for youth
❑ Children's publications (like Ranger Rick® magazine)
❑ Educator Workshops
❑ Gardening for Wildlife
❑ NWF television and film programs
❑ Volunteerism
❑ After School programs for teens
❑ Distance learning
❑ Inclusive environmental education curricula
❑ Programs for college students
❑ Turning your work or school grounds into a home for wildlife

Would you like to be on our education mailing list? ❑ Yes ❑ No

Would you like to receive free Wildlife Week materials and information? ❑ Yes ❑ No

Organization: ______________________________

Are you a:
❑ School Administrator
❑ College/University Faculty
❑ Green Coordinator
❑ Non-Formal Educator
❑ Librarian or Resource Specialist
❑ Teacher (if so, what do you teach): Grade ____________
- ❑ All Disciplines
- ❑ AP Education
- ❑ Art/Fine Arts
- ❑ Computer Science
- ❑ English/Reading
- ❑ Foreign Language
- ❑ Home School
- ❑ Mathematics
- ❑ Music
- ❑ Physical Education
- ❑ Science
- ❑ Social Studies
- ❑ Special Education

Primary Address (work or school)

Address

City State Zip Country

Secondary Address (home)

Address

City State Zip Country

Day Phone ______________ Evening Phone ______________

Fax ______________ E-mail ______________

Office Use Only
Original Source: Conservation 2003 Directory Evaluation

2003

CONSERVATION DIRECTORY

48TH EDITION

The Guide to Worldwide Environmental Organizations

Bill Street, *Editor*

ISLAND PRESS

Washington • Covelo • London

ISBN 1-55963-996-2

NATIONAL WILDLIFE FEDERATION

11100 Wildlife Center Drive • Reston • VA 20190-5362

www.nwf.org

The mission of the National Wildlife Federation is to educate, inspire, and assist individuals and organizations of diverse cultures to conserve wildlife and other natural resources, and to protect the Earth's environment in order to achieve a peaceful, equitable, and sustainable future.

The *Conservation Directory* is published as a public service. Organization are included on the basis of their stated objectives and other information provided. Inclusion does not imply confirmation of the information nor does it imply any endorsement of the organizations listed by the National Wildlife Federation.

To purchase the *Conservation Directory*, call Island Press at (800) 828-1302. If you have any general questions about the *Conservation Directory*, call the National Wildlife Federation at (703) 438-6000. To update your listing, please visit our Web site at www.nwf.org.

Library of Congress Cataloging-in-Publication Data is available on file. British Cataloguing-in-Publication Data is also available.

Printed on recycled, acid-free paper containing a minimum of 30 percent postconsumer recycled content. 

Manufactured in the United States of America

09 08 07 06 05 04 03   8 7 6 5 4 3 2 1

LETTER FROM THE EDITOR

Dear Conservation Directory Reader:

The National Wildlife Federation is pleased to present the 48th edition of the ***Conservation Directory***. The National Wildlife Federation is the only conservation education organization currently providing an annually updated directory of conservation organizations.

Since its debut in 1955, the information contained in this publication has helped a wide variety of people. Over the years we have heard from research scientists, professional resource managers, wildlife biologists, non-profit groups and their staff members, citizen activists, librarians, and students looking for internships and other job opportunities who have found what they were looking for within these pages. We sincerely hope that this will be your experience as well.

The ***2003 Conservation Directory***, by its very nature, displays constant growth and change in natural resource-related organizations, both private and governmental. When the first directory was published, it was only one-fourth the size it is today. In many ways, pages added over the years track the popular development of personal commitment to environmental stewardship in America.

This commitment is what the National Wildlife Federation is all about and we will be satisfied if our publication helps you to make a vital contact in your search to contribute to this essential stewardship ethic.

NWF is proud to have Island Press as the publisher of the ***Conservation Directory***. It is only fitting that this valuable resource is published by a leader in environmental publications. I also wish to thank Artech Group, Inc. for their expertise in the design and editing of this Directory.

As always, we welcome your comments, suggestions, additions, or corrections for next year's edition. You may visit the online ***Conservation Directory*** at **www.nwf.org/conservationdirectory** and update your organization's information automatically.

Sincerely,

Bill Street
Senior Director of Education
National Wildlife Federation

National Wildlife Federation Executive Staff

Conservation Directory Editorial and Production Staff

TABLE OF CONTENTS

INTRODUCTION

This is the forty-eighth edition of the National Wildlife Federation's ***Conservation Directory***. It has been published every year since 1955. The first directory listed National Wildlife Federation's state affiliate organizations and was expanded in 1960 to include other conservation organizations. The directory now lists U.S. and state government agencies, international, national, regional organizations and commissions, international government agencies non-governmental organizations from around the world. The Directory has over 4,000 entries, nearly twice the number of the 2001 edition.

USER'S GUIDE

The Conservation Directory is divided into three parts:

• Part One: Introduction

The introduction provides information about the Directory and other National Wildlife Federation programs. The Table of Contents is an excellent resource for beginning a search, listing all section headings with corresponding page numbers.

• Part Two: Descriptive Listings

Entries are arranged alphabetically according to sections:

- ***US Congress, Committees, and Subcommittees***
- ***US Federal and International Government Agencies*****:** Consists of executive branch organizations, independent government agencies, Commissions and international Government Agencies.
- ***State and Provincial Government Agencies*****:** consists of state agencies that deal with conservation issues, organized by state.
- ***Non-Governmental Organizations (Non-Profit & For-Profit)*****:** consists of American and international organizations that are not affiliated with any government agency whose mission is to help protect, preserve and defend the natural world. Subdivided into non-profit organizations. Listed in alphabetical order.
- ***Educational Institutions*****:** consists of colleges and universities with conservation programs and research centers, organized by state.

National Wildlife Federation Affiliates are listed in the front of the book. Governors are listed first for each state in address, founding date, membership, senior staff by name and title and description of the organization's primary goals and mission as provided by the organizations.

• Part Three: Indices

Organization Index
This is a quick and easy way to locate an organization. The index includes the name of every organization included in the directory in alphabetical order with the corresponding page number.

Keyword Index
This useful reference tool lists various subject areas and gives the name of those organizations whose work is related to that keyword. Index citations contain page numbers.

Staff Name Index
The Conservation Directory is very helpful if you know the name of an individual involved with an organization but do not know the specific name of the organization. This index lists all individuals cited in directory listings. Each citation contains the individual's name and page numbers where it appears.

Geographic Index
This index lists agencies and organizations by geographic regions. It is a great way to locate organizations that can be found in a certain state or province.

NWF AFFILIATES

National Wildlife Federation Affiliates are autonomous, statewide organizations that support the purposes and objectives of the National Wildlife Federation. Each affiliate is governed by its own board of directors and develops its own membership on a local level. Affiliates provide NWF with an organized grassroots network nationwide. The elected delegates from the state affiliates determine the conservation policy for NWF through a resolution process at the NWF Annual Meeting. The delegates also elect NWF's Chair, Vice Chairs, and 13 Regional Directors. Detailed descriptions can be found in the Non-Governmental Organization section.

ALABAMA WILDLIFE FEDERATION
46 Commerce Street
Montgomery, AL 36104
phone: (334) 832-9453
fax: (334) 832-9454
email: awf@mindspring.com
web: www.alawild.org

ARIZONA WILDLIFE FEDERATION
644 N. Country Club Drive, Suite E
Mesa, AZ 85201-4983
phone: (480) 644-0077
fax: (480) 644-0078
email: awf@azwildlife.org
web: www.azwildlife.org

ARKANSAS WILDLIFE FEDERATION
9700 Rodney Parham Road, Suite I-2
Little Rock, AR 72227-6212
phone: (501) 224-9200
fax: (501) 224-9214
email: arkwildlifefed@aristotle.net
web: www.arkansaswildlifefederation.org

PLANNING AND CONSERVATION LEAGUE
926 J Street, Suite 612
Sacramento, CA 95814
phone: (916) 444-8726
fax: (916) 448-1789
email: pclmail@pcl.org
web: www.pcl.org

COLORADO WILDLIFE FEDERATION
445 Union Blvd, #302
Lakewood, CO 80228-1243
phone: (303) 987-0400
fax: (303) 987-0200
email: cwf@coloradowildlife.org
web: www.coloradowildlife.org

CONNECTICUT FOREST AND PARK ASSOCIATION, INC.
16 Meriden Road
Rockfall, CT 06481-2961
phone: (860) 346-2372
fax: (860) 347-7463
email: amoore@ctwoodlands.org
web: www.ctwoodlands.org

DELAWARE NATURE SOCIETY
P.O. Box 700
Hockessin, DE 19707-0700
phone: (302) 239-2334
fax: (302) 239-2473
email: email@dnsashland.org
web: www.delawarenaturesociety.org

FLORIDA WILDLIFE FEDERATION
P.O. Box 6870
Tallahassee, FL 32314-6870
phone: (850) 656-7113
fax: (850) 942-4431
email: wildfed@aol.com
web: www.flawildlife.org

GEORGIA WILDLIFE FEDERATION
11600 Hazelbrand Road
Covington, GA 30014
phone: (770) 787-7887
fax: (770) 787-9229
email: gwf@gwf.org
web: www.gwf.org

CONSERVATION COUNCIL FOR HAWAII
PMB-203, 111 E. Puainako Street
Suite 585
Hilo, HI 96720
phone: (808) 968-6360
fax: (808) 968-0896
email: cch@aloha.net
web: www.conservation-hawaii.org

IDAHO WILDLIFE FEDERATION
P.O. Box 6426
Boise, ID 83707-6426
phone: (208) 342-7055
fax: (208) 342-7097
email: iwfboise@micron.net

PRAIRIE RIVERS NETWORK
809 South Fifth Street
Champaign, IL 61820
phone: (217) 344-2371
fax: (217) 344-2381
email: robmoore@prairierivers.org
web: www.prairierivers.org

INDIANA WILDLIFE FEDERATION
950 North Rangeline Rd., Suite A
Carmel, IN 46032-1315
phone: (317) 571-1220
fax: (317) 571-1223
email: iwf@indy.net
web: www.indianawildlife.org

IOWA WILDLIFE FEDERATION
P.O. Box 3332
Des Moines, IA 50316-0332
phone: (319) 624-3107

KANSAS WILDLIFE FEDERATION
P.O. Box 8237
Wichita, KS 67208-0237

LEAGUE OF KENTUCKY SPORTSMEN, INC.
P.O. Box 8527
Lexington, KY 40533
phone: (859) 276-3518
email: office@kentuckysportsmen.com
web: www.kentuckysportsmen.com

LOUISIANA WILDLIFE FEDERATION, INC.
P.O. Box 65239 Audubon Station
Baton Rouge, LA 70896-5239
phone: (225) 344-6762
fax: (225) 344-6707
email: lawildfed@aol.com

NATURAL RESOURCES COUNCIL OF MAINE
3 Wade Street
Augusta, ME 04330-6351
phone: (207) 622-3101
fax: (207) 622-4343
email: nrcm@nrcm.org
web: www.maineenvironment.org

ENVIRONMENTAL LEAGUE OF MASSACHUSETTS
14 Beacon Street, Suite 714
Boston, MA 02108
phone: (617) 742-2553
fax: (617) 742-9656
email: elm@environmentalleague.org
web: www.environmentalleague.org

MICHIGAN UNITED CONSERVATION CLUBS, INC.
2101 Wood St.
Lansing, MI 48912-3728
phone: (517) 371-1041
fax: (517) 371-1505
email: mucc@mucc.org
web: www.mucc.org

MINNESOTA CONSERVATION FEDERATION
551 South Snelling Avenue, Suite B
St. Paul, MN 55116-1525
phone: (651) 690-3077
fax: (651) 690-3077
email: mncf@mtn.org
web: www.mncf.org

MISSISSIPPI WILDLIFE FEDERATION
855 S. Pear Orchard Road, Suite 500
Ridgeland, MS 39157-5138
phone: (601) 206-5703
fax: (601) 206-5705
email: cshropshire@mswf.org
web: www.mswildlife.org

CONSERVATION FEDERATION OF MISSOURI
728 West Main Street
Jefferson City, MO 65101-1159
phone: (573) 634-2322
fax: (573) 634-8205
email: confedmo@socket.net
web: www.confedmo.com

MONTANA WILDLIFE FEDERATION
P.O. Box 1175
Helena, MT 59624-1175
phone: (406) 458-0227
fax: (406) 458-0373
email: mwf@mtwf.org
web: www.montanawildlife.com

NEBRASKA WILDLIFE FEDERATION, INC.
P.O. Box 81437
Lincoln, NE 68501-1437
phone: (402) 994-2001
fax: (402) 994-2021
email: NebraskaWildlife@alltel.net

NEVADA WILDLIFE FEDERATION, INC.
P.O. Box 71238
Reno, NV 89570
phone: (775) 885-7965
fax: (775) 885-0405
email: nvwf@nvwf.org
web: www.nvwf.org

NEW HAMPSHIRE WILDLIFE FEDERATION
54 Portsmouth Street
Concord, NH 03766
phone: (603) 224-5953
fax: (603) 226-7147
email: nhwf@aol.com
web: www.nhwf.org

NEW MEXICO WILDLIFE FEDERATION, INC.
2921 Carlisle Blvd. NE
Albuquerque, NM 87110
phone: (505) 299-5404

ENVIRONMENTAL ADVOCATES
353 Hamilton Street
Albany, NY 12210
phone: (518) 462-5526
fax: (518) 427-0381
email: info@eany.org
web: www. eany.org

NORTH CAROLINA WILDLIFE FEDERATION
P.O. Box 10626
Raleigh, NC 27605
phone: (919) 833-1923
fax: (919) 829-1192
email: ncwf_chuck@mindspring.com
web: www.ncwildlifefed.org

NORTH DAKOTA WILDLIFE FEDERATION
P.O. Box 7248
Bismarck, ND 58507-7248
phone: (701) 845-0812
fax: (701) 222-0334
email: ndwf@gcentral.com
web: www.ndwf.org

LEAGUE OF OHIO SPORTSMEN
3953 Indianola Avenue
Columbus, OH 43214
phone: (614) 268-9924
fax: (614) 268-9925
email: info@leaugeofohiosportsmen.org
web: www.leagueofohiosportsmen.org

OKLAHOMA WILDLIFE FEDERATION
P.O. Box 60126
Oklahoma City, OK 73146-0126
phone: (405) 521-9270
fax: (405) 524-7009
email: owf@nstar.net
(405) 524-7009
web: www.okwildlife.org

PENNSYLVANIA FEDERATION OF SPORTSMEN'S CLUBS
2426 N. Second Street
Harrisburg, PA 17110-1104
phone: (717) 232-3480
fax: (717) 231-3524
web: www.pfsc.org

ENVIRONMENT COUNCIL OF RHODE ISLAND
P.O. Box 9061
Providence, RI 02940
phone: (401) 621-8048
fax: (401) 331-5266
email: environmentcouncil@earthlink.net
web: www.environmentcouncilri.org

SOUTH CAROLINA WILDLIFE FEDERATION
2711 Middleburg Drive, Suite 104
Columbia, SC 29204
phone: (803) 256-0670
fax: (803) 256-0690
email: mail@scwf.org
web: www.scwf.org

SOUTH DAKOTA WILDLIFE FEDERATION
P.O. Box 7075
Pierre, SD 57501-7075
phone: (605) 224-7524
fax: (605) 224-7524
email: sdwf@sbtc.net
web: www.sdwf.org

TENNESSEE CONSERVATION LEAGUE
300 Orlando Avenue
Nashville, TN 37209-3257
phone: (615) 353-1133
fax: (615) 353-0083
email: tcl@conservetn.com
web: www.conservetn.com

TEXAS COMMITTEE ON NATURAL RESOURCES
1301 South IH-35, Suite 301
Austin, TX 78741
phone: (512) 441-1122
fax: (512) 328-3399
email: tconr@texas.net
web: tconr.home.texas.net

UTAH WILDLIFE FEDERATION
P.O. Box 526367
Salt Lake City, UT 84152-6367
phone: (801) 487-1946
fax: (801) 773-0412
email: uwfhall@xmission.com

VERMONT NATURAL RESOURCES COUNCIL
9 Bailey Avenue
Montpelier, VT 05602-2100
phone: (802) 223-2328
fax: (802) 223-0287
email: info@vnrc.org
web: www.vnrc.org

VIRGIN ISLANDS CONSERVATION SOCIETY, INC.
Arawak Building, Suite 3, Gallows Bay
Christiansted, VI 00820
phone: (340) 773-1989
fax: (340) 773-7545
email: sea@viaccess.net

WASHINGTON WILDLIFE FEDERATION
P.O. Box 1966
Olympia, WA 98507-1966
phone: (360) 705-1903
email: wwf@washingtonwildlife.org
web: www.washingtonwildlife.org

WEST VIRGINIA WILDLIFE FEDERATION, INC.
P.O. Box 275
Paden City, WV 26159
phone: (304) 455-6401
fax: (304) 455-6401
email: pleinbach@aol.com

WISCONSIN WILDLIFE FEDERATION, INC.
2036 West 9th Street
Oshkosh, WI 54904
phone: (920) 235-9136
fax: (920) 235-6030
email: wiwf@execpc.com
web: www.execpc.com/~wiwf/

WYOMING WILDLIFE FEDERATION
P.O. Box 106
Cheyenne, WY 82003-0106
phone: (307) 637-5433
fax: (307) 637-6629
web: www.wyomingwildlife.org

U.S. CONGRESS, COMMITTEES, AND SUBCOMMITTEES

Updated as of September 1, 2002

ALABAMA

Senators:

Jeff Sessions
Phone: 202-224-4124 Fax: 202-224-3149
E-mail: senator@sessions.senate.gov
Website: www.senate.gov/~sessions

Richard Shelby
Phone: 202-224-5744 Fax: 202-224-3416
E-mail: senator@shelby.senate.gov
Website: www.senate.gov/~shelby

Representatives:

Sonny Callahan
Phone: 202-225-4931 Fax: 202-225-0562
Website: www.house.gov/callahan

Terry Everett
Phone: 202-225-2901 Fax: 202-225-8913
E-mail: terry.everett@mail.house.gov
Website: www.house.gov/everett

Bob Riley
Phone: 202-225-3261 Fax: 202-225-6827
E-mail: bob.riley@mail.house.gov
Website: www.house.gov/riley

Robert B. Aderholt
Phone: 202-225-4876 Fax: 202-225-5587
E-mail: robert.aderholt@mail.house.gov
Website: www.house.gov/aderholt

Robert E. "Bud" Cramer Jr.
Phone: 202-225-4801 Fax: 202-225-4392
E-mail: budmail@mail.house.gov
Website: www.house.gov/cramer

Spencer Bachus
Phone: 202-225-4921 Fax: 202-225-2082
Website: www.house.gov/bachus

Earl F. Hillard
Phone: 202-225-2665 Fax: 202-226-0772
Website: www.house.gov/hillard

ALASKA

Senators:

Ted Stevens
Phone: 202-224-3004 Fax: 202-224-2354
Website: www.senate.gov/~stevens

Frank H. Murkowski
Phone: 202-224-6665 Fax: 202-224-5301
E-mail: email@murkowski.senate.gov
Website: www.senate.gov.~murkowski

Representatives:

Don Young
Phone: 202-225-5765 Fax: 202-225-0425
E-mail: donyoung@mail.house.gov
Website: www.house.gov/donyoung

ARIZONA

Senators:

John McCain
Phone: 202-224-2235 Fax: 202-228-2862
E-mail: senator_mccain@mccain.senate.gov
Website: www.senate.gov/~mccain

Jon L. Kyl
Phone: 202-224-4521 Fax: 202-224-2207
E-mail: info@kyl.senate.gov
Website: www.senate.gov/~kyl

Representatives:

Jeff Flake
Phone: 202-225-2635 Fax: 202-226-4386
E-mail: jeff.flake@mail.house.gov
Website: www.house.gov/flake

Ed Pastor
Phone: 202-225-4065 Fax: 202-225-1655
E-mail: ed.pastor@mail.house.gov
Website: www.house.gov/pastor

Bob Stump
Phone: 202-225-4576 Fax: 202-225-6328
Website: www.house.gov/stump

John B. Shadegg
Phone: 202-225-3361 Fax: 202-225-3462
E-mail: shadegg@mail.house.gov
Website: www.house.gov/shadegg

Jim Kolbe
Phone: 202-225-2542 Fax: 202-225-0378
Website: www.house.gov/kolbe

J.D. Hayworth
Phone: 202-225-2190 Fax: 202-225-3263
E-mail: jdhayworth@mail.house.gov
Website: www.house.gov/hayworth

ARKANSAS

Senators:

Tim Hutchinson
Phone: 202-224-2353 Fax: 202-228-3973
E-mail: senator.hutchinson@hutchinson.senate.gov
Website: www.senate.gov/~hutchinson

Blanche L. Lincoln
Phone: 202-224-4843 Fax: 202-228-1371
E-mail: info@lincoln.senate.gov
Website: www.senate.gov/~lincoln

Representatives:

Marion Berry
Phone: 202-225-4076 Fax: 202-225-5602
Website: www.house.gov/berry

Vic Snyder
Phone: 202-225-2506 Fax: 202-225-5903
E-mail: snyder.congress@mail.house.gov
Website: www.house.gov/snyder

John Boozman
Phone: 202-225-4301 Fax: 202-225-5713
Website: www.house.gov/boozman

Mike Ross
Phone: 202-225-3772 Fax: 202-225-1314
Website: www.house.gov/ross

CALIFORNIA

Senators:

Dianne Feinstein
Phone: 202-224-3841 Fax: 202-228-3954
E-mail: feinstein.senate.gov/email.html
Website: feinstein.senate.gov

Barbara Boxer
Phone: 202-224-3553 Fax: 415-956-6701
E-mail: senator@boxer.senate.gov
Website: www.senate.gov/~boxer

Representatives:

Mike Thompson
Phone: 202-225-3311 Fax: 202-225-4335
E-mail: m.thompson@mail.house.gov
Website: www.house.gov/mthompson

Wally Herger
Phone: 202-225-3076 Fax: 202-225-1740
Website: www.house.gov/herger

Doug Ose
Phone: 202-225-5716 Fax: 202-226-1298
E-mail: doug.ose@mail.house.gov
Website: www.house.gov/ose

John T. Doolittle
Phone: 202-225-2511 Fax: 202-225-5444
E-mail: doolittle@mail.house.gov
Website: www.house.gov/doolittle

Robert T. Matsui
Phone: 202-225-7163 Fax: 202-225-0566
Website: www.house.gov/matsui

Lynn Woolsey
Phone: 202-225-5161 Fax: 202-225-5163
E-mail: lynn.woolsey@mail.house.gov
Website: www.house.gov/woolsey

George Miller
Phone: 202-225-2095 Fax: 202-225-5609
E-mail: george.miller@mail.house.gov
Website: www.house.gov/georgemiller

Nancy Pelosi
Phone: 202-225-4965 Fax: 202-225-8259
E-mail: sf.nancy@mail.house.gov
Website: www.house.gov/pelosi

Barbara Lee
Phone: 202-225-2661 Fax: 202-225-9817
E-mail: barbara.lee@mail.house.gov
Website: www.house.gov/lee

Ellen O. Tauscher
Phone: 202-225-1880 Fax: 202-225-5914
E-mail: ellen.tauscher@mail.house.gov
Website: www.house.gov/tauscher

Richard Pombo
Phone: 202-225-1947 Fax: 202-225-0861
E-mail: rpombo@mail.house.gov
Website: www.house.gov/pombo

Tom Lantos
Phone: 202-225-3531 Fax: 202-226-9789
Website: www.house.gov/lantos

Fortney H. "Pete" Stark
Phone: 202-225-5065 Fax: 202-226-3805
Website: www.house.gov/stark

Anna Eshoo
Phone: 202-225-8104 Fax: 202-225-8890
E-mail: annagram@mail.house.gov
Website: www.house.gov/eshoo

Michael M. Honda
Phone: 202-225-2631 Fax: 202-225-2699
E-mail: mike.honda@mail.house.gov
Website: www.house.gov/honda

Zoe Lofgren
Phone: 202-225-3072 Fax: 202-225-3336
E-mail: zoe@lofgren.house.gov
Website: www.house.gov/lofgren

Sam Farr
Phone: 202-225-2861 Fax: 202-225-6791
E-mail: samfarr@mail.house.gov
Website: www.house.gov/farr

Gary Condit
Phone: 202-225-6131 Fax: 202-225-0819
Website: www.house.gov/gcondit

George P. Randovich
Phone: 202-225-4540 Fax: 202-225-3402
Website: www.house.gov/radanovich

Calvin Dooley
Phone: 202-225-3341 Fax: 202-225-9308
Website: www.house.gov/dooley

William M. Thomas
Phone: 202-225-2915 Fax: 202-225-8798
Website: www.house.gov/billthomas

Lois Capps
Phone: 202-225-3601 Fax: 202-225-5632
E-mail: loiscapps@mail.house.gov
Website: www.house.gov/capps

Elton Gallegly
Phone: 202-225-5811 Fax: 202-225-1100
Website: www.house.gov/gallegly

Brad Sherman
Phone: 202-225-5911 Fax: 202-225-5879
Website: www.house.gov/sherman

Howard "Buck" McKeon
Phone: 202-225-1956 Fax: 202-226-0683
E-mail: tellbuck@mail.house.gov
Website: www.house.gov/mckeon

Howard L. Berman
Phone: 202-225-4695 Fax: 202-225-3196
E-mail: howard.berman@mail.house.gov
Website: www.house.gov/berman

Adam Schiff
Phone: 202-225-4176 Fax: 202-225-5828
E-mail: congressman.schiff@mail.house.gov
Website: www.house.gov/schiff

David Dreier
Phone: 202-225-2305 Fax: 202-225-7018
Website: www.house.gov/dreier

Henry A. Waxman
Phone: 202-225-3976 Fax: 202-225-4099
Website: www.house.gov/waxman

Xavier Becerra
Phone: 202-225-6235 Fax: 202-225-2202
Website: www.house.gov/becerra

Hilda L. Solis
Phone: 202-225-5464 Fax: 202-225-5467
Website: www.house.gov/solis

Diane Watson
Phone: 202-225-7084 Fax: 202-225-2422

Lucille Roybal-Allard
Phone: 202-225-1766 Fax: 202-226-0350
Website: www.house.gov/roybal-allard

Grace F. Napolitano
Phone: 202-225-5256 Fax: 202-225-0027
E-mail: grace@mail.house.gov
Website: www.house.gov/napolitano

Maxine Waters
Phone: 202-225-2201 Fax: 202-225-7854
Website: www.house.gov/waters

Jane F. Harman
Phone: 202-225-8220 Fax: 202-226-7290
E-mail: jane.harman@mail.house.gov
Website: www.house.gov/harman

Juanita Millender-McDonald
Phone: 202-225-7924 Fax: 202-225-7926
E-mail: millender.mcdonald@mail.house.gov
Website: www.house.gov/millender-mcdonald

Steve Horn
Phone: 202-225-6676 Fax: 202-226-1012
E-mail: steve.hon@mail.house.gov
Website: www.house.gov/horn

Edward Royce
Phone: 202-225-4111 Fax: 202-226-0335
Website: www.house.gov/royce

Jerry Lewis
Phone: 202-225-5861 Fax: 202-225-6498
Website: www.house.gov/jerrylewis

Gary G. Miller
Phone: 202-225-3201 Fax: 202-226-6962
E-mail: publicca41@mail.house.gov
Website: www.house.gov/garymiller

Joe Baca
Phone: 202-225-6161 Fax: 202-225-8671
E-mail: cong.baca@mail.house.gov
Website: www.house.gov/baca

Ken Calvert
Phone: 202-225-1986 Fax: 202-225-2004
Website: www.house.gov/calvert

Mary Bono
Phone: 202-225-5330 Fax: 202-225-2961
Website: www.house.gov/bono

Dana Rohrabacher
Phone: 202-225-2415 Fax: 202-225-0145
E-mail: dana@mail.house.gov
Website: www.house.gov/rohrabacher

Loretta L. Sanchez
Phone: 202-225-2965 Fax: 202-225-5859
E-mail: loretta@mail.house.gov
Website: www.house.gov/sanchez

Christopher Cox
Phone: 202-225-5611 Fax: 202-225-9177
E-mail: christopher.cox@mail.house.gov
Website: cox.house.gov

Darrell Issa
Phone: 202-225-3906 Fax: 202-225-3303
E-mail: congressman.issa@mail.house.gov
Website: www.house.gov/issa

Susan A. Davis
Phone: 202-225-2040 Fax: 202-225-2948
E-mail: susan.davis@mail.house.gov
Website: www.house.gov/susandavis

Bob Filner
Phone: 202-225-8045 Fax: 202-225-9073
Website: www.house.gov/filner

Randy "Duke" Cunningham
Phone: 202-225-5452 Fax: 202-225-2558
Website: www.house.gov/cunningham

Duncan Hunter
Phone: 202-225-5672 Fax: 202-225-0235
Website: www.house.gov/hunter

COLORADO

Senators:

Ben Nighthorse Campbell
Phone: 202-224-5852 Fax: 202-224-1933
Website: www.senate.gov/~campbell

Wayne Allard
Phone: 202-224-5941 Fax: 202-224-6471
Website: www.senate.gov/~allard

Representatives:

Diana L. DeGette
Phone: 202-225-4431 Fax: 202-225-5657
E-mail: degette@mail.house.gov
Website: www.house.gov/degette

Mark Udall
Phone: 202-225-2161 Fax: 202-226-7840
Website: www.house.gov/markudall

Scott McInnis
Phone: 202-225-4761 Fax: 202-226-0622
Website: www.house.gov/mcinnis

Bob Schaffer
Phone: 202-225-4676 Fax: 202-225-5870
E-mail: rep.schaffer@mail.house.gov
Website: www.house.gov/schaffer

Joel Hefley
Phone: 202-225-4422 Fax: 202-225-1942
Website: www.house.gov/hefley

Thomas G. Tancredo
Phone: 202-225-7882 Fax: 202-226-4623
E-mail: tom.tancredo@mail.house.gov
Website: www.house.gov/tancredo

CONNECTICUT

Senators:

Christopher J. Dodd
Phone: 202-224-2823 Fax: 202-228-1683
E-mail: senator@dodd.senate.gov
Website: dodd.senate.gov

Joseph I. Lieberman
Phone: 202-224-4041 Fax: 202-224-9750
E-mail: senator_lieberman@liberman.senate.gov
Website: www.senate.gov/~lieberman

Representatives:

John B. Larson
Phone: 202-225-2265 Fax: 202-225-1031
Website: www.house.gov/larson

Robert R. Simmons
Phone: 202-225-2076 Fax: 202-225-4977
Website: www.house.gov/simmons

Rosa DeLauro
Phone: 202-225-3661 Fax: 202-225-4890
Website: www.house.gov/delauro

Christopher Shays
Phone: 202-225-5541 Fax: 202-225-9629
E-mail: rep.shays@mail.house.gov
Website: www.house.gov/shays

James H. Maloney
Phone: 202-225-3822 Fax: 202-225-5746
Website: www.house.gov/jimmaloney

Nancy L. Johnson
Phone: 202-225-4476 Fax: 202-225-4488
Website: www.house.gov/nancyjohnson

DELAWARE

Senators:

Joseph R. Biden Jr.
Phone: 202-224-5402 Fax: 202-224-0139
E-mail: senator@biden.senate.gov
Website: www.senate.gov/~biden

Thomas R. Carper
Phone: 202-224-2441 Fax: 202-228-2190
Website: carper.senate.gov

Representatives:

Michael Castle
Phone: 202-225-4165 Fax: 202-225-2291
E-mail: delaware@mail.house.gov
Website: www.house.gov/castle

FLORIDA

Senators:

Bob Graham
Phone: 202-224-3041 Fax: 202-224-2237
E-mail: bob_graham@graham.senate.gov
Website: www.senate.gov/~graham

Bill Nelson
Phone: 202-224-5274 Fax: 202-228-2183
E-mail: senator@billneslon.senate.gov
Website: billnelson.senate.gov

Representatives:

Jeff Miller
Phone: 202-225-4136 Fax: 202-225-3414
Website: www.house.gov/jeffmiller

F. Allen Boyd Jr.
Phone: 202-225-5235 Fax: 202-225-5615
Website: www.house.gov/boyd

Corrine Brown
Phone: 202-225-0123 Fax: 202-225-2256
Website: www.house.gov/corrinebrown

Ander Crenshaw
Phone: 202-225-2501 Fax: 202-225-2504
Website: www.house.gov/crenshaw

Karen Thurman
Phone: 202-225-1002 Fax: 202-226-0329
Website: www.house.gov/thurman

Cliff Stearns
Phone: 202-225-5744 Fax: 202-225-3973
E-mail: csterns@mail.house.gov
Website: www.house.gov/stearns

John Mica
Phone: 202-225-4035 Fax: 202-226-0821
E-mail: john.mica@mail.house.gov
Website: www.house.gov/mica

Ric Keller
Phone: 202-225-2176 Fax: 202-225-0999
Website: www.house.gov/keller

Michael Bilirakis
Phone: 202-225-5755 Fax: 202-225-4085
Website: www.house.gov/bilirakis

C.W. "Bill" Young
Phone: 202-225-5961 Fax: 202-225-9764
Website: www.house.gov/young

Jim Davis
Phone: 202-225-3376 Fax: 202-225-5652
Website: www.house.gov/jimdavis

Adam Putnam
Phone: 202-225-1252 Fax: 202-226-0585
E-mail: ask.adam@mail.house.gov
Website: www.house.gov/putnam

Dan Miller
Phone: 202-225-5015 Fax: 202-226-0828
Website: www.house.gov/danmiller

Porter J. Goss
Phone: 202-225-2536 Fax: 202-225-6820
E-mail: porter.goss@mail.house.gov
Website: www.house.gov/goss

Dave Weldon
Phone: 202-225-3671 Fax: 202-225-3516
Website: www.house.gov/weldon

Mark Foley
Phone: 202-225-5792 Fax: 202-225-3132
E-mail: mark.foley@mail.house.gov
Website: www.house.gov/foley

Carrie Meek
Phone: 202-225-4506 Fax: 202-226-0777
Website: www.house.gov/meek

Ileana Ros-Lehtinen
Phone: 202-225-3931 Fax: 202-225-5620
Website: www.house.gov/ros-lehtinen

Robert I. Wexler
Phone: 202-225-3001 Fax: 202-225-5974
Website: www.house.gov/wexler

Peter Deutsch
Phone: 202-225-7931 Fax: 202-225-8456
E-mail: pdeutsch.pub@mail.house.gov
Website: www.house.gov/deutsch

Lincoln Diaz-Blart
Phone: 202-225-4211 Fax: 202-225-8576
Website: www.house.gov/diaz-balart

E. Clay Shaw Jr.
Phone: 202-225-3026 Fax: 202-225-8398
Website: www.house.gov/shaw

Alcee L. Hastings
Phone: 202-225-1313 Fax: 202-225-1171
E-mail: alcee.pubhastings@mail.house.gov
Website: www.house.gov/alceehastings

GEORGIA

Senators:

Max Cleland
Phone: 202-224-3521 Fax: 202-224-0072
Website: www.senate.gov/~cleland

Zell B. Miller
Phone: 202-224-3643 Fax: 202-228-2090
Website: miller.senate.gov

Representatives:

Jack Kingston
Phone: 202-225-5831 Fax: 202-226-2269
E-mail: jack.kingston@mail.house.gov
Website: www.house.gov/kingston

Sanford Bishop Jr.
Phone: 202-225-3631 Fax: 202-225-2203
E-mail: bishop.email@mail.house.gov
Website: www.house.gov/bishop

Michael "Mac" Collins
Phone: 202-225-5901 Fax: 202-225-2515
E-mail: mac.collins@mail.house.gov
Website: www.house.gov/maccollins

Cynthia McKinney
Phone: 202-225-1605 Fax: 202-226-0691
E-mail: cymck@mail.house.gov
Website: www.house.gov/mckinney

John Lewis
Phone: 202-225-3801 Fax: 202-225-0351
E-mail: john.lewis@mail.house.gov
Website: www.house.gov/johnlewis

Johnny Isakson
Phone: 202-225-4501 Fax: 202-225-4656
E-mail: ga06@mail.house.gov
Website: www.house.gov/isakson

Bob Barr
Phone: 202-225-2931 Fax: 202-225-2944
E-mail: barr.ga@mail.house.gov
Website: www.house.gov/barr

Saxby Chambliss
Phone: 202-225-6531 Fax: 202-225-3013
E-mail: saxby.chambliss@mail.house.gov
Website: www.house.gov/chambliss

Nathan Deal
Phone: 202-225-5211 Fax: 202-225-8272
Website: www.house.gov/deal

Charles Norwood
Phone: 202-225-4101 Fax: 202-226-5995
E-mail: rep.charlie.norwood@mail.house.gov
Website: www.house.gov/norwood

John Linder
Phone: 202-225-4272 Fax: 202-225-4696
E-mail: john.linder@mail.house.gov
Website: www.house.gov/linder

HAWAII

Senators:

Daniel K. Inouye
Phone: 202-224-3934 Fax: 202-224-6747
E-mail: senate@inouye.senate.gov
Website: www.senate.gov/~inouye

Daniel K. Akaka
Phone: 202-224-6361 Fax: 202-224-2126
E-mail: senator@akaka.senate.gov
Website: www.senate.gov/~akaka

Representatives:

Neil Abercrombie
Phone: 202-225-2726 Fax: 202-225-4580
E-mail: neil.abercrombie@mail.house.gov
Website: www.house.gov/abercrombie

Patsy T. Mink
Phone: 202-225-4906 Fax: 202-225-4987
Website: www.house.gov/mink

IDAHO

Senators:

Larry E. Craig
Phone: 202-224-2752 Fax: 202-228-1067
Website: www.senate.gov/~craig

Michael D. Crapo
Phone: 202-224-6142 Fax:
Website: crapo.senate.gov

Representatives:

C.L. "Butch" Otter
Phone: 202-225-6611 Fax: 202-225-3029
E-mail: butch.otter@mail.house.gov
Website: www.house.gov/otter

Mike Simpson
Phone: 202-225-5531 Fax: 202-225-8216
E-mail: mike.simpson@mail.house.gov
Website: www.house.gov/simpson

ILLINOIS

Senators:

Richard J. Durbin
Phone: 202-224-2152 Fax: 202-228-0400
E-mail: dick@durbin.senate.gov
Website: www.senate.gov/~durbin

Peter G. Fitzgerald
Phone: 202-224-2854 Fax: 202-228-1372
E-mail: senator_fitzgerald@fitzgerald.senate.gov
Website: www.senate.gov/~fitzgerald

Representatives:

Bobby L. Rush
Phone: 202-225-4372 Fax: 202-226-0333
E-mail: bobby.rush@mail.house.gov
Website: www.house.gov/rush

Jesse L. Jackson, Jr.
Phone: 202-225-0773 Fax: 202-225-0899
Website: www.jessejacksonjr.org

William O. Lipinski
Phone: 202-225-5701 Fax: 202-225-1012
Website: www.house.gov/lipinski

Luis V. Gutierrez
Phone: 202-225-8203 Fax: 202-225-7810
Website: www.house.gov/gutierrez

Rod R. Blagojevich
Phone: 202-225-4061 Fax: 202-225-5603
E-mail: rod.blagojevich@mail.house.gov
Website: www.house.gov/blagojevich

Henry J. Hyde
Phone: 202-225-4561 Fax: 202-225-1166
Website: www.house.gov/hyde

Danny K. Davis
Phone: 202-225-5006 Fax: 202-225-5641
Website: www.house.gov/dannydavis

Philip M. Crane
Phone: 202-225-3711 Fax: 202-225-7830
Website: www.house.gov/crane

Janice D. Schakowsky
Phone: 202-225-2111 Fax: 202-226-6890
E-mail: jan.schakowsky@mail.house.gov
Website: www.house.gov/schakowsky

Mark S. Kirk
Phone: 202-225-4835 Fax: 202-225-3521
E-mail: rep.kirk@mail.house.gov
Website: www.house.gov/kirk

Jerry Weller
Phone: 202-225-3635 Fax: 202-225-3521
Website: www.house.gov/weller

Jerry F. Costello
Phone: 202-225-5661 Fax: 202-225-0285
Website: www.house.gov/costello

Judy Biggert
Phone: 202-225-3515 Fax: 202-225-9420
Website: www.house.gov/biggert

J. Dennis Hastert
Phone: 202-225-2976 Fax: 202-225-0697
E-mail: dhastert@mail.house.gov
Website: www.house.gov/hastert

Timothy V. Johnson
Phone: 202-225-2371 Fax: 202-226-0791
E-mail: rep.johnson@mail.house.gov
Website: www.house.gov/timjohnson

Donald A. Manzullo
Phone: 202-225-5676 Fax: 202-225-5284
Website: www.house.gov/manzullo

Lane Evans
Phone: 202-225-5905 Fax: 202-225-5396
E-mail: lane.evans@mail.house.gov
Website: www.house.gov/evans

Ray LaHood
Phone: 202-225-6201 Fax: 202-225-9249
Website: www.house.gov/lahood

David Phelps
Phone: 202-225-5201 Fax: 202-225-1541
E-mail: david.phelps@mail.house.gov
Website: www.house.gov/phelps

John M. Shimkus
Phone: 202-225-5271 Fax: 202-225-5880
Website: www.house.gov/shimkus

INDIANA

Senators:

Richard G. Lugar
Phone: 202-224-4814 Fax: 202-228-0360
E-mail: senator_lugar@lugar.senate.gov
Website: www.senate.gov/senator/~lugar

Evan Bayh
Phone: 202-224-5623 Fax: 202-228-1377
E-mail: senator@bayh.senate.gov
Website: www.senate.gov/~bayh

Representatives:

Peter J. Visclosky
Phone: 202-225-2461 Fax: 202-225-2493
Website: www.house.gov/visclosky

Mike Pence
Phone: 202-225-3021 Fax: 202-225-3382
E-mail: mike.pence@mail.house.gov
Website: mikepence.house.gov

Tim J. Roemer
Phone: 202-225-3915 Fax: 202-225-6798
E-mail: tim.roemer@mail.house.gov
Website: www.house.gov/roemer

Mark Souder
Phone: 202-225-4436 Fax: 202-225-3479
E-mail: souder@mail.house.gov
Website: www.house.gov/souder

Steve Buyer
Phone: 202-225-5037 Fax: 202-225-2267
Website: www.house.gov/buyer

Dan Burton
Phone: 202-225-2276 Fax: 202-225-0016
Website: www.house.gov/burton

Brian D. Kerns
Phone: 202-225-5805 Fax:
Website: www.house.gov/kerns

John N. Hostettler
Phone: 202-225-4636 Fax: 202-225-3284
E-mail: john.hostettler@mail.house.gov
Website: www.house.gov/hostettler

Baron Hill
Phone: 202-225-5315 Fax: 202-226-6866
Website: www.house.gov/baronhillf

Julia M. Carson
Phone: 202-225-4011 Fax: 202-225-5633
E-mail: rep.carson@mail.house.gov
Website: www.house.gov/carson

IOWA

Senators:

Charles E. Grassley
Phone: 202-224-3744 Fax: 202-224-6020
E-mail: chuck_grassley@grassley.senate.gov
Website: www.senate.gov/~grassley

Tom Harkin
Phone: 202-224-3254 Fax: 202-224-9369
E-mail: tom_harkin@harkin.senate.gov
Website: www.senate.gov/~harkin

Representatives:

Jim Leach
Phone: 202-225-6576 Fax: 202-226-1278
E-mail: talk2jim@mail.house.gov
Website: www.house.gov/leach

Jim Nussle
Phone: 202-225-2911 Fax: 202-225-9129
E-mail: nussleia@mail.house.gov
Website: www.house.gov/nussle

Leonard L. Boswell
Phone: 202-225-3806 Fax: 202-225-5608
E-mail: rep.boswell.ia03@mail.house.gov
Website: www.house.gov/boswell

Greg Ganske
Phone: 202-225-4426 Fax: 202-225-3193
E-mail: rep.ganske@mail.house.gov
Website: www.house.gov/ganske

Tom Latham
Phone: 202-225-5476 Fax: 202-225-3301
E-mail: latham.ia05@mail.house.gov
Website: www.house.gov/latham

KANSAS

Senators:

Sam Brownback
Phone: 202-224-6521 Fax: 202-228-1265
E-mail: sam_brownback@brownback.senate.gov
Website: www.senate.gov/~brownback

Pat Roberts
Phone: 202-224-4774 Fax: 202-224-3514
Website: www.senate.gov/senator/roberts.html

Representatives:

Jerry Moran
Phone: 202-225-2715 Fax: 202-225-5124
E-mail: jerry.moran@mail.house.gov
Website: www.house.gov/moranks01

Jim R. Ryun
Phone: 202-225-6601 Fax: 202-225-7986
Website: www.house.gov/ryun

Dennis Moore
Phone: 202-225-2865 Fax: 202-225-2807
Website: www.house.gov/moore

Todd Tiahrt
Phone: 202-225-6216 Fax: 202-225-3489
E-mail: tiahrt@mail.house.gov
Website: www.house.gov/tiahrt

KENTUCKY

Senators:

Mitch McConnell
Phone: 202-224-2541 Fax: 202-224-2499
E-mail: senator@mcconnell.senate.gov
Website: www.senate.gov/~mcconnell

Jim Bunning
Phone: 202-224-4343 Fax: 202-228-1373
E-mail: jim_bunning@bunning.senate.gov
Website: www.senate.gov/~bunning

Representatives:

Edward Whitfield
Phone: 202-225-3115 Fax: 202-225-3547
Website: www.house.gov/whitfield

Ron Lewis
Phone: 202-225-3501 Fax: 202-226-2019
E-mail: ron.lewis@mail.house.gov
Website: www.house.gov/ronlewis

Anne M. Northup
Phone: 202-225-5401 Fax: 202-225-5776
E-mail: rep.northup@mail.house.gov
Website: www.house.gov/northup

Ken R. Lucas
Phone: 202-225-3465 Fax: 202-225-0003
E-mail: 24i53.k3nludqw@mail.house.gov
Website: www.house.gov/kenlucas

Harold Rogers
Phone: 202-225-4601 Fax: 202-225-0940
Website: www.house.gov/rogers

Ernest Lee Fletcher
Phone: 202-225-4706 Fax: 202-225-2122
Website: www.house.gov/fletcher

LOUISIANA

Senators:

John B. Breaux
Phone: 202-224-4623 Fax: 202-228-2577
E-mail: senator@breaux.senate.gov
Website: www.senate.gov/breaux

Mary Landrieu
Phone: 202-224-5824 Fax: 202-224-9735
E-mail: senator@landrieu.senate.gov
Website: www.senate.gov/~landrieu

Representatives:

David Vitter
Phone: 202-225-3015 Fax: 202-225-0739
E-mail: david.vitter@mail.house.gov
Website: www.house.gov/vitter

William J. Jefferson
Phone: 202-225-6636 Fax: 202-225-1988
E-mail: jeffersonmc@mail.house.gov
Website: www.house.gov/jefferson

W.J. "Billy" Tauzin
Phone: 202-225-4031 Fax: 202-225-0563
Website: www.house.gov/tauzin

Jim McCrery
Phone: 202-225-2777 Fax: 202-225-8039
E-mail: jim.mccrery@mail.house.gov
Website: www.house.gov/mccrery

John C. Cooksey
Phone: 202-225-8490 Fax: 202-225-5639
E-mail: congressman.cooksey@mail.house.gov
Website: www.house.gov/cooksey

Richard H. Baker
Phone: 202-225-3901 Fax: 202-225-7313
Website: www.house.gov/baker

Chris John
Phone: 202-225-2031 Fax: 202-225-5724
E-mail: christopher.john@mail.house.gov
Website: www.house.gov/john

MAINE

Senators:

Olympia J. Snowe
Phone: 202-224-5344 Fax: 202-224-1946
E-mail: olympia@snowe.senate.gov
Website: www.senate.gov/~snowe

Susan M. Collins
Phone: 202-224-2523 Fax: 202-224-2693
E-mail: senator@collins.senate.gov
Website: www.senate.gov/senator/collins.html

Representatives:

Thomas H. Allen
Phone: 202-225-6166 Fax: 202-225-5590
E-mail: rep.tomallen@mail.house.gov
Website: www.tomallen.house.gov

John E. Baldacci
Phone: 202-225-6306 Fax: 202-225-2943
E-mail: baldacci@me02.house.gov
Website: www.house.gov/baldacci

MARYLAND

Senators:

Paul S. Sarbanes
Phone: 202-224-4524 Fax: 202-224-1651
E-mail: senator@sarbanes.senate.gov
Website: www.senate.gov/~sarbanes

Barbara A. Mikulski
Phone: 202-224-4654 Fax: 202-224-8858
E-mail: senator@mikulski.senate.gov
Website: www.senate.gov/~mikulski

Representatives:

Wayne Gilchrest
Phone: 202-225-5311 Fax: 202-225-0254
Website: www.house.gov/gilchrest

Robert Ehrlich Jr
Phone: 202-225-3061 Fax: 202-225-3094
E-mail: ehrlich@mail.house.gov
Website: www.house.gov/ehrlich/index.html

Benjamin L. Cardin
Phone: 202-225-4016 Fax: 202-225-9219
E-mail: rep.cardin@mail.house.gov
Website: www.house.gov/cardin

Albert Wynn
Phone: 202-225-8699 Fax: 202-225-8714
Website: www.house.gov/wynn

Steny H. Hoyer
Phone: 202-225-4131 Fax: 202-225-4300
Website: www.house.gov/hoyer

Roscoe Bartlett
Phone: 202-225-2721 Fax: 202-225-2193
Website: www.house.gov/bartlett

Elijah Cummings
Phone: 202-225-4741 Fax: 202-225-3178
Website: www.house.gov/cummings

Connie A. Morella
Phone: 202-225-5341 Fax: 202-225-1389
E-mail: rep.morella@mail.house.gov
Website: www.house.gov/morella

MASSACHUSETTS

Senators:

Edward M. Kennedy
Phone: 202-224-4543 Fax: 202-224-2417
Website: www.senate.gov/~kennedy

John F. Kerry
Phone: 202-224-2742 Fax: 202-224-8525
E-mail: john_kerry@kerry.senate.gov
Website: www.senate.gov/~kerry

Representatives:

John W. Olver
Phone: 202-225-5335 Fax: 202-226-1224
E-mail: john.olver@mail.house.gov
Website: www.house.gov/olver

Richard E. Neal
Phone: 202-225-5601 Fax: 202-225-8112
Website: www.house.gov/neal

James P. McGovern
Phone: 202-225-6101 Fax: 202-225-5759
Website: www.house.gov/mcgovern

Barney Frank
Phone: 202-225-5931 Fax: 202-225-0182
Website: www.house.gov/frank

Marty Meehan
Phone: 202-225-3411 Fax: 202-226-0771
Website: www.house.gov/meehan

John F. Tierney
Phone: 202-225-8020 Fax: 202-225-5915
Website: www.house.gov/tierney

Edward J. Markey
Phone: 202-225-2836 Fax:
Website: www.house.gov/markey

Michael Capuano
Phone: 202-225-5111 Fax: 202-225-9322
Website: www.house.gov/capuano

Stephen F. Lynch
Phone: 202-225-8273 Fax: 202-225-3984

William Delahunt
Phone: 202-225-3111 Fax: 202-225-5658
E-mail: willian.delhunt@mail.house.gov
Website: www.house.gov/delahunt

MICHIGAN

Senators:

Carl Levin
Phone: 202-224-6221 Fax: 202-224-1388
E-mail: senator@levin.senate.gov
Website: www.senate.gov/~levin

Debbie A. Stabenow
Phone: 202-224-4822 Fax: 202-228-0325
E-mail: senator@stabenow.senate.gov
Website: stabenow.senate.gov

Representatives:

Bart Stupak
Phone: 202-225-4735 Fax: 202-225-4744
E-mail: stupak@mail.house.gov
Website: www.house.gov/stupak

Peter Hoekstra
Phone: 202-225-4401 Fax: 202-226-0779
E-mail: tellhoek@mail.house.gov
Website: www.house.gov/hoekstra

Vernon Ehlers
Phone: 202-225-3831 Fax: 202-225-5144
E-mail: rep.ehlers@mail.house.gov
Website: www.house.gov/ehlers

Dave Camp
Phone: 202-225-3561 Fax: 202-225-9679
Website: www.house.gov/camp

James Barcia
Phone: 202-225-8171 Fax: 202-225-2168
E-mail: jim.barcia-pub@mail.house.gov
Website: www.house.gov/barcia

Fred Upton
Phone: 202-225-3761 Fax: 202-225-4986
E-mail: tellupton@mail.house.gov
Website: www.house.gov/upton

Nick Smith
Phone: 202-225-6276 Fax: 202-225-6281
E-mail: rep.smith@mail.house.gov
Website: www.house.gov/nicksmith

Michael J. Rogers
Phone: 202-225-4872 Fax: 202-225-5820
Website: www.house.gov/mikerogers

Dale E. Kildee
Phone: 202-225-3611 Fax: 202-225-6393
E-mail: dkildee@mail.house.gov
Website: www.house.gov/kildee

David E. Bonior
Phone: 202-225-2106 Fax: 202-226-1169
E-mail: david.bonior@mail.house.gov
Website: davidbonior.house.gov

Joseph Knollenberg
Phone: 202-225-5802 Fax: 202-226-2356
E-mail: rep.knollenberg@mail.house.gov
Website: www.house.gov/knollenberg

Sander M. Levin
Phone: 202-225-4961 Fax: 202-226-1033
E-mail: slevin@mail.house.gov
Website: www.house.gov/levin

Lynn Rivers
Phone: 202-225-6261 Fax: 202-225-3404
E-mail: lynn.rivers@mail.house.gov
Website: www.house.gov/rivers

John Conyers Jr.
Phone: 202-225-5126 Fax: 202-225-0072
E-mail: john.conyers@mail.house.gov
Website: www.house.gov/conyers

Carolyn C. Kilpatrick
Phone: 202-225-2261 Fax: 202-225-5730
Website: www.house.gov/kilpatrick

John D. Dingell
Phone: 202-225-4071 Fax: 202-226-0371
E-mail: public.dingell@mail.house.gov
Website: www.house.gov/dingell

MINNESOTA

Senators:

Paul David Wellstone
Phone: 202-224-5641 Fax: 202-224-8438
E-mail: senator@wellstone.senate.gov
Website: www.senate.gov/~wellstone

Mark Dayton
Phone: 202-224-3244 Fax: 202-228-2186
Website: dayton.senate.gov

Representatives:

Gil Gutknecht
Phone: 202-225-2472 Fax: 202-225-3246
E-mail: gil@mail.house.gov
Website: www.house.gov/gutknecht

Mark R. Kennedy
Phone: 202-225-2331 Fax: 202-225-6475
E-mail: mark.kennedy@mail.house.gov
Website: markkennedy.house.gov

Jim Ramstad
Phone: 202-225-2871 Fax: 202-225-6351
E-mail: mn03@mail.house.gov
Website: www.house.gov/ramstad

Betty McCollum
Phone: 202-225-6631 Fax: 202-225-1968
Website: www.house.gov/mccollum

Martin Olav Sabo
Phone: 202-225-4755 Fax: 202-225-4886
E-mail: martin.sabo@mail.house.gov
Website: www.house.gov/sabo

Bill Luther
Phone: 202-225-2271 Fax: 202-225-3368
E-mail: bill.luther@mail.house.gov
Website: www.house.gov/luther

Collin Peterson
Phone: 202-225-2165 Fax: 202-225-1593
E-mail: tocollin.peterson@mail.house.gov
Website: www.house.gov/collinpeterson

James L. Oberstar
Phone: 202-225-6211 Fax: 202-225-0699
Website: www.house.gov/oberstar

MISSISSIPPI

Senators:

Thad Cochran
Phone: 202-224-5054 Fax: 202-224-9450
E-mail: senator@cochran.senate.gov
Website: www.senate.gov/~cochran

Trent Lott
Phone: 202-224-6253 Fax: 202-224-2262
E-mail: senatorlott@lott.senate.gov
Website: www.senate.gov/~lott

Representatives:

Roger F. Wicker
Phone: 202-225-4306 Fax: 202-225-3549
E-mail: roger.wicker@mail.house.gov
Website: www.house.gov/wicker

Bennie G. Thompson
Phone: 202-225-5876 Fax: 202-225-5898
E-mail: thompsonms2nd@mail.house.gov
Website: www.house.gov/thompson

Charles "Chip" Pickering Jr.
Phone: 202-225-5031 Fax: 202-225-5797
Website: www.house.gov/pickering

Ronnie Shows
Phone: 202-225-5865 Fax: 202-225-5886
E-mail: ronnie.shows@mail.house.gov
Website: www.house.gov/shows

Gene Taylor
Phone: 202-225-5772 Fax: 202-225-7074
Website: www.house.gov/Taylor

MISSOURI

Senators:

Christopher S. "Kit" Bond
Phone: 202-224-5721 Fax: 202-224-8149
E-mail: kit_bond@bond.senate.gov
Website: www.senate.gov/~bond/comm.html

Jean Carnahan
Phone: 202-224-6154 Fax: 202-228-1518
E-mail: senator_carahan@carnahan.senate.gov
Website: carnahan.senate.gov

Representatives:

William L. Clay Jr
Phone: 202-225-2406 Fax: 202-225-1725
Website: www.house.gov/clay

Todd Akin
Phone: 202-225-2561 Fax: 202-225-2563
E-mail: rep.akin@mail.house.gov
Website: www.house.gov/akin

Richard A. Gephardt
Phone: 202-225-2671 Fax: 202-225-7452
E-mail: gephardt@mail.house.gov
Website: dickgephardt.house.gov

Ike Skelton
Phone: 202-225-2876 Fax: 202-225-2695
E-mail: ike.skelton@mail.house.gov
Website: www.house.gov/skelton

Karen McCarthy
Phone: 202-225-4535 Fax: 202-225-4403
Website: www.house.gov/karenmccarthy

Samuel B. Graves
Phone: 202-225-7041 Fax: 202-225-8221
E-mail: sam.graves@mail.house.gov
Website: www.house.gov/graves

Roy Blunt
Phone: 202-225-6536 Fax: 202-225-5604
E-mail: blunt@mail.house.gov
Website: www.house.gov/blunt

Jo Ann H. Emerson
Phone: 202-225-4404 Fax: 202-226-0326
E-mail: joann.emerson@mail.house.gov
Website: www.house.gov/emerson

Kenny C. Hulshof
Phone: 202-225-2956 Fax: 202-225-5712
Website: www.house.gov/hulshof

MONTANA

Senators:

Max Baucus
Phone: 202-224-2651 Fax: 202-228-3687
E-mail: max@baucus.senate.gov
Website: www.senate.gov/~baucas

Conrad Burns
Phone: 202-224-2644 Fax: 202-224-8594
Website: burns.senate.gov

Representative:

Dennis Rehberg
Phone: 202-225-3211 Fax: 202-225-5687
Website: www.house.gov/rehberg

NEBRASKA

Senators:

Chuck Hagel
Phone: 202-224-4224 Fax: 202-224-5213
E-mail: chuck_hagel@hagel.senate.gov
Website: www.senate.gov/~hagel

Ben Nelson
Phone: 202-224-6551 Fax: 202-228-0012
E-mail: senator@bennelson.senate.gov
Website: www.senate.gov/~bennelson

Representatives:

Doug Bereuter
Phone: 202-225-4806 Fax: 202-225-5686
Website: www.house.gov/bereuter

Lee Terry
Phone: 202-225-4155 Fax: 202-226-5452
E-mail: talk2lee@mail.house.gov
Website: www.house.gov/terry

Thomas W. Osborne
Phone: 202-225-6435 Fax: 202-226-1385
Website: www.house.gov/osborne

NEVADA

Senators:

Harry Reid
Phone: 202-224-3542 Fax: 202-224-7327
E-mail: senator_reid@reid.senate.gov
Website: www.senate.gov/~reid

John Ensign
Phone: 202-224-6244 Fax: 202-228-2193
Website: ensign.senate.gov

Representatives:

Shelley Berkley
Phone: 202-225-5965 Fax: 202-225-3119
E-mail: shelley.berkley@mail.house.gov
Website: www.house.gov/berkley

James A. Gibbons
Phone: 202-225-6155 Fax: 202-225-5679
E-mail: mail.gibbons@mail.house.gov
Website: www.house.gov/gibbons

NEW HAMPSHIRE

Senators:

Robert C. Smith
Phone: 202-224-2841 Fax: 202-224-1353
E-mail: opinion@smith.senate.gov
Website: www.senate.gov/~smith

Judd Gregg
Phone: 202-224-3324 Fax: 202-224-4952
E-mail: mailbox@gregg.senate.gov
Website: www.senate.gov/~gregg

Representatives:

John E. Sununu
Phone: 202-225-5456 Fax: 202-225-5822
E-mail: rep.sununu@mail.house.gov
Website: www.house.gov/sununu

Charles Bass
Phone: 202-225-5206 Fax: 202-225-2946
E-mail: cbass@mail.house.gov
Website: www.house.gov/bass

NEW JERSEY

Senators:

Robert G. Torricelli
Phone: 202-224-3224 Fax: 202-224-8567
E-mail: senator_torricelli@torricelli.senate.gov
Website: www.senate.gov/~torricelli

Jon Corzine
Phone: 202-224-4744 Fax: 202-228-2197
Website: corzine.senate.gov

Representatives:

Robert E. Andrews
Phone: 202-225-6501 Fax: 202-225-6583
E-mail: andrews@mail.house.gov
Website: www.house.gov/andrews

Frank A. LoBiondo
Phone: 202-225-6572 Fax: 202-225-3318
E-mail: lobiondo@mail.house.gov
Website: www.house.gov/lobiondo

Jim Saxton
Phone: 202-225-4765 Fax: 202-225-0778
E-mail: jim.saxton@mail.house.gov
Website: www.house.gov/saxton

Christopher H. Smith
Phone: 202-225-3765 Fax: 202-225-7768
Website: www.house.gov/smith

Marge Roukema
Phone: 202-225-4465 Fax: 202-225-9048
E-mail: rep.roukema@mail.house.gov
Website: www.house.gov/roukema

Frank Pallone Jr.
Phone: 202-225-4671 Fax: 202-225-9665
E-mail: frank.pallone@mail.house.gov
Website: www.house.gov/pallone

Michael A. Ferguson
Phone: 202-225-5361 Fax: 202-225-9460
Website: www.house.gov/ferguson

William J. Pascrell, Jr.
Phone: 202-225-5751 Fax: 202-225-5782
E-mail: bill.pascrell@mail.house.gov
Website: www.house.gov/pascrell

Steven R. Rothman
Phone: 202-225-5061 Fax: 202-225-5851
E-mail: steven.rothman@mail.house.gov
Website: www.house.gov/rothman

Donald M. Payne
Phone: 202-225-3436 Fax: 202-225-4160
Website: www.house.gov/payne

Rodney Frelinghuysen
Phone: 202-225-5034 Fax: 202-225-3186
E-mail: rodney.frelinghuysen@mail.house.gov
Website: www.house.gov/frelinghuysen

Rush Holt
Phone: 202-225-5801 Fax: 202-225-6025
E-mail: rush.holt@mail.house.gov
Website: www.house.gov/rholt

Robert Menendez
Phone: 202-225-7919 Fax: 202-226-0792
E-mail: menendez@mail.house.gov
Website: www.house.gov/menendez

NEW MEXICO

Senators:

Pete V. Domenici
Phone: 202-224-6621 Fax: 202-228-0900
Website: domenici.senate.gov

Jeff Bingaman
Phone: 202-224-5521 Fax: 202-224-2852
E-mail: senator_bingaman@bingaman.senate.gov
Website: www.senate.gov/~bingaman

Representatives:

Heather A. Wilson
Phone: 202-225-6316 Fax: 202-225-4975
E-mail: ask.heather@mail.house.gov
Website: www.house.gov/wilson

Joe Skeen
Phone: 202-225-2365 Fax: 202-225-9599
E-mail: joe.skeen@mail.house.gov
Website: www.joeskeen.house.gov

Tom Udall
Phone: 202-225-6190 Fax: 202-226-1331
E-mail: tom.udall@mail.house.gov
Website: www.house.gov/tomudall

NEW YORK

Senators:

Charles E. Schumer
Phone: 202-224-6542 Fax: 202-228-3027
E-mail: senator@schumer.senate.gov
Website: schumer.senate.gov

Hillary Rodham Clinton
Phone: 202-224-4451 Fax: 202-228-0282
Website: clinton.senate.gov

Representatives:

Felix J. Grucci, Jr.
Phone: 202-225-3826 Fax: 202-225-3143
Website: www.house.gov/grucci

Steve J. Israel
Phone: 202-225-3335 Fax: 202-225-4669
Website: www.house.gov/israel

Peter King
Phone: 202-225-7896 Fax: 202-226-2279
E-mail: peter.king@mail.house.gov
Website: www.house.gov/king

Carolyn McCarthy
Phone: 202-225-5516 Fax: 202-225-5758
Website: www.house.gov/carolynmccarthy

Gary L. Ackerman
Phone: 202-225-2601 Fax: 202-225-1589
E-mail: gary_ackerman@mail.house.gov
Website: www.house.gov/ackerman

Gregory W. Meeks
Phone: 202-225-3461 Fax: 202-226-4169
E-mail: congmeeks@mail.house.gov
Website: www.house.gov/meeks

Joseph Crowley
Phone: 202-225-3965 Fax: 202-225-1909
E-mail: write2joecrowley@mail.house.gov
Website: www.house.gov/crowley

Jerrold Nadler
Phone: 202-225-5635 Fax: 202-225-6923
E-mail: jerrold.nadler@mail.house.gov
Website: www.house.gov/nadler

Anthony David Weiner
Phone: 202-225-6616 Fax: 202-226-7253
E-mail: weiner@mail.house.gov
Website: www.house.gov/weiner

Edolphus Towns
Phone: 202-225-5936 Fax: 202-225-1018
E-mail: edolphus.towns@mail.house.gov
Website: www.house.gov/towns

Major R. Owens
Phone: 202-225-6231 Fax: 202-226-0112
Website: www.house.gov/owens

Nydia Velazquez
Phone: 202-225-2361 Fax: 202-226-0327
Website: www.house.gov/velazquez

Vito Fossella
Phone: 202-225-3371 Fax: 202-226-1272
E-mail: vito.fossella@mail.house.gov
Website: www.house.gov/fossella

Carolyn Maloney
Phone: 202-225-7944 Fax: 202-225-4709
E-mail: rep.carolyn.maloney@mail.house.gov
Website: www.house.gov/maloney

Charles B. Rangel
Phone: 202-225-4365 Fax: 202-225-0816
Website: www.house.gov/rangel

Jose E. Serrano
Phone: 202-225-4361 Fax: 202-225-6001
E-mail: jserrano@mail.house.gov
Website: www.house.gov/serrano

Eliot Engel
Phone: 202-225-2464 Fax: 202-225-5513
Website: www.house.gov/engel

Nita M. Lowey
Phone: 202-225-6506 Fax: 202-225-0546
E-mail: nita.lowey@mail.house.gov
Website: www.house.gov/lowey

Sue W. Kelly
Phone: 202-225-5441 Fax: 202-225-3289
E-mail: dearsue@mail.house.gov
Website: www.house.gov/suekelly

Benjamin A. Gilman
Phone: 202-225-3776 Fax: 202-225-2541
Website: www.house.gov/gilman

Michael R. McNulty
Phone: 202-225-5076 Fax: 202-225-5077
E-mail: mike.mcnulty@mail.house.gov
Website: www.house.gov/mcnulty

John E. Sweeney
Phone: 202-225-5614 Fax: 202-225-6234
E-mail: john.sweeney@mail.house.gov
Website: www.house.gov/sweeney

Sherwood L. Boehlert
Phone: 202-225-3665 Fax: 202-225-1891
E-mail: rep.boehlert@mail.house.gov
Website: www.house.gov/boehlert

John McHugh
Phone: 202-225-4611 Fax: 202-226-0621
Website: www.house.gov/mchugh

James T. Walsh
Phone: 202-225-3701 Fax: 202-225-4042
E-mail: rep.james.walsh@mail.house.gov
Website: www.house.gov/walsh

Maurice Hinchey
Phone: 202-225-6335 Fax: 202-226-0774
E-mail: www.house.gov/writerep
Website: www.house.gov/hinchey

Thomas Reynolds
Phone: 202-225-5265 Fax: 202-225-5910
Website: www.house.gov/reynolds

Louise McIntosh Slaughter
Phone: 202-225-3615 Fax: 202-225-7822
E-mail: louiseny@mail.house.gov
Website: www.house.gov/slaughter

John J. LaFalce
Phone: 202-225-3231 Fax: 202-226-9911
Website: www.house.gov/lafalce

Jack Quinn
Phone: 202-225-3306 Fax: 202-226-0347
Website: www.house.gov/quinn

Amory Houghton Jr.
Phone: 202-225-3161 Fax: 202-225-5574
Website: www.house.gov/houghton

NORTH CAROLINA

Senators:

Jesse Helms
Phone: 202-224-6342 Fax: 202-228-1339
E-mail: jeese_helms@helms.senate.gov
Website: www.senate.gov/~helms

John R. Edwards
Phone: 202-224-3154 Fax: 202-228-1374
E-mail: senator@edwards.senate.gov
Website: www.senate.gov/~edwards

Representatives:

Eva M. Clayton
Phone: 202-225-3101 Fax: 202-225-3354
Website: www.house.gov/clayton

Bob Etheridge
Phone: 202-225-4531 Fax: 202-225-5662
E-mail: bob.etheridge@mail.house.gov
Website: www.house.gov/etheridge

Walter Jones Jr.
Phone: 202-225-3415 Fax: 202-225-3286
E-mail: conjones@mail.house.gov
Website: www.house.gov/jones

David E. Price
Phone: 202-225-1784 Fax: 202-225-2014
E-mail: david.price@mail.house.gov
Website: www.house.gov/price

Richard M. Burr
Phone: 202-225-2071 Fax: 202-225-2995
E-mail: richard.burrnc05@mail.house.gov
Website: www.house.gov/burr

Howard Coble
Phone: 202-225-3065 Fax: 202-225-8611
E-mail: howard.coble@mail.house.gov
Website: www.house.gov/coble

Mike McIntyre
Phone: 202-225-2731 Fax: 202-225-5773
E-mail: congmcintyre@mail.house.gov
Website: www.house.gov/mcintyre

Robin Hayes
Phone: 202-225-3715 Fax: 202-225-4036
Website: www.house.gov/hayes

Sue Myrick
Phone: 202-225-1976 Fax: 202-225-3389
E-mail: myrick@mail.house.gov
Website: www.house.gov/myrick

Cass Ballenger
Phone: 202-225-2576 Fax: 202-225-0316
E-mail: cass.ballenger@mail.house.gov
Website: www.house.gov/ballenger

Charles H. Taylor
Phone: 202-225-6401 Fax:
E-mail: repcharles.taylor@mail.house.gov
Website: www.house.gov/charlestaylor

Melvin L. Watt
Phone: 202-225-1510 Fax: 202-225-1512
E-mail: nc12.public@mail.house.gov
Website: www.house.gov/watt

NORTH DAKOTA

Senators:

Kent Conrad
Phone: 202-224-2043 Fax: 202-224-7776
E-mail: senator@conrad.senate.gov
Website: www.senate.gov/~conrad

Byron L. Dorgan
Phone: 202-224-2551 Fax: 202-224-1193
E-mail: senator@dorgan.senate.gov
Website: www.senate.gov/~dorgan

Representatives:

Earl Pomeroy
Phone: 202-225-2611 Fax: 202-226-0893
E-mail: rep.earl.pomeroy@mail.house.gov
Website: www.house.gov/pomeroy

OHIO

Senators:

Mike DeWine
Phone: 202-224-2315 Fax: 202-224-6519
E-mail: senator_dewine@dewine.senate.gov
Website: dewine.senate.gov

George V. Voinovich
Phone: 202-224-3353 Fax: 202-228-1382
E-mail: senator_voinovich@voinovich.senate.gov
Website: www.senate.gov/~voinovich

Representatives:

Steve Chabot
Phone: 202-225-2216 Fax: 202-225-3012
Website: www.house.gov/chabot

Rob J. Portman
Phone: 202-225-3164 Fax: 202-225-1992
E-mail: portmail@mail.house.gov
Website: www.house.gov/portman

Tony P. Hall
Phone: 202-225-6465 Fax: 202-226-1443
Website: www.house.gov/tonyhall

Michael G. Oxley
Phone: 202-225-2676 Fax: 202-226-0577
E-mail: mike.oxley@mail.house.gov
Website: www.house.gov/oxley

Paul E. Gillmor
Phone: 202-225-6405 Fax: 202-225-1985
E-mail: paul.gillmor@mail.house.gov
Website: www.house.gov/gillmor

Ted Strickland
Phone: 202-225-5705 Fax: 202-225-5907
Website: www.house.gov/strickland

David Hobson
Phone: 202-225-4324 Fax: 202-225-1984
Website: www.house.gov/hobson

John A. Boehner
Phone: 202-225-6205 Fax: 202-225-0704
E-mail: john.boehner@mail.house.gov
Website: www.house.gov/boehner

Marcy Kaptur
Phone: 202-225-4146 Fax: 202-225-7711
E-mail: rep.kaptur@mail.house.gov
Website: www.house.gov/kaptur

Dennis J. Kucinich
Phone: 202-225-5871 Fax: 202-225-5745
Website: www.house.gov/kucinch

Stephanie Tubbs Jones
Phone: 202-225-7032 Fax: 202-225-1339
E-mail: stephanie.tubbs.jones@mail.house.gov
Website: www.house.gov/tubbsjones

Patrick J. Tiberi
Phone: 202-225-5355 Fax: 202-226-4523
Website: www.house.gov/tiberi

Sherrod Brown
Phone: 202-225-3401 Fax: 202-225-2266
E-mail: sherrod@mail.house.gov
Website: www.house.gov/sherrodbrown

Thomas C. Sawyer
Phone: 202-225-5231 Fax: 202-225-5278
Website: www.house.gov/sawyer

Deborah Pryce
Phone: 202-225-2015 Fax: 202-225-3529
E-mail: pryce.oh15@mail.house.gov
Website: www.house.gov/pryce

Ralph Regula
Phone: 202-225-3876 Fax: 202-225-3059
Website: www.house.gov/regula

James A. Traficant Jr
Phone: 202-225-5261 Fax: 202-225-3719
E-mail: telljim@mail.house.gov
Website: www.house.gov/traficant

Bob Ney
Phone: 202-225-6265 Fax: 202-225-3394
E-mail: bobney@mail.house.gov
Website: www.house.gov.ney

Steven C. laTourette
Phone: 202-225-5731 Fax: 202-225-3307
Website: www.house.gov/latourette

OKLAHOMA

Senators:

Don Nickles
Phone: 202-224-5754 Fax: 202-224-6008
E-mail: senator@nickles.senate.gov
Website: www.senate.gov/~nickles

James M. Inhofe
Phone: 202-224-4721 Fax: 202-228-0380
E-mail: jim_inhofe@inhofe.senate.gov
Website: www.senate.gov/~inhofe

Representatives:

Steve Largent
Phone: 202-225-2211 Fax: 202-225-9187
Website: www.house.gov/largent

Brad Carson
Phone: 202-225-2701 Fax: 202-225-3038
E-mail: brad.carson@mail.house.gov
Website: www.house.gov/bradcarson

Wes W. Watkins
Phone: 202-225-4565 Fax: 202-225-5966
E-mail: wes.watkins@mail.house.gov
Website: www.house.gov/watkins

J.C. Watts Jr.
Phone: 202-225-6165 Fax: 202-225-3512
E-mail: rep.jcwatts@mail.house.gov
Website: www.house.gov/watts

Ernest Istook Jr.
Phone: 202-225-2132 Fax: 202-226-1463
E-mail: istook@mail.house.gov
Website: www.house.gov/istook/welcome.htm

Frank D. Lucas
Phone: 202-225-5565 Fax: 202-225-8698
E-mail: replucas@mail.house.gov
Website: www.house.gov/lucas

OREGON

Senators:

Ron Wyden
Phone: 202-224-5244 Fax: 202-228-2717
E-mail: senator@wyden.senate.gov
Website: www.senate.gov/~wyden

Gordon Smith
Phone: 202-224-3753 Fax: 202-228-3997
E-mail: oregon@gsmith.senate.gov
Website: www.senate.gov/~gsmith

Representatives:

David Wu
Phone: 202-225-0855 Fax: 202-225-9497
E-mail: david.wu@mail.house.gov
Website: www.house.gov/wu

Greg Walden
Phone: 202-225-6730 Fax: 202-225-5774
E-mail: greg.walden@mail.house.gov
Website: www.house.gov/walden

Earl Blumenauer
Phone: 202-225-4811 Fax: 202-225-8941
Website: www.house.gov/blumenauer

Peter A. DeFazio
Phone: 202-225-6416 Fax: 202-225-0032
Website: www.house.gov/defazio/index.htm

Darlene Hooley
Phone: 202-225-5711 Fax: 202-225-5699
Website: www.house.gov/hooley

PENNSYLVANIA

Senators:

Arlen Specter
Phone: 202-224-4254 Fax: 202-228-1229
E-mail: senator_specter@specter.senate.gov
Website: www.senate.gov/~specter

Rick Santorum
Phone: 202-224-6324 Fax: 202-228-0604
Website: www.senate.gov/~santorum

Representatives:

Robert A. Brady
Phone: 202-225-4731 Fax: 202-225-0088
E-mail: robert.brady@mail.house.gov
Website: www.house.gov/robertbrady

Chaka Fattah
Phone: 202-225-4001 Fax: 202-225-5392
Website: www.house.gov/fattah

Robert A. Borski
Phone: 202-225-8251 Fax: 202-225-4628
E-mail: robert.borski@mail.house.gov
Website: www.house.gov/borski

Melissa A. Hart
Phone: 202-225-2565 Fax: 202-226-2274
E-mail: rep.hart@mail.house.gov
Website: www.house.gov/hart

John E. Peterson
Phone: 202-225-5121 Fax: 202-225-5796
E-mail: john.peterson@mail.house.gov
Website: www.house.gov/johnpeterson

Tim Holden
Phone: 202-225-5546 Fax: 202-226-0996
Website: www.house.gov/holden

Curt Weldon
Phone: 202-225-2011 Fax: 202-225-8137
E-mail: curtpa07@mail.house.gov
Website: www.house.gov/weldon

Jim Greenwood
Phone: 202-225-4276 Fax: 202-225-9511
E-mail: greenwoodpa@mail.house.gov
Website: www.house.gov/greenwood

Bill Shuster
Phone: 202-225-2431 Fax: 202-225-2486
Website: www.house.gov/shuster

Don Sherwood
Phone: 202-225-3731 Fax: 202-225-9594
Website: www.house.gov/sherwood

Paul E. Kanjorski
Phone: 202-225-6511 Fax: 202-225-0764
E-mail: paul.kanjorski@mail.house.gov
Website: www.house.gov/kanjorski

John P. Murtha
Phone: 202-225-2065 Fax: 202-225-5709
E-mail: murtha@mail.house.gov
Website: www.house.gov/murtha

Joseph M. Hoeffel III
Phone: 202-225-6111 Fax: 202-226-0611
Website: www.house.gov/hoeffel

William J. Coyne
Phone: 202-225-2301 Fax: 202-225-1844
Website: www.house.gov/coyne

Pat Toomey
Phone: 202-225-6411 Fax: 202-226-0778
E-mail: rep.toomey.pa15@mail.house.gov
Website: www.house.gov/toomey

Joseph R. Pitts
Phone: 202-225-2411 Fax: 202-225-2013
E-mail: pitts.pa16@mail.house.gov
Website: www.house.gov/pitts

George W. Gekas
Phone: 202-225-4315 Fax: 202-225-8440
E-mail: askgeorge@mail.house.gov
Website: www.house.gov/gekas

Mike Doyle
Phone: 202-225-2135 Fax: 202-225-3084
E-mail: rep.doyle@mail.house.gov
Website: www.house.gov/doyle

Todd R. Platts
Phone: 202-225-5836 Fax: 202-226-1000
Website: www.house.gov/platts

Frank R. Mascara
Phone: 202-225-4665 Fax: 202-225-3377
Website: www.house.gov/mascara

Philip S. English
Phone: 202-225-5406 Fax: 202-225-3103
E-mail: phil.english@mail.house.gov
Website: www.house.gov/english

RHODE ISLAND

Senators:

Jack Reed
Phone: 202-224-4642 Fax: 202-224-4680
E-mail: jack@reed.senate.gov
Website: www.senate.gov/senator/reed.html

Lincoln D. Chafee
Phone: 202-224-2921 Fax: 202-228-2853
E-mail: senator_chafee@chafee.senate.gov
Website: www.senate.gov/~chafee

Representatives:

Patrick J. Kennedy
Phone: 202-225-4911 Fax: 202-225-3290
E-mail: patrick.kennedy@mail.house.gov
Website: www.house.gov/patrickkennedy

James R. Langevin
Phone: 202-225-2735 Fax: 202-225-5976
E-mail: james.langevin@mail.house.gov
Website: www.house.gov/langevin

SOUTH CAROLINA

Senators:

Strom Thurmond
Phone: 202-224-5972 Fax: 202-224-1300
E-mail: senator@thurmond.senate.gov
Website: www.senate.gov/~thurmond

Ernest F. Hollings
Phone: 202-224-6121 Fax: 202-224-4293
E-mail: senator@hollings.senate.gov
Website: www.senate.gov/~hollings

Representatives:

Henry E. Brown, Jr.
Phone: 202-225-3175 Fax: 202-225-3407
E-mail: writehenrybrown@mail.house.gov
Website: www.house.gov/henrybrown

[Floyd Spence]
Phone: 202-225-2452 Fax: 202-225-2455
(died on 8/16/2001)

Lindsey Graham
Phone: 202-225-5301 Fax: 202-225-3216
Website: www.house.gov/graham

Jim DeMint
Phone: 202-225-6030 Fax: 202-226-1177
E-mail: jim.demint@mail.house.gov
Website: www.demint.house.gov

John M. Spratt, Jr.
Phone: 202-225-5501 Fax: 202-225-0464
Website: www.house.gov/spratt

James Clyburn
Phone: 202-225-3315 Fax: 202-225-2313
E-mail: jclyburn@mail.house.gov
Website: www.house.gov/clyburn

SOUTH DAKOTA

Senators:

Thomas A. Daschle
Phone: 202-224-2321 Fax: 202-224-7895
E-mail: tom_daschle@daschle.senate.gov
Website: www.senate.gov/~daschle

Tim Johnson
Phone: 202-224-5842 Fax: 202-228-5765
E-mail: tim@johnson.senate.gov
Website: johnson.senate.gov

Representatives:

John R. Thune
Phone: 202-225-2801 Fax: 202-225-5823
E-mail: jthune@mail.house.gov
Website: www.housae.gov/thune

TENNESSEE

Senators:

Fred Thompson
Phone: 202-224-4944 Fax: 202-228-3679
E-mail: senator_thompson@thompson.senate.gov
Website: www.senate.gov/~thompson

Bill Frist
Phone: 202-224-3344 Fax: 202-228-1264
E-mail: senator_frist@frist.senate.gov
Website: frist.senate.gov

Representatives:

William L. Jenkins
Phone: 202-225-6356 Fax: 202-225-5714
Website: www.house.gov/jenkins

John J. Duncan, Jr.
Phone: 202-225-5435 Fax: 202-225-6440
E-mail: jjduncan@mail.house.gov
Website: www.house.gov/duncan

Zach Wamp
Phone: 202-225-3271 Fax: 202-225-3494
Website: www.house.gov/wamp

Van Hilleary
Phone: 202-225-6831 Fax: 202-225-3272
E-mail: van.hilleary@mail.house.gov
Website: www.house.gov/hilleary

Bob Clement
Phone: 202-225-4311 Fax: 202-226-1035
E-mail: bob.clement@mail.house.gov
Website: www.house.gov/clement

Bart Gordon
Phone: 202-225-4231 Fax: 202-225-6887
E-mail: bart.gordon@mail.house.gov
Website: www.house.gov/gordon

Ed Bryant
Phone: 202-225-2811 Fax: 202-225-2989
Website: www.house.gov/bryant

John S. Tanner
Phone: 202-225-4714 Fax: 202-225-1765
Website: www,house.gov/tanner/index.htm

Harold E. Ford, Jr.
Phone: 202-225-3265 Fax: 202-225-5663
E-mail: rep.harold.ford.jr.@mail.house.gov
Website: www.house.gov/ford

TEXAS

Senators:

Phil Gramm
Phone: 202-224-2934 Fax: 202-228-2856
E-mail: phil_gramm@gramm.senate.gov
Website: www.senate.gov/senator/gramm.html

Kay Bailey Hutchison
Phone: 202-224-5922 Fax: 202-224-0776
E-mail: senator@hutchison.senate.gov
Website: www.senate.gov/~hutchison

Representatives:

Max A. Sandlin
Phone: 202-225-3035 Fax: 202-225-5866
Website: www.house.gov/sandlin

Jim Turner
Phone: 202-225-2401 Fax: 202-225-5955
E-mail: tx02wyr@mail.house.gov
Website: www.house.gov/turner

Sam Johnson
Phone: 202-225-4201 Fax: 202-225-1485
Website: www.house.gov/samjohnson

Ralph M. Hall
Phone: 202-225-6673 Fax: 202-225-3332
E-mail: rmhall@mail.house.gov
Website: www.house.gov/ralphhall

Pete Sessions
Phone: 202-225-2231 Fax: 202-225-5878
E-mail: petes@mail.house.gov
Website: wwww.house.gov/sessions

Joe Barton
Phone: 202-225-2002 Fax: 202-225-3052
Website: www.house.gov/barton

John A. Culberson
Phone: 202-225-2571 Fax: 202-225-4381
Website: www.house.gov/culberson

Kevin P. Brady
Phone: 202-225-4901 Fax: 202-225-5524
E-mail: rep.brady@mail.house.gov
Website: www.house.gov/brady

Nicholas V. Lampson
Phone: 202-225-6565 Fax: 202-225-5547
E-mail: nick.lampson@mail.house.gov
Website: www.house.gov/lampson

Lloyd Doggett
Phone: 202-225-4865 Fax: 202-225-3073
E-mail: lloyd.doggett@mail.house.gov
Website: www.house.gov/doggett

Chet Edwards
Phone: 202-225-6105 Fax: 202-225-0350
Website: www.house.gov/edwards

Kay Granger
Phone: 202-225-5071 Fax: 202-225-5683
E-mail: texas.granger@mail.house.gov
Website: www.house.gov/granger

Willliam "Mac" Thornberry
Phone: 202-225-3706 Fax: 202-225-3486
Website: www.house.gov/thornberry

Ron E. Paul
Phone: 202-225-2831 Fax: 202-226-4871
E-mail: rep.paul@mail.house.gov
Website: www.house.gov/paul

Ruben E. Hinojosa
Phone: 202-225-2531 Fax: 202-225-5688
E-mail: rep.hinojosa@mail.house.gov
Website: www.house.gov/hinojosa

Silvestre Reyes
Phone: 202-225-4831 Fax: 202-225-2016
E-mail: talk2silver@mail.house.gov
Website: www.house.gov/reyes

Charles W. Stenholm
Phone: 202-225-6605 Fax: 202-225-2234
Website: www.hosue.gov/stenholm

Sheila Jackson Lee
Phone: 202-225-3816 Fax: 202-225-3317
E-mail: tx18@mail.house.gov
Website: www.house.gov/jacksonlee

Larry Combest
Phone: 202-225-4005 Fax: 202-225-9615
Website: www.house.gov/combest

Charles A. Gonzalez
Phone: 202-225-3236 Fax: 202-225-1915
Website: www.house.gov/gonzalez

Lamar S. Smith
Phone: 202-225-4236 Fax: 202-225-8628
Website: lamarsmith.house.gov

Tom DeLay
Phone: 202-225-5951 Fax: 202-225-5241
Website: tomdelay.house.gov

Henry Bonilla
Phone: 202-225-4511 Fax: 202-225-2237
Website: www.house.gov/bonilla

Martin Frost
Phone: 202-225-3605 Fax: 202-225-4951
E-mail: martin.frost@mail.house.gov
Website: www.house.gov/frost

Ken Bentsen
Phone: 202-225-7508 Fax: 202-225-2947
E-mail: ken.bentsen@mail.house.gov
Website: www.house.gov/bentsen

Richard K. Armey
Phone: 202-225-7772 Fax: 202-226-8100
Website: armey.house.gov

Solomon P. Ortiz
Phone: 202-225-7742 Fax: 202-226-1134
Website: www.house.gov/ortiz

Ciro D. Rodriguez
Phone: 202-225-1640 Fax: 202-225-1641
Website: www.house.gov/rodriguez

Gene Green
Phone: 202-225-1688 Fax: 202-225-9903
E-mail: ask.gene@mail.house.gov
Website: www.house.gov/green

Eddie Bernice Johnson
Phone: 202-225-8885 Fax: 202-226-1477
E-mail: rep.e.b.johnson@mail.house.gov
Website: www.house.gov/ebjohnson

UTAH

Senators:

Orrin G. Hatch
Phone: 202-224-5251 Fax: 202-224-6331
E-mail: senator_hatch@hatch.senate.gov
Website: www.senate.gov/~hatch

Robert Bennett
Phone: 202-224-5444 Fax: 202-228-1168
E-mail: senator@bennett.senate.gov
Website: www.senate.gov/~bennett

Representatives:

James V. Hansen
Phone: 202-225-0453 Fax: 202-225-5857
Website: www.house.gov/hansen

James David Matheson
Phone: 202-225-3011 Fax: 202-225-5638
E-mail: jim.matheson@mail.house.gov
Website: www,house.gov/matheson

Chris Cannon
Phone: 202-225-7751 Fax: 202-225-5629
E-mail: cannon.ut03@mail.house.gov
Website: www.house.gov/cannon

VERMONT

Senators:

Patrick J. Leahy
Phone: 202-224-4242 Fax: 202-224-3479
E-mail: senator_leahy@leahy.senate.gov
Website: www.senate.gov/~leahy

James M. Jeffords
Phone: 202-224-5141 Fax: 202-228-0776
E-mail: vermont@jeffords.senate.gov
Website: www.senate.gov/~jeffords

Representatives:

Bernard Sanders
Phone: 202-225-4115 Fax: 202-225-6790
E-mail: bernie@mail.house.gov
Website: bernie.house.gov

VIRGINIA

Senators:

John W. Warner
Phone: 202-224-2023 Fax: 202-224-6295
E-mail: senator@warner.senate.gov
Website: warner.senate.gov

George Allen
Phone: 202-224-4024 Fax: 202-224-5432
E-mail: senator_allen@allen.senate.gov
Website: allen.senate.gov

Representatives:

Jo Ann S. Davis
Phone: 202-225-4261 Fax: 202-225-4382
E-mail: joann.davis@mail.house.gov
Website: www.house.gov/joanndavis

Edward L. Schrock
Phone: 202-225-4215 Fax: 202-225-4218
E-mail: ed.schrock@mail.house.gov
Website: schrock.house.gov

Bobby Scott
Phone: 202-225-8351 Fax: 202-225-8354
Website: www.house.gov/scott

Randy Forbes
Phone: 202-225-6365 Fax: 202-226-1170
Website: www.house.gov/forbes

Virgil H. Goode, Jr.
Phone: 202-225-4711 Fax: 202-225-5681
E-mail: rep.goode@mail.house.gov
Website: www.house.gov/goode

Bob Goodlatte
Phone: 202-225-5431 Fax: 202-225-9681
E-mail: talk2bob@mail.house.gov
Website: www.house.gov/goodlatte

Eric I. Cantor
Phone: 202-225-2815 Fax: 202-225-0011
E-mail: eric.cantor@mail.house.gov
Website: www.house.gov/cantor

James P. Moran
Phone: 202-225-4376 Fax: 202-225-0017
E-mail: jim.moran@mail.house.gov
Website: www.house.gov/moran

Rick Boucher
Phone: 202-225-3861 Fax: 202-225-0442
E-mail: ninthnet@mail.house.gov
Website: www.house.gov/boucher

Frank R. Wolf
Phone: 202-225-5136 Fax: 202-225-0437
Website: www.house.gov/wolf

Thomas M. Davis III
Phone: 202-225-1492 Fax: 202-225-3071
E-mail: tom.davis@mail.house.gov
Website: www.house.gov/tomdavis

WASHINGTON

Senators:

Patty Murray
Phone: 202-224-2621 Fax: 202-224-0238
E-mail: senator_murray@murray.senate.gov
Website: www.senate.gov/~murray

Maria Cantwell
Phone: 202-224-3441 Fax: 202-228-0514
Website: cantwell.senate.gov

Representatives:

Jay Inslee
Phone: 202-225-6311 Fax: 202-226-1606
E-mail: jay.inslee@mail.house.gov
Website: www.house.gov/inslee

Richard R. Larsen
Phone: 202-225-2605 Fax: 202-225-4420
E-mail: rick.larsen@mail.house.gov
Website: www.house.gov/larsen

Brian Baird
Phone: 202-225-3536 Fax: 202-225-3478
E-mail: brian.baird@mail.house.gov
Website: www.house.gov/baird

Doc Hastings
Phone: 202-225-5816 Fax: 202-225-3251
Website: www.house.gov/dochastings

George R. Nethercutt, Jr.
Phone: 202-225-2006 Fax: 202-225-3392
E-mail: george.nethercutt-pub@mail.house.gov
Website: www.house.gov/nethercutt

Norman D. Dicks
Phone: 202-225-5916 Fax: 202-226-1176
Website: www.house.gov/dicks

Jim McDermott
Phone: 202-225-3106 Fax: 202-225-6197
Website: www.house.gov/mcdermott

Jennifer Dunn
Phone: 202-225-7761 Fax: 202-225-8673
E-mail: dunnwa08@mail.house.gov
Website: www.house.gov/dunn

Adam Smith
Phone: 202-225-8901 Fax: 202-225-5893
E-mail: adam.smith@mail.house.gov
Website: www.house.gov/adamsmith

WEST VIRGINIA

Senators:

Robert C. Byrd
Phone: 202-224-3954 Fax: 202-228-0002
E-mail: senator_byrd@byrd.senate.gov
Website: www.senate.gov/~byrd

John D. Rockefeller
Phone: 202-224-6472 Fax: 202-224-7665
E-mail: senator@rockefeller.senate.gov
Website: www.senate.gov/~rockefeller

Representatives:

Alan B. Mollohan
Phone: 202-225-4172 Fax: 202-225-7564
Website: www.house.gov/mollohan

Shelley Moore Capito
Phone: 202-225-2711 Fax: 202-225-7856
Website: www.house.gov/capito

Nick J. Rahall II
Phone: 202-225-3452 Fax: 202-225-9061
E-mail: nrahall@mail.house.gov
Website: www.house.gov/rahall

WISCONSIN

Senators:

Herbert H. Kohl
Phone: 202-224-5653 Fax: 202-224-9787
E-mail: senator_kohl@kohl.senate.gov
Website: www.senate.gov/~kohl

Russ Feingold
Phone: 202-224-5323 Fax: 202-224-2725
Website: www.senate.gov/~feingold

Representatives:

Paul D. Ryan
Phone: 202-225-3031 Fax: 202-225-3393
Website: www.house.gov/ryan

Tammy Baldwin
Phone: 202-225-2906 Fax: 202-225-6942
E-mail: tammy.baldwin@mail.house.gov
Website: www.house.gov/baldwin

Ron J. Kind
Phone: 202-225-5506 Fax: 202-225-5739
E-mail: ron.kind@mail.house.gov
Website: www.house.gov/kind

Jerry Kleczka
Phone: 202-225-4572 Fax: 202-225-8135
Website: www.house.gov/kleczka

Thomas Barrett
Phone: 202-225-3571 Fax: 202-225-2185
E-mail: telltom@mail.house.gov
Website: www.house.gov/barrett

Thomas E. Petri
Phone: 202-225-2476 Fax: 202-225-2356
Website: www.house.gov/petri

David R. Obey
Phone: 202-225-3365
Website: www.house.gov/obey

Mark Green
Phone: 202-225-5665 Fax: 202-225-5729
E-mail: mark.green@mail.house.gov
Website: www.house.gov/markgreen

F. James Sensenbrenner, Jr.
Phone: 202-225-5101 Fax: 202-225-3190
E-mail: sensen09@mail.house.gov
Website: www.house.gov/sensenbrenner

WYOMING

Senators:

Craig Thomas
Phone: 202-224-6441 Fax: 202-224-1724
E-mail: craig@thomas.senate.gov
Website: www.senate.gov/~thomas

Michael B. Enzi
Phone: 202-224-3424 Fax: 202-228-0359
E-mail: senator@enzi.senate.gov
Website: enzi.senate.gov

Representative:

Barbara Cubin
Phone: 202-225-2311 Fax: 202-225-3057
E-mail: barbara.cubin@mail.house.gov
Website: www.house.gov/cubin

DISTRICT OF COLUMBIA

Representative:

Eleanor Holmes Norton
Phone: 202-225-8050 Fax: 202-225-3002
Website: www.house.gov/norton

AMERICAN SAMOA

Representative:

Eni F.H. Faleomavaega
Phone: 202-225-8577 Fax: 202-225-8757
E-mail: faleomavaega@mail.house.gov
Website: www.house.gov/faleomavaega

GUAM

Representative:

Robert A. Underwood
Phone: 202-225-1188 Fax: 202-226-0341
E-mail: guamtodc@mail.house.gov
Website: www.house.gov/underwood

PUERTO RICO

Representative:

Anibal Acevedo-Vila
Phone: 202-225-2615 Fax: 202-225-2154
E-mail: anibal@mail.house.gov
Website: www.house.gov/acevedo-vila

VIRGIN ISLANDS

Representative:

Donna M. Christian-Christensen
Phone: 202-225-1790 Fax: 202-225-5517
E-mail: donna.christensen@mail.house.gov
Website: www.house.gov/christian-christensen

HOUSE COMMITTEES

HOUSE COMMITTEE ON AGRICULTURE

DEPARTMENT OPERATIONS, OVERSIGHT, NUTRITION AND FORESTRY; GENERAL FARM COMMODITIES, RESOURCE CONSERVATION AND CREDIT; LIVESTOCK AND HORTICULTURE; RISK MANAGEMENT, RESEARCH AND SPECIALTY CROPS
Washington, DC 20515
Phone: 202-225-2171 Fax: 202-225-0917
Website: www.agriculture.house.gov

Founded: 1820
Membership: 52
Scope: National

Description: Adulteration of seeds, insect pests, and protection of birds and animals in forest reserves; agriculture generally; agricultural and industrial chemistry; agricultural colleges and experiment stations; agricultural economics and research; agricultural education extension services; agricultural production and marketing and stabilization of prices of agricultural products; animal industry and diseases of animals; crop insurance and soil conservation; dairy industry; entomology and plant quarantine; extension of farm credit and farm security; forestry in general, and forest reserves other than those created from the public domain; human nutrition and home economics; inspection of livestock and meat products; plant industry, soils, and agricultural engineering; rural electrification; commodities exchanges and rural development.

Contact(s):
Larry Combest, CHAIR

HOUSE COMMITTEE ON APPROPRIATIONS

AGRICULTURE, RURAL DEVELOPMENT, FOOD AND DRUG ADMINISTRATION; COMMERCE, JUSTICE, STATE, AND JUDICIARY; DISTRICT OF COLUMBIA; ENERGY AND WATER DEVELOPMENT; FOREIGN OPERATIONS, EXPORT FINANCING, AND RELATED PROGRAMS; INTERIOR; LABOR, HEALTH AND HUMANS
Washington, DC 20515
Phone: 202-225-2771
Website: www.house.gov

Founded: NA
Membership: 60
Scope: National

Description: Consists of 60 members: Appropriation of the revenue for the support of the government, rescissions of appropriations contained in appropriation acts, and transfers of unexpended balances.

Contact(s):
Bill Young, CHAIR

HOUSE COMMITTEE ON ENERGY AND COMMERCE

TELECOMMUNICATIONS, TRADE, AND CONSUMER PROTECTION; FINANCE AND HAZARDOUS MATERIALS; HEALTH AND ENVIRONMENT; ENERGY AND POWER; OVERSIGHT AND INVESTIGATIONS
Washington, DC 20515
Phone: 202-225-2927 Fax: 202-225-1919

Founded: NA
Membership: 125
Scope: National

Description: Jurisdiction: Interstate and foreign commerce generally; national energy policy generally; measures relating to the exploration, production, storage, supply, marketing, pricing, and regulation of energy resources, including all fossil fuels, solar energy, and other unconventional or renewable energy resources; measures relating to the conservation of energy resources; measures relating to the commercial application of energy technology; measures relating to energy information generally; measures relating to: (A) the generation and marketing of power (except by federally chartered or federal regional power marketing authorities), (B) the reliability and interstate transmission of, and ratemaking for, all power, and (C) the citing of generation facilities (except the installation of interconnections between government waterpower projects); interstate energy compacts; measures relating to general management of the Department of Energy, and the management and all functions of the Federal Energy Regulatory Commission; regulation of interstate and foreign communications; securities and exchanges; consumer affairs and consumer protection; travel and tourism; public health and quarantine; health and health facilities, except health care supported by payroll deductions; and biomedical research and development. The committee shall have the same jurisdiction with respect to regulation of nuclear facilities and of use of nuclear energy as it has with respect to regulation of non-nuclear facilities and of use of non-nuclear energy.

Contact(s):
Billy Tauzin, CHAIR
Dave Marventano, CHIEF OF STAFF
James Barnette, GENERAL COUNSEL

HOUSE COMMITTEE ON EDUCATION AND THE WORKFORCE

Washington, DC 20515
Phone: 202-225-4527 Fax: 202-225-9571
Website: edwrksorce.house.gov

Founded: NA
Membership: 47
Scope: national

Description: Jurisdiction: Measures relating to education or labor generally; child labor; Gallaudet College; Howard University; convict labor and the entry of goods made by convicts into interstate commerce; labor standards; labor statistics; mediation and arbitration of labor disputes; regulation or prevention of importation of foreign laborers under contract; food programs for children in schools; United States Employees' Compensation Commission; vocational rehabilitation; wages and hours of labor; welfare of miners; and work incentive programs.

Contact(s):
John Boehner, CHAIR
202-225-6205

HOUSE COMMITTEE ON INTERNATIONAL RELATIONS

AFRICA; ASIA AND THE PACIFIC; THE WESTERN HEMISPHERE; INTERNATIONAL ECONOMIC POLICY AND TRADE; INTERNATIONAL OPERATIONS AND HUMAN RIGHTS
Washington, DC 20515
Phone: 202-225-5021 Fax: 202-225-0225
E-mail: hirc@mail.house.gov
Website: www.house.gov/International_relations

Founded: NA
Membership: 50
Scope: National

Description: Jurisdiction: Foreign policy; international economic and environmental policy; international conferences and congresses; United Nations organizations; fishing agreements; nuclear export policy.

Contact(s):
Henry Hyde, CHAIR

HOUSE COMMITTEE ON RESOURCES

Washington, DC 20515
Phone: 202-225-2761
Website: www.house.gov/resources

Founded: NA
Membership: 52
Scope: National

Description: Consists of 52 members: Forest reserves and national parks created from the public domain; national parks lands; forfeiture of land grants and alien ownership, including alien ownership of mineral lands; geological survey; interstate compacts relating to apportionment of waters for irrigation purposes; irrigation and reclamation, including water supply for reclamation projects, and easements on public lands for irrigation projects, and acquisition of private lands when necessary to complete irrigation projects; measures relating to the care and management of Indians, including the care and allotment of Indian lands and general and special measures relating to Indian claims; measures (including funding measures) relating generally to the U.S. territories, commonwealths, and successor governments of the Trust Territory of the Pacific Islands, except measures concerning the federal tax system and federal appropriations; military parks and battlefields; national cemeteries administered by the Secretary of the Interior, and parks within the District of Columbia; mineral land laws and claims and entries thereunder; mineral resources of the public lands; mining interests generally; mining schools and experimental stations; petroleum conservation on the public lands and conservation of the radium supply in the U.S.; preservation of prehistoric ruins and objects of interest on the public domain; public lands generally, including entry, easements, and grazing thereon; relations of the U.S. with the Indians and the Indian tribes; regulation of the domestic nuclear energy industry, including regulation of research and development of reactors and nuclear regulatory research. Also special oversight functions with respect to all programs affecting Indians and nonmilitary nuclear energy and research and development, including the disposal of nuclear waste.

Contact(s):
James Hansen, CHAIR
Allen Freemyer, CHIEF OF STAFF

HOUSE COMMITTEE ON RULES

Washington, DC 20515
Phone: 202-225-9191 Fax: 202-225-6763
Website: www.house.gov/rules

Founded: NA
Membership: 13
Scope: National

Description: Consists of 13 members: Grants rules outlining conditions for floor debate on legislation reported by regular standing committees, which includes granting emergency waivers under the Congressional Budget Act of 1974; also has legislative authority to create committees, change the rules of the House, and provide order of business of the House.

Contact(s):
David Drier, CHAIR
Porter Goss, VICE CHAIR

HOUSE COMMITTEE ON TRANSPORTATION AND INFRASTRUCTURE

Washington, DC 20515
Phone: 202-225-4472 Fax: 202-226-1270
Website: www.house.gov/transportation

Founded: NA
Membership: 20
Scope: National
Description: Consists of 73 members.

Contact(s):
Don Young, CHAIRMAN

SENATE COMMITTEES

SENATE COMMITTEE ON AGRICULTURE, NUTRITION, AND FORESTRY

PRODUCTION AND PRICE COMPETITIVENESS; MARKETING, INSPECTION, AND PRODUCT PROMOTION; FORESTRY, CONSERVATION, AND RURAL REVITALIZATION; RESEARCH, NUTRITION, AND GENERAL LEGISLATION
Washington, DC 20510
Phone: 202-224-2035
Website: agriculture.senate.gov

Founded: NA
Scope: National

Description: Concerned with agriculture and agricultural commodities; inspection of livestock, meat, and agricultural products; animal industry and diseases; pests and pesticides; agricultural extension services and experiment stations; forestry in general and forest reserves and wilderness areas other than those created from the public domain; agricultural economics and research; human nutrition; home economics; farm credit and farm security; rural development, rural electrification and watersheds; agricultural production, marketing, and stabilization of prices; crop insurance and soil conservation; school nutrition programs; food stamp programs; food from fresh waters; plant industry, soils, and agricultural engineering. Such committee shall also study and review, on a comprehensive basis, matters relating to food, nutrition, and hunger, both in the United States and foreign countries, and rural affairs and report thereon from time to time.

Contact(s):
Tom Harkin, CHAIRMAN
Robert Sturm, CHIEF CLERK
Mark Halverson, CHIEF OF STAFF
David Johnson, COUNSEL
Keith Luse, MINORITY STAFF DIRECTOR
Richard Lugar, RANKING REPUBLICAN MEMBER

SENATE COMMITTEE ON APPROPRIATIONS

Washington, DC 20510
Phone: 202-224-3471 Fax: 202-224-8553
Website: www.appropriations.senate.gov

Founded: NA
Scope: National

Description: Concerned with all proposed legislation, messages, petitions, memorials, and other matters relating to appropriation of the revenue for the support of the federal government.

Contact(s):
Robert Byrd, CHAIR
Terry Sauvain, STAFF DIRECTOR

SENATE COMMITTEE ON COMMERCE, SCIENCE AND TRANSPORTATION

AVIATION; COMMUNICATIONS; CONSUMER AFFAIRS, FOREIGN COMMERCE AND TOURISM; SCIENCE, TECHNOLOGY, AND SPACE; SURFACE TRANSPORTATION AND MERCHANT MARINE; OCEANS AND FISHERIES
Washington, DC 20510
Phone: 202-224-5115 Fax: 202-228-5769
Website: commerce.senate.gov

Founded: NA

Description: Concerned with interstate commerce; transportation; regulation of interstate common carriers, including railroads, buses, trucks, vessels, pipelines, and civil aviation; merchant marine and navigation; marine and ocean navigation, safety and transportation, including navigational aspects of deepwater ports; Coast Guard; inland waterways, except construction; communications; regulation of consumer products and services, except for credit, financial services, and housing; the Panama Canal, except for maintenance, operation, administration, sanitation, and government, and interoceanic canals generally; standards and measurements; highway safety; science, engineering and technology research, and development and policy; nonmilitary aeronautical and space sciences; transportation and commerce aspects of Outer Continental Shelf lands; marine fisheries; coastal zone management; oceans, weather, and atmospheric activities; sports.

Contact(s):
Ernest Hollings, CHAIR

SENATE COMMITTEE ON ENERGY AND NATURAL RESOURCES

Washington, DC 20510
Phone: 202-224-4971 Fax: 202-224-6163

Founded: NA
Membership: 22
Scope: National

Description: Concerned with the comprehensive study and review of matters relating to energy and resources development. Jursdiction: Coal production, distribution, and utilization; energy policy; energy regulation and conservation; energy related aspects of deepwater ports; energy research and development; extraction of minerals from oceans and Outer Continental Shelf lands; hydroelectric power, irrigation, and reclamation; mining education and research; mining, mineral lands, mining claims, and mineral conservation; national parks, recreation areas, wilderness areas, wild and scenic rivers, historical sites, military parks and battlefields, and on the public domain, preservation of prehistoric ruins and objects of interest; naval petroleum reserves in Alaska; nonmilitary development of nuclear energy; oil and gas production and distribution; public lands and forests, including farming and grazing thereon, and mineral extraction therefrom; solar energy systems; and territorial possessions of the United States, including trusteeships.

Contact(s):
Jeff Bingaman, CHAIR

SENATE COMMITTEE ON ENVIRONMENT AND PUBLIC WORKS

TRANSPORTATION AND INFRASTRUCTURE; SUPERFUND; WASTE CONTROL AND RISK ASSESMENT; CLEAN AIR, WETLANDS, PRIVATE PROPERTY, AND NUCLEAR SAFETY; DRINKING WATER, FISHERIES, AND WILDLIFE
Washington, DC 20510
Phone: 202-224-6176 Fax: 202-224-1273
Website: www.senate.gov/~epw

Founded: NA
Membership: 50
Scope: National

Description: Committee on Environment and Public Works, to which shall be referred all proposed legislation, messages, petitions, memorials, and other matters relating to the following subjects: environmental policy; environmental research and development; ocean dumping; fisheries and wildlife; environmental aspects of Outer Continental Shelf lands; solid waste disposal and recycling; environmental effects of toxic substances, other than pesticides; water resources; flood control and improvements of rivers and harbors, including environmental aspects of deepwater ports; public works, bridges, and dams; water pollution; air pollution; noise pollution; nonmilitary environmental regulation and control of nuclear energy; regional economic development; construction and maintenance of highways; public buildings and improved grounds of the United States generally, including federal buildings in the District of Columbia. Such committee shall also study and review on a comprehensive basis matters relating to environmental protection and resource utilization and conservation, and report thereon from time to time.

Contact(s):
Jim Jeffords, CHAIR
Ken Connolly, DEMOCRAT STAFF DIRECTOR
J. Sliter, MINORITY STAFF DIRECTOR
Dave Conover, REPUBLICAN STAFF DIRECTOR

SENATE COMMITTEE ON FOREIGN RELATIONS

AFRICAN AFFAIRS; EAST ASIAN AND PACIFIC AFFAIRS; EUROPEAN AFFFAIRS; INTERNATIONAL ECONOMIC POLICY, EXPORT AND TRADE PROMOTION; INTERNATIONAL OPERATIONS; NEAR EASTERN AND SOUTH ASIAN AFFAIRS; WESTERN HEMISPHERE, PEACE CORPS, NARCOTICS AND TERRORISM
Washington, DC 20510-6225
Phone: 202-224-4651 Fax: 202-228-1608
Website: www.foreign.state.gov

Founded: NA
Membership: 10
Scope: National

Description: Jurisdiction: Foreign and national security policy; international treaties, conferences, and congresses; World Bank and International Monetary Fund; oceans and international environmental and scientific affairs; humanitarian assistance and hunger; and United Nations and its affiliated organizations.

Contact(s):
Russel Feingold, CHAIR, SUBCOMMITTEE ON AFRICAN AFFAIRS
Paul Sarbanes, CHAIR, SUBCOMMITTEE ON INTERNATIONAL ECONOMIC POLICY, EXPORT AND TRADE PROMOTION
Barbara Boxer, CHAIR, SUBCOMMITTEE ON INTERNATIONAL OPERATIONS AND TERRORISM
Paul Wellstone, CHAIR, SUBCOMMITTEE ON NEAR EASTERN AND SOUTH ASIAN AFFAIRS
Christopher Dodd, CHAIR, SUBCOMMITTEE ON WESTERN HEMISPHERE, PEACE CORPS AND NARCOTICS

SENATE COMMITTEE ON HEALTH, EDUCATION, LABOR, AND PENSIONS

AGING; CHILDREN, FAMILY, DRUGS, AND ALCOHOLISM; EDUCATION, ARTS, AND HUMANITIES; EMPLOYMENT AND PRODUCTIVITY; HANDICAPPED; LABOR
Washington, DC 20510
Phone: 202-224-5375
Website: labor.senate.gov

Founded: NA
Contact(s):
Edward Kennedy, CHAIR

U.S. FEDERAL AND INTERNATIONAL GOVERNMENT AGENCIES

A

ADVISORY COUNCIL ON HISTORIC PRESERVATION

1100 Pennsylvania Ave., NW, #809,
The Old Post Office Bldg.
Washington, DC 20004 United States
Phone: 202-606-8503 Fax: 202-606-8672
E-mail: achp@achp.gov
Website: www.achp.gov

Founded: N/A
Membership: 1–100
Scope: National
Description: An independent federal agency, the Council is the primary policy advisor to the President and Congress on historic preservation matters and guides, and other federal agencies to ensure their actions do not result in unnecessary harm to the nation's historic properties. The Council, established by the National Historic Preservation Act of 1966, is made up of the heads of seven federal departments whose actions regularly affect historic properties.
Keyword(s): Land Issues, Pollution (general), Public Health, Reduce/Reuse/Recycle
Contact(s):
John Fowler, Executive Director

APPALACHIAN REGIONAL COMMISSION

1666 Connecticut Ave., NW., Suite 700
Washington, DC 20009 United States
Phone: 202-884-7700 Fax: 202-884-7691
Website: www.arc.gov

Founded: 1965
Membership: 1–100
Scope: Regional
Description: To promote economic and human development in the 13-state Appalachian region and to provide a framework for joint federal and state efforts. Includes 406 counties in Alabama, Georgia, Kentucky, Maryland, Mississippi, New York, North Carolina, Ohio, Pennsylvania, South Carolina, Tennessee, Virginia and West Virginia.
Publication(s): Appalachia-Quarterly
Contact(s):
Tom Hunter, Executive Director; 202-884-7700
Michael Kiernan, Public Information; 202-884-7771
Paul Patton, States Co-Chairman
Bill Walker, States Washington Representative; 202-884-7746
Jesse White, Federal Co-Chairman; 202-884-7660

C

C AND O CANAL NATIONAL HISTORICAL PARK

NATURAL RESOURCES DIVISION
P.O. Box 4
Sharpsburg, MD 21782 United States
Phone: 301-739-4200 Fax: 301-739-5275
E-mail: CHOH_Superintendent@nps.gov
Website: www.nps.gov/choh/

Founded: N/A

CALIFORNIA COOPERATIVE FISHERY RESEARCH UNIT (USGS)

CO-OP FISH UNIT
Humboldt State University
1 Harpst Street
Arcata, CA 95521 United States
Phone: 707-826-3268 Fax: 707-826-3269
E-mail: cuca@humboldt.edu
Website: www.humboldt.edu/~cuca

Founded: 1967
Membership: 1–100
Scope: National
Description: A cooperative research and education group consisting of Humboldt State Univ., Calif. Dept. of Fish and Game and U.S. Geological Survey.
Publication(s): See publication website
Keyword(s): Ecosystems (precious), Water Habitats & Quality
Contact(s):
Walter Duffy, Leader; 707-826-5644; wgd7001@humboldt.edu
Kenneth Cummins, Senior Advisory Scientist; kenwcummins@aol.com
Margaret Wilzbach, Assistant Leader; 707-826-5645; paw7002@humboldt.edu

CANADIAN WILDLIFE SERVICE

3rd Fl., Place Vincent Massey, 351 St. Joseph Blvd.
Hull, K1A 0H3 Quebec Canada
Phone: 819-997-1301 Fax: 819-953-7177

Founded: N/A
Membership: 1–100
Scope: Regional
Publication(s): The Canadian Field Naturalist
Contact(s):
David Brackett, Director General; 819-997-1301; Fax: 819-953-7177

CANADIAN WILDLIFE SERVICE

ENVIRONMENT CANADA
Ottawa, K1A 0H3 Ontario Canada
Phone: 819-997-1095 Fax: 819-997-2754
Website: www.cws-scf.ec.gc.ca/

Founded: N/A
Description: Canada Wildlife Service is a federal agency devoted to the protection and management of migratory birds and nationally important wildlife habitat, endangered species, research on nationally important wildlife issues, control of international trade in endangered species, and international treaties.
Publication(s): Full list of publications is available on the organization's website.
Contact(s):
Ken Sato, Director General; 819-953-8065; Fax: 819-994-2724

COLUMBIA RIVER INTER-TRIBAL FISH COMMISSION

729 NE Oregon, Suite 200
Portland, OR 97232 United States
Phone: 503-238-0667 Fax: 503-235-4228
Website: www.critfc.org

Founded: 1977
Scope: Regional
Description: The Commission was formed to return salmon to Columbia basin rivers and to protect the Indian tribes' treaty-reserved fishing rights.
Contact(s):
Don Sampson, Executive Director

COLUMBIA RIVER INTER-TRIBAL FISH COMMISSION

STREAMNET LIBRARY
729 NE Oregon St., Suite 190
Portland, OR 97232 United States
Phone: 503-731-1304 Fax: 503-731-1260
E-mail: fishmail@critfc.org
Website: www.fishlib.org

Founded: N/A
Description: The StreamNet Library is a cooperative venture of the region's fish and wildlife agencies and tribes and serves these organizations. It is a fisheries and aquatic species library emphasizing management and restoration of the Columbia

River salmon and sturgeon, providing data and data services. Open to the public.

Keyword(s): Wildlife & Species

Contact(s):

David Liberty, Library Technician; libd@critfc.org
Laurie Nock, Assistant Librarian; nocl@critfc.org
Lenora Ofterdahl, Head Librarian; oftl@critfc.org

CONSERVATION COUNCIL OF WESTERN AUSTRALIA, INC.

2 Delhi St.
West Perth, West Australia, 6000 Australia
Phone: 08-9420-7266 Fax: 08-9420-7273
E-mail: conswa@conservationwa.asn.au
Website: www.conservationwa.asn.au/

Founded: 1970
Membership: 101–1,000
Scope: State
Description: To promote the cause of conservation and environmentalism throughout the state of Western Australia; and to serve as a liaison to other bodies dealing with conservation and environmental issues.

Contact(s):

Rachel Siewert, Contact

COUNCIL ON ENVIRONMENTAL QUALITY

722 Jackson Pl., NW
Washington, DC 20503 United States
Phone: 202-456-6224 Fax: 202-456-2710
Website: www.eop.gov/ceq

Founded: 1970
Membership: 1–100
Scope: International
Description: CEQ serves as the source of environmental expertise and policy analysis for the President and other organizations within the Executive Office of the President, and provides for coordination between departments and agencies. It is also charged with implementing statutory or regulatory requirements and programs.
Publication(s): CEQ Annual Report

Contact(s):

Philip Cooney, Chief of Staff
Dave Anderson, Associate Director Congressional Affairs
Cameron Bailey, Special Assistant
Dinah Bear, General Counsel
Jim Connaughton, Chairman
Bill Leary, Associate Director for Natural Resources
Elizabeth Slotpe, Associate Director
V. Stevens, Associate Director
Sam Thurstrom, Associate Director of Communications

D

DELAWARE RIVER BASIN COMMISSION

P.O. Box 7360
West Trenton, NJ 08628-0360 United States
Phone: 609-883-9500, ext. 200 Fax: 609-883-9522
E-mail: drbc@drbc.state.nj.us
Website: www.drbc.net

Founded: 1961
Membership: 1–100
Scope: Regional
Description: Delaware River Basin Commission (DRBC) is an interstate/federal compact organization managing water resources without regard to political boundaries. The basin includes area in NY, NJ, PA & DE. DRBC adopts and promotes "uniform and coordinated policies for water conservation, control, use, and management in the basin." Priorities include: PCB TMDL-Delaware Estuary; anti-deg. program; fair allocation of water, and comprehensive water resources plan.
Publication(s): Administrative Manual and Water Code, Water Resources Program, Annual Report, Delaware River Basic Compact

Contact(s):

Carol Collier, Executive Director
Christopher Roberts, Public Information Officer

DEPARTMENT OF CANADIAN HERITAGE

PORTFOLIO AND CORPORATE AFFAIRS
15 Eddy St. Room 12G (15-12-8)
Hull, K1A 0M5 Quebec Canada
Phone: 819-994-3046 Fax: 819-953-4796

Founded: N/A
Scope: National

Contact(s):

Yazmime Laroche, Assistant Deputy Minister; 819-994-3046

DEPARTMENT OF FISHERIES AND OCEANS

CANADA DIVISION
200 Kent St. Centennial Towers, 13th Floor
Ottawa, K1A 0E6 Ontario Canada
Phone: 613-993-0999 Fax: 613-990-1866
Website: www.dfo-mpo.gc.ca

Founded: N/A
Scope: National
Description: Fisheries and Oceans Canada is responsible for policies and programs in support of Canada's economic, ecological, and scientific interests in oceans and inland water; and for safe, effective and environmentally sound marine services responsive to the needs of Canadians in a global economy.

Contact(s):

Herb Dhaliwal, Minister; 613-992-3474
Wayne Wouters, Deputy Minister; 613-993-2200

DEPARTMENT OF FISHERIES AND OCEANS

CANADIAN COAST GUARD
200 Kent St.
Ottawa, K1A 0E6 Ontario Canada
Phone: 613-998-1571 Fax: 613-990-2780
Website: www.ccg-gcc.gc.ca

Founded: N/A
Membership: 101–1,000
Scope: International

Contact(s):

Dave Faulkner, Director General: Integrated Technical Support; 613-998-1638; Fax: 613-993-5333
Charles Gadula, Director of Fleet; 613-993-1849; gadulac@dfo-mpo-gc.ca
Debra Normoyle, Director General: Marine Programs; 613-990-5508; Fax: 613-991-4982
Anne O'Toole, Director General: Integrated Business Management; 613-998-1440; Fax: 613-990-3480
John Adams, Assistant Deputy Minister, Marine Services/ Commissioner; 613-998-1571; Fax: 613-990-2780
Guy Bujold, Deputy Commissioner; 613-998-1570; Fax: 613-990-2780

DEPARTMENT OF FISHERIES AND OCEANS

CORPORATE SERVICES
200 Kent St.
Ottawa, K1A 0E6 Ontario Canada
Phone: 613-993-0868 Fax: 613-990-3604
Website: www.intra.dfo-mpo.gc.ca/index.htm

Founded: N/A
Membership: 101–1,000
Scope: National

Contact(s):

Robert Bergeron, Director General: Small Craft Harbours; 613-993-1937

Yves Dupuis, Director General: Human Resources; 613-990-0023
Mike Hawkes, Director General: Finance and Administration; 613-993-9372
Paul Hession, Director General: Information Management and Technology Services; 613-993-2051
Donna Petrachenko, Assistant Deputy Minister; 613-993-0868

DEPARTMENT OF FISHERIES AND OCEANS

LEGAL SERVICES
200 Kent St.
Ottawa, K1A 0E6 Ontario Canada
Phone: 613-993-0966
Website: www.dfo-mpo.gc.ca

Founded: N/A
Scope: National
Description: Canadian Government

DEPARTMENT OF FISHERIES AND OCEANS

OCEANS
200 Kent St.
Ottawa, K1A 0E6 Ontario Canada
Phone: 613-993-0850-000 Fax: 613-990-2768
Website: www.intra.dfo-mpo.gc.ca

Founded: N/A
Contact(s):
Paul Cuillerier, Director General: Habitat Management and Environmental Science; 613-991-1280
Daniel McDougall, Director General: Oceans Directorate; 613-990-0001
Matthew King, Assistant Deputy Minister; 613-993-0850

DEPARTMENT OF FISHERIES AND OCEANS

POLICY
200 Kent St.
Ottawa, K1A 0E6 Ontario Canada
Phone: 613-993-1808 Fax: 613-993-6958

Founded: N/A
Membership: 1–100
Scope: National
Contact(s):
Sharon Ashley, Director General: Policy, Coordination and Liaison; 613-990-0007
Lori Ridgeway, Director General: Economic and Policy Analysis; 613-993-1914
Paul Thompson, Director General: Strategic Priorities and Planning; 613-990-0146
Richard Wex, Director General: Office of Sustainable Aquaculture; 613-993-1872
Liseanne Forand, Assistant Deputy Minister; 613-993-1808

DEPARTMENT OF FISHERIES AND OCEANS

SCIENCE
200 Kent St.
Ottawa, K1A 0E6 Ontario Canada
Phone: 613-990-5123 Fax: 613-990-5113
Website: www.intra.dfo-mpo.gc.ca

Founded: N/A
Scope: National
Contact(s):
Serge Labonte, Director General: Fisheries and Biodiversity Science Director; 613-990-9082
Elizabeth Marsollier, Director General: Ocean and Aquaculture Science Directorate; 613-990-0271
Tony O'Connor, Director General: Canadian Hydrography Services; 613-995-4413
Brian Wilson, Director General: Program Planning and Coordination; 613-990-0149
John Davis, Assistant Deputy Minister; 613-990-5123

E

EGYPTIAN ENVIRONMENTAL AFFAIRS AGENCY

30, Misr Helwan St., Maadi
Cairo, Egypt
Phone: 25256442 Fax: 02-525-6451

Founded: N/A
Publication(s): Annual Report; EAS, National Workplan and Law
Contact(s):
Nadia Ebeid, H.E. Minister
Nirvana Khadr; 025256447

ENVIRONMENT CANADA

351 St. Joseph Boulevard
Hull, K1A 0H3 Quebec Canada
Website: www.ec.ga.ca

Founded: N/A
Description: Purpose is to formulate and take action to meet threats to environment arising through adverse impacts of human activities. Priority responsibilities include toxic chemicals, acid rain ozone depletion, urban smog, and the ongoing management of concerns such as hazardous wastes.
Contact(s):
David Anderson, Minister of the Environment; 819-997-1441; David.Anderson@ec.ga.ca

ENVIRONMENTAL CONSERVATION SERVICE

1 Place Vincent Massey
351 St. Joseph Blvd.
Hull, K1A 0H3 Quebec Canada
Phone: 819-994-4750 Fax: 819-997-1541
Website: www.infolane.ec.gc.ca

Founded: N/A
Membership: 1–100
Scope: International
Description: In Environmental Conservation Service (ECS) our goal is to ensure that future generations of Canadians inherit a natural environment as rich as the one we enjoy today. We work with many partners—individual Canadians, environmental and community groups, aboriginal peoples, industry, other levels of government, and international organizations. We provide information on the natural environment to Canadians.
Contact(s):
Ken Sato, Director General; 819-953-8065; Fax: 819-994-2724
Karen Brown, Assistant Deputy Minister; 819-997-2161; Fax: 819-997-1541

ENVIRONMENTAL CONSERVATION SERVICE

ATLANTIC REGION ENVIRONMENT CANADA
17 Waterfowl Lane
Sackville, E4L 4N1 New Brunswick Canada
Phone: 506-364-5044 Fax: 506-364-5062
E-mail: nature@ec.gc.ca
Website: www.ec.gc.ca

Founded: N/A
Scope: International
Contact(s):
George Finney, Regional Director

ENVIRONMENTAL CONSERVATION SERVICE

ECOSYSTEM AND ENVIRONMENTAL RESOURCES DIRECTORATE
6th Fl., Place Vincent Massey, 351 St. Joseph Blvd.
Hull, K1A 0H3 Quebec Canada
Phone: 819-997-5674 Fax: 819-994-2541

Founded: N/A
Scope: International

Contact(s):
Jennifer Moore, Director General; 819-997-5674; Fax: 819-994-2541

ENVIRONMENTAL CONSERVATION SERVICE
PACIFIC AND YUKON REGION
ENVIRONMENT CANADA
Suite 700, 1200 West 73rd Ave.
Vancouver, V6P 6H9 British Columbia Canada
Phone: 604-664-4065 Fax: 604-664-9195
Website: www.ec.gc.ca

Founded: N/A

Contact(s):
Don Fast, Regional Director, Acting

ENVIRONMENTAL CONSERVATION SERVICE
PRAIRIE AND NORTHERN REGION
CANADIAN WILDLIFE SERVICE
4999-98th Ave.
Edmonton, T6B 2X3 Alberta Canada
Phone: 780-951-8853 Fax: 780-495-2615
Website: www.ec.gc.ca

Founded: N/A
Membership: 1–100
Scope: Regional

Contact(s):
Gerald McKeating, Regional Director

ENVIRONMENTAL CONSERVATION SERVICE
QUEBEC REGION ENVIRONMENT CANADA
Canadian Wildlife Service, 1141 Route de l'Eglise, P.O. Box 10100, 9th Floor
Sainte-Foy, G1V 4H5 Quebec Canada
Phone: 418-648-2543 Fax: 418-649-6475

Founded: N/A

Contact(s):
Albin Tramblay, Regional Director; 418-648-7808

ENVIRONMENTAL PROTECTION AGENCY
1200 Pennsylvania Ave. NW
Washington, DC 20460 United States
Phone: 202-260-2090 Fax: 202-564-4613
Website: www.epa.gov

Founded: N/A
Membership: 10,001–100,000
Scope: State
Description: The Environmental Protection Agency (EPA) was established as an independent agency in the Executive Branch of the U.S. Government, pursuant to Reorganization Plan No. 3 of 1970, effective December 2, 1970. EPA endeavors to achieve systematic control and abatement of pollution, by properly administering and integrating a variety of research, monitoring, standard-setting, and enforcement activities.

Contact(s):
Donald Barnes, Science Advisory Board Director; 202-260-4125
Jeanette Brown, Small and Disadvantaged Business Utilization Director; 202-260-4100
Jay Benforado, Associate Administrator for Reinvention, Acting; 202-260-1849
Joseph Crapa, Associate Administrator for Congressional Affairs; 202-260-5200
Linda Fisher, Deputy Administrator
Scott Fulton, General Counsel, Acting; 202-260-8064
Sallyanne Harper, Chief Financial Officer, Acting; 202-260-1151
W. Ryan, Comptroller; 202-260-9674
Nikki Tinsley, Inspector General, Acting; 202-260-3137
Loretta Ucelli, Associate Administrator for Communications; 202-260-9828
Christie Whitman, Administrator

ENVIRONMENTAL PROTECTION AGENCY
901 N. 5th St.
Kansas City, KS 66101 United States
Phone: 913-551-7000
Website: www.epa.gov/region/

Founded: N/A
Membership: 101–1,000
Scope: Regional

Contact(s):
William Rice, Regional Administrator

ENVIRONMENTAL PROTECTION AGENCY
1650 Arch St.
Philadelphia, PA 19103 United States
Phone: 215-814-5000 Fax: 215-814-5103
Website: www.epa.gov/region/

Founded: N/A
Membership: 1,001–10,000
Scope: Regional

Contact(s):
Donald Welsh, Regional Administrator

ENVIRONMENTAL PROTECTION AGENCY
ADMINISTRATION AND RESOURCES MANAGEMENT
1200 Pennsylvania Avenue NW
Washington, DC 20460 United States
Phone: 202-564-4700
Website: www.epa.gov

Founded: N/A

Contact(s):
Mark Day, Director of Information Resources Management, Acting; 202-260-4465
William Henderson, Director of Administration, Cincinnati, Oh; 513-569-7910
William Laxton, Director of Administration and Resources Management; 919-541-2258
David O'Connor, Human Resources and Organizational Services Director; 202-260-4467
Christie Whitman, Administrator; 202-260-4600

ENVIRONMENTAL PROTECTION AGENCY
AIR AND RADIATION
1200 Pennsylvania Ave. NW
Washington, DC 20460 United States
Phone: 202-564-4700
Website: www.epa.gov/oeca

Founded: N/A

Contact(s):
Margo Oge, Mobile Sources Director; 202-233-7645
John Seitz, Air Quality Planning and Standards Director; 919-541-5504
Paul Stoplman, Atmospheric Programs Director; 202-564-9150
Lawrence Weinstock, Radiation and Indoor Air Director, Acting; 202-564-9370
Robert Perciasepe, Assistant Administrator; 202-260-7400
Richard Wilson, Deputy Administrator; 202-260-7400

ENVIRONMENTAL PROTECTION AGENCY
ENFORCEMENT AND COMPLIANCE
1200 Pennsylvania Avenue NW
Washington, DC 20460 United States
Phone: 202-564-4700
Website: www.epa.gov/oeca/

Founded: N/A

Contact(s):
Barry Breen, Site Remediation Enforcement Director; 202-564-5110
Barry Hill, Environmental Justice Director, Acting; 202-564-2515; Fax: 202-501-0740

Richard Sanderson, Federal Activities Director; 202-564-2400
Eric Schaffer, Regulatory Enforcement Director; 202-564-2220
Gregory Snyder, Compliance Director; 202-564-2461

ENVIRONMENTAL PROTECTION AGENCY
PREVENTION, PESTICIDES, AND TOXIC SUBSTANCES
1200 Pennsylvania Avenue NW
Ariel Rios Bldg.
Washington, DC 20460 United States
Website: www.epa.gov/opptsfrs

Founded: N/A

Contact(s):
Marcia Mulkey, Pesticide Programs Director; 703-305-7090
William Sanders, Pollution Prevention and Toxics Director; 202-260-3810
Stephen Johnson, Assistant Administrator; 202-260-2902

ENVIRONMENTAL PROTECTION AGENCY
REGION I (CT, ME, MA, NH, RI, VT)
1 Congress Street, Suite 1100
Boston, MA 02203-0001 United States
Phone: 617-918-1111
Website: www.epa.gov/region/01

Founded: N/A

Contact(s):
John Devillars, Regional Administrator; 617-918-1010

ENVIRONMENTAL PROTECTION AGENCY
REGION II (NJ, NY, PR, VI)
290 Broadway
New York, NY 10007-1866 United States
Phone: 212-637-3000 Fax: 212-637-5046
Website: www.epa.gov/region/02

Founded: 1970
Membership: N/A
Scope: Local, State, Regional, National, International
Description: This regional office of the U.S. Environmental Protection Agency serves New Jersey, New York, Puerto Rico and the seven federally recognized Tribal Nations located within the region.

Contact(s):
Jane Kenny, Regional Administrator; 212-367-5000
William Muszynski, Deputy Regional Administrator

ENVIRONMENTAL PROTECTION AGENCY
REGION IV (AL, FL, GA, KY, MS, NC, SC, TN)
61 Forsyth St., S.W.
Atlanta, GA 30303 United States
Phone: 404-562-9900 Fax: 404-562-8174
Website: www.epa.gov/region/04

Founded: N/A
Membership: 1,001–10,000
Scope: Regional

Contact(s):
Stanley Meiburg, Contact

ENVIRONMENTAL PROTECTION AGENCY
REGION V (IL, IN, MI, NM, OH, WI)
77 West Jackson Blvd.
Chicago, IL 60604-3507 United States
Phone: 312-353-2000 Fax: 312-353-1120
Website: www.epa.gov/region05/

Founded: N/A

Scope: Regional

Contact(s):
Thomas Skinner, Regional Administrator
David Ulrich, Deputy Regional Administrator; 312-886-3000

ENVIRONMENTAL PROTECTION AGENCY
REGION VI (AR, LA, NM, OK, TX)
Fountain Place, 12th Fl., Suite 1200, 1445 Ross Ave.
Dallas, TX 75202-2733 United States
Phone: 214-665-6444
Website: www.epa.gov/region06/

Founded: N/A
Membership: 101–1,000
Scope: International

Contact(s):
Gregg Cooke, Regional Adminstrator; 214-665-2100

ENVIRONMENTAL PROTECTION AGENCY
REGION VIII (CO, MT, ND, SD, UT, WY)
999 18th St.
Denver, CO 80202-2466 United States
Phone: 303-312-6312 Fax: 303-312-6363
Website: www.epa.gov/region08/

Founded: N/A
Membership: 101–1,000
Scope: Regional

Contact(s):
Jack McGraw, Regional Administrator (Acting)

ENVIRONMENTAL PROTECTION AGENCY
REGION IX (GU, AS, NV, HI, CA, AZ)
75 Hawthorne St.
San Francisco, CA 94105 United States
Phone: 415-744-1702
Website: www.epa.gov/region/09

Founded: N/A

Scope: International

Contact(s):
Laura Yoshii, Regional Administrator; yoshii.laura@epa.gov

ENVIRONMENTAL PROTECTION AGENCY
REGION X (WA, OR, ID, AK)
1200 Sixth Ave.
Seattle, WA 98101 United States
Phone: 206-553-1200 Fax: 206-553-0149
E-mail: epa-seattle@epamail.epa.gov
Website: www.epa.gov/region10/

Founded: 1970
Membership: 101–1,000
Scope: Local, State, Regional, National, International
Description: Responsible for implementing federal programs in Alaska, Oregon, Idaho and Washington.
Keyword(s): Agriculture/Farming, Air Quality/Atmosphere, Ecosystems (precious), Ethics/Environmental Justice, Forests/Forestry, Oceans/Coasts/Beaches, Pollution (general), Public Health, Reduce/Reuse/Recycle, Water Habitats & Quality

Contact(s):
L. Iani, Regional Administrator; 206-553-1234

ENVIRONMENTAL PROTECTION AGENCY
RESEARCH AND DEVELOPMENT
USEPA Ariel Rios Building (5101)
1200 Pennsylvania Avenue NW
Washington, DC 20460 United States
Phone: 202-564-4700
Website: www.epa.gov/ord

Founded: N/A

Scope: National

Contact(s):
William Farland, Acting Deputy Assistant Administrator

ENVIRONMENTAL PROTECTION AGENCY
SCIENCE POLICY
1200 Pennsylvania Avenue NW
Washington, DC 20460 United States
Phone: 202-564-4700
Website: www.epa.gov/science

Founded: N/A

Contact(s):

Leonard Fleckenstein, Sustainable Ecosystems and Communities Director, Acting; 202-260-4002
Thomas Kelly, Regulatory Management and Information Director; 202-260-4335
Albert McGarland, Economy and Environment Director; 202-260-3354
Pamela Sterling, Program Support and Resource Management Director; 202-260-4335

ENVIRONMENTAL PROTECTION AGENCY
SOLID WASTE AND EMERGENCY RESPONSE
1200 Pennsylvania Avenue NW
Washington, DC 20460 United States
Phone: 202-564-4700
Website: www.epa.gov/swerrins

Founded: N/A

Contact(s):

Elizabeth Cotsworth, Solid Waste Director, Acting; 703-308-8895
Walter Kovalick, Technology Innovation Director; 703-603-9910
Stephen Luftig, Director Emergency and Remedial Response, Superfund; 703-603-8960
James Makris, Chief Preparedness and Prevention Director; 202-260-8600
Timothy Fields, Assistant Administrator, Acting; 202-260-4610

ENVIRONMENTAL PROTECTION AGENCY
WATER
United States
Website: www.epa.gov/ow

Founded: N/A

Contact(s):

Jeff Besougloff, American Indian Environmental Directory; 202-260-7939
Michael Cook, Wastewater Management Director; 202-260-5850
Cynthia Dougherty, Ground Water and Drinking Water Director; 202-260-5543
Geoffery Grubbs, Science and Technology Director; 202-260-5400
Robert Wayland, Wetlands, Oceans, and Watersheds Director; 202-260-7166
Tracy Mehan, Assistant Administrator; 202-260-5700

ENVIRONMENTAL PROTECTION SERVICE
AIR POLLUTION PREVENTION DIRECTORATE
P.O. Box 1320
Yellowknife, X1A 2L9 Northwest Territories Canada
Phone: 867-873-7654 Fax: 867-873-0221
E-mail: lisette_self@gov.nt.ca
Website: www.gov.nt.ca/RWED/eps/index.htm

Founded: N/A

Contact(s):

D. Egar, Director General; Place Vincent Massey, 10e et., 351 Blvd., St. Joseph, Hull, Quebec K1A 0H3; 819-997-1298; Fax: 819-953-9547

F

FISH AND WILDLIFE REFERENCE SERVICE
KRA CORPORATION
5430 Grosvenor Ln. Suite 110
Bethesda, MD 20814 United States
Phone: 301-492-6403 Fax: 301-564-4059
E-mail: fw9_fa_reference_service@fws.gov
Website: fa.r9.fws.gov/r9fwrs/

Founded: 1965
Membership: 10,001–100,000
Scope: National
Description: Produces "Fish and Wildlife Reference Service Databases", bibliographic database of primarily state fish and wildlife agency research reports; some USFWS publications; COOP Unit Theses and dissertations and some USNBS publications.

Contact(s):

Paul Wilson, Project Manager; 800-582-3421; Fax: 301-564-4059; paul_wilson@fws.gov
Geoffrey Yeadon, Senior Indexer; 800-582-3421; Fax: 301-564-4059; geoffrey_yeadon@fws.gov

FISHERIES AND OCEANS CANADA
COMMUNICATIONS DIRECTORATE
200 Kent St.
Ottawa, K1A 0E6 Ontario Canada
Phone: 613-993-0999 Fax: 613-990-1866
E-mail: info@dfo-mpo.gc.ca
Website: www.dfo-mpo.gc.ca

Founded: N/A
Scope: Local, Regional, National
Description: The Communications Branch houses the Department's expertise in internal and external communications. Communications advisors meet regularly with internal clients to discuss their communication objectives and to recommend appropriate strategies and tools for effective communication.

Contact(s):

Paul Schubert, Director General; 613-993-0989

FISHERIES AND OCEANS CANADA
FISHERIES AND MANAGEMENT
200 Kent St., 13th Floor Station 13228
Ottawa, K1A 0E6 Ontario Canada
Phone: 613-993-0999 Fax: 613-990-1866
E-mail: info@dfo-mpo.gc.ca
Website: www.dfo-mpo.gc.ca

Founded: N/A

Contact(s):

Mike Alexander, Director General: Aboriginal Affairs; 613-993-8598
David Balfour, Director General: Program Planning and Coordination; 613-993-2574
David Bezan, Director General: Resource Management; 613-990-0189
Dennis Brock, Director General: Conservation and Protection; 613-990-6012
Earl Wiseman, Director General: International; 613-993-1873
Pat Chamut, Assistant Deputy Minister; 613-990-9864
Paul Sprout, Associate Assistant Deputy Minister; 613-990-7203

G

GENERAL SERVICES ADMINISTRATION
GSA Bldg., 1800 F St., NW
Washington, DC 20405 United States
Phone: 202-501-1231
Website: www.gsa.gov

Founded: N/A

Description: Concerned with the conveyance of surplus real property for wildlife conservation purposes to the Secretary of Interior or to a state, pursuant to Public Law 537, 80th Congress.

Contact(s):
John Martin, Director of Redeployment Services Division/Property Disposal; 202-501-4671
Ronald Rice, Director of Program Development and Outreach; 202-501-0052
David Barram, Administrator

GEORGIA COOPERATIVE FISH AND WILDLIFE RESEARCH UNIT (USDI)

Warnell School of Forest Resources,
University of Georgia
Athens, GA 30602-2152 United States
Phone: 706-542-5260 Fax: 706-542-8356
E-mail: coopunit@smokey.forestry.uga.edu
Website: www.uga.edu/~gacoop

Founded: 1984
Membership: 1–100
Scope: State

Description: The Unit is supported by the Biological Resources Division, USGS; Georgia Department of Natural Resources; and the Wildlife Management Institute; and the University of Georgia. Fisheries and wildlife research, graduate education and training, technical assistance, and extension are the main missions of the Unit.

Keyword(s): Land Issues, Water Habitats & Quality, Wildlife & Species

Contact(s):
Michael Conroy, Assistant Unit Leader Wildlife
Cecil Jennings, Unit Leader
James Peterson, Assistant Unit Leader, Fisheries

GREAT LAKES FISHERY COMMISSION

2100 Commonwealth Blvd.
Ann Arbor, MI 48105 United States
Phone: 734-662-3209 Fax: 734-741-2010
Website: www.glfc.org

Founded: N/A
Membership: 1–100
Scope: International

Description: The 1955 Canada-U.S. Convention on Great Lakes Fisheries established the Commission to advise governments on ways to improve the fisheries, to develop and coordinate fishery research programs, to develop measures and implement programs to manage sea lamprey, and to improve and perpetuate fishery resources.

Publication(s): Fish Community Objectives for Lake Huron, Fish Community Objectives for Lake Superior, Economics of Great Lakes Fisheries: A 1985 Assessment

Contact(s):
Chris Goddard, Executive Secretary; cgoddard@glfc.org

GREAT LAKES INDIAN FISH AND WILDLIFE COMMISSION

P.O. Box 9
Odanah, WI 54861 United States
Phone: 715-682-6619 Fax: 715-682-9294
E-mail: jgilbert@glifwc.org
Website: www.glifwc.org

Founded: 1983

Description: Provide biological, enforcement, and legal services to our member tribes in matters related to off-reservation treaty gathering rights in Wisconsin, Michigan, and Minnesota.

Publication(s): Technical reports, Masinaigan

Contact(s):
Gerald Deperry, Deputy Administrator
Tom Maulson, Chairman of the Board
James Schlender, Executive Administrator

GULF STATES MARINE FISHERIES COMMISSION

P.O. Box 726
Ocean Springs, MS 39566-0726 United States
Phone: 228-875-5912 Fax: 228-875-6604
E-mail: lsimpson@gsmfc.org
Website: www.gsmfc.org

Founded: 1949
Membership: 1–100
Scope: National

Description: The GSMFC is an interstate compact of the states of Alabama, Florida, Louisiana, Mississippi, and Texas. The compact was authorized by the U.S. Congress. The Commission has 15 commissioners. The purpose of the Commission is to promote better utilization of the fisheries, marine, shell, and anadromous, of the seaboard of the Gulf of Mexico by cooperative programs for the promotion and protection of such fisheries and the prevention of the physical waste of the fisheries from any cause.

Publication(s): Publications on line

Contact(s):
Larry Simpson, Executive Director
Ronald Lukens, Assistant Director
Virginia Vail, Chairman

H

HELSINKI COMMISSION/ BALTIC MARINE ENVIRONMENT PROTECTION COMMISSION

Katajanokanlaituri 6 B FIN-00160
Helsinki, 150 Finland
Phone: 358-9-6220220 Fax: 358-9-62202239
E-mail: helcom@helcom.fi
Website: www.helcom.fi

Founded: 1980
Scope: International

Description: To protect the marine environment of the Baltic Sea against pollution from all sources.

Publication(s): Baltic Sea Environment Proceedings (BSEP)

Keyword(s): Agriculture/Farming, Ecosystems (precious), Executive/Legislative/Judicial Reform, Land Issues, Oceans/Coasts/Beaches, Pollution (general), Transportation, Water Habitats & Quality, Wildlife & Species

Contact(s):
Anne Brusendorff, Professional Secretary
Christine Fvll, Project Manager
Kaj Forsius, Professional Secretary
Claus Hagebro, Professional Secretary
Ulrike Hassink, Information Officer
Ritva Kostakow-Kampe, Administrative Officer
Juha-Markku LeppSnen, Professional Secretary
Mieczyslaw Ostojski, Executive Secretary

HOUSE COMMITTEE ON AGRICULTURE

DEPARTMENT OPERATIONS, OVERSIGHT, NUTRITION AND FORESTRY; GENERAL FARM COMMODITIES, RESOURCE CONSERVATION AND CREDIT; LIVESTOCK AND HORTICULTURE; RISK MANAGEMENT, RESEARCH AND SPECIALTY CROPS
Rm. 1301, Longworth House Office Bldg.
Washington, DC 20515 United States
Phone: 202-225-2171 Fax: 202-225-0917
Website: www.agriculture.house.gov

Founded: 1820
Membership: 1–100
Scope: National

Description: Adulteration of seeds, insect pests, and protection of birds and animals in forest reserves; agriculture generally; agricultural and industrial chemistry; agricultural colleges and experiment stations; agricultural economics and research; agricultural education extension services; agricultural production and marketing and stabilization of prices of agricultural products; animal industry and diseases of animals; crop insurance and soil conservation; dairy industry; entomology and plant quarantine.

Contact(s):
Larry Combest, Chair

HOUSE COMMITTEE ON APPROPRIATIONS

AGRICULTURE, RURAL DEVELOPMENT, FOOD AND DRUG ADMINISTRATION; COMMERCE, JUSTICE, STATE, AND JUDICIARY; DISTRICT OF COLUMBIA ENERGY AND WATER DEVELOPMENT; FOREIGN OPERATIONS, EXPORT FINANCING, AND RELATED PROGRAMS; INTERIOR; LABOR, HEALTH AND HUMAN SVCS
Rm. H-218, Capitol Bldg.
Washington, DC 20515 United States
Phone: 202-225-2771
Website: www.house.gov

Founded: N/A
Membership: 1–100
Scope: National
Description: Consists of 60 members: Appropriation of the revenue for the support of the government, rescissions of appropriations contained in appropriation acts, and transfers of unexpended balances.

Contact(s):
Bill Young, Chair

HOUSE COMMITTEE ON COMMERCE

TELECOMMUNICATIONS, TRADE, AND CONSUMER PROTECTION; FINANCE AND HAZARDOUS MATERIALS; HEALTH AND ENVIRONMENT; ENERGY AND POWER; OVERSIGHT AND INVESTIGATIONS
2125 Rayburn House Office Bldg.
Washington, DC 20515 United States
Phone: 202-225-2927 Fax: 202-225-1919

Founded: N/A
Membership: 101–1,000
Scope: National
Description: Jurisdiction: Interstate and foreign commerce generally; national energy policy generally; measures relating to the exploration, production, storage, supply, marketing, pricing, and regulation of energy resources, including all fossil fuels, solar energy, and other unconventional or renewable energy resources; measures relating to the conservation of energy resources; measures relating to the commercial application of energy technology; measures relating to energy information generally.

Contact(s):
Dave Marventano, Chief of Staff
James Barnette, General Counsel
Billy Tauzin, Chair

HOUSE COMMITTEE ON EDUCATION AND THE WORKFORCE

2181 Rayburn House Office Bldg.
Washington, DC 20515 United States
Phone: 202-225-4527 Fax: 202-225-9571
Website: edwrksorce.house.gov

Founded: N/A
Membership: 1–100
Scope: National
Description: Jurisdiction: Measures relating to education or labor generally; child labor; Gallaudet College; Howard University; convict labor and the entry of goods made by convicts into interstate commerce; labor standards; labor statistics; mediation and arbitration of labor disputes; regulation or prevention of importation of foreign laborers under contract; food programs for children in schools; United States Employees' Compensation Commission; vocational rehabilitation; wages and hours of labor.

Contact(s):
John Boehner, Chairman; 202-225-6205

HOUSE COMMITTEE ON INTERNATIONAL RELATIONS

AFRICA; ASIA AND THE PACIFIC; THE WESTERN HEMISPHERE; INTERNATIONAL ECONOMIC POLICY AND TRADE; INTERNATIONAL OPERATIONS AND HUMAN RIGHTS
2170 Rayburn House Office Bldg.
Washington, DC 20515 United States
Phone: 202-225-5021 Fax: 202-225-0225
E-mail: hirc@mail.house.gov

Founded: N/A
Membership: 1–100
Scope: National
Description: Jurisdiction: Foreign policy; international economic and environmental policy; international conferences and congresses; United Nations organizations; fishing agreements; nuclear export policy.

Contact(s):
Henry Hyde, Chairman

HOUSE COMMITTEE ON RESOURCES

Rm. 1324, Longworth House Office Bldg.
Washington, DC 20515 United States
Phone: 202-225-2761
Website: www.resourcecommittee.house.gov

Founded: N/A
Scope: National
Description: Consists of 52 members: Forest reserves and national parks created from the public domain; national parks lands; forfeiture of land grants and alien ownership, including alien ownership of mineral lands; geological survey; interstate compacts relating to apportionment of waters for irrigation purposes; irrigation and reclamation, including water supply for reclamation projects, and easements on public lands for irrigation projects, and acquisition of private lands.

Contact(s):
Allen Freemyer, Chief of Staff
James Hansen, Chair

HOUSE COMMITTEE ON RULES

Capitol Bldg.
Washington, DC 20515 United States
Phone: 202-225-9191 Fax: 202-225-6763
Website: www.house.gov/rules

Founded: N/A
Membership: 1–100
Scope: National
Description: Consists of 13 members: Grants rules outlining conditions for floor debate on legislation reported by regular standing committees, which includes granting emergency waivers under the Congressional Budget Act of 1974; also has legislative authority to create committees, change the rules of the House, and provide order of business of the House.

Contact(s):
David Drier, Chair
Porter Gross, Vice Chair

HOUSE COMMITTEE ON TRANSPORTATION AND INFRASTRUCTURE

Rm. 2163 Rayburn House Office Bldg.
Washington, DC 20515 United States
Phone: 202-225-4472 Fax: 202-226-1270
Website: www.house.gov/transportation/democrats/

Founded: N/A
Membership: 1–100
Scope: National
Description: Consists of 73 members.
Keyword(s): Air Quality/Atmosphere, Energy, Land Issues, Oceans/Coasts/Beaches, Pollution (general), Sprawl/Urban Planning, Transportation, Water Habitats & Quality
Contact(s):
Don Young, Chairman

I

INSTITUTO NACIONAL DE BIODIVERSIDAD (INBIO)

Apdo. #22-3100
Santo Domingo, Costa Rica
Phone: 5062440690 Fax: 5062442816
E-mail: inbioparque@inbio.ac.cr
Website: www.inbio.ac.cr

Founded: 1989
Description: INBIO is conducting a biodiversity inventory in Costa Rica's protected areas. Through this knowledge, society will be able to appreciate and value the resources contained in the wildlands, and use this information in a sustainable manner.
Publication(s): Mariposas Heliconius de Costa Rica, Guia de Aves de Costa Rica, Biodiversity Prospecting, Biodiversidad de Costa Rica: Lecturas para Ecoturistas
Contact(s):
Rodrigo Gamez, General Director; rgamez @inbio.ac.cr
Ana Gueuvara, Prospecting Coordinator; agueuvara@inbio.ac.cr
Eric Mata, Management Coordinator; emata@inbio.ac.cr
Vanessa Matamorros, Public Relations; vmatamorros@inbio.ac.cr
Alfio Piva, Deputy Director; apiva@inbio.ac.cr
Sonia Rojas, Biodiversity Education; srojas@inbio.ac.cr
Jesus Ugalde, Biodiversity Inventory; jugalde@inbio.ac.cr
Natalia Zamora, Biodiversity & Garden; nzamora@inbio.ac.cr
Karla Zanabria, Communications; kzanabria@inbio.ac.cr

INTER-AMERICAN TROPICAL TUNA COMMISSION

c/o Scripps Institution of Oceanography
8604 La Jolla Shores Drive
La Jolla, CA 92037-1508 United States
Phone: 858-546-7100 Fax: 858-546-7133
Website: www.ihttc.org

Founded: 1949
Membership: 1–100
Scope: International
Description: Charged with the investigation and conservation of the tuna and dolphin resources of the eastern Pacific Ocean. Member nations: U.S., Costa Rica, El Salvador, Ecuador, France, Japan, Mexico, Nicaragua, Panama, Vanuatu and Venezuela. Established by convention between the U.S. and Costa Rica.
Publication(s): Special Report of the Inter-American Tropical Tuna Commission, Bulletin of the Inter-American Tropical Tuna Commission
Keyword(s): Other
Contact(s):
Robin Allen, Director; 858-546-7019
William Bayliff, Editor; 858-546-7025

INTERNATIONAL BOUNDARY AND WATER COMMISSION, UNITED STATES AND MEXICO

UNITED STATES SECTION
4171 North Mesa Street, Suite C-310
El Paso, TX 79902 United States
Phone: 915-832-4175 Fax: 915-832-4195
E-mail: sallyspener@ibwc.state.gov
Website: www.ibwc.state.gov

Founded: 1889
Membership: N/A
Scope: Regional, International
Description: International commission of the United States and Mexican governments. Responsible for applying the boundary and water treaties between the two countries. The Commission is involved in water quality and water quantity issues.
Keyword(s): Development/Developing Countries, Recreation/Ecotourism, Water Habitats & Quality

INTERNATIONAL JOINT COMMISSION

National Headquarters, 1250 23rd St., NW, Suite 100
Washington, DC 20440 United States
Phone: 202-736-9000 Fax: 202-736-9015
Website: www.ijc.org

Founded: 1909
Membership: 1–100
Scope: International
Description: Established by the Boundary Waters Treaty of 1909 to prevent and resolve disputes regarding the use of the waters on the U.S.- Canadian Boundary, and to act as an independent advisor on issues referred by both countries. Regional office monitors, evaluates, and reports on compliance with the Great Lakes Water Quality Agreement of November 22, 1978. Commission functions in quasi-judicial, investigative, and coordination capacities.
Publication(s): Focus
Contact(s):
Thomas Behlen, Director, Regional Office; 519-257-6700; Fax: 519-257-6740
Frank Bevacqua, Public Information Officer; 202-736-9024; Fax: 202-736-9015; bevacquaf@washington.ijc.org
Murray Clamen, Canadian Section Secretary; 613-995-2984
Jennifer Day, Public Information Officer; 313-226-2170, ext. 6733; Fax: 519-257-6740; DayJ@windsor.ijc.org.

INTERNATIONAL JOINT COMMISSION

CANADIAN SECTION
234 Laurier Ave. W., 22nd Floor
Ottawa, K1P 6K6 Ontario Canada
Phone: 613-995-2984 Fax: 613-993-5583
Website: www.ijc.org

Founded: N/A
Membership: 1–100
Scope: International
Publication(s): Focus
Contact(s):
Mary Gusella, Chairman, Canadian Section

INTERNATIONAL JOINT COMMISSION

GREAT LAKES REGIONAL OFFICE
100 Ouellette Ave.
Windsor, N9A 6T3 Ontario Canada
Phone: 519-257-6700 Fax: 519-257-6740
E-mail: commission@windsor.ijc.org
Website: www.ijc.org

Founded: N/A
Membership: 1–100
Scope: Regional
Publication(s): Focus (newsletter), Biannual Reports
Contact(s):
Jennifer Day, Director of Public Affairs

INTERNATIONAL PACIFIC HALIBUT COMMISSION

P.O. Box 95009
Seattle, WA 98145-2009 United States
Phone: 206-634-1838 Fax: 206-632-2983
Website: www.iphc.washington.edu

Founded: 1923
Membership: N/A
Scope: International
Description: Scientific investigation and management of the Pacific halibut resource. Established by a convention between Canada and the United States.
Keyword(s): Oceans/Coasts/Beaches
Contact(s):
Bruce Leaman, Executive Director; 206-634-1838; Fax: 206-632-2983; bruce@iphc.washington.edu

INTERNATIONAL WHALING COMMISSION

The Red House 135 Station Rd.
Impington, Cambridge+132, CB4 9NP United Kingdom
Phone: 01223-233971 Fax: 01223-232876
E-mail: iwcoffice@compuserve.com

Founded: 1946
Description: Established under the International Convention for the Regulation of Whaling in 1946 to provide for the conservation of whale stocks and the orderly development of the whaling industry.
Publication(s): International Journal of Cetacean Research and Management, Special Issues Series on specialist cetacean subjects, Annual reports of the Commission (including reports and papers of the Scientific Committee)
Contact(s):
J. Baker, U.S. Commissioner; U.S. Department of Commerce, Rm. 5128, Herbert C. Hoover Bldg., 14th and Constitution Ave., NW, Washington, DC 20230
M. Canny, Chairman, Ireland
Bo Fernholm, Vice Chairman, Sweden
R. Gambell, Secretary, Cambridge
M. Harvey, Executive Officer, Cambridge

INTERSTATE COMMISSION ON THE POTOMAC RIVER BASIN

6110 Executive Blvd., Suite 300
Rockville, MD 20852-3903 United States
Phone: 301-984-1908 Fax: 301-984-5841
E-mail: info@ICPRB.org
Website: www.potomacriver.org

Founded: 1940
Scope: Regional
Description: Interstate compact, established by Maryland, Pennsylvania, Virginia, West Virginia, and the District of Columbia. Coordinates, tabulates, and summarizes existing data on condition of streams in Potomac Watershed; promotes uniform legislation; disseminates information; cooperates in studies; promotes coordination of program in Basin states. Areas of interest are water quality, water supply, and land resources associated with the Potomac and its tributaries.
Publication(s): In the Anacostia Watershed, Potomac Basin Reporter
Contact(s):
Joseph Hoffman, Executive Director
James Cummins, Associate Director of Living Resources
Curtis Dalpra, Communications Manager
Carlton Haywood, Associate Director of Water Quality

M

MARINE MAMMAL COMMISSION

4340 East-West Highway
Room 905
Bethesda, MD 20814 United States
Phone: 301-504-0087 Fax: 301-504-0099
E-mail: mmc@mmc.gov

Founded: 1972
Membership: N/A
Scope: State, Regional, National, International
Description: Established by the Marine Mammal Protection Act of 1972, P.L. 92-522, the Marine Mammal Commission, in consultation with its Committee of Scientific Advisors on Marine Mammals, periodically reviews the status of marine mammal populations; manages a research program concerned with their conservation; and develops, reviews, and makes recommendations on federal activities and policies which affect the protection and conservation of marine mammals.
Publication(s): Research Reports, Annual Report
Contact(s):
Robert Mattlin, Executive Director; rmattlin@mmc.gov
Timothy Ragen, Scientific Program Director
Michael Gosliner, General Counsel
David Laist, Policy and Program Analyst

MIGRATORY BIRD CONSERVATION COMMISSION

1849 C St., NW (ARL SQ. 622)
Washington, DC 20240 United States
Phone: 703-358-1716 Fax: 703-358-2223
E-mail: Jeffrey-M-Donahoe@fws.gov

Founded: 1929
Membership: 1–100
Scope: National
Description: Considers, passes upon, and fixes the prices for lands recommended by the Secretary of the Interior for purchase or lease by him under the Migratory Bird Conservation Act of February 18, 1929, as amended, as migratory bird refuges in the National Wildlife Refuge System.
Contact(s):
Jeffery Donahoe, Secretary; 703-358-1716; Fax: 703-358-2223

MINISTRY OF THE ENVIRONMENT OF THE CZECH REPUBLIC

Vrsovicka 65
100 10 Prague 10, Czech Republic
Phone: 420-2-6712-2769 Fax: 420-2-6731-0370
E-mail: roudna@env.cz

Founded: N/A
Contact(s):
Peter Roth, Chairman; roth@env.cz
Milena Roudna, Minister; roudna@env.cz

MINISTRY OF THE ENVIRONMENT OF THE CZECH REPUBLIC

ENVIRONMENTAL COMMISSION
Academy of Sciences of The Czech Republic, Narodni 3
11720 Praha 1, Czech Republic
Phone: 420-2-2420538 Fax: 420-2-24220944
E-mail: info@env.cz

Founded: N/A
Contact(s):
Milos Kuzvart, Secretary; petr.kuzvart@enc.cz

MINNESOTA-WISCONSIN BOUNDARY AREA COMMISSION

619 2nd St.
Hudson, WI 54016 United States
Phone: 651-436-7131 Fax: 715-386-9571
E-mail: mwbac@mwbac.org
Website: www.mwbac.org

Founded: 1965
Membership: 1–100
Scope: Regional
Description: To conduct studies, develop recommendations, and coordinate planning for protection, use, and development in the public interest of lands, river valleys, and waters that form the boundary between Minnesota and Wisconsin, principally on the St. Croix and Mississippi rivers.
Publication(s): River Steward Journal
Contact(s):
Robin Grawe, Mississippi Valley Director
Buck Malick, Executive Director
Rosetta Herricks, Office Manager
Judith Olson, Secretary

N

NATIONAL AGRICULTURAL LIBRARY

10301 Baltimore Ave
Beltsville, MD 20705 United States
Phone: 301-504-6813 Fax: 301-504-6968
E-mail: agref@nal.usda.gov
Website: www.nal.usda.gov

Founded: 1862
Membership: 1–100
Scope: National, International
Description: Produces "Agricola", a database of bibliographic citations covering all aspects of agricultural and food sciences, including natural resources, animal welfare, pollution, pesticides and land and water management. The database has over 4 million records.

NATIONAL SCIENCE FOUNDATION

4201 Wilson Blvd.
Arlington, VA 22230 United States
Phone: 703-191-5111
Website: www.nsf.gov

Founded: 1950
Description: Responsible for the support of science and engineering research and the development of science education programs. Policy is set by the National Science Board, which is composed of 24 part-time members appointed by the President, with the consent of the Senate, and includes the Director of the Foundation.
Publication(s): Where Discoveries Begin, NSF in a Changing World: The National Science Foundation Strategic Plan, Grant Proposal Guide, Guide to Programs
Contact(s):
Rita Colwell, Director; 703-306-1000
Julia Moore, Director of Office of Legislative and Public Affairs; 703-306-1070
Stephanie Bianchi, Head Librarian; 703-306-0658
Joseph Bordogna, Deputy Director; 703-306-1000
Eamon Kelly, Chairman of National Science Board; 703-306-2000

NATIONAL TRANSPORTATION SAFETY BOARD

490 L'Enfant Plaza East, SW
Washington, DC 20594 United States
Phone: 202-314-6000 Fax: 202-314-6148
Website: www.ntsb.gov

Founded: N/A
Scope: National
Description: The Safety Board is an independent federal accident investigation agency. The Board's mission is to determine the "probable cause" of transportation accidents and to formulate safety recommendations to improve transportation safety.
Contact(s):
Ron Battocchi, Director of Office of General Counsel
Jamie Finch, Director of Office of Government, Public, and Family Affairs

NATURAL RESOURCES CANADA, CANADIAN FOREST SERVICE

PACIFIC FORESTRY CENTRE
580 Booth St.
Ottawa, K1A 0E4 Ontario Canada
Phone: 250-363-0600 Fax: 250-363-0775
Website: www.NRCan.gc.ca/cfs

Founded: N/A
Description: CFS promotes sustainable development of Canada's forests and competitiveness of the Canadian forest sector for the well-being of present and future generations of Canadians. The CFS also establishes links with other non-governmental organizations to better address issues such as international trade, market access and the sustainable management of forests world-wide.
Contact(s):
Paul Addison, Director General; 506 West Burnside Rd., Victoria, British Columbia V8Z 1M5; 604-363-0608; Fax: 604-363-6088
Jacques Carette, Director General of Policy, Planning and International Affai; 613-947-9100; Fax: 613-947-9038
Boyd Case, Director General; 5320 122 St., Edmonton, Alberta T6H 3S5; 403-435-7202; Fax: 403-435-7396
Doug Ketcheson, Director General for Industry, Economics and Programs Branch; 613-947-9052; Fax: 613-947-9038
Ed Kondo, Director General; P.O. Box 490, 1219 Queen St. East, Sault Ste. Marie, Ontario P6A 5M7; 705-949-9461, ext. 2039; Fax: 705-759-5714
Normand Lafreniere, Director General; 1055 du P.E.P.S. St., P.O. Box 3800, Sainte-Foy, Quebec G1V-4C7; 418-648-3957; Fax: 418-648-7317
Sylvie Letellier, Director of Communications and Executive Services; 613-947-7404; Fax: 613-947-7396
Gordon Miller, Director General of Science Branch; 613-947-8984; Fax: 613-947-9090
Gerrit Van Raalte, Director General; P.O. Box 4000, Regent St., Fredericton, New Brunswick E3B 5P7; 506-452-3508; Fax: 506-452-3140
Sylvia Frehner, Manager of Sector Human Resources Unit; 613-947-7386; Fax: 613-947-7409
Yvan Hardy, Assistant Deputy Minister of Canadian Forest Service; 613-947-7400; Fax: 613-947-7395
Anne McLellan, Minister; 613-996-2007; Fax: 613-996-4516
Jean McLoskey, Deputy Minister; 613-992-3456; Fax: 613-992-3828

NEW ENGLAND WATER POLLUTION CONTROL COMMISSION

Boott Mills South, 100 Foot of John St.
Lowell, MA 01852-1124 United States
Phone: 978-323-7929 Fax: 978-323-7919
E-mail: general@neiwpcc.org
Website: www.neiwpcc.org

Founded: 1947
Scope: Regional
Description: The Commission provides a forum for interstate communication on high priority water-related environmental issues; provides training opportunities for state environmental staff and wastewater treatment plant operators; and provides the public with outreach and training materials on a wide range of environmental issues.

Publication(s): NEI Environmental Information Catalog, Annual Report, LUSTLine (bulletin on underground storage tanks), Water Connection (newsletter)

Keyword(s): Oceans/Coasts/Beaches

Contact(s):
Ronald Poltak, Executive Director

NORTH AMERICAN DEVELOPMENT BANK

NADB
203 South St. Mary's, Suite 300
San Antonio, TX 78205 United States
Phone: 210-231-8000 Fax: 210-231-6232
E-mail: webmaster@nadb.org
Website: www.nadb.org

Founded: 1993

Scope: Local, State, Regional, International

Description: The NADB is an international financial institution established and capitalized in equal parts by the U.S. and Mexico for the purpose of financing environmental infrastructure projects. All NADB-financed environmental projects must be certified by the BECC, be related to potable water supply, wastewater treatment or municipal solid waste management and be located within the border region, defined as 100 km. (62 miles) north and south of the international boundary between the two countries.

Publication(s): BECC-NADB Quarterly Status Reports, U.S. Mexico 5-Year Outlook 2001 Edition, NADB Annual Reports

Keyword(s): Air Quality/Atmosphere, Development/Developing Countries, Energy, Finance/Banking/Trade, Pollution (general), Public Health, Reduce/Reuse/Recycle, Water Habitats

Contact(s):
Raul Rodriguez, Managing Director; 210-231-8000; Fax: 210-231-6232
Jorge Garcias, Deputy Managing Director; 210-231-8000; Fax: 21-231-6232
Suzanne Gallagher, Director of Program Development; 210-231-8000; Fax: 210-231-6232; sgallagher@nadb.org
Armando Perez-Gea, Director of Project Development; 210-231-8000; Fax: 210-231-6232; aperez-gea@nadb.org

NORTH AMERICAN WETLANDS CONSERVATION COUNCIL

UNITED STATES DEPARTMENT OF THE INTERIOR
UNITED STATES FISH AND WILDLIFE SERVICE
DIVISION OF BIRD HABITAT CONSERVATION
4401-4501 North Fairfax Dr., Suite 110
Arlington, VA 22203 United States
Phone: 703-358-1784 Fax: 703-358-2282
E-mail: birdhabitat@fws.gov
Website: www.birdhabitat.fws.gov

Founded: 1989
Membership: N/A
Scope: International

Description: On behalf of the Secretary of the Interior, The North American Wetlands Conservation Council encourages public-private partnerships to conserve wetland ecosystems for waterfowl, other migratory birds, fish, and wildlife. Grant projects with a 1-1 match are funded to acquire, restore, and enhance wetlands and associated habitats in Canada, the U.S., and Mexico.

Publication(s): "Birdscapes", North American Wetlands Conservation Act; Highlights Habitat Projects, Progress Report 2000-2001

Keyword(s): Oceans/Coasts/Beaches, Public Lands/Greenspace, Water Habitats & Quality, Wildlife & Species

Contact(s):
John Berry, Member; National Fish and Wildlife Foundation, 1120 Connecticut Avenue, NW, Suite 900, Washington, DC 20036; 202-857-0166; Fax: 202-857-0162; berry@nfwf.org
John Cooper, Vice-Chair; South Dakota Game, Fish & Parks Department, 523 East Capitol, Pierre, SD 57501-3182; 605-773-3387; Fax: 605-773-7201; john.cooper@state.sd.us
Michael Dennis, Esq., Member; The Nature Conservancy, 4245 North Fairfax Drive, Suite 100, Arlington, VA 22203; 703-841-5318; Fax: 703-841-8796
Jean Hocker, Member; 20 West Chapman Street, Alexandria, VA 22301; 703-683-0506; Fax: 703-683-4940; jean@hockers.com
Wayne MacCallum, Member; Massachusetts Division of Fisheries and Wildlife, 1 Rabbit Hill Road, Westborough, MA 01581; 508-792-7270, ext. 143; Fax: 508-792-7275; wayne.maccallum@state.ma.us
Steve Miller, Member; Wisconsin Dept of National Resources, Madison, WI 53707; 608-266-5782; Fax: 608-266-6983; millesw@dnr.state.wi.us
David Nomsen, Alternate Member; Pheasants Forever, Inc, 2101 Ridgewood Drive, Alexandria, MN 56308; 320-763-6103; Fax: 320-763-6103; pfnomsen@rea-alp.com
Duane Shroufe, Chairperson; Arizona Game and Fish Department, 2221 West Greenway Road, Phoenix, AZ 85023-4399; 602-789-3278; Fax: 602789-3299; dshroufe@gf.state.az.us
David Smith, Council Coordinator & Division Chief; U.S. Fish & Wildlife Service, 4401 North Fairfax Drive,, Suite 110, Arlington, VA 22203; 703-358-1784; Fax: 703-358-2282; david_a_smith@fws.gov
W. Wentz, Member; Ducks Unlimited, Inc., One Waterfowl Way, Memphis, TN 38120-2351; 901-758-3784; Fax: 901-758-3855; awentz@ducks.org
Steve Williams, Member; U.S. Fish & Wildlife Service, Department of the Interior, 1849 C Street, NW, Washington, DC 20240-0001; 202-208-4717; Fax: 202-208-6965; Steven_A_Williams@fws.gov

NORTH PACIFIC ANADROMOUS FISH COMMISSION

889 W. Pender Street, Suite 502
Vancouver, V6C 3B2 British Columbia Canada
Phone: 604-775-5550 Fax: 604-775-5577
E-mail: secretariat@npafc.org
Website: www.npafc.org

Founded: 1993
Membership: 1–100
Scope: International

Description: Established by a Convention between Canada, Japan, Russia, and the U.S. for the conservation of the anadromous fish resources of the North Pacific Ocean.

Publication(s): North Pacific Anadromous Commission-newsletter

Contact(s):
Anatoly Makoedov Dr., President
Koji Imamura, Vice President, Russia
Vladimir Fedorenko, Executive Director

NORTHEAST ATLANTIC FISHERIES COMMISSION

22 Berners St.
London, WIP 4DY United Kingdom
Phone: 0207-631-0016 Fax: 2076369225
E-mail: info@neafc.org

Founded: 1980

Description: To promote the conservation and optimum utilization of the fishery resources of the northeast Atlantic, within a framework appropriate to the regime of extended coastal state jurisdiction over fisheries, and to encourage international cooperation and consultation with respect to these resources.

Publication(s): Handbook of Basic Texts, Annual Report

Contact(s):
O. Tougaard, President
E. Lemche, Vice President

V. Sokolov, Vice President
Sigmund Engesaeter, Secretary

NORTHEASTERN FOREST FIRE PROTECTION COMMISSION

36 Roslyn Ave.
Warner, NH 03278-4021 United States
Phone: 603-456-3474 Fax: 603-456-3474
Website: www.nffpc.com

Founded: N/A
Membership: 1,001–10,000
Scope: International
Description: International forest fire protection mutual aid organization composed of three commissioners each from CT, ME, MA, NH, RI, VT, NY, and the Canadian Provinces of Quebec, New Brunswick, and Nova Scotia plus New England national forests (Green Mountain and White Mountain). Uniform fire organization planning and suppression technique training carried out annually by the members. The Northeastern Interstate Forest Fire Protection Compact is the governing document that established the organization.
Contact(s):
Clark Davis, Executive Director; 36 Roslyn Ave., Warner, NH 03278-4021; 603-456-3474

NUCLEAR REGULATORY COMMISSION

2120 L Street
Washington, DC 20555 United States
Phone: 301-415-7000

Founded: 1975
Scope: National
Description: Five-member commission responsible for regulating all commercial uses of nuclear energy to protect the health and safety of the public and the environment.
Keyword(s): Energy
Contact(s):
William Beecher, Director of Office of Public Affairs; 301-415-8200
Paul Bird, Director of Office of Personnel; 301-415-7516
Bruce Boger, Director of Division of Reactor Controls and Human Factors; 301-415-1004
Guy Caputo, Director of Office of Investigations; 301-415-2373
Frank Congel, Director of Incident Response Division; 301-415-7476
Donald Cool, Director of Division of Industrial/Medical/Nuclear Safety; 301-415-7197
John Cordes, Director of Office of Commission Appellate Adjudication; 301-415-1600
Gerald Cranford, Director of Office of Information Resources Management; 301-415-7585
Lloyd Donnelly, Director of Financial Management, and Procurement; 301-415-5828
Francis Gillespie, Director of Division of Inspection and Support Programs; 301-415-1275
John Greeves, Director of Division of Waste Management; 301-415-7358
Brian Grimes, Director; 301-415-1193
Edward Halman, Associate Director of Contract and Security; 301-415-7305
M. Hodges, Director of Division of Systems Technology; 301-415-5728
Gary Holahan, Director of Division of Systems Safety and Analysis; 301-415-2884
Edward Jordan, Director of Office for Analysis and Evaluation; 301-415-7472
John Larkins, Executive Director; 301-415-7360
James Lieberman, Director of Office of Enforcement; 301-415-2741
John Linehan, Director of Program Management and Policy Development; 301-415-7780
Irene Little, Director of Office of Small Business and Civil Rights; 301-415-7380
Paul Lohaus, Director; 301-415-2326
Thomas Martian, Deputy Director of Division of Reactor Programs; 301-415-1199
James Milhoan, Deputy Executive Director for Nuclear Reactor Regulation; 301-415-1705
Frank Miraglia, Director of Office of Nuclear Reactor Regulation, Acting; 301-415-1270
Bill Morris, Director of Division of Regulatory Applications; 301-415-6207
David Morrison, Director of Office of Nuclear Regulatory Research; 301-415-6641
Carl Paperiello, Director of Office of Nuclear Material Safety and Safeguards; 301-415-7800
Kenneth Raglin, Director of Technical Training Division; 423-855-6500
Dennis Rathbun, Director of Office of Congressional Affairs; 301-415-1776
C. Rossi, Director of Safety Programs Division; 301-415-7499
Lawrence Shao, Director of Division of Engineering Technology; 301-415-5678
Brian Sheron, Director of Division of Engineering; 301-415-2722
Carlton Stoiber, Director of Office of International Programs; 301-415-1780
James Taylor, Executive Director for Operations; 301-415-1700
Elizabeth Teneyck, Director of Division of Fuel Cycle Safety and Safeguards; 301-415-7212
Hugh Thompson, Deputy Executive Director for Nuclear Materials, Safety, Saf; 301-504-1713
William Travers, Director of Spent Fuel Project Office; 301-415-8500
Richard Bangart, Deputy Director of Office of State Programs; 301-415-3340
Arthur Beach, Deputy; 708-829-9658
Arthur Beach, Regional Administrator, Region 3; 801 Warrenville Rd., Lisle, IL 60532-4351; 708-829-9500
Hubert Bell, Inspector General; 301-415-5930
Stephen Burns, Associate General Counsel for Hearing, and Enforcement; 301-415-1740
Leonard Callan, Regional Administrator, Region 4; 611 Ryan Plaza Dr., Suite 4000, Arlington, TX 76011-8064; 817-860-8225
Samuel Collins, Deputy; 817-860-8226
B. Cotter, Chief Administrative Judge and Chairman of Atomic Safety; 301-415-7450
Karen Cyr, General Counsel; 301-415-1743
Greta Dirus, Commissioner; 301-415-1820
Stewart Ebneter, Regional Administrator, Region 2; 101 Marietta St., Suite 2900, Atlanta, GA 30323-0199; 404-331-5500
Roger Fortuna, Deputy Director; 301-415-3476
Jesse Funches, Deputy Controller; 301-415-7322
Elizabeth Hayden, Deputy Director; 301-415-8200
John Hoyle, Secretary of the Commission; 301-415-1969
Shirley Jackson, Chairman; 301-415-1820
William Kane, Deputy; 610-337-5340
Malcolm Knapp, Deputy Director; 301-415-8468
Arnold Levin, Deputy Director of Licensing Support Systems Administrator; 301-415-7458
Martin Malsch, Deputy General Counsel; 301-415-1740
James McDermott, Deputy Director; 301-415-7516
Richard Meserve, Chairman of Commission
Hubert Miller, Regional Administrator, Region 1; 475 Allendale Rd., King of Prussia, PA 19406-1415; 610-337-5299
Patricia Norry, Associate Director of Office of Administration; 301-415-7443
William Olmstead, Licensing and Regulation; 301-415-1740
Paul Pomeroy, Vice Chairman; 301-415-7360
Linda Portner, Associate Director; 301-415-1776
Luis Reyes, Deputy; 404-331-5610

Kenneth Rogers, Commissioner; 301-415-1855
Denwood Ross, Deputy Director; 301-415-7473
Ronald Scroggins, Deputy Chief Financial Officer/Controller; 301-415-7501
Robert Seale, Vice Chairman; 301-415-7360
Frederick Shon, Deputy Chief Administrative Judge; 301-415-7468
Themis Speis, Deputy Director; 301-415-6802
Michael Springer, Associate Director of Facilities and Property Management; 301-415-8080
Martin Steindler, Chairman of Advisory Committee on Nuclear Waste; 301-415-7360
Ashok Thadani, Associate Director, Insp. and Tech. Review; 301-415-1274
Roy Zimmerman, Associate Director of Projects; 301-415-1284

O

OHIO RIVER VALLEY WATER SANITATION COMMISSION

5735 Kellogg Ave.
Cincinnati, OH 45228-1112 United States
Phone: 513-231-7719 Fax: 513-231-7761
E-mail: info@orsanco.org
Website: www.orsanco.org

Founded: 1948

Scope: State, Regional

Description: An interstate agency representing Illinois, Indiana, Kentucky, New York, Ohio, Pennsylvania, Virginia, and West Virginia for control of water pollution in the Ohio River Valley Compact District.

Publication(s): Publications of general or technical interest such as Ohio River fish populations, Annual Report, ORSANCO Quality Monitor

Contact(s):
Alan Vicory, Executive Director and Chief Engineer
Jeanne Ison, Public Information Programs Manager
Rhonda Barnes-Cloth, Communications Coordinator

P

PACIFIC SALMON COMMISSION

1155 Robson St., Suite 600
Vancouver, V6E 1B5 British Columbia Canada
Phone: 604-684-8081 Fax: 604-666-8707
Website: www.psc.org

Founded: N/A
Membership: 1–100
Scope: International

Description: Charged with implementation of the Pacific Salmon Treaty signed by Canada and the United States in 1985, the Commission provides regulatory advice and recommendations to the U.S. and Canada relative to their management of salmon originating in one country, but subject to interception by the other. The Commission is also charged with conserving Pacific Salmon stocks in order to achieve optimum production.

Contact(s):
Don Kowal, Executive Secretary

PACIFIC STATES MARINE FISHERIES COMMISSION

45 SE 82nd Dr., Suite 100
Gladstone, OR 97027-2522 United States
Phone: 503-650-5400 Fax: 503-650-5426
Website: www.psmfc.org

Founded: 1947
Membership: 1–100
Scope: State

Description: The Commission serves the Pacific states of Alaska, California, Idaho, Oregon, and Washington to promote conservation, development, and management of marine and anadromous fisheries of mutual concern through a coordinated regional approach to fisheries research, monitoring, and utilization. Activities focus on multistate databases, interjurisdiction fishery management plans, marine debris, saving fisheries habitat, and marine mammal/fishery interactions.

Contact(s):
Randy Fisher, Executive Director

PEACE CORPS

1111 20th St., NW
Washington, DC 20526 United States
Phone: 202-692-2100
E-mail: volunteer@peacecorps.gov
Website: www.peacecorps.gov

Founded: 1961
Membership: 1,001–10,000
Scope: International

Description: The Peace Corps was established in 1961. More than 165,000 Americans have joined the Peace Corps and have served in 135 countries. The Peace Corps has three goals: to help the people of interested countries in meeting their need for trained men and women; to help promote a better understanding of Americans on the part of the peoples served; and to help promote a better understanding of other peoples on the part of Americans.

Publication(s): The Peace Corps Times

Contact(s):
Charles Baquet, Acting Director; 202-692-2100

PEACE CORPS

ECUADOR
Avenida 6 de Diciembre 2269
Quito, Ecuador
Phone: 5932561224
E-mail: fgarces@ec.peacecorps.gov

Founded: 1960

Description: Peace Corps Ecuador provides technical assistance and cultural exchange in rural communites, through conservation NGO's and government agencies. Technical assistance is provided in the fields of EE, Agroforestry, and Conservation of Protected Areas.

Publication(s): Remedios Naturales Contra Plagas, Algunes alternativas para el desarrallo, Agroforesteria en los Audes del Ecuador

Contact(s):
Francisco Garces, Natural Resources Program Director; 593-256-1224; fgarces@ec.peacecorps.gov
Marcy Kelly, Peace Corps Ecuador Director; 593-256-1224; mkelly@ec.peacecorps.gov
Tim Criste, Program and Training Officer; 593-256-1224; tcriste@ec.peacecorps.gov

S

SENATE COMMITTEE ON AGRICULTURE, NUTRITION, AND FORESTRY

PRODUCTION AND PRICE COMPETITIVENESS; MARKETING, INSPECTION, AND PRODUCT PROMOTION; FORESTRY, CONSERVATION, AND RURAL REVITALIZATION; RESEARCH, NUTRITION, AND GENERAL LEGISLATION
Rm. 328-A, Russell Bldg.
Washington, DC 20510 United States
Phone: 202-224-2035
Website: www.senate.gov/~agriculture

Founded: N/A

Scope: National

Description: Concerned with agriculture and agricultural commodities; inspection of livestock, meat, and agricultural products; animal industry and diseases; pests and pesticides; agricultural extension services and experiment stations; forestry in general and forest reserves and wilderness areas other than those created from the public domain; agricultural economics and research; human nutrition; home economics; farm credit and farm security; rural development, rural electrification and watersheds.

Contact(s):
Keith Luse, Minority Staff Director
Mark Halverson, Chief of Staff
Tom Harkin, Chairman
David Johnson, Counsel
Richard Lugar, Ranking Republican Member
Robert Sturm, Chief Clerk

SENATE COMMITTEE ON APPROPRIATIONS

S128 Capitol Bldg.
Washington, DC 20510 United States
Phone: 202-224-3471 Fax: 202-224-8553
Website: www.appropriations.senate.gov

Founded: N/A
Scope: National
Description: Concerned with all proposed legislation, messages, petitions, memorials, and other matters relating to appropriation of the revenue for the support of the federal government.

Contact(s):
Terry Sauvain, Staff Director
Robert Byrd, Chairman

SENATE COMMITTEE ON COMMERCE, SCIENCE AND TRANSPORTATION

AVIATION; COMMUNICATIONS; CONSUMER AFFAIRS, FOREIGN COMMERCE AND TOURISM; SCIENCE, TECHNOLOGY, AND SPACE; SURFACE TRANSPORTATION AND MERCHANT MARINE; OCEANS AND FISHERIES
U.S. Senate SD508
Washington, DC 20510 United States
Phone: 202-224-5115 Fax: 202-228-5769
Website: www.senate.gov/~commerce/

Founded: N/A
Description: Concerned with interstate commerce; transportation; regulation of interstate common carriers, including railroads, buses, trucks, vessels, pipelines, and civil aviation; merchant marine and navigation; marine and ocean navigation, safety and transportation, including navigational aspects of deepwater ports; Coast Guard; inland waterways, except construction; communications; regulation of consumer products and services, except for credit, financial services, and housing.

Contact(s):
John McCain, Chair

SENATE COMMITTEE ON ENERGY AND NATURAL RESOURCES

Rm. SD-364 Dirksen Bldg.
Washington, DC 20510 United States
Phone: 202-224-4971 Fax: 202-224-6163

Founded: N/A
Membership: 1–100
Scope: National
Description: Concerned with the comprehensive study and review of matters relating to energy and resources development. Jursdiction: Coal production, distribution, and utilization; energy policy; energy regulation and conservation; energy related aspects of deepwater ports; energy research and development; extraction of minerals from oceans and Outer Continental Shelf lands; hydroelectric power, irrigation, and reclamation; mining education and research.

Contact(s):
Frank Murkowski, Chair

SENATE COMMITTEE ON ENVIRONMENT AND PUBLIC WORKS

TRANSPORTATION AND INFRASTRUCTURE; SUPERFUND; WASTE CONTROL AND RISK ASSESSMENT; CLEAN AIR, WETLANDS, PRIVATE PROPERTY, AND NUCLEAR SAFETY; DRINKING WATER, FISHERIES, AND WILDLIFE
Dirksen Bldg.
Washington, DC 20510 United States
Phone: 202-224-6176 Fax: 202-224-1273
Website: epw.senate.gov

Founded: N/A
Membership: 1–100
Scope: National
Description: Committee on Environment and Public Works, to which shall be referred all proposed legislation, messages, petitions, memorials, and other matters relating to the following subjects: environmental policy; environmental research and development; ocean dumping; fisheries and wildlife; environmental aspects of Outer Continental Shelf lands; solid waste disposal and recycling; environmental effects of toxic substances, other than pesticides; water resources.

Contact(s):
Ken Connolly, Democrat Staff Director
Dave Conover, Republican Staff Director
J. Sliter, Minority Staff Director
Jim Jeffords, Chair

SENATE COMMITTEE ON FOREIGN RELATIONS

AFRICAN AFFAIRS; EAST ASIAN AND PACIFIC AFFAIRS; EUROPEAN AFFAIRS; INTERNATIONAL ECONOMIC POLICY, EXPORT AND TRADE PROMOTION, INTERNATIONAL OPERATIONS; NEAR EASTERN AND SOUTH ASIAN AFFAIRS; WESTERN HEMISPHERE, PEACE CORPS, NARCOTICS AND TERRORISM
U.S. Senate
Washington, DC 20510-6225 United States
Phone: 202-224-4651 Fax: 202-228-1608
Website: www.foreign.state.gov

Founded: N/A
Membership: 1–100
Scope: National
Description: Jurisdiction: Foreign and national security policy; international treaties, conferences, and congresses; World Bank and International Monetary Fund; oceans and international environmental and scientific affairs; humanitarian assistance and hunger; and United Nations and its affiliated organizations.

Contact(s):
Sam Brownback, Chair, Subcommittee on Near Eastern and South Asian Affairs
Christopher Dodd, Chair, Subcommittee on Western Hemisphere, Peace Corps, Narco
Bill Frist, Chair, Subcommittee on African Affairs
Rod Grams, Chair, Subcommittee on International Operations
Chuck Hagel, Chair, Subcommittee on International Economic Policy, Export

SENATE COMMITTEE ON HEALTH, EDUCATION, LABOR, AND PENSIONS

AGING; CHILDREN, FAMILY, DRUGS, AND ALCOHOLISM; EDUCATION, ARTS, AND HUMANITIES; EMPLOYMENT AND PRODUCTIVITY; HANDICAPPED; LABOR
SD-428 Dirksen Bldg.
Washington, DC 20510 United States
Phone: 202-224-5375
Website: www.access.gpo.gov

Founded: N/A

Contact(s):
James Jeffords, Chair

SOUTH ATLANTIC FISHERY MANAGEMENT COUNCIL

One Southpark Circle
Charleston, SC 29407-4699 United States
Phone: 843-571-4366 Fax: 843-769-4520
E-mail: safmc@safmc.net
Website: www.safmc.net

Founded: 1976
Membership: 1–100
Scope: Regional
Description: Responsible for the conservation and management of fish stocks within the 200-mile limit (federal waters) of the Atlantic off the coasts of North Carolina, South Carolina, Georgia, and Florida.
Publication(s): South Atlantic Update, Fishery Management Plans
Keyword(s): Oceans/Coasts/Beaches, Wildlife & Species
Contact(s):
Robert Mahood, Executive Director
Fulton Love, Chairman

SOUTH DAKOTA COOPERATIVE FISH AND WILDLIFE RESEARCH UNIT (USDI-USGS)

Department of Wildlife and Fisheries Sciences
P.O. Box 2140B
South Dakota State University
Brookings, SD 57007 United States
Phone: 605-688-6121 Fax: 605-688-4515
E-mail: charles_berry@sdstate.edu
Website: wfs.sdstate.edu

Founded: 1963
Scope: Local, State, Regional, National, International
Description: Conducts fish and wildlife research and provides educational experiences for fishery and wildlife biologists. Cooperators: South Dakota Department of Game, Fish and Parks, South Dakota State University, US Geological Survey, USDI, and Wildlife Management Institute.
Contact(s):
Charles Berry, Leader; 605-688-6121; Fax: 605-688-4515; charles_berry@sdstate.edu
Steven Chipps, Assistant Leader for Fisheries; steven_chipps@sdstate.edu
Kenneth Higgins, Assistant Leader for Wildlife; kenneth_higgins@sdstate.edu

SUSQUEHANNA RIVER BASIN COMMISSION

1721 N. Front St.
Harrisburg, PA 17102 United States
Phone: 717-238-0422 Fax: 717-238-2436
E-mail: srbc@srbc.net
Website: www.srbc.net

Founded: 1970
Membership: 1–100
Scope: Local, State, Regional
Description: Conservation and development of water resources and water-related resources in the river basin, comprising parts of Maryland, New York, and Pennsylvania.
Publication(s): Susquehanna Guardian (newsletter), Annual Report
Contact(s):
Paul Swartz, Executive Director; 1721 N. Front St., Harrisburg, PA 17102; 717-238-0422

SWAZILAND ENVIRONMENT AUTHORITY (SEA)

Ministry of Natural Resources Building
Mbabane, Swaziland
Phone: 2684041719

Founded: 1993
Description: SEA is the responsible government agency for environmental management in Swaziland (policy, EIA, legislation, monitoring, developing standards, environmental ed/public awareness)
Publication(s): Environment Management Act, Solid Waste Regulations, etc., Swaziland's Environment Action Plan
Contact(s):
J. Vilakati, Director; 268-404-1719
Irma Allen, Chair/Board; 268-404-1719; Fax: 268-518-6284; szallen@iafrica.sz
Stephen Zuke, Senior Environmental Officer; 268-404-1719

T

TANZANIA COASTAL MANAGEMENT PARTNERSHIP

Haile Selassie St., P.O. Box 71886
Dar Es Salaam, Tanzania
Phone: 255-51-667589 Fax: 255-51-668611
E-mail: gluhikula@epog.or.tz

Founded: N/A
Description: Integrated coastal management policy process in Tanzania.
Keyword(s): Oceans/Coasts/Beaches
Contact(s):
G. Luhikula, Contact

TENNESSEE VALLEY AUTHORITY

400 W. Summit Hill Dr.
Knoxville, TN 37902-1499 United States
Phone: 865-632-2101
E-mail: tvainfo@tva.gov
Website: www.tva.gov

Founded: 1933
Scope: Regional
Description: TVA was created by an Act of Congress for the regional development of the Tennessee Valley region in Tennessee, Kentucky, Mississippi, Alabama, Virginia, Georgia, and North Carolina. In 1964, TVA opened Land Between the Lakes as a national demonstration project for outdoor recreation, environmental education, and resource management.
Publication(s): Recreation on TVA Lakes, RiverPulse, various others on different subjects
Keyword(s): Air Quality/Atmosphere, Energy, Forests/Forestry, Land Issues, Pollution (general), Recreation/Ecotourism, Water Habitats & Quality, Wildlife & Species

TENNESSEE VALLEY AUTHORITY

KNOXVILLE AND CHATTANOOGA CORPORATE LIBRARY
400 W. Summit Hill Dr., ET PC
Knoxville, TN 37902-1499 United States
Phone: 865-632-3464
E-mail: corplibknox@tva.gov
Website: www.tva.gov

Founded: 1933

Scope: Local, State, Regional, National, International

Description: TVA achieves excellence in public service for the good of the people of the Tennessee Valley by supporting sustainable economic development, supplying affordable, reliable power, and managing a thriving river system. TVA's Knoxville and Chattanooga libraries support the agency's mission by providing research services and access to engineering, environmental and historical materials.

TENNESSEE VALLEY AUTHORITY

MUSCLE SHOALS TECHNICAL LIBRARY
CTR 1E
P.O.Box 1010
Muscle Shoals, AL 35662-1010 United States
Phone: 256-386-2872
E-mail: whclark@tva.gov

Founded: N/A

Scope: Local, State, Regional, National

Description: We are a technical library which specializes in environmental research.

TEXAS COOPERATIVE FISH AND WILDLIFE RESEARCH UNIT

Texas Tech. University
P.O. Box 42120
Lubbock, TX 79409-2120 United States
Phone: 806-742-2851 Fax: 806-742-2946
E-mail: txcoop@hobbes.tcru.ttu.edu
Website: www.tcru.ttu.edu/tcru/

Founded: 1988

Membership: 1–100

Scope: Local, State, Regional, National, International

Description: To conduct research, train graduate students, and provide technical assistance in the maintenance and management of fish and wildlife biodiversity, biological informatics, wetland ecology, molecular (genetic) biology, aquatic and wildlife ecology, general and reproductive physiology, and fish culture using the technical expertise of three federal staff members and collaborators.

Publication(s): www.tcru.ttu.edu/tcru

Keyword(s): Agriculture/Farming, Ecosystems (precious), Energy, Land Issues, Pollution (general), Public Health, Reduce/Reuse/Recycle, Sprawl/Urban Planning, Wildlife & Species

Contact(s):
Clint Boal, Assistant Leader—Wildlife; 806-742-2851; Fax: 806-742-2946
Nick Parker, Leader; 806-742-2851; Fax: 806-742-2946
Reynaldo Patino, Assistant Leader - Fisheries; 806-742-2851; Fax: 806-742-2946

U

UNITED NATIONS RESEARCH INSTITUTE FOR SOCIAL DEVELOPMENT (UNRISD)

Palais des Nations, CH 1211
Geneva 10, Switzerland
Phone: 41-22-798-8400 Fax: 41-22-740-0791
E-mail: info@UNRISD.org
Website: www.unrisd.org

Founded: 1963

Description: UNRISD is an autonomous agency that researches the social dimensions of contemporary development problems. The Institute provides governments, development agencies, grassroots organizations, and scholars with a better understanding of how development policies and processes of economic, social, and environmental change affect different social groups. UNRISD promotes original research and strengthens research capacity in developing countries.

Publication(s): Discussion Papers, Focus on Integrating Gender into The Politics of Development, The Challenge of Peace, UNRISD News

Keyword(s): Agriculture/Farming, Development/Developing Countries, Forests/Forestry, Land Issues, Reduce/Reuse/Recycle, Sprawl/Urban Planning, Wildlife & Species

Contact(s):
Dharam Ghai, Director

UNITED STATES DEPARTMENT OF AGRICULTURE

1400 Independence Ave. SW
Washington, DC 20250 United States
Phone: 202-720-8732
Website: www.usca.gov

Founded: 1862

Scope: National

Description: Created by Congress to acquire and disperse "useful" information on subjects connected with agriculture in the most general and comprehensive sense of that word, and to procure, propagate, and distribute among the people new and valuable seeds and plants. Today, in addition to managing the national forests and grasslands, USDA manages a variety of research, regulatory, domestic and foreign marketing, food and nutrition, and many other programs.

Contact(s):
Ann Beneman

UNITED STATES DEPARTMENT OF AGRICULTURE

AGRICULTURAL RESEARCH SERVICE
1400 Independence Ave., SW, Suite 302A
Washington, DC 20250 United States
Phone: 202-720-3656 Fax: 202-720-5427
Website: www.ars.usda.gov

Founded: N/A

Scope: Local, Regional

Description: Conducts research in natural resources, plant sciences, animal sciences, food sciences and human nutrition.

Contact(s):
Dwayne Buxton, Deputy Administrator; 301-504-5084
Allen Dedrick, Associate Deputy Administrator for Natural Resources; 301-504-7987
Floyd Horn, Administrator; 202-720-3656
Edward Knipling, Associate Administrator; 202-720-3658
Caird Rexroad, Associate Deputy Administrator for Animal Production; 301-504-7050
Judith St. John, Associate Deputy Administrator for Crop Production; 301-504-6252

UNITED STATES DEPARTMENT OF AGRICULTURE

ANIMAL AND PLANT HEALTH INSPECTION SERVICE
ANIMAL CARE
4700 River Road, Unit 84
Riverdale, MD 20737-0123 United States
Phone: 301-734-4980 Fax: 301-734-4978
E-mail: ace@usda.gov
Website: www.aphif.usda.gov/ac

Founded: N/A

Membership: 1–100

Scope: Local, Regional, National

Description: Investigates and prosecutes violations of federal laws governing the movement of animals and plants between states or into and out of the United States and regulates the humane care and treatment of warmblooded animals used for purposes of research or exhibiition, for sale as pets at the wholesale level, or transported in commerce.

Publication(s): List of Licensed Dealers, List of Licensed Exhibitors, List of Registered Research Facilities

Contact(s):
W. Dehaven, Deputy Administrator for Animal Care; 301-734-4980

Richard Watkins, Assitant Deputy Administrator for Animal Care; 301-734-7833

UNITED STATES DEPARTMENT OF AGRICULTURE
ANIMAL AND PLANT HEALTH INSPECTION SERVICE
ANIMAL CARE EASTERN REGIONAL OFFICE
920 Main Campus Drive, Suite 200
Raleigh, NC 27606 United States
Phone: 919-716-5532 Fax: 919-716-5696
E-mail: ace@usda.gov
Website: www.aphis.usda.gov/animalcare

Founded: N/A
Membership: 1–100
Scope: Regional
Contact(s):
Elizabeth Goldentyer, Regional Director

UNITED STATES DEPARTMENT OF AGRICULTURE
ANIMAL AND PLANT HEALTH INSPECTION SERVICE
ANIMAL CARE REGIONAL CENTRAL OFFICE
P.O. BOX 915004
Ft. Worth, TX 76115-9104 United States
Phone: 817-885-6923 Fax: 817-885-6917
E-mail: ace@usda.gov
Website: www.aphis.usda.gov/ac

Founded: N/A
Membership: 1–100
Scope: National
Contact(s):
Walter Christensen, Assistant Regional Director

UNITED STATES DEPARTMENT OF AGRICULTURE
ANIMAL AND PLANT HEALTH INSPECTION SERVICE
ANIMAL CARE WESTERN REGIONAL OFFICE
9580 Micron Ave., Suite J
Sacramento, CA 95827-2623 United States
Phone: 916-857-6205 Fax: 916-857-6212
Website: www.aphif.usda.gov/ac

Founded: N/A
Contact(s):
Robert Gibbons, Regional Director; 916-857-6205

UNITED STATES DEPARTMENT OF AGRICULTURE
ANIMAL AND PLANT HEALTH INSPECTION SERVICE
INTERNATIONAL SERVICES ASIA AND PACIFIC OFFICE
USDA-APHIS-IS American Embassy, Tokyo Unit 45004, Box 226 APO AP
Tokyo, 96337-5004 Japan
Phone: 81332245457 Fax: 81332245291

Founded: N/A
Contact(s):
Gary Green, Regional Director

UNITED STATES DEPARTMENT OF AGRICULTURE
ANIMAL AND PLANT HEALTH INSPECTION SERVICE
INTERNATIONAL SERVICES CENTRAL AMERICA, CARIBBEAN AND PANAMA OFFICE
USDA-APHIS-IS, American Embassy, Guatemala, Unit 3319
APO, 34024-3319 United States
Phone: 502-331-2036

Founded: N/A

UNITED STATES DEPARTMENT OF AGRICULTURE
ANIMAL AND PLANT HEALTH INSPECTION SERVICE
INTERNATIONAL SERVICES EUROPE, AFRICA, RUSSIA, NEAR EAST OFFICE
USDA-APHIS-IS FAS-USEU, PSC 82, Box 002
APO, 9724 United States
Phone: 322-508-2762

Founded: N/A

UNITED STATES DEPARTMENT OF AGRICULTURE
ANIMAL AND PLANT HEALTH INSPECTION SERVICE
INTERNATIONAL SERVICES MEXICO OFFICE
USDA-APHIS-IS, P.O. Box 3087
Laredo, TX 78044 United States

Founded: N/A
Contact(s):
Gordon Tween, Regional Director

UNITED STATES DEPARTMENT OF AGRICULTURE
ANIMAL AND PLANT HEALTH INSPECTION SERVICE
INTERNATIONAL SERVICES SCREWWORM ERADICATION PROGRAM OFFICE
USDA-APHIS-IS, P.O. Box 3087
Laredo, TX 78044 United States

Founded: N/A
Contact(s):
John Wyss, Regional Director

UNITED STATES DEPARTMENT OF AGRICULTURE
ANIMAL AND PLANT HEALTH INSPECTION SERVICE
INTERNATIONAL SERVICES SOUTH AMERICA OFFICE
USDA-APHIS-IS
American Embassy Santiago, Unit 4113
APO, NY 34033 United States
Phone: 562-638-1989

Founded: N/A

UNITED STATES DEPARTMENT OF AGRICULTURE
ANIMAL AND PLANT HEALTH INSPECTION SERVICE
NATIONAL WILDLIFE RESEARCH CENTER
4101 LaPorte Ave.
Fort Collins, CO 80521 United States
Phone: 970-266-6000 Fax: 970-266-6032
Website: www.aphis.usda.gov/ws/nwrc

Founded: N/A
Scope: National
Contact(s):
Richard Curnow, Director

UNITED STATES DEPARTMENT OF AGRICULTURE
ANIMAL AND PLANT HEALTH INSPECTION SERVICE
PLANT PROTECTION AND QUARANTINE
4700 River Road
Riverdale, MD 20737 United States
Phone: 301-734-8261
Website: www.aphis.usda.gov/ppq/

Founded: N/A
Description: Regulates the importation of plants, plant products, and animal products from foreign countries. Regulates the movement of such products between U.S. possessions and the mainland and the importation and interstate movement of plant pests. Inspects and certifies plants and plant products for export. Administers cooperative programs with states to control

and eradicate insects, diseases, weeds, and nematodes of economic importance.

Contact(s):
Richard Dunkle, Deputy Administrator; 202-720-5601; Richard.L.Dunkle@usda.gov

UNITED STATES DEPARTMENT OF AGRICULTURE
ANIMAL AND PLANT HEALTH INSPECTION SERVICE REGULATORY ENFORCEMENT EASTERN REGIONAL OFFICE
2568A Riva Rd., Suite 302
Annapolis, MD 21401-7400 United States
Phone: 410-571-9480 Fax: 410-962-0008
Website: www.aphis.usda.gov/ws/nwrc

Founded: N/A

Contact(s):
John Kinsella, Regional Director; Fax: 919-716-5626; john.s.kinsella@usda.gov

UNITED STATES DEPARTMENT OF AGRICULTURE
ANIMAL AND PLANT HEALTH INSPECTION SERVICE VETERINARY SERVICES
4700 River Road
Riverdale, MD 20737 United States
Phone: 301-734-8093
Website: www.aphis.usda.gov

Founded: N/A

Description: Regulates the importation of animals, animal semen, embryos, and animal products from foreign countries and the interstate movement of animals. Inspects and certifies animals for export. Administers cooperative federal-state programs to control and eradicate animal pests and diseases. Provides laboratory support for animal health programs and diagnostic referral assistance for private and state laboratories.

Contact(s):
Joseph Annelli, Chief Staff Veterinarian; 301-734-8073; joseph.f.annelli@usda.gov
Gary Colgrove, Assistant Director; 301-734-4356; gary.s.colgrove@usda.gov
Alfonso Torres, Deputy Administrator for Veterinary Services; 202-720-5193; alfonso.torres@usda.gov

UNITED STATES DEPARTMENT OF AGRICULTURE
CSREES-NATURAL RESOURCES AND ENVIRONMENT
Waterfront, Mail Stop 2210, 800 9TH St.
Washington, DC 20250-2210 United States
Phone: 202-401-4555 Fax: 202-401-1706

Founded: N/A
Membership: 1–100
Scope: Local
Description: NRE is the operational staff of the CSREES. NRE is responsible for providing leadership and administering research and educational programs that ensure the efficient use and conservation of the Nation's natural resources and protection of the environment.

Contact(s):
Larry Biles, National Program Leader, Forestry Management; 202-401-4926; ibiles@reeusda.gov
Catalino Blanche, National Program Leader, Forestry Biology; 202-401-4190; cblanche@reeusda.gov
Greg Crosby, National Program Leader, Sustainable Development; 202-401-6050; gcrosby@reeusda.gov
Jane Dodds, National Program Leader, Environmental Health; 202-401-4044; jdodds@reeusda.gov
Raymond Knighton, National Program Leader, Soils Science; 202-401-6417; knighton@reeusda.gov
Chuck Krueger, Liaison, State Ag. Experiment Station; 202-401-6516; ckrueger@psu.edu
Michael O'Neill, National Program Leader, Water Quality; 202-205-5952
Ralph Otto, Deputy Administrator; rotto@reeusda.gov
Mary Rozum, National Program Leader, Water Quality and Animal Waste; 202-401-4533; mrozum@reeusda.gov
Fred Swader, National Program Leader, Water Quality and Extension; 202-401-5853; fswader@reeusda.gov
Joe Wysocki, National Program Leader, Housing and Environment; 202-401-4980; jwysocki@reeusda.gov

UNITED STATES DEPARTMENT OF AGRICULTURE
ECONOMIC RESEARCH CENTER
1800 M St., NW
Washington, DC 20036 United States
Phone: 202-694-5050 Fax: 202-694-5734
Website: www.ers.usda.gov

Founded: N/A

Scope: Regional

Description: Provides a program of agricultural, economic, and social research and analysis, statistical programs, technical consultation, planning assistance, and associated services. Conducts research and staff work relating to natural resources and environmental quality, including supplies, uses, and projected future requirements for land and water; effects of environmental quality improvement measures on agricultural production and agricultural resource use.

Publication(s): Various research monographs on natural resources use, conservation, agricultural inputs, pest control

Contact(s):
Paul Chen, Director of Information Services Division, Acting
Adrie Custer, Director of Publication Services Branch
Kitty Smith, Director of Resource Economics Division
Susan Offutt, Administrator

UNITED STATES DEPARTMENT OF AGRICULTURE
FARM SERVICE AGENCY (FSA)
CONSERVATION AND ENVIRONMENTAL PROGRAMS DIVISION
USDA/FSA/CEPD/STOP 0513
1400 Independence Ave., S.W.
Washington, DC 20250-0513 United States
Phone: 202-720-6221 Fax: 202-720-4619
Website: www.fsa.usda.gov

Founded: 1936
Membership: 10,001–100,000
Scope: National
Description: Formerly known as AGRICULTURAL STABILIZATION AND CONSERVATION SERVICE. Administers the following: Conservation Reserve Program, Conservation Reserve Enhancement Program, Emergency Conservation Program, various commodity and farm loan programs, production flexibility contracts, and various farm loan and disaster assistance programs.

Keyword(s): Agriculture/Farming, Air Quality/Atmosphere, Climate Change, Ecosystems (precious), Energy, Water Habitats & Quality, Wildlife & Species

Contact(s):
Grady Bilberry, Director of Price Support Division
Diane Sharp, Director of Production, Emergencies and Compliance Division
Robert Stephenson, Director, Conservation and Environmental Programs
Tade Sullivan, Director of Public Affairs
Carolyn Cooksie, Deputy Administrator for Farm Loan Programs
James Little, Acting Administrator
Larry Mitchell, Deputy Administrator for Farm Programs

UNITED STATES DEPARTMENT OF AGRICULTURE
FOREST SERVICE
P.O. Box 96090
Washington, DC 20090-6090 United States
Phone: 202-205-8333 Fax: 202-205-1599
Website: www.fs.fed.us

Founded: N/A

Scope: National

Description: Administers National Forests and National Grasslands and is responsible for the management of their resources. Cooperates with federal and state officials in the enforcement of game laws on the National Forests and in the development and maintenance of wildlife resources; cooperates with the state and private owners in the application of sound forest management practices, in protection of forest lands against fire, insects, diseases, and in the distribution of planting stock.

Publication(s): See publications on website

Contact(s):
- Hilda Diaz-Stero, Director of Pacific SW Research Station Region 5; 202-205-1491
- Kathy Gause, Civil Rights Director; 202-205-1585
- Phil Janik, Director of Wildlife, Fish, Water & Air Research; 202-205-1661
- George Lennon, Director of Office Communications; 202-205-8333
- Randy Phillips, Executive Director of Forest County Payments; 202-205-1663
- Michael Rains, Director North East Research Station; 202-205-1657
- Dale Bosworth, Chief; 202-205-1661
- Paul Brouha, Associate Deputy National Forest System; 202-205-1465
- Sally Collins, Deputy Chief for Natural Resources; 202-205-1465
- Jim Furnish, Deputy National Forest System; 202-205-1523
- Vincette Goerl, Chief Financial Officer; 202-205-1784
- Robert Lewis, Deputy Research and Development; 202-205-1665
- Valdis Mezainis, International Programs; 202-205-1650
- Clyde Thompson, Business Operations; 202-205-1707
- Bill Wasley, Law Enforcement and Investigations; 703-605-4690
- Barbara Weber, Associate Deputy Research and Development; 202-205-1702

UNITED STATES DEPARTMENT OF AGRICULTURE
FOREST SERVICE
ALLEGHENY NATIONAL FOREST
222 Liberty St., Box 847
Warren, PA 16365 United States
Phone: 814-723-5150 Fax: 814-726-1465
Website: fs.fed.us/r9/allegheny

Founded: N/A

Membership: 101–1,000

Scope: Regional, National

Description: Managing the resources of the Allegheny National Forest

Keyword(s): Ecosystems (precious), Forests/Forestry

UNITED STATES DEPARTMENT OF AGRICULTURE
FOREST SERVICE
ANGELES NATIONAL FORESTS
701 N. Santa Anita Ave.
Arcadia, CA 91006-2725 United States
Phone: 626-574-1613 Fax: 626-574-5233

Founded: N/A

Scope: Regional

UNITED STATES DEPARTMENT OF AGRICULTURE
FOREST SERVICE
ANGELINA, DAVY CROCKETT, SABINE AND SAM HOUSTON NATIONAL FOREST
National Forest in Texas, Homer Garrison Federal Bldg., 701 N. 1st St.
Lufkin, TX 75901 United States

Founded: N/A

Scope: Regional

UNITED STATES DEPARTMENT OF AGRICULTURE
FOREST SERVICE
ANGELINA NATIONAL FOREST
Rt. 2 Box 242
Zavalla, TX 75980 United States
Phone: 936-897-1068 Fax: 936-897-3406
Website: www.r8web.com/texas

Founded: N/A

Scope: Local, State

Description: Angelina National Forest within the National Forests and Grasslands of Texas

Keyword(s): Ecosystems (precious), Forests/Forestry, Water Habitats & Quality, Wildlife & Species

UNITED STATES DEPARTMENT OF AGRICULTURE
FOREST SERVICE
APACHE-SITGREAVES NATIONAL FOREST
Federal Bldg., Box 640
Springville, AZ 85938 United States
Phone: 928-333-4301 Fax: 928-333-6357

Founded: N/A

Scope: Regional

UNITED STATES DEPARTMENT OF AGRICULTURE
FOREST SERVICE
ARAPAHO AND ROOSEVELT NATIONAL FORESTS
240 W. Prospect St.
Fort Collins, CO 80526 United States
Phone: 970-498-1375

Founded: N/A

Scope: Regional

UNITED STATES DEPARTMENT OF AGRICULTURE
FOREST SERVICE
ASHLEY NATIONAL FOREST
355 N. Vernal Ave.
Vernal, UT 84078 United States
Phone: 801-789-1181

Founded: N/A

Scope: Regional

UNITED STATES DEPARTMENT OF AGRICULTURE
FOREST SERVICE
BEAVERHEAD—DEERLODGE NATIONAL FOREST
420 Barrett St.
Dillon, MT 59725-3572 United States
Phone: 406-683-3900
Founded: N/A
Scope: Regional

UNITED STATES DEPARTMENT OF AGRICULTURE
FOREST SERVICE
BIENVILLE, DELTA, DESOTO, HOLLY SPRINGS, HOMOCHITTO, AND TOMBIGBEE NATIONAL FORESTS
National Forests in Mississippi, 100 W. Capital St., Ste. 1141
Jackson, MS 39269-1199 United States
Phone: 601-965-4391 Fax: 601-965-5519
Website: www.fs.fed.us/r8/miss
Founded: N/A
Scope: Regional

UNITED STATES DEPARTMENT OF AGRICULTURE
FOREST SERVICE
BIGHORN NATIONAL FOREST
1969 S. Sheridan Ave.
Sheridan, WY 82801 United States
Phone: 307-672-0751
Founded: N/A
Scope: Regional

UNITED STATES DEPARTMENT OF AGRICULTURE
FOREST SERVICE
BITTERROOT NATIONAL FOREST
1801 N. 1st St.
Hamilton, MT 59840 United States
Phone: 406-363-7121
Founded: N/A
Scope: Regional

UNITED STATES DEPARTMENT OF AGRICULTURE
FOREST SERVICE
BLACK HILLS NATIONAL FOREST
Hwy. 385 N. R.R. 2, Box 200
Custer, SD 57730-9501 United States
Phone: 605-673-9200 Fax: 605-673-9350
Founded: N/A
Scope: Regional

UNITED STATES DEPARTMENT OF AGRICULTURE
FOREST SERVICE
BOISE NATIONAL FOREST
1249 S. Vinnell Way, Ste. 200
Boise, ID 83709 United States
Phone: 208-373-4100
Website: www.fs.fed.us/r4/boise/
Founded: N/A
Scope: Regional

UNITED STATES DEPARTMENT OF AGRICULTURE
FOREST SERVICE
BRIDGER-TETON NATIONAL FOREST
Forest Service Bldg., 340 N. Cache
Jackson, WY 83001 United States
Phone: 307-739-5500 Fax: 307-739-5503
E-mail: r4_b-t_info@fs.fed.us
Website: www.fs.fed.us/btnf/
Founded: N/A
Scope: Regional

UNITED STATES DEPARTMENT OF AGRICULTURE
FOREST SERVICE
BUFFALO GAP NATIONAL GRASSLAND, FALL RIVER RANGER DISTRICT
P.O. Box 732
1801 Highway 18 Bypass
Hot Springs, SD 57747 United States
Phone: 605-745-4107
Founded: N/A
Scope: Local, State, Regional
Description: District office Buffalo Gap National Grasslands, Nebraska National Forest, U.S. Forest Service

UNITED STATES DEPARTMENT OF AGRICULTURE
FOREST SERVICE
BUFFALO GAP NATIONAL GRASSLAND, WALL RANGER DISTRICT / NATIONAL GRASSLANDS VISITOR CENTER
708 Main St., P.O. Box 425
Wall, SD 57790 United States
Phone: 605-279-2125
Founded: N/A
Scope: Regional

UNITED STATES DEPARTMENT OF AGRICULTURE
FOREST SERVICE
BUTTE VALLEY NATIONAL GRASSLAND
Goosewest Ranger District, 37805 Hwy. 97
Macdoel, CA 96058 United States
Phone: 530-398-4391
Founded: N/A
Scope: Regional

UNITED STATES DEPARTMENT OF AGRICULTURE
FOREST SERVICE
CARIBBEAN NATIONAL FOREST
Call Box 490
Palmer, PR 00721 United States
Phone: 787-888-1810 Fax: 787-888-5622
Website: www.r8web.com/caribbean/
Founded: N/A
Scope: Regional

UNITED STATES DEPARTMENT OF AGRICULTURE
FOREST SERVICE
CARIBOU—TARGHEE NATIONAL FOREST
1405 Hollipark Drive
Idaho Falls, ID 83401 United States
Phone: 208-524-7500
Founded: N/A
Scope: Regional

UNITED STATES DEPARTMENT OF AGRICULTURE
FOREST SERVICE
CARSON NATIONAL FOREST
Fed. Bldg., 208 Cruz Alta Rd., Box 558
Taos, NM 87571 United States
Phone: 505-758-6200

Founded: N/A

Scope: Regional

UNITED STATES DEPARTMENT OF AGRICULTURE
FOREST SERVICE
CEDAR RIVER / GRAND RIVER NATIONAL GRASSLAND
1005 5th Ave. W., P.O. Box 390
Lemmon, SD 57638 United States
Phone: 605-374-3592

Founded: N/A

Scope: Regional

UNITED STATES DEPARTMENT OF AGRICULTURE
FOREST SERVICE
CHATTAHOOCHEE AND OCONEE NATIONAL FORESTS
1755 Cleveland Hwy.
Gainesville, GA 30501 United States
Phone: 770-297-3000
Website: www.fs.fed.us/conf/

Founded: N/A

Scope: State

Description: Government Agency - Natural Resource Management

UNITED STATES DEPARTMENT OF AGRICULTURE
FOREST SERVICE
CHEQUAMEGON—NICOLET NATIONAL FOREST
1170 4th Ave., S.
Park Falls, WI 54552 United States
Phone: 715-762-2461

Founded: N/A

Scope: Regional

Contact(s):
Anne Archie, n/a

UNITED STATES DEPARTMENT OF AGRICULTURE
FOREST SERVICE
CHEROKEE NATIONAL FOREST
P.O. Box 2010
Cleveland, TN 37320 United States
Phone: 423-476-9700

Founded: N/A

Scope: Regional

UNITED STATES DEPARTMENT OF AGRICULTURE
FOREST SERVICE
CHEYENNE NATIONAL GRASSLAND
Box 946
Lisbon, ND 58054 United States
Phone: 701-683-4342

Founded: N/A

Scope: Regional

Contact(s):
Coleen Rufsvold, Manager; 701-683-4342; crufsvold@fs.fed.us

UNITED STATES DEPARTMENT OF AGRICULTURE
FOREST SERVICE
CHIPPEWA NATIONAL FOREST
200 Ash Ave., NW
Cass Lake, MN 56633 United States
Phone: 218-720-5324 Fax: 218-335-8637
Website: www.fs.fed.us/r9/chippewa/

Founded: N/A

Scope: Regional

UNITED STATES DEPARTMENT OF AGRICULTURE
FOREST SERVICE
CHUGACH NATIONAL FOREST
3301 C St., Ste. 300
Anchorage, AK 99503-3956 United States
Phone: 907-271-2525

Founded: N/A

Scope: Regional

UNITED STATES DEPARTMENT OF AGRICULTURE
FOREST SERVICE
CIBOLA NATIONAL FOREST
2113 Osuna Rd. NE, Ste. A
Albuquerque, NM 87111–1001 United States
Phone: 505-761-4650

Founded: N/A

Scope: Regional

UNITED STATES DEPARTMENT OF AGRICULTURE
FOREST SERVICE
CIMARRON NATIONAL GRASSLAND
242 Hwy. 56 E., P.O. Box 300
Elkhart, KS 67950 United States
Phone: 620-697-4621 Fax: 620-697-4340
Website: www.fs.fed.us/r2/psicc/cim

Founded: N/A

Scope: Regional

Description: National Grassland management

UNITED STATES DEPARTMENT OF AGRICULTURE
FOREST SERVICE
CLEARWATER NATIONAL FOREST
12730 Highway 12
Orofino, ID 83544 United States
Phone: 208-476-4541

Founded: N/A

Scope: Regional

UNITED STATES DEPARTMENT OF AGRICULTURE
FOREST SERVICE
CLEVELAND NATIONAL FOREST
10845 Rancho Bernardo Rd., Ste. 200
San Diego, CA 92127 United States
Phone: 858-674-2901 Fax: 858-673-6192

Founded: N/A

Scope: Regional

UNITED STATES DEPARTMENT OF AGRICULTURE
FOREST SERVICE
COCONINO NATIONAL FOREST
2323 E. Greenlaw Ln.
Flagstaff, AZ 86004 United States
Phone: 928-527-3600 Fax: 928-527-3620
Website: www.fs.fed.us/r3/coconino

Founded: 1908

Scope: Regional

Description: USDA, Forest Service, National Forest

UNITED STATES DEPARTMENT OF AGRICULTURE
FOREST SERVICE
COLVILLE NATIONAL FOREST
716 S. Main
Colville, WA 99114 United States
Phone: 509-662-4335

Founded: N/A

Scope: Regional

UNITED STATES DEPARTMENT OF AGRICULTURE
FOREST SERVICE
COMANCHE NATIONAL GRASSLAND
27204 Hwy. 287, P.O. Box 127
Springfield, CO 81073 United States
Phone: 719-523-6591

Founded: N/A

Scope: Regional

Contact(s):
Ben Garcia, Manager; 719-523-6591; bgarcia02@fs.fed.us

UNITED STATES DEPARTMENT OF AGRICULTURE
FOREST SERVICE
CORONADO NATIONAL FOREST
300 W. Congress
Tucson, AZ 85701 United States
Phone: 520-670-4552 Fax: 520-670-4567

Founded: N/A

Scope: Regional

UNITED STATES DEPARTMENT OF AGRICULTURE
FOREST SERVICE
CROATAN, NANTAHALA, PISGAH AND UWHARRIE NATIONAL FORESTS
National Forests in North Carolina, P.O. Box 2750
Asheville, NC 28802 United States
Phone: 828-257-4200 Fax: 828-257-4263
Website: www.cs.unca.edu/nfsnc

Founded: N/A

Scope: National, International

Description: National Forests

Contact(s):
Larry Hayden, Ecosystems & Planning Staff Officer; 828-257-4200, ext. 864; Fax: 828-257-4263

UNITED STATES DEPARTMENT OF AGRICULTURE
FOREST SERVICE
CROOKED RIVER NATIONAL GRASSLAND
813 SW Hwy. 97
Madras, OR 97741 United States
Phone: 541-475-9272

Founded: N/A

Scope: Local, Regional

Description: District Manager, Range Conservationist, Range Techs, Wildlife Biologist, Office Manager

Keyword(s): Agriculture/Farming, Ecosystems (precious), Forests/Forestry, Land Issues, Recreation/Ecotourism, Water Habitats & Quality, Wildlife & Species

Contact(s):
Robert Rock, District Manager
Glenn Adams, Range Conservationist
Anne Alford, Wildlife Biologist

UNITED STATES DEPARTMENT OF AGRICULTURE
FOREST SERVICE
CURLEW NATIONAL GRASSLAND
P.O. Box 146
Malad, ID 83252 United States
Phone: 208-766-6474
Website: www.fs.fed.us/r4/caribou/

Founded: N/A

Scope: Regional

UNITED STATES DEPARTMENT OF AGRICULTURE
FOREST SERVICE
CUSTER NATIONAL FOREST
P.O. Box 50760
Billings, MT 59105 United States
Phone: 406-657-6361

Founded: N/A

Scope: Regional

UNITED STATES DEPARTMENT OF AGRICULTURE
FOREST SERVICE
DANIEL BOONE NATIONAL FOREST
1700 Bypass Rd.
Winchester, KY 40391 United States
Phone: 606-745-3100

Founded: N/A

Scope: Regional

UNITED STATES DEPARTMENT OF AGRICULTURE
FOREST SERVICE
DESCHUTES NATIONAL FOREST
1645 Highway 20 East
Bend, OR 97701 United States
Phone: 541-388-2715

Founded: N/A

Scope: Regional

UNITED STATES DEPARTMENT OF AGRICULTURE
FOREST SERVICE
DIXIE NATIONAL FOREST
82 N. 100 E St.
Cedar City, UT 84720-2686 United States
Phone: 435-865-3701
Website: www.fs.fed.us/dxnf

Founded: N/A

Scope: Regional

UNITED STATES DEPARTMENT OF AGRICULTURE
FOREST SERVICE
ELDORADO NATIONAL FOREST
100 Forni Rd.
Placerville, CA 95667 United States
Phone: 530-622-5061 Fax: 530-621-5297

Founded: N/A
Scope: Regional

UNITED STATES DEPARTMENT OF AGRICULTURE
FOREST SERVICE
FINGER LAKES NATIONAL FOREST
5218 State Route 414
Hector, NY 14841 United States
Phone: 607-546-4470 Fax: 607-546-4474
Website: www.fs.fed.us/r9/gmfl

Founded: 1958
Membership: N/A
Scope: Local, State, Regional, National, International
Description: The mission of the Finger Lakes National Forest is to sustain, protect and enhance forest ecosystems. We understand that our greatest asset is the land, our greatest strength is our work force, and we will strive to gain public understanding, trust, and confidence in all that we do through demonstration and education.
Keyword(s): Forests/Forestry
Contact(s):
Paul Brewster, Forest Supervisor; 802-747-6704; Fax: 802-747-6766; pbrewster@fs.fed.us
Michael Dockry, Forest Planner; 607-546-4470, ext. 316; Fax: 607-546-4474; mdockry@fs.fed.us
Martha Twarkins, Hector District Ranger; 607-546-4470, ext. 314; Fax: 607-546-4474; mtwarkins@fs.fed.us

UNITED STATES DEPARTMENT OF AGRICULTURE
FOREST SERVICE
FISHLAKE NATIONAL FOREST
115 East 900 North
Richfield, UT 84701 United States
Phone: 435-896-9233

Founded: N/A
Scope: Regional
Contact(s):
May Erickson, Manager; 435-896-1001; mcerickson@fs.fed.us

UNITED STATES DEPARTMENT OF AGRICULTURE
FOREST SERVICE
FLATHEAD NATIONAL FOREST
1935 3rd. Ave., E.
Kalispell, MT 59901 United States
Phone: 406-758-5251
Website: www.fs.fed.us/r1/flathead

Founded: 1905
Membership: 101–1,000
Scope: State
Description: Manage the Flathead National Forest

UNITED STATES DEPARTMENT OF AGRICULTURE
FOREST SERVICE
FORT PIERRE NATIONAL GRASSLAND
124 South Euclid Ave., P.O. Box 417
Pierre, SD 57501 United States
Phone: 605-224-5517 Fax: 605-224-6517

Founded: N/A
Scope: Regional
Contact(s):
Anthony Detoy, n/a; 605-224-5517; adetoy@fs.fed.us

UNITED STATES DEPARTMENT OF AGRICULTURE
FOREST SERVICE
FRANCIS MARION AND SUMTER NATIONAL FOREST
4931 Broad River Rd.
Columbia, SC 29212-3530 United States
Phone: 803-561-4000 Fax: 803-561-4004
Website: www.fs.fed.us/r8/fms

Founded: N/A
Scope: Local, State, Regional, National
Description: Natural Resource

UNITED STATES DEPARTMENT OF AGRICULTURE
FOREST SERVICE
FREMONT NATIONAL FOREST
1301 S. G St.
Lakeview, OR 97630 United States
Phone: 541-947-2151

Founded: N/A
Scope: Regional

UNITED STATES DEPARTMENT OF AGRICULTURE
FOREST SERVICE
GALLATIN NATIONAL FOREST
10 E. Babcock Ave., Federal Bldg., Box 130
Bozeman, MT 59771 United States
Phone: 406-587-6701 Fax: 406-587-6758

Founded: N/A
Scope: Regional
Contact(s):
Becki Heath, Forest Supervisor
Rich Inman, Deputy Forest Supervisor

UNITED STATES DEPARTMENT OF AGRICULTURE
FOREST SERVICE
GEORGE WASHINGTON AND JEFFERSON NATIONAL FORESTS
5162 Valleypointe Pkwy.
Roanoke, VA 24019 United States
Phone: 540-265-5100
Website: www.southernregion.fs.fed.us/gwj/

Founded: N/A
Scope: Regional
Description: Manage 1.8 million acres of National Forest land in Virginia and West Virginia.

UNITED STATES DEPARTMENT OF AGRICULTURE
FOREST SERVICE
GIFFORD PINCHOT NATIONAL FOREST
6926 E. 4th Plain Blvd.
Vancouver, WA 98668-8944 United States
Phone: 360-891-5000
Website: www.fs.fed.us/gpnf

Founded: N/A
Scope: Regional

UNITED STATES DEPARTMENT OF AGRICULTURE
FOREST SERVICE
GILA NATIONAL FOREST
3005 E. Camino del Bosque
Silver City, NM 88061 United States
Phone: 505-388-8201 Fax: 505-388-8204
Website: www.fs.fed.us/r3/gila

Founded: 1905

Scope: National

Description: The Gila National Forest is part of the Southwestern Region of National Forests and Grasslands

Keyword(s): Air Quality/Atmosphere, Ecosystems (precious), Forests/Forestry, Land Issues, Public Lands/Greenspace, Recreation/Ecotourism, Water Habitats & Quality, Wildlife & Species

UNITED STATES DEPARTMENT OF AGRICULTURE
FOREST SERVICE
GRAND MESA, UNCOMPAHGRE AND GUNNISON NATIONAL FORESTS
2250 Highway 50
Delta, CO 81416 United States
Phone: 970-874-6600

Founded: N/A

Scope: Regional

UNITED STATES DEPARTMENT OF AGRICULTURE
FOREST SERVICE
GREEN MOUNTAIN NATIONAL FOREST
231 N. Main Street
Rutland, VT 05701 United States
Phone: 802-747-6700 Fax: 802-747-6766
Website: www.fs.fed.us/r9/gmfl

Founded: 1932
Membership: N/A
Scope: Local, State, Regional, National, International

Description: The mission of the Green Mountain National Forest is to sustain, protect and enhance forest ecosystems. We understand that our greatest asset is the land, our greatest strength is our work force, and we will strive to gain public understanding, trust, and confidence in all that we do through demonstration and education.

Keyword(s): Air Quality/Atmosphere, Development/Developing Countries, Ecosystems (precious), Forests/Forestry, Land Issues, Pollution (general), Public Lands/Greenspace, Reduce/Reuse/Recycle, Water Habitats & Quality

Contact(s):

Paul Brewster, Forest Supervisor; 802-747-6704; Fax: 802-747-6766; pbrewster@fs.fed.us

Kathleen Diehl, Public Affairs Officer; 802-747-6709; Fax: 802-747-6766; kdiehl@fs.fed.us

Melissa Reichert, Forest Planner; 802-747-6754; Fax: 802-747-6766; mmreichert@fs.fed.us

UNITED STATES DEPARTMENT OF AGRICULTURE
FOREST SERVICE
HELENA NATIONAL FOREST
2880 Skyway Dr.
Helena, MT 59602 United States
Phone: 406-449-5201

Founded: N/A

UNITED STATES DEPARTMENT OF AGRICULTURE
FOREST SERVICE
HIAWATHA NATIONAL FOREST
2727 N. Lincoln Rd.
Escanaba, MI 49829 United States
Phone: 906-786-4062

Founded: N/A

Scope: Regional

UNITED STATES DEPARTMENT OF AGRICULTURE
FOREST SERVICE
HOOSIER NATIONAL FOREST
811 Constitution Ave.
Bedford, IN 47421 United States
Phone: 812-275-5987

Founded: N/A

Scope: Regional

UNITED STATES DEPARTMENT OF AGRICULTURE
FOREST SERVICE
HUMBOLDT—TOIYABE NATIONAL FOREST
2035 1200 Franklin Way
Sparks, NV 89431 United States
Phone: 775-331-6444

Founded: N/A

Scope: Regional

UNITED STATES DEPARTMENT OF AGRICULTURE
FOREST SERVICE
HURON-MANISTEE NATIONAL FOREST
1755 S. Mitchell St.
Cadillac, MI 49601 United States
Phone: 616-775-2421

Founded: N/A

Scope: Regional

UNITED STATES DEPARTMENT OF AGRICULTURE
FOREST SERVICE
IDAHO PANHANDLE NATIONAL FORESTS
83815 Schreiber Way
Coeur d'Alene, ID 83815-8863 United States
Phone: 208-765-7223

Founded: N/A

UNITED STATES DEPARTMENT OF AGRICULTURE
FOREST SERVICE
INYO NATIONAL FOREST
873 N. Main St.
Bishop, CA 93514 United States
Phone: 760-873-2400 Fax: 760-873-2458

Founded: N/A

Scope: Regional

UNITED STATES DEPARTMENT OF AGRICULTURE
FOREST SERVICE
KAIBAB NATIONAL FOREST
800 South 6th St.
Williams, AZ 86046 United States
Phone: 928-635-2681 Fax: 928-635-8208

Founded: N/A

Scope: Regional

Contact(s):
Mike Williams, Director; 928-635-2681

UNITED STATES DEPARTMENT OF AGRICULTURE
FOREST SERVICE
KIOW / RITA BLANCA NATIONAL GRASSLAND
714 Main St.
Clayton, NM 88415 United States
Phone: 505-374-9652
Founded: N/A
Scope: Regional

UNITED STATES DEPARTMENT OF AGRICULTURE
FOREST SERVICE
KISATCHIE NATIONAL FOREST
2500 Shreveport Hwy.
Pineville, LA 71360 United States
Phone: 318-473-7160 Fax: 318-473-7117
Founded: N/A
Scope: Regional

UNITED STATES DEPARTMENT OF AGRICULTURE
FOREST SERVICE
KLAMATH NATIONAL FOREST
1312 Fairlane Rd.
Eureka, CA 96097 United States
Phone: 530-842-6131 Fax: 530-841-4571
Founded: N/A
Scope: Regional

UNITED STATES DEPARTMENT OF AGRICULTURE
FOREST SERVICE
KOOTENAI NATIONAL FOREST
506 US Highway 2 West
Libby, MT 59923 United States
Phone: 406-293-6211
Founded: N/A
Scope: Regional

UNITED STATES DEPARTMENT OF AGRICULTURE
FOREST SERVICE
LAKE TAHOE BASIN MANAGEMENT UNIT
870 Emerald Bay Rd., Ste. 1
South Lake Tahoe, CA 96150 United States
Phone: 530-573-2600 Fax: 530-573-2780
Founded: N/A
Scope: Regional

UNITED STATES DEPARTMENT OF AGRICULTURE
FOREST SERVICE
LEWIS AND CLARK NATIONAL FOREST
Box 869, 1101 15th St., N.
Great Falls, MT 59403 United States
Phone: 406-791-7700
Founded: N/A
Scope: Regional

UNITED STATES DEPARTMENT OF AGRICULTURE
FOREST SERVICE
LINCOLN NATIONAL FOREST
Fed. Bldg., 1101 New York Ave.,
Alamogordo, NM 88310-6992 United States
Phone: 505-434-7200
Founded: N/A
Scope: Regional

UNITED STATES DEPARTMENT OF AGRICULTURE
FOREST SERVICE
LITTLE MISSOURI NATIONAL FOREST, MCKENZIE RANGER DISTRICT
1901 S. Main Street
Watford City, ND 58854 United States
Phone: 701-842-2393
Founded: N/A
Scope: Regional
Contact(s):
Frank Guzman, n/a; 701-842-2393; fguzman@fs.fed.us

UNITED STATES DEPARTMENT OF AGRICULTURE
FOREST SERVICE
LITTLE MISSOURI NATIONAL GRASSLANDS, MEDORA RANGER DISTRICT
161 21st St. W.
Dickinson, ND 58601 United States
Phone: 701-225-5151
Website: www.fs.fed.us/r1/dakotaprairie
Founded: N/A
Scope: Regional

UNITED STATES DEPARTMENT OF AGRICULTURE
FOREST SERVICE
LOLO NATIONAL FOREST
Bldg. 24, Ft. Missoula
Missoula, MT 59801 United States
Phone: 406-329-3797
Founded: N/A
Scope: Regional

UNITED STATES DEPARTMENT OF AGRICULTURE
FOREST SERVICE
LOS PADRES NATIONAL FOREST
6755 Hollister Avenue
Suite 150
Goleta, CA 93117 United States
Phone: 805-968-6640
Website: www.r5.fs.fed.us/lospadres
Founded: N/A
Scope: Regional
Description: 1.75 million acre national forest in the central coastal mountains of California. Five ranger districts with offices in King City, Santa Maria, Santa Barbara, Ojai and Frazier Park, CA. Forest Supervisor's Office is in Goleta, CA. Forest consists of a wide variety of landscapes and habitats from coastal, to oak savannah and high elevation conifer forest, to arid badlands.
Keyword(s): Ecosystems (precious), Energy, Forests/Forestry, Land Issues, Oceans/Coasts/Beaches, Public Lands/Greenspace, Recreation/Ecotourism, Water Habitats & Quality, Wildlife & Species

Contact(s):
Maeton Freel, Wildlife Biologist; 805-961-5764; mfreel@fs.fed.us
Jeff Saley, Human Resource/Volunteer Program Coordinator; 805-961-5771; jsaley@fs.fed.us
Rich Tobin, Director of Conservation Partnerships; 805-961-5748; rtobin@fs.fed.us

UNITED STATES DEPARTMENT OF AGRICULTURE
FOREST SERVICE
LYNDON B. JOHNSON / CADDO NATIONAL FOREST
1400 N. US. 81/287 Hwy., P.O. Box 507
Decatur, TX 76234 United States
Phone: 940-627-5475
Website: southernregion.fs.fed.us.fordtexas.com
Founded: N/A
Scope: Regional
Contact(s):
Tim Crooks, n/a; 940-627-5475; jcrooks@fs.fed.us

UNITED STATES DEPARTMENT OF AGRICULTURE
FOREST SERVICE
MALHEUR NATIONAL FOREST
139 NE Dayton St.
John Day, OR 97845 United States
Phone: 541-575-1731
Founded: N/A
Scope: Regional

UNITED STATES DEPARTMENT OF AGRICULTURE
FOREST SERVICE
MANTI-LASAL NATIONAL FOREST
599 West Price River Dr.
Price, UT 84501 United States
Phone: 435-637-2817 Fax: 435-637-4940
Website: www.fs.fed.us/r4/mantilasal/
Founded: N/A
Scope: Regional

UNITED STATES DEPARTMENT OF AGRICULTURE
FOREST SERVICE
MARK TWAIN NATIONAL FOREST
410 Fairgrounds Rd.
Rolla, MO 65401 United States
Phone: 573-364-4621
Website: www.fs.fed.us/r9/marktwain/
Founded: N/A
Scope: Regional

UNITED STATES DEPARTMENT OF AGRICULTURE
FOREST SERVICE
MCCLELLAN CREEK/BLACK KETTLE NATIONAL GRASSLAND
Rt. 1, Box 55B
Cheyenne, OK 73628 United States
Phone: 580-497-2143
Founded: N/A
Scope: Regional
Contact(s):
Bryan Hajny, Wildlife Biologist; 580-497-2143; bhajny@fs.fed.us

UNITED STATES DEPARTMENT OF AGRICULTURE
FOREST SERVICE
MEDICINE BOW-ROUTT NATIONAL FOREST
2468 Jackson St.
Laramie, WY 82070-6535 United States
Phone: 307-745-2300 Fax: 307-745-2398
Website: www.fs.fed.us/r2/mbr/
Founded: N/A
Scope: Regional

UNITED STATES DEPARTMENT OF AGRICULTURE
FOREST SERVICE
MENDOCINO NATIONAL FOREST
825 N. Humboldt Ave.
Willows, CA 95988 United States
Phone: 530-233-5811
Founded: N/A
Scope: Regional

UNITED STATES DEPARTMENT OF AGRICULTURE
FOREST SERVICE
MODOC NATIONAL FOREST
800 W. 12th St.
Alturas, CA 96101 United States
Phone: 530-233-5811 Fax: 530-233-8709
Founded: N/A
Scope: Regional

UNITED STATES DEPARTMENT OF AGRICULTURE
FOREST SERVICE
MONONGAHELA NATIONAL FOREST
USDA Bldg., 200 Sycamore St.
Elkins, WV 26241-3962 United States
Phone: 304-636-1800
Founded: N/A
Scope: Regional
Description: USDA Forest Service

UNITED STATES DEPARTMENT OF AGRICULTURE
FOREST SERVICE
MT. HOOD NATIONAL FOREST
2955 Division St.
Gresham, OR 97030 United States
Phone: 503-666-1700
Founded: N/A
Scope: Regional

UNITED STATES DEPARTMENT OF AGRICULTURE
FOREST SERVICE
NATIONAL FORESTS IN ALABAMA
2946 Chestnut St.
Montgomery, AL 36107 United States
Phone: 334-832-4470
Founded: N/A
Scope: Regional

UNITED STATES DEPARTMENT OF AGRICULTURE
FOREST SERVICE
NATIONAL FORESTS IN FLORIDA
Woodcrest Office Park, 325 John Knox Rd., Ste. F-100
Tallahassee, FL 32303 United States
Phone: 850-942-9300

Founded: N/A

Scope: Regional

UNITED STATES DEPARTMENT OF AGRICULTURE
FOREST SERVICE
NEBRASKA NATIONAL FOREST
125 N. Main St.
Chadron, NE 69337 United States
Phone: 308-432-0300

Founded: N/A

Scope: Regional

UNITED STATES DEPARTMENT OF AGRICULTURE
FOREST SERVICE
NEZ PERCE NATIONAL FOREST
Rt. 2, Box 475
Grangeville, ID 83530 United States
Phone: 208-983-1950 Fax: 208-983-4099
Website: www.fs.fed.us/r1/nezperce

Founded: 1906
Membership: 101–1,000
Scope: Regional
Description: USDA Forest Service Northern Region, Nez Perce National Forest, Forest Supervisor's Office
Keyword(s): Ecosystems (precious), Forests/Forestry, Land Issues, Public Lands/Greenspace, Recreation/Ecotourism, Water Habitats & Quality, Wildlife & Species
Contact(s):
Laura Smith, Public Affairs Officer; 208-983-1950, ext. 4102; lasmith@fs.fed.us

UNITED STATES DEPARTMENT OF AGRICULTURE
FOREST SERVICE
NORTH CENTRAL RESEARCH STATION
1992 Folwell Ave.
St. Paul, MN 55108 United States
Phone: 651-649-5000 Fax: 651-649-5285
Website: ncrs.fs.fed.us

Founded: N/A
Membership: N/A
Scope: Local, State, Regional, National, International
Description: The Station, part of the Forest Service's Research & Development branch, employs 45 scientists and more than 200 technical and support people located in 7 Midwestern states. The Station strives to enhance the quality of people's lives by providing the knowledge and tools to help people make informed choices about natural resources. We supply the scientific and technical foundation for actions that ensure clean air, sparkling water, rich soil, healthy economies, and a diverse living landscape.
Contact(s):
Linda Donoghue, Director

UNITED STATES DEPARTMENT OF AGRICULTURE
FOREST SERVICE
NORTHEASTERN RESEARCH STATION
100 Matsonford Rd., 5 Radnor Corporate Center, Suite 200
Radnor, PA 19087-4585 United States
Phone: 610-975-4017

Founded: N/A

Contact(s):
Bob Eav, Director

UNITED STATES DEPARTMENT OF AGRICULTURE
FOREST SERVICE
OCHOCO NATIONAL FOREST
P.O. Box 490
Prineville, OR 97754 United States
Phone: 541-416-6500 Fax: 541-416-6695
Website: www.fs.fed.us/r6/centraloregon

Founded: N/A

Scope: Regional

UNITED STATES DEPARTMENT OF AGRICULTURE
FOREST SERVICE
OGLALA NATIONAL GRASSLAND
16524 Hwy. 385
Chadron, NE 69337 United States
Phone: 308-432-4475

Founded: N/A

Scope: Regional

UNITED STATES DEPARTMENT OF AGRICULTURE
FOREST SERVICE
OKANOGAN NATIONAL FOREST
1240 S. Second
Okanogan, WA 98840 United States
Phone: 509-826-3275

Founded: N/A

Scope: Regional

UNITED STATES DEPARTMENT OF AGRICULTURE
FOREST SERVICE
OLYMPIC NATIONAL FOREST
1835 Blacklake Blvd., SW
Olympia, WA 98512 United States
Phone: 360-956-2300

Founded: N/A

Scope: Regional

UNITED STATES DEPARTMENT OF AGRICULTURE
FOREST SERVICE
OTTAWA NATIONAL FOREST
2100 E. Cloverland Dr.
Ironwood, MI 49938 United States
Phone: 906-932-1330

Founded: N/A

Scope: Regional

UNITED STATES DEPARTMENT OF AGRICULTURE
FOREST SERVICE
OUACHITA NATIONAL FOREST
Box 1270, Federal Bldg.
Hot Springs National Park, AR 71902 United States
Phone: 501-321-5202 Fax: 501-321-5353
Website: www.fs.fed.us/oont/ouach.ta.htm

Founded: 1890

Scope: Regional

Contact(s):
Maureen Hyzer, Deputy Supervisor; 501-321-5202

UNITED STATES DEPARTMENT OF AGRICULTURE
FOREST SERVICE
OZARK—ST. FRANCIS NATIONAL FOREST
605 West Main St.
Russellville, AR 72801 United States
Phone: 479-968-2354 Fax: 479-964-7255
E-mail: r8.ozark.forinfo@fs.fed.us
Website: www.fs.fed.us/ooonf/ozark/welcome.html

Founded: N/A

Scope: Regional

UNITED STATES DEPARTMENT OF AGRICULTURE
FOREST SERVICE
PACIFIC NORTHWEST RESEARCH STATION
P.O. Box 3890
Portland, OR 97208 United States
Phone: 503-808-2592
Website: www.fs.fed.us.pnw

Founded: N/A

Contact(s):
Robert Szaro, Director; 503-808-2100

UNITED STATES DEPARTMENT OF AGRICULTURE
FOREST SERVICE
PACIFIC SOUTHWEST RESEARCH STATION
800 Buchanan St., West Annex Building
Albany, CA 94710-0011 United States
Phone: 510-559-6310 Fax: 510-559-6440
E-mail:
mailroom_pacificsouthwest_research_station@fs.fed.us
Website: www.psw.fs.fed.us

Founded: N/A

Scope: National

Publication(s): See publications on website

Contact(s):
Garland Mason, Director, Acting

UNITED STATES DEPARTMENT OF AGRICULTURE
FOREST SERVICE
PAWNEE NATIONAL GRASSLAND
660 O St.
Greeley, CO 80631 United States
Phone: 970-353-5004

Founded: N/A

Scope: Regional

Contact(s):
Steve Currey, Manager; 970-353-5004; scurrey@fs.fed.us

UNITED STATES DEPARTMENT OF AGRICULTURE
FOREST SERVICE
PAYETTE NATIONAL FOREST
Payette National Forest, Box 1026
McCall, ID 83638 United States
Phone: 208-634-0700

Founded: N/A

Scope: Regional

UNITED STATES DEPARTMENT OF AGRICULTURE
FOREST SERVICE
PIKE AND SAN ISABEL NATIONAL FORESTS
2840 Kachina Dr.
Pueblo, CO 81008 United States
Phone: 719-553-1400

Founded: N/A

UNITED STATES DEPARTMENT OF AGRICULTURE
FOREST SERVICE
PLUMAS NATIONAL FOREST
159 Lawrence St., Box 11500
Quincy, CA 95971 United States
Phone: 530-283-2050 Fax: 530-283-7746

Founded: N/A

Scope: Regional

UNITED STATES DEPARTMENT OF AGRICULTURE
FOREST SERVICE
PRESCOTT NATIONAL FOREST
344 S. Cortez Street
Prescott, AZ 86303 United States
Phone: 928-771-4700 Fax: 928-771-4884
Website: www.fs.fed.us/r3/prescott

Founded: 1898

Scope: Regional

Description: The Prescott National Forest lies in west Central Arizona. Total acreage is approximately 1.25 million acres. At the lowest elevation, the vegetation is of the Sonoran Desert type. As the elevation rises, chaparral becomes common, followed by pinon pine and juniper. Above that, ponderosa pine dominates. The forest offers many activities including hiking, mountain biking, camping, wildlife viewing, OHV use, hunting and fishing to name just a few.

Keyword(s): Forests/Forestry

UNITED STATES DEPARTMENT OF AGRICULTURE
FOREST SERVICE
REGION 01 (NORTHERN)
200 E. Broadway, P.O. Box 7669
Missoula, MT 59807 United States
Phone: 406-329-3316 Fax: 406-329-3411
Website: www.fs.fed.us

Founded: N/A

Scope: National

Contact(s):
Brad Powell, Regional Forester

UNITED STATES DEPARTMENT OF AGRICULTURE
FOREST SERVICE
REGION 02 (ROCKY MOUNTAIN)
P.O. Box 25127
Lakewood, CO 80225 United States
Phone: 303-275-5450

Founded: N/A
Membership: 101–1,000
Scope: Regional
Contact(s):
Rick Cables, Regional Forester

UNITED STATES DEPARTMENT OF AGRICULTURE
FOREST SERVICE
REGION 04 (INTERMOUNTAIN)
Federal Office Bldg. 324, 25th St.
Ogden, UT 84401 United States
Phone: 801-625-5605 Fax: 801-625-5359
Website: www.fs.fed.us

Founded: N/A
Scope: Regional
Contact(s):
Jack Troyer, Regional Forester
Glenna Prevado, Assistant

UNITED STATES DEPARTMENT OF AGRICULTURE
FOREST SERVICE
REGION 05 (PACIFIC SOUTHWEST)
Mare Island, 1323 Club Dr.
Vallejo, CA 94592 United States
Phone: 707-562-9000
Website: www.r.fs.fed.us

Founded: N/A
Contact(s):
Bradley Powell, Regional Forester

UNITED STATES DEPARTMENT OF AGRICULTURE
FOREST SERVICE
REGION 06 (PACIFIC NORTHWEST)
333 SW 1st Ave.
Portland, OR 97208 United States
Phone: 503-808-2200
Website: www.fs.fed.us

Founded: N/A
Scope: Regional
Contact(s):
Harvey Forsgren, Regional Forester

UNITED STATES DEPARTMENT OF AGRICULTURE
FOREST SERVICE
REGION 08 (SOUTHERN)
1720 Peachtree Rd., NW,
Atlanta, GA 30309 United States
Phone: 404-347-4178 Fax: 404-347-4821

Founded: N/A
Scope: Regional
Contact(s):
Elizabeth Estill, Regional Forester

UNITED STATES DEPARTMENT OF AGRICULTURE
FOREST SERVICE
REGION 09 (EASTERN)
310 W. Wisconsin Ave., Suite 580
Milwaukee, WI 53203 United States
Phone: 414-297-3600 Fax: 414-297-3778
Website: www.fs.fed.us.

Founded: N/A
Scope: State
Contact(s):
Robert Jacobs, Regional Forester

UNITED STATES DEPARTMENT OF AGRICULTURE
FOREST SERVICE
REGION 10 (ALASKA)
P.O. Box 21628
709 W. 9th St.
Juneau, AK 99802-1628 United States
Phone: 907-586-8863 Fax: 907-586-7840
Website: www.fs.fed.us

Founded: N/A
Scope: Regional
Contact(s):
Paul Forward, Acting Regional Forester

UNITED STATES DEPARTMENT OF AGRICULTURE
FOREST SERVICE
RIO GRANDE NATIONAL FOREST
1803 West Highway 160
Monte Vista, CO 81144 United States
Phone: 719-852-5941

Founded: N/A
Scope: Regional

UNITED STATES DEPARTMENT OF AGRICULTURE
FOREST SERVICE
ROCKY MOUNTAIN RESEARCH STATION
2150 Centre Ave., Bldg. A, Suite 376
Ft. Collins, CO 80526-2098 United States
Phone: 970-295-5926 Fax: 970-295-5927
Website: www.fs.fed.us/rm

Founded: N/A
Membership: 101–1,000
Scope: Local, State, Regional, National, International
Description: The Rocky Mountain Research Station develops scientific information and technology to improve management, protection, and use of the forests and rangelands. Research is designed to meet the needs of National Forest managers, Federal and State agencies, public and private organizations, academic institutes, industry, and individuals.
Keyword(s): Air Quality/Atmosphere, Climate Change, Ecosystems (precious), Forests/Forestry, Land Issues, Pollution (general), Public Lands/Greenspace, Recreation/ Ecotourism, Water Habitats & Quality, Wildlife & Species
Contact(s):
Marcia Patton-Mallory, Director; 970-295-5925; Fax: 970-295-5927; mpattonmallory@fs.fed.us

UNITED STATES DEPARTMENT OF AGRICULTURE
FOREST SERVICE
ROGUE RIVER NATIONAL FOREST
Fed. Bldg., 333 W. 8th St., Box 520
Medford, OR 97501 United States
Phone: 541-776-3600

Founded: N/A
Scope: Regional

UNITED STATES DEPARTMENT OF AGRICULTURE
FOREST SERVICE
ROUTT NATIONAL FOREST
925 Wiess Dr.
Steamboat Springs, CO 80487-9550 United States
Phone: 970-879-1870
Founded: N/A
Scope: Local

UNITED STATES DEPARTMENT OF AGRICULTURE
FOREST SERVICE
SALMON-CHALLIS NATIONAL FOREST
Forest Service
50 Highway 93 South
Salmon, ID 83467 United States
Phone: 208-756-5100
Founded: N/A
Scope: Regional

UNITED STATES DEPARTMENT OF AGRICULTURE
FOREST SERVICE
SAN BERNARDINO NATIONAL FOREST
1824 S. Commercenter Cir.
San Bernardino, CA 92408 United States
Phone: 909-383-5588 Fax: 909-383-5770
Founded: N/A
Scope: Regional

UNITED STATES DEPARTMENT OF AGRICULTURE
FOREST SERVICE
SAN JUAN NATIONAL FOREST
San Juan Public Land Center
Federal Bldg., 15 Burnett Court
Durango, CO 81301-3647 United States
Phone: 970-247-4874
Founded: N/A
Scope: Regional

UNITED STATES DEPARTMENT OF AGRICULTURE
FOREST SERVICE
SANTA FE NATIONAL FOREST
1220 St. Francis Dr.
Santa Fe, NM 87504 United States
Phone: 505-438-7834 Fax: 505-438-7834
Website: www.fs.fed.us/r3/sfe/
Founded: N/A
Scope: Regional

UNITED STATES DEPARTMENT OF AGRICULTURE
FOREST SERVICE
SAWTOOTH NATIONAL FOREST
2647 Kimberly Rd., East
Twin Falls, ID 83301-7976 United States
Phone: 208-737-3200
Founded: N/A
Scope: Regional

UNITED STATES DEPARTMENT OF AGRICULTURE
FOREST SERVICE
SEQUOIA NATIONAL FOREST
900 W. Grand Ave.
Porterville, CA 93257 United States
Phone: 209-784-1500
Founded: N/A
Scope: Regional

UNITED STATES DEPARTMENT OF AGRICULTURE
FOREST SERVICE
SHASTA-TRINITY NATIONAL FOREST
2400 Washington Ave.
Redding, CA 96001 United States
Phone: 530-244-2978 Fax: 530-242-2233
Founded: N/A
Scope: Local
Description: Federal Agency managing the Shasta-Trinity National Forest

UNITED STATES DEPARTMENT OF AGRICULTURE
FOREST SERVICE
SHAWNEE NATIONAL FOREST
901 S. Commercial St.
Harrisburg, IL 62946 United States
Phone: 618-253-7114
E-mail: mailroom_r9_shawnee@fs.fed.us
Website: www.fs.fed.us/r9/shawnee/
Founded: 1933
Scope: Regional

UNITED STATES DEPARTMENT OF AGRICULTURE
FOREST SERVICE
SHOSHONE NATIONAL FOREST
808 Meadow Ln.
Cody, WY 82414-4516 United States
Phone: 307-527-6241
Founded: N/A
Scope: Regional
Contact(s):
Rebecca Aus, Manager; 307-527-6241; raus@fs.fed.us

UNITED STATES DEPARTMENT OF AGRICULTURE
FOREST SERVICE
SIERRA NATIONAL FOREST
1600 Tollhouse Rd.
Clovis, CA 93611 United States
Phone: 559-297-0706, ext. 4800 Fax: 559-294-4809
Founded: N/A
Scope: Regional

UNITED STATES DEPARTMENT OF AGRICULTURE
FOREST SERVICE
SISKIYOU NATIONAL FOREST
Box 440
Grants Pass, OR 97526 United States
Phone: 541-471-6500
Founded: N/A
Scope: Regional

UNITED STATES DEPARTMENT OF AGRICULTURE
FOREST SERVICE
SIUSLAW NATIONAL FOREST
P.O. Box 1148
Corvallis, OR 97339 United States
Phone: 541-750-7000 Fax: 541-750-7234
Founded: N/A
Scope: Regional
Keyword(s): Agriculture/Farming, Air Quality/Atmosphere, Ecosystems (precious), Forests/Forestry, Land Issues, Oceans/Coasts/Beaches, Recreation/Ecotourism, Water Habitats & Quality, Wildlife & Species

UNITED STATES DEPARTMENT OF AGRICULTURE
FOREST SERVICE
SIX RIVERS NATIONAL FOREST
1330 Bayshore Way
Eureka, CA 95501 United States
Phone: 707-442-1721
Founded: N/A
Scope: Regional

UNITED STATES DEPARTMENT OF AGRICULTURE
FOREST SERVICE
SOUTHERN RESEARCH STATION
P.O. Box 2750
Asheville, NC 28802 United States
Phone: 828-257-4832 Fax: 828-257-4263
Website: www.cs.unca.edu/nfsnc
Founded: N/A
Scope: State
Contact(s):
Rob McClanahan, Forest Wildlife Biologist

UNITED STATES DEPARTMENT OF AGRICULTURE
FOREST SERVICE
SOUTHWESTERN REGION 3
333 Broadway S.E.
Albuquerque, NM 87102 United States
Phone: 505-842-3300 Fax: 505-842-3110
Founded: N/A
Contact(s):
Eleanor Towns, Regional Forester

UNITED STATES DEPARTMENT OF AGRICULTURE
FOREST SERVICE
STANISLAUS NATIONAL FOREST
19777 Greenley Rd.
Sonora, CA 95370 United States
Phone: 209-532-3671 Fax: 209-533-1890
Founded: N/A
Scope: Regional

UNITED STATES DEPARTMENT OF AGRICULTURE
FOREST SERVICE
SUPERIOR NATIONAL FOREST
8901 Grand Avenue Place
Duluth, MN 55808-1102 United States
Phone: 218-626-4300
Website: www.superiornationalforest.org
Founded: N/A
Scope: Regional

UNITED STATES DEPARTMENT OF AGRICULTURE
FOREST SERVICE
TAHOE NATIONAL FOREST
631 Coyote St.
Nevada City, CA 95959-6003 United States
Phone: 530-265-4531 Fax: 530-478-6109
Founded: N/A
Scope: Regional

UNITED STATES DEPARTMENT OF AGRICULTURE
FOREST SERVICE
THUNDER BASIN NATIONAL GRASSLANDS
2250 East Richards
Douglas, WY 82633 United States
Phone: 307-358-4690
Website: www.fs.fed.us/r2/mbr
Founded: N/A
Scope: Regional
Contact(s):
Norman Wagoner, District Ranger; 307-358-4690

UNITED STATES DEPARTMENT OF AGRICULTURE
FOREST SERVICE
TONGASS NATIONAL FOREST
SITKA OFFICE
204 Siginaka Way
Sitka, AK 99835-7316 United States
Phone: 907-747-6671 Fax: 907-747-4331
Website: www.fs.fed.us/r10/tongass/
Founded: N/A
Scope: Regional
Description: Manages land and resources of the Tongass National Forest

UNITED STATES DEPARTMENT OF AGRICULTURE
FOREST SERVICE
TONGASS-KETCHIKAN AREA NATIONAL FOREST
Federal Bldg.
Ketchikan, AK 99901-6591 United States
Phone: 907-228-6281
Founded: N/A
Scope: Regional

UNITED STATES DEPARTMENT OF AGRICULTURE
FOREST SERVICE
TONGASS-PETERSBURG OFFICE NATIONAL FOREST
Box 309
Petersburg, AK 99833-0309 United States
Phone: 907-772-3841 Fax: 907-772-5895
Website: www.fs.fed.us/r10/tongass/
Founded: N/A
Scope: Regional
Description: Land and resource management agency

UNITED STATES DEPARTMENT OF AGRICULTURE
FOREST SERVICE
TONTO NATIONAL FOREST
2324 E. McDowell Rd.
Phoenix, AZ 85006 United States
Phone: 602-225-5200 Fax: 602-225-5295
Founded: N/A
Scope: Regional

UNITED STATES DEPARTMENT OF AGRICULTURE
FOREST SERVICE
UINTA NATIONAL FOREST
88 West 100 North
Provo, UT 84601 United States
Phone: 801-342-5100
Founded: N/A
Scope: Regional
Contact(s):
Peter Karp, Manager; 801-342-5100; peterkarp@fs.fed.us

UNITED STATES DEPARTMENT OF AGRICULTURE
FOREST SERVICE
UMATILLA NATIONAL FOREST
2517 SW Hailey Ave.
Pendleton, OR 97801 United States
Phone: 541-278-3716
Website: www.fs.fed.us/r6/uma
Founded: N/A
Scope: Regional

UNITED STATES DEPARTMENT OF AGRICULTURE
FOREST SERVICE
UMPQUA NATIONAL FOREST
Box 1008
Roseburg, OR 97470 United States
Phone: 541-672-6601
Founded: N/A
Scope: Regional

UNITED STATES DEPARTMENT OF AGRICULTURE
FOREST SERVICE
WALLOWA WHITMAN NATIONAL FORESTS
Box 907
Baker City, OR 97814 United States
Phone: 541-523-6391
Website: www.fs.fed.us/r6/w-w
Founded: N/A
Scope: Regional

UNITED STATES DEPARTMENT OF AGRICULTURE
FOREST SERVICE
WASATCH-CACHE NATIONAL FOREST
8236 Federal Bldg., 125 S. State St.
Salt Lake City, UT 84138 United States
Phone: 801-524-5030
Founded: N/A
Scope: Regional

UNITED STATES DEPARTMENT OF AGRICULTURE
FOREST SERVICE
WAYNE NATIONAL FOREST
219 Columbus Rd.
Athens, OH 45701 United States
Phone: 740-592-6644
Founded: N/A
Scope: Regional

UNITED STATES DEPARTMENT OF AGRICULTURE
FOREST SERVICE
WENATCHEE NATIONAL FOREST
215 Melody Lane
Wenatchee, WA 98801 United States
Phone: 509-662-4335 Fax: 509-662-4368
Website: www.fs.fed.us/r6/wenatchee/
Founded: N/A
Scope: Regional

UNITED STATES DEPARTMENT OF AGRICULTURE
FOREST SERVICE
WHITE MOUNTAIN NATIONAL FOREST
Federal Bldg. 719 Main St., Box 638
Laconia, NH 03247 United States
Phone: 603-528-8721
Founded: N/A
Scope: Regional

UNITED STATES DEPARTMENT OF AGRICULTURE
FOREST SERVICE
WHITE RIVER NATIONAL FOREST
Old Federal Bldg., P.O. Box 948
Glenwood Springs, CO 81602 United States
Phone: 970-945-2521
Founded: N/A
Scope: Regional

UNITED STATES DEPARTMENT OF AGRICULTURE
FOREST SERVICE
WILLAMETTE NATIONAL FOREST
Box 10607
Eugene, OR 97440 United States
Phone: 541-465-6521
Founded: N/A
Scope: Regional

UNITED STATES DEPARTMENT OF AGRICULTURE
FOREST SERVICE
WINEMA NATIONAL FOREST
2819 Dahlia
Klamath Falls, OR 97601 United States
Phone: 541-883-6714
Founded: N/A
Scope: Regional

UNITED STATES DEPARTMENT OF AGRICULTURE
RESEARCH EDUCATION AND ECONOMICS
1400 Independence Ave., SW
Washington, DC 20250-0110 United States
Phone: 202-720-5923 Fax: 202-690-2842
Website: www.usda.gov
Founded: N/A
Membership: 1–100
Scope: National
Contact(s):
Joseph Jen, Under Secretary

UNITED STATES DEPARTMENT OF AGRICULTURE
RESEARCH EDUCATION AND ECONOMICS
ARS BELTSVILLE AREA
10300 Baltimore Rm. 223, B-003 BARC-West
Beltsville, MD 20705 United States
Phone: 301-504-6078 Fax: 301-504-5863
Website: www.ba.ars.usda.gov

Founded: N/A

Scope: National

Contact(s):
Phyllis Johnson, Area Director
Ronald Korcak, Associate Area Director

UNITED STATES DEPARTMENT OF AGRICULTURE
RESEARCH EDUCATION AND ECONOMICS
ARS MID SOUTH OFFICE
P.O. Box 225
Stoneville, MS 38776 United States
Phone: 662-686-5265 Fax: 662-686-5459
E-mail: atucker@ars.usda.gov
Website: www.ars.usda.gov

Founded: N/A
Membership: 101–1,000
Scope: Regional

Contact(s):
Edgar King, Area Director

UNITED STATES DEPARTMENT OF AGRICULTURE
RESEARCH EDUCATION AND ECONOMICS
ARS MIDWEST OFFICE
1815 N. University St.
Peoria, IL 61604 United States
Phone: 309-681-6602 Fax: 309-681-6684
Website: www.mva.arf.usda.gov

Founded: N/A
Membership: 1–100
Scope: Regional
Publication(s): Midwest Area Research Highlights 2000

Contact(s):
Adrianna Hewings, Area Director

UNITED STATES DEPARTMENT OF AGRICULTURE
RESEARCH EDUCATION AND ECONOMICS
ARS NORTH ATLANTIC OFFICE
600 E. Mermaid Ln.
Windmoor, PA 19038 United States
Phone: 215-233-6593 Fax: 215-233-6719

Founded: N/A
Membership: 101–1,000
Scope: National

Contact(s):
Wilda Martinez, Area Director

UNITED STATES DEPARTMENT OF AGRICULTURE
RESEARCH EDUCATION AND ECONOMICS
ARS NORTHERN PLAINS AREA OFFICE
1201 Oakridge Dr.
Fort Collins, CO 80525 United States
Phone: 970-229-5500 Fax: 970-229-5565
Website: www.npa.ars.usda.gov

Founded: N/A
Membership: 1–100
Scope: State, National

Contact(s):
Wilbert Blackburn, Area Director

UNITED STATES DEPARTMENT OF AGRICULTURE
RESEARCH EDUCATION AND ECONOMICS
ARS PACIFIC WEST AREA
800 Buchanan St.
Albany, CA 94710 United States
Phone: 510-559-6060 Fax: 510-559-5779
E-mail: abetschart@pw.ars.usda.gov
Website: www.pwa.ars.usda.gov

Founded: 1890
Membership: 1,001–10,000
Scope: National, International
Description: The USDA ARS Pacific West Area consists of 52 Research Programs in the eight western states of AK, AR, CA, HI, ID, NV, OR and WA. Research is conducted by some 1400 employees at 25 centers. The $145 million budget is appropriated by the U.S.Congress. Research projects are issue-driven and the outcome of the research is directed to the customers and beneficiaries through technology transfer. Scientific excellence with impact is the hallmark of USDA ARS research in the Pacific West Area.

Contact(s):
A. Betschart, Area Director

UNITED STATES DEPARTMENT OF AGRICULTURE
RESEARCH EDUCATION AND ECONOMICS
ARS SOUTH ATLANTIC OFFICE
Russell Agr. Res. Center, P.O. Box 5677,
College Station Rd.
Athens, GA 30604-5677 United States
Phone: 706-546-3311 Fax: 706-546-3398
Website: www.ars-grin.gov/ars/soatlantic

Founded: N/A

Contact(s):
Karl Narang, Area Director

UNITED STATES DEPARTMENT OF AGRICULTURE
RESEARCH EDUCATION AND ECONOMICS
ARS SOUTHERN PLAINS OFFICE
7607 Eastmark Dr., Suite 230
College Station, TX 77840 United States

Founded: N/A

UNITED STATES DEPARTMENT OF AGRICULTURE
RESEARCH EDUCATION AND ECONOMICS
COOPERATIVE STATE RESEARCH, EDUCATION, AND EXTENSION SERVICE
1400 Independence Ave., SW., 305A
Washington, DC 20250 United States
Phone: 202-720-7441 Fax: 202-720-8987
Website: www.reeusda.gov

Founded: N/A
Description: The Cooperative State Research, Education, and Extension Service links the research and education resources and programs of the U.S. Department of Agriculture and works with land-grant institutions in each state, territory, and the District of Columbia.

Contact(s):
George Cooper, Deputy Administrator for Partnerships; 202-720-5623; george.cooper@usda.gov
Jane Coulter, Deputy Administrator for Science and Education Resources; 202-720-3377
Colien Hefferan, Administrator; 202-720-7441; colien.hefferan@usda.gov

Alma Hobbs, Deputy Administrator for Families, 4-H and Nutrition; 202-720-2908; alma.hobbs@usda.gov
Sally Rockey, Deputy Administrator for Competitive Research Grants; 202-401-1761

UNITED STATES DEPARTMENT OF AGRICULTURE NATURAL RESOURCES CONSERVATION SERVICES

NATURAL RESOURCES CONSERVATION SERVICE
USDA, 14th and Independence Ave., SW, P.O. Box 2890
Washington, DC 20013 United States
Phone: 202-720-3210 Fax: 202-720-1564
Website: www.nrcs.usda.gov

Founded: 1935
Membership: N/A
Scope: National
Description: (formerly Soil Conservation Service) NRCS provides leadership in a partnership effort to help people conserve, maintain, and improve our natural resources and environment. NRCS is the technical delivery arm for conservation of the United States Department of Agriculture. It provides technical assistance and conservation programs through a unique partnership with America's conservation districts and state agencies.
Contact(s):
Terry Bish, Director, Conservation Communications Staff; Room 6121-S, Washington, DC 20013
Renae Anderson, WI Public Affairs Specialist; 6515 Watts Rd., Suite 200, Madison, WI 53719-2726; 608-276-8732; Fax: 608-276-5890; randerso@wi.nrcs.usda.gov
Nancy Atkinson, WY Public Affairs Specialist; Federal Office Bldg., 100 East B St., Room 3124, Casper, WY 82601; 307-261-6482; Fax: 307-261-6490; nla@wy.nrcs.usda.gov
Petra Barnes, CO Public Affairs Specialist; 655 Parfet St., Rm. E 200C, Lakewood, CO 80215-5517; 303-236-2886, ext. 216; Fax: 303-236-2896; pbarnes@co.nrcs.usda.gov
Lynn Betts, IA Public Affairs Specialist; 693 Federal Bldg., 210 Walnut St., Des Moines, IA 50309-2180; 515-284-4262; Fax: 515-284-4394; lynn.betts@ia.nrcs.usda.gov
Chris Bieker, WA Public Affairs Specialist; Rock Pointe Tower 2, Suite 450, West 316 Boone Ave., Spokane, WA 99201-2348; 509-323-2912; Fax: 509-323-2909; cbieker@wa.nrcs.usda.gov
Larry Blick, TN Public Affairs Specialist; 675 U.S. Courthouse, 801 Broadway St., Nashville, TN 37203-3878; 615-736-5490; Fax: 615-736-7764; lblick@tn.nrcs.usda.gov
Herb Bourque, LA Public Affairs Specialist; 3737 Government St., Alexandria, LA 71302-3727; 318-473-7762; Fax: 318-473-7682; hbourque@laso2.la.nrcs.usda.gov
Anita Brown, CA Public Affairs Specialist; 2121-C 2nd St., Suite 102, Davis, CA 95616-5475; 530-792-5644; Fax: 530-792-5791; anita.brown@ca.usda.gov
Harold Bryant, TX Public Affairs Specialist; W.R. Poage Federal Bldg., 101 S. Main St., Temple, TX 76501-7682; 254-742-9811; Fax: 254-742-9819; hbryant@tx.nrcs.usda.gov
Paige Buck, IL Public Affairs Specialist; 1902 Fox Dr., Champaign, IL 61820-7335; 217-398-5273; Fax: 217-398-5310; paige.mitchell@il.nrcs.usda.gov
Kathy Carpenter, NY Public Affairs Specialist; 441 S. Salilna Street, Suite 354, Syracuse, NY 13202; 315-477-6524; kathy.carpenter@ny.nrcs.usda.gov
Sonja Coderre, AR Public Affairs Specialist; Federal Office Bldg., Rm. 5404, 700 W. Capitol Ave., Little Rock, AR 72201-3228; 501-301-3133; Fax: 501-301-3189; scoderre@ar.usda.gov
Jeanne Comerford, RI Public Affairs Specialist; 60 Quaker Ln., Suite 46, Warwick, RI 02886-0111; 401-828-1300; Fax: 401-828-0433; jcomerford@ri.nrcs.usda.gov
Christina Coulon, MI Public Affairs Specialist; 1405 S. Harrison Rd., Rm. 101, East Lansing, MI 48823-5243; 517-337-6701; Fax: 517-337-6905; ccoulon@miso.mi.nrcs.usda.gov
Arlene Deutscher, ND Public Affairs Specialist; Federal Bldg., 220 E. Rosser Ave., Rm. 278, 220 E. Rosser Ave., Bismarck, ND 58502-1458; 701-250-4768; Fax: 701-250-4778; ajd@nd.nrcs.usda.gov
Carol Donzella, CT Public Affairs Specialist; 344 Merrow Rd, Tolland, CT 06084; 203-787-0390; caroldonzella@ct.usda.gov
Becky Fraticelli, Puerto Rico Public Affairs Specialist; IBM Bldg., 6th Flr., 654 Munoz Rivera Ave., Hato Rey, PR 00918-7013; 787-766-5206, ext. 236; Fax: 787-766-5987; becky@pr.nrcs.usda.gov
Joyce Hawkins, Program Assistant; Room 6121-S, Washington, DC 20013; 202-720-3210; Fax: 202-720-1564; joyce.hawkins@usda.gov
Anne Hillard, VT Public Affairs Specialist; 69 Union St., Winooski, VT 05404-1999; 802-951-6796; Fax: 802-951-6327; ahillard@vt.nrcs.usda.gov
Carol Hollingsworth, MD Public Affairs Specialist; John Hanson Business Center, 339 Busch's Frontage Rd., Suite 30, Annapolis, MD 21401-5534; 410-757-0861, ext. 313; Fax: 410-757-0687; carol.hollingsworth@md.usda.gov
Lynn Howell, HI Public Affairs Specialist; 300 Ala Moana Blvd., Rm. 4316, Honolulu, HI 96850-0002; 808-541-2600; Fax: 808-541-2652; lhowell@hi.nrcs.usda.gov
Lois Jackson, KY Public Affairs Specialist; 771 Corporate Dr., Suite 110, Lexington, KY 40503-5479; 606-224-7372; Fax: 606-224-7399; ljackson@kystate.ky.nrcs.usda.gov
Betty Joubert, NM Public Affairs Specialist; 6200 Jefferson St., NE, Suite 305, Albuquerque, NM 87109-3734; 505-761-4406; Fax: 505-761-4463; betty.joubert@nm.usda.gov
Norm Klopfenstein, MO Public Affairs Specialist; Parkade Center, Suite 250, 601 Business Loop, 70 West, Columbia, MO 65203-2546; 573-876-0911; Fax: 573-876-0913; normk@mo.nrcs.usda.gov
Wendi Kroll, MA Public Affairs Specialist; 451 West St., Amherst, MA 01002-2995; 413-253-4351; Fax: 413-253-4375; wkroll@ma.nrcs.usda.gov
Irene Lieberman, NJ Public Affairs Specialist; 1370 Hamilton St., Somerset, NJ 08873-3157; 732-246-1171, ext. 124; Fax: 732-246-2358; ilieberman@nj.nrcs.usda.gov
Jeanine May, MS Public Affairs Specialist; Federal Bldg., Suite 1321, 100 W. Capitol St., Jackson, MS 39269-1399; 601-965-4337; Fax: 601-965-4536; jbm@ms.nrcs.usda.gov
Michael McGovern, IN Public Affairs Specialist; 6013 Lakeside Blvd., Indianapolis, IN 46278-2933; 317-290-3222, ext. 324; Fax: 317-290-3225; mmcgover@in.nrcs.usda.gov
Pat McGrane, NE Public Affairs Specialist; Federal Bldg., Rm. 152, 100 Centennial Mall, N., Lincoln, NE 68508-3866; 402-437-5328; Fax: 402-437-5327; pat.mcgrane@ne.usda.gov
Mary McQuinn, AZ Public Affairs Specialist; 3003 N. Central Ave., Suite 800, Phoenix, AZ 85012-2945; 602-280-8778; Fax: 602-280-8809; mmcquinn@az.nrcs.usda.gov
Stacy Mitchell, PA Public Affairs Specialist; One Credit Union Pl., Suite 340, Harrisburg, PA 17110-2993; 717-237-2208; Fax: 717-237-2238; smitchell@pa.nrcs.usda.gov
Laura Morton, NH Public Affairs Specialist; Federal Bldg. 2 Madbury Rd, Durham, NH 03824; 732-246-1171
Marie Mundheim, Pacific Basin Public Affairs Specialist; 671-472-7490, ext. 21; Fax: 671-472-7298; pacbas@ite.net
Gayle Norman, OR Public Affairs Specialist; 101 SW Main Street, Suite 1300, Portland, OR 97204-3221; 503-414-3236; Fax: 503-414-3101; gnorman@or.nrcs.usda.gov
Sharon Norris, ID Public Affairs Specialist; 3244 Elder St., Room 124, Boise, ID 83705-4711; 208-378-5725; Fax: 208-378-5735; snorris@id.nrcs.usda.gov
Pat Paul, VA Public Affairs Specialist; Culpeper Bldg., 1606 Santa Rosa Rd., Suite 209, Richmond, VA 23229-5014; 804-287-1681; Fax: 804-287-1737; ppaul@va.nrcs.usda.gov

Paul Petrichenko, DE Public Affairs Specialist; 1203 College Park Dr., Suite 101, Dover, DE 19904-8713; 302-678-4178; Fax: 302-678-0843; ppetrichencko@de.nrcs.usda.gov
Dwain Phillips, OK Public Affairs Specialist; 100 USDA Agriculture Center Bldg., Suite 203, Stillwater, OK 74074-2624; 405-742-1243; Fax: 405-742-1201; dwain.phillip@ok.usda.gov
Sylvia Rainford, MN Public Affairs Specialist; 600 Farm Credit Services Bldg., 375 Jackson St., St. Paul, MN 55101-1854; 612-602-7859; Fax: 612-602-7914; str@mn.nrcs.usda.gov
Peg Reese, WV Public Affairs Specialist; 75 High St., Rm. 301, Morgantown, WV 26505; 304-291-4152, ext. 168; Fax: 304-291-4628; preese@wv.nrcs.usda.gov
Mary Schaffer, KS Public Affairs Specialist; 760 S. Broadway, Salina, KS 67401; 785-823-4571; Fax: 785-823-4540; mary.shaffer@ks.nrcs.usda.gov
Andrew Smith, NC Public Affairs Specialist; 4405 Bland Rd., Suite 205, Raleigh, NC 27609-6293; 919-873-2107; Fax: 919-873-2156; asmith@nc.nrcs.usda.gov
Dorothy Staley, FL Public Affairs Specialist; 2614 NW 43rd St., Gainesville, FL 32606-6611; 352-338-9565; Fax: 352-338-9574; dstaley@fl.nrcs.usda.gov
Elaine Tremble, ME Public Affairs Specialist; 5 Godfrey Dr., Orono, ME 04473; 207-866-7241; Fax: 207-866-7262; etremble@me.nrcs.usda.gov
Lori Valdez, MT Public Affairs Specialist; Federal Bldg., Rm. 443, 10 E. Babcock St., Bozeman, MT 59715-4704; 406-587-6842; Fax: 406-587-6761; lvaldez@mt.nrcs.usda.gov
Liz Warner, NV Public Affairs Specialist; 5301 Langley Ln., Bldg. F, Suite 201, Reno, NV 89511; 775-784-5288; Fax: 702-784-5939; ewarner@nv.nrcs.usda.gov
Joyce Watkins, SD Public Affairs Specialist; 200 4th St., SW, Federal Bldg., Huron, SD 57350-2475; 605-352-1228; Fax: 605-352-1261; joyce.watkins@sdso1.sd.nrcs.usda.gov

UNITED STATES DEPARTMENT OF COMMERCE

Herbert C. Hoover Bldg., Rm. 5610, 14th St. and Constitution Ave., NW
Washington, DC 20230 United States
Phone: 202-219-3605 Fax: 202-482-5168
Website: www.doc.gov

Founded: N/A

Scope: International

Description: The Department of Commerce promotes job creation, economic growth, sustainable development, and improved living standards for all Americans, by working in partnership with business, universities, communities, and workers.

Contact(s):
Donald Evans, Secretary; 202-482-4883
Robert Mallett, Deputy Secretary

UNITED STATES DEPARTMENT OF COMMERCE

ECONOMIC DEVELOPMENT ADMINISTRATION
Department of Commerce
Herbert C. Hoover Bldg.
14th St. and Constitution Ave., NW
Washington, DC 20230 United States
Phone: 202-482-5081 Fax: 202-273-4781
E-mail: edawebmaster@eda.eoc.gov
Website: www.doc.gov/eda

Founded: N/A

Scope: National

Description: Conducts programs to help stimulate private enterprise and create permanent jobs in economically distressed areas of the Nation. Provides public works grants and planning and technical assistance in areas with high unemployment or low median family income.

Contact(s):
David Sampson, Assistant Secretary

UNITED STATES DEPARTMENT OF COMMERCE

NATIONAL ENVIRONMENTAL SATELLITE, DATA, AND INFORMATION SERVICE
1335 East-West Highway
Silver Spring, MD 20910-3284 United States
Phone: 301-713-3578 Fax: 301-713-1249
Website: www.noah.gov

Founded: N/A

Scope: State

Description: Manages satellites which observe the natural variability of the global Earth systems - the ocean, atmosphere, features of the solid earth, and the near-space system.

Contact(s):
Gregory Withee, Assistant Administrator; 301-713-3578, ext. 101; Fax: 301-713-1249; greg.withee@noaa.gov

UNITED STATES DEPARTMENT OF COMMERCE

NATIONAL OCEANIC AND ATMOSPHERIC ADMINISTRATION
Department of Commerce
Herbert C. Hoover Bldg., Rm. 5128
14th and Constitution Ave., NW
Washington, DC 20230 United States
Phone: 202-482-3436 Fax: 202-408-9674
Website: www.noaa.gov

Founded: 1970
Membership: 1–100
Scope: Regional

Description: NOAA was created within the Department of Commerce to promote global environmental stewardship and to describe and predict changes in the Earth's environment. NOAA conducts oceanic and atmospheric research; maintains environmental databases and disseminates environmental information products; manages living marine resources and the marine environment; and operates environmental satellites, ships, aircraft, and buoys.

Contact(s):
Scott Gudes, Deputy Under Secretary; 202-482-4569

UNITED STATES DEPARTMENT OF COMMERCE

NATIONAL OCEANIC AND ATMOSPHERIC ADMINISTRATION
GRAY'S REEF NATIONAL MARINE SANCTUARY
10 Ocean Science Cir.
Savannah, GA 31411 United States
Phone: 912-598-2345
Website: www.graysreef.nos.noaa.gov

Founded: 1981

Scope: Local, State, Regional, National, International

Description: Marine protected area

Keyword(s): Ecosystems (precious), Oceans/Coasts/Beaches, Water Habitats & Quality, Wildlife & Species

UNITED STATES DEPARTMENT OF COMMERCE

NATIONAL OCEANIC AND ATMOSPHERIC ADMINISTRATION
NATIONAL MARINE FISHERIES SERVICE
Silver Spring Metro Center 3, 1315 East-West Hwy.
Silver Spring, MD 20910 United States
Phone: 301-713-2239 Fax: 301-703-1940
Website: www.nmfs.noaa.gov

Founded: N/A

Scope: International

Description: Provides management, research, and services for the protection and rational use of living marine resources for their aesthetic, economic, and recreational value. Determines the consequences of the natural environment and human activities on living marine resources and provides knowledge and services to achieve efficient and judicious domestic and international management, use, and conservation of the resources.

Publication(s): Publications on line

Contact(s):
William Hogarth, Assistant Administrator

UNITED STATES DEPARTMENT OF COMMERCE

NATIONAL OCEANIC AND ATMOSPHERIC ADMINISTRATION
NATIONAL OCEAN SERVICE
1305 East-West Highway
Silver Spring, MD 20910 United States
Phone: 301-713-3074 Fax: 301-713-4269
Website: www.noaa.gov

Founded: N/A

Scope: International

Description: Administers the National Geodetic Survey, Nautical and Aeronautical Charting, National Estuarine Research Reserves, National Marine Sanctuaries, Coastal Zone Management, Marine Assessments, and Coastal Ocean Programs.

Contact(s):
Dan Dewell, Public Affairs Officer; 301-713-3070
Nancy Foster, Assistant Administrator; 301-713-3074

UNITED STATES DEPARTMENT OF COMMERCE

NATIONAL OCEANIC AND ATMOSPHERIC ADMINISTRATION
NATIONAL WEATHER SERVICE
Silver Spring Metro Center 2, 1325 East-West Hwy.
Silver Spring, MD 20910 United States
Phone: 301-713-0689 Fax: 301-713-0662
Website: www.nws.noaa.gov

Founded: N/A

Scope: Local, Regional

Description: Observes, describes, and predicts the natural variability of the atmosphere, and to some extent the ocean and the earth, in order to protect life and property and enhance the national economy.

Contact(s):
Robert Burpee, Director of National Hurricane Center; 305-229-4470
John Kelly, Director and Assistant Administrator for Weather Service
Jerry McCall, Director of National Data Buoy Center; 601-688-2800
Ronald McPherson, Director of National Centers for Environmental Prediction; 301-713-8016
Frederick Ostby, Director of Severe Storm Forecast Center; 816-426-5922
Richard Augulis, National Weather Service Central Region; 816-426-5400
Louis Boezi, Deputy Assistant Administrator for Modernization; 301-713-0397
Randee Exter, Public Affairs Officer of Weather; 301-713-0622
John Forsing, National Weather Service Eastern Region; 516-244-0100
Richard Hagemeyer, National Weather Service Pacific Region; 808-541-1641
Harry Hassel, Southern Region; 817-334-2651
Richard Hutcheon, National Weather Service Alaska Region; 907-271-5136
Thomas Potter, National Weather Service Western Region; 801-524-5122
Susan Zevin, Deputy Assistant Administrator for Operations; 301-713-0711

UNITED STATES DEPARTMENT OF COMMERCE

NATIONAL OCEANIC AND ATMOSPHERIC ADMINISTRATION
STELLWAGEN BANK NATIONAL MARINE SANCTUARY
175 Edward Foster Rd.
Scituate, MA 02066 United States
Phone: 781-545-8026 Fax: 781-545-8036
E-mail: stellwagen@noaa.gov
Website: stellwagen.nos.noaa.gov

Founded: 1992

Scope: Regional

Description: New England's only National Marine Sanctuary

Keyword(s): Ecosystems (precious), Oceans/Coasts/Beaches, Recreation/Ecotourism

UNITED STATES DEPARTMENT OF COMMERCE

NATIONAL OCEANIC AND ATMOSPHERIC ASSOCIATION
OFFICE OF GLOBAL PROGRAM
1100 Wayne Ave.
Silver Spring, MD 20910 United States
Phone: 301-427-2089 Fax: 301-427-2222
Website: www.ogp.noaa.gov

Founded: N/A

Scope: State

Description: Provides the primary focus for coordination with national and international scientific communities in the areas of global warming, Tropical Oceans and Global Atmosphere Project, and worldwide climate research.

Contact(s):
J. Hall, Director; 301-427-2089

UNITED STATES DEPARTMENT OF COMMERCE

NATIONAL OCEANOGRAPHIC AND ATMOSPHERIC ADMINISTRATION
ACE BASIN NATIONAL ESTUARINE RESEARCH RESERVE
South Carolina Department of Natural Resources,
P.O. Box 12559
Charleston, SC 29412 United States
Phone: 803-762-5412 Fax: 803-762-5412

Founded: N/A

Scope: Regional

UNITED STATES DEPARTMENT OF COMMERCE

NATIONAL OCEANOGRAPHIC AND ATMOSPHERIC ADMINISTRATION
APALACHICOLA NATIONAL ESTUARINE RESEARCH RESERVE
Department of Environmental Protection, 350 Carroll St.
Eastpoint, FL 32328 United States
Phone: 850-670-4783 Fax: 850-670-4324

Founded: N/A

Scope: Regional

UNITED STATES DEPARTMENT OF COMMERCE

NATIONAL OCEANOGRAPHIC AND ATMOSPHERIC ADMINISTRATION
CHANNEL ISLANDS NATIONAL MARINE SANCTUARY
113 Harbor Way
Santa Barbara, CA 93109 United States
Phone: 805-966-7107 Fax: 805-568-1582

Founded: 1980

Scope: Regional

UNITED STATES DEPARTMENT OF COMMERCE
NATIONAL OCEANOGRAPHIC AND ATMOSPHERIC ADMINISTRATION
CHESAPEAKE BAY NATIONAL ESTUARINE RESEARCH RESERVE
MARYLAND OFFICE
Department of Natural Resources, Tawes State Office Bldg., E-2, 580 Taylor Ave.
Annapolis, MD 21401 United States
Phone: 410-260-8730 Fax: 410-260-8739
Founded: N/A
Scope: Regional

UNITED STATES DEPARTMENT OF COMMERCE
NATIONAL OCEANOGRAPHIC AND ATMOSPHERIC ADMINISTRATION
CHESAPEAKE BAY NATIONAL ESTUARINE RESEARCH RESERVE
VIRGINIA OFFICE
Virginia Institute of Marine Science
P.O. Box 1346
Greate Road
Gloucester Point, VA 23062 United States
Phone: 804-684-7135 Fax: 804-684-7120
E-mail: cbnerr@vims.edu
Website: www.vims.edu/cbnerr
Founded: 1991
Membership: N/A
Scope: Local, State, Regional, National
Description: CBNERRVA strives to be a national leader in demonstrating how science, education and coastal resource stewardship can solve coastal management problems and improve the awareness and understanding of estuaries. Our Reserve system located along the York River estuary is a key resource that supports all aspects of Reserve activities. Reserve components include Sweet Hall Marsh, Taskinas Creek, Catlett Island, and Goodwin Islands.
Keyword(s): Ecosystems (precious), Oceans/Coasts/Beaches, Water Habitats & Quality

UNITED STATES DEPARTMENT OF COMMERCE
NATIONAL OCEANOGRAPHIC AND ATMOSPHERIC ADMINISTRATION
CORDELL BANK NATIONAL MARINE SANCTUARY
P.O. Box 159
Olema, CA 94950 United States
Phone: 415-464-5248 Fax: 415-868-1202
E-mail: cordellbank@noaa.gov
Website: www.sanctuaries.nos.noaa.gov/oms/omscordell/omscordellvisit.html
Founded: 1989
Scope: Regional

UNITED STATES DEPARTMENT OF COMMERCE
NATIONAL OCEANOGRAPHIC AND ATMOSPHERIC ADMINISTRATION
DELAWARE NATIONAL ESTUARINE RESEARCH RESERVE
DEPARTMENT OF NATURAL RESOURCES AND ENVIRONMENTAL CONTROL
818 Kitts Hummock Rd.
Dover, DE 19011 United States
Phone: 302-739-3436 Fax: 302-739-3446
Website: www.dnrec.state.de.us/DNREC2000/Divisions/Soil/DNERR
Founded: N/A
Scope: Regional
Description: The DNERR's mission is to preserve and manage the natural resources within the Reserve as a place for research, to provide education and outreach programs that promote better understanding of Delaware's estuarine and coastal areas, and to promote informed coastal decision-making.
Keyword(s): Ecosystems (precious), Oceans/Coasts/Beaches, Public Lands/Greenspace, Recreation/Ecotourism, Sprawl/Urban Planning, Water Habitats & Quality, Wildlife & Species

UNITED STATES DEPARTMENT OF COMMERCE
NATIONAL OCEANOGRAPHIC AND ATMOSPHERIC ADMINISTRATION
ELKHORN SLOUGH NATIONAL ESTUARINE RESEARCH RESERVE
1700 Elkhorn Rd.
Watsonville, CA 95076 United States
Phone: 831-728-2822 Fax: 831-728-1056
Founded: N/A
Scope: Regional

UNITED STATES DEPARTMENT OF COMMERCE
NATIONAL OCEANOGRAPHIC AND ATMOSPHERIC ADMINISTRATION
FLORIDA KEYS NATIONAL MARINE SANCTUARY
P.O. Box 500368, 5550 Overseas Hwy.
Marathon, FL 33050 United States
Phone: 305-743-2437
Website: www.fknms.nos.noaa.gov/
Founded: N/A
Scope: Regional

UNITED STATES DEPARTMENT OF COMMERCE
NATIONAL OCEANOGRAPHIC AND ATMOSPHERIC ADMINISTRATION
FLOWER GARDEN BANKS NATIONAL MARINE SANCTUARY
216 W. 26th St., Suite 104
Bryan, TX 77803 United States
Phone: 979-779-2705 Fax: 979-779-2334
E-mail: flowergarden@noaa.gov
Website: www.flowergarden.nos.noaa.gov
Founded: 1992
Scope: Regional
Description: Mission is to serve as trustee for the Flower Garden Banks National Marine Sanctuary in conserving, protecting, and enhancing the marine biodiversity, ecological integrity and cultural legacy.
Publication(s): 100 Common Fishes
Keyword(s): Ecosystems (precious), Oceans/Coasts/Beaches

UNITED STATES DEPARTMENT OF COMMERCE
NATIONAL OCEANOGRAPHIC AND ATMOSPHERIC ADMINISTRATION
GREAT BAY NATIONAL ESTUARINE RESEARCH RESERVE
Department of Fish and Game, 225 Main St.
Durham, NH 03824 United States
Phone: 603-868-1095 Fax: 603-868-3305
Founded: N/A
Scope: Regional

UNITED STATES DEPARTMENT OF COMMERCE
NATIONAL OCEANOGRAPHIC AND ATMOSPHERIC ADMINISTRATION
GULF OF FARALLONES NATIONAL MARINE SANCTUARY
Fort Mason Building 201
San Francisco, CA 94123 United States
Phone: 415-561-6622 Fax: 415-561-6616
E-mail: farallones@noaa.gov
Website: farallones.nos.noaa.gov

Founded: 1981
Membership: N/A
Scope: Regional, National
Description: The Gulf of the Farallones National Marine Sanctuary was designated to protect the unique marine wildlife and habitats off the California coast west of San Francisco. The Sanctuary encompasses 948 square nautical miles of open ocean and the nearshore waters of Bodega Bay, Tomales Bay, Estero Americano, Estero de San Antonio, and Bolinas Lagoon. National Marine Sanctuaries are administered by the National Oceanic and Atmospheric Administration (NOAA).
Publication(s): Beyond the Golden Gate, Hydrosphere
Keyword(s): Ecosystems (precious), Oceans/Coasts/Beaches, Recreation/Ecotourism, Water Habitats & Quality, Wildlife & Species
Contact(s):
Edward Ueber, Sanctuary Manager; 415-561-6622
Paul Wong, Education Specialist; 415-561-6622, ext. 201; farallones@noaa.gov

UNITED STATES DEPARTMENT OF COMMERCE
NATIONAL OCEANOGRAPHIC AND ATMOSPHERIC ADMINISTRATION
HAWAIIAN ISLANDS HUMPBACK WHALE NATIONAL SANCTUARY
726 South Kihei Road
Kihei, HI 96753 United States
Phone: 808-879-2818 Fax: 808-874-3815

Founded: 1997
Scope: Regional, National
Description: One of 13 marine sanctuaries. Mission is to protect the humpback whale and its Hawaiian habitat.

UNITED STATES DEPARTMENT OF COMMERCE
NATIONAL OCEANOGRAPHIC AND ATMOSPHERIC ADMINISTRATION
HUDSON RIVER NATIONAL ESTUARINE RESEARCH RESERVE
c/o Bard College Field Station, Annandale-on-Hudson
Annandale, NY 12504 United States
Phone: 845-758-7010

Founded: N/A
Scope: Regional

UNITED STATES DEPARTMENT OF COMMERCE
NATIONAL OCEANOGRAPHIC AND ATMOSPHERIC ADMINISTRATION
JACQUES COUSTEAU NATIONAL ESTUARINE RESEARCH RESERVE INSTITUTE OF MARINE AND COASTAL SCIENCES
71 Dudley Road
New Brunswick, NJ 08901 United States
Phone: 732-932-6555 Fax: 732-932-8578
Website: http://marine.rutgers.edu/pt/home.htm

Founded: N/A
Scope: Regional
Description: The JCNERR program goals are to (1) ensure a stable environment for research through long-term protection of the NERR resources; (2) address coastal management issues indentified as significant through coordinated estuarine research within the system; (3) enhance the public awareness and understanding of esturine areas; (4) conduct and coordinate estuarine research within the system, gathering and making available information necessary for improving understanding and management of esturine areas.

UNITED STATES DEPARTMENT OF COMMERCE
NATIONAL OCEANOGRAPHIC AND ATMOSPHERIC ADMINISTRATION
JOBOS BAY NATIONAL ESTUARINE RESEARCH RESERVE
Department of Natural Resources, Call Box B
Aquirre, PR 00704 United States
Phone: 787-853-4617 Fax: 787-853-4618
Website: www.ocrm.nos.noaa.gov/nerr/reserves/nerrjobos.html

Founded: N/A
Scope: Regional

UNITED STATES DEPARTMENT OF COMMERCE
NATIONAL OCEANOGRAPHIC AND ATMOSPHERIC ADMINISTRATION
KACHEMAK BAY NATIONAL ESTUARINE RESEARCH RESERVE
2181 Kachemak Drive
Homer, AK 99603 United States
Phone: 907-235-6377 Fax: 907-267-4794

Founded: N/A
Scope: Regional

UNITED STATES DEPARTMENT OF COMMERCE
NATIONAL OCEANOGRAPHIC AND ATMOSPHERIC ADMINISTRATION
MONITOR NATIONAL MARINE SANCTUARY
c/o the Mariners' Museum, 100 Museum Dr.
Newport News, VA 23606 United States
Phone: 757-599-3122
Website: monitor.nos.noaa.gov/

Founded: N/A
Scope: Regional

UNITED STATES DEPARTMENT OF COMMERCE
NATIONAL OCEANOGRAPHIC AND ATMOSPHERIC ADMINISTRATION
MONTEREY BAY NATIONAL MARINE SANCTUARY
299 Foam St., Suite D
Monterey, CA 93940 United States
Phone: 831-647-4201 Fax: 831-647-4250
E-mail: montereybay@noaa.gov
Website: www.sanctuaries.nos.noaa.gov/oms/omsmonterey/omsmontereyvisit.html

Founded: 1992
Scope: Regional

UNITED STATES DEPARTMENT OF COMMERCE
NATIONAL OCEANOGRAPHIC AND ATMOSPHERIC ADMINISTRATION
NARRAGANSETT BAY NATIONAL ESTUARINE RESEARCH RESERVE
Department of Environmental Management, 55 South Reserve Dr.
Prudence Island, RI 02872 United States
Phone: 401-683-6780 Fax: 401-682-1936

Founded: N/A
Scope: Regional

UNITED STATES DEPARTMENT OF COMMERCE
NATIONAL OCEANOGRAPHIC AND ATMOSPHERIC ADMINISTRATION
NORTH CAROLINA NATIONAL ESTUARINE RESEARCH RESERVE
1 Harvin Moss Ln.
Willmington, NC 28409 United States
Phone: 910-962-2470 Fax: 910-962-2410

Founded: N/A

Scope: Regional

UNITED STATES DEPARTMENT OF COMMERCE
NATIONAL OCEANOGRAPHIC AND ATMOSPHERIC ADMINISTRATION
NORTH INLET NATIONAL ESTUARINE RESEARCH RESERVE
Winyah Bay NERR, Baruch Marine Field Lab, P.O. Box 1630
Georgetown, SC 29442 United States
Phone: 843-546-3623

Founded: N/A

Scope: Regional

UNITED STATES DEPARTMENT OF COMMERCE
NATIONAL OCEANOGRAPHIC AND ATMOSPHERIC ADMINISTRATION
OLD WOMAN CREEK NATIONAL ESTUARINE RESEARCH RESERVE
2514 Cleveland Rd., East
Huron, OH 44839 United States
Phone: 419-433-4601 Fax: 419-433-2851

Founded: N/A

Scope: Regional

UNITED STATES DEPARTMENT OF COMMERCE
NATIONAL OCEANOGRAPHIC AND ATMOSPHERIC ADMINISTRATION
OLYMPIC COAST NATIONAL MARINE SANCTUARY
138 W. First St.
Port Angeles, WA 98362-2600 United States
Phone: 360-457-6622

Founded: N/A

Scope: Regional

UNITED STATES DEPARTMENT OF COMMERCE
NATIONAL OCEANOGRAPHIC AND ATMOSPHERIC ADMINISTRATION
PADILLA BAY NATIONAL ESTUARINE RESEARCH RESERVE
10441 Bayview-Edison Rd.
Mt. Vernon, WA 98273-9668 United States
Phone: 360-428-1558 Fax: 360-428-1491
E-mail: alex@padillabay.gov
Website: inlet.geol.sc.edu

Founded: 1980

Scope: Regional

UNITED STATES DEPARTMENT OF COMMERCE
NATIONAL OCEANOGRAPHIC AND ATMOSPHERIC ADMINISTRATION
ROOKERY BAY NATIONAL ESTUARINE RESEARCH RESERVE
Department of Environmental Protection
300 Tower Road
Naples, FL 34113 United States
Phone: 941-417-6310 Fax: 941-417-6315

Founded: 1972
Membership: 101–1,000
Scope: Regional

Description: Coastal stewards of 110,000 acres, providing science-based data for more informed coastal decisions.

Keyword(s): Ecosystems (precious), Forests/Forestry, Land Issues, Oceans/Coasts/Beaches, Public Lands/Greenspace, Recreation/Ecotourism, Water Habitats & Quality, Wildlife & Species

UNITED STATES DEPARTMENT OF COMMERCE
NATIONAL OCEANOGRAPHIC AND ATMOSPHERIC ADMINISTRATION
SAPELO ISLAND NATIONAL ESTUARINE RESEARCH RESERVE
P.O. BOX 19
Sapelo Island, GA 31327 United States
Phone: 912-485-2251

Founded: N/A

Scope: Regional

UNITED STATES DEPARTMENT OF COMMERCE
NATIONAL OCEANOGRAPHIC AND ATMOSPHERIC ADMINISTRATION
SEA GRANT PROGRAM - ALABAMA
Mississippi and Alabama Sea Grant Consortium
Caylor Bldg., Gulf Coast Research Lab.
P.O. Box 7000
Ocean Springs, MS 39566-7000 United States
Phone: 228-875-9341 Fax: 228-875-0528
Website: www.masgc.org

Founded: N/A
Membership: 1–100
Scope: State
Contact(s):

Richard Wallace, Coordinator and Extension Marine Specialist; Alabama Sea Grant Extension Program: 4170 Commanders Dr., Mobile, AL 36615; 334-438-5690; Fax: 334-438-5670

UNITED STATES DEPARTMENT OF COMMERCE
NATIONAL OCEANOGRAPHIC AND ATMOSPHERIC ADMINISTRATION
SEA GRANT PROGRAM - ALASKA
UNIVERSITY OF ALASKA
University of Alaska, P.O. Box 755040
Fairbanks, AK 99775-5040 United States
Phone: 907-474-7086 Fax: 907-474-6285
E-mail: fygrant@uaf.edu
Website: www.uaf.edu/seagrant/

Founded: N/A

Scope: State

Description: A state/federal partnership administered by the National Oceanic and Atmospheric Administration and the University of Alaska that sponsors and conducts marine research, graduate education, marine industry advisory services, and formal and nonformal public education aimed at promoting the wise use and conservation of Alaska's coastal and marine resources.

Publication(s): Free catalog, posters, videos, SeaWeek Curriculum Series, Biennial Program Report, Management Strategies for Exploited Fish, Guide to Marine Mammals of Alaska

Keyword(s): Oceans/Coasts/Beaches, Wildlife & Species

Contact(s):

Ronald Dearborn, Director; fnrkd@uaf.edu

Donald Kramer, Director of Marine Advisory Program; University of Alaska, Carlton Trust Bldg., Suite 110, 2221 E. Northern Lights Blvd., Anchorage, AK 99508-4140; 907-274-9691; Fax: 907-277-5242; afdek@uaa.alaska.edu

Kurt Byers, Communications Manager; Alaska Sea Grant College Program, University of Alaska, P.O. Box 755040, Fairbanks, AK 99775-5040; 907-474-6702; fnkmb1@uaf.edu

Sue Keller, Publications Manager; P.O. Box 755040, Fairbanks, AK 99775-5040; 907-474-6703; fnsk@uaf.edu
Sherri Pristash, Publications Manager; 888-789-0090; fypubs@uaf.edu

UNITED STATES DEPARTMENT OF COMMERCE
NATIONAL OCEANOGRAPHIC AND ATMOSPHERIC ADMINISTRATION
SEA GRANT PROGRAM - CALIFORNIA
UNIVERSITY OF CALIFORNIA
9500 Gilman Drive
La Jolla, CA 92093-0232 United States
Phone: 858-534-4440 Fax: 858-534-2231
E-mail: caseagrant@ucsd.edu
Website: www-csgc.ucsd.edu/

Founded: N/A
Scope: Local, State, Regional
Description: A university-based program of marine research, extension services, and education that contributes to the growing body of knowledge about coastal and marine resources. Through its Extension and Communications components, transfers information and technology to industry, government, and the public.
Publication(s): Publication List, Sea Grant in Brief, Program Directory
Contact(s):
Linda Duguay, Director, USC Sea Grant Program; University of Southern California, University Park, Los Angeles, CA 90089-0373; 213-740-1961; Fax: 213-740-5936; seagrant@usc.edu
Russell Moll, Director; California Sea Grant, University of California, 9500 Gilman Drive, La Jolla, CA 92093-0232; 858-534-4440; Fax: 858-534-2231
Judy Lemus, Leader, USC Sea Grant Marine Advisory Program and Associat; USC Sea Grant Program Marine Advisory Service, University of Southern California, University Park, Los Angeles, CA 90089-0373; 213-740-1965; Fax: 213-740-5936
Paul Olin, Interim Extension Leader; Sea Grant Extension, UC Cooperative Extension, 2604 Ventura Avenue, Room 100, Santa Rosa, CA 95403; 707-565-2621; Fax: 707-565-2623

UNITED STATES DEPARTMENT OF COMMERCE
NATIONAL OCEANOGRAPHIC AND ATMOSPHERIC ADMINISTRATION
SEA GRANT PROGRAM - CONNECTICUT
UNIVERSITY OF CONNECTICUT
1080 Shennecossett Rd.
Groton, CT 06340-6048 United States
Phone: 860-405-9110 Fax: 860-405-9109
Website: www.seagrant.uconn.edu

Founded: N/A
Membership: 1–100
Scope: National
Contact(s):
Edward Monahan, Director; sgoadm01@uconnvm.uconn.edu

UNITED STATES DEPARTMENT OF COMMERCE
NATIONAL OCEANOGRAPHIC AND ATMOSPHERIC ADMINISTRATION
SEA GRANT PROGRAM - DELAWARE
UNIVERSITY OF DELAWARE
College of Marine Studies
Marine Public Education Office
222 S. Chapel Street, Rm. 103
Newark, DE 19716-3530 United States
Phone: 302-831-8083 Fax: 302-831-2005
E-mail: marinecom@udel.edu
Website: www.ocean.udel.edu/seagrant/

Founded: 1968
Scope: Local, State, Regional, National
Description: The University of Delaware Sea Grant College Program conducts research, education, and outreach projects to help people from all walks of life wisely use, manage, and conserve Delaware's ocean and coastal resources. The program is a partnership involving the National Sea Grant College Program in the National Oceanic and Atmospheric Administration (NOAA), U.S. Department of Commerce; the State of Delaware; and the University of Delaware.
Publication(s): Publications Catalog
Keyword(s): Agriculture/Farming, Ecosystems (precious), Oceans/Coasts/Beaches, Pollution (general), Recreation/Ecotourism, Transportation, Water Habitats & Quality, Wildlife & Species
Contact(s):
David McCarren, Executive Director; University of Delaware, College of Marine Studies, 118 Robinson Hall, Newark, DE 19716-3501; 302-831-8255; Fax: 302-831-1487; mccarren@udel.edu
Carolyn Thoroughgood, Director; University of Delaware, College of Marine Studies, 111 Robinson Hall, Newark, DE 19716-3501; 302-831-2841; Fax: 302-831-4389; ctgood@udel.edu
Tracey Bryant, Communications Director; University of Delaware, Marine Public Education Office, 222 S. Chapel Street, Rm 103, Newark, DE 19716-3530; 302-831-8185; Fax: 302-831-2005; tbryant@udel.edu
James Falk, MAS Director; University of Delaware, Sea Grant College Program, 700 Pilottown Road, 204H Cannon Lab, Lewes, DE 19958; 302-645-4235; Fax: 302-645-4213; jfalk@udel.edu

UNITED STATES DEPARTMENT OF COMMERCE
NATIONAL OCEANOGRAPHIC AND ATMOSPHERIC ADMINISTRATION
SEA GRANT PROGRAM - FLORIDA
UNIVERSITY OF FLORIDA
P.O. Box 110400
Gainesville, FL 32611-0400 United States
Phone: 352-392-5870 Fax: 352-392-5113
Website: www.flseagrant.org

Founded: N/A
Membership: 1–100
Scope: State
Description: A statewide university-based program of coastal and ocean research, education, and public service to enhance productivity, conservation, and long-term use and management of marine systems and resources.
Publication(s): Fathom Magazine, listing of various publications availabl
Keyword(s): Agriculture/Farming, Ecosystems (precious), Oceans/Coasts/Beaches, Sprawl/Urban Planning, Water Habitats & Quality
Contact(s):
James Cato, Director: Florida Sea Grant College Program; jcato@mail.ifas.ufl.edu
William Seaman, Associate Director: Florida Sea Grant College Program; seaman @mail.ifas.ufl.edu
Michael Spranger, Assistant Dean and Coordinator: Sea Grant Extension Program; P.O. Box 110405, University of Florida, Gainesville, FL 32611-0405; 352-392-1837; msspranger@mail.ifas.ufl.edu

UNITED STATES DEPARTMENT OF COMMERCE

NATIONAL OCEANOGRAPHIC AND ATMOSPHERIC ADMINISTRATION
SEA GRANT PROGRAM - GEORGIA
UNIVERSITY OF GEORGIA
Marine Sciences Bldg.
Rm. 220
Athens, GA 30602-3636 United States
Phone: 706-542-5954 Fax: 706-542-3652
Website: www.alpha.marsci.uga.edu/gaseagrant.html

Founded: 1971

Scope: State

Description: A part of the National Sea Grant College Program, the Georgia program fosters the sustainable development and environmental stewardship of the nation's marine resources. It is a competitive grant program funding applied marine research, education, and advisory service projects at universities in Georgia.

Keyword(s): Development/Developing Countries, Oceans/Coasts/Beaches, Reduce/Reuse/Recycle

Contact(s):

Mac Rawson, Director, Sea Grant College Program; mrawson@arches.uga.edu
Randy Walker, Marine Extension; 706-542-5956; rwalker@arches.uga.edu
David Bryant, Communicator
Keith Gates, Leader, Marine Advisory Service

UNITED STATES DEPARTMENT OF COMMERCE

NATIONAL OCEANOGRAPHIC AND ATMOSPHERIC ADMINISTRATION
SEA GRANT PROGRAM - HAWAII
UNIVERSITY OF HAWAII
2525 Correa Rd., HIG 238
Honolulu, HI 96822 United States
Phone: 808-956-7031 Fax: 808-956-3014
E-mail: seagrant@soest.hawaii.edu
Website: www.soest.hawaii.edu/seagrant/

Founded: 1968

Membership: 1–100

Scope: International

Description: The University of Hawaii Sea Grant College Program supports research projects in coastal and marine-related areas. Its extension service has agents and specialists located in Honolulu, Maui, the Big Island of Hawaii, Kauai, and American Samoa. Agents help marine users benefit from the Sea Grant-supported research, especially in the areas of commercial and recreational fishing, aquaculture, coastal nearshore resources, marine recreation and tourism development, marine biotechnology.

Contact(s):

Priscilla Billig, Director of Communications Program; 808-956-2414; Fax: 808-956-2880
Dr. Richard Brock, Director of Sea Grant Extension Service
Gordon Grau, Director: Sea Grant College Program; sg-dir@soest.hawaii.edu
Richard Brock, Fisheries Extension Agent; 808-956-2859; Fax: 808-956-2858
Alan Kam, Fisheries Extension Agent; 808-956-2865; Fax: 808-956-2858
Elizabeth Kumabe, Education Specialist; 808-956-2860; Fax: 808-956-2858
Jeff Kuwabara, Hanauma Bay Educational Program Volunteer Coordinator; 808-396-1319; Fax: 808-956-2858
Peter Rappa, Coastal Resource Management Extension Agent; 808-956-2868; Fax: 808-956-2858
Raymond Tabata, Coastal Recreation & Tourism Extension Agent; 808-956-2866; Fax: 808-956-2858
Clyde Tamaru, Aquaculture Extension Specialist; 808-956-2869; Fax: 808-956-2858
Christine Woolaway, Coastal Recreation & Tourism Extension Agent; 808-956-2872; Fax: 808-956-2858

UNITED STATES DEPARTMENT OF COMMERCE

NATIONAL OCEANOGRAPHIC AND ATMOSPHERIC ADMINISTRATION
SEA GRANT PROGRAM - ILLINOIS-INDIANA
PURDUE UNIVERSITY
Department of Forestry and Natural Resources
1200 Forest Products Bldg.
West Lafayette, IA 47907-1200 United States
Phone: 765-494-3573 Fax: 765-496-6026
Website: www.iisgcp.org

Founded: N/A

Membership: 1–100

Scope: Local, State, Regional, National

Description: Illinois-Indiana Sea Grant College Program fosters the creation and stewardship of an enhanced and sustainable environment and economy along Southern Lake Michigan and in the Great Lakes region through research, education, and outreach.

Keyword(s): Land Issues, Oceans/Coasts/Beaches, Pollution (general), Public Health, Public Lands/Greenspace, Sprawl/Urban Planning

Contact(s):

Richard Warner, Interim Director; University of Illinois, 211 Mumford Hall, 1301 West Gregory Drive, Urbana, IL 61801; 217-333-0240; dickw@uiuc.edu
Patrice Charlebois, Biological Resources Specialist; Lake Michigan Biological Station, Illinois Natural History Survey, 400 17th Street, Zion, IL 60099; 847-872-0140; Fax: 847-872-8679; charlebo@uiuc.edu
Leslie Dorworth, Aquatic Ecology Specialist; Purdue University Calumet, Department of Biology, Hammond, IN 46323-2094; 219-989-2726; Fax: 219-989-2130; dorworth@calumet.purdue.edu
Martin Jaffe, Coastal Business & Environmental Interim Specialist; University of Illinois Chicago, Great Cities Institute (MC348), 412 South Peoria Street, Suite 400, Chicago, IL 60607-7067; 312-996-2178; Fax: 312-413-2314; mjaffe@uic.edu
Robert McCormick, Planning with POWER Coordinator; Purdue University, 1200 Forest Products Building, West Lafayette, IN 47907; 765-494-3627; Fax: 765-496-6026; rmccormick@fnr.purdue.edu
Brian Miller, Associate Director and Outreach Coordinator; Purdue University, 1200 Forest Products Building, West Lafayette, IN 47907-1200; 765-494-3573; Fax: 765-496-6026; bmiller@fnr.purdue.edu
Richard Sparks, Research Coordinator; University of Illinois, National Soybean Research Center, Room 350, 1101 West Peabody Drive, MC-635, Urbana, IL 61801-4723; 217-333-0536; Fax: 217-333-8046; rsparks@uiuc.edu
Robin Goettel, Communications Coordinator; University of Illinois, 63 Mumford Hall, Urbana, IL 61801; 217-333-9448; Fax: 217-333-2614; goettel@uiuc.edu

UNITED STATES DEPARTMENT OF COMMERCE

NATIONAL OCEANOGRAPHIC AND ATMOSPHERIC ADMINISTRATION
SEA GRANT PROGRAM - LOUISIANA
LOUISIANA STATE UNIVERSITY
Baton Rouge, LA 70803 United States
Phone: 225-388-6710 Fax: 225-578-6331
Website: www.laseagrant.org/

Founded: 1968

Scope: National

Description: The Louisiana Sea Grant College Program is a research, education, and public service organization supported by federal, state, and private sector funds. The Program provides the knowledge, trained personnel, and public

Federal Government Agencies

awareness needed to wisely and effectively develop and manage coastal and marine areas and resources in a manner that will assure sustainable economic and societal benefits.

Publication(s): Coast and Sea

Keyword(s): Development/Developing Countries, Oceans/Coasts/Beaches, Reduce/Reuse/Recycle, Water Habitats & Quality

Contact(s):

Jack Vanlopik, Executive Director; Louisiana State University, Baton Rouge, LA 70803; 225-388-6710; Fax: 225-388-6331; jvl@lsu.edu

Ronald Becker, Associate Director; Sea Grant College Program, Louisiana State University, Baton Rouge, LA 70803; 225-388-6345

Elizabeth Coleman, Communications Coordinator; Louisiana Sea Grant College Program, Louisiana State University, Baton Rouge, LA 70803; 225-388-6448

Michael Liffmann, Assistant Director

UNITED STATES DEPARTMENT OF COMMERCE

NATIONAL OCEANOGRAPHIC AND ATMOSPHERIC ADMINISTRATION
SEA GRANT PROGRAM - MAINE
UNIVERSITY OF MAINE
5715 Coburn Hall #14
Orono, ME 04469-5715 United States
Phone: 207-581-1435 Fax: 207-581-1426
E-mail: umseagrant@umaine.edu
Website: www.seagrant.umaine.edu

Founded: N/A

Membership: 1–100

Scope: National

Description: Part of a National Network funding reasearch on marine issues.

Keyword(s): Oceans/Coasts/Beaches, Water Habitats & Quality, Wildlife & Species

Contact(s):

Paul Anderson, Director; 207-581-1435; Fax: 207-581-1426; panderson@maine.edu

Paul Anderson, Director & Marine Extension Leader; 207-581-1422; panderson@maine.edu

Chris Bartlett, Finfish Aquaculture Specialist; Marine Technology Center, Washington County Technical College, 16 Deep Cove Road, Eastport, ME 04631-0618; 207-853-2518; Fax: 207-853-0940; chris.bartlett@umit.maine.edu

Dana Morse, Extension Associate, Darling Marine Center; Clarks Cove, Walpole, ME 04573; 207-563-3146, ext. 205; Fax: 207-563-3119; dana.l.morse@umit.maine.edu

Natalie Springuel, Extension Associate

Kristen Whiting-Grant, Extension Agent; Wells Reserve, 342 Laudholm Farm Rd., Wells, ME 04090; 207-646-1555; Fax: 207-646-2930; kristen.whiting-grant@maine.edu

UNITED STATES DEPARTMENT OF COMMERCE

NATIONAL OCEANOGRAPHIC AND ATMOSPHERIC ADMINISTRATION
SEA GRANT PROGRAM - MARYLAND
UNIVERSITY OF MARYLAND
4321 Hartwick Rd.
Suite 300
College Park, MD 20740 United States
Phone: 301-403-4220 Fax: 301-403-4255
E-mail: mdsg@mdsg.umd.edu
Website: www.mdsg.umd.edu/

Founded: 1977

Membership: 1–100

Scope: National

Description: Maryland Sea Grant supports marine research, education, and outreach activities, especially in connection with the Chesapeake Bay. It currently supports research at four of the region's marine laboratories, and on the campuses of the University System of Maryland, the Johns Hopkins University, and other institutions of higher learning.

Publication(s): Chesapeake Quarterly, Maryland Marine Notes, Maryland Sea Grant Books and Videos, Watershed, Aquafarmer —quarterly newsletters

Keyword(s): Oceans/Coasts/Beaches, Public Health, Water Habitats & Quality, Wildlife & Species

Contact(s):

Jonathan Kramer, Director; 301-403-4220, ext. 10; Fax: 301-403-4255; kramer@mdsg.umd.edu

Jack Greer, Assistant Director; 301-403-4220, ext. 18; Fax: 301-403-4255

UNITED STATES DEPARTMENT OF COMMERCE

NATIONAL OCEANOGRAPHIC AND ATMOSPHERIC ADMINISTRATION
SEA GRANT PROGRAM - MASSACHUSETTS
MASSACHUSETTS INSTITUTE OF TECHNOLOGY
E38-330, 292 Main St.
Cambridge, MA 02139-9910 United States
Phone: 617-253-7131 Fax: 617-258-5730
Website: www.mit.edu/seagrant/

Founded: N/A

Scope: National

Contact(s):

Chrys Chryssostomidis, Director; chrys@deslab.mit.edu

UNITED STATES DEPARTMENT OF COMMERCE

NATIONAL OCEANOGRAPHIC AND ATMOSPHERIC ADMINISTRATION
SEA GRANT PROGRAM - MASSACHUSETTS
WOODS HOLE OCEANOGRAPHIC INSTITUTION
193 Oyster Pond Rd.
Mail Stop #2
Woods Hole, MA 02543-1525 United States
Phone: 508-289-2398 Fax: 508-457-2172
E-mail: seagrant@whoi.edu
Website: www.whoi.edu/seagrant/

Founded: 1973

Membership: 1–100

Scope: National

Description: The WHOI Sea Grant Program supports research, education, and advisory projects to promote the wise use and understanding of ocean and coastal resources for the public benefit. It is part of the National Sea Grant College Program of the National Oceanic and Atmospheric Administration, a network of 30 individual programs located in each of the coastal and Great Lakes states to foster cooperation among government, academia, and industry.

Keyword(s): Agriculture/Farming, Oceans/Coasts/Beaches, Wildlife & Species

Contact(s):

Judith McDowell, Director; 508-289-2557; jmcdowell@whoi.edu

Tracey Crago, Communicator; 508-289-2665; tcrago@whoi.edu

Sheri Derosa, Program Assistant; 508-289-2398; sderosa@whoi.edu

Dale Leavitt, Fisheries Aquaculture Specialist; 508-289-2997; dleavitt@whoi.edu

UNITED STATES DEPARTMENT OF COMMERCE

NATIONAL OCEANOGRAPHIC AND ATMOSPHERIC ADMINISTRATION
SEA GRANT PROGRAM - MICHIGAN
MICHIGAN STATE UNIVERSITY
2200 Bonisteel Boulevard
IST (Institute of Science & Technology Building)
Ann Arbor, MI 48109-2099 United States
Phone: 734-763-1437 Fax: 734-647-0768
Website: www.miseagrant.org

Founded: 1969
Membership: 1–100
Scope: Local, State, Regional, National
Description: To promote the understanding and wise use of the Great Lakes through research, education and extension.
Contact(s):
George Carignan, Director; Michigan Sea Grant College Program, 2200 Bonisteel Blvd., Suite 4103, University of Michigan, Ann Arbor, MI 48109-2099; 734-763-1437; Fax: 734-647-0768; carignan@engin.umich.edu
Jennifer Read, Assistant Director; 734-936-3622; Fax: 734-647-0768; jenread@umich.edu
Dave Brenner, Web Designer; 734-764-2421; Fax: 734-647-0768
Joyce Daniels, Editor; 734-647-0766; Fax: 734-647-0768; joydan@umich.edu
Minuet Henderson, Publications Assistant; 734-764-1118; Fax: 734-647-0768; minti@umich.edu
Elizabeth Laporte, Communication Coordinator; 734-647-0767; Fax: 734-647-0768; elzblap@umich.edu
Elyse Larsen, Fiscal Officer; 734-763-1438; Fax: 734-647-0768; elarsen@umich.edu
John Schwartz, Program Leader: Sea Grant Extension; Michigan Sea Grant College Program, 334 Natural Resources Bldg., Michigan State University, East Lansing, MI 48824; 517-355-9637; Fax: 517-353-6496; schwartj@msue.msu.edu
William Taylor, Associate Director; Michigan Sea Grant College Program, 13 Natural Resources Bldg., Michigan State University, East Lansing, MI 48824; 517-355-0233; taylorw@msu.edu

UNITED STATES DEPARTMENT OF COMMERCE
NATIONAL OCEANOGRAPHIC AND ATMOSPHERIC ADMINISTRATION
SEA GRANT PROGRAM - MINNESOTA
UNIVERSITY OF MINNESOTA
208 Washburn Hall
2305 E. 5th St.
Duluth, MN 55812-1445 United States
Phone: 218-726-8106 Fax: 218-726-6556
E-mail: seagrant@umn.edu
Website: www.seagrant.umn.edu

Founded: N/A
Membership: 1–100
Scope: State
Description: A statewide program that supports research, outreach, and educational programs related to Lake Superior and Minnesota's inland waters. Research areas include: water quality, fisheries, biotechnology, aquaculture, exotic species, and coastal tourism.
Publication(s): Seiche, The Newsletter, see publication web site
Keyword(s): Development/Developing Countries, Oceans/Coasts/Beaches, Public Health, Water Habitats & Quality, Wildlife & Species
Contact(s):
Carl Richards, Director; crichard@d.umn.edu
Doug Jensen, Coordinator, Exotic Species Information Center; 218-726-8712; djensen1@d.umn.edu
Sharon Moen, Editor; 218-726-6195; smoen@d.umn.edu

UNITED STATES DEPARTMENT OF COMMERCE
NATIONAL OCEANOGRAPHIC AND ATMOSPHERIC ADMINISTRATION
SEA GRANT PROGRAM - MISSISSIPPI-ALABAMA CONSORTIUM
MISSISSIPPI-ALABAMA SEA GRANT CONSORTIUM
Caylor Bldg., Gulf Coast Research Laboratory
P.O. Box 7000
Ocean Springs, MS 39566-7000 United States
Phone: 228-875-9341 Fax: 228-875-0528
Website: www.masgc.org

Founded: N/A
Scope: State
Contact(s):
Barry Costa-Pierce, Director; b.costapierce@usm.edu
Ladon Swann, Assoc. Director Office of Alabama Prog.; P.O. Box 369-370 D, Dauphin Island, AL 36528; 334-861-7544; Fax: 334-861-4646; swanndl@auburn.edu

UNITED STATES DEPARTMENT OF COMMERCE
NATIONAL OCEANOGRAPHIC AND ATMOSPHERIC ADMINISTRATION
SEA GRANT PROGRAM - NEW HAMPSHIRE
UNIVERSITY OF NEW HAMPSHIRE
Kingman Farm
Durham, NH 03824-3512 United States
Phone: 603-749-1565 Fax: 603-743-3997
Website: www.seagrant.unh.edu

Founded: N/A
Scope: National
Keyword(s): Development/Developing Countries, Oceans/Coasts/Beaches, Recreation/Ecotourism, Reduce/Reuse/Recycle, Water Habitats & Quality, Wildlife & Species
Contact(s):
Ann Bucklin, Director; 603-862-0122; acb@cisunix.unh.edu
Steve Adams, Coordinator, Communications; steve.adams@unh.edu
Brian Doyle, Associate Director and Program Leader; brian.doyle@unh.edu

UNITED STATES DEPARTMENT OF COMMERCE
NATIONAL OCEANOGRAPHIC AND ATMOSPHERIC ADMINISTRATION
SEA GRANT PROGRAM - NEW JERSEY
NEW JERSEY MARINE SCIENCES CONSORTIUM
Bldg. 22
Fort Hancock, NJ 07732 United States
Phone: 732-872-1300 Fax: 732-291-4483
Website: www.njmsc.org/seagrant.htm

Founded: N/A
Description: The New Jersey Marine Sciences Consortium is an alliance of 29 institutions from New Jersey, New York, and Pennsylvania formed for the purposes of conducting sponsored research in marine and coastal sciences, technology development through group action; and assembling material resources which lie beyond the capabilities of the individual member institutions. The consortium manages the Sea Grant College Program and the Sea Grant Extension Program.
Contact(s):
Eleanor Bochenek, Associate Sea Grant Director/Sea Grant Extension Director; Eleanor@njmsc.org
Michael Weinstein, Director; mikew@njmsc.org

UNITED STATES DEPARTMENT OF COMMERCE
NATIONAL OCEANOGRAPHIC AND ATMOSPHERIC ADMINISTRATION
SEA GRANT PROGRAM - NEW YORK
SUNY AT STONY BROOK
121 Discovery Hall
Stony Brook, NY 11794-5001 United States
Phone: 631-632-6905 Fax: 631-632-6917
E-mail: NYSeaGrant@notes.cc.sunysb.edu
Website: www.nyseagrant.org

Founded: 1971
Membership: 1–100
Scope: Local, State, Regional, National
Description: A cooperative program of the State University of New York and Cornell University fostering the wise use and development of coastal resources through research grants, extension advisory services, education, training, and informational materials.

Keyword(s): Climate Change, Oceans/Coasts/Beaches, Recreation/Ecotourism, Sprawl/Urban Planning, Water Habitats & Quality, Wildlife & Species

Contact(s):

Jack Mattice, Director; 121 Discovery Hall, Stony Brook University, Stony Brook, NY 11794-5001; 631-632-6905; Fax: 631-632-6917; Jack.Mattice@stonybrook.edu

Dale Baker, Associate Director and Program Leader; New York Sea Grant, 348 Roberts Hall, Cornell University, Ithaca, NY 14853-4203; 607-255-2832; Fax: 607-255-2812; drb17@cornell.edu

Barbara Branca, Communicator; 115 Discovery Hall, Stony Brook University, Stony Brook, NY 11794-5001; 631-632-6956; Fax: 631-632-6917; Barbara.Branca@stonybrook.edu

Paul Focazio, Assistant Communicator; 115 Discovery Hall, Stony Brook University, Stony Brook, NY 11794-5001; 631-632-6910; Fax: 631-632-6917; Paul.Focazio@stonybrook.edu

Robert Kent, Marine Program Coordinator; New York Sea Grant, Cornell University Research and Extension Center, 3059 Sound Ave., Riverhead, NY 11901-1098; 631-727-3910; Fax: 631-369-5944; rjk13@cornell.edu

Stefanie Massucci, Fiscal Officer of New York Sea Grant; 121 Discovery Hall, Stony Brook University, Stony Brook, NY 11794-5001; 631-632-6905; Fax: 631-632-6917; smassucci@sunysb.edu

Cornelia Schlenk, Assistant Director; 121 Discovery Hall, Stony Brook University, Stony Brook, NY 11794-5001; 631-632-6905; Fax: 631-632-6917; Cornelia.Schlenk@stonybrook.edu

David White, Great Lakes Program Coordinator; New York Sea Grant, SUNY College at Oswego, Oswego, NY 13126-3599; 315-312-3042; Fax: 315-312-2954; dgw9@cornell.edu

UNITED STATES DEPARTMENT OF COMMERCE

NATIONAL OCEANOGRAPHIC AND ATMOSPHERIC ADMINISTRATION
SEA GRANT PROGRAM - NORTH CAROLINA
NORTH CAROLINA STATE UNIVERSITY
Box 8605
100B 1911 Bldg.
Raleigh, NC 27695-8605 United States
Phone: 919-515-2454 Fax: 919-515-7095
Website: www.ncsu.edu/seagrant

Founded: N/A

Scope: State

Publication(s): Marine Extension News, Water Wise, Coast Watch

Keyword(s): Agriculture/Farming, Oceans/Coasts/Beaches, Recreation/Ecotourism, Water Habitats & Quality, Wildlife & Species

Contact(s):

Ronald Hodson, Director; ronald_hodson@ncsu.edu

Jack Thigpen, Extension Director

Katie Mosher, Assistant Director for Communications

Steve Rebach, Associate Director

UNITED STATES DEPARTMENT OF COMMERCE

NATIONAL OCEANOGRAPHIC AND ATMOSPHERIC ADMINISTRATION
SEA GRANT PROGRAM - OHIO
1314 Kinnear Rd.
Columbus, OH 43212-1194 United States
Phone: 614-292-8949 Fax: 614-292-4364
Website: www.sg.ohio-state.edu/

Founded: 1977

Membership: 1–100

Scope: State, Regional

Description: The Ohio Sea Grant College Program is dedicated to the goal of promoting the understanding and management, development, utilization, and conservation of ocean, coastal, and Great Lakes resources, specifically Lake Erie, through research, education, outreach, and communications. The program is administrated by The Ohio State University. Stone Laboratory is Ohio's biological field station located on Gibraltar Island at Put-in-Bay, Ohio.

Publication(s): Twine Line

Keyword(s): Oceans/Coasts/Beaches, Pollution (general), Water Habitats & Quality, Wildlife & Species

Contact(s):

Jeffrey Reutter, Director; reutter.1@osu.edu

Karen Ricker, Assistant Director and Communications Coordinator; ricker.15@osu.edu

UNITED STATES DEPARTMENT OF COMMERCE

NATIONAL OCEANOGRAPHIC AND ATMOSPHERIC ADMINISTRATION
SEA GRANT PROGRAM - OREGON
OREGON STATE UNIVERSITY
500 322 Kerr Administration Bldg.
Corvallis, OR 97331-2131 United States
Phone: 541-737-2714 Fax: 541-737-7958
E-mail: seagrant.admin@orst.edu
Website: seagrant.orst.edu/

Founded: N/A

Scope: State

Description: Oregon Sea Grant takes an integrated approach to addressing the problems and opportunities of Oregon's marine resources through three related primary activities—research, education, and extension services. Oregon Sea Grant responds to the needs of ocean users.

Publication(s): Catalogue available upon request from Sea Grant Communications.

Keyword(s): Oceans/Coasts/Beaches, Public Health, Wildlife & Species

Contact(s):

Robert Malouf, Program Director; maloufr@ccmail.orst.edu

Jan Auyong, Assistant Director for Programs; jan.auyong@orst.edu

Joseph Cone, Assistant Director for Communications; 402 Kerr Admin. Bldg. OSU, Corvallis, OR 97331-2134; 541-737-2716; Fax: 541-737-7958; joe.cone@orst.edu

Jay Rasmussen, Extension Program Leader; Hatfield Marine Science Center, 2030 S. Marine Science Dr., Newport, OR 97365; 541-867-0370; Fax: 541-867-0369; jay.rasmussen@hmsc.orst.edu

UNITED STATES DEPARTMENT OF COMMERCE

NATIONAL OCEANOGRAPHIC AND ATMOSPHERIC ADMINISTRATION
SEA GRANT PROGRAM - PUERTO RICO
UNIVERSITY OF PUERTO RICO
UPRM P.O. Box 9011
Mayagnez, PR 00681 United States
Phone: 787-832-3585 Fax: 787-265-2880
Website: http://seagrant.uprm.edu/seagrant/main.html

Founded: 1985

Scope: International

Description: Promote marine education activities among pre-college teachers and students. Faciliate interdisciplinary teaching and learning experience using the marine environment as a resource.

Publication(s): The Boletin Marino, Seagrant in the Caribbean

Keyword(s): Oceans/Coasts/Beaches, Water Habitats & Quality, Wildlife & Species

Contact(s):

Manuel Valdes Pizzini, Director of UPR Sea Grant College Program; 787-832-3585; Fax: 787-265-2880; ma_valdes@rumac.uprm.edu

UNITED STATES DEPARTMENT OF COMMERCE

NATIONAL OCEANOGRAPHIC AND ATMOSPHERIC ADMINISTRATION
SEA GRANT PROGRAM - RHODE ISLAND
UNIVERSITY OF RHODE ISLAND COASTAL INSTITUTE
Narragansett Bay Campus
Narragansett, RI 02882-1197 United States
Phone: 401-874-6800 Fax: 401-789-8340
Website: seagrant.gso.uri.edu/

Founded: N/A
Membership: N/A
Scope: Local, State, Regional, National
Description: The Rhode Island Sea Grant College Program conducts research and outreach on important marine issues. Outreach topics include coastal management and fisheries, aquaculture, and seafood safety.
Keyword(s): Ecosystems (precious), Oceans/Coasts/Beaches, Public Lands/Greenspace, Sprawl/Urban Planning, Water Habitats & Quality, Wildlife & Species
Contact(s):
Barry Costa-Pierce, Director
Malia Schwartz, Communications Director; 401-874-6842

UNITED STATES DEPARTMENT OF COMMERCE

NATIONAL OCEANOGRAPHIC AND ATMOSPHERIC ADMINISTRATION
SEA GRANT PROGRAM - SOUTH CAROLINA
287 Meeting St.
Charleston, SC 29401 United States
Phone: 843-727-2078 Fax: 843-727-2080
Website: www.scseagrant.org

Founded: N/A
Membership: 1–100
Scope: National
Description: A Universtiy-based state agency that supports research, education and outreach to conserve coastal and marine reserves and provide economic oppurtunities for the cities of South Carolina and the region.
Publication(s): Coastal Heritage, coastal hazard information., aquaculture handbooks, marine education publications and slide, extension materials, Inside SeaGrant
Keyword(s): Development/Developing Countries, Oceans/Coasts/Beaches, Water Habitats & Quality, Wildlife & Species
Contact(s):
Linda Blackwell, Director of Communications; blackwlj@musc.edu
M. Devoe, Executive Director; devoemr@musc.edu
Bob Bacon, Extension Program Leader; baconrh@musc.edu
Elaine Knight, Assistant Director; knightel@musc.edu

UNITED STATES DEPARTMENT OF COMMERCE

NATIONAL OCEANOGRAPHIC AND ATMOSPHERIC ADMINISTRATION
SEA GRANT PROGRAM - TEXAS
TEXAS A & M UNIVERSITY
1716 Briarcrest, Suite 702
Bryan, TX 77802 United States
Phone: 409-845-3854
Website: texas-sea-grant.tamu.edu/

Founded: N/A
Scope: State, National
Publication(s): Texas Shores, Marine Education
Keyword(s): Agriculture/Farming, Ethics/Environmental Justice, Land Issues, Oceans/Coasts/Beaches, Reduce/Reuse/Recycle, Water Habitats & Quality, Wildlife & Species
Contact(s):
Robert Stickney, Director; 2700 Earl Rudder Frwy. S, Suite 1800, College Station, TX 77845; 979-845-3854; Fax: 979-845-7525; stickne@unix.tamu.edu
Amy Broussard, Associate Director, Marine Information Service; 2700 Earl Rudder Frwy. S, Suite 1800, College Station, TX 77845; 979-862-3767; Fax: 979-845-7525; abrouss@unix.tamu.edu
Jim Hiney, Editor, Texas Shores Magazine; 2700 Earl Rudder Frwy. S, Suite 1800, College Station, TX 77845; 409-862-3773; Fax: 409-862-3786; bohiney@unix.tamu.edu
Russell Miget, Marine Advisory Service; Texas A&M University, Natural Resources Center, 6300 Ocean Dr., Suite 2800, Corpus Christi, TX 78412; 361-825-3460; Fax: 361-825-3465; rmiget@falcon.tamucc.edu

UNITED STATES DEPARTMENT OF COMMERCE

NATIONAL OCEANOGRAPHIC AND ATMOSPHERIC ADMINISTRATION
SEA GRANT PROGRAM - VIRGINIA
UNIVERSITY OF VIRGINIA
Virginia Graduate Marine Science Consortium
170 Rugby Rd.
Madison House
Charlottesville, VA 22903 United States
Phone: 804-924-5965 Fax: 804-982-3694
Website: www.virginia.edu/virginia-sea-grant/

Founded: N/A
Scope: State
Keyword(s): Oceans/Coasts/Beaches, Reduce/Reuse/Recycle, Water Habitats & Quality
Contact(s):
William Rickards, Director; rickards@virginia.edu
William Dupaul, Staff of Marine Advisory Program; Virginia Institute of Marine Science, Gloucester Point, VA 23062; 804-684-7163

UNITED STATES DEPARTMENT OF COMMERCE

NATIONAL OCEANOGRAPHIC AND ATMOSPHERIC ADMINISTRATION
SEA GRANT PROGRAM - WASHINGTON
3716 Brooklyn Ave., NE
Seattle, WA 98105-6716 United States
Phone: 206-543-6600 Fax: 206-685-0380
E-mail: seagrant@u.washington.edu
Website: www.wsg.washington.edu/

Founded: 1971
Scope: State
Description: Since 1968, Washington Sea Grant Program has supported research, advisory, and communication activities for the benefit of marine resources, users, and communities. It is part of a national network of universities meeting the changing environmental and economic needs of people in our coastal and Great Lakes regions.
Publication(s): El Nino North: Nino Effects in the East, Shape and Form of Puget Sound, The, Guide to Manila Clam Culture in WA, Ocean Ecology of North Pacific Salmonids
Keyword(s): Development/Developing Countries, Oceans/Coasts/Beaches, Public Health, Water Habitats & Quality, Wildlife & Species
Contact(s):
Louie Echols, Director; echols@u.washington.edu
Melissa O'Neill, Communications Manager; 206-685-9215; Fax: 206-685-0380; nboneill@u.washington.edu
Susan Cook, Publications Coordinator/Web Master; 206-685-2606; Fax: 206-685-0380
Andrea Copping, Assistant Director; 206-685-8209

UNITED STATES DEPARTMENT OF COMMERCE
NATIONAL OCEANOGRAPHIC AND ATMOSPHERIC ADMINISTRATION
SEA GRANT PROGRAM - WISCONSIN
UNIVERSITY OF WISCONSIN
1975 Willow Dr.
Madison, WI 53706-1177 United States
Phone: 608-262-0905 Fax: 608-262-0591
E-mail: administrator@seagrant.wisc.edu
Website: www.seagrant.wisc.edu/

Founded: 1968

Scope: National

Description: The University of Wisconsin Sea Grant Institute is a statewide program of basic and applied research, education, and technology transfer dedicated to the wise stewardship and sustainable use of Great Lakes and ocean resources.

Keyword(s): Oceans/Coasts/Beaches, Public Health, Water Habitats & Quality, Wildlife & Species

Contact(s):
Anders Andren, Director; awandren@seagrant.wisc.edu
Mary Reeb, Assistant Director for Administration and Information Technology; 608-263-3296; mlreeb@seagrant.wisc.edu
Stephen Wittman, Assistant Director of Communications; 608-263-5371; swittman@seagrant.wisc.edu

UNITED STATES DEPARTMENT OF COMMERCE
NATIONAL OCEANOGRAPHIC AND ATMOSPHERIC ADMINISTRATION
SOUTH SLOUGH NATIONAL ESTUARINE RESEARCH RESERVE
P.O. Box 5471
Charleston, OR 97420 United States
Phone: 541-888-5559 Fax: 541-888-5559

Founded: N/A

Scope: Regional

UNITED STATES DEPARTMENT OF COMMERCE
NATIONAL OCEANOGRAPHIC AND ATMOSPHERIC ADMINISTRATION
TIJUANA RIVER NATIONAL ESTUARINE RESEARCH RESERVE
301 Caspian Way
Imperial Beach, CA 91932 United States
Phone: 619-575-3613 Fax: 619-575-6913
E-mail: trnerr@ixpres.com
Website: www.tijuanaestuary.com

Founded: 1982

Membership: N/A

Scope: Regional, International

Description: The Tijuana River NERR emcompasses 2500 acres of protected southern California wetland, upland and riparian habitat and is located on the U.S./Mexico border. It includes Border Field State Park and Tijuana Slough National Wildlife Refuge and is jointly managed by California State Parks and U.S. Fish & Wildlife Service with additional support from NOAA. It is home to over 300 species of birds and 7 endangered species. The Visitor Center is open from 10-5 seven days a week.

UNITED STATES DEPARTMENT OF COMMERCE
NATIONAL OCEANOGRAPHIC AND ATMOSPHERIC ADMINISTRATION
WAQUOIT BAY NATIONAL ESTUARINE RESEARCH RESERVE
Department of Environmental Management,
P.O. Box 3092
Waquoit, MA 02536 United States
Phone: 508-457-0495 Fax: 617-727-5537
E-mail: waquoit.bay@state.ma.us
Website: www.waquoitbayreserve.org

Founded: N/A

Scope: Regional

Description: Our mission is to work with commmunities to provide and promote improved understanding and management of coastal resources through integrated programs of research, education and stewardship.

UNITED STATES DEPARTMENT OF COMMERCE
NATIONAL OCEANOGRAPHIC AND ATMOSPHERIC ADMINISTRATION
WEEKS BAY NATIONAL ESTUARINE RESEARCH RESERVE
11300 U.S. Highway 98
Fairhope, AL 36532 United States
Phone: 251-928-9792 Fax: 334-928-1792

Founded: N/A

Scope: Regional

Contact(s):
L. Adams, n/a; 251-928-9792

UNITED STATES DEPARTMENT OF COMMERCE
NATIONAL OCEANOGRAPHIC AND ATMOSPHERIC ADMINISTRATION
WELLS NATIONAL ESTUARINE RESEARCH RESERVE
342 Laudholm Farm Rd.
Wells, ME 04090 United States
Phone: 207-646-1555 Fax: 207-646-2930

Founded: N/A

Scope: Regional

UNITED STATES DEPARTMENT OF COMMERCE
OFFICE OF OCEANIC AND ATMOSPHERIC RESEARCH
Silver Spring Metro Center 3, 1315 East-West Hwy.
Silver Spring, MD 20910 United States
Phone: 301-713-2458 Fax: 301-713-0163
Website: www.oar.noaa.gov

Founded: N/A

Membership: 101–1,000

Scope: International

Description: Conducts environmental research in the oceans, atmosphere, and space. Administers the National Sea Grant College Program, which provides grants to academic institutions for research, education, and advisory/extension services in the marine environment.

Keyword(s): Air Quality/Atmosphere, Climate Change

Contact(s):
Ronald Baird, Director of National Sea Grant College Program of Extension; 301-713-2448
Barbara Moore, Director of National Undersea Research Program; 301-713-2427
David Evans, Assistant Administrator; David.Evans@noaa.gov
Louisa Koch, Deputy Assistant Administrator
Dane Konop, Public Affairs Officer; 301-713-2483
Maryann Whitcomb, Resource Management; 301-713-2454

UNITED STATES DEPARTMENT OF DEFENSE

The Pentagon, Office of the Secretary, 3400 Defense Pentagon
Washington, DC 20301-3400 United States
Phone: 703-697-1013 Fax: 703-693-7011
Website: www.denix.osd.mil

Founded: N/A

Scope: International

Description: Responsible for the security of the U.S. by establishing policies and procedures relating to national defense. The Department of Defense conducts programs to prevent pollution, enhance the environment, and conserve the natural and cultural resources on military lands.

Publication(s): DOD Commanders' Guide to Biodiversity, Legacy Resource Management Program Report to Congress, Cultural Resources in the Department of Defense, Natural Resources in the Department of Defense

Contact(s):
Sarah Hagan, Key Contact

UNITED STATES DEPARTMENT OF DEFENSE

AIR FORCE MAJOR AIR COMMANDS
AFBCA/EV HEADQUARTERS
HQ AFBCA/EV
1700 N. Moore St., Ste. 2300
Arlington, VA 22209-2802 United States
Phone: 703-696-5536

Founded: N/A

Contact(s):
Jerry Cleaver, Conservation Manager; HQ AFBCA/EV, 1700 N. Moore St., Ste. 2300, Arlington, VA 22209-2802; 703-696-5536

UNITED STATES DEPARTMENT OF DEFENSE

AIR FORCE MAJOR AIR COMMANDS
AFSOC EV HEADQUARTERS
HQ AFSOC EV, 427 Cody Ave.
Hurlburt Field, FL 32544 United States
Phone: 850-884-2260 Fax: 850-884-5982

Founded: N/A

Scope: International

Contact(s):
Michael Applegate, Natural Resource Manager and Entomologist; 850-884-2562

UNITED STATES DEPARTMENT OF DEFENSE

AIR FORCE MAJOR AIR COMMANDS
AIR MOBILITY COMMAND (AMC)
HQ AMC/CEVP,
507 Symington Drive
Scott AFB, IL 62225-5022 United States
Phone: 618-229-0842 Fax: 618-229-0257
E-mail: will.summers@scott.af.mil

Founded: 1947

Membership: 101–1,000

Scope: National

Description: U.S. Air Force Air Mobility Command natural resources manager is a function of the Environmental Programs Division which oversees natural resources management on twelve USAF military bases and related outlying airfields and airspace.

Keyword(s): Agriculture/Farming, Ecosystems (precious), Forests/Forestry, Land Issues, Pollution (general), Public Lands/Greenspace, Recreation/Ecotourism, Water Habitats & Quality, Wildlife & Species

Contact(s):
William Summers, Natural Resources Manager, HQ AMC/CEVP

UNITED STATES DEPARTMENT OF DEFENSE

AIR FORCE MAJOR AIR COMMANDS
ANDREWS AFB, MD
3500 Fetchet Ave.
Andrews AFB, MD 20331-5157 United States
Phone: 301-836-8798

Founded: N/A

Contact(s):
Pat Richerson, Natural Resources Manager, HQ ANG/CEVP

UNITED STATES DEPARTMENT OF DEFENSE

AIR FORCE MAJOR AIR COMMANDS
BOLLING AFB, DC
3700 Brookley Ave.
Washington, DC 20332 United States
Phone: 202-767-8600 Fax: 202-767-1160

Founded: N/A

Contact(s):
Mark Dickerson, Chief of Environmental Planning Branch

UNITED STATES DEPARTMENT OF DEFENSE

AIR FORCE MAJOR AIR COMMANDS
GERMANY AFB
Unit 3050, Box 10
APO, AE, 09094-5010 Germany
Phone: 011-49-6371-47-6482

Founded: N/A

Contact(s):
Edwin Worth, Natural/Cultural Resources Manager, HQ USAFE/CEVP

UNITED STATES DEPARTMENT OF DEFENSE

AIR FORCE MAJOR AIR COMMANDS
HICKAM AFB, HI
25 E St.
Hickam AFB, HI 96853-5412 United States
Phone: 808-449-9695 Fax: 808-448-4209
E-mail: pacf.csv@exchange.hickam.af.mil
Website: www.hqpacif.af.mil/ce/cevindx/cevindx.htm

Founded: N/A

Membership: 1–100

Scope: National

Contact(s):
Arthur Buckman, Natural Resources Manager, HQ PACAF/CEVEP

UNITED STATES DEPARTMENT OF DEFENSE

AIR FORCE MAJOR AIR COMMANDS
KIRTLAND AFB, NM
9700 Avenue G S.E.
Suite 266
Kirtland AFB, NM 87117-5671 United States
Phone: 505-846-5674 Fax: 505-846-0684

Founded: N/A

Contact(s):
Peter Windler, Chief, USAF Bash Team

UNITED STATES DEPARTMENT OF DEFENSE

AIR FORCE MAJOR AIR COMMANDS
LANGLEY AFB, VA
129 Andrews St., Suite 102, Major Air Commands
Langley AFB, VA 23665-2769 United States
Phone: 757-764-9338
Website: www.acc.af.mil/

Founded: N/A

Scope: Regional

Description: Provide natural resource conservation leadership to 18 AF installations, protecting threatened and endangered species, migratory birds, neotropical birds in an ecoystem management approach.

Contact(s):
Roy Barker, Natural Resources Manager, HQ ACC/CEVA

UNITED STATES DEPARTMENT OF DEFENSE
AIR FORCE MAJOR AIR COMMANDS
PETERSON AFB, CO
150 Vandenberg St., Suite 1105
Peterson AFB, CO 80914-4150 United States
Phone: 719-554-9915 Fax: 719-554-3849

Founded: N/A

Scope: Local, State, Regional, National, International

Description: AFSPC is a Major Command with over 14 installations in the U.S. and overseas.

Keyword(s): Agriculture/Farming, Ecosystems (precious), Forests/Forestry, Land Issues, Oceans/Coasts/Beaches, Public Lands/Greenspace, Recreation/Ecotourism, Sprawl/Urban Planning, Water Habitats & Quality, Wildlife & Species

Contact(s):
Stanley Rogers, Natural Resources Manager, HQ AFSPC/CEVP; stanley.rogers@peterson.af.mil

UNITED STATES DEPARTMENT OF DEFENSE
AIR FORCE MAJOR AIR COMMANDS
POPE AFB, NC
43 CES/CEV
560 Interceptor Rd.
Pope AFB, NC 28308 United States
Phone: 910-394-4195
Website: www.pope.af.mil

Founded: N/A
Membership: 1–100
Scope: Local

Description: Pope Air Force Base Environmental Flight Supports the 43rd Airlift Wing with Environmental Programs including Mandatory Recycling, Stormwater Management, Review of Construction Projects, Pollution Prevention, Installation Restoration (Cleanup of Sites/Soils), Asbestos and Lead-based Paint Abatement Programs, Tanks, Spill Response, Natural Resources, Historic Properties, Hazardous Wastes, and NEPA.

Keyword(s): Air Quality/Atmosphere, Ecosystems (precious), Land Issues, Pollution (general), Public Health, Recreation/Ecotourism, Reduce/Reuse/Recycle, Water Habitats & Quality, Wildlife & Species

Contact(s):
Viola Walker, Natural/Cultural Resources Manager; 910-394-4195

UNITED STATES DEPARTMENT OF DEFENSE
AIR FORCE MAJOR AIR COMMANDS
RANDOLPH AFB, TX
266 F St., West, Bldg. 901
Randolph AFB, TX 78150-4321 United States
Phone: 210-652-3959
Website: www.aetc.randolph.af.mil/

Founded: N/A

Contact(s):
Carl Lahsher, Natural Resources Manager, HQ AETC/CEV

UNITED STATES DEPARTMENT OF DEFENSE
AIR FORCE MAJOR AIR COMMANDS
ROBINS AFB, GA
155 Richard Ray Blvd.
Robins AFB, GA 31098-1635 United States

Founded: N/A

UNITED STATES DEPARTMENT OF DEFENSE
AIR FORCE MAJOR AIR COMMANDS
SPECIAL OPERATIONS COMMAND
Building 90333
427 Cody Avenue
Suite 225
Hurlburt Field, FL 32404 United States
Phone: 850-884-2977 Fax: 850-884-5982
E-mail: ronald.nasca@hurlburt.af.mil
Website: www.hurlburt.af.mil

Founded: 1990
Membership: 1,001–10,000
Scope: Local, International

Description: Hurlburt Field, home of the AF Special Operations Command

Contact(s):
Philip Pruit, Natural Resources Manager; 850-884-4651

UNITED STATES DEPARTMENT OF DEFENSE
AIR FORCE MAJOR AIR COMMANDS
USAF ACADEMY
8120 Edgerton Dr., Suite 40
USAF Academy, CO 80840-2400 United States
Phone: 719-333-3308 Fax: 719-333-3337
E-mail: brian.mihlbachler@usafa.af.mil
Website: www.usafa.af.mil

Founded: N/A

Scope: Local

Description: Range, Wildlife, and Forestry Management

Contact(s):
Brian Mihlbachler, Natural Resource Planner A/CEVP; 719-333-3308; Fax: 719-333-3337; brian.mihlbachler@usafa.af.mil
Jim McDermott, Natural Resource Planner; 719-333-3308; Fax: 719-333-3337; james.mcdermott@usafa.af.mil

UNITED STATES DEPARTMENT OF DEFENSE
AIR FORCE MAJOR AIR COMMANDS
USAF/ILEV HEADQUARTERS
Environmental Division, HQ USAF/ILEV, 1260 Air Force Pentagon
Washington, DC 20330-1260 United States
Phone: 703-604-0632 Fax: 703-604-3740

Founded: N/A

Scope: National

Description: A comprehensive natural resources conservation program focusing on fish and wildlife management, forestry, outdoor recreation, and soil and water conservation has been conducted on Air Force lands since the mid-1950's. Current policy requires all installations with significant land and water resources to develop integrated natural resource management plans as part of the base comprehensive planning process.

Contact(s):
Alan Holck, Natural and Cultural Resources Program Manager

UNITED STATES DEPARTMENT OF DEFENSE
AIR FORCE MAJOR AIR COMMANDS
WRIGHT PATTERSON AFB, OH
HQ AFMC/CEVQ
4225 Logistics Ave., Rm. A128
Wright Patterson AFB, OH 45433-5747 United States
Phone: 937-656-1409 Fax: 937-587-5875
E-mail: mike.cornelius@wpafb.af.mil
Website: https://www.afmc-mil.wpafb.af.mil/HQ-AFMC/CE/

Founded: N/A
Membership: N/A
Scope: National

Description: Provides natural resources program and budget support for AFMC installations.

Contact(s):

Mike Cornelius, Natural Resources Manager; HQ AFMC/CEVQ,

UNITED STATES DEPARTMENT OF DEFENSE
AIR FORCE MAJOR U.S. INSTALLATIONS
EGLIN AIR FORCE BASE
NATURAL RESOURCE MANAGEMENT UNIT
Jackson Guard
107 Highway 85N
Niceville, FL 32578 United States
Phone: 850-882-4164, ext. 301 Fax: 850-882-5321

Founded: 1945

Scope: Local, State, Regional, National

Description: Natural Resource managers for 464,000 acre Eglin AFB, one of The Nature Conservancy's hotspots of national biodiversity. Natural Resource managers sections cover Forestry, Fire and Wildlife.

Keyword(s): Ecosystems (precious), Forests/Forestry, Public Lands/Greenspace, Recreation/Ecotourism, Water Habitats & Quality, Wildlife & Species

UNITED STATES DEPARTMENT OF DEFENSE
AIR FORCE MAJOR U.S. INSTALLATIONS
ALTUS AFB, OK
97 CES/CEV
607 South First Street
Altus AFB, OK 73523-5106 United States

Founded: N/A

Contact(s):

Jim Bellon, Natural Resources Manager; 580-481-7606

UNITED STATES DEPARTMENT OF DEFENSE
AIR FORCE MAJOR U.S. INSTALLATIONS
ANDERSON AFB, GUAM, UNITED STATES

Founded: N/A

Contact(s):

Heidi Hirsh, Natural Resources Manager; 671-366-2549

UNITED STATES DEPARTMENT OF DEFENSE
AIR FORCE MAJOR U.S. INSTALLATIONS
ANDREWS AFB, MD, UNITED STATES

Founded: N/A

Contact(s):

Carol Devier-Heemey, Cultural/Natural Resources Manager; 301-981-2579

UNITED STATES DEPARTMENT OF DEFENSE
AIR FORCE MAJOR U.S. INSTALLATIONS
ARNOLD AFB, TN, UNITED STATES

Founded: N/A

Contact(s):

Clark Brandon, Natural/Cultural Resources Manager; 615-454-7115

UNITED STATES DEPARTMENT OF DEFENSE
AIR FORCE MAJOR U.S. INSTALLATIONS
AVON PARK AFB, FL, UNITED STATES

Founded: N/A

Contact(s):

Paul Ebersbach, Chief of Conservation Programs; 941-452-7119, ext. 301

UNITED STATES DEPARTMENT OF DEFENSE
AIR FORCE MAJOR U.S. INSTALLATIONS
BARKSDALE AFB, LA, UNITED STATES

Founded: N/A

Contact(s):

Bruce Holland, Natural Resources Manager; 318-456-1981

UNITED STATES DEPARTMENT OF DEFENSE
AIR FORCE MAJOR U.S. INSTALLATIONS
BEALE AFB, CA, UNITED STATES

Founded: N/A

Contact(s):

Kristen Christopherson, Natural Resouces Manager; 916-634-2643

UNITED STATES DEPARTMENT OF DEFENSE
AIR FORCE MAJOR U.S. INSTALLATIONS
BOLLING AFB, DC, UNITED STATES

Founded: N/A

Contact(s):

Fioravante Gaetano, Natural Resources Manager; 202-767-8603

UNITED STATES DEPARTMENT OF DEFENSE
AIR FORCE MAJOR U.S. INSTALLATIONS
BROOKS AFB, TX, UNITED STATES

Founded: N/A

Contact(s):

Hamid Kamalpour, Natural Resources Manager; 210-536-6703

UNITED STATES DEPARTMENT OF DEFENSE
AIR FORCE MAJOR U.S. INSTALLATIONS
CANNON AFB, NM, UNITED STATES

Founded: N/A

Contact(s):

Rick Crow, Cultural/Natural Resources Manager; 505-784-6383

UNITED STATES DEPARTMENT OF DEFENSE
AIR FORCE MAJOR U.S. INSTALLATIONS
CHARLESTON AFB, SC, UNITED STATES

Founded: N/A

Contact(s):

Al Urrutia, Cultural/Natural Resources Manager; 843-963-4978

UNITED STATES DEPARTMENT OF DEFENSE
AIR FORCE MAJOR U.S. INSTALLATIONS
COLUMBUS AFB, MS, UNITED STATES
14 CES/CEV
555 Simler Boulevard
Columbus AFB, MS 39701-6010 United States

Founded: N/A

Contact(s):

Ryan Nelson, Cultural/Natural Resources Manager; 601-434-7315

UNITED STATES DEPARTMENT OF DEFENSE
AIR FORCE MAJOR U.S. INSTALLATIONS
DAVIS-MONTHAN AFB, AZ, UNITED STATES

Founded: N/A

Contact(s):

Gwen Lisa, Cultural/Natural Resources Manager; 520-228-3215

UNITED STATES DEPARTMENT OF DEFENSE
AIR FORCE MAJOR U.S. INSTALLATIONS
DOVER AFB, DE, UNITED STATES

Founded: N/A

Contact(s):

Charles Mikula, Cultural/Natural Resources Manager; 302-677-6820

UNITED STATES DEPARTMENT OF DEFENSE
AIR FORCE MAJOR U.S. INSTALLATIONS
DYESS AFB, TX UNITED STATES
Phone: 915-696-5049 Fax: 915-696-2899
Website: https://www.mil.dyess.af.mil

Founded: N/A

Contact(s):
Jim Robertson, Cultural/Natural Resources Director

UNITED STATES DEPARTMENT OF DEFENSE
AIR FORCE MAJOR U.S. INSTALLATIONS
EDWARDS AFB, CA, UNITED STATES

Founded: N/A

Contact(s):
Mark Hagan, Natural Resources Manager; 805-277-1418

UNITED STATES DEPARTMENT OF DEFENSE
AIR FORCE MAJOR U.S. INSTALLATIONS
EIELSON AFB, AK, UNITED STATES

Founded: N/A

Contact(s):
Gerald Von Rueden, Natural Resources Manager; 907-377-5182

UNITED STATES DEPARTMENT OF DEFENSE
AIR FORCE MAJOR U.S. INSTALLATIONS
ELLSWORTH AFB, SD, UNITED STATES

Founded: N/A

Contact(s):
Jim Stengler, Cultural/Natural Resources Manager; 605-385-6677

UNITED STATES DEPARTMENT OF DEFENSE
AIR FORCE MAJOR U.S. INSTALLATIONS
ELMENDORF AFB, AK, UNITED STATES

Founded: N/A

Contact(s):
Alan Richmond, Natural Resources Manager; 907-552-1609

UNITED STATES DEPARTMENT OF DEFENSE
AIR FORCE MAJOR U.S. INSTALLATIONS
F.E. WARREN AFB, WY, UNITED STATES
Phone: 307-773-5494

Founded: N/A

Contact(s):
Catherine Pazenti, Natural Resources Manager; 307-773-5494

UNITED STATES DEPARTMENT OF DEFENSE
AIR FORCE MAJOR U.S. INSTALLATIONS
FAIRCHILD AFB, WA, UNITED STATES

Founded: N/A

Contact(s):
Gerald Johnson, Natural Resources Manager; 509-247-2313

UNITED STATES DEPARTMENT OF DEFENSE
AIR FORCE MAJOR U.S. INSTALLATIONS
GOODFELLOW AFB, TX, UNITED STATES
17 CES/CEV
460 Kearney Boulevard
Goodfellow AFB, TX 37608-4122 United States

Founded: N/A

Contact(s):
Lyndal Fisher, Natural Resources Manager; 915-654-3451

UNITED STATES DEPARTMENT OF DEFENSE
AIR FORCE MAJOR U.S. INSTALLATIONS
GRAND FORKS AFB, ND, UNITED STATES

Founded: N/A

UNITED STATES DEPARTMENT OF DEFENSE
AIR FORCE MAJOR U.S. INSTALLATIONS
HANSCOM AFB, MA, UNITED STATES

Founded: N/A

Contact(s):
Don Morris, Natural Resources Manager; 617-377-4667

UNITED STATES DEPARTMENT OF DEFENSE
AIR FORCE MAJOR U.S. INSTALLATIONS
HICKAM AFB, HI, UNITED STATES

Founded: N/A

Contact(s):
Gary O'Donnell, Natural Resources Manager; 808-449-9695, ext. 205

UNITED STATES DEPARTMENT OF DEFENSE
AIR FORCE MAJOR U.S. INSTALLATIONS
HILL AFB, UT, UNITED STATES
Phone: 801-777-4618

Founded: N/A

Contact(s):
Marcus Blood, Cultural/Natural Resources Manager; 801-777-4618

UNITED STATES DEPARTMENT OF DEFENSE
AIR FORCE MAJOR U.S. INSTALLATIONS
HOLLOMAN AFB, NM, UNITED STATES

Founded: N/A

Contact(s):
Hildy Reiser, Natural Resources Manager; 505-475-3931

UNITED STATES DEPARTMENT OF DEFENSE
AIR FORCE MAJOR U.S. INSTALLATIONS
HURLBURT FIELD, FL, UNITED STATES

Founded: N/A

Contact(s):
Philip Pruit, Natural/Cultural Resources Manager; 850-884-4651

UNITED STATES DEPARTMENT OF DEFENSE
AIR FORCE MAJOR U.S. INSTALLATIONS
KEESLER AFB, MS, UNITED STATES
81 CES/CEV
508 L Street
Keesler AFB, MS 39534-2115 United States
Phone: 228-377-2489

Founded: N/A

Contact(s):
George Daniels, Natural Resources Manager; 228-377-2489

UNITED STATES DEPARTMENT OF DEFENSE
AIR FORCE MAJOR U.S. INSTALLATIONS
KIRTLAND AFB, NM, UNITED STATES
Phone: 505-280-7604

Founded: N/A

Contact(s):
Bob Dow, Natural Resources Manager; 505-280-7604

UNITED STATES DEPARTMENT OF DEFENSE
AIR FORCE MAJOR U.S. INSTALLATIONS
LACKLAND AFB, TX, UNITED STATES
Phone: 210-671-4843

Founded: N/A

Contact(s):
Robert Johnson, Natural Resources Manager; 210-671-4843

UNITED STATES DEPARTMENT OF DEFENSE

AIR FORCE MAJOR U.S. INSTALLATIONS
LANGLEY AFB, VA, UNITED STATES
Phone: 757-764-1090

Founded: N/A

Contact(s):
Patsy Kerr, Natural Resources Manager; 757-764-1090

UNITED STATES DEPARTMENT OF DEFENSE

AIR FORCE MAJOR U.S. INSTALLATIONS
LAUGHLIN AFB, TX, UNITED STATES
47 CES/CEV
251 Fourth Street
Laughlin AFB, TX 78843-5143 United States
Phone: 830-298-5694

Founded: N/A

Contact(s):
Jadee Bell, Natural Resources Manager; 830-298-4298

UNITED STATES DEPARTMENT OF DEFENSE

AIR FORCE MAJOR U.S. INSTALLATIONS
LITTLE ROCK AFB, AR, UNITED STATES
314 CES/CEV
528 Thomas Avenue
Little Rock AFB, AR 72099-5005 United States
Phone: 501-987-3681

Founded: N/A

Contact(s):
James Popham, Cultural/Natural Resources Manager; 501-987-3681

UNITED STATES DEPARTMENT OF DEFENSE

AIR FORCE MAJOR U.S. INSTALLATIONS
LUKE AFB (AND THE BARRY M. GOLDWATER AFR), AZ, UNITED STATES
56 CES/CEV
13970 Lightning
Luke AFB, AZ 85309-1149 United States
Phone: 623-856-3823

Founded: N/A

Contact(s):
Robert Barry, Chief of Conservation Programs; 623-856-3823, ext. 242

UNITED STATES DEPARTMENT OF DEFENSE

AIR FORCE MAJOR U.S. INSTALLATIONS
MACDILL AFB, FL, UNITED STATES
Jason Kirkpatrick
2610 Pink Flamingo Avenue
MacDill AFB, FL 33621 United States
Phone: 813-828-0459

Founded: N/A

Membership: N/A

Scope: Local

Description: Natural/Cultural Resources Program for MacDill AFB. Responsible for environmental compliance, and protection/improvement of natural and cultural resources on base.

Keyword(s): Air Quality/Atmosphere, Ecosystems (precious), Ethics/Environmental Justice, Pollution (general), Reduce/Reuse/Recycle, Water Habitats & Quality, Wildlife & Species

Contact(s):
Jason Kirkpatrick, Natural Resources Manager; 813-828-2567

UNITED STATES DEPARTMENT OF DEFENSE

AIR FORCE MAJOR U.S. INSTALLATIONS
MALMSTROM AFB, MT, UNITED STATES
Phone: 406-731-6438

Founded: N/A

Contact(s):
Rudy Berzuh, Cultural/Natural Resources Manager; 406-731-6437

UNITED STATES DEPARTMENT OF DEFENSE

AIR FORCE MAJOR U.S. INSTALLATIONS
MAXWELL AFB, AL, UNITED STATES
42 CES/CEV
400 Cannon Street
Maxwell AFB, AL 36112-6523 United States
Phone: 334-953-3892

Founded: N/A

Contact(s):
Ruth Vandiver, Natural Resources Manager; 334-953-3892

UNITED STATES DEPARTMENT OF DEFENSE

AIR FORCE MAJOR U.S. INSTALLATIONS
MCCHORD AFB, WA, UNITED STATES
62 DES/CEVN
555 A Street
McChord AFB, WA 98438 United States
Phone: 253-982-3913

Founded: N/A

Contact(s):
Valerie Elliott, Natural Resources Manager

UNITED STATES DEPARTMENT OF DEFENSE

AIR FORCE MAJOR U.S. INSTALLATIONS
MCCLELLAN AFB, CA, UNITED STATES
Phone: 916-643-1742

Founded: N/A

Contact(s):
Molly Enloe, Natural Resources Manager; 919-643-1742

UNITED STATES DEPARTMENT OF DEFENSE

AIR FORCE MAJOR U.S. INSTALLATIONS
MCCONNELL AFB, KS, UNITED STATES
Phone: 316-759-3884

Founded: N/A

Contact(s):
John Hafker, Cultural/Natural Resources Manager; 316-759-3884

UNITED STATES DEPARTMENT OF DEFENSE

AIR FORCE MAJOR U.S. INSTALLATIONS
MCGUIRE AFB, NJ, UNITED STATES

Founded: N/A

UNITED STATES DEPARTMENT OF DEFENSE

AIR FORCE MAJOR U.S. INSTALLATIONS
MOODY AFB, GA, UNITED STATES
347 CES/CEVA
3485 Georgia Street
Moody AFB, GA 31699-1707 United States
Phone: 229-257-5881 Fax: 229-257-5811
E-mail: gregory.lee@moody.af.mil

Founded: N/A

Scope: Local, State, Regional, National

Description: The Environmental Flight at Moody AFB is charged with the professional stewardship of the natural resources entrusted to the installation.

Contact(s):
Gregory Lee, Natural Resources Manager; 229-257-5881; Fax: 229-257-5811; gregory.lee@moody.af.mil

UNITED STATES DEPARTMENT OF DEFENSE

AIR FORCE MAJOR U.S. INSTALLATIONS
MOUNTAIN HOME AFB, ID, UNITED STATES
Phone: 208-828-6351

Founded: N/A

Contact(s):

Angelia Martin, Cultural/Natural Resources Manager; 208-828-6351

UNITED STATES DEPARTMENT OF DEFENSE

AIR FORCE MAJOR U.S. INSTALLATIONS
NELLIS AFB, NV, UNITED STATES
Phone: 702-652-3173

Founded: N/A

Contact(s):

Shelia Amos, Natural Resources Manager; 702-652-3173

UNITED STATES DEPARTMENT OF DEFENSE

AIR FORCE MAJOR U.S. INSTALLATIONS
OFFUT AFB, NE, UNITED STATES

Founded: N/A

Contact(s):

Gene Svensen, Cultural/Natural Resource Manager; 402-294-7619

UNITED STATES DEPARTMENT OF DEFENSE

AIR FORCE MAJOR U.S. INSTALLATIONS
PATRICK AFB, FL, UNITED STATES
Phone: 321-494-7288

Founded: N/A

Contact(s):

Mike Camardese, Cultural/Natural Resources Manager; 321-853-0910

UNITED STATES DEPARTMENT OF DEFENSE

AIR FORCE MAJOR U.S. INSTALLATIONS
PETERSON AFB, CO, UNITED STATES
Phone: 719-554-9915

Founded: N/A

Contact(s):

Dan Rogers, Natural Resource Manager

UNITED STATES DEPARTMENT OF DEFENSE

AIR FORCE MAJOR U.S. INSTALLATIONS
RANDOLPH AFB, TX, UNITED STATES
12 CES/CEV
1651 Fifth Street West
Randolph AFB, TX 78150-4513 United States
Phone: 210-652-4668

Founded: N/A

Contact(s):

Catherine Vornberg, Natural Resources Manager; 210-652-4668

UNITED STATES DEPARTMENT OF DEFENSE

AIR FORCE MAJOR U.S. INSTALLATIONS
REMOTE SITES (611 SUPPORT GROUP), AK, UNITED STATES

Founded: N/A

Contact(s):

Gene Augustine, Natural Resources Manager; 907-552-0788

UNITED STATES DEPARTMENT OF DEFENSE

AIR FORCE MAJOR U.S. INSTALLATIONS
SCOTT AFB, IL, UNITED STATES

Founded: N/A

Contact(s):

William Calvert, Cultural/Natural Resources Manager; 618-256-2092

UNITED STATES DEPARTMENT OF DEFENSE

AIR FORCE MAJOR U.S. INSTALLATIONS
SEYMOUR JOHNSON AFB (AND DARE COUNTY AFR), NC, UNITED STATES

Founded: N/A

Contact(s):

Brian Henderson, Cultural/Natural Resources Manager; 919-722-5173

UNITED STATES DEPARTMENT OF DEFENSE

AIR FORCE MAJOR U.S. INSTALLATIONS
SHAW AFB, SC, UNITED STATES

Founded: N/A

Contact(s):

Terry Madewell, Cultural/Natural Resources Manager; 803-895-5193

UNITED STATES DEPARTMENT OF DEFENSE

AIR FORCE MAJOR U.S. INSTALLATIONS
SHEPPARD AFB, TX, UNITED STATES
82 CES/CEV
231 Ninth Street
Sheppard AFB, TX, 76311-2254 United States
Phone: 940-676-5698

Founded: N/A

Contact(s):

Tim Hunter, Cultural/Natural Resources Manager; 940-676-5698

UNITED STATES DEPARTMENT OF DEFENSE

AIR FORCE MAJOR U.S. INSTALLATIONS
SHRIEVER AFB, CO, UNITED STATES
Phone: 719-567-3360

Founded: N/A

Contact(s):

Melissa Trenchik, Natural Resource Manager

UNITED STATES DEPARTMENT OF DEFENSE

AIR FORCE MAJOR U.S. INSTALLATIONS
TINKER AFB, OK, UNITED STATES

Founded: N/A

Contact(s):

John Krupovage, Natural Resources Manager; 405-734-3093

UNITED STATES DEPARTMENT OF DEFENSE

AIR FORCE MAJOR U.S. INSTALLATIONS
TRAVIS AFB, CA, UNITED STATES
Phone: 707-424-7515

Founded: N/A

Contact(s):

Robert Holmes, Natural Resources Manager

UNITED STATES DEPARTMENT OF DEFENSE

AIR FORCE MAJOR U.S. INSTALLATIONS
TYNDALL AFB, AL, UNITED STATES
325 CES/CEV
119 Alabama Avenue
Tyndall AFB, FL 32403-5014 United States
Phone: 850-283-2641

Founded: N/A

Contact(s):

Bob Bates, Natural Resources Manager; 850-283-2641

UNITED STATES DEPARTMENT OF DEFENSE

AIR FORCE MAJOR U.S. INSTALLATIONS
VANCE AFB, OK, UNITED STATES

Founded: N/A

Contact(s):
Mark Buthman, Cultural/Natural Resources Manager

UNITED STATES DEPARTMENT OF DEFENSE
AIR FORCE MAJOR U.S. INSTALLATIONS
VANDENBERG AFB, CA, UNITED STATES

Founded: N/A

Contact(s):
Allan Naydol, Natural Resources Manager

UNITED STATES DEPARTMENT OF DEFENSE
AIR FORCE MAJOR U.S. INSTALLATIONS
WHITEMAN AFB, MO, UNITED STATES

Founded: N/A

Contact(s):
Neil Bass, Cultural/Natural Resources Manager
Angela Corson, Natural Resources Manager

UNITED STATES DEPARTMENT OF DEFENSE
AIR FORCE MAJOR U.S. INSTALLATIONS
WRIGHT-PATTERSON AFB, OH, UNITED STATES
Phone: 937-257-5535, ext. 262

Founded: N/A

Contact(s):
Terri Lucas, Natural Resources Planner; 937-257-5535, ext. 262

UNITED STATES DEPARTMENT OF DEFENSE
AIR FORCE
CENTER FOR ENVIRONMENTAL EXCELLENCE
3207 North Rd.
Brooks AFB, TX 78235-5344 United States
Phone: 210-536-3823 Fax: 210-536-3890
Website: www.afcee.brooks.af.mil/

Founded: N/A

Scope: National, International

Description: Provides program and project support for Air Force installations worldwide.

Contact(s):
Edward Bakunas, Chief, Program Support Division; 210-536-3334; ed.bakunas@brooks.af.mil
Mary Anderson, Botanist; 210-536-3808; mary.anderson@brooks.af.mil
Daniel Friese, Natural Resource Specialist; 210-536-3823; daniel.friese@brooks.af.mil
Kevin Porteck, Forester; 210-536-5631; kevin.porteck@brooks.af.mil

UNITED STATES DEPARTMENT OF DEFENSE
AIR FORCE
CIVIL ENGINEERING SUPPORT AGENCY HQ
139 Barnes Dr.
Tyndall AFB, FL 32403-5319 United States
Phone: 850-283-6465 Fax: 850-283-6219

Founded: N/A

Membership: 1–100

Scope: International

Contact(s):
Wayne Fordham, Management Agronomist, AFCESA/CEM

UNITED STATES DEPARTMENT OF DEFENSE
ARMY
Pentagon Environmental Dept.
Washington, DC 20310 United States
Phone: 703-695-7824 Fax: 703-693-8149

Founded: N/A

Scope: State

Contact(s):
Raymond Fatz, Deputy Assistant Secretary of the Army; 703-695-7824
Phil Huber, Assistant for Environmental Quality; 703-614-9555

UNITED STATES DEPARTMENT OF DEFENSE
ARMY CORPS OF ENGINEERS
441 G St.
Washington, DC 20314-1000 United States
Phone: 202-761-0001
Website: www.usace.army.mil

Founded: 1775

Membership: 10,001–100,000

Scope: Local, State, Regional, National, International

Description: The mission of the Corps of Engineers is to provide quality, responsive engineering and environmental services to the nation. The Corps plans, designs, builds, and operates water resources and other civil works projects. The Corps designs and manages the construction of military facilities and activities for the Army and Air Force and provides design and construction management support for other defense and federal agencies.

Keyword(s): Development/Developing Countries, Energy, Oceans/Coasts/Beaches, Pollution (general), Public Health, Public Lands/Greenspace, Recreation/Ecotourism, Reduce/Reuse/Recycle, Transportation, Water Habitats & Quality, Wildlife & Species

Contact(s):
John Bellinger, Endangered Species/NEPA Coordinator; 202-761-0166
Darrell Lewis, Chief, Natural Resources; 202-761-0247
Robert Mirelson, Chief, Public Affairs; 202-761-0010
Paul Rubenstein, Cultural Resources Coordinator; 202-761-1257
Lloyd Saunders, Executive Secretary, Environmental Advisory Board; 202-761-8731
Robert Soots, Chief, Office of Environmental Policy; 703-428-6491
John Studt, Chief, Regulatory; 202-761-1785
Timothy Toplisek, Fish and Wildlife Coordinator; 202-761-1789
James Wolcott, Chief, Environmental Compliance; 202-761-0200

UNITED STATES DEPARTMENT OF DEFENSE
ARMY CORPS OF ENGINEERS
ALASKA ENGINEER DISTRICT
Anchorage, AK 99506-0898 United States
Phone: 907-753-2520 Fax: 907-753-2526
Website: www.poa.usace.army.mil

Founded: N/A

Membership: 101–1,000

Scope: National

UNITED STATES DEPARTMENT OF DEFENSE
ARMY CORPS OF ENGINEERS
ALBUQUERQUE ENGINEER DISTRICT
4101 Jefferson Plaza NE
Albuquerque, NM 87109-3435 United States
Phone: 505-342-3116 Fax: 505-342-3199

Founded: N/A

Membership: 101–1,000

Scope: National

UNITED STATES DEPARTMENT OF DEFENSE
ARMY CORPS OF ENGINEERS
BALTIMORE ENGINEER DISTRICT
P.O. Box 1715
Baltimore, MD 21203 United States
Phone: 410-962-2809 Fax: 410-962-3660
Website: nab.usace.army.mil

Founded: N/A

Membership: 1,001–10,000
Scope: Local, State, Regional, National
Description: Provides quality engineering, technical and environmental services to a variety of Department of Defense and non-Defense customers throughout the mid-Atlantic region.
Contact(s):
Charles Fiala, District Engineer

UNITED STATES DEPARTMENT OF DEFENSE
ARMY CORPS OF ENGINEERS
BUFFALO ENGINEER DISTRICT
1766 Niagara Street
Buffalo, NY 14207-3199 United States
Phone: 716-879-4200 Fax: 716-879-4195
Website: www.lrb.usace.army.mil
Founded: N/A
Scope: State
Contact(s):
Nancy Sticht, Public Affairs Officer; 716-879-4410; nancy.j.sticht@usace.army.mil

UNITED STATES DEPARTMENT OF DEFENSE
ARMY CORPS OF ENGINEERS
CHARLESTON ENGINEER DISTRICT
P.O. Box 919
Charleston, SC 29401-0919 United States
Phone: 843-329-8000
Founded: N/A
Contact(s):
Peter Mueller

UNITED STATES DEPARTMENT OF DEFENSE
ARMY CORPS OF ENGINEERS
CHICAGO ENGINEER DISTRICT
111 N. Canal Street, Suite 600
Chicago, IL 60606-7206 United States
Phone: 312-353-6400 Fax: 312-353-2525
Website: www.lrc.usace.army.mil
Founded: N/A
Membership: 101–1,000
Scope: National
Contact(s):
Mark Roncoli, District Commander

UNITED STATES DEPARTMENT OF DEFENSE
ARMY CORPS OF ENGINEERS
COLD REGIONS RESEARCH AND ENGINEERING LABORATORY
72 Lyme Road
Hanover, NH 03755-1290 United States
Phone: 603-646-4200 Fax: 603-646-4178
Website: www.crrel.usace.army.mil
Founded: N/A
Membership: 101–1,000
Scope: International
Publication(s): Technical Reports
Contact(s):
Barbara Sotirin, Director; 603-646-4200

UNITED STATES DEPARTMENT OF DEFENSE
ARMY CORPS OF ENGINEERS
CONSTRUCTION ENGINEERING RESEARCH LABORATORIES
P.O. Box 9005
Champaign, IL 61826-9005 United States
Phone: 217-373-7201 Fax: 217-373-7222
Website: www.cecer.army.mil
Founded: N/A
Membership: 101–1,000
Scope: International

UNITED STATES DEPARTMENT OF DEFENSE
ARMY CORPS OF ENGINEERS
DETROIT ENGINEER DISTRICT
P.O. Box 1027
Detroit, MI 48231-1027 United States
Phone: 313-226-6762 Fax: 313-226-6009
Founded: N/A
Membership: 101–1,000
Scope: State
Contact(s):
Richard Polo, Commander & District Engineer

UNITED STATES DEPARTMENT OF DEFENSE
ARMY CORPS OF ENGINEERS
ENGINEER RESEARCH AND DEVELOPMENT CENTER
ARMY ENGINEER WATERWAYS EXPERIMENT STATION
3909 Halls Ferry Road
Vicksburg, MS 39180-6199 United States
Phone: 601-634-2000 Fax: 601-634-2388
E-mail: james.r.houston@erdc.usace.army.mil
Website: www.erdc.usace.army.mil
Founded: 1929
Membership: 1,001–10,000
Scope: National
Description: All of the research and development laboratories of the Corps of Engineers.
Keyword(s): Climate Change, Ecosystems (precious), Oceans/Coasts/Beaches, Water Habitats & Quality, Wildlife & Species
Contact(s):
Dr. James Houston, Director
Edwin Theriot, Director, Environmental Laboratory; 601-634-2678; edwin.a.theriot@erdc.usace.army.mil

UNITED STATES DEPARTMENT OF DEFENSE
ARMY CORPS OF ENGINEERS
FORT WORTH ENGINEER DISTRICT
Fort Worth, TX 76102-0300 United States
Phone: 817-978-2300 Fax: 817-978-3311
Website: www.usace.army.mil
Founded: N/A
Membership: 101–1,000
Scope: Regional

UNITED STATES DEPARTMENT OF DEFENSE
ARMY CORPS OF ENGINEERS
GALVESTON ENGINEER DISTRICT
Galveston, TX 77553-1229 United States
Phone: 409-766-3001 Fax: 409-766-3951
Website: www.usace.army.mil
Founded: N/A
Membership: 101–1,000
Scope: Local
Contact(s):
Mary Ann Patlan, Secretary

UNITED STATES DEPARTMENT OF DEFENSE
ARMY CORPS OF ENGINEERS
GREAT LAKES AND OHIO ENGINEER DISTRICT
P.O. Box 1159
Cincinnati, OH 45201-1159 United States
Phone: 513-684-3002 Fax: 513-684-2085
E-mail: celrd-de@usace.army.mil
Website: www.lrd.usace.army.mil
Founded: N/A
Membership: 1–100
Scope: State

Contact(s):
Steven Hawkins, Division Commander of the Great Lakes & Ohio River

UNITED STATES DEPARTMENT OF DEFENSE
ARMY CORPS OF ENGINEERS
HONOLULU ENGINEER DISTRICT
Building 230
Fort Shafter, HI 96858-5440 United States
Phone: 808-438-1069 Fax: 808-438-8351
Website: www.poh.usace.army.mil

Founded: N/A
Membership: 101–1,000
Scope: State
Contact(s):
Alex Skinner, Executive Assistant

UNITED STATES DEPARTMENT OF DEFENSE
ARMY CORPS OF ENGINEERS
HUNTINGTON ENGINEER DISTRICT
502 8th Street
Huntington, WV 25701-2070 United States
Phone: 304-529-5395 Fax: 304-529-5591
Website: www.intra.lrh.usace.army.mil

Founded: N/A
Membership: 101–1,000
Scope: Regional
Contact(s):
John Ridenburg, Colonel

UNITED STATES DEPARTMENT OF DEFENSE
ARMY CORPS OF ENGINEERS
JACKSONVILLE ENGINEER DISTRICT
P.O. Box 4970
Jacksonville, FL 32232-0019 United States
Phone: 904-232-2241 Fax: 904-232-1213

Founded: N/A
Membership: 101–1,000
Scope: State
Contact(s):
James May, District Engineer

UNITED STATES DEPARTMENT OF DEFENSE
ARMY CORPS OF ENGINEERS
KANSAS CITY ENGINEER DISTRICT
601 E. 12th Street
Kansas City, MO 64106-2896 United States
Phone: 816-983-3201 Fax: 806-426-5575

Founded: N/A
Membership: 101–1,000
Scope: Regional

UNITED STATES DEPARTMENT OF DEFENSE
ARMY CORPS OF ENGINEERS
LITTLE ROCK ENGINEER DISTRICT
P.O. Box 867
Little Rock, AR 72203-0867 United States
Phone: 501-324-5531 Fax: 501-324-6968
Website: www.swl.usace.army.mil

Founded: N/A
Membership: 101–1,000
Scope: Regional
Contact(s):
Dale Leggett, Chief Natural Resources Branch

UNITED STATES DEPARTMENT OF DEFENSE
ARMY CORPS OF ENGINEERS
LOS ANGELES ENGINEER DISTRICT
P.O. Box 532711
Los Angeles, CA 90053-2325 United States
Phone: 213-452-3840 Fax: 213-452-4219
Website: www.spl.usace.army.mil

Founded: N/A
Scope: Local, State, Regional
Description: Environmental Resources Branch
Contact(s):
Paul Rose, Chief of Environmental Resources Branch; 213-452-3840; Fax: 213-452-4219; prose@spl.usace.army.mil

UNITED STATES DEPARTMENT OF DEFENSE
ARMY CORPS OF ENGINEERS
LOUISVILLE ENGINEER DISTRICT
P.O. Box 59
Louisville, KY 40201-0059 United States
Phone: 502-315-6768 Fax: 502-315-6771
E-mail: todd.j.hornback@lrl02usace.army.mil
Website: www.lrl.usace.army.mil/default.htm

Founded: N/A
Scope: Local, State, Regional, National
Description: The U.S. Army Corps of Engineers, Louisville District, has a civil mission in Indiana, Kentucky and Ohio. The military mission also includes Michigan and Illinois. The District's civil mission includes navigation, flood reduction, regulatory and emergency response. The military mission includes military construction, world-wide support for the Army Reserve Centers and environmental cleanup up at Formerly Used Defense Sites and military sites under the Installation Restoration Program.

UNITED STATES DEPARTMENT OF DEFENSE
ARMY CORPS OF ENGINEERS
MEMPHIS ENGINEER DISTRICT
167 N. Main Street, Rm. B202 Attn: Environmental Branch
Memphis, TN 38103-1894 United States
Phone: 901-544-3221 Fax: 901-544-3955

Founded: N/A
Scope: International

UNITED STATES DEPARTMENT OF DEFENSE
ARMY CORPS OF ENGINEERS
MISSISSIPPI VALLEY ENGINEER DIVISION
Vicksburg, MS 39181-0080 United States
Phone: 601-634-5750 Fax: 601-634-5666
E-mail: cemvd-de@mvd02.usace.army.mil
Website: www.mvd.usace.army.mil

Founded: N/A
Membership: 101–1,000
Scope: National
Contact(s):
Patti Beard, Executive Secretary

UNITED STATES DEPARTMENT OF DEFENSE
ARMY CORPS OF ENGINEERS
MOBILE, AL ENGINEER DISTRICT
P.O. Box 2288
Mobile, AL 36628-0001 United States
Phone: 334-690-2511 Fax: 334-690-2525
Website: www.sam.usace.army.mil

Founded: N/A
Scope: National
Contact(s):
Janet Shelby, Public Affairs Specialist

UNITED STATES DEPARTMENT OF DEFENSE

ARMY CORPS OF ENGINEERS
NASHVILLE ENGINEER DISTRICT
P.O. Box 1070
Nashville, TN 37202-1070 United States
Phone: 615-736-7161 Fax: 615-736-7065
E-mail: edward.m.evans@usace.army.mil
Website: www.orn.usace.army.mil

Founded: 1888
Membership: 101–1,000
Scope: Regional
Description: Covers 59,000 square miles and parts of seven states throughout the Cumberland and Tennessee River basins for navigation, hydropower, flood control, recreation, and environmental stewardship.
Publication(s): Navigation Maps & Charts
Keyword(s): Energy, Land Issues, Public Lands/Greenspace, Recreation/Ecotourism
Contact(s):
Steve Gay, District Engineer; P.O. Box 1070, Nashville, TN 37202-1070

UNITED STATES DEPARTMENT OF DEFENSE

ARMY CORPS OF ENGINEERS
NEW ENGLAND ENGINEER DISTRICT
696 Virginia Rd.
Concord, MA 01742-2751 United States
Phone: 978-318-8220 Fax: 978-318-8821

Founded: N/A
Membership: 1–100
Scope: International
Contact(s):
Joe Bocchino, Executive Assistant

UNITED STATES DEPARTMENT OF DEFENSE

ARMY CORPS OF ENGINEERS
NEW ORLEANS ENGINEER DISTRICT
New Orleans, LA 70160-0267 United States
Phone: 504-862-2204 Fax: 504-862-1259
E-mail: cemvn-de@mvn02.usace.army.mil
Website: www.mvn.usace.army.mil

Founded: N/A
Membership: 1,001–10,000
Scope: Regional

UNITED STATES DEPARTMENT OF DEFENSE

ARMY CORPS OF ENGINEERS
NEW YORK ENGINEER DISTRICT
Jacob K. Javits Federal Building, 26 Federal Plaza, Room 2109
New York, NY 10278-0090 United States
Phone: 212-264-0100 Fax: 212-264-5947
Website: www.nan.usace.army.mil

Founded: N/A
Membership: 101–1,000
Scope: Local, State, Regional, National
Description: Federal agency

UNITED STATES DEPARTMENT OF DEFENSE

ARMY CORPS OF ENGINEERS
NORFOLK ENGINEER DISTRICT
Waterfield Building, 803 Front Street
Norfolk, VA 23510-1096 United States
Phone: 757-441-7601 Fax: 757-441-7678
E-mail: neo@usace.army.mil
Website: www.nao.usace.army.mil

Founded: N/A
Membership: 101–1,000
Scope: Regional
Contact(s):
Bob Hume, Chief Regulatory Branch

UNITED STATES DEPARTMENT OF DEFENSE

ARMY CORPS OF ENGINEERS
NORTH ATLANTIC ENGINEER DIVISION
Fort Hamilton Military Community
General Lee Ave.
Building 302
Brooklyn, NY 11252-6000 United States
Phone: 718-765-7018 Fax: 718-765-7173
E-mail: david.j.lipsky@usace.army.mil
Website: www.nad.usace.army.mil

Founded: 1775
Membership: 1,001–10,000
Scope: Regional
Description: The North Atlantic Division of the U.S. Army Corps of Engineers is made up of about 4,000 team members in six districts and a division HQ. We plan, design and build for the Army and Air Force in the northeastern states and Europe. Our districts develop and manage water resources, in addition to protecting and restoring the environment. When asked, we work for other federal, state and local agencies and foreign nations.

UNITED STATES DEPARTMENT OF DEFENSE

ARMY CORPS OF ENGINEERS
NORTHWESTERN ENGINEER DIVISION
Regional Headquarters, P.O. Box 2870
Portland, OR 97208-2870 United States
Phone: 503-808-3700 Fax: 503-808-3706

Founded: N/A

UNITED STATES DEPARTMENT OF DEFENSE

ARMY CORPS OF ENGINEERS
OMAHA ENGINEER DISTRICT
106 S. 15th St.
Omaha, NE 68102-1618 United States
Phone: 402-221-3900 Fax: 402-221-3229
E-mail: karenl.stefeno@usace.army.mil

Founded: N/A
Membership: 1,001–10,000
Scope: National

UNITED STATES DEPARTMENT OF DEFENSE

ARMY CORPS OF ENGINEERS
PACIFIC OCEAN ENGINEER DISTRICT
Building 525
Fort Shafter, HI 96858-5440 United States
Phone: 808-438-1500 Fax: 808-438-8387

Founded: N/A
Membership: 1–100
Scope: Regional
Contact(s):
Frank Oliva, Key Contact

UNITED STATES DEPARTMENT OF DEFENSE

ARMY CORPS OF ENGINEERS
PHILADELPHIA ENGINEER DISTRICT
Wanamaker Building
100 Penn Square East
Philadelphia, PA 19107-3390 United States
Phone: 215-656-6515 Fax: 215-656-6820
E-mail: webmaster@nap02.usace.army.mil
Website: www.nap.usace.army.mil

Founded: 1775
Membership: 10,001–100,000
Scope: National, International
Description: Federal engineering and project management agency.

Publication(s): District Observer

Keyword(s): Ecosystems (precious), Oceans/Coasts/Beaches, Recreation/Ecotourism, Transportation, Water Habitats & Quality, Wildlife & Species

Contact(s):

Timothy Brown, District Commander
John Vickers, Deputy District Commander

UNITED STATES DEPARTMENT OF DEFENSE
ARMY CORPS OF ENGINEERS
PITTSBURGH ENGINEER DISTRICT
U.S. Army Corps of Engineers, William S. Moorhead Fed. Bldg., 1000 Liberty Avenue
Pittsburgh, PA 15222-4186 United States
Phone: 412-395-7103 Fax: 412-644-4093
Website: www.lrp.usace.army.mil/

Founded: N/A
Membership: 101–1,000
Scope: Regional
Description: Civil works, navigation, ecosystem restoration, infrastructure rehabilitation.
Keyword(s): Ecosystems (precious), Recreation/Ecotourism, Transportation, Water Habitats & Quality, Wildlife & Species

UNITED STATES DEPARTMENT OF DEFENSE
ARMY CORPS OF ENGINEERS
PORTLAND ENGINEER DISTRICT
P.O. Box 2946
Portland, OR 97208-2946 United States
Phone: 503-808-4500 Fax: 503-808-4505

Founded: N/A

UNITED STATES DEPARTMENT OF DEFENSE
ARMY CORPS OF ENGINEERS
ROCK ISLAND ENGINEER DISTRICT
Clock Tower Building
Rock Island, IL 61204-2004 United States
Phone: 309-794-5759 Fax: 309-794-5181
E-mail: mvr@usace.army.mil
Website: www.mvr.usace.army.mil

Founded: N/A
Scope: State, Regional
Contact(s):

Bob Romic, Key Contact

UNITED STATES DEPARTMENT OF DEFENSE
ARMY CORPS OF ENGINEERS
SACRAMENTO ENGINEER DISTRICT
1325 J Street
Sacramento, CA 95814-2922 United States
Phone: 916-557-7490 Fax: 916-557-7859

Founded: N/A

UNITED STATES DEPARTMENT OF DEFENSE
ARMY CORPS OF ENGINEERS
SAN FRANCISCO ENGINEER DISTRICT
333 Market St.
San Francisco, CA 94105-2195 United States
Phone: 415-977-8500 Fax: 415-977-8316

Founded: N/A
Contact(s):

Timothy O'Rourke, LTC

UNITED STATES DEPARTMENT OF DEFENSE
ARMY CORPS OF ENGINEERS
SEATTLE ENGINEER DISTRICT
Seattle, WA 98124-3755 United States
Phone: 206-764-3690 Fax: 206-764-6544
E-mail: paoteam@usace.army.mil
Website: www.nws.usace.army.mil/index.cfm

Founded: N/A
Membership: 101–1,000
Scope: Regional
Publication(s): Flagship

UNITED STATES DEPARTMENT OF DEFENSE
ARMY CORPS OF ENGINEERS
SOUTH ATLANTIC ENGINEER DIVISION
Room 9M15, 60 Forsyth Street, SW
Atlanta, GA 30303-8801 United States
Phone: 404-562-5003 Fax: 404-562-5002
Website: www.sad.usace.army.mil

Founded: N/A
Membership: 101–1,000
Scope: Regional

UNITED STATES DEPARTMENT OF DEFENSE
ARMY CORPS OF ENGINEERS
SOUTH PACIFIC ENGINEER DIVISION
333 Market Street, Room 1101
San Francisco, CA 94105-2195 United States
Phone: 415-977-8001 Fax: 415-977-8316

Founded: N/A

UNITED STATES DEPARTMENT OF DEFENSE
ARMY CORPS OF ENGINEERS
SOUTHWESTERN ENGINEER DISTRICT
1100 Commerce Street
Dallas, TX 75242-0216 United States
Phone: 214-767-2502 Fax: 214-767-6499

Founded: N/A
Scope: National

UNITED STATES DEPARTMENT OF DEFENSE
ARMY CORPS OF ENGINEERS
ST. LOUIS ENGINEER DISTRICT
1222 Spruce Street
St. Louis, MO 63103-2833 United States
Phone: 314-331-8010 Fax: 314-331-8770
Website: www.mvs.usce.army.mil

Founded: N/A
Membership: 101–1,000
Scope: National
Contact(s):

Linda Collins, Executive Secretary

UNITED STATES DEPARTMENT OF DEFENSE
ARMY CORPS OF ENGINEERS
ST. PAUL ENGINEER DISTRICT
Army Corps of Engineers Centre, 190 5th Street East
St. Paul, MN 55101-1638 United States
Phone: 651-290-5300 Fax: 651-290-5478
Website: www.mvp.usace.army.mil

Founded: N/A
Membership: 101–1,000
Scope: Local
Description: Federal government

UNITED STATES DEPARTMENT OF DEFENSE
ARMY CORPS OF ENGINEERS
TULSA ENGINEER DISTRICT
1645 South 101st East Avenue
Tulsa, OK 74128-4609 United States
Phone: 918-669-7201 Fax: 918-669-7207
E-mail: stephen.l.nolen@usace.army.mil
Website: www.swt.usafe.army.mil

Founded: N/A
Membership: 101–1,000
Scope: National

UNITED STATES DEPARTMENT OF DEFENSE
ARMY CORPS OF ENGINEERS
U.S.A.E.R.D.C. TOPOGRAPHIC ENGINEERING CENTER
7701 Telegraph Rd.
Alexandria, VA 22315-3864 United States
Phone: 703-428-6600 Fax: 703-428-8154
Website: www.tech.army.mil

Founded: N/A
Membership: 101–1,000
Scope: National

UNITED STATES DEPARTMENT OF DEFENSE
ARMY CORPS OF ENGINEERS
VICKSBURG ENGINEER DISTRICT
4155 Clay Street
Vicksburg, MS 39183 United States
Phone: 601-631-5010 Fax: 601-631-5296
Website: www.usace.army.mil

Founded: N/A
Membership: 101–1,000
Scope: National

UNITED STATES DEPARTMENT OF DEFENSE
ARMY CORPS OF ENGINEERS
WALLA WALLA ENGINEER DISTRICT
201 North 3rd Avenue
Walla Walla, WA 99362-1876 United States
Phone: 509-527-7700 Fax: 509-527-7804

Founded: N/A

UNITED STATES DEPARTMENT OF DEFENSE
ARMY CORPS OF ENGINEERS
WATER RESOURCES SUPPORT CENTER
7701 Telegraph Road, Casey Building
Alexandria, VA 22315-3868 United States
Phone: 703-428-8250 Fax: 703-428-8171
Website: www.iwr.usce.army.mil

Founded: N/A
Membership: 101–1,000
Scope: State

UNITED STATES DEPARTMENT OF DEFENSE
ARMY CORPS OF ENGINEERS
WILMINGTON ENGINEER DISTRICT
P.O. Box 1890
Wilmington, NC 28402-1890 United States
Phone: 910-251-4501 Fax: 910-251-4185
Website: www.saw.usace.army.mil

Founded: N/A
Membership: 101–1,000
Scope: State
Publication(s): Wilmington District Newsletter
Contact(s):
Penny Schmidt, Chief of Public Affairs

UNITED STATES DEPARTMENT OF DEFENSE
ARMY ENGINEER RESEARCH AND DEVELOPMENT CENTER
Champaign, IL 61826-9005 United States
Phone: 217-352-6511 Fax: 217-373-7222

Founded: 1969
Scope: National
Description: CERL conducts research on infrastructure and environmental problems facing the operations of military facilities. CERL also conducts research on innovative materials and engineering procedures; energy reduction measures and equipment; management systems; air and water pollution; environmental compliance; and natural resource management.
Publication(s): The Cutting Edge, Index to Publications, CERL Abstracts
Contact(s):
Dana Finney, Champaign Public Affairs

UNITED STATES DEPARTMENT OF DEFENSE
ARMY FORCES COMMAND
Forester, HQ USAFORSCOM
Attn: AFEN-EN (Mr. Cannon)
1777 Hardee Ave, SW
Fort McPherson, GA 30330-1062 United States
Phone: 404-464-5762 Fax: 404-464-7827
E-mail: cannons@forscom.army.mil

Founded: N/A
Membership: 1–100
Scope: National
Description: Administer evvironmental policy and budgets for selected Army installaitons across the country.
Keyword(s): Agriculture/Farming, Air Quality/Atmosphere, Ecosystems (precious), Forests/Forestry, Land Issues, Pollution (general), Public Lands/Greenspace, Recreation/Ecotourism, Reduce/Reuse/Recycle, Sprawl/Urban Planning, Water Habitats & Quality
Contact(s):
Albert Bivings, Wildlife Biologist; bivingsb@forscom.army.mil
Stuart Cannon, Forester

UNITED STATES DEPARTMENT OF DEFENSE
ARMY MATERIAL COMMAND
Alexandria, VA 22333-0001 United States

Founded: N/A
Contact(s):
Billye Haslett, Land Manager of Blue-Grass Army Depot; 606-625-6669
Ken Knouf, Natural Resources Manager of Jefferson Proving Ground, India; 812-273-7436
Randy Quinn, Natural Resources Manager of Letterkenny Army Depot, Ohio; 717-267-8438
Bob Speaker, Natural Resources Manager of Savanna Army Depot, Illinois; 815-273-8533
James Bailey, Wildlife Biologist of U.S. Army Aberdeen Proving Ground; 410-278-6748
William Burns, Forester of Anniston Army Depot, Alabama; 205-235-4217
Robert Burton, Archeologist of White Sands Missile Range, New Mexico; 505-678-8731
Richard Clewell, Natural Resources Specialist, Installations and Services Act; 309-782-8252
Tom Coleman, Agronomist of Red River Army Depot, Texas; 903-334-2385
Jesse Horton, Forester of Redstone Arsenal Support Activity, Alabama; 205-876-3122
Junior Kerns, Wildlife Biologist of Yuma Proving Ground, Arizona; 602-328-2148
John Martin, Chief of Conservation and Preservation of Dugway Proving Ground; 801-831-2986

Timothy McNamara, Environmental Protection Specialist of U.S. Army Aberdeen Proving Ground; Directorate of Safety, Health and Environment; 410-278-5622
Valerie Morrill, Wildlife Biologist of Yuma Proving Ground, Arizona; 602-328-2244
Patrick Morrow, Wildlife Biologist of White Sands Missile Range, New Mexico; 505-678-7095
Bennie Murray, Forester, Chief Lm of Red River Army Depot, Texas; 903-334-2379
James Pottie, Wildlife Biologist of U.S. Army Aberdeen Proving Ground; 410-278-6772
Terry Ruth, Forester of Red River Army Depot, Texas; 903-334-2379
Abdul Shiek, Entomologist of U.S. Army Aberdeen Proving Ground; 410-278-3303
Roger Stoflet, Forester of U.S. Army Aberdeen Proving Ground; 410-278-4915
Daisan Taylor, Wildlife Biologist of White Sands Missile Range, New Mexico; 505-678-6140
Tom Vorac, Forester, Installations and Services Activity, Illinois; 309-782-4062
Mason Walker, Project Engineer of Tooele Army Depot, Utah; 801-833-2891
Steve Wampler, Environmental Protection Specialist of U.S. Army Aberdeen Proving Ground; Directorate of Safety, Health and Environment; 410-671-4843
Bob Wardwell, Agronomist of U.S. Army Research Laboratory, Maryland; 301-394-1060

UNITED STATES DEPARTMENT OF DEFENSE

ARMY MILITARY ACADEMY
NATURAL RESOURCES BRANCH
DHPW
U.S. Military Academy
West Point, NY 10996-1592 United States
Phone: 845-938-2314 Fax: 845-938-2324

Founded: N/A
Membership: 1–100
Scope: Local
Description: Natural resources management on the 16,000-acre West Point Military Reservation
Keyword(s): Ecosystems (precious), Forests/Forestry, Water Habitats & Quality, Wildlife & Species
Contact(s):
Catherine Coleman, ITAM Program Manager; 1 Bn, 1 Inf, U.S. Military Academy, West Point, NY 10996; 845-938-5453; Catherine.Coleman@usma.army.mil
James Beemer, Fish and Wildlife Biologist; 845-938-3857; Fax: 845-938-2324; yj6936@exmail.usma.army.mil
Joe Deschenes, Branch Chief and Forester; 845-938-2314; Fax: 845-938-2324; Joseph.Deschenes@usma.army.mil
Robert Jones, Agronomist; 845-938-6789

UNITED STATES DEPARTMENT OF DEFENSE

ARMY TRAINING AND DOCTRINE COMMAND
ATBO-SE
Fort Monroe, VA 23651 United States

Founded: N/A
Contact(s):
Ron Levy, Director of Environment of Fort McClellan; 205-848-3539
Charles Ford, Chief Natural Resources Manager of Fort Benning; 706-544-7319
Don Hack, Natural Resources Manager of Navajo Depot Activity; 602-774-7161, ext. 274
Mark Imlay, Natural Resources Manager of Army National Guard Bureau; 703-756-5794
Ronald Moore, Natural Resources Manager of Camp Atterbury; 812-526-1250
Bob Anderson, Natural Resources Specialist; 804-727-2077
Dave Apsley, Forester of Fort Knox; 502-624-8147
Edna Barber, Environmental Officer of U.S. Army Military District of Washington; 202-696-3815
Joyce Beelman, Environmental Protection Specialist of Fort Greeley; 907-451-2141
Scott Belfit, Natural Resources Team of U.S. Army Environmental Center; 410-612-6831
Kenneth Boyd, Wildlife Biologist of Fort Gordon; 706-791-2403
Allen Braswell, Forester of Fort Gordon; 706-791-2327
Patrick Ching, Agronomist of Schofield Barracks; 808-655-6383
Bob Coleman, Chief Environment Branch of Fort Chaffee; 501-484-2516
Marie Cottrell, Archeologist; 804-727-2389
Doug Dasher, Environmental Protection Specialist of Fort Greeley; 907-451-2172
Bob Decker, Natural Resources Team of U.S. Army Environmental Center; 410-612-6831
Glen Degarmo, Archeologist of Fort Bliss; 915-568-5140
Joe Deschenes, Chief of Natural Resources of U.S. Military Academy; 914-938-2314
Chris Dunn, Entomologist of Fort Benning; 706-545-3224
Mark Dutton, Chief of Natural Resources; 803-751-4103
Al Freeland, Chief Environmental Management Division of Fort Knox; 502-624-3629
Brad Fristoe, Environmental Protection Specialist of Fort Greeley; 907-451-2159
Bill Garland, Forester of Fort McClellan; 205-848-3758
Bill Gates, Wildlife Biologist; 803-751-4793
Hershel Gaw, Forester of Military Traffic Management Command, Military Oc; 919-457-8292
Tom Glueck, Wildlife Biologist of Fort Leonard Wood; 314-596-0871
William Gossweiler, Wildlife Biologist of Fort Richardson; 907-384-3017
Jack Greenlee, Forester of Fort Benning; 706-544-7319
Stuart Hayashi, Entomologist of Headquarters of U.S. Army Pacific; 808-438-2180
William Herb, Natural Resources Team of U.S. Army Environmental Center; 410-671-1234
Lawrence Hirai, Environmental Protection Specialist; 808-438-8997
Mike Hudson, Forester of Fort Belvoir; 703-806-4007
Wayne Johndrown, Natural Resources Specialist of Fort Chaffee; 501-484-2231
Robert Jones, Agronomist of U.S. Military Academy, Natural Resources Branch; 914-938-3467
Dorothy Keough, Acting Chief of Environmental and Natural Resources Division; 703-806-4007
Robert King, Wildlife Biologist of Fort Benning; 706-544-7319
Pamela Klinger, Natural Resources Team of U.S. Army Environmental Center; 410-612-6832
James Loewen, Biologist of Fort Lee; 804-734-5080
Paul Lukowski, Archeologist of Fort Bliss; 915-568-6999
James McCracken, Biologist of Da Headquarters; 803-751-4622
Kevin McCurdy, Biological Tech./Game Warden of Fort Sill; 405-351-4324
Robert Mcguire, Chief of Environmental Resources Management; 703-756-5794
Roger Meyers, Wildlife Biologist of Fort Dix; 609-562-2040
John Miller, Forester of Information Systems Command; 602-533-7083
James Murphy, Agronomist of U.S. Army Military District of Washington; 202-696-3815
Marvin Myers, Agronomist of Fort Leonard Wood; 314-596-0871
Matt Nowak, Forester of Fort Leavenworth; 913-684-2749
Luther Owen, Natural Resources Specialist of Fort McClellan; 205-848-5663
Delarie Parmer, Agronomist of Fort Rucker; 205-255-9363

William Pittman, Agronomist of Health Services Command; 512-221-4411
Bill Quirk, Environmental Specialist of Fort Richardson; 907-384-3021
Clark Reames, Wildlife Biologist of Fort Chaffee; 501-484-2231
Tony Rizzio, Forester of Fort Eustis; 804-878-4152
Mark Salley, Environmental Protection Specialist of Schofield Barracks; 808-656-2878
John Schenck, Entomologist of Fort Eustis; 804-878-2585
Eric Seaborn, Natural Resources Team of U.S. Army Environmental Center; 410-612-6833
Steve Sekscienski, Natural Resources Team of U.S. Army Environmental Center; 410-612-6832
Thomas Shafer, Chief of Environment of Fort Benjamin Harrison; 317-549-5386
Donald Sheroan, Wildlife Biologist Tech. of Fort Knox; 502-624-7373
Bob Shuffield, Forester of Fort Rucker; 205-255-9368
Roger Smith, Agronomist of Fort Dix; 609-562-2040
Sheridan Stone, Wildlife Biologist of Information Systems Command; 602-538-7340
Gene Stout, Chief of Natural/Environmental Resources of Fort Sill; 405-351-4324
Jerry Sturdy, Chief Natural Resources Section of Fort Chaffee; 501-484-2231
Joe Tarnopol, Entomologist of U.S. Army Military District of Washington; 202-475-1003
Donald Teig, Entomologist; 804-727-2366
Steve Thurman, Forester of Fort Leonard Wood; 314-596-0871
Robert Turnbow, Entomologist of Fort Rucker; 205-255-3710
Kevin Von Finger, Ecologist of Fort Bliss; 915-568-7031
Glen Wampler, Fish and Wildlife Administrator of Fort Sill; 405-442-8111
Steve Willard, Chief of Environmental and Natural Resources of Fort Gordon; 706-791-2403
Jerry Williamson, Natural Resources Team of U.S. Army Environmental Center; 410-612-6833

UNITED STATES DEPARTMENT OF DEFENSE

ARMY TRAINING AND DOCTRINE COMMAND
Department of the Army, HQ TRADOC, ATBO-SE, Environmental Division
Fort Monroe, VA 23651 United States

Founded: N/A

Description: Manages conservation programs for 2 million acres at 16 Army installations nationwide. It also provides for compliance with federal, state, and local environmental regulations.

Publication(s): Endangered Species Law Sourcebook, Army Leader's Guide to NEPA, Historic Preservation Sourcebook

Contact(s):
Robert Anderson, Natural Resources Specialist; 757-727-2077
Jack Damron, NEPA Consultant; 757-727-4135
Frances Doyle
John Esson, NEPA Consultant; 757-727-3335
Shawn Holsinger, Conservation and Analysis Branch; 757-727-3045
Jim White, NEPA Consultant; 757-727-5896

UNITED STATES DEPARTMENT OF DEFENSE

ASSISTANT CHIEF OF STAFF FOR INSTALLATION MANAGEMENT, OFFICE OF THE DIRECTOR OF ENVIRONMENTAL PROGRAMS, AND CONSERVATION TEAM
Attn: DAIM-ED-N, 600 Army Pentagon
Washington, DC 20310-0600 United States

Founded: N/A

Description: Natural and cultural resources professionals are responsible for the management of approximately 12 million acres of land on Army military installations. Management objectives include: Compliance with environmental laws, conservation and protection of resources, support to the military mission uses of the land, and contributions to programs which support the public needs. Resources managed include: Land, forest, wildlife, soils, vegetation, and historical and archaeological sites.

Contact(s):
Bob Decker, Natural Resources Specialist; 703-693-0673
Joe Dudley, Conservation Specialist; 703-693-9423
Vic Diersing, Conservation Team Leader; 703-693-0677
Lee Foster, Cultural Resources Specialist; 703-693-0675
Bill Woodson, Natural Resource Specialist; 703-693-0680

UNITED STATES DEPARTMENT OF DEFENSE

MARINE CORPS
Headquarters, U.S. Marine Corps, 2 Navy Annex
Washington, DC 20380-4775 United States
Phone: 703-695-8332

Founded: N/A

Description: The Marine Corps, as America's premier crisis response force, trains as it fights. Accordingly, Marine Corps cultural and natural resources managers provide and maintain a variety of landscapes to support military training, while protecting and preserving the cultural and natural resources the American people cherish for their intrinsic value.

Contact(s):
Jim Omans, Head of Natural Resources Section; 703-695-8232

UNITED STATES DEPARTMENT OF DEFENSE

MARINE CORPS INSTALLATIONS, UNITED STATES

Founded: N/A

Contact(s):
Lupe Armas, MCB Camp Pendleton, CA: Head of Environmental Management Department; 619-725-3561
Mark Brannan, MCAS Cherry Point, NC: Head of Environmental Department
Bruce Frizzell, MCCDC Quantico, VA: Head of Environmental Management Department; 703-640-4030
Alice Howard, MCAS Beaufort, SC: Head of Environmental Management Department; 803-522-7370
Roy Madden, MCAGCC Twentynine Palms, CA: Head of Natural Resources Branch; 619-830-5719
Johnsie Nabors, MCRD Parris Island, SC: Head of Environmental Management Department; 803-525-2779
Jerry Palmer, MCLB Albany, GA: Head of Environmental Management Department; 912-439-6261
Ron Pearce, MCAS Yuma, AZ: Head of Natural Resources Branch; 802-341-3318
Jack Stormo, MCLB Barstow, CA: Head of Environmental Management Department; 619-577-6111
Bob Warren, MCB Camp Lejeune, NC: Head of Environmental Management Department; 910-451-5003

UNITED STATES DEPARTMENT OF DEFENSE

NAVY
1000 Navy Pentagon, Department of the Navy
Washington, DC 20350-1000 United States
Website: www.navy.mil

Founded: N/A

Description: The mission of the Navy is to maintain, train, and equip combat-ready Naval forces capable of winning wars, deterring aggression and maintaining freedom of the seas.

Contact(s):
Richard Danzig, Secretary
Jerry Hultin, Undersecretary

UNITED STATES DEPARTMENT OF DEFENSE

OFFICE OF THE CIVIL ENGINEER
AF/ILE, 1260 Air Force Pentagon
Washington, DC 20330-1260 United States
Phone: 703-604-0632

Founded: N/A

UNITED STATES DEPARTMENT OF EDUCATION

400 Maryland Ave., SW
Washington, DC 20202-0498 United States
Phone: 202-401-3000
E-mail: customerservice@inet.ed.gov
Website: www.ed.gov

Founded: N/A

Contact(s):

Roderick Paige, Secretary; 202-401-3000

UNITED STATES DEPARTMENT OF ENERGY

Forrestal Bldg., 1000 Independence Ave., SW
Washington, DC 20585 United States
Phone: 202-586-5000 Fax: 202-586-5049
Website: www.energy.gov

Founded: N/A

Description: Provides the framework for a comprehensive and balanced national energy strategy through the coordination and administration of the energy functions of the federal government. The department is responsible for research, development, and demonstration of energy technology; the marketing of federal power; energy conservation programs; the nuclear weapons program; energy regulatory programs; and a central energy data collection and analysis program.

Publication(s): Assessment of Costs and Benefits of Flexible and Alternative Fuel Use in the United States Transportation Sector, Report to the Congress of the United States: Limiting New Greenhouse Gas Emissions in the United States

UNITED STATES DEPARTMENT OF ENERGY

CARBON DIOXIDE INFORMATION ANALYSIS CENTER
OAK RIDGE NATIONAL LABORATORY
Oak Ridge National Laboratory, P.O. Box 2008 MS-6335
Oak Ridge, TN 37831-6335 United States
Phone: 865-574-0390 Fax: 865-574-2232
E-mail: cdiac@ornl.gov
Website: cdiac.ornl.gov/

Founded: 1982

Membership: 1–100

Scope: International

Description: The Carbon Dioxide Information Analysis Center (CDIAC) provides data and information support for the United States Department of Energy's global change research program and makes these data and information products available to a multidisciplinary community of researchers, policymakers, and educators at no cost.

Publication(s): CDIAC Communications, Trends Online, Annual Report

Keyword(s): Air Quality/Atmosphere, Climate Change

Contact(s):

Robert Cushman, Director; 865-574-4791; Fax: 865-574-2232; cushmanrm@ornl.gov
Sonja Jones, Information Services; 865-574-3645; Fax: 865-574-2232; cdiac@ornl.gov

UNITED STATES DEPARTMENT OF ENERGY

FEDERAL ENERGY REGULATORY COMMISSION
888 First Street, NE
Washington, DC 20426 United States
Phone: 202-208-1088
Website: www.ferc.gov

Founded: 1977

Membership: 1,001–10,000

Scope: National

Description: The Federal Energy Regulatory Commission regulates the interstate aspects of the electric power and natural gas industries and establishes rates for transporting oil by pipeline. The Commission issues and enforces licenses for construction and operation of nonfederal hydroelectric power projects. The FERC also advises federal agencies on the merits of proposed federal multiple-purpose water development projects.

Contact(s):

Shelton Cannon, Director of Electric Power Regulation; 202-208-1200
Thomas Herlihy, Director and Chief Financial Officer of Finance, Accounting; 202-208-0300
Kevin Madden, Director of Pipeline Regulation; 202-208-0700
Richard O'Neill, Director of Economic Policy; 202-208-0100
Carol Sampson, Director of Hydropower Licensing; 202-219-2700
Rebecca Schaffer, Director of Office of External Affairs; 202-208-0004
Virginia Strasser, Director of Office of Administrative Litigation; 202-219-2600
Vicky Bailey, Commissioner; 202-208-0388
David Boergers, Secretary; 202-208-0400
Linda Breathitt, Commissioner; 202-208-0377
Curtis Herbert, Commisioner; 202-208-0601
Thomas Herlihy, Chief Information Officer, Acting; 202-208-1055
James Hoecker, Chair; 202-208-0000
William Massey, Commissioner; 202-208-0366
Douglas Smith, General Counsel; 202-208-1000
Curtis Wagner, Chief Administrative Law Judge; 202-219-2500

UNITED STATES DEPARTMENT OF HEALTH AND HUMAN SERVICES

200 Independence Ave., SW
Washington, DC 20201 United States
Phone: 202-690-7000 Fax: 202-690-7203
Website: www.hhs.gov

Founded: N/A

Scope: National

Description: The Department of Health and Human Services is the United States government's principal agency for protecting the health of all Americans and providing essential human services, especially for those who are least able to help themselves.

Contact(s):

William Corr, Chief of Staff; 202-690-7431
Tommy Thompson, Secretary; 202-690-7000

UNITED STATES DEPARTMENT OF HEALTH AND HUMAN SERVICES

FOOD AND DRUG ADMINISTRATION
5600 Fishers Ln.
Rockville, MD 20857 United States
Phone: 410-433-1544
Website: www.fda.gov

Founded: N/A

Description: Protects the health of American consumers by enforcing federal laws which require that foods must be safe, pure, and wholesome; human and veterinary drugs, biologies, and therapeutic devices must be safe and effective; cosmetics and radiation-emitting products must be harmless; and that all these products must be honestly and informatively labeled and packaged.

Contact(s):

Betsy Adams, Director of Press Relations for Staff of Office of Public Affairs; 410-443-4177
D. Burlington, Director; 410-443-4690
Mary Danello, Director; 410-443-1565

Rosamelia De la Rocha, Director of Office of Equal Employment and Civil Rights; 410-443-5541
Marlene Haffner, Director of Office of Orphan Products Development
Joseph Levitt, Director of Office of Executive Operations; 410-443-5004
Gerald Meyer, Director; 410-443-2894
Henry Miller, Director of Office of Biotechnology; 410-443-7573
Bernard Schwetz, Director; 501-543-7517
Fred Shank, Director; 202-205-4850
Richard Teske, Director; 410-594-1740
Randolph Wykoff, Director of Aids Coordination Staff
Kathryn Zoon, Director; 410-496-3556
Ronald Chesemore, Associate Commissioner for Regulatory Affairs; 410-433-1594
Paul Coppinger, Associate Commissioner for Planning and Evaluation; 410-433-4230
R. Grant, Associate Commissioner for Consumer Affairs; 410-443-5006
Sharon Holston, Associate Commissioner for Management and Operations; 410-443-3370
Jack Martin, Special Assistant to the Commissioner for Program Policy; 410-443-6776
Stuart Nightingale, Associate Commissioner for Health Affairs; 410-433-6143
James O'Hara, Associate Commissioner for Public Affairs; 410-443-1130
Amanda Pedersen, Ombudsman; 410-443-1306
Mary Porter, Chief Counsel for Office of General Counsel; 410-443-4370
Carol Scheman, Deputy Commissioner for External Affairs; 410-443-2400
Michael Taylor, Deputy Commissioner for Policy; 410-443-2854
Dianne Thompson, Associate Commissioner for Legislative Affairs; 410-443-3793
Mary Veverka, Deputy Commissioner for Management and Systems; 410-443-1263

UNITED STATES DEPARTMENT OF HOUSING AND URBAN DEVELOPMENT

HUD Bldg., 451 7th St., SW
Washington, DC 20410 United States
Phone: 202-708-1600
Website: www.hud.gov

Founded: N/A

Scope: National

Contact(s):

Philip Musser, Chief of Staff; 202-708-2236
Vicker Meadows, General Deputy Assistant Secretary for Administration; 202-708-0940
Kenneth Donohue Sr., Inspector General; 202-708-0430
Michael Liu, Assistant Secretary for Public & Indian Housing; 202-708-0950
Mel Martinez, Secretary; 202-708-0417
John Weicher, Assistant Secretary; 202-708-3600

UNITED STATES DEPARTMENT OF JUSTICE

ENVIRONMENT AND NATURAL RESOURCES
10th St. and Constitution Ave., NW
Washington, DC 20530 United States
Phone: 202-514-2701 Fax: 202-514-0557
Website: www.usdoj.gov/enrd/

Founded: 1909

Membership: 101–1,000

Scope: International

Description: The Environment and Natural Resources Division of the Department of Justice handles litigation involving America's pollution control, land use, wildlife, resource management and Indian laws. Nearly one-half of the Division's lawyers bring cases against those who violate the nation's civil and criminal pollution control laws. Others defend legal challenges to government programs and activities and represent the U.S. in matters concerning stewardship of natural resources and public lands.

Contact(s):

Thomas Sansonetti, Assistant Attorney General; 202-514-2701
Kelly Johnson, Principal Deputy Assistant Attorney General; 202-514-2701
Craig Alexander, Indian Resources Section Chief; 202-514-9080
Robert Bruffy, Executive Officer; 202-616-3100
Virginia Butler, Land Acquisition Section Chief; 202-305-0316
Jeffrey Clark, Deputy Assistant Attorney General; 202-514-2701
John Cruden, Deputy Assistant Attorney General; 202-514-2718
Bruce Gilber, Environmental Enforcement Section Chief
Letitia Grishaw, Environmental Defense Section Chief; 202-514-2219
Jack Haugrud, General Litigation Section Chief
James Kilbourne, Appellate Section Chief; 202-514-2748
Pauline Milius, Policy of Legislation and Special Litigation Section Chief; 202-514-2586
Eileen Sobeck, Deputy Assistant Attorney General; 202-514-0943
Jean Williams, Wildlife and Marine Resources Section Chief; 202-305-0228

UNITED STATES DEPARTMENT OF LABOR

200 Constitution Ave., NW
Washington, DC 20210 United States
Phone: 202-219-5000
Website: www.dol.gov

Founded: N/A

Contact(s):

Alexis Herman, Secretary; 202-693-6000
J. McAteer, Mine Safety and Health Administrator; 703-235-1385
Edward Montgomery, Deputy Secretary, Acting; 202-693-6002

UNITED STATES DEPARTMENT OF LABOR

JOB CORPS
Department of Labor, Employment and Training Administration, Office of Job Corps
Frances Perkins Bldg.
200 Constitution Ave., NW
Washington, DC 20210 United States
Phone: 202-693-3000 Fax: 202-693-2767
Website: jobcorps.doleta.gov

Founded: 1964

Scope: National

Description: Authorized by the Workforce Investment Act, the program includes conservation centers known as Civilian Conservation Centers, located primarily in rural areas and operated for the Department of Labor by the Departments of Agriculture and Interior. Job Corps is a residential,vocational and educational training program for economically disadvantaged youth ages 16-24.

UNITED STATES DEPARTMENT OF LABOR

MINE SAFETY AND HEALTH ADMINISTRATION
Department of Labor
Mine Safety and Health Administration
4015 Wilson Boulevard
Arlington, VA 22203 United States
Phone: 703-235-2600 Fax: 703-235-4369
E-mail: asmsha@msha.gov
Website: www.msha.gov

Founded: N/A

Scope: National

Description: Objectives are to administer the Federal Mine Safety and Health Act, thereby promoting safety and health in the mining industry, preventing disasters, and protecting the health and safety of the nation's miners.

Contact(s):

Gordon Burke, Director of Administration and Management; 703-235-1383; Fax: 703-235-1634; Burke-Gordon@msha.gov
Jeffrey Duncan, Director of Educational Policy and Development; 703-235-1515; Fax: 703-235-1634; Duncan-Jeffrey@msha.gov
Katharine Snyder, Director, Office of Information and Public Affairs; 703-235-1452; Fax: 703-235-4323; Snyder-Katharine@msha.gov
Carol Jones, Chief, Metal and Nonmetal Safety and Health; 703-235-8307; Fax: 703-235-9173; Jones-Carol@msha.gov
Dave Lauriski, Assistant Secretary, Mine Safety and Health Administration; 703-235-2600; Fax: 703-235-4369; ASMSHA@msha.gov

UNITED STATES DEPARTMENT OF STATE

Harry S. Truman Bldg., 2201 C St., NW
Washington, DC 20520 United States
Phone: 202-647-4000 Fax: 202-736-7720
E-mail: secretary@state.gov
Website: www.state.gov

Founded: N/A
Membership: 1,001–10,000
Scope: State

Contact(s):

Colin Powell, U.S. Secretary of State; 202-647-6575; secretary@state.gov

UNITED STATES DEPARTMENT OF STATE

BUREAU OF OCEANS AND INTERNATIONAL ENVIRONMENTAL AND SCIENTIFIC AFFAIRS
Department of State, 2201 C St., NW
Washington, DC 20520 United States
Phone: 202-647-3004 Fax: 202-647-0217
Website: www.state.gov/g/oes/

Founded: N/A

Description: OES has the principal responsibility for formulating and implementing U.S. policies for oceans, environmental, scientific, and technological aspects of U.S. relations with other governmental and multilateral institutions. The Bureau's activities cover a broad range of foreign policy issues relating to environment, pollution, tropical forests, biological diversity, wildlife, oceans policy, fisheries, global climate change, atmospheric ozone-depletion, space, and advanced technologies.

Contact(s):

David Balton, Office of Marine Conservation, Director; 202-647-2335
Ralph Braibanti, Office of Space and Advanced Technology, Director; 202-647-2433
Nancy Foster, Office of Emerging Infectious Diseases, Director; 202-647-2435
Leslie Gerson, Office of Science and Environmental Initiative, Director; 202-647-3625
Stephanie Kinney, Executive Assistant/Executive Director of Administration; 202-647-3622
Mary McLead, Office of Ecology and Terrestrial Conservation, Director; 202-647-2418
Michael Mtelits, Office of Environment Policy, Director; 202-647-9266
Daniel Reifsnyder, Office of Global Change, Director; 202-647-4069
R. Scully, Office of Oceans Affairs, Director; 202-647-3262
Roger Soles, U.S. Man and The Biosphere Program, Director; 703-235-2948
Kenneth Brill, Acting Assistant Secretary; 202-647-1554
Mark Hambley, Special Negotiator
Melinda Kimble, Principal Department Assisting Secretary
Rafe Pomerance, Deputy Assistant Secretary of Environment and Development; 202-647-2232
Mary West, Deputy Assistant Secretary of Oceans, Fisheries and Space; 202-647-2396

UNITED STATES DEPARTMENT OF STATE

UNITED STATES MAN AND THE BIOSPHERE PROGRAM (U.S. MAB)
U.S. MABUSDA-Forest Service, Yates Federal Bldg. (1-NW) P.O. Box 96090
Washington, DC 20090 United States
Phone: 202-776-8318 Fax: 202-776-8367
E-mail: usmab@state.gov
Website: www.mabnet.org

Founded: N/A

Description: The mission of the United States Man and the Biosphere Program (U.S. MAB) is to explore, demonstrate, promote, and encourage harmonious relationships between people and their environments, building on the MAB network of Biosphere Reserves and interdisciplinary research. The long-term goal of the U.S. MAB Program is to contribute to achieving a sustainable society early in the 21st century.

Publication(s): Conferences, proceedings of symposia, research reports from U.S. MAB, U.S. MAB Bulletin

Contact(s):

Roger Soles, Executive Director of U.S. MAB; 202-776-8318
David Hales, Chairman of U.S. MAB National Committee

UNITED STATES DEPARTMENT OF THE INTERIOR

U.S. Department of the Interior, 1849 C St., NW
Washington, DC 20240 United States
Phone: 202-208-6843 Fax: 202-219-0910
E-mail: waso-public-affairs@nps.gov
Website: www.nps.gov

Founded: N/A

Scope: National

Description: Administers 1,378 parks, monuments, and other administrative classifications of national significance for their recreational, historical, and natural values. Manages landmarks programs for natural and historic properties; coordinates Wild and Scenic Rivers System and National Trail System; administers study and grants programs.

Contact(s):

Rob Arnberger, Alaska Regional Director
Jerry Belson, Southeast Regional Director; 100 Alabama St., SW, Atlanta Federal Center, Atlanta, GA 30303; 404-562-3100
Terry Carlstrom, National Capital Regional Director; 1100 Ohio Dr., SW, Washington, DC 20242; 202-619-7256
Fran Mainella, Director of The National Park Service
John Reynolds, Pacific West Regional Director; 600 Harrison St., Suite 600, San Francisco, CA 94107; 415-427-1300
Marie Rust, Northeast Regional Director; U.S. Customs House, 5th Fl., 200 Chestnut St., Philadelphia, PA 19106; 215-597-7013
William Schenk, Midwest Regional Director; 1709 Jackson St., Omaha, NE 68102; 402-221-3471
Karen Wade, Intermountain Regional Director
David Barna, Chief of Office of Public Affairs; 202-208-6843
Terrell Emmons, Associate Director of Professional Services
Denis Galvin, Deputy Director; 202-208-3818
Sue Masica, Associate Director of Budget and Administration; 202-208-6953
Dick Ring, Associate Director of Park Operations
Bill Shaddox, Associate Director of Professional Services; 202-208-3264
C. Sheaffer, Comptroller; 202-208-4566
Michael Soukup, Associate Director of Natural Resources; 202-208-3884

Kate Stevenson, Associate Director of Cultural Resources; 202-208-7625

UNITED STATES DEPARTMENT OF THE INTERIOR
Interior Bldg., 1849 C St., NW
Washington, DC 20240 United States
Phone: 202-208-3100
Website: www.doi.gov

Founded: N/A

Description: The mission of the Department of the Interior is to protect and provide access to our Nation's natural and cultural heritage and honor our trust responsibilities to tribes.

UNITED STATES DEPARTMENT OF THE INTERIOR
BUREAU OF INDIAN AFFAIRS
1849 C St., NW
Washington, DC 20240 United States
Phone: 202-208-5116 Fax: 202-208-6334
E-mail: jamesmcdivitt@bia.gov
Website: www.doi.gov

Founded: 1824

Membership: 1–100

Scope: National

Description: An agency charged with carrying out the major portion of the trust responsibility of the United States to Indian tribes. This trust includes the protection and enhancement of Indian lands and the conservation and development of natural resources, including fish, wildlife, and outdoor recreation resources.

Contact(s):

Terry Virden, Director of Office of Trust Responsibilities; 202-208-5831
Daphne Berwald, Administrative Assistant; 202-208-7163
Sharon Blackwell, Deputy Commissioner; 202-208-5116
Gary Rankel, Chief of Branch of Fish, Wildlife and Recreation; 202-208-4088

UNITED STATES DEPARTMENT OF THE INTERIOR
BUREAU OF LAND MANAGEMENT
ALBUQUERQUE FIELD OFFICE
435 Montano Rd., NE
Albuquerque, NM 87107 United States
Phone: 505-761-8700 Fax: 505-761-8911

Founded: N/A

Scope: Regional

Contact(s):

Andy Iskra, Manager; 505-761-8789; Fax: 505-761-8911; aiskra@blm.gov

UNITED STATES DEPARTMENT OF THE INTERIOR
BUREAU OF LAND MANAGEMENT
ALTURAS FIELD OFFICE
708 West 12th Street
Alturas, CA 96101 United States
Phone: 530-233-4666 Fax: 530-233-5696

Founded: N/A

Scope: Regional

UNITED STATES DEPARTMENT OF THE INTERIOR
BUREAU OF LAND MANAGEMENT
AMARILLO FIELD OFFICE
801 S. Fillmore St., Ste. 500
Amarillo, TX 79101-3545 United States
Phone: 806-324-2617 Fax: 806-324-2633

Founded: N/A

Scope: Regional

Contact(s):

Paul Tanner, n/a; 806-324-2641; Paul_Tanner@Blm.gov

UNITED STATES DEPARTMENT OF THE INTERIOR
BUREAU OF LAND MANAGEMENT
ANASAZI HERITAGE CENTER
27501 Highway 184
Dolores, CO 81323 United States
Phone: 970-882-4811 Fax: 970-882-7035

Founded: N/A

Scope: Regional

UNITED STATES DEPARTMENT OF THE INTERIOR
BUREAU OF LAND MANAGEMENT
ANCHORAGE DISTRICT
6881 Abbott Loop Road
Anchorage, AK 99507-2599 United States
Phone: 907-267-1246 Fax: 907-267-1267

Founded: N/A

Scope: Regional

UNITED STATES DEPARTMENT OF THE INTERIOR
BUREAU OF LAND MANAGEMENT
ARCATA FIELD OFFICE
1695 Heindon Road
Arcata, CA 95521 United States
Phone: 707-825-2300 Fax: 707-825-2301

Founded: N/A

Scope: Regional

UNITED STATES DEPARTMENT OF THE INTERIOR
BUREAU OF LAND MANAGEMENT
ARIZONA STATE OFFICE
222 North Central Avenue
Phoenix, AZ 85004-2203 United States
Phone: 602-417-9200 Fax: 602-417-9556

Founded: N/A

Scope: Regional

Contact(s):

Lucy Ontiveros, Manager; 602-417-9500; Fax: 602-417-9556; lucy_ontiveros@blm.gov

UNITED STATES DEPARTMENT OF THE INTERIOR
BUREAU OF LAND MANAGEMENT
ARIZONA STRIP FIELD OFFICE
345 East Riverside Drive
St. George, UT 84790-9000 United States
Phone: 801-688-3301 Fax: 435-688-3258

Founded: N/A

Scope: Regional

UNITED STATES DEPARTMENT OF THE INTERIOR
BUREAU OF LAND MANAGEMENT
BAKERSFIELD DISTRICT
3801 Pegasus Drive
Bakersfield, CA 93308-6837 United States
Phone: 661-391-6000 Fax: 661-391-6040

Founded: N/A

Scope: Regional

UNITED STATES DEPARTMENT OF THE INTERIOR
BUREAU OF LAND MANAGEMENT
BARSTOW FIELD OFFICE
2601 Barstow Road
Barstow, CA 92311 United States
Phone: 760-252-6000 Fax: 760-252-6099
Founded: N/A
Scope: Regional

UNITED STATES DEPARTMENT OF THE INTERIOR
BUREAU OF LAND MANAGEMENT
BATTLE MOUNTAIN FIELD OFFICE
50 Bastian Rd.
Battle Mountain, NV 89820 United States
Phone: 775-635-4000 Fax: 775-635-4034
Founded: N/A
Scope: Regional

UNITED STATES DEPARTMENT OF THE INTERIOR
BUREAU OF LAND MANAGEMENT
BILLINGS FIELD OFFICE
5001 Southgate Dr.
Billings, MT 59101 United States
Phone: 406-896-5013 Fax: 406-896-5281
Founded: N/A
Scope: Regional

UNITED STATES DEPARTMENT OF THE INTERIOR
BUREAU OF LAND MANAGEMENT
BISHOP FIELD OFFICE
785 North Main Street, Suite E
Bishop, CA 93514 United States
Phone: 760-872-4881 Fax: 760-872-2894
Website: www.ca.blm.gov/bishop/
Founded: N/A
Scope: Regional

UNITED STATES DEPARTMENT OF THE INTERIOR
BUREAU OF LAND MANAGEMENT
BRUNEAU FIELD OFFICE
3948 Development Ave.
Boise, ID 83705-5389 United States
Phone: 208-384-3300 Fax: 208-384-3493
Founded: N/A
Scope: Regional

UNITED STATES DEPARTMENT OF THE INTERIOR
BUREAU OF LAND MANAGEMENT
BUFFALO FIELD OFFICE
1425 Fort St.
Buffalo, WY 82834-2436 United States
Phone: 307-684-1100 Fax: 307-684-1122
Founded: N/A
Scope: Regional

UNITED STATES DEPARTMENT OF THE INTERIOR
BUREAU OF LAND MANAGEMENT
BURLEY FIELD OFFICE
15 E. 200 South
Burley, ID 83318 United States
Phone: 208-677-6641 Fax: 208-677-6699
Founded: N/A
Scope: Regional

UNITED STATES DEPARTMENT OF THE INTERIOR
BUREAU OF LAND MANAGEMENT
BURNS DISTRICT
HC 74-12533, Hwy. 20 West
Hines, OR 97738 United States
Phone: 541-574-4400
Founded: N/A
Scope: Regional

UNITED STATES DEPARTMENT OF THE INTERIOR
BUREAU OF LAND MANAGEMENT
BUTTE DISTRICT
106 N. Parkmont
Butte, MT 59701 United States
Phone: 406-494-5059 Fax: 406-533-7660
Founded: N/A
Scope: Regional

UNITED STATES DEPARTMENT OF THE INTERIOR
BUREAU OF LAND MANAGEMENT
CARLSBAD FIELD OFFICE
620 E. Greene St.
Carlsbad, NM 88220-6292 United States
Phone: 505-887-6544 Fax: 505-885-9264
Founded: N/A
Scope: Regional

UNITED STATES DEPARTMENT OF THE INTERIOR
BUREAU OF LAND MANAGEMENT
CARSON CITY FIELD OFFICE
5665 Morgan Mill Rd.
Carson City, NV 89701 United States
Phone: 775-885-6000 Fax: 775-885-6147
Founded: N/A
Scope: Regional

UNITED STATES DEPARTMENT OF THE INTERIOR
BUREAU OF LAND MANAGEMENT
CASCADE FIELD OFFICE
3948 Development Ave.
Boise, ID 83705-5389 United States
Phone: 208-384-3300 Fax: 208-384-3493
Founded: N/A
Scope: Regional

UNITED STATES DEPARTMENT OF THE INTERIOR
BUREAU OF LAND MANAGEMENT
CASPER DISTRICT
1701 East E St.
Casper, WY 82601 United States
Phone: 307-261-7600 Fax: 307-234-1525
Founded: N/A
Scope: Regional

UNITED STATES DEPARTMENT OF THE INTERIOR
BUREAU OF LAND MANAGEMENT
CEDAR CITY DISTRICT FIELD OFFICE
176 East D.L. Sargent Dr.
Cedar City, UT 84720 United States
Phone: 435-586-2401 Fax: 435-865-3058
Website: www.ut.blm.gov/cedarcity_fo

Founded: N/A

Scope: Regional

UNITED STATES DEPARTMENT OF THE INTERIOR
BUREAU OF LAND MANAGEMENT
CHALLIS FIELD OFFICE
50 Highway 93 South
Salmon, ID 83467 United States
Phone: 208-756-5400 Fax: 208-756-5436

Founded: N/A

Scope: Regional

UNITED STATES DEPARTMENT OF THE INTERIOR
BUREAU OF LAND MANAGEMENT
CODY FIELD OFFICE
1002 Blackburn
P.O. Box 518
Cody, WY 82414-0518 United States
Phone: 307-578-5900 Fax: 307-578-5939
Website: www.wy.blm.gov

Founded: N/A

Scope: Regional

UNITED STATES DEPARTMENT OF THE INTERIOR
BUREAU OF LAND MANAGEMENT
COEUR D'ALENE FIELD OFFICE
1808 North Third Street
Coeur d'Alene, ID 83814-3407 United States
Phone: 208-769-5030 Fax: 208-769-5050
Website: www.id.blm.gov/offices/coeurd'alene/

Founded: N/A

Scope: Regional

UNITED STATES DEPARTMENT OF THE INTERIOR
BUREAU OF LAND MANAGEMENT
COLORADO STATE OFFICE
2850 Youngfield Street
Lakewood, CO 80215 United States
Phone: 303-239-3600 Fax: 303-239-3933

Founded: N/A

Scope: Regional

UNITED STATES DEPARTMENT OF THE INTERIOR
BUREAU OF LAND MANAGEMENT
COOS BAY FIELD OFFICE
1300 Airport Lane Rd.
North Bend, OR 97459 United States
Phone: 541-756-0100 Fax: 541-751-4303

Founded: N/A

Scope: Regional

UNITED STATES DEPARTMENT OF THE INTERIOR
BUREAU OF LAND MANAGEMENT
COTTONWOOD FIELD OFFICE
Route 3
Box 181
Cottonwood, ID 83522-9498 United States
Phone: 208-962-3245 Fax: 208-962-3275

Founded: N/A

Scope: Regional

UNITED STATES DEPARTMENT OF THE INTERIOR
BUREAU OF LAND MANAGEMENT
DILLON FIELD OFFICE
1005 Selway Dr.
Dillon, MT 59725-9431 United States
Phone: 406-683-2337 Fax: 406-683-8066

Founded: N/A

Scope: Regional

UNITED STATES DEPARTMENT OF THE INTERIOR
BUREAU OF LAND MANAGEMENT
EAGLE LAKE FIELD OFFICE
2950 Riverside Drive
Susanville, CA 96130 United States
Phone: 530-257-0456 Fax: 530-257-4831

Founded: N/A

Scope: Regional

UNITED STATES DEPARTMENT OF THE INTERIOR
BUREAU OF LAND MANAGEMENT
EASTERN STATES OFFICE
7450 Boston Blvd.
Springfield, VA 22153 United States
Phone: 703-440-1713 Fax: 703-440-1722
E-mail: terry_lewis@es.blm.gov
Website: www.es.blm.gov/index.html

Founded: N/A

Scope: Regional

Description: The U.S. Department of Interior, Bureau of Land Management (BLM), Eastern States is responsible for the stewardship of the public lands and resources under the jurisdiction of the BLM in the 31 states east of and bordering the Mississippi River.

UNITED STATES DEPARTMENT OF THE INTERIOR
BUREAU OF LAND MANAGEMENT
EL CENTRO FIELD OFFICE
1661 South Fourth Street
El Centro, CA 92243 United States
Phone: 760-337-4400 Fax: 760-337-4490

Founded: N/A

Scope: Regional

UNITED STATES DEPARTMENT OF THE INTERIOR
BUREAU OF LAND MANAGEMENT
ELKO FIELD OFFICE
3900 E. Idaho St.
Elko, NV 89801 United States
Phone: 775-753-0200 Fax: 775-753-0255

Founded: N/A

Scope: Regional

UNITED STATES DEPARTMENT OF THE INTERIOR
BUREAU OF LAND MANAGEMENT
ELY FIELD OFFICE
702 N. Industrial Way
HC 33, Box 33500
Ely, NV 89301 United States
Phone: 775-289-1800 Fax: 775-289-1810
Website: www.nv.blm.gov/ely
Founded: N/A
Scope: Regional

UNITED STATES DEPARTMENT OF THE INTERIOR
BUREAU OF LAND MANAGEMENT
EUGENE DISTRICT OFFICE
WILDLIFE WORKING GROUP
2890 Chad Drive
P.O. Box 10226
Eugene, OR 97440-2226 United States
Phone: 541-683-6114 Fax: 541-683-6981
E-mail: eric_greenquist@or.blm.gov
Founded: N/A
Scope: Regional
Description: Comprised of professional staff biologists, the Wildlife Working Group guides the implementation of the District wildlife habitat and endangered species programs. In addition to wildlife management activities, the Working Group advises the District supervisory and professional staffs on wildlife resources, laws, policies and methods, coordinates program work, handles special issues, and provides information and educational materials to schools, private organizations and members of the public.
Keyword(s): Forests/Forestry, Land Issues, Recreation/Ecotourism, Water Habitats & Quality, Wildlife & Species

UNITED STATES DEPARTMENT OF THE INTERIOR
BUREAU OF LAND MANAGEMENT
EUGENE FIELD OFFICE
2890 Chad Dr.
Eugene, OR 97408 United States
Phone: 541-683-6600 Fax: 541-683-6981
Founded: N/A
Scope: Regional

UNITED STATES DEPARTMENT OF THE INTERIOR
BUREAU OF LAND MANAGEMENT
FARMINGTON FIELD OFFICE
1235 La Plata Hwy., Suite A
Farmington, NM 87401 United States
Phone: 505-599-8911 Fax: 505-599-6377
E-mail: lotteni@blm.gov
Website: www.nm.blm.gov/www/ffo/ffo_home.html
Founded: N/A
Scope: Regional
Description: Renewable Energy Resource Development on Public Land

UNITED STATES DEPARTMENT OF THE INTERIOR
BUREAU OF LAND MANAGEMENT
FILLMORE FIELD OFFICE
35 E. 500 North
Fillmore, UT 84631 United States
Phone: 435-743-6811
Founded: N/A
Scope: Regional
Contact(s):
Rex Rowley, Manager; 435-743-3100; rex_rowley@blm.gov

UNITED STATES DEPARTMENT OF THE INTERIOR
BUREAU OF LAND MANAGEMENT
FOLSOM FIELD OFFICE
63 Natoma Street
Folsom, CA 95630 United States
Phone: 916-985-4474 Fax: 916-985-3259
Founded: N/A
Scope: Regional

UNITED STATES DEPARTMENT OF THE INTERIOR
BUREAU OF LAND MANAGEMENT
GLENNALLEN DISTRICT
P.O. Box 147
Glennallen, AK 99588 United States
Phone: 907-822-3217 Fax: 907-822-3120
Founded: N/A
Scope: Regional

UNITED STATES DEPARTMENT OF THE INTERIOR
BUREAU OF LAND MANAGEMENT
GLENWOOD SPRINGS FIELD OFFICE
50629 Hwys. 6 & 24; P.O. Box 1009
Glenwood Springs, CO 81602 United States
Phone: 970-947-2800 Fax: 970-947-2829
Founded: N/A
Scope: Regional
Contact(s):
Tom Fresques, Wildlife Biologist; 970-947-2814; thomas_fresques@blm.gov

UNITED STATES DEPARTMENT OF THE INTERIOR
BUREAU OF LAND MANAGEMENT
GRAND JUNCTION FIELD OFFICE/
NORTHWEST CENTER
2815 H Rd.
Grand Junction, CO 81506 United States
Phone: 970-244-3000 Fax: 970-244-3083
Website: www.co.blm.gov/gjra/gjra.html
Founded: N/A
Scope: Regional

UNITED STATES DEPARTMENT OF THE INTERIOR
BUREAU OF LAND MANAGEMENT
GUNNISON FIELD OFFICE
216 N. Colorado
Gunnison, CO 81230 United States
Phone: 970-641-0471 Fax: 970-641-1928
Founded: N/A
Scope: Regional

UNITED STATES DEPARTMENT OF THE INTERIOR
BUREAU OF LAND MANAGEMENT
HOLLISTER FIELD OFFICE
20 Hamilton Court
Hollister, CA 95023 United States
Phone: 831-630-5000 Fax: 831-630-5050
Founded: N/A
Scope: Regional

UNITED STATES DEPARTMENT OF THE INTERIOR
BUREAU OF LAND MANAGEMENT
IDAHO FALLS FIELD OFFICE
1405 Hollypark Dr.
Idaho Falls, ID 83401 United States
Phone: 208-524-7500 Fax: 208-524-7505
Founded: N/A
Scope: Regional

UNITED STATES DEPARTMENT OF THE INTERIOR
BUREAU OF LAND MANAGEMENT
JACKSON FIELD OFFICE
411 Briarwood Dr., Suite 404
Jackson, MS 39206 United States
Phone: 601-977-5400
Founded: N/A
Scope: Regional

UNITED STATES DEPARTMENT OF THE INTERIOR
BUREAU OF LAND MANAGEMENT
JARBRIDGE FIELD OFFICE
2620 Kimberly Road
Twin Falls, ID 83301 United States
Phone: 208-736-2350 Fax: 208-736-2375
Founded: N/A
Scope: Regional

UNITED STATES DEPARTMENT OF THE INTERIOR
BUREAU OF LAND MANAGEMENT
KANAB
318 N. First East
Kanab, UT 84741 United States
Phone: 435-644-2672
Website: www.ut.blm.gov/kanab_fo/information.htm
Founded: N/A
Scope: Regional

UNITED STATES DEPARTMENT OF THE INTERIOR
BUREAU OF LAND MANAGEMENT
KEMMERER FIELD OFFICE
312 Highway 189 N.
Kemmerer, WY 83101-9710 United States
Phone: 307-828-4500 Fax: 307-828-4539
Founded: N/A
Scope: Regional

UNITED STATES DEPARTMENT OF THE INTERIOR
BUREAU OF LAND MANAGEMENT
KINGMAN FIELD OFFICE
2475 Beverly Avenue
Kingman, AZ 86401-3629 United States
Phone: 928-692-4400 Fax: 928-692-4414
Founded: N/A
Scope: Regional

UNITED STATES DEPARTMENT OF THE INTERIOR
BUREAU OF LAND MANAGEMENT
KREMMLING FIELD OFFICE
2103 East Park Avenue
P.O. Box 68
Kremmling, CO 80459 United States
Phone: 970-724-3437 Fax: 970-724-9590
Founded: N/A
Scope: Regional

UNITED STATES DEPARTMENT OF THE INTERIOR
BUREAU OF LAND MANAGEMENT
LA JARA FIELD OFFICE
15571 County Rd. T5
La Jara, CO 81140 United States
Phone: 719-274-8971 Fax: 719-274-6301
Founded: N/A
Scope: Regional

UNITED STATES DEPARTMENT OF THE INTERIOR
BUREAU OF LAND MANAGEMENT
LAKE HAVASU FIELD OFFICE
2610 Sweetwater Avenue
Lake Havasu City, AZ 86406-9071 United States
Phone: 928-505-1200 Fax: 928-505-1208
Founded: N/A
Scope: Regional

UNITED STATES DEPARTMENT OF THE INTERIOR
BUREAU OF LAND MANAGEMENT
LAKEVIEW FIELD OFFICES
HC10 Box 337, 1301 S. G St
Lakeview, OR 97630 United States
Phone: 541-947-2177 Fax: 541-947-6399
Website: www.or.blm.gov/orwadir.htm
Founded: N/A
Scope: Regional

UNITED STATES DEPARTMENT OF THE INTERIOR
BUREAU OF LAND MANAGEMENT
LANDER FIELD OFFICE
1335 Main; P.O. Box 589
Lander, WY 82520-0589 United States
Phone: 307-332-8400 Fax: 307-332-8447
Founded: N/A
Scope: Regional

UNITED STATES DEPARTMENT OF THE INTERIOR
BUREAU OF LAND MANAGEMENT
LAS CRUCES DISTRICT
1800 Marquess
Las Cruces, NM 87005-3371 United States
Phone: 505-525-4300 Fax: 505-525-4412
Founded: N/A
Scope: Regional

UNITED STATES DEPARTMENT OF THE INTERIOR
BUREAU OF LAND MANAGEMENT
LAS VEGAS FIELD OFFICE
4701 No. Torrey Pines Drive
Las Vegas, NV 89130 United States
Phone: 702-515-5000 Fax: 702-515-5060
Website: www.nv.blm.gov
Founded: N/A
Scope: Regional
Description: Federal land management agency

UNITED STATES DEPARTMENT OF THE INTERIOR
BUREAU OF LAND MANAGEMENT
LEWISTOWN FIELD OFFICE
P.O. Box 1160
Lewistown, MT 59457-1160 United States
Phone: 406-538-7461 Fax: 406-538-1904
Founded: N/A
Scope: Regional

UNITED STATES DEPARTMENT OF THE INTERIOR
BUREAU OF LAND MANAGEMENT
LITTLE SNAKE FIELD OFFICE
455 Emerson St.
Craig, CO 81625 United States
Phone: 970-826-5000 Fax: 970-826-5002
Founded: N/A
Scope: Regional

UNITED STATES DEPARTMENT OF THE INTERIOR
BUREAU OF LAND MANAGEMENT
MALAD FIELD OFFICE
138 South Main
Malad City, ID 83252-1346 United States
Phone: 208-766-4766 Fax: 208-766-4087
Founded: N/A
Scope: Regional

UNITED STATES DEPARTMENT OF THE INTERIOR
BUREAU OF LAND MANAGEMENT
MALTA FIELD OFFICE
501 S. 2nd St. E.
Malta, MT 59538 United States
Phone: 406-654-1240 Fax: 406-654-5150
Founded: N/A
Scope: Regional

UNITED STATES DEPARTMENT OF THE INTERIOR
BUREAU OF LAND MANAGEMENT
MEDFORD DISTRICT OFFICE
3040 Biddle Rd.
Medford, OR 97504 United States
Phone: 541-618-2200 Fax: 541-618-2400
Founded: N/A
Scope: Regional
Contact(s):
Ron Wenker, District Manager

UNITED STATES DEPARTMENT OF THE INTERIOR
BUREAU OF LAND MANAGEMENT
MILES CITY FIELD OFFICE
111 Garryowen Rd.
Miles City, MT 59301 United States
Phone: 406-233-2800 Fax: 406-233-2921
Founded: N/A
Scope: Regional
Contact(s):
Dave McIlnay, Field Manager; 406-233-2800

UNITED STATES DEPARTMENT OF THE INTERIOR
BUREAU OF LAND MANAGEMENT
MILWAUKEE FIELD OFFICE
310 W. Wisconsin Ave., Suite 450
Milwaukee, WI 53203 United States
Phone: 414-297-4400
Founded: N/A
Scope: Regional

UNITED STATES DEPARTMENT OF THE INTERIOR
BUREAU OF LAND MANAGEMENT
MISSOULA FIELD OFFICE
3255 Ft. Missoula Rd.
Missoula, MT 59804-7293 United States
Phone: 406-329-3914 Fax: 406-329-3721
Founded: N/A
Scope: Regional

UNITED STATES DEPARTMENT OF THE INTERIOR
BUREAU OF LAND MANAGEMENT
MOAB DISTRICT FIELD OFFICE
82 E. Dogwood
Moab, UT 84532 United States
Phone: 435-259-2100
Founded: N/A
Scope: Regional
Contact(s):
Maggie Wyatt, Manager; 435-259-2100;
maggie_wyatt@blm.gov

UNITED STATES DEPARTMENT OF THE INTERIOR
BUREAU OF LAND MANAGEMENT
MONTICELLO FIELD OFFICE
435 N. Main, P.O. Box 7
Monticello, UT 84535 United States
Phone: 435-587-1502
Founded: N/A
Scope: Regional

UNITED STATES DEPARTMENT OF THE INTERIOR
BUREAU OF LAND MANAGEMENT
NATIONAL APPLIED RESOURCE CENTER
BLM
1859 C Street
Washington, DC 80225 United States
Phone: 202-452-7761 Fax: 202-452-7702
Website: www.blm.gov
Founded: N/A
Membership: N/A
Scope: National

Contact(s):
Robert Abbey, NV State Director; 1340 Financial Blvd., Reno, NV 89502-7147; 702-861-6590
Lee Barkow, Director of National Science & Tech Center; P.O. Box 25047, Building 50, Dever Federal Center, Denver, CO 80225-0047; lee_barkow@blm.gov
Henri Bisson, AK State Director; 222 W. 7th Ave., #13, Anchorage, AK 99513; 907-271-5080
Elaine Marquis-Borng, OR State Director; 1515 SW 5th Ave., Portland, OR 97208; 503-952-6024
Mike Nedd, Eastern States Director; 7450 Boston Blvd, Springfield, VA 22153; 703-440-1700; Fax: 703-440-1599
Michael Pool, CA State Director; 28 Cottage Way, Rm. W-1834, Sacramento, CA 95825; 916-978-4600; Fax: 916-978-4699
Position Vacant, WY State Director; 5353 Yellowstone Rd., Cheyenne, WY 82003
Position Vacant, NM State Director; 1474 Rodeo Rd., Santa Fe, NM 87505
Position Vacant, MT State Director; 5001 Southgate Dr, Billings, MT 59107
Position Vacant, ID State Director; 1387 S. Vinnell Way, Boise, ID 83709-1657
Position Vacant, CO State Director; 2850 Youngfield St., Lakewood, CO 80215
Sally Wisely, UT State Director; 324 S. State St., Ste. 301, Salt Lake City, UT 84145; 801-539-4010
Elaine Zielinski, AZ State Director; 222 North Central Avenue, Phoenix, AZ 85004; 602-417-9500

UNITED STATES DEPARTMENT OF THE INTERIOR

BUREAU OF LAND MANAGEMENT
NATIONAL INTERAGENCY FIRE CENTER
NATIONAL OFFICE OF FIRE AND AVIATION
3833 S. Development Ave.
Boise, ID 83705 United States
Phone: 208-387-5512 Fax: 208-387-5797
Website: www.nifc.gov

Founded: N/A
Membership: 101–1,000
Scope: National
Publication(s): Burning Issues-newsletter bi-quarterly
Contact(s):
Larry Hamilton, Director; 208-387-5446

UNITED STATES DEPARTMENT OF THE INTERIOR

BUREAU OF LAND MANAGEMENT
NATIONAL TRAINING CENTER
9828 North 31st Avenue
Phoenix, AZ 85051-2517 United States
Phone: 602-906-5500 Fax: 602-906-5555

Founded: N/A
Scope: Regional

UNITED STATES DEPARTMENT OF THE INTERIOR

BUREAU OF LAND MANAGEMENT
NEEDLES FIELD OFFICE
101 West Spikes Road
Needles, CA 92363 United States
Phone: 760-326-7000 Fax: 760-326-7099

Founded: N/A
Scope: Regional

UNITED STATES DEPARTMENT OF THE INTERIOR

BUREAU OF LAND MANAGEMENT
NEWCASTLE FIELD OFFICE
1101 Washington Blvd.
Newcastle, WY 82701-2972 United States
Phone: 307-746-6600 Fax: 307-746-6639
Website: www.wy.blm.gov/index.html

Founded: N/A
Scope: Regional

UNITED STATES DEPARTMENT OF THE INTERIOR

BUREAU OF LAND MANAGEMENT
NORTH DAKOTA FIELD OFFICE
2933 Third Ave., W.
West Dickinson, ND 58601-2619 United States
Phone: 701-225-9148 Fax: 701-227-8510

Founded: N/A
Scope: Regional

UNITED STATES DEPARTMENT OF THE INTERIOR

BUREAU OF LAND MANAGEMENT
NORTHERN DISTRICT
1150 University Avenue
Fairbanks, AK 99709 United States
Phone: 907-474-2200

Founded: N/A
Scope: Regional

UNITED STATES DEPARTMENT OF THE INTERIOR

BUREAU OF LAND MANAGEMENT
OWYHEE FIELD OFFICE
3948 Development Ave.
Boise, ID 83705-5389 United States
Phone: 208-384-3300 Fax: 208-384-3493

Founded: N/A
Scope: Regional

UNITED STATES DEPARTMENT OF THE INTERIOR

BUREAU OF LAND MANAGEMENT
PALM SPRINGS / SOUTH COAST FIELD OFFICE
690 West Garnet Avenue
P.O. Box 1260
North Palm Springs, CA 92258-1260 United States
Phone: 760-251-4800 Fax: 760-251-4899

Founded: N/A
Scope: Regional

UNITED STATES DEPARTMENT OF THE INTERIOR

BUREAU OF LAND MANAGEMENT
PHOENIX FIELD OFFICE
21605 North 7th Street
Phoenix, AZ 85027 United States
Phone: 623-580-5500 Fax: 623-580-5580

Founded: N/A
Scope: Regional

UNITED STATES DEPARTMENT OF THE INTERIOR
BUREAU OF LAND MANAGEMENT
PINEDALE FIELD OFFICE
432 E. Mill Street; P.O. Box 768
Pinedale, WY 82941-0768 United States
Phone: 307-367-5300 Fax: 307-367-5329

Founded: N/A

Scope: Regional

UNITED STATES DEPARTMENT OF THE INTERIOR
BUREAU OF LAND MANAGEMENT
POCATELLO FIELD OFFICE
1111 N. 8th Ave.
Pocatello, ID 83201 United States
Phone: 208-236-6860 Fax: 208-234-0246

Founded: N/A

Scope: Regional

UNITED STATES DEPARTMENT OF THE INTERIOR
BUREAU OF LAND MANAGEMENT
PRICE FIELD OFFICE
125 S. 600 West
Price, UT 84501 United States
Phone: 435-636-3601

Founded: N/A

Scope: Regional

Contact(s):
Thomas Rasmussen, Manager; 435-636-3600; tom_rasmussen@blm.gov

UNITED STATES DEPARTMENT OF THE INTERIOR
BUREAU OF LAND MANAGEMENT
PRINEVILLE DISTRICT FIELD OFFICE
P.O. Box 550
Prineville, OR 97754 United States
Phone: 541-416-6700 Fax: 541-416-6798

Founded: N/A

Scope: Regional

UNITED STATES DEPARTMENT OF THE INTERIOR
BUREAU OF LAND MANAGEMENT
PUBLIC AFFAIRS
1849 C St., NW, LS-406
Washington, DC 20240 United States
Phone: 202-208-3801 Fax: 202-208-5242
Website: www.blm.gov

Founded: 1946

Membership: 101–1,000

Scope: National

Description: Administers the public lands which are located primarily in the Western states and which amount to about 48 percent over 272 million acres of all federally owned lands. These lands and resources are managed under multiple-use principles, including outdoor recreation, fish and wildlife production, livestock grazing, timber, industrial development, watershed protection, and onshore mineral production.

Contact(s):
Nina Hatfield, Director, Acting
Henri Bisson, Assistant Director of Renewable Resources & Planning; 202-208-4896
Carson Culp, Assistant Director of Minerals, Realty, & Resource Protection; 202-208-4201
Bob Doyle, Assistant Director of Business and Fiscal Services; 202-208-4864
Larry Finfer, Assistant Director of Communications; 202-208-6913
Gayle Gordon, Assistant Director of Information Resources Management
Warren Johnson, Assistant Director of Human Resources; 202-501-6724
Carol Macdonald, Environmental, NEPA Issues; 202-452-5111
W. Tipton, Information Resource

UNITED STATES DEPARTMENT OF THE INTERIOR
BUREAU OF LAND MANAGEMENT
RAWLINS FIELD OFFICE
1300 North Third St.; P.O. Box 2407
Rawlins, WY 82301-2407 United States
Phone: 307-328-4200 Fax: 307-328-4224
E-mail: rawlins_wymail@blm.gov

Founded: 1946

Scope: Local, State, Regional

Description: One of ten BLM field offices in Wyoming

Keyword(s): Agriculture/Farming, Air Quality/Atmosphere, Energy, Forests/Forestry, Land Issues, Public Lands/Greenspace, Recreation/Ecotourism, Water Habitats & Quality, Wildlife & Species

UNITED STATES DEPARTMENT OF THE INTERIOR
BUREAU OF LAND MANAGEMENT
REDDING FIELD OFFICE
355 Hemsted Drive
Redding, CA 96002 United States
Phone: 530-224-2100 Fax: 530-224-2172

Founded: N/A

Scope: Regional

UNITED STATES DEPARTMENT OF THE INTERIOR
BUREAU OF LAND MANAGEMENT
RICHFIELD DISTRICT FIELD OFFICE
150 E. 900, N
Richfield, UT 84701 United States
Phone: 435-896-1523
Website: www.ut.blm.gov/richfield/index.html

Founded: N/A

Scope: Regional

UNITED STATES DEPARTMENT OF THE INTERIOR
BUREAU OF LAND MANAGEMENT
RIDGECREST FIELD OFFICE
300 South Richmond Road
Ridgecrest, CA 93555 United States
Phone: 760-384-5400 Fax: 760-384-5499

Founded: N/A

Scope: Regional

UNITED STATES DEPARTMENT OF THE INTERIOR
BUREAU OF LAND MANAGEMENT
ROCK SPRINGS FIELD OFFICE
280 Highway 191 N.
Rock Springs, WY 82901-3448 United States
Phone: 307-352-0256 Fax: 307-352-0329

Founded: N/A

Scope: Regional

UNITED STATES DEPARTMENT OF THE INTERIOR
BUREAU OF LAND MANAGEMENT
ROSEBURG DISTRICT
777 NW Garden Valley Blvd.
Roseburg, OR 97470 United States
Phone: 541-440-4930 Fax: 541-440-4948

Founded: N/A

Scope: Regional

UNITED STATES DEPARTMENT OF THE INTERIOR
BUREAU OF LAND MANAGEMENT
ROSWELL DISTRICT
2909 West Second Street
Roswell, NM 88201-2019 United States
Phone: 505-627-0272 Fax: 505-627-0276

Founded: N/A

Scope: Regional

Description: Field office location serving seven-county area in southeastern NM

Contact(s):
Tim Kreager, Manager; 505-627-0272; Fax: 505-627-0276; tim_kreager@blm.gov

UNITED STATES DEPARTMENT OF THE INTERIOR
BUREAU OF LAND MANAGEMENT
ROYAL GORGE FIELD OFFICE/
FRONT RANGE CENTER
3170 E. Main St.
Canon City, CO 81212 United States
Phone: 719-269-8500 Fax: 719-269-8599

Founded: N/A
Membership: N/A
Scope: Local

Description: The Bureau of Land Management sustains the health, diversity and productivity of the public lands for the use and enjoyment of present and future generations.

UNITED STATES DEPARTMENT OF THE INTERIOR
BUREAU OF LAND MANAGEMENT
SAFFORD FIELD OFFICE
711 South 14th Avenue
Safford, AZ 85546-3321 United States
Phone: 928-348-4400 Fax: 928-348-4450

Founded: N/A

Scope: Regional

UNITED STATES DEPARTMENT OF THE INTERIOR
BUREAU OF LAND MANAGEMENT
SAGUACHE FIELD OFFICE
46525 Hwy. 114, P.O. Box 67
Saguache, CO 81149 United States
Phone: 719-655-2547 Fax: 719-655-2502

Founded: N/A

Scope: Regional

UNITED STATES DEPARTMENT OF THE INTERIOR
BUREAU OF LAND MANAGEMENT
SALEM DISTRICT FIELD OFFICE
1717 Fabry Rd., SE
Salem, OR 97306 United States
Phone: 503-375-5646 Fax: 503-375-5622
Website: www.or.blm.gov/salem

Founded: N/A

Scope: Regional

UNITED STATES DEPARTMENT OF THE INTERIOR
BUREAU OF LAND MANAGEMENT
SALMON FIELD OFFICE
Hwy. 93, South / Route 2, Box 610
Salmon, ID 83467 United States
Phone: 208-756-5400 Fax: 208-756-5436

Founded: N/A

Scope: Regional

UNITED STATES DEPARTMENT OF THE INTERIOR
BUREAU OF LAND MANAGEMENT
SALT LAKE DISTRICT
2370 S. 2300, W
Salt Lake City, UT 84119 United States
Phone: 801-977-4300 Fax: 801-997-4397

Founded: N/A

Scope: Regional

UNITED STATES DEPARTMENT OF THE INTERIOR
BUREAU OF LAND MANAGEMENT
SAN JUAN FIELD OFFICE
15 Burnett Ct.
Durango, CO 81301 United States
Phone: 970-247-4874 Fax: 970-385-1375

Founded: N/A

Scope: Regional

UNITED STATES DEPARTMENT OF THE INTERIOR
BUREAU OF LAND MANAGEMENT
SAN PEDRO PROJECT OFFICE
1763 Paseo San Luis
Sierra Vista, AZ 85635-2240 United States
Phone: 520-458-3559 Fax: 520-439-6422

Founded: N/A

Scope: Regional

UNITED STATES DEPARTMENT OF THE INTERIOR
BUREAU OF LAND MANAGEMENT
SHOSHONE FIELD OFFICE
400 W. F St., P.O. Box 2-B
Shoshone, ID 83352 United States
Phone: 208-732-7200 Fax: 208-732-7317

Founded: N/A

Scope: Regional

UNITED STATES DEPARTMENT OF THE INTERIOR
BUREAU OF LAND MANAGEMENT
SOCORRO FIELD OFFICE
198 Neel Ave., NW
Socorro, NM 87801-4648 United States
Phone: 505-835-0412 Fax: 505-835-0223

Founded: N/A

Scope: Regional

Contact(s):
David Heft, Manager; 505-838-1267; Fax: 505-835-0223; dheft@nm.blm.gov

UNITED STATES DEPARTMENT OF THE INTERIOR
BUREAU OF LAND MANAGEMENT
SOUTH DAKOTA FIELD OFFICE
310 Roundup St.
Belle Fourche, SD 57717-1698 United States
Phone: 605-892-7000 Fax: 605-892-4742
Founded: N/A
Scope: Regional

UNITED STATES DEPARTMENT OF THE INTERIOR
BUREAU OF LAND MANAGEMENT
SPOKANE DISTRICT
1103 N. Fancher
Spokane, WA 99212 United States
Phone: 509-536-1200 Fax: 509-536-1275
Website: www.or.blm.gov/spokane
Founded: N/A
Scope: Regional

UNITED STATES DEPARTMENT OF THE INTERIOR
BUREAU OF LAND MANAGEMENT
ST. GEORGE FIELD OFFICE
345 East Riverside Dr.
St. George, UT 84720 United States
Phone: 435-688-3200
Founded: N/A
Scope: Regional
Contact(s):
James Crisp, Manager; 435-688-3201; james_crisp@blm.gov

UNITED STATES DEPARTMENT OF THE INTERIOR
BUREAU OF LAND MANAGEMENT
STATE OFFICE FOR CA
2800 Cottage Way, RM W-1834
Sacramento, CA 95825 United States
Phone: 916-978-4400 Fax: 916-978-4305
Founded: N/A
Scope: Regional

UNITED STATES DEPARTMENT OF THE INTERIOR
BUREAU OF LAND MANAGEMENT
STATE OFFICE FOR ID
1387 S. Vinnell Way
Boise, ID 83709-1657 United States
Phone: 208-373-4000 Fax: 208-373-4005
Founded: N/A
Scope: Regional
Description: The BLM is responsible for the stewardship of almost 12 million acres of public land in Idaho. It is committed to manage these lands to serve the needs of the American people for all times. The BLM bases its management on the principles of multiple use and sustained yield.

UNITED STATES DEPARTMENT OF THE INTERIOR
BUREAU OF LAND MANAGEMENT
STATE OFFICE FOR MT, ND AND SD
P.O. Box 36800
Billings, MT 59107-6800 United States
Phone: 406-896-5012 Fax: 406-896-5299
Founded: N/A
Scope: Regional

UNITED STATES DEPARTMENT OF THE INTERIOR
BUREAU OF LAND MANAGEMENT
STATE OFFICE FOR NM, TX, OK AND KS
P.O. Box 27115
Santa Fe, NM 87502-0115 United States
Phone: 505-438-7400 Fax: 505-438-7435
Founded: N/A
Scope: Regional

UNITED STATES DEPARTMENT OF THE INTERIOR
BUREAU OF LAND MANAGEMENT
STATE OFFICE FOR NV
P.O. Box 12000
Reno, NV 89520-0006 United States
Phone: 775-861-6586
Founded: N/A
Scope: Regional

UNITED STATES DEPARTMENT OF THE INTERIOR
BUREAU OF LAND MANAGEMENT
STATE OFFICE FOR OR AND WA
P.O. Box 2965
Portland, OR 97208 United States
Phone: 503-808-6002 Fax: 503-808-6308
E-mail: or912mb@or.blm.gov
Website: www.or.blm.gov
Founded: N/A
Scope: Regional

UNITED STATES DEPARTMENT OF THE INTERIOR
BUREAU OF LAND MANAGEMENT
STATE OFFICE FOR UT
324 S. State St.
Salt Lake City, UT 84145-0155 United States
Phone: 801-539-4001
Founded: N/A
Scope: Regional
Contact(s):
Sally Wisely, Manager; 801-539-4010; sally_wisely@blm.gov

UNITED STATES DEPARTMENT OF THE INTERIOR
BUREAU OF LAND MANAGEMENT
STATE OFFICE FOR WY AND NE
5353 Yellowstone; P.O.Box 1828
Cheyenne, WY 82003 United States
Phone: 307-775-6256
Founded: N/A
Scope: Regional

UNITED STATES DEPARTMENT OF THE INTERIOR
BUREAU OF LAND MANAGEMENT
SURPRISE FIELD OFFICE
602 Cressler Street
P.O. Box 460
Cedarville, CA 96104 United States
Phone: 530-279-6101 Fax: 530-279-2171
Founded: N/A
Scope: Regional

UNITED STATES DEPARTMENT OF THE INTERIOR
BUREAU OF LAND MANAGEMENT
TAOS FIELD OFFICE
226 Cruz Alta Rd.
Taos, NM 87571-5983 United States
Phone: 505-758-8851 Fax: 505-758-1620

Founded: N/A

Scope: Regional

UNITED STATES DEPARTMENT OF THE INTERIOR
BUREAU OF LAND MANAGEMENT
TUCSON FIELD OFFICE
12661 East Broadway
Tucson, AZ 85748-7208 United States
Phone: 520-722-4289 Fax: 520-258-7238

Founded: N/A

Scope: Regional

UNITED STATES DEPARTMENT OF THE INTERIOR
BUREAU OF LAND MANAGEMENT
TULSA DISTRICT
7906 East 33rd St.
Tulsa, OK 74145-1352 United States
Phone: 918-621-4100 Fax: 918-621-4130

Founded: N/A

Scope: Regional

Contact(s):
Phil Keasling, n/a; 405-790-1016

UNITED STATES DEPARTMENT OF THE INTERIOR
BUREAU OF LAND MANAGEMENT
UKIAH FIELD OFFICE
2550 North State Street
Ukiah, CA 95482 United States
Phone: 707-468-4000 Fax: 707-468-4027

Founded: N/A

Scope: Regional

UNITED STATES DEPARTMENT OF THE INTERIOR
BUREAU OF LAND MANAGEMENT
UNCOMPAHGRE FIELD OFFICE/
SOUTHWEST CENTER
2505 S. Townsend Ave.
Montrose, CO 81401 United States
Phone: 970-240-5300 Fax: 970-240-5367

Founded: N/A

Scope: Regional

UNITED STATES DEPARTMENT OF THE INTERIOR
BUREAU OF LAND MANAGEMENT
VALE DISTRICT
100 Oregon St.
Vale, OR 97918 United States
Phone: 541-473-3144 Fax: 541-473-6213

Founded: N/A

Scope: Regional

UNITED STATES DEPARTMENT OF THE INTERIOR
BUREAU OF LAND MANAGEMENT
VERNAL DISTRICT
170 S. 500 St., East
Vernal, UT 84078 United States
Phone: 801-781-4400 Fax: 801-781-4410

Founded: N/A

Scope: Regional

UNITED STATES DEPARTMENT OF THE INTERIOR
BUREAU OF LAND MANAGEMENT
WHITE RIVER FIELD OFFICE
73544 Hwy. 64
Meeker, CO 81641 United States
Phone: 970-878-3800 Fax: 970-878-3805

Founded: N/A

Scope: Regional

UNITED STATES DEPARTMENT OF THE INTERIOR
BUREAU OF LAND MANAGEMENT
WINNEMUCCA FIELD OFFICE
5100 E. Winnemucca Blvd.
Winnemucca, NV 89445 United States
Phone: 775-623-1500 Fax: 775-623-1503

Founded: N/A

Scope: Regional

UNITED STATES DEPARTMENT OF THE INTERIOR
BUREAU OF LAND MANAGEMENT
WORLAND FIELD OFFICE
S. 23rd St., P.O. Box 119
Worland, WY 82401-0119 United States
Phone: 307-347-5100 Fax: 307-347-6195

Founded: N/A

Scope: Regional

UNITED STATES DEPARTMENT OF THE INTERIOR
BUREAU OF LAND MANAGEMENT
YUMA FIELD OFFICE
2555 East Gila Ridge Road
Yuma, AZ 85365-2240 United States
Phone: 928-317-3200 Fax: 928-317-3250

Founded: N/A

Scope: Regional

UNITED STATES DEPARTMENT OF THE INTERIOR
BUREAU OF RECLAMATION
U.S. Department of the Interior 1849 C St., NW
Washington, DC 20240 United States

Founded: N/A

Description: The Bureau of Reclamation was created by the Reclamation Act of 1902 to reclaim arid lands in the 17 Western states. This has been accomplished by the development of a system of works for the storage, diversion, and development of water. Reclamation's future role entails a shift in emphasis from development to total resource management and more effective use of existing facilities. Nonstructural means of meeting future water and power needs is now being emphasized.

Contact(s):
Stephen Magnussen, Director of Operations; 202-208-4082
Steven Richardson, Chief of Staff; 202-208-4292
Paul Bledsoe, Chief of Public Affairs Division; 202-208-4662
Eluid Martinez, Commissioner; 202-208-4157

UNITED STATES DEPARTMENT OF THE INTERIOR

BUREAU OF RECLAMATION
DENVER OFFICE
Bldg. 67, Denver Federal Center, P.O. Box 25007
Denver, CO 80225 United States

Founded: N/A

Contact(s):

Kathy Gordon, Director of Management Services; 303-445-3002
David Montoya, Director of Human Resources; 303-445-2670
Neal Stessman, Director of Reclamation Service Center; 303-445-2692
Wayne Deason, Deputy Director of Office of Policy; 303-445-2781

UNITED STATES DEPARTMENT OF THE INTERIOR

BUREAU OF RECLAMATION
LOWER COLORADO REGION
P.O. Box 61470
Boulder City, NV 89006-1470 United States
Phone: 702-293-8411 Fax: 702-293-8614
E-mail: rwalsh@oc.usbr.gov
Website: www.lc.usbr.gov

Founded: N/A
Membership: 101–1,000
Scope: Regional

Contact(s):

Bob Johnson, Director
Bob Walsh, External Affairs Officer

UNITED STATES DEPARTMENT OF THE INTERIOR

BUREAU OF RECLAMATION
MID PACIFIC REGION
Federal Office Bldg., 2800 Cottage Way
Sacramento, CA 95825 United States
Phone: 916-978-5000 Fax: 916-978-5599

Founded: N/A
Membership: 101–1,000
Scope: Regional

Contact(s):

Kirk Rodgers, Director, Acting

UNITED STATES DEPARTMENT OF THE INTERIOR

BUREAU OF RECLAMATION
PACIFIC NORTHWEST REGION
1150 N. Curtis Rd., Suite 100
Boise, ID 83706-1234 United States
Phone: 208-378-503612 Fax: 208-378-5066
E-mail: mmcclendon@pn.usbr.gov
Website: www.pn.usbr.gov

Founded: 1902
Membership: 1,001–10,000
Scope: National

Description: The Bureau of Reclamation is a federal water management agency. Water projects managed by the agency are authorized for irrigation, flood control, hydro-electric power, fish & wildlife, and recreation.

Contact(s):

Bill Macdonald, Director

UNITED STATES DEPARTMENT OF THE INTERIOR

BUREAU OF RECLAMATION
UPPER COLORADO REGION
125 South State St., Rm. 6107
Salt Lake City, UT 84138 United States
Phone: 801-524-3600 Fax: 801-524-5499
Website: www.uc.usbr.gov

Founded: N/A
Membership: 101–1,000
Scope: Regional

Contact(s):

Rick Gold, Regional Director
Tony Morton, Chief of Environmental Resources Group; 801-524-3679
Barry Wirth, Public Affairs Officer; 801-524-3774

UNITED STATES DEPARTMENT OF THE INTERIOR

FISH AND WILDLIFE SERVICE
Department of Interior, 1849 C St., Rm. 3359
Washington, DC 20240 United States
Phone: 202-208-5634 Fax: 202-208-7407
Website: www.fws.gov

Founded: N/A
Scope: National

Description: Effective July 1, 1974, an act of Congress (Public Law 93-271, April 22, 1974) renamed the Bureau of Sport Fisheries and Wildlife, the United States Fish and Wildlife Service, under the Assistant Secretary for Fish and Wildlife and Parks. The Service is the lead federal agency in the conservation of the nation's migratory birds, threatened and endangered species, certain marine mammals, and sport fishing. The Service administers fish and wildlife restoration grant programs to state governments,

Contact(s):

Robert Lesino, Program Manager of Federal Duck Stamp Program; 202-208-4354
Kevin Adams, Chief of Division of Law Enforcement; 703-358-1949
Jon Andrew, Chief of Office of Migratory Bird Management; 703-358-1714
Daniel Ashe, Assistant Director of Refuges and Wildlife; 202-208-5333
Kent Baum, Chief of Division of Personnel Management; 202-208-6104
Hannibal Bolton, Chief of Division of Fish and Wildlife Management Assistance; 703-358-1718
William Brooks, Chief of Division of Information Resources Management; 703-358-1729
Jerome Butler, Chief of Office for Human Resources; 202-208-3195
Paul Camp, Chief of Division of Engineering; 303-275-2300
Jeffery Donahoe, Chief of Division of Realty; 703-358-1713
Megan Durham, Chief of Office of Public Affairs; 202-208-4131
Arthur Ford, Chief of FWS Finance Center; Denver Federal Center, P.O. Box 25207, Denver, CO 80225-0207
Gary Frazer, Assistant Director of Ecological Services; 202-208-4646
Nancy Gloman, Chief of Division of Endangered Species; 703-358-2171
Paul Henne, Assistant Director of Administration; 202-208-4888
David Holland, Chief of Division of Finance; 703-358-1742
Marshall Jones, Assistant Director of International Affairs; 202-208-6393
William Knapp, Chief of Division of National Fish Hatcheries; 703-358-1715
Jim Kurth, Chief of Division of Refuge; 703-358-1744

Robert Lange, Chief of Office of Federal Aid; 703-358-2156
Thomas Melius, Assistant Director of External Affairs; 202-208-4500
Alexandra Pitts, Chief of Office of Congressional and Legislative Services; 202-208-5403
Herbert Raffaele, Chief of Office of International Affairs; 703-358-1754
Cathleen Short, Assistant Director of Fisheries; 202-208-6394
Kenneth Stansell, Chief of Office of Management Authority; 703-358-2093
Benjamin Tuggle, Chief of Division of Habitat Conservation; 703-358-2161
Juanita Williams, Chief of Division of Contracting and General Services; 703-358-1901
Everett Wilson, Chief of Division of Environmental Contaminants; 703-358-2148

UNITED STATES DEPARTMENT OF THE INTERIOR

FISH AND WILDLIFE SERVICE
ACE BASIN NATIONAL WILDLIFE REFUGE
P.O. Box 848
Hollywood, SC 29449 United States
Phone: 843-889-3084 Fax: 843-889-3282
E-mail: acebasin@fws.gov
Website: acebasin.fws.gov

Founded: N/A
Scope: Regional
Description: National Wildlife Refuge
Keyword(s): Ecosystems (precious)

UNITED STATES DEPARTMENT OF THE INTERIOR

FISH AND WILDLIFE SERVICE
AGASSIZ NATIONAL WILDLIFE REFUGE
22996 290th Street NE
Middle River, MN 56737 United States
Phone: 218-449-4115 Fax: 218-449-3241

Founded: N/A
Scope: National

UNITED STATES DEPARTMENT OF THE INTERIOR

FISH AND WILDLIFE SERVICE
ALAMOSA/MONTE VISTA
NATIONAL WILDLIFE REFUGE
9383 El Rancho Ln.
Alamosa, CO 81101-9003 United States
Phone: 719-589-4021, ext. 103 Fax: 719-587-6595

Founded: N/A
Scope: Regional

UNITED STATES DEPARTMENT OF THE INTERIOR

FISH AND WILDLIFE SERVICE
ALASKA MARITIME NATIONAL WILDLIFE REFUGE
2355 Kachemak Bay Dr., Ste. 101
Homer, AK 99603-8021 United States
Phone: 907-235-6546 Fax: 907-235-7783

Founded: N/A
Scope: Regional

UNITED STATES DEPARTMENT OF THE INTERIOR

FISH AND WILDLIFE SERVICE
ALASKA PENINSULA/BECHAROF
NATIONAL WILDLIFE REFUGE
P.O. Box 277
King Salmon, AK 99613 United States
Phone: 907-246-3339 Fax: 907-246-6696

Founded: N/A
Scope: Regional

UNITED STATES DEPARTMENT OF THE INTERIOR

FISH AND WILDLIFE SERVICE
ALASKA REGIONAL OFFICE 7
1011 E. Tudor Rd.
Anchorage, AK 99503 United States
Phone: 907-786-3542 Fax: 907-786-3306
Website: www.fws.gov

Founded: N/A
Scope: National
Publication(s): See publications on website
Contact(s):
David Allen, Regional Director; 907-786-3542

UNITED STATES DEPARTMENT OF THE INTERIOR

FISH AND WILDLIFE SERVICE
ALLIGATOR RIVER/PEA ISLAND
NATIONAL WILDLIFE REFUGE
P.O. Box 1969
Manteo, NC 27954 United States
Phone: 252-473-1131, ext. 230 Fax: 252-473-1668
E-mail: alligatorriver@fws.gov
Website: alligatorriver.fws.gov/

Founded: 1937
Membership: N/A
Scope: Regional, National
Description: Two National Wildlife Refuges on the coast of NE NC
Keyword(s): Agriculture/Farming, Ecosystems (precious), Forests/Forestry, Oceans/Coasts/Beaches, Recreation/ Eco-tourism, Wildlife & Species

UNITED STATES DEPARTMENT OF THE INTERIOR

FISH AND WILDLIFE SERVICE
ANAHUAC NATIONAL WILDLIFE REFUGE
P.O. Box 278
Anahuac, TX 77514 United States
Phone: 409-267-3337 Fax: 409-267-4314

Founded: N/A
Scope: Regional

UNITED STATES DEPARTMENT OF THE INTERIOR

FISH AND WILDLIFE SERVICE
ANKENY NATIONAL WILDLIFE REFUGE
10995 Hwy. 22
Dallas, OR 97338-9343 United States
Phone: 503-623-2749 Fax: 503-623-7812

Founded: N/A
Scope: Regional

UNITED STATES DEPARTMENT OF THE INTERIOR

FISH AND WILDLIFE SERVICE
ANTIOCH DUNES NATIONAL WILDLIFE REFUGE
c/o Don Edwards
San Francisco Bay NWR Complex
P.O. Box 524
Newark, CA 94560-0524 United States

Founded: N/A
Scope: Regional
Contact(s):
Anne Badgley, Regional Director; 510-792-0222

UNITED STATES DEPARTMENT OF THE INTERIOR
FISH AND WILDLIFE SERVICE
ARAPAHO NATIONAL WILDLIFE REFUGE
P.O. Box 457
Walden, CO 80480 United States
Phone: 970-723-8202 Fax: 970-723-8528

Founded: N/A

Scope: Regional

UNITED STATES DEPARTMENT OF THE INTERIOR
FISH AND WILDLIFE SERVICE
ARCHIE CARR NATIONAL WILDLIFE REFUGE
1339 20th Street
Vero Beach, FL 32960-3559 United States
Phone: 772-562-3909 Fax: 772-299-3101
E-mail: fw4_rw_pelican_island@fws.gov
Website: archiecarr.fws.gov

Founded: 1991
Membership: N/A
Scope: National
Description: The Carr refuge stretches 20 miles along Florida's central Atlantic coast. The Carr refuge is the Nation's only refuge designated to protect sea turtles. The Carr refuge provides nesting habitat for approximately one-fourth of all sea turtle nesting in the United States. The Carr refuge provides habitat for several other threatened or endangered species.

UNITED STATES DEPARTMENT OF THE INTERIOR
FISH AND WILDLIFE SERVICE
ARCTIC NATIONAL WILDLIFE REFUGE
101 12th Ave., Box 20
Fairbanks, AK 99701 United States
Phone: 907-456-0250 Fax: 907-456-0428

Founded: N/A

Scope: Regional

UNITED STATES DEPARTMENT OF THE INTERIOR
FISH AND WILDLIFE SERVICE
ARKANSAS NATIONAL WILDLIFE REFUGE
P.O. Box 100
Austwell, TX 77950 United States
Phone: 361-286-3559 Fax: 361-286-3722

Founded: N/A

Scope: Regional

UNITED STATES DEPARTMENT OF THE INTERIOR
FISH AND WILDLIFE SERVICE
ARROWWOOD NATIONAL WILDLIFE REFUGE COMPLEX
7745 11th St. SE
Pingree, ND 58476 United States
Phone: 701-285-3341 Fax: 701-285-3350
E-mail: R6RW_ARR@fws.gov
Website: www.fws.gov

Founded: 1935
Membership: N/A
Scope: Local, State, Regional, National
Description: National Wildlife Refuge
Keyword(s): Agriculture/Farming, Recreation/Ecotourism, Reduce/Reuse/Recycle, Water Habitats & Quality, Wildlife & Species
Contact(s):
Kim Hanson, Project Leader; 701-285-3341; kim_hanson@fws.gov
Stacy Adolf-Whipp, Refuge Operations Specialist; 701-285-3341; Fax: 701-285-3350; stacy_whipp@fws.gov
Mark Vaniman, Deputy Project Leader; 701-285-3341; Fax: 701-285-3350; mark_vaniman@fws.gov
Paulette Scherr, Wildlife Biologist; 701-285-3341; Fax: 701-285-3350; paulette_scherr@fws.gov

UNITED STATES DEPARTMENT OF THE INTERIOR
FISH AND WILDLIFE SERVICE
ARTHUR R. MARSHALL LOXAHATCHEE/HOPE SOUND NATIONAL WILDLIFE REFUGE
10216 Lee Rd.
Boynton Beach, FL 33437-4796 United States
Phone: 561-732-3684 Fax: 561-369-7190
E-mail: Loxahatchee@fws.gov
Website: Loxahatchee.fws.gov

Founded: 1951
Membership: N/A
Scope: Local, State, Regional, National
Description: National Wildlife Refuge
Publication(s): Refuge Newsletter
Keyword(s): Air Quality/Atmosphere, Ecosystems (precious), Land Issues, Pollution (general), Public Lands/Greenspace, Recreation/Ecotourism, Water Habitats & Quality, Wildlife & Species

UNITED STATES DEPARTMENT OF THE INTERIOR
FISH AND WILDLIFE SERVICE
ASH MEADOWS NATIONAL WILDLIFE REFUGE
HCR 70, Box 610-Z
Amargosa Valley, NV 89020 United States
Phone: 775-372-5435 Fax: 775-372-5436
E-mail: eric_hopson@fws.gov
Website: http://desertcomplex.fws.gov/

Founded: 1984
Membership: N/A
Scope: Regional
Description: Ash Meadows NWR encompasses over 22,000 acres of spring-fed wetlands and desert uplands which are managed by the U.S. Fish & Wildlife Service primarily for the benefit of 13 threatened and endangered species. The refuge also provides habitat for at least 24 plants and animals found nowhere else in the world.
Keyword(s): Land Issues, Public Health, Recreation/Ecotourism, Wildlife & Species

UNITED STATES DEPARTMENT OF THE INTERIOR
FISH AND WILDLIFE SERVICE
ATTWATER PRAIRIE CHICKEN NATIONAL WILDLIFE REFUGE
P.O. Box 519
Eagle Lake, TX 77434-0519 United States
Phone: 979-234-3021 Fax: 979-234-3278

Founded: N/A

Scope: Regional

UNITED STATES DEPARTMENT OF THE INTERIOR
FISH AND WILDLIFE SERVICE
AUDUBON COMPLEX NATIONAL WILDLIFE REFUGE
RR 1, P.O. Box 16
Coleharbor, ND 59531 United States
Phone: 701-442-5474 Fax: 701-442-5546

Founded: N/A

Scope: Regional

UNITED STATES DEPARTMENT OF THE INTERIOR
FISH AND WILDLIFE SERVICE
BACK BAY/PLUM TREE ISLAND NATIONAL WILDLIFE REFUGE
4005 Sandpiper Rd.
Virginia Beach, VA 23456 United States
Phone: 757-721-2412 Fax: 757-721-6141

Founded: N/A
Scope: Regional

UNITED STATES DEPARTMENT OF THE INTERIOR
FISH AND WILDLIFE SERVICE
BALCONES CANYONLANDS NATIONAL WILDLIFE REFUGE
10711 Burnet Rd., Ste. 201
Austin, TX 78758 United States
Phone: 512-339-9432 Fax: 512-339-9453
E-mail: FW2_RW_Balcones@fws.gov

Founded: 1992
Membership: N/A
Scope: Regional
Description: Balcones is a National Wildlife Refuge established to protect the nesting habitat of the Golden-cheeked Warbler and Black-capped Vireo, 2 endangered neotropical migrants, as well as endangered cave invertebrates. The Refuge has 3 areas open to the public that provide hiking and wildlife observation. The Refuge also hosts a dove hunt and several deer hunts. The Friends of Balcones Canyonlands NWR is a grass roots organization dedicated to helping the Refuge achieve its objectives.
Keyword(s): Public Lands/Greenspace, Wildlife & Species
Contact(s):
Deborah Holle, Refuge Manager; 512-339-9432; fw2_rw_balcones@fws.gov

UNITED STATES DEPARTMENT OF THE INTERIOR
FISH AND WILDLIFE SERVICE
BALD KNOB NATIONAL WILDLIFE REFUGE
Rt. 2, Box 126-T
Augusta, AR 72006 United States
Phone: 870-347-2614 Fax: 870-347-2908

Founded: N/A
Scope: Regional

UNITED STATES DEPARTMENT OF THE INTERIOR
FISH AND WILDLIFE SERVICE
BAYOU COCODRIE NATIONAL WILDLIFE REFUGE
P.O. Box 1772
Ferriday, LA 71334 United States
Phone: 318-336-7119 Fax: 318-336-5610

Founded: N/A
Scope: Regional

UNITED STATES DEPARTMENT OF THE INTERIOR
FISH AND WILDLIFE SERVICE
BEAR LAKE NATIONAL WILDLIFE REFUGE
P.O. Box 9
Montpelier, ID 83253-1019 United States
Phone: 208-847-1757 Fax: 208-847-1319

Founded: N/A
Scope: Regional

UNITED STATES DEPARTMENT OF THE INTERIOR
FISH AND WILDLIFE SERVICE
BEAR RIVER MIGRATORY BIRD NATIONAL WILDLIFE REFUGE
58 South 950 West
Brigham City, UT 84302 United States
Phone: 435-723-5887 Fax: 435-723-8873
E-mail: 6DE-RWBRR@fws.gov
Website: http://mountain-prairie.fws.gov/bearriver/

Founded: N/A
Scope: Regional

UNITED STATES DEPARTMENT OF THE INTERIOR
FISH AND WILDLIFE SERVICE
BENTON LAKE NATIONAL WILDLIFE REFUGE
922 Bootlegger Trail
Great Falls, MT 59404 United States
Phone: 406-727-7400 Fax: 406-727-7432
E-mail: fw6_rw_benton_lake_nwr@fws.gov

Founded: 1929
Membership: N/A
Scope: National
Description: National Wildlife Refuge and Wetland Management District. Important Bird Area.
Keyword(s): Land Issues, Pollution (general), Recreation/Ecotourism, Water Habitats & Quality

UNITED STATES DEPARTMENT OF THE INTERIOR
FISH AND WILDLIFE SERVICE
BIG LAKE NATIONAL WILDLIFE REFUGE
P.O. Box 67
Manila, AR 72442 United States
Phone: 870-564-2429 Fax: 870-564-2573

Founded: N/A
Scope: Regional
Contact(s):
Brian Braudis

UNITED STATES DEPARTMENT OF THE INTERIOR
FISH AND WILDLIFE SERVICE
BIG MUDDY NATIONAL WILDLIFE AND FISH REFUGE
4200 New Haven Rd.
Columbia, MO 65201 United States
Phone: 573-876-1826 Fax: 573-876-1839

Founded: N/A
Scope: Regional
Contact(s):
Tom Bell, Refuge Manager; 573-876-1826, ext. 2; tom_bell@fws.gov

UNITED STATES DEPARTMENT OF THE INTERIOR
FISH AND WILDLIFE SERVICE
BIG STONE NATIONAL WILDLIFE REFUGE
Rt. 1 Box 25
44843 County Rd. 19
Odessa, MN 56276 United States
Phone: 320-273-2191 Fax: 320-273-2231

Founded: N/A
Scope: National
Contact(s):
Carole Gerber, Manager

UNITED STATES DEPARTMENT OF THE INTERIOR
FISH AND WILDLIFE SERVICE
BITTER CREEK NATIONAL WILDLIFE REFUGE
c/o Hopper Mountain Complex, P.O. Box 5839
Ventura, CA 93005-0839 United States
Phone: 805-644-5185 Fax: 805-644-1732

Founded: N/A
Scope: National

UNITED STATES DEPARTMENT OF THE INTERIOR
FISH AND WILDLIFE SERVICE
BITTER LAKE NATIONAL WILDLIFE REFUGE
4065 Bitter Lakes Road
Roswell, NM 88201-0007 United States
Phone: 505-622-6755, ext. 19 Fax: 505-622-9039
E-mail: fw2_rw_bitterlake@fws.gov
Website: southwest.fws.gov

Founded: 1937
Membership: N/A
Scope: Local, State, Regional
Description: A 25,000-acre refuge w/unique wetlands, waterfowl, shorebirds, dragonflies, scenery. Public use facilities include 8-mi. auto tour, hiking trails, bike trail, overlooks, observation platforms, and limited public hunting (call for details).

UNITED STATES DEPARTMENT OF THE INTERIOR
FISH AND WILDLIFE SERVICE
BLACKWATER NATIONAL WILDLIFE REFUGE
2145 Key Wallace Dr.
Cambridge, MD 21613 United States
Phone: 410-228-2692 Fax: 410-228-3261

Founded: N/A
Scope: National

UNITED STATES DEPARTMENT OF THE INTERIOR
FISH AND WILDLIFE SERVICE
BLUE RIDGE NATIONAL WILDLIFE REFUGE
2493-A Portola Rd
Ventura, CA 93003 United States
Phone: 805-644-5185 Fax: 805-644-1732
Website: http://pacific.fws.gov/hoppermtn/blue.htm

Founded: N/A
Scope: National

UNITED STATES DEPARTMENT OF THE INTERIOR
FISH AND WILDLIFE SERVICE
BOMBAY HOOK NATIONAL WILDLIFE REFUGE
2591 Whitehall Neck Rd.
Smyrna, DE 19977 United States
Phone: 302-653-9345 Fax: 302-653-0684
E-mail: FW5RW_BHNWR@FWS.GOV
Website: http://bombayhook.fws.gov

Founded: 1937
Membership: N/A
Scope: National
Description: Bombay Hook NWR was established in 1937 to provide habitat for migratory birds. The refuge includes 15,978 acres with tidal marsh, freshwater impoundments, cropland fields, forestland, and grasslands. The refuge provides habitat for thousands of migrating shorebirds in the Spring and waterfowl in the Fall and Winter. The Refuge hosts 170,000 visitors annually for wildlife-dependent recreation including wildlife observation, interpretation and environmental education, photography, and hunting.
Keyword(s): Public Lands/Greenspace, Recreation/Ecotourism, Wildlife & Species
Contact(s):
L. Villanueva, Refuge Manager; 302-653-9345; Fax: 302-653-0684

UNITED STATES DEPARTMENT OF THE INTERIOR
FISH AND WILDLIFE SERVICE
BON SECOUR NATIONAL WILDLIFE REFUGE
12295 State Highway 180
Gulf Shores, AL 36542 United States
Phone: 251-540-7720 Fax: 251-540-7301

Founded: N/A
Scope: Regional

UNITED STATES DEPARTMENT OF THE INTERIOR
FISH AND WILDLIFE SERVICE
BOSQUE DE APACHE NATIONAL WILDLIFE REFUGE
P.O. Box 1246
Socorro, NM 87801 United States
Phone: 505-835-1828 Fax: 505-835-0314

Founded: N/A
Scope: Regional

UNITED STATES DEPARTMENT OF THE INTERIOR
FISH AND WILDLIFE SERVICE
BOWDOIN NATIONAL WILDLIFE REFUGE
HC 65, Box 5700
Malta, MT 59538 United States
Phone: 406-654-2863 Fax: 406-654-2866

Founded: N/A
Scope: National

UNITED STATES DEPARTMENT OF THE INTERIOR
FISH AND WILDLIFE SERVICE
BRAZORIA NATIONAL WILDLIFE REFUGE
1212 N. Velasco, Ste. 200
Angleton, TX 77515-1088 United States
Phone: 979-849-7771 Fax: 979-849-5118

Founded: N/A
Scope: Regional

UNITED STATES DEPARTMENT OF THE INTERIOR
FISH AND WILDLIFE SERVICE
BROWNS PARK NATIONAL WILDLIFE REFUGE
1318 Highway 318
Maybell, CO 81640 United States
Phone: 970-365-3613 Fax: 970-365-3614
E-mail: brownspark@fws.gov

Founded: N/A
Scope: Regional
Description: National Wildlife Refuge charged with managing for a diversity of habitat and animals along the Green River. Wetland, riparian, grassland, and upland shrub habitats.
Keyword(s): Recreation/Ecotourism, Wildlife & Species

UNITED STATES DEPARTMENT OF THE INTERIOR
FISH AND WILDLIFE SERVICE
BUENOS AIRES NATIONAL WILDLIFE REFUGE
P.O. Box 109
Sasabe, AZ 85633 United States
Phone: 520-823-4251 Fax: 520-823-4247
E-mail: r2rw_bw@fws.gov
Website:
http://southwest.fws.gov/refuges/arizona/buenos.html
Founded: N/A
Scope: Regional

UNITED STATES DEPARTMENT OF THE INTERIOR
FISH AND WILDLIFE SERVICE
BUFFALO LAKE NATIONAL WILDLIFE REFUGE
P.O. Box 179
Umbarger, TX 79091 United States
Phone: 806-499-3382
Founded: N/A
Scope: Regional

UNITED STATES DEPARTMENT OF THE INTERIOR
FISH AND WILDLIFE SERVICE
CABEZA PRIETA NATIONAL WILDLIFE REFUGE
1611 N. Second Ave.
Ajo, AZ 85321 United States
Phone: 520-387-6483 Fax: 520-387-5359
Founded: N/A
Scope: Regional

UNITED STATES DEPARTMENT OF THE INTERIOR
FISH AND WILDLIFE SERVICE
CACHE RIVER NATIONAL WILDLIFE REFUGE
26320 Hwy. 33 South
Augusta, AR 72006 United States
Phone: 870-347-2614 Fax: 870-347-2908
Founded: N/A
Scope: Regional

UNITED STATES DEPARTMENT OF THE INTERIOR
FISH AND WILDLIFE SERVICE
CALIFORNIA-NEVADA OPERATIONS
2800 Cottage Way, Rm. W-2606
Sacramento, CA 95825 United States
Phone: 916-414-6464 Fax: 916-414-6486
Founded: N/A
Contact(s):
Steve Thompson, Manager

UNITED STATES DEPARTMENT OF THE INTERIOR
FISH AND WILDLIFE SERVICE
CAMAS NATIONAL WILDLIFE REFUGE
2150 E. 2350 N.
Hamer, ID 83425 United States
Phone: 208-662-5423 Fax: 208-662-5525
Founded: N/A
Scope: Regional

UNITED STATES DEPARTMENT OF THE INTERIOR
FISH AND WILDLIFE SERVICE
CAMERON PRAIRIE NATIONAL WILDLIFE REFUGE
1428 Highway 27
Bell City, LA 70630 United States
Phone: 318-598-2216 Fax: 318-598-2492
Founded: N/A
Scope: Regional

UNITED STATES DEPARTMENT OF THE INTERIOR
FISH AND WILDLIFE SERVICE
CANAAN VALLEY NATIONAL WILDLIFE REFUGE
HC 70, Box 200
Davis, WV 26260 United States
Phone: 304-866-3858 Fax: 304-866-3852
E-mail: fw5rw_cvnwr@fws.gov
Website: northeast.fws.gov/wv/can.htm
Founded: 1994
Scope: Regional
Description: Tucked in the mountains of West Virginia is the largest high elevation valley east of the Rockies. Northern plants and animals have found a niche here far south of their normal range. The valley also holds the largest wetland complex in West Virginia. The refuge works to conserve these wetlands and adjacent upland habitats for the fish, wildlife and plants that depend on them.
Keyword(s): Ecosystems (precious), Public Lands/Greenspace, Water Habitats & Quality, Wildlife & Species

UNITED STATES DEPARTMENT OF THE INTERIOR
FISH AND WILDLIFE SERVICE
CAPE MAY NATIONAL WILDLIFE REFUGE
24 Kimbles Beach Rd.
Cape May Courthouse, NJ 08210-4207 United States
Phone: 609-463-0994 Fax: 609-463-1667
Founded: N/A
Scope: Regional

UNITED STATES DEPARTMENT OF THE INTERIOR
FISH AND WILDLIFE SERVICE
CAPE ROMAIN/SANTEE NATIONAL WILDLIFE REFUGE
5801 Hwy. 17 N.
Awendaw, SC 29429 United States
Phone: 843-928-3264 Fax: 843-928-3803
Founded: N/A
Scope: Regional

UNITED STATES DEPARTMENT OF THE INTERIOR
FISH AND WILDLIFE SERVICE
CARIBBEAN ISLANDS NATIONAL WILDLIFE REFUGE
P.O. Box 510
Boqueron, PR 00622 United States
Phone: 787-851-7258 Fax: 787-851-7440
Founded: N/A
Scope: Regional

UNITED STATES DEPARTMENT OF THE INTERIOR
FISH AND WILDLIFE SERVICE
CAROLINA SANDHILLS NATIONAL WILDLIFE REFUGE
Rt. 2, Box 100
McBee, SC 29101 United States
Phone: 803-335-8401 Fax: 803-335-8406
Website: carolinasandhills.fws.gov/

Founded: N/A
Scope: Regional

UNITED STATES DEPARTMENT OF THE INTERIOR
FISH AND WILDLIFE SERVICE
CATAHOULA NATIONAL WILDLIFE REFUGE
P.O. Drawer Z
Rhinehart, LA 71363-0201 United States
Phone: 318-992-5261 Fax: 318-992-6023
Founded: N/A
Scope: Regional

UNITED STATES DEPARTMENT OF THE INTERIOR
FISH AND WILDLIFE SERVICE
CHARLES M. RUSSELL NATIONAL WILDLIFE REFUGE
P.O. Box 110
Lewistown, MT 59457 United States
Phone: 406-538-8706 Fax: 406-538-7521
Founded: N/A
Scope: National

UNITED STATES DEPARTMENT OF THE INTERIOR
FISH AND WILDLIFE SERVICE
CHASE LAKE NATIONAL WILDLIFE REFUGE
5924 19th St. SE
Woodworth, ND 58496 United States
Phone: 701-752-4218 Fax: 701-752-4216
Founded: N/A
Scope: Regional
Contact(s):
Mick Erickson, n/a; 701-752-4218; Fax: 701-752-4216; michael_erickson@fws.gov

UNITED STATES DEPARTMENT OF THE INTERIOR
FISH AND WILDLIFE SERVICE
CHASSAHOWITZKA NATIONAL WILDLIFE REFUGE
1502 S.E. Kings Bay Dr.
Crystal River, FL 34429 United States
Phone: 352-563-2088 Fax: 352-795-7961
Founded: N/A
Scope: Regional

UNITED STATES DEPARTMENT OF THE INTERIOR
FISH AND WILDLIFE SERVICE
CHICKASAW NATIONAL WILDLIFE REFUGE
1505 Sandy Bluff Rd.
Ripley, TN 38063 United States
Phone: 731-635-7621 Fax: 731-635-0178
Founded: N/A
Scope: Regional

UNITED STATES DEPARTMENT OF THE INTERIOR
FISH AND WILDLIFE SERVICE
CHINCOTEAGUE/WALLOPS ISLAND NATIONAL WILDLIFE REFUGE
P.O. Box 62
Chincoteague, VA 23336 United States
Phone: 757-336-6122 Fax: 757-336-5273
Founded: N/A
Scope: Regional

UNITED STATES DEPARTMENT OF THE INTERIOR
FISH AND WILDLIFE SERVICE
CHOCTAW NATIONAL WILDLIFE REFUGE
P.O. Box 808
Jackson, AL 36545 United States
Phone: 251-246-3583 Fax: 251-246-5414
Founded: N/A
Scope: Regional

UNITED STATES DEPARTMENT OF THE INTERIOR
FISH AND WILDLIFE SERVICE
CLARKS RIVER NATIONAL WILDLIFE REFUGE
P.O. Box 89
Benton, KY 42025 United States
Phone: 502-527-5770
Founded: N/A
Scope: Regional

UNITED STATES DEPARTMENT OF THE INTERIOR
FISH AND WILDLIFE SERVICE
COLUMBIA NATIONAL WILDLIFE REFUGE
P.O. Drawer F, 735 E. Main St.
Othello, WA 99344 United States
Phone: 509-488-2668 Fax: 509-488-0705
E-mail: bob_flores@fws.gov
Website: www.fws.gov
Founded: N/A
Scope: Regional, National
Description: National Wildlife Refuge
Keyword(s): Recreation/Ecotourism, Water Habitats & Quality, Wildlife & Species

UNITED STATES DEPARTMENT OF THE INTERIOR
FISH AND WILDLIFE SERVICE
CONBOY LAKE NATIONAL WILDLIFE REFUGE
Box 5
Glenwood, WA 98619-0005 United States
Phone: 509-364-3410 Fax: 509-364-3667
Founded: N/A
Scope: Regional

UNITED STATES DEPARTMENT OF THE INTERIOR
FISH AND WILDLIFE SERVICE
CRAB ORCHARD NATIONAL WILDLIFE REFUGE
8588 Rt. 148
Marion, IL 62959 United States
Phone: 618-997-3344 Fax: 618-997-8961
Founded: N/A
Scope: Regional

UNITED STATES DEPARTMENT OF THE INTERIOR
FISH AND WILDLIFE SERVICE
CRESCENT LAKE NATIONAL WILDLIFE REFUGE
Phone: 308-762-4893
Founded: N/A
Scope: Regional

UNITED STATES DEPARTMENT OF THE INTERIOR
FISH AND WILDLIFE SERVICE
CRESCENT LAKE/NORTH PLATTE COMPLEX NATIONAL WILDLIFE REFUGE
115 Railway Street
Scottsbluff, NE 69361-3190 United States
Phone: 308-635-7851 Fax: 308-635-7841

Founded: N/A

Scope: Regional

UNITED STATES DEPARTMENT OF THE INTERIOR
FISH AND WILDLIFE SERVICE
CROCODILE LAKE NATIONAL WILDLIFE REFUGE
P.O. Box 370
Key Largo, FL 33037 United States
Phone: 305-451-4223 Fax: 305-451-1508
Website: southeast.fws.gov/CrocodileLake/index.html

Founded: N/A

Scope: National

UNITED STATES DEPARTMENT OF THE INTERIOR
FISH AND WILDLIFE SERVICE
CROSBY WMD/LAKE ZAHL NATIONAL WILDLIFE REFUGE
P.O. Box 148
Crosby, ND 58730-0148 United States
Phone: 701-965-6488 Fax: 701-965-6487

Founded: N/A

Scope: Regional

UNITED STATES DEPARTMENT OF THE INTERIOR
FISH AND WILDLIFE SERVICE
CROSS CREEKS NATIONAL WILDLIFE REFUGE
643 Wildlife Rd.
Dover, TN 37058 United States
Phone: 931-232-7477 Fax: 931-232-5958

Founded: N/A

Scope: Regional

UNITED STATES DEPARTMENT OF THE INTERIOR
FISH AND WILDLIFE SERVICE
CULEBRA NATIONAL WILDLIFE REFUGE
P.O. Box 190
Culebra, PR 00622 United States
Phone: 787-742-0115
Website: http://southeast.fws.gov/Culebra/index.html

Founded: N/A

Scope: Regional

UNITED STATES DEPARTMENT OF THE INTERIOR
FISH AND WILDLIFE SERVICE
CYPRESS CREEK NATIONAL WILDLIFE REFUGE
137 Rustic Campus Dr.
Ullin, IL 62992 United States
Phone: 618-634-2231 Fax: 618-634-9656

Founded: N/A

Scope: Regional

UNITED STATES DEPARTMENT OF THE INTERIOR
FISH AND WILDLIFE SERVICE
DEEP FORK NATIONAL WILDLIFE REFUGE
P.O. Box 816
Okmulgee, OK 74447 United States
Phone: 918-756-0815 Fax: 918-756-0275

Founded: N/A

Scope: Regional

Contact(s):
Mike Oldham, Refuse Manager; 918-756-0815; Mike_Oldham@fws.gov

UNITED STATES DEPARTMENT OF THE INTERIOR
FISH AND WILDLIFE SERVICE
DEER FLAT NATIONAL WILDLIFE REFUGE
13751 Upper Embankment Rd.
Nampa, ID 83686 United States
Phone: 208-467-9278 Fax: 208-467-1019

Founded: N/A
Membership: N/A
Scope: Regional
Description: Deer Flat National Wildlife Refuge is located outside of Nampa, ID. The refuge is a prime nesting area and wintering spot for Canada Geese and migratory waterfowl of various species. Bird watching, nature trails and educational presentations are available on the refuge and at the visitor center.

UNITED STATES DEPARTMENT OF THE INTERIOR
FISH AND WILDLIFE SERVICE
DELAWARE BAY ESTUARY PROJECT
2610 Whitehall Neck Rd.
Smyrna, DE 19977 United States
Phone: 302-653-9152 Fax: 302-653-9421

Founded: N/A

Scope: National

Description: The Delaware Estuary Project was established to coordinate, complement, and support existing U.S. Fish and Wildlife Service programs, focusing on important natural resource issues in the Delaware River watershed. The office provides technical assistance to the EPA's National Estuary Program for the Delaware Bay and Delaware's Inland Bays Estuary programs (started in 1988)

UNITED STATES DEPARTMENT OF THE INTERIOR
FISH AND WILDLIFE SERVICE
DE SOTO (BOYER CHUTE NATIONAL WILDLIFE REFUGE)
1434 316th Ln.
Missouri Valley, IA 51555 United States
Phone: 712-642-4121 Fax: 712-642-2877

Founded: N/A

Scope: Regional

Contact(s):
Larry Klimek, Manager; larry.klimek@fws.gov

UNITED STATES DEPARTMENT OF THE INTERIOR
FISH AND WILDLIFE SERVICE
DES LACS NATIONAL WILDLIFE REFUGE
P.O. Box 578
Kenmare, ND 58746-0578 United States
Phone: 701-385-4046 Fax: 701-385-3214

Founded: N/A

Scope: Regional

UNITED STATES DEPARTMENT OF THE INTERIOR
FISH AND WILDLIFE SERVICE
DETROIT LAKES WMD
26624 N. Tower Rd.
Detroit Lakes, MN 56501-7959 United States
Phone: 218-847-4431 Fax: 218-847-4156
Founded: N/A
Scope: National

UNITED STATES DEPARTMENT OF THE INTERIOR
FISH AND WILDLIFE SERVICE
DEVILS LAKE WMD NATIONAL WILDLIFE REFUGE
P.O. Box 908
Devil's Lake, ND 58301 United States
Phone: 701-662-8611 Fax: 701-662-8612
Founded: N/A
Scope: Regional

UNITED STATES DEPARTMENT OF THE INTERIOR
FISH AND WILDLIFE SERVICE
EASTERN MASSACHUSETTS NATIONAL WILDLIFE REFUGE COMPLEX
GREAT MEADOWS NATIONAL WILDLIFE REFUGE
73 Weir Hill Rd.
Sudbury, MA 01776 United States
Phone: 508-443-4661 Fax: 508-443-2898
Website: greatmeadows.fws.gov
Founded: 1944
Scope: Local, State, Regional, National
Description: Just twenty miles west of Boston lies an oasis for wildlife—Great Meadows NWR. Roughly 85 percent of the refuge's more than 3,600 acres is composed of valuable freshwater wetlands stretching along 12 miles of the Concord and Sudbury Rivers. The refuge also houses an environmental education center, visitor center, and auditorium which are available for groups upon request.
Keyword(s): Agriculture/Farming, Ecosystems (precious), Ethics/Environmental Justice, Land Issues, Public Lands/Greenspace, Recreation/Ecotourism, Water Habitats & Quality, Wildlife & Species

UNITED STATES DEPARTMENT OF THE INTERIOR
FISH AND WILDLIFE SERVICE
EASTERN NECK NATIONAL WILDLIFE REFUGE
1730 Eastern Neck Rd.
Rock Hall, MD 21661 United States
Phone: 410-639-7056 Fax: 410-639-2516
Founded: N/A
Scope: Regional

UNITED STATES DEPARTMENT OF THE INTERIOR
FISH AND WILDLIFE SERVICE
EASTERN SHORE OF VA/FISHERMAN ISLAND NATIONAL WILDLIFE REFUGE
5003 Hallett Circle
Cape Charles, VA 23310 United States
Phone: 757-331-2760 Fax: 757-331-3424
Founded: N/A
Scope: Regional

UNITED STATES DEPARTMENT OF THE INTERIOR
FISH AND WILDLIFE SERVICE
EDWIN B. FORSYTHE NATIONAL WILDLIFE REFUGE
70 Collinstown Rd., P.O. Box 544
Barnegat, NJ 08005 United States
Phone: 609-698-1378 Fax: 609-698-0109
Founded: N/A
Scope: Regional

UNITED STATES DEPARTMENT OF THE INTERIOR
FISH AND WILDLIFE SERVICE
EDWIN B. FORSYTHE NATIONAL WILDLIFE REFUGE
P.O. Box 72, Great Creek Rd., Box 72
Oceanville, NJ 08231 United States
Phone: 609-652-1665 Fax: 609-652-1474
Website: forsythe.fws.gov/
Founded: N/A
Scope: Regional

UNITED STATES DEPARTMENT OF THE INTERIOR
FISH AND WILDLIFE SERVICE
ERIE NATIONAL WILDLIFE REFUGE
11296 Wood Duck Ln.
Guys Mills, PA 16327 United States
Phone: 814-789-3585 Fax: 814-789-2909
Website: erie.fws.gov/
Founded: N/A
Scope: Regional

UNITED STATES DEPARTMENT OF THE INTERIOR
FISH AND WILDLIFE SERVICE
EUFAULA NATIONAL WILDLIFE REFUGE
509 Old Highway 165
Eufaula, AL 36027 United States
Phone: 334-687-4065 Fax: 334-687-5906
Founded: N/A
Scope: Regional

UNITED STATES DEPARTMENT OF THE INTERIOR
FISH AND WILDLIFE SERVICE
FELSENTHAL NATIONAL WILDLIFE REFUGE
P.O. Box 1157
Crossett, AR 71635 United States
Phone: 870-364-3167 Fax: 870-364-3757
Founded: N/A
Scope: Regional

UNITED STATES DEPARTMENT OF THE INTERIOR
FISH AND WILDLIFE SERVICE
FERGUS FALLS WMD NATIONAL WILDLIFE REFUGE
21932 State Highway 210 E
Fergus Falls, MN 56537 United States
Phone: 218-739-2291 Fax: 218-739-9534
Founded: N/A
Scope: National

UNITED STATES DEPARTMENT OF THE INTERIOR
FISH AND WILDLIFE SERVICE
FISH SPRINGS NATIONAL WILDLIFE REFUGE
P.O. Box 568
Dugway, UT 84022 United States
Phone: 801-831-5353 Fax: 801-831-5354

Founded: N/A
Scope: Regional
Description: National Wildlife Refuge

UNITED STATES DEPARTMENT OF THE INTERIOR
FISH AND WILDLIFE SERVICE
FLINT HILLS (MARAIS DES CYGNES) NATIONAL WILDLIFE REFUGE
P.O. Box 128, 530 W. Maple
Hartford, KS 66854 United States
Phone: 316-392-5553 Fax: 316-392-5554

Founded: N/A
Scope: Regional

UNITED STATES DEPARTMENT OF THE INTERIOR
FISH AND WILDLIFE SERVICE
FLORIDA PANTHER/TEN THOUSAND ISLAND NATIONAL WILDLIFE REFUGE
3860 Tollgate Blvd., Ste. 300
Naples, FL 34114 United States
Phone: 941-353-8442 Fax: 941-353-8640

Founded: N/A
Scope: Regional

UNITED STATES DEPARTMENT OF THE INTERIOR
FISH AND WILDLIFE SERVICE
FORT NIOBRARA/VALENTINE NATIONAL WILDLIFE REFUGE
HC 14, Box 67
Valentine, NE 69201 United States
Phone: 402-376-3789 Fax: 402-376-3217

Founded: N/A
Scope: Regional

UNITED STATES DEPARTMENT OF THE INTERIOR
FISH AND WILDLIFE SERVICE
GRAYS LAKE NATIONAL WILDLIFE REFUGE
74 Grays Lake Rd.
Wayan, ID 83285 United States
Phone: 208-574-2755 Fax: 208-574-2756

Founded: N/A
Scope: Regional

UNITED STATES DEPARTMENT OF THE INTERIOR
FISH AND WILDLIFE SERVICE
GREAT DISMAL SWAMP/NANSEMOND NATIONAL WILDLIFE REFUGE
P.O. Box 349
Suffolk, VA 23434 United States
Phone: 757-986-3705 Fax: 757-986-2353

Founded: N/A
Scope: Regional

UNITED STATES DEPARTMENT OF THE INTERIOR
FISH AND WILDLIFE SERVICE
GREAT LAKES-BIG RIVERS REGION
1 Federal Drive
Ft. Snelling, MN 55111 United States
Phone: 612-713-5301 Fax: 612-713-5284
E-mail: William_Hartwig@fws.gov
Website: midwest.fws.gov

Founded: N/A
Scope: Local, State, Regional, National, International
Description: Provide the public with opportunities to enjoy their native fish and wildlife now and in the future.
Contact(s):
William Hartwig, Regional Director; 612-713-5301; Fax: 612-713-5284; William_Hartwig@fws.gov

UNITED STATES DEPARTMENT OF THE INTERIOR
FISH AND WILDLIFE SERVICE
GREAT LAKES-BIG RIVERS REGIONAL OFFICE 3
1 Federal Dr., Federal Bldg.
Fort Snelling, MN 55111 United States
Phone: 612-713-5301 Fax: 612-713-5284

Founded: N/A
Scope: Regional
Contact(s):
William Hartwig, Regional Director; 612-713-5301
Marvin Moriarty, Deputy Regional Director; 612-713-5201
Brian Norris, Assistant Regional Director of External Affairs; 612-713-5310

UNITED STATES DEPARTMENT OF THE INTERIOR
FISH AND WILDLIFE SERVICE
GREAT RIVER NATIONAL WILDIFE REFUGE
CLARENCE CANNON NATIONAL WILDLIFE REFUGE
P.O. Box 88
Annada, MO 63330 United States
Phone: 573-847-2333 Fax: 573-847-2269

Founded: N/A
Scope: Regional
Description: These refuges are scattered along 100 miles of the Mississippi River. Managed wetlands, forests and fields provide habitat for over 230 species of birds.

UNITED STATES DEPARTMENT OF THE INTERIOR
FISH AND WILDLIFE SERVICE
GREAT SWAMP NATIONAL WILDLIFE REFUGE
152 Pleasant Plains Rd.
Basking Ridge, NJ 07920 United States
Phone: 973-425-1222 Fax: 973-425-7309
E-mail: FW5RW_GSNWR@fws.gov
Website: northeast.fws.gov/nj/grs.htm

Founded: N/A
Scope: Local, State, Regional, National
Description: National Wildlife Refuge

UNITED STATES DEPARTMENT OF THE INTERIOR
FISH AND WILDLIFE SERVICE
GUADALUPE-NIPOMO DUNES NATIONAL WILDLIFE REFUGE
1045 Guadalupe Street
Guadalupe, CA 93434 United States
Phone: 805-343-9151
Website: http://pacific.fws.gov/hoppermtn/guadalupe.htm

Founded: N/A
Scope: National

UNITED STATES DEPARTMENT OF THE INTERIOR
FISH AND WILDLIFE SERVICE
GUAM NATIONAL WILDLIFE REFUGE
P.O. Box 8134, MOU-3
Dededo, GU 96912 United States
Phone: 671-355-5096 Fax: 671-355-5098
Website: www.r1.fws.gov/refuges/office/guam.htm
Founded: N/A
Scope: Regional

UNITED STATES DEPARTMENT OF THE INTERIOR
FISH AND WILDLIFE SERVICE
HAGERMAN NATIONAL WILDLIFE REFUGE
6465 Refuge Rd.
Sherman, TX 75092 United States
Phone: 903-786-2826 Fax: 903-786-3327
Founded: N/A
Scope: Regional

UNITED STATES DEPARTMENT OF THE INTERIOR
FISH AND WILDLIFE SERVICE
HAKALAU FOREST NATIONAL WILDLIFE REFUGE
32 K Kincole St, Suite 101
Hilo, HI 96720 United States
Phone: 808-933-6915 Fax: 808-933-6917
Founded: N/A
Scope: Regional

UNITED STATES DEPARTMENT OF THE INTERIOR
FISH AND WILDLIFE SERVICE
HANFORD COMPLEX/SADDLE MOUNTAIN NATIONAL WILDLIFE REFUGE
3520 Port of Benton Blvd.
Richland, WA 99352 United States
Phone: 509-371-1801 Fax: 509-371-0196
Founded: N/A
Scope: National

UNITED STATES DEPARTMENT OF THE INTERIOR
FISH AND WILDLIFE SERVICE
HART MOUNTAIN NATIONAL ANTELOPE REFUGE NATIONAL WILDLIFE REFUGE
P.O. Box 111
Lakeview, OR 97630 United States
Phone: 541-947-3315
Founded: N/A
Scope: Regional

UNITED STATES DEPARTMENT OF THE INTERIOR
FISH AND WILDLIFE SERVICE
HATCHIE NATIONAL WILDLIFE REFUGE
P.O. Box 1031
Brownsville, TN 38012 United States
Phone: 731-772-0501, ext. 25 Fax: 731-772-7839
Website: hatchie.fws.gov
Founded: 1964
Membership: 1–100
Scope: Regional
Description: Acres: 11,556. Location: 1 mile S of Brownsville, TN on the S bank of 23.5 miles of the state-designated Hatchie Scenic River; 50 miles E of Memphis and 130 miles W of Nashville, TN. Calendar of Events March: refuge birthday. April: disabled fishing tourney, spring turkey hunting. June: Jr. / Sr. Fishing Rodeo. September-October: archery/gun deer hunting, Wildlife Refuge Week Celebration. September-February: small game hunting. September and December-January: waterfowl hunting.
Contact(s):
Marvin Nichols, n/a; 731-772-0501, ext. 25; Fax: 731-772-7839; Marvin_Nichols@fws.gov

UNITED STATES DEPARTMENT OF THE INTERIOR
FISH AND WILDLIFE SERVICE
HAWAIIAN AND PACIFIC ISLANDS NATIONAL WILDLIFE REFUGE COMPLEX
P.O. Box 50167
Honolulu, HI 96850 United States
Phone: 808-541-1201 Fax: 808-541-1216
Founded: N/A
Scope: Regional

UNITED STATES DEPARTMENT OF THE INTERIOR
FISH AND WILDLIFE SERVICE
HILLSIDE NATIONAL WILDLIFE REFUGE
1562 Providence Rd.
Cruger, MS 35924 United States
Phone: 662-235-4989 Fax: 662-235-5303
Founded: N/A
Scope: Regional

UNITED STATES DEPARTMENT OF THE INTERIOR
FISH AND WILDLIFE SERVICE
HOBE SOUND NATIONAL WILDLIFE REFUGE
P.O. Box 645
Hobe Sound, FL 33475-0645 United States
Phone: 561-546-6141 Fax: 561-545-7572
E-mail: margo_stahl@fws.gov
Founded: 1969
Membership: 10,001–100,000
Scope: Regional
Description: Hobe Sound NWR is a coastal refuge consisting of two separate tracts of land located in Martin County, Florida. Over 1000 acres of coastal sand dune, mangrove swamps and sand pine-oak scrub forest can be explored. The refuge was established through the generosity of conservation minded Jupiter Island residents. As a result a unique remnant of South Florida's ecology is being preserved from the encroachment of civilization that is rapidly expanding northward along the South Florida coast.
Keyword(s): Ecosystems (precious), Forests/Forestry, Oceans/Coasts/Beaches, Recreation/Ecotourism

UNITED STATES DEPARTMENT OF THE INTERIOR
FISH AND WILDLIFE SERVICE
HOLLA BEND/LOGAN CAVE NATIONAL WILDLIFE REFUGE
Rt. 1, Box 59
Dardanelle, AR 72834-9704 United States
Phone: 870-229-4300 Fax: 870-229-4302
Founded: N/A
Scope: Regional

UNITED STATES DEPARTMENT OF THE INTERIOR
FISH AND WILDLIFE SERVICE
HOPPER MOUNTAIN COMPLEX NATIONAL WILDLIFE REFUGE
P.O. Box 5839
Ventura, CA 93005 United States
Phone: 805-644-5158 Fax: 805-644-1732

Founded: N/A

Scope: Regional

UNITED STATES DEPARTMENT OF THE INTERIOR
FISH AND WILDLIFE SERVICE
HORICON COMPLEX NATIONAL WILDLIFE REFUGE
W 4279 Headquarters Rd.
Mayville, WI 53050 United States
Phone: 920-387-2658 Fax: 920-387-2973
E-mail: patti_meyers@fws.gov

Founded: N/A

Scope: Regional

UNITED STATES DEPARTMENT OF THE INTERIOR
FISH AND WILDLIFE SERVICE
HUMBOLDT BAY NATIONAL WILDLIFE REFUGE
1020 Ranch Rd.
Loleta, CA 95551 United States
Phone: 707-733-5406 Fax: 707-733-1946

Founded: N/A

Scope: Regional

UNITED STATES DEPARTMENT OF THE INTERIOR
FISH AND WILDLIFE SERVICE
HURON WMD NATIONAL WILDLIFE REFUGE
200 4th St., SW, Rm. 317 Federal Bldg.
Huron, SD 57350-2470 United States
Phone: 605-352-5894 Fax: 605-352-6709

Founded: N/A

Scope: Regional

Contact(s):
Harris Hoistad, Project Leader; 605-352-5894, ext. 11; harris_hoistad@fws.gov

UNITED STATES DEPARTMENT OF THE INTERIOR
FISH AND WILDLIFE SERVICE
ILLINOIS RIVER NATIONAL WILDLIFE AND FISH REFUGE (CHAUTAUQUA, EMIQUON, MEREDOSIA)
19031 E. County Rd. 2110 N
Havana, IL 62644 United States
Phone: 309-535-2290 Fax: 309-535-3023

Founded: N/A

Scope: Regional

UNITED STATES DEPARTMENT OF THE INTERIOR
FISH AND WILDLIFE SERVICE
IMPERIAL NATIONAL WILDLIFE REFUGE
P.O. Box 72217
Yuma, AZ 85365 United States
Phone: 928-783-3371 Fax: 928-783-0652

Founded: N/A

Scope: Regional

UNITED STATES DEPARTMENT OF THE INTERIOR
FISH AND WILDLIFE SERVICE
INNOKO NATIONAL WILDLIFE REFUGE
P.O. Box 69
McGrath, AK 99627 United States
Phone: 907-524-3251 Fax: 907-524-3141

Founded: N/A

Scope: Regional

UNITED STATES DEPARTMENT OF THE INTERIOR
FISH AND WILDLIFE SERVICE
IROQUOIS NATIONAL WILDLIFE REFUGE
1101 Casey Rd.
Alabama, NY 14003 United States
Phone: 716-948-9154 Fax: 716-948-9538

Founded: N/A

Scope: Regional

UNITED STATES DEPARTMENT OF THE INTERIOR
FISH AND WILDLIFE SERVICE
IZEMBEK NATIONAL WILDLIFE REFUGE
P.O. Box 127, #1 Izembek Dr.
Cold Bay, AK 99571 United States
Phone: 907-532-2445 Fax: 907-532-2549

Founded: N/A

Scope: Regional

UNITED STATES DEPARTMENT OF THE INTERIOR
FISH AND WILDLIFE SERVICE
J. CLARK SALYER NATIONAL WILDLIFE REFUGE
P.O. Box 66
Upham, ND 58789 United States
Phone: 701-768-2548 Fax: 701-768-2834

Founded: N/A

Scope: Regional

Contact(s):
Robert Howard, Refuse Manager; 701-768-2548; rgrw_jcs@fws.gov

UNITED STATES DEPARTMENT OF THE INTERIOR
FISH AND WILDLIFE SERVICE
J.N. (DING) DARLING NATIONAL WILDLIFE REFUGE
One Wildlife Dr.
Sanibel, FL 33957 United States
Phone: 941-472-1100 Fax: 941-472-4061

Founded: N/A

Scope: Regional

UNITED STATES DEPARTMENT OF THE INTERIOR
FISH AND WILDLIFE SERVICE
JOHN HEINZ NATIONAL WILDLIFE REFUGE AT TINICUM
Ste. 104, Scott Plaza 2
Philadelphia, PA 19113 United States
Phone: 610-521-0662 Fax: 610-521-0611
Website: heinz.fws.gov/

Founded: N/A

Scope: Regional

UNITED STATES DEPARTMENT OF THE INTERIOR
FISH AND WILDLIFE SERVICE
JOHNSTON ISLAND NATIONAL WILDLIFE REFUGE
Box 396
APO, AP, HI 96558-0396 United States
Phone: 808-421-0011 Fax: 808-422-6905
Founded: N/A
Scope: Regional

UNITED STATES DEPARTMENT OF THE INTERIOR
FISH AND WILDLIFE SERVICE
JULIA BUTLER HANSEN REFUGE FOR THE COLUMBIA WHITE-TAILED DEER NATIONAL WILDLIFE REFUGE
P.O. Box 566
Cathlamet, WA 98612-0566 United States
Phone: 509-795-3915 Fax: 360-795-0803
Founded: N/A
Scope: Regional

UNITED STATES DEPARTMENT OF THE INTERIOR
FISH AND WILDLIFE SERVICE
KANUTI NATIONAL WILDLIFE REFUGE
101 12th Ave., Box 11; Rm. 262
Fairbanks, AK 99701 United States
Phone: 907-456-0329 Fax: 907-456-0506
Founded: N/A
Scope: Regional

UNITED STATES DEPARTMENT OF THE INTERIOR
FISH AND WILDLIFE SERVICE
KEALIA POND NATIONAL WILDLIFE REFUGE
P.O. Box 1042
Kihei, HI 96753-1042 United States
Phone: 808-875-1582 Fax: 808-875-2945
Founded: N/A
Scope: Regional

UNITED STATES DEPARTMENT OF THE INTERIOR
FISH AND WILDLIFE SERVICE
KENAI NATIONAL WILDLIFE REFUGE
P.O. Box 2139
Soldotna, AK 99669-2139 United States
Phone: 907-262-7021 Fax: 907-262-3599
Founded: N/A
Scope: Regional

UNITED STATES DEPARTMENT OF THE INTERIOR
FISH AND WILDLIFE SERVICE
KERN/BLUE RIDGE/PIXLEY NATIONAL WILDLIFE REFUGE
P.O. Box 670
Delano, CA 93216-0670 United States
Phone: 661-725-2767 Fax: 661-725-6041
Founded: N/A
Scope: Regional

UNITED STATES DEPARTMENT OF THE INTERIOR
FISH AND WILDLIFE SERVICE
KETERSON NATIONAL WILDLIFE REFUGE
P.O. Box 2176
Los Banos, CA 93635-2176 United States
Phone: 209-826-3508 Fax: 209-826-1445
Founded: N/A
Scope: Regional

UNITED STATES DEPARTMENT OF THE INTERIOR
FISH AND WILDLIFE SERVICE
KILAUEA POINT (HANALEI, HULEIA) NATIONAL WILDLIFE REFUGE
P.O. Box 1128
Kilauea, Kauai, HI 96754-1128 United States
Phone: 808-828-1413 Fax: 808-828-6634
Founded: N/A
Scope: Regional

UNITED STATES DEPARTMENT OF THE INTERIOR
FISH AND WILDLIFE SERVICE
KIRWIN NATIONAL WILDLIFE REFUGE
702 E. Xavier Road
Kirwin, KS 67644 United States
Phone: 785-543-6673 Fax: 785-543-5464
Founded: N/A
Scope: Regional

UNITED STATES DEPARTMENT OF THE INTERIOR
FISH AND WILDLIFE SERVICE
KLAMATH BASIN COMPLEX NATIONAL WILDLIFE REFUGE
4009 Hill Road
Tule Lake, CA 96134-9715 United States
Phone: 530-667-2231 Fax: 530-667-2231
Founded: N/A
Scope: Regional

UNITED STATES DEPARTMENT OF THE INTERIOR
FISH AND WILDLIFE SERVICE
KODIAK NATIONAL WILDLIFE REFUGE
1390 Buskin River Rd.
Kodiak, AK 99615 United States
Phone: 907-487-2600 Fax: 907-487-2144
Founded: N/A
Scope: Regional

UNITED STATES DEPARTMENT OF THE INTERIOR
FISH AND WILDLIFE SERVICE
KOFA NATIONAL WILDLIFE REFUGE
356 W. 1st St.
Yuma, AZ 85364 United States
Phone: 928-783-7861 Fax: 928-783-8611
E-mail: FW2_RW_kofa@fws.gov
Website: southwest.fws.gov/refuges/arizona/kofa.html
Founded: 1939
Membership: 1–100
Scope: Local, State, Regional, National
Description: Kofa NWR contains 665,400-acres of pristine Sonoran Desert. Its primary objective is to preserve habitat for desert bighorn sheep. Approximately 80% of the refuge is designated wilderness.

Keyword(s): Ecosystems (precious), Public Lands/Greenspace, Recreation/Ecotourism, Reduce/Reuse/Recycle, Water Habitats & Quality, Wildlife & Species

Contact(s):

Susanna Henry, Assistant Manager
Ron Kearns, Biologist
Michelle Willcox, Administrative Technician

UNITED STATES DEPARTMENT OF THE INTERIOR
FISH AND WILDLIFE SERVICE
KOOTENAI NATIONAL WILDLIFE REFUGE
HCR 60, Box 283
Bonners Ferry, ID 83805 United States
Phone: 208-267-3888 Fax: 208-267-5570

Founded: N/A

Scope: Regional

UNITED STATES DEPARTMENT OF THE INTERIOR
FISH AND WILDLIFE SERVICE
KULM WMD NATIONAL WILDLIFE REFUGE
P.O. Box E
Kulm, ND 58456-0170 United States
Phone: 701-647-2866 Fax: 701-647-2221

Founded: N/A

Scope: Regional

UNITED STATES DEPARTMENT OF THE INTERIOR
FISH AND WILDLIFE SERVICE
LACASSINE NATIONAL WILDLIFE REFUGE
209 Nature Road
Lake Arthur, LA 70549 United States
Phone: 337-774-5923 Fax: 337-774-9913
Website: lacassine.fws.gov

Founded: N/A

Scope: National

Description: Wildlife Refuge

Keyword(s): Agriculture/Farming, Ecosystems (precious), Land Issues

UNITED STATES DEPARTMENT OF THE INTERIOR
FISH AND WILDLIFE SERVICE
LACREEK/BEAR BUTTE NATIONAL WILDLIFE REFUGE
HC 5, Box 114
Martin, SD 57551 United States
Phone: 605-685-6508 Fax: 605-685-1173
Website: lacreek@fws.gov

Founded: N/A

Scope: Regional

UNITED STATES DEPARTMENT OF THE INTERIOR
FISH AND WILDLIFE SERVICE
LAGUNA ATASCOSA NATIONAL WILDLIFE REFUGE
P.O. Box 450
Rio Hondo, TX 78583 United States
Phone: 956-748-3607 Fax: 956-748-3609

Founded: N/A

Scope: Regional

UNITED STATES DEPARTMENT OF THE INTERIOR
FISH AND WILDLIFE SERVICE
LAKE ANDES/KARL E. MUNDT NATIONAL WILDLIFE REFUGE
38627 291st St.
Lake Andes, SD 57356 United States
Phone: 605-487-7603 Fax: 605-487-7604

Founded: N/A

Scope: Regional

Contact(s):

Gene Williams, Project Leader; 605-487-7603; Gene_Williams@fws.gov

UNITED STATES DEPARTMENT OF THE INTERIOR
FISH AND WILDLIFE SERVICE
LAKE OPHELIA/GRAND COLE NATIONAL WILDLIFE REFUGE
401 Island Rd.
Marksville, LA 71351 United States
Phone: 318-253-4238 Fax: 318-253-7139

Founded: N/A

Scope: Regional

UNITED STATES DEPARTMENT OF THE INTERIOR
FISH AND WILDLIFE SERVICE
LAKE UMBAGOG NATIONAL WILDLIFE REFUGE
Box 240
Errol, NH 03579 United States
Phone: 603-482-3415 Fax: 603-482-3308

Founded: N/A

Scope: Regional

UNITED STATES DEPARTMENT OF THE INTERIOR
FISH AND WILDLIFE SERVICE
LAKE WOODRUFF NATIONAL WILDLIFE REFUGE
P.O. Box 488
DeLeon Springs, FL 32130-0488 United States
Phone: 386-985-4673 Fax: 386-985-0926

Founded: N/A

Scope: Regional

UNITED STATES DEPARTMENT OF THE INTERIOR
FISH AND WILDLIFE SERVICE
LAS VEGAS NATIONAL WILDLIFE REFUGE
Rt. 1 Box 399
Las Vegas, NM 87701 United States
Phone: 505-425-3581 Fax: 505-454-8510

Founded: N/A

Scope: Regional

UNITED STATES DEPARTMENT OF THE INTERIOR
FISH AND WILDLIFE SERVICE
LEE METCALF NATIONAL WILDLIFE REFUGE
P.O. Box 247
Stevensville, MT 59870 United States
Phone: 406-777-5552 Fax: 406-777-4344

Founded: N/A

Scope: National

UNITED STATES DEPARTMENT OF THE INTERIOR
FISH AND WILDLIFE SERVICE
LEOPOLD NATIONAL WILDLIFE REFUGE
Phone: 920-387-0336 Fax: 920-387-2973
Founded: N/A
Scope: National

UNITED STATES DEPARTMENT OF THE INTERIOR
FISH AND WILDLIFE SERVICE
LITCHFIELD WMD
22274 615th Avenue
Litchfield, MN 55355 United States
Phone: 320-693-2849 Fax: 320-693-7207
Founded: N/A
Scope: National

UNITED STATES DEPARTMENT OF THE INTERIOR
FISH AND WILDLIFE SERVICE
LITTLE PEND OREILLE NATIONAL WILDLIFE REFUGE
1310 Bear Creek Rd.
Colville, WA 99114-9713 United States
Phone: 509-684-8384 Fax: 509-684-8381
Founded: N/A
Scope: Regional

UNITED STATES DEPARTMENT OF THE INTERIOR
FISH AND WILDLIFE SERVICE
LITTLE RIVER/LITTLE SANDY NATIONAL WILDLIFE REFUGE
P.O. Box 340
Broken Bow, OK 74728 United States
Phone: 580-584-6211 Fax: 580-584-2034
Founded: N/A
Scope: Regional

UNITED STATES DEPARTMENT OF THE INTERIOR
FISH AND WILDLIFE SERVICE
LONG ISLAND NATIONAL WILDLIFE REFUGE COMPLEX
P.O. Box 21
Shirley, NY 11967 United States
Phone: 631-286-0485 Fax: 631-286-4003
Website: northeast.fws.gov/ny/lirc.htm
Founded: N/A
Scope: Local, State, Regional, National, International
Description: The Long Island NWR Complex is comprised of nine units, totalling almost 6,500 acres. The purpose for each is to protect & benefit wildlife. These nine units protect many of Long Island's habitat types which are critical to migratory birds, endangered species and other wildlife. Long Island's strategic location along the Atlantic Flyway and within the Long Island Pine Barrens provides important nesting, wintering & migratory stop-over areas for hundreds of bird species.
Keyword(s): Ecosystems (precious), Recreation/Ecotourism, Water Habitats & Quality, Wildlife & Species
Contact(s):
Mark Maghini, Biologist; 631-286-0485; Fax: 631-286-4003
Andrea Stewart, Outdoor Recreation Planner; 631-286-0485; Fax: 631-286-4003

UNITED STATES DEPARTMENT OF THE INTERIOR
FISH AND WILDLIFE SERVICE
LONG LAKE NATIONAL WILDLIFE REFUGE
1200 353rd St. SE
Moffit, ND 58560-9740 United States
Phone: 701-387-4397 Fax: 701-387-4767
Founded: N/A
Scope: Regional
Contact(s):
Paul Van Ningen, n/a; 701-387-4397, ext. 14; Paul_vanningen@fws.gov

UNITED STATES DEPARTMENT OF THE INTERIOR
FISH AND WILDLIFE SERVICE
LOUISIANA WMD/HANDY BRAKE NATIONAL WILDLIFE REFUGE
1428 Hwy. 143
Farmerville, LA 71241 United States
Phone: 318-726-4400 Fax: 318-726-4667
Founded: N/A
Scope: Regional

UNITED STATES DEPARTMENT OF THE INTERIOR
FISH AND WILDLIFE SERVICE
LOWER COLORADO RIVER COMPLEX NATIONAL WILDLIFE REFUGE
c/o Bureau of Reclamation
P.O. Box D
Yuma, AZ 85364 United States
Phone: 928-343-8112 Fax: 928-343-8320
Founded: N/A
Scope: Regional

UNITED STATES DEPARTMENT OF THE INTERIOR
FISH AND WILDLIFE SERVICE
LOWER HATCHIE NATIONAL WILDLIFE REFUGE
1505 Sandy Bluff Rd.
Ripley, TN 38063 United States
Phone: 731-635-7621 Fax: 731-635-0178
Founded: N/A
Scope: Regional

UNITED STATES DEPARTMENT OF THE INTERIOR
FISH AND WILDLIFE SERVICE
LOWER RIO GRANDE/SANTA ANNA COMPLEX NATIONAL WILDLIFE REFUGE
Rt. 2, Box 202A
Alamo, TX 78516 United States
Phone: 210-787-3079 Fax: 210-787-8338
Founded: N/A
Scope: Regional

UNITED STATES DEPARTMENT OF THE INTERIOR
FISH AND WILDLIFE SERVICE
LOWER SUWANNEE/CEDAR KEYS NATIONAL WILDLIFE REFUGE
16450 NW 31st Pl.
Chiefland, FL 32626 United States
Phone: 352-493-0238 Fax: 352-493-1935
Founded: N/A
Scope: Regional

UNITED STATES DEPARTMENT OF THE INTERIOR
FISH AND WILDLIFE SERVICE
MACKAY ISLAND/CURRITUCK NATIONAL WILDLIFE REFUGE
P.O. Box 39
Knotts Island, NC 27950 United States
Phone: 919-429-3100 Fax: 919-429-3185
Website: alligatorriver.fws.gov/mackayisland/

Founded: 1960
Scope: Regional
Description: National Wildlife Refuges. Mackay Island NWR established in 1960 for wintering migratory birds, Currituck NWR established in 1983 for wintering migratory birds and to preserve the fragile barrier island habitat.

UNITED STATES DEPARTMENT OF THE INTERIOR
FISH AND WILDLIFE SERVICE
MADISON WMD NATIONAL WILDLIFE REFUGE
P.O. Box 48
Madison, SD 57042 United States
Phone: 605-256-2974 Fax: 605-256-9432

Founded: N/A
Scope: Regional

UNITED STATES DEPARTMENT OF THE INTERIOR
FISH AND WILDLIFE SERVICE
MALHEUR NATIONAL WILDLIFE REFUGE
HC 72, Box 245
Princeton, OR 97721-9505 United States
Phone: 541-493-2612 Fax: 541-493-2405

Founded: N/A
Scope: Regional

UNITED STATES DEPARTMENT OF THE INTERIOR
FISH AND WILDLIFE SERVICE
MARK TWAIN NATIONAL WILDLIFE REFUGE
1704 N. 24th St.
Quincy, IL 62301 United States
Phone: 217-224-8580 Fax: 217-224-8583

Founded: N/A
Scope: Regional

UNITED STATES DEPARTMENT OF THE INTERIOR
FISH AND WILDLIFE SERVICE
MARK TWAIN/BRUSSELS DISTRICT NATIONAL WILDLIFE REFUGE
HCR 82, Box 107
Brussels, IL 62013-9711 United States
Phone: 618-883-2524 Fax: 618-883-2201

Founded: N/A
Scope: Regional

UNITED STATES DEPARTMENT OF THE INTERIOR
FISH AND WILDLIFE SERVICE
MARK TWAIN/WAPELLO DISTRICT NATIONAL WILDLIFE REFUGE
10728 County Rd. X-61
Wapello, IA 52653-9477 United States
Phone: 319-523-6982 Fax: 319-523-6960

Founded: N/A
Scope: Regional

UNITED STATES DEPARTMENT OF THE INTERIOR
FISH AND WILDLIFE SERVICE
MATTAMUSKEET NATIONAL WILDLIFE REFUGE
38 Mattamuskeet Road
Swan Quarter, NC 27885 United States
Phone: 919-926-4021 Fax: 919-926-1743
Website: mattamuskeet.fws.gov/index.html

Founded: 1934
Membership: N/A
Scope: Regional
Description: 50,180 acre national wildlife refuge in northeastern North Carolina serving as a major wintering and migration area for waterfowl in the Atlantic Flyway. Main feature is the 40,000 acre Lake Mattamuskeet.
Keyword(s): Agriculture/Farming, Air Quality/Atmosphere, Public Lands/Greenspace, Recreation/Ecotourism, Water Habitats & Quality, Wildlife & Species

UNITED STATES DEPARTMENT OF THE INTERIOR
FISH AND WILDLIFE SERVICE
MAXWELL NATIONAL WILDLIFE REFUGE
P.O. Box 276
Maxwell, NM 87728 United States
Phone: 505-375-2331 Fax: 505-375-2332

Founded: N/A
Scope: Regional

UNITED STATES DEPARTMENT OF THE INTERIOR
FISH AND WILDLIFE SERVICE
MEDICINE LAKE NATIONAL WILDLIFE REFUGE COMPLEX
MEDICINE LAKE/LAMESTEER NWR, NE MONTANA WETLAND MANAGEMENT DISTRICT
223 Northshore Rd.
Medicine Lake, MT 59247-9600 United States
Phone: 406-789-2305 Fax: 406-789-2350
E-mail: medicinelake@fws.gov

Founded: 1935
Membership: N/A
Scope: Local, State, Regional, National
Description: Medicine Lake NWR Complex is part of the NWR System, and the U.S. Fish and Wildlife Service. The Complex includes the 31,660 acre Medicine Lake NWR, the 800 acre Lamesteer easement NWR, and the 3-county NE Montana WMD with 45 Waterfowl Production Areas encompassing 12,000 acres.

UNITED STATES DEPARTMENT OF THE INTERIOR
FISH AND WILDLIFE SERVICE
MERRITT ISLAND NATIONAL WILDLIFE REFUGE
P.O. Box 6504
Titusville, FL 32782 United States
Phone: 407-861-0667 Fax: 407-861-1276

Founded: N/A
Scope: Regional

UNITED STATES DEPARTMENT OF THE INTERIOR
FISH AND WILDLIFE SERVICE
MICHIGAN WMD NATIONAL WILDLIFE REFUGE
2651 Coolidge Rd.
East Lansing, MI 48823 United States
Phone: 517-351-4230

Founded: N/A
Scope: National

UNITED STATES DEPARTMENT OF THE INTERIOR
FISH AND WILDLIFE SERVICE
MID-COLUMBIA RIVER NATIONAL WILDLIFE REFUGE COMPLEX
P.O. Box 2527
2805 St. Andrews Loop
Pasco, OR 99301 United States
Phone: 509-545-8588 Fax: 509-545-8670

Founded: N/A
Scope: Regional

UNITED STATES DEPARTMENT OF THE INTERIOR
FISH AND WILDLIFE SERVICE
MIDWAY ATOLL NATIONAL WILDLIFE REFUGE
P.O. Box 29460, Midway Island Station #4
Honolulu, HI 96820-1860 United States
Phone: 808-599-3914

Founded: N/A
Scope: Regional

UNITED STATES DEPARTMENT OF THE INTERIOR
FISH AND WILDLIFE SERVICE
MILLE LACS NATIONAL WILDLIFE REFUGE
36289 State Hwy. 65
McGregor, MN 55760 United States
Phone: 218-768-2402 Fax: 218-768-3040
E-mail: Mary_Stefanski@fws.gov
Website: midwest.fws.gov/millelacs/

Founded: 1915
Scope: National
Description: One of over 540 National Wildlife Refuges in the country. Mille Lacs is the smallest refuge in the country at less than 0.5 acre. It is the site of a colony of common terns.
Contact(s):
Mary Stefanski, Refuge Manager; 218-768-2402; Fax: 218-768-3040; Mary_Stefanski@fws.gov

UNITED STATES DEPARTMENT OF THE INTERIOR
FISH AND WILDLIFE SERVICE
MINGO NATIONAL WILDLIFE REFUGE
24279 State Highway 51
Puxico, MO 63960 United States
Phone: 573-222-3589 Fax: 573-222-6343
Website: www.fws.gov/r3pao/ming_nwr

Founded: 1945
Scope: National
Keyword(s): Water Habitats & Quality, Wildlife & Species
Contact(s):
Kathleen Maycroft, Refuge Manager

UNITED STATES DEPARTMENT OF THE INTERIOR
FISH AND WILDLIFE SERVICE
MINIDOKA NATIONAL WILDLIFE REFUGE
961 E. Minidoka Dam
Rupert, ID 83350 United States
Phone: 208-436-3589 Fax: 208-436-1570

Founded: N/A
Scope: Regional

UNITED STATES DEPARTMENT OF THE INTERIOR
FISH AND WILDLIFE SERVICE
MINNESOTA VALLEY NATIONAL WILDLIFE REFUGE
3815 E. 80th St.
Bloomington, MN 55425-1600 United States
Phone: 952-854-5900 Fax: 612-725-3279
Website: midwest.fws.gov/minnesotavalley.com

Founded: 1976
Membership: N/A
Scope: National
Description: Minnesota Valley National Wildlife Refuge is part of the National Wildlife Refuge System located in the urban areas of Minneapolis and St. Paul. The Refuge comprises 14,000 acres along a 34-mile portion of the Minnesota River. The Refuge provides high quality production and migration habitat for bald eagles, waterfowl, water birds, song birds, and several species of resident wildlife. The Refuge also provides environmental education and interpretive programs to Twin Cities residents.
Keyword(s): Public Lands/Greenspace, Recreation/Ecotourism, Wildlife & Species

UNITED STATES DEPARTMENT OF THE INTERIOR
FISH AND WILDLIFE SERVICE
MISSISQUOI NATIONAL WILDLIFE REFUGE
371 North River St.
Swanton, VT 05488 United States
Phone: 802-868-4781 Fax: 802-868-2379

Founded: 1943
Scope: Regional, National
Description: This 6,592-acre refuge includes most of the Missisquoi River delta where it flows into Missisquoi Bay. The refuge consists of quiet waters and wetlands which attracts large flocks of migratory birds.
Keyword(s): Recreation/Ecotourism
Contact(s):
Mark Sweeny, Refuge Manager

UNITED STATES DEPARTMENT OF THE INTERIOR
FISH AND WILDLIFE SERVICE
MISSISSIPPI SANDHILL CRANE/GRAND BAY NATIONAL WILDLIFE REFUGE
7200 Crane Ln.
Gautier, MS 39553 United States
Phone: 601-497-6322 Fax: 601-497-5407

Founded: N/A
Scope: Regional

UNITED STATES DEPARTMENT OF THE INTERIOR
FISH AND WILDLIFE SERVICE
MISSISSIPPI WMD NATIONAL WILDLIFE REFUGE
P.O. Box 1070, 16736 Hwy. 8 West
Grenada, MS 38902 United States
Phone: 601-226-8286 Fax: 601-226-8488

Founded: N/A
Scope: Regional

UNITED STATES DEPARTMENT OF THE INTERIOR
FISH AND WILDLIFE SERVICE
MOAPA VALLEY NATIONAL WILDLIFE REFUGE
HCR 38, Box 700
Las Vegas, NV 89124 United States
Phone: 702-879-6110 Fax: 702-879-6115
Website: desertcomplex.fws.gov

Founded: N/A
Scope: Local, State, Regional, National
Description: Moapa Valley National Wildlife Refuge, part of the Desert National Wildlife Refuge Complex.
Keyword(s): Wildlife & Species
Contact(s):
Amy Sprunger-Allworth, Refuge Manager; 702-879-6110; Fax: 702-879-6115; amy_sprunger-allworth@fws.gov

UNITED STATES DEPARTMENT OF THE INTERIOR
FISH AND WILDLIFE SERVICE
MODOC NATIONAL WILDLIFE REFUGE
P.O. Box 1610
Alturas, CA 96101 United States
Phone: 530-233-3572 Fax: 530-233-4143
Founded: N/A
Scope: Regional

UNITED STATES DEPARTMENT OF THE INTERIOR
FISH AND WILDLIFE SERVICE
MONOMOY NATIONAL WILDLIFE REFUGE
Wikis Way, Morris Island
Chatham, MA 02633 United States
Phone: 508-945-0594 Fax: 508-945-9559
Founded: N/A
Scope: National

UNITED STATES DEPARTMENT OF THE INTERIOR
FISH AND WILDLIFE SERVICE
MONTEZUMA NATIONAL WILDLIFE REFUGE
3395 Rt. 5/20 East
Seneca Falls, NY 13148 United States
Phone: 315-568-5987 Fax: 315-568-8835
Founded: N/A
Scope: Regional

UNITED STATES DEPARTMENT OF THE INTERIOR
FISH AND WILDLIFE SERVICE
MOOSEHORN NATIONAL WILDLIFE REFUGE
R.R. 1, Box 202, Suite 1
Baring, ME 04694 United States
Phone: 207-454-7161 Fax: 207-454-2550
Founded: N/A
Scope: National

UNITED STATES DEPARTMENT OF THE INTERIOR
FISH AND WILDLIFE SERVICE
MORRIS WETLAND MANAGEMENT DISTRICT
43875 230th St.
Morris, MN 56267 United States
Phone: 320-589-1001 Fax: 320-589-2624
Website: midwest.fws.gov/Morris/
Founded: N/A
Scope: National
Description: A part of the Fish and Wildlife Service's Refuge division devoted to migratory bird and habitat conservation.
Keyword(s): Agriculture/Farming, Ecosystems (precious), Land Issues, Public Lands/Greenspace, Recreation/Ecotourism, Water Habitats & Quality, Wildlife & Species
Contact(s):
Steve Delehanty, Manager; 320-589-4961; Fax: 320-589-2624; steve_delehanty@fws.gov
Rodney Ahrndt, Maintenance; 320-589-4967; Fax: 320-589-2624; rodney_ahrndt@fws.gov
Victor Gades, Maintenance; 320-589-4966; Fax: 320-589-2624; victor_gades@fws.gov
Deb Gaunitz, Assistant Manager; 320-589-4962; Fax: 320-589-2624; debbie_gaunitz@fws.gov
Darrell Haugen, Wildlife Biologist; 320-589-4963; Fax: 320-589-2624; darrell_haugen@fws.gov
Wayne Henderson, Wildlife Biologist; 320-589-4964; Fax: 320-589-2624; wayne_henderson@fws.gov
Katie Kramer, Refuge Operations Specialist; 320-589-4971; Fax: 320-589-2624; katie_kramer@fws.gov
Don Lantz, Prescribe Fire Specialist; 320-589-4972; Fax: 320-589-2624; donald_lantz@fws.gov
Kenton Moos, Refuge Operations Specialist; 320-589-4970; Fax: 320-589-2624; kenton_moos@fws.gov
Donna Oglesby, Biological Technician; 320-589-4965; Fax: 320-589-2624; donna_oglesby@fws.gov
Karen Stettner, Administrative Technician; 320-589-1001; Fax: 320-589-2624; karen_stetner@fws.gov
Sara Vacek, Wildlife Biologist; 320-589-4973; Fax: 320-589-2624; sara_vacek@fws.gov
Michelle Zastrow, Biological Technician; 320-589-4976; Fax: 320-589-2624; michelle_zastrow@fws.gov

UNITED STATES DEPARTMENT OF THE INTERIOR
FISH AND WILDLIFE SERVICE
MOUNTAIN-PRAIRIE REGIONAL OFFICE 6
134 Union Blvd., P.O. Box 25486
Denver, CO 80225 United States
Phone: 303-236-7920 Fax: 303-236-8295
Website: www.fws.gov
Founded: N/A
Scope: Regional
Contact(s):
Ralph Morgenweck, Regional Director; 303-236-7920; Fax: 303-236-8295

UNITED STATES DEPARTMENT OF THE INTERIOR
FISH AND WILDLIFE SERVICE
MULESHOE/GRULLA NATIONAL WILDLIFE REFUGE
P.O. Box 549
Muleshoe, TX 79347 United States
Phone: 806-946-3341 Fax: 806-946-3317
Founded: N/A
Scope: Regional

UNITED STATES DEPARTMENT OF THE INTERIOR
FISH AND WILDLIFE SERVICE
MUSCATATUCK NATIONAL WILDLIFE REFUGE
12985 E. U.S. Hwy. 50
Seymour, IN 47274 United States
Phone: 812-522-4352 Fax: 812-522-6826
Founded: N/A
Scope: Regional

UNITED STATES DEPARTMENT OF THE INTERIOR
FISH AND WILDLIFE SERVICE
NATIONAL BISON RANGE NATIONAL WILDLIFE REFUGE
132 Bison Range Rd.
Moiese, MT 59824 United States
Phone: 406-644-2211 Fax: 406-644-2661
Founded: N/A
Scope: Regional

UNITED STATES DEPARTMENT OF THE INTERIOR
FISH AND WILDLIFE SERVICE
NATIONAL CONSERVATION TRAINING CENTER
Rt. 1 Box 166
Shepherdstown, WV 25443 United States
Phone: 304-876-1600 Fax: 304-876-7227
Website: www.fws.gov

Founded: N/A
Membership: 1–100
Scope: National
Description: The mission of the Center is to advance conservation of fish, wildlife, and their habitats through leadership in conservation education for the public, training for the conservation and resource management community, and fostering alliances among diverse interests.
Contact(s):
John Lemon, Director; 304-876-7263
Todd Jones, Chief, Division of Training; 304-876-7431
Mona Womack, Deputy Director; 304-876-7263

UNITED STATES DEPARTMENT OF THE INTERIOR
FISH AND WILDLIFE SERVICE
NATIONAL ELK NATIONAL WILDLIFE REFUGE
675 E. Broadway, P.O. Box 510
Jackson, WY 83001 United States
Phone: 307-733-9212 Fax: 307-733-9729

Founded: N/A
Scope: Regional

UNITED STATES DEPARTMENT OF THE INTERIOR
FISH AND WILDLIFE SERVICE
NATIONAL FISH AND WILDLIFE FORENSICS LABORATORY
1490 East Main St.
Ashland, OR 97520 United States
Phone: 541-482-4191 Fax: 541-482-4989
Website: www.labs.fws.gov

Founded: N/A
Description: The mission of the Laboratory is to provide forensic crime lab support for wildlife law enforcement investigations at the federal, state, and international levels.
Contact(s):
Ken Goddard, Director

UNITED STATES DEPARTMENT OF THE INTERIOR
FISH AND WILDLIFE SERVICE
NATIONAL KEY DEER WILDLIFE REFUGE
P.O. Box 43510
Big Pine Key, FL 33043-0510 United States
Phone: 305-872-0774 Fax: 305-872-2154
E-mail: fw4rwkeydeer@fws.gov
Website: nationalkeydeer.fws.gov/index.html

Founded: 1957
Membership: N/A
Scope: Local, State, Regional
Description: National Wildlife Refuge established to protect the endangered Key deer in the Florida Keys

UNITED STATES DEPARTMENT OF THE INTERIOR
FISH AND WILDLIFE SERVICE
NATIONAL WILDLIFE REFUGE SYSTEM
REGION 1 OFFICE
911 NE 11th Ave., Eastside Federal Complex
Portland, OR 97232-4181 United States
Phone: 503-231-6214 Fax: 503-231-2364

Founded: N/A
Scope: National

UNITED STATES DEPARTMENT OF THE INTERIOR
FISH AND WILDLIFE SERVICE
NATIONAL WILDLIFE REFUGE SYSTEM
REGION 2 OFFICE
500 Gold Avenue
Albuquerque, NM 87102 United States
Phone: 505-248-6911 Fax: 505-248-6803

Founded: N/A
Scope: National

UNITED STATES DEPARTMENT OF THE INTERIOR
FISH AND WILDLIFE SERVICE
NATIONAL WILDLIFE REFUGE SYSTEM
REGION 3 OFFICE
1 Federal Dr., Federal Bldg.
Fort Snelling, MN 55111-4056 United States
Phone: 612-713-5401 Fax: 612-713-5288

Founded: N/A
Scope: National

UNITED STATES DEPARTMENT OF THE INTERIOR
FISH AND WILDLIFE SERVICE
NATIONAL WILDLIFE REFUGE SYSTEM
REGION 4 OFFICE
1875 Century Blvd., NE, Rm. 324
Atlanta, GA 30345 United States
Phone: 404-679-7166 Fax: 404-679-7081
Website: southeast.fws.gov/index.html

Founded: N/A
Scope: National

UNITED STATES DEPARTMENT OF THE INTERIOR
FISH AND WILDLIFE SERVICE
NATIONAL WILDLIFE REFUGE SYSTEM
REGION 5 OFFICE
300 Westgate Center Dr.
Hadley, MA 01035-9589 United States
Phone: 413-253-8306 Fax: 413-253-8309
Website: ortheast.fws.gov/index.html

Founded: N/A
Scope: National

UNITED STATES DEPARTMENT OF THE INTERIOR
FISH AND WILDLIFE SERVICE
NATIONAL WILDLIFE REFUGE SYSTEM
REGION 6 OFFICE
134 Union Blvd.
Lakewood, CO 80228 United States
Phone: 303-236-8145 Fax: 303-236-4792

Founded: N/A
Scope: National

UNITED STATES DEPARTMENT OF THE INTERIOR
FISH AND WILDLIFE SERVICE
NATIONAL WILDLIFE REFUGE SYSTEM
REGION 7 OFFICE
1011 E. Tudor Rd.
Anchorage, AK 99503 United States
Phone: 907-786-3545 Fax: 907-786-3640

Founded: N/A
Scope: National

UNITED STATES DEPARTMENT OF THE INTERIOR
FISH AND WILDLIFE SERVICE
NEAL SMITH NATIONAL WILDLIFE REFUGE
P.O. Box 399
Prairie City, IA 50228 United States
Phone: 515-994-3400 Fax: 515-944-3459
Website: tallgrass.org

Founded: 1990
Membership: N/A
Scope: Local, State, Regional, National
Description: Neal Smith National Wildlife Refuge/Prairie Learning Center involved in tallgrass prairie reconstruction and restoration; environmental education facility; interpretation; research and monitoring; private lands assistance.

UNITED STATES DEPARTMENT OF THE INTERIOR
FISH AND WILDLIFE SERVICE
NECEDAH NATIONAL WILDLIFE REFUGE
W7996 20th Street West
Necedah, WI 54646-7531 United States
Phone: 608-565-2551 Fax: 608-565-3160
E-mail: larry_wargowsky@fws.gov
Website: midwest.fws.gov/Necedah/

Founded: 1937
Scope: Regional
Description: Necedah National Wildlife Refuge consists of nearly 44,000 acres in central Wisconsin. The refuge is home to more than 220 bird species, the southernmost pack of gray/timber wolves, the endangered Karner Blue butterfly, and many more. The refuge also hosts the training of whooping crane chicks as part of the Whooping Crane Reintroduction Project.
Keyword(s): Ecosystems (precious), Forests/Forestry, Land Issues, Public Lands/Greenspace, Recreation/Ecotourism, Water Habitats & Quality, Wildlife & Species

UNITED STATES DEPARTMENT OF THE INTERIOR
FISH AND WILDLIFE SERVICE
NISQUALLY/GRAYS HARBOR NATIONAL WILDLIFE REFUGE
100 Brown Farm Rd.
Olympia, WA 98516-2302 United States
Phone: 360-753-9467 Fax: 360-534-9302
Website: nisqually.r1.fws.gov

Founded: N/A
Scope: Regional
Description: National Wildlife Refuge

UNITED STATES DEPARTMENT OF THE INTERIOR
FISH AND WILDLIFE SERVICE
NORTHEAST REGION (CT, DE, ME, MD, MA, NH, NJ, NY, PA, RI, VT, VA, WV)
300 Westgate Center Drive
Hadley, MA 01035-9589 United States
Phone: 413-253-8200 Fax: 413-253-8308
Website: northeast.fws.gov

Founded: N/A
Membership: N/A
Scope: Local, State, Regional, National, International
Description: Our mission is working with others to conserve, protect, and enhance fish, wildlife, and plants and their habitats for the continuing benefit of the American people.
Contact(s):
Richard Bennett, Deputy Regional Director
Mamie Parker, Regional Director

UNITED STATES DEPARTMENT OF THE INTERIOR
FISH AND WILDLIFE SERVICE
NORTHEAST REGIONAL OFFICE 5
300 Westgate Center Dr.
Hadley, MA 01035 United States
Phone: 413-253-8200 Fax: 413-253-8482
Website: www.fws.gov

Founded: N/A
Membership: 101–1,000
Scope: Regional
Contact(s):
Mamie Parker, Regional Director; 413-253-8300

UNITED STATES DEPARTMENT OF THE INTERIOR
FISH AND WILDLIFE SERVICE
NORTH LOUISIANA COMPLEX NATIONAL WILDLIFE REFUGE
11372 Hwy. 143
Farmerville, LA 71241 United States
Phone: 318-726-4222 Fax: 318-726-4667

Founded: N/A
Scope: National

UNITED STATES DEPARTMENT OF THE INTERIOR
FISH AND WILDLIFE SERVICE
NOWITNA/KOYUKUK NATIONAL WILDLIFE REFUGE
P.O. Box 287
Galena, AK 99741 United States
Phone: 907-656-1231 Fax: 907-656-1708

Founded: N/A
Scope: Regional

UNITED STATES DEPARTMENT OF THE INTERIOR
FISH AND WILDLIFE SERVICE
NOXUBEE NATIONAL WILDLIFE REFUGE
Rt. 1, Box 142
Brooksville, MS 39739 United States
Phone: 601-323-5548 Fax: 601-323-5806
Website: noxubee.fws.gov/

Founded: N/A
Scope: Regional

UNITED STATES DEPARTMENT OF THE INTERIOR
FISH AND WILDLIFE SERVICE
OAHU NATIONAL WILDLIFE REFUGE COMPLEX
66-590 Kamehameha Hwy., Rm. 2C/D
Haleiwa, HI 96712 United States
Phone: 808-637-6330 Fax: 808-637-3578

Founded: N/A
Membership: N/A
Scope: Regional
Description: Part of the national refuge lands system under the Departatment of the Interior.

UNITED STATES DEPARTMENT OF THE INTERIOR
FISH AND WILDLIFE SERVICE
OHIO RIVER ISLANDS NATIONAL WILDLIFE REFUGE
P.O. Box 1811
Parkersburg, WV 26102-1811 United States
Phone: 304-422-0752 Fax: 304-422-0754

Founded: N/A

Scope: Regional

UNITED STATES DEPARTMENT OF THE INTERIOR

FISH AND WILDLIFE SERVICE
OKEFENOKEE (BANKS LAKE) NATIONAL WILDLIFE REFUGE
Rt. 2, Box 3330
Folkston, GA 31537 United States
Phone: 912-496-7366 Fax: 912-496-3332

Founded: N/A

Scope: Regional

UNITED STATES DEPARTMENT OF THE INTERIOR

FISH AND WILDLIFE SERVICE
OREGON COAST NATIONAL WILDLIFE REFUGE COMPLEX
2127 SE OSU Dr.
Newport, OR 97365-5258 United States
Phone: 541-867-4550 Fax: 541-867-4551

Founded: N/A

Scope: Regional

UNITED STATES DEPARTMENT OF THE INTERIOR

FISH AND WILDLIFE SERVICE
OTTAWA NATIONAL WILDLIFE REFUGE
14000 W. State, Rt. 2
Oak Harbor, OH 43449 United States
Phone: 419-898-0014 Fax: 419-898-7895

Founded: N/A

Scope: Regional

UNITED STATES DEPARTMENT OF THE INTERIOR

FISH AND WILDLIFE SERVICE
OURAY NATIONAL WILDLIFE REFUGE
HC 69 Box 232
Randlett, UT 84063 United States
Phone: 435-545-2522 Fax: 435-545-2369
E-mail: r6rw_ory@fws.gov
Website: http://mountain-prairie.fws.gov/ouray/

Founded: N/A

Scope: Regional

UNITED STATES DEPARTMENT OF THE INTERIOR

FISH AND WILDLIFE SERVICE
OVERFLOW NATIONAL WILDLIFE REFUGE
c/o Felsenthal NWR, P.O. Box 1157
Crossett, AR 71635 United States
Phone: 870-364-3167 Fax: 870-364-3757

Founded: N/A

Scope: Regional

UNITED STATES DEPARTMENT OF THE INTERIOR

FISH AND WILDLIFE SERVICE
OXFORD SLOUGH WPA NATIONAL WILDLIFE REFUGE COMPLEX
4428 Burley Drive
Chussack, ID 83202 United States
Phone: 208-237-6616 Fax: 208-237-6617

Founded: N/A

Scope: Regional

UNITED STATES DEPARTMENT OF THE INTERIOR

FISH AND WILDLIFE SERVICE
PACIFIC REGIONAL OFFICE 1
911 North East 11th Avenue
Portland, OR 97232-4181 United States
Phone: 503-231-6828

Founded: N/A

Scope: Regional

Description: The Pacific Region of USFWS includes the states of California, Hawaii, Idaho, Nevada, Oregon, Washington and the U.S. Trust Territories in the Pacific Ocean, and spans 9 time zones. Approximately half the country's threatened and endangered species are found in the Pacific Region. The Region employs approximately 2,100 people at 105 field stations (as of April, 2002).

Publication(s): Endangered Species Information, Brochures and Fact Sheets

Keyword(s): Ecosystems (precious), Land Issues, Oceans/Coasts/Beaches, Public Lands/Greenspace, Recreation/Ecotourism, Water Habitats & Quality, Wildlife & Species

Contact(s):

Anne Badgley, Regional Director; 503-231-6118; Fax: 503-231-2716
Cynthia Barry, Assistant Regional Director - Ecological; 503-231-6151; Fax: 503-231-2240
Carolyn Bohan, Regional Chief, National Wildlife Refuge System; 503-231-6214; Fax: 503-231-6837
Daniel Diggs, Assistant Regional Director - Fisheries; 503-872-2763; Fax: 503-231-2062
Rowan Gould, Deputy Regional Director; 503-231-6122; Fax: 503-231-2716
David Patte/ Joan Jewett, Acting Assistant Regional Director - External Affairs; 503-231-6120; Fax: 503-231-2122
Benito Perez, Assistant Regional Director - Law Enforcement; 503-231-6125; Fax: 503-231-6197
Steve Thompson, California/Nevada Operations Manager; 2800 Cottage Way, Room W-2606, Sacramento, CA 95825; 916-414-6464; Fax: 916-414-6486
Don Weathers, Assistant Regional Director - Budget & Administration; 503-231-6115; Fax: 503-231-2811
David Wesley, Assistant Regional Director - Migratory Birds, State Programs; 503-231-6159; Fax: 503-231-2019
Paul Henson, Pacific Islands Field Supervisor; 300 Ala Moana Blvd., Box 50088, Honolulu, HI 96850; 808-541-3441; Fax: 808-541-3470

UNITED STATES DEPARTMENT OF THE INTERIOR

FISH AND WILDLIFE SERVICE
PACIFIC/REMOTE ISLANDS COMPLEX (HAWAIIAN ISLANDS, BAKER ISLAND, HOWLAND ISLAND, JARVIS ISLAND, ROSE ATOLL) NATIONAL WILDLIFE REFUGE
P.O. Box 50167
Honolulu, HI 96850-5167 United States
Phone: 808-541-1201 Fax: 808-541-1216

Founded: N/A

Scope: Regional

UNITED STATES DEPARTMENT OF THE INTERIOR

FISH AND WILDLIFE SERVICE
PAHRANAGAT NATIONAL WILDLIFE REFUGE
Box 510
Almo, NV 89001 United States
Phone: 725-725-3417 Fax: 725-725-3389

Founded: N/A

Scope: Regional

UNITED STATES DEPARTMENT OF THE INTERIOR
FISH AND WILDLIFE SERVICE
PANTHER SWAMP NATIONAL WILDLIFE REFUGE
13695 River Rd.
Yazoo City, MS 39194 United States
Phone: 662-746-5060 Fax: 662-839-2619

Founded: N/A

Scope: National

UNITED STATES DEPARTMENT OF THE INTERIOR
FISH AND WILDLIFE SERVICE
PARKER RIVER/THATCHER ISLAND NATIONAL WILDLIFE REFUGE
161 Northern Blvd., Plum Island
Newburyport, MA 01950 United States
Phone: 508-465-5753 Fax: 508-465-2807

Founded: N/A

Scope: National

UNITED STATES DEPARTMENT OF THE INTERIOR
FISH AND WILDLIFE SERVICE
PATOKA RIVER NATIONAL WETLANDS PROJECT NATIONAL WILDLIFE REFUGE
P.O. Box 217
510 1/2 West Morton Street
Oakland City, IN 47660 United States
Phone: 812-749-3199 Fax: 812-749-3059
E-mail: bill_mccoy@fws.gov

Founded: 1994
Membership: N/A
Scope: Local, State, Regional
Description: National Wildlife Refuge - 5131 acres purchased out of 22,089 authorized. River bottom project.
Keyword(s): Forests/Forestry, Land Issues, Pollution (general), Public Lands/Greenspace, Recreation/Ecotourism, Water Habitats & Quality, Wildlife & Species

UNITED STATES DEPARTMENT OF THE INTERIOR
FISH AND WILDLIFE SERVICE
PATUXENT RESEARCH REFUGE
NATIONAL WILDLIFE VISITOR CENTER
10901 Scarlet Tanager Loop
Laurel, MD 20708-4027 United States
Phone: 301-497-5760 Fax: 301-497-5765
Website: patuxent.fws.gov

Founded: 1936
Membership: N/A
Scope: Local, State, Regional, National, International
Description: National Wildlife Visitor Center has interactive exhibits featuring natural areas and endangered species found throughout the United States. Seasonal tram tours are available for a nominal fee.
Keyword(s): Recreation/Ecotourism, Wildlife & Species

Contact(s):
Brad Knudsen, Refuge Manager

UNITED STATES DEPARTMENT OF THE INTERIOR
FISH AND WILDLIFE SERVICE
PEE DEE NATIONAL WILDLIFE REFUGE
Rt.1, Box 92
Wadesboro, NC 28170 United States
Phone: 704-694-4424 Fax: 704-694-6570
Website: peedee.fws.gov/index.html

Founded: N/A
Scope: Regional
Description: Wildlife Refuge

UNITED STATES DEPARTMENT OF THE INTERIOR
FISH AND WILDLIFE SERVICE
PELICAN ISLAND NATIONAL WILDLIFE REFUGE
1339 20th Street
Vero Beach, FL 32960 United States
Phone: 772-562-3909 Fax: 772-299-3101
E-mail: fw4_rw_pelican_island@fws.gov
Website: pelicanisland.fws.gov

Founded: 1903
Membership: N/A
Scope: National
Description: America's first National Wildlife Refuge. A 5.5 acre mangrove island in Florida's Indian River Lagoon, established as a preserve and breeding ground for native birds in 1903 by President Theodore Roosevelt. This was the birth of the National Wildlife Refuge System, which today encompasses 538 refuges on over 94 million acres.
Keyword(s): Public Lands/Greenspace, Wildlife & Species

UNITED STATES DEPARTMENT OF THE INTERIOR
FISH AND WILDLIFE SERVICE
PETIT MANAN NATIONAL WILDLIFE REFUGE
P.O. Box 279
Millbridge, ME 04658 United States
Phone: 207-546-2124 Fax: 207-546-7805

Founded: N/A

Scope: National

UNITED STATES DEPARTMENT OF THE INTERIOR
FISH AND WILDLIFE SERVICE
PIEDMONT AND BOND SWAMP NATIONAL WILDLIFE REFUGES
718 Juliette Rd.
Round Oak, GA 31038 United States
Phone: 478-986-5441 Fax: 478-986-9646
E-mail: piedmont@fws.gov
Website: piedmont.fws.gov

Founded: N/A

Scope: Regional
Description: Piedmont National Wildlife Refuge consists of 35,000 acres of beautiful forest. It boasts loblolly pine ridges and hardwoods situated along creek bottoms. Clear streams and green fields are abundant. Bond Swamp NWR consists of 6,500 acres situated along the Fall Line separating the Piedmont from the coastal plain. It hosts a great diversity of habitat types ranging from mixed hardwood/pine ridges to bottomland hardwoods and swamp forests with creeks, beaver swamps and oxbow lakes.
Publication(s): Piedmont and Bond Swamp Bird Lists
Keyword(s): Ecosystems (precious), Recreation/Ecotourism, Wildlife & Species

Contact(s):
Ronnie Shell, Refuge Manager

UNITED STATES DEPARTMENT OF THE INTERIOR
FISH AND WILDLIFE SERVICE
PIERCE NATIONAL WILDLIFE REFUGE
Columbia River Gorge Refuges, 36062 SR 14
Stevenson, WA 98648-9541 United States
Phone: 509-427-5208 Fax: 509-427-4707

Founded: N/A

Scope: Regional

UNITED STATES DEPARTMENT OF THE INTERIOR
FISH AND WILDLIFE SERVICE
POCOSIN LAKES NATIONAL WILDLIFE REFUGE
205 South Ludington Drive
P.O. Box 329
Columbia, NC 27925 United States
Phone: 252-796-3004 Fax: 252-796-3010
E-mail: fw4_rw_pocosin_lakes@fws.gov
Website: /pocosinlakes.fws.gov/
Founded: N/A
Scope: Local
Description: National Wildlife Refuge

UNITED STATES DEPARTMENT OF THE INTERIOR
FISH AND WILDLIFE SERVICE
POND CREEK NATIONAL WILDLIFE REFUGE
c/o Felsenthal NWR, P.O. Box 1157
Crossett, AR 71635 United States
Phone: 870-364-3167 Fax: 870-364-3757
Founded: N/A
Scope: Regional

UNITED STATES DEPARTMENT OF THE INTERIOR
FISH AND WILDLIFE SERVICE
POTOMAC RIVER COMPLEX NATIONAL WILDLIFE REFUGE
14344 Jefferson Davis Hwy.
Woodbridge, VA 22191 United States
Phone: 703-490-4979 Fax: 703-490-5631
Founded: N/A
Scope: Regional

UNITED STATES DEPARTMENT OF THE INTERIOR
FISH AND WILDLIFE SERVICE
PRIME HOOK NATIONAL WILDLIFE REFUGE
R.D. 3, Box 195
Milton, DE 19968 United States
Phone: 302-684-8419 Fax: 302-684-8504
Founded: N/A
Scope: Regional

UNITED STATES DEPARTMENT OF THE INTERIOR
FISH AND WILDLIFE SERVICE
QUIVIRA NATIONAL WILDLIFE REFUGE
R.R. 3, Box 48A
Stafford, KS 67530 United States
Phone: 316-486-2393 Fax: 316-486-2394
Founded: N/A
Scope: Regional

UNITED STATES DEPARTMENT OF THE INTERIOR
FISH AND WILDLIFE SERVICE
RACHEL CARSON NATIONAL WILDLIFE REFUGE
Box 751
Wells, ME 04090 United States
Phone: 207-646-9226 Fax: 207-646-6554
Founded: N/A
Scope: National

UNITED STATES DEPARTMENT OF THE INTERIOR
FISH AND WILDLIFE SERVICE
RAINWATER BASIN WMD NATIONAL WILDLIFE REFUGE
P.O. Box 1686
Kearney, NE 68848 United States
Phone: 308-236-5015, ext. 27 Fax: 308-236-3899
E-mail: rainwater@fws.gov
Website: rainwater.fws.gov
Founded: N/A
Scope: Regional
Description: Rainwater Basin Wetland Management District is responsible for the management of 24,000 acres scattered over 62 tracts of land. Each tract contains a large wetland used for staging waterfowl and shorebirds. Each spring over 10 million birds use these areas.
Keyword(s): Water Habitats & Quality, Wildlife & Species
Contact(s):
Gene Mack, Project Leader; 308-236-5015, ext. 27; Fax: 308-236-3899; gene_mack@fws.gov

UNITED STATES DEPARTMENT OF THE INTERIOR
FISH AND WILDLIFE SERVICE
RAPPAHANNOCK RIVER VALLEY NATIONAL WILDLIFE REFUGE
P.O. Box 189
Prince George, VA 23875 United States
Phone: 804-733-8042
Founded: N/A
Scope: Regional

UNITED STATES DEPARTMENT OF THE INTERIOR
FISH AND WILDLIFE SERVICE
RED ROCK LAKES NATIONAL WILDLIFE REFUGE
27820 Southside Centennial Road
Lima, MT 59739 United States
Phone: 406-276-3536 Fax: 406-276-3538
E-mail: redrocks@fws.gov
Founded: N/A
Scope: Regional

UNITED STATES DEPARTMENT OF THE INTERIOR
FISH AND WILDLIFE SERVICE
REELFOOT NATIONAL WILDLIFE REFUGE
Fed. Bldg. Rm. 201, 309 N. Church St.
Dyersburg, TN 38024 United States
Phone: 731-287-0650 Fax: 731-286-0468
Founded: N/A
Scope: Regional

UNITED STATES DEPARTMENT OF THE INTERIOR
FISH AND WILDLIFE SERVICE
RHODE ISLAND NATIONAL WILDLIFE REFUGE COMPLEX
3769 Old Post Road
P.0. Box 307
Charlestown, RI 02813 United States
Phone: 401-364-9124 Fax: 401-364-0170
Founded: N/A
Scope: Regional

UNITED STATES DEPARTMENT OF THE INTERIOR

FISH AND WILDLIFE SERVICE
RICE LAKE NATIONAL WILDLIFE REFUGE
36289 State Hwy. 65
McGregor, MN 55760 United States
Phone: 218-768-2402 Fax: 218-768-3040
E-mail: Mary_Stefanski@fws.gov
Website: midwest.fws.gov/ricelake/

Founded: 1935

Scope: National

Description: One of over 540 National Wildlife Refuges in the country. Rice Lake has over 18,000 acres of bog, forest and grassland open to the public.

Contact(s):
- Mary Stefanski, Refuge Manager; 218-768-2402; Fax: 218-768-3040; Mary_Stefanski@fws.gov
- John Francis, Refuge Operations Specialist; 218-768-2402; Fax: 218-768-3040; John_Francis@fws.gov
- Dean Huhta, Maintenance Mechanic; 218-768-7028; Fax: 218-768-3040; Dean_Huhta@fws.gov
- Duane King, Biological Technician - Fire; 218-768-2402; Fax: 218-768-3040; Duane_King@fws.gov
- Sharon Young, Administrative Technician; 218-768-2402; Fax: 218-768-3040; Sharon_Young@fws.gov

UNITED STATES DEPARTMENT OF THE INTERIOR

FISH AND WILDLIFE SERVICE
RIDGEFIELD NATIONAL WILDLIFE REFUGE
P.O. Box 1022
Ridgefield, WA 98642-0457 United States
Phone: 360-887-9495 Fax: 360-887-4109

Founded: N/A

Scope: Regional

Contact(s):
- Liza Halpenny, EE Coordinator

UNITED STATES DEPARTMENT OF THE INTERIOR

FISH AND WILDLIFE SERVICE
ROANOKE RIVER NATIONAL WILDLIFE REFUGE
P.O. Box 430
Windsor, NC 27983 United States
Phone: 919-794-5326 Fax: 919-794-5338
E-mail: sherrie_jager@fws.gov
Website: roanokeriver.fws.gov/index.html

Founded: 1989

Scope: Local, State

Description: Department of the Interior, Fish & Wildlife Service Roanoke River National Wildlife Refuge

Keyword(s): Ecosystems (precious), Forests/Forestry, Land Issues, Public Lands/Greenspace, Reduce/Reuse/Recycle, Wildlife & Species

Contact(s):
- Jerry Holloman, Refuge Manager; 252-794-3808, ext. 26; jerry_holloman@fws.gov
- Mike Canada, Assistant Refuge Manager; 252-794-3808, ext. 24; mike_canada@fws.gov
- Sherrie Jager, Office Assistant; 252-794-3808, ext. 21; sherrie_jager@fws.gov
- Jean Richter, Fish & Wildlife Biologist; 252-794-3808, ext. 22; jean_richter@fws.gov
- Doak Wilkins, Engineering Equipment Operator; 252-794-5755; doak_wilkins@fws.gov

UNITED STATES DEPARTMENT OF THE INTERIOR

FISH AND WILDLIFE SERVICE
ROCKY MOUNTAIN ARSENAL NATIONAL WILDLIFE REFUGE
USF&WS, Bldg. 111
Commerce City, CO 80022-1748 United States
Phone: 303-289-0232 Fax: 303-289-0579

Founded: N/A

Scope: Regional

UNITED STATES DEPARTMENT OF THE INTERIOR

FISH AND WILDLIFE SERVICE
RUBY LAKE NATIONAL WILDLIFE REFUGE
HC 60, Box 860
Ruby Valley, NV 89833 United States
Phone: 775-779-2237 Fax: 775-779-2370

Founded: N/A

Scope: Regional

Contact(s):
- Martha Collins, Office Manager; 775-779-2237; marti_collins@fws.gov

UNITED STATES DEPARTMENT OF THE INTERIOR

FISH AND WILDLIFE SERVICE
SABINE NATIONAL WILDLIFE REFUGE
3000 Holly Beach Hwy
Hackberry, LA 70645 United States
Phone: 337-762-3816 Fax: 337-762-3780

Founded: N/A

Scope: National

UNITED STATES DEPARTMENT OF THE INTERIOR

FISH AND WILDLIFE SERVICE
SACRAMENTO NATIONAL WILDLIFE REFUGE
752 County Rd. 99W
Willows, CA 95988 United States
Phone: 530-934-2801 Fax: 530-934-7814
Website: sacramentovalleyrefuges.fws.gov

Founded: N/A

Scope: Regional

Description: Administered by the U.S. Fish and Wildlife Service, the Sacramento National Wildlife Refuge is located in the Sacramento Valley of north central California

UNITED STATES DEPARTMENT OF THE INTERIOR

FISH AND WILDLIFE SERVICE
SALT PLAINS NATIONAL WILDLIFE REFUGE
Rt. 1, Box 76
Jet, OK 73749 United States
Phone: 580-626-4794 Fax: 580-626-4793

Founded: N/A

Scope: Regional

UNITED STATES DEPARTMENT OF THE INTERIOR

FISH AND WILDLIFE SERVICE
SAN ANDRES NATIONAL WILDLIFE REFUGE
P.O. Box 756
Las Cruces, NM 88004 United States
Phone: 505-382-5047 Fax: 505-382-5454

Founded: N/A

Scope: Regional

UNITED STATES DEPARTMENT OF THE INTERIOR
FISH AND WILDLIFE SERVICE
SAN BERNARDINO/LESLIE CANYON NATIONAL WILDLIFE REFUGE
P.O. Box 3509
Douglas, AZ 85607 United States
Phone: 520-364-2104 Fax: 520-364-2130
Website: southwest.fws.gov/refuges/arizona/sanb.html
Founded: N/A
Scope: Regional

UNITED STATES DEPARTMENT OF THE INTERIOR
FISH AND WILDLIFE SERVICE
SAN FRANCISCO BAY NATIONAL WILDLIFE REFUGE
P.O. Box 524
Newark, CA 94560 United States
Phone: 510-792-0222 Fax: 510-792-5828
Founded: N/A
Scope: Regional

UNITED STATES DEPARTMENT OF THE INTERIOR
FISH AND WILDLIFE SERVICE
SAN LUIS NATIONAL WILDLIFE REFUGE COMPLEX
P.O. Box 2176
Los Banos, CA 93635-2176 United States
Phone: 209-826-3508 Fax: 209-826-1445
Website: sanluis.fws.gov/
Founded: N/A
Scope: Regional

UNITED STATES DEPARTMENT OF THE INTERIOR
FISH AND WILDLIFE SERVICE
SAND LAKE NATIONAL WILDLIFE REFUGE
39650 Sand Lake Dr.
Columbia, SD 57433 United States
Phone: 605-885-6320 Fax: 605-885-6401
E-mail: r6rw_sdl@fws.gov
Website: sandlake.fws.gov
Founded: 1935
Membership: N/A
Scope: Regional, National, International
Description: National Wildlife Refuge totalling 21,500 acres located in northeastern South Dakota.

UNITED STATES DEPARTMENT OF THE INTERIOR
FISH AND WILDLIFE SERVICE
SANDY POINT NATIONAL WILDLIFE REFUGE
3013 Estate Golden Rock, Ste. 167
Christiansted, VI 00820-4355 United States
Phone: 340-773-4554
Website: http://southeast.fws.gov/SandyPoint/index.html
Founded: N/A
Scope: Regional

UNITED STATES DEPARTMENT OF THE INTERIOR
FISH AND WILDLIFE SERVICE
SAVANNAH COASTAL REFUGES NATIONAL WILDLIFE REFUGE
1000 Business Center Dr., Ste. 10
Savannah, GA 31405 United States
Phone: 912-652-4415 Fax: 912-652-4385
Founded: N/A
Scope: Regional

UNITED STATES DEPARTMENT OF THE INTERIOR
FISH AND WILDLIFE SERVICE
SEEDSKADEE/COKEVILLE MEADOWS NATIONAL WILDLIFE REFUGE
P.O. Box 700
Green River, WY 82935 United States
Phone: 307-875-2187 Fax: 307-875-4425
Founded: N/A
Scope: Regional

UNITED STATES DEPARTMENT OF THE INTERIOR
FISH AND WILDLIFE SERVICE
SELAWIK NATIONAL WILDLIFE REFUGE
P.O. Box 270
Kotzebue, AK 99752-3799 United States
Phone: 907-442-3799 Fax: 907-442-3124
Founded: N/A
Scope: Regional

UNITED STATES DEPARTMENT OF THE INTERIOR
FISH AND WILDLIFE SERVICE
SENEY NATIONAL WILDLIFE REFUGE
1674 Refuge Entrance Road
Seney, MI 49883 United States
Phone: 906-586-9851 Fax: 906-586-3800
Founded: N/A
Scope: National
Contact(s):
Tracy Casselman, Refuge Manager; 906-586-9851, ext. 11

UNITED STATES DEPARTMENT OF THE INTERIOR
FISH AND WILDLIFE SERVICE
SEQUOYAH/OZARK PLATEAU NATIONAL WILDLIFE REFUGE
Rt. 1, Box 18A
Vian, OK 74962 United States
Phone: 918-773-5251 Fax: 918-773-5598
Founded: N/A
Scope: Regional
Description: Waterfowl
Contact(s):
Craig Heflebower, Biologist; 918-773-5251; Fax: 918-773-5598

UNITED STATES DEPARTMENT OF THE INTERIOR
FISH AND WILDLIFE SERVICE
SEVILLETA NATIONAL WILDLIFE REFUGE
P.O. Box 1248
Socorro, NM 87801 United States
Phone: 505-864-4021 Fax: 505-864-7761
Founded: N/A
Scope: Regional

UNITED STATES DEPARTMENT OF THE INTERIOR
FISH AND WILDLIFE SERVICE
SHELDON/HART MOUNTAIN NATIONAL WILDLIFE REFUGE
P.O. Box 111
Lakeveiw, OR 97630-0107 United States
Phone: 541-947-3315
Founded: N/A
Scope: Regional

UNITED STATES DEPARTMENT OF THE INTERIOR
FISH AND WILDLIFE SERVICE
SHERBURNE/CRANE MEADOWS NATIONAL WILDLIFE REFUGE
17076 293rd Ave.
Zimmerman, MN 55398 United States
Phone: 763-389-3323 Fax: 612-389-3493

Founded: N/A

Scope: National

Contact(s):
Charles Blair, Refuge Manager; 763-398-3323

UNITED STATES DEPARTMENT OF THE INTERIOR
FISH AND WILDLIFE SERVICE
SHIAWASSEE NATIONAL WILDLIFE REFUGE
6975 Mower Rd.
Saginaw, MI 48601 United States
Phone: 517-777-5930 Fax: 517-777-9200

Founded: N/A

Scope: National

UNITED STATES DEPARTMENT OF THE INTERIOR
FISH AND WILDLIFE SERVICE
SILVIO O. CONTE NATIONAL WILDLIFE AND FISH REFUGE
38 Ave. A
Turners Falls, MA 01376 United States
Phone: 413-863-0209 Fax: 413-863-3070

Founded: N/A

Scope: National

UNITED STATES DEPARTMENT OF THE INTERIOR
FISH AND WILDLIFE SERVICE
SONNY BONO SALTON SEA NATIONAL WILDLIFE REFUGE
906 W. Sinclair
Calipatria, CA 92233 United States
Phone: 760-348-5278 Fax: 760-348-7245

Founded: 1930

Scope: Regional

Description: Established in 1930, this 37,600 acre refuge is home to over 400 avian species. It is of great importance to birds of the Pacific Flyway with 95% of California's inland wetlands gone. 90% of the North American population of eared grebes; 30% of the North American breeding population of American white pelicans; 40% of the U.S. population of endangered Yuma clapper rails; 25% of the endangered California brown pelican population reside on the Sea.

UNITED STATES DEPARTMENT OF THE INTERIOR
FISH AND WILDLIFE SERVICE
SOUTHEAST LOUISIANA COMPLEX NATIONAL WILDLIFE REFUGE
1010 Gause Blvd., Bldg. 936
Slidell, LA 70458 United States
Phone: 504-646-7555 Fax: 504-646-7588

Founded: N/A

Scope: National

UNITED STATES DEPARTMENT OF THE INTERIOR
FISH AND WILDLIFE SERVICE
SOUTHEAST REGIONAL OFFICE 4
1875 Century Blvd.
Atlanta, GA 30345 United States
Phone: 404-679-4000 Fax: 404-679-4006
E-mail: fw4_dir@fws.gov
Website: www.fws.gov

Founded: 1903

Membership: 1,001–10,000

Scope: Regional, National

Description: Government agency whose purpose is to preserve and protect habitats and species.

Contact(s):
Sam Hamilton, Regional Director; 404-679-4000; Fax: 404-679-4006; fw4_dir@fws.gov

UNITED STATES DEPARTMENT OF THE INTERIOR
FISH AND WILDLIFE SERVICE
SOUTHWEST REGION
P.O. Box 1306500 Gold Ave SW, Room 8526
Albuquerque, NM 87102 United States
Phone: 505-248-6282 Fax: 505-248-6845

Founded: N/A

UNITED STATES DEPARTMENT OF THE INTERIOR
FISH AND WILDLIFE SERVICE
SOUTHWEST REGIONAL OFFICE 2
P.O. Box 1306
Albuquerque, NM 87103 United States
Phone: 505-248-6911 Fax: 505-248-6915
Website: www.southwest.fws.gov

Founded: N/A

Membership: 101–1,000

Scope: Regional

Contact(s):
Nancy Kaufman, Regional Director; 505-248-6282
Tom Bauer, Assistant Director of External Affairs; 505-248-6911; Fax: 505-248-6915

UNITED STATES DEPARTMENT OF THE INTERIOR
FISH AND WILDLIFE SERVICE
SQUAW CREEK NATIONAL WILDLIFE REFUGE
P.O. Box 158
Mound City, MO 64470 United States
Phone: 660-442-3187 Fax: 660-442-5248
Website: www.squawcreek.org

Founded: 1935

Scope: National

Keyword(s): Ecosystems (precious)

Contact(s):
Ronald Bell, Refuge Manager

UNITED STATES DEPARTMENT OF THE INTERIOR
FISH AND WILDLIFE SERVICE
ST. CATHERINE CREEK NATIONAL WILDLIFE REFUGE
P.O. Box 117
Sibley, MS 39165 United States
Phone: 601-442-6696 Fax: 601-446-8990

Founded: N/A

Scope: Regional

UNITED STATES DEPARTMENT OF THE INTERIOR
FISH AND WILDLIFE SERVICE
ST. CROIX WMD NATIONAL WILDLIFE REFUGE
1764 95th St.
New Richmond, WI 54017 United States
Phone: 715-246-7784 Fax: 715-246-4670
E-mail: chet_mccarty@fws.gov
Founded: N/A
Scope: Regional

UNITED STATES DEPARTMENT OF THE INTERIOR
FISH AND WILDLIFE SERVICE
ST. LAWRENCE NATIONAL WILDLIFE REFUGE
127 N. Water St., C/O U.S. Customs House
Ogdensburg, NY 13669 United States
Phone: 315-393-9002 Fax: 315-393-8570
Founded: N/A
Scope: Regional

UNITED STATES DEPARTMENT OF THE INTERIOR
FISH AND WILDLIFE SERVICE
ST. MARKS NATIONAL WILDLIFE REFUGE
P.O. Box 68
St. Marks, FL 32355 United States
Phone: 850-925-6121 Fax: 850-925-6930
Founded: N/A
Scope: Regional

UNITED STATES DEPARTMENT OF THE INTERIOR
FISH AND WILDLIFE SERVICE
ST. VINCENT NATIONAL WILDLIFE REFUGE
P.O. Box 447
Apalachicola, FL 32329-0447 United States
Phone: 850-653-8808 Fax: 850-653-9893
Founded: N/A
Scope: Regional

UNITED STATES DEPARTMENT OF THE INTERIOR
FISH AND WILDLIFE SERVICE
STILLWATER NATIONAL WILDLIFE REFUGE
P.O. Box 1236
Fallon, NV 89407-1236 United States
Phone: 775-423-5128 Fax: 775-423-0146
Website: stillwater.fws.gov/
Founded: N/A
Scope: Regional

UNITED STATES DEPARTMENT OF THE INTERIOR
FISH AND WILDLIFE SERVICE
STONE LAKES NATIONAL WILDLIFE REFUGE
1624 Hood-Franklin Rd.
Elk Grove, CA 95758-9774 United States
Phone: 916-775-4421 Fax: 916-775-4407
Founded: N/A
Scope: Regional

UNITED STATES DEPARTMENT OF THE INTERIOR
FISH AND WILDLIFE SERVICE
SUNKHAZE MEADOWS NATIONAL WILDLIFE REFUGE/CARLTON POND WATERFOWL PRODUCTION AREA
1033 S. Main St.
Old Town, ME 04468-2023 United States
Phone: 207-827-6138, ext. 17 Fax: 207-827-6099
E-mail: Tom_Comish@fws.gov
Website: www.Sunkhaze.org
Founded: 1966
Membership: 1–100
Scope: National
Description: Two units of the National Wildlife Refuge System
Keyword(s): Recreation/Ecotourism, Wildlife & Species

UNITED STATES DEPARTMENT OF THE INTERIOR
FISH AND WILDLIFE SERVICE
SUPAWNA MEADOWS NATIONAL WILDLIFE REFUGE
197 Lighthouse Rd.
Pennsville, NJ 08070 United States
Phone: 609-935-1487 Fax: 609-935-1198
Website: northeast.fws.gov/nj/spm.htm
Founded: N/A
Scope: Regional

UNITED STATES DEPARTMENT OF THE INTERIOR
FISH AND WILDLIFE SERVICE
SWAN LAKE NATIONAL WILDLIFE REFUGE
Rt. 1, Box 29 A
Sumner, MO 64681 United States
Phone: 660-856-3323 Fax: 660-856-3687
Founded: N/A
Scope: National

UNITED STATES DEPARTMENT OF THE INTERIOR
FISH AND WILDLIFE SERVICE
TAMARAC NATIONAL WILDLIFE REFUGE
35704 County Hwy. 26
Rochert, MN 56578 United States
Phone: 218-847-2641 Fax: 218-847-9141
Founded: N/A
Scope: National
Contact(s):
Jay Johnson, Refuse Manager; 218-847-2641

UNITED STATES DEPARTMENT OF THE INTERIOR
FISH AND WILDLIFE SERVICE
TENNESSEE NATIONAL WILDLIFE REFUGE
3006 Dinkins Ln.
Paris, TN 38242 United States
Phone: 731-642-2091 Fax: 731-644-3351
Founded: N/A
Scope: Regional

UNITED STATES DEPARTMENT OF THE INTERIOR
FISH AND WILDLIFE SERVICE
TENSAS RIVER NATIONAL WILDLIFE REFUGE
Rt. 2, Box 295
Tallulah, LA 71282 United States
Phone: 318-574-2664 Fax: 318-574-1624
Founded: N/A
Scope: National

UNITED STATES DEPARTMENT OF THE INTERIOR
FISH AND WILDLIFE SERVICE
TETLIN NATIONAL WILDLIFE REFUGE
P.O. Box 779
Tok, AK 99780 United States
Phone: 907-883-5312 Fax: 907-883-5747

Founded: N/A

Scope: Regional

UNITED STATES DEPARTMENT OF THE INTERIOR
FISH AND WILDLIFE SERVICE
TEWAUKON NATIONAL WILDLIFE REFUGE
9754 143 1/2 Ave. SE
Cayuga, ND 58013 United States
Phone: 701-724-3598 Fax: 701-724-3683

Founded: N/A

Scope: Regional

UNITED STATES DEPARTMENT OF THE INTERIOR
FISH AND WILDLIFE SERVICE
TISHOMINGO NATIONAL WILDLIFE REFUGE
12000 S. Refuge Rd.
Tishomingo, OK 73460 United States
Phone: 580-371-2402 Fax: 580-371-9312

Founded: N/A

Scope: Regional

UNITED STATES DEPARTMENT OF THE INTERIOR
FISH AND WILDLIFE SERVICE
TOGIAK NATIONAL WILDLIFE REFUGE
P.O. Box 270
Dillingham, AK 99576 United States
Phone: 907-842-1063 Fax: 907-842-5402

Founded: N/A

Scope: Regional

UNITED STATES DEPARTMENT OF THE INTERIOR
FISH AND WILDLIFE SERVICE
TREMPEALEAU NATIONAL WILDLIFE REFUGE
W28488 Refuge Rd.
Trempealeau, WI 54661 United States
Phone: 608-539-2311 Fax: 608-539-2703
E-mail: bob_drieslein@fws.gov

Founded: N/A

Scope: Regional

UNITED STATES DEPARTMENT OF THE INTERIOR
FISH AND WILDLIFE SERVICE
TRINITY RIVER NATIONAL WILDLIFE REFUGE
P.O. Box 10015
Liberty, TX 77575 United States
Phone: 409-336-9786 Fax: 409-336-9847

Founded: N/A

Scope: Regional

UNITED STATES DEPARTMENT OF THE INTERIOR
FISH AND WILDLIFE SERVICE
TUALATIN RIVER NATIONAL WILDLIFE REFUGE
16340 SW Beef Bend Rd.
Sherwood, OR 97140-8306 United States
Phone: 503-590-5811 Fax: 503-590-6702

Founded: N/A

Scope: Regional

UNITED STATES DEPARTMENT OF THE INTERIOR
FISH AND WILDLIFE SERVICE
TURNBULL NATIONAL WILDLIFE REFUGE
26010 S. Smith Rd.
Cheney, WA 99004-9326 United States
Phone: 509-235-4723 Fax: 509-235-4703

Founded: N/A

Scope: Regional

UNITED STATES DEPARTMENT OF THE INTERIOR
FISH AND WILDLIFE SERVICE
TWO PONDS C/O ROCKY MOUNTAIN ARSENAL NATIONAL WILDLIFE REFUGE
USF&WS, Bldg. 111
Commerce City, CO 80022-1748 United States
Phone: 303-289-0232 Fax: 303-289-0579

Founded: N/A

Scope: Regional

UNITED STATES DEPARTMENT OF THE INTERIOR
FISH AND WILDLIFE SERVICE
UNION SLOUGH (IOWA WMD) NATIONAL WILDLIFE REFUGE
1710 360th St.
Titonka, IA 50480 United States
Phone: 515-928-2523 Fax: 515-928-2230

Founded: N/A

Scope: Regional

UNITED STATES DEPARTMENT OF THE INTERIOR
FISH AND WILDLIFE SERVICE
UPPER MISSISSIPPI RIVER
WINONA DISTRICT NATIONAL WILDLIFE REFUGE
51 E. 4th St., Rm. 203
Winona, MN 55987 United States
Phone: 507-452-4232 Fax: 507-452-0851

Founded: N/A

Scope: National

UNITED STATES DEPARTMENT OF THE INTERIOR
FISH AND WILDLIFE SERVICE
UPPER SOURIS NATIONAL WILDLIFE REFUGE
17705 212th Ave., NW
Berthold, ND 58718-9666 United States
Phone: 701-468-5467 Fax: 701-468-5600
E-mail: usr@fws.gov

Founded: 1935

Membership: N/A

Scope: Regional

Description: Upper Souris National Wildlife Refuge lies in the picturesque Souris River Valley of north central North Dakota. The 35 mile long corridor is comprised of steep native prairie-covered hills, brush-covered coulees, and wooded river bottomlands. This 32,084-acre Refuge is managed by the U.S. Fish and Wildlife Service. The Refuge was established by Executive Order on August 27, 1935, "... as a refuge and breeding ground for migratory birds and other wildlife...".

Keyword(s): Wildlife & Species

UNITED STATES DEPARTMENT OF THE INTERIOR

FISH AND WILDLIFE SERVICE
VALLEY CITY WETLAND MANAGEMENT DISTRICT
11515 River Road
Valley City, ND 58072-9619 United States
Phone: 701-845-3466 Fax: 701-845-3482
Website: www.fws.gov

Founded: N/A

Scope: Regional

Description: The Valley City WMD manages Waterfowl Production Areas and Wetland Easements in Barnes, Cass, Griggs, Steele and Trail Counties in Southeast North Dakota.

Contact(s):
Kory Richardson, Staff; 701-845-3466; kory_richardson@fws.gov

UNITED STATES DEPARTMENT OF THE INTERIOR

FISH AND WILDLIFE SERVICE
WALLKILL RIVER NATIONAL WILDLIFE REFUGE
1547 County Rt. 565
Sussex, NJ 07461 United States
Phone: 973-702-7266 Fax: 973-702-7286
E-mail: wallkillriver@fws.gov
Website: wallkillriver.fws.gov

Founded: 1990
Membership: N/A
Scope: Regional

Description: National Wildlife Refuge in Sussex County, New Jersey and Orange County, New York focused on migratory bird protection and management.

Keyword(s): Public Lands/Greenspace, Recreation/Ecotourism, Wildlife & Species

UNITED STATES DEPARTMENT OF THE INTERIOR

FISH AND WILDLIFE SERVICE
WAPANOCCA NATIONAL WILDLIFE REFUGE
P.O. Box 279
Turrell, AR 72384 United States
Phone: 870-343-2595 Fax: 870-343-2416

Founded: N/A

Scope: Regional

Contact(s):
Geln Miller, Refuge Manager; 870-343-2595; Glen_Miller@fws.gov

UNITED STATES DEPARTMENT OF THE INTERIOR

FISH AND WILDLIFE SERVICE
WASHINGTON MARITIME NATIONAL WILDLIFE REFUGE COMPLEX
33 S. Barr Rd.
Port Angeles, WA 98362-9202 United States
Phone: 360-457-8451 Fax: 360-457-9778

Founded: N/A

Scope: National

UNITED STATES DEPARTMENT OF THE INTERIOR

FISH AND WILDLIFE SERVICE
WASHITA/OPTIMA NATIONAL WILDLIFE REFUGE
Rt. 1, Box 68
Butler, OK 73625 United States
Phone: 405-664-2205 Fax: 405-664-2206

Founded: N/A

Scope: Regional

UNITED STATES DEPARTMENT OF THE INTERIOR

FISH AND WILDLIFE SERVICE
WAUBAY WMD NATIONAL WILDLIFE REFUGE
Rural Route 1, P.O. Box 39
Waubay, SD 57273 United States
Phone: 605-947-4521 Fax: 605-947-4524

Founded: N/A

Scope: Regional

UNITED STATES DEPARTMENT OF THE INTERIOR

FISH AND WILDLIFE SERVICE
WESTERN OREGON NATIONAL WILDLIFE REFUGE COMPLEX
26208 Finley Refuge Rd.
Corvallis, OR 97333-9533 United States
Phone: 541-757-7236 Fax: 541-757-4450

Founded: N/A

Scope: Regional

UNITED STATES DEPARTMENT OF THE INTERIOR

FISH AND WILDLIFE SERVICE
WHEELER NATIONAL WILDLIFE REFUGE
2700 Refuge Hq. Rd.
Decatur, AL 35603 United States

Founded: N/A

Scope: Regional

UNITED STATES DEPARTMENT OF THE INTERIOR

FISH AND WILDLIFE SERVICE
WHITE RIVER NATIONAL WILDLIFE REFUGE
P.O. Box 308
DeWitt, AR 72042-0308 United States
Phone: 870-946-1468 Fax: 870-946-2591

Founded: N/A

Scope: Regional

UNITED STATES DEPARTMENT OF THE INTERIOR

FISH AND WILDLIFE SERVICE
WICHITA MOUNTAINS NATIONAL WILDLIFE REFUGE
RR 1, Box 448
Indiahoma, OK 73552 United States
Phone: 580-429-3222 Fax: 580-429-9323

Founded: N/A

Scope: Regional

UNITED STATES DEPARTMENT OF THE INTERIOR

FISH AND WILDLIFE SERVICE
WILLAPA/LEWIS AND CLARK NATIONAL WILDLIFE REFUGE
3888 SR 101
Ilwaco, WA 98624-9707 United States
Phone: 360-484-3482 Fax: 360-484-3109

Founded: N/A
Scope: Regional

UNITED STATES DEPARTMENT OF THE INTERIOR

FISH AND WILDLIFE SERVICE
WINDOM WMD NATIONAL WILDLIFE REFUGE
49663 Tony Rd. 17
Windom, MN 56101-3026 United States
Phone: 507-831-2220 Fax: 507-831-5524

Founded: N/A
Scope: Regional

UNITED STATES DEPARTMENT OF THE INTERIOR

FISH AND WILDLIFE SERVICE
YAZOO NATIONAL WILDLIFE REFUGE
728 Yazoo Refuge Road
Hollandale, MS 38748 United States
Phone: 662-839-2638 Fax: 662-839-2619
E-mail: yazoo@fws.gov
Website: www.fws.gov

Founded: N/A
Scope: Regional
Description: National Wildlife Refuge

UNITED STATES DEPARTMENT OF THE INTERIOR

FISH AND WILDLIFE SERVICE
YUKON DELTA NATIONAL WILDLIFE REFUGE
P.O. Box 346
Bethel, AK 99559-0346 United States
Phone: 907-543-3151 Fax: 907-543-4413

Founded: N/A
Scope: Regional

UNITED STATES DEPARTMENT OF THE INTERIOR

FISH AND WILDLIFE SERVICE
YUKON FLATS NATIONAL WILDLIFE REFUGE
101 12th Ave., Rm. 264
Fairbanks, AK 99701 United States
Phone: 907-456-0440 Fax: 907-456-0447

Founded: N/A
Scope: Regional

UNITED STATES DEPARTMENT OF THE INTERIOR

GREAT PLAINS REGION
P.O. Box 36900
Billings, MT 59107-6900 United States
Phone: 406-247-7610 Fax: 406-247-7393
Website: www.gp.usbr.gov

Founded: N/A
Scope: Regional
Description: Federal water agency
Contact(s):
Maryanne Bach, Regional Director
Mark Andersen, Director of Public Affairs

UNITED STATES DEPARTMENT OF THE INTERIOR

IOWA COOPERATIVE FISH AND WILDLIFE RESEARCH UNIT
11 Science Hall II
Department of Animal Ecology
Iowa State University
Ames, IA 50011-3221 United States
Phone: 515-294-3056 Fax: 515-294-5468
E-mail: coopunit@iastate.edu
Website: www.cfwru.iastate.edu

Founded: 1932
Membership: 1–100
Scope: State, Regional, National
Description: The Iowa Cooperative Fish and Wildlife Research Unit is a joint venture of the U.S. Geological Survey, the Iowa Department of Natural Resources, Iowa State University, and the Wildlife Management Institute. The Unit was established do research and to provide education for fisheries and wildlife professionals.
Publication(s): Annual Report
Keyword(s): Water Habitats & Quality, Wildlife & Species
Contact(s):
David Otis, Unit Leader
Rolf Koford, Assistant Unit Leader - Wildlife
Clay Pierce, Assistant Unit Leader - Fisheries

UNITED STATES DEPARTMENT OF THE INTERIOR

KANSAS STATE COOPERATIVE FISH AND WILDLIFE RESEARCH UNIT
205 Leasure Hall
Manhattan, KS 66506-3501 United States
Phone: 785-532-6070 Fax: 785-532-7159
E-mail: kscfwru@ksu.edu
Website: www.ksu.edu/kscfwru

Founded: 1991
Membership: 1–100
Scope: Local, State, Regional
Description: Provides graduate training and research in fisheries and wildlife biology, research, management, ecology, population dynamics, genetics, and related areas. Supported cooperatively by Kansas State University, the Kansas Department of Wildlife and Parks, the National Biological Service and the Wildlife Management Institute.
Publication(s): Annual Report of Activities
Contact(s):
Jack Cully, Assistant Leader of Wildlife
Philip Gipson, Leader
Christopher Guy, Assistant Leader of Fisheries

UNITED STATES DEPARTMENT OF THE INTERIOR

MISSOURI COOPERATIVE FISH AND WILDLIFE RESEARCH UNIT
302 Anheuser Busch Natural Resources Building
Fisheries and Wildlife
University of Missouri
Columbia, MO 65211-7240 United States
Phone: 573-882-3634 Fax: 573-884-5070
E-mail: CoopUnit@missouri.edu

Founded: 1985
Membership: 1–100
Scope: Local, State, Regional, National, International
Description: Established by cooperative agreement among the U.S. Geological Survey, Missouri Department of Conservation, University of Missouri, and Wildlife Management Institute. Primary purpose is research and graduate student education in wildlife conservation, aquatic ecology, and fisheries management areas.

Keyword(s): Water Habitats & Quality, Wildlife & Species
Contact(s):
Sandy Clark, Administrative Officer; 573-882-3634
Ronald Drobney, Assistant Leader: Wildlife; 573-882-9420
David Galat, Assistant Leader: Fisheries; 573-882-9426
Charles Rabeni, Leader; 573-882-3524

UNITED STATES DEPARTMENT OF THE INTERIOR
MONTANA STATE EXTENSION SERVICES
219 Linfield Hall
Montana State University
Bozeman, MT 59717-2230 United States
Phone: 406-994-5579 Fax: 406-994-5589
E-mail: jknight@montana.edu
Website: www.extn.msu.montana.edu/
Founded: N/A
Membership: N/A
Scope: State
Publication(s): MontGuides - Newsletter
Contact(s):
David Bryant, Vice Provost Director; dbryant@montana.edu
Jim Johannes, Statewide Director of Programming
Jim Knight, Extension Wildlife Specialist; Dept. of Animal and Range Science, Montana State University, Bozeman, MT 59717; 406-994-5579; Fax: 406-944-5589

UNITED STATES DEPARTMENT OF THE INTERIOR
NATIONAL PARK SERVICE
ACADIA NATIONAL PARK
P.O. Box 177
Bar Harbor, ME 04609 United States
Phone: 207-288-0374
Founded: N/A
Scope: National

UNITED STATES DEPARTMENT OF THE INTERIOR
NATIONAL PARK SERVICE
ARCHES NATIONAL PARK
P.O. Box 907
Moab, UT 84532-0907 United States
Phone: 435-259-8161
E-mail: archinfo@nps.gov
Website: www.nps.gov/arch/
Founded: 1928
Scope: National

UNITED STATES DEPARTMENT OF THE INTERIOR
NATIONAL PARK SERVICE
ASSATEAGUE ISLAND NATIONAL SEASHORE
7206 National Seashore Ln.
Berlin, MD 21811 United States
Phone: 410-641-1443
Founded: N/A
Scope: National

UNITED STATES DEPARTMENT OF THE INTERIOR
NATIONAL PARK SERVICE
BADLANDS NATIONAL PARK
P.O. Box 6, Rt. 240
Interior, SD 57750 United States
Phone: 605-433-5280
Founded: N/A
Scope: National

UNITED STATES DEPARTMENT OF THE INTERIOR
NATIONAL PARK SERVICE
BIG BEND NATIONAL PARK
P.O. Box 129
Big Bend National Park, TX 79834 United States
Phone: 915-477-2251 Fax: 915-477-1175
E-mail: BIBEInformation@nps.gov
Website: www.nps.gov/bibe
Founded: 1944
Membership: 1–100
Scope: National, International

UNITED STATES DEPARTMENT OF THE INTERIOR
NATIONAL PARK SERVICE
BISCAYNE NATIONAL PARK
9700 SW 328th St.
Homestead, FL 33033 United States
Phone: 305-230-7275
E-mail: BISC_information@nps.gov
Website: www.nps.gov/bisc
Founded: 1968
Membership: N/A
Scope: Local, State, Regional, National, International
Description: Turquoise waters, emerald islands and fish-bejeweled reefs make Biscayne National Park a paradise for wildlife-watching, snorkeling, diving, boating, fishing and other activities. The Park protects a 20 mile stretch of mangrove forest, the clear shallow waters of Biscayne Bay, the northern-most Florida Keys, and a spectacular living coral reef. Superimposed on all of this natural beauty is 10,000 years of human history, including stories of native peoples, shipwrecks, pirates, and pioneers.

UNITED STATES DEPARTMENT OF THE INTERIOR
NATIONAL PARK SERVICE
BRYCE CANYON NATIONAL PARK
P.O. Box 170001
Bryce Canyon, UT 84717-0001 United States
Phone: 435-834-5322 Fax: 435-834-4102
E-mail: brca_reception_area@nps.gov
Website: nps.gov/brca/index.htm
Founded: N/A
Scope: National
Description: National Park Service "to conserve the scenery and the natural and historic objects and the wild life therein, and to provide for their enjoyment in such manner as will leave them unimpaired for the enjoyment of furture generations" NPS Organic Act of 1916

UNITED STATES DEPARTMENT OF THE INTERIOR
NATIONAL PARK SERVICE
CANAVERAL NATIONAL SEASHORE
308 Julia St.
Titusville, FL 32796-3521 United States
Phone: 321-267-1110 Fax: 321-264-2906
Founded: N/A
Scope: National

UNITED STATES DEPARTMENT OF THE INTERIOR

NATIONAL PARK SERVICE
CANYONLANDS NATIONAL PARK
2282 SW Resource Blvd.
Moab, UT 84532-3298 United States
Phone: 435-719-2313 Fax: 435-719-2300
E-mail: canyinfo@nps.gov
Website: www.nps.gov/cany/index.htm

Founded: 1964
Scope: National
Description: Supervises National Park areas in southeast Utah

UNITED STATES DEPARTMENT OF THE INTERIOR

NATIONAL PARK SERVICE
CAPE COD NATIONAL SEASHORE
99 Marconi Site Rd.
Wellfleet, MA 02667 United States
Phone: 508-349-3785 Fax: 508-349-9052

Founded: N/A
Scope: National

UNITED STATES DEPARTMENT OF THE INTERIOR

NATIONAL PARK SERVICE
CAPE HATTERAS NATIONAL SEASHORE
1401 National Park Dr.
Manteo, NC 27954 United States
Phone: 252-473-2111 Fax: 252-473-2595
Website: www.nps.gov/caha

Founded: N/A
Scope: National
Description: Cape Hatteras National Seashore was authorized in 1937 and includes 74 miles of the barrier islands in northeastern North Carolina.

UNITED STATES DEPARTMENT OF THE INTERIOR

NATIONAL PARK SERVICE
CAPE LOOKOUT NATIONAL SEASHORE
131 Charles St.
Harkers Island, NC 28531 United States
Phone: 252-728-2250 Fax: 252-728-2160
E-mail: CALO_Information@nps.gov
Website: www.nps.gov/calo/

Founded: N/A
Membership: N/A
Scope: National
Description: A unit of the National Park Service; the seashore encompasses 56 miles of undeveloped beach on three barrier islands along the North Carolina Outer Banks coastline. Protected within the boundaries are nesting grounds for endangered species such as plovers and sea turtles as well as two historic districts.

UNITED STATES DEPARTMENT OF THE INTERIOR

NATIONAL PARK SERVICE
CAPITOL REEF NATIONAL PARK
HC 70, Box 15
Torrey, UT 84775-9602 United States
Phone: 435-425-3791

Founded: N/A
Scope: National

UNITED STATES DEPARTMENT OF THE INTERIOR

NATIONAL PARK SERVICE
CARLSBAD CAVERNS NATIONAL PARK
3225 National Park Hwy.
Carlsbad, NM 88220 United States
Phone: 505-785-2232
E-mail: cave_interpretation@nps.gov
Website: www.nps.gov/cave/home.htm

Founded: 1930
Scope: National

UNITED STATES DEPARTMENT OF THE INTERIOR

NATIONAL PARK SERVICE
CHANNEL ISLANDS NATIONAL PARK
1901 Spinnaker Dr.
Ventura, CA 93001 United States
Phone: 805-658-5700

Founded: N/A
Scope: National

UNITED STATES DEPARTMENT OF THE INTERIOR

NATIONAL PARK SERVICE
CHIHUAHUAN DESERT NETWORK
Chihuahuan Desert Network
c/o William Reid, Coordinator
HC 60 Box 400
Salt Flat, TX 79847 United States
Phone: 915-828-3251, ext. 250 Fax: 915-828-3269
E-mail: bill_reid@nps.gov

Founded: N/A
Membership: 1–100
Scope: Local, State, Regional
Description: A network of six Chihuahuan Desert national park units coordinating inventory and monitoring work initially to produce a common database.
Keyword(s): Air Quality/Atmosphere, Climate Change, Development/Developing Countries, Ecosystems (precious), Forests/Forestry, Pollution (general), Recreation/Ecotourism, Wildlife & Species

UNITED STATES DEPARTMENT OF THE INTERIOR

NATIONAL PARK SERVICE
CRATER LAKE NATIONAL PARK
P.O. Box 7
Crater Lake, OR 97604 United States
Phone: 541-594-2211 Fax: 541-594-3010
E-mail: CRLA_Information_Requests@nps.gov
Website: www.nps.gov/crla/

Founded: 1902
Scope: National

UNITED STATES DEPARTMENT OF THE INTERIOR

NATIONAL PARK SERVICE
CUMBERLAND ISLAND NATIONAL SEASHORE
P.O. Box 806
Saint Marys, GA 31558 United States
Phone: 888-817-3421 Fax: 912-673-7747

Founded: N/A
Scope: National
Description: Cumberland Island National Seashore is one of the best preserved barrier islands on the U. S. Atlantic coast.

UNITED STATES DEPARTMENT OF THE INTERIOR
NATIONAL PARK SERVICE
DEATH VALLEY NATIONAL PARK
P.O. Box 579
Death Valley, CA 92328 United States
Phone: 760-786-2331 Fax: 760-786-3283
Website: www.nps.gov/deva
Founded: N/A
Scope: National

UNITED STATES DEPARTMENT OF THE INTERIOR
NATIONAL PARK SERVICE
DENALI NATIONAL PARK
P.O. Box 74680
Denali Park, AK 99755 United States
Phone: 907-683-9581
Founded: N/A
Scope: National

UNITED STATES DEPARTMENT OF THE INTERIOR
NATIONAL PARK SERVICE
DRY TORTUGAS NATIONAL PARK
P.O. Box 6208
Key West, FL 33041 United States
Phone: 305-242-7700 Fax: 305-242-7711
Founded: N/A
Scope: National

UNITED STATES DEPARTMENT OF THE INTERIOR
NATIONAL PARK SERVICE
EVERGLADES NATIONAL PARK
40001 State Rd. 9336
Homestead, FL 33034 United States
Phone: 305-242-7700
Founded: N/A
Scope: National

UNITED STATES DEPARTMENT OF THE INTERIOR
NATIONAL PARK SERVICE
FIRE ISLAND NATIONAL SEASHORE
120 Laurel St
Patchogue, NY 11772 United States
Phone: 631-289-4810 Fax: 631-289-4898
Founded: N/A
Scope: National

UNITED STATES DEPARTMENT OF THE INTERIOR
NATIONAL PARK SERVICE
GATES OF THE ARCTIC NATIONAL PARK
201 First Ave., Doyon Bldg.
Fairbanks, AK 99701 United States
Phone: 907-456-0281
Founded: N/A
Scope: National

UNITED STATES DEPARTMENT OF THE INTERIOR
NATIONAL PARK SERVICE
GLACIER BAY NATIONAL PARK
One Park Rd.
Gustavus, AK 99826-0140 United States
Phone: 907-697-2230
Founded: N/A
Scope: National

UNITED STATES DEPARTMENT OF THE INTERIOR
NATIONAL PARK SERVICE
GLACIER NATIONAL PARK
P.O. Box 128
West Glacier, MT 59936 United States
Phone: 406-888-7901
Founded: N/A
Scope: National

UNITED STATES DEPARTMENT OF THE INTERIOR
NATIONAL PARK SERVICE
GRAND CANYON NATIONAL PARK
P.O. Box 129
Grand Canyon, AZ 86023 United States
Phone: 928-638-7945 Fax: 928-638-7797
Website: www.nps.gov/grca/
Founded: 1919
Scope: National

UNITED STATES DEPARTMENT OF THE INTERIOR
NATIONAL PARK SERVICE
GRAND TETON NATIONAL PARK
P.O. Drawer 170
Moose, WY 83012-0170 United States
Phone: 307-739-3300
Founded: N/A
Scope: National
Contact(s):
Stephen Martin, Manager; 307-739-3410; jackie_skaggs@nps.gov

UNITED STATES DEPARTMENT OF THE INTERIOR
NATIONAL PARK SERVICE
GREAT BASIN NATIONAL PARK
100 Great Basin National Park
Baker, NV 89311 United States
Phone: 775-234-7331 Fax: 775-234-7269
Founded: N/A
Scope: National

UNITED STATES DEPARTMENT OF THE INTERIOR
NATIONAL PARK SERVICE
GREAT SMOKY MOUNTAINS NATIONAL PARK
107 Park Headquarters Rd.
Gatlinburg, TN 37738 United States
Phone: 865-436-1200
Founded: N/A
Scope: National

UNITED STATES DEPARTMENT OF THE INTERIOR
NATIONAL PARK SERVICE
GUADALUPE MOUNTAINS NATIONAL PARK
HC 60, Box 400
Salt Flat, TX 79847-9400 United States
Phone: 915-828-3251
Founded: N/A
Scope: National

UNITED STATES DEPARTMENT OF THE INTERIOR
NATIONAL PARK SERVICE
GULF ISLANDS NATIONAL SEASHORE
1801 Gulf Breeze Pkwy.
Gulf Breeze, FL 32563-5000 United States
Phone: 850-934-2600 Fax: 850-932-9654
Website: www.nps.gov/guis

Founded: 1971
Membership: N/A
Scope: National
Description: One of ten National Seashores in the National Park System

UNITED STATES DEPARTMENT OF THE INTERIOR
NATIONAL PARK SERVICE
HALEAKALA NATIONAL PARK
P.O. Box 369, Makawao
Maui, HI 96768 United States
Phone: 808-572-9306

Founded: N/A
Scope: National

UNITED STATES DEPARTMENT OF THE INTERIOR
NATIONAL PARK SERVICE
HAWAII VOLCANOES NATIONAL PARK
P.O. Box 52
Hawaii Volcanoes, HI 96718 United States
Phone: 808-985-6025

Founded: N/A
Scope: National

UNITED STATES DEPARTMENT OF THE INTERIOR
NATIONAL PARK SERVICE
HOT SPRINGS NATIONAL PARK
P.O. Box 1860
Hot Springs, AR 71902 United States
Phone: 501-624-3383

Founded: N/A
Scope: National

UNITED STATES DEPARTMENT OF THE INTERIOR
NATIONAL PARK SERVICE
ISLE ROYALE NATIONAL PARK
800 E. Lakeshore Dr.
Houghton, MI 49931-1895 United States
Phone: 906-482-0984 Fax: 906-482-8753
E-mail: ISRO_ParksInfo@nps.gov
Website: www.nps.gov/isro

Founded: N/A
Scope: National
Description: National Parks Service

UNITED STATES DEPARTMENT OF THE INTERIOR
NATIONAL PARK SERVICE
JOSHUA TREE NATIONAL PARK
74485 National Park Dr.
Twenty-nine Palms, CA 92277 United States
Phone: 760-367-5502 Fax: 760-367-6392
Website: www.nps.gov/jotr

Founded: N/A
Scope: National

UNITED STATES DEPARTMENT OF THE INTERIOR
NATIONAL PARK SERVICE
KATMAI NATIONAL PARK
One King Salmon Mall
King Salmon, AK 99613 United States
Phone: 907-246-3305

Founded: N/A
Scope: National

UNITED STATES DEPARTMENT OF THE INTERIOR
NATIONAL PARK SERVICE
KENAI FJORDS NATIONAL PARK
1212 4th Ave.
Seward, AK 99664 United States
Phone: 907-224-3175

Founded: N/A
Scope: National

UNITED STATES DEPARTMENT OF THE INTERIOR
NATIONAL PARK SERVICE
KOBUK VALLEY NATIONAL PARK
P.O. Box 1029
Kotzebue, AK 99752 United States
Phone: 907-442-3890

Founded: N/A
Scope: National

UNITED STATES DEPARTMENT OF THE INTERIOR
NATIONAL PARK SERVICE
LAKE CLARK NATIONAL PARK
4230 University Dr., Ste. 311
Anchorage, AK 99508 United States
Phone: 907-271-3751

Founded: N/A
Scope: National

UNITED STATES DEPARTMENT OF THE INTERIOR
NATIONAL PARK SERVICE
LASSEN VOLCANIC NATIONAL PARK
P.O. Box 100, 38050 Hwy. 36E
Mineral, CA 96063 United States
Phone: 530-595-4444 Fax: 530-595-3262
E-mail: LAVO_information@nps.gov
Website: www.nps.gov/lavo/

Founded: 1916
Scope: National

UNITED STATES DEPARTMENT OF THE INTERIOR
NATIONAL PARK SERVICE
MAMMOTH CAVE NATIONAL PARK
P.O. Box 7
Mammoth Cave, KY 42259 United States
Phone: 270-758-2328 Fax: 270-758-2349
E-mail: maca_park_information@nps.gov
Website: www.nps.gov/maca/home.htm

Founded: 1941
Scope: National, International
Description: Mammoth Cave National Park was established to preserve the cave system, including Mammoth Cave (the world's longest cave), scenic river valleys of Green and Nolin Rivers, and a section of the hilly country of south central Kentucky. Designated a World Heritage Site in 1981, and an International Biosphere Reserve in 1990.

Keyword(s): Air Quality/Atmosphere, Ecosystems (precious), Forests/Forestry, Public Lands/Greenspace, Recreation/Ecotourism, Reduce/Reuse/Recycle, Water Habitats & Quality, Wildlife & Species

UNITED STATES DEPARTMENT OF THE INTERIOR

NATIONAL PARK SERVICE
MESA VERDE NATIONAL PARK
NATURAL RESOURCE OFFICE
P.O. Box 8
Mesa Verde, CO 81330 United States
Phone: 970-529-5069 Fax: 970-529-5071
E-mail: george_san_miguel@nps.gov
Website: www.nps.gov/meve

Founded: 1906
Membership: N/A
Scope: National
Description: The park's branch of natural resource management is responsible for ensuring that Mesa Verde's native plant and animal life, waters, air, soil, mineral, paleontological resources, and the natural processes that sustain them are left unimpaired for this and future generations.
Keyword(s): Air Quality/Atmosphere, Ecosystems (precious), Forests/Forestry, Recreation/Ecotourism, Water Habitats & Quality, Wildlife & Species

UNITED STATES DEPARTMENT OF THE INTERIOR

NATIONAL PARK SERVICE
MOUNT RAINIER NATIONAL PARK
Tahoma Woods, Star Route
Ashford, WA 98304-9751 United States
Phone: 360-569-2211

Founded: 1899
Scope: Local, State, Regional, National
Description: Unit of the National Park System, icon of the Pacific Northwest
Keyword(s): Air Quality/Atmosphere, Ecosystems (precious), Forests/Forestry, Land Issues, Public Lands/Greenspace, Recreation/Ecotourism, Reduce/Reuse/Recycle, Water Habitats & Quality, Wildlife & Species

UNITED STATES DEPARTMENT OF THE INTERIOR

NATIONAL PARK SERVICE
NATIONAL PARK OF AMERICAN SAMOA
Superintendent
National Park of American Samoa
Pago Pago, AS 96799 United States
Phone: 011-684-633-7082 Fax: 011-684-633-7085
E-mail: NPSA_administration@nps.gov
Website: www.nps.gov/npsa/home.htm

Founded: N/A
Scope: National

UNITED STATES DEPARTMENT OF THE INTERIOR

NATIONAL PARK SERVICE
NORTH CASCADES NATIONAL PARK
810 State Rte. 20
Sedro Woolley, WA 98284-9314 United States
Phone: 360-856-5700

Founded: N/A
Scope: National

UNITED STATES DEPARTMENT OF THE INTERIOR

NATIONAL PARK SERVICE
OLYMPIC NATIONAL PARK
600 E. Park Ave.
Port Angeles, WA 98362-6798 United States
Phone: 360-452-4501

Founded: N/A
Scope: National

UNITED STATES DEPARTMENT OF THE INTERIOR

NATIONAL PARK SERVICE
PADRE ISLAND NATIONAL SEASHORE
P.O. Box 181300
Corpus Christi, TX 78480-1300 United States
Phone: 361-949-8173 Fax: 361-949-8023
Website: www.nps.gov/pais/

Founded: N/A
Scope: National
Contact(s):
Jack Whitworth, Superintendent; 361-949-8173; pais_superintendent@nps.gov

UNITED STATES DEPARTMENT OF THE INTERIOR

NATIONAL PARK SERVICE
PETRIFIED FOREST NATIONAL PARK
One Park Rd.
Petrified Forest, AZ 86028 United States
Phone: 928-524-6228 Fax: 928-524-3567
Website: www.nps.gov/pefo/

Founded: 1962
Scope: National

UNITED STATES DEPARTMENT OF THE INTERIOR

NATIONAL PARK SERVICE
POINT REYES NATIONAL SEASHORE
Point Reyes, CA 94956 United States
Phone: 415-464-5100 Fax: 415-663-8132
Website: www.nps.gov/pore

Founded: 1962
Scope: National
Publication(s): Visitors Guide
Contact(s):
Don Neubacher, Superintendent

UNITED STATES DEPARTMENT OF THE INTERIOR

NATIONAL PARK SERVICE
REDWOOD NATIONAL PARK
1111 Second St.
Crescent City, CA 95531 United States
Phone: 707-464-6101, ext. 5001

Founded: N/A
Scope: National

UNITED STATES DEPARTMENT OF THE INTERIOR

NATIONAL PARK SERVICE
ROCKY MOUNTAIN NATIONAL PARK
1000 U.S. Hwy. 36
Estes Park, CO 80517 United States
Phone: 970-586-1206 Fax: 970-586-1310
E-mail: ROMO_Superintendent@nps.gov
Website: www.nps.gov/ROMO

Founded: 1915

Scope: National

Description: Rocky Mountain National Park, located in Colorado, preserves one of the most scenic stretches of the southern Rocky Mountains

UNITED STATES DEPARTMENT OF THE INTERIOR

NATIONAL PARK SERVICE
SEQUOIA AND KINGS CANYON NATIONAL PARK
47050 Generals Hwy.
Three Rivers, CA 93271-9651 United States
Phone: 559-565-3341
Website: www.nps.gov

Founded: N/A

Scope: National

UNITED STATES DEPARTMENT OF THE INTERIOR

NATIONAL PARK SERVICE
SHENANDOAH NATIONAL PARK
3655 U.S. Hwy. 211-E
Luray, VA 22835-9036 United States
Phone: 540-999-3400

Founded: N/A

Scope: National

UNITED STATES DEPARTMENT OF THE INTERIOR

NATIONAL PARK SERVICE
SONORAN DESERT NETWORK
125 Biological Sciences East
University of Arizona
Tucson, AZ 85719 United States
Phone: 520-670-5834 Fax: 520-670-5612
E-mail: Andy_Hubbard@nps.gov

Founded: 2001

Scope: Regional

Description: The Sonoran Desert Network conducts long-term monitoring of ecological resources on 11 national parks in southern Arizona and New Mexico: Casa Grande Ruins National Monument, Chiricahua National Monument, Coronado National Memorial, Fort Bowie National Historic Site, Gila Cliff Dwellings National Monument, Montezuma Castle National Monument, Organ Pipe Cactus National Monument, Saguaro National Park, Tonto National Monument, Tumacacori National Historic Park, and Tuzigoot National Monument.

Keyword(s): Air Quality/Atmosphere, Ecosystems (precious), Public Lands/Greenspace, Water Habitats & Quality, Wildlife & Species

Contact(s):

Andy Hubbard, Ecologist; Andy_Hubbard@nps.gov
Debbie Angell, Data Manager; Deborah_Angell@nps.gov

UNITED STATES DEPARTMENT OF THE INTERIOR

NATIONAL PARK SERVICE
THEODORE ROOSEVELT NATIONAL PARK
P.O. Box 7, 315 2nd Ave.
Medora, ND 58645-0007 United States
Phone: 701-623-4466 Fax: 701-623-4840
E-mail: Thro_Information@nps.gov
Website: www.nps.gov

Founded: 1947

Membership: N/A

Scope: National

Description: The colorful North Dakota Badlands provides the scenic backdrop to Theodore Roosevelt National Park, which memorializes the 26th president for his outstanding contributions to conservation and environmental efforts. The Little Missouri River has shaped this land which is home to variety of plants and animals.

Keyword(s): Air Quality/Atmosphere, Land Issues, Recreation/ Ecotourism, Wildlife & Species

UNITED STATES DEPARTMENT OF THE INTERIOR

NATIONAL PARK SERVICE
VIRGIN ISLANDS NATIONAL PARK
P.O. Box 710, Cruz Bay
Saint John, VI 00830 United States
Phone: 340-775-6201 Fax: 340-693-9301
E-mail: viis_superintendent@nps.gov
Website: www.virgin.islands.national-park.com/

Founded: N/A

Scope: National

UNITED STATES DEPARTMENT OF THE INTERIOR

NATIONAL PARK SERVICE
VOYAGEURS NATIONAL PARK
3131 Hwy. 53
International Falls, MN 56649 United States
Phone: 218-283-9821

Founded: N/A

Scope: National

UNITED STATES DEPARTMENT OF THE INTERIOR

NATIONAL PARK SERVICE
WIND CAVE NATIONAL PARK
RR 1, Box 190
Hot Springs, SD 57747-9430 United States
Phone: 605-745-4600

Founded: N/A

Scope: National

UNITED STATES DEPARTMENT OF THE INTERIOR

NATIONAL PARK SERVICE
WRANGELL-ST. ELIAS NATIONAL PARK
P.O.Box 439
Copper Center, AK 99573 United States
Phone: 907-822-5234

Founded: N/A

Scope: National

UNITED STATES DEPARTMENT OF THE INTERIOR

NATIONAL PARK SERVICE
YELLOWSTONE NATIONAL PARK
P.O. Box 168
Yellowstone, WY 82190 United States
Phone: 307-344-2002 Fax: 307-344-2005
E-mail: yell_superintendent@nps.gov
Website: www.nps.gov/yell

Founded: N/A

Scope: National

Description: National Park

Keyword(s): Air Quality/Atmosphere, Ecosystems (precious), Forests/Forestry, Land Issues, Pollution (general), Recreation/ Ecotourism, Reduce/Reuse/Recycle, Transportation, Water Habitats & Quality, Wildlife & Species

Contact(s):

Suzanne Lewis, Superintendent; 307-344-7381; yell_superintendent@nps.gov

UNITED STATES DEPARTMENT OF THE INTERIOR

NATIONAL PARK SERVICE
YOSEMITE NATIONAL PARK
P.O. Box 577, Administration Bldg.
Yosemite National Park, CA 95389 United States
Phone: 209-372-0200

Founded: N/A

Scope: National

UNITED STATES DEPARTMENT OF THE INTERIOR

NATIONAL PARK SERVICE
ZION NATIONAL PARK
Springdale, UT 84767 United States
Phone: 435-772-3256

Founded: N/A

Scope: National

Contact(s):

Marty Ott, Manager; 435-772-0142; marty_ott@nps.gov

UNITED STATES DEPARTMENT OF THE INTERIOR

NORTH DAKOTA STATE UNIVERSITY
EXTENSION SERVICE
North Dakota State University
Fargo, ND 58105-5437 United States
Phone: 701-231-7173 Fax: 701-231-8378
Website: www.ndsuext.nodak.edu

Founded: N/A

Scope: State

Contact(s):

Sharon Anderson, Director, Extension Service; ext-dir@ndsuext.nodak.edu
Cole Gustafson, Director, North Dakota Agricultural Experiment Station; NDSU, Box 5655, Fargo, ND 58105-5655; 701-231-7655; Fax: 701-231-8520; exp-dir@ndsuext.nodak.edu
Kevin Sedivec, Natural Resource Information; NDSU, P.O. Box 5053, Fargo, ND 58105

UNITED STATES DEPARTMENT OF THE INTERIOR

OFFICE OF SURFACE MINING RECLAMATION AND ENFORCEMENT
Department of Interior, Interior South Bldg.,
1951 Constitution Ave., NW
Washington, DC 20240 United States
Phone: 202-208-2719
E-mail: getinfo@osmre.gov
Website: www.osmre.gov/

Founded: N/A

Description: Established by the Surface Mining Control and Reclamation Act of 1977 to administer the nationwide program to protect society and the environment from adverse effects of coal mining operations, to establish national standards for regulating the surface environmental effects of coal mining, to support state implementation of such regulatory programs, and to promote reclamation of abandoned mine lands.

UNITED STATES DEPARTMENT OF THE INTERIOR

UNITED STATES GEOLOGICAL SURVEY
12201 Sunrise Valley Drive National Center
Reston, VA 20192 United States
Phone: 703-648-4000
Website: www.usgs.gov

Founded: 1879

Scope: National

Description: The Geological Survey works in cooperation with more than 2,000 organizations across the country to provide reliable, impartial, scientific information to resource managers, planners, and other customers.

Contact(s):

John Buffington, Western Regional Director; 909 First Ave., 8th Flr., Seattle, WA 98104; 206-220-4600
Thomas Casadevall, Central Regional Director; Denver Federal Center, Mail Stop 150, Denver, CO 80225; 303-202-4740
Charles Groat, Director; 703-648-7411
Bonnie McGregor, Eastern Regional Director; 1700 Leetown Rd., Kearneysville, WV 25430; 304-724-4521
S. Cook, Chief, Office of Equal Opportunity; 703-648-7770
James Devine, Senior Advisor, Science Applications; 703-648-4423
Dennis Fenn, Associate Director for Biology; 703-648-4050
Trudy Harlow, Public Affairs Officer; 703-648-4483
Robert Hirsch, Associate Director for Water; 703-648-5215
Amy Holley, Senior Advisor to the Director; 703-648-4411
Robert Hosenfeld, Chief, Office of Personnel; 703-648-7442
P. Leahy, Associate Director for Geology; 703-648-6600
Barbara Ryan, Associate Director of Operations; 703-648-7413
Carl Shapiro, Strategic Chief Planning, Analysis
Barbara Wainman, Chief, Office of Communications; 703-648-5750
Timothy West, Congressional Liaison Officer; 703-648-4300

UNITED STATES DEPARTMENT OF THE INTERIOR

UNITED STATES GEOLOGICAL SURVEY
BIOLOGICAL RESOURCES DIVISION
12201 Sunrise Valley Dr., MS-300
Reston, VA 20192 United States
Phone: 703-648-4050 Fax: 703-648-4042
Website: biology.usgs.gov/

Founded: N/A

Description: The Biological Resources Division works with others to provide the scientific understanding and technologies needed to manage the Nation's biological resources.

Contact(s):

Dennis Fenn, Chief Biologist; 703-648-4050
William Gregg, Chief of International Affairs; 703-648-4067
Susan Haseltine, Deputy Chief Biologist for Science; 703-648-4060
Suzzette Kimball, Regional Biologist; Eastern Regional Office, 1700 Leestown Rd., Kearneysville, WV 25430; 304-724-4500
J. Ludke, Regional Biologist; Central Regional Office, Denver Federal Center, P.O. Box 25046, Bldg. 20, Mailstop 300, Denver, CO 80225-0046; 303-236-2730

UNITED STATES DEPARTMENT OF THE INTERIOR

UNITED STATES GEOLOGICAL SURVEY
NEW MEXICO COOPERATIVE FISH AND WILDLIFE RESEARCH UNIT
P.O. Box 30003, MSC 4901
New Mexico State University
Las Cruces, NM 88003-0003 United States
Phone: 505-646-6053 Fax: 505-646-1281
E-mail: coopunit@nmsu.edu
Website: leopold.nmsu.edu/fwscoop

Founded: 1988

Membership: N/A

Scope: National

Description: Supported cooperatively by U.S.G.S. Biological Resources, New Mexico State University, New Mexico Department of Game and Fish, the Wildlife Management Institute, and U.S. Fish and Wildlife Service, the New Mexico Research Unit's primary purpose is research on management and conservation of fish and wildlife species and graduate research training in fisheries and wildlife resources.

Keyword(s): Land Issues, Pollution (general), Water Habitats & Quality, Wildlife & Species

Contact(s):
Louis Bender, Assistant Leader - Wildlife; lbender@nmsu.edu
Colleen Caldwell, Assistant Leader - Fisheries; ccaldwel@nmsu.edu
Bruce Thompson, Unit Leader; bthompso@nmsu.edu

UNITED STATES DEPARTMENT OF THE INTERIOR

UNITED STATES GEOLOGICAL SURVEY WESTERN REGION
909 First Avenue
Suite 704
Seattle, WA 98104 United States
Phone: 206-220-4573 Fax: 206-220-4570
Website: www.usgs.gov/

Founded: 1878
Membership: 1,001–10,000
Scope: State, Regional, National, International
Description: The Western Region includes 9 Western states: CA, OR, WA, ID, UT, NV, AZ, Alaska, Hawaii and U.S. Pacific Territories. Science includes Geological, Hazards, Water Resources, Biological and Geographic disciplines.
Keyword(s): Agriculture/Farming, Air Quality/Atmosphere, Climate Change, Ecosystems (precious), Energy, Forests/Forestry, Land Issues, Oceans/Coasts/Beaches, Population, Public Lands/Greenspace, Recreation/Ecotourism, Water Habitats & Quality, Wildlife & Species
Contact(s):
John Buffington, Regional Director

Federal Government Agencies

UNITED STATES DEPARTMENT OF TRANSPORTATION

Office of Public Affairs, Nassif Bldg., 400 7th St., SW
Washington, DC 20590 United States
Phone: 202-366-4000
Website: www.dot.gov

Founded: 1967
Membership: 10,001–100,000
Scope: National
Description: Composed of these main elements: The United States Coast Guard, Federal Aviation Administration, Federal Highway Administration, Federal Railroad Administration, Maritime Administration, St. Lawrence Seaway Development Corporation, National Highway Traffic Safety Administration, Federal Transit Administration, and Research and Special Programs Administration.
Publication(s): Merchant Vessels of the United States
Contact(s):
Norm Mineta, Assistant to the Secretary and Director of Public Affairs
Mortimer Downey, Deputy Secretary; 202-366-2222

UNITED STATES DEPARTMENT OF TRANSPORTATION

COAST GUARD
2100 2nd St., SW
Washington, DC 20593-0001 United States
Phone: 202-267-2229 Fax: 202-267-4696

Founded: N/A
Scope: State
Contact(s):
Timothy Josiah, Chief of Staff; 202-267-1642

UNITED STATES DEPARTMENT OF TRANSPORTATION

FEDERAL AVIATION ADMINISTRATION
FOB 10A 800 Independence Ave., SW
Washington, DC 20591 United States
Phone: 202-267-3484
Website: www.faa.gov

Founded: N/A
Description: Charged with regulating air commerce to foster aviation safety; promoting civil aviation and a national system of airports; achieving efficient use of navigable airspace; and developing and operating a common system of air traffic control and air navigation for both civilian and military aircraft.
Contact(s):
Jane Garvey, Administrator; 202-267-3111

UNITED STATES DEPARTMENT OF TRANSPORTATION

FEDERAL HIGHWAY ADMINISTRATION
Attn: Executive Director, Washington Headquarters,
400 7th St., SW
Washington, DC 20590 United States

Founded: N/A
Description: Charged with carrying out the Department of Transportation responsibilities concerned with the highway mode of land transport, including intermodal connections, has the primary missions of ensuring the safety of the motor carrier industry and that the Nation's highway transportation system is safe, economic, and efficient with respect to the movement of people and goods, while giving full consideration to the highway's impact on the environment and social and economic conditions.
Keyword(s): Transportation
Contact(s):
Fred Hempel, Director, Office of Corporate Management; 202-366-9393
Dennis Judycki, Director, Office of Research, Development, and Technology; 202-493-3165
Anthony Kane, Executive Director; 202-366-2242
George Moore, Director, Office of Administration; 202-366-0604
Edward Morris, Director, Office of Civil Rights; 202-366-0693
Gail Shibley, Director, Office of Public Affairs; 202-366-0660
Walter Sutton, Director, Office of Policy; 202-366-0585
Joseph Toole, Director, Office of Professional Development; 703-235-0519
Cynthia Burbank, Program Manager, Office of Planning and Environment; 202-366-0342
Julie Cirillo, Program Manager, Office of Motor Carrier and Highway Safety; 202-366-2519
Arthur Hamilton, Program Manager, Office of Federal Lands; 202-366-9494
Christine Johnson, Program Manager, Office of Operations; 202-366-0408
Vincent Schimmoler, Program Manager, Office of Infrastructure; 202-366-0371
Gloria Jeff, Deputy Administrator; 202-366-2240
Karen Skelton, Chief Counsel; 202-366-0740
Kenneth Wykle, Administrator; 202-366-0650

UNITED STATES DEPARTMENT OF TRANSPORTATION

FEDERAL RAILROAD ADMINISTRATION
1120 Vermont Ave, NW
Washington, DC 20590 United States
Phone: 202-366-4000 Fax: 202-493-6169
Website: www.fra.dot.gov

Founded: 1967
Scope: National
Description: The FRA promulgates and enforces rail safety regulations, administers financial assistance programs for

designated railroads, conducts research and development in support of improved railroad safety and national rail transportation policy, as well as monitors rail passenger service nationwide, and consolidates government support of rail transportation activities.

Contact(s):
S. Lindsey, Chief Counsel
Allan Rutter, Administrator of Federal RR Adminstrations

UNITED STATES DEPARTMENT OF TRANSPORTATION
FEDERAL TRANSIT ADMINISTRATION
400 7th St., SW
Washington, DC 20590 United States
Phone: 202-366-4043
Website: www.fta.dot.gov/

Founded: N/A
Description: Seeks to improve the environmental standards of American cities through grant programs which extend and modernize existing urban mass transit equipment and facilities and which study, develop, and test new equipment and concepts in urban mass transit applications and operations.
Keyword(s): Transportation
Contact(s):
Bruce Frame, Director, Office of Public Affairs; 202-366-4319
Arthur Lopez, Director, Office of Civil Rights; 202-366-4018
Charlotte Adams, Associate Administrator for Planning; 202-366-4033
Dorrie Aldrich, Associate Administrator for Administration; 202-366-4007
Nuria Fernandez, Deputy Administrator of Office of Administration; 202-366-4325
Mary Knapp, Executive Information, Office of Public Affairs; 202-366-9788
Gordon Linton, Administrator of Office of the Administrator; 202-366-4040
Gregory McBride, Deputy Chief Counsel; 202-366-4063
Patrick Reilly, Chief Counsel; 202-366-4063
Janet Sahaj, Deputy Associate Administrator; 202-366-4020
John Spencer, Deputy Associate Administrator; 202-366-1691
Edward Thomas, Associate Administrator for Research Demonstration and Innovation; 202-366-4052
Hiram Walker, Associate Administrator for Program Management; 202-366-4020
Michael Winter, Associate Administrator for Budget and Policy; 202-366-4050
Timothy Wolgast, Deputy Associate Administrator; 202-366-4007
A. Yen, Deputy Associate Administrator; 202-366-4991

UNITED STATES DEPARTMENT OF TRANSPORTATION
NATIONAL HIGHWAY TRAFFIC SAFETY ADMINISTRATION
Nassif Bldg., 400 7th St., SW
Washington, DC 20590 United States
Phone: 202-366-9550 Fax: 202-366-7402

Founded: N/A
Scope: State
Contact(s):
Donald Bischoff, Executive Director; 202-366-2111
Ricardo Martinez, Administrator; 202-366-1836
James Nichols, Associate Administrator for Traffic Safety Programs, Acting; 202-366-1755
Raymond Owings, Associate Administrator for Research and Development; 202-366-1537
Philip Recht, Deputy Director; 202-366-2775
Frank Seales, Chief Counsel; 202-366-9511
L. Shelton, Associate Administrator for Safety Performance Standards; 202-366-1810
Herman Simms, Associate Administrator for Administration, Acting; 202-366-1788
William Walsh, Associate Administrator for Plans and Policy; 202-366-2550
Kenneth Weinstein, Associate Administrator for Safety Assurance; 202-366-9700

UNITED STATES DEPARTMENT OF TRANSPORTATION
SAINT LAWRENCE SEAWAY DEVELOPMENT CORPORATION
400 7th St. SW
Washington, DC 20590 United States
Phone: 202-366-0091 Fax: 202-366-7047
Website: www.greatlakes-seaway.com

Founded: N/A
Membership: 1–100
Scope: State
Publication(s): Seaway Compass
Contact(s):
Tim Downey, Deputy Director of Office of Congressional and Public Affairs; P.O. Box 44090, Washington, DC 20026-4090; 202-366-0110
Albert Jacquez, Administrator; 202-366-0091

UNITED STATES DEPARTMENT OF TREASURY
1500 Pennsylvania Ave., NW
Washington, DC 20220 United States
Phone: 202-622-2000 Fax: 202-622-1999
Website: www.ustreas.gov

Founded: N/A
Scope: National
Description: The basic functions of the Department of the Treasury include: economic and fiscal policy; government accounting, cash, and debt management; international economic policy; and enforcement of customs and trade laws.

UNITED STATES DEPARTMENT OF TREASURY
UNITED STATES CUSTOMS SERVICE
EAST TEXAS CMC
2323 S. Shepard St., Suite 1200
Houston, TX 77019 United States
Phone: 713-387-7200 Fax: 713-387-7202

Founded: N/A
Contact(s):
John Babb, Director

UNITED STATES DEPARTMENT OF TREASURY
UNITED STATES CUSTOMS SERVICE
GULF CMC
423 Canal St.
New Orleans, LA 70130 United States
Phone: 504-670-2404 Fax: 504-670-2286

Founded: N/A
Membership: 101–1,000
Scope: Regional
Contact(s):
Leticia Moran, Director

UNITED STATES DEPARTMENT OF TREASURY
UNITED STATES CUSTOMS SERVICE
MID AMERICA CMC
610 S. Canal St., Suite 900
Chicago, IL 60607 United States
Phone: 312-983-9100 Fax: 312-886-4921
Website: www.uscustoms.treas.gov

Founded: N/A
Membership: 1–100
Scope: Regional

UNITED STATES DEPARTMENT OF TREASURY

UNITED STATES CUSTOMS SERVICE
NEW YORK CMC
6 World Trade Center, Rm. 716
New York, NY 10048 United States
Phone: 212-637-7900
Website: www.customs.treas.gov

Founded: N/A
Membership: 1,001–10,000
Scope: International
Contact(s):
John Martuge, Director

UNITED STATES DEPARTMENT OF TREASURY

UNITED STATES CUSTOMS SERVICE
NORTH ATLANTIC CMC
10 Causeway St.
Boston, MA 02222 United States
Phone: 617-565-6210 Fax: 617-565-6277
Website: www.uscustoms.treas.gov

Founded: N/A
Scope: International
Contact(s):
Philip Spayd, Director

UNITED STATES DEPARTMENT OF TREASURY

UNITED STATES CUSTOMS SERVICE
OFFICE OF PUBLIC AFFAIRS
1300 Pennsylvania Ave., NW,
Washington, DC 20229 United States
Phone: 202-927-1770 Fax: 202-927-1393
Website: www.customs.gov

Founded: 1789
Membership: 10,001–100,000
Scope: National, International
Description: The United States Customs Service is responsible for the enforcement of the U.S. laws regarding the importation and exportation of injurious and endangered species.
Publication(s): U.S. Customs Today - Monthly Newsletter
Keyword(s): Wildlife & Species
Contact(s):
Robert Bonner, Commissioner
Ben Devane, Special Agent In Charge, Acting
Allan Doody, Special Agent In Charge
Bobby Fernandez, Special Agent In Charge, Acting
Frank Figueroa, Special Agent In Charge, Acting
Gary Hillberry, Special Agent In Charge
Ken Kilroy, Special Agent In Charge
James Lewis, Special Agent In Charge, Acting
Leonard Lindheim, Special Agent In Charge
Bruce Murray, Special Agent In Charge, Acting
Charlie Simonsen, Special Agent In Charge
Jeremiah Sullivan, Special Agent In Charge
Bonni Tischler, Assistant Commissioner for Office of Field Operations; 202-927-0100
Awilda Villafane, Special Agent In Charge, Acting; 555 E. River Rd., Tucson, AZ 85704
Gary Waugh, Special Agent In Charge
Joe Webber, Special Agent In Charge, Acting

UNITED STATES DEPARTMENT OF TREASURY

UNITED STATES CUSTOMS SERVICE
SOUTHEAST
909 SE 1st Ave.
Miami, FL 33131 United States
Phone: 305-810-5120 Fax: 305-810-5143

Founded: N/A

UNITED STATES DEPARTMENT OF TREASURY

UNITED STATES CUSTOMS SERVICE
SOUTH PACIFIC CMC
One World Trade Center, P.O. Box 32639
Long Beach, CA 90831 United States
Phone: 562-980-3100 Fax: 562-980-3107

Founded: N/A
Scope: National
Contact(s):
Audrey Adams, Director

UNITED STATES INSTITUTE FOR ENVIRONMENTAL CONFLICT RESOLUTION

110 S. Church Ave.
Suite 3350
Tucson, AZ 85701 United States
Phone: 520-670-5299 Fax: 520-670-5530
E-mail: usiecr@ecr.gov
Website: www.ecr.gov

Founded: 1998
Membership: N/A
Scope: Local, State, Regional, National, International
Description: The U.S. Institute for Environmental Conflict Resolution is a federal program established by the U.S. Congress to assist parties in resolving environmental, natural resource, and public lands conflicts. The Institute is part of the Morris K. Udall Foundation, an independent federal agency of the executive branch overseen by a board of trustees appointed by the President. The Institute serves as an impartial, non-partisan institution providing professional expertise, services, and resources.
Publication(s): Roster of ECR Professionals
Keyword(s): Agriculture/Farming, Air Quality/Atmosphere, Ecosystems (precious), Energy, Ethics/Environmental Justice, Executive/Legislative/Judicial Reform, Forests/Forestry, Land Issues, Oceans/Coasts/Beaches, Pollution (general), Public Lands/Greenspace, Recreation
Contact(s):
Joan Calcagno, Roster Manager, National Roster of ECR Professionals; 520-670-5299; roster@ecr.gov
Michael Eng, Senior Program Manager, Protected Areas & Resources; 520-670-5299; eng@ecr.gov
Larry Fisher, Senior Program Manager, Public Lands & Natural Resource Mgmt.; 520-670-5299; fisher@ecr.gov
Dale Keyes, Senior Program Manager, Transportation, Energy & Env. Quality; 520-670-5299; keyes@ecr.gov
Sarah Palmer, Program Manager, Native American & Alaskan Native program; 520-670-5299; palmer@ecr.gov
Cherie Shanteau, Program Manager/Senior Mediator, Litigation program; 520-670-5299; shanteau@ecr.gov
Melanie Emerson, Program Associate, Public Education & Outreach; 520-670-5659; memerson@ecr.gov

UPPER COLORADO RIVER COMMISSION

355 S. 400 East St.
Salt Lake City, UT 84111 United States
Phone: 801-531-1150 Fax: 801-531-9705

Founded: 1949
Scope: Regional
Description: An administrative agency composed of commissioners appointed by the states of the Upper Division of the Colorado River - Colorado, New Mexico, Utah, and Wyoming, and by the President of the U.S.
Contact(s):
Wayne Cook, Executive Director and Secretary
Frank Maynes, Chairman; P.O. Drawer 2717, Durango, CO 81501

USAID/TANZANIA

So Mirambo
Dar-Es-Salaam, Tanzania
Phone: 255-511-1753 Fax: 255-111-6559

Founded: N/A

Description: International Development

Contact(s):
Z. Kristos Minja, Training Officer; 255-511-1753; Fax: 255-111-6559

USDA FOREST PRODUCTS LABORATORY

UNITED STATES FOREST SERVICE
FOREST PRODUCTS LABORATORY
One Gifford Pinchot Dr.
Madison, WI 53705-2398 United States
Phone: 608-231-9200 Fax: 608-231-9592
E-mail: mailroom_forest_products_laboratory@fs.fed.us
Website: www.fpl.fs.fed.us./

Founded: 1910

Membership: 101–1,000

Scope: National, International

Description: Uses science and technology to conserve and extend our Nation's forest resources. We promote healthy forest and forest-based economies through the sustainable use of our wood resources.

Publication(s): Dividends, NewsLine

Keyword(s): Climate Change, Development/Developing Countries, Energy, Forests/Forestry, Pollution (general), Public Health, Reduce/Reuse/Recycle, Water Habitats & Quality

Contact(s):
Chris Risbrudt, Director; 608-231-9318
Gordie Blum, Public Affairs Director; 608-231-9325; gblum@fs.fed.us

USGS FOREST AND RANGELAND ECOSYSTEM SCIENCE CENTER

3200 SW Jefferson Way
Corvallis, OR 97331 United States
Phone: 541-750-7307
Website: fresc.usgs.gov

Founded: 1994

Scope: Regional, International

Description: The Forest and Rangeland Ecosystem Science Center provides scientific understanding and the technology needed to support sound management and conservation of our nation's natural resources, with emphasis on western ecosystems.

Contact(s):
Ruth Jacobs, Technical Information Specialist; ruth_jacobs@usgs.gov

W

WESTERN PACIFIC REGIONAL FISHERY MANAGEMENT COUNCIL

1164 Bishop St., Suite 1400
Honolulu, HI 96813 United States
Phone: 808-522-8220 Fax: 808-522-8226
E-mail: info.wpcouncil@noaa.gov
Website: www.wpcouncil.org

Founded: 1977

Membership: 1–100

Scope: National

Description: The Council is the policy-making organization for the management of fisheries in and around the EEZs of American Samoa, Guam, Hawaii, and the Northern Mariana Islands, and U.S. possessions in the Pacific Ocean. Council members and members of its advisory bodies: Scientific and Statistical Committee, Plan Teams, and Advisory Panels represent the fishing community, government agencies, and national international fisheries management organizations throughout the region.

Publication(s): Pacific Islands Fishery News

Keyword(s): Recreation/Ecotourism, Wildlife & Species

Contact(s):
Kitty Simonds, Executive Director
Frank Farm, Chairman

WESTERN SNOWY PLOVER WORKING TEAM

OREGON/WASHINGTON SUBGROUP
Coos Bay BLM
1300 Airport Lane
North Bend, OR 97459 United States
Phone: 541-756-0100
E-mail: kerrie_palermo@or.blm.gov

Founded: 1992

Membership: 1–100

Scope: State

Description: Group of agency biologists working in a coordinated effort to recover western snowy plovers on the coast of Oregon and Washington through habitat restoration, education, recreation management and predator control.

Publication(s): Plover brochure; describes plover issues and management on the Oregon Coast

Keyword(s): Ecosystems (precious), Oceans/Coasts/Beaches, Wildlife & Species

STATE AND PROVINCIAL GOVERNMENT AGENCIES

A

ADIRONDACK PARK AGENCY
P.O. Box 99
Route 86
Ray Brook, NY 12977 United States
Phone: 518-891-4050, ext. 173 Fax: 518-891-3938
E-mail: vxhristo@gw.dec.state.ny.us
Website: www.northnet.org/adirondackparkagency/

Founded: 1971
Membership: N/A
Scope: International
Description: Created by state law and charged with developing a state Land Master Plan for the 40% of the park that is public land and a Private Land Use and Development Plan for the private lands within the six-million-acre Adirondack Park. The agency also administers the state's Wild, Scenic, and Recreational Rivers System Act for private lands within the park and the state's Freshwater Wetlands Act for both state and private lands within the park.
Publication(s): State Land Master Plan, Adirondack Park, Land Use Planning, publications list available upon request
Keyword(s): Land Issues, Water Habitats & Quality
Contact(s):
Daniel Fitts, Executive Director
Richard Lefebvre, Chairman
John Banta, Director of Planning
William Curran, Deputy Director, Regulatory Programs
Victoria Hristovski, Director, Public Information
Andy Flynn, Senior Information Specialist, Interpretive Centers

AGENCY OF NATURAL RESOURCES
103 S. Main St.
Waterbury, VT 05671 United States
Phone: 802-241-3600 Fax: 802-241-1102
Website: www.anr.state.vt.us

Founded: 1970
Scope: State
Description: The Agency's mission is to act as a steward of Vermont's natural resources. We work to manage Vermont's natural systems and to foster public understanding so that the integrity, vitality, and diversity of these natural systems are sustained or restored.
Contact(s):
James Bressor, Director of Media and Public Relations; 802-241-3600
Stephen Sease, Director of Planning; 802-241-3620
Scott Johnstone, Secretary; 802-241-3600
Salvatore Spinosa, Enforcement; 802-241-3820

AGENCY OF NATURAL RESOURCES
DEPARTMENT OF ENVIRONMENTAL CONSERVATION
Waterbury Complex, 103 S. Main St. Bldg. 10 N
Waterbury, VT 05671 United States
Phone: 802-241-3770 Fax: 802-241-3287
Website: www.decweb.anr.state.vt.us

Founded: N/A
Scope: State
Contact(s):
Marilyn Davis, Director of Wastewater; 802-241-3822
Larry Fitch, Director of Facilities; 802-241-3742
P. Flanders, Director of Waste Management; 802-241-3888
Wallace McLean, Director of Water Quality; 802-241-3770
Richard Phillips, Director of Environmental Assistance; 802-241-3470
Jay Rutherford, Director of Water Supply; 802-241-3434
Richard Valentinetti, Director of Air Quality; 802-241-3860
Canute Dalmasse, Commissioner; 802-241-3800

AGENCY OF NATURAL RESOURCES
DEPARTMENT OF FISH AND WILDLIFE
103 S. Main, 10 South
Waterbury, VT 05671-0501 United States
Phone: 802-241-3700 Fax: 802-241-3295
Website: www.vt.fishandwildlife.com

Founded: N/A
Scope: National
Keyword(s): Air Quality/Atmosphere, Reduce/Reuse/Recycle, Wildlife & Species
Contact(s):
Angelo Incerpi, Director of Operations
Eric Palmer, Director of Fisheries
Linda Eldredge, Business Manager
John Hall, Information and Education
Dave Mallory, Chair of Fish and Wildlife Board
Ron Regan, Commissioner
Lisa Wright, Hunter Education

AGENCY OF NATURAL RESOURCES
DEPARTMENT OF FORESTS, PARKS, AND RECREATION
Commissioners Office, 103 South Main St.
Waterbury, VT 05671 United States
Phone: 802-241-3670 Fax: 802-244-1481
Website: www.vtstateparks.com

Founded: N/A
Membership: 101–1,000
Scope: State
Contact(s):
Michael Fraysier, State Land Director
Larry Simino, Director of State Parks; 802-241-3644
David Stevens, Director of Forests; 802-241-3678
Ed Leary, Chief of Operations
Conrad Motyka, Commissioner
M. Stone, Chief of Forest Resource Management; 802-241-3675
H. Teillon, Chief of Forest Resource Protection; 802-241-3676
Craig Whipple, Chief of Park Operations; 802-241-3663

AGENCY OF NATURAL RESOURCES
VERMONT GEOLOGICAL SURVEY
103 S. Main St., Old Laundry Bldg.
Waterbury, VT 05671-0301 United States
Phone: 802-241-3496 Fax: 802-241-3273
E-mail: laurence.becker@anrmail.anr.state.vt.us
Website: www.anr.state.vt.us/geologyvgshmpg.htm

Founded: 1844
Membership: 1–100
Scope: State
Description: The Vermont Geological Survey encompasses two divisions. The State Geologist provides surveys of the geology, mineral resources, topography and geological information services to citizens, industry, and state and federal agencies. The Radioactive Waste Management Program manages the disposal of low-level radioactive waste generated in Vermont.
Publication(s): Price list sent upon request or visit the website.
Keyword(s): Energy, Land Issues, Pollution (general)
Contact(s):
Laurence Becker, State Geologist; laurencebecker@anrmail.anr.state.vt.us
Marjorie Gale, Geologist; marjieg@dec.anr.state.vt.us

AGRICULTURE AND FISHERIES
P.O. Box 2223
Halifax, B3J 3C4 Nova Scotia Canada
Phone: 902-424-4560 Fax: 902-424-4671
Website: www.gov.ns.ca/nsaf/home.htm

Founded: N/A
Scope: International

Description: The Department is involved in almost all aspects of the province's fishing industry. It has significant input into some of the policies and programs legislated and administered by the federal government, which has jurisdiction over much of the fishery. The department has jurisdictional responsibility for developing and regulating aquaculture and freshwater recreational fisheries. It is also responsible for the licensing and inspection of fish processing plants.

Publication(s): See publication web site

Contact(s):

Jim Sarty, Ceo/Fisheries & Aquaculture Loan Board; 902-424-0312
Dave Hansen, Executive Director; 902-424-0337
Murray Hill, Director of Inland Fisheries; 902-485-7021
Leo Muise, Director of Aquaculture; 902-424-3664
Janis Raymond, Acting Director of Marketing Services; 902-424-0330
Greg Roach, Executive Director, Fisheries & Aquaculture Services; 902-424-0348
Ernest Fage, Minister; 902-424-8953
Peter Underwood, Deputy Minister; 902-424-0300

ALABAMA COOPERATIVE EXTENSION SYSTEM

109 Duncan Hall
Auburn, AL 36849-5612 United States
Phone: 334-844-4444
Website: www.aces.edu

Founded: 1914

Scope: National

Description: The extension system (Alabama A&M and Auburn Universities), through its statewide network of County Extension Offices, conducts informal education programs using research-based knowledge and techniques. Programs are offered in agriculture and forestry profitability; developing, conserving, and managing natural resources; enhancing family and individual well being; developing human resources; and community development.

Publication(s): Contact Extension Communications

Keyword(s): Agriculture/Farming, Forests/Forestry, Wildlife & Species

Contact(s):

James Armstrong, Extension Wildlife Specialist; Dept. of Forestry & Wildlife Science, 331 Funchess Hall, Auburn University, AL 36849; 334-844-9233; Fax: 334-844-0234
Martha Johnson, Assistant Director/Family Programs; ACES, 107-A Duncan Hall, Auburn University, AL 36849; 334-844-5514; mjohnson@acesag.auburn.edu
Carolyn Whatley, Co-Leader Communications; ACES, 122 Duncan Hall Annex, Auburn University, AL 36849; 334-844-5690; cwhatley@acesag.auburn.edu

ALABAMA COOPERATIVE FISH AND WILDLIFE RESEARCH UNIT (USDI)

108 White Smith Hall, Auburn University
Auburn, AL 36849 United States
Phone: 334-844-4796 Fax: 334-887-4509
Website: www.ag.auburn.edu/alcfwru

Founded: 1935

Membership: 1–100

Scope: National

Description: The unit is sponsored by the Biological Resources Division, U.S. Geological Survey; Alabama Department of Conservation and Natural Resources, Division of Game and Fish; Auburn University; and the Wildlife Management Institute. Fish and wildlife research, graduate education, and technical assistance are the unit's primary purposes.

Keyword(s): Wildlife & Species

Contact(s):

James Grand, Leader
Elise Irwin, Assistant Leader of Fisheries
Michael Mitchell, Assistant Leader of Wildlife

ALABAMA DEPARTMENT OF AGRICULTURE AND INDUSTRIES

The Richard Beard Bldg., P.O. Box 3336
Montgomery, AL 36109-0336 United States
Phone: 334-240-7100 Fax: 334-240-7190
E-mail: commtwo@agi.state.al.us
Website: www.agi.state.al.us

Founded: N/A

Membership: 101–1,000

Scope: State

Description: The Alabama Department of Agriculture and Industries is responsible for enforcing the laws of Alabama relating to agriculture. It also works to provide agribusiness assistance such as marketing, loan mediation, and trade information. The department strives to ensure consumer safety and to promote all of Alabama agriculture.

Publication(s): Alabama Farmers Bulletin, Livestock Mkt. News

Contact(s):

Charles Bishop, Commissioner; commone@agi.state.al.us

ALABAMA DEPARTMENT OF CONSERVATION AND NATURAL RESOURCES

64 North Union Street, Suite 567P.O. Box 301456
Montgomery, AL 36130 United States
Phone: 334-242-3486 Fax: 334-242-3489
E-mail: commissioner@dcnr.state.al.us
Website: www.dcnr.state.al.us

Founded: 1905

Scope: State

Description: The program goal of the Alabama Department of Conservation and Natural Resources is to protect and, where possible, enhance or restore Alabama's natural resources for this and succeeding generations.

Publication(s): Alabama's Coastal Connection, Outdoor Alabama

Keyword(s): Oceans/Coasts/Beaches, Reduce/Reuse/Recycle

Contact(s):

Don Cooley, Division Director of State Parks; 334-242-3334
William Garner, Division Director of Marine Police; 334-353-2628
Gil Gilder, Division Director of Coastal Programs; 334-242-5502
James Griggs, Division Director of State Lands; 334-242-3484
R. Vernon Minton, Division Director of Marine Resources; P.O. Box 458, Gulf Shores, AL 36542; 251-968-7576
Corky Pugh, Division Director of Wildlife and Freshwater Fisheries; 334-242-3848
Richard Liles, Assistant Commissioner
Riley Smith, Commissioner

ALABAMA DEPARTMENT OF ENVIRONMENTAL MANAGEMENT

P.O. Box 301463
Montgomery, AL 36130-1463 United States
Phone: 334-271-7700 Fax: 334-271-7950
E-mail: Cab@adem.state.al.us
Website: www.adem.state.al.us/

Founded: 1982

Description: To respond in an efficient, comprehensive, and coordinated manner to environmental problems, thereby assuring a safe, healthful, and productive environment. Encompasses water quality, public water supply, underground injection control, solid waste, hazardous waste, air pollution control, well water standards, operator certification, and coastal area functions.

Publication(s): Environmental Update

Keyword(s): Air Quality/Atmosphere, Oceans/Coasts/Beaches, Reduce/Reuse/Recycle, Water Habitats & Quality

Contact(s):

James Warr, Director
Clark Bruner, Staff of Public Affairs

Gerald Hardy, Staff of Land Division
Charles Horn, Staff of Water Division
Steve Jenkins, Staff of Field Operations
Jim Moore, Staff of Office of Education and Outreach
John Poole, Staff of Permits and Services
Marilyn Elliott, Deputy Director
Ron Gore, Staff of Air Division
Olivia Jenkins, Office of General Counsel

ALABAMA FORESTRY COMMISSION

Montgomery, AL 36130 United States
Phone: 334-240-9300 Fax: 334-240-9390
Website: www.forestry.state.al.us

Founded: N/A

Scope: Local, State, Regional

Description: The FC was created by the 1969 regular session of the Alabama Legislature and is charged by law to protect, conserve, and increase the timber and forest resources of this state. A seven-member board is the policymaking body of the Commission. The State Forester is Chief Administrative Officer. Fire prevention and suppression, educational programs and materials, and free forest management assistance are some of the services which the Commission offers to the general public.

Publication(s): Alabama's Treasured Forests

Keyword(s): Development/Developing Countries, Forests/ Forestry, Reduce/Reuse/Recycle

Contact(s):

Gary Cole, Director of Administration Division; 334-240-9333
David Frederick, Fire Division Director; 334-240-9335
Timothy Boyce, State Forester; 334-240-9304
Richard Cumbie, Assistant State Forester; 334-240-9367
David Long, Commissioner
Coleen Vansant, Editor; 334-240-9355

ALABAMA SOIL AND WATER CONSERVATION COMMITTEE

Executive Director
Montgomery, AL 36130 United States
Phone: 334-242-2620 Fax: 334-242-0551

Founded: N/A

Membership: 1–100

Scope: State

Contact(s):

Stephen Cauthen, Executive Director; P.O. Box 304800, Montgomery, AL 36130-4800
Beverly Riker, Executive Assistant
Micky Smith, Chair; Rt. 1, Box 85A, Emelle, AL 35459; 205-652-7459

ALASKA COOPERATIVE FISH AND WILDLIFE RESEARCH UNIT

209 Irving I Bldg., P.O. Box 757020,
University of Alaska Fairbanks
Fairbanks, AK 99775-7020 United States
Phone: 907-474-7661 Fax: 907-474-6716

Founded: 1950

Membership: 1–100

Scope: State

Description: Sponsored jointly by the U.S. Geological Service, Alaska Department of Fish and Game, University of Alaska Fairbanks, U.S. Fish and Wildlife Service and Wildlife Management Institute, the Unit conducts graduate education and research programs on the ecology and management of Alaskan fish and wildlife, and their habitats.

Keyword(s): Water Habitats & Quality, Wildlife & Species

Contact(s):

Brad Griffith, Assistant Leader of Wildlife
F. Margraf, Leader
A. Mcguire, Assistant Leader of Ecology

ALASKA DEPARTMENT OF ENVIRONMENTAL CONSERVATION

410 Willoughby Ave.
Juneau, AK 99801-1795 United States
Phone: 907-465-5000 Fax: 907-465-5770
Website: www.state.ak.us/dec

Founded: 1971

Scope: State

Description: Created by the Seventh Alaska Legislature to protect the quality of the state's natural resources and the health and quality of life of its people. The department has broad regulatory authority in the areas of water quality, drinking water, air quality, solid waste disposal, oil spills, subsurface pollution, pesticides, food safety, seafood wholesomeness, sanitation, and radiation.

Keyword(s): Air Quality/Atmosphere, Public Health, Reduce/Reuse/Recycle, Water Habitats & Quality

Contact(s):

Janice Adair, Director of Division of Environmental Health; 907-269-7644
Tom Chapple, Director of Division of Air and Water Quality; 907-269-7686
Mike Conway, Director of Statewide Public Service; 907-465-5337
Larry Dietrick, Director of Spill Prevention and Response; 907-465-5250
Dan Easton, Director of Division of Facilities Construction and Operations; 907-465-5180
Barbara Frank, Director of Division of Administrative Services; 907-465-5256
Michele Brown, Commissioner; 907-465-5065
Charles Fedullo, Public Information; 907-269-3784
Kurt Fredriksson, Deputy Commissioner, Acting; 907-465-5065

ALASKA DEPARTMENT OF FISH AND GAME

P.O. Box 25526
Juneau, AK 99802 United States
Phone: 907-465-4100 Fax: 907-465-2332
Website:
www.state.ak.us/local/akpages/fish.game/adfghome.htm

Founded: N/A

Scope: State

Description: A research and management agency whose mission is to develop and organize its technical, human, and fiscal assets to maintain, rehabilitate, and enhance the fish and wildlife resources of the state, and to provide for their sustained optimum use consistent with the social, cultural, environmental, and economic needs of the public.

Keyword(s): Recreation/Ecotourism, Reduce/Reuse/Recycle, Wildlife & Species

Contact(s):

Kevin Brooks, Director of Division of Administration; 907-465-5999
Diana Cote, Executive Director of Board of Game and Board of Fish; 907-465-6095
Kelly Hepler, Director of Division of Sport Fish; 907-465-4180
Doug Mecom, Director of Commercial Fisheries Management and Development; 907-465-4210
Mary Pete, Director of Division of Subsistence; 907-465-4147
Wayne Regelin, Director of Division of Wildlife Conservation; 907-465-4190
Ken Taylor, Director of Habitat and Restoration Division; 907-465-4105
Robert Bosworth, Deputy Commissioner
Dan Coffey, Board of Fisheries Vice Chair; 207 E. Northern Lights Blvd., Suite 200, Anchorage, AK 99503
Kevin Duffy, Deputy Commissioner
Nancy Long, Public Communications Section; 907-465-6167
Lori Quakenbush, Board of Game Chair; P.O. Box 82391, Fairbanks, AK 99708

Greg Roczicka, Board of Game Vice Chairman; P.O. Box 513, Bethel, AK 99559
Frank Rue, Commissioner
John White, Board of Fisheries Chairman; Bering Sea Dental Center, P.O. Box 190, Bethel, AK 99559
Gordy Williams, Special Assistant for Legislative Liaision; 907-465-6143

ALASKA DEPARTMENT OF NATURAL RESOURCES

400 Willoughby
Juneau, AK 99801 United States
Phone: 907-465-3400 Fax: 907-586-2954
Website: www.dnr.state.ak.us

Founded: N/A
Scope: State
Keyword(s): Agriculture/Farming, Forests/Forestry, Land Issues, Public Lands/Greenspace, Reduce/Reuse/Recycle
Contact(s):
Bob Loeffler, Director of Division of Mining and Water Management; 3601 C St., Anchorage, AK 99503-5935; 907-269-8600
Mark Myers, Director of Division of Oil and Gas; 3601 C St. Suite 1380, Anchorage, AK 99503-5948; 907-269-8800
Jim Stratton, Director of Division of Parks and Outdoor Recreation; 3601 C St. Suite 1200, Anchorage, AK 99503-5921; 907-269-8700
Rob Wells, Director of Division of Agriculture; 1800 Glenn Hwy. Suite 12, P.O. Box 949, Palmer, AK 99645-0949; 907-745-7200
Milton Wiltse, Director of Division of Geological and Geophysical Surveys; 794 University Ave. Suite 200, Fairbanks, AK 99709-3654; 907-451-5000
Jeff Jahnke, State Forester of Division of Forestry; 3601 C St. Suite 1030, Anchorage, AK 99503; 907-269-8463
Pat Pourchot, Commissioner

ALASKA DEPARTMENT OF PUBLIC SAFETY

P.O. Box 111200
Juneau, AK 99811 United States
Phone: 907-465-4322 Fax: 907-465-4362
Website: www.dps.state.ak.us

Founded: N/A
Membership: 1–100
Scope: State
Description: Responsible for enforcing all of the Fish and Game laws and regulations of the state.
Publication(s): The Quarterly
Keyword(s): Recreation/Ecotourism
Contact(s):
Joel Hard, Director of Fish and Wildlife Protection
Al Cain, Operations Commander
James Cockrell, Deputy Director
Del Smith, Commissioner; 907-465-4322; Fax: 907-465-4362

ALASKA DEPARTMENT OF PUBLIC SAFETY

ALASKA STATE TROOPERS
DIVISION OF FISH AND WILDLIFE PROTECTION
5700 E. Tudor Rd.
Anchorage, AK 99507 United States
Phone: 907-269-5509 Fax: 907-269-5616
Website: www.dps.state.ak.us/fwp

Founded: N/A
Membership: 1–100
Scope: State
Description: Our primary mission is the protection of Alaska's fish and wildlife resources through enforcement of laws and regulations governing use of natural resources within Alaska and its adjacent waters, as well as through increasing the knowledge of, and respect for, fish and wildlife laws and regulations.
Contact(s):
Joel Hard, Director

ALASKA HEALTH PROJECT

218 East 4th Avenue
Anchorage, AK 99501 United States
Phone: 907-276-2864 Fax: 907-279-3089

Founded: 1980
Description: To provide information and advocacy on occupational and environmental health issues in Alaska, the Pacific Northwest, and Canada.
Publication(s): Involve waste management and worker health, and are inclusive of a 22 edition list.
Keyword(s): Reduce/Reuse/Recycle
Contact(s):
Daniel Middaugh, Executive Director
R. Gryder, Instructor

ALBERTA DEPARTMENT OF ENVIRONMENTAL PROTECTION

COMMUNICATIONS DIVISION
9th Floor, Petroleum Plaza, S. Tower, 9945-108 St.
Edmonton, T5K 2C6 Alberta Canada

Founded: N/A
Contact(s):
Bob Scott, Director; 403-427-8636

ALBERTA DEPARTMENT OF ENVIRONMENTAL PROTECTION

ENVIRONMENTAL SERVICE
Alberta Canada
Phone: 780-427-6247 Fax: 780-427-6247
E-mail: doug.tupper@gov.abc.ca
Website: www.gov.ab.ca/env/

Founded: N/A
Contact(s):
Doug Tupper, Assistant Deputy Minister; 403-427-6247

ALBERTA DEPARTMENT OF ENVIRONMENTAL PROTECTION

LAND AND FOREST SERVICE
Alberta Canada
Phone: 780-427-3542 Fax: 780-422-6068
E-mail: cliff.henderson@gov.ab.ca
Website: www.gov.ab.ca/env/

Founded: N/A
Contact(s):
Cliff Henderson, Assistant Deputy Minister

ALBERTA DEPARTMENT OF ENVIRONMENTAL PROTECTION

NATURAL RESOURCES SERVICE
Alberta Canada
Website: www.gov.ab.ca/env/

Founded: N/A
Contact(s):
Morley Barret, Deputy Minister; 780-427-6749; Fax: 780-427-8884; morley.barrett@gov.ab.ca

ALBERTA DEPARTMENT OF SUSTAINABLE RESOURCE DEVELOPMENT

FISH AND WILDLIFE DIVISION
Main Fl., South Tower
9915 - 108 Street
Edmonton, T5K 2G8 Alberta Canada
Phone: 780-944-0313 Fax: 780-422-9557
E-mail: env.infocent@gov.ab.ca
Website: www3.gov.ab.ca/srd/fishwl.html

Founded: 1964

Membership: 101–1,000
Scope: State
Description: The Fish and Wildlife Division of Alberta Sustainable Resource Development is committed to the wise use and conservation of fish and wildlife resources. The Division seeks to preserve the intrinsic value these resources add to the environment as well as the enjoyment of Albertans now and in the future.
Publication(s): Guide to Trapping Regulations, Guide to Hunting Regulations, Guide to Sportfishing Regulations, Species at Risk series, State of Alberta's Wildlife Report
Keyword(s): Ecosystems (precious), Executive/Legislative/Judicial Reform, Land Issues, Recreation/Ecotourism, Water Habitats & Quality, Wildlife & Species
Contact(s):
Mike Cardinal, Minister

AMERICAN SAMOA DEPARTMENT OF AGRICULTURE

American Samoa Government
Pago Pago, AS 96799 United States
Phone: Fax: 684-699-4031
E-mail: josephmatua@samoa.as
Founded: N/A
Contact(s):
Philo Maluia, Director

ARIZONA STATE LAND DEPARTMENT

1616 W. Adams St.
Phoenix, AZ 85007 United States
Phone: 602-542-4621 Fax: 602-542-2590
Website: www.land.state.az.us
Founded: 1915
Membership: 101–1,000
Scope: Regional
Description: The purpose of the Arizona State Land Department is to manage 9.4 million acres of Trust lands, through leasing and sale, in order to generate revenue for 14 state institutions. Resource protection and preservation is an integral part of trust land management.
Keyword(s): Development/Developing Countries, Land Issues, Public Lands/Greenspace, Reduce/Reuse/Recycle
Contact(s):
Bill Dowdle, Director of Natural Resources Division; 602-542-4625; Fax: 602-542-3507
T. Hart, Director of Forestry Division; 602-542-4627; Fax: 602-542-2590
Lynn Larson, Director of Administration and Resource Analysis Division; 602-542-4621
Richard Oxford, Director of Operations Division; 602-542-4602; Fax: 602-542-5223
Kirk Rowdabaugh, Director of Fire Management Division; 602-255-4059; Fax: 602-255-1781
Ron Ruzifka, Director of Planning and Land Disposition Division; 602-542-1704
Michael Anable, Deputy Commissioner of State Land
Jody Latimer, NRCD Administrator; 602-542-2699; Fax: 602-542-3507

ARIZONA COOPERATIVE FISH AND WILDLIFE RESEARCH UNIT (USDI)

Rm. 104, Biological Sciences East, University of Arizona
Tucson, AZ 85721 United States
Phone: 520-621-1959 Fax: 520-621-8801
Founded: N/A
Membership: 1–100
Scope: State
Description: The Unit is a cooperative effort by the U.S. Department of Interior, the Arizona Game and Fish Department, the University of Arizona, and the Wildlife Management Institute. The Unit conducts research on fish and wildlife questions for client agencies.
Contact(s):
Scott Bonar, Leader

ARIZONA COOPERATIVE STATE EXTENSION SERVICES

University of Arizona, P.O. Box 210036
Tucson, AZ 85721-0036 United States
Phone: 520-621-7205 Fax: 520-621-1314
Website: www.ag.arizona.edu/extension/
Founded: N/A
Membership: 1–100
Scope: State
Publication(s): See publication website
Contact(s):
James Christenson, Associate Dean and Director of Cooperative Extension; 520-621-7209; jimc@ag.arizona.edu
Kevin Fitzsimmons, Aquaculture Specialist; Soil, Water, and Environmental Science, P.O. Box 210038, University of Arizona, Tucson, AZ 85721; 520-626-3324; kevfitz@ag.arizona.edu
Richard Hawkins, Watershed Management Specialist; School of Renewable Natural Resources: College of Agriculture, P.O. Box 210043, University of Arizona, Tucson, AZ 85721; 520-621-7273; rhawkins@ag.arizona.edu
Bill Peterson, Assistant Director, 4-H; 520-621-3623; bpeters@ag.arizona.edu
George Ruyle, Range Management and Forest Resources Program Chair; School of Renewable Natural Resources: College of Agriculture, P.O. Box 210043, University of Arizona, Tucson, AZ 85721; 520-621-1384; gruyle@ag.arizona.edu
Larry Sullivan, Natural Resources Specialist, Wildlife; School of Renewable Natural Resources: College of Agriculture, P.O. Box 210043, University of Arizona, Tucson, AZ 85721; 520-621-7998; Fax: 520-621-8801; sullivan@ag.arizona.edu
Deborah Young, Associate Director, Programs; 520-621-5308; djyoung@ag.arizona.edu

ARIZONA DEPARTMENT OF AGRICULTURE

1688 W. Adams
Phoenix, AZ 85007 United States
Phone: 602-542-4373 Fax: 602-542-5420
Website: www.agriculture.state.az.us
Founded: N/A
Scope: International
Description: The ADA regulates and supports Arizona agriculture in a manner that encourages farming, ranching, and agribusiness while protecting consumers and natural resources. The ADA provides a number of services to its regulated industry, as well as the general public.
Contact(s):
Sheldon Jones, Director; 602-542-0998

ARIZONA DEPARTMENT OF AGRICULTURE

ANIMAL SERVICES DIVISION
1688 W. Adams
Phoenix, AZ 85007 United States
Phone: 602-542-6309 Fax: 602-542-3244
Website: www.agriculture.state.az.us/ASD/asd.htm
Founded: N/A
Scope: State
Description: The Animal Services Division is responsible for the protection of livestock from theft and disease and for the regulation of the state's aquaculture, dairy, egg, and slaughtering and meat-processing industries.

Contact(s):
Sheldon Jones, Director
Al Davis, Associate Director

ARIZONA DEPARTMENT OF AGRICULTURE
ENVIRONMENTAL SERVICES DIVISION
1688 W. Adams
Phoenix, AZ 85007 United States
Phone: 602-542-2579 Fax: 602-542-0466
Website: www.agriculture.state.az.us

Founded: N/A
Scope: State
Description: The Environmental Services Division is responsible for regulating the agricultural industry to ensure the safe use of pesticides, and to ensure the quality of feed, fertilizer, and pesticide formulations.
Contact(s):
Jack Peterson, Associate Director

ARIZONA DEPARTMENT OF AGRICULTURE
PLANT SERVICES DIVISION
1688 W. Adams St.
Phoenix, AZ 85007 United States
Phone: 602-542-0998 Fax: 602-542-0999
Website: www.agriculture.state.ac.us

Founded: N/A
Membership: 1–100
Scope: State
Description: The Plant Services Division is responsible for enforcement of state plant regulatory statutes, state agricultural industry plants, and plant health service programs.
Contact(s):
John Caravetta, Associate Director; 602-542-0994

ARIZONA DEPARTMENT OF ENVIRONMENTAL QUALITY
3033 N. Central Ave.
Phoenix, AZ 85012 United States
Phone: 602-207-2300 Fax: 602-207-2218
Website: www.adeq.state.az.us

Founded: 1987
Membership: 101–1,000
Scope: Regional
Description: The Arizona Department of Environmental Quality shall preserve, protect, and enhance the environment and the public health, and shall be a leader in the development of public policy to maintain and improve the quality of Arizona's air, land, and water resources.
Keyword(s): Air Quality/Atmosphere, Oceans/Coasts/Beaches, Pollution (general), Reduce/Reuse/Recycle, Water Habitats & Quality
Contact(s):
Jean Calhoun, Director of Waste Programs Division; 602-207-2381
Robert Rocha, Director of Administration Services Division; 602-207-4867
Jacquelin Schafer, Director; 602-207-2203
Karen Smith, Director of Water Quality Division; 602-207-2306
Nancy Wrona, Director of Air Quality Division; 602-207-2308
Charles Matthewson, Southern Regional Office; 400 W. Congress Suite 433, Tucson, AZ; 520-628-6733

ARIZONA GAME AND FISH DEPARTMENT
2221 W. Greenway Rd.
Phoenix, AZ 85023-4312 United States
Phone: 602-942-3000 Fax: 602-789-3924
Website: www.azgfd.com

Founded: 1929
Membership: 101–1,000
Scope: Local, State
Description: The mission of the Arizona Game and Fish Department is to conserve, enhance, and restore Arizona's diverse wildlife resources and habitats through aggressive protection and management programs, and to provide wildlife resources and safe watercraft and off-highway vehicle recreation for the enjoyment, appreciation, and use by present and future generations.
Publication(s): Arizona Wildlife Views
Keyword(s): Recreation/Ecotourism, Wildlife & Species
Contact(s):
Duane Shroufe, Director
Dick Maze, Heritage Program Coordinator
Diana Shaffer, Personnel Manager
Kerry Baldwin, (Acting) Assistant Director of Information and Education Div.
Steve Ferrell, Deputy Director
W. Gilstrap, Commissioner
Bob Miles, Publications Editor
Richard Rico, Assistant Director of Special Services Division
Mike Senn, Assistant Director of Field Operations Division
Alan Silverberg, Funds and Contracts
Bruce Taubert, Assistant Director of Wildlife Management Division

ARIZONA GEOLOGICAL SURVEY
416 W. Congress St.
Tucson, AZ 85701 United States
Phone: 520-770-3500 Fax: 520-770-3505
E-mail: azgs@azgs.az.gov
Website: www.azgs.az.gov

Founded: 1881
Membership: 1–100
Scope: State
Description: Develops, maintains, and disseminates information related to the geologic framework, geological hazards and limitations, and mineral and energy resources. Provides staff support for the Arizona Oil and Gas Conservation Commission, which regulates the drilling and production of oil, gas, geothermal, carbon dioxide and helium resources.
Publication(s): Down-To-Earth, digital information, contributed maps and reports, miscellaneous maps, open-file reports, maps, bulletins, special papers, circulars, Arizona Geology
Keyword(s): Energy, Land Issues
Contact(s):
Larry Fellows, Director and State Geologist; 520-770-3500; fellows_larry@pop.state.az.us

ARIZONA STATE PARKS BOARD
1300 W. Washington Ave.
Phoenix, AZ 85007 United States
Phone: 602-542-4174 Fax: 602-542-4188
Website: www.pr.state.az.us

Founded: 1957
Scope: State
Description: The purposes and objectives of the Arizona State Parks Board are to select, acquire, preserve, establish, and maintain areas of natural features, scenic beauty, historical and scientific interest, zoos, and botanical gardens, for the education, pleasure, recreation, and health of the people.
Publication(s): Access Arizona (disabled/seniors), Arizona Wildlife Viewing Guides, Arizona State Trails Guides, Arizona Rivers and Streams Guide
Keyword(s): Ethics/Environmental Justice, Recreation/Ecotourism, Wildlife & Species
Contact(s):
Kenneth Travous, Executive Director
Walter Armer, Chairperson
Ellen Bilbrey, Public Information Officer; 602-542-1996

ARKANSAS COOPERATIVE RESEARCH UNIT

Department of Interior, U.S. Geological Survey
Biological Sciences
University of Arkansas
Fayetteville, AR 72701 United States
Phone: 479-575-6709 Fax: 479-575-3330
E-mail: coopunit@uark.edu
Website: www.biology.uakr.edu/coop

Founded: 1988
Membership: 1–100
Scope: Local, State, Regional, National
Description: Primary purpose is field research, graduate research training in fisheries and wildlife resources, technical assistance, and extension activities. Areas of research include habitat selection, life history and demographics, ecology, animal behavior, and fisheries and wildlife biology.
Publication(s): Peer reviewed journals
Keyword(s): Agriculture/Farming, Population, Wildlife & Species
Contact(s):
David Krementz, Unit Leader; 479-575-7560; Fax: 479-575-3330; krementz@uark.edu
Dan Magoulick, Assistant Unit Leader - Fisheries; 479-575-5449; Fax: 479-575-3330; danmag@uark.edu
William Thompson, Assistant Unit Leader - Wildlife; 479-575-4266; Fax: 479-575-3330; thompson@uark.edu

ARKANSAS DEPARTMENT OF PARKS AND TOURISM

One Capitol Mall
Little Rock, AR 72201 United States
Phone: 501-682-7777 Fax: 501-682-1364
E-mail: info@arkansas.com
Website: www.arkansas.com

Founded: N/A
Membership: 101–1,000
Scope: State
Description: Develop, maintain and operate 50 state parks and four museums; advertise and promote all the state's recreation and travel potentials; provide information to attract retirees and others wanting to relocate; and assist communities in establishing local litter prevention and recycling projects.
Publication(s): The Arkansas Tour Guide, The Arkansas Adventure Guide, Arkansas State Parks Guide, The Arkansas Calendar of Events
Keyword(s): Ethics/Environmental Justice, Land Issues, Recreation/Ecotourism
Contact(s):
Greg Butts, Director of Parks Division; 501-682-7743; greg.butts@mail.state.ar.us
R. Cargile, Director of Administration; 501-682-2039; rl.cargile@mail.state.ar.us
Nancy Clark, Director of Great River Road Division; 501-682-1120; nancy.clark@mail.state.ar.us
Richard Davies, Executive Director; 501-682-2535; richardw.davies@mail.state.ar.us
John Ferguson, Director of History Commission; 501-682-6900; johnl.ferguson@mail.state.ar.us
Patricia Murphy, Director of Historical Resources and Museum Services Section; 501-682-3603; patriciam.murphy@mail.state.ar.us
Joe Rice, Director of Tourism Division; 501-682-1088; joedavid.rice@mail.state.ar.us
Bryan Kellar, Outdoor Recreation Grants; 501-682-1301; bryan.kellar@mail.stste.ar.us
Robert Phelps, Keep Arkansas Beautiful; 501-682-3507; robert.phelps@mail.state.ar.us

ARKANSAS GAME AND FISH COMMISSION

2 Natural Resources Dr.
Little Rock, AR 72205 United States
Phone: 501-223-6300 Fax: 501-223-6444
Website: www.agfc.com

Founded: 1915
Membership: 1–100
Scope: State
Description: The mission of the Arkansas Game and Fish Commission is to wisely manage the fish and wildlife resources of Arkansas while providing maximum enjoyment for the people.
Publication(s): Arkansas Wildlife, Explore Arkansas, Arkansas Outdoors Newsletter
Contact(s):
Len Pitcock, Director of Communications; 501-223-6473
Mary Smith, Educational Director; 501-223-6317
Mike Gibson, Chief of Fisheries Management; 501-223-6371
Jim Goodhart, Legal Counsel; 501-223-6327
Donny Harris, Chief of Wildlife Management; 501-223-6359
Scott Henderson, Assistant Director; 501-223-6309; Fax: 501-223-6448; shenderson@agfc.state.ar.us
Loren Hitchcock, Chief of Enforcement; 501-223-6384
Marcus Kilburn, Chief of Educational Services; 501-223-6402
Marion McCollum, Chairman; POB 8509, Pinebluff, AK 71611; 807-535-9000; Fax: 870-535-8544
Bill Robinson, Chief of Computer Services; 501-223-6368
Ray Sebren, Chief of Fiscal Services; 501-223-6341
Jim Spencer, Editor; 501-223-6336
Keith Sutton, Editor; 501-223-6406
Stephen Wilson, Public Affairs Coordinator; 501-223-6408

ARKANSAS NATURAL HERITAGE COMMISSION

1500 Tower Building
323 Center Street
Little Rock, AR 72201 United States
Phone: 501-324-9619 Fax: 501-324-9618
E-mail: arkansas@naturalheritage.org
Website: www.naturalheritage.com

Founded: 1979
Membership: 1–100
Scope: Local, State, Regional
Description: The Arkansas Natural Heritage Commission (ANHC) is responsible for maintaining the most up-to-date and comprehensive source of information concerning the rare plant and animal species, and high-quality natural communities of Arkansas. To protect rare species and habitats, the ANHC maintains a System of Natural Areas. Along with comprising remnants of the original natural landscape, lands within the System of Natural Areas provide vital habitat for imperiled plant and animal species.
Publication(s): Natural Area Brochures, Natural Diversity in Arkansas
Keyword(s): Ecosystems (precious), Wildlife & Species
Contact(s):
Karen Smith, Director; 501-324-9614; Fax: 501-324-9618; karen@arkansasheritage.org
Chris Colclasure, Chief of Acquisitions and Stewardship; 501-324-9760; Fax: 501-324-9618; chrisc@arkansasheritage.org
Douglas Fletcher, Chief of Stewardship; 501-324-9612; Fax: 501-324-9618; douglas@arkansasheritage.org
Tom Foti, Chief of Research; 501-324-9761; Fax: 501-324-9618; tom@arkansasheritage.org
Jane Jones-Schulz, Information and Education Coordinator; 501-324-9159; Fax: 501-324-9618; jane@arkansasheritage.org
Cindy Osborne, Data Manager; 501-324-9762; Fax: 501-324-9618; cindy@arkansasheritage.org
Bill Holimon, Zoologist/Grants Coordinator; 501-324-9636; Fax: 501-324-9618; billh@arkansasheritage.org

Jasa Holt, Assistant Data Manager; 501-324-9617; Fax: 501-324-9618; jasa@arkansasheritage.org
Amy Thiele, Assistant Data Manager; 501-324-9763; Fax: 501-324-9618; amyt@arkansasheritage.org
Michael Warriner, Invertebrate Zoologist/Information Officer; 501-324-9634; Fax: 501-324-9618; michaelw@arkansasheritage.org
Samuel Wilkes, Stewardship Field Ecologist; 501-324-9581; Fax: 501-324-9618; samuel@arkansasheritage.org
Theo Witsell, Botanist; 501-324-9615; Fax: 501-324-9618; theo@arkansasheritage.org

ARKANSAS STATE EXTENSION SERVICES

FOUR H CENTER
1 4-H Way
Little Rock, AR 72223 United States
Phone: 501-821-4444 Fax: 501-821-2545
Website: www.arkansashcenter.org

Founded: N/A
Membership: 1–100
Scope: State
Description: An off-campus education organization with faculty and offices in each county with the basic mission to disseminate and encourage the application of research-generated knowledge and leadership techniques to individuals, families, and communities. The county faculty is backed by subject matter specialists and their research counterparts.
Publication(s): Brochures
Keyword(s): Agriculture/Farming, Forests/Forestry, Reduce/Reuse/Recycle
Contact(s):
Leslie Gall, Assistant Extension Specialist, Environmental Education; #1, Four-H Way, Little Rock, AR 72211; 501-821-4444; lgall@uaex.edu
Kevin Jones, Program Specialist for Outdoor Recreation
Lucy Moreland, Natural Resources Instructor; #1, Four-H Way, Little Rock, AR 72211; 501-821-4444; lmoreland@uaex.edu
J.J. Pitman, 4-H Assistant Specialist-Outdoor Education

ATLANTIC STATES MARINE FISHERIES COMMISSION

1444 Eye St., NW, 6th Fl.
Washington, DC 20005 United States
Phone: 202-289-6400 Fax: 202-289-6051
E-mail: info@asmfc.org
Website: www.asmfc.org

Founded: 1942
Membership: 1–100
Scope: Regional
Description: The Commission was established by the Atlantic States Marine Fisheries Compact to promote better utilization of the fisheries, marine and shell, of the 15 Atlantic seaboard states, Maine to Florida, through the development of a joint program for the promotion and protection of such fisheries, and by the prevention of physical waste of the fisheries from any cause.
Publication(s): Focus
Contact(s):
John Dunnigan, Executive Director
David Borden, Past-Chairman
John Nelson, Vice-Chairman
Susan Shipman, Chairman

B

BOARD OF MINERALS AND ENVIRONMENT

523 E. Capitol Avenue
Pierre, SD 57501 United States
Phone: 605-773-3153 Fax: 605-773-6035
Website: www.state.sd.us/denr

Founded: 1981
Scope: State
Description: The Board of Minerals and Environment promulgates rules and issues permits in the areas of air quality, solid waste, hazardous waste, mineral exploration and mining, and oil and gas exploration and production.
Keyword(s): Air Quality/Atmosphere, Land Issues, Pollution (general)
Contact(s):
Steven Pirner, Secretary of the Department; 605-773-5559; Fax: 605-773-6035

BOTANICAL SOCIETY OF WESTERN PENNSYLVANIA

5837 Nicholson St.
Pittsburgh, PA 15217-2309 United States
Phone: 412-521-9425
E-mail: speedy@kiski.net
Website: home.kiski.net/~speedy/b.html

Founded: N/A
Scope: Local
Description: Botanical Society of Western Pennsylvania brings together those who are interested in botany and encourages the study of botany and knowledge of plants.
Publication(s): Wildflowers of Pennsylvania
Keyword(s): Agriculture/Farming, Reduce/Reuse/Recycle, Wildlife & Species
Contact(s):
Mary Haywood, President; 412-578-6175
Walter Gardill, Treasurer; 412-364-5308
Loree Speedy, Secretary

BRITISH COLUMBIA CONSERVATION DATA CENTRE

MINISTRY OF SUSTAINABLE RESOURCE MANAGEMENT
P.O. Box 9993 Station Provincial Gov.
Victoria, V8W 9R71 British Columbia Canada
Phone: 250-356-0928 Fax: 250-387-2733
E-mail: cdcdata@victoria1.gov.bc.ca
Website: srmwww.gov.bc.ca/cdc

Founded: N/A
Scope: International
Description: Providing information on rare organisms and ecosystems.
Publication(s): See publications on website
Contact(s):
Andrew Harcombe, Coordinator; andrewharcombe@gems2.gov.bc.ca

BUREAU OF ECONOMIC GEOLOGY

University of Texas at Austin, University Station, Box X
Austin, TX 78713-7508 United States
Phone: 512-471-1534 Fax: 512-471-0140
E-mail: beg@utexas.edu
Website: www.beg.utexas.edu

Founded: 1909
Membership: 101–1,000
Scope: State, International
Description: Functions as a state geological survey. Program includes basic research; application of geology to resources, conservation, and engineering problems; and publication of varied reports and maps. Maintains an extensive environmental mapping program.
Publication(s): University of Texas Report of Investigations, mineral resource circular, annual reports, handbooks, guidebooks, Geological Quadrangle Maps, Geological Atlas of Texas, Environmental Geologic Atlases, Special Publications, Geological Circulars
Keyword(s): Energy

Contact(s):
Scott Tinker, Director; 512-471-1534
D. Ratcliff, Associate Director for Administration

C

CALIFORNIA DEPARTMENT OF EDUCATION
OFFICE OF ENVIRONMENTAL EDUCATION
721 Capitol Mall, P.O. Box 944272
Sacramento, CA 94244-2720 United States
Phone: 916-322-9503 Fax: 916-322-9360
Website: www.cde.ca.gov

Founded: 1970
Description: The California Department of Education provides technical assistance and curriculum leadership in environmental education for counties and schools in California. The department offers an annual competitive grant program and provides curriculum and other publications related to environmental education in California.
Publication(s): Endangered Species Resource Guide, Greatest Hits of Environment, A Child's Place in the Environment, Environmental Education Compendia
Keyword(s): Air Quality/Atmosphere, Wildlife & Species
Contact(s):
Bill Andrews, Environmental Education Consultant; 916-657-5374; Fax: 916-657-3682; bandrews@cde.ca.gov

CALIFORNIA DEPARTMENT OF FOOD AND AGRICULTURE
1220 N St.
Sacramento, CA 95814 United States
Phone: 916-654-0462 Fax: 916-657-4240
E-mail: officeofpublicaffairs@bdfa.ca.gov
Website: www.cdfa.ca.gov

Founded: N/A
Membership: 1,001–10,000
Scope: National
Description: To assure public health, safety, and welfare; protects agriculture by administering, directing and enforcing the state's agricultural laws and regulations.
Publication(s): See publications on website
Contact(s):
Richard Breitmeyer, Director of Animal Industry; 916-654-0881
Mike Cleary, Director of Measurement Standards; 916-229-3000
John Donahue, Director of Inspection Services; 916-654-0792
Don Henry, Director of Plant Industry; 916-654-0317
Elizabeth Houser, Director of Fairs and Expositions; 916-263-2952
Kelly Krug, Director of Marketing Services; 916-654-1240
Les Lombardo, Planning Information Technology Director; 916-653-7643
Steve Lyle, Director of Public Affairs; 916-654-0462
Janice Strong, Legislative Director; 916-654-0326
Francine Kammeyer, Chief Counsel; 916-654-1393
William Lyons, Secretary; 916-654-0433
Dan Webb, Deputy Secretary; 916-654-0321

CALIFORNIA DEPARTMENT OF PESTICIDE REGULATION
1001 I Street
P.O. Box 4015
Sacramento, CA 95812-4015 United States
Phone: 916-445-4300 Fax: 916-324-1452
Website: www.cdpr.ca.gov

Founded: 1991
Membership: N/A
Scope: State
Description: Mission: To protect human health and the environment by regulating pesticide sales and use, and by fostering reduced-risk pest management.
Keyword(s): Agriculture/Farming, Air Quality/Atmosphere, Pollution (general)
Contact(s):
Paul Helliker, Director; 916-445-4000; Fax: 916-324-1452

CALIFORNIA ENERGY COMMISSION
ENVIRONMENTAL DEPARTMENT
1516 9th St.
Sacramento, CA 95814 United States
Phone: 916-654-4287 Fax: 916-654-4420
Website: www.energy.ca.gov

Founded: 1975
Membership: 101–1,000
Scope: State
Description: To ensure continuation of a reliable and affordable supply of energy for California at a level consistent with the state's needs.
Contact(s):
Steve Larson, Executive Director; 916-654-4996
Nancy Deller, Deputy Director of Energy Technology Division; 916-654-4628; Fax: 916-654-4676
William Keese, Chairman; 916-654-5000
Scott Matthews, Deputy Director of Energy Efficiency Division; 916-654-5013; Fax: 916-654-4304
Robert Pernell, Commissioner; 530-654-5036
Art Rosenfeld, Vice Chair; 916-654-4930
Robert Therkelsen, Deputy Director of Energy Facilities Siting; 916-654-3924; Fax: 916-654-3882

CALIFORNIA ENVIRONMENTAL PROTECTION AGENCY
P.O. Box 2815
Sacramento, CA 95812 United States
Phone: 916-445-3846 Fax: 916-445-6401
Website: www.calepa.ca.gov

Founded: 1991
Scope: State
Description: The Secretary for Environmental Protection, a member of the Governor's Cabinet, serves as the Governor's principal advisor on environmental protection issues and oversees the activities of the Air Resources Board, Water Resources Control Board, and Integrated Waste Management Board, the Department of Toxic Substances Control, the Office of Environmental Health Hazard Assessment, and the Department of Pesticide Regulation.
Contact(s):
William Rukeyser, Director of Communications; 916-324-9670
Patty Zwarts, Director of Legislative Affairs, Acting; 916-322-7315
Deborah Barnes, Deputy Secretary of Law Enforcement and Counsel; 916-327-2064
C. Haddix, Undersecretary
Winston Hickox, Secretary; 916-445-3846

CALIFORNIA ENVIRONMENTAL PROTECTION AGENCY
CALIFORNIA AIR RESOURCES BOARD
P.O. Box 2815
Sacramento, CA 95812 United States
Phone: 916-322-2990 Fax: 916-445-5025
Website: www.arb.ca.gov

Founded: 1968
Scope: National
Description: The California Air Resources Board is responsible for the adoption and enforcement of the state's ambient air quality standards, rules, and regulations for the control of vehicular air pollution and toxic air contaminants throughout the state. Oversees the efforts of 34 air pollution control districts that regulate emissions from industrial facilities. Conducts studies of the causes of air pollution and evaluates its effort upon human, plant, and animal life.

Contact(s):
Tom Cackette, Chief Deputy Executive Officer; 916-322-2892
Bart Croes, Research Division Chief; 916-445-0753
Robert Fletcher, Technical Support Division Chief; 916-322-5350
Michael Kenny, Executive Officer; 916-445-4383
Alan Lloyd, Chairman
William Loscutoff, Monitoring and Laboratory Division Chief; 916-445-3742
Jerry Martin, Public Information Officer; 916-322-2990
Larry Morris, Administrative Services Division Chief; 916-322-8198
Rob Oglesby, Legislative Office Chief; 916-322-2896
Michael Scheible, Deputy Executive Officer; 916-322-2890
Lynn Terry, Assistant Executive Officer; 916-322-2739
Kathleen Tschogl, Office of Ombudsman Chief; 916-323-6791
Peter Venturini, Stationary Division Chief; 916-445-0650
Kathleen Walsh, Office of Legal Affairs General Counsel; 916-322-2884

CALIFORNIA ENVIRONMENTAL PROTECTION AGENCY

DEPARTMENT OF TOXIC SUBSTANCES CONTROL
P.O. Box 806
Sacramento, CA 95812-0806 United States
Phone: 916-323-9723 Fax: 916-324-1788
Website: www.dtsc.ca.gov

Founded: N/A
Membership: 101–1,000
Scope: State
Description: Responsible for overseeing the cleanup of hazardous waste sites; monitoring and regulatory management of hazardous waste transportation, treatment, storage and disposal; and promotion of hazardous waste reduction in California.
Contact(s):
Edwin Lowry, Director; 916-322-0504; elowry@dtsc.ca.gov
Bob Borzeueri, Chief Deputy Director; 916-322-0449; bborzeuri@dtsc.ca.gov

CALIFORNIA ENVIRONMENTAL PROTECTION AGENCY

INTEGRATED WASTE MANAGEMENT BOARD, IWMB
1001 I Street, P.O.B. 4025
Sacramento, CA 95812 United States
Phone: 916-341-6000
Website: www.calepa.ca.gov

Founded: 1990
Description: The CIWMB is comprised of six members; four appointed by the governor and two by the legislature. CIWMB's goal is to protect the public's health and safety and the environment through waste prevention, waste diversion, and safe waste processing and disposal.
Contact(s):
Linda Moulton-Patterson, Chairman; 916-341-6024; lmoulton@ciwmb.ca.gov

CALIFORNIA ENVIRONMENTAL PROTECTION AGENCY

OFFICE OF ENVIRONMENTAL HEALTH HAZARD ASSESSMENT
P.O. Box 4010
Sacramento, CA 95812-4010 United States
Phone: 916-324-7572 Fax: 916-327-1097
Website: www.oehha.ca.gov

Founded: N/A
Membership: 1–100
Scope: State
Description: The Office of Environmental Health Hazard Assessment is charged with assessing human health risks posed by chemicals in the environment. The office is also the lead agency for implementation of the Safe Drinking Water and Toxic Enforcement Act of 1986 (Proposition 65).
Contact(s):
Joan Denton, Director

CALIFORNIA ENVIRONMENTAL PROTECTION AGENCY

STATE WATER RESOURCES CONTROL BOARD
1001 I St.
Sacramento, CA 95814 United States
Phone: 916-341-5250 Fax: 916-341-5252
Website: www.swrcb.ca.gov

Founded: N/A
Scope: State
Description: To protect water quality and allocate water rights. These objectives are achieved through two action programs: water quality and water rights.
Contact(s):
Celeste Cantu, Executive Director, Acting
Arthur Baggett, Chairman, Acting
Loretta Barsamian, Regional Executive Officer of the San Francisco Bay Region; San Francisco Bay Region, 1515 Clay Street, Suite 1400, Oakland, CA 94612; 510-622-2300; Fax: 510-622-2460
Roger Briggs, Regional Executive Officer of the Central Coast Region; Central Coast Region, 81 Higuera St., Ste. 200, San Luis Obispo, CA 93401; 805-549-3147; Fax: 805-543-0397
Gary Carlton, Regional Executive Officer of the Central Valley Region; Central Valley Region, 3443 Routier Road, Suite A, Sacramento, CA 95827; 916-255-3000; Fax: 916-255-3015
Dennis Dickerson, Regional Executive Officer of the Los Angeles Region; Los Angeles Region, 320 West 4th Street, Ste. 200, Los Angeles, CA 90013; 213-266-7500; Fax: 213-576-6640
Phil Gruenberg, Regional Executive Officer of the Colorado River Basin Regio; Colorado River Basin Region, 73-720 Fred Waring Dr., Suite 100, Palm Desert, CA 92260; 760-241-6583; Fax: 760-241-7308
Richard Katz, Board Member
John Robertus, Regional Executive Officer of the San Diego Region; San Diego Region, 9174 Sky Park Court, Suite 100, San Diego, CA 92123; 858-467-2952; Fax: 858-571-6972
Harry Schueller, Deputy Director
Peter Silva, Board Member
Harold Singer, Regional Executive Officer of the Lahontan Region; Lahontan Region, 2501 Lake Tahoe Blvd., South Lake Tahoe, CA 96150; 916-542-5400; Fax: 530-544-2271
Gerald Thibeault, Regional Executive Officer of the Santa Ana Region; Santa Ana Region, 3737 Main Street, Suite 500, Riverside, CA 92501; 909-782-4130; Fax: 909-781-6288
Susan Warner, Regional Executive Officer of the North Coast Region; North Coast Region, 5550 Skylane Blvd., Ste. A, Santa Rosa, CA 95403; 707-576-2220; Fax: 707-523-0135

CALIFORNIA FISH AND GAME COMMISSION

FISH AND GAME COMMISSION
1416 9th St., Rm. 1320,
P.O. Box 944209
Sacramento, CA 94244 United States
Phone: 916-653-4899 Fax: 916-653-5040
E-mail: fgc@dfg.ca.gov
Website: www.dfg.ca.gov/fg_comm/

Founded: 1870
Membership: 1–100
Scope: State
Description: Adopts fish, game, and plant regulations as authorized by the Fish and Game Code and sets policies for the Department of Fish and Game.
Contact(s):
Michael Flores, President
Mike Chrisman, Vice President
Robert Treanor, Executive Director; fgc@dfg.ca.gov

CALIFORNIA STATE LANDS COMMISSION

100 Howe Avenue
Suite 100-South
Sacramento, CA 95825-8202 United States
Phone: 916-574-1800 Fax: 916-574-1810
Website: www.slc.ca.gov

Founded: 1938
Membership: 101–1,000
Scope: State
Description: Jurisdiction over and management responsibility for state-owned sovereign and legislatively granted lands. Handles related land leases, exchanges, and associated transactions. Conducts oil, gas, geothermal, and leasing of other minerals on state-owned lands. Related activities include boundary and ownership determination, granted lands administration, and maintaining land information systems.
Keyword(s): Oceans/Coasts/Beaches, Public Lands/Greenspace
Contact(s):
Cruz Bustamante, Commissioner & Lieutenant Governor; 916-445-8994
Kathleen Connell, Commissioner & State Controller (Chair); 916-445-2636
B. Gage, Commissioner & State Director of Finance; 916-445-4141
Paul Thayer, Executive Officer; 916-574-1800; Fax: 916-574-1810; thayerp@slc.ca.gov
William Morrison, Legislative Liaison; 916-574-1800; Fax: 916-574-1810; morrisb@slc.ca.gov
Jack Rump, Chief Counsel; 916-574-1850; Fax: 916-574-1855; rumpj@slc.ca.gov
Dwight Sanders, Chief, Environmental Planning and Management Division; 916-574-1890; Fax: 916-574-1885; sanderd@slc.ca.gov
Robert Lynch, Chief, Land Management Division; 916-574-1940; Fax: 916-574-1945; lynchr@slc.ca.gov
Gary Gregory, Chief, Marine Facilities Division; 200 Oceangate, Suite 900, Long Beach, CA 90802; 562-499-6312; Fax: 562-499-6317; gregorg@slc.ca.gov
Paul Mount, Chief, Mineral Resources Management Division; 200 Oceangate, Suite 1200, Long Beach, CA 90802; 562-590-5205; Fax: 562-590-5210; mountp@slc.ca.gov

CLEMSON UNIVERSITY EXTENSION SERVICE

Clemson University, Rm. 103 Barre Hall
Clemson, SC 29634-0110 United States
Phone: 864-656-3382 Fax: 864-656-5819
Website: www.clemson.edu/extension/

Founded: N/A
Scope: State
Contact(s):
Allen Dunn, Director of School of Natural Resources; 130 Lehotsky Hall, Clemson University, Clemson, SC 29634; 864-656-3215; adunn@clemson.edu
Daniel Smith, Director of Extension Service; 103 Barre Hall, Clemson University, Clemson, SC 29634-0310; 864-656-3382; dbsmith@clemson.edu
P. Horton, Extension Entomologist; 103 Barre Hall, Clemson, SC 29634; 864-656-3382; mhorton@clemson.edu
Larry Nelson, Extension Forester; 272-E Lehotsky Hall, Clemson University, Clemson, SC 29634-1003; 864-656-4866; lnelson@clemson.edu
John Sweeney, Extension Fish Specialist; Department Head of Aquaculture, Fisheries, and Wildlife, Lehotsky Hall, Clemson University, Clemson, SC 29634-0362; 864-656-3117; jswny@clemson.edu
Greg Yarrow, Extension Wildlife Specialist; 864-656-7370; gyarrow@clemson.edu

COASTAL RESOURCE MANAGEMENT PROJECT

5th Floor CIFC Towers North Reclamation Area
Cebu City, Cebu, 6000 Philippines
Phone: 63322321822 Fax: 63322321825
E-mail: crmhot@mozcom.com
Website: www.oneocean.org

Founded: 1996
Membership: N/A
Scope: International
Description: Technical assistance project of the Department of Environment and Natural Resources in the Philippines supported by USAID
Keyword(s): Development/Developing Countries, Ecosystems (precious), Ethics/Environmental Justice, Executive/Legislative/Judicial Reform, Land Issues, Oceans/Coasts/Beaches, Recreation/Ecotourism, Water Habitats & Quality, Wildlife & Species
Contact(s):
Catherine Courtney, Chief of Party; 633-223-2182; courtney@mozcom.com
Alan White, Deputy Chief of Party; 633-223-2182; awhite@mozcom.com

COLORADO COOPERATIVE FISH AND WILDLIFE RESEARCH UNIT (USDI)

201 Wagar Bldg.
Dept. of Fishery and Wildlife Biology
Colorado State University
Ft. Collins, CO 80523-1484 United States
Phone: 970-491-5396 Fax: 970-491-1413

Founded: 1947
Membership: 1–100
Scope: International
Description: Offers expertise and training facilities in fish and wildlife population ecology, aquatic habitat analysis, conservation biology, sampling and analysis theory, and biostatistics.
Keyword(s): Wildlife & Species
Contact(s):
David Anderson, Leader
Eric Bergersen, Assistant Leader
Kenneth Burnham, Assistant Leader

COLORADO DEPARTMENT OF AGRICULTURE

700 Kipling St., Suite 4000
Lakewood, CO 80215 United States
Phone: 303-239-4100 Fax: 303-239-4176
Website: www.ag.state.co.us

Founded: 1949
Scope: State
Description: Strives to meet the increasingly complex needs of agriculture through work on marketing problems, technological changes in pest and insect control, and rapidly changing patterns in crop and livestock operations.

Keyword(s): Agriculture/Farming, Pollution (general), Public Lands/Greenspace

Contact(s):
Jerry Bohlender, Director of Animal Industry Division
John Gerhardt, Director of Plant Industry Division
Jim Rubingh, Director of Markets Development Division
Ronald Turner, Director of Division of Inspection and Consumer Services
Don Ament, Commissioner
David Carlson, Resource Analyst
Robert McLavey, Deputy Commissioner
Gary Shoun, Brand Commissioner of Board of Stock Inspection Division

COLORADO DEPARTMENT OF EDUCATION

STATE OFFICE
201 E. Colfax Ave.
Denver, CO 80203 United States
Phone: 303-866-6600 Fax: 303-830-0793
Website: www.cde.state.co.us

Founded: N/A
Scope: State
Description: Conservation Education Services, jointly with the Colorado Division of Wildlife.
Keyword(s): Ethics/Environmental Justice, Pollution (general), Reduce/Reuse/Recycle
Contact(s):
Don Hollums, Environmental Education Consultant; 303-866-6787; hollums_d@cde.state.co.us

COLORADO DEPARTMENT OF NATURAL RESOURCES

1313 Sherman St.
Denver, CO 80203 United States
Phone: 303-866-3311 Fax: 303-866-2115
Website: www.dnr.state.co.us

Founded: 1968
Membership: 1,001–10,000
Scope: State
Description: Responsible for mineral and energy, land, water, wildlife, and park resources management for the state. Also responsible for major environmental conservation and management programs.
Publication(s): See publication website
Keyword(s): Ecosystems (precious), Energy, Executive/Legislative/Judicial Reform, Forests/Forestry, Land Issues, Pollution (general), Public Lands/Greenspace, Recreation/Ecotourism, Water Habitats & Quality, Wildlife & Species
Contact(s):
Cindy Horiuchi, Human Resources Director
Greg Walcher, Executive Director
Ronald Cattany, Deputy Director
Bill Daley, Deputy Director

COLORADO DEPARTMENT OF NATURAL RESOURCES

COLORADO GEOLOGIC SURVEY
1313 Sherman St., Rm. 715
Denver, CO 80203 United States
Phone: 303-866-2611 Fax: 303-866-2461
E-mail: cgspubs@state.co.us
Website: www.geosurvey.state.co.us

Founded: N/A
Membership: 1–100
Scope: State
Description: State Geological Survey.
Publication(s): Rock Talk - quarterly newsletters
Contact(s):
Vicki Cowart, State Geologist

COLORADO DEPARTMENT OF NATURAL RESOURCES

DIVISION OF MINERALS AND GEOLOGY
1313 Sherman St., Rm. 215 Geology
Denver, CO 80203 United States
Phone: 303-866-3567 Fax: 303-832-8106
E-mail: dmg_pio@state.co.us
Website: www.mining.state.co.us

Founded: N/A
Membership: 1–100
Scope: State
Contact(s):
Michael Long, Director; michael.long@state.co.us

COLORADO DEPARTMENT OF NATURAL RESOURCES

DIVISION OF PARKS AND OUTDOOR RECREATION
1313 Sherman St., Rm. 618
Denver, CO 80203 United States
Phone: 303-866-3437 Fax: 303-866-3206
Website: www.parks.state.co.us

Founded: N/A
Membership: 101–1,000
Scope: State
Description: Colorado State Parks operates 40 state parks offering camping, fishing, hiking etc. Staffed with 250+ permanent FTEs.
Keyword(s): Recreation/Ecotourism, Water Habitats & Quality, Wildlife & Species
Contact(s):
Lyle Laverty, Director; 303-866-3437; Fax: 303-866-3206; lyle.laverty@state.co.us
Tom Kenyon, Deputy Director; 303-866-3437; Fax: 303-866-3206; tom.kenyon@state.co.us

COLORADO DEPARTMENT OF NATURAL RESOURCES

DIVISION OF WATER RESOURCES
STATE ENGINEER'S OFFICE
1313 Sherman St., Room 818
Denver, CO 80203 United States
Phone: 303-866-3581 Fax: 303-866-3589
Website: www.water.state.co.us

Founded: N/A
Membership: 1–100
Scope: State
Description: The Colorado Division of Water Resources issues water well permits, administers water rights, monitors streamflow and water use, inspects dams for safety, maintains databases of Colorado water information and represents Colorado in interstate water compact proceedings. Designated ground water basins are regulated by the 12-member Colorado Ground Water Commission. The safe and proper construction of water wells and pump installation activities are regulated by the 5-member Board of Examiners.
Publication(s): StreamLines - Newsletter
Contact(s):
Hal Simpson, State Engineer; 303-866-3581
Will Burt, Deputy State Engineer; 303-866-3581

COLORADO DEPARTMENT OF NATURAL RESOURCES

DIVISION OF WILDLIFE
6060 Broadway
Denver, CO 80216 United States
Phone: 303-297-1192 Fax: 303-294-0894
E-mail: AskDOW@state.co.us
Website: www.wildlife.state.co.us

Founded: N/A
Scope: State

Contact(s):
Russell George, Director

COLORADO DEPARTMENT OF NATURAL RESOURCES

OIL AND GAS CONSERVATION COMMISSION
1120 Lincoln St., Suite 801
Denver, CO 80203 United States
Phone: 303-894-2100 Fax: 303-894-2109
E-mail: dnr.ogcc@state.co.us
Website: www.oil-gas.state.co.us

Founded: N/A
Scope: State
Description: Promotes the responsible development of Colorado's oil and gas natural resources.
Contact(s):
Richard Griebling, Director

COLORADO DEPARTMENT OF NATURAL RESOURCES

STATE BOARD OF LAND COMMISSIONERS
1313 Sherman St., Rm. 621
Denver, CO 80203 United States
Phone: 303-866-3454 Fax: 303-866-3152
Website: www.trustlands.state.co.us

Founded: N/A
Membership: 1–100
Scope: State
Publication(s): Available on web
Contact(s):
John Brejcha, Acting Director; 303-866-3454

COLORADO DEPARTMENT OF PUBLIC HEALTH AND ENVIRONMENT

4300 Cherry Creek Dr., S.
Denver, CO 80246-1530 United States
Phone: 303-692-2035 Fax: 303-691-7702
E-mail: cdphe.information@state.co.us
Website: www.cdphe.state.co.us/

Founded: N/A
Scope: State
Description: The Colorado Department of Public Health and Environment has the responsibility for improving and protecting the health and environment for Colorado's citizens by: assuring a healthy working and living environment, protecting people against exposure to diseases, establishing preventive health services, and providing a quality environment through air, waste, water, radiation, and other environmental protection activities.
Contact(s):
Jane Norton, Executive Director

COLORADO GOVERNOR'S OFFICE OF ENERGY MANAGEMENT AND CONSERVATION

OEMC
225 East 16th Avenue
Suite 650
Denver, CO 80203 United States
Phone: 303-894-2383 Fax: 303-894-2388
E-mail: oemc@state.co.us
Website: www.state.co.us/oemc/

Founded: 1977
Scope: State
Description: OEC's mission includes leading the citizens of Colorado by promoting the efficient use of energy and resources. OEC develops, implements, and monitors energy conservation programs and offers services for individuals, community organizations, institutions, businesses, and government. Those services are designed to reduce energy consumption and increase awareness of the environmental, economic, and personal benefit to efficient energy use.
Publication(s): Recycle Colorado Bulletin
Keyword(s): Energy, Reduce/Reuse/Recycle, Water Habitats & Quality
Contact(s):
Rick Grice, Director; 303-894-2383; Fax: 303-894-2388; rick.grice@state.co.us
Ed Lewis, Deputy Director of Programs; 303-894-2383, ext. 1204; Fax: 303-894-2388; ed.lewis@state.co.us
Megan Castle, Public Information Officer; 303-894-2383, ext. 1211; Fax: 303-894-2388; megan.castle@state.co.us

COLORADO STATE FOREST SERVICE

203 Forestry Building
Ft. Collins, CO 80523-5060 United States
Phone: 970-491-6303 Fax: 970-491-7736
Website: www.colostate.edu/Depts/CSFS

Founded: 1885
Membership: 101–1,000
Scope: State
Description: The mission of the State Forest Service is to achieve stewardship of Colorado's environment through forestry outreach and service.
Keyword(s): Forests/Forestry, Land Issues
Contact(s):
James Hubbard, Director
Phil Hoefer, Community Forestry
Rich Homann, Wildfire Protection
Phil Schwolert, Forest Management
Bob Sturtevant, Conservation Education

COLORADO STATE SOIL CONSERVATION BOARD

COLORADO DEPARTMENT OF AGRICULTURE
1313 Sherman St., Rm. 219
Denver, CO 80203-2243 United States
Phone: 303-866-3351 Fax: 303-832-8106
Website: www.ag.state.co.us

Founded: N/A
Membership: 1–100
Scope: State
Contact(s):
Robert Zebroski, Director; robert.zebroski@ag.state.co.us

COLORADO STATE UNIVERSITY COOPERATIVE EXTENSION

1 Administration Bldg., Colorado State University
Ft. Collins, CO 80523 United States
Phone: 970-491-6281 Fax: 970-491-6208
Website: www.colostate.edu/Depts/CoopExt/

Founded: 1914
Membership: 101–1,000
Scope: State
Description: A branch of Colorado State University. Conducts statewide noncredit educational programs off campus.
Publication(s): Publications listed on website; www.cerc1@ur.colostate.edu
Keyword(s): Agriculture/Farming, Development/Developing Countries, Pollution (general), Public Health, Recreation/Ecotourism, Reduce/Reuse/Recycle, Sprawl/Urban Planning
Contact(s):
Milan Rewerts, Director of Cooperative Extension; mrewerts@coop.ext.colostate.edu
William Andelt, Extension Wildlife Specialist: Animal Damage Control; Dept. of Fishery and Wildlife Biology: 109 Wagar: Colorado State University, Ft. Collins, CO 80523; 970-491-7093

Delwin Benson, Extension Wildlife Specialist: Wildlife Management; Dept. of Fishery and Wildlife Biology: 109 Wagar: Colorado State University, Ft. Collins, CO 80523; 970-491-6411; Fax: 970-491-5091
Mary Gray, Associate Director of Programs; gray@coop.ext.colostate.edu
Shelley Stanley, Extension Agent-Natural Resources; 15200 W. Sixth Ave., Golden, CO 80401; 303-271-6620

COLORADO WATER CONSERVATION BOARD

WATER CONSERVATION BOARD
1313 Sherman St.
Denver, CO 80203 United States
Phone: 303-866-3441 Fax: 303-866-4474
Website: www.dnr.state.co.us

Founded: N/A
Scope: State
Keyword(s): Public Lands/Greenspace, Recreation/Ecotourism
Contact(s):
Rod Kuharich, Director

COLUMBIA RIVER GORGE COMMISSION

P.O. Box 730
White Salmon, WA 98672 United States
Phone: 509-493-3323 Fax: 509-493-2229
E-mail: crgc@gorge.net
Website: www.gorgecommission.org

Founded: N/A
Membership: 1–100
Scope: Regional
Description: Established by the states of Oregon and Washington to implement the Columbia River Gorge National Scenic Area Act by developing a regional management plan, in cooperation with the U.S. Forest Service. The commission is composed of three members from Oregon, three from Washington, and one from each of the six local Gorge counties. A Secretary of Agriculture appointee is a thirteenth nonvoting member.
Keyword(s): Land Issues, Recreation/Ecotourism
Contact(s):
Maratha Bennett, Executive Director; bennett@gorgecommission.org
Anne Squier, Chairman
Wayne Wooster, Vice Chairman; 509-493-3724; wooster@gorge.net

COMITE DESPERTAR CIDRENO

Box 1714
Cidra, PR 00739 United States
Phone: 787-739-5492

Founded: 1987
Description: Primarily devoted to educate and organize communities in the east-central part of the island to deal with water pollution and wildlife habitat. Also deals with toxic waste problems.
Publication(s): Despertar Cidreno
Keyword(s): Air Quality/Atmosphere, Reduce/Reuse/Recycle, Water Habitats & Quality, Wildlife & Species
Contact(s):
Olga Rodriguez Berrios, President
Juanita Garcia, Treasurer
Vivian Santiago, Secretary

CONNECTICUT COUNCIL ON ENVIRONMENTAL QUALITY

79 Elm Street
Hartford, CT 06106 United States
Phone: 860-424-4000 Fax: 860-424-4070
E-mail: karl.wagener@po.state.ct.us
Website: www.ceq.state.ct.us

Founded: 1971
Membership: 1–100
Scope: State
Description: Prepares annual reports to the Governor on the status of Connecticut's environment; receives and investigates citizen complaints pertaining to the environment; and reviews environmental assessments of construction activities of state agencies. The council is composed of nine appointed members who serve without compensation.
Publication(s): Environmental Quality in Connecticut (Annual Report)
Contact(s):
Karl Wagener, Executive Director
Donal O'Brien, Chairman

CONNECTICUT DEPARTMENT OF AGRICULTURE

765 Asylum Ave.
Hartford, CT 06105 United States
Phone: 860-713-2500 Fax: 860-713-2514
E-mail: ctdeptag@po.state.ct.us
Website: www.state.ct.us/doag

Founded: 1971
Membership: 1–100
Scope: State
Description: State Department of Agriculture
Publication(s): Connecticut Weekly
Contact(s):
Emilie Andrews, Director: Personnel; 860-713-2501; Fax: 860-713-2585; emilie.andrews@po.state.ct.us
David Carey, Executive Director: Connecticut Marketing Authority; 101 Reserve Rd., Hartford, CT 06114; 860-566-3699; Fax: 860-566-2944; ct.mktg.authority@snet.net
Dawn Cassada, Director: Administration; 860-713-2502; Fax: 860-713-2585; dawn.cassada@po.state.ct.us
Joseph Dippel, Director: Farmland Preservation; 860-713-2511; Fax: 860-713-2514; joseph.dippel@po.state.ct.us
Robert Pellegrino, Director: Marketing and Technology; 860-713-2503; Fax: 860-713-2516; robert.pellegrino@po.state.ct.us
Bruce Sherman, Director: Regulation and Inspection; 860-713-2504; Fax: 860-713-2515; bruce.sherman@po.state.ct.us
John Volk, Director: Aquaculture Division; P.O. Box 97, Milford, CT 06460; 203-874-2855; Fax: 203-783-9976; dept.agric@snet.net
Shirley Ferris, Commissioner; 860-713-2500; Fax: 860-713-2514; commissioner.ctdeptag@po.state.ct.us
Bruce Gresczyk, Deputy Commissioner; 860-713-2526; Fax: 860-713-2514; commissioner.ctdeptag@po.state.ct.us
Frank Intino, Deputy Director: Marketing and Technology; 860-713-2503; Fax: 860-713-2516; frank.intino@po.state.ct.us
Mary Lis, State Veterinarian; 860-713-2505; Fax: 860-713-2515; mary.lis@po.state.ct.us
Gabriel Moquin, Deputy Director: Regulation and Inspection; 860-713-2508; Fax: 860-713-2515; gabriel.moquin@po.state.ct.us

CONNECTICUT DEPARTMENT OF ENVIRONMENTAL PROTECTION

79 Elm St.
Hartford, CT 06106-5127 United States
Phone: 860-424-3000 Fax: 860-424-4078
Website: www.dep.state.ct.us

Founded: N/A
Membership: 1–100
Scope: State
Description: Created by the Connecticut General Assembly to conserve, protect, and improve the state's environment and to manage the basic resources of air, water, and land for the benefit of present and future generations.
Publication(s): Connecticut Wildlife

Contact(s):
Pamela Adams, Director, Parks Division; 860-424-3200
George Barone, Director, Law Enforcement Division; 860-424-3012
Ernest Beckwith, Director, Fisheries Division; 860-424-3474
Dail May, Director, Wildlife Division; 860-424-3011
Charles Reed, Director, Land Acquisition and Management; 860-424-3016
Donald Smith, Director, Forestry Division; 860-424-3630
Michele Sullivan, Director, Communications, Education and Publications; 860-424-4100
Richard Barlow, Chief, Bureau of Waste Management; 860-424-3021
Richard Clifford, Chief, Bureau of Outdoor Recreation; 860-424-3200
Carmine DiBattista, Chief, Bureau of Air Management; 860-424-3026
David Leff, Deputy Commissioner Environmental Conservations; 860-424-3005
Edward Parker, Chief, Bureau of Natural Resources; 860-424-3010
Arthur Rocque, Commissioner; 860-424-3001
Robert Smith, Chief, Bureau of Water Management; 860-424-3704
Jane Stahl, Assistant Commissioner, Air, Water and Waste; 860-424-3009

COOPERATIVE EXTENSION SERVICE

UNIVERSITY OF ALASKA FAIRBANKS
COLLEGE OF RURAL ALASKA
CES Bldg., University of Alaska
Fairbanks, AK 99775-6180 United States
Phone: 907-474-7246 Fax: 907-474-6971
E-mail: fyace@uaf.edu
Website: www.uaf.edu/coop-ext

Founded: N/A
Membership: 1–100
Scope: State
Contact(s):
Anthony Nakazawa, Director; anatn@uaa.alaska.edu
Robert Gorman, Land Resources Program Chair; 907-786-6323; ffrfg@uaf.edu
Michele Hebert, Land Resources Agent; 907-474-1530; ffmah@uaf.edu
Peter Stortz, Fish and NR Specialist; CES/Palmer Research Center, 533 E. Fireweed Ln., Palmer, AK 99645; 907-746-9459; Fax: 907-746-2677; ffpjs@ufa.edu

COUNCIL ON RESOURCES AND DEVELOPMENT

c/o Office of State Planning, 2 1/2 Beacon St.
Concord, NH 03301 United States
Phone: 603-271-2155 Fax: 603-271-1728
Website: www.state.nh.us/osp/planning

Founded: 1963
Membership: 1–100
Scope: State
Description: The ten members on the council represent the state's development and resource agencies. The council conducts studies and presents recommendations concerning problems in the fields of environmental protection, natural resources, and growth management; consults with, negotiates with, and obtains information from other state and federal agencies; offers guidance and recommendations to the Governor and Council or the General Court; recommends disposition or lease of state-owned surplus real property.
Contact(s):
Jeffrey Taylor, Chairman

COUNTY OF SAN DIEGO

DEPARTMENT OF PLANNING AND LAND USE
MULTIPLE SPECIES CONSERVATION PROGRAM
5201 Ruffin Road
Suite B
San Diego, CA 92123 United States
Phone: 858-694-3075 Fax: 858-694-2555
E-mail: mscp@sdcounty.ca.gov
Website: www.mscp-sandiego.org

Founded: N/A
Scope: Local, Regional
Description: Working with the Federal, State, local and regional governments to protect the region's biodiversity and 85 sensitive species by linking together large blocks of habitat with County, State and Federal parks, open space and watershsed protection areas to preserve biological core areas and connecting corridors.
Keyword(s): Ecosystems (precious), Land Issues, Public Lands/Greenspace, Wildlife & Species
Contact(s):
Trish Boaz, Environmental Resource Manager; 858-694-3075; Fax: 858-694-2555; trish.boaz@sdcounty.ca.gov

D

DELAWARE COOPERATIVE EXTENSION SERVICES

Delaware Cooperative Extension, Townsend Hall, University of Delaware
Newark, DE 19717-1303 United States
Phone: 302-831-2504 Fax: 302-831-6758
E-mail: pbarber@udel.edu
Website: www.bluehen.ags.udel.edu/deces/

Founded: N/A
Scope: State
Keyword(s): Agriculture/Farming, Energy, Forests/Forestry, Land Issues, Pollution (general), Public Health, Wildlife & Species
Contact(s):
Robin Morgan, Dean, College of Agricultural Sciences and Director, Agricul
Patricia Barber, Associate Dean for Extension and Outreach; pbarber@udel.edu
John Ewart, Aquaculture Specialist; University of Delaware Aquac. Research Center, 700 Pilottown Rd., Lewes, DE 19958; 302-645-4060; Fax: 302-645-4007

DELAWARE DEPARTMENT OF AGRICULTURE

FOREST SERVICE
2320 S. DuPont Hwy.
Dover, DE 19901 United States
Phone: 302-739-4811 Fax: 302-697-6287
E-mail: kay@dda.state.de.us
Website: www.state.de.us/deptagri/

Founded: 1982
Scope: State
Description: A statewide organization affiliated with the National Woodland Owners Association, dedicated to promote good forest practices and multiple use of private forest lands in Delaware.
Publication(s): DFA Newsletter
Keyword(s): Forests/Forestry
Contact(s):
W. Jones, President and Editor; 410-742-3163
Jim Bennett, Vice President

DELAWARE DEPARTMENT OF NATURAL RESOURCES AND ENVIRONMENTAL CONTROL

DIVISION OF AIR AND WASTE MANAGEMENT
89 Kings Hwy., P.O. Box 1401
Dover, DE 19901 United States
Phone: 302-739-4403 Fax: 302-739-6242

Founded: N/A

Scope: State

Contact(s):

Denise Ferguson-Southard, Director; 302-739-4764
Nancy Marker, Manager, Hazardous Waste; 302-739-3689
Jamie Rutherford, Manager, Solid Waste; 302-739-3820
Kathleen Stiller, Manager, Underground Storage Tanks; 302-323-4588
Christina Wirtz, Manager, Site Investigation and Remediation; 302-395-2600
William Hill, Administrator Enforcement; 302-739-5072

DELAWARE DEPARTMENT OF NATURAL RESOURCES AND ENVIRONMENTAL CONTROL

DIVISION OF FISH AND WILDLIFE
89 Kings Hwy.
Dover, DE 19901 United States
Phone: 302-739-5295 Fax: 302-739-6157
Website: www.dnrec.state.de.us-fw-index.htm

Founded: N/A
Membership: 101–1,000
Scope: Local
Publication(s): The Observer
Contact(s):

Andrew Manus, Director; 302-739-5295
Phil Carpenter, Manager, Acquisitions; 302-739-3441
Lacy Nichols, Manager, Construction; 302-739-3441
H. Alexander, Administrator, Wildlife; 302-739-5297
James Graybeal, Administrator, Enforcement; 302-739-3440
Lynn Herman, Federal Aid Coordinator and Senior Planner; 302-739-5296
Charles Lesser, Administrator, Fisheries; 302-739-3441
William Meredith, Administrator of Mosquito Control; 302-739-3493

DELAWARE DEPARTMENT OF NATURAL RESOURCES AND ENVIRONMENTAL CONTROL

DIVISION OF FISH AND WILDLIFE
89 Kings Highway
Dover, DE 19901 United States
Phone: 302-739-4431 Fax: 302-739-6157
Website: www.dnrec.state.de.us

Founded: 1970
Membership: 101–1,000
Scope: State
Description: The mission of the Delaware Department of Natural Resources and Environmental Control is to protect and manage the state's natural resources, protect public health and safety, provide quality outdoor recreation and to serve and educate the citizens of Delaware to promote the wise use, conservation, and enhancement of Delaware's environment.
Publication(s): Outdoor Delaware, DNREC News
Keyword(s): Air Quality/Atmosphere, Land Issues, Oceans/Coasts/Beaches, Reduce/Reuse/Recycle, Water Habitats & Quality, Wildlife & Species
Contact(s):

Melinda Carl, Editor, DNREC News; 302-739-4506
Nicholas DiPasquale, Secretary; ndipasquale@state.de.us
Kathleen Jamison, Editor, Outdoor Delaware; 302-739-4506
David Small, Deputy Secretary

DELAWARE DEPARTMENT OF NATURAL RESOURCES AND ENVIRONMENTAL CONTROL

DIVISION OF PARKS AND RECREATION
89 Kings Hwy.
Dover, DE 19901 United States
Phone: 302-739-4401 Fax: 302-739-3817
Website: www.destateparks.com

Founded: 1951

Scope: State

Description: State Park Agency

Contact(s):

Charles Salkin, Director; 302-739-4401
Mark Chura, Manager, Planning, Preservation and Development; 302-739-5285
James Oneill, Manager, Cultural & Recreation Services; 302-739-4413
Clyde Shipman, Manager, Park Operations; 302-739-4406

DELAWARE DEPARTMENT OF NATURAL RESOURCES AND ENVIRONMENTAL CONTROL

DIVISION OF SOIL AND WATER CONSERVATION
89 Kings Highway
Dover, DE 19901 United States
Phone: 302-739-4411 Fax: 302-739-6724

Founded: N/A

Scope: State

Keyword(s): Air Quality/Atmosphere, Land Issues, Water Habitats & Quality

Contact(s):

John Hughes, Director; jhughes@dnrec.state.de.us
Sarah Cooksey, Administrator: Delaware Coastal Management Program; 302-739-3451
Robert Henry, Administrator: Shoreline and Waterway Management

DELAWARE DEPARTMENT OF NATURAL RESOURCES AND ENVIRONMENTAL CONTROL

DIVISION OF WATER RESOURCES
89 Kings Hwy.
Dover, DE 19901 United States
Phone: 302-739-4403
Website: www.dnrc.state.de.us

Founded: N/A

Scope: State

Contact(s):

Kevin Donnelly, Director; 302-739-4860
Peder Hansen, Manager, Surface Water Discharges; 302-739-5731
Stewart Lovell, Manager, Water Supply; 302-739-4793
William Moyer, Manager, Wetlands and Subaqueous Lands; 302-739-4691
John Schneider, Manager, Watershed Assessment; 302-739-4590
Rodney Wyatt, Manager, Ground Water Discharges; 302-739-4761
Sergio Huerta, Administrator, Environmental Services

DELAWARE FOREST SERVICE

2320 S. DuPont Highway
Dover, DE 19901-5515 United States
Phone: 302-698-4500 Fax: 302-697-6245
E-mail: austin@dda.state.de.us
Website: www.state.de.us/deptagri/

Founded: 1927
Membership: N/A
Scope: State
Description: The DDA works to provide mandated services which protect the health and welfare of Delaware consumers and to advertise those services; to promote the sound utilization of resources, especially agricultural lands; and to advance the

economic viability of the food, fiber, and agricultural industries of Delaware.

Keyword(s): Agriculture/Farming, Forests/Forestry, Land Issues, Pollution (general)

Contact(s):

Teresa Crenshaw, Agriculture Compliance Laboratory; teresa@dda.state.de.us
Anne Fitzgerald, Community Relations Officer; anne.dda.state.de.us
Michael Scuse, Secretary
Bruce Walton, Executive Assistant; brucew@dda.state.de.us

DELAWARE GEOLOGICAL SURVEY

DGS Bldg., University of Delaware
Newark, DE 19716 United States
Phone: 302-831-2833 Fax: 302-831-3579
E-mail: delgeosurvey@udel.edu
Website: www.udel.edu/dgs

Founded: 1951
Membership: 1–100
Scope: State
Description: The survey was formed to study the geology, water, and other earth resources of Delaware; also to prepare reports, maps, and otherwise disseminate its findings, and to provide assistance in its area to other agencies and individuals.

Contact(s):

Robert Jordan, State Geologist and Director
John Talley, Associate Director; waterman@udel.edu
Dorothy Windish, Librarian

DELAWARE SOLID WASTE AUTHORITY

1128 S. Bradford St., P.O. Box 455
Dover, DE 19903 United States
Phone: 302-739-5361 Fax: 302-739-4287
E-mail: dra@dswa.com
Website: www.dswa.com

Founded: 1975
Membership: 101–1,000
Scope: Local
Description: To define, develop, and implement cost-effective plans and programs for solid waste management which best serve Delaware and protect our public health and environment.
Publication(s): Statewide Solid Waste Management Plan and Executive Summary, Trash Tracks (DSWA Newsletter), Marketing Research Findings and Executive Summary, Great Waste Mystery Curriculum
Keyword(s): Public Health, Reduce/Reuse/Recycle

Contact(s):

Pasquale Canzano, Chief Operating Officer; psc@dswa.com
Thomas Houska, Chief of Administrative/ Services Officer; teh@dswa.com
N. Vasuki, Chief Executive Officer; ncv@dswa.com

DEPARTAMENTO DE RECURSOS NATURALES Y AMBIENTALES

AREA DE PLANIFICACION INTEGRAL
DIVISION DE PATRIMONIO NATURAL
P.O.BOX 9066600 PUERTA DE TIERRA STATION
San Juan, 00906-6600 Puerto Rico
Phone: 787-724-8774, ext. 4037 Fax: 787-725-9526
E-mail: dpn@caribe.net
Website: http://www.natureserve.org/nhp/lacarb/pr/

Founded: 1988
Membership: N/A
Scope: State
Description: Identify and protect priority conservation areas
Keyword(s): Ecosystems (precious), Wildlife & Species

Contact(s):

Aida Martinez, Division Director
Daniel Davila-Casanova, Zoologist/Data Manager; 787-724-8774, ext. 2230; dpn@caribe.net

DEPARTMENT FOR ENVIRONMENT AND HERITAGE

Level 9 Chesser House
91 97 Grenfell Street
Adelaide, 5000 Australia
Phone: 8204-1910, ext. 8
E-mail: environmentshop@saugov.sa.gov.au
Website: www.environment.sa.gov.au

Founded: 1990
Membership: N/A
Scope: Local, State, Regional, National
Description: State Government body representing Land, Water, Biodiversity, Conservation, National Parks and Wildlife SA and environmental policy.
Keyword(s): Air Quality/Atmosphere, Ecosystems (precious), Land Issues, Oceans/Coasts/Beaches, Pollution (general), Recreation/Ecotourism, Reduce/Reuse/Recycle, Water Habitats & Quality, Wildlife & Species

Contact(s):

Alan Holmes, Chief Executive

DEPARTMENT OF CONSERVATION

NORTHEASTERN REGION
Box 28, 59 Elizabeth Rd.
Thompson, R8N 1X4 Manitoba Canada
Phone: 204-677-6628 Fax: 204-677-6359

Founded: N/A
Scope: Regional

Contact(s):

Don Cook, Regional Director; 204-677-6628
Steve Kearney, Regional Superintendent; 204-677-6629

DEPARTMENT OF CULTURE, HERITAGE, AND TOURISM

Travel Manitoba, Department RHO, 7th Fl., 155 Carlton St.
Winnipeg, R3C 3H8 Manitoba Canada
Phone: 204-945-3777 Fax: 204-945-2302
Website: www.travelmanitoba.com

Founded: N/A
Scope: State
Description: Coordinates visits to Manitoba by travel and outdoor editors; produces and distributes travel and outdoor literature and films.

Contact(s):

Statia Elliot, Director of Marketing; 204-945-6777
Colette Fontaine, Marketing Consultant; 204-945-4045
Hubert Messman, Assistant Deputy Minister of Tourism and Business Developmen; 204-945-4204

DEPARTMENT OF ENVIRONMENT AND CONSERVATION (TENNESSEE)

401 Church St., 21st Fl.
Nashville, TN 37243 United States
Phone: 615-532-0109 Fax: 615-532-0120
E-mail: ask.tdec@state.tn.us
Website: www.tdec.org

Founded: N/A
Membership: 1,001–10,000
Scope: State
Description: To plan, promote, protect, and conserve this state's natural, cultural, recreational, and historical resources, and to enforce environmental laws and regulations which protect the state's land and water.

Contact(s):

Mike Apple, Director of Solid Waste Management; 615-532-0780; Fax: 615-532-0886

Charles Brewton, Director of Resort Operations; 615-532-0263; Fax: 615-532-0740
Paul Davis, Director of Water Pollution Control; 615-532-0625; Fax: 615-532-0046
David Draughon, Director of Water Supply; 615-532-0191; Fax: 615-532-0503
Tim Eagle, Director of Land Reclamation; 865-594-5609
Wayne Gregory, Director of Underground Storage Tanks; 615-532-0945; Fax: 615-532-0938
Herbert Harper, Director of Historical Commission; 615-532-1550; Fax: 615-532-1549
Jim Haynes, Director of Superfund; 615-532-0900; Fax: 615-532-0938
Toye Heape, Director of Indian Affairs; 615-532-0745; Fax: 615-532-0732
Joyce Hoyle, Director of Recreation Resources; 615-742-0748; Fax: 615-532-0778
Eddie Nanney, Director of Radiological Health; 615-532-0364
Reggie Reeves, Director of Natural Heritage Division; 615-532-0431; Fax: 615-532-0231
Barry Stephens, Director of Air Pollution Control; 615-532-0554; Fax: 615-532-0614
Kent Taylor, Director of Groundwater Protection; 615-532-0762; Fax: 615-532-0778
Ron Zurawski, Director of Geology; 615-532-1500; Fax: 615-532-1517
Tom Callery, Asst. Commissioner for Conservation; 615-532-4511; Fax: 615-532-0231
Nick Fielder, State Archaeologist of Archaeology Division; 615-741-1588; Fax: 615-741-7329
Dodd Galbreagh, Environmental Policy Office; 615-532-8545; Fax: 615-532-0120
Milton Hamilton, Commissioner; 615-532-0109; Fax: 615-532-0120
John Leonard, Asst. Commissioner for Environment; 615-532-0225; Fax: 615-532-0120
Kim Olson, Public Information Officer; 615-532-0288; Fax: 615-532-0740
Joe Sanders, General Counsel; 615-532-0131; Fax: 615-532-0145
Mark Williams, Asst. Commissioner for State Parks; 615-532-0022; Fax: 615-532-0732

DEPARTMENT OF ENVIRONMENT AND WILDLIFE (QUEBEC)

Edifice Marie-Guyart, 675, Blvd. Rene-Levesque East
Quebec City, G1R 5V7 Quebec Canada
Phone: 418-521-3830 Fax: 418-646-5974
E-mail: info@menv.gouv.qc.ca
Website: www.menv.gouv.qc.ca

Founded: N/A

Contact(s):

George Arsenault, Vice-President of Society of Faune and Parks of Quebec; 418-521-3851
Claudette Blais, Vice-President of Parks for Quebec; 418-521-3850
Luc Berthiaume, Director of Internal Affairs; 418-521-3828
Andre Martel, Director of Wildlife Protection In Outaouais; 418-622-0313
Andre Taillon, Director General of Wildlife Protection; 819-623-1981
Paul Begin, Minister; 418-521-3911
Herve Bolduc, General Secretary; 418-521-3850
Diane Gian, Deputy Minister; 418-521-3860

DEPARTMENT OF ENVIRONMENTAL MANAGEMENT (RHODE ISLAND)

235 Promenade St.
Providence, RI 02908 United States
Phone: 401-222-2774 Fax: 401-222-6174
Website: www.state.ri.us/dem

Founded: N/A

Membership: 101–1,000

Scope: State

Description: The Department of Environmental Management's top priorities include the preservation and protection of the environmental quality of Rhode Island. Air pollution, water pollution, and waste disposal problems are handled by the DEM. The DEM develops, administers, and enforces programs designed to preserve and manage Rhode Island's forests, parks, farms, wildlife, fisheries, and coastline. DEM is also responsible for providing, on the average, 750 full-time jobs for the people of Rhode Island.

Contact(s):

Jan Reitsma, Director; 235 Promenade St., Providence, RI 02908; 401-222-2771
Dean Albro, Compliance and Inspection; 235 Promenade St., Providence, RI 02908; 401-277-6820
Kenneth Ayers, Chief of Agriculture; 83 Park St., Providence, RI 02903; 401-222-2781
Susan Bundy, Chief of Watershed and Standards; 235 Promenade St., Providence, RI 02908
Russell Chateauneuf, Chief of Permitting; 235 Promenade St., Providence, RI 02908; 401-222-2306
Thomas Dupree, Chief of Forest Environment; R.F.D. #2 Box 851, North Scituate, RI 02859; 401-222-1414
Ronald Gagnon, Chief of Technical and Customer Assistance; 291 Promenade St., Providence, RI 02908; 401-277-2797
Alicia Good, Assistant Director of Water Resources; 235 Promenade St., Providence, RI 02908; 401-222-3961
Malcolm Grant, Associate Director for Natural Resource Management; 235 Promenade St., Providence, RI 02908; 401-222-6605
Terrence Gray, Asst. Director for Air, Waste & Compliance; 235 Promenade St., Providence, RI 02908; 401-222-6677
Steven Hall, Chief of Enforcement; 83 Park St., Providence, RI 02903; 401-222-2284
Leo Hellested, Chief of Waste Management; 235 Promenade St., Providence, RI 02908; 401-277-2797
Janet Keller, Chief of Strategic Planning and Policy; 235 Promenade St., Providence, RI 02908; 401-277-3434
Kathleen Lanphear, Chief Hearing Officer of Administrative Adjudication; 235 Promenade, Providence, RI 02908; 401-222-1357
Stephen Majkut, Chief of Air Resources; 235 Promenade St., Providence, RI 02908; 401-222-2808
Melanie Marcaccio, Chief of Office of Human Resources; 235 Promenade St., Providence, RI 02908; 401-222-2774
Donald McGovern, Chief of Coastal Resources; 83 Park St., Providence, RI 02903; 401-222-3429
Glenn Miller, Chief of Management Services; 235 Promenade St., Providence, RI 02908; 401-222-6825
Larry Mouradjian, Chief of Parks and Recreation; 2321 Hartford Ave., Johnston, RI 02919; 401-222-2632
Kurt Schatz, Chief of Criminal Investigation Office; 235 Promenade St., Providence, RI 02908; 401-222-6768
John Stolgitis, Chief of Fish and Wildlife; Stedman Government Center, Wakefield, RI 02879; 401-222-3075
Robert Sutton, Chief of Planning and Development; 235 Promenade St., Providence, RI 02908; 401-222-2776
Frederick Vincent, Associate Director for Planning and Administration; 235 Promenade St., Providence, RI 02908; 401-222-2776

DEPARTMENT OF ENVIRONMENTAL QUALITY (ARKANSAS)

8001 National Dr., P.O. Box 8913
Little Rock, AR 72219-8913 United States
Phone: 501-682-0744 Fax: 501-682-0798
E-mail: help-cuspsvs@adeq.state.ar.us
Website: www.adeq.state.ar.us

Founded: 1949

Membership: 101–1,000

Scope: State

Description: To prevent, abate, and control all types of pollution and maintain the state's natural environment.

Publication(s): Arkansas Waste Line

Keyword(s): Air Quality/Atmosphere, Oceans/Coasts/Beaches, Reduce/Reuse/Recycle

Contact(s):

Richard Weiss, Director
Mike Bates, Chief of Hazardous Waste Division
Chuck Bennett, Chief of Water Division
Dennis Burks, Chief of Solid Waste Division
Richard Cassat, Chief of Technical Services Division
Leigh Ann Chrouch, Chief of Fiscal Division
Al Eckert, Chief of Legal Division
Sandy Formica, Chief of Environmental Preservation Division
Robert Gage, Chief of Computer Services Division
James Gilson, Chief of Customer Service Division
Becky Keogh, Deputy Director
Mary Leath, Chief Deputy Director; 501-682-0959
Keith Michaels, Chief of Air Division
Ed Morris, Administrator of Management Services
Jim Shell, Chief of Regulated Storage Tank Division

DEPARTMENT OF ENVIRONMENTAL QUALITY

INDUSTRIAL SITING DIVISION
State of Wyoming, 3rd Fl, E Herschler Bldg.
Cheyenne, WY 82002 United States
Phone: 307-777-4369
E-mail: vforse@missc.state.wy.us
Website: www.dequ.state.wy.us/

Founded: 1975

Description: Administers the Wyoming Industrial Development Information and Siting Act, which deals with the social, economic, and environmental impacts of large-scale industrial development. Responsibilities consist of investigating, reviewing, processing, and serving notice of permit applications.

Contact(s):

Gary Beach, Administrator; 307-777-7369

DEPARTMENT OF GEOLOGY AND MINERAL INDUSTRIES

800 NE Oregon St., Suite 965, #28
Portland, OR 97232-2162 United States
Phone: 503-731-4100 Fax: 503-731-4066
Website: www.oregongeology.com

Founded: N/A
Membership: 1–100
Scope: State
Publication(s): Oregon Geology - quarterly

Contact(s):

John Beaulieu, State Geologist; john.beaulieu@state.or.us
Klaus Nevendorf, Librarian; 800 NE Oregon St., Suite 965, #28, Portland, OR 97232-2162

DEPARTMENT OF LAND AND NATURAL RESOURCES (HAWAII)

P.O Box 621
Honolulu, HI 96809 United States
Phone: 808-587-0400 Fax: 808-587-0390
E-mail: dlnr@pixie.com

Founded: N/A

Scope: State

Contact(s):

Gilbert Coloma-Agaran, Chairman, Commission on Water Resources Management; 808-587-0401
Janet Kawelo, Deputy to Chairperson; 805-870-0403
Linnel Nishioka, Deputy Director Commission on Water Resouce Management; 808-587-0214

DEPARTMENT OF LAND AND NATURAL RESOURCES (HAWAII)

601 Kamokila Blvd.
Kapolei, HI 96707 United States
Phone: 808-692-8015 Fax: 808-692-8020
Website: www.state.hi.us-dlnr-hpd-hpgreeting.htm

Founded: N/A
Membership: 1–100
Scope: Local

Contact(s):

Don Hibbard, Administrator; 808-587-0045

DEPARTMENT OF LAND AND NATURAL RESOURCES (HAWAII)

DIVISION OF AQUATIC RESOURCES
1151 Punchbowl St.
Honolulu, HI 96813 United States
Phone: 808-587-0100 Fax: 808-587-0115
Website: www.state.hi.us/dlnr/dnr

Founded: N/A

Scope: State

Contact(s):

Michael Fugimoto, Program Manager: Commercial Fisheries Aquaculture Branch; 808-587-0085
William Devick, Administrator, Acting; 808-587-0110

DEPARTMENT OF LAND AND NATURAL RESOURCES (HAWAII)

DIVISION OF BOATING AND OCEAN RECREATION
333 Queen Street
Honolulu, HI 96813 United States
Phone: 808-587-1963 Fax: 808-587-1977
Website: www.hawaii.gov/dlnr/ddor

Founded: N/A

Scope: State

Contact(s):

Mason Young, Administrator, Acting

DEPARTMENT OF LAND AND NATURAL RESOURCES (HAWAII)

DIVISION OF CONSERVATION AND RESOURCES ENFORCEMENT
1151 Punchbowl St., Rm. 311
Honolulu, HI 96813 United States
Phone: 808-587-0077 Fax: 808-587-0080
Website: www.state.hi.us/dlnr.html

Founded: N/A

Scope: State

Publication(s): Hunter Education

Contact(s):

Wendell Kam, Manager: Hunter Education Program; 808-587-0200
Gary Moniz, Administrator, Acting

DEPARTMENT OF LAND AND NATURAL RESOURCES (HAWAII)

DIVISION OF FORESTRY AND WILDLIFE
1151 Punchbowl St.
Honolulu, HI 96813 United States
Phone: 808-587-0166 Fax: 808-587-0160

Founded: N/A
Membership: 1–100
Scope: State

Contact(s):

Carl Masaki, Manager, Forestry Program
Michael Buck, Administrator

DEPARTMENT OF LAND AND NATURAL RESOURCES (HAWAII)

DIVISION OF STATE PARKS
P.O. Box 621
Honolulu, HI 96809 United States
Phone: 808-587-0300

Founded: N/A

Contact(s):
Ralston Nagata, Administrator: State Parks

DEPARTMENT OF LAND AND NATURAL RESOURCES (HAWAII)

DIVISION OF WATER RESOURCE MANAGEMENT
P.O. Box 621
Honolulu, HI 96809 United States
Phone: 808-587-0214 Fax: 808-587-0219
Website: www.state.hi.us/dlnr/cwrm

Founded: N/A

Scope: State

Description: Protect and enhance the water resources of the state of Hawaii through wise and responsible management.

Keyword(s): Land Issues, Wildlife & Species

Contact(s):
Linnel Nishioka, Deputy

DEPARTMENT OF LAND AND NATURAL RESOURCES (HAWAII)

LAND DIVISION
P. O. Box 621
Honolulu, HI 96809 United States
Phone: 808-587-0446 Fax: 808-587-0455
Website: www.state.hi.us

Founded: N/A
Membership: 1–100
Scope: State

Contact(s):
Harry Yada, Administrator

DEPARTMENT OF LANDS (IDAHO)

P.O. Box 83720
Boise, ID 83720-0050 United States
Phone: 208-334-0200 Fax: 208-334-2339
E-mail: boise@idl.state.id.us
Website: www.state.id.us.lands

Founded: N/A
Membership: 101–1,000
Scope: State

Description: The State Board of Land Commissioners is a constitutional board charged with administering the trust under which endowment lands are held. These lands were granted to the state at the time of statehood for the financial support of nine beneficiaries, the largest being the common schools.

Publication(s): Sentinel Newsletter Quarterly, Public Involvement Brochure

Contact(s):
Dirk Kempthorne, State Board of Land Commissioner President; 208-334-2100
Winston Wiggins, Secretary of Board & Director of the Idaho Dept. of Lands
Pete Cenarrusa, Secretary of State; 208-334-2300
Marilyn Howard, Superintendent of Public Instruction; 208-332-6800
Alan Lance, Attorney General; 208-334-2400
J. Williams, State Controller; 208-334-3100

DEPARTMENT OF PARKS AND RECREATION

DEPARTMENT OF PARKS AND RECREATION
1416 9th Street
Room 1405
Sacramento, CA 95814 United States
Phone: 916-653-8380 Fax: 916-657-3903
Website: www.cal-parks.ca.gov

Founded: N/A

Scope: Local, State

Description: Responsible for the acquisition, preservation, development, interpretation, and operation of the state park system; also responsible for the administration of grants for recreation to local government and for development of the California Outdoor Recreation Resources Plan.

Keyword(s): Recreation/Ecotourism

Contact(s):
Ruth Coleman, Director; 916-653-8380
Bill Berry, Chief Deputy Director of Park Stewardship; 916-653-8288
Ron Brean, Chief of Northern Division; 916-657-4042
George Cook, Central Field Division Chief; 916-653-2021
Tim Lafranchi, Legal Office; 916-653-6884
John McMahon, Deputy Director of Marketing and Revenue Generation; 916-653-5841; jmcma@parks.ca.gov
Knox Mellon, Deputy Director of Historic Preservation Office; 916-653-6624
Pilar Onate, Deputy Director of Legislation; 916-653-6887
Richard Rayburn, Natural Heritage Division; 916-653-6745
Mark Schrader, Acquisition and Development; 916-653-7475; mschrader@parks.ca.gov
Steven Treanor, Chief of Southern Division; 916-657-4042; strea@parks.ca.gov
Denzil Verardo, Chief Deputy Director of Administration; 916-653-0528
Ray Watson, Human Rights; 916-653-9990
Dave Widell, Deputy Director of Off Highway Motor Vehicle Recreation; 916-324-5801

DEPARTMENT OF PARKS AND RECREATION (GUAM)

Building 13-8
Tiyan, GU 96913 United States
Phone: 671-475-9620 Fax: 671-472-9626

Founded: N/A
Keyword(s): Public Lands/Greenspace, Recreation/Ecotourism
Contact(s):
A. Shelton, Director
Franklin Gutierrez, Deputy Director

DEPARTMENT OF PARKS, RECREATION AND TOURISM

Edgar A. Brown Bldg.
1205 Pendleton St.
Columbia, SC 29201 United States
Phone: 803-734-1700 Fax: 803-734-0138
E-mail: fulfillment@scprt.com
Website: www.discoversouthcarolina.com

Founded: N/A

Scope: State

Contact(s):
Curt Cottle, Director of Heritage Tourism Development Office
Terri Cowling, Director of Marketing Office
Roger Deaton, Director of Internal Operations
John Durst, Director
David Elwart, Director of Information Technology
Charles Harrison, Director of Division of Parks and Recreation
Isabel Hill, Director of Division of Tourism Development
Robert Liming, Director of New Market Development
Beth McClure, Director of Office of Recreation, Planning, and Engineering

R. McGowan, Director of Tourism
Toni Nance, Director of Business Development Office
Beverly Shelley, Director of Sales Office
Yvette Sistare, Director of Finance Office
Van Stickles, Director of State Park Service
Ronald Carter, Deputy Director
Amy Duffy, Deputy Director
Marion Edmonds, Agency Spokesperson

DEPARTMENT OF PLANNING AND NATURAL RESOURCES

DIVISION OF ENVIRONMENTAL PROTECTION
Cyril E. King Airport, 2nd Floor
St. Thomas, VI 00802 United States
Phone: 340-774-3320 Fax: 340-714-9549
E-mail: stt-office@vidpnr-dep.org
Website: www.dpnr.gov.vi/dep/home.htm

Founded: 1970

Description: Responsible for: Fish and wildlife; trees, vegetation and water resources; air and water pollution control; flood control; sewers and sewage disposal; culture and the arts; libraries and museums; minerals and other natural resources; historical preservation; submerged lands; earth change permits; and oil spill prevention and control.

Publication(s): Annual Report, Species Technical Bulletin, Natural History Atlas to the Cays of the Virgin Islands, Wildlife Plant booklet, Proceedings - Fisheries in Crisis Conference (Division of Fish and Wildlife), Blue Book, Zone Management Notes (CZM Notes)

Keyword(s): Water Habitats & Quality, Wildlife & Species

Contact(s):
Hollis Griffin, Director, Division of Environmental Protection
Dean Plaskett, Esq., Commissioner, Department of Planning & Natural Resources
Leonard Reed, Esq., Assistant Director, Division of Environmental Protection

DEPARTMENT OF PLANNING AND NATURAL RESOURCES

DIVISION OF FISH AND WILDLIFE
UNITED STATES VIRGIN ISLANDS
6291 Estate Nazareth, 101
St. Thomas, VI 00802 United States
Phone: 340-775-6762 Fax: 340-775-3972

Founded: N/A

Membership: 1–100

Scope: Regional

Publication(s): Wildlife Viewing Guide

Contact(s):
Barbara Kojis, Director; bkojis@telecom.net
Judy Pierce, Chief of Wildlife; sula@vitelcom.net

DEPARTMENT OF PUBLIC WORKS

2000 14th St., NW
Washington, DC 20009 United States
Phone: 202-727-1000
Website: dpw.dc.gov/main.shtml

Founded: N/A

Keyword(s): Oceans/Coasts/Beaches, Reduce/Reuse/Recycle, Transportation

Contact(s):
Leslie Hotaling, Director

DEPARTMENT OF RENEWABLE RESOURCES

Box 2703
Whitehorse, Y1A 2C6 Yukon Canada
Phone: 867-667-5652 Fax: 867-393-6213
Website: www.renres.gov.yk.ca

Founded: N/A

Contact(s):
Karyn Armour, Acting Director of Policy and Planning; 403-667-5634
Joe Ballantyne, Director of Environmental Protection and Assessment; 403-667-8177
Dave Beckman, Director of Agriculture; 403-667-5838
Stan Marinoske, Director of Finance and Administration; 403-667-5197
Jim McIntyre, Director of Parks and Outdoor Recreation; 403-667-5261
Don Toews, Acting Director of Fish and Wildlife; 403-667-5715
Jim Connell, Acting Assistant Deputy Minister; 402-667-8955
Bill Oppen, Deputy Minister; 403-667-5460

DEPARTMENT OF RESOURCES AND ECONOMIC DEVELOPMENT

172 Pembroke Rd.
Concord, NH 03302-1856 United States
Phone: 603-271-2411 Fax: 603-271-2629
E-mail: gbald@dred.state.nh.us
Website: www.dred.state.nh. us

Founded: N/A

Scope: State

Contact(s):
Stuart Arnett, Director of Division of Economic Development; 603-271-2341
Philip Bryce, Director of Division of Forests and Lands; 603-271-2214
Lauri Klefos, Director of Division of Travel and Tourism Developement
Richard McLeod, Director of Division of Parks; 603-271-3556
George Bald, Commissioner; 603-271-2411
J. Cullen, Urban Forester of Urban Forestry Center; 603-431-6774
Paul Gray, Chief of Bureau of Off-Highway Recreational Vehicles; 603-271-3254

DEPARTMENT OF RESOURCES, WILDLIFE AND ECONOMIC DEVELOPMENT, GOVERNMENT OF THE NORTHWEST TERRITORIES

P.O. Box 1320
Yellowknife, X1A 2L9 Northwest Territories Canada
Phone: 867-873-7379 Fax: 867-873-0114
Website: www.rwed-hq.gov.nt.ca

Founded: N/A

Scope: State

Description: Has broad responsibility for wildlife, environmental protection, forest management, parks and tourism, trade and investment, and minerals, oil, and gas in the Northwest Territories, and provides assistance to people dependent on these resources to harvest wildlife in a manner which will ensure continued availability of the resource.

Publication(s): Safety in Bear Country, Sport Fishing Guide, NWT Wildlife Sketches, NWT Explorers Guide, Summary of Hunting Regulations

Keyword(s): Agriculture/Farming, Air Quality/Atmosphere, Climate Change, Energy, Executive/Legislative/Judicial Reform, Forests/Forestry, Land Issues, Pollution (general), Public Lands/Greenspace, Recreation/Ecotourism, Reduce/Reuse/Recycle, Wildlife & Species

Contact(s):
Susan Corey, Director of Forest Management; Box 7, Fort Smith, Northwest Territories X0E 0P0; 867-872-7700; Fax: 867-872-2077
Doris Eggers, Director of Policy and Legislation/Communications; 867-920-8046; Fax: 867-873-0114
Martin Irving, Director of Diamond Projects; 867-920-3125; Fax: 867-873-0224
Jim Kennedy, Director of Corporate Service; 867-873-7532; Fax: 867-920-2756

Gerry LePrieur, Director of Parks and Tourism; 867-873-7902; Fax: 867-873-0163
Doug Matthews, Director of Minerals, Oil and Gas; 867-920-3222; Fax: 867-873-0254
Otto Olah, Director of Investment and Economic Analysis; 867-873-7361; Fax: 867-873-0101
Emery Paquin, Director of Environmental Protection; 867-873-7654; Fax: 867-873-0221
Doug Stewart, Director of Wildlife and Fisheries; 867-920-8064; Fax: 867-873-0293
Jim Antoine, Minister; 867-669-2388; Fax: 867-873-0306; jim_antoine@gov.nt.ca
Robert Bailey, Assistant Deputy Minister, Operations; 867-920-6389; Fax: 867-873-0638
Doug Doan, Assistant Deputy Minister of Resources; 867-873-7115; Fax: 867-873-0114
Lloyd Jones, Regional Superintendent; Box 390, Fort Smith, Northwest Territories X0E 0P0; 867-872-6400; Fax: 879-872-4250
Paul Kraft, Regional Superintendent; Box 240, Fort Simpson, Northwest Territories X0E 0N0; 879-695-2231; Fax: 897-695-2442
Robert McLeod, Deputy Minister; 867-920-8048; Fax: 867-873-0563; bob-mcleod@gov.mt.ca
Ron Morrison, Regional Superintendent; Bag 1, Inuvik, Northwest Territories X0E 0T0; 879-777-7286; Fax: 879-777-7321
Robert Murphy, Regional Superintendent, Acting; Box 2668, Yellowknife, Northwest Territories X1A 2P9; 879-920-6134; Fax: 879-873-6230
Celina Stroeder, Regional Superintendent; Box 130, Normal Wells, Northwest Territories X0E 0V0; 879-587-3501; Fax: 879-587-2204
Alison Welch, Librarian; NWT Resources, Wildlife and Economic Development Library, P.O. Box 1320, Yellowknife, Northwest Territories X1A 2L9; 867-920-8606; Fax: 867-873-0293

DEPARTMENT OF THE ENVIRONMENT

2500 Broening Highway
Baltimore, MD 21224 United States
Phone: 410-631-3000 Fax: 410-631-3966
Website: www.mde.state.md.us

Founded: 1987

Scope: State

Description: The Department of the Environment is charged with protection of the state's land, air, and water resources, to ensure the long-term protection of public health and quality of life.

Publication(s): Regulatory Calendar, List of Potential Hazardous Waste Sites, Biennial Water Report, Annual Air Quality Data Report

Keyword(s): Air Quality/Atmosphere, Oceans/Coasts/Beaches, Pollution (general), Reduce/Reuse/Recycle

Contact(s):

Richard Collins, Director of Waste Management Administration; 410-631-3304
Ann Marie Debiase, Director of Air and Radiation Management Administration
Allan Jensen, Director of Administrative and Employee Services; 410-631-3116
Robert Summers, Director of Water Management Administration
Denise Ferguson-Southard, Assistant Secretary
Etta Lyles, Librarian; 410-631-3818
Jane Nishida, Secretary; 410-631-3084
Merrylin Zaw-Mon, Deputy Director

DEPARTMENT OF TOURISM, CULTURE AND RECREATION

Commerce Court
Cornerbrook, A2H 6J8 Newfoundland Canada
Phone: 709-729-2817 Fax: 709-637-2004

Founded: N/A

Membership: 1–100

Scope: State

Contact(s):

Kevin Aylward, Minister; 709-729-4715
Clyde Granter, Deputy Minister
Keith Healey, Associate Deputy Minister

DEPARTMENT OF TRANSPORTATION (RHODE ISLAND)

Two Capitol Hill
Providence, RI 02903 United States
Phone: 401-222-1362

Founded: N/A

Description: To provide a safe, efficient, effective, and environmentally responsible intermodal transportation system that supports economic development and improves our quality of life.

Keyword(s): Transportation

Contact(s):

William Ankner, Director

DEPARTMENT OF WILDLIFE CONSERVATION

1801 N. Lincoln, P.O. Box 53465
Oklahoma City, OK 73152 United States
Phone: 405-521-3851 Fax: 405-521-6535
E-mail: pmoore@odwc.state.ok.us
Website: www.wildlifedepartment.com

Founded: 1909

Membership: 101–1,000

Scope: Regional

Publication(s): Outdoor Oklahoma

Keyword(s): Recreation/Ecotourism, Water Habitats & Quality, Wildlife & Species

Contact(s):

Greg Duffy, Director; 405-521-4660
Ed Abel, Commission Secretary
Kyle Eastham, Human Resorces Administrator; 405-521-4640
Kim Erickson, Chief of Fisheries; 405-521-3721
Richard Hatcher, Assistant Director; 405-522-6279
Vyrl Keeter, Vice Chairman
Alan Peoples, Chief Wildlife Division; 405-521-2739
Nels Rodefeld, Editor; 405-521-4635
Harlan Stonecipher, Commissioner Chairman
John Streich, Chief of Law Enforcement; 405-521-3719
Melinda Sturgess-Striech, Chief of Administation; 405-521-4640
Ron Suttles, Natural Resources Coordinator; 405-521-4616
David Warren, Chief of Information-Education; 405-521-3855

DISTRICT OF COLUMBIA DEPARTMENT OF HEALTH

ENVIRONMENTAL HEALTH ADMINISTRATION, WATERSHED PROTECTION DIVISION
51 N Street NE 5th Floor
Washington, DC 20002 United States
Phone: 202-535-2240
Website:
www.dchealth.com/eha/watersheds/welcome.htm

Founded: N/A

DIVISION DE PATRIMONIO NATURAL

DEPARTMENTO DE RECURSOS NATURALES Y AMBIENTALES DE PUERTO RICO
P.O. Box 9066600
Puerta de Tierra Station
San Juan, 00906-6600 Puerto Rico
Phone: 787-724-8774, ext. 4037 Fax: 787-725-9526
E-mail: dpn@caribe.net
Website: www.natureserve.org/nhp/lacarb/pr/

Founded: N/A

Scope: State

Description: Puerto Rico Natural Heritage Program and Conservation Data Center

Contact(s):
Aida Martinez-Medina, Division Director
Carmen Hernandez-Serrano, Chief, Planning and Acquisitions
Vicente Quevedo-Bonilla, Chief, Research and Data Analysis
Luis Beltran-Burgos, Biologist and Environmental Planner
Amparo Chavez-Quiroga, Environmental Planner
Daniel Davila-Casanova, Biologist and Data Manager
Eliu Rivera-Lucena, Environmental Planner

DIVISION OF FORESTRY AND SOIL RESOURCES OF GUAM

192 Dairy Road
Mangilao, GU 96923 United States
Phone: 671-735-3949 Fax: 671-734-0111

Founded: 1953

Description: The DFSR was formed for the management, protection, and enhancement of the territory's forest and land resources to produce ample amounts of water, wood, fiber, and recreation to benefit the most number of people.

Keyword(s): Forests/Forestry

Contact(s):
Joseph Acfalle, Urban and Community Forester; jacfalle@ns.gu
Rodolfo Ando, Management Forester; rlando@ns.gu
Louann Guzman, Forester I; lcguzman@ns.gu
David Limtiaco, Chief; dlimti@ns.gu
Belmina Soliva, Forester I; bsoliva@ns.gu

E

ENERGY, MINERALS, AND NATURAL RESOURCES DEPARTMENT

Pinon Building
1220 South St. Francis Drive
Santa Fe, NM 87505 United States
Phone: 505-476-3200 Fax: 505-476-3220
Website: www.emnrd.state.nm.us/default.htm

Founded: N/A

Scope: State

Description: As the steward for New Mexico's natural resources, the department seeks to preserve the unique natural beauty of New Mexico and to facilitate the beneficial development and use of its resources in an environmentally responsible manner.

Contact(s):
Betty Rivera, Cabinet Secretary

ENERGY, MINERALS, AND NATURAL RESOURCES DEPARTMENT

ADMINISTRATIVE SERVICES DIVISION
1220 South St. Francis Drive
Santa Fe, NM 87505 United States
Phone: 505-476-3200 Fax: 505-476-3220
Website: www.emnrd.state.nm.us/default.htm

Founded: N/A

Scope: State

Description: Provides clerical, recordkeeping, and administrative support to the department in the areas of personnel, budget, procurement and contracting, and administration of federal and state grants.

Keyword(s): Energy, Land Issues, Recreation/Ecotourism, Reduce/Reuse/Recycle

Contact(s):
Dale Lucero, Director

ENERGY, MINERALS, AND NATURAL RESOURCES DEPARTMENT

ENERGY CONSERVATION AND MANAGEMENT DIVISION
1220 S. St. Francis Drive
P.O. Box 6429
Santa Fe, NM 87505 United States
Phone: 505-476-3310 Fax: 505-476-3322
Website: www.emnrd.state.nm.us/ecmd

Founded: 1978

Membership: 1–100

Scope: Local, State, Regional, National, International

Description: Administers state and federally funded energy efficiency, renewable energy, and alternative transportation programs to state agencies, political subdivisions, regional organizations, nonprofit community service agencies, and New Mexico energy consumers, by providing engineering and technical assistance, and informational, financial, and programmatic support.

Keyword(s): Agriculture/Farming, Air Quality/Atmosphere, Climate Change, Energy, Forests/Forestry, Pollution (general), Reduce/Reuse/Recycle, Transportation, Water Habitats & Quality

Contact(s):
Chris Wentz, Divisional Director; 505-476-3312; cwentz@state.nm.us

ENERGY, MINERALS, AND NATURAL RESOURCES DEPARTMENT

FORESTRY DIVISION
1220 St. Francis Dr., Rm 112
Santa Fe, NM 87505 United States
Phone: 505-476-3325 Fax: 505-476-3330
Website: www.emnrd.state.nm.us/forestry/

Founded: N/A

Scope: State

Description: Provides management and protection of New Mexico's renewable forest, rangeland, soil, and water resources through professional forest, pest, fire, and land management; provides law enforcement and administration, public education in conservation; and supports to enhance the environment and quality of resources to protect jobs and maintain social and economic benefits.

Publication(s): See publication website

Contact(s):
Toby Martinez, State Forester

ENERGY, MINERALS, AND NATURAL RESOURCES DEPARTMENT

MINING AND MINERALS DIVISION
1220 S. St. Francis Drive
Santa Fe, NM 87505 United States
Phone: 505-476-3405
Website: www.emnrd.state.nm.us/mining/

Founded: N/A

Scope: State

Description: Provides for the study, development, and optimum production of the mineral and energy resources within the state; the reduction of hazards associated with these processes consistent with the conservation of these resources; the protection of public health, safety, and the environment, and the economic well-being of the citizens.

Contact(s):
Douglas Bland, Director

ENERGY, MINERALS, AND NATURAL RESOURCES DEPARTMENT
OIL CONSERVATION DIVISION
1240 S. Pacheco
Santa Fe, NM 87505 United States
Phone: 505-827-7133 Fax: 505-827-8177
Website: www.emnrd.state.nm.us

Founded: N/A

Scope: State

Description: Regulates and sets standards for operations related to the drilling and production of crude oil, natural gas, and geothermal resources and promotes the development and conservation of these resources while ensuring the prevention of waste and protection. Cares for the prevention of loss and contamination of freshwater supplies.

Contact(s):
Lori Wrotenberry, Director

ENERGY, MINERALS, AND NATURAL RESOURCES DEPARTMENT
STATE PARKS AND RECREATION DIVISION
1220 St. Francis, P.O. Box 1147
Santa Fe, NM 87505 United States
Phone: 505-827-7173 Fax: 505-827-1376
E-mail: nmparks@state.nm.us
Website: www.emnrd.state.nm.us/nmparks/

Founded: N/A

Scope: State

Description: Provides and cares for the recreational resources, facilities, and opportunities, and promotes user safety on recreational land and water to benefit and enrich the lives of New Mexico residents and visitors alike.

Contact(s):
Tom Trujillo, Director

ENVIRONMENTAL BOARD
WATER RESOURCE BOARD
National Life Records Center Building, Drawer 20
Montpelier, VT 05620 United States
Phone: 802-828-3309
E-mail: bbartlett@envboard.state.vt.us
Website: www.state.vt.us/envboard/

Founded: N/A

Scope: State

Contact(s):
Marcy Harding, Chairman of the Board; 802-828-5440

ENVIRONMENTAL PROTECTION BUREAU
DEPARTMENT OF LAW
120 Broadway
New York City, NY 10271 United States
Phone: 212-416-8446 Fax: 212-416-6007
Website: www.oag.state.ny.us

Founded: N/A

Scope: State, Regional, National

Description: Institutes legal actions on behalf of the people of New York State in cases involving air and water pollution, protection of wildlife, waste site remediation, and protection of scenic and natural resources. Has responsibility for enforcement of laws protecting endangered species of wildlife, as well as public nuisance actions to restrain pollution and other environmental damage. Defends environmental decisions of state agencies.

Contact(s):
Peter Lehner, Bureau Chief
Peter Skinner, Environmental Scientist; 518-474-2432

ENVIRONMENTAL PROTECTION MASSACHUSETTS
DEPARTMENT OF ENVIRONMENTAL PROTECTION
One Winter St.
Dept. of Environmental Affairs
Boston, MA 02108 United States
Phone: 617-292-5500 Fax: 617-556-1049
Website: www.state.ma.us/dep

Founded: N/A

Membership: 1,001–10,000

Scope: State

Publication(s): Publications on line

Contact(s):
Barbara Kwetz, Director of Planning and Evaluation; 617-292-5593
James Coleman, Assistant Commissioner: Waste Prevention; 617-292-5570
Lauren Liss, Commissioner

ENVIRONMENTAL QUALITY DEPARTMENT
122 W. 25th St., Herschler Bldg.
Cheyenne, WY 82002 United States
Phone: 307-777-7937 Fax: 307-777-7682
E-mail: deqwyo@state.wy.us
Website: www.deq.state.wy.us

Founded: 1973

Membership: 101–1,000

Scope: State

Description: Established to plan the development, use, reclamation, preservation, and enhancement of the air, land, and water resources of the state.

Publication(s): Outreach

Contact(s):
Dennis Hemmer, Director; 307-777-7938
David Finley, Manager of Solid Waste Program; 307-777-7752
Gary Beach, Administrator of Water Quality; 307-777-7781
Richard Chancellor, Administrator of Land Quality; 307-777-7756
Evon Green, Administrator of Abandoned Mine Land; 307-777-6145
Dan Olson, Administrator of Air Quality; 307-777-7391
James Uzzell, Administrator of Management Services; 307-777-7937

ENVIRONMENTAL REVIEW APPEALS COMMISSION
236 E. Town St., Rm. 300
Columbus, OH 43215 United States
Phone: 614-466-8950

Founded: N/A

Membership: 1–100

Scope: Regional

Description: The Environmental Review Appeals Commission is an administrative commission designed to review the actions of the Ohio EPA, State Fire Marshal, and the various county boards of health charged with environmental jurisdiction in order to determine that the agencies' actions have been reasonable and lawful.

Contact(s):
Maria Armstrong, Member

F

FLORIDA COOPERATIVE EXTENSION SERVICE
1038 McCarty Hall, P.O. Box 110210, University of Florida
Gainesville, FL 32611-0210 United States
Phone: 352-392-1761 Fax: 352-392-3583
Website: www.ifas.ufl.edu

Founded: N/A

Scope: Regional

Publication(s): See publications on website
Keyword(s): Forests/Forestry, Water Habitats & Quality, Wildlife & Species
Contact(s):
Pierce Jones, Director of Energy Extension Service, Acting; Box 110570, 102 Rogers Hall, University of Florida, Gainesville, FL 32611-0570; 352-392-8074; Fax: 352-392-4092; ez@agen.ufl.edu
Joesph Schaefer, Director of Natural Resources; Univ. of Florida, Wildlife Ecology and Conservation, P.O. Box 110430, Gainesville, FL 32611-0430; 352-846-0568; Fax: 352-392-6984
Nat Frazer, Assistant Extension Scientist, Wildlife; Pinellas County Extension Office, 12175 125th St. North, Largo, FL 33774-3695; 813-582-2100; Fax: 813-582-2149; whk@gnv.ifas.ufl.edu
Christine Waddill, Dean of Extension; 1038 McCarty Hall, P.O. Box 110210, University of Florida, Gainesville, FL 32611-0210

FLORIDA COOPERATIVE FISH AND WILDLIFE RESEARCH UNIT (USDI)

P.O. Box 110485, Building 810
University of Florida
Gainesville, FL 32611-0485 United States
Phone: 352-392-1861 Fax: 352-846-0841
E-mail: hatfieldd@wec.ufl.edu
Website: www.wec.ufl.edu/coop/

Founded: 1979
Scope: Local, State, Regional, National
Description: Established by cooperative agreement among the National Biological Survey, Florida Game and Fresh Water Fish Commission, and the University of Florida. Primary purpose is research, graduate education, and extension activities integrating fish and wildlife ecology and management in Florida's unique ecosystems, particularly wetlands.
Keyword(s): Water Habitats & Quality, Wildlife & Species
Contact(s):
Raymond Carthy, Assistant Unit Leader: Wildlife; 352-392-1861; Fax: 352-846-0841; rayc@zoo.ufl.edu
Wiley Kitchens, Research Ecologist; 352-392-1861; Fax: 352-846-0841; kitchensw@wec.ufl.edu
H. Percival, Unit Leader; 352-392-1861; Fax: 352-846-0841; percivalf@wec.ufl.edu

FLORIDA DEPARTMENT OF AGRICULTURE AND CONSUMER SERVICES

The Capitol, PL 10
Tallahassee, FL 32399-0800 United States
Phone: 850-488-3022 Fax: 850-488-7585
Website: www.doacs.state.fl.us

Founded: N/A
Membership: 1–100
Scope: State
Contact(s):
Charles Bronson, Commissioner; 850-488-3022

FLORIDA DEPARTMENT OF AGRICULTURE AND CONSUMER SERVICES

DIVISION OF FORESTRY
3125 Conner Blvd.
Tallahassee, FL 32399-1650 United States
Phone: 850-488-4274 Fax: 850-488-0863
Website: www.fl-dof.com

Founded: 1927
Membership: 1,001–10,000
Scope: Regional
Description: To protect and manage Florida's forest resources through a stewardship ethic to assure these resources will be available for future generations. Current number of employees: 1,100.
Contact(s):
L. Peterson, Director; 850-922-0135
Rich Ashley, Chief of Planning and Support Services; 850-414-0843
Raymond Geiger, Chief, Field Operations; 850-414-9969
James Karels, Bureau of Forest Protection; 850-488-6106
Mike Long, Assistant Director; 850-414-9967
C. Maynard, Chief of Forest Management; 850-488-6611

FLORIDA DEPARTMENT OF AGRICULTURE AND CONSUMER SERVICES

OFFICE OF AGRICULTURAL WATER POLICY
1203 Governor Square Blvd.
Tallahassee, FL 32301 United States
Phone: 850-488-6249 Fax: 850-921-2153

Founded: N/A
Membership: 1,001–10,000
Scope: State
Description: Provides administrative, legislative, and promotional assistance to 63 Soil and Water Conservation Districts in Florida.
Contact(s):
Chuck Aller, Director
John Folks, Environmental Administrator; 850-488-6249

FLORIDA DEPARTMENT OF AGRICULTURE AND CONSUMER SERVICES

SOIL AND WATER CONSERVATION COUNCIL
3125 Conner Blvd., Suite C, Mail Stop C28
Tallahassee, FL 32399 United States
Phone: 850-488-5321 Fax: 850-921-2153

Founded: N/A
Scope: State
Contact(s):
Clegg Hooks, SWC Administrator; 3125 Conner Blvd., Suite C, Conner Bldg, Tallahassee, FL 32399; 850-488-6249; Fax: 850-921-2153
Richard Machek, Chair; 17 NW 16th St., Delray Beach, FL 33444

FLORIDA DEPARTMENT OF ENVIRONMENTAL PROTECTION

3900 Commonwealth Blvd.
M.S. 49
Tallahassee, FL 32399-3000 United States
Phone: 850-921-1222 Fax: 850-487-3267
E-mail: ingrid.king@dep.state.fl.us
Website: www.dep.state.fl.us

Founded: N/A
Membership: 1,001–10,000
Scope: State
Description: More Protection, Less Process. Lead agency in Florida state government for environmental management and stewardship. Administers regulatory programs and issues permits for air, water and waste management. It oversees the State's land and water conservation program, Florida Forever, and manages the Florida Park Service.
Keyword(s): Air Quality/Atmosphere, Ecosystems (precious), Land Issues, Oceans/Coasts/Beaches, Pollution (general), Public Lands/Greenspace, Recreation/Ecotourism, Reduce/Reuse/Recycle, Water Habitats & Quality
Contact(s):
Denver Stutler, Chief of Staff; 850-488-7131
Teri Donalson, General Counsel; 850-488-9314
Pinky Hall, Inspector General; 850-488-2287
David Struhs, Secretary; 850-488-1154

FLORIDA DEPARTMENT OF ENVIRONMENTAL PROTECTION

AIR RESOURCES MANAGEMENT DIVISION
2600 Blair Stone Rd. MS 5500
Tallahassee, FL 32399-2400 United States
Phone: 850-488-0114 Fax: 850-922-6979

Founded: N/A

FLORIDA DEPARTMENT OF ENVIRONMENTAL PROTECTION

BUREAU OF BEACHES WETLAND RESOURCES
3900 Commonwealth Blvd.
Mail Station 300
Tallahassee, FL 32399-3000 United States
Phone: 850-488-31815 Fax: 850-488-5257
Website: www.dep.state.fl.us/beaches

Founded: N/A
Scope: State
Description: State Agency
Contact(s):
Michael Sole, Bureau Chief; 850-488-3181
Gene Chelecki, P.E. Administrator; 850-488-3181, ext. 111
Mark Leadon, Research Analysis & Policy P.E.; 850-487-4475
Tom Watters, Coastal Data Acquisition; 850-487-4475
Paden Woodruff, Environmental Administrator; 850-487-1262

FLORIDA DEPARTMENT OF ENVIRONMENTAL PROTECTION

COASTAL AND AQUATIC MANAGED AREAS
3900 Commonwealth Blvd.
Mail Station 235
Tallahassee, FL 32399 United States
Phone: 850-488-3456 Fax: 850-488-3896

Founded: N/A
Contact(s):
Anna Hartman, Director; 850-488-3456
Dennis Raley, Program Administrator; 850-488-3456

FLORIDA DEPARTMENT OF ENVIRONMENTAL PROTECTION

DIVISION OF STATE LANDS
3900 Commonwealth Blvd.
Mail Station 100
Tallahassee, FL 32399 United States
Phone: 850-488-2725
E-mail: eva.armstrong@dep.state.fl.us
Website: www.dep.state.fl.us/lands

Founded: 1979
Membership: 101–1,000
Scope: Local, State, Regional
Description: Responsible for managing Florida's public lands.
Keyword(s): Agriculture/Farming, Ecosystems (precious), Forests/Forestry, Land Issues, Public Lands/Greenspace, Sprawl/Urban Planning, Wildlife & Species
Contact(s):
Eva Armstrong, Director
Rob Lovern, Assistant Director

FLORIDA DEPARTMENT OF ENVIRONMENTAL PROTECTION

FLORIDA STATE PARKS
FLORIDA STATE PARKS AMERICORPS
3900 Commonwealth Boulevard
Mail Stop 535
Tallahassee, FL 32399 United States
Phone: 850-488-8243, ext. 183
Website: www.floridastateparks.org/americorps

Founded: 1997
Membership: 1–100
Scope: Local, State
Description: To serve and strengthen Florida State Parks' natural and cultural resources by addressing critical environmental and human needs.
Keyword(s): Ecosystems (precious), Forests/Forestry, Oceans/Coasts/Beaches, Public Lands/Greenspace, Recreation/Ecotourism, Water Habitats & Quality, Wildlife & Species
Contact(s):
Phillip Werndli, Coordinator of Volunteer Programs; 850-488-8243, ext. 142

FLORIDA DEPARTMENT OF ENVIRONMENTAL PROTECTION

LAW ENFORCEMENT DIVISION
3900 Commonwealth Blvd.
Mail Stop 600
Tallahassee, FL 32399 United States
Phone: 850-488-5757
Website: www.dep.state.fl.us/law

Founded: N/A
Contact(s):
Thomas Tramell III, Division Director; 850-488-5757, ext. 132

FLORIDA DEPARTMENT OF ENVIRONMENTAL PROTECTION

RECREATION AND PARKS DIVISION
3900 Commonwealth Blvd.
Tallahassee, FL 32399 United States
Website: www.myflorida.com/communities/learn/stateparks

Founded: N/A
Contact(s):
Joe Bakker, Staff of Mine Reclamation; 904-488-8217
Tom Brown, Staff of Aquatic Plant Management; 904-488-5631
Walter Schmidt, Staff of Geology; 904-488-4191

FLORIDA DEPARTMENT OF ENVIRONMENTAL PROTECTION

RESOURCE ASSESSMENT AND MANAGEMENT
3900 Commonwealth Blvd
Tallahassee, FL 32399 United States
Phone: 850-922-6407
Website: www.dep.state.fl.us/resource

Founded: N/A
Contact(s):
Ed Conklin, Director; 850-922-6407

FLORIDA DEPARTMENT OF ENVIRONMENTAL PROTECTION

WASTE MANAGEMENT DIVISION
3900 Commonwealth Blvd.
Tallahassee, FL 32399 United States
Phone: 850-488-0300 Fax: 850-414-0414
Website: www.dep.state.fl.us/waste/

Founded: N/A
Contact(s):
Bill Hinkley, Staff of Solid and Hazardous Waste; 904-488-0300
Doug Jones, Staff of Waste Cleanup; 904-488-0190
John Ruddell; 904-487-3299

FLORIDA DEPARTMENT OF ENVIRONMENTAL PROTECTION

WATER RESOURCE MANAGEMENT
3900 Commonwealth Blvd.
Tallahassee, FL 32399 United States
Phone: 850-487-1855

Founded: N/A

Contact(s):
Mimi Drew, Director; 850-487-1855
Jerry Brooks, Deputy Director; 850-487-1855

FLORIDA FISH AND WILDLIFE CONSERVATION COMMISSION

620 S. Meridian St.
Tallahassee, FL 32399-1600 United States
Phone: 850-488-3641 Fax: 850-414-8212
Website: www.state.fl.us/fwc

Founded: N/A
Membership: 1–100
Scope: State
Publication(s): Florida Wildlife
Keyword(s): Recreation/Ecotourism, Water Habitats & Quality, Wildlife & Species
Contact(s):
Robert Edwards, Director: Division of Law Enforcement; 850-488-6251
Allan Egbert, Executive Director; 850-487-3796
Brad Hartman, Director: Office of Environmental Services; 850-488-6661
Victor Heller, Assistant Executive Director; 850-488-3084
Frank Montalbano, Director: Division of Wildlife; 850-488-3831
Edwin Moyer, Director: Division of Freshwater Fisheries; 850-488-0331
Sandra Porter, Director: Division of Administrative Services; 850-488-6551
James Antista, General Counsel; 850-487-1764
Dick Sublette, Editor; 850-488-5564
Susan Weaver, Bureau of Licensing and Permitting

FLORIDA STATE DEPARTMENT OF HEALTH

State Health Office, 2020 Capital Circle SE, BIN # AOO
Tallahassee, FL 32399-1701 United States
Phone: 904-487-2945 Fax: 850-410-1375
Website: www.doh.state.fl.us/

Founded: N/A
Keyword(s): Pollution (general), Public Health
Contact(s):
Sharon Heber, Division Director of Environmental Health; 850-488-6811
Bart Bibler, Environmental Programs; 850-488-4070
Eric Grimm, Environmental Programs; 850-487-0004
Richard Hunter, Deputy State Health Officer for Prevention and Control Programs; 850-487-2945
Roger Inman, Environmental Hazards; 850-488-3385
Russell Mardon, Epidemiology Programs, Acting Chief; 850-488-3370

FORESTRY COMMISSION (ARKANSAS)

3821 W. Roosevelt Rd.
Little Rock, AR 72204-6395 United States
Phone: 501-296-1940 Fax: 501-296-1949
Website: www.forestry.state.ar.us

Founded: N/A
Membership: 1–100
Scope: Regional
Description: To prevent and suppress forest fires; control forest insects and diseases; grow and distribute forest planting stock; and collect and disseminate information concerning growth, utilization, and renewal of forests.
Keyword(s): Forests/Forestry
Contact(s):
O. Darling, Commission Chairman
James Grant, Conservation Education; 501-296-1940
Don McBride, Fire Control; 501-296-1940
Faustine McDowell, Fiscal Department; 501-296-1931
Alan Murray, Baucum Nursery; 501-907-2485
Larry Nance, Deputy State Forester; 501-296-1943
George Rheinhardt, Forest Management; 501-296-1940
John Shannon, State Forester

FORESTRY COMMISSION (SOUTH CAROLINA)

Box 21707
Columbia, SC 29221-1707 United States
Phone: 803-896-8800 Fax: 803-798-8097
E-mail: scsc@forestry.state.sc.us
Website: www.state.sc.us/forest

Founded: 1927
Scope: State
Description: Provides basic forest fire protection on all state and private forest lands in South Carolina; assists landowners in proper management and utilization of forest lands; promotes forest fire prevention and other forestry practices through an information and education program; and operates forest tree nursery, seed orchards, and state forests.
Keyword(s): Forests/Forestry, Sprawl/Urban Planning, Water Habitats & Quality
Contact(s):
Tim Adams, Director of Field Operations Support; 803-896-8802
Joe Richbourg, Director of Administration Division; 803-896-8858
Bill Boykin, Deputy State Forester; 803-896-8832
Cecil Campbell, Coastal Regional Forester; 843-538-3708
C. Carson, Technical Assistant to the State Forester; 803-896-8822
Ken Hill, Commission Vice Chairman; 308 Fuller St., Manning, SC 29102; 803-435-8133
Ed Muckenfuss, Commission Chairman; P.O. Box 1950, Summerville, SC 29484; 843-871-5000
Charles Ramsey, Piedmont Regional Forester; 803-276-0205
Steve Scott, Pee Dee Regional Forester; 843-662-5571
Robert Showalter, State Forester
Judy Weston, Executive Assistant to State Forester; 803-896-8875

G

GEORGIA DEPARTMENT OF AGRICULTURE

19 Martin Luther King Dr., Capitol Sq.
Atlanta, GA 30334 United States
Phone: 404-656-3600 Fax: 404-656-9380
Website: www.agr.state.ga.us

Founded: 1874
Membership: 101–1,000
Scope: State
Description: The department serves farmers and consumers in the state by verifying and enforcing the accuracy and quality of both products and services in many areas including food products, seed, fertilizers, pesticides, fuel, weights and measures, and bedding, and by overseeing the health and well-being of Georgia's livestock, poultry, and commercial pet industry.
Publication(s): Farmers and Consumers Market Bulletin, Georgia Poultry Facts, Georgia Agricultural Facts
Keyword(s): Agriculture/Farming, Pollution (general), Public Health
Contact(s):
Bobby Harris, Assistant Commissioner of Marketing; 404-656-3368
Earl Harris, Assistant Commissioner of Administration; 404-656-3608
Tommy Irvin, Commissioner of Agriculture
Brenda James-Griffin, Assistant Commissioner for Public Affairs; 404-656-3689
Phil Kea, Assistant Commissioner of Finance; 404-656-3608
Lee Meyers, Assistant Commissioner of Animal Industry; 404-656-3671
Cameron Smoak, Assistant Commissioner for Consumer Protection Field Forces; 404-656-3627

GEORGIA DEPARTMENT OF AGRICULTURE
CONSUMER SERVICES LIBRARY
Agriculture Bldg., Capitol Square
Atlanta, GA 30334 United States
Phone: 404-656-3645 Fax: 404-651-7957
Website: www.agr.state.ga.us

Founded: 1874

Scope: State

Description: The Georgia Department of Agriculture has the distinction of being the nation's oldest such agency. The Department operates as a regulatory and enforcement agency, with the major goal of protecting the consuming public and promoting the farming sector. Under the office of Public Affairs, we respond to consumer inquiries on the department's areas of jurisdiction or student requests for project information. The Farmers and Consumers Market Bulletin has been serving Georgia citizens since 1917.

Publication(s): Farmers and Consumers Market Bulletin

Contact(s):
Arty Schronce, Director, Public Affairs; 1-800-282-5852; Fax: 404-651-7957; aschronce@agr.state.ga.us
Teresa Jenkins, Manager, Consumer Services; 1-800-282-5852; tjenkins@agr.state.ga.us
Brenda Griffin, Assistant Commissioner; bgriffin@agr.state.ga.us
Tommy Irvin, Commissioner; bgriffin@agr.state.ga.us

GEORGIA DEPARTMENT OF EDUCATION
1766 Twin Towers, East
Atlanta, GA 30334-5040 United States
Phone: 404-656-0913 Fax: 404-651-8582
E-mail: bmoore@doe.k12.ga.us
Website: www.doe.k.ga.us

Founded: N/A
Membership: 1,001–10,000
Scope: State
Publication(s): Observation - newsletter, Georgia Science Teacher

Contact(s):
Bob Moore, Science Program Specialist

GEORGIA DEPARTMENT OF NATURAL RESOURCES
205 Jesse Hill, Jr. Dr., SE, East Tower
Suite 1252
Atlanta, GA 30334 United States
Phone: 404-656-3500 Fax: 404-656-0770
Website: www.dnr.state.ga.us

Founded: N/A

Scope: State

Description: Natural Resources

Keyword(s): Air Quality/Atmosphere, Ethics/Environmental Justice, Land Issues, Oceans/Coasts/Beaches, Pollution (general), Public Lands/Greenspace, Recreation/Ecotourism, Reduce/Reuse/Recycle, Water Habitats & Quality, Wildlife & Species

Contact(s):
Lonice Barrett, Commissioner

GEORGIA DEPARTMENT OF NATURAL RESOURCES
COASTAL RESOURCES DIVISION
One Conservation Way
Brunswick, GA 31520 United States
Phone: 912-264-7218 Fax: 912-262-3143
Website: www.dnr.state.ga.us

Founded: N/A
Membership: 1–100
Scope: State
Description: The Coastal Resource Division administers many different programs to ensure wise management of Georgia's marshlands, barrier islands and marine commercial and sport species.

Contact(s):
Susan Shipman, Director; 912-264-7218

GEORGIA DEPARTMENT OF NATURAL RESOURCES
ENVIRONMENTAL PROTECTION DIVISION
2 Martin Luther King, Jr. Drive, SE, Suite 1152 - East Tower
Atlanta, GA 30334 United States
Phone: 404-657-5947 Fax: 404-651-5778
Website: www.ganet.org/dnr/environ

Founded: N/A
Membership: N/A
Scope: Local, State
Description: EPD is responsible for enforcing 23 state laws. In addition, EPD is delegated to carry out the Congressionally mandated permitting and compliance programs for four Federal laws: the Clean Air Act, the Clean Water Act, the Safe Drinking Water Act, and the Resource Conservation and Recovery Act.

Contact(s):
Harold Reheis, Director; 404-656-4713

GEORGIA DEPARTMENT OF NATURAL RESOURCES
ENVIRONMENTAL PROTECTION DIVISION
1 Conservation Way
Brunswick, GA 31520 United States
Phone: 912-264-7284

Founded: N/A

Contact(s):
Harold Reheis, Director; 404-656-4713
Alan Hallum, Chief: Water Protection Branch
Nolton Johnson, Chief: Water Resources Branch
Jennifer Kaduck, Chief: Hazardous Waste Branch
Ron Methier, Chief: Air Protection Branch
Jim Setser, Chief: Program Coordination Branch
Mark Smith, Chief: Land Protection Branch
David Word, Assistant Director

GEORGIA DEPARTMENT OF NATURAL RESOURCES
HISTORIC PRESERVATION DIVISION
156 Trinity Ave., SW, Suite 101
Atlanta, GA 30303 United States
Phone: 404-656-2840 Fax: 404-651-8739
Website: www.gashpo.org

Founded: N/A
Membership: 1–100
Scope: State
Description: Georgia's State Historic Preservation Office
Publication(s): Publications on line

Contact(s):
Ray Luce, Director; 404-656-2840

GEORGIA DEPARTMENT OF NATURAL RESOURCES
PARKS, RECREATION AND HISTORIC SITES DIVISION
205 Butler, SE, Suite 1352
Atlanta, GA 30334 United States
Phone: 404-656-2770 Fax: 404-651-5871

Founded: N/A

Scope: State

Contact(s):
Burt Weerts, Director; 404-656-2770

Wayne Escoe, Chief, Parks Operation Section
David Freedman, Chief, Maintenance and Engineering Section

GEORGIA DEPARTMENT OF NATURAL RESOURCES

POLLUTION PREVENTION ASSISTANCE DIVISION
7 Martin Luther King Jr. Dr., SW, Suite 450
Atlanta, GA 30334-9004 United States
Phone: 404-651-5120 Fax: 404-651-5130
E-mail: info@p2ad.org
Website: www.pad.org

Founded: 1993
Membership: N/A
Scope: State
Description: P2AD is a non-regulatory division of DNR. We provide free, confidential technical assistance on cost-effective ways to prevent, reduce, reuse or recycle wastes, and conserve natural resources. Services are available to all Georgia businesses, industries, governmental agencies, institutions, and individual citizens.
Contact(s):
Robert Kerr, Director; 404-651-5120

GEORGIA DEPARTMENT OF NATURAL RESOURCES

WILDLIFE RESOURCES DIVISION
2070 U.S. Highway 278, SE
Social Circle, GA 30025 United States
Phone: 770-918-6400 Fax: 706-557-3030
Website: www.georgiawildlife.com

Founded: N/A
Membership: N/A
Scope: State
Description: The Georgia Department of Natural Resources (DNR) was established in 1972 to manage and protect the state's natural resources. The DNR Wildlife Resources Division is charged with managing, protecting and encouraging the conservation of all wildlife, including game and nongame animals, fish and protected plants.
Publication(s): WRD Website
Contact(s):
David Waller, Director; 770-918-6401
Noel Holcomb, Assistant Director; 770-918-6401
Ron Bailey, Chief: Law Enforcement; 770-918-6408
Chuck Coomer, Chief: Fisheries Management; 770-918-6406
Mike Harris, Chief: Nongame Wildlife/Natural Heritage; 770-761-3035
Todd Holbrook, Chief: Game Management; 770-918-6404

GEORGIA FORESTRY COMMISSION

P.O. Box 819
Macon, GA 31202-0819 United States
Phone: 478-751-3500 Fax: 478-751-3465
E-mail: slong@gfc.state.ga.us
Website: www.gfc.state.ga.us

Founded: 1925
Scope: State
Description: To foster, improve, and encourage reforestation; to engage in research and other projects for better forestry practices; to inform the public of the values and benefits of forestry; and to detect, prevent, and combat forest fires.
Publication(s): Georgia Forestry, Wood Using Industries
Contact(s):
J. Allen, Director; 478-751-3480
Sharon Dolliver, Chief of Information and Education; 478-751-3530
Alan Dozier, Chief of Forest Protection; 478-751-3488
Robert Farris, Field Supervisor
Jim Gillis, Board of Commissioner Chairman
William Lazenby, Deputy Director; 478-751-3480
Garland Nelson, Chief of Forest Administration; 478-751-3464
Randall Perry, Personnel Officer; 404-298-4949
Russ Pohl, Chief of Reforestation; 478-751-3530
Larry Thompson, Chief of Forest Management; 478-751-3458
Lynn Walton, Editor; 478-751-3530

GEORGIA STATE EXTENSION SERVICE

College of Agricultural and Environmental Sciences
101 Conner Hall
The University of Georgia
Athens, GA 30602-7501 United States
Phone: 706-542-3924 Fax: 706-542-0803
E-mail: caesdean@arches.uga.edu
Website: www.uga.edu/caes/

Founded: N/A
Membership: 1–100
Scope: International
Contact(s):
Gale Buchanan, Dean and Director; 706-542-3924; caesdean@arches.uga.edu
Jeffery Jackson, Wildlife Specialist; University of Georgia, Warnell School of Forest Resources, Athens, GA 30602-2152; 706-542-9054; Fax: 706-542-3342
George Lewis, Aquaculture and Fisheries Specialist; 706-542-9038
Tony Tyson, Interim Associate Dean for Extension; 111 Conner Hall, Athens, GA 30602; 706-542-3824; Fax: 706-542-8815; caesext@arches.uga.edu

GOVERNORS OFFICE OF PLANNING AND RESEARCH (CALIFORNIA)

STATE CLEARINGHOUSE
P.O.Box 3044
Sacramento, CA 95812-3044 United States
Phone: 916-445-0613 Fax: 916-323-3018
Website: www.opr.ca.gov

Founded: 1970
Scope: State
Description: Primary areas of concentration are the development of environmental and related land use goals and policies; growth management; evaluation of state plans and programs; and preparation of statewide environmental goals and policies statements.
Keyword(s): Ethics/Environmental Justice, Land Issues, Population, Sprawl/Urban Planning
Contact(s):
Tal Finney, Acting Director
Terry Roberts, State Clearinghouse Senior Planner; 916-445-0613

GUADALUPE-BLANCO RIVER AUTHORITY

933 East Court Street
Seguin, TX 78155 United States
Phone: 800-413-4130 Fax: 830-379-9718
Website: www.gbra.org

Founded: 1933
Membership: 101–1,000
Scope: Local, State, Regional
Description: Responsibility to develop, conserve, and protect the water resources within a ten county statutory district and to aid in the prevention of soil erosion and flooding. Actively engaged in water supply, irrigation, hydroelectric power generation, water and wastewater treatment, and outdoor recreation operations.
Publication(s): Water Resources Report—Quarterly
Keyword(s): Agriculture/Farming, Ecosystems (precious), Energy, Land Issues, Public Lands/Greenspace, Recreation/Ecotourism, Water Habitats & Quality
Contact(s):
Debbie Magin, Director of Water Quality

Alvin Schuerg, Director of Accounting and Finance
Todd Votteler, Director of Water Policy
David Welsch, Director of Project Development
Judy Gardner, Manager of Communications and Education
Bryan Serold, Manager of Lower Basin
John Smith, Manager of Upper Basin
W. West, General Manager
Fred Blumberg, Deputy General Manager
Thomas Hill, Chief Engineer

GUAM COASTAL MANAGEMENT PROGRAM

Bureau of Planning
P.O. Box 2950
Agana, GU 96932 United States
Phone: 671-472-4201 Fax: 671-477-1812
Website: www.ocrm.nos.noaa.gov/czm/czmguam.html

Founded: 1979

Publication(s): Public Television Show: Man, Land, and Sea (Guam only), list of publications, posters, and fliers available upon request.

Keyword(s): Development/Developing Countries, Oceans/Coasts/Beaches

Contact(s):
Vincent Arriola, Director: Bureau of Planning
Susan Ham, Library Services: Bureau of Planning: Supervisor
Michael Ham, Administrator: Guam Coastal Management Program

GUAM COOPERATIVE EXTENSION SERVICE

College of Agriculture and Life Sciences (CALS) Bldg.
Rm. 206, University of Guam
303 University Dr., University of Guam Station
Mangilao, GU 96923 United States
Phone: 671-735-2000 Fax: 671-734-6842
Website: www.uog.uog.edu/cals/GCE/mission.html

Founded: N/A

Contact(s):
Jeff Barcinas, Dean of CALS and Director of Extension Service and Agricultu; 671-735-2002; jbarcina@uog9.uog.edu
Victor Artero, Associate Dean, Cooperative Extension, Acting; 671-735-2004; vartero@uog9.uog.edu
John Brown, Associate Director of the Agricultural Experiment Station; 671-735-2140; Fax: 671-734-4600; gwall@uog9.uog.edu
David Chrisotomo, Aquaculturist; 303 University Dr., UOG Station, Mangilao, GU 96923; 671-735-2080; Fax: 706-734-5600
Clarissa San Nicholas, Extension Assistant; cdsannic@uog9.uog.edu

GUAM DEPARTMENT OF AGRICULTURE

192 Dairy Rd.
Mangilao, GU 96923 United States
Phone: 671-734-3942 Fax: 671-734-6569

Founded: 1950

Description: Charged with responsibility for the conservation and management of Guam's fish, wildlife, soil, and forestry resources, together with development of agricultural and fishery production for food purposes.

Contact(s):
Michael Kuhlmann, Director; 192 Dairy Rd., Mangilao, GU 96923; 671-734-3942; Fax: 671-734-6569
Joseph Sablan, Deputy Director

GUAM DEPARTMENT OF AGRICULTURE

DIVISION OF AQUATIC AND WILDLIFE RESOURCES
192 Dairy Rd.
Mangilao, GU 96923 United States
Phone: 671-734-3944 Fax: 671-734-6570

Founded: N/A

Contact(s):
Robert Anderson, Chief
Alan Van Aken, Administrative Officer

GUAM ENVIRONMENTAL PROTECTION AGENCY

P.O. Box 22439
Guam Main Facility
Barrigada, GU 96921 United States
Phone: 671-477-9402

Founded: 1973

Description: Activities include: land-use planning; review of environmental impact assessments and environmental protection plans; supervision, planning, and regulation of all new or modified wastewater sources; and the development and protection of potable water supplies; solid and hazardous waste management, pesticides importation, distribution, and use; and air pollution sources. Provide field and laboratory support for the agency's water, air, and land regulatory programs.

Publication(s): Annual Report, list available on request.

Contact(s):
Ben Machol, Guam Program Manager; 415-972-3770
Grace Garces, Public Information Officer; 671-477-9402

GULF COAST RESEARCH LABORATORY

703 East Beach Drive
Ocean Springs, MS 39566-7000 United States
Phone: 228-872-4200 Fax: 228-872-4204
Website: www.cms.usm.edu/gindex.htm

Founded: 1947

Description: Conducts research in marine biology, fisheries, geology, chemistry, and oceanography, and conducts an academic program in the marine sciences.

Publication(s): Marine Briefs Newsletter, Gulf Research Reports-Scientific Journal

Contact(s):
Robert Vanaller, Interim Director
Robert Vanaller, Editor
William Walker, Assistant Director: Research

H

HAWAII COOPERATIVE FISHERY RESEARCH UNIT (USDI)

2538 The Mall, University of Hawaii
Honolulu, HI 96822 United States
Phone: 808-956-8350 Fax: 808-956-4238

Founded: N/A

Scope: State, National, International

Description: Activities include research, graduate program teaching, and public service regarding inshore marine and inland waters with emphasis on native fishes and invertebrates.

Publication(s): Scientic Reports (irregular)

Keyword(s): Oceans/Coasts/Beaches, Water Habitats & Quality, Wildlife & Species

Contact(s):
Dr. Charles Birkeland, Assistant Leader
James Parrish, Leader

HAWAII DEPARTMENT OF AGRICULTURE

P.O. Box 22159
Honolulu, HI 96823-2159 United States
Phone: 808-973-9560
E-mail: holoa-info@exec.state.hi.us
Website: www.hawaiiag.org/hdoa

Founded: N/A

Description: Promotes the best use of Hawaii's agricultural resources. Concerned with the protection of agricultural lands and water and diversification of the state's agricultural economy. Functions include agricultural planning, agricultural credit, product promotion and market development, plant and animal quarantine, plant and animal disease and pest control, milk control, livestock and market reporting service, commodities grading, pesticide use enforcement, and enforcement of weights and measures standards.

Contact(s):
Elaine Abe, Chief: Administrative Services; 808-973-9606
Samuel Camp, Head: Quality Assurance Division; 808-586-0870
Samuel Camp, Head: Agriculture Development Division; 808-973-9566
Paul Matsuo, Head: Agricultural Resource Management Division; 808-973-9475
James Nakatani, Chairperson; 808-973-9551
Doreen Shishido, Head: Agricultural Loan Division; 808-973-9460
Letitia Uyehara, Deputy to the Chairperson; 808-973-9553

HAWAII DEPARTMENT OF HEALTH

OFFICE OF ENVIRONMENTAL QUALITY CONTROL
235 S. Beretania St.
Suite 702
Honolulu, HI 96813 United States
Phone: 808-586-4185 Fax: 808-586-4186
E-mail: OEQC@HEALTH.STATE.HI.US
Website: www.state.hi.us/health/oeqc/index.html

Founded: 1974
Membership: 1–100
Scope: Local, State
Description: OEQC advises the Governor on environmental quality control matters; implements Hawaii's EIS law; reviews all documents required by Hawaii's EIS process; and informs the public of proposed actions through The Environmental Notice (OEQC Bulletin). The director of OEQC is also responsible for environmental education projects, and proposing and encouraging legislation supporting the preservation of environmental resources.
Publication(s): A Guidebook for the Hawaii State Environmental Review Process, Annual Report—Environmental Indicators and Report Card, OEQC Bulletin
Keyword(s): Other
Contact(s):
Genevieve Salmonson, Director

HAWAII INSTITUTE OF MARINE BIOLOGY

University of Hawaii
Kaneohe, HI 96744-1346 United States
Phone: 808-236-7401 Fax: 808-236-7443
Website: www.hawaii.edu/HIMB

Founded: N/A
Scope: State
Description: Concerned with research in tropical marine biology and oceanography with emphasis on coral reef biology, aquaculture, fish endocrinology, and behavior of reef organisms. Provides research facilities for investigations in tropical marine biology. Offers annual summer program in selected topics for graduate students.
Contact(s):
Joann Leong, Director

I

IDAHO DEPARTMENT OF FISH AND GAME

600 S. Walnut, Box 25
P.O. Box 25
Boise, ID 83707 United States
Phone: 208-334-3700 Fax: 208-334-2114
E-mail: idfginfo@idfg.state.id.us
Website: www2.state.id.us/fishgame

Founded: 1938
Scope: State
Description: To preserve, protect, perpetuate, and manage all wildlife within the state of Idaho; to make and declare such rules and regulations, and to employ personnel necessary to administer and enforce the harvest of wildlife.
Publication(s): Idaho Fish & Game News
Keyword(s): Land Issues, Recreation/Ecotourism, Water Habitats & Quality, Wildlife & Species
Contact(s):
Steve Huffaker, Director; 208-334-3771
Terry Mansfield, Deputy Director; 208-334-5159
Jack Trueblood, Acting Chief of Information and Education; 208-334-3746; Fax: 208-334-2148
Stephen Barton, Bureau Chief of Administration; 208-334-3782
Phil Jeppson, Chief of Engineering; 208-334-3730
Virgil Moore, Chief of Fisheries; 208-334-3791
Al Nicholson, Chief of Enforcement; 208-334-3736
Bob Royce, Chief of DP Management; 208-334-3700
Tracey Trent, Chief of Natural Resources Policy; 208-334-2595
Jack Trueblood, Editor; 208-334-3746; jtrueblood@idfg.state.id.us

IDAHO DEPARTMENT OF PARKS AND RECREATION

P.O. Box 83720
Boise, ID 83720-0065 United States
Phone: 208-334-4199 Fax: 208-334-3741
Website: www.idahoparks.org

Founded: 1965
Membership: N/A
Scope: State, Regional
Description: To formulate and put into execution a long-range program for the acquisition, planning, protection, operation, maintenance, development, and wise use of parks; and to provide state leadership in recreation.
Publication(s): Idaho State Parks Guide
Keyword(s): Ethics/Environmental Justice, Land Issues, Public Lands/Greenspace, Recreation/Ecotourism, Water Habitats & Quality
Contact(s):
Rick Cummins, Division Administrator, Management Services; 208-334-4180, ext. 253; rcummins@idpr.state.id.us
Rick Collignon, Director
Ernest Lombard, Chairman of the Board; 208-939-3311

IDAHO DEPARTMENT OF WATER RESOURCES

1301 North Orchard
Boise, ID 83706-2237 United States
Phone: 208-327-7900 Fax: 208-327-7866
Website: www.idwr.state.id.us

Founded: N/A
Membership: 101–1,000
Scope: State
Description: Administration of State Water Plan and Energy Plan; allocation and planning of water resources and energy programs and projects; permit and license procedures for water rights, dams, and mine tailing impoundment structures, well construction, injection wells, and stream channel alterations.
Publication(s): Water and Energy Information Bulletins, State Water Plan, and Newsletter
Contact(s):
Karl Dreher, Director; 208-327-7910
Hal Anderson, Administrator of Planning and Technical Services Division; 208-327-7910
Robert Hoppie, Administrator of Energy Division; 208-327-7910
Joe Jordan, Chairman of The Board; 208-253-1103
Norman Young, Administrator of Water Management Division; 208-327-7910

IDAHO DEPARTMENT OF WATER RESOURCES

WATER AWARENESS WEEK
c/o Catherine Chertudi
Boise Public Works
P.O. Box 500
Boise, ID 83701-0500 United States
Phone: 208-384-3901
E-mail: cchertudi@cityofboise.org
Website: www.idwr.state.id.us

Founded: 1994
Membership: N/A
Scope: Local, State
Description: The Idaho Department of Water Resources hosts the water education program, Water Awareness Week, for sixth grade students in Idaho.
Publication(s): Idaho Water Education Brochure
Keyword(s): Water Habitats & Quality

IDAHO FISH AND WILDLIFE FOUNDATION

P.O. Box 2254
Boise, ID 83701 United States
Phone: 208-334-2648 Fax: 208-334-2148
Website: www.idfishnhunt.com/~ifwf

Founded: 1990
Membership: 1–100
Scope: State
Description: To facilitate the organization and funding of natural resource projects: fish, wildlife, habitat, and education. Work with Idaho Department of Fish and Game and other entities to build public and private partnerships for wildlife projects.
Publication(s): Steelhead Fishing Economic Survey (1996), Salmon Fishing Economic Survey (1998), Steelhead Fishing Economic Values brochure
Keyword(s): Wildlife & Species
Contact(s):
Gayle Valentine, Executive Director

IDAHO GEOLOGICAL SURVEY

Morrill Hall, Third Floor, University of Idaho
Moscow, ID 83844-3014 United States
Phone: 208-885-7991 Fax: 208-885-5826
E-mail: igf@uidaho.edu
Website: www.idahogeology.org

Founded: 1919
Membership: 1–100
Scope: State
Description: The Survey is the lead state agency for the collection, interpretation, and dissemination of all geologic and mineral data for Idaho. Conducts field investigations and laboratory studies; assists in preparation of geologic maps, derivative land-use planning, and geologic hazards maps; provides expertise to individuals and governmental and private groups in planning land use.
Contact(s):
Earl Bennett, Director; 208-885-7991
Roy Breckenridge, Associate Director; 208-885-7991
Kurt Othberg, Associate Director

IDAHO STATE DEPARTMENT OF AGRICULTURE

P.O. Box 790
Boise, ID 83701 United States
Phone: 208-332-8500
Website: www.agri.state.id.us

Founded: N/A
Keyword(s): Agriculture/Farming, Land Issues, Oceans/Coasts/Beaches, Pollution (general), Public Health, Reduce/Reuse/Recycle, Water Habitats & Quality, Wildlife & Species
Contact(s):
Patrick Takasugi, Director
Bob Hillman, Division of Animal Industries Administrator; 208-332-8541
Laura Johnson, Div. of Agr. Res., Mar., & Dev. Bureau Chief; 208-332-8531

IDAHO STATE SOIL CONSERVATION COMMISSION

P.O. Box 790
Boise, ID 83701-0790 United States
Phone: 208-332-8650 Fax: 208-334-2386
E-mail: bthomass@agri.state.id.us
Website: www.scc.state.id.us

Founded: 1939
Membership: 1–100
Scope: State
Description: Coordinates programs and activities of Soil Conservation Districts in Idaho. Concerned with overall leadership and administration of districts in development, wise use, and conservation of soil and water and other closely related resources. Participates in the National Cooperative Soil Survey Program through employment of soil scientists and has been designated the state water quality management agency for private and state agricultural lands.
Keyword(s): Agriculture/Farming, Land Issues, Reduce/Reuse/Recycle
Contact(s):
Tom Johnston, Chairman; 22410 Ten Davis Rd., Parma, ID 83660; 208-722-6224; Fax: 208-722-6090; tj@widaho.net
Jerry Nicolescu, Administrator; 208-332-8649; Fax: 208-334-2386; jnicoles@agri.state.id.us
Tony Bennett, Technical Program Manager; 208-332-8651; Fax: 208-334-2386; abennett@agri.state.id.us
David Coburn, RCRDP Program Manager; 208-332-8653; Fax: 208-334-2386; dcoburn@agri.state.id.us
Brenda Thomasson, Management Assistant; 208-332-8646; Fax: 208-334-2386; bthomass@agri.state.id.us
Kathy Weaver, District Operations Manager; 3563 Ririe Highway, Idaho Falls, ID 83401; 208-525-7269; Fax: 208-525-7178; kweaver@agri.state.id.us
David Ferguson, Agricultural Program Specialist; 208-332-8654; Fax: 208-334-2386; dferguso@agri.state.id.us
Kathie Shea, Program Coordinator; 208-332-8647; Fax: 208-334-2386; khassels@agri.state.id.us

ILLINOIS DEPARTMENT OF AGRICULTURE

State Fairgrounds, P.O. Box 19281
Springfield, IL 62794-9281 United States
Phone: 217-782-2172
Website: www.agr.state.il.us/

Founded: 1917
Description: The Illinois Department of Agriculture protects and promotes the state's agricultural and natural resources. The agency provides services that benefit consumers, farmers, and agribusinesses.
Publication(s): Illinois Agricultural Guide, Illinois Food Products, Illinois Grain and Livestock Market News, Illinois Agricultural Organizations Directory
Keyword(s): Agriculture/Farming, Land Issues, Pollution (general), Reduce/Reuse/Recycle
Contact(s):
Becky Doyle, Director
Dave Bender, Executive Office: Assistant Director
Chet Boruff, Deputy Director for Natural Resources
Jim Reynolds, Superintendent for Fairs and Promotions

ILLINOIS DEPARTMENT OF AGRICULTURE

BUREAU OF LAND AND WATER RESOURCES
P.O. Box 19281
State Fairgrounds
Springfield, IL 62794-9281 United States
Phone: 217-782-6297 Fax: 217-557-0993
Website: www.agr.state.il.us

Founded: N/A

Scope: State

Description: Responsible for administering the laws and programs relating to the conservation of Illinois' agricultural, land and water resources.

Keyword(s): Agriculture/Farming, Land Issues, Public Health, Sprawl/Urban Planning, Water Habitats & Quality

Contact(s):

Steve Frank, Bureau Chief; Fax: 217-557-0993

ILLINOIS DEPARTMENT OF NATURAL RESOURCES

One Natural Resources Way
Springfield, IL 62702-1271 United States
Phone: 217-782-6302 Fax: 217-785-9236
Website: www.dnr.state.il.us

Founded: 1913

Membership: 1,001–10,000

Scope: State

Description: Provide leadership to manage, protect, sustain, and promote Illinois' natural and cultural resources.

Keyword(s): Ecosystems (precious), Ethics/Environmental Justice, Forests/Forestry, Land Issues, Public Lands/ Greenspace, Recreation/Ecotourism, Reduce/Reuse/ Recycle, Sprawl/Urban Planning, Water Habitats & Quality, Wildlife & Species

Contact(s):

Brent Manning, Director; 217-785-0075; Fax: 217-785-9236
Diane Giannone, Contact; 217-785-0075; Fax: 217-785-9236
Andrea Moore, Assistant Director; 217-782-6302; Fax: 217-785-9236

ILLINOIS DEPARTMENT OF NATURAL RESOURCES

One Natural Resources Way
Springfield, IL 62702-1271 United States
Phone: 217-782-6302 Fax: 217-785-9236
Website: www.dnr.state.il.us

Founded: 1913

Membership: 1,001–10,000

Scope: State

Description: The mission of the Illinois Department of Natural Resources is to promote an understanding and appreciation of the state's natural resources and work with the people of Illinois to protect and manage those resources to ensure a high quality of life for present and future generations.

Publication(s): Digest of Hunting and Trapping Regulations, Outdoor Illinois Magazine, State Park Magazine, Illinois Fishing Information Book

Keyword(s): Ecosystems (precious), Energy, Forests/Forestry, Land Issues, Pollution (general), Recreation/Ecotourism, Reduce/Reuse/Recycle, Sprawl/Urban Planning, Water Habitats & Quality, Wildlife & Species

Contact(s):

Brian Anderson, Director, Office of Scientific Research & Analysis; 217-524-9506
Jerry Beverlin, Director of Office of Land Management and Education; 217-782-6752
Bruce Clark, Director of Office of Capital Development; 217-782-1807
Kirby Cottrell, Director of Resource Conservation Office; 217-785-8547
Tom Flattery, Director of Realty and Environmental Planning Office; 217-782-7940
Jim Fulgenzi, Director of Public Services Office; 217-782-7454
Diane Hendren, Director of Legislation and Constituency Services; 217-785-0073
Carol Knowles, Director of Public Affairs Office; 217-785-0970
Brent Manning, Director; 217-782-6302; Fax: 217-785-9236
Neal Merrifield, Director of Office Mines and Minerals; 217-782-0031
Andrea Moore, Assistant Director; 217-782-6302
John Schmitt, Conservation Foundation Executive Director; 100 W. Randolph, Chicago, IL 60601; 312-814-7237
Kevin Sronce, Director, Office of Administration; 217-782-0179
Don Vonnahme, Director of Water Resources Office; 217-782-2152
Tom Wakolbinger, Acting Director, Office of Law Enforcement; 217-782-6431
Brad Hammond, Division Manager of Internal Audit Office; 217-785-0853
John Bandy, Chief Fiscal Officer; 217-785-8552
Theresa Cummings, Equal Employment Opportunity Officer; 217-785-0067
Jim Garner, Deputy Director
Robert Lawley, Chief Legal Counsel; 217-782-1809
Jim Riemer, Deputy Director; 217-782-1824
Tom Wakolbinger, Chief of Law Enforcement Office; 217-782-6431

ILLINOIS DEPARTMENT OF TRANSPORTATION

2300 S. Dirksen Pkwy.
Springfield, IL 62764 United States
Phone: 217-782-7820
Website: www.dot.state.il.us

Founded: N/A

Scope: State

Keyword(s): Transportation

Contact(s):

James Easterly, Director: Division of Highways; 217-782-2151; Fax: 217-524-2972
Kirk Brown, Secretary; 217-782-6828
Mike Hines, Chief: Bureau of Design and Environment; 217-782-7526; Fax: 217-524-0989

ILLINOIS ENVIRONMENTAL PROTECTION AGENCY

P.O. Box 19276
Springfield, IL 62794-9276 United States
Phone: 217-782-3397 Fax: 217-782-9039
Website: www.epa.state.us

Founded: 1970

Membership: 1,001–10,000

Scope: State

Description: Responsible for implementing the environmental program for the State of Illinois. Administers a variety of programs to protect the air, land, and water.

Publication(s): Digester/Over the Spillway, Environmental Progress

Keyword(s): Air Quality/Atmosphere, Land Issues, Oceans/Coasts/ Beaches, Pollution (general)

Contact(s):

Renee Cipriano, Director
Dennis McMurray, Manager: Public Information
William Child, Chief: Bureau of Land; 217-785-9407
Dave Kolaz, Chief: Bureau of Air; 217-785-4140
Joan Muraro, Editor; 217-785-7209
James Park, Chief: Bureau of Water; 217-782-1654
William Seith, Deputy Director
Nancy Simpson, Head Librarian; 1021 N. Grand Ave. E., P.O. Box 19276, Springfield, IL 62794-9276; 217-782-9691
Marcia Willhite, Bureau Chief

ILLINOIS NATURE PRESERVES COMMISSION (INPC)

524 S. Second St., Lincoln Tower Plaza
Springfield, IL 62701-1787 United States
Phone: 217-785-8686 Fax: 217-785-6040
Website: www.dnr.state.il.us/inpc/index.htm

Founded: 1963
Membership: N/A
Scope: Local, State, Regional
Description: The mission of the Illinois Nature Preserves Commission (INPC) is to assist private and public landowners in protecting high quality natural areas and habitats of endangered and threatened species in perpetuity, through voluntary dedication or registration of such lands into the Illinois Nature Preserves System. The commission promotes the preservation of these significant lands and provides leadership in their stewardship, management, and protection.
Publication(s): Directory of Illinois Nature Preserves Volume 1 & 2
Keyword(s): Ecosystems (precious), Land Issues, Wildlife & Species
Contact(s):

Carolyn Grosboll, Director
Jill Allread, Secretary
Carolyn Grosboll, Legal Counsel
Randy Heidorn, Deputy Director for Stewardship
Don McFall, Deputy Director for Protection
Joyce O' Keefe, Chairperson
Jonathon Schwegman, Vice-Chair

INDIANA DEPARTMENT OF ENVIRONMENTAL MANAGEMENT

Indianapolis, IN 46206 United States
Phone: 317-232-8560 Fax: 317-233-6647
Website: www.in.gov/idem

Founded: N/A
Membership: 101–1,000
Scope: State
Description: The Indiana Department of Environmental Management is dedicated to conserving, protecting, enhancing, restoring, and managing Indiana's environment. We strive to fairly but vigorously enforce laws and standards; promulgate regulations consistent with the law and public policy; and promote conservation, pollution prevention, and a healthy and sustainable ecosystem. We are committed to making Indiana a cleaner, healthier place to live.
Contact(s):

Adriane Blaesing, Director of Northwest Regional Office; 219-881-6712; ablaesin@dem.state.in.us
Terry Coleman, Director of Northern Regional Office; 219-245-4870
Phillip Schermerhorn, Director of Media & Communication Services; 317-232-8560
Ericka Seydel, Director of Business & Legislative Relations; 317-232-8598
Paula Smith, Director of Planning & Assessment; 317-233-1210
Karen Terrell, Director of Community Relations; 317-233-6648; kterrell@dem.state.in.us
Judy Thomann, Director of Southwest Regional Office; 812-436-2570
Kristin Whittington, Director of Agricultural Relations; 317-232-8587
Dana Reed-Wise, Chief of Staff; 317-233-2773
Cynthia Collier, Assistant Commissioner for Public Policy and Planning; 317-233-5965
Bill Divine, Assistant Commissioner Office of Legal Counsel; 317-233-5546
Lori Kaplan, Commissioner; 317-232-8611
Jim Mahern, Assistant Commissioner for Office of Pollution Prevention; 317-233-6658
Janet McCabe, Assistant Commissioner of Air Management; 317-233-6861
Timothy Method, Deputy Commissioner for Environmental and Regulatory Affairs; 317-233-3706
Bruce Palin, Deputy Commissioner, Office of Land Quality; 317-233-6591
Felicia Robinson, Deputy Commissioner of Legal Affairs; 317-233-3706; frobinso@dem.state.in.us
Mary Tuohy, Assistant Commissioner, Office of Land Quality; 317-234-0337

INDIANA DEPARTMENT OF NATURAL RESOURCES

402 W. Washington St., Rm. W255B
Indianapolis, IN 46204-2748 United States
Phone: 317-232-4200
Website: www.state.in.us/dnr

Founded: N/A
Scope: State
Description: The DNR administers more than 100 properties throughout Indiana, comprising more than 400,000 acres. The DNR provides recreational opportunities for millions of Hoosiers and out-of-state visitors annually at its state parks, forests, reservoirs, and fish and wildlife areas. The DNR also has wide-ranging responsibilities for various programs such as maintaining the Indiana State Museum and more than a dozen historic sites throughout the state.
Publication(s): Outdoor Indiana
Keyword(s): Forests/Forestry, Recreation/Ecotourism
Contact(s):

John Bacone, Director: Division of Nature Preserves; 317-232-4052
Thomas Barton, Director: Division of Accounting; 317-232-4041
John Davis, Director: Division of Land Acquisition; 317-232-4050
Gary Doxtater, Director: Division of Fish and Wildlife; 317-232-4080
Daniel Fogerty, Director: Division of Historic Preservation and Archaeology; 317-232-1646
Richard Gantz, Director: Division of State Museum and Historical Sites; 317-232-1637
Emily Kress, Director: Division of Outdoor Recreation; 317-232-4070
James Liverett, Director: Division of Internal Audit; 317-232-8092
Gerald Pagac, Director: Division of State Parks; 317-232-4124
Mike Quigley, Director: Management Information Systems; 317-232-4007
Patrick Ralston, Director; 317-232-4020
Stephen Sellers, Director: Division of Public Information and Education; 317-232-4200
John Simpson, Director: Division of Water; 317-232-4160
Jim Slutz, Director: Division of Oil and Gas; 317-232-4055
Mike Sponsler, Director: Division of Reclamation; 812-665-2207
J. Taylor, Director: Division of Reservoir Management; 317-232-4060
Philip Wagner, Director: Division of Safety and Training; 317-232-4145
Charles Walker, Director: Division of Law Enforcement; 317-232-4010
Robert Waltz, State Entomologist Director; 317-232-4120
John Costello, Deputy Director: Bureau of Lands and Cultural Resources; 317-232-4020
Paul Ehret, Deputy Director: Bureau of Mine Reclamation; 317-232-4020
Burnell Fischer, State Forester: Head: Division of Forestry; 317-232-4105
David Herbst, Deputy Director: Bureau of Water and Resource Regulation; 317-232-4020

Tom Hohman, Head Chief Engineer: Division of Engineering; 317-232-4150
Lori Kaplan, Chief Counsel; 317-232-4020
Michael Kiley, Chairman: Natural Resources Commission; 317-232-4020
Steven Lucas, Chief Hearings Officer; 317-232-0156
Jerry Miller, Chairman: Lands and Cultural Resources Advisory Council; 317-232-4020
Stephen Sellers, Editor; 317-232-4200
Joseph Siener, Chairman: Water and Resource Regulation Advisory Council; 317-232-4020
David Vice, Deputy Director: Law Enforcement and Administration; 317-232-4020

INDIANA DEPARTMENT OF NATURAL RESOURCES

DIVISION OF SOIL CONSERVATION
402 W. Washington St., Rm. W265
Indianapolis, IN 46204-2782 United States
Phone: 317-233-3870 Fax: 317-233-3882
Website: www.state.in.us/dnr

Founded: N/A
Membership: 1–100
Scope: Regional
Description: The Division's mission is to facilitate the protection, wise use, and enhancement of Indiana's soil and water resources by: coordinating implementation of the state's T-by-2000 soil conservation/water quality protection program and providing assistance to local soil and water conservation districts.
Publication(s): Indiana Handbook for Erosion Control in Developing Areas, Erosion Control for the Home Builder, Urban Conservation Program, Lake and River Enhancement Program, Topsoil
Keyword(s): Agriculture/Farming, Land Issues, Water Habitats & Quality
Contact(s):
Harry Nikides, Director
David Avery, Vice Chairman
Peter Hippensteel, Chairman of the Board

INDIANA GEOLOGICAL SURVEY

Institute of Indiana University, 611 N. Walnut Grove
Bloomington, IN 47405 United States
Phone: 812-855-7636 Fax: 812-855-2862
E-mail: igsinfo@indiana.edu
Website: www.indiana.edu/~igs/

Founded: 1869
Membership: 1–100
Scope: State
Description: Conducts basic and applied research in geology and disseminates geologic information as published reports and maps; consults with industry, academia, and the public on the geologic makeup, mineral and energy resources, and geologic hazards of the state.
Publication(s): Geologic Publications
Keyword(s): Land Issues
Contact(s):
John Stenmetz, Director and State Geologist; 812-855-5067
John Hill, Assistant Director; 812-855-6067

INDIANA STATE DEPARTMENT OF HEALTH

Two North Meridian St.
Indianapolis, IN 46204 United States
Phone: 317-233-1325
E-mail: rfeldman@isdh.state.in.us
Website: www.state.in.us/isdh

Founded: N/A
Scope: State
Keyword(s): Energy, Pollution (general), Public Health
Contact(s):
Richard Feldman, State Health Commissioner

INDUSTRIAL COMMISSION OF NORTH DAKOTA

NORTH DAKOTA GEOLOGICAL SURVEY
600 E. Blvd.
Bismarck, ND 58505-0840 United States
Phone: 701-328-8000 Fax: 701-328-8010
Website: www.state.nd.us/ndgs

Founded: 1895
Membership: 1–100
Scope: State
Description: Responsible for collecting and disseminating geologic information.
Publication(s): NDGS Newsletter
Keyword(s): Energy, Land Issues, Oceans/Coasts/Beaches
Contact(s):
John Bluemle, State Geologist

INSTITUTE FOR ECOLOGICAL STUDIES UNIVERSITY OF NORTH DAKOTA

P.O. Box 7110,
Grand Forks, ND 58202 United States
Phone: 701-777-2851 Fax: 701-777-2623

Founded: 1965
Membership: 1–100
Scope: Local
Description: A nonprofit university research center devoted to ecology, policy analysis, and environmental biology. A interdisciplinary staff composed of university faculty, biologists, and associates conducts basic and applied research centering in the upper Midwest, and provides technical services for government and corporate agencies, and the public.
Publication(s): Contributions, Research Reports
Keyword(s): Water Habitats & Quality, Wildlife & Species
Contact(s):
Richard Crawford, Director

INTERAGENCY COMMITTEE FOR OUTDOOR RECREATION (IAC)

1111 Washington St., SE, P.O. Box 40917
Olympia, WA 98504-0917 United States
Phone: 360-902-3000 Fax: 360-902-3026
E-mail: info@iac.wa.gov
Website: www.wa.gov/iac

Founded: 1965
Scope: State
Description: IAC administers grants and technical assistance programs for public recreation, open space, and conservation projects in Washington state. The agency assists local, state, federal, and nonprofit organizations in planning, acquiring, and developing recreation resources. IAC also writes the state's outdoor recreation and open space plan, as well as plans on trails and nonhighway off-road vehicle recreation.
Publication(s): Refer to Website for publication listings: www.wa.gov/iappleconnie
Keyword(s): Land Issues, Public Lands/Greenspace, Recreation/Ecotourism, Wildlife & Species
Contact(s):
Laura Johnson, Director; 360-902-3000
Gregory Lovelady, Manager of Applied Planning; 360-902-3008
Jim Fox, Special Assistant to the Director; 360-902-3021
Debra Wilhelmi, Deputy Director of Management Services; 360-902-3005

IOWA ASSOCIATION OF COUNTY CONSERVATION BOARDS

405 SW 3rd, Suite 1
Ankeny, IA 50021 United States
Phone: 515-963-9582 Fax: 515-963-9582
E-mail: iaccb@ecity.net
Website: www.george.ecity.net/iacob

Founded: N/A

Description: Promotes the objectives of Iowa's County Conservation Boards, board member education, information exchange, legislation, and public awareness.

Publication(s): Iowa Board Member, Board Member Handbook, Outdoor Adventure Guide (Area Directory), IACCB Legislative Update, IACCB Newsletter

Contact(s):
Dan Heissel, President
Steve Lekwa, Vice President
Ann Adkins, Secretary
Don Brazelton, Executive Secretary

IOWA DEPARTMENT OF AGRICULTURE AND LAND STEWARDSHIP

BUREAU OF FIELD SERVICES
E. 9th and Grand Ave., Wallace Bldg.
Des Moines, IA 50319-0034 United States
Phone: 515-281-5321
Website: www.state.ia.us/agriculture

Founded: N/A

Contact(s):
James Gillespie; 515-281-5258

IOWA DEPARTMENT OF AGRICULTURE AND LAND STEWARDSHIP

BUREAU OF FINANCIAL INCENTIVE PROGRAM
E. 9th and Grand Ave., Wallace Bldg
Des Moines, IA 50319-0034 United States
Phone: 515-281-5851 Fax: 515-281-6170

Founded: N/A

Scope: State

Contact(s):
William McGill, Bureau Chief; 515-281-5851

IOWA DEPARTMENT OF AGRICULTURE AND LAND STEWARDSHIP

BUREAU OF WATER RESOURCES
E. 9th and Grand Ave., Wallace Bldg.
Des Moines, IA 50319-0050 United States
Phone: 515-281-5851 Fax: 515-281-6170
Website: www.state.ia.us/agriculture

Founded: N/A
Membership: 1–100
Scope: State

Contact(s):
Dean Lemke, Cheif Water Resource Bureau; 515-281-3963

IOWA DEPARTMENT OF AGRICULTURE AND LAND STEWARDSHIP

DIVISION OF SOIL CONSERVATION
502 E. 9th
Wallace State Office Bldg.
Des Moines, IA 50319-0034 United States
Phone: 515-281-5851 Fax: 515-281-6170
Website: www.agriculture.state.ia.us

Founded: 1939
Membership: N/A
Scope: State

Description: The Division of Soil Conservation is responsible for state leadership in the protection and management of soil, water and mineral resources; assisting soil and water conservation districts and private landowners to achieve their agricultural and environmental objectives.

Keyword(s): Agriculture/Farming, Ethics/Environmental Justice, Land Issues, Pollution (general), Water Habitats & Quality

Contact(s):
William Ehm, Director; 515-281-6146; Fax: 515-281-6170; william.ehm@idals.state.ia.us
Jim Gillespie, Bureau Chief, Field Services Bureau; 515-281-5258; Fax: 515-281-6170; jim.gillespie@idals.state.ia.us
Dean Lemke, Bureau Chief, Water Resource Bureau; 515-281-6146; Fax: 515-281-6170; dean.lemke@idals.state.ia.us
Bill McGill, Bureau Chief, Financial Incentives Bureau; 515-281-5851; Fax: 515-281-6170; bill.mcgill@idals.state.ia.us
Kenneth Tow, Bureau Chief, Mines and Minerals Bureau; 515-281-4246; Fax: 515-281-6170; ken.tow@idals.state.ia.us

IOWA DEPARTMENT OF NATURAL RESOURCES

E. 9th and Grand Ave., Wallace Bldg.
Des Moines, IA 50319-0034 United States
Phone: 515-281-5145 Fax: 515-281-8895
E-mail: webmaster@dnr.state.ia.us
Website: www.state.ia.us/government/dnr

Founded: 1986

Scope: State

Description: Established with the merging of the following state agencies: Iowa Conservation Commission, Department of Water, Air and Waste Management; Iowa Geological Survey; and the resources/conservation functions of the Energy Policy Council. The seven-member Natural Resources Commission is a policy and rule-setting authority over the Fish and Wildlife Division, Parks, Recreation, and Preserves Division, and the Forestry Division

Keyword(s): Air Quality/Atmosphere, Energy, Pollution (general), Recreation/Ecotourism, Reduce/Reuse/Recycle, Water Habitats & Quality, Wildlife & Species

Contact(s):
Jeffrey Vonk, Director
Liz Christiansen, Deputy Director
William Ehm, Environmental Protection Commission Chair
Ross Harrison, Chief of Information-Education Bureau
Joan Schneider, Natural Resource Commission Chair
Julie Sparks, Editor of Iowa Conservationist

IOWA DEPARTMENT OF NATURAL RESOURCES

ADMINISTRATIVE SERVICES DIVISION
502 E. 9th St.
Wallace State Office Building
Des Moines, IA 50319-0034 United States
Phone: 515-281-5918 Fax: 515-281-6794
E-mail: webmaster@dnr.state.ia.us
Website: www.state.ia.us/dnr

Founded: N/A

Scope: State

Description: The Administrative Services Division (ASD) is comprised of four bureaus: Administrative Services, Acquisition and Construction, Budget and Finance, and Information Technology. The Volunteer Program is also a part of the ASD. The common goal of these areas is to enable and support the Department of Natural Resources in its efforts to provide the highest level of customer service through the most efficient and cost-effective methods.

Contact(s):
Linda Hanson, Administrator
Sally Jagnandan, Chief of Administrative Support Bureau
Basil Nimry, Chief of Construction Services Bureau
Mark Slatterly, Chief of Budget and Finance Bureau

IOWA DEPARTMENT OF NATURAL RESOURCES

COOPERATIVE NORTH AMERICAN SHOTGUNNING EDUCATION PROGRAM
Wallace State Office Bldg.
Des Moines, IA 50319 United States
Phone: 515-281-5918 Fax: 503-884-2974
Website: www.state.ia.us/dnr

Founded: 1982

Scope: Regional

Description: The Cooperative North American Shotgunning Program is a research, information, and education program designed to assist wildlife professionals, hunters, and sportsmen in making a successful transition from lead shot to nontoxic shot, as well as educating sportsmen on improving shooting skills and harvest efficiency, thereby reducing wounding losses.

Publication(s): CONSEP Newsletter, Periodic Ballistics Reports

Keyword(s): Recreation/Ecotourism, Wildlife & Species

Contact(s):

Jeffrey Zonk, Director; 515-281-5918; jeff.zonk@dnr.state.ia.us
Lloyd Alexander, Contact for Atlantic Flyway; 89 Kings Highway, P.O. Box 1401, Dover, DE; 302-739-5287
Richard Bishop, Wildlife Bureau Chief; Wallace State Bldg., Des Moines, IA 50319; 515-281-6156
Don Childress, Contact for Pacific Flyway; 1420 E. 6th, Box 20071, Helena, MT 59601; 406-444-2612
Bob McLean, Contact for Canadian Wildlife Service; 17th Fl., Place Vincent Massey, Ottawa, Ontario K1A 0H3; 819-997-2957
Tom Roster, Consultant; 1190 Lynnewood Blvd., Klamath Falls, OR 97601; 503-884-2974
John Smith, Contact for Mississippi Flyway; P.O. Box 180, Jefferson City, MO 65102-0180; 573-751-4115
George Vandel, Contact for Central Flyway; 445 E. Capitol, Pierre, SD; 605-773-3381

IOWA DEPARTMENT OF NATURAL RESOURCES

ENERGY AND GEOLOGICAL RESOURCES DIVISION
Wallace State Office Building
502 E 9th St
Des Moines, IA 50319 United States
Phone: 515-281-6558 Fax: 515-281-6794
Website: www.state.ia.us/dnr/energy

Founded: N/A

Scope: Local, State

Description: The Energy and Geological Resources Division (EGRD) assists Iowans in adopting energy and geology practices which are environmentally and economically sound. The EGRD assists Iowans in adopting cost-effective energy management practices and using renewable energy resources while maintaining energy emergency preparedness. The EGRD collects geologic information on Iowa's mineral & groundwater resources that is applied to resource development, management and protection.

Contact(s):

Liz Christiansen, Deputy Director
Jeffrey Vonk, Director
Wayne Gieselman, Administrator, Environmental Services Division
Brian Tormey, Chief, Energy and Waste Management Bureau

IOWA DEPARTMENT OF NATURAL RESOURCES

ENVIRONMENTAL PROTECTION DIVISION
Wallace State Office Building
East 9 & Grand Avenue
Des Moines, IA 50319 United States
Phone: 515-281-5918
E-mail: webmaster@dnr.state.ia.us

Founded: N/A

Contact(s):

Mike Brandup, Division Administrator, Conservation Resources
Richard Bishop, Chief of Wildlife Bureau
Marion Conover, Chief of Fisheries Bureau
Lowell Joslin, Chief of Law Enforcement Bureau
Steve Pennington, Chief of Parks Bureau
John Walkowiak, Chief of Forestry Bureau

IOWA DEPARTMENT OF NATURAL RESOURCES

FISH AND WILDLIFE DIVISION
Wallace State Office Building
East 9 & Grand Avenue
Des Moines, IA 50319 United States
Phone: 515-281-4687 Fax: 515-281-6794
E-mail: webmaster@dnr.state.ia.us

Founded: N/A

Contact(s):

Mike Brandup, Division Administrator, Conservation Resources
Richard Bishop, Chief of Wildlife Bureau
Marion Conover, Chief of Fisheries Bureau
Allen Farris, Administrator
Lowell Joslin, Chief of Law Enforcement Bureau

IOWA DEPARTMENT OF NATURAL RESOURCES

FORESTS AND PRAIRIES DIVISION
Wallace State Office Building
East 9 & Grand Avenue
Des Moines, IA 50319 United States
Phone: 515-281-8657
E-mail: mike.brandrup@dnr.state.ia.us

Founded: N/A

Contact(s):

Mike Brandrup, Administrator
Jim Bulman, Chief of State Forests Management Bureau
John Walkowiak, Chief of Forestry Services Bureau

IOWA DEPARTMENT OF NATURAL RESOURCES

PARKS
Wallace State Office Building
502 E. 9th St.
Des Moines, IA 50319 United States
Phone: 515-281-5207 Fax: 515-281-6794
E-mail: janet.ott@dnr.state.ia.us
Website: www.exploreiowaparks.com

Founded: N/A

Scope: State

Description: Parks, Recreation and Preserves management

Contact(s):

Mike Brandrup, Division Administrator; 515-281-8657
Stephen Pennington, Bureau Chief; 515-281-5207

IOWA DEPARTMENT OF NATURAL RESOURCES

WASTE MANAGEMENT DIVISION
Wallace State Office Building
East 9 & Grand Avenue
Des Moines, IA 50319 United States
Phone: 515-281-4367 Fax: 515-281-8895
E-mail: teresa.barrie@dnr.state.ia.us

Founded: N/A

Contact(s):

Brent Laning, Executive Officer
Roya Stanley, Administrator

IOWA STATE EXTENSION SERVICES

1099 Court Avenue P.O.Box 146
Marengo, IA 52301 United States
Phone: 319-642-5504 Fax: 319-642-5505
E-mail: xiowa@iastate.edu
Website: www.extension.iastate.edu

Founded: N/A

Scope: State

Description: ISU Extension is a client-centered organization that provides research-based, unbiased information and education to help people make better decisions in their personal, community, and professional lives.

Contact(s):

James Pease, Extension Wildlife Conservationist; 103 Science II, Iowa State University, Ames, IA 50011; 515-294-7429; Fax: 515-294-7874
Paul Wray, Extension Forester; 251 Bessey Hall, Iowa State University, Ames, IA 50011; 515-294-1168

K

KANSAS BIOLOGICAL SURVEY

2021 Constant Ave. Foley Hall
Lawrence, KS 66047-2729 United States
Phone: 785-864-7725 Fax: 785-864-5093
Website: www.kbs.ukans.edu

Founded: 1959
Membership: 1–100
Scope: State
Description: A research and development branch of the University of Kansas whose purpose is to survey and inventory the native plants and animals of Kansas, report on its findings, and develop and administer lands for the study and preservation of native animal and plant resources.
Publication(s): Publications on website
Keyword(s): Land Issues, Water Habitats & Quality, Wildlife & Species
Contact(s):

Edward Martinko, Director and State Biologist
Frank Denoyelles, Associate Director
Paul Liechti, Assistant Director

KANSAS COOPERATIVE FISH AND WILDLIFE RESEARCH UNIT

205 Leasure Hall, Kansas State University
Manhattan, KS 66506-3501 United States
Phone: 785-532-6070 Fax: 785-532-7159
Website: www.ksu.edu/kscfwru/

Founded: 1991

Scope: National

Contact(s):

Jack Cully, Assistant Leader of Wildlife
Philip Gipson, Leader
Christopher Guy, Assistant Leader of Fisheries

KANSAS DEPARTMENT OF AGRICULTURE

109 SW 9th St., 2nd Fl.
Topeka, KS 66612-1280 United States
Phone: 785-296-3717 Fax: 785-296-1176
Website: www.ink.org/public/kda/dwr

Founded: N/A
Membership: 1–100
Scope: State
Keyword(s): Agriculture/Farming, Reduce/Reuse/Recycle, Water Habitats & Quality
Contact(s):

Tom Huntzinger, Water Appropriations Program Manager
Steve Stankiewicz, Operations Manager for Water Resources Division
Jamie Adams, Secretary of Agriculture; 785-296-3902; Fax: 785-296-8389
David Pope, Chief Engineer; 785-296-3717

KANSAS DEPARTMENT OF HEALTH AND ENVIRONMENT

1000 SW Jackson Street, Suite 400
Topeka, KS 66612-1367 United States
Phone: 785-296-1535 Fax: 785-296-8464
E-mail: rhammersc@kdhe.state.ks.us
Website: www.kdhe.state.ks.us

Founded: N/A
Membership: 101–1,000
Scope: State
Description: The Kansas Department of Health and Environment is responsible for administering a diverse collection of programs that enhance public health and state wildlife protection efforts. The path of the department is defined by strengthening programs and developing initatives on pollutant releases, spill cleanup, air and water quality, water resources, pollution prevention, waste management, and general health and environmental protection.
Keyword(s): Air Quality/Atmosphere, Pollution (general), Public Health, Reduce/Reuse/Recycle, Water Habitats & Quality
Contact(s):

Bill Bider, Director: Bureau of Waste Management
Gary Blackburn, Director: Bureau of Environmental Remediation; 785-296-1660
Ron Hammerschmidt, Director: Division of Environment; 785-296-1535
Mike Heideman, Director: Office of Public Information; 785-296-5795
Theresa Hodges, Director: Bureau of Environmental Field Services; 785-296-5572
Michael Moser, Director: Bureau of Environmental Health Services; 785-296-1086
Karl Mueldener, Director: Bureau of Water; 785-296-5500
Clyde Graber, Secretary; 785-296-0461

KANSAS DEPARTMENT OF WILDLIFE AND PARKS

OFFICE OF THE SECRETARY
900 SW Jackson St., Suite 502
Topeka, KS 66612 United States
Phone: 785-296-2281 Fax: 785-296-6953
Website: www.kdwp.state.ks.us

Founded: N/A
Membership: 101–1,000
Scope: State
Description: Charged with the conservation of state wildlife and fishery resources, provision of environmental services and habitat protection, and park development and management. Administers state boating law, hunter education programs, Land and Water Conservation Funds, and other related functions.
Publication(s): Kansas Wildlife & Parks Magazine
Keyword(s): Agriculture/Farming, Public Lands/Greenspace, Recreation/Ecotourism, Reduce/Reuse/Recycle, Water Habitats & Quality, Wildlife & Species
Contact(s):

Terry Denker, Federal Aid Coordinator
John Dykes, Commissioner Members Chairman; 913-831-3058
J. Michael Hayden, Secretary
Richard Koerth, Assistant Secretary for Administration
Cheryl Swayne, Boating Education, Topeka Office

KANSAS DEPARTMENT OF WILDLIFE AND PARKS

OPERATIONS OFFICE
512 SE 25th Ave.
Pratt, KS 67124-8174 United States
Phone: 620-672-5911 Fax: 620-672-2972
E-mail: feedback@wp.state.ks.us
Website: www.kdwp.state.ks.us

Founded: N/A
Membership: 101–1,000
Scope: State
Description: State agency responsible for management and protection of fish and wildlife resources
Publication(s): Kansas Wildlife and Parks Magazine
Keyword(s): Agriculture/Farming, Public Lands/Greenspace, Recreation/Ecotourism, Reduce/Reuse/Recycle, Water Habitats & Quality, Wildlife & Species
Contact(s):
Jerold Hover, Parks Division Director
Kevin Jones, Law Enforcement Division Director
Joe Kramer, Fisheries and Wildlife Division Director
Wayne Doyle, Coordinator, Hunter Education/Furharvester Education Service
Bob Mathews, Information and Education
Bob Mathews, Public Information
Mike Miller, Editor
Keith Sexson, Assistant Secretary for Operations
Roland Stein, Coordinator, Wildlife Education Service
Mike Theurer, Administrative Services Division

KANSAS DEPARTMENT OF WILDLIFE AND PARKS

REGION 1
1426 Hwy. 183 Alt.
Hays, KS 67601 United States
Phone: 785-628-8614 Fax: 785-623-2945
Website: www.kdwp.state.ks.us

Founded: N/A
Membership: 101–1,000
Scope: State
Description: Northwest Regional Office of state agency responsible for management and protection of fish and wildlife resources.
Keyword(s): Agriculture/Farming, Public Lands/Greenspace, Recreation/Ecotourism, Reduce/Reuse/Recycle, Water Habitats & Quality, Wildlife & Species
Contact(s):
Jerry Bump, Law Enforcement Regional Supervisor
Melody Burkholder, Parks Division Regional Supervisor
Vacant Position, F&W Division Regional Supervisor
Bruce Taggart, Public Lands Regional Supervisor

KANSAS DEPARTMENT OF WILDLIFE AND PARKS

REGION 2
3300 SW 29th St.
Topeka, KS 66614 United States
Phone: 785-273-6740 Fax: 785-273-6757
Website: www.kdwp.state.ks.us

Founded: N/A
Membership: 101–1,000
Scope: State
Description: Northeast Regional Office of state agency responsible for management and protection of fish and wildlife resources.
Keyword(s): Agriculture/Farming, Public Lands/Greenspace, Recreation/Ecotourism, Reduce/Reuse/Recycle, Water Habitats & Quality, Wildlife & Species
Contact(s):
Rob Ladner, Law Enforcement Regional Supervisor
Ron Little, Public Lands Regional Supervisor
Bill Porter, Parks Division Regional Supervisor
Roger Wolfe, F&W Division Regional Supervisor

KANSAS DEPARTMENT OF WILDLIFE AND PARKS

REGION 3
1001 W. McArtor Drive
Dodge City, KS 67801 United States
Phone: 620-227-8609 Fax: 620-227-8600
Website: www.kdwp.state.ks.us

Founded: N/A
Membership: 101–1,000
Scope: State
Description: Southwest Regional Office of state agency responsible for management and protection of fish and wildlife resources
Keyword(s): Agriculture/Farming, Public Lands/Greenspace, Recreation/Ecotourism, Reduce/Reuse/Recycle, Water Habitats & Quality, Wildlife & Species
Contact(s):
Scotty Baugh, F&W Division Regional Supervisor
Jim Kellenberger, Law Enforcement Regional Supervisor
Mark Sexson, Public Lands Regional Supervisor

KANSAS DEPARTMENT OF WILDLIFE AND PARKS

REGION 4
6232 E. 29th St., N
Wichita, KS 67220 United States
Phone: 316-683-8069 Fax: 316-683-4664
Website: www.kdwp.state.ks.us

Founded: N/A
Membership: 101–1,000
Scope: State
Description: South Central Regional Office of state agency responsible for management and protection of fish and wildlife resources
Keyword(s): Agriculture/Farming, Public Lands/Greenspace, Recreation/Ecotourism, Reduce/Reuse/Recycle, Wildlife & Species
Contact(s):
Randy Clark, Public Lands Regional Supervisor
Val Jansen, Law Enforcement Regional Supervisor
J. Alan Stark, Parks Division Regional Supervisor
Tom Swan, F&W Division Regional Supervisor

KANSAS DEPARTMENT OF WILDLIFE AND PARKS

REGION 5
1500 W. 7th, P.O. Box 777
Chanute, KS 66720-0777 United States
Phone: 620-431-0380 Fax: 620-431-0381
Website: www.kdwp.state.ks.us

Founded: N/A
Membership: 101–1,000
Scope: State
Description: Southeast Regional Office of state agency responsible for management and protection of fish and wildlife resources
Keyword(s): Agriculture/Farming, Public Lands/Greenspace, Recreation/Ecotourism, Reduce/Reuse/Recycle, Water Habitats & Quality, Wildlife & Species
Contact(s):
C. Doug Blex, Public Lands Regional Supervisor
Larry Tiemann, F&W Division Regional Supervisor
Charles Ward, Law Enforcement Regional Supervisor

KANSAS FOREST SERVICE

2610 Claflin Rd.
Manhattan, KS 66502-2798 United States
Phone: 785-532-3300 Fax: 785-532-3305
E-mail: kfs@lists.oznet.ksu.edu
Website: www.kansasforests.org

Founded: N/A
Membership: N/A
Scope: State
Description: Provides technical forestry assistance to landowners, wood industries, and communities; conducts a tree distribution program, and a rural fire protection program.
Keyword(s): Forests/Forestry, Reduce/Reuse/Recycle, Water Habitats & Quality
Contact(s):
Casey McCoy, Fire Manager
Raymond Aslin, State Forester
Robert Atchison, Rural Forestry Coordinator
William Loucks, Conservation Forester

KANSAS GEOLOGICAL SURVEY

1930 Constant Ave., Campus West, Kansas University
Lawrence, KS 66047 United States
Phone: 785-864-3965 Fax: 785-864-5317
Website: www.kgs.ku.edu

Founded: 1889
Membership: 101–1,000
Scope: State
Description: Purpose is to research and develop information about minerals, water resources, and geologic hazards of Kansas, and to publish reports on those subjects.
Publication(s): Bulletin, public information circulars, educational series, technical series, maps, journals.
Keyword(s): Energy, Oceans/Coasts/Beaches
Contact(s):
M. Allison, Director and State Geologist; lallison@kgs.ku.edu
Pieter Berendsen, Chief: Geologic Investigations
Timothy Carr, Chief: Petroleum Research
John Davis, Chief: Mathematical Geology
William Harrison, Deputy Director
Don Whittemore, Chief: Geohydrology

KANSAS STATE CONSERVATION COMMISSION

109 SW Ninth St.
Topeka, KS 66612-1215 United States
Phone: 785-296-3600 Fax: 785-296-6172
E-mail: tstreeter@scc.state.ks.us
Website: www.ink.org/public/kscc

Founded: 1937
Membership: 1–100
Scope: State
Description: The SCC administrative responsibility is to provide leadership, direction, and support to the conservation districts, watershed districts, and other special purpose districts for the protection and enhancement of Kansas' natural resources. It administers a total of ten programs: seven are financial assistance programs funded by appropriations from the Special Revenue Fund of the State Water Plan.
Keyword(s): Land Issues, Oceans/Coasts/Beaches, Water Habitats & Quality
Contact(s):
Tracy Streeter, Executive Director; 913-296-3600; Fax: 913-296-6172

KANSAS STATE EXTENSION SERVICES

Wildlife Damage Control, Department of Animal Sciences and Industry
131 Call Hall
Kansas State University
Manhattan, KS 66506-1600 United States
Phone: 785-532-5734 Fax: 785-532-5681
Website: www.oznet.ksu.edu

Founded: 1914
Scope: Local, State, Regional
Keyword(s): Recreation/Ecotourism, Water Habitats & Quality, Wildlife & Species
Contact(s):
Charles Lee, Extension Specialist; 785-532-5734; clee@oznet.ksu.edu

KANSAS WATER OFFICE

901 S. Kansas Ave.
Topeka, KS 66612-1249 United States
Phone: 785-296-3185 Fax: 785-296-0878
Website: www.kwo.org/

Founded: N/A
Description: State water planning, policy, and coordination agency. Prepares state plan of water resources management; conservation; fish and wildlife, and recreation and development; reviews water laws, and recommends new or amendatory legislation. Administers the state water monitoring program.
Keyword(s): Development/Developing Countries, Water Habitats & Quality
Contact(s):
Al Ledoux, Director
Clark Duffy, Assistant Director

KENTUCKY DEPARTMENT OF AGRICULTURE

7th Fl., 500 Mero St.
Frankfort, KY 40601 United States
Phone: 502-564-4696 Fax: 502-564-2133
Website: www.kyagr.com

Founded: 1876
Scope: State
Description: The service, regulatory, and promotional agency for Kentucky's agriculture industry.
Publication(s): Kentucky Agricultural News, Kentucky Agricultural Statistics (Yearly), see publications on website.
Keyword(s): Agriculture/Farming, Land Issues, Pollution (general), Water Habitats & Quality
Contact(s):
Doug Thomas, Director: Division of Communications; 502-564-4696, ext. 248
Ted Sloan, Editor; 502-564-4696, ext. 247
Billy Smith, Commissioner

KENTUCKY DEPARTMENT OF FISH AND WILDLIFE RESOURCES

#1 Game Farm Rd.
Frankfort, KY 40601 United States
Phone: 800-858-1549 Fax: 502-564-6508
E-mail: info.center@mail.state.ky.us
Website: kyafield.com/

Founded: 1944
Membership: 101–1,000
Scope: State
Description: We are stewards of Kentucky's fish and wildlife resources and their habitats. We manage for the perpetuation of these resources and their use by present and future generations. Through partnerships, we will enhance wildlife diversity and promote sustainable use, including hunting, fishing, boating, and other nature-related recreation.

Publication(s): Kentucky Wildlife Viewing Guide, Hunting and Fishing Regulation Guides, Kentucky Fish, Kentucky Afield Magazine
Keyword(s): Wildlife & Species
Contact(s):
Robert Bates, Director of Administrative Services Division
Charles Bush, Director of Engineering Division
Lee Carolan, Director of Division of Information and Education
Lynn Garrison, Director of Public Affairs Division
Roy Grimes, Director of Division of Wildlife
David Loveless, Director of Division of Law Enforcement
Peter Pfeiffer, Director of Division of Fisheries
John Akers, Superintendent of State Game Farm
Gerald Alexander, Regional Law Enforcement Supervisor; 6575 Beech Grove Rd., Farmington, KY 42040
James Axon, Coordinator of Sport Fish Restoration Section
Tom Baker, District 2 Commissioner; 661 A U.S. 31 W. By-Pass, Bowling Green, KY 42101
Charles Bale, District 4 Commissioner; 855 Parkers Grove Rd., Hodgenville, KY 42748
C. Bennett, Commissioner
Mike Boatwright, District 1 Commissioner; 2601 N. 10th St., Paducah, KY 42001
Frank Brown, District 6 Commissioner; 124 Lancaster Ave., Richmond, KY 40475; Fax: 606-624-0820
Allen Gailor, District 3 Commissioner; 730 W. Market, Louisville, KY 40202
David Godby, District 9 Commissioner; P.O. Box 1277, Somerset, KY 42502; Fax: 606-677-0115
K. Henderson, Regional Boating Supervisor; P.O. Box 131, Clarkson, KY 42726
Doug Hensley, District 7 Commissioner; P.O. Box 480, Hazard, KY 41701; Fax: 606-436-5180
Steve Owens, Regional Boating Supervisor; 338 Candlelite Drive, Almo, KY 42020
James Rich, District 5 Commissioner; 5975 Taylor Mill Rd., Covington, KY 41015
Reed Sanders, Regional Boating Supervisor; 185 Gwinn Island Circle, Danville, KY 40422
Don Walker, Coordinator of Pittman-Robertson Section
Dennis Watson, Regional Boating Supervisor; Route 1 Sand Knob, Falls of Rough, KY 40119
Robert Webb, District 8 Commissioner; 45 Webb Circle, Grayson, KY 41143
Thomas Young, Deputy Commissioner

KENTUCKY DEPARTMENT OF PARKS
10th Fl., Capital Plaza Tower
Frankfort, KY 40601 United States
Phone: 502-564-2172 Fax: 502-564-9015
Website: www.kystateparks.com
Founded: N/A
Membership: 1,001–10,000
Scope: Regional
Publication(s): Kentucky Hiking Trails, Kentucky State Parks Booklet
Keyword(s): Land Issues, Public Lands/Greenspace, Recreation/Ecotourism
Contact(s):
Jim Goodman, Director of Resort Parks
Danny Reed, Director: Rangers
Bob Bender, Deputy Commissioner
Kenny Rapier, Commissioner
Carey Tichenor, State Naturalist

KENTUCKY GEOLOGICAL SURVEY
228 Mining and Mineral Resources Bldg., University of Kentucky
Lexington, KY 40506-0107 United States
Phone: 859-257-5500 Fax: 859-257-1147
Website: www.uky.edu/kgs
Founded: 1854
Membership: 1–100
Scope: State
Description: Investigates the geology and mineral and water resources of Kentucky and makes this information available to the public. It is a research and service organization.
Publication(s): See publication website
Contact(s):
James Cobb, Director and State Geologist; cobb@kgs.mm.uky.edu
Steven Cordiviola, Head: Computer and Laboratory Services Section; cordiviola@kgs.mm.uky.edu
James Dinger, Head: Water Resources Section; dinger@kgs.mm.uky.edu
James Drahovzal, Head: Energy & Mineral Section; drahovzal@kgs.mm.uky.edu
John Kiefer, Assistant State Geologist for Administration; kiefer@kgs.mm.uky.edu

KENTUCKY NATURAL RESOURCES AND ENVIRONMENTAL PROTECTION CABINET
DEPARTMENT FOR ENVIRONMENTAL PROTECTION
14 Reilly Road
Frankfort, KY 40601 United States
Phone: 502-564-2150 Fax: 502-564-4245
Website: www.kyenvironment.org
Founded: N/A
Scope: State
Description: The mission of the Kentucky Natural Resources and Environmental Protection Cabinet is to protect and preserve Kentucky's land, air, and water resources.
Contact(s):
Ralph Collins, Deputy Commissioner
Rob Daniell, Division of Waste Management; 502-564-6716
William Davis, Environmental Services; 502-564-6120
Robert Logan, Commissioner
John Lyons, Division for Air Quality; 502-573-3382
Jeff Pratt, Division of Water; 502-564-3410

KENTUCKY SOIL AND WATER CONSERVATION COMMISSION
663 Teton Trail
Frankfort, KY 40601 United States
Phone: 502-564-3080 Fax: 502-564-9195
E-mail: steve.coleman@mail.state.ky.us
Website:
www.kyenvironment.org/nrepc/dnr/Conserve/doc2.htm
Founded: 1946
Scope: Local, State, Regional
Description: Set policy for state soil and water conservation programs and assist 121 local conservation districts.
Keyword(s): Agriculture/Farming, Land Issues, Pollution (general), Sprawl/Urban Planning
Contact(s):
Stephen Coleman, Director of Division of Conservation; 502-564-3080; Fax: 502-564-9195
David Gerrein, Chair; 606-623-3960

KENTUCKY STATE COOPERATIVE EXTENSION SERVICES
307 WP Garrigus Building
Lexington, KY 40546-0091 United States
Phone: 859-257-4302 Fax: 859-323-1991
Website: www.ca.uky.edu/coopext/
Founded: N/A
Membership: 101–1,000
Scope: State
Publication(s): Extension Today

Contact(s):
Curtis Absher, Assistant Extension Director of Agriculture; 309 Garrigus Bldg., University of Kentucky, Lexington, KY 40546; 606-257-1846; cabsher@ca.uky.edu
Thomas Barnes, Wildlife Specialist; Univ. of Kentucky, Dept. of Forestry, Lexington, KY 40546-0073; 606-257-8633; Fax: 606-323-1031
Rick Maurer, Assistant Director, Rural and Economic Development; 500 Garrigus Bldg., University of Kentucky, Lexington, KY 40546-0215; 606-257-7585; rmaurer@ca.uky.edu
Paul Warner, Interim Associate Director of Extension Service; wwalla@ca.uky.edu

KENTUCKY STATE NATURE PRESERVES COMMISSION

801 Schenkel Ln.
Frankfort, KY 40601 United States
Phone: 502-573-2886 Fax: 502-573-2355
E-mail: nrepc.ksnpcemail@mail.state.ky.us
Website: www.kynaturepreserves.org

Founded: 1976
Membership: 1–100
Scope: State
Description: KSNP's mission is to protect Kentucky's natural heritage by (1) identifying, acquiring, and managing natural areas that represent the best known occurences of rare native species, natural communitites, and significant natural features in a statewide nature preserve system; (2) working with others to protect biological diveristy; and (3) educating Kentuckians as to the value and purpose of nature preserves and biodiversity conservation.
Publication(s): Naturally Kentucky
Keyword(s): Ecosystems (precious), Forests/Forestry, Land Issues, Public Lands/Greenspace, Recreation/Ecotourism, Water Habitats & Quality, Wildlife & Species
Contact(s):
Donald Dott, Director; 502-573-2886; Fax: 502-573-2355; don.dott@mail.state.ky.us
Ken Jackson, Secretary of Commission; 606-734-4436
Clara Wheatley, Chair of Commission; 502-358-8643

L

LEE COUNTY PARKS AND RECREATION

LEE COUNTY MANATEE PARK
Manatee Park Program Office, 7330 Gladiolus Dr.
Fort Myers, FL 33908 United States
Phone: 941-432-2038 Fax: 941-432-2032
E-mail: kisedajb@leegov.com
Website: www.lee-county.com/parksandrec/

Founded: 1990
Membership: N/A
Scope: Local, State, Regional
Description: To promote and develop environmental awareness in Southwest Florida by conducting educational programs which teach ecological concepts and outdoor skills, and by coordinating informational events which alert citizens and community leaders of environmental concerns.
Publication(s): Florida Native Plant Habitat Guide, Elements Newsletter
Keyword(s): Ecosystems (precious), Land Issues, Public Lands/Greenspace, Recreation/Ecotourism, Reduce/Reuse/Recycle, Water Habitats & Quality, Wildlife & Species
Contact(s):
John Kiseda, Environmental Educator; kisedajb@leegov.com

LOUISIANA COOPERATIVE FISH AND WILDLIFE RESEARCH UNIT (USDI)

U.S. Geological Survey, School of Forestry, Wildlife and Fisheries
FWF Building, Rm. 124
Louisiana State University
Baton Rouge, LA 70803-6202 United States
Phone: 225-388-4179 Fax: 225-388-4144

Founded: N/A
Membership: 1–100
Scope: National
Contact(s):
Alan Afton, Assistant Leader; 225-388-4212; aafton@lsu.edu
Charles Bryan, Leader; 225-388-4184; Fax: 225-388-4144; cbryan@lsu.edu
Megan Lapeyre, Assistant Leader Fisheries; 225-578-4180

LOUISIANA DEPARTMENT OF AGRICULTURE AND FORESTRY

P.O. Box 631
Baton Rouge, LA 70821-0631 United States
Phone: 225-922-1234 Fax: 225-922-1253
E-mail: info@ldaf.state.la.us
Website: www.ldaf.state.la.us/

Founded: N/A
Contact(s):
Bud Courson, Deputy Commissioner; 504-922-1238; Fax: 504-922-1253
Bob Odom, Commissioner
Skip Rhorer, Assistant Commissioner: Office of Management and Finance

LOUISIANA DEPARTMENT OF AGRICULTURE AND FORESTRY

OFFICE OF FORESTRY
Baton Rouge, LA 70821-1628 United States
Phone: 225-925-4500 Fax: 225-922-1356
Website: www.ldaf.state.la.us

Founded: 1944
Membership: 1–100
Scope: State
Description: Charged with: Detection and suppression of wildfire on forest lands; providing technical management assistance to forest landowners; and dissemination of materials and information for education of the public. Produces approximately 50 million seedlings annually (pine and hardwood) for Louisiana landowners, operates a 400-acre seed orchard that produces improved slash and loblolly pine seed that are genetically improved. Actively engaged in promoting urban forestry activities.
Publication(s): Publications on website
Keyword(s): Forests/Forestry, Recreation/Ecotourism, Reduce/Reuse/Recycle
Contact(s):
Donald Feduccia, Chief: Forest Management; 225-925-8010
Paul Frey, State Forester; 225-952-8002; paul_f@ldaf.state.la.us
Louis Heaton, Chief: Forest Protection; 225-952-8013; louis_h@ldaf.state.la.us
Cyril Lejeune, Associate State Forester; 225-952-8002; cyril_l@ldaf.state.la.us
Charles Matherne, Chief: Reforestation; 225-925-4515
Burton Weaver, Chairman

LOUISIANA DEPARTMENT OF AGRICULTURE AND FORESTRY

OFFICE OF SOIL AND WATER CONSERVATION, STATE SOIL AND WATER CONSERVATION COMMITTEE
P.O. Box 3554
Baton Rouge, LA 70821-3554 United States
Phone: 225-922-1269 Fax: 225-922-2577

Founded: 1938

Description: To assist soil and water conservation districts in carrying out their conservation programs, to coordinate activities among districts, and to secure the cooperation and assistance of state and federal agencies in the work of such districts.

Contact(s):

Bradley Spicer, Executive Director; 504-922-1269; Fax: 504-922-2577
A. Allee, Secretary and Treasurer
Pedro Angelle, Chairman; 4879 Main Hwy., St. Martinville, LA 70582; 318-332-2910; Fax: 318-332-6563
Thad Spurlock, Vice Chairman

LOUISIANA DEPARTMENT OF NATURAL RESOURCES

P.O. Box 94396
Baton Rouge, LA 70804 United States
Phone: 225-342-4500 Fax: 225-342-4471
E-mail: webmaster@dnr.state.la.us
Website: www.dnr.state.la.us

Founded: 1975
Membership: 101–1,000
Scope: State

Description: This is a cabinet-level organization within the State of Louisiana charged with responsibilities related to coastal restoration, mineral conservation, and energy conservation.

Keyword(s): Energy, Oceans/Coasts/Beaches

Contact(s):

Katherine Vaughan, Assistant Secretary; 225-342-1375; Fax: 225-342-5861

LOUISIANA DEPARTMENT OF NATURAL RESOURCES

617 North Third Street
P. O. Box 94396
Baton Rouge, LA 70802 United States
Phone: 225-342-8955 Fax: 224-342-3442
Website: www.dnr.state.la.us

Founded: N/A

Scope: State

Contact(s):

Jack Caldwell, Secretary; 225-342-4503; Fax: 225-342-5861
Robert Harper, Undersecretary
Katherine Vaughan, Deputy Secretary; 225-342-1375

LOUISIANA DEPARTMENT OF NATURAL RESOURCES

OFFICE OF CONSERVATION
P.O. Box 94275
Baton Rouge, LA 70804-9275 United States
Phone: 225-342-5540 Fax: 225-342-3705
Website: www.dnr.state.la.us/cons/conserv.ssi

Founded: 1901
Membership: 101–1,000
Scope: Local, State, Regional

Description: State regulatory agency for oil and gas matters.

Contact(s):

James Welsh, Commissioner of Conservation

LOUISIANA DEPARTMENT OF NATURAL RESOURCES

OFFICE OF MINERAL RESOURCES
625 North Fourth Street, P.O. Box 2827
Baton Rouge, LA 70804 United States
Phone: 225-342-4615
Website: www.dnr.state.la.us

Founded: N/A

Contact(s):

Gus Rodemacher, Assistant Secretary

LOUISIANA DEPARTMENT OF WILDLIFE AND FISHERIES

P.O. Box 98000
Baton Rouge, LA 70898-9000 United States
Phone: 225-765-2800
Website: www.wlf.state.la.us

Founded: 1872

Scope: State

Description: Established as a part of state government to protect, conserve, and replenish the natural resources of the state, including wild game and nongame quadrupeds or animals, oysters, fish, and other aquatic life.

Publication(s): Louisiana Conservationist

Keyword(s): Wildlife & Species

Contact(s):

Phil Bowman, Assistant Secretary: Office of Wildlife; 225-765-2806
Bill Busbice, Chairman
Bennie Fontenot, Administrator: Inland Fisheries Division; 225-765-2330
Karen Foote, Administrator: Marine Fisheries Division; 225-765-2384
James Jenkins, Secretary; 225-765-2623
James Patton, Undersecretary: Office of Management and Finance; 225-765-2860
Tommy Prickett, Administrator: Wildlife Division; 225-765-2346
John Roussel, Assistant Secretary: Office of Fisheries; 225-765-2801
Brandt Savioe, Administrator: Fur & Refuge Division; 225-765-2811
Winton Vidrine, Administrator: Colonel, Law Enforcement Division; 225-765-2989

LOUISIANA GEOLOGICAL SURVEY

208 Howe-Russell
Louisana State University
Baton Rouge, LA 70803 United States
Phone: 225-578-5320 Fax: 225-578-3662
E-mail: hammer@isu.edu
Website: www.lgs.lsu.edu

Founded: 1934

Description: The Survey is charged with conducting geologic investigations and preparing technical reports that assist in finding and developing new reserves of natural resources in the state and in protecting the state's environment.

Keyword(s): Energy, Oceans/Coasts/Beaches, Water Habitats & Quality

Contact(s):

Chacko John, Director

LOUISIANA OFFICE OF STATE PARKS, DEPARTMENT OF CULTURE, RECREATION, AND TOURISM

P.O. Box 44426
Baton Rouge, LA 70804 United States
Phone: 225-342-8111 Fax: 225-342-8107
E-mail: parks@crt.state.la.us
Website: www.lastateparks.com

Founded: 1934

Scope: State
Description: Created to plan, design, construct, operate, and maintain the state's parks, natural areas, recreational facilities, and commemorative sites. Office has 17 parks or recreational areas, 16 historic sites, and one preservation area open to the public. The Office is assisted by the Parks and Recreation Commission, an advisory board appointed by the Governor.
Keyword(s): Ecosystems (precious), Ethics/Environmental Justice, Land Issues, Public Lands/Greenspace, Recreation/Ecotourism, Wildlife & Species
Contact(s):
Bo Boehringer, Public Information Director; 225-342-2443; Fax: 225-219-9429; bboehringer@crt.state.la.us
Dwight Landreneau, Assistant Secretary; dlandreneau@crt.state.la.us

LSU AGCENTER - LOUISIANA COOPERATIVE EXTENSION SERVICE

P.O. Box 25100
Baton Rouge, LA 70894-5100 United States
Phone: 225-578-6083 Fax: 504-578-2478
Website: www.lsu.edu.center.edu
Founded: N/A
Scope: State
Publication(s): See publications on website
Contact(s):
Paul Coriel, Director of Extension Service; jlngent@agctr.lsu.edu
Rex Caffey, Assistant Specialist for Wetland and Coastal Resources; 225-388-2266; Fax: 225-388-2478; rcaffey@agctr.lsu.edu
Michael Dunn, Specialist: Forestry; 225-578-4087; Fax: 225-388-2478; mdunn@agctr.lsu.edu
Charles Lutz, Associate Specialist of Aquaculture; 225-388-2152; Fax: 225-388-2478; glutz@agctr.lsu.edu
Michael Moody, Specialist for Seafood Technology; 225-388-2152; Fax: 225-388-2478; mmoody@agctr.lsu.edu
Donald Reed, Assistant Specialist for Forestry and Wildlife; 225-388-4087; Fax: 225-388-2478; dreed@agctr.lsu.edu
Kenneth Roberts, Project Leader of Aquaculture: Fisheries: Wetland & Coastal; 225-388-2145; Fax: 225-388-2478; kroberts@agctr.lsu.edu
Todd Shupe, Assistant Specialist for Forestry; 225-388-4087; Fax: 225-388-2478; tshupe@agctr.lsu.edu

M

MAINE ATLANTIC SALMON COMMISSION

650 State St.
Bangor, ME 04401-5654 United States
Phone: 207-941-4449 Fax: 207-941-4443
Website: www.state.me.us/asa
Founded: 1948
Membership: 1–100
Scope: State
Description: (formerly Maine Atlantic Salmon Authority) The Atlantic Salmon Commission was established for the purposes of undertaking research, planning, management, restoration, and propagation of the Atlantic sea run salmon in the state. The Commission has authority to adopt and amend regulations to promote the conservation and propagation of Atlantic salmon in all Maine waters.
Keyword(s): Recreation/Ecotourism, Water Habitats & Quality, Wildlife & Species
Contact(s):
Frederick Kircheis, Executive Director
Paul Frinsko, Member At Large
George Lapointe, Commissioner of Marine Resources
Henry Nichols, Policy Development Specialist
Lee Perry, Commissioner of Inland Fisheries and Wildlife

MAINE COOPERATIVE FISH AND WILDLIFE RESEARCH UNIT (USDI)

USGS Biological Resources Division, 5755 Nutting Hall, University of Maine
Orono, ME 04469-5755 United States
Phone: 207-581-2870 Fax: 207-581-2858
Founded: 1935
Membership: 1–100
Scope: Regional
Description: Provide graduate training and research experience in wildlife and fish ecology and management. Supported cooperatively by the University of Maine in Orono, ME, Maine Department of Inland Fisheries and Wildlife, U.S. Geological Survey, and the Wildlife Management Institute.
Keyword(s): Water Habitats & Quality, Wildlife & Species
Contact(s):
William Krohn, Leader; 258 Nutting Hall, University of Maine, Orono, ME 04469; 207-581-2870; Fax: 207-581-2858
Cynthia Loftin, Assistant Leader: Wildlife; 230 Nutting Hall, University of Maine, Orono, ME 04469; 207-581-2843; Fax: 207-581-2858
John Moring, Assistant Leader: Fisheries; 310 Murray Hall, University of Maine, Orono, ME 04469; 207-581-2582

MAINE DEPARTMENT OF AGRICULTURE, FOOD, AND RURAL RESOURCES

DEPARTMENT OF AGRICULTURE, FOOD AND RURAL RESOURCES
Office of Agricultural, Natural and Rural Resources
28 State House Station
Augusta, ME 04333-0028 United States
Phone: 207-287-1132 Fax: 207-287-7548
Website: www.state.me.us/agriculture
Founded: N/A
Membership: 101–1,000
Scope: State
Description: The Department was established to improve Maine agriculture through: the conservation and improvements of the soil and cropland of the State; the development, compilation and dissemination of scientific and practical knowledge; the marketing and promotion of agricultural products; the detection, prevention and eradication of plant and animal diseases; the protection of the consuming public against harmful and unsanitary products and practices; and the sound development of the natural resources.
Keyword(s): Agriculture/Farming, Water Habitats & Quality
Contact(s):
Peter Mosher, Director; 207-287-1132; Fax: 207-287-7548; peter.mosher@state.me.us
Robert Spear, Commissioner; 207-287-3419

MAINE DEPARTMENT OF CONSERVATION

22 State House Station
Augusta, ME 04333-0022 United States
Phone: 207-287-2211 Fax: 208-287-2216
Website: www.doc.state.me.us
Founded: 1973
Scope: State
Description: To preserve, protect, and enhance the land resources of the State of Maine; to encourage the wise use of the scenic, mineral, and forest resources; to ensure that coordinated planning for the future allocation of lands for recreational, forest production, mining, and other public and private uses is effectively accomplished; and to provide for the effective management of public lands.
Contact(s):
Susan Benson, Director of Public Information
Will Harris, Director of General Services
Dawn Gallagher, Deputy Commissioner

Ronald Lovaglio, Commissioner
Gale Ross, Administrative Assistant

MAINE DEPARTMENT OF CONSERVATION

BUREAU OF GEOLOGY AND NATURAL AREAS
22 State House Station
Augusta, ME 04333 United States
Phone: 207-287-2801 Fax: 207-287-2353
E-mail: mgs@state.me.us
Website: www.state.me.us/doc/nrimc.mgs/mgs.htm

Founded: N/A
Membership: 1–100
Scope: State
Publication(s): See publications on website
Contact(s):
Molly Docherty, Director, Maine Natural Areas Program; 207-287-8045
Robert Marvinney, State Geologist and Director; 207-287-2804; Fax: 207-287-2353; robert.g.marvinney@state,me.us
Robert Tucker, Director, Earth Resources Information
Tom Weddle, Hydrogeologist & Divison Director

MAINE DEPARTMENT OF CONSERVATION

BUREAU OF PARKS AND LANDS
22 State House Station
Augusta, ME 04333 United States
Phone: 207-287-3821 Fax: 207-287-3823
Website: www.state.me.us/doc

Founded: N/A
Scope: State
Publication(s): Outdoors & Maine - brochure
Contact(s):
Tom Morrison, Director; 207-287-3821; tom.morrison@state.me.us
Marlene Bowman, Resource Administrator; 207-287-4912; marlene.bowman@state.me.us
Herb Hartman, Deputy Director; 207-287-4961; herb.hartman@state.me.us
Ralph Knoll, Planning & Land Use Acquisition; 207-287-4911; ralph.knoll@state.me.us
Scott Ramsay, Off-Road Vehicle Program; 207-287-4956; scott.ramsay@state.me.us
Richard Skinner, Boating Facilities; 207-287-4953; richard.skinner@state.me.us
Marilyn Tourtelotte, Allagash Wilderness Waterway; 207-941-4014; marilyn.tourtelotte@state.me.us

MAINE DEPARTMENT OF CONSERVATION

FOREST SERVICE
22 State House Station
Augusta, ME 04333 United States
Phone: 207-287-2791 Fax: 207-287-8422
Website: www.state.me.us/doc/mfs

Founded: N/A
Membership: 101–1,000
Scope: State
Contact(s):
Tom Doak, Director
Peter Beringer, Resource Administrator
Don Mansius, Forest Policy and Management
Tom Parent, Forest Protection
Dave Struble, State Entomologist

MAINE DEPARTMENT OF CONSERVATION

LAND USE REGULATION COMMISSION
State House, Station #22
Augusta, ME 04333 United States
Phone: 207-287-2631 Fax: 207-287-7439
Website: www.state.me.us/doc/lurc/lurchome.htm

Founded: N/A
Membership: 1–100
Scope: State
Publication(s): Available on Web
Contact(s):
John Williams, Director
Peggy Dwyer, Resource Administrator; 207-287-4924

MAINE DEPARTMENT OF ENVIRONMENTAL PROTECTION

State House Station 17
Augusta, ME 04333 United States
Phone: 207-287-7688 Fax: 207-287-7826
Website: www.state.me.us/dep

Founded: 1972
Membership: 101–1,000
Scope: State
Description: DEP is charged with the protection and improvement of Maine's natural environment and acting in the best interests of the citizens' health and quality of life.
Publication(s): A Citizen's Guide to Lake Watershed Surveys, Planning Guides for Municipalities (series), Watershed: An Action Guide to Improving Maine Waters, The Quality of Maine Waters—A Condensed Version of the 1996 Maine Water Quality Assessment
Keyword(s): Air Quality/Atmosphere, Pollution (general), Reduce/Reuse/Recycle, Water Habitats & Quality
Contact(s):
James Brooks, Director: Bureau of Air Quality
David Lenette, Director: Bureau of Remediation and Waste Management
David Van Wie, Director: Bureau of Land and Water Quality
Brooke Barnes, Deputy Commissioner
Martha Kirkpatrick, Commissioner

MAINE DEPARTMENT OF INLAND FISHERIES AND WILDLIFE

284 State St.
Augusta, ME 04333-0041 United States
Phone: 207-287-8000 Fax: 207-287-6395
E-mail: webmaster_ifw@state.me.us
Website: www.mefishwildlife.com

Founded: 1880
Membership: 1–100
Scope: State
Publication(s): Maine Fish and Wildlife
Keyword(s): Public Lands/Greenspace, Recreation/Ecotourism, Wildlife & Species
Contact(s):
Vesta Billing, Director: Licensing and Registration Division; 207-287-5225
Peter Bourque, Director of Fisheries and Hatcheries Division; 207-287-5261
Kenneth Elowe, Director: Bureau of Resource Management; 207-287-5252
Donald Kleiner, Director: Bureau of Information and Education; 207-287-5244
Richard Record, Director: Bureau of Administrative Service; 207-287-5210
Andrea Erskine, Rules and Regulations Officer; 207-287-5201
Frederick Hurley, Deputy Commissioner; 207-287-5202
Timothy Peabody, Colonel: Bureau of Warden Service; 207-287-2766
Lee Perry, Commissioner; 207-287-5202
G. Stadler, Chief: Wildlife Research and Management Division; 207-287-5252
Ron Taylor, Chief, Engineering & Realty Division

MAINE DEPARTMENT OF MARINE RESOURCES

21 State House Station
Augusta, ME 04333-0021 United States
Phone: 207-624-6550 Fax: 207-624-6024
Website: www.state.me.us/dmr

Founded: 1867
Membership: 1–100
Scope: State
Description: Responsible for research, development, promotion, planning, and enforcement of laws relating to conservation of Maine's marine resources. The department was established to conserve and develop marine and estuarine resources of the State of Maine by conducting and sponsoring scientific research, promoting and developing the Maine commercial fishing industry, and by advising agencies of government concerned with development or activity in coastal waters.
Keyword(s): Public Health, Water Habitats & Quality, Wildlife & Species
Contact(s):

Gilbert Bilodeau, Director of Division of Administrative Services; gilbert.m.bilodeau@state.me.us
Dr. Mercer, Director of Bureau of Resource Management; 207-633-9500; Fax: 207-633-9579; linda.mercer@state.me.us
E. Estabrook, Deputy Commissioner
Joseph Fessenden, Chief of Bureau of Marine Patrol; Fax: 207-624-6024
George Lapointe, Commissioner

MANITOBA CONSERVATION

Rm. 333, Legislative Bldg.
Winnipeg, R3C 0V8 Manitoba Canada
Phone: 204-945-3730 Fax: 204-945-3586
E-mail: mancon@leg.gov.mb.ca

Founded: N/A
Scope: State
Description: The purpose of Manitoba Natural Resources is to encourage wise use of Manitoba's natural resources and preserve them for future generations.
Contact(s):

Wayne Fisher, Director of Headquarters Operations; Box 44, 200 Saulteaux Cres., Winnipeg, Manitoba R3J 3W3; 204-945-6647
Brian Gillespie, Director of Wildlife; Box 24, 200 Saulteaux Cres., Winnipeg, Manitoba R3J 3W3; 204-945-7761
Harley Jonasson, Director of Lands Branch; 123 Main St., W., Box 20000, Neepawa, Manitoba R0J 1H0; 204-476-3441
Gord Jones, Director of Forestry; Box 70, 200, Saulteaux Cres., Winnipeg, Manitoba R3J 3W3; 204-945-7998
Wayne Leeman, Director of Surveys and Mapping; 1007 Century St., Winnipeg, Manitoba R3H 0W4; 204-945-0011
Peter Lockett, Director of Financial Services; Box 85,200 Saulteaux, Winnipeg, Manitoba; 204-945-4187
Blair Mctavish, Director of Policy Coordination; Box 38, 200 Saulteaux Cres., Winnipeg, Manitoba R3J 3W3; 204-945-6658
Lorraine Metz, Director of Human Resources; 500-326 Broadway WPG MB, R3C 0S5; 204-945-2810
Joe O'Connor, Director of Fisheries Branch; Box 20, 200 Saulteaux Cres., Winnipeg, Manitoba R3J 3W3; 204-945-7814
W. Podolsky, Executive Director of Management Services; Box 85,200 Saulteaux, Winnipeg, Manitoba R3J 3W3; 204-945-4056
Kerry Poole, Director of Resource Information Systems; Box 90, 200 Saulteaux Cres., Winnipeg, Manitoba R3J 3W3; 204-945-2929
C. Prouse, Director of Parks and Natural Areas; Box 50, 200 Saulteaux Cres., Winnipeg, Manitoba R3J 3W3; 204-945-4362
Jack Schreuder, Executive Director of Land Information Centre; 1007 Century St., Winnipeg, Manitoba R3H 0W4; 204-945-6613
Steven Topping, Director of Water Resources Branch; Box 11 200 Saulteaux, Winnipeg, Manitoba R3E 3J5; 204-945-7488
Harvey Boyle, Assistant Deputy Minister; Box 80,200 Saulteaux, Winnipeg; 204-945-4842
Norm Brandson, Deputy Minister; Rm. 327, Legislative Bldg., Winnipeg, Manitoba R3C 0V8; 204-945-3785
Glen Holmes, Special Assistant to the Minister
Oscar Lathlin, Minister
Merlin Shoesmith, Assistant Deputy Minister; Box 80, 200 Saulteaux Cres., Winnipeg, Manitoba R3J 3W3; 204-945-6829

MANITOBA CONSERVATION

EASTERN REGION
Box 4000
Lac du Bonnet, R0E 1A0 Manitoba Canada
Phone: 204-345-1433 Fax: 204-345-1440

Founded: N/A
Scope: National
Contact(s):

Bob Enns, Regional Director
Bob Cameron, Regional Superintendent

MANITOBA CONSERVATION

NORTHWESTERN REGION
Box 2550, 3rd St. and Ross Ave.
The Pas, R9A 1M4 Manitoba Canada
Phone: 204-627-8261 Fax: 204-623-5733

Founded: N/A
Scope: Regional
Contact(s):

Albert King, Regional Director
Craig Asseltine, Regional Superintendent; 204-627-8353

MANITOBA CONSERVATION

OPERATIONS WESTERN
1129 Queens Ave., Box 13
Brandon, R7A 1L9 Manitoba Canada
Phone: 204-726-6296 Fax: 204-726-6301

Founded: N/A
Scope: Regional
Contact(s):

Bob Wooley, Regional Director
Blair Bastian, Regional Superintendent

MANITOBA CONSERVATION DATA CENTRE

DEPARTMENT OF CONSERVATION
WILDLIFE AND ECOSYSTEM PROTECTION BRANCH
Box 24, 200 Saulteaux Crescent
Winnipeg, R3J 3W3 Manitoba Canada
Phone: 204-645-7743 Fax: 204-945-3077
E-mail: cdc_wildlife@gov.mb.ca
Website: web2.gov.mb.ca/conservation/cdc

Founded: 1994
Membership: 101–1,000
Scope: Local, State, Regional, National, International
Description: The Manitoba Conservation Data Centre is part of an international network of data centres throughout North America and parts of Latin America.

MANITOBA DEPARTMENT OF NATURAL RESOURCES

CENTRAL REGION
Box 6000
Gimli, R0C1B0 Manitoba Canada
Phone: 204-642-6096 Fax: 204-642-6108

Founded: N/A

Scope: National

Contact(s):

Worth Hayden, Regional Director
Syd Robak, Regional Superintendent

MARINE LABORATORY (FLORIDA)

Florida State University, Rt. 1, Box 219A
Sopchoppy, FL 32358 United States
Phone: 904-697-4095 Fax: 904-697-4098
Website: www.fsu.edu/~fsuml/

Founded: N/A

Description: Includes studies on the biology, chemistry, and geology of coastal communities, physical oceanography of near-shore waters, aquatic and terrestrial ecosystems, and aquaculture.

Keyword(s): Oceans/Coasts/Beaches, Water Habitats & Quality, Wildlife & Species

Contact(s):

Nancy Marcus, Director

MARYLAND DEPARTMENT OF AGRICULTURE

50 Harry S. Truman Pkwy.
Annapolis, MD 21401 United States
Phone: 410-841-5700 Fax: 410-841-5914
Website: www.mda.state.md.us

Founded: 1972

Membership: 101–1,000

Scope: State

Description: Created as a cabinet-level state agency, the department is charged with assisting soil conservation districts to protect state waters from agricultural nonpoint source pollution, overseeing numerous inspection, testing, grading, and marketing programs, mosquito control and gypsy moth control, and forest pest management under various laws. The department also has responsibility for regulatory functions, such as pesticide applicators, weights and measures, nursery inspection, seed and turf regulations.

Publication(s): MDA Annual Report, Agricultural in Maryland Brochure, MDA News

Contact(s):

Don Vandrey, Director of Communications
Robert Halman, Assistant Secretary: Marketing
Hagner Mister, Secretary
Craig Nielsen, Counsel; 410-841-5883
Roger Olson, State Veterinarian; 410-841-5810
Royden Powell, Assistant Secretary: Office of Resource Conservation; 410-841-5865
Bradley Powers, Deputy Secretary
Charles Puffinberger, Assistant Secretary: Office of Plant Industries; 410-841-5870

MARYLAND DEPARTMENT OF AGRICULTURE

STATE SOIL CONSERVATION COMMITTEE
50 Harry S. Truman Pkwy.
Annapolis, MD 21401 United States
Phone: 410-841-5863 Fax: 410-841-5736
Website: www.mda.state.md.us

Founded: 1937

Membership: 1–100

Scope: State

Description: Established to organize soil conservation districts and to establish policy, resolve problems to give guidance and assistance to districts. The SSCC membership includes representatives from the Maryland Departments of Natural Resources, Agriculture, and Environment, Maryland Agricultural Commission, University of Maryland, Maryland Association of Soil Conservation Districts, and five soil conservation district supervisors. The committee is a unit of the Maryland Dept. of Agriculture.

Publication(s): SSCC Reporter Newsletter

Keyword(s): Agriculture/Farming, Ecosystems (precious), Land Issues, Pollution (general), Water Habitats & Quality, Wildlife & Species

Contact(s):

Robert Fitzgerald, Chairman; 410-841-5863
Louise Lawrence, Executive Secretary; 410-841-5863; Fax: 410-841-5914; lawrenl@mda.state.md.us
Royden Powell, Assistant Secretary; 410-841-5865; Fax: 410-841-5914

MARYLAND DEPARTMENT OF NATURAL RESOURCES

580 Taylor Avenue
Annapolis, MD 21401 United States
Phone: 410-260-8021 Fax: 410-260-8024
E-mail: customerservice@dnr.state.md.us
Website: www.dnr.state.md.us

Founded: N/A

Membership: 1,001–10,000

Scope: Regional

Description: for today and tomorrow the Department of Natural Resources inspires people to enjoy and live in harmony with their environment, and to protect what makes Maryland unique — our treasured Chesapeake Bay, our diverse landscapes and our living and natural resources.

Publication(s): Natural Resource Magazine, Streams, Trib Team Monitor

Keyword(s): Forests/Forestry, Land Issues, Oceans/Coasts/Beaches, Public Lands/Greenspace, Recreation/Ecotourism, Sprawl/Urban Planning, Water Habitats & Quality, Wildlife & Species

Contact(s):

J. Charles Fox, Secretary; 410-260-8105; Fax: 410-260-8111; customerservice@dnr.state.md.us
Sumita Chaudhuri, Assistant Secretary for Management Service; 410-260-8107; Fax: 410-260-8111; customerservice@dnr.state.md.us
James W. Dunmyer, Assistant Secretary for Public Lands; 410-260-8108; Fax: 410-260-8111; customerservice@dnr.state.md.us
Verna E. Harrison, Assistant Secretary for Chesapeake Bay & Watershed Programs; 410-260-8116; Fax: 410-260-8111; customerservice@dnr.state.md.us
Michael J. Nelson, Assistant Secretary for Capital Grants and Loans; 410-260-8446; Fax: 410-260-8111; customerservice@dnr.state.md.us
Wilson H. Parran, Chief of Information Technology; 410-260-8369; Fax: 410-260-8111; customerservice@dnr.state.md.us
Carolyn V. Watson, Assistant Secretary for Resource Management Service; 410-260-8113; Fax: 410-260-8111; customerservice@dnr.state.md.us
Karen M. White, Deputy Secretary; 410-260-8105; Fax: 410-260-8111; customerservice@dnr.state.md.us

MARYLAND-NATIONAL CAPITAL PARK AND PLANNING COMMISSION

6611 Kenilworth Ave.
Riverdale, MD 20737 United States
Phone: 301-454-1740 Fax: 301-454-1750
Website: www.mncppc.org

Founded: 1927

Membership: 101–1,000

Scope: National

Description: Established by the General Assembly of the State of Maryland to provide for the orderly development of Montgomery and Prince George's counties; to provide a system of parks to serve the residents of this bi-county region; and to provide recreation programs and services in Prince George's County.

Contact(s):

Donald Cochran, Montgomery County Director: Parks; 301-495-2500
Trudye Johnson, Executive Director; 301-454-1740
Charles Loehr, Director of Montgomery County Department of Parks and Planni; 301-495-4500
Fern Piret, Director: Prince George's County Planning; 301-952-3595
Mary Wells-Harley, Acting Director of Prince George's County Parks and Recreati; 301-699-2582
Patricia Barney, Secretary of Treasurer
Elizabeth Hewlett, Vice Chairman; 14741 Governor Oden Bowie Dr., Upper Marlboro, MD 20772; 301-952-3560
William Hussmann, Vice Chairman; 8787 Georgia Ave., Silver Spring, MD 20910; 301-495-4605
Richard Romine, General Counsel, Legal Department; 301-454-1670

MASSACHUSETTS COOPERATIVE FISH AND WILDLIFE RESEARCH UNIT (USDI)

Box 34220, Holdsworth Natural Resources Ctr., University of Massachusetts
Amherst, MA 01003-4220 United States
Phone: 413-545-0398 Fax: 413-545-4358

Founded: 1948

Scope: National

Description: Provides graduate training and research experience in fisheries and wildlife research management, ecology, habitat, population dynamics, and management. Supported cooperatively by the University of Massachusetts, Massachusetts Division of Fisheries and Wildlife, Massachusetts Division of Marine Fisheries, the U.S. Department of Interior, U.S.G.S.-BRD, and the Wildlife Management Institute.

Keyword(s): Wildlife & Species

Contact(s):

Steve Destefano, Leader
Martha Mather, Assistant Leader: Fisheries
Paul Sievert, Assistant Leader: Wildlife

MASSACHUSETTS DIVISION OF FISHERIES AND WILDLIFE

MASSWILDLIFE
251 Causeway Street
4th floor
Boston, MA 02114 United States
Phone: 617-626-1590 Fax: 617-626-1517
E-mail: mass.wildlife@state.ma.us
Website: www.masswildlife.org

Founded: 1863

Scope: State

Description: State wildlife agency with a mandate to conserve wildlife and natural resources for the benefit and enjoyment of the citizens.

Publication(s): Guidelines for Vernal Pool Certification, Massachusetts Natural Heritage Atlas, BioMap, Field Guide to Animals in Vernal Pools, Critters of Massachusetts, Fishing & Hunting Abstracts, Massachusetts Wildlife

Keyword(s): Ecosystems (precious), Forests/Forestry, Land Issues, Public Lands/Greenspace, Recreation/Ecotourism, Water Habitats & Quality, Wildlife & Species

Contact(s):

Wayne MacCallum, Director; 617-626-1590; Fax: 617-626-1517; wayne.maccallum@state.ma.us

MASSACHUSETTS EXECUTIVE OFFICE OF ENVIRONMENTAL AFFAIRS

Leverett Saltonstall Bldg.
100 Cambridge St.
Rm. 2000
Boston, MA 02202 United States
Phone: 617-626-1000 Fax: 617-626-1181
E-mail: env.internet@state.ma.us
Website: www.state.ma.us/envir/

Founded: N/A

Description: The cabinet-level environmental agency in the state and includes within the secretariat all state environmental agencies.

Contact(s):

Joel Lerner, Director: Conservation Services; 617-727-1552
Tom Skinner, Director: Coastal Zone Management; 617-727-9530
Jay Wickersham, Director: Impact Review Unit, MEPA; 617-727-5830
Steve Bernard, Under Secretary: Administration & Finance
Bob Durand, Secretary

MASSACHUSETTS EXECUTIVE OFFICE OF ENVIRONMENTAL AFFAIRS

251 Causeway St., 9th Floor
Boston, MA 02114 United States
Phone: 617-626-1000 Fax: 617-626-1181
Website: www.state.ma.us/envir/

Founded: N/A

Scope: State

Description: Commonwealth of Massachusetts' cabinet department on environmental issues.

Keyword(s): Agriculture/Farming, Air Quality/Atmosphere, Climate Change, Development/Developing Countries, Ecosystems (precious), Energy, Ethics/Environmental Justice, Executive/Legislative/Judicial Reform, Forests/Forestry, Land Issues, Oceans/Coasts/Beaches

Contact(s):

Bob Durand, Secretary; 617-626-1000; Fax: 617-626-1181; bob.durand@state.ma.us

MASSACHUSETTS EXECUTIVE OFFICE OF ENVIRONMENTAL AFFAIRS

BUREAU OF PESTICIDES
251 Causeway St., Suite 900
Boston, MA 02114 United States
Phone: 617-626-1000 Fax: 617-262-1181
Website: www.state.ma.us/envir

Founded: N/A

Scope: State

Description: State Agency

Publication(s): State of Our Environment

Contact(s):

Brad Mitchell, Chief; 617-727-7712

MASSACHUSETTS EXECUTIVE OFFICE OF ENVIRONMENTAL AFFAIRS

DEPARTMENT OF ENVIRONMENTAL MANAGEMENT
251 Causeway St. Suite 700
Boston, MA 02114 United States
Phone: 617-973-8700

Founded: N/A

Contact(s):

Todd Fredericks, Director: Division of Forests and Parks; 617-626-1000
Ralph Silva, Director of Engineering
Richard Thibedeau, Deputy Commissioner, Resource Conservation, Acting; 617-727-3267
Peter Webber, Commissioner

MASSACHUSETTS EXECUTIVE OFFICE OF ENVIRONMENTAL AFFAIRS

DEPARTMENT OF FOOD AND AGRICULTURE
100 Cambridge St., Rm. 2103
Boston, MA 02202 United States
Phone: 617-727-3000
Website: www.state.ma.us/envir/

Founded: N/A

MASSACHUSETTS EXECUTIVE OFFICE OF ENVIRONMENTAL AFFAIRS

DIVISION OF CONSERVATION SERVICES
251 Causeway St., 9th Floor
Boston, MA 02114 United States
Website: www.state.ma.us/envir/conservation

Founded: N/A

MASSACHUSETTS EXECUTIVE OFFICE OF ENVIRONMENTAL AFFAIRS

GEOGRAPHIC INFORMATION SYSTEM
251 Causeway St., 9th Floor
Boston, MA 02114 United States
Website: www.state.ma.us/mgis

Founded: N/A

Contact(s):
Christian Jacqz, Director; 617-626-1056

MASSACHUSETTS EXECUTIVE OFFICE OF ENVIRONMENTAL AFFAIRS

MASSACHUSETTS COASTAL ZONE MANAGEMENT
251 Causeway St. Suite 900
Boston, MA 02114 United States
Phone: 617-626-1200 Fax: 617-626-1240
Website: www.state.ma.us/czm

Founded: N/A

Contact(s):
Tom Skinner, Director; 617-626-1201

MASSACHUSETTS EXECUTIVE OFFICE OF ENVIRONMENTAL AFFAIRS

MASSACHUSETTS ENVIRONMENTAL POLICY ACT
251 Causeway St., Suite 900
Boston, MA 02114 United States
Phone: 617-626-1020 Fax: 617-626-1181
Website: www.state.ma.us/envir/mepa

Founded: N/A

Contact(s):
Jay Wickersham, Director; 617-626-1022

MASSACHUSETTS EXECUTIVE OFFICE OF ENVIRONMENTAL AFFAIRS

MASSACHUSETTS ENVIRONMENTAL TRUST
33 Union Street, 4th Floor
Boston, MA 02108 United States
Phone: 617-727-0249 Fax: 617-367-1616
E-mail: env.trust@state.ma.us
Website: www.MassEnvironmentalTrust.org

Founded: 1988
Membership: N/A
Scope: State
Description: The Trust is a quasi-public environmental philanthropy established by the state legislature in 1988 with proceeds from the Boston Harbor pollution settlement. The Trust gives grants to a variety of entities working on issues dealing with the Commonwealth's water and related resources.
Keyword(s): Ecosystems (precious), Oceans/Coasts/Beaches, Water Habitats & Quality, Wildlife & Species

MASSACHUSETTS EXECUTIVE OFFICE OF ENVIRONMENTAL AFFAIRS

OFFICE OF TECHNICAL ASSISTANCE FOR TOXIC USE REDUCTION
251 Causeway St., 9th Floor
Boston, MA 02114 United States
Phone: 617-626-1060 Fax: 617-626-1095
Website: www.state.ma.us/ota

Founded: N/A

Contact(s):
Paul Richard, Director; 617-626-1042

MASSACHUSETTS EXECUTIVE OFFICE OF ENVIRONMENTAL AFFAIRS

WETLANDS AND WATERWAYS PROGRAM
1 Winter St.
Boston, MA 02108 United States
Phone: 617-292-5695 Fax: 617-292-5696
Website: www.state.ma.us/dep

Founded: N/A

Scope: State

Contact(s):
Glenn Haas, Director
Michael Stroman, Acting Director of Wetlands

MASSACHUSETTS HIGHWAY DEPARTMENT

10 Park Plaza
Boston, MA 02116 United States
Phone: 617-973-7800 Fax: 617-973-8040
Website: www.state.ma.us/mhd

Founded: N/A

Scope: State

Description: The mission of the Massachusetts Highway Department is to provide a safe, efficient, quality highway system in a cost-effective and environmentally sensitive manner that continuously meets the diverse needs of its users.

Keyword(s): Air Quality/Atmosphere, Ethics/Environmental Justice, Pollution (general), Reduce/Reuse/Recycle, Transportation, Water Habitats & Quality

Contact(s):
Matthew Amorello, Commissioner; 617-973-7800; matthew.amorello@state.ma.us
David Anderson, Deputy Chief Engineer: Construction; 817-973-7491; david.anderson@state.ma.us
Henry Barbaro, Supervisor: Wetlands and Water Resources; 617-973-7419; henry.barbaro@state.ma.us
John Blundo, Deputy Chief Engineer: Highway Engineering; 617-973-7521; john.blundo@state.ma.us
Thomas Broderick, Chief Engineer; 617-973-7830; thomas.broderick@state.ma.us
Gordon Broz, Deputy Chief Engineer: Operations; 617-973-7741; gordon.broz@state.ma.us
James Elliott, Supervisor: Cultural Resources Unit; 617-973-7494; james.elliott@state.ma.us
Steven Miller, Supervisor: Permitting and Regulatory Compliance; 617-973-7582; steven.miller@state.ma.us
Gregory Prendergast, Deputy Chief Engineer: Environmental Division; 617-973-7484; gregory.prendergast@state.ma.us
Kevin Walsh, Project Development; 617-973-7529; kevin.walsh@state.ma.us

MECKLENBURG COUNTY PARK AND RECREATION DEPARTMENT

DIVISION OF NATURAL RESOURCES
5841 Brookshire Boulevard
Charlotte, NC 28216 United States
Phone: 704-336-8798
Website: www.parkandrec.com/nature

Founded: 1993
Membership: 1,001–10,000

State Government Agencies

Scope: Local

Description: The Division of Natural Resources is the principal government agency responsible for the protection, conservation, and management of Mecklenburg County's natural areas. The Division operates three nature centers - Reedy Creek, McDowell, and Latta Plantation - and offers environmental education programs to students of all ages, manages over 7,500 acres of nature preserves & greenways, monitors wildlife populations, restores habitats for endangered plant species, and conserves natural communities.

Publication(s): Natural Connections

Keyword(s): Public Lands/Greenspace, Recreation/Ecotourism, Water Habitats & Quality, Wildlife & Species

Contact(s):

Steve Law, Division Manager; 704-336-8798; Fax: 704-336-5472; lawsh@co.mecklenburg.nc.us

Bridget Hanifin, Greenways and Trails Planner; 704-336-8466; Fax: 704-336-5472; hanifbe@co.mecklenburg.nc.us

Don Seriff, Conservation Section Supervisor; 2900 Rocky River Road, Charlotte, NC 28215; 704-432-1391; Fax: 704-432-1420; serifdw@co.mecklenburg.nc.us

Marek Smith, Environmental Education Supervisor; 2900 Rocky River Road, Charlotte, NC 28215; 704-598-8857; Fax: 704-599-1770; smithmk@co.mecklenburg.nc.us

Sarah Kiser, Environmental Education Specialist; Reedy Creek Nature Center, 2900 Rocky River Road, Charlotte, NC 28215; 704-598-8857; Fax: 704-599-1770; kisersm@co.mecklenburg.nc.us

Karen McKenzie, Environmental Education Specialist; McDowell Nature Center, 15222 York Road, Charlotte, NC 28278; 704-588-5224; Fax: 704-588-5226; mckenak@co.mecklenburg.nc.us

Charles Yelton, Environmental Education Specialist; Latta Plantation Nature Center, 6211 Sample Road, Huntersville, NC 28078; 704-875-1391; Fax: 704-875-1394; yeltocw@co.mecklenburg.nc.us

METROPOLITAN DISTRICT COMMISSION

METROPOLITAN DISTRICT COMMISSION
20 Somerset St.
Boston, MA 02108 United States
Phone: 617-727-5114 Fax: 617-727-0891
Website: www.state.ma.us

Founded: 1919

Membership: 101–1,000

Scope: State

Description: Operates and maintains 19 swimming pools, 17 salt water beaches, 3 fresh water beaches, 23 skating rinks, and various other recreational facilities; also maintains a network of parkways and main traffic roadways and a police force for protection of its property and people using its facilities.

Contact(s):

Brian Broderick, Director: Reservations and Historic Sites Unit; 617-727-2744

Gary Doak, Director: Division of Recreation; 617-727-9547

David Balfour, Commissioner

MICHIGAN DEPARTMENT OF AGRICULTURE

P.O. Box 30017
Lansing, MI 48909 United States
Phone: 517-373-1052 Fax: 517-373-9146
Website: www.mda.state.mi.us

Founded: N/A

Scope: Regional

Keyword(s): Agriculture/Farming, Land Issues, Pollution (general), Wildlife & Species

Contact(s):

Ken Rauscher, Director of Pesticide & Plant Pest Management Division; 517-373-1087

Dan Wyant, Director

MICHIGAN DEPARTMENT OF ENVIRONMENTAL QUALITY

525 West Allegan St.
Constitution Hall 6th Fl., South
P.O. Box 30473
Lansing, MI 48909-7973 United States
Phone: 517-373-7917 Fax: 517-241-7401
Website: www.michigan.gov/deq

Founded: 1995

Scope: State

Description: Our mission is to drive improvements in environmental quality for the protection of public health and natural resources to benefit current and future generations. This will be accomplished through effective administration of agency programs, and providing for the use of innovative strategies, while helping to foster a strong and sustainable economy.

Publication(s): See publications on website

Keyword(s): Air Quality/Atmosphere, Land Issues, Oceans/Coasts/Beaches, Pollution (general), Reduce/Reuse/ Recycle, Water Habitats & Quality

Contact(s):

Russell Harding, Director; 517-373-7917

David K. Ladd, Director of Office of The Great Lakes; 517-335-4056; Fax: 517-335-4053

Dennis Fedewa, Chief of Financial and Business Services Division; 517-241-7427; Fax: 517-241-7428

Gary Hughes, Deputy Director for Operations; 517-241-7394; Fax: 517-241-7401

Arthur Nash, Deputy Director for Programs and Regulations; 517-241-7392; Fax: 517-241-7401

MICHIGAN DEPARTMENT OF NATURAL RESOURCES

P.O. Box 30028
Lansing, MI 48909 United States
Phone: 517-373-2329 Fax: 517-335-4242
E-mail: dnr-wld-webpages@state.mi.us
Website: www.michigandnr.com

Founded: 1921

Scope: State

Description: State agency for administration, including enforcement of laws and regulations, regarding the state's natural resources; and for enhancing recreational opportunities and quality. Derived from the Department of Conservation.

Keyword(s): Forests/Forestry, Public Lands/Greenspace, Recreation/Ecotourism, Wildlife & Species

Contact(s):

K. Cool, Director; P.O. Box 30028, Lansing, MI 48909; 517-373-2329; Fax: 517-335-4242

Guy Gordon, Chief of Staff; P.O. Box 30028, Lansing, MI 48909; 517-373-2329; Fax: 517-335-4242

Bradley Wurfel, Press Secretary; P.O. Box 30028, Lansing, MI 48909; 517-335-3014; Fax: 517-335-4242

Rob Abent, Chief of Finance and Operations Service Bureau; P.O. Box 30028, Lansing, MI 48909; 517-373-1750; Fax: 517-335-6807

Rick Asher, Chief of Law Enforcement; P.O. Box 30031, Lansing, MI 48909; 517-373-1230; Fax: 517-373-6816

Carol Bambery, Legislative Liaison; P.O. Box 30028, Lansing, MI 48909; 517-373-0023; Fax: 517-335-4242

Thomas Benson, Chief of Office of Internal Audit; P.O. Box 30028, Lansing, MI 48909; 517-373-0755; Fax: 517-241-2986

George Burgoyne, Deputy for Resource Management; P.O. Box 30028, Lansing, MI 48909; 517-373-0046; Fax: 517-335-4242

James Ekdahl, Upper Peninsula Field Deputy; 1990 US-41 South, Marquette, MI 49855; 906-228-6561; Fax: 906-228-9441

Teresa Gloden, Executive Assistant to the Natural Resources Commission; P.O. Box 30028, Lansing, MI 48909; 517-373-2352; Fax: 517-335-4242
Gerald Harris, Chief of Human Resources; P.O. Box 30028, Lansing, MI 48909; 517-373-1207; Fax: 517-373-8063
Rebecca Humphries, Chief of Wildlife; P.O. Box 30444, Lansing, MI 48909; 517-373-1263; Fax: 517-373-6705
Mindy Koch, Forest, Mineral and Fire Management; P.O. Box 30452, Lansing, MI 48909; 517-373-1275; Fax: 517-373-2443
Lowen Schuett, Chief of Property Management Division; P.O. Box 30448, Lansing, MI 48909; 517-241-2438; Fax: 517-241-4278
Kelley Smith, Chief of Fisheries; P.O. Box 30446, Lansing, MI 48909; 517-373-1280; Fax: 517-373-0381
Kelli Sobel, Deputy for Administrative Services; P.O. Box 30028, Lansing, MI 48909; 517-373-2425; Fax: 517-335-4242
Rodney Stokes, Chief of Parks and Recreation; P.O. Box 30257, Lansing, MI 48909; 517-373-9900; Fax: 517-373-4625

MICHIGAN STATE UNIVERSITY EXTENSION
Bulletin Office, 10-B Agric. Hall
East Lansing, MI 48824 United States
Phone: 517-355-0240
E-mail: msue@msue.msu.edu
Website: www.msue.msu.edu/msue/

Founded: N/A
Membership: 1–100
Scope: State
Description: Helps people improve their lives through an educational process that applies knowledge to critical issues, needs, and opportunities. Publications, instructional videos, and microcomputer software are listed in a catalogue which is available by writing to the Bulletin Office.
Keyword(s): Agriculture/Farming, Forests/Forestry, Pollution (general)
Contact(s):
Margaret Bethel, Acting Director

MINISTRY OF AGRICULTURE FOOD AND FISHERIES
BC FISHERIES
780 Blanshard St., 3rd. Fl.
Victoria, V8V 1X4 British Columbia Canada
Phone: 250-387-3190 Fax: 307-954-3291
Website: www.gov.bc.ca/fish

Founded: N/A
Membership: 1–100
Scope: State
Contact(s):
Jamie Alley, Director of Fisheries Management; 250-387-9711
Joyce Murray, Minister of Water, Land, Air Protection

MINISTRY OF COMMUNITY, ABORIGINAL AND WOMEN SERVICES
P.O. Box 9805, Stn. Prov. Govt.
Victoria, V8W 9W1 British Columbia Canada
Phone: 250-356-6305 Fax: 250-387-3798
Website: www.gov.bc.ca/mcaws

Founded: N/A
Membership: 1–100
Scope: Regional
Contact(s):
George Abbott, Minister; 250-356-3089

MINISTRY OF NATURAL RESOURCES
300 Water St., 2nd Fl., North Tower
Peterborough, K9J 8M5 Ontario Canada
Phone: 705-755-2363 Fax: 705-755-1640
E-mail: nric@mnr.gov.on.ca
Website: www.mnr.gov.on.ca

Founded: N/A
Scope: State
Description: Provides the ministry with leadership in the development and application of scientific knowledge, information management, and information technology. The division also plays a lead role in the provision of land-related information.
Contact(s):
Jim Hamilton, Director; 705-755-2139
Des Mckee, Adm. of Science of Information Division; 705-755-1401
Collin Turnpenny, Associate Director of Zimbabwe Natural Resource Management; 416-314-1550

MINISTRY OF NATURAL RESOURCES
ALGONQUIN FORESTRY AUTHORITY
222 Main St. W
Huntsville, P1H 1Y1 Ontario Canada
Phone: 705-789-9647 Fax: 705-789-3353
E-mail: huntsville.office@algonquinforestry.on.ca
Website: www.algonquinforestry.on.ca

Founded: N/A
Scope: Regional
Contact(s):
Carl Corbett, General Manager

MINISTRY OF NATURAL RESOURCES
CORPORATE SERVICES DIVISION
POB 7000 300 Water Street
Peterborough, K9J 8M5 Ontario Canada
Phone: 705-755-2505 Fax: 705-755-2508

Founded: N/A
Scope: Regional
Description: This division facilitates the delivery of ministry programs by providing leadership, strategic advice, and responsive results-oriented services to ministry clients. These services include business planning, audit and evaluation, financial, administrative, legal, and human resources. The division also develops corporate and administrative policies and gives advice on standards, guidelines, planning, and management.
Contact(s):
Anne Marie Gutierrez, Director of Legal Services Branch; 416-314-2025
John Kenrick, Director of Finance and Business Branch; 705-755-2505
Dave Lynch, Director of Human Resources Branch; 705-755-3131
Fadia Mishrigi, Communications Services Branch; 416-314-2119

MINISTRY OF NATURAL RESOURCES
FIELD SERVICES DIVISION
435 S. James St., Ste. 221
Ontario, P7E 6S8 Canada

Founded: N/A
Description: Delivering resource management programs for Ontario's fisheries, wildlife, forests and provincial lands is the responsibility of this division. It is also responsible for the Aviation, Flood, and Fire Management Branch and the Provincial Enforcement Section. The division's structure is highly decentralized with three regional offices, 25 district offices, and 17 area offices located across the province.

Contact(s):
Charlie Lauer, Director of Northwest Region; 807-475-1264
Jack McFadden, Director of Aviation, Flood, and Fire Management; 705-945-5937
Gregg Sons, Director of Enforcement Branch, Acting; 705-755-1750

MINISTRY OF NATURAL RESOURCES

FISH AND WILDLIFE BRANCH
300 Water St.
Peterborough, K9J 8M5 Ontario Canada
Phone: 705-755-1909 Fax: 705-755-1900

Founded: N/A
Membership: 1–100
Scope: Regional
Contact(s):
Cameron Mack, Director; 705-755-1909; cameron.mack@mnr.gov.on.ca
Dave Maraldo, Manager of Fisheries; dave.maraldo@mnr.gov.on.ca
Deborah Stetson, Manager of Wildlife; 705-755-1925; deb.stetson@mnr.gov.on.ca

MINISTRY OF NATURAL RESOURCES

NATURAL RESOURCE MANAGEMENT DIVISION
99 Wellesley St. W
Toronto, M7A 1W3 Ontario Canada
Phone: 416-314-2624 Fax: 416-314-1994
E-mail: mnr.nric@mnr.gov.on.ca
Website: www.mnr.gov.on.ca/MNR/

Founded: N/A
Scope: Local, Regional, International
Description: The division is responsible for ensuring that natural resource programs are responsive to the needs of Ontarians and consistent with the ministry's vision of sustainable development and its mission of ecological sustainability. Its mandate covers lands, waters, forests, fish, wildlife, and parks, and includes fish hatcheries, tree nurseries, and the management of the Great Lakes.
Publication(s): Annual Parks Guide, Fishing Regulations Summary, Hunting Regulations Summary, Fish Ontario, Hunt Ontario
Contact(s):
David de Launay, Director of Lands and Waters Branch; Lands and Waters Branch, 300 Water Street, 5th Fl. South Tower, Peterborough, Ontario K9J 8M5; 705-755-1620; Fax: 705-755-1201; david.delaunay@mnr.gov.on.ca
Adair Ireland-Smith, Managing Director of Ontario Parks; Ontario Parks, 300 Water Street, 6th Fl. South Tower, P.O. Box 7000, Peterborough, Ontario K9J 8M5; 705-755-1702; Fax: 705-755-1701; adair.ireland-smith@mnr.gov.on.ca
Cameron Mack, Director of Fish and Wildlife Branch; Fish and Wildlife Branch, 300 Water Street, 5th Floor North Tower, P.O. Box 7000, Peterborough, Ontario K9J 8M5; 705-755-1909; Fax: 705-755-1845; cameron.mack@mnr.gov.on.ca
Peter Wallace, Assistant Deputy Minister; 99 Wellesley St. W., Toronto, Ontario M7A 1W3; 416-314-6131; Fax: 416-314-1994; peter.wallace@mnr.gov.on.ca

MINISTRY OF NATURAL RESOURCES

NORTHEAST REGION
Ontario Government Complex, Highway 101 East
P.O. Bag 3020
South Porcupine, P0N 1H0 Ontario Canada
Phone: 705-235-1154 Fax: 705-235-1226

Founded: N/A
Scope: International
Publication(s): North Science & Technology Newsletter
Contact(s):
Rob Galloway, Regional Director
Mary Ellen Stoll, Manager of Science & Technology

MINISTRY OF NATURAL RESOURCES

NORTHWEST REGION
435 James St.,S
Thunder Bay, P7E 6S8 Ontario Canada
Phone: 807-475-1261 Fax: 807-473-3023
Website: www.mnr.gov.on.ca

Founded: N/A
Membership: 1–100
Scope: Regional
Contact(s):
Charlie Lauer, Regional Director

MINISTRY OF NATURAL RESOURCES

SOUTH CENTRAL REGION
P.O. Box 7000 4th Floor, South Tower, 300 Water Street
Huntsville, K9J 8M5 Ontario Canada
Phone: 705-755-2500

Founded: N/A
Contact(s):
Allan Stewart, Regional Director

MINISTRY OF WATER, LAND AND AIR PROTECTION

P.O . Box 9360
Victoria, V8W 9M2 British Columbia Canada
Phone: 250-387-9422 Fax: 250-356-6464
E-mail: wlapmail@gems5.gov.bc.ca
Website: www.giv.bc.ca/wlap

Founded: N/A
Membership: 1–100
Scope: Regional
Description: The Ministry of Environment's mission is to provide leadership in building environmental principles into day-to-day decisions of governments, corporations, and private individuals; to monitor and report on the state of the environment, and to ensure that defensible environmental standards are set and complied with; and to manage natural habitats, fish, wildlife, and water resources for ecological diversity and the economic and recreational opportunities they provide.
Contact(s):
Rod Davis, Director of Resource Stewardship Branch; 250-356-7725
Doug Dryden, Director of Wildlife; 250-387-9731
Jim Mattison, Director of Resources Inventory Branch; 250-387-1112
Margaret Eckenfelder, Assistant Deputy Minister, Environment & Land Headquarters
Dana Hayden, Assistant Deputy Minister, Corporate Services
Joyce Murray, Minister
Denis O'Gorman, Assistant Deputy Minister, Parks Division; 250-387-9997
Dick Roberts, Assistant Deputy Minister, Regions Division
Derek Thompson, Deputy Minister; 250-387-5429
Jim Walker, Assistant Deputy Minister for Wildlife and Habitat; 250-356-0139

MINNESOTA BOARD OF WATER AND SOIL RESOURCES

One W. Water St., Suite 200
St. Paul, MN 55107 United States
Phone: 651-296-3767 Fax: 651-297-5615
Website: www.bwsr.state.mn.us

Founded: 1987
Membership: 1–100
Scope: State
Description: Formed under M.S. chapter 103B to develop the capabilities of local governments in resource management. Works most often with soil and water conservation districts, watershed districts, watershed management organizations, and counties. Provides these local governments with financial

and technical assistance. Administers programs focusing on erosion control and water quality.

Publication(s): Water BillBoard, various brochures, reports, and fact sheets, Directory of local governments.

Keyword(s): Land Issues, Water Habitats & Quality

Contact(s):

Ronald Harnack, Director; Fax: 651-297-5615; ron.harnack@bwsr.state.mn.us

Lee Coe, Chairman

MINNESOTA COOPERATIVE FISH AND WILDLIFE RESEARCH UNIT

U.S. Geological Survey, Biological Resources Division
University of Minnesota, Department of Fisheries and Wildlife
200 Hodson Hall, 1980 Folwell Ave.
St. Paul, MN 55108 United States
Phone: 612-624-3421 Fax: 612-625-5299
Website: www.fw.umn.edu/co-op/co-op.html

Founded: 1987

Scope: Regional

Description: The research mission of the Minnesota Cooperative Fish and Wildlife Research Unit (MNCFWRU) is to address the biological, social, and economic aspects of both game and nongame wildlife and fisheries management in the context of conservation of biological diversity, and integrity and sustainability of ecosystems.

Keyword(s): Pollution (general), Water Habitats & Quality, Wildlife & Species

Contact(s):

David Andersen, Unit Leader

David Fulton, Assistant Leader: Wildlife

Loralee Kerr, Librarian; 375 Hodson Hall, 1980 Folwell Ave., St. Paul, MN 55108; 612-624-9288

Bruce Vondracek, Assistant Leader: Fisheries

MINNESOTA DEPARTMENT OF AGRICULTURE

90 W. Plato Blvd.
St. Paul, MN 55107 United States
Phone: 651-297-2200 Fax: 651-297-7868
Website: www.mda.state.mn.us

Founded: 1919

Scope: State

Description: Enforces laws to protect the public health, promote family farming and marketing of Minnesota farm products, conserve soil and water, and prevent fraud and deception in the manufacture and distribution of foods, animal feeds, fertilizers, pesticides, seeds, and other items.

Keyword(s): Agriculture/Farming, Development/Developing Countries, Oceans/Coasts/Beaches, Pollution (general), Wildlife & Species

Contact(s):

Shirley Bohm, Director of Dairy and Food Inspection; 651-296-1590

Greg Buzicky, Director: Agronomy and Plant Protection; 651-297-7121

James Gryniewski, Director: Agriculture Certification; 651-297-2230

Gerald Heil, Director: Agriculture Marketing and Development; 651-296-1486

Dale Heimermann, Director of Grain and Produce Inspection; 612-341-7190

Mike Hunst, Director: Agricultural Statistics; 651-296-3896

William Krueger, Director: Laboratory Services; 651-296-3273

Becky Leschner, Director of Accounting Division; 651-215-5770

Larry Palmer, Director: Information Services; 651-296-4659

Curtis Pietz, Director: Agriculture Finance; 651-297-3557

Perry Aasness, Assistant Commissioner

Sharon Clark, Deputy Commissioner

Gene Hugoson, Commissioner

Tom Masso, Assistant Commissioner

MINNESOTA DEPARTMENT OF NATURAL RESOURCES

500 Lafayette Rd.
St. Paul, MN 55155-4040 United States
Phone: 651-296-6157
E-mail: info@dnr.state.mn.us
Website: www.dnr.state.mn.us/

Founded: 1931

Scope: Local, State, Regional

Description: The Department of Conservation was renamed the Department of Natural Resources (DNR) in 1971. The DNR's goal is to achieve optimum natural resources planning, protection, and development responsive to public need, consistent with resource potentials, and for the social and economic well-being of both present and future generations.

Publication(s): Minnesota Conservation Volunteer, The

Contact(s):

Dennis Asmussen, Director: Trails and Waterways Division; 651-297-1151; Fax: 651-297-5475; dennis.asmussen@dnr.state.mn.us

Michelle Beeman, Director: Regulatory and Legislative Services; 651-296-0915; Fax: 651-296-46-4799; michelle.beeman@dnr.state.mn.us

Bill Bernhjelm, Director: Division of Enforcement; 651-296-4828; Fax: 651-297-3727; bill.bernhjelm@dnr.state.mn.us

Tim Bremicker, Director: Wildlife Division; 651-297-4960; Fax: 651-297-4961; tim.bremicker@dnr.state.mn.us

William Brice, Director: Division of Lands and Minerals; 651-296-4807; Fax: 651-296-5939; william.brice@dnr.state.mn.us

Mike Carroll, Director: Division of Forestry; 651-296-4491; Fax: 651-296-5954; mike.carroll@dnr.state.mn.us

Charlotte Cohn, Director: Professional Standards Office; 651-284-3340; charlotte.cohn@dnr.state.mn.us

Wayne Edgerton, Director: Agricultural Policy; 651-297-8341; Fax: 651-296-4799; wayne.edgerton@dnr.state.mn.us

Char Feist, Library Director; 651-297-4929; Fax: 651-297-4946; char.feist@dnr.state.mn.us

Kent Lokkesmoe, Director: Division of Waters; 651-296-4800; Fax: 651-296-0445; kent.lokkesmoe@dnr.state.mn.us

William Morrissey, Director: Division of Parks and Recreation; 651-296-9223; Fax: 651-297-2257; bill.morrissey@dnr.state.mn.us

Ron Payer, Director: Fisheries Division; 651-296-3325; Fax: 651-297-4916; ron.payer@dnr.state.mn.us

Lee Pfannmuller, Director: Ecological Services Division; 651-296-2835; Fax: 651-296-2835; lee.pfannmuller@dnr.state.mn.us

Peggy Adelmann, Administrator: Management and Budget Services; 651-296-8340; Fax: 651-296-6047; peggy.adelman@dnr.state.mn.us

Allen Garber, Commissioner; 651-296-2549; Fax: 651-296-4799; allen.garber@dnr.state.mn.us

John Guenther, Regional Administrator; 1201 E. Highway 2, Grand Rapids, MN 55744; 218-327-4455; Fax: 218-327-4263; john.guenther@dnr.state.mn.us

Cheryl Heide, Regional Administrator; 261 Highway 15 S, New Ulm, MN 56073; 507-359-6000; Fax: 507-359-60018; cheryl.heide@dnr.state.mn.us

Mark Heywood, Regional Administrator; 2300 Silver Creek Rd NE, Rochester, MN 55906; 507-285-7418; Fax: 507-285-7144; mark.heywood@dnr.state.mn.us

Elaine Johnson, Administrator:Facilities & Operations Support Bureau; 651-297-3758; Fax: 651-297-1542; elaine.johnson@dnr.state.mn.us

Colleen Miecoch, Administrator: Bureau of Management Information Services; 651-297-3906; Fax: 651-297-4946; colleen.mlecoch@dnr.state.mn.us

Brad Moore, Assistant Commissioner: Operations; 651-296-5229; Fax: 651-296-4799; brad.moore@dnr.state.mn.us
Steve Morse, Deputy Commissioner; 651-296-2540; Fax: 651-296-4799; steve.morse@dnr.state.mn.us
Mary O'Neill, Administrator: Bureau of Human Resources; 651-296-6493; Fax: 651-296-6494; mary.o'neill@dnr.state.mn.us
Paul Swenson, Regional Administrator; 2115 Birchmont Beach Rd NE, Bemidji, MN 56601; 218-755-3955; Fax: 218-755-4024; paul.swenson@dnr.state.mn.us
Kurt Ulrich, Administrator: Information, Education & Licensing; 651-296-0997; Fax: 651-296-0902; kurt.ulrich@dnr.state.mn.us
Kathleen Wallace, Regional Administrator; 1200 Warner Road, St. Paul, MN 55106; 651-772-7900; Fax: 651-772-7977; kathleen.wallace@dnr.state.mn.us

MINNESOTA ENVIRONMENTAL QUALITY BOARD
500 Lafayette Road
St. Paul, MN 55155 United States
Phone: 651-296-1305

Founded: 1973
Description: The EQB is Minnesota's principal forum for discussing environmental issues. The EQB provides an opportunity for the public to have direct input into the development of the state's environmental policy. The EQB is an independent decisionmaking body and is staffed by the Minnesota Office of Strategic and Long Range Planning.
Publication(s): EQB Monitor
Keyword(s): Development/Developing Countries, Energy
Contact(s):
Michael Sullivan, Executive Director; 3rd Fl. Centennial Bldg., 658 Cedar St., St. Paul, MN 55155; 612-296-9027
Rod Sando, Commissioner; 3rd Fl. Centennial Bldg., 658 Cedar St., St. Paul, MN 55155; 612-297-1257

MINNESOTA GEOLOGICAL SURVEY
University of Minnesota,
2642 University Ave.
St. Paul, MN 55114-1057 United States
Phone: 612-627-4780, ext. 0 Fax: 612-627-4778
E-mail: mgs@umn.edu
Website: www.geo.umn.edu/mgs

Founded: 1872
Membership: 1–100
Scope: State
Description: Established as a Geological and Natural History Survey, reconstituted in 1911 as the Minnesota Geological Survey to investigate the geology of the state; describe, classify and map the geological formations and mineral and water resources; and investigate all aspects of the geology affecting the environment.
Publication(s): List available on request.
Keyword(s): Other
Contact(s):
Val Chandler, Acting Director; 612-627-4780, ext. 0; Fax: 612-627-4778; mgs@umn.edu

MINNESOTA POLLUTION CONTROL AGENCY
BAXTER, MN
1800 College Road South
Baxter, MN 56425 United States
Phone: 218-828-2492 Fax: 218-828-2594
Website: www.pca.state.mn.us

Founded: N/A
Scope: State
Publication(s): See publications on website
Contact(s):
Reed Larson, Regional Manager

MINNESOTA POLLUTION CONTROL AGENCY
DETROIT LAKES, MN
Lake Avenue Plaza, 714 Lake Ave. Suite 220
Detroit Lakes, MN 56501 United States
Phone: 218-847-1519 Fax: 218-846-0719
Website: www.pca.state.mn.us

Founded: N/A
Membership: 1–100
Scope: State
Contact(s):
Jeff Lewis, Director; 218-846-0730; jeff.lewis@pca.state.mn.us

MINNESOTA POLLUTION CONTROL AGENCY
DULUTH, MN
525 S. Lake Ave., Suite 400
Duluth, MN 55802 United States
Phone: 218-723-4660 Fax: 218-723-4727
Website: www.pca.state.mn.us

Founded: N/A
Membership: 1–100
Scope: Local, State, Regional
Contact(s):
Suzanne Hanson, Director

MINNESOTA POLLUTION CONTROL AGENCY
MARSHALL, MN
1420 East College
Suite 900
Marshall, MN 56258 United States
Phone: 507-537-7146 Fax: 507-537-6001
Website: www.pca.state.mn.us

Founded: N/A
Membership: 1–100
Scope: Regional
Contact(s):
Mark Jacobs, Supervisor

MINNESOTA POLLUTION CONTROL AGENCY
ROCHESTER, MN
18 Wood Lake Dr., SE
Rochester, MN 55904 United States
Phone: 507-285-7343 Fax: 507-280-5513
Website: www.pca.state.mn.us

Founded: N/A
Membership: 1–100
Scope: Regional
Description: Helping Minnesotans protect the environment.
Contact(s):
Larry Landherr, Director

MINNESOTA POLLUTION CONTROL AGENCY
ST. PAUL, MN
520 Lafayette Rd.
St. Paul, MN 55155 United States
Phone: 612-296-6300 Fax: 651-297-8687
E-mail: barb.hannegan@tca.state.mn
Website: www.pca.state.mn.us

Founded: 1967
Membership: 101–1,000
Scope: State
Description: Administers the state statutes covering water pollution, air pollution, and solid and hazardous waste control.
Contact(s):
James Warner, Director: Division of Groundwater and Solid Waste; 612-296-7777
Karen Studders, Chairman of The Board and Commissioner; 612-296-7301
Lisa Thorvig, Deputy Commissioner; 612-296-7331
Gordon Wegwart, Assistant Commissioner; 612-296-7319

MINNESOTA STATE EXTENSION SERVICES

University of Minnesota, 240 Coffey Hall
1420 Eckles Ave.
St. Paul, MN 55108-6070 United States
Phone: 612-625-1915 Fax: 612-625-6227
E-mail: info@mes.umn.edu
Website: www.extension.umn.edu

Founded: N/A
Membership: 1–100
Scope: State
Contact(s):

Charles Casey, Dean and Director Extension Service; 612-624-2703; casey002@umn.edu
Melvin Baughman, Forest Resources Specialist; 612-624-0734
Stephan Carlson, Youth Specialist; 612-626-1259
James Cooper, Wildlife Specialist; 104 Hodson, University of Minnesota, St. Paul, MN 55108; 612-624-1223; Fax: 612-625-5299; jac@umn.edu
Steven Daley Laursen, Associate Dean and Collegiate Program Leader; 612-624-9298
Jeffrey Gunderson, Sea Grant Extension and Fisheries Educator
Cynthia Hagley, Water Quality Educator Specialist
Patrick Huelman, Housing Specialist; 612-624-1286
Steven Taff, Public Policy Specialist; 612-625-3103

MISSISSIPPI COOPERATIVE FISH AND WILDLIFE RESEARCH UNIT

MISSISSIPPI STATE UNIVERSITY
Mailstop 9691
Mississippi State, MS 39762 United States
Phone: 662-325-2643 Fax: 662-325-8276

Founded: 1978
Membership: 1–100
Scope: State
Description: The Unit is sponsored by the U.S.G.S. Biological Resources Division; Mississippi Department of Wildlife, Fisheries, and Parks; Mississippi State University; and the Wildlife Management Institute. Fisheries and wildlife research, graduate education, technical assistance, and extension are the Unit's main missions.
Keyword(s): Recreation/Ecotourism, Water Habitats & Quality, Wildlife & Species
Contact(s):

L. Miranda, Assistant Leader: Fisheries
Harold Schramm, Leader; hschramm@cfr.msstate.edu
Francisco Vilella, Assistant Leader: Wildlife

MISSISSIPPI DEPARTMENT OF AGRICULTURE AND COMMERCE

P.O. Box 1609
Jackson, MS 39215-1609 United States
Phone: 601-354-7050
Website: www.mdac.state.me.us

Founded: 1906
Membership: 101–1,000
Scope: State
Description: The department was created to foster and promote the business of agriculture. Duties include: Regulatory, consumer protection, marketing, and a wide range of service activities.
Publication(s): Mississippi Market Bulletin
Contact(s):

Roger Barlow, Director of Market Development; 601-359-1158
Billy Carter, Director of Farmers Market; 601-354-6818
Billy Carter, Director of Market News; 601-354-6818
Tommy Gregory, Director of National Agricultural Statistics; 601-965-4575
Robert Louys, Director of Petroleum; 601-359-1101
Julia Mclemore, Director of Regulatory Services; 601-359-1144
Jim Meadows, Director of Meat Inspection
Keith Pouncy, Director of Grain Inspection
Russell Robbins, Director of Weights and Measures; 601-359-1117
Donnis Roberson, Director of Fruit & Vegetable Inspections; 601-354-6573
Rodney Sanders, Director of Administration and Finance; 601-359-1132
Umesh Sanjanwala, Director of Information Systems; 601-359-1151
John Tillson, Director of Consumer Protection; 601-359-1148
Jim Watson, Director of Board of Animal Health; 601-359-1170
Stella Cessna, Personnel Officer; 601-359-1152
Claude Nash, Editor; 601-359-1123
Chris Sparkman, Deputy Commissioner; 601-359-1138
Lester Spell, Commissioner

MISSISSIPPI DEPARTMENT OF ENVIRONMENTAL QUALITY

OFFICE OF LAND AND WATER RESOURCES
Southport Mall, P.O. Box 10631
Jackson, MS 39289 United States
Phone: 601-961-5200 Fax: 601-354-6938
Website: www.deq.state.ms.us

Founded: 1956
Scope: State
Description: Administers Water Use Permitting Act of 1985, licensing of water well drillers, and the 1978 Dam Safety Act; inventories water resources; coordinates water and land resources planning; and conducts reviews of proposed water resources development.
Contact(s):

Charles Branch, Head
Patricia Phillips, Chief: Division of Hydrologic Investigation and Reporting; 601-961-5213

MISSISSIPPI DEPARTMENT OF ENVIRONMENTAL QUALITY

OFFICE OF POLLUTION CONTROL
P.O. Box 10385
Jackson, MS 39289-0385 United States
Phone: 601-961-5171 Fax: 601-354-6612
Website: www.deq.state.ms.us

Founded: N/A
Scope: State
Contact(s):

P. Harkins, Head; 601-961-5002

MISSISSIPPI DEPARTMENT OF WILDLIFE, FISHERIES, AND PARKS

1505 Eastover Drive
Jackson, MS 39211 United States
Phone: 601-432-2400
Website: www.mdwfp.com

Founded: N/A
Description: The purpose of the MDWFP is to manage, conserve, develop, and protect Mississippi's outdoors, state parks, wildlife and marine resources, and their habitats; and to provide continuing recreational, economic, educational, ecological, aesthetic, social and scientific benefits for present and future generations.
Publication(s): Mississippi Outdoors, Mississippi Soundings
Keyword(s): Recreation/Ecotourism, Water Habitats & Quality, Wildlife & Species

Contact(s):
Robert Cook, Director: Administrative Services; 601-364-2006
Libby Hartfield, Director: Museum of Natural Science; 601-354-7303
Ellen Morgan, Director of Marketing; 601-364-2152
Sam Polles, Executive Director; 601-364-2000
Al Tuck, Director: Support Services Division; 601-364-2046
Jim Walker, Director: Public Information; 601-364-2124
Steve Adcock, Hunter Education; 601-364-2192
Ron Garavelli, Chief: Fisheries; 601-364-2202
Jimmy Laird, Boating Enforcement; 601-364-2182
Randall Miller, Chief: Law Enforcement; 601-364-2232
Bill Quisenberry, Executive Assistant; 601-364-2005
Tommy Shropshire, Coordinator: Planning and Policy; 601-364-2107
Mary Stevens, Head Librarian; Museum of Natural Science, 111 N. Jefferson, Jackson, MS 39202-2897; 601-354-7303
Mitiz Stubbs, Outdoor Recreation Grants; 601-364-2156
Bill Thomason, Chief: Game; 601-364-2212
Bob Tyler, Deputy Administrator; 601-364-2004
David Watts, Editor; 601-364-2129

MISSISSIPPI FORESTRY COMMISSION
301 N. Lamar St., Suite 300
Jackson, MS 39201 United States
Phone: 601-359-1386 Fax: 601-359-1349
Website: www.mfc.state.ms.us

Founded: 1926

Scope: State

Description: Basic duties are forest protection against wildfire, insects, and disease; operation of tree-seedlings nurseries for reforestation; provision of forest resource management assistance to private landowners; and creation of interest in forestry.

Publication(s): Forestry Forum Magazine, various forest management brochures

Keyword(s): Forests/Forestry, Public Lands/Greenspace, Reduce/Reuse/Recycle

Contact(s):
Harold Anderson, Editor and Education Director
Kent Grizzard, Information Director
Lezlin Proctor, Director of Finance & Administration
Everard Baker, Deputy State Forester: Management Chief
William Lambert, Deputy State Forester: Protection Chief
James Mordica, Deputy State Forester Services
James Sledge, State Forester

MISSISSIPPI SOIL AND WATER CONSERVATION COMMISSION
Attn: Public Relations Director, P.O. Box 23005
Jackson, MS 39225 United States
Phone: 601-354-7645 Fax: 601-354-6628
E-mail: gmartin@mswcc.state.ms.us
Website: www.mswcc.state.ms.us

Founded: 1938

Scope: Local, State

Description: Originally established as the state agency for the control of soil erosion. Current statutory responsibilities include assistance to local soil and water conservation districts in the areas of water and soil quality projects, qualifications and elections of Commissioners, and administration of programs. Other responsibilities include reviewing and commenting on surface mining reclamation efforts. Serves as the state resource agency for agricultural nonpoint source pollution issues and projects.

Keyword(s): Agriculture/Farming, Ecosystems (precious), Forests/Forestry, Land Issues, Oceans/Coasts/Beaches, Pollution (general), Public Lands/Greenspace, Reduce/Reuse/ Recycle, Sprawl/Urban Planning, Water Habitats & Quality

Contact(s):
Emma Connolly, Public Relations Director; P.O. Box 23005, Jackson, MS 39225-3005
Gale Martin, Executive Director; P.O. Box 23005, Jackson, MS 39225-3005; 601-354-7645; Fax: 601-354-6628
Paul Myrick, Chairman

MISSISSIPPI STATE DEPARTMENT OF HEALTH
P.O. Box 1700
Jackson, MS 39215-1700 United States
Phone: 601-576-7400 Fax: 601-576-7364
Website: www.msdh.state.ms.us

Founded: N/A

Scope: State

Contact(s):
Mary Currier, Director: Division of Epidemiology / State Epidemiologist; 601-576-7725
Rick Harrington, Director: Environmental Health; 601-576-7680
F. Thompson, State Health Officer; 601-576-7633

MISSOURI DEPARTMENT OF AGRICULTURE
P.O. Box 630, 1616 Missouri Blvd.
Jefferson City, MO 65102 United States
Phone: 573-751-4211 Fax: 573-751-1784
Website: www.mda.state.mo.us

Founded: N/A
Membership: 101–1,000
Scope: State

Contact(s):
Lowell Mohler, Director; lowell_mohler@mail.mda.state.mo.us
Peter Hosherr, Deputy Director; 573-751-3376
Sally Oxenhandler, Public Information Officer; 573-751-4645

MISSOURI DEPARTMENT OF CONSERVATION
P.O. Box 180
Jefferson City, MO 65102-0180 United States
Phone: 573-751-4115 Fax: 573-751-4467
Website: www.conservation.state.mo.us/

Founded: 1937

Scope: State

Description: The department is responsible for the control, management, restoration, conservation and regulation of the bird, fish, game, forestry, and all wildlife resources of the state. These responsibilities are met through a wide variety of programs encompassing fish, wildlife, and forest management, regulations and enforcement, conservation education and interpretation, endangered species, and policy development.

Publication(s): Missouri Conservationist

Keyword(s): Agriculture/Farming, Ecosystems (precious), Forests/Forestry, Recreation/Ecotourism, Water Habitats & Quality, Wildlife & Species

Contact(s):
Jerry Conley, Director, ext. 3212
Robbie Briscoe, Internal Auditor, ext. 3356
Dave Erickson, Administrative Services Division Administrator, ext. 3142
Debbie Goff, Human Resources Division Administrator, ext. 3225
John Hoskins, Protection Division Administrator, ext. 3261
Bob Krepps, Forestry Division Administrator, ext. 3300
Kathy Love, Outreach and Education Division Administrator, ext. 3246
Bill Lueckenhoff, Design and Development Division Administrator; 573-522-2323, ext. 2234
Gerald Ross, Assistant Director, ext. 3209
George Seek, Private Land Services Division Administrator, ext. 3873
Jane Smith, General Counsel, ext. 3210
John Smith, Deputy Director, ext. 3217
Norm Stucky, Fisheries Division Administrator, ext. 3159

Rick Thom, Natural History Division Administrator, ext. 3193
Ollie Torgerson, Wildlife Division Administrator, ext. 3149

MISSOURI DEPARTMENT OF CONSERVATION
ADMINISTRATIVE SERVICES DIVISION
2901 W. Truman Blvd.
Jefferson City, MO United States
Phone: 573-751-4115 Fax: 573-751-4467
Website: http://www.conservation.state.mo.us

Founded: N/A

Contact(s):
David Erickson, Administrator

MISSOURI DEPARTMENT OF CONSERVATION
DESIGN AND DEVELOPMENT DIVISION
2901 W. Truman Blvd.
Jefferson City, MO 65109 United States
Phone: 573-522-2323 Fax: 573-522-2324

Founded: N/A

Contact(s):
William Lueckenhoff, Administrator

MISSOURI DEPARTMENT OF CONSERVATION
FISHERIES DIVISION
P.O.Box 180
Jefferson City, MO 65102-0180 United States
Phone: 573-751-4115 Fax: 573-526-4047
Website: www.conservation.state.mo.us/

Founded: N/A

Contact(s):
Norman Stucky, Administrator

MISSOURI DEPARTMENT OF CONSERVATION
FORESTRY DIVISION
P.O Box 180
Jefferson City, MO 65102-0180 United States

Founded: N/A

Contact(s):
Bob Krepps, Administrator

MISSOURI DEPARTMENT OF CONSERVATION
HUMAN RESOURCES SECTION
P.O. Box 180
Jefferson City, MO 65102-0180 United States
Phone: 573-751-4115 Fax: 573-751-9099
Website: www.conservation.state.mo.us/

Founded: N/A

Contact(s):
Deborah Goff, Chief

MISSOURI DEPARTMENT OF CONSERVATION
NATURAL HISTORY DIVISION
2901 W. Truman Blvd.
Jefferson City, MO 65109 United States
Phone: 573-751-4115 Fax: 573-751-4467

Founded: N/A

Contact(s):
Richard Thom, Chief

MISSOURI DEPARTMENT OF CONSERVATION
OUTREACH AND EDUCATION DIVISION
P.O.Box 180
Jefferson City, MO 65102-0180 United States
Phone: 573-751-4115 Fax: 573-751-2260
Website: www.conservation.state.mo.us/

Founded: N/A

Contact(s):
Kathryn Love, Administrator

MISSOURI DEPARTMENT OF CONSERVATION
PROTECTION DIVISION
P.O. Box 180
Jefferson City, MO 65102-0180 United States
Phone: 573-751-4115 Fax: 573-751-8971
Website: www.conservation.state.mo.us/

Founded: N/A

Contact(s):
Dennis Steward, Administrator

MISSOURI DEPARTMENT OF CONSERVATION
WILDLIFE DIVISION
P.O. Box 180
Jefferson City, MO 65102-0180 United States
Phone: 573-751-4115 Fax: 573-526-4663
Website: www.conservation.state.mo.us/

Founded: N/A

Contact(s):
Oliver Torgerson, Administrator

MISSOURI DEPARTMENT OF NATURAL RESOURCES
P.O. Box 176
Jefferson City, MO 65102 United States
Phone: 573-751-4422 Fax: 573-526-3878
Website: www.dnr.state.mo.us

Founded: N/A

Scope: State

Description: The Missouri Department of Natural Resources is the state resource management agency responsible for addressing environmental and natural resource-related issues. Areas of responsibility include: protecting Missouri's air, land and water resources, enforcing related laws where applicable; managing and maintaining the state's 80 state parks and state historic sites while protecting and promoting Missouri's cultural heritage and recreational opportunities.

Publication(s): Missouri Resources

Keyword(s): Energy, Land Issues, Public Lands/Greenspace, Recreation/Ecotourism

Contact(s):
Douglas Eiken, Director of Division of State Parks; 573-751-9392
Mimi Garstang, Director of Geological Survey and Resource Assessment; 573-368-2101; garsm@mail.dnr.state.mo.us
Gary Heimericks, Director of Division of Administrative Support; 573-751-7961
Connie Patterson, Communications Director; 573-751-1010; nrpattc@mail.dnr.state.mo.us
Thomas Welch, Director of Environmental Improvement and Energy Resources; P.O. Box 744, Jefferson City, MO 65102-0176; 573-751-4919
John Young, Director of Division of Air and Land Resources; 573-751-0763; younj@mail.dnr.state.mo.us
Sara Parker, Outreach and Assistance; 573-522-8796; parks@mail.dnr.state.mo.us
Scott Totten, Division of Water Quality/Soil Conservation; totts@mail.dnr.state.mo.us

MISSOURI STATE EXTENSION SERVICES
University of Missouri, 309 University Hall
Columbia, MO 65211 United States
Phone: 573-882-7754 Fax: 573-884-4204
Website: outreach.missouri.edu

Founded: N/A
Membership: 1–100
Scope: State

Contact(s):
Ronald Turner, Director: Extension Service

John Slusher, Extension Forester; 203 Natural Resources Bldg., Columbia, MO 65211; 573-882-4444; Fax: 573-882-1977

MONTANA BUREAU OF MINES AND GEOLOGY

GEOLOGY SURVEY
Montana Tech of the University of Montana
Butte, MT 59701-8997 United States
Phone: 406-496-4167 Fax: 406-496-4451
E-mail: pubsales@mtech.edu
Website: mbmgsun.mtech.edu

Founded: 1919
Membership: 1–100
Scope: State
Description: Established by law to aid the development and wise use of the state's mineral, energy, and groundwater resources by geologic and hydrogeologic studies of their occurrence and potential. Publishes formal reports and maps on Montana geology and groundwater.
Keyword(s): Energy
Contact(s):
Edmond Deal, Director and State Geologist; 406-496-4180; edeal@mbmgsun.mtech.edu

MONTANA COOPERATIVE WILDLIFE RESEARCH UNIT (USGS/BRD)

University of Montana
Missoula, MT 59812 United States
Phone: 406-243-5372 Fax: 406-243-6064
E-mail: mtcwru@selway.umt.edu
Website: www.pica.wru.umt.edu/mtcwru

Founded: 1950
Membership: 1–100
Scope: International
Description: Conducts basic and applied research, trains graduate students in wildlife biology and management, and disseminates information. Research specialties include breeding productivity, nest predation, and habitat use by birds (particularly nongame and waterfowl species) in relation to land use practices, predator populations, and natural variation in the environment.
Keyword(s): Forests/Forestry, Land Issues, Water Habitats & Quality, Wildlife & Species
Contact(s):
I. Ball, Leader; ball1@selway.umt.edu
Thomas Martin, Assistant Leader; tmartin@selway.umt.edu

MONTANA DEPARTMENT OF AGRICULTURE

P.O. Box 200201
Helena, MT 59620-0201 United States
Phone: 406-444-3144 Fax: 406-444-5409
E-mail: agr@state.mt.us
Website: www.agr.state.mt.us

Founded: N/A
Membership: 1–100
Scope: State
Keyword(s): Agriculture/Farming, Pollution (general), Water Habitats & Quality, Wildlife & Species
Contact(s):
W. Peck, Director
Gregory Ames, Administrator, Agricultural Sciences Division
Will Kissinger, Administrator: Agricultural Development Division; 406-444-2402

MONTANA DEPARTMENT OF FISH, WILDLIFE, AND PARKS

P.O. Box 200701
Helena, MT 59620-0701 United States
Phone: 406-444-3186 Fax: 406-444-4952
E-mail: fwpgen@state.mt.us
Website: www.fwp.state.mt.us

Founded: N/A
Membership: 101–1,000
Scope: State
Publication(s): Montana Outdoors
Keyword(s): Recreation/Ecotourism
Contact(s):
Jeff Hagener, Director; 406-444-3186; Fax: 406-444-4952
Larry Peterman, Chief of Field Operations; 406-444-3186; Fax: 406-444-4952
Christian Smith, Chief of Staff; 406-444-3186; Fax: 406-444-4952
Ron Aasheim, Administrator: Conservation Education; 406-444-4038
Don Childress, Administrator: Wildlife; 406-444-2612
Tom Dickson, Editor; Montana Outdoors, 930 Custer Ave. W, Helena, MT 59601; 406-444-2474; Fax: 406-443-4619; tdickson@state.mt.us
Spence Hegstad, Foundation Liaison
Chris Hunter, Administrator: Fisheries; 406-444-2449
Jim Kropp, Administrator: Enforcement; 406-444-5657
Doug Monger, Administrator: Parks; 406-444-3750
Paul Sihler, Field Service Administrator; 406-444-3196; Fax: 406-444-3023

MONTANA DEPARTMENT OF NATURAL RESOURCES AND CONSERVATION

1625 11th Ave., P.O. Box 201601
Helena, MT 59620-1601 United States
Phone: 406-444-2074 Fax: 406-444-2684
Website: www.dnrc.state.mt.us

Founded: 1971
Membership: 101–1,000
Scope: State
Description: Administers state-owned water projects; plans, regulates, and coordinates the development and use of 5.2 million acres of state school trust, land, and forest resources; wildland fire suppression and protection; service forestry; water-right adjudication; floodplain management; supervision, assistance, and coordination for local conservation and grazing districts; and regulation of oil and gas production.
Keyword(s): Agriculture/Farming, Energy, Forests/Forestry, Land Issues
Contact(s):
Bud Clinch, Director; 406-444-2074
Don Artley, Administrator: Forestry Division; 2705 Spurgin Rd., Missoula, MT 59801; 406-542-4300
Ann Bauchman, Administrator for Central Services Division; 406-444-6734
Ray Beck, Administrator: Conservation and Resource Development Division; 1520 E. 6th Ave., Helena, MT 59620; 406-444-6667; Fax: 406-444-6721; rbeck@mt.gov
Susan Cottingham, Administrator: Reserved Water Rights Compact Commission; 406-444-6841
Donald MacIntyre, Chief Legal Counsel; 406-444-6713
Carole Massman, Supervisor and Editor for Information Services; 406-444-6737
Mike Mikota, Personnel and EEO Officer
Terri Perrigo, Administrator: Oil and Gas Conservation Division
Tom Schultz, Administration Trust Land Management Division
Jack Stults, Administrator: Water Resources Division; 1520 E. 6th Ave., Helena, MT 59620; 406-444-6605

MONTANA ENVIRONMENTAL QUALITY COUNCIL

State Capitol
P.O.Box 201704
Room 171
Helena, MT 59620-1704 United States
Phone: 406-444-3742 Fax: 406-444-3971
E-mail: teverts@state.mt.us
Website: www.leg.state.mt.us

Founded: 1971
Membership: N/A
Scope: State
Description: The Environmental Quality Council is a state legislative committee created by the 1971 Montana Environmental Policy Act.
Keyword(s): Air Quality/Atmosphere, Land Issues, Water Habitats & Quality
Contact(s):
Todd Everts, Legislative Environmental Analyst
Bea McCarthy, Chair
Doug Mood, Vice-Chair

MONTANA NATURAL HERITAGE PROGRAM

1515 E 6th Ave.
Helena, MT 59620-1800 United States
Phone: 406-444-5354 Fax: 406-444-0581
E-mail: mtnhp@state.mt.us
Website: nhp.nris.state.mt.us/

Founded: 1985
Scope: Local, State
Description: The Montana Natural Heritage Program serves as the state's clearinghouse for information on Montana's native species and habitats, emphasizing those of conservation concern. We collect, validate, and distribute this information, and assist natural resource managers and others in applying it effectively. Established by the Montana State Legislature in 1983, the program is located in the Montana State Library, where it is part of the Natural Resource Information System.
Publication(s): Montana Bird Distribution, Montana Animal Species of Special Concern, Montana Plant Species of Special Concern
Keyword(s): Wildlife & Species
Contact(s):
Susan Crispin, Director

N

NATIVE AMERICAN HERITAGE COMMISSION

915 Capitol Mall, Rm. 364
Sacramento, CA 95814 United States
Phone: 916-653-4082 Fax: 916-657-5390
E-mail: nahc@pacbell.net
Website: www.nahc.ca.gov

Founded: N/A
Membership: 1–100
Scope: State
Description: The preservation and protection of Native American human remains and associated grave goods.
Publication(s): A Professional Guide
Keyword(s): Other
Contact(s):
Larry Myers, Executive Secretary; 916 653-4082; Fax: 916 657-5390; nahc@pacbell.net

NATURAL RESOURCES AND ENVIRONMENTAL PROTECTION CABINET

2 Hudson Hollow
Frankfort, KY 40601 United States
Phone: 502-564-6940 Fax: 502-564-6764
E-mail: blaine.fennell@mail.state.ky.us

Founded: N/A
Membership: 1–100
Scope: State
Contact(s):
Larry Adams, Director: Division of Permits; 502-564-2320; Fax: 502-564-6764; larry.adams@mail.state.ky.us
Stephen Hohmann, Director: Division of Abandoned Lands; 502-564-2141; Fax: 502-564-6544; stevehohmann@mail.state.ky.us
Mark Thompson, Director: Division of Field Services; 502-564-2340; Fax: 502-564-5848; markw.thompson@mail.state.ky.us
Carl Campbell, Commissioner
Allen Luttrell, Deputy Commissioner

NATURAL RESOURCES AND ENVIRONMENTAL PROTECTION CABINET

14 Reilly Rd.
Frankfort, KY 40601 United States
Phone: 502-564-2150 Fax: 502-564-4245
Website: www.nr.state.ky.us

Founded: N/A
Membership: 1,001–10,000
Scope: State
Description: Natural Resources and Environmental Protection Cabinet.
Contact(s):
Robert Daniell, Director: Division of Waste Management; 502-564-6716; Fax: 502-564-4049
William Davis, Director: Division of Environmental Services; 502-564-6120; Fax: 502-564-8930
John Hornback, Director: Division for Air Quality; 502-573-3382; Fax: 502-573-3787
Jeff Pratt, Director: Division of Water; 502-564-3410; Fax: 502-564-4245
Ralph Collins, Deputy Commissioner
Robert Logan, Commissioner

NATURAL RESOURCES AND ENVIRONMENTAL PROTECTION CABINET

Capital Plaza Tower
Frankfort, KY 40601 United States
Phone: 502-564-3350 Fax: 502-564-3354
Website: www.kyenvironment.org

Founded: N/A
Scope: State
Contact(s):
James Bickford, Secretary
Barbara Foster, General Counsel: Office of Legal Services; 502-564-5576; Fax: 502-564-6131
Hank List, Deputy Secretary

NATURAL RESOURCES AND ENVIRONMENTAL PROTECTION CABINET

DEPARTMENT FOR NATURAL RESOURCES
663 Teton Trail
Frankfort, KY 40601 United States
Phone: 502-564-2184 Fax: 502-564-9195
E-mail: steve.coleman@mail.state.ky.us
Website: www.nr.state.ky.us/nrepc/dnr/dnrhome.htm

Founded: N/A
Membership: 1–100
Scope: Regional
Publication(s): Publications on website
Contact(s):
Steve Coleman, Director: Division of Conservation; 502-564-3080; Fax: 502-564-9195
John Davies, Director: Division of Energy; 502-564-7192; Fax: 502-564-7484

Leah Macswords, Director: Division of Forestry; 502-564-4496; Fax: 502-564-6553
Hugh Archer, Commissioner

NATURAL RESOURCES AND ENVIRONMENTAL PROTECTION CABINET

ENVIRONMENTAL QUALITY COMMISSION
14 Reilly Rd.
Frankfort, KY 40601 United States
Phone: 502-564-2150 Fax: 502-567-4245
Website: www.kyeqc.net

Founded: N/A

Scope: State

Publication(s): Kentucky's Environment - bimonthly newsletter, State of Kentucky's Environment - biyearly book

Contact(s):
Leslie Cole, Executive Director
Aloma Dew, Chair

NATURAL RESOURCES AND ENVIRONMENTAL PROTECTION CABINET

KENTUCKY STATE NATURE PRESERVES COMMISSION
801 Schenkel Ln.
Frankfort, KY 40601 United States
Phone: 502-573-2886 Fax: 502-573-2355
E-mail: nrepc.ksnpcmail@mail.state.ky.us
Website: www.kynaturepreserves.org

Founded: 1976

Scope: State

Description: KSNP's mission is to protect Kentucky's natural heritage by (1) identifying, acquiring, and managing natural areas that represent the best known occurrences of rare native species, natural communitites, and significant natural features in a statewide nature preserve system; (2) working with others to protect biological diverisity; and (3) educating Kentuckians as to the value and purpose of nature preserves and biodiversity conservation..

Publication(s): Naturally Kentucky.

Keyword(s): Ecosystems (precious), Forests/Forestry, Land Issues, Public Lands/Greenspace, Recreation/Ecotourism, Water Habitats & Quality, Wildlife & Species

Contact(s):
Don Dott, Director; 502-573-2886; Fax: 502-573-2355; don.dott@mail.state.ky.us
Clara Wheatley, Chairman, KSNPC Citizen Commission

NATURAL RESOURCES CANADA

ONTARIO
Toronto, M7A 1W3 Ontario Canada
Phone: 705-755-2000 Fax: 416-314-2102
Website: www.nrcan-rncan.gc.ca/inter/index.html

Founded: N/A

Scope: State

Description: The ministry's business plan establishes the following as MNR's core businesses: natural resource management; Crown land management; public safety and enforcement; parks and protected areas; and geographic information. In pursuing these core businesses, the ministry contributes to the environmental, social, and economic well-being of Ontario through the biological features of provincial interest, and protects human life, the resource base, and physical property from the threats of forest fires,

Contact(s):
Jeff Krantzberg, Director of Communications Services Branch; 416-314-2119
John McHugh, Director of Communications Services; 416-314-2119
Gail Beggs, Assistant Deputy Minister for Field Services
John Burke, Deputy Minister
Ted Chudleigh, Parliamentary Assistant; 416-314-2193
Ann-Marie Guttier, Assistant Deputy Minister for Corporate Services
Linda Kemerman, Commissioner of Mining and Lands; 700 Bay St., 24th Fl.
Patricia Malcolmson, Assistant Deputy Minister for Science and Information Resources
John Snobelen, Minister

NAVAJO NATION DEPARTMENT OF FISH AND WILDLIFE

NAVAJO NATURAL HERITAGE PROGRAM
P.O. Box 1480
Window Rock, AZ 86515 United States
Phone: 520-871-7068 Fax: 520-871-7069
E-mail: jcole@navajofishandwildlife.org
Website: www.navajofishandwildlife.org

Founded: 1984
Membership: 1–100
Scope: Regional

Description: The Navajo Nation Department of Fish and Wildlife is responsible for conserving, protecting, enhancing and restoring the Navajo Nation's fish, wildlife and plants for the spiritual, cultural and material benefit of present and future generations of the Navajo Nation.

Publication(s): Newsletter- Proclamation (Annually)

Keyword(s): Development/Developing Countries, Ecosystems (precious), Ethics/Environmental Justice, Recreation/Ecotourism, Water Habitats & Quality, Wildlife & Species

Contact(s):
Jeff Cole, Coordinator

NEBRASKA CONSERVATION AND SURVEY DIVISION

University of Nebraska-Lincoln,
113 Nebraska Hall, 901 N. 17th St.
Lincoln, NE 68588 United States
Phone: 402-472-3471 Fax: 402-472-4608
Website: www.csd.unl.edu

Founded: N/A

Scope: State

Description: CSD, the state geological, water, soil and land cover survey, has state-mandated responsibilities to inventory and investigate geologically related natural resources of the state; to record the results of these investigations; to assist non-profit, private and governmental agencies working to conserve the state's natural resources; to study the geologic history and geography of the state to aid sustainable economic development; and to publish maps, reports and electronic information about these

Publication(s): See publication website

Contact(s):
Mark Kuzila, Director; 402-472-7537

NEBRASKA DEPARTMENT OF AGRICULTURE

301 Centennial Mall S., P.O. Box 94947
Lincoln, NE 68509-4947 United States
Phone: 402-471-2341 Fax: 402-471-2759
E-mail: joannelk@agr.state.ne.us
Website: www.agr.state.ne.us

Founded: N/A
Membership: 1–100
Scope: State

Contact(s):
Merlyn Carlson, Director
Greg Ibach, Assistant Director; Fax: 402-471-6876

NEBRASKA DEPARTMENT OF ENVIRONMENTAL QUALITY

1200 N St.
Lincoln, NE 68509-8922 United States
Phone: 402-471-2186 Fax: 402-471-2909
Website: www.deq.state.ne.us

Founded: 1971

Scope: State

Description: Created by the Nebraska Environmental Protection Act. Administers and enforces rules and regulations, and monitors the quality of the environment in Nebraska.

Publication(s): Environmental Update

Contact(s):

Michael Linder, Director
Tom Lamberson, Deputy Director, Administration and Hearing Officer, State E
Brian McManus, Public Information Officer and Publications Editor
Jay Ringenberg, Deputy Director, Programs

NEBRASKA DEPARTMENT OF NATURAL RESOURCES

301 Centennial Mall South
Lincoln, NE 68509-4676 United States
Phone: 402-471-2363 Fax: 402-471-2900
E-mail: dnr@dnr.state.ne.us
Website: www.dnr.state.ne.us

Founded: 1937

Membership: 1–100

Scope: State

Description: The state agency responsible for comprehensive water resources planning, flood plain management, administration of state financial assistance for water resources, flood control, and soil and water conservation. It also has advisory and administrative responsibility for Natural Resources Districts throughout the state.

Publication(s): Nebraska Resources - quarterly newsletter

Keyword(s): Land Issues, Water Habitats & Quality

Contact(s):

Richard Jiskra, Chairperson; 2342 County Rd. 1600, Swanton, NE 68445; 402-448-5305

NEBRASKA DEPARTMENT OF NATURAL RESOURCES

301 Centennial Mall South
Lincoln, NE 68509 United States
Phone: 402-471-2363 Fax: 402-471-2900
E-mail: rpatterson@dnr.state.ne.us
Website: www.dnr.state.ne.us

Founded: N/A

Membership: 1–100

Scope: State

Description: DNR is a state agency with responsibilities in the areas of: Ground Water, Surface Water, Floodplain Management, Dam Safety, Natural Resources Planning, Storage of Natural Resources and Related Data, Administration of State Funds. Administers and enforces the state water laws and all matters pertaining to water rights; measuring and recording the flow of various streams and canals; approving plans and specifications for dam construction; inspection of dams; and registration of wells.

Publication(s): Nebraska Resources, newsletter, Hydrographic Report, Biannual Report

Keyword(s): Climate Change, Land Issues, Population, Water Habitats & Quality

Contact(s):

Roger Patterson, Director
Ann Bleed, Deputy Director
James Cook, Legal Counsel
Susan France, Permits and Adjudications

NEBRASKA GAME AND PARKS COMMISSION

2200 N. 33rd St., P.O. Box 30370
Lincoln, NE 68503-0370 United States
Phone: 402-471-0641 Fax: 402-471-5528
E-mail: ngpc@state.ne.us
Website: www.ngpc.state.ne.us

Founded: 1929

Membership: 101–1,000

Scope: State

Description: The commission has sole charge of state parks, game and fish, and all things pertaining thereto; boating; and administration of the Land and Water Conservation Fund. Complete information on Game and Parks Commission facilities is available on the WWW at: www.ngpc.state.ne.us.

Publication(s): Nebraskaland Magazine

Keyword(s): Ecosystems (precious), Executive/Legislative/Judicial Reform, Forests/Forestry, Land Issues, Public Lands/Greenspace, Recreation/Ecotourism, Water Habitats & Quality, Wildlife & Species

Contact(s):

Rex Amack, Director; 402-471-5539
Ted Blume, Administrator: Law Enforcement; 402-471-4010; tblume@ngpc.state.ne.us
Mark Brohman, Administrator: Administration; 402-471-5539; mbrohman@ngpc.state.ne.us
James Carney, Central Region Parks Manager; 402-471-5547; jcarney@ngpc.state.ne.us
Patrick Cole, Administrator: Budget and Fiscal; 402-471-5523; pcole@ngpc.state.ne.us
James Douglas, Administrator: Wildlife; 402-471-5411; jdouglas@ngpc.state.ne.us
James Fuller, Administrator: Parks; 402-471-5550; jfuller@ngpc.state.ne.us
Don Gabelhouse, Administrator: Fisheries; 402-471-5515; dgabel@ngpc.state.ne.us
Paul Horton, Administrator: Information and Education; 402-471-5481; phorton@ngpc.state.ne.us
Noelyn Isom, Assistant Director; 402-471-5539; nisom@ngpc.state.ne.us
Earl Johnson, Administrator: Operations and Construction; 402-471-5525
Roger Kuhn, Assistant Director; 402-471-5512; rkuhn@ngpc.state.ne.us
Kirk Nelson, Assistant Director; 402-471-5539; knelson@ngpc.state.ne.us
Bruce Sackett, Administrator: Realty; 402-471-5536; bsackett@ngpc.state.ne.us
Jim Sheffield, Administrator: Engineering; 402-471-5557; jsheff@ngpc.state.ne.us
Jim Swenson, Eastern Region Parks Manager; 402-471-5499; jswenson@ngpc.state.ne.us
Larry Voecks, Western Region Parks Manager; 308-665-2900; lvoecks@ngpc.state.ne.us
Barbara Voeltz, Librarian; 2200 N 33rd St., P.O. Box 30370, Lincoln, NE 68503; 402-471-5587; Fax: 402-471-5528; bvoeltz@ngpc.state.ne.us
Duane Westerholt, Administrator: Planning and Development; 402-471-5511; dwester@ngpc.state.ne.us
Tom White, Editor; 402-471-5471; twhite@ngpc.state.ne.us

NEBRASKA GAME AND PARKS COMMISSION

OMAHA OFFICE
1212 Bob Gibson Blvd.
Omaha, NE 68108 United States
Phone: 402-595-2144 Fax: 402-595-2569
Website: www.ngpc.state.ne.us

Founded: N/A

Scope: Local

NEBRASKA STATE EXTENSION SERVICES

211 Agricultural Hall, University of Nebraska
Lincoln, NE 68583-0703 United States
Phone: 402-472-2966 Fax: 402-472-5557
Website: www.unl.edu/ianr/coopext/coopext.htm

Founded: N/A
Membership: 101–1,000
Scope: International
Keyword(s): Agriculture/Farming, Reduce/Reuse/Recycle, Sprawl/Urban Planning
Contact(s):

John Allen, Director, Center for Rural Community Revitalization and Dev.; 58C H.C. Filley Hall, University of Nebraska, Lincoln, NE 68583-0947; 402-472-8012; Fax: 402-472-3460; jallen1@unl.edu
Elbert Dickey, Dean and Director of Cooperative Extension; edickey1@unl.edu
Susan Fritz, Dept. Head of Agricultural Leadership, Education and Communication; 300 Agricultural Hall, University of Nebraska, Lincoln, NE 68583-0709; 402-472-9559; Fax: 402-472-5863
Scott Hygnstrom, Vertebrate Pest Specialist; 202 Natural Resources Hall, University of Nebraska, Lincoln, NE 68583-0819; 402-472-6822; Fax: 402-472-2946

NEVADA BUREAU OF MINES AND GEOLOGY

Mail Stop 178, University of Nevada, Reno
Reno, NV 89557-0088 United States
Phone: 775-784-6691 Fax: 775-784-1709
E-mail: nbmginfo@unr.edu
Website: www.nbmg.unr.edu

Founded: N/A
Membership: 1–100
Scope: State
Description: Conducts research on Nevada geology and mineral resources. Collects and disseminates information (including published maps and reports) on Nevada geology, mineral resources, base maps, and airphotos.
Publication(s): Nevada Mineral Industry, Major Mines of Nevada, Living with Earthquakes in Nevada
Keyword(s): Land Issues, Public Lands/Greenspace
Contact(s):

Jonathan Price, Director and State Geologist; jprice@unr.edu
David Davis, Geologic Information Specialist, ext. 133

NEVADA DEPARTMENT OF AGRICULTURE

350 Capitol Hill Ave.
Reno, NV 89502-2923 United States
Phone: 775-688-1180 Fax: 775-688-1178
Website: www.agri.state.nv.us

Founded: N/A
Membership: 1–100
Scope: State
Publication(s): Test Alert
Contact(s):

Paul Iverson, Director, ext. 222
Robert Gronowski, Administrator, Division of Plant Industry
Edward Hoganson, Administrator Division of Measurment Standards; 775-688-1166; Fax: 775-688-2533
David Thain, Administrator and State Veterinarian

NEVADA DEPARTMENT OF CONSERVATION AND NATURAL RESOURCES

Office of the Director
123 West Nye Lane, Room 230
Carson City, NV 89706-0818 United States
Phone: 775-687-4360 Fax: 775-687-6122
Website: www.state.nv.us/cnr

Founded: N/A
Membership: 1,001–10,000
Scope: State
Description: State of Nevada Department of Conservation & Natural Resources
Contact(s):

R. Michael Turnipseed, P.E., Director
Glenn Clemmer, Program Manager: Nevada Natural Heritage Program; 775-687-4245
Allen Biaggi, Administrator: Division of Environmental Protection; 775-687-4670
Terry Crawforth, Administrator: Division of Wildlife; 775-688-1500
Wayne Perock, Administrator: Division of State Parks; 775-687-4384
Hugh Ricci, State Engineer: Division of Water Resources; 775-687-4278
Steve Robinson, Administrator: Division of Forestry; 775-684-2500
Pamela Wilcox, Administrator: Division of State Lands; 775-687-4363

NEVADA DIVISION OF WILDLIFE

1100 Valley Rd.
Reno, NV 89512 United States
Phone: 775-688-1500 Fax: 775-688-1595
Website: www.nevadadivisionofwildlife.org

Founded: N/A
Scope: State
Description: A regulatory and policymaking body, administering laws, regulations, and policies. Mission is the protection, propagation, restoring, introduction, transplanting, and management of wildlife throughout the state.
Contact(s):

Thomas Atkinson, Chief, Enforcement
Steve Bremer, Administrative
Terry Crawforth, Administrator
David Rice, Chief, Conservation Education
Boyd Spratling, Board of Wildlife Commissioner Vice Chairman
Gregg Tanner, Chief, Game
Gene Weller, Chief, Fisheries

NEVADA NATURAL HERITAGE PROGRAM

1550 E. College Parkway, Suite 145
Carson City, NV 89706-7921 United States
Phone: 775-687-4245 Fax: 775-687-1288
Website: www.state.nv.us/nvnhp/

Founded: 1986
Membership: N/A
Scope: State, National
Description: The program represents an ongoing effort to collect and standardize data on Nevada's sensitive biodiversity and share this information with developers, researchers, and decision-makers for environmentally wise planning.
Keyword(s): Wildlife & Species
Contact(s):

Glenn Clemmer, Program Manager

NEW BRUNSWICK DEPARTMENT OF NATURAL RESOURCES AND ENERGY

P.O. Box 6000
Fredericton, E3B 5H1 New Brunswick Canada
Phone: 506-453-2207 Fax: 506-453-2930

Founded: N/A
Scope: State
Contact(s):

Arnold Boer, Executive Director of Fish and Wildlife; P.O. Box 6000, Fredericton, New Brunswick E3B 5H1; 506-453-2433
David Ferguson, Deputy Minister; 506-453-2501
Jeannot Volpe, Minister; 506-453-2510

NEW HAMPSHIRE DEPARTMENT OF AGRICULTURE, MARKETS, AND FOOD

P.O. Box 2042
Concord, NH 03302-2042 United States
Phone: 603-271-3551 Fax: 603-271-1109
E-mail: marketbulletin@agr.state.nh.us

Founded: 1913

Scope: State

Description: The department is responsible for a broad range of activities, including protecting the environment, food safety, market integrity, animal and plant health, and the economic security of the New Hampshire agricultural industry.

Publication(s): Weekly Market Bulletin

Keyword(s): Agriculture/Farming, Development/Developing Countries, Ethics/Environmental Justice, Land Issues, Sprawl/Urban Planning

Contact(s):
Stephen Taylor, Commissioner; 603-271-3551; Fax: 603-271-1109

NEW HAMPSHIRE DEPARTMENT OF AGRICULTURE, MARKETS, AND FOOD

STATE CONSERVATION COMMITTEE
P.O. Box 2042
Concord, NH 03302-2042 United States
Phone: 603-271-3551
Website: www.state.nh.us/agric/aghome.html

Founded: 1945

Scope: State

Description: The SCC consists of twelve members. Six members represent state agencies, five are appointed, and one represents the NH Association of Conservation Commissions. Duties are to offer assistance to supervisors of the ten conservation districts, keep supervisors of each district informed of other district activities, and coordinate the conservation of New Hampshire activities.

Keyword(s): Agriculture/Farming, Land Issues, Water Habitats & Quality

Contact(s):
Samuel Doyle, Chair; P.O. Box 4, North Sutton, NH 03260; 603-927-4163; Fax: 603-224-8260
Joanna Pellerin, Coordinator; 118 North Rd., Brentwood, NH 03833-6614; 603-679-2790; Fax: 603-679-2860

NEW HAMPSHIRE DEPARTMENT OF ENVIRONMENTAL SERVICES

6 Hazen Dr.
P.O. Box 95
Concord, NH 03302-0095 United States
Phone: 603-271-3503 Fax: 603-271-2867
E-mail: pip@des.state.nh.us
Website: www.des.state.nh.us

Founded: 1987

Membership: 101–1,000

Scope: Local, State, Regional, National, International

Description: The DES is a result of a legislatively-mandated state environmental agency. The DES consists of three divisions: Water Division; Waste Management Division; and Air Resources Division.

Keyword(s): Agriculture/Farming, Air Quality/Atmosphere, Climate Change, Ecosystems (precious), Energy, Ethics/Environmental Justice, Land Issues, Oceans/Coasts/Beaches, Pollution (general), Public Health, Reduce/Reuse/Recycle, Sprawl/Urban Planning, Transportation

Contact(s):
Timothy Drew, Administrator, Public Information and Permitting Unit; 603-271-3306; Fax: 603-271-8013; tdrew@des.state.nh.us
Kenneth Colburn, Director of Air Resources Division; 603-271-1370; Fax: 603-271-1381
Philip O'Brien, Director of Waste Management Division; 603-271-2900; Fax: 603-271-2456
Harry Stewart, Director of Water Division; 603-271-3503; Fax: 603-271-2982
G. Bisbee, Assistant Commissioner

NEW HAMPSHIRE FISH AND GAME DEPARTMENT

2 Hazen Dr.
Concord, NH 03301 United States
Phone: 603-271-3422 Fax: 603-271-1438
E-mail: info@wildlife.state.nh.us
Website: www.wildlife.state.nh.us

Founded: 1865

Scope: State

Description: Fish and wildlife management.

Publication(s): New Hampshire Wildlife Journal

Keyword(s): Recreation/Ecotourism, Wildlife & Species

Contact(s):
Wayne Vetter, Executive Director; wvetter@wildlife.state.nh.us
Eric Aldrich, Media Contact; 603-271-3211; ealdrich@wildlife.state.nh.us
Ronald Alie, Chief: Law Enforcement Division; 603-271-3127; ralie@wildlife.state.nh.us
Richard Cunningham, Business Administrator; 603-271-2741; rcunningham@wildlife.state.nh.us
Ellis Hatch, Commission Vice Chairman; 31 Harding Street, Rochester, NH 03867
Jim Jones, Commissioner Secretary; 501 Beanhill Rd., Norfield, NH 03276
Daniel Lynch, Assistant Director; dlynch@wildlife.state.nh.us
Charles Miner, Chief of Access and Engineering; cminer@wildlife.state.nh.us
Richard Moquin, Commission Chairman; 212 Coolidge Ave., Manchester, NH 03102
John Nelson, Chief: Marine Fisheries Division; 603-868-1095
Stephen Perry, Chief: Inland Fisheries; sperry@wildlife.state.nh.us
Judy Stokes, Chief: Public Affairs Division; 603-271-3211; jstokes@wildlife.state.nh.us
Steven Weber, Chief: Wildlife Division; 603-271-2461; sweber@wildlife.state.nh.us

NEW HAMPSHIRE NATURAL HERITAGE INVENTORY

P.O. Box 1856
Concord, NH 03302-1856 United States
Phone: 603-271-3623 Fax: 603-271-2629
Website: www.dred.state.nh.us

Founded: 1987

Membership: N/A

Scope: Local, State, Regional

Description: New Hampshire Natural Heritage Inventory is responsible for finding, tracking, and providing information about the state's rare species and exemplary ecosystems.

Publication(s): Checklist of New Hampshire's Vascular Plants, List of New Hampshire's Rare Animal Species, List of New Hampshire's Rare Plant Species

Keyword(s): Ecosystems (precious), Forests/Forestry, Land Issues, Wildlife & Species

Contact(s):
Lionel Chute, Coordinator

NEW JERSEY DEPARTMENT OF AGRICULTURE

P.O. Box 330
Trenton, NJ 08625 United States
Phone: 609-292-5530 Fax: 609-292-3978
Website: www.state.nj.us/agriculture/index.html

Founded: N/A

Membership: 101–1,000

Scope: Local

Keyword(s): Agriculture/Farming

Contact(s):

Robert Balaam, Director of Division of Plant Industry; 609-292-5441
John Gallagher, Director of Division of Administration; 609-292-6931
George Horzepa, Director of Division of Rural Resources; 609-292-5532
P. Mullen, Director of Division of Dairy and Commodity Regulation; 609-292-5575
A. Murray, Director of Division of Markets, Acting; 609-292-5536
Gregory Romano, Executive Director of State Agriculture Development Committee; 609-984-2504
Ernest Zirkle, Director of Division of Animal Health; 609-292-3965
Carol Shipp, Chief of Staff; 609-633-7794
Samuel Garrison, Assistant Secretary; 609-292-5530

NEW JERSEY DEPARTMENT OF AGRICULTURE STATE SOIL AND CONSERVATION COMMITTEE

DIVISION OF RURAL RESOURCES
STATE SOIL CONSERVATION COMMITTEE
P.O. Box 330
Trenton, NJ 08625 United States
Phone: 609-292-5540 Fax: 609-633-7229
E-mail: james.sadley@ag.state.nj.us
Website: www.state.nj.us

Founded: 1937
Membership: 1–100
Scope: State
Description: A unit of state government administered by the state Dept. of Agriculture. Responsible for conservation of soil resources and control and prevention of soil erosion and nonpoint source pollution, prevention of damage by floodwater or sediment, and conservation of water for agricultural purposes. Provides direction, leadership, standards, rules, funding, and administrative assistance; coordinates local district conservation programs; and is interagency with 12 members.
Publication(s): Standards for Soil Erosion and Sediment
Keyword(s): Agriculture/Farming, Land Issues, Oceans/Coasts/Beaches, Pollution (general), Reduce/Reuse/Recycle, Water Habitats & Quality

Contact(s):

Charles Kuperus, Chairman; 609-292-3976; charles.kuperus@ag.state.nj.us
Jim Sadley, Executive Secretary; 609-292-5540; Fax: 609-633-7229; james.sadley@ag.state.nj.us

NEW JERSEY DEPARTMENT OF ENVIRONMENTAL PROTECTION

401 E. State St.,
Trenton, NJ 08625-0402 United States
Phone: 609-292-2885 Fax: 609-292-7695
E-mail: askdep@dep.state.nj.us
Website: www.state.nj.us/dep

Founded: N/A
Membership: 101–1,000
Scope: State
Description: To assist the residents of New Jersey in preserving, sustaining, protecting and enhancing the environment to ensure the integration of high environmental quality, public health and economic vitality.
Publication(s): New Jersey Outdoors

Contact(s):

Leslie McGeorge, Director, Div. of Science & Research/Assistant Commissioner; 609-984-6070
Peter Page, Director: Communications; 609-777-1344; Fax: 609-292-1410
Gary Sondermeyer, Chief of Staff; 609-292-2795; Fax: 609-292-7695
Sue Boyle, Assistant Commissioner: Site Remediation; 609-292-1250; Fax: 609-777-1914
Ray Cantor, Assistant Commissioner: Land Use Mangement; 401 E. State St., P.O. Box 439; 609-292-2178
Marlen Dooley, Assistant Commissioner: Enforcement; 609-984-3285
Denise Mikics, Editor; 609-777-4182
Robert Shinn, Commissioner
Cari Wild, Assistant Commissioner: Natural and Historic Resources; 609-292-3541

NEW JERSEY DEPARTMENT OF ENVIRONMENTAL PROTECTION

DIVISION OF FISH AND WILDLIFE
P.O. Box 400
Trenton, NJ 08625-0400 United States
Phone: 609-292-2965 Fax: 609-984-1414
Website: www.njfishandwildlife.com

Founded: N/A
Membership: N/A
Scope: State
Description: The mission of the New Jersey Division of Fish and Wildlife is to protect and manage the state's fish and wildlife to maximize their long-term biological, recreational and economic values for all New Jerseyans.

Contact(s):

Robert McDowell, Director; 609-292-9410
David Chanda, Assistant Director; 609-292-0891
Lawrence Herrighty, Chief: Rural Wildlife Management; 609-292-6685
Jim Joseph, Chief: Shellfisheries; 609-984-5546
Tom McCloy, Chief: Marine Fisheries; 609-984-5546
Martin McHugh, Assistant Director; 609-292-0891
Larry Niles, Chief: Endangered and Nongame Species Program; 609-292-9101
Tony Petrongolo, Chief: Lands Management; 609-292-1599
Jim Sciascia, Chief: Wildlife Information/Education; 609-292-9450; jsciasci@dep.state.nj.us
Robert Soldwedel, Chief: Freshwater Fisheries; 609-292-8642
Rob Winkel, Chief: Law Enforcement; 609-292-9430

NEW JERSEY DEPARTMENT OF ENVIRONMENTAL PROTECTION

DIVISION OF PARKS AND FORESTRY
P.O. Box 404
Trenton, NJ 08625-0404 United States
Phone: 609-292-2733 Fax: 609-984-0503
Website: www.state.nj.us/dep/forestry/parknj/divhome.htm

Founded: N/A
Scope: Regional

Contact(s):

Gregory Marshall, Director
Richard Barker, Assistant Director: State Park Service; 609-292-2772
James Barresi, Assistant Director: State Park Service; 609-292-2530
Maris Gabliks, Chief: Bureau of Forest Fire Management and State Firewarden; 609-292-2977
Frank Gallagher, Administrator, Office of Interpretive & Educational Services; 609-292-8190
Dorothy Guzzo, Administrator: Office of Historic Preservation; 609-984-0176
Edward Lempicki, Chief: Bureau of Forest Management: State Forester; 609-292-2531
Carl Nordstrom, Deputy Director; 609-292-5990

NEW JERSEY DEPARTMENT OF ENVIRONMENTAL PROTECTION

DIVISION OF PUBLICLY FUNDED SITE REMEDIATION
P.O. Box 402
Trenton, NJ 08625-0402 United States
Phone: 609-984-3081 Fax: 609-777-0756
Website: www.state.nj.us/dep/index.html

Founded: N/A

Scope: State

Description: To assist the residents of New Jersey in preserving, sustaining, protecting and enhancing the environment to ensure the integration of high environmental quality, public health and economic vitality.

Contact(s):
Anthony Farro, Director

NEW JERSEY DEPARTMENT OF ENVIRONMENTAL PROTECTION

DIVISION OF SOLID AND HAZARDOUS WASTE
P.O. Box 414
Trenton, NJ 08625-0414 United States
Phone: 609-984-6880 Fax: 609-984-6874
E-mail: dshweb@dep.state.nj.us
Website: www.state.nj.us/dep

Founded: N/A

Scope: State

Description: The Division of Solid and Hazardous Waste is dedicated to the environmentally sound and cost effective management of solid and hazardous wastes and recyclable materials, to protect the public health, preserve the environment, and enhance the quality of life for the citizens of the State of New Jersey.

Contact(s):
John Castler, Director

NEW JERSEY DEPARTMENT OF ENVIRONMENTAL PROTECTION

GEOLOGICAL SURVEY
P.O. Box 427
Trenton, NJ 08625-0427 United States
Phone: 609-292-1185 Fax: 609-633-1004
Website: www.state.nj.us/dep/njgs/

Founded: 1835

Membership: 1–100

Scope: State, Regional

Description: Formed to study, evaluate, and prepare maps and reports on New Jersey's resources. In addition to a geologic map and information on the mineral industry and water resources, the survey provides geologic and ground water reports, geologic and topographic maps, ground water monitoring, and other resource information.

Publication(s): Geologic Survey Reports & Maps

Keyword(s): Climate Change, Land Issues, Oceans/Coasts/Beaches, Pollution (general), Public Lands/Greenspace, Sprawl/Urban Planning, Water Habitats & Quality

Contact(s):
Richard Dalton, Chief of Bureau of Geology and Topography; 609-292-2576
Karl Muessig, State Geologist; 609-292-1185
David Pasicznyk, Chief, Ground Water Resource Evaluations; 609-984-6587
Thomas Seckler, Editor; 609-292-1185

NEW JERSEY DEPARTMENT OF ENVIRONMENTAL PROTECTION

GREEN ACRES PROGRAM
State of New Jersey/Department of Environmental Protection
Green Acres Program
P.O. Box 412
Trenton, NJ 08625-0412 United States
Phone: 609-984-0500 Fax: 609-984-0608
Website: www.state.nj.us/dep/greenacres

Founded: 1961

Membership: N/A

Scope: State

Description: Green Acres protects open space to enhance New Jersey's natural environment and its historic, scenic, and recreational resources. As the land acquisition agent for NJDEP, Green Acres acquires land, which becomes part of the system of state parks, forests, natural areas and wildlife management areas. Green Acres also provides low interest (2%) loans and partial grants to municipal and county governments to acquire open space and develop outdoor recreation facilities.

Keyword(s): Public Lands/Greenspace, Recreation/Ecotourism

Contact(s):
Dennis Davidson, Deputy Administrator; 609-984-0555; Fax: 609-984-0608; ddavidso@dep.state.nj.us
Thomas Wells, Administrator; 609-984-0508; Fax: 609-984-0608; twells@dep.state.nj.us
Gary Rice, Chief, Local Assistance Program; 609-984-0570; Fax: 609-984-0608; grice@dep.state.nj.us
Robert Stokes, Chief, Planning and Information Management; 609-984-0495; Fax: 609-984-0608; rstokes@dep.state.nj.us
John Watson, Chief, State Land Acquisition; 609-984-0609; Fax: 609-984-0608; jwatson@dep.state.nj.us
Judith Yeany, Chief, Legal Services and Stewardship; 609-984-0631; Fax: 609-984-0608; jyeany@dep.state.nj.us

NEW JERSEY PINELANDS COMMISSION

P.O. Box 7
New Lisbon, NJ 08064 United States
Phone: 609-894-7300 Fax: 609-894-7330
E-mail: info@njpines.state.nj.us
Website: www.nj.gov/pinelands/

Founded: 1979

Membership: 1–100

Scope: State, Regional

Description: State planning and regulatory agency with jurisdiction over land use and development in the million-acre Pinelands national reserve; 53 municipalities in the state Pinelands area have and revise local master plans and zoning ordinances to incorporate standards of regional conservation plan.

Publication(s): Pinelander, The Newsletter, a list of reports and studies is available upon request.

Keyword(s): Land Issues

Contact(s):
Annette Barbaccia, Executive Director
Elizabeth Carpenter, Educational Coordinator
William Harrison, Assistant Director of Development Review and Enforcement
Jerrold Jacobs, Chairman
John Stokes, Assistant Director of Planning and Management

NEW MEXICO BUREAU OF GEOLOGY AND MINERAL RESOURCES

GEOLOGICAL INFORMATION CENTER LIBRARY
801 Leroy Place
Socorro, NM 87801 United States
Phone: 505-835-5145 Fax: 505-835-6333
E-mail: bureau@gis.nmt.edu
Website: www.geoinfo.nmt.edu/

Founded: N/A
Membership: 1–100
Scope: State
Publication(s): New Mexico Geology-quarterly newsletter
Contact(s):
Peter Scholle, Contact

NEW MEXICO BUREAU OF GEOLOGY AND MINERAL RESOURCES

801 Leroy Pl.
Socorro, NM 87801 United States
Phone: 505-835-5420 Fax: 505-835-6333
E-mail: pubsosc@gis.nmt.edu
Website: www.geoinfo.nmt.edu

Founded: 1927
Membership: 1–100
Scope: Local
Description: Charged with investigating and reporting on all types of mineral resources and the geology of the state, including environmental geology, water resources, and geological hazards; responsible for conducting applied research on all aspects of geology and mineral resources.
Publication(s): Bulletins, Databases on CD-ROM and home page, Scenic Trips to the Geologic Past, Lite Geology, New Mexico Geology, Geologic Maps, Ground Water Reports, Memoirs, Circulars, Topological Maps.
Keyword(s): Energy
Contact(s):
Peter Scholle, Director and State Geologist; 505-835-5302; pscholle@gis.nmt.edu
Susan Welch, Manager of Geological Extension Service; 505-835-5112; susie@gis.nmt.edu
Bruce Allen, Environmental Geologist; 505-255-0317; allenb@gis.nmt.edu
Jane Love, Editor; jane@gisnmt.edu
David Love, Environmental Geologist; 505-835-5146; dave@gis.nmt.edu

NEW MEXICO DEPARTMENT OF AGRICULTURE

MSC 3189, P.O. Box 30005
Las Cruces, NM 88003-8005 United States
Phone: 505-646-3007
Website: www.nmdaweb.nmsu.edu

Founded: 1955
Membership: 101–1,000
Scope: State
Description: Organized to protect state agriculture from importation of plant diseases and insects and help control those that gain entrance; to ensure products offered for sale meet quality standards as advertised and labeled; maintain inspection of agricultural products for interstate shipping; laboratory analyses of animal diseases and deaths on fee basis; promote state agricultural commodities; provide market news; and conduct consumer and producer service activities designated by law.
Publication(s): Biennial Report, New Mexico Agricultural Statistics
Contact(s):
Edward Avalos, Director of Marketing and Development Division; 505-646-4929
Larry Dominguez, Director of Agricultural and Environmental Services Division; 505-646-3208
Frank Dubois, Director and Secretary; 505-646-3007
Richard Larock, Director of Veterinary Diagnostic Services; 505-841-2576
Gary West, Director of Standards and Consumer Services Division; 505-646-1616
Ronald White, Director of Agricultural Programs and Resources Division; 505-646-2642
Rick Janecka, State Chemist of Laboratory; 505-646-3318
Richard Kochevar, State Seed Analyst of Laboratory; 505-646-3407
Jeff Witte, Assistant Director; 505-646-3007

NEW MEXICO DEPARTMENT OF GAME AND FISH

P.O. Box 25112
Santa Fe, NM 87504 United States
Phone: 505-827-7911 Fax: 505-476-8124
E-mail: iispa@state.nm.us
Website: www.gmfsh.state.nm.us

Founded: N/A
Membership: 101–1,000
Scope: State
Description: The State Game Commission and the Game and Fish Department are administratively attached to the Energy, Minerals, and Natural Resources Department. The responsibility of the State Game Commission is to develop policy for the Game and Fish Department.
Publication(s): Publications on line
Contact(s):
Larry Bell, Director; P.O. Box 25112, Santa Fe, NM 87504; 505-827-6333; lbell@state.nm.us
Dan Brook, Chief of Law Enforcement; 505-827-7934; dbrook@state.nm.us
Scott Brown, Assistant Director of Resource Divisions; 505-827-6333; sbrown@state.nm.us
Lydia Duran, Chief of Administrative Services, Acting; 505-827-7920; lduran@state.nm.us
Steven Emery, Chairman of State Game Commission; 505-856-0963; semery@state.nm.us
Barry Hale, Chief of Wildlife Division; 505-827-7885; bhale@state.nm.us
Jack Kelly, Chief of Fish Management; 505-827-7905; jkelly@state.nm.us
Don MacCarter, Chief of Public Affairs
Roberta Salazar-Henry, Assistant Director of Administrative Services; 505-827-6333; rhenry@state.nm.us
Jennifer Salisbury, Cabinet Secretary of Energy, Minerals, and Natural Resources; 505-827-5950; jsalisbury@state.nm.us
Tod Stevenson, Chief of Conservation Services; 505-827-7882; tstevenson@state.nm.us

NEW MEXICO DEPARTMENT OF GAME AND FISH

ALBUQUERQUE NM OFFICE
3481 Midway Pl., NE
Albuquerque, NM 87109 United States
Phone: 505-841-8881 Fax: 505-841-8885
Website: www.gmfsh.state.nm.us

Founded: N/A
Membership: 1–100
Scope: State
Contact(s):
Chris Chadwick, Public Affairs Specialist
Luke Shelby, Chief of Operations NW Area

NEW MEXICO DEPARTMENT OF GAME AND FISH

RATON NM OFFICE
P.O. Box 1145, 215 York Canyon Rd.
Raton, NM 87740 United States
Phone: 505-445-2311 Fax: 505-445-5651
E-mail: gmfsh@state.nm.us
Website: www.gmfsh.state.nm.us

Founded: N/A
Scope: State
Description: NM Department of Game & Fish
Contact(s):
Joanna Lackey, Chief; jlackey@state.nm.us

NEW MEXICO DEPARTMENT OF GAME AND FISH

ROSWELL NM OFFICE
1912 West 2nd St.
Roswell, NM 88201 United States
Phone: 505-624-6135 Fax: 505-624-6136
Website: www.gmfsh.state.nm.us

Founded: N/A
Scope: State
Contact(s):
Roy Hayes, Chief

NEW MEXICO DEPARTMENT OF GAME AND FISH

SW AREA OPERATIONS
566 N. Telshor Blvd.
Las Cruces, NM 88011 United States
Phone: 505-522-9796 Fax: 505-522-8382
E-mail: jveo@state.nm.us
Website: www.gmfsh.state.nm.us

Founded: N/A
Membership: 1–100
Scope: Regional
Description: State agency responsible for managing New Mexico's wildlife.
Contact(s):
Steve Henry, Chief

NEW MEXICO ENVIRONMENT DEPARTMENT

1190 Saint Francis Dr., P.O. Box 26110
Santa Fe, NM 87502 United States
Phone: 505-827-2855 Fax: 505-827-2836
Website: www.nmenv.state.nm.us

Founded: N/A
Membership: 101–1,000
Scope: State
Description: To preserve, protect, and perpetuate New Mexico's environment for present and future generations.
Contact(s):
Ralph Gruebel, Director of Environmental Protection Division
Robert Horwitz, Director of Administrative Services Division; 505-827-2773; robert_horwitz@nmenv.state.nm.us
Mike Koranda, Director of Field Operations Division; 505-827-1080; mike_koranda@nmenv.state.nm.us
Greg Lewis, Director of Water and Waste Management Division; 505-827-2886; greg_lewis@nmenv.state.nm.us
Darwin Pattengale, Manager of District IV; 505-624-6046; darwin_pattengale@nmenv.state.nm.us
Ken Smith, Manager of District III 505-524-6300; ken_smith@nmenv.state.nm.us
Courte Vohres, Manager of District II; 505-827-1840; courte_vohres@nmenv.state.nm.us
James Bearzi, Chief of Hazardous & Radioactive Materials Bureau; 505-827-1557; james_bearzi@nmenv.state.nm.us
Sandra Eli, Chief of Air Quality Bureau; 505-827-1494; sandra_eli@nmenv.state.nm.us
Cliff Hawley, Chief of Program Support Bureau; 505-827-2844; cliff_hawley@nmenv.state.nm.us
Marcy Leavitt, Chief of Ground Water Protection and Remediation Bureau; 505-827-2919; marcy_leavitt@nmenv.state.nm.us
Pete Maggiore, Secretary; 505-827-2855; pete_maggiore@nmenv.state.nm.us
John Parker, Chief of Department of Energy Oversight Bureau; 505-827-4252; john_parker@nmenv.state.nm.us
Sam Rogers, Chief of Occupational Health and Safety Bureau; 505-827-2877; sam_rogers@nmenv.state.nm.us
Jerry Scheppner, Chief of Underground Storage Tank Bureau; 505-827-0188; jerry_sheppner@nmenv.state.nm.us
Butch Tongate, Chief of Solid Waste Bureau; 505-827-2775; butch_tongate@nmenv.state.nm.us

NEW MEXICO SOIL AND WATER CONSERVATION COMMISSION

MSC APR P.O. Box 30005
Las Cruces, NM 88003-8005 United States
Phone: 505-646-2642 Fax: 505-646-1540
E-mail: acoleman@nmda-bubba.nmsu.edu

Founded: N/A
Membership: 1–100
Scope: State
Description: Policy making organization for soil and water conservation districts.
Keyword(s): Agriculture/Farming, Ecosystems (precious), Ethics/Environmental Justice, Forests/Forestry, Land Issues, Public Lands/Greenspace, Sprawl/Urban Planning, Water Habitats & Quality, Wildlife & Species
Contact(s):
Ron White, Division Director; P.O. Box 30005 MSC APR, Mexico Department of Agriculture, Las Cruces, NM 88003-8005; 505-524-6210; Fax: 505-524-6211
Ron White, Division Director

NEW MEXICO STATE UNIVERSITY

COOPERATIVE EXTENSION SERVICES
COLLEGE OF AG AND HOME ECONOMICS
Box 30003, Campus Box 3AG
Las Cruces, NM 88003 United States
Phone: 505-646-3748 Fax: 505-646-5975
E-mail: agdean@nmsu.edu
Website: www.cahe.nmsu.edu/ces/

Founded: N/A
Scope: State
Contact(s):
Billy Dickson, Associate Dean and Director CES; NM State University, Box 3AE, Las Cruces, NM 88003; 505-646-3015
Chris Allison, Extension Range Management Specialist; Box 3AE, NM State University, Las Cruces, NM 88003; 505-646-1944
Jon Boren, Extension Wildlife Specialist; Box 3AE, NM State University, Las Cruces, NM 88003; 505-646-1164; Fax: 505-646-1281
Ron Byford, Extension Department Head of Plant Sciences; Box 3AE, NM State University, Las Cruces, NM 88003; 505-646-2458
Ron Parker, Extension Department Head of Animal Resources; Box 3AE, NM State University, Las Cruces, NM 88003; 505-646-1709
Jerry Schickedanz, Dean and Chief Administrative Officer

NEW YORK COOPERATIVE FISH AND WILDLIFE RESEARCH UNIT

Department of Natural Resources, Fernow Hall, Cornell University
Ithaca, NY 14853 United States
Phone: 607-255-2839 Fax: 607-255-1895
E-mail: dnrcru-mailbox@cornell.edu
Website: www.dnr.cornell.edu

Founded: 1961
Scope: Local, State, Regional, National
Description: Primary purpose is field and laboratory research on management and conservation of a variety of fish and wildlife species, and graduate research training in fisheries and wildlife resources. Supported cooperatively by U.S. Geological Survey, Cornell University, New York State Department of Environmental Conservation, and the Wildlife Management Institute.
Publication(s): See publication website
Contact(s):
Mark Bain, Assistant Leader of Fisheries; 607-255-2840; mbb1@cornell.edu

Richard Malecki, Assistant Leader of Wildlife; 607-255-2836; ram26@cornell.edu
Milo Richmond, Leader; 607-255-2151; mer6@cornell.edu

NEW YORK DEPARTMENT OF AGRICULTURE AND MARKETS

1 Winners Cir.
Albany, NY 12235 United States
Phone: 518-457-3880 Fax: 518-457-3087
E-mail: info@agmkt.state.ny.us
Website: www.agmkt.state.ny.us

Founded: 1884
Membership: 101–1,000
Scope: State
Description: Promotes and regulates production, manufacturing, marketing, storing, and distribution of food. Supervises quality of plant materials, health of animals, and regulates dogs. Also, represents agricultural interests before NY Public Service Commission on siting of transmission lines and power plants.
Publication(s): Available on website
Keyword(s): Agriculture/Farming, Land Issues, Pollution (general), Public Health, Wildlife & Species
Contact(s):
Kim Blot, Director of Division of Agricultural Protection and Support
Robert Mungari, Director of Division of Plant Industry
Jessica Chittenden, Public Information Officer
Nathan Rudgers, Commissioner

NEW YORK DEPARTMENT OF AGRICULTURE AND MARKETS

STATE SOIL AND WATER CONSERVATION COMMITTEE
1 Winners Circle
Albany, NY 12235 United States
Phone: 518-457-3738 Fax: 518-457-3412
Website: www.agmkt.state.ny.us

Founded: N/A
Membership: 1–100
Scope: State
Publication(s): Newsletter - Down to Earth
Contact(s):
John Wildeman, Director; 518-457-3738; Fax: 518-457-1204
Philip Griffen, Chair; 28 Spook Hollow Rd., Stillwater, NY 12170; 518-664-5038

NEW YORK DEPARTMENT OF ENVIRONMENTAL CONSERVATION

625 Broadway 12th Fl.
Albany, NY 12233 United States
Phone: 518-474-2121 Fax: 518-402-9392
Website: www.dec.state.ny.us

Founded: 1970
Scope: State
Description: The mission of the New York State Department of Environmental Conservation is to conserve, improve, and protect its natural resources and environment, and control water, land and air pollution, in order to enhance the health, safety and welfare of the people of the state and their overall economic and social well-being.
Publication(s): Environmental Notice Bulletin
Contact(s):
Jim Austin, Special Projects; 518-485-8437
Frank Bifera, Deputy Commissioner and Counsel; 518-457-4415
Gordon Colvin, Marine Resources; 631-444-0430
Erin Crotty, Commissioner; 518-402-8540
Peter Duncan, Deputy Commissioner for Natural Resources; 518-457-0975
Fran Dunwell, Hudson River; 914-256-3017
James Ferreira, Assistant Commissioner of Office of Hearings and Mediation Services
Linda Frick, Special Assistant to the Commissioner; 518-457-0904
Carl Johnson, Deputy Commissioner Air and Waste Management
Thomas Kelly, Environmental Facilities Corporation; 518-402-6951
John Kelly, Adirondacks; 518-623-3671
Tom Kunkel, Special Projects; 718-482-4949
John McKeon, Assistant Commissioner for Office of Bond Act; 518-402-9401
Francis Sheehan, Natural Resources Planning; 518-457-4208
Susan Taluto, Assistant Commissioner for Administrative Services; 518-457-6533
James Tuftey, Assistant Commissioner for the Office of Public Protection
Fran Verdoliva, Salmon River; 315-298-7605

NEW YORK DEPARTMENT OF ENVIRONMENTAL CONSERVATION

DIVISION OF PUBLIC AFFAIRS AND EDUCATION
625 Broadway
Second Floor
Albany, NY 12233 United States
Phone: 518-402-8013
Website: www.dec.state.ny.us

Founded: N/A
Scope: State
Description: Public Affairs unit representing the New York State government department responsible for environmental quality and natural resource management programs.
Publication(s): Environmental Notice Bulletin, The New York State Conservationist.
Contact(s):
Laurel Remus, Director; 518-457-0840

NEW YORK DEPARTMENT OF ENVIRONMENTAL CONSERVATION

DIVISION OF SOLID AND HAZARDOUS MATERIALS
625 Broadway
Albany, NY 12232 United States
Phone: 518-402-8540
Website: dec.state.ny.us/website/dshm

Founded: N/A
Membership: N/A
Scope: State
Description: We regulate and monitor solid and hazardous waste facilities and generators of hazardous waste; control disposal of radioactive materials and use of pesticides; and promote sound management of wastes by communities, businesses and industries.
Contact(s):
Stephen Hammond, Director, Division of Solid & Hazardous Materials; 518-402-8651
Erin Crotty, Commissioner; 518-402-8540

NEW YORK DEPARTMENT OF ENVIRONMENTAL CONSERVATION

DIVISION OF WATER
50 Wolf Rd.
Albany, NY 12233 United States
Phone: 518-402-8233 Fax: 518-402-8230

Founded: N/A
Scope: State
Contact(s):
N. Kaul, Director; 518-457-6674

NEW YORK DEPARTMENT OF ENVIRONMENTAL CONSERVATION

REGIONAL DIRECTORS

Founded: N/A

Contact(s):

Stuart Buchanan, Region 5; Route 86, P.O. Box 296, Ray Brook, NY 12977; 518-897-1200
Raymond Cowen, Region 1; Bldg. 40, State University of New York, Stony Brook, NY 11794; 516-444-0354
John Hicks, Region 8; 6274 E. Avon-Lima Road, Avon, NY 14414; 716-226-2466
Mary Kris, Region 2; Hunters Point Plaza, Long Island City, NY 11101; 718-482-4900
Sandy Lebarron, Region 6; 317 Washington Street, Watertown, NY 13204; 315-785-2239
Kenneth Lynch, Region 7; 615 Erie Blvd., W, Syracuse, NY 13204; 315-426-7400
Gerald Mikol, Region 9; 270 Michigan Avenue, Buffalo, NY 14203; 716-851-7000
Marc Moran, Region 3; 21 S. Putt Corners Rd., New Paltz, NY 12561; 845-256-3000
Steve Schassler, Region 4; 11 North Westcott Road, Schenectady, NY 12306; 518-357-2234

NEW YORK DEPARTMENT OF HEALTH

Tower Bldg., Empire State Plaza
Albany, NY 12237 United States
Phone: 800-458-1158
Website: health.state.ny.us

Founded: N/A

Contact(s):

Ronald Trammontano, Director of Center for Environmental Health; 518-458-1158

NEW YORK GEOLOGICAL SURVEY AND STATE MUSEUM

Cultural Education Center
Albany, NY 12230 United States
Phone: 518-474-5816 Fax: 518-486-2034
Website: www.nysm.nysed.gov

Founded: 1836

Scope: State

Description: The Geological Survey and State Museum serves as a clearinghouse for information concerning bedrock and surficial geology within the state. The survey conducts regular mapping projects and investigations in basic, environmental, and applied geology and publishes maps and reports of investigations.

Publication(s): New York State Geogram, publications list of the New York State Geological Survey

Keyword(s): Energy, Land Issues, Oceans/Coasts/Beaches

Contact(s):

Richard Nyahay, Oil and Gas Office Director; 518-486-2161
Robert Fakundiny, State Geologist and Chief Scientist; 518-474-5816
Robert Fickies, Engineering and Environmental Geology, Geologic Information; 518-474-5810

NEW YORK STATE COOPERATIVE EXTENSION

New York State
College of Agriculture and Life Sciences, and Human Ecology
365 Roberts Hall, Cornell University
Ithaca, NY 14853-4203 United States
Phone: 607-255-2237 Fax: 607-255-2473
E-mail: cce@cornell.edu
Website: www.cce.cornell.edu/

Founded: N/A
Membership: 1–100
Scope: State

Keyword(s): Agriculture/Farming, Forests/Forestry, Reduce/Reuse/Recycle, Water Habitats & Quality, Wildlife & Species

Contact(s):

D. Ewert, Director of Cooperative Extension
Steve Brown, Sportfishing and Aquatic Resources Education; Director, Extension Associate, Dept. of Natural Resources, 120 Fernow Hall, Cornell University, Ithaca, NY 14853-3001; 607-255-9370
Tommy Brown, Human Dimensions Research Unit; Sr. Res. Assoc., Dept. of Natural Resources, 122B Fernow Hall, Cornell University, Ithaca, NY 14853-3001; 607-255-7695
Paul Curtis, Wildlife Management; Sr. Extension Associate, Dept. of Natural Resources, 114 Fernow Hall, Cornell University, Ithaca, NY 14853-3001; 607-255-2835; Fax: 607-255-2815
Gary Goff, Forestry/Wildlife; Extension Associate/Director Master Forest Owners/, COVERTS Volunteer Program, Dept. of Natural Resources, 104 Fernow Hall, Cornell University, Ithaca, NY 14853-3001; 607-255-2824
David Gross, Protected Area Planning and Management; Sr. Extension Associate & Environmental Program Leader, Department of Natural Resources, 112 Fernow Hall, Cornell University, Ithaca, NY 14853-3001; 607-255-2825
Marianne Krasny, Environmental/Conservation Youth Education; Associate Professor, Dept. of Natural Resources, 16 Fernow Hall, Cornell University, Ithaca, NY 14853-3001; 607-255-2827
Rebecca Schneider, Wetlands; Assistant Professor, Dept. of Natural Resources, 122C Fernow Hall, Cornell University, Ithaca, NY 14853-3001; 607-255-2110
Peter Smallidge, Forestry Resource Management; Sr. Extension Associate, Dept. of Natural Resources, 116 Fernow Hall, Cornell University, Ithaca, NY 14853-3001; 607-255-4696
R. Smith, Agriculture

NEW YORK STATE FISH AND WILDLIFE MANAGEMENT BOARD

625 Broadway
Albany, NY 12233 United States
Phone: 518-402-8924 Fax: 518-402-9027
E-mail: fwinfo@gw.dec.state.ny.us
Website: www.dec.state.ny.us

Founded: 1957

Scope: State

Description: Membership composed of sportsmen, landowners, and local government representatives. State and regional boards advise the Department of Environmental Conservation in programs designed to improve resource management by landowners and increase public access to private lands.

Keyword(s): Public Lands/Greenspace, Recreation/Ecotourism

Contact(s):

Emory Green, Chairman; 519 Rte. 247, Rushville, NY 14544; 716-554-3362
Lewis Nagy, Vice Chairman; Rte. 1, Box 271-A1, Glenfield, NY 13343; 315-376-3389
Clark Pell, Secretary; 50 Wolf Rd., Albany, NY 12233; 518-457-5420

NEW YORK STATE FISH AND WILDLIFE MANAGEMENT BOARD

REGION 3
2 Ridgeway
Goshen, NY 10924 United States
Phone: 914-294-9360

Founded: N/A

Contact(s):

Rudy Vallet, Board Chairman

State Government Agencies

NEW YORK STATE FISH AND WILDLIFE MANAGEMENT BOARD

REGION 4
1150 Westcott Rd.
Schenectady, NY 12306 United States
Phone: 518-357-2234 Fax: 607-547-8814

Founded: N/A

Scope: State

Contact(s):
Dean Winsor, Board Chairman

NEW YORK STATE FISH AND WILDLIFE MANAGEMENT BOARD

REGION 5
P.O. Box 123
Paradox, NY 12858 United States
Phone: 518-585-7250 Fax: 518-585-9799

Founded: N/A

Scope: State, Regional

Contact(s):
Don Sage, Board Chairman

NEW YORK STATE FISH AND WILDLIFE MANAGEMENT BOARD

REGION 6
Harrisville, NY 13648 United States
Phone: 315-543-2781 Fax: 315-543-2781

Founded: N/A
Membership: 1–100
Scope: State

Contact(s):
Kelley Dickinson, Board Chairman

NEW YORK STATE FISH AND WILDLIFE MANAGEMENT BOARD

REGION 7
NYSDEC
1285 Fisher Avenue
Cortland, NY 13045-1090 United States
Phone: 607-753-3095, ext. 298 Fax: 607-753-8532
E-mail: taphelps@gw.dec.state.ny.us

Founded: N/A
Membership: 1–100
Scope: Regional
Description: This board is an independent, grass-roots organization, consisting of representatives of landowners, sportsmen, and county legislatures from each county and appointed by each county in the state. Board members identify problems related to access, habitat management, and good landowner-sportsman relations in their local areas. They discuss and consider possible solutions to these problems at board meetings, and then seek to resolve them through meaningful action.
Keyword(s): Land Issues

Contact(s):
Craig Tryon, Board Chairman

NEW YORK STATE FISH AND WILDLIFE MANAGEMENT BOARD

REGION 8
6274 E. Avon-Lima Rd
Avon, NY 14414 United States
Phone: 585-226-5333 Fax: 585-226-3905

Founded: N/A
Membership: 1–100
Scope: Regional
Description: Deals with access and habitat related issues involving private lands.

Contact(s):
James Runyan, Board Chairman; 22 Woodland Park, Pine City, NY 14871-9006; 607-732-6397; jjrunyan@aol.com
Ron Schroder, Secretary; 6274 E. Avon-Lima RD, Avon, NY 14414; 585-226-5333; Fax: 585-226-3905; rlschrod@gw.dec.state.ny.us

NEW YORK STATE OFFICE OF PARKS, RECREATION AND HISTORIC PRESERVATION

Empire State Plaza Agency Bldg.1
Albany, NY 12238 United States
Phone: 518-474-0456 Fax: 518-486-2924
Website: www.nysparks.state.ny.us

Founded: N/A
Membership: 1,001–10,000
Scope: Regional
Description: Administers and operates 151 parks, park preserves, and recreational facilities, three arboretums, and 35 historic sites throughout the state; administers 15 heritage areas in partnership with local communities. Acquires and protects public lands and open space; coordinates athletic programs; develops environmental interpretive programs; maintains a field services bureau which oversees historic resources and National Historic Register entries; administers boating and snowmobiling laws.
Publication(s): New York State Operated Parks, New York State Boat Launching Sites, New York State Boater's Guide, Exploring New York's Past, Historic Sites and Their Programs.
Keyword(s): Ethics/Environmental Justice, Land Issues, Recreation/Ecotourism

Contact(s):
Anthony Ellis, Director of Law Enforcement; 518-474-0456
Wendy Gibson, Director of Public Affairs; 518-486-1868
Dominic Jacangelo, Director of Marine, Coastal, and Legislative Programs; 518-474-7336
Margaret Reilly, Regional Director Long Island Region; 631-669-1000
Winthrop Aldrich, Deputy Commissioner for Historic Preservation; 518-473-5385
Albert Caccese, Deputy Commissioner for Land Management; 518-474-0402
Bernadette Castro, Commissioner; 518-474-0443
Nancy Palumbo, Deputy Commissioner for Administration; 518-474-0430
Julia Stokes, Deputy Commissioner for Operations, Saratoga/Taconic/Palisad; 518-584-2000

NEWFOUNDLAND DEPARTMENT OF FOREST RESOURCES AND AGRIFOODS

ECOSYSTEM HEALTH DIVISION
P.O. Box 8700
St. John's, A1B 4J6 Newfoundland Canada
E-mail: info@gov.nf.ca
Website: gov.nf.ca/forest

Founded: N/A

Contact(s):
D. Fong, Director; 709-729-1804
J. Brazil, Senior Biologist, Endangered Species; 709-729-3773
C. Butler, Senior Biologist, Environmental/Land Use; 709-729-2543

NEWFOUNDLAND DEPARTMENT OF FOREST RESOURCES AND AGRIFOODS

INLAND FISH AND WILDLIFE DIVISION
Bldg. 810, Pleasantville, P.O. Box 8700
St. John's, A1B 4J6 Newfoundland Canada

Founded: N/A
Description: Objective is to maintain diverse and abundant wildlife populations and wildlife habitat; provide for the safe and sustainable use of wildlife, both consumptive and noncon-

State Government Agencies

sumptive; and help create a social environment conducive to effective wildlife conservation.

Publication(s): Newfoundland and Labrador Hunting and Trapping Guide, Endangered Species Poster and brochure series, Newfoundland and Labrador Hunter Education Manual (student and instructor editions)

Contact(s):

J. Hancock, Director; 709-729-2817
J. Blake, Manager of Conservation Services; 709-729-3509
R. Jarvis, Manager of Salmonier Nature Park and Environmental Education; 709-729-6974
M. Cahill, Chief of Wildlife Management Planning; 709-729-2548
L. Croke, Supervisor of Administration; 709-729-2636
K. Curnew, Chief of Inland Fish; 709-729-2540
R. Gulliver, Supervisor of Licencing; 709-729-2630
S. Mahoney, Chief of Research and Inventory; 709-729-3593
M. Mcgrath, Senior Biologist, Small Game; 709-729-0748
M. Vanzyll de Jong, Senior Biologist, Inland Fish; 709-729-4306

NEWFOUNDLAND DEPARTMENT OF FOREST RESOURCES AND AGRIFOODS

LEGISLATION AND COMPLIANCE DIVISION
P.O. Box 8700
St. Johns, A1B 4J6 Newfoundland Canada
Phone: 709-729-2647 Fax: 709-729-6108

Founded: N/A

Scope: State

Contact(s):

R. Whitten, Director; 709-729-2647

NEWFOUNDLAND DEPARTMENT OF FOREST RESOURCES AND AGRIFOODS

REGIONAL OFFICES
P.O. Box 2222
Gander, A1V 2N9 Newfoundland Canada
Phone: 709-256-1450 Fax: 709-256-1459

Founded: N/A

Membership: 1–100

Scope: State

Contact(s):

K. Colbert, Labrador Director, Goose Bay; 709-896-3405
David Fong, Eastern Director, Gander; 709-256-1451
A. Masters, Western Director, Corner Brook; 709-637-2370
D. Leboubon, Regional Compliance Manager; 709-896-2541
R. Trask, Regional Compliance Manager; 709-256-1461

NIAGARA ESCARPMENT COMMISSION

232 Guelph St.
3rd Floor
Georgetown, L7G 4B1 Ontario Canada
Phone: 905-877-5191 Fax: 905-873-7452
E-mail: nec@escarpment.org
Website: www.escarpment.org

Founded: 1973

Scope: State

Description: Maintains the Niagara Escarpment and land in its vicinity substantially as a continuous natural environment, and ensures that only such development occurs as is compatible with that natural environment. The commission was established under the Niagara Escarpment Planning and Development Act. In 1990, the Niagara Escarpment was designated a World Biosphere Reserve.

Publication(s): Explorer Brochures, Ontario Niagara Escarpment, Annual Reports.

Contact(s):

Mark Frawley, Director, ext. 224
Richard Murzin, Manager of Commission
Shannon Cassidy, Public Affairs Officer; webmaster@escarpment.org
Don Scott, Chair, ext. 222

NORTH CAROLINA COOPERATIVE EXTENSION SERVICE

North Carolina State University,
Raleigh, NC 27695 United States
Phone: 919-515-2811 Fax: 919-515-3135
Website: www.ces.ncsu.edu

Founded: N/A

Scope: State

Keyword(s): Agriculture/Farming, Wildlife & Species

Contact(s):

Ronald Hodson, Director of Sea Grant Program; Sea Grant, Box 8605, North Carolina State University, Raleigh, NC 27695; 919-515-2455; Fax: 919-515-7095; ronald_hodson@ncsu.edu
Jon Ort, Director of Extension Service; jon_ort@ncsu.edu
Peter Bromley, Wildlife Specialist; Zoology Dept., Box 7646, North Carolina State University, Raleigh, NC 27695; 919-515-7587; Fax: 919-515-5110; pete_bromley@ncsu.edu
Roger Crickenberger, Assistant Director and State Program Leader; NCSU, Box 7602, Raleigh, NC 27695-7602; 919-515-3252; Fax: 919-515-5950; roger_crickenberger@ncsu.edu
Harry Daniels, Aquaculture Specialist; Vernon James Research and Extension Center, 207 Research Station Rd., Plymouth, NC 27962; 252-793-4428; Fax: 252-793-5142; harry_daniels@ncsu.edu
Jeffrey Hinshaw, Extension Trout Specialist; Research and Extension Center, Box 9628, 2016 Fanning Bridge Rd., Fletcher, NC 28732-9216; 828-684-3562; Fax: 828-684-8715; jeff_hinshaw@ncsu.edu
Thomas Losordo, Aquaculture Specialist; Box 7646, North Carolina State University, Raleigh, NC 29695; 919-515-7587; Fax: 919-515-5110; tlosordo@unity.ncsu.edu
Chris Moorman, Extension Wildlife Specialist; North Carolina State University, Box 8003, Raleigh, NC 27695; 919-515-5578; Fax: 919-515-6883; chris_moorman@ncsu.edu
James Rice, Extension Fisheries Specialist; Box 7617, North Carolina State University, Raleigh, NC 27695; 919-515-4592; Fax: 919-515-5327; jim_rice@ncsu.edu

NORTH CAROLINA COOPERATIVE FISH AND WILDLIFE RESEARCH UNIT (USDI)

201 David Clark Lab
Raleigh, NC 27695 United States
Phone: 919-515-2631 Fax: 919-515-4454
Website: www.scsu.edu/nccoopunit

Founded: N/A

Membership: 1–100

Scope: State

Contact(s):

Tom Kwak, Unit Leader
Wendy Moore, Administrative Assistant

NORTH CAROLINA DEPARTMENT OF AGRICULTURE AND CONSUMER SERVICES

P.O. Box 27647
Raleigh, NC 27611 United States
Phone: 919-733-7125 Fax: 919-733-1141
Website: www.agr.state.nc.us

Founded: N/A

Membership: 1,001–10,000

Scope: State

Keyword(s): Agriculture/Farming, Land Issues, Pollution (general), Public Health

Contact(s):

Mike Blanton, Director; 919-733-4216
Jim Burnette, Pesticide Section Staff; 919-733-3556

Bill Dickerson, Plant Industry Division Staff; 919-733-3933
Tom Ellis, Aquaculture & Natural Resources Staff; 919-733-7125
Carl Falco, Structural Pest Staff; 919-733-6100
Cecil Frost, Plant Conservation Program Staff; 919-733-3610
David Marshall, Veterinary Services Staff; 919-733-7601
William McClelland, Pesticide Disposal Staff; 919-733-7366
David McLeod, Legal Staff; 919-733-7125
Richard Reich, Agronomic Services Staff; 919-733-2655
Carl Tart, Research Stations Staff; 919-733-3236
Bruce Williams, Food and Drug Protection Staff; 919-733-7366
Meg Phipps, Commissioner; 919-733-7125

NORTH CAROLINA DEPARTMENT OF ENVIRONMENT AND NATURAL RESOURCES

1601 Mail Services Center
Raleigh, NC 27699-1601 United States
Phone: 919-733-4984 Fax: 919-715-3060
E-mail: denr.csc@ncmail.net
Website: www.enr.state.nc.us

Founded: N/A
Membership: N/A
Scope: State
Description: The N.C. Department of Environment and Natural Resources (DENR) is the lead stewardship agency for the preservation and protection of North Carolina's natural resources. The organization administers regulatory and technical assistance programs designed to protect air quality, water quality, and the public's health. Through its natural resource divisions, DENR works to protect fish, wildlife and wilderness areas.
Keyword(s): Executive/Legislative/Judicial Reform
Contact(s):

Stanford Adams, Director of Forest Resources; 919-733-2162
Betsy Bennett, Director of Museum of Natural Sciences; 919-733-7450
Laura DeVivo, Director Legislative Affairs; 715-4189
Charles Fullwood,, Executive Director of Wildlife Resources Commission; 919-733-3391
Charles Gardner, Director of Land Resources; 919-733-3833
Beverley Hall, Acting Director of Division of Radiation Protection; 919-571-4141
Gary Hunt, Director of Office of Pollution Prevention; 919-715-4100
David Jones, Director of Zoological Park; 910-879-7102
Dexter Matthews, Director of Division of Waste Management; 919-733-4996
Phil McKnelly, Director of State Parks and Recreation; 919-733-4181
Donna Moffitt, Director of Coastal Management; 919-733-2293
John Morris, Director of Division of Water Resources; 919-733-4064
Preston Pate, Director of Division of Marine Fisheries; 919-726-7021
Don Reuter, Director of Public Affairs; 919-715-4112
Richard Rogers, Director of Open Spaces; 715-4152
Anne Taylor, Director of Office of Environmental Education; 919-733-0711
Greg Thorpe, Acting Director of Environmental Water Quality; 919-733-7015
David Vogel, Director of Soil and Water Conservation; 919-733-2302
Rhett White, Director of North Carolina Aquariums; 919-733-2290
Dempsey Benton, Chief Deputy Secretary; 919-733-4984
Melanie Buckingham, Librarian
Jimmy Carter, Assistant Secretary, Operations and Development; 919-733-4908
Dan Oakley, General Counsel; 919-715-4142
Bill Ross, Secretary; 919-715-4101
Robin Smith, Assistant Secretary for Planning/Policy; 919-715-4141

NORTH CAROLINA DIVISION OF SOIL AND WATER

STATE SOIL AND WATER CONSERVATION COMMISSION
1614 Mail Service Center
Raleigh, NC 27699-1614 United States
Phone: 919-733-2302 Fax: 919-715-3559
Website: www.dern.com

Founded: 1937
Membership: 1–100
Scope: State
Description: A unit of state government administered by the Division of Soil and Water Conservation in the Department of Environment and Natural Resources. To organize soil and water conservation districts; grant funds for operations, technical assistance, and the NC Agriculture Cost-Share Program for Nonpoint Source Pollution Control—a water quality program; provide for control of soil erosion and improvement of water quality; accept PL566 Small Watershed applications.
Contact(s):

David Vogel, Director; 919-715-6097; Fax: 919-715-3559; david.vogel@ncmail.net
James Ferguson, Chairman; 11571 Betsy Gap Rd., Clyde, NC 28721; 704-627-6458

NORTH CAROLINA WILDLIFE RESOURCES COMMISSION

1701 Mail Service Center
Raleigh, NC 27699-1701 United States
Phone: 919-733-3391 Fax: 919-733-7083
Website: www.ncwildlife.org

Founded: 1947
Membership: 101–1,000
Scope: State
Description: The commission has the function, purpose, and duty to manage, restore, develop, cultivate, conserve, protect, and regulate the wildlife resources of the state, and to administer the laws relating to boating, hunting, fishing, and other wildlife resources, including nongame.
Publication(s): Wildlife in North Carolina
Keyword(s): Agriculture/Farming, Ecosystems (precious), Forests/Forestry, Land Issues, Oceans/Coasts/Beaches, Public Lands/Greenspace, Recreation/Ecotourism, Water Habitats & Quality, Wildlife & Species
Contact(s):

Charles Fullwood, Executive Director
Carol Batker, Personnel Officer; 919-733-2241
David Cobb, Chief of Division of Wildlife Management; 919-733-7291
Cecilia Edgar, Deputy Director; 1702 Mail Service Center, Raleigh, NC 27699-1702; 919-733-3391, ext. 235; Fax: 919-715-2532; edgarcf@mail.wildlife.state.nc.us
Rodney Foushee, Editor, Wildlife in North Carolina; 919-733-7123, ext. 268; Fax: 919-715-2381; foushee.rodney@coned.wildlife.state.nc.us
Richard Hamilton, Chief Deputy Director; 919-733-3391, ext. 222; Fax: 919-733-7083; hamiltrb@mail.wildlife.state.nc.us
Fred Harris, Chief of Division of Inland Fisheries; 919-733-3633, ext. 275; Fax: 919-715-7643; harrisfa@mail.wildlife.state.nc.us
Roger Lequire, Chief of Division of Enforcement; 919-733-7191
Gordon Myers, Division of Engineering Services; 919-715-3155
John Pechmann, Commission Chairman; 910-483-0107
Wes Seegars, Commission Vice Chairman; 919-735-8211

Ginger Williams, Chief of Division of Conservation Education; 1712 Mail Service Center, Raleigh, NC 27699-1712; 919-733-7123, ext. 258; Fax: 919-715-2381; williams.ginger@coned.wildlife.state.nc.us

NORTH DAKOTA DEPARTMENT OF AGRICULTURE

600 E. Blvd. Ave., Department 602
Bismarck, ND 58505-0020 United States
Phone: 701-328-2231 Fax: 701-328-4567
Website: www.agdepartment.com

Founded: N/A
Membership: 1–100
Scope: State
Description: The North Dakota Department of Agriculture is the regulating and licensing agency for the agricultural industry in North Dakota.
Contact(s):
Roger Johnson, Commissioner; 701-328-2231; Fax: 701-328-4567; rojohnso@state.nd.us

NORTH DAKOTA DEPARTMENT OF HEALTH

600 E. Blvd. Ave.
Bismarck, ND 58506-5520 United States
Phone: 701-328-2372 Fax: 701-328-4727
Website: www.health.state.nd.us

Founded: N/A
Membership: 101–1,000
Scope: State
Description: State pollution control programs.
Keyword(s): Air Quality/Atmosphere, Ethics/Environmental Justice, Public Health, Reduce/Reuse/Recycle, Water Habitats & Quality
Contact(s):
Dennis Fewless, Director of Division of Water Quality; P.O. Box 5520, Bismarck, ND 58506-5520; 701-328-5210; Fax: 701-328-5200
L. David Glatt, Director of Division of Waste Management; P.O. Box 5520, Bismarck, ND 58506-5520; 701-328-5166; Fax: 701-328-5200
Jack Long, Director of Division of Municipal Facilities; P.O. Box 5520, Bismarck, ND 58506-5520; 701-328-5211; Fax: 701-328-5200
Terry O'Clair, Director of Divison of Air Quality
Francis Schwindt, Chief Environmental Health Section; P.O. Box 5520, Bismarck, ND 58506-5520; 701-328-5150; Fax: 701-328-5200

NORTH DAKOTA FOREST SERVICE

307 First St. E.
Bottineau, ND 58318-1100 United States
Phone: 701-228-5422 Fax: 701-228-5448
E-mail: forest@state.nd.us
Website: www.state.nd.us/forest

Founded: 1891
Membership: 1–100
Scope: State
Description: Mission Statement: Caring for, protecting, and improving forest resources for future generations.
Publication(s): Prairie Forester, The
Keyword(s): Forests/Forestry, Public Lands/Greenspace, Wildlife & Species
Contact(s):
Roy Laframboise, Towner Nursery Manager; 878 Nursery Rd., Towner, ND 58788; 701-537-5636; Fax: 701-537-5680
Thomas Berg, Staff Forester; 701-228-5483
Thomas Claeys, Sustainable Forestry Coordinator; 701-228-5486; Fax: 701-228-5448
Glenda Fauske, Information and Education Coordinator; 701-228-5446
W. Jackson Bird, Community Forestry Coordinator; 1511 E. Interstate Ave., Bismarck, ND 58501; 701-328-9945; Fax: 701-250-4454
Thomas Karch, State Forest Coordinator
Larry Kotchman, State Forester; 701-228-5422
Michael Santucci, Fire Management Coordinator; 1511 E. Interstate Ave., Bismarck, ND 58501; 701-328-9946

NORTH DAKOTA GAME AND FISH DEPARTMENT

100 N. Bismarck Expressway
Bismarck, ND 58501 United States
Phone: 701-328-6300 Fax: 701-328-6352
Website: www.discovernd.com/gnf/

Founded: N/A
Membership: 101–1,000
Scope: Regional
Publication(s): North Dakota Outdoors
Keyword(s): Recreation/Ecotourism, Wildlife & Species
Contact(s):
Dean Hildebrand, Director
Ray Goetz, Chief of Enforcement
Randy Kreil, Chief of Wildlife
Mike McKenna, Chief of Conservation & Communicaton
Roger Rostvet, Deputy Director; srrostvet@state.nd.us
Paul Schadewald, Chief of Administrative Services
Terry Steinwand, Chief of Fisheries
Harold Umber, Editor

NORTH DAKOTA PARKS AND RECREATION DEPARTMENT

1835 Bismarck Expressway
Bismarck, ND 58504 United States
Phone: 701-328-5357 Fax: 701-328-5363
E-mail: parkrec@state.nd.us
Website: www.ndparks.com

Founded: 1993
Membership: 1–100
Scope: State
Description: Plan and coordinate government programs encouraging the full development and preservation of existing and future parks, outdoor recreation areas, nature preserves, rare plant and animal species, and unique natural communities.
Publication(s): Discover Newspaper
Keyword(s): Land Issues, Public Lands/Greenspace, Wildlife & Species
Contact(s):
Douglass Prchal, Director
Kathy Duttenhefner, Coordinator of Nature Preserve/Natural Heritage Programs
Jesse Hanson, Coordinator of Planning and Natural Resources

NORTH DAKOTA STATE SOIL CONSERVATION COMMITTEE

4023 North State St., Suite 30
Bismarck, ND 58503-0620 United States
Phone: 701-328-5125 Fax: 701-328-5123
Website: www.ag.ndsu.nodak.edu/ndsscc/sscc

Founded: 1937
Scope: State
Description: To organize soil conservation districts and provide for control and prevention of soil erosion; represent the state in soil conservation matters; accept P.L. 566 Small Watershed applications and assign planning priority; and administer the Surface Mining Reports Law; and soil conservation technician grants program.
Keyword(s): Agriculture/Farming, Land Issues, Pollution (general), Water Habitats & Quality

Contact(s):
Thomas Christensen, Vice Chair; 7114 110th Ave. SE, Verona, ND 58490; 701-432-5685; ctomrun@yahoo.com
Keith Bartholomay, Member; 14618 57th St. SE, Sheldon, ND 58068; 701-882-3460; kbarth@mlgc.com
Lowell Disrud, Member; 1106 14th St. N, Fargo, ND 58102; 701-293-1505; lowell.disrud@ndsu.nodak.edu
Russell Fauske, Member; RR1, Box 143, Dunseith, ND 58329; 701-263-4742; rfranch@ndak.net
Dennis Reich, Member; 4181 82nd Ave. SW, Richardton, ND 58652; 701-878-4397; dreich@westriv.com
Carol Zuther, Member; 2921 19th Ave. SE, Martin, ND 58758; 701-693-2341; zuther@martin.ndak.net
Scott Hochhalter, Soil Conservation Specialist; 701-328-5125; Fax: 701-328-5123; shochhal@ndsuext.nodak.edu
Curtiss Klein, Chairperson; 6025 4th St. SE, Carrington, ND 58421; 701-984-2669; cklein@daktel.com

NORTH DAKOTA WATER COMMISSION
900 E. Blvd.
Bismarck, ND 58505-0850 United States
Phone: 701-328-2750 Fax: 701-328-3696
Website: www.water.swc.state.nd.us

Founded: 1905
Membership: 1–100
Scope: State
Description: State Agency: water rights, water development, floodplain management, dam safety.
Contact(s):
Dale Frink, State Engineeer

NORTHERN VIRGINIA REGIONAL PARK AUTHORITY
5400 Ox Rd.
Fairfax Station, VA 22039 United States
Phone: 703-352-5900 Fax: 703-273-0905
E-mail: info@nvrpa.org
Website: www.nvrpa.org

Founded: 1959
Scope: Regional
Description: To preserve open and wooded areas and provide outdoor recreation to meet the needs of a growing population.
Publication(s): Discover Your Regional Parks, Washington and Old Dominion Railroad Regional Park Trail Guide, Policy Plan, Calendar of Events
Keyword(s): Land Issues, Recreation/Ecotourism, Wildlife & Species
Contact(s):
Gary Fenton, Executive Director; 703-359-4605; gfenton@nvrpa.org
Walter Mess, Chairman

NOVA SCOTIA DEPARTMENT OF NATURAL RESOURCES
P.O. Box 698
Halifax, B3J 2T9 Nova Scotia Canada
Phone: 902-424-4103 Fax: 902-424-7735
Website: www.gov.ns.ca

Founded: N/A
Scope: State
Contact(s):
Harold Carroll, Director of Parks and Recreation
Nancy Leek, Director of Forestry; P.O. Box 68, Truro, Nova Scotia B2N 5B8; 902-893-5749; Fax: 902-893-5662
Ed Macaulay, Executive Director; 902-424-4103
Barry Sabean, Director of Wildlife; 136 Exhibition St., Kentville, Nova Scotia B4N 4E5; 902-679-6139; Fax: 902-679-6176
Bert Vissers, Manager of Wildlife Parks; P.O. Box 299, Shubenacadie, Nova Scotia B0N 2H0; 902-758-2040; Fax: 902-758-7011

NOVA SCOTIA DEPARTMENT OF NATURAL RESOURCES
LAND SERVICES BRANCH
Halifax, B3J 2T9 Nova Scotia Canada
Phone: 902-424-4267 Fax: 902-424-7735
E-mail: rcpenfou@gov.ns.ca
Website: www.gov.ns.ca/natr

Founded: N/A
Scope: State
Contact(s):
Jo-Ane Himmelman, Director Land Administration; 902-424-4267
Rosalind Penfound, Executive Director; 902-424-4267; rcpenfou.gov.ns.ca

NOVA SCOTIA DEPARTMENT OF NATURAL RESOURCES
REGIONAL SERVICES BRANCH
P.O. Box 698
Halifax, B3J 2T9 Nova Scotia Canada
Phone: 902-424-3949 Fax: 902-424-7735
Website: www.gov.ns.ca

Founded: N/A
Membership: 101–1,000
Scope: Regional
Contact(s):
Dan Eidt, Director of Crown Lands Management; 902-424-7594
Brian Gilbert, Executive Director; 902-424-3949
John Mombourquette, Director; 902-424-5254
Bill Smith, Director of Extension Services; 902-424-4445
Arden Whidden, Director of Private Lands Management; 902-424-5703

NOVA SCOTIA DEPARTMENT OF NATURAL RESOURCES CORPORATE SERVICE UNIT
CORPORATE SERVICE UNIT
P.O. Box 698
Halifax, B3J 2T9 Nova Scotia Canada
Phone: 902-424-5935 Fax: 902-424-7735
Website: www.gov.ns.ca

Founded: N/A
Membership: 1–100
Scope: State
Publication(s): Magazine - Nature's Resources
Contact(s):
Frank Dunn, Director of Finance; 902-424-3288
Susan Zinck, Information Officer; 902-424-2354

O

OFFICE OF ENERGY EFFICIENCY AND ENVIRONMENT
New York State Dept. of Public Service, 3 Empire State Plaza
Albany, NY 12223 United States
Phone: 518-473-7248

Founded: 1970
Description: The Office of Energy Efficiency and Environment provides staff support in developing and administering policies that assure appropriate consideration of energy efficiency and environmental protection in utility regulation, management, and restructuring. The office also plays a major role in the development of systems and procedures necessary to introduce retail competition in the state.
Keyword(s): Air Quality/Atmosphere, Energy, Land Issues, Reduce/Reuse/Recycle
Contact(s):
Paul Powers, Director

OHIO DEPARTMENT OF AGRICULTURE

8995 E. Main Street
Reynoldsburg, OH 43068 United States
Phone: 614-466-2732 Fax: 614-728-6226
Website: www.state.oh.us/agr

Founded: N/A
Membership: 101–1,000
Scope: Regional
Contact(s):
Mark Anthony, Communication Director; 614-752-4505
Fred Dailey, Director

OHIO DEPARTMENT OF DEVELOPMENT

OFFICE OF ENERGY EFFICIENCY
77 S. High St.
Columbus, OH 43215 United States
Phone: 614-466-6797 Fax: 614-466-1864
Website: www.odod.state.oh.us

Founded: 1979
Membership: 1–100
Scope: Regional
Description: The Office of Energy Efficiency, Ohio's state energy office, develops policies and programs that use energy efficiency and renewable energy to enhance economic benefits and better Ohio's environment.
Publication(s): 1999 Energy Efficiency Bookmark Contest Winners, Ohio's Home Weatherization Assistance Program (brochure), Ohio's Home Weatherization Assistance Program: An Independent Evaluation
Keyword(s): Air Quality/Atmosphere, Energy, Public Health, Reduce/Reuse/Recycle, Sprawl/Urban Planning, Transportation
Contact(s):
Tim Lenahan, Residential Programs; 614-466-8434; tlenahan@odod.state.oh.us
Bill Manz, Commercial/Industrial Programs; 614-466-7429; wmanz@odod.state.oh.us
Dawn Smith, Assistant Chief; 614-466-1835; dsmith@odod.state.oh.us
Stjepan Vlahovich, Education Programs; 614-466-0545; svlahovich@odod.state.oh.us
Sara Ward, Chief; 614-466-8396; sward@odod.state.oh.us

OHIO DEPARTMENT OF NATURAL RESOURCES

1930 Belcher Dr. Fountain Square
Bldg. D
Columbus, OH 43224-1387 United States
Phone: 614-265-6565 Fax: 614-261-9601
E-mail: dnrmail@dnr.state.oh.us
Website: www.ohiodnr.com

Founded: 1949
Membership: N/A
Scope: State
Description: The mission of the Ohio Department of Natural Resources is to ensure a balance between the wise use and protection of Ohio's natural resources for the benefit of all.
Publication(s): Wild Ohio
Keyword(s): Ecosystems (precious), Energy, Forests/Forestry, Land Issues, Oceans/Coasts/Beaches, Pollution (general), Public Lands/Greenspace, Recreation/Ecotourism, Reduce/Reuse/Recycle, Water Habitats & Quality, Wildlife & Species
Contact(s):
Samuel Speck, Director; 614-265-6875; Fax: 614-261-9601
J. Moody, Assistant Director; 614-265-6877
Lori Houpe, Deputy Director; 614-265-6845
David Pagnard, Chief of Office of Communications; 614-265-6787; Fax: 614-267-9165
Scott Zody, Deputy Director; 614-265-6845
Jim Lynch, Media Relations Mgr.; 614-265-6886; Fax: 614-268-1943
Ken Alvey, Acting Chief of Division of Watercraft; 614-265-6480
Paul Baldridge, Chief of Division of Real Estate and Land Management; 614-265-6395
Thomas Berg, Chief of Division of Geological Survey; 614-265-6576
Mike Budzik, Chief of Division of Wildlife; 614-265-6300
John Dorka, Chief of Division of Forestry; 614-265-6694
David Hanselmann, Chief of Division of Soil and Water Conservation; 614-265-6618
Ron Kolbash, Chief of Office of Recycling and Litter Prevention; 614-265-6333
Stu Lewis, Chief of Division of Natural Areas and Preserves; 614-265-6453
David Mackey, Chief of Office of Coastal Management; 1634 Sycamore Line Road, Sandusky, OH 44870-4132; 419-626-4670; Fax: 419-626-7983
Steve Manilla, Chief of Division of Engineering; 614-265-6948
Jim Morris, Chief of Division of Water; 614-265-6717
Mike Sponsler, Chief of Division of Mineral Resources Management; 614-265-6633
Terrie TerMeer, Acting Chief of Division of Civilian Conservation; 614-265-6423
Dan West, Chief of Division of Parks and Recreation; 614-265-6561
Michele Willis, Asst. to Director for Water and Great Lakes Issues; 614-265-6894

OHIO ENVIRONMENTAL PROTECTION AGENCY

122 South Front Street
Columbus, OH 43215 United States
Phone: 614-644-3020 Fax: 614-644-3184
Website: www.epa.state.oh.us

Founded: 1972
Membership: N/A
Scope: State
Description: The mission of the Ohio Environmental Protection Agency is to protect the environment and public health by ensuring compliance with environmental laws and demonstrating leadership in environmental stewardship. This state agency implements laws and regulations regarding air and water quality; solid, hazardous and infectious waste disposal; water quality planning; sewage treatment and public drinking water supplies; and cleanup of unregulated hazardous waste sites.
Keyword(s): Air Quality/Atmosphere, Oceans/Coasts/Beaches, Reduce/Reuse/Recycle, Water Habitats & Quality
Contact(s):
Christopher Jones, Director; 614-644-2782
John Albrecht, Chief of Data and Systems; 614-644-2990
Michael Baker, Chief of Division of Drinking and Ground Waters; 614-644-2752
Stuart Bruny, Chief of Southeast District Office; 740-385-8501
Bruce Coleman, Chief of Central District Office; 614-782-3778
Bonnie Crocket, Chief of Operations and Facilities; 614-644-2089
Al Franks, Chief of Strategic Management; 614-644-2782
Linda Friedman, Chief of Division of Environmental Services; 614-644-4247
Chris Geyer, Chief of Office of Fiscal Administration; 614-644-2339
Cindy Hafner, Chief of Division of Emergency and Remedial Response; 614-644-2924
Edwin Hammett, Chief of Northwest District Office; 419-352-8461
Daniel Harris, Chief of Division of Solid and Infectious Waste; 614-644-2621
Carol Hester, Chief of Public Interest Center; 614-644-2166
Robert Hodanbosi, Chief of Division of Air Pollution Control; 614-644-2270
Jacqueline Hymes, Chief of Equal Employment Opportunity; 614-644-3553
Mike Kelley, Chief of Office of Pollution Prevention; 614-644-3467
William Kirk, Chief of Office of Employee Services; 614-644-2100

Joseph Koncelik, Assistant Director; 614-644-2782
Patricia Madigan, Deputy Director of Policy; 614-644-2782
Lisa Morris, Chief of Division of Surface Water; 614-644-2001
Laura Powell, Deputy Director of Policy; 614-644-2782
Michael Savage, Chief of Division of Hazardous Waste Management; 614-644-2917
Bill Skowronski, Chief of Northeast District Office; 330-425-9171
Greg Smith, Chief of Division of Environmental and Financial Assistance; 614-644-2798
Edmund Tormey, Chief of Legal Affairs; 614-644-1037
Carolyn Watkins, Chief of Office of Environmental Education; 614-644-2873
Tom Winston, Chief of Southwest District Office; 937-285-6357

OHIO STATE UNIVERSITY EXTENSION

2120 Fyffe Rd.
Columbus, OH 43210 United States
Phone: 614-292-6181 Fax: 614-688-3807
Website: www.ag.ohio-state.edu/

Founded: N/A
Membership: 1–100
Scope: State
Description: To help people improve their lives through an educational process using scientific knowledge focused on identified issues and needs.
Contact(s):
Gary Mullins, Director of School of Natural Resources; Ohio State University, 210 Kottman Hall, 2021 Coffey Rd., Columbus, OH 43210; 614-292-2265; Fax: 614-292-7432; mullins.2@osu.edu
Keith Smith, Director of Extensions; smith.150@osu.edu
Erik Norland, Extension Specialist of Natural Resources; School of Natural Resources, 2021 Coffey Rd., Columbus, OH 43210; 614-292-6544; Fax: 614-292-7432; norland.1@osu.edu
Robert Roth, Associate Director of Environmental Education; School of Natural Resources, 207 Kottman Hall, 2021 Coffey Rd., Columbus, OH 43210; 614-292-2265; Fax: 614-292-7432; roth.3@osu.edu

OKLAHOMA BIOLOGICAL SURVEY

OKLAHOMA NATURAL HERITAGE INVENTORY
SUTTON AVIAN RESEARCH CENTER
ROBERT BEBB HERBARIUM
111 E. Chesapeake St., University of Oklahoma
Norman, OK 73019 United States
Phone: 405-325-4034 Fax: 405-325-7702
Website: www.biosurvey.ou.edu

Founded: 1927
Membership: N/A
Scope: State
Description: State office and organized research unit of university. Acquires information on biological resources and natural areas, conducts research on natural biota, jointly maintains Bebb Herbarium, has responsibility for Oklahoma Natural Heritage Inventory, and provides training for students. Jointly operates Oklahoma Fishery Research Laboratory with Oklahoma Department of Wildlife Conservation.
Keyword(s): Reduce/Reuse/Recycle, Wildlife & Species
Contact(s):
Steve Sherrod, Executive Director of Sutton Avian Research Center; G.M. Sutton Avian Research Center, P.O.Box 2007, Bartlesville, OK 74005-2007; 918-336-7778; Fax: 918-336-7783; gmsarc@aol.com
Caryn Vaughn, Director; 405-325-4034; Fax: 405-325-7702; cvaughn@ou.edu
Bruce Hoagland, Coordinator of Oklahoma Natural Heritage Inventory; 405-325-1985; Fax: 405-325-7702; bhoagland@ou.edu
Wayne Elisens, Interim Curator, Robert Bebb Herbarium; Dept. of Botany/Microbiology, 770 Van Vleet Oval, University of Oklahoma, Norman, OK 73019; 405-325-5923; Fax: 405-325-7619; elisens@ou.edu

OKLAHOMA CONSERVATION COMMISSION

2800 N. Lincoln Blvd., Suite 160
Oklahoma City, OK 73105 United States
Phone: 405-521-2384 Fax: 405-521-6686
E-mail: markh@okcc.state.ok.us
Website: www.okcc.state.ok.us

Founded: 1937
Membership: 1–100
Scope: Local, State
Description: To assist and supervise the state's 88 local conservation districts in carrying out conservation practices of all renewable natural resources.
Publication(s): Conservation Conversation Newsletter, Geographic Information Systems Newsletter.
Keyword(s): Agriculture/Farming, Land Issues, Pollution (general), Water Habitats & Quality
Contact(s):
Mike Thralls, Executive Director; 405-521-2384; Fax: 405-521-6686; miket@okcc.state.ok.us
Ben Pollard, Assistant Director; benp@okcc.state.ok.us
Lawrence Edmison, Director of Water Quality Division; larrye@okcc.state.ok.us
Mike Kastl, Director of Abandoned Mine Land Reclamation Program Division; mikek@okcc.state.ok.us
Lisa Knauf, Director of District Services Division; lisak@okcc.state.ok.us
Dan Sebert, Director of Conservation Programs Division; dans@okcc.state.ok.us
Mike Sharp, Director of Information Technology Division; mikes@okcc.state.ok.us
Mark Harrison, Information Officer; markh@okcc.state.ok.us
Terry Wyatt, Commission Board Chair

OKLAHOMA COOPERATIVE FISH AND WILDLIFE RESEARCH UNIT (USDI)

404 Life Sciences West Bldg., Oklahoma State University
Stillwater, OK 74078-3051 United States
Phone: 405-744-6342 Fax: 405-744-5006

Founded: 1948
Membership: 1–100
Scope: State, Regional, National, International
Description: Involved in graduate education in resource conservation.
Keyword(s): Wildlife & Species
Contact(s):
William Fisher, Assistant Leader, Ecology
David Leslie, Leader
Dana Winkleman, Assistant Leader, Fisheries

OKLAHOMA DEPARTMENT OF AGRICULTURE

P.O. Box 528804
Oklahoma City, OK 73152-8804 United States
Phone: 405-521-3864 Fax: 405-522-0909
Website: www.state.ok.us/~okag/

Founded: N/A
Membership: 101–1,000
Scope: State
Description: The Oklahoma Department of Agriculture is principally a service agency, but it is also a promotional and cooperative agency for segments of agriculture and forestry. Major divisions of the department are forestry, animal industry, legal, plant industry, marketing, water quality, agriculture laboratory, and the federal-state cooperative programs of wildlife services and agricultural statistics.
Keyword(s): Agriculture/Farming, Forests/Forestry, Pollution (general), Reduce/Reuse/Recycle

Contact(s):
Barry Bloyd, Director of Agricultural Statistics; 405-525-9226
Roger Davis, Director of Forestry Services; 405-521-3864
Burke Healey, Director of Animal Industry Services; 405-521-3864
Rick Maloney, Director of Market Development 414 Services
John Steuber, Director of Wildlife Services; 405-521-4039
Janet Stewart, Director of Legal Services
Mike Talkington, Director of Agricultural Laboratory
David Ligon, Administration Staff; 405-521-3864, ext. 220
Jack Carson, Information Officer; 405-521-3864, ext. 220
Lynn Davis, Assistant Director; 405-522-5486
Charles Freeman, Deputy Commissioner; 405-521-3864
Dennis Howard, Secretary of Agriculture

OKLAHOMA DEPARTMENT OF ENVIRONMENTAL QUALITY

1000 NE 10th St.
Oklahoma City, OK 73117-1212 United States
Phone: 405-271-8056
Website: www.deq.state.ok.us

Founded: N/A

Description: The Department of Environmental Quality is dedicated to providing quality service to the people of Oklahoma through comprehensive environmental protection and management programs. Those programs are designed to assist the people of the state in sustaining a clean sound environment and in preserving and enhancing our natural surroundings.

Publication(s): Clear View, Air Quality Annual Report, Superfund Program Sites Status Report, Certified Operator News Letter (Waterworks and Wastewater)

Keyword(s): Air Quality/Atmosphere, Pollution (general), Reduce/Reuse/Recycle, Water Habitats & Quality

Contact(s):
Ellen Bussert, Director of Public Information and Education; 405-271-8056
Larry Byrum, Director of Air Quality; 405-271-5220
H.A. Caves, Director of Waste Management; 405-271-5338
Mark Coleman, Executive Director; 405-271-8056
Jon Craig, Director of Water Quality; 405-271-5205
Judy Duncan, Director of Customer Services; 405-271-1400
Lawrence Gales, Director of Support Services; 405-271-8062
Larry McKee, Director of Complaints and Local Services; 405-271-7363
Steven Thompson, Deputy Executive Director; 405-271-8056
Bob Kellogg, General Counsel; 405-271-8056

OKLAHOMA GEOLOGICAL SURVEY

University of Oklahoma, Sarkeys Energy Center, 100 E. Boyd, Rm. N-131
Norman, OK 73019-0628 United States
Phone: 405-325-3031 Fax: 405-325-7069
Website: www.ou.edu/special/ogs-pttc/

Founded: 1908

Membership: 1–100

Scope: State

Description: To investigate and disseminate information on the geology of the state, with special reference to mineral resources and environmental issues. Investigations include: geologic mapping, evaluation of metallic and nonmetallic mineral deposits, and studies of earthquakes, groundwater, and fossil fuels, plus basic research and environmental studies.

Publication(s): Oklahoma Geology Notes, bulletins, circulars, guidebooks, geologic map series, educational publications series, hydrologic atlases

Keyword(s): Energy, Land Issues

Contact(s):
Charles Mankin, Director
Claren Kidd, Librarian; 100 E. Boyd, Rm. 220, Norman, OK 73019-0628
Connie Smith, Promotion and Information Specialist
Joyce Stiehler, Chief Publications Clerk; 405-360-2886; ogssales@ou.edu

OKLAHOMA STATE EXTENSION SERVICES

DIVISION OF AGRICULTURE
Oklahoma State University, Rm. 139, Agricultural Hall
Stillwater, OK 74078 United States
Phone: 405-744-5398 Fax: 405-744-5339
E-mail: securl@okstate.edu
Website: www.dasnr.okstate.edu

Founded: 1946

Scope: International

Description: Extension Forestry and Wildlife are a unit of the Oklahoma Cooperative Extension Service and the Department of Forestry, Division of Agricultural Sciences and Natural Resources, Oklahoma State University. The Department of Forestry provides accredited education in forest resources management, conducts forestry research through the Oklahoma Agricultural Experiment Station, and brings forest resources education to the citizens of Oklahoma through its extension efforts.

Publication(s): Oklahoma Renewable Resources newsletter, Natural Resources Speakers Bureau, Oklahoma Forest Industry bulletin.

Keyword(s): Forests/Forestry, Wildlife & Species

Contact(s):
Sam Curl, Director of Cooperative Extension Service
D. Coston, Associate Director for Oklahoma Agricultural Experiment
Kenneth Hitch, Assistant Extension Forester and Wildlife Specialist; Oklahoma State University, Rm. 008C, Agricultural Hall, Stillwater, OK 74078; 405-744-5442
Ronald Masters, Extension Wildlife Specialist; Oklahoma State University, Rm. 240, Agricultural Hall, Stillwater, OK 74078; 405-744-8065
Craig McKinley, Department Head of Forestry; Oklahoma State University, Rm. 011, Agricultural Hall, Stillwater, OK 74078; 405-744-5438

OKLAHOMA TOURISM AND RECREATION DEPARTMENT

15 N. Robinson
Oklahoma City, OK 73102 United States
Phone: 405-521-2409 Fax: 405-521-3992
Website: www.touroklahoma.com

Founded: 1972

Membership: 1–100

Scope: State

Description: To encourage residents and travelers to "Native America" as a vacation destination; and to develop human and natural resources for the purpose of promoting tourism, recreation, wildlife preservation, and environmental conservation. An annual industry conference is held each fall.

Publication(s): Oklahoma Today, Oklahoma Vacation Guide

Keyword(s): Public Lands/Greenspace, Recreation/Ecotourism, Wildlife & Species

Contact(s):
Jayne Jayroe, Cabinet Secretary and Executive Director; 405-521-2413
Betty Koehn, Director of Administration; 405-520-4031
John Ressmeyer, Director of State Parks; 405-521-4291
Doug Enevoldsen, Chief of Operations; 405-521-4678
Jeff Erwin, Resort Division
Joan Henderson, Publisher; 405-521-2496
Kristina Marek, Division of Planning and Development; 405-521-2973
Kathleen Marks, Division of Travel and Tourism; 405-521-3981
Amos Moses, Division of Human Resources; 405-522-4523

OKLAHOMA WATER RESOURCES BOARD

3800 N. Classen Blvd.
Oklahoma City, OK 73118 United States
Phone: 405-530-8800 Fax: 405-530-8900
Website: www.state.ok.us/~owrb

Founded: 1957
Membership: 1–100
Scope: State
Description: Promulgates water quality standards for state; lead agency in Clean Lakes Program; investigates pollution complaints; assesses water quality, quantity of groundwater, and stream water; issues permits for water use; administers dam safety, floodplain management programs, and plans for adequate supplies of good quality water for all beneficial uses; updates plans; administers financial assistance programs for water and wastewater systems.
Publication(s): The Well Drillers Log Newsletter, Oklahoma Water News
Keyword(s): Agriculture/Farming, Land Issues, Pollution (general), Water Habitats & Quality
Contact(s):
Duane Smith, Executive Director
Michael Melton, Assistant to the Director

OREGON DEPARTMENT OF AGRICULTURE

NATURAL RESOURCES DIVISION
635 Capitol St., NE
Salem, OR 97310-2532 United States
Phone: 503-986-4700

Founded: 1939
Membership: N/A
Scope: Local, State
Description: The Natural Resources Divisions mission is to conserve, protect, and develop natural resources on public and private land so agriculture will continue to be productive and economically viable. Primary program areas include Water Quality, Confined Animal Feeding Operations, Smoke Management, Land Use, Soil and Water Conservation Districts, Plant Conservation Biology and Shellfish.
Contact(s):
John Byers, Public Information/Outreach Specialist; 503-986-4700
Debbie Gorham, Administrator; 503-986-4700
Bob Graham, Advisory Member; Natural Resource Conservation Service, 101 SW Main St. Suite 1300, Portland, OR 97204-3221; 503-326-2751
Ray Jaindl, Assistant Administrator; 503-986-4700

OREGON DEPARTMENT OF ENVIRONMENTAL QUALITY (DEQ)

811 S.W. 6th Ave.
Portland, OR 97204 United States
Phone: 503-229-5696 Fax: 503-229-6124
Website: www.deq.state.or.us

Founded: 1969
Scope: State
Description: Our mission is to be an active leader in restoring, maintaining, and enhancing the quality of Oregon's air, water, and land.
Publication(s): Recycling Newsletter, Tankline, Beyond Waste
Keyword(s): Air Quality/Atmosphere, Pollution (general), Reduce/Reuse/Recycle, Water Habitats & Quality
Contact(s):
Langdon Marsh, Director; 503-229-5300
Rick Gates, Laboratory Administrator; 503-229-5983
Steve Greenwood, Western Region Administrator; 541-686-7838
Stephanie Hallock, Eastern Region Administrator; 541-338-6146
Michael Llewelyn, Water Quality Administrator; 503-229-5324
Neil Mullane, Northwest Region Administrator; 503-229-5372
Sally Puent, Intern

OREGON DEPARTMENT OF FISH AND WILDLIFE (ODFW)

2501 SW 1st Ave.
Portland, OR 97201 United States
Phone: 503-872-5310 Fax: 503-872-5302
E-mail: odfwinfo@state.or.us
Website: www.dfw.state.or.us

Founded: 1975
Scope: State
Description: Responsibilities include management of fish and wildlife resources and regulation of commercial and recreational harvest.
Publication(s): Oregon Wildlife
Contact(s):
Brian Alula, Director of Information Services; 503-872-5267
Lindsay Ball, Director
Carol Brown, Human Resources Division Director; 503-872-5262
Chip Dale, High Desert Region Director; 61374 Parrell Rd., Bend, OR 97702; 541-388-6363; Fax: 541-388-6281
Steve Denney, SW Region Director, Acting
Craig Ely, NE Region Director; 107 20th St., LaGrande, OR 97850; 541-963-2138; Fax: 541-963-6670
Dave McAllister, Habitat Division Director; 503-872-5255
Chris Wheaton, NW Region Director; 17330 SE Evelyn St., Clackamas, OR 97015; 503-657-2000; Fax: 503-657-2050
Wayne Rawlins, Manager of Business Services/Realty; 503-872-5310
Susan Adams Gunn, Information and Education
Ron Anglin, Deputy Director
Pat Wray, Editor; 7118 NE Vandenberg Ave., Corvallis, OR 97330; 541-757-4186; Fax: 541-757-4252

OREGON DEPARTMENT OF FORESTRY

2600 State St.
Salem, OR 97310 United States
Phone: 503-945-7200 Fax: 503-945-7212
Website: www.odf.state.or.us

Founded: 1911
Membership: 101–1,000
Scope: State
Description: The department is responsible for fire protection of 15.8 million acres of private and public forests; directs insect and disease management on 11 million acres of state and private forests; manages 789,000 acres of state-owned forests; provides forestry assistance to private forest landowners; enforces other Oregon forest laws; provides forestry information to schools, organizations, and individuals; and advises Governor and State Legislature on forestry matters.
Publication(s): Forest Log, The, The Oregon Forests Report (Annual), CommuniTree News (Quarterly)
Keyword(s): Forests/Forestry, Wildlife & Species
Contact(s):
Rick Gibson, Director of Fire Prevention; 503-945-7440
Cary Greenwood, Director of Public Affairs; 503-945-7420
Lanny Quackenbush, Director of Fire Protection; 503-945-7435
Wallace Rutledge, Director of Forestry Assistance; 503-945-7392
Gayle Birch, Board of Forestry
James Brown, Secretary; 503-945-7211
Dave Gilbert, Chairman
Ted Lorensen, Assistant State Foresters
Charlie Stone, Assistant State Forester of Forest Protection; 503-945-7205
Steve Thomas, Assistant State Foresters

Roy Woo, Deputy State Forrester; 801 Gales Creek Rd., Forest Grove, OR 97117-1199; 503-357-2191; Fax: 503-357-4548

OREGON DEPARTMENT OF TRANSPORTATION

Oregon Department of Transportation
1158 Chemeketa NE
Salem, OR 97301-2528 United States
Phone: 503-986-3477 Fax: 503-986-3524

Founded: N/A
Membership: 1–100
Scope: State
Description: ODOT avoids, minimizes and mitigates the environmental impacts of its highway construction and maintenance activities.
Keyword(s): Ethics/Environmental Justice, Forests/Forestry, Sprawl/Urban Planning, Transportation, Water Habitats & Quality, Wildlife & Species
Contact(s):

Lori Sundstrom, Environmental Services Section Manager; Oregon Department of Transportation, 1158 Chemeketa St., NE, Salem, OR 97310; 503-986-3477

OREGON FISH AND WILDLIFE DIVISION/DEPARTMENT OF STATE POLICE

400 Public Service Bldg.
Salem, OR 97310 United States
Phone: 503-378-3720 Fax: 503-363-5475
E-mail: first.last@state.or.us
Website: www.osp.state.or.us

Founded: N/A
Scope: State
Description: The Fish and Wildlife Division is charged with the enforcement of fish and game, commercial fish, shellfish, environmental protection laws, and all endangered species laws, rules, and regulations. Also provides general law enforcement services in rural areas. Provides law enforcement services on contract with the Oregon Department of Fish and Wildlife, the Department of Environmental Quality, and the Department of Forestry.
Publication(s): See publication website
Keyword(s): Recreation/Ecotourism, Wildlife & Species
Contact(s):

Lindsay Ball, C & D Director, Captain; 503-378-3720
D. Cleary, Staff of Commercial Fisheries; 503-378-3720
C. Kok, Staff of Wildlife; 503-378-3720
K. Allison, District I Supervisor of Portland, Or; 503-731-3027
J. Hunsaker, Aircraft Supervisor; 503-378-3720
S. Lane, District II Supervisor of Salem, Or; 503-378-2110
W. Markee, Special Investigations Unit Supervisor; 503-378-3387
S. Ross, District III Supervisor of Medford, Or; 503-776-6114
R. Scorby, District IV Supervisor of Baker City, Or; 503-523-5848

OREGON PARKS AND RECREATION DEPARTMENT

1115 Commercial St., NE, Suite 1
Salem, OR 97301–1002 United States
Phone: 503-378-6305 Fax: 503-378-6447
Website: www.oregonparks.org

Founded: 1921
Membership: 1–100
Scope: State
Description: To provide and protect outstanding natural, scenic, cultural, historic, and recreational sites for the enjoyment and education of present and future generations.
Keyword(s): Oceans/Coasts/Beaches, Recreation/Ecotourism, Water Habitats & Quality
Contact(s):

Michael Carrier, Director; 503-378-5019

OREGON STATE EXTENSION SERVICES

Oregon State University, 101 Ballard Extension Hall
Corvallis, OR 97331-3606 United States
Phone: 541-737-2713 Fax: 541-737-4423
Website: www.osu.orst.edu/extension/

Founded: N/A
Scope: State
Contact(s):

Lyla Houglum, Dean and Director
Deborah Maddy, Regional Director; 541-737-2711; deborah.maddy@orst.edu
Michael Stoltz, Regional Director; 541-737-2711; michael.stoltz@orst.edu
Peter Bloome, Associate Director; peter.bloome@orst.edu
William Braunworth, Extension Program Coordinator, Agriculture; Stag Hall, Room 138, Oregon State University, Corvallis, OR 97331; 541-737-4251; Fax: 541-737-3178; bill.braunworth@orst.edu
W. Edge, Natural Resources Information; 104 Nash Hall, Oregon State University, Corvallis, OR 97331-3803; 541-737-1953; Fax: 541-737-3590
A. Reed, Program Leader, Forestry; 119 Peavy Hall, Oregon State University, Corvallis, OR 97331; 541-737-3700; Fax: 541-737-3008

OREGON WATER RESOURCES DEPARTMENT

158 12th St., NE
Salem, OR 97301-4172 United States
Phone: 503-378-8455 Fax: 503-378-2496
Website: www.wrd.state.or.us

Founded: N/A
Membership: 101–1,000
Scope: State
Description: The Water Resources Department is the steward of the state's water resources. The agency enforces state water laws and policies; promotes actions that restore and protect streamflows and watersheds in order to ensure the long-term sustainability of Oregon's ecosystems, economy, and quality of life; addresses water supply needs; and increases the understanding of the resource and the demands on it.
Contact(s):

Paul Cleary, Director; 503-378-2982
Dick Bailey, Administrator of Water Rights and Adjudications; 503-378-8455
Bruce Moyer, Administrator of Administrative Services Division; 503-378-8455
Barry Norris, Administrator of Technical Services Division; 503-378-8455
Tom Paul, Administrator of Field Services Division; 503-378-8455

P

PENNSYLVANIA COOPERATIVE FISH AND WILDLIFE RESEARCH UNIT

UNITED STATES GEOLOGICAL SURVEY
BIOLOGICAL RESOURCES DIVISION
Merkle Bldg., Pennsylvania State University
University Park, PA 16802 United States
Phone: 814-865-4511 Fax: 814-863-4710
E-mail: klc2@psu.edu
Website: pacfwru.cas.psu.edu

Founded: 1938
Membership: 1–100
Scope: National
Description: Established as a cooperative activity among Pennsylvania State University, Pennsylvania Fish and Boat Commission, Wildlife Management Institute, Pennsylvania Game Commission, and the Department of the Interior. Areas of research are: The effects of natural and manmade forces on aquatic and terrestrial ecosystems, animal-habitat interactions,

State Government Agencies

acid precipitation effects, fish and wildlife management, and health profiles of game animals. Graduate training is also provided.

Publication(s): Annual Report available on request.

Contact(s):
Robert Carline, Leader; f7u@psu.edu
Duane Diefenbach, Assistant Leader for Wildlife; drd11@psu.edu
Erin Snyder, Assistant Unit Leader for Fisheries; ems19@psu.edu

PENNSYLVANIA DEPARTMENT OF AGRICULTURE

REGION I
13410 Dunham Rd. Region 1
Meadville, PA 16335 United States
Phone: 814-332-6890 Fax: 814-333-1431
Website: www.tda.state.pa.us

Founded: N/A
Membership: 1–100
Scope: State

Contact(s):
George Gregg, Director

PENNSYLVANIA DEPARTMENT OF AGRICULTURE

REGION II
542 County Farm Rd., Suite 102
Montoursville, PA 17754-9685 United States
Phone: 570-433-2640 Fax: 570-433-4770
Website: www.pda.state.pa.us

Founded: N/A
Scope: State

Contact(s):
Dean Ely, Director

PENNSYLVANIA DEPARTMENT OF AGRICULTURE

REGION III
Rt. 92 South, P.O. Box C
Tunkhannock, PA 18657 United States
Phone: 570-836-2181 Fax: 570-836-6266

Founded: N/A
Membership: 1–100
Scope: State

Contact(s):
Russell Gunton, Director

PENNSYLVANIA DEPARTMENT OF AGRICULTURE

REGION IV
5349 William Flynn Hwy.
Gibsonia, PA 15044 United States
Phone: 724-443-1585 Fax: 724-443-8150

Founded: N/A
Membership: 1–100
Scope: Local

Contact(s):
R. Nehrig, Director

PENNSYLVANIA DEPARTMENT OF AGRICULTURE

REGION V
1307 7th St.
Altoona, PA 16601-4701 United States
Phone: 814-946-7315 Fax: 814-946-7354

Founded: N/A
Scope: Regional

Contact(s):
Kenneth Mowry, Director

PENNSYLVANIA DEPARTMENT OF AGRICULTURE

REGION VI
P.O. Box 419
Summerdale, PA 17093 United States
Phone: 717-728-2570
Website: www.pda.state.pa.us/

Founded: N/A

Contact(s):
Sam Hayes, Secretary

PENNSYLVANIA DEPARTMENT OF AGRICULTURE

REGION VII
P.O. Box 300
Creamery, PA 19430 United States
Phone: 610-489-1003 Fax: 610-489-6119
E-mail: pstarr@state.pa.us
Website: www.pda.state.pa.us

Founded: N/A
Membership: 1–100
Scope: Regional

Contact(s):
Frank Stearns, Director

PENNSYLVANIA DEPARTMENT OF AGRICULTURE STATE CONSERVATION COMMISSION

STATE CONSERVATION COMMISSION
2301 N. Cameron St.
Harrisburg, PA 17110-9408 United States
Phone: 717-787-8821 Fax: 717-705-3778
E-mail: kbrown@state.pa.us
Website: www.pascc.org

Founded: 1945
Membership: 1–100
Scope: State

Description: To establish policy for Pennsylvania's 66 local conservation districts. Programs administered by the commission include: a $2,850,000 annual grant program, which provides funds to conservation districts for the employment of managerial and technical staff; a $5.2 million annual Chesapeake Bay Program, which provides technical and financial assistance to farmers to install soil conservation and nutrient management practices, and more.

Publication(s): Highlights Newsletter

Keyword(s): Agriculture/Farming, Land Issues

Contact(s):
Karl Brown, Executive Secretary; Fax: 717-705-3778; kbrown@agric.state.us

PENNSYLVANIA DEPARTMENT OF CONSERVATION AND NATURAL RESOURCES

7th Floor
Rachel Carson State Office Bldg.
Harrisburg, PA 17105-8551 United States
Phone: 717-787-2869 Fax: 717-705-2832
Website: www.dcnr.state.pa.us

Founded: 1995
Scope: State

Description: To maintain and preserve state parks; to manage state forest lands to assure their long-term health, sustainability and economic use; to provide information on Pennsylvania's ecological and geologic resources; and to administer grant and technical assistance programs that will benefit river conservation, trails and greenways, local recreation, regional heritage conservation and environmental education programs across Pennsylvania.

Publication(s): Resource, Become a Conservation Volunteer, Discover DCNR, Penn's Woods, PA State Park Recreation Guide

Keyword(s): Forests/Forestry, Land Issues, Public Lands/Greenspace, Recreation/Ecotourism, Reduce/Reuse/Recycle, Wildlife & Species

Contact(s):

Damon Anderson, Director of Information Technology; 717-783-9732
Frederick Carlson, Director of Policy
Eugene Comoss, Director, Bureau of Facility Design and Construction; 717-787-7398
Dana Datres, Director, Bureau of Administrative Services; 717-787-2362
Joan Dlippinger, Director of Environmental Education; 717-705-2862
Dennis Farley, Director, Bureau of Personnel; 717-787-5496
Roger Fickes, Director, Bureau of State Parks; 717-787-6640
James Grace, Director, Bureau of Forestry; 717-787-2703
Kurt Leitholf, Executive Director, Conservation and Natural Resources; 8th Fl., Rachel Carson State Office Bldg., P.O. Box 8773, Harrisburg, PA 17105-8773; 717-705-0031
Jay Parrish, Director of Dept. of Topographic & Geological Survey
Geralyn Umstead, Director of Community Relations; 717-772-9087
Larry Williamson, Director, Bureau of Recreation and Conservation; 717-783-2658
Karen Deklinski, Deputy Secretary for Administration; 717-772-9100
Joseph Graci, Legislative Liaison; 717-772-9101
Sally Just, Senior Advisor to Secretary; 717-787-2869
Gretchen Leslie, Press Secretary; 717-772-9101
John Oliver, Secretary; 717-787-2869
John Plonski, Executive Deputy Secretary for Parks and Forestry; 717-772-9104
William Shakely, Chief Counsel; 717-772-4171
Richard Sprenkle, Deputy Secretary for Conservation and Engineering Services; 717-787-9306

PENNSYLVANIA DEPARTMENT OF ENVIRONMENTAL PROTECTION

P.O. Box 2063
Harrisburg, PA 17105-2063 United States
Phone: 717-787-2815 Fax: 717-705-4980
Website: www.dep.state.pa.us

Founded: 1995

Scope: State

Description: The Department of Environmental Protection's mission is to protect Pennsylvania's air, land, and water from pollution and to provide for the health and safety of its citizens through a cleaner environment. We will work as partners with individuals, organizations, governments, and businesses to prevent pollution and restore our natural resources.

Keyword(s): Land Issues, Public Health.

Contact(s):

Christopher Allen, Acting Director of Local Government Relations; 717-787-9580
Irene Brooks, Office for River Basin Cooperation Executive Director; 717-772-4785
Larry Brown, Director, Bureau of Network Operations; 717-772-5909
Michael Conway, Director, Bureau of Waterways Engineering; 717-787-3411
James Erb, Director, Bureau of Oil and Gas Management; 717-772-2199
Roderick Fletcher, Director, Bureau of Abandoned Mine Reclamation; 717-783-2267
Ronald Flory, Director, Bureau of Fiscal Management; 717-787-1319
Stuart Gansell, Director, Bureau of Watershed Conservation; 717-787-5267
Jeffrey Jarrett, Director, District Mining Operations; 724-942-7204
Richard Mather, Director, Bureau of Regulatory Counsel; 717-787-7060
Gary Niland, Director, Bureau of Investigations; 717-787-0453
Helen Olena, Director of Environmental Education; 717-772-1828
Jay Roberts, Director, Bureau of Mining and Reclamation; 717-787-5103
James Salvaggio, Director, Bureau of Air Quality; 717-787-9702
Barbara Sexton, Director, The Policy Office; 717-783-8727
James Snyder, Director, Bureau of Land Recycling and Waste Management; 717-783-2388
Richard Stickler, Director, Bureau of Deep Mine Safety; 724-439-7469
Robert Barkanic, Deputy Secretary for Pollution Prevention and Compliance; 717-783-0540
Michael Bedrin, Chief Counsel; 717-787-4449
Denise Chamberlain, Deputy Secretary for Air, Recycling and Radiation Protection; 717-772-2724
Robert Dolence, Deputy Secretary for Mineral Resources Management; 717-783-5338
Terry Fabian, Deputy Secretary for Field Operations; 717-787-5028
Kenwood Giffhorn, Deputy Secretary for Management and Technical Services; 717-787-7116
David Hess, Executive Deputy Secretary; 717-772-1856
Gregory Mahon, Legistlative Liaison; 717-783-8303
Kimberly Nelson, Chief Information Officer; 717-772-0801
James Seif, Secretary; 717-787-2814
Lawrence Tropea, Deputy Secretary for Water Management; 717-787-4686
Donald Welsh, Deputy Secretary for Federal/State Relations; 717-783-1566

PENNSYLVANIA FISH AND BOAT COMMISSION

P.O. Box 67000
Harrisburg, PA 17106-7000 United States
Phone: 717-705-7800 Fax: 717-705-7802
Website: www.fish.state.pa.us

Founded: 1866

Scope: State

Description: To conduct and support public education and information efforts related to aquatic resource protection, improvement, and management programs, and enhance public understanding of the wise and safe use of our fishing and boating resources.

Publication(s): Pennsylvania Angler and Boater

Keyword(s): Recreation/Ecotourism, Water Habitats & Quality, Wildlife & Species

Contact(s):

Ted Keir, President
Leon Reed, Vice President
Peter Colangelo, Executive Director; 717-657-4515
Delano Graff, Director of Bureau of Fisheries; 814-359-5169
Dennis Guise, Deputy Executive Director/Chief Counsel; 717-657-4525
Thomas Kamerzel, Director of Bureau of Law Enforcement; 717-657-4542
Wasyl Polischuk, Director of Bureau of Administration Services; 717-657-4522
John Simmons, Director of Bureau of Boating and Education; 717-657-4538
Ted Walke, Art Director; 717-564-6846
James Young, Director of Bureau of Engineering and Development; 814-359-5152
Thomas Ford, Planning Coordinator; 717-657-4394

Joseph Greene, Legislative Liaison; 717-657-4517
Arthur Michaels, Editor; 717-657-4520

PENNSYLVANIA FISH AND BOAT COMMISSION

BUREAU OF LAW ENFORCEMENT
NORTHCENTRAL REGION HEADQUARTERS
466 Robinson Ln.
P.O.Box 5306
Pleasant Gap, PA 16823 United States
Phone: 814-359-5250 Fax: 814-359-5254
E-mail: ra-ncregion@state.pa.us
Website: www.fish.state.pa.us

Founded: 1866
Membership: 1–100
Scope: Regional
Description: Regional headquarters for agency's law enforcement staff and field operations in a 14 county area of NC Pennsylvania - Cameron, Centre, Clearfield, Clinton, Elk, Jefferson, Lycoming, McKean, Montour, Northumberland, Potter, Snyder, Tioga & Union.
Contact(s):
Gerald Barton, Assistant Manager; 814-359-5250; Fax: 814-359-5254; ra-ncregion@state.pa.us
Brian Burger, Region Manager; 814-359-5250; Fax: 814-359-5254; ra-ncregion@state.pa.us
Barbara Walker, Office Administrator; 814-359-5250; Fax: 814-359-5254; ra-ncregion@state.pa.us

PENNSYLVANIA FISH AND BOAT COMMISSION

REGION 1, NORTHWEST
11528 State Highway 98
Meadville, PA 16335 United States
Phone: 814-337-0444 Fax: 814-337-0579
Website: www.fish.state.pa.us

Founded: N/A
Membership: 1–100
Scope: State
Contact(s):
Frank Parise, Asistant Regional Manager
Gary Deiger, Law Enforcement Supervisor
Robert Nestor, Assistant Regional Manager

PENNSYLVANIA FISH AND BOAT COMMISSION

REGION 2 SOUTHWEST
236 Lake Rd. Region 2 SW
Somerset, PA 15501-1644 United States
Phone: 814-445-8974 Fax: 814-445-3497
E-mail: pfbcsw1@twd.net
Website: www.fish.state.pa.us

Founded: N/A
Membership: 1–100
Scope: Regional
Contact(s):
Rick Lorson, Area Fisheries Biologist
Emil Svetahor, Law Enforcement Supervisor; 814-445-3554
Dennis Tubbs, Aquatic Resource Program Specialist; 814-443-9841

PENNSYLVANIA FISH AND BOAT COMMISSION

REGION 3 NORTHEAST
P.O. Box 88
Sweet Valley, PA 18656-0008 United States
Phone: 570-477-5717 Fax: 570-477-3221
E-mail: pfbcne1@ptd.net
Website: www.pda.state.pa.us

Founded: N/A
Contact(s):
Kerry Messerle, Law Enforcement Supervisor

PENNSYLVANIA FISH AND BOAT COMMISSION

REGION 4, SOUTHEAST
Box 9
Brubaker Valley Road & Lakeview Drive
Elm, PA 17521-0009 United States
Phone: 717-626-0228 Fax: 717-626-0486
Website: www.fish.state.pa.us

Founded: N/A
Membership: 1–100
Scope: Regional
Description: Region Law Enforcement Office

PENNSYLVANIA FISH AND BOAT COMMISSION

REGION 6 SOUTHCENTRAL
1704 Pine Rd.
Newville, PA 17241-9544 United States
Phone: 717-486-7087 Fax: 717-486-8227
E-mail: psbcsc1@epix.net
Website: www.fish.state.pa.us

Founded: N/A
Scope: State
Publication(s): Pennsylvania Angler & Boater Magazine
Contact(s):
George Geisler, Regional Manager Southcentral; 1704 Pine Rd., Newville, PA 17241

PENNSYLVANIA FISH AND BOAT COMMISSION: REGION 1

REGION 1, NORTHWEST,
11528 State Highway 98
Meadville, PA 16335 United States
Phone: 814-337-0444 Fax: 814-337-0579
Website: www.fish.state.pa.us

Founded: N/A
Membership: 1–100
Scope: State
Contact(s):
Gary Deiger, Regional Manager; 814-337-0444; gdeiger@state.pa.us

PENNSYLVANIA FISH AND BOAT COMMISSION: REGION 2

REGION 2 SOUTHWEST
236 Lake Rd. Region 2 SW
Somerset, PA 15501-1644 United States
Phone: 814-445-8974 Fax: 814-445-3497
Website: www.fish.state.pa.us

Founded: N/A
Scope: Regional
Contact(s):
Emil Svetahor, Contact

PENNSYLVANIA FISH AND BOAT COMMISSION: REGION 3

REGION 3 NORTHEAST
Sweet Valley, PA 18656-0008 United States
Phone: 570-477-5717 Fax: 570-477-3221
Website: www.fish.state.pa.us

Founded: N/A
Membership: 1–100
Scope: State

PENNSYLVANIA FISH AND BOAT COMMISSION: REGION 6

SOUTHCENTRAL REGION
1704 Pine Rd.
Newville, PA 17241-9544 United States
Phone: 717-486-7087 Fax: 717-486-8227
Website: www.fish.state.pa.us

Founded: N/A
Membership: 1–100
Scope: Regional
Contact(s):
George Geisler, Regional Manager

PENNSYLVANIA FOREST STEWARDSHIP PROGRAM

DCNR-BUREAU OF FORESTRY
DCNR, Bureau of Forestry
P.O. Box 8552
400 Market Street
Harrisburg, PA 17105-8552 United States
Phone: 717-787-2106 Fax: 717-783-5109
E-mail: godato@state.pa.us
Website: dcnr.state.pa.us

Founded: 1990
Membership: 1,001–10,000
Scope: State, Regional
Description: To educate Pennsylvania forest landowners and citizens about the importance of sound forest management and the need to conserve our forest resources for future generations through wise use today. Works in conjunction with the Stewardship Incentive Program, which provides cost-share assistance to landowner's forest management practices.
Publication(s): Forest Stewardship Bulletin Series
Keyword(s): Forests/Forestry, Land Issues, Wildlife & Species
Contact(s):
James Grace, Director
Gene Odato, Chief of Stewardship & Education Program

PINE BLUFF COOPERATIVE FISHERY RESEARCH PROJECT

USGS-BRG-University of Arkansas
Ag. Exp. Station, 1200 N. University
P.O. Box 4005
Pine Bluff, AR 71611-2799 United States
Phone: 501-543-8165

Founded: N/A
Description: The Pine Bluff Cooperative Fishery Research Project is a cooperative educational effort between the U.S. Geological Survey-Biological Resources Division, Cooperative Research Units Division, and the University of Arkansas - Pine Bluff. The project provides undergraduate training in fisheries science and biology and conducts research on environmental problems, fisheries, and related topics.
Keyword(s): Water Habitats & Quality, Wildlife & Species
Contact(s):
Steve Lochmann, Project Leader

PRINCE EDWARD ISLAND DEPARTMENT OF FISHERIES, AQUACULTURE AND ENVIRONMENT

P.O. Box 2000
Charlottetown, C1A 7N8 Prince Edward Island Canada
Phone: 902-368-5000 Fax: 902-368-5830
Website: www.gov.pe.ca

Founded: N/A
Scope: State
Description: To work with individuals, businesses, groups and communities to protect, enhance and enjoy in a sustainable way the province's environment and natural resources.
Publication(s): Tracks in the Snow, Our Land and Water, The Bald Eagle in Prince Edward Island, Wildlife Policy, Patterns of the Pond
Contact(s):
Arthur Smith, Director of Fish and Wildlife Division; 902-368-6083
Clare Birch, Firearm Safety Coordinator; 902-368-4686
Lewie Creed, Deputy Minister; 902-368-5340
Rosemary Curley, Habitat and Natural Areas Biologist; 902-368-4807
Randall Dibblee, Waterfowl and Furbearer Biologist; 902-368-4666
Chester Gillan, Minister; 902-368-4863
Gerald MacDougall, Head of Investigations and Enforcement; 902-368-4808
Alan McLennan, Eastern Habitat Joint Venture Coordinator

PUERTO RICO DEPARTMENT OF AGRICULTURE

Box 10163
Santurce, PR 00908-1163 United States
Phone: 787-721-2120 Fax: 787-722-0291
Website: www.nass.usda.gov/pr/de_ag_PR.htm

Founded: N/A
Contact(s):
Brenda Marrero, Executive Secretary

PUERTO RICO DEPARTMENT OF NATURAL AND ENVIRONMENTAL RESOURCES

P.O. Box 5887, Puerta de Tierra Sta.
San Juan, PR 00906 United States
Phone: 787-724-8774 Fax: 787-723-3090
E-mail: reglamentos@drna.gobierno.pr
Website: www.drna.gobierno.pr

Founded: 1973
Description: To develop, protect, manage, evaluate, and administer the natural resources of Puerto Rico; and to derive maximum public benefits.
Keyword(s): Forests/Forestry, Wildlife & Species
Contact(s):
Salvador Salas, Secretary; 787-723-3090; ssalas@drna.gobierno.pr

PURDUE UNIVERSITY EXTENSION SERVICES

1140 Agriculture Administration Bldg., Purdue University
West Lafayette, IN 47907-1140 United States
Phone: 888-398-4636 Fax: 765-494-5876
E-mail: extension@ces.purdue.edu
Website: www.ces.purdue.edu/

Founded: N/A
Contact(s):
David Petritz, Director, Cooperative Extension Service; david.petritz@ces.purdue.edu
Janet Ayres, Program Leader, Leadership and Community Development; 765-494-4215; ayres@agecon.purdue.edu
Linda Chezem, Program Leader, 4-H/Youth; 765-494-8422; lchezem@.four-h.purdue.edu
Brian Miller, Wildife Specialist and Sea Grant Coordinator; Purdue Univ., 1159 Forestry Building, West Lafayette, IN 47907-1159; 765-494-3586; Fax: 765-496-2422

R

RESOURCES AGENCY, THE

1416 9th St., Rm. 1311
Sacramento, CA 95814 United States
Phone: 916-653-5656 Fax: 916-653-8102
Website: www.resources.ca.gov

Founded: N/A
Scope: State
Description: Responsible for ensuring an adequate and properly balanced management of government functions related to California's natural environment.
Contact(s):
Jennifer Galehause, Deputy Secretary for Legislative Affairs
Margaret Kim, General Counsel
Mary Nicholas, Secretary of Resources
Michael Sweeney, Under Secretary of Resources

Don Wallace, Assistant Secretary of Administration and Finance
Stanley Young, Communication Director Public Information

RESOURCES AGENCY, THE
CALIFORNIA COASTAL COMMISSION
45 Fremont St.,
San Francisco, CA 94105-2219 United States
Phone: 415-904-5200 Fax: 415-904-5400
Website: www.coastal.ca.gov

Founded: N/A
Scope: State
Description: A coastal management agency which carries out mandated policies on coastal conservation and development through regulation and planning programs. These policies deal with public access to the coast, coastal recreation, the California marine environment, coastal land resources, and coastal development of various types, including power plant and other energy installation.
Contact(s):
Peter Douglas, Executive Director
Ralph Faust, Chief Counsel
Susan Hansch, Chief Deputy Director
Jaime Kooser, Deputy Director for Energy, Ocean Resources and Water Quality
Chris Parry, Public Education and Activities Coordinator
Steve Scholl, Deputy Director for North Coast District
Lane Yee, Chief of Administrative Services Division

RESOURCES AGENCY, THE
CALIFORNIA COASTAL CONSERVANCY
1330 Broadway, Suite 1100
Oakland, CA 94612 United States
Phone: 510-286-1015 Fax: 510-286-0470
E-mail: dwayman@scc.ca.gov
Website: www.coastalconservancy.ca.gov

Founded: N/A
Membership: 1–100
Scope: State
Description: A state agency using planning, land-use conflict resolution, acquisition, and development techniques in the restoration, enhancement, and preservation of coastal resources. Program areas include agricultural preservation, lot consolidation, urban waterfront restoration, coastal resource enhancement, the reservation of significant resource sites, provision of public access, and assistance to nonprofit organizations.
Publication(s): Coast and Ocean
Contact(s):
Sam Schuchat, Executive Officer

RESOURCES AGENCY, THE
CALIFORNIA CONSERVATION CORPS
1719 24th St.
Sacramento, CA 95814 United States
Phone: 916-341-3100 Fax: 916-324-3347

Founded: 1976
Description: The CCC was created with a dual mission: the employment and development of the state's youth, and the protection and enhancement of California's natural resources. Some 42 million hours of public service conservation work and emergency assistance have been provided by the Corps in its twenty years of existence.
Contact(s):
H. Pratt, Director
Buzz Breedlove, Deputy Director of External Affairs
Patti Keating, Chief Deputy Director
Marie Mijares, Special Assistant to the Director

RESOURCES AGENCY, THE
CALIFORNIA WATER COMMISSION
1416 9th St., Rm. 1118
Sacramento, CA 95814 United States
Phone: 916-653-5137 Fax: 916-653-9745
Website: ceres.ca.gov/cra/

Founded: 1913
Scope: State
Description: Serves as a policy advisory body to the Director of Water Resources on matters within the Department's jurisdiction and coordinates state and local views on federal appropriations for water projects in California. The commission also conducts public hearings and investigations statewide for the department and provides an open forum for interested citizens to voice their opinion on water development issues.
Keyword(s): Water Habitats & Quality, Wildlife & Species

RESOURCES AGENCY, THE
COLORADO RIVER BOARD OF CALIFORNIA
770 Fairmont Ave., Suite 100
Glendale, CA 91203-1035 United States
Phone: 818-543-4676 Fax: 818-543-4685
E-mail: crb@crb.ca.gov
Website: www.crb.ca.gov

Founded: 1937
Membership: 1–100
Scope: State
Description: The board was established to represent California, its agencies, and citizens in matters concerning the water and power resources provided by the Colorado River and its tributaries. Working with federal and state agencies, Congress, courts, and other Colorado River Basin states, the board analyzes engineering, legal, and economic matters concerning the use of Colorado River resources within the United States.
Publication(s): Western Water, California Journal
Contact(s):
Gerald Zimmerman, Executive Director

RESOURCES AGENCY, THE
DEPARTMENT OF BOATING AND WATERWAYS
2000 Evergreen, Suite 100
Sacramento, CA 95815-3888 United States
Phone: 888-326-2822 Fax: 916-263-0648
E-mail: pubinfo@dbw.ca.gov
Website: www.dbw.ca.gov/

Founded: 1958
Membership: N/A
Scope: Local, State, Regional
Description: Makes loans to public agencies and small businesses for small craft harbor development and grants to public agencies for boat launching facilities; licenses yacht and ship brokers and for-hire vessel operators; conducts programs of boating safety, education, and regulation; and grants funds to local entities for boating law enforcement activities. Participates with the Corps of Engineers and local agencies in the construction of beach erosion control projects.
Keyword(s): Oceans/Coasts/Beaches, Recreation/Ecotourism, Water Habitats & Quality
Contact(s):
Raynor Tsuneyoshi, Director; 916-263-4326; Fax: 916-263-0648; pubinfo@dbw.ca.gov
Dolores Farrell, Chief of Boating Operations Division; 916-262-8181
David Johnson, Public Information; 916-263-0780; Fax: 916-263-0648; pubinfo@dbw.ca.gov
Don Waltz, Boating Facilities Chief; 916-263-8122; Fax: 916-263-0648; pubinfo@dbw.ca.gov

RESOURCES AGENCY, THE

DEPARTMENT OF CONSERVATION
801 K St., MS 24-01
Sacramento, CA 95814 United States
Phone: 916-322-1080 Fax: 916-445-0732
Website: www.consrv.ca.gov

Founded: N/A
Membership: 101–1,000
Scope: State
Description: The mission of the department is to protect health and safety, ensure environmental quality, and support the states's long-term economic viability in the use of California's land and mineral resources.
Contact(s):
Darryl Young, Director
Pat Meehan, Deputy Director

RESOURCES AGENCY, THE

DEPARTMENT OF FISH AND GAME
1416 9th St. Fl. 112
Sacramento, CA 95814 United States
Phone: 916-653-7664 Fax: 916-653-1856
Website: www.dfg.ca.gov

Founded: N/A
Membership: 1,001–10,000
Scope: State
Description: Responsible for the protection and management of fish and wildlife and threatened native plants in California. Enforces the laws pertaining to fish and game and threatened native plants enacted by the legislature and the regulations of the Fish and Game Commission.
Publication(s): Track Magazine, Outdoor California Magazine
Contact(s):
Robert Hight, Director; 916-653-7667
L. Boydstun, Intergovernmental Affairs Representative; 916-653-3136
Gene Fleming, Chief, Fisheries Programs; 916-653-4280
Michael Harris, Deputy Director of Administration; 916-653-4633
Perry Herrgesell, Chief, Central Valley Bay-Delta; 209-948-7800
Greg Laret, Chief of Conservation & Education & Enforcement Branch
Sonke Mastrup, Deputy Director of Wildlife & Inland Fisheries Division
Sandra Morey, Chief Habitat Conservation Planning
Julie Oltmann, Legislative Representative; 916-653-5581
Ron Rempel, Deputy Director of Habitat Conservation Division; 916-653-1070
Jim Steele, Native Anadromous Fish & Watershed Branch,Technical Assistant.; 916-653-2459
Michael Valentine, General Counsel, Acting; 916-654-3821
Larry Week, Native Anadromous Fish & Watershed Branch; 916-327-8847

RESOURCES AGENCY, THE

DEPARTMENT OF FISH AND GAME
WILDLIFE CONSERVATION BOARD
1807 13th St., Suite 103
Sacramento, CA 95814-7117 United States
Phone: 916-445-8448 Fax: 916-323-0280
Website: www.dfg.ca.gov

Founded: 1947
Membership: 1–100
Scope: State
Description: In concert with the Department of Fish and Game, the board authorizes the acquisition, restoration, and enhancement of land and water for wildlife conservation and related recreational purposes. The board also administers the Inland Wetlands Conservation Program and the California Riparian Habitat Conservation Program to protect, restore, and enhance wetland and riparian habitats.
Contact(s):
Georgia Lipphardt, Assistant Executive Director of Development Program
James Sarro, Assistant Executive Director of Land Acquisition
Al Wright, Executive Director

RESOURCES AGENCY, THE

DEPARTMENT OF FORESTRY AND FIRE PROTECTION
1416 9th St., P.O. Box 944246
Sacramento, CA 94244-2460 United States
Phone: 916-653-5121 Fax: 916-653-4171
Website: www.fire.ca.gov

Founded: N/A
Scope: State
Description: The department protects the people of California from fires, responds to emergencies, and protects and enhances forest, range, and watershed values providing social, economic, and environmental benefits to rural and urban citizens.
Contact(s):
Andrea Tuttle, Director; 916-653-7772; andrea_tuttle@fire.ca.gov
Ross Johnson, Deputy Director, Resource Management; 916-653-4298; ross_johnson@fire.ca.gov

RESOURCES AGENCY, THE

DEPARTMENT OF WATER RESOURCES
P.O. Box 942836
Sacramento, CA 95814 United States
Phone: 916-653-5791 Fax: 916-653-5028
Website: www.dwr.water.ca.gov

Founded: N/A
Scope: Regional
Description: To manage the water resources of California in cooperation with other agencies, to benefit the state's people, and to protect, restore, and enhance the natural and human environments.
Contact(s):
Thomas Hannigan, Director; 916-653-7007
Naser Bateni, Division of Planning and Local Assistance; 1020 9th St., Sacramento, CA 95814; 916-327-1646
Randall Brown, Environmental Services Office; 3252 S St., Sacramento, CA 95816; 916-227-7531
L. Chipponeri, Assistant Director of Legislation; 916-653-0488
Frank Conti, Division of Land and Right of Way; 916-653-7891
Les Harder, Division of Engineering; 916-653-3927
Kathy Kelly, State Water Project Planning Office; 916-653-1099
Paula Landis, District Chief of San Joaquin; 559-230-3310
James Libonati, Division of Management Services; 916-653-6743
Steve Macaulay, Chief Deputy Director; 916-653-6055
Jonas Minton, Deputy Director; 916-653-7092
George Qualley, Division of Flood Management; 916-653-7572
Steve Verigin, Division of Safety of Dams; 916-445-7606
Susan Weber, Chief Counsel; 916-653-6186
Pete Weisser, Office of Water Education
Charles White, District Chief of Southern; 818-543-4610
Karl Winkler, District Chief of Central; 916-227-7566
Chester Winn, Division of Fiscal Services; 916-653-4413

RESOURCES AGENCY, THE

SAN FRANCISCO BAY CONSERVATION AND DEVELOPMENT COMMISSION
50 California St., Ste. 2600
San Francisco, CA 94111 United States
Phone: 415-352-3600 Fax: 415-352-3606
E-mail: info@bcdc.ca.gov
Website: www.bcdc.ca.gov/

Founded: 1965

Description: To implement a planning and regulatory program designed to conserve and use beneficially the environmental, economic, social, and aesthetic values of San Francisco Bay through carefully considered and democratically determined policies. Composed of 27 commissioners, representing the public and state, federal, and local governmental agencies.

Contact(s):
Will Travis, Executive Director; 415-352-3653; travis@bcdc.ca.gov
Barbara Kaufman, Chairman; 415-352-3663; barbarakaufman01@aol.com

RESOURCES AGENCY, THE

STATE RECLAMATION BOARD
1416 9th St., Rm. 1601
Sacramento, CA 95814 United States
Phone: 916-653-5434 Fax: 916-653-5805
E-mail: lorib@water.ca.gov
Website: www.recbd/

Founded: 1911
Membership: 1–100
Scope: State

Description: Agency provides flood protection along the Sacramento and San Joaquin Rivers and their tributaries by planning, constructing, operating, and maintaining flood control projects in cooperation with local, state, and federal agencies, and by implementing nonstructural flood control measures.

Contact(s):
Barbara Levake, President
Frances Mizuno, Vice President
Peter Rabbon, General Manager
Brenda Jahns-Shwick, Secretary

RHODE ISLAND COOPERATIVE EXTENSION SERVICE

Woodward Hall, University of Rhode Island
Kingston, RI 02881 United States
Phone: 401-874-2900 Fax: 401-874-2259
E-mail: ceec@etal.uri.edu
Website: www.uri.edu/ce/ceec

Founded: N/A
Scope: Local, State, National
Publication(s): Publication on website
Keyword(s): Agriculture/Farming, Pollution (general), Water Habitats & Quality

Contact(s):
Jeffrey Seemann, Director
Joseph Dealteris, Aquaculture and Fisheries Leader; 401-874-5333; Fax: 401-789-8930; jdealteris@uri.edu
Art Gold, Natural Resources Leader; 401-874-2903; Fax: 401-874-4561; agold@uri.edu
Patrick Logan, Community Economic Development Leader; 401-874-2970; Fax: 401-874-4017; mayfly@uri.edu

RIVERSIDE COUNTY CONSERVATION AGENCY

4080 Lemon Street
Riverside, CA 92506-6247 United States
Phone: 909-955-6625 Fax: 909-955-1817

Founded: N/A
Membership: N/A
Scope: Local

Description: The Riverside County Habitat Conservation Agency (RCHCA) was established in 1990 for the purpose of planning, acquiring, and managing habitat for the SKR, a federal and state listed species. The RCHCA is a Joint Powers Agency comprised of 8 cities and the County of Riverside.

Keyword(s): Wildlife & Species

RUTGERS COOPERATIVE EXTENSION

Rutgers Cooperative Extension, 88 Lipman Dr.
New Brunswick, NJ 08901 United States
Phone: 732-932-5000 Fax: 732-932-6633
Website: www.rce.rutgers.edu

Founded: N/A
Membership: 1–100
Scope: State
Keyword(s): Agriculture/Farming, Pollution (general), Reduce/Reuse/Recycle

Contact(s):
Zane Helsel, Director; helsel@aesop.rutgers.edu
David Drake, Extension Specialist In Wildlife; 732-932-1509, ext. 12; Fax: 732-932-3222
Mark Vodak, Specialist In Forest Resources; Rutgers Cooperative Extension, 80 Nichol Ave, New Brunswick, NJ 08901-2828; 732-932-8993, ext. 10

S

SALTON SEA AUTHORITY

78-401 Highway 111
Suite T
La Quinta, CA 92253-2066 United States
Phone: 760-564-4888 Fax: 760-564-5288
Website: www.saltonsea.ca.gov

Founded: N/A
Membership: 1–100
Scope: Regional

Description: The Authority is a joint powers agency comprised of the Counties of Imperial and Riverside, the Coachella Valley Water District and the Imperial Irrigation District. The Authority is working with the U.S.Bureau of Reclamation and other agencies to restore the Salton Sea.

Keyword(s): Water Habitats & Quality

SAN DIEGUITO RIVER PARK JOINT POWERS AUTHORITY

18372 Sycamore Creek Road
Escondido, CA 92025 United States
Phone: 858-674-2275, ext. 15 Fax: 858-674-2280
E-mail: dbobertz@sdrp.org
Website: www.sdrp.org

Founded: 1989
Membership: N/A
Scope: Local

Description: Five cities and a county cooperating to establish a 55-mile long natural open space park that will preserve an entire river corridor.

Keyword(s): Agriculture/Farming, Ecosystems (precious), Public Lands/Greenspace, Recreation/Ecotourism, Water Habitats & Quality, Wildlife & Species

Contact(s):
Dick Bobertz, Executive Director; 858-674-2275, ext. 15; Fax: 858-674-2280; dbobertz@sdrp.org

SASKATCHEWAN CONSERVATION DATA CENTRE (SKCDC)

SASKATCHEWAN ENVIRONMENT AND RESOURCE MANAGEMENT
FISH AND WILDLIFE BRANCH
3211 Albert St
Regina, S4S 5W6 Saskatchewan Canada
Phone: 306-787-7196 Fax: 306-787-9544
E-mail: jkeith@serm.gov.sk.ca
Website: www.biodiversity.sk.ca

Founded: N/A

Scope: Local, Regional

Description: SKCDC serves the Saskatchewan public by gathering, interpreting and distributing standardized information on the ecological status of provincial wild species and communities.

Contact(s):
Jeff Keith, Information Manager

SASKATCHEWAN ENVIRONMENT AND RESOURCE MANAGEMENT

3211 Albert St.
Regina, S4S 5W6 Saskatchewan Canada
Phone: 306-787-2700

Founded: 1930

Description: To manage, enhance, and protect Saskatchewan's natural and environmental resources - fish, forests, parks, lands, wildlife, air and water for conservation, recreation, social, and economic purposes, all to be sustained for future generations.

Publication(s): State of the Environment Report, Annual Report

Contact(s):
Rick Bates, Director of Communication Services; 306-787-0114
Stuart Kramer, Deputy Minister; 306-787-2930
Lorne Scott, Minister; 361 Legislative Bldg., Regina, Saskatchewan S4S 0B3; 306-787-0393

SASKATCHEWAN ENVIRONMENT AND RESOURCE MANAGEMENT

CORPORATE SERVICES
3211 Albert St.
Regina, S4S 5W6 Saskatchewan Canada
Website: serm.gov.sk.ca

Founded: N/A

Publication(s): State of the Environment Report, Annual Report

Contact(s):
Mike Dumelie, Director of Information Mangement; 306-787-3194
Donna Kellsey, Director of Service Bureau; 306-787-6121
Lynn Tulloch, Executive Director of Corporate Services; 306-787-1176
Sue Mitten, Corporate Development; 306-787-2336
Al Parenteau, Corporate Development; 306-787-8449
Dave Tulloch, Corporate Development; 306-787-1095

SASKATCHEWAN ENVIRONMENT AND RESOURCE MANAGEMENT

DIRECTOR OF FISH AND WILDLIFE BRANCH
436-3211 Albert Street
Regina, S4S 5W6 Saskatchewan Canada
Phone: 306-787-2309 Fax: 306-787-9544
E-mail: dsherratt@serm.gov.sk.ca
Website: serm.gov.sk.ca

Founded: 1930

Scope: State

Description: To manage, enhance, and protect Saskatchewan's natural and environmental resources - fish, forests, parks, lands, wildlife, air and water for conservation, recreation, social and economic purposes, all to be sustained for future generations.

Keyword(s): Wildlife & Species

SASKATCHEWAN ENVIRONMENT AND RESOURCE MANAGEMENT

EAST BOREAL ECOREGION
Box 3003
Prince Albert, S6V 6G1 Saskatchewan Canada
Phone: 306-953-2896 Fax: 306-953-2502
E-mail: hyggen@derm.gov.sk.ca
Website: www.gov.sk.ca

Founded: N/A

Scope: Regional

Contact(s):
Ron Erickson, Regional Director; erickson@derm.gov.sk.ca

SASKATCHEWAN ENVIRONMENT AND RESOURCE MANAGEMENT

ENFORCEMENT AND COMPLIANCE BRANCH
Box 3003
Prince Albert, S6V 6G1 Saskatchewan Canada
Phone: 306-953-2991 Fax: 306-953-2999
Website: www.serm.gov.sk.ca

Founded: N/A
Membership: 1–100
Scope: International

Contact(s):
Dave Harvey, Regional Director; Box 3003, Prince Albert, Saskatchewan S6V 6G1; 306-953-2993

SASKATCHEWAN ENVIRONMENT AND RESOURCE MANAGEMENT

FIRE MANAGEMENT AND FOREST PROTECTION BRANCH
P.O. Box 3003
Prince Albert, S6V 6G1 Saskatchewan Canada
Phone: 306-425-7625 Fax: 306-953-3447
E-mail: utcoop@cc.usu.edu
Website: www.nr.usu.edu/utcfwru/index.html

Founded: N/A
Membership: 1–100
Scope: International

Contact(s):
Murdoch Carrierre, Regional Director; Box 3003, Prince Albert, Saskatchewan S6V 6G1; 306-953-2206

SASKATCHEWAN ENVIRONMENT AND RESOURCE MANAGEMENT

GRASSLAND ECOREGION
350 Cheadle St. W.
Swift Current, S9H 4G3 Saskatchewan Canada
Phone: 306-778-8207 Fax: 306-778-8212

Founded: N/A

Scope: State

Contact(s):
Syd Barber, Regional Director

SASKATCHEWAN ENVIRONMENT AND RESOURCE MANAGEMENT

OPERATIONS
Rm. 524, 3211 Albert St.
Regina, SK, S4S 5W6
Phone: 306-787-9075 Fax: 306-787-2947
Website: www.serm.gov.sk.ca

Founded: N/A

Scope: State

Contact(s):
Hugh Hunt, Director of Regional Services; 306-787-9117
Dave Phillips, Assistant Deputy Minister; 306-787-9079

SASKATCHEWAN ENVIRONMENT AND RESOURCE MANAGEMENT
PARKLAND ECOREGION
112 Research Dr.
Saskatoon, S7K 2H6 Saskatchewan Canada
Phone: 306-933-6240 Fax: 306-933-5773
Website: www.serm.gov.sk.ca

Founded: N/A

Scope: Regional

Contact(s):
Merv Swanson, Regional Director

SASKATCHEWAN ENVIRONMENT AND RESOURCE MANAGEMENT
POLICY AND ASSESSMENT
3211 Albert St.
Regina, S4S 5W6 Saskatchewan Canada
Phone: 306-787-4931 Fax: 306-787-2947

Founded: N/A

Scope: State

Contact(s):
Larry Lechner, Director of Environmental Assessment Branch; 306-787-5786; larry.lechner.erm@govmail.gov.sk.ca
Seonaid Macpherson, Director of Public Involvement and Aboriginal Affairs; 306-787-8103; seonaid.macpherson.erm@govmail.gov.sk.ca
Ron Zukowsky, Executive Director; 306-787-6285; ron.zukowsky.erm@govmail.gov.sk.ca
Lynda Langford, Senior Manager of Policy and Legislation; 306-787-6868; lynda.langford.erm@govmail.gov.sk.ca

SASKATCHEWAN ENVIRONMENT AND RESOURCE MANAGEMENT
SHIELD ECOREGION
Box 5000
La Ronge, S0J 1L0 Saskatchewan Canada
Phone: 306-425-4231 Fax: 306-425-2580

Founded: N/A

Scope: State

Contact(s):
John Schisler, Regional Director; 306-425-4231
Tim Trottier, Wildlife Biologist; 306-425-4237

SASKATCHEWAN ENVIRONMENT AND RESOURCE MANAGEMENT
WEST BOREAL ECOREGION
201-2nd St. W
Meadow Lake, S9X 1C7 Saskatchewan Canada
Phone: 306-236-7540 Fax: 306-236-7677

Founded: N/A

Scope: International

Contact(s):
Tom Harrison, Regional Director

SOIL CONSERVATION COMMITTEE OF PUERTO RICO
P.O. Box 10163
Santurce, PR 00908 United States
Phone: 787-725-3040 Fax: 787-721-7350

Founded: N/A

Scope: State

Contact(s):
Ivan Lockward, Executive Secretary; 787-725-3040; Fax: 787-721-7350
Miguel Munoz, Secretary of Agriculture; 787-721-2120; Fax: 787-722-0812

SOUTH CAROLINA COOPERATIVE FISH AND WILDLIFE RESEARCH UNIT
G27 Lehotsky Hall, Clemson University
Clemson, SC 29634 United States
Phone: 864-656-0168 Fax: 864-656-1034
E-mail: sccoop_l@clemson.edu
Website: www.clemson.edu

Founded: 1988

Scope: National

Description: The Unit conducts ecological research of importance to its cooperators, i.e., the Department of Interior, Clemson University, and the state of South Carolina. Its mission also involves training of graduate students in fish and wildlife biology and related fields.

Keyword(s): Land Issues, Recreation/Ecotourism, Water Habitats & Quality, Wildlife & Species

Contact(s):
Craig Allen, Assistant Leader of Wildlife
J. Isely, Assistant Leader of Fisheries

SOUTH CAROLINA DEPARTMENT OF AGRICULTURE
Wade Hampton Office Bldg., P.O. Box 11280
Columbia, SC 29211 United States
Phone: 803-734-2210 Fax: 803-734-2192
Website: www.scda.state.sc.us

Founded: 1904

Scope: State

Description: Administers more than 30 state laws relating to agriculture and the consumer. Represents the farmer in national, regional, and state policy matters and is involved in local and international programs of commodity promotion. Enforces regulatory programs affecting the consumer on a statewide basis.

Publication(s): South Carolina Market Bulletin, The

Keyword(s): Agriculture/Farming, Water Habitats & Quality

Contact(s):
Larry Boyleston, Director of Agribusiness Development
William Brooks, Director of Laboratory Services
Carol Fulmer, Director of Consumer Services
Wayne Mack, Director of Marketing
Becky Walton, Director of Public Information
Daniel Breazeale, Administrative Manager
Kay Rike, Executive Assistant to the Commissioner
D. Tindal, Commissioner
David Tompkins, Farmers Markets Administrator
Sidney Whalen, Assistant Editor

SOUTH CAROLINA DEPARTMENT OF HEALTH AND ENVIRONMENTAL CONTROL
J. Marion Sims Bldg., 2600 Bull St.
Columbia, SC 29201 United States
Phone: 803-896-8940 Fax: 803-896-8941
Website: www.scdhec.net/eqc/

Founded: N/A

Publication(s): A General Guide to Environmental Permitting in South Carolina

Keyword(s): Air Quality/Atmosphere, Pollution (general), Public Health, Reduce/Reuse/Recycle

Contact(s):
Douglas Bryant, Commissioner; 803-734-4880
James Joy, Bureau of Air Quality; 803-734-4750
R. Shaw, Deputy Commissioner of Environmental Quality Control Office; 803-734-5360

SOUTH CAROLINA DEPARTMENT OF HEALTH AND ENVIRONMENTAL CONTROL

OFFICE OF OCEAN AND COASTAL RESOURCE MANAGEMENT (OCRM)
Suite 400, 1362 McMillan Avenue
Charleston, SC 29405 United States
Phone: 803-744-5838 Fax: 803-744-5847
Website: www.scdhec.net/

Founded: 1975

Scope: Local, State

Description: OCRM is a division of South Carolina's Department of Health and Environmental Control. OCRM has the dual responsibility of protecting the coastal environment while promoting responsible development within the eight coastal counties.

Publication(s): Carolina Currents, Legislature Update

Keyword(s): Land Issues, Oceans/Coasts/Beaches, Water Habitats & Quality

Contact(s):
Steve Moore, Director of Permitting
Steve Snyder, Director of Planning
Christopher Brooks, Bureau Chief

SOUTH CAROLINA DEPARTMENT OF NATURAL RESOURCES

Rembert C. Dennis Bldg.
1000 Assembly Street
P.O. Box 167
Columbia, SC 29202 United States
Phone: 803-734-3888 Fax: 803-734-6310
Website: www.dnr.state.sc.us

Founded: 1994

Membership: 101–1,000

Scope: State

Description: SCDNR was created by Act 181 of 1993 for the conservation, management, utilization, and protection of SC's natural resources. It also administers SC's Heritage Trust Program for significant natural areas and historical sites. On July 1, 1994, the former Wildlife & Marine Resources Dept.; SC Geological Survey; Migratory Waterfowl Committee; and non-regulatory portions of Water Resources and Land Resources Commissions combined to form SCDNR.

Publication(s): South Carolina Wildlife, South Carolina Weekly Climate Summary, South Carolina Geology

Keyword(s): Climate Change, Land Issues, Oceans/Coasts/Beaches, Recreation/Ecotourism, Water Habitats & Quality, Wildlife & Species

Contact(s):
Paul Sandifer, Director; 803-734-4007
James Timmerman, Director Emeritus; 803-798-2858
Cary Chamblee, Associate Director; 803-734-9102
Carole Collins, Deputy Director Conservation Education & Communication; 803-734-3957
Joab Lesesne, Board Chairman; 864-597-4010
William McTeer, Deputy Director of Wildlife and Freshwater Fisheries Division; 803-734-3889
John Miglarese, Deputy Director of Marine Resources Division; P.O. Box 12559, Charleston, SC 29422-2559; 843-762-5000
Alfred Vang, Deputy Director of Land, Water and Conservation Division; 2221 Devine St., Suite 222, Columbia, SC 29205; 803-734-9101
Alvin Wright, Deputy Director of Law Enforcement Division; 803-734-4021

SOUTH CAROLINA ENERGY OFFICE

1201 Main St., Suite 600
Columbia, SC 29201 United States
Phone: 803-737-8030 Fax: 803-737-9846
E-mail: energy@ogs.state.sc.us
Website: www.state.sc.us/energy/

Founded: N/A

Scope: State

Description: The SC Energy Office is responsible for the statewide promotion of energy conservation and cost effective use of new energy sources.

Publication(s): Energy Connection Newsletter, The, The Energy Factbook, Energy Savers, How to Reduce Your Energy Costs—A Guide, $aving Money in Your Manufactured Home T, Landscaping for Energy Efficiency, Passive Solar Home Designs for South Carolina.

Keyword(s): Energy, Reduce/Reuse/Recycle, Transportation

Contact(s):
Mitch Perkins, Director; 803-737-8030; Fax: 803-737-9846; mperkins@ogs.state.sc.us
Renee Daggerhart, Public Information Coordinator; 803-737-8030; Fax: 803-737-9846; rdaggerhart@ogs.state.sc.us

SOUTH DAKOTA COOPERATIVE EXTENSION SERVICE

South Dakota State University, AgH, 154
Brookings, SD 57007 United States
Phone: 605-688-4792 Fax: 605-688-6347
Website: www.abs.sdstate.edu/CES/index.htm

Founded: N/A

Membership: 101–1,000

Scope: Regional

Publication(s): See publication website

Keyword(s): Agriculture/Farming, Pollution (general), Reduce/Reuse/Recycle

Contact(s):
Larry Tidemann, Director of Cooperative Extension Service
Barry Bunn, Range Livestock Production Specialist; 605-688-5455
Patricia Johnson, Range Management Specialist; West River Ag Center, South Dakota State University, 1905 Plaza Blvd., Rapid City, SD 57702-9302

SOUTH DAKOTA DEPARTMENT OF AGRICULTURE

523 E. Capitol, Foss Bldg.
Pierre, SD 57501-3182 United States
Phone: 605-773-5425 Fax: 605-773-5926
E-mail: agmail@state.sd.us
Website: www.state.sd.us/doa/doa.html

Founded: N/A

Scope: State

Publication(s): See publication website

Contact(s):
Larry Gabriel, Secretary
Raymond Sowers, State Forester; 605-773-3623; raymond.sowers@state.sd.us

SOUTH DAKOTA DEPARTMENT OF AGRICULTURE

DIVISION OF RESOURCE CONSERVATION AND FORESTRY
523 E. Capitol Ave.
Pierre, SD 57501-3182 United States
Phone: 605-773-3623 Fax: 605-773-4003
Website: www.state.sd.us/doa/forestry/index.htm

Founded: N/A

Scope: State

Contact(s):
Raymond Sowers, Director; 605-773-3623

SOUTH DAKOTA DEPARTMENT OF AGRICULTURE

STATE CONSERVATION COMMISSION
523 E. Capitol Ave.
Pierre, SD 57501-3182 United States
Phone: 605-773-3623 Fax: 605-773-4003
Website: www.state.sd.us/state/doa/doa

Founded: N/A

Scope: State

Contact(s):

Robert Gab, Chairman

SOUTH DAKOTA DEPARTMENT OF ENVIRONMENT AND NATURAL RESOURCES

523 East Capitol Ave.
Joe Foss Building
Pierre, SD 57501 United States
Phone: 605-773-3151 Fax: 605-773-6035
E-mail: denrinternet@state.sd.us
Website: www.state.sd.us/denr

Founded: 1979

Membership: 101–1,000

Scope: State

Description: Our mission is to provide environmental and natural resources assessment, financial assistance, and regulation in a customer service manner that protects the public health, conserves natural resources, preserves the environment, and promotes economic development.

Keyword(s): Air Quality/Atmosphere, Land Issues, Pollution (general), Reduce/Reuse/Recycle, Water Habitats & Quality

Contact(s):

Steven Pirner, Secretary; 605-773-5559; Fax: 605-773-6035; denrinternet@state.sd.us

David Templeton, Director of Division of Financial and Technical Assistance; 605-773-4216; Fax: 605-773-4068; dave.templeton@state.sd.us

Tim Tollefsrud, Director of Division of Environmental Services; 605-773-3153; Fax: 605-773-6035; tim.tollefsrud@state.sd.us

SOUTH DAKOTA DEPARTMENT OF GAME, FISH, AND PARKS

523 East Capitol
Joe Foss Office Bldg.
Pierre, SD 57501-3182 United States
Phone: 605-773-3485 Fax: 605-773-6245
E-mail: wildinfo@state.sd.us
Website: www.state.sd.us

Founded: N/A

Membership: 1–100

Scope: State

Description: To provide environmental and natural resources assessment, financial assistance, and regulation in a customer service orientated manner which provides protection of public health, conservation of natural resources, preservation of the environment, and promotes economic development.

Publication(s): South Dakota Conservation Digest.

Keyword(s): Land Issues, Recreation/Ecotourism, Water Habitats & Quality, Wildlife & Species

Contact(s):

Ken Anderson, Director of Administration Division; 605-773-3396

Doug Hansen, Director of Wildlife Division; 605-773-3381

Doug Hofer, Director of Parks and Recreation Division; 605-773-3391

Rollie Noem, Director of Custer State Park Division; 605-255-4515

Paul Coughlin, Habitat Program Administrator; 605-773-4194; Fax: 605-773-6245; paul.coughlin@state.sd.us

Ron Fowler, Game Program Administrator; 605-773-4193

Dave McCrea, Law Enforcement Program Administrator; 605-773-4243

Chuck Schlueter, Communications Program Administrator; 605-773-3485; Fax: 605-773-6245; chuck.schlueter@state.sd.us

Dennis Unkenholz, Fisheries Program Administrator; 605-773-4508; Fax: 605-773-6245; dennis.unkenholz@state.sd.us

Wayne Winter, Federal Aid Manager; 605-773-6228

Amy Brady, Editor; Game, Fish & Parks, 412 West Missouri Ave, Pierrre, SD 57501; 605-773-3486; Fax: 605-773-6921; amy.brady@state.sd.us

John Cooper, Secretary; 605-773-3387

Emmett Keyser, Operations Assistant Director of Wildlife Division; 605-773-4607

John Kirk, Specialist of Environmental Review; 605-773-4501

Robert Schuurmans, Turn In Poachers, Training Coordinator; Game, Fish & Parks, 412 West Missouri Ave, Pierre, SD 57501; 605-773-5906; Fax: 605-773-6921

William Shattuck, Boating and Hunting Safety; 412 West Missouri Ave, Pierre, SD 57501; 605-773-4506; Fax: 605-773-6921; bill.shattuck@state.sd.us

George Vandel, Technical Services Assistant Director of Wildlife Division; 605-773-4192

SOUTH FLORIDA WATER MANAGEMENT DISTRICT

3301 Gun Club Rd., P.O. Box 24680
West Palm Beach, FL 33416-4680 United States
Phone: 561-686-8800 Fax: 561-682-6200
Website: www.sfwmd.gov

Founded: 1949

Membership: 1,001–10,000

Scope: State

Description: Responsible for local cooperation in the Federal-State Central and Southern Florida flood Control Project. Goals include: Flood control, water supply, water quality, and environmental protection for sixteen counties in south Florida. Additional benefits are preservation of natural conditions in the Everglades, land purchases under Save Our Rivers program and enhancement of wetlands, fish, wildlife, waterfowl and public recreation.

Keyword(s): Ecosystems (precious), Water Habitats & Quality

Contact(s):

Henry Dean, Executive Director, ext. 6136; lsori@sfwmd.gov

Alvin Jackson, Deputy Executive Director - Corporate Resources, ext. 2805; rsandhau@sfwmd.gov

Chip Merriam, Deputy Executive Director - Water Resource Management, ext. 6597; lelias@sfwmd.gov

Joseph Schweigart, Deputy Exec. Dir. - Public Works, ext. 6102; cberger@sfwmd.gov

SOUTHWEST FLORIDA WATER MANAGEMENT DISTRICT (SWFWMD)

2379 Broad St., U.S. 41 South
Brooksville, FL 34604-6899 United States
Phone: 352-796-7211 Fax: 352-754-6883
Website: www.watermatters.org

Founded: 1961

Membership: 101–1,000

Scope: State

Description: A governmental agency dedicated to resource protection conservation programs, which are supported through regulatory and nonregulatory initiatives and cooperative funding projects.

Publication(s): Fifty Ways to Do Your Part, various residential and commercial water conservation education resources, list of vendors and manufacturers of water conservation devices and services, Plant Guide and associated technical bulletins

Keyword(s): Water Habitats & Quality

Contact(s):

Kathy Scott, Conservation Project Manager; 352-796-7211, ext. 4247; kathy.scott@swfwmd.state.fl.us

Kathy Scott, Water Resource Analyst Staff and Secretary of The Florida Water Wise Council; 352-796-7211, ext. 4247; kathy.scott@swfwmd.state.fl.us

STATE ENGINEER OFFICE/INTERSTATE STREAM COMMISSION

Bataan Memorial Bldg., P.O. Box 25102
Santa Fe, NM 87504 United States
Phone: 505-827-6160 Fax: 505-827-6188
Website: www.seo.state.nm.us

Founded: N/A
Membership: 1–100
Scope: State, Regional
Description: Administration, development, protection, and conservation of the water resources of the State of New Mexico.
Publication(s): Water Line
Contact(s):

Norman Gaume, Director of Interstate Stream Commission/Interstate Stream E; 505-827-6160
Elaine Pacheco, Acting Chief of Technical Division
Hoyt Pattison, Vice Chairman
Paul Saavedra, Chief of Water Rights Division
Thomas Turney, State Engineer and Secretary; 505-827-6160

STATE FORESTRY DIVISION (WYOMING)

1100 W. 22nd St.
Cheyenne, WY 82002 United States
Phone: 307-777-7586
E-mail: forestry@state.wy.us

Founded: 1952
Membership: 1–100
Scope: National
Description: Has direction of all forestry matters within the jurisdiction of the State of Wyoming; manages state-owned forest land; coordinates fire protection on twenty-nine million acres of state and private rural lands; assists landowners and communities in proper management of woody vegetation and forested lands; and provides forestry information to schools, organizations, and individuals.
Publication(s): Wyoming State Forest Resource Program
Keyword(s): Forests/Forestry, Public Health, Reduce/Reuse/Recycle, Wildlife & Species
Contact(s):

Thomas Ostermann, State Forester
Daniel Perko, Deputy State Forester
Howard Pickerd, Assistant State Forester of Forest Management
Ray Weidenhaft, Assistant State Forester of Fire Management

STATE MARINE BOARD (OREGON)

P.O. Box 14145
Salem, OR 97309-5065 United States
Phone: 503-378-8587 Fax: 503-378-4597
Website: www.boatoregon.com

Founded: N/A
Scope: State
Keyword(s): Recreation/Ecotourism, Water Habitats & Quality
Contact(s):

Paul Donheffner, Director

STATE OF IDAHO DEPARTMENT OF ENVIRONMENTAL QUALITY

1410 N. Hilton St.
Boise, ID 83706-1255 United States
Phone: 208-373-0502 Fax: 208-373-0417
Website: www2.state.id.us/deq

Founded: N/A
Scope: State
Description: Administers and directs programs designed to protect and enhance the environment and public health. Emphasis is placed on monitoring, technical assistance, and environmental education at the community level. The agency is additionally responsible for all permitting and permit review functions.
Publication(s): Hazardous Waste Report, Performance Partnership Agreement, State of the Environment Report, Strategic Plan, Groundwater Report, Drinking Water Report
Keyword(s): Air Quality/Atmosphere, Pollution (general), Reduce/Reuse/Recycle, Water Habitats & Quality
Contact(s):

C. Allred, Director of Enviromental Quality; 208-373-0240; Fax: 208-373-0417; callred@deq.state.id.us
J. Sandoval, Chief of Staff; 208-373-0240; Fax: 208-3730417; jsandova@deq.state.id.us
Orville Green, State Waste Mgmt. & Remediation Administrator; 208-373-0418; Fax: 208-373-0154; ogreen@deq.state.id.us
Katherine Kelly, State Air Quality Administrator; 208-373-0440; Fax: 208-373-0154; kkelly@deq.state.id.us
David Mabe, State Water Quality Administrator; 208-373-0413; Fax: 208-373-0576; dmabe@deq.state.id.us

STATE PARKS AND RECREATION COMMISSION (WASHINGTON)

7150 Cleanwater Ln., P.O. Box 42650
Olympia, WA 98504-2650 United States
Phone: 360-902-8500

Founded: 1912
Scope: State
Description: To acquire, develop, improve, and maintain state parks and recreation areas. Involvement includes but is not limited to state parks, seashore conservation, water and boating safety, snowmobile safety, and natural and historic heritage interpretation.
Keyword(s): Ethics/Environmental Justice, Public Lands/Greenspace, Recreation/Ecotourism
Contact(s):

Cleve Pinnix, Director; 360-902-8501
Frank Boteler, Deputy Director; 360-902-8502
Tom Boyer, Chief Engineer; 360-902-8616
Art Brown, Chief of Information Processing; 360-902-8585
Rita Cooper, Assistant Director of Administrative Services; 360-902-8525
Rex Derr, Legislative Liaison; 306-902-8504
Larry Fairleigh, Assistant Director of Resources Development; 360-902-8642
Jim French, Chief of Boating Programs; 360-902-8515
Bill Gansberg, Chief of Visitor Protection and Law Enforcement; 360-902-8598
Paul George, Chief of Parks Maintenance; 360-902-8540
Ann Hersley, Administrator of Public Affairs; 360-902-8562
James Horan, Chief of Programs Management; 360-902-8580
Dan Ingman, Chief of Natural Resource Management; 360-902-8592
Judy Johnson, Chief of Employee Services; 360-902-8568
Bill Jolly, Chief of Environmental Coordination; 360-902-8636
William Jolly, Chief of Research and Long Range Planning; 360-902-8641
Bill Koss, Chief of Site Planning; 360-902-8629
Pam McConkey, Chief of Visitor Services; 360-902-8595
Wayne McLaughlin, Contracts Specialist; 360-902-8599
Sandy Rees, Chief of Fiscal Services; 360-902-8575
Marsh Taylor, Chief of Budget Services; 360-902-8532

STATE PARKS AND RECREATION COMMISSION (WASHINGTON)

EASTERN REGION HEADQUARTERS
2201 N. Duncan Dr.
Wenatchee, WA 98801–1007 United States
Phone: 509-662-0420 Fax: 509-663-9754
Website: www.parks.wa.gov

Founded: N/A

Membership: 101–1,000
Scope: State, Regional
Description: Regional Office for Eastern State Parks
Publication(s): Call information # 1-800-233-0321
Contact(s):
Jim Harris, Regional Manager; 2201 N. Duncan Dr., Wenatchee, WA 98801; 509-662-0420

STATE PARKS AND RECREATION COMMISSION (WASHINGTON)

NORTHWEST REGION
220 Walnut St.
P.O. Box 487
Burlington, WA 98233 United States
Phone: 360-755-9231 Fax: 360-428-1094
Website: www.parks.wa.gov

Founded: N/A
Membership: 1–100
Scope: State
Contact(s):
Terry Doran, Region Mngr.; P.O. Box 487, Burlington, WA 98801–1007; 360-755-9231

STATE PARKS AND RECREATION COMMISSION (WASHINGTON)

SOUTHWEST REGION
11838 Tilley Rd. S
Olympia, WA 98512 United States
Phone: 360-753-7143 Fax: 360-586-4272
Website: www.parks.wa.gov/

Founded: N/A
Scope: State
Contact(s):
Paul Malmberg; 11838 Tilley Rd., S., Olympia, WA 98512-9167; 360-753-7143

STATE PLANT BOARD (ARKANSAS)

1 Natural Resources Dr., P.O. Box 72203
Little Rock, AR 72205 United States
Phone: 501-225-1598 Fax: 501-225-3590
Website: www.naturallyarkansas.org

Founded: N/A
Membership: 101–1,000
Scope: State
Publication(s): Plant Board News
Keyword(s): Wildlife & Species
Contact(s):
Don Alexander, Director
Darryl Little, Assistant Director

STATE SOIL AND WATER CONSERVATION COMMISSION (GEORGIA)

P.O. Box 8024
Athens, GA 30603 United States
Phone: 706-542-3065 Fax: 706-542-4242
Website: www.gaswcc.org

Founded: 1937
Membership: 1–100
Scope: Local, Regional
Description: Established under the Soil Conservation Districts Act to work with and assist the 40 Soil and Water Conservation Districts and their 370 District Supervisors throughout Georgia.
Publication(s): Conservation Commission, Conservation Contact
Keyword(s): Agriculture/Farming, Land Issues, Reduce/Reuse/Recycle, Water Habitats & Quality
Contact(s):
F. Liles, Executive Director; 706-542-3065; Fax: 706-542-4242
David Bennett, Deputy Director
Garland Thompson, Chairman

STATE WATER RESOURCES BOARD (RHODE ISLAND)

100 North Main Street, 5th Floor
Providence, RI 02903 United States
Phone: 401-222-2217 Fax: 401-222-4707

Founded: 1967
Description: The Water Resources Board is the key agency in water-supply planning, financing, regulation, and development. The Board also plans for the future water needs of cities and towns.
Publication(s): RI Public Water Supply, RI Legal and Legislative Aspects of Water Supply, RI Industrial Water, RI Fish and Wildlife.
Keyword(s): Land Issues, Public Health, Reduce/Reuse/Recycle, Water Habitats & Quality
Contact(s):
M. Sams, General Manager and Secretary and Treasurer
Daniel Schatz, Chairman
Maurice Trudeau, Vice Chairman

T

TAHOE REGIONAL PLANNING AGENCY

P.O. Box 1038
308 Dorla Ct.
Zephyr Cove, NV 89448-1038 United States
Phone: 775-588-4547 Fax: 775-588-4527
E-mail: trpa@trpa.org
Website: www.trpa.org

Founded: 1969
Membership: 1–100
Scope: Regional
Description: To establish and implement land use and environmental plans and regulations in the Lake Tahoe Region. Established by Public Law No. 91-148, December 1969, amended by Public Law No. 96-551, December 1980.
Keyword(s): Air Quality/Atmosphere, Forests/Forestry, Land Issues, Transportation, Water Habitats & Quality, Wildlife & Species
Contact(s):
Juan Palma, Executive Director
Jordan Kahn, Legal Counsel
John Marshall, Legal Counsel

TENNESSEE AGRICULTURAL EXTENSION SERVICE

121 Morgan Hall
Knoxville, TN 37996-4530 United States
Phone: 865-974-7114 Fax: 865-974-1068
E-mail: clnorman@utk.edu
Website: www.utextension.utk.edu

Founded: N/A
Membership: 101–1,000
Scope: State
Description: The Tennessee Agricultural Extension Service is an off-campus division of The University of Tennessee Institute of Agriculture. It is a statewide educational organization, funded by federal, state and local governments, that brings research-based information about agriculture, family and consumer sciences, and resource development to the people of Tennessee where they live and work.
Keyword(s): Agriculture/Farming, Air Quality/Atmosphere, Forests/Forestry, Land Issues, Recreation/Ecotourism, Reduce/Reuse/Recycle, Water Habitats & Quality, Wildlife & Species
Contact(s):
Craig Harper, General Wildlife Specialist; 865-974-7346; Fax: 865-974-4714; charper@utk.edu
Thomas Hill, General Fish and Wildlife Specialist; 865-974-7164; Fax: 865-974-4714; tkhill@utk.edu
George Hopper, Head, Forestry, Wildlife & Fisheries; 865-974-7126; Fax: 865-974-0957

Charles Norman, Dean of Extension Service; 865-974-7114; Fax: 865-974-1068; clnorman@utk.edu

TENNESSEE COOPERATIVE FISHERY RESEARCH UNIT (USDI)

Tennessee Technological University, Box 5114
Cookeville, TN 38505 United States
Phone: 931-372-3094 Fax: 931-382-6257

Founded: N/A
Keyword(s): Wildlife & Species
Contact(s):
James Layzer, Leader

TENNESSEE DEPARTMENT OF AGRICULTURE

Ellington Agricultural Center
Nashville, TN 37204 United States
Phone: 615-360-0103 Fax: 615-837-5333
E-mail: dwheeler@mail.state.tn.us
Website: www.state.tn.us/agriculture

Founded: N/A
Scope: State
Contact(s):
Dan Wheeler, Commissioner

TENNESSEE DEPARTMENT OF AGRICULTURE

STATE SOIL CONSERVATION COMMITTEE
Ellington Agriculture Center, P.O. Box 40627
Nashville, TN 37204 United States
Phone: 615-837-5225
E-mail: myra.lilly@state.tn.us

Founded: N/A
Keyword(s): Agriculture/Farming, Land Issues, Pollution (general), Water Habitats & Quality
Contact(s):
Barry Lake, Chair; P.O. Box 107, Hickory Valley, TN 38042; 901-764-2909
Jim Nance, Executive Secretary; 615-360-0108

TEXAS DEPARTMENT OF AGRICULTURE

Austin, TX 78711 United States
Phone: 512-463-7476 Fax: 512-463-1104
Website: www.agr.state.tx.us

Founded: 1904
Scope: State
Description: Our mission is to make Texas the nation's leader in agriculture while providing efficient and extraordinary service.
Contact(s):
Delane Caeser, Assistant Commissioner, Marketing and Promotion; Fax: 512-463-7843
Susan Combs, Commissioner
Lee Deviney, Assistant Commissioner, Finance & Agribusiness; Fax: 512-475-1762
Donnie Dippel, Assistant Commissioner, Pesticide Division; Fax: 512-475-1618
Raette Hearne, Assistant Commissioner, Administrative Services; Fax: 512-463-7582
Martin Hubert, Deputy Commissioner
David Kostroun, Assistant Commissioner, Regulatory Division; Fax: 512-463-8225
Brian Murray, Special Assistant of Producer Relations; 512-463-7553; brian.murray@agr.state.tx.us
Allen Spelce, Assistant Commissioner, Communications

TEXAS DEPARTMENT OF HEALTH

1100 W. 49th St.
Austin, TX 78756 United States
Phone: 512-458-7111
Website: www.tdh.state.tx.us

Founded: 1879
Scope: State
Description: The Department of Health was created to protect and promote the health of the people of Texas.
Keyword(s): Energy, Pollution (general), Public Health.
Contact(s):
Kirk Wiles, Director of Seafood Safety Division; 512-719-0215
Joseph Fuller, Associate Commissioner of Environmental and Consumer Health; 512-458-7541
Debra Stabeno, Deputy Commissioner of Public Health Sciences and Quality; 512-458-7437

TEXAS FOREST SERVICE

301 Tarrow, Suite 364
College Station, TX 77840-7896 United States
Phone: 979-458-6600 Fax: 979-458-6610
E-mail: joverhouse@tfs.tamu.edu
Website: txforestservice.tamu.edu

Founded: 1915
Membership: 1–100
Scope: State
Description: To encourage and aid private landowners to practice multiple-use forestry; to protect private forest land against wildfire, insects, and diseases; and to inform the public of the contribution that forests make.
Keyword(s): Forests/Forestry, Public Lands/Greenspace, Reduce/Reuse/Recycle, Water Habitats & Quality, Wildlife & Species
Contact(s):
James Hull, Director; 979-458-6600; Fax: 979-458-6610; jhull@tfs.tamu.edu
Edwin Barron, Associate Director of Forest Resource Development; 979-458-6650; Fax: 979-458-6655; ebarron@tfs.tamu.edu
Tom Boggus, Associate Director for Administration; 979-458-6600; Fax: 979-458-6610; tboggus@tfs.tamu.edu
Robert Fewin, Regional Forester of West Texas; Rt. 3 Box 216, Lubbock, TX 79401; 806-746-5801
William Oates, Regional Forester of Southern Region; 1825 Sycamore, Huntsville, TX 77340; 409-435-0852
Ernest Smith, Regional Forester of Northern Region; P.O. Box 3527, Longview, TX 75606-3527; 903-234-2829
I. Weldon, Head of Forest Products Department; 409-639-8180
Bobby Young, Associate Director of Forest Resources Protection; 409-639-8100

TEXAS GENERAL LAND OFFICE

Stephen F. Austin State Office Bldg., 1700 N. Congress Ave.
Austin, TX 78701-1495 United States
Phone: 512-463-5001 Fax: 512-475-1415
Website: www.glo.state.tx.us

Founded: N/A
Scope: State
Description: Serves as the custodian of approximately 20.5 million acres of state-owned land including 4.25 million acres of submerged coastal land. Responsibilities include: protecting state land from unlawful use; managing special projects which protects the state's natural resources; and providing the public with information pertaining to the state's land resources.
Publication(s): Public Information Office
Keyword(s): Oceans/Coasts/Beaches, Public Lands/Greenspace
Contact(s):
David Dewhurst, Commissioner; 512-463-5256; david.dewhurst@glo.state.tx.us
Ashley Wadick, Deputy Commissioner, Resource Management; 512-305-9121; ashley.wadick@glo.state.tx.us

TEXAS PARKS AND WILDLIFE DEPARTMENT

4200 Smith School Rd.
Austin, TX 78744 United States
Phone: 512-389-4800 Fax: 512-389-4814
E-mail: webcomments@tpwd.state.tx.us
Website: www.tpwd.state.tx.us

Founded: N/A

Scope: State

Description: The agency manages and conserves natural and cultural resources of Texas for the use and enjoyment of future generations.

Publication(s): Texas Parks and Wildlife Magazine

Contact(s):

Walter Dabney, Director of State Parks; 512-389-4866; walter.dabney@tpwd.state.tx.us
Annette Dominguez, Director of Human Resources; 512-389-4809
Phil Durocher, Director of Inland Fisheries; 512-389-8110
Gary Graham, Director of Wildlife; 512-389-4971; gary.graham@tpwd.state.tx.us
Larry McKinney, Director of Resource Protection; 512-389-4864
Dan Patton, Director of Infrastructure; 512-389-4995
Jim Robertson, Director of Law Enforcement; 512-389-4845; jim.robertson@tpwd.state.tx.us
Lydia Saldana, Director of Communications; 512-389-4994
Andrew Sansom, Executive Director; 512-389-4802; andrew.sansom@tpwd.state.tx.us
Gene McCarty, Chief of Staff; 512-389-4418; gene.mccarty@tpwd.state.tx.us
Lee Bass, Commission Chairman; Fax: 817-390-8408; lee.bass@tpwd.state.tx.us
Robert Cook, Chief Operating Officer; 512-389-4976; robert.cook@tpwd.state.tx.us
Carol Dinkins, Commission Vice Chairman; Fax: 713-615-5311; carol.dinkins@tpwd.state.tx.us
Susan Ebert, Editor, Texas Parks and Wildlife Magazine; 512-912-7000
Tom Harvey, Media and News Coordinator; 512-389-4453
Hal Osborne, Chief Financial Officer; 512-389-4862; hal.osborne@tpwd.state.tx.us

TEXAS STATE SOIL AND WATER CONSERVATION BOARD

P.O. Box 658
Temple, TX 76503-0658 United States
Phone: 254-773-2250 Fax: 254-773-3311
Website: www.tsswcb.state.tx.us

Founded: N/A

Scope: Regional

Description: The Texas State Soil and Water Conservation Board is a state agency established to administer and carry out Texas' soil and water conservation law. The Board is charged with the responsibility of administering and coordinating Texas' soil and water conservation program with the state's 216 local soil and water conservation districts. The Board is also the agency responsible for planning, implementing, and managing programs and practices for abating agricultural and silvicultural nonpoint source

Keyword(s): Agriculture/Farming, Land Issues, Reduce/Reuse/Recycle

Contact(s):

Robert Buckley, Executive Director; 311 N. 5th St., Temple, TX 76501-3107; Fax: 254-773-3311

TEXAS WATER DEVELOPMENT BOARD

1700 N. Congress
Austin, TX 78701 United States
Phone: 512-463-7847 Fax: 512-475-2053
Website: www.twdb.state.tx.us

Founded: 1957

Membership: 1–100

Scope: State

Description: Texas Water Development Board provides loans to local governments for water supply projects; water quality projects, including wastewater treatment, municipal solid waste management, and nonpoint source pollution control; agricultural water conservation projects; and flood control projects. Provides water related research and planning and agricultural water conservation funding.

Publication(s): Water for Texas - Today and Tomorrow, bay and estuary reports since 1967, ground water reports since 1957, Texas Water Facts, Rainwater Harvesting - brochure

Keyword(s): Water Habitats & Quality

Contact(s):

Wales Madden, Chairman
Jack Hunt, Vice Chairman
Hugh Bender, Director of Texas Natural Resources Information System; 512-463-8051; hugh.bender@twdb.state.tx.us
Bill Mullican, Director of Water Resources Information; 512-936-0813; bill.mullican@twdb.state.tx.us
George Green, Northern Project Management Division; 512-463-7853; george.green@twdb.state.tx.us
Tommy Knowles, Deputy Executive Administrator for Planning; 512-463-8043; tommy.knowles@twdb.state.tx.us
Ignacio Madera, Border Project Management Division; 512-463-7509; ignacio.madera@twdb.state.tx.us
Leonard Olson, Special Assistant for Intergovernmental Customers; 512-463-7931; leonard.olson@twdb.state.tx.us
Suzanne Schwartz, General Counsel; 512-463-7981; suzanne.schwartz@twdb.state.tx.us
J. Ward, Deputy Executive Administrator for Office of Project Finance; 512-463-0991; kevin.ward@twdb.state.tx.us

THE ENVIRONMENT SHOP

DEPARTMENT FOR ENVIRONMENT AND HERITAGE
77 Grenfell St.
Adelaide, South Australia, 5000 Australia
Phone: 8204-1910, ext. 618 Fax: 8204-1919
E-mail: environmentshop@saugov.sa.gov.au
Website: www.environment.sa.gov.au

Founded: 1999

Membership: N/A

Scope: Local, State, Regional, National

Description: The Environment Shop is the Department of Environment and Heritage's one stop shopping offering products and services that relate to the activities of the department. Products include: park passes, fauna and hunting license renewal, mapping and spatial information, environmental management and retail products. The Shop is the key interface with South Australia National Park visitors and offers information relating to parks, bush-walking trails and more.

Publication(s): Environmental Publications, EPA Reports, products for sale, mapping and spatial information.

Keyword(s): Air Quality/Atmosphere, Climate Change, Ecosystems (precious), Energy, Land Issues, Oceans/ Coasts/Beaches, Pollution (general), Recreation/Ecotourism, Reduce/Reuse/Recycle, Water Habitats & Quality, Wildlife & Species

Contact(s):

Allan Holmes, Chief Executive

TUG HILL COMMISSION

317 Washington St.
Watertown, NY 13601 United States
Phone: 315-785-2380 Fax: 315-785-2574
E-mail: tughill@tughill.org
Website: www.tughill.org

Founded: 1972

Membership: 1–100

Scope: Local

Description: The Tug Hill Commission is a nonregulatory state agency charged with helping local governments, organizations, and citizens shape the future of this rural, 2,100-square-mile region in northern New York State, especially its environment and economy.

Publication(s): Headwaters, Issue Paper series, Cooperative Rural Planning, Tug Hill Program, The

Keyword(s): Agriculture/Farming, Energy, Forests/Forestry, Land Issues, Recreation/Ecotourism, Sprawl/Urban Planning, Water Habitats & Quality

Contact(s):
Robert Quinn, Executive Director

U

UNITED STATES DEPARTMENT OF THE INTERIOR
IDAHO COOPERATIVE FISH AND WILDLIFE RESEARCH UNIT
COLLEGE OF NATURAL RESOURCES
P.O. Box 44-1141
Moscow, ID 83844-1141 United States
Phone: 208-885-2750 Fax: 208-885-9080
Website: www.its.uidaho.edu/coop

Founded: 1963
Membership: 101–1,000
Scope: National, International
Description: An interagency organization which conducts research, graduate level training, and extension in the fields of fish, wildlife, and conservation biology.
Keyword(s): Wildlife & Species
Contact(s):
James Congleton, Assistant Leader
J. Scott, Leader
R. Wright, Assistant Leader

UNITED STATES DEPARTMENT OF THE INTERIOR
MISSISSIPPI STATE UNIVERSITY EXTENSION SERVICES
WILDLIFE FISHERIES
Box 9690
Mississippi State, MS 39762 United States
Phone: 662-325-3133 Fax: 662-325-8750
E-mail: wildlife@ext.msstate.edu
Website: www.msucares.com

Founded: 1878
Membership: 1–100
Scope: Local, State, Regional, National
Description: State Cooperative Extension Program in Natural Resources
Keyword(s): Forests/Forestry, Water Habitats & Quality, Wildlife & Species
Contact(s):
Joe Mcgilberry, Director Interim
Martin Brunson, Extension Leader Professer Wildlife & Fisheries; martyb@ext.mstate.edu

UNITED STATES DEPARTMENT OF THE INTERIOR
MONTANA COOPERATIVE FISHERY RESEARCH UNIT
Dept. Ecology, Montana State University
Bozeman, MT 59717-3460 United States
Phone: 406-994-4549 Fax: 406-994-7479
Website: www.montana/ecology/facility

Founded: N/A
Scope: National
Description: Applied Fisheries Research

UNITED STATES DEPARTMENT OF THE INTERIOR
OREGON COOPERATIVE FISH AND WILDLIFE RESEARCH UNIT
104 Nash Hall
Oregon State University
Corvallis, OR 97331-3803 United States
Phone: 541-737-4531 Fax: 541-737-3590
E-mail: or_sfwru@orst.edu
Website: www.orst.edu/dept/fish_wild/

Founded: N/A
Membership: 1–100
Scope: State, Regional, National
Description: Research focus on physiological, ecological, and genetic factors affecting production and performance of freshwater fishes. The staff consists of two permanent and two-three other Ph.D. level scientists, as well as graduate students and technicians.
Keyword(s): Water Habitats & Quality, Wildlife & Species
Contact(s):
Carl Schreck, Leader
Hiram Li, Assistant Leader
Robert Anthony, Wildlife Leader
Daniel Roby, Wildlife Assistant Leader

UNITED STATES DEPARTMENT OF THE INTERIOR
UTAH COOPERATIVE FISH AND WILDLIFE RESEARCH UNIT
College of Natural Resources, Utah State University
Logan, UT 84322-5210 United States
Phone: 435-797-2509 Fax: 435-797-4025
E-mail: utcoop@cc.usu.edu
Website: www.ella.nr.usu.edu/utcop/index.html

Founded: 1935
Membership: 1–100
Scope: National
Description: The unit conducts research and training in all aspects of fishery and wildlife biology and management.
Keyword(s): Land Issues, Recreation/Ecotourism, Reduce/Reuse/Recycle, Water Habitats & Quality, Wildlife & Species
Contact(s):
Esther Biesinger, Financial Assistant; 435-797-2467
John Bissonette, Leader; 435-797-2511; johnbissonette@cnor.usu.edu
Thomas Edwards,, Assistant Leader of Wildlife; 435-797-2529

UNITED STATES DEPARTMENT OF THE INTERIOR
WASHINGTON COOPERATIVE FISH AND WILDLIFE RESEARCH UNIT
SCHOOL OF AQUATIC AND FISHERY SCIENCES
Box 355020 University of Washington
Seattle, WA 98195 United States
Phone: 206-543-6475 Fax: 206-616-9012
E-mail: washcoop@u.washington.edu
Website: www.fish.washington.edu/wacfwru

Founded: 1988
Scope: National
Description: The goals of the WCFWRU are: (1) conduct research in support of the Department of the Interior and Washington State; (2) train graduate students in fisheries and wildlife science through research support and by teaching; and (3) disseminate research results to the scientific community, management agencies, and the general public.
Keyword(s): Pollution (general), Water Habitats & Quality, Wildlife & Species
Contact(s):
David Beauchamp, Assistant Unit Leader of Fishery

Christian Grue, Leader
Glenn Vanblaricom, Assistant Leader of Wildlife

UNIVERSITY OF CONNECTICUT COOPERATIVE EXTENSION

COLLEGE OF AGRICULTURE AND NATURAL RESOURCES
Unit 4066 1376 Storrs Rd., University of Connecticut
West Hartford, CT 06117 United States
Phone: 860-570-9010 Fax: 860-570-9008
Website: www.canr.uconn.edu

Founded: N/A

Scope: State

Description: Natural resource components includes forest management, forest stewardship, urban forestry, water resources, and wildlife managment.

Contact(s):

John Barclay, Extension Specialist: Wildlife; Natural Resources Management and Engineering, Box U-87, University of Connecticut, Storrs, CT 06269-4087; 860-486-0143; Fax: 860-486-5875
Norman Bender, Program Leader: Marine Advisory Program; University of CT-MAS: 1084 Shennecossett Rd., Groton, CT 06340-6097; 860-445-8664
Stephen Broderick, Extension Educator: Forest Managment; 139 Wolf Den Rd., Brooklyn, CT 06234; 860-774-9600
Glenn Warner, Extension Specialist: Water Resources; Natural Resources Managment and Engineering: Box U-87: University of Connecticut, Storrs, CT 06269-4087; 860-486-2840
Xiusheng Yang, State Climatologist; Natural Resources Management and Engineering, Box U-87, University of Connecticut, Storrs, CT 06269-4087; 860-486-2840

UNIVERSITY OF HAWAII

ENVIRONMENTAL CENTER
WATER RESOURCES RESEARCH CENTER
Krauss Annex 19
2500 Dole St.
Honolulu, HI 96822 United States
Phone: 808-956-7361 Fax: 808-956-3980
E-mail: envctr@hawaii.edu
Website: www2.hawaii.edu/~envctr/

Founded: 1970

Membership: 1–100

Scope: State

Description: To stimulate, expand, and coordinate education, research, and service efforts of the university related to ecological relationships, natural resources, and environmental quality, with special relation to human needs and social institutions, particularly with regard to the state. for information on Liberal Studies BA Degree in Environmental Studies, check the University of Hawaii website: www.hawaii.edu/catalog/special-pgms-files/inter-progs.html#es

Keyword(s): Water Habitats & Quality

Contact(s):

James Moncur, Director
John Harrison, Environmental Coordinator; jth@hawaii.edu
Jacquelin Miller, Associate Environmental Coordinator; jackiem@hawaii.edu

UNIVERSITY OF HAWAII COOPERATIVE EXTENSION PROGRAM

COLLEGE OF TROPICAL AGRICULTURE AND HUMAN RESOURCES
College of Tropical Agriculture and Human Resources
Gilmore Hall 203, 3050 Maile Way
Univ. of Hawaii at Manoa
Honolulu, HI 96822 United States
Phone: 808-956-8397 Fax: 808-956-9105
E-mail: extension@ctahr.hawaii.edu
Website: www.ctahr.hawaii.edu/extout/extout.asp

Founded: 1907

Membership: 101–1,000

Scope: State

Description: The University of Hawaii (UH) Cooperative Extension Service (CES) covers areas of agriculture, natural resources and environment, home economics, community resource development and 4-H and youth development.

Contact(s):

Andrew Hashimoto, Dean and Director of Cooperative Extension, Interim
Richard Brock, Researcher/Fisheries Specialist; Univ. of Hawaii Sea Grant Program, 1000 Pope Rd./MSB 204, Honolulu, HI 96822; 808-956-2859; Fax: 808-956-2858
Ronald Mau, Associate Dean and Associate Director for Cooperative Extensions

UNIVERSITY OF MARYLAND COOPERATIVE EXTENSION

1296 Symons Hall
College Park, MD 20742 United States
Phone: 301-405-2072 Fax: 301-405-2963
E-mail: tf.43@umail.umd.edu
Website: www.agnr.umc.edu

Founded: N/A

Membership: 101–1,000

Scope: National

Publication(s): Located on website

Contact(s):

Thomas Fretz, Dean and Director of Agricultural Experiment Station; 301-405-2072; Fax: 301-314-9146; tf43@umail.umd.edu
James Hanson, Program Leader and Assistant Director of Agriculture and Nat; University of Maryland, Cooperative Extension, 1200 Symons Hall, College Park, MD 20742-5565; 301-405-7992; Fax: 301-405-2963
Jonathan Kays, Regional Natural Resource Specialist; University of Maryland, Cooperative Extension, Western Maryland Research and Education Center, 18330 Keedysville Road, Keedysville, MD 21756; 301-432-2735, ext. 323; Fax: 301-432-4089
Doug Lipton, Coordinator: Sea Grant Extension Program; University of Maryland, Cooperative Extension, 2218B Symons Hall, College Park, MD 20742; 301-405-1280
Bob Tjaden, Regional Natural Resource Specialist; University of Maryland, Cooperative Extension, Wye Research and Education Center, P.O. Box 169, Queenstown, MD 21658; 410-827-8056; Fax: 410-827-9039
James Wade, Associate Dean & Associate Director Maryland Cooperative Ext; University of Maryland, Cooperative Extension, 1200 Symons Hall, College Park, MD 20742-5565; 301-405-2907; Fax: 301-405-2963

UNIVERSITY OF MASSACHUSETTS EXTENSION

Stockbridge Hall, Box 30099, University of Massachusetts
Amherst, MA 01003 United States
Phone: 413-545-6555 Fax: 413-545-4800
E-mail: umextadm@umext.umass.edu
Website: www.umass.edu/umext/

Founded: N/A

Keyword(s): Forests/Forestry, Reduce/Reuse/Recycle, Wildlife & Species

Contact(s):

John Gerber, Director; jgerber@umext.umass.edu

Anna Hicks, Natural Resources and Environmental Conservation Program; Holdsworth Hall, University of Massachusetts, Amherst, MA 01003; 413-545-4743; Fax: 413-545-4358; ahicks@umext.umass.edu

Scott Jackson, Conservation Specialist; University of Massachusetts, Department of Forestry and Wildlife Management, Holdsworth Natural Resources Center, Amherst, MA 01003; 413-545-2665

UNIVERSITY OF NEW HAMPSHIRE COOPERATIVE EXTENSION

FORESTRY AND WILDLIFE PROGRAM
214 Nesmith Hall
131 Main Street
Durham, NH 03824-3597 United States
Phone: 603-862-1028 Fax: 603-862-0107
Website: www.ceinfo.unh.edu

Founded: 1925
Membership: N/A
Scope: State

Description: The natural resource components include Wildlife, Forest Stewardship, Community Forestry, Rural Economic Well-Being, Agriculture, and Natural Resource Conservation Education.

Keyword(s): Forests/Forestry, Land Issues, Public Lands/Greenspace, Water Habitats & Quality, Wildlife & Species

Contact(s):

Robert Edmonds, Program Leader: Forestry/Wildlife; 603-862-2619; bob.edmonds@unh.edu

Karen Bennett, Extension Specialist, Forest Resources; 603-862-4861; karen.bennett@unh.edu

Darrel Covell, Extension Specialist, Wildlife; 603-862-3594; darrel.covell@unh.edu

Frank Mitchell, Extension Specialist: Land and Water Conservation; 603-862-1067; frank.mitchell@unh.edu

Ellen Snyder, Extension Specialist, Biodiversity; 603-862-4277; ellen.snyder@unh.edu

Jeffrey Schloss, Extension Specialist: Water Resources Lakes Lay Monitoring; 603-862-3848; jeff.schloss@unh.edu

UNIVERSITY OF VERMONT EXTENSION

601 Main St.
Burlington, VT 05401-3439 United States
Phone: 802-656-2990 Fax: 802-656-8642
Website: www.uvm.edu/~uvmext/

Founded: 1914
Membership: 101–1,000
Scope: State

Description: UVM Extension is a system of nonformal education, bringing research information in a practical form to Vermonters. Extension with the specific expertise of our state university meets the needs of agriculture, communities, families, and youth. Programs are specifically focused on natural resource conservation, sustainable agriculture and rural development, health care in rural areas, resource distribution in communities, and the contemporary stresses on the American family.

Keyword(s): Air Quality/Atmosphere, Development/Developing Countries, Public Health

Contact(s):

Lawrence Forcier, Director

Vern Grubinger, Director of Sustainable Agriculture Center; 802-257-7967

Gary Deziel, Program Leader of Agriculture; 802-524-6501

Lois Frey, Family and Community Resource and Economic Development; 802-223-2389

Doug Lantagne, Natural Resources and Environmental Management; 802-656-2990

Thom McEvoy, Extension Forester; School of Natural Resources, 345 Aiken Center, Burlington, VT 05405; 802-656-2913; Fax: 802-656-8683

Ellen Rowe, Family and Community Resource and Economic Development; 802-751-8307

Dale Steen, Nutrition, Food Safety, and Health; 802-751-8307

UNIVERSITY OF VERMONT EXTENSION

PUBLICATIONS OFFICE
Communications Technology Resources
Agr. Eng. Bldg. 63 Carrigg Dr.
Burlington, VT 05405-0004 United States
Phone: 802-656-3024 Fax: 802-656-5878
Website: cpr.uvm.edu/ext

Founded: N/A
Membership: 1–100
Scope: Local, Regional

UTAH DEPARTMENT OF AGRICULTURE

P.O. Box 146500
Salt Lake City, UT 84114-6500 United States
Phone: 801-538-7100 Fax: 801-538-7126
Website: www.ag.state.ut.us

Founded: N/A
Membership: 101–1,000
Scope: State

Contact(s):

Renee Matsuura, Director of Administrative Services
Randy Parker, Director of Marketing
G. Wilson, Director of Plant Industry
James Christensen, Staff of Agricultural Development and Conservation
Bob Smoot, Staff of Weights and Measures
Kyle Stephens, Staff of Food and Dairy
Van Burgess, Deputy Commissioner
Miles Ferry, Commissioner
Michael Marshall, State Veterinarian
Ahmad Salari, State Chemist
El Shaffer, Information Officer

UTAH DEPARTMENT OF HEALTH

P.O. Box 14100
Salt Lake City, UT 84114-1011 United States
Phone: 801-538-6003 Fax: 801-538-6306
Website: www.dhrn.state.ut.us

Founded: N/A
Scope: State
Publication(s): Health Data Programs, Baby Your Baby
Keyword(s): Pollution (general), Public Health

Contact(s):

Rod Betit, Executive Director

Jana Kettering, Department of Health Public Information Officer; 801-538-6339

UTAH DEPARTMENT OF NATURAL RESOURCES

DIVISION OF UTAH STATE PARKS AND RECREATION
1594 W. North Temple, Suite 116
P.O. Box 146001
Salt Lake City, UT 84114-6001 United States
Phone: 801-538-7220 Fax: 801-538-7378
E-mail: parkcomment@utah.gov
Website: www.stateparks.utah.gov

Founded: N/A
Membership: 101–1,000
Scope: State

Description: Utah State Parks and Recreation is steward of many of Utah's natural and cultural resources.

Publication(s): Utah State Field Guide

Keyword(s): Public Lands/Greenspace, Recreation/Ecotourism

State Government Agencies

Contact(s):
Courtland Nelson, Director
Terry Green, Park Planning Manager; 801-538-7346
Jim Harland, Regional Manager of Northwest; 1084 North Redwood Road, Salt Lake City, UT 84116; 801-533-5127; Fax: 801-533-4229
Tim Smith, Regional Manager of Southeast; 435-259-3750
Gordon Topham, Regional Manager of Southwest; 585 North Main, Cedar City, UT 84720; 435-586-4497; Fax: 435-586-2789
Dennis Weaver, Regional Manager of Northeast; 435-649-9109
Jay Christianson, Chief of Law Enforcement; 801-538-7326
Dave Morrow, Deputy Director
Mary Tullius, Deputy Director
Ted Woolley, Boating Coordinator

UTAH FORESTRY, FIRE AND STATE LANDS

1594 W. North Temple, Suite 3520
P.O. Box 145703
Salt Lake City, UT 84114-5703 United States
Phone: 801-538-5555 Fax: 801-533-4111
Website: www.nr.utah.gov/slf/slfhome.htm

Founded: N/A
Membership: N/A
Scope: State
Description: The Utah Division of Forestry, Fire and State Lands manages all state-owned non-trust lands, and manages state forestry and fire control programs.
Contact(s):
Arthur Dufault, State Forester and Director
Karl Kappe, Strategic Planner

UTAH GEOLOGICAL SURVEY

1594 W. North Temple, Suite 3110, P.O. Box 146100
Salt Lake City, UT 84114-6100 United States
Phone: 801-537-3300 Fax: 801-537-3400
Website: www.ugs.state.ut.us

Founded: N/A
Scope: State
Publication(s): Geologic
Contact(s):
Richard Allis, Director

UTAH STATE DEPARTMENT OF NATURAL RESOURCES

1594 W. North Temple, Suite 3710, P.O. Box 145610
Salt Lake City, UT 84114-5610 United States
Phone: 801-538-7200 Fax: 801-538-7315
Website: www.nr.utah.gov

Founded: 1967
Membership: 100,001–500,000
Scope: State
Description: Sustain and enhance the quality of life for people today and tomorrow through the coordinated and balanced stewardship of our natural resources.
Keyword(s): Energy, Forests/Forestry, Land Issues, Public Lands/Greenspace, Recreation/Ecotourism, Water Habitats & Quality, Wildlife & Species
Contact(s):
Robert Morgan, Executive Director; 801-538-7200; Fax: 801-538-7315; nradm.bbarela@state.ut.us
Darin Bird, Assistant Director
Sherm Hoskins, Deputy Director
Hugh Thompson, Deputy Director

UTAH STATE DEPARTMENT OF NATURAL RESOURCES

DIVISION OF WATER RESOURCES
1594 W. North Temple, Suite 310
P.O.Box 146201
Salt Lake City, UT 84114-6201 United States
Phone: 801-538-7230 Fax: 801-538-7279
Website: www.nr.utah.gov

Founded: N/A
Membership: 1–100
Scope: State
Description: State Agency
Contact(s):
D. Anderson, Director

UTAH STATE DEPARTMENT OF NATURAL RESOURCES

DIVISION OF WILDLIFE RESOURCES
1594 W. North Temple, Suite 2110, P.O. Box 146301
Salt Lake City, UT 84114-6301 United States
Phone: 801-538-4700 Fax: 801-538-4745
Website: www.nr.state.ut.us

Founded: N/A
Scope: State
Publication(s): Weekly Wildlife News (Weekly), Wildlife Review (Quarterly)
Contact(s):
Kevin Conway, Director of Division of Wildlife Resources

UTAH STATE DEPARTMENT OF NATURAL RESOURCES

DIVISION OF WILDLIFE RESOURCES
1594 W. North Temple, Suite 2110, P.O. Box 146301
Salt Lake City, UT 84114-6301 United States
Phone: 801-538-4700 Fax: 801-538-4745
E-mail: wcomment.nrdwr@state.ut.us
Website: www.wildlife.utah.gov

Founded: N/A
Scope: State
Contact(s):
John Kimball, Director
J. Allan, Board Member
Connie Brooks, Board Member
Kevin Conway, Assistant Director
Rick Danvir, Board Member
B. Dastrup, Board Member
Walt Donaldson, Supervisor of Northeast Region; 152 E. 100 N., Vernal, UT 84078; 435-789-3103; Fax: 435-789-8343
Brenda Freeman, Board Member
Jim Guymon, Supervisor of Southern Region; P.O. Box 606, Cedar City, UT 84721; 435-865-6100; Fax: 435-586-2457
Robert Hasenyager, Supervisor of Northern Region; 515 E. 5300 S., Ogden, UT 84405; 435-476-2740; Fax: 435-479-4010
Raymond Heaton, Board Member
Miles Moretti, Supervisor of Southeastern Region; 475 W. Price River Dr., Suite C, Price, UT 84501; 435-636-0260; Fax: 435-637-7361
Max Morgan, Chair Person
Jordan Pedersen, Supervisor of Central Region; 115 N. Main St., Springfield, UT 84663; 435-489-5678; Fax: 435-489-7000

UTAH STATE DEPARTMENT OF NATURAL RESOURCES

UTAH ENERGY OFFICE
1594 W. North Temple, Suite 3610, P.O. Box 146480
Salt Lake City, UT 84114-6480 United States
Phone: 801-538-5428 Fax: 801-538-4795
E-mail: gfleisch.ueo@state.ut.us
Website: www.nr.utah.gov/energy/home.htm

Founded: N/A

Scope: State

Description: The Utah Energy Office is a state government office that works to promote energy efficiency and conservation.

Keyword(s): Energy

Contact(s):
Michael Glenn, Manager; 801538787; Fax: 801538795; mglenn.ueo@state.ut.us

UTAH STATE SOIL CONSERVATION COMMISSION

350 N. Redwood Rd.
Salt Lake City, UT 84116 United States
Phone: 801-538-7120 Fax: 801-538-4949
E-mail: sadginton@state.ut.us
Website: www.ag.state.ut.us

Founded: 1938

Scope: State

Description: Assists Utah's 39 soil conservation districts (SCD) in encouraging land operators to implement measures and practices; to prevent soil deterioration; restore depleted soil; prevent flood damage; improve irrigation water efficiency; and to encourage nonpoint water pollution control programs. The commission has 12 members; 5 ex-officio, and 7 governor-appointed SCD members with their alternates.

Keyword(s): Agriculture/Farming, Development/Developing Countries, Land Issues, Reduce/Reuse/Recycle

Contact(s):
Miles Ferry, Chairman
K. Jacobson, Executive

V

VERMONT DEPARTMENT OF AGRICULTURE, FOOD, AND MARKETS

116 State St., Drawer 20
Montpelier, VT 05620-2901 United States
Phone: 802-828-2500 Fax: 802-828-2361
Website: www.state.vt.us/agric

Founded: 1908

Membership: 1–100

Scope: State

Publication(s): Agriview, list available on request.

Contact(s):
Philip Benedict, Director of Plant Industry; 802-828-2431
Rudolph Polli, Business Manager of Administrative Services; 802-828-3567
Louise Calderwood, Deputy Commissioner of Administration
Leon Graves, Commissioner; 802-828-2430
Todd Johnson, State Veterinarian; 802-828-2421

VERMONT DEPARTMENT OF AGRICULTURE, FOOD, AND MARKETS

NATURAL RESOURCES CONSERVATION COUNCIL
116 State St.
Montpelier, VT 05620-2901 United States
Phone: 802-828-2416 Fax: 802-828-2361
E-mail: jwa@agr.state.vt.us

Founded: N/A

Membership: 1–100

Scope: Local

Description: The Conservation Council is the administrative body for the 14 conservation districts in Vermont. The goal of conservation districts is to ensure the wise use, protection and enhancement of Vermont soil, water, and related natural resources; to foster public awareness and appreciation of the need for conservation; and to advance the concept that we are all stewards of the living earth.

Keyword(s): Agriculture/Farming, Land Issues, Oceans/Coasts/Beaches

VERMONT DEPARTMENT OF AGRICULTURE, FOOD, AND MARKETS

STATE CONSERVATION COMMISSION
48 Bushey Dr.
Shelburne, VT 05482 United States
Phone: 802-985-2048

Founded: N/A

Scope: State

Contact(s):
Jon Anderson, Executive Secretary; 802-828-3529; Fax: 802-828-2361; jwa@agr.state.vt.us
Thomas Bushey, Chair; 802-985-2048; Fax: 802-951-6327

VERMONT DEPARTMENT OF HEALTH

108 Cherry St.
Burlington, VT 05402 United States
Phone: 802-863-7280 Fax: 802-863-7425
Website: www.state.vt.us/health

Founded: N/A

Membership: 101–1,000

Scope: State

Keyword(s): Air Quality/Atmosphere, Pollution (general), Public Health

Contact(s):
Larry Crist, Director of Health Protection; 802-863-7223
Jan Carney, Commissioner; 802-863-7280

VIRGIN ISLANDS COOPERATIVE EXTENSION SERVICE

University of Virgin Islands, R.R. 2, Box 10,000, Kingshill
St. Croix, VI 00850 United States
Phone: 340-692-4080 Fax: 340-692-4085
Website: www.rps.uvi.edu/cds

Founded: N/A

Scope: National

Contact(s):
Kwame Garcia, Director of CES
James Rakocy, Director of Agricultural Experiment Station; Univeristy of VI, RR2, Box 10,000, Kingshill, VI 00850; 340-692-4031; Fax: 340-692-4035
Clinton George, Program Leader of Agriculture and Natural Resources
Jozef Keularts, Coordinator, Integrated Pest Management of Pesticide Impact

VIRGIN ISLANDS SOIL AND WATER CONSERVATION DIVISION

Founded: N/A

Contact(s):
Henry Schuster, Commissioner; 809-778-0997

VIRGINIA COOPERATIVE EXTENSION

VIRGINIA POLYTECHNIC INSTITUTE AND STATE UNIVERSITY
Blacksburg, VA 24061-0402 United States
Phone: 540-231-5299 Fax: 540-231-4370
Website: www.ext.vt.edu/

Founded: N/A

Membership: 101–1,000

Scope: National

Contact(s):
J. Barrett, Director of Cooperative Extension; davebarr@vt.edu
Gerald Cross, Extension Wildlife Specialist; Department of Fisheries and Wildlife Sciences, Virginia Polytechnic Institute and State University, Blacksburg, VA 24061-0321; 540-231-8844; gecross@vt.edu
George Flick, Sea Grant Extension Seafood Technologist; Dept. of Food Science and Technology, Virginia Polytechnic Institute and State University, Blacksburg, VA 24061-0418; 540-231-6965; flickg@vt.edu
Louis Helfrich, Extension Fisheries Specialist; Department of Fisheries and Wildlife Sciences, Virginia Polytechnic Institute and State University, Blacksburg, VA 24061-0321; 540-231-5059; lhelfric@vt.edu
James Johnson, Project Leader of Forestry and Wildlife Extension; College of Natural Resources, Virginia Polytechnic Institute and State University, Blacksburg, VA 24061-0324; 540-231-7679; jej@vt.edu
Brian Nerrie, Extension Aquaculture Specialist; Virginia State University, P.O. Box 9081, Petersburg, VA 23806; 804-524-5903; bnerrie@vsu.edu
James Parkhurst, Extension Wildlife Specialist; Department of Fisheries & Wildlife Sciences, Virginia Polytechnic Institute and State University, Blacksburg, VA 24061-0321; 540-231-9283; Fax: 540-231-7265; jparkhur@vt.edu

VIRGINIA COOPERATIVE FISH AND WILDLIFE RESEARCH UNIT (USDI)

100 Cheatham Hall, Virginia Polytechnic Institute and State University
Blacksburg, VA 24061 United States
Phone: 540-231-5573 Fax: 540-231-7580
E-mail: vsutherl@vt.edu
Website: www.cnr.vt.edu/fisheries/

Founded: 1935
Scope: State
Description: Founded for training graduate students in fisheries and wildlife; with teaching and extension in fisheries and wildlife biology. Cooperatively supported by the Biological Resources Division of U.S.G.S., Department of Game and Inland Fisheries, and Virginia Polytechnic Institute and State University.
Publication(s): Annual reports, research publications., journal articles
Keyword(s): Water Habitats & Quality, Wildlife & Species

VIRGINIA DEPARTMENT OF AGRICULTURE AND CONSUMER SERVICES

1100 Bank Street
Suite 203
Richmond, VA 23219 United States
Phone: 804-786-2373 Fax: 804-371-7679
E-mail: webmaster@vdacs.state.va.us
Website: www.vdacs.state.va.us

Founded: 1877
Membership: 101–1,000
Scope: State
Description: To promote the economic growth and development of Virginia agriculture, encourage environmental stewardship, and provide consumer protection. Thirteen-member board appointed by Governor.
Publication(s): Bulletin
Keyword(s): Agriculture/Farming, Pollution (general), Wildlife & Species
Contact(s):
Elaine Lidholm, Director of Communication; 804-786-7686
Roy Seward, Director of Policy Planning and Research; 804-786-3535
Marvin Lawson, Manager of Pesticides Services; 804-371-6558
J. Courter, Department Commissioner; 804-786-3501
Elaine Lidholm, Editor

VIRGINIA DEPARTMENT OF CONSERVATION AND RECREATION

203 Governor St., Suite 302
Richmond, VA 23219 United States
Phone: 804-786-5046 Fax: 804-786-6141
E-mail: dcr@state.va.us
Website: www.dcr.state.va.us

Founded: N/A
Membership: 101–1,000
Scope: Local
Publication(s): Chesapeake Bay, Susquehanna River & Tidal Tributaries Public Access Guide, Virginia Outdoors Plan
Contact(s):
David Brickley, Director

VIRGINIA DEPARTMENT OF CONSERVATION AND RECREATION

203 Governor St., Suite 302
Richmond, VA 23219 United States
Phone: 804-786-1712 Fax: 804-786-6141
E-mail: pco@dcr.state.va.us
Website: www.dcr.state.va.us

Founded: N/A
Scope: State
Description: The Department's mission is to conserve, protect, enhance, and advocate wise use of Virginia's natural, recreational, and scenic resources in order to maintain and improve the quality of life for present and future generations. The Department is responsible for administrative support of various state collegial bodies including: The Board of Conservation and Recreation, the Virginia Cave Board, the Virginia Soil and Water Conservation Board, and the Breaks Interstate Park Commission.
Contact(s):
David Brickley, Director; 804-786-2123; dgbrickley@dcr.state.va.us
Linda Cox, Administrative Staff Specialist; 804-786-2123; ljcox@dcr.state va.us
Leon App, Chief Deputy, Acting; 804-786-4570; leonapp@dcr.state.va.us
David Dowling, Conservation & Development Programs Supervisor; 804-786-2291; Fax: 804-786-2291; ddowling@dcr.state.va.us

VIRGINIA DEPARTMENT OF CONSERVATION AND RECREATION

BOARD OF CONSERVATION AND RECREATION
203 Governor St., Suite 302
Richmond, VA 23219 United States

Founded: N/A
Contact(s):
W. Wingo, Chairman; 203 Governor St., Suite 302, Richmond, VA 23219

VIRGINIA DEPARTMENT OF CONSERVATION AND RECREATION

BREAKS INTERSTATE PARK COMMISSION
203 Governor St., Suite 302
Richmond, VA 23219 United States

Founded: N/A
Contact(s):
Joseph Elton, Advisor
Jack Sykes, Chairman; 101 Summitt Drive, Pikesville, KY 41501; 606-432-1447

VIRGINIA DEPARTMENT OF CONSERVATION AND RECREATION

CHIPPOKES PLANTATION FARM FOUNDATION
101 North 14th Street
Monroe Building, 11th Floor
Richmond, VA 23219 United States
Phone: 804-786-7950 Fax: 804-371-8500
E-mail: cffmuseum@dcr.state.va.us
Website: www.dcr.state.va.us

Founded: 1977
Membership: N/A
Scope: Local, State, Regional
Description: Chippokes Plantation Farm Foundation mission is to provide the public with educational experiences that focus on agriculture, forestry and conservation. The Chippokes Farm & Forestry Museum tells the story of life on a farm in rural Virginia through its extensive collection of tools, farm equipment, household items and other artifacts. Other educational offerings include demonstration gardens, a Forestry Interpretive Trail and an authenic 1930's Sawmill.
Contact(s):
Frederick Quayle, Chairman; Member, Senate of Virginia, 3808 Poplar Hill Road, Chesapeake, VA 23321
Katherine Wright, Advisor

VIRGINIA DEPARTMENT OF CONSERVATION AND RECREATION

CONSERVATION AND DEVELOPMENT OF PUBLIC BEACHES BOARD
203 Governor St., Suite 302
Richmond, VA 23209 United States

Founded: N/A
Contact(s):
Donald Campen, Chairman; 7603 Hillside Avenue, Richmond, VA 23229
Carlton Hill, Advisor

VIRGINIA DEPARTMENT OF CONSERVATION AND RECREATION

DIVISION OF ADMINISTRATION
203 Governor St., Suite 302
Richmond, VA 23219 United States
Phone: 804-786-6124 Fax: 804-786-6141
Website: www.dcr.state.va.us

Founded: N/A
Membership: 101–1,000
Scope: State
Contact(s):
Timothy Bishton, Director of Finance
Donald Bryne, Director of ADP
Karen Carey, Director of Human Resources
William Price, Director of Adminstration; 203 Governor St, Suite 204, Richmond, VA 23219; 804-786-0001
Gary Waugh, Public Relations Manager; 804-786-5045

VIRGINIA DEPARTMENT OF CONSERVATION AND RECREATION

DIVISION OF DAM SAFETY
203 Governor St., Suite 302
Richmond, VA 23219 United States
Phone: 804-786-1369 Fax: 804-786-0536
E-mail: dam@dcr.state.va.us
Website: www.dcr.va.us

Founded: N/A
Membership: 1–100
Scope: State

VIRGINIA DEPARTMENT OF CONSERVATION AND RECREATION

DIVISION OF NATURAL HERITAGE
217 Governor St.
Richmond, VA 23219 United States
Phone: 804-786-7951 Fax: 804-371-2674
Website: www.dcr.state.va.us/dnh

Founded: 1986
Membership: N/A
Scope: State
Description: The Division of Natural Heritage works to conserve VA's biodiversity through inventory, protection, and stewardship. Scientists collect field data on the location and status of natural communities and rare plant and animal species. Staff manage an information system to facilitate land management and conservation decisions, protect natural areas and manage the State Natural Area Preserve System.
Keyword(s): Ecosystems (precious), Land Issues, Public Lands/Greenspace, Wildlife & Species
Contact(s):
Thomas Smith, Director; 217 Governor St., Richmond, VA 23219; 804-786-7951
Rene Hypes, Project Review Coordinator; 804-371-2708; Fax: 804-371-2674; srhypes@dcr.state.va.us

VIRGINIA DEPARTMENT OF CONSERVATION AND RECREATION

DIVISION OF SOIL AND WATER CONSERVATION
203 Governor St., Suite 213
Richmond, VA 23219 United States
Phone: 804-786-1712
E-mail: pco@dcr.state.va.us
Website: www.dcr.state.va.us

Founded: N/A
Scope: State
Contact(s):
David Brickley, Director; dordswc@erols.com

VIRGINIA DEPARTMENT OF CONSERVATION AND RECREATION

DIVISION OF STATE PARKS
203 Governor St., Suite 306
Richmond, VA 23219 United States
Phone: 804-692-0403 Fax: 804-786-9294
Website: www.dcr.state.va.us

Founded: N/A
Scope: State
Publication(s): Virginia State Parks
Contact(s):
Joseph Elton, Director; 203 Governor St., Suite 306, Richmond, VA 23219; 804-786-4377

VIRGINIA DEPARTMENT OF CONSERVATION AND RECREATION

VIRGINIA CAVE BOARD
217 Governor Street, 3rd Floor
Richmond, VA 23219 United States
Phone: 804-786-7951 Fax: 804-371-2674

Founded: N/A
Contact(s):
Bill Keith, Chairman; Rt. 1 Box 17, Cleveland, VA 24225
Lawrence Smith, Advisor

VIRGINIA DEPARTMENT OF ENVIRONMENTAL QUALITY

629 E. Main St.
Richmond, VA 23219 United States
Phone: 804-698-4000 Fax: 804-698-4500
E-mail: vanaturally@deq.state.va.us
Website: www.deq.state.va.us

Founded: 1993

Scope: State

Description: The Department of Environmental Quality strives to provide efficient, cost-effective services that promote a proper balance between environmental improvement and economic vitality.

Keyword(s): Air Quality/Atmosphere, Reduce/Reuse/Recycle

Contact(s):

Robert Burnley, Director; 804-698-4020; rgburnley@deq.state.va.us
Ann Regan, Environmental Education Coordinator

VIRGINIA DEPARTMENT OF FORESTRY

900 Natural Resources Dr., Suite 800
Charlottesville, VA 22903 United States
Phone: 804-977-6555 Fax: 804-296-2369
Website: www.dof.state.va.us

Founded: 1914

Scope: State

Description: The mission of the Department of Forestry is to protect and develop healthy, sustainable forest resources for Virginians. The Department assists private landowners with the management and protection of forest resources. We also provide at-cost seedlings for reforestation of the state's forestlands, and management of public state forests and other state public forest lands.

Contact(s):

Faye Difazio, Fiscal Director
Ellie Whinnery, Human Resources Director
Edwina Blalock, Team Leader for Information Technology
James Garner, State Forester
Ronald Jenkins, Team Leader for General Services
Bettina Ring, Deputy State Forester
Lou Southard, Forest Protection
James Starr, Team Leader for Forest Management
Timothy Tigner, Team Leader for Resource Information

VIRGINIA DEPARTMENT OF GAME AND INLAND FISHERIES

4010 West Broad Street
Post Office Box 11104
Richmond, VA 23230 United States
Phone: 804-367-1000 Fax: 804-367-9147
E-mail: dgifweb@dgif.state.va.us
Website: www.dgif.state.va.us

Founded: 1916

Membership: 101–1,000

Scope: State

Description: To provide for the management, conservation, restoration, and enhancement of the Commonwealth's fish and wildlife resources. The Department also provides boat registration and titling services and boating law administration and enforcement, as well as providing public informational and educational services related to wildlife resources and recreational boating. Our major publication is Virginia Wildlife magazine, published monthly.

Publication(s): Virginia Wildlife Magazine

Keyword(s): Recreation/Ecotourism, Water Habitats & Quality, Wildlife & Species

Contact(s):

Bill Woodfin, Department Director; 804-367-9231; Fax: 804-367-0405; bwoodfin@dgif.state.va.us
Ray Davis, Director of Administration; 804-367-2387; Fax: 804-367-0405; rdavis@dgif.state.va.us
Bob Duncan, Wildlife Division Director; 804-367-6878; Fax: 804-367-0262; bduncan@dgif.state.va.us
Herb Foster, Law Enforcement Operations; 804-367-0957; Fax: 804-367-2430; hfoster@dgif.state.va.us
Gary Martel, Fisheries Division Director; 804-367-1004; Fax: 804-367-2628; gmartel@dgif.state.va.us
Charles Sledd, Program Development Director; 804-367-6481; Fax: 804-367-0405; csledd@dgif.state.va.us
Jeff Uerz, Law Enforcement Administration; 804-367-1005; Fax: 804-367-2430; juerz@dgif.state.va.us
David Whitehurst, Wildlife Diversity Division Director; 804-367-0940; Fax: 804-367-2427; dwhitehurst@dgif.state.va.us
James Adams, Capital Programs Director; 804-367-0183; Fax: 804-367-2311; jadams@dgif.state.va.us
Terry Bradberry, Outdoor Education Program Manager; 804-367-0076; Fax: 804-367-2430; tbradbery@dgif.state.va.us
Larry Harizanoff, Human Resources Director; 804-367-0849; Fax: 804-367-0256; lharizanoff@dgif.state.va.us
Larry Hart, Boating Section Manager; 804-367-1295; Fax: 804-367-1064; lhart@dgif.state.va.us
Virgil Kopf, IMS Director; 804-367-0639; Fax: 804-367-0336; vkopf@dgif.state.va.us
Rick Busch, Wildlife Federal Aid Coordinator; 804-367-1215; Fax: 804-367-0262; rbusch@dgif.state.va.us
Jeff Decker, Boating Education Coordinator; 804-367-8693; Fax: 804-367-2311; jdecker@dgif.state.va.us
Fred Leckie, Fisheries Federal Aid Coordinator; 804-367-8994; Fax: 804-367-2628; fleckie@dgif.state.va.us
Julia Smith, Media Relations Coordinator; 804-367-0991; Fax: 804-367-4391; jsmith@dgif.state.va.us
Lee Walker, Virginia Wildlife Magazine Editor; 804-367-0486; Fax: 804-367-0488; lwalker@dgif.state.va.us

VIRGINIA DEPARTMENT OF GAME AND INLAND FISHERIES

REGION II (LYNCHBURG)
1121 Thomas Jefferson Rd.
Forest, VA 24551-9223 United States
Phone: 804-525-7522 Fax: 804-525-7720
Website: www.dgif.state.va.us

Founded: N/A

Scope: State

VIRGINIA DEPARTMENT OF GAME AND INLAND FISHERIES

REGION III
1796 Highway Sixteen
Marion, VA 24354 United States
Phone: 540-783-4860 Fax: 540-783-6115
E-mail: vjessee@dgif.state.va.us
Website: www.dgif.state.va.us

Founded: 1917

Scope: State

Description: Coordination of wildlife management, fisheries management, and wildlife law enforcement in region.

VIRGINIA DEPARTMENT OF GAME AND INLAND FISHERIES

REGION IV (STAUNTON)
Verona, VA 24482 United States
Phone: 540-248-9360 Fax: 540-248-9399
Website: www.dgif.state.va.us

Founded: N/A

Membership: 1–100

Scope: Regional

VIRGINIA DEPARTMENT OF GAME AND INLAND FISHERIES

REGIONAL OFFICE - LYNCHBURG
1132 Thomas Jefferson Road
Forest, VA 24551-9223 United States
Phone: 434-525-7522 Fax: 434-525-7720
Website: www.dgif.state.va.us

Founded: N/A

Scope: State

Description: To provide for the management, conservation, restoration, and enhancement of the Commonwealth's fish and wildlife resources. The department also provides boat registration and titling services and boating law administration and enforcement; as well as providing public informational and educational services related to wildlife resources and recreational boating.

Publication(s): Virginia Wildlife

Keyword(s): Recreation/Ecotourism, Water Habitats & Quality, Wildlife & Species

Contact(s):

James Adams, Capital Programs Director
Raymond Davis, Director of Administration; 804-367-2387; rdavis@dgif.state.va.us
Robert Duncan, Director of Wildlife Division; 804-367-9588; rduncan@dgif.state.va.us
Larry Harizanoff, Director of Human Resources; 804-367-8195; lharizanoff@dgif.state.va.us
Virgil Kopf, Director of Information Management Systems; 804-367-0787; vkopf@dgif.state.va.us
Gary Martel, Director of Fisheries Division; 804-367-0509; gmartel@dgif.state.va.us
Charles Sledd, Director of Program Development; 804-367-6481; csledd@dgif.state.va.us
Jeffrey Uerz, Director of Law Enforcement Division; 804-367-0776; juerz@dgif.state.va.us
David Whitehurst, Director of Wildlife Diversity Division; 804-367-4335; dwhitehurst@dgif.state.va.us
Terry Bradberry, Outdoor Education
Rick Busch, Federal Aid Coordinator of Wildlife; 804-367-1215; rbusch@dgif.state.va.us
Larry Hart, Boat Registration Section, Title; 804-367-1295; lhart@dgif.state.va.us
Fred Leckie, Federal Aid Coordinator of Fisheries; 804-367-8629; fleckie@dgif.state.va.us
Charles Sledd, Boating Law Administrator; 804-367-6481; csledd@dgif.state.va.us
Julia Smith, Media Relations Coordinator; 804-367-0991; jsmith@dgif.state.va.us
Lee Walker, Editor; 804-367-0486; Fax: 804-367-0488; lwalker@dgif.state.va.us

VIRGINIA DEPARTMENT OF HEALTH

Commissioners Office, Suite 214, Main St. Station
Richmond, VA 23219 United States
Phone: 804-786-3561 Fax: 804-786-4616
Website: www.vdh.state.va.us

Founded: 1872

Scope: State

Description: The department carries out protective and preventive public health services for all citizens of the Commonwealth and provides public health care services to the indigent.

Publication(s): Virginia's Health

Contact(s):

Anne Peterson, Commissioner
Helen Tarantino, Deputy Commissioner of Administration

VIRGINIA DEPARTMENT OF MINES, MINERALS AND ENERGY

Ninth St. Office Bldg., 8th Fl., 202 N. Ninth St.
Richmond, VA 23219 United States
Phone: 804-692-3200 Fax: 804-692-3237
E-mail: dmmeinfo@mme.state.va.us
Website: www.mme@state.va.us

Founded: 1985

Membership: 101–1,000

Scope: State

Description: The department is committed to enhancing the development and conservation of energy and mineral resources in a safe and environmentally sound manner in order to support a more productive economy in Virginia.

Contact(s):

O. Dishner, Director

VIRGINIA DEPARTMENT OF MINES, MINERALS AND ENERGY

DIVISION OF ENERGY

Founded: N/A

Description: The Division of Energy promotes the efficient use and conservation of energy and the use of alternative energy sources.

Contact(s):

Stephen Walz, Director; Ninth St. Office Bldg., 8th Fl., 202 N. Ninth St., Richmond, VA 23219; 540-692-3211

VIRGINIA DEPARTMENT OF MINES, MINERALS AND ENERGY

DIVISION OF GAS AND OIL
Abingdon, VA 24210 United States
Phone: 540-676-5423 Fax: 540-676-5459
Website: www.mme.state.va.us

Founded: N/A

Membership: 1–100

Scope: State

Description: The Division of Gas and Oil regulates the operation and reclamation of gas and oil extractions.

Contact(s):

Bob Wilson, Director

VIRGINIA DEPARTMENT OF MINES, MINERALS AND ENERGY

DIVISION OF MINED LAND RECLAMATION
P.O. Drawer 900
Big Stone Gap, VA 24219 United States
Phone: 276-523-8100 Fax: 276-523-8163
E-mail: mmeinfo@mme.state.va.us
Website: www.mme.state.va.us

Founded: N/A

Scope: State

Description: The Division of Mined Land Reclamation regulates the operation of coal surface-mining activities, enforces the reclamation laws and regulations, and administers financial resources for reclaiming abandoned coal mining sites.

VIRGINIA DEPARTMENT OF MINES, MINERALS AND ENERGY

DIVISION OF MINERAL MINING
P.O. Box 3727
Charlottesville, VA 22903 United States
Phone: 434-951-6310 Fax: 434-951-6325
E-mail: mmeinfo@mme.state.va.us
Website: www.mme.state.va.us

Founded: N/A

Scope: State

Description: The Division of Mineral Mining regulates the operation of noncoal mining activities for environmental protection and worker safety.

Contact(s):

Conrad Spangler, Director; P.O. Box 3727, Charlottesville, VA 22903; 804-951-6310

VIRGINIA DEPARTMENT OF MINES, MINERALS, AND ENERGY

DIVISION OF MINES
Big Stone Gap, VA 24219 United States
Phone: 276-523-8224 Fax: 276-523-8239
Website: www.mme.state.va.us

Founded: N/A

Scope: State

Description: The Division of Mines enforces the coal mining laws of the Commonwealth to promote the safety and health of coal miners.

Contact(s):

Frank Linkous, Chief; P.O. Drawer 900, Big Stone Gap, VA 24219; 540-523-8100

VIRGINIA MARINE RESOURCES COMMISSION

2600 Washington Avenue, 3rd Floor
Newport News, VA 23607 United States
Phone: 757-247-2200 Fax: 757-247-2020
Website: www.state.va.us/vmrc

Founded: 1875

Membership: 101–1,000

Scope: State

Description: This state agency holds regulatory jurisdiction over all commercial and sports fishing, marine fish, marine shellfish, and marine organisms in the tidal waters of Virginia. Holds permit jurisdiction on all projects involving use of state-owned submerged lands and authority over use or development in vegetated and nonvegetated tidal wetlands and coastal primary sand dunes.

Publication(s): Virginia Landings Bulletin

Contact(s):

Erik Barth, Chief of Management Information Systems
Steven Bowman, Chief of Law Enforcement
Robert Craft, Chief of Administration and Finance
Robert Grabb, Chief, Habitat Management
William Pruitt, Commissioner
Jack Travelstead, Chief of Fisheries Management
Jim Wesson, Chief of Conservation and Replenishment

VIRGINIA MUSEUM OF NATURAL HISTORY

1001 Douglas Ave.
Martinsville, VA 24112 United States
Phone: 540-666-8600 Fax: 276-632-6487
Website: www.vmnh.org

Founded: 1988

Membership: 1–100

Scope: State

Description: Preserves, studies, and interprets Virginia's natural and cultural heritage. Statewide system of museum facilities, research sites, and educational programs. The museum has more than eleven million specimens in collections.

Publication(s): Virginia Explorer, The, Children's Activity Books, Scientific Publication Series, Books, Virginia Naturally

Keyword(s): Wildlife & Species

Contact(s):

Stephen Pike, Executive Director; spike@ngocomm.net
Judy Winston, Research Director; 540-666-8609; jwinston@vmnh.org

VIRGINIA OUTDOORS FOUNDATION

NORTHERN VIRGINIA OFFICE- ALDIE
CHARLOTTESVILLE OFFICE
SOUTHWESTERN VIRGINIA OFFICE- BLACKSBURG
203 Governor St., Suite 317
Richmond, VA 23219 United States
Phone: 804-225-2147 Fax: 804-371-4810
E-mail: ldt@dcr.state.va.us
Website: www.virginiaoutdoorsfoundation.org

Founded: 1966

Membership: N/A

Scope: State

Description: To preserve Virginia's natural scenic, historic, scientific, open space, and recreational areas by means of private philanthropy. The Foundation accepts gifts of cash, stock, real property, or open spaces easements to achieve its purpose.

Keyword(s): Agriculture/Farming, Ecosystems (precious), Land Issues, Public Lands/Greenspace, Reduce/Reuse/Recycle

Contact(s):

Sherry Buttrick, Charlottesville Office Director; 1010 Harris St, Suite 4, Charlottesville, VA 22903; 434-293-3423; Fax: 434-293-3859; vofsherryb@aol.com
Faye Cooper, Staunton Office Director; 11 E. Beverly Street, Staunton, VA 24401; 540-886-2460; Fax: 540-886-2464; fcooper@virginiaoutdoorsfoundation.org
Leslie Grayson, Northern Virginia Office Director; P.O.Box 322, Aldie, VA 20105; 703-327-6118; Fax: 703-327-6444; voflgray@aol.com
Leslie Trew, Richmond Office Director; 203 Governor St, Richmond, VA 22319; 804-225-2147; Fax: 804-371-4810; ldt@dcr.state.va.us
Tamara Vance, Executive Director; 302 Royal Lane, Blacksburg, VA 24060; 540-951-2822; Fax: 540-951-2695; voftvance@aol.com

VIRGINIA SOIL AND CONSERVATION BOARD

7293 Hanover Green Dr., Suite B-101
Mechanicsville, VA 23111 United States
Phone: 804-559-0324 Fax: 804-559-0325
E-mail: vaswcd@erols.com
Website: www.vaswcd.erols.com

Founded: N/A

Scope: Regional

Contact(s):

Stephanie Martin, Executive Director; 804-786-3914; Fax: 804-786-1798
Jack Frye, Advisor
Charles Horn, Chairman; 203 Governor St., Suite 206, Richmond, VA 23219; 804-786-2064

W

WASHINGTON DEPARTMENT OF AGRICULTURE

Olympia, WA 98504-2560 United States
Phone: 360-902-1800
Website: www.wa.gov/agr

Founded: N/A

Scope: State

Keyword(s): Agriculture/Farming, Pollution (general)

Contact(s):

Jim Jesernig, Director; 360-902-1801
Bob Arrington, Assistant Director of Pesticide Management Division; 360-902-2011
Bill Brookerson, Deputy Director; 360-902-1810
John Daley, Assistant Director of Food Safety and Animal Health Division
Bob Gore, Assistant Director of Commodity Inspection; 360-902-1827
Robert Mead, State Veterinarian; 360-902-1881

Mary Toohey, Assistant Director of Laboratory Services; 360-902-1907
Linda Waring, Information Officer; 360-902-1815

WASHINGTON DEPARTMENT OF ECOLOGY

P.O. Box 47600
Olympia, WA 98504-7600 United States
Phone: 360-407-6000
Website: www.ecy.wa.gov

Founded: 1970

Description: Charged with programs of air quality control, water pollution control, solid waste management, management of water resources, hazardous waste management, reduction, and cleanup, shoreline management, coastal zone management, and State Environmental Policy Act (SEPA).

Contact(s):

Tom Fitzsimmons, Director; 360-407-7001; Fax: 360-407-6989; tfit@461.us.gov
Carol Fleskes, Administrative Services Manager; 360-407-7012
Bill Alkire, Assistant Director of Legislative Relations; 360-407-7003
Sandy Howard, Public Information Officer
David Mears, Attorney General of Office of Attorney General; 360-459-6158
Phyllis Shafer, Librarian; 206-407-6150
Dan Silver, Deputy Director; 360-407-7011; Fax: 360-407-6989
Nancy Stevenson, Chief Financial Officer; 360-407-7005

WASHINGTON DEPARTMENT OF ECOLOGY

CENTRAL REGIONAL OFFICE
15 West Yakima Ave., Suite 200
Yakima, WA 98902 United States
Phone: 509-575-2490 Fax: 509-575-2809
Website: www.ecy.wa.gov

Founded: N/A

Scope: State

Contact(s):

Polly Zehm

WASHINGTON DEPARTMENT OF ECOLOGY

EASTERN REGIONAL OFFICE
4601 North Monroe
Spokane, WA 99205 United States
Phone: 509-456-2926 Fax: 509-456-6175
Website: www.ecy.wa.gov

Founded: N/A

Scope: State

Contact(s):

Tony Grover; 509-456-6149; agro461@ecy.wa.gov

WASHINGTON DEPARTMENT OF ECOLOGY

NORTHWEST REGIONAL OFFICE
3190 160th Ave., SE
Bellevue, WA 98008 United States
Phone: 425-649-7000 Fax: 425-649-7098
Website: www.ecy.wa.gov

Founded: N/A

Scope: Regional

Description: Environmental Agency

Contact(s):

Ray Hellwig, Regional Director; 425-649-7010

WASHINGTON DEPARTMENT OF ECOLOGY SOUTHWEST REGIONAL OFFICE

SOUTHWEST REGIONAL OFFICE
P.O. Box 47775
Olympia, WA 98504-7775 United States
Phone: 360-407-6300 Fax: 360-407-6305
Website: www.ecy.wa.gov

Founded: N/A

Membership: 101–1,000

Scope: Regional

Contact(s):

Sue Mauermann, Regional Director; 360-407-6307; smau461@ecy.wa.gov

WASHINGTON DEPARTMENT OF FISH AND WILDLIFE

WASHINGTON FISH AND WILDLIFE COMMISSION
600 Capitol Way N.
Olympia, WA 98501-1091 United States
Phone: 360-902-2200 Fax: 360-902-2947
E-mail: webmaster@dfw.wa.gov
Website: www.wa.gov/wdfw

Founded: 1933

Membership: 1,001–10,000

Scope: State

Description: Mission: "Sound Stewardship of Fish and Wildlife". The department is responsible for preservation, protection, and perpetuation of wildlife, fish, shellfish, and fish and wildlife habitat; maximizing fishing, hunting, and recreational opportunities compatible with healthy and diverse fish and wildlife populations; maintaining the economic well-being and stability of the fishing industry; promoting orderly fisheries; and enhancing recreational and commercial fishing.

Keyword(s): Ecosystems (precious), Land Issues, Oceans/Coasts/Beaches, Pollution (general), Population, Recreation/Ecotourism, Water Habitats & Quality, Wildlife & Species

Contact(s):

Russ Cahill, Chair, Fish and Wildlife Commission; 360-902-2267; Fax: 360-902-2448; commission@dfw.wa.gov
Jeff Koenings, Ph.D., Director; 360-902-2225; Fax: 360-902-2947; koenijpk@dfw.wa.gov
Larry Peck, Deputy Director; 360-902-2650; Fax: 360-902-2224; peckrlp@dfw.wa.gov
Phil Anderson, Staff Director of Intergovernmental Policy Group; 360-902-2720; Fax: 360-902-2158; anderpma@dfw.wa.gov
John Andrews, Regional Director, Region 1; 8702 N.Division St., Spokane, WA 99218-1199; 509-456-4082; Fax: 509-456-4071; anderjga@dfw.wa.gov
Lew Atkins, Assistant Director of Fish Program; 360-902-2651; Fax: 360-902-2183; atkinlja@dfw.wa.gov
Dennis Beich, Regional Director, Region 2; 1550 Alder St. NW, Ephrata, WA 98823-9699; 509-754-4624; Fax: 509-754-5257; beichdvb@dfw.wa.gov
Bruce Bjork, Assistant Director of Enforcement Program; 360-902-2373; Fax: 360-902-2942; bjorkbb@dfw.wa.gov
Dave Brittell, Assistant Director of Wildlife Program; 360-902-2515; Fax: 360-902-2162; brittjdb@dfw.wa.gov
Penny Cusick, Personnel Manager; 360-902-2276; Fax: 360-902-2392; cusicprc@dfw.wa.gov
Bob Everitt, Regional Director, Region 4; 16018 Mill Creek Blvd., Mill Creek, WA 98012-1296; 425-775-1311; Fax: 425-338-1066; everide@dfw.wa.gov
Greg Hueckel, Assistant Director of Habitat Program; 360-902-2416; Fax: 360-902-2946; hueckgjh@dfw.wa.gov
Jim Lux, Assisant Director of Business Services Program; 360-902-2200; Fax: 360-902-2230; luxjjl@dfw.wa.gov
Sue Patnude, Regional Director, Region 6; 48 Devonshire Rd., Montesano, WA 98563-9618; 360-249-4628; Fax: 360-664-0689; patnusm@dfw.wa.gov

Jeff Tayer, Regional Director, Region 3; 1701 S. 24th Ave., Yakima, WA 98902-5720; 509-575-2740; Fax: 509-575-2474; tayerjjt@dfw.wa.gov
Lee Van Tussenbrook, Regional Director, Region 5; 2108 Grand Blvd., Vancouver, WA 98661-4624; 360-696-6211; Fax: 360-906-6776; vantulv@dfw.wa.gov
Sara LaBorde, Special Assistant of Quality Initiatives; 360-902-2224; Fax: 360-902-2947; laborsgl@dfw.wa.gov
Tim Smith, Special Asst., Nearshore Project & Salmon Recovery Grants; 360-902-2223; Fax: 360-902-2947; smithtrs@dfw.wa.gov
Tim Waters, Special Assistant of Public Affairs; 360-902-2250; Fax: 360-902-2171; watertrw@dfw.wa.gov
Josh Weiss, Special Assistant of Legislative Affairs; 360-902-2226; Fax: 360-902-2157; weissjw@dfw.wa.gov

WASHINGTON DEPARTMENT OF NATURAL RESOURCES

P.O. Box 47001
Olympia, WA 98504-7001 United States
Phone: 360-902-1000 Fax: 360-902-1775
Website: www.wa.gov/dnr

Founded: N/A
Membership: N/A
Scope: State, Regional
Publication(s): DNR News
Keyword(s): Ecosystems (precious), Forests/Forestry, Land Issues, Oceans/Coasts/Beaches, Pollution (general), Public Lands/Greenspace, Recreation/Ecotourism, Water Habitats & Quality, Wildlife & Species
Contact(s):

Bonnie Bunning, Executive Director
Pat McElroy, Executive Director
Randy Acker, Manager of Resource Protection Division; 360-902-1300
Al Bloomberg, Manager of Information Technology Division; 360-902-1500
Bill Boyum, Manager of Agricultural Resources Division, Acting; 360-902-1130
Catherine Elliott, Manager of Forest Practices Division; 360-902-1400
Meg Grimaldi, Manager of Employee Services Division; 360-902-1150
Tony Ifie, Manager of Engineering Division; 360-920-1200
Ray Lasmanis, Region Manager; 360-577-2025
Connie Manson, Geology Library Manager; 360-902-1472
Loren Stern, Manager of Financial Management Division; 360-902-1250
Chuck Turley, Manager of Aquatic Resources Division; 360-902-1100
Jennifer Belcher, Commissioner of Public Lands; 360-902-1004; Fax: 360-902-1775
Michelle Benton, Executive Assistant; 360-902-1004
Julie Boyer, Department Supervisor; 360-902-1034
Kaleen Cottingham, Deputy Commissioner; 360-902-1003
Terry Kirkpatrick, Business System Support; 360-902-1600
Bruce McKay, Land Steward
Fran McNair, Aquatic Steward
Doug Sutherland, Commissioner
Sue Zemek, Communications; 360-902-1023

WASHINGTON DEPARTMENT OF NATURAL RESOURCES

CENTRAL REGION
1405 Rush Rd.
Chehalis, WA 98532-8763 United States
Phone: 360-748-2383 Fax: 360-748-2387
Website: www.wadnr.gov

Founded: N/A
Membership: 101–1,000
Scope: Regional
Contact(s):

Vicky Christenson, Central Region Manager

WASHINGTON DEPARTMENT OF NATURAL RESOURCES

NORTHEAST REGION
P.O. Box 47001
Olympia, WA 98504 United States
Phone: 360-902-1000 Fax: 360-902-1775
E-mail: information@wadnr.gov

Founded: N/A
Scope: State

WASHINGTON DEPARTMENT OF NATURAL RESOURCES

NORTHWEST REGION
919 N Township St.
Sedro Woolley, WA 98284 United States
Phone: 360-856-3500 Fax: 360-856-2150
Website: www.wadnr.gov

Founded: N/A
Membership: 101–1,000
Scope: Local
Contact(s):

Bill Wallace, Regional Manager; 360-856-3500

WASHINGTON DEPARTMENT OF NATURAL RESOURCES

SOUTH PUGET SOUND REGION
950 Farming Avenue N.
Enumclaw, WA 98022 United States
Phone: 360-825-1631 Fax: 360-825-1672

Founded: N/A
Scope: State
Contact(s):

Gretchen Nicholas, Staff; 360-825-1631

WASHINGTON DEPARTMENT OF NATURAL RESOURCES

SOUTHEAST REGION
713 Bowers Road
Ellensburg, WA 98926 United States
Phone: 509-925-8510

Founded: N/A
Scope: State

WASHINGTON DEPARTMENT OF NATURAL RESOURCES

SOUTHWEST REGION
P.O. Box 280
Castle Rock, WA 98611-0280 United States
Phone: 360-577-2025 Fax: 360-274-4196
E-mail: tami.riepe@wadnr.gov

Founded: N/A
Membership: 1–100
Scope: Regional
Description: Scientific Consulting
Contact(s):

Rick Cooper; 360-577-2025

WASHINGTON NATURAL HERITAGE PROGRAM

P.O. Box 47014
Olympia, WA 98504-7014 United States
Phone: 360-902-1600 Fax: 360-902-1789
Website: www.wa.gov/dnr/

Founded: 1978
Scope: State
Description: Identify and evaluate native ecosystems and species, set conservation priorities, provide information to

protect these irreplaceable resources for the benefit of current and future generations.

Publication(s): Endangered, Threatened, and Sensitive Vascular Plants of Washington with working list of Rare Non-vascular Species, State of Washington Natural Heritage Plan

Keyword(s): Wildlife & Species

Contact(s):

John Gamon, Program Manager and Botanist; 360-902-1661

WASHINGTON STATE

DEPARTMENT OF NATURAL RESOURCES
OLYMPIC REGION
411 Tillicum Lane
Forks, WA 98331 United States
Phone: 360-374-6131 Fax: 360-374-5446
Website: www.wa.gov/dnr/

Founded: N/A

Scope: State, Regional

Description: On Washington's Olympic Peninsula: administer State Forest Practices Rules for non-federal landowners; manage 376,000 acres of State Forests for environmental and social values as well as for income to public beneficiaries; manage 13 Natural Areas (15,000 acres).

Keyword(s): Ecosystems (precious), Forests/Forestry, Oceans/Coasts/Beaches, Public Lands/Greenspace, Recreation/Ecotourism, Water Habitats & Quality, Wildlife & Species

Contact(s):

Charlie Cortelyou, Regional Manager; 360-374-6131
Scott Horton, Wildlife Biologist; 360-374-6131

WASHINGTON STATE CONSERVATION COMMISSION

P.O. Box 47721
300 Desmond Drive
Olympia, WA 98504-7721 United States
Phone: 206-407-6200 Fax: 206-407-6215
Website: www.scc.wa.gov

Founded: 1939

Membership: N/A

Scope: Local, State

Description: The mission of the Washington State Conservation Commission is to protect, conserve and enhance the natural resources of the state. The Commission provides leadership, partnerships and resources to support 48 locally governed conservation districts in promoting conservation stewardship by all. The Commission encourages the cooperation and collaboration of the federal, state, regional, interstate, and local public agencies which assist them.

Keyword(s): Agriculture/Farming, Land Issues, Pollution (general), Water Habitats & Quality

Contact(s):

Steven Meyer, Executive Director; 206-407-6201; Fax: 360-407-6215; smey461@ecy.wa.gov
Kristin Bettridge, Adminstrative Manager; 360-407-6209; Fax: 360-407-6215; kbet461@ecy.wa.gov
Lynn Brown, Commission Chair; P.O. Box 775, Ellensburg, WA 98926

WASHINGTON STATE DEPARTMENT OF ECOLOGY

WASHINGTON CONSERVATION CORPS
P.O. Box 47600
Olympia, WA 98599-7600 United States
Phone: 360-407-7038 Fax: 360-407-6902
E-mail: lbam461@ecy.wa.gov
Website: www.ecy.wa.gov/programs/sea/wcc/index.html

Founded: 1983

Membership: 101–1,000

Scope: Local, State, Regional

Description: We are an AmeriCorps Program affiliated with Washington State Government. We conduct environmental restoration and recreational trails construction projects in National Parks, Wilderness Areas, and other Federal, State, and local lands. Our philosophy is hard work, beautiful locations, and the time of your life. We hire 150 members each year. Call or e-mail for applications.

Keyword(s): Ecosystems (precious), Forests/Forestry, Recreation/Ecotourism, Wildlife & Species

WASHINGTON STATE EXTENSION SERVICES

Director, WA State U., P.O. Box 646230
Pullman, WA 99164 United States
Phone: 509-335-2933 Fax: 509-335-2926
Website: www.ext.wsu.edu/

Founded: N/A

Scope: State

Description: Washington State University Cooperative Extension helps people develop leadership skills and use research-based knowledge to improve their economic status and quality of life.

Keyword(s): Agriculture/Farming, Forests/Forestry, Reduce/Reuse/Recycle

Contact(s):

Edward Adams, Program Leader; Washington State University Cooperative Extension, 668 N. Riverpoint Blvd., Box B, Spokane, WA 99202-1662; 509-358-7960; Fax: 509-358-7900; adamse@wsu.edu
David Baumgartner, Extension Forester; Department of Natural Resource Sciences, P.O. Box 646410, Washington State University, Pullman, WA 99164-6410; 509-335-2964
Sheila Gray, Extension Urban and Community Horticulture, Interim; Washington State University, 207 4th Ave. N., Kelso, WA 98262-4124; 360-577-3014
Donald Hanley, Extension Forester; College of Forest Resources, University of Washington, Box 352100, Seattle, WA 98195-2100; 206-685-4960
John Munn, Extension Naturalist; Washington State University CES, 600 128th St., SE, Everett, WA 98208; 425-388-2400; Fax: 425-338-3994
Michael Tate, Associate Dean and Associate Director of Extension Services

WASHINGTON STATE OFFICE OF ENVIRONMENTAL EDUCATION

Office of Superintendent of Public Instruction, 2800 NE 200th St.
Seattle, WA 98155-1418 United States
Phone: 206-365-3893 Fax: 206-367-4540
E-mail: wsoee@earthlink.net
Website: www.k.wa.us/envedu

Founded: N/A

Membership: 1–100

Scope: Regional

Description: To provide curriculum resources and training for teachers in environmental education, and to evaluate these programs pursuant to improving content and effectiveness. The office is responsible for E.E. program coordination and cooperation as it applies to K-12 public school programs and to state mandate requiring E.E. integrated into the K-12 curriculum.

Publication(s): Clean Water, Streams and Fish: A Holistic View of Watersheds, Closing the Achievement Gap: Using the Environment as an Integrating Context for Learning, Puget Sound Habitats Teachers Guide and Charts, Environmental Education Guidelines for Washington Schools

Keyword(s): Reduce/Reuse/Recycle, Water Habitats & Quality

Contact(s):

Tony Angell, State Supervisor of Environmental Education
Michele Halfhill, Administrative Assistant

WEST VIRGINIA COOPERATIVE FISH AND WILDLIFE RESEARCH UNIT

DIVISION OF FORESTRY
Division of Forestry, West Virginia University
Morgantown, WV 26506-6125 United States
Phone: 304-293-3794, ext. 2430 Fax: 304-293-4826
E-mail: wvcoop@wvu.edu
Website: www.forestry.caf.wvu.edu

Founded: N/A

Scope: State, National

Description: A cooperative research and graduate education organization sponsored by the Biological Resources Division of USGS, West Virginia Division of Natural Resources, West Virginia University, and Wildlife Management Institute. The role of the unit is to conduct natural resources research of state, regional, or national scope, and to train graduate-level researchers in natural resources.

Keyword(s): Pollution (general), Water Habitats & Quality, Wildlife & Species

Contact(s):

Joseph McNeel, Director Division of Forestry; jmcneel@wvu.edu
Patricia Mazik, Unit Leader: Fisheries
Stuart Welsh, Assistant Leader: Fisheries
Petra Wood, Assistant Leader: Wildlife

WEST VIRGINIA DEPARTMENT OF AGRICULTURE

1900 Kanawha Blvd. E
Charleston, WV 25305 United States
Phone: 304-558-2201 Fax: 304-558-2203
Website: www.state.wv.us/agriculture

Founded: N/A

Scope: State

Keyword(s): Agriculture/Farming, Land Issues, Pollution (general), Public Health

Contact(s):

Charles Coffman, Director of Plant Industries Division
Gus Douglass, Commissioner
Janet Fisher, Deputy Commissioner
Richard Hannah, Deputy Commissioner

WEST VIRGINIA DEPARTMENT OF ENVIRONMENTAL PROTECTION

Division of Environmental Protection, #10, McJunkin Rd.
Nitro, WV 25143-2546 United States
Phone: 304-759-0515 Fax: 304-759-0562
Website: www.dp.state.wv.us

Founded: 1991

Membership: 101–1,000

Scope: State

Description: The Division of Environmental Protection is charged with the protection of West Virginia's environment through the regulation and administration of the state's abandoned mine lands, air quality, mining & reclamation, oil & gas, waste management, and water resources programs.

Contact(s):

Michael Callaghan, Director, ext. 301; mcallaghan@mail.dep.state.wv.us
Matthew Crum, Chief of Mining & Reclamation; 304-759-0510; mcrum@mail.dep.state.wv.us
Ken Ellison, Chief of Waste Management; 304-558-2508; kellison@mail.dep.state.wv.us
Andy Gallagher, Chief Communications Officer; 304-558-4253; agallagher@mail.dep.state.wv.us
Randy Huffman, Chief of Administration; 304-558-5529; rhuffman@mail.dep.state.wv.us
Perry McDaniel, Chief of Legal Services; 304-558-9160; pmcdaniel@mail.dep.state.wv.us
Alan Turner, Chief of Water Resources; 304-558-2107; aturner@mail.dep.state.wv.us

WEST VIRGINIA DIVISION OF NATURAL RESOURCES

1900 Kanawha Blvd., East Building 3
Charleston, WV 25305 United States
Phone: 304-558-2754 Fax: 304-558-3147
Website: www.dnr.state.wv.us

Founded: 1933

Scope: State

Description: The Division's objective is to provide a comprehensive program for the exploration, conservation, development, protection, enjoyment, and use of the natural resources of the State of West Virginia. The commission was the forerunner of the Department of Natural Resources, created by the legislature in 1961 and modified to the Division of Natural Resources in 1993.

Publication(s): Wonderful West Virginia, West Virginia Wildlife

Keyword(s): Recreation/Ecotourism, Water Habitats & Quality, Wildlife & Species

Contact(s):

Ed Hamrick, Director; 1900 Kanawha Boulevard, East, Charleston, WV 25305; 304-558-2754; Fax: 304-558-2768; ehamrick@dnr.state.wv.us
Jeffrey Bowers, District I Commissioner; HC 70 Box 40 A, Sugar Grove, WV 26815; 304-358-3333; Fax: 304-358-3334
Charles Capito, District I Commissioner; Suite #3 2619 Pennsylvania Ave., Weirton, WV 26062; 304-723-3355; Fax: 304-723-5638
Kenneth Caplinger, Deputy Chief, Parks and Recreation; 1900 Kanawha Boulevard, East, Charleston, WV 25305; 304-558-2764; Fax: 304-558-0077; kcaplinger@dnr.state.wv.us
William Daniel, Deputy Chief, Law Enforcement; 1900 Kanawha Boulevard, East, Charleston, WV 25305; 304-558-2784; Fax: 304-558-1170; wdaniel@dnr.state.wv.us
Dr. Thomas Dotson, District III Commissioner; The Greenbrier Clinic, 320 West Main Street, White Sulphur Springs, WV 24986; 304-536-4870; Fax: 304-536-1664
Bernard Dowler, Deputy Director; 1900 Kanawha Boulevard, East, Charleston, WV 25305; 304-558-2754; Fax: 304-558-2768; bdowler@dnr.state.wv.us
James Fields, Chief of Law Enforcement; 1900 Kanawha Boulevard, East, Charleston, WV 25305; 304-558-2784; Fax: 304-558-1170; jfields@dnr.state.wv.us
Emily Fleming, Chief of Environmental Resources; 1900 Kanawha Boulevard, East, Charleston, WV 25305; 304-558-3370; Fax: 304-558-6207; efleming@dnr.state.wv.us
Carl Gainer, District II Commissioner; P.O. Box 670, Richwood, WV 26261; 304-846-6247; Fax: 304-846-6145
Charles Hooten, District II Commissioner; 1570 Summit Drive, Charleston, WV 25302; 304-346-0521; Fax: 304-346-3421
Arnout Hyde, Editor; 1900 Kanawha Boulevard, East, Charleston, WV 25305; 304-558-9152; Fax: 304-558-2768
Paul Johansen, Assistant Chief In Charge of Game Management; 1900 Kanawha Boulevard, East, Charleston, WV 25305; 304-558-2771; Fax: 304-558-3147; pjohansen@dnr.state.wv.us
James Jones, Chief of Real Estate Management; 1900 Kanawha Boulevard, East, Charleston, WV 25305; 304-558-3225; Fax: 304-558-3680; jjones@dnr.state.wv.us
Walt Kordek, Assistant Chief in Charge of Planning and Biometrics; P.O. Box 67, Elkins, WV 26241; 304-637-0245; Fax: 304-637-0250; wkordek@dnr.state.wv.us
Twila Metheney, District II Commission; 848 Pleasant Hill Road, Morgantown, WV 26508; 304-267-2389
David Milne, District I Commissioner; Route 5, Box 16, Bruceton Mills, WV 26525; 304-292-3339; Fax: 304-292-0093

Hoy Murphy, Public Information Officer; 1900 Kanawha Boulevard, East, Charleston, WV 25305; 304-558-3380; Fax: 304-558-2768; hmurphy@dnr.state.wv.us
Donald Phares, Assistant Chief In Charge of Special Projects; P.O. Box 67, Elkins, WV 26241; 304-637-0245; Fax: 304-637-0250
J. R. Pope, Chief of Parks; 1900 Kanawha Boulevard, East, Charleston, WV 25305; 304-558-2764; Fax: 304-558-0077; jpope@dnr.state.wv.us
Bret Preston, Assistant Chief In Charge of Warmwater Fisheries; 1900 Kanawha Boulevard, East, Charleston, WV 25305; 304-558-2771; Fax: 304-558-3147; bpreston@dnr.state.wv.us
Harry Price, Executive Secretary; 1900 Kanawha Boulevard, East, Charleston, WV 25305; 304-558-3315; Fax: 304-558-2768; hprice@dnr.state.wv.us
Gordon Robertson, Deputy Chief, Wildlife Resources; 304-558-2771; Fax: 304-558-3147; grobertson@dnr.state.wv.us
Michael Shingleton, Assistant Chief In Charge of Coldwater Fisheries; P.O. Box 67, Elkins, WV 26241; 304-637-0245; Fax: 304-637-0250; mshingleton@dnr.state.wv.us
Curtis Taylor, Chief of Wildlife; 1900 Kanawha Boulevard, East, Charleston, WV 25305; 304-558-2771; Fax: 304-558-3147; ctaylor@dnr.state.wv.us

WEST VIRGINIA GEOLOGICAL AND ECONOMIC SURVEY

Box 879
Morgantown, WV 26507-0879 United States
Phone: 304-594-2331 Fax: 304-594-2575
E-mail: info@geosrv.wvnet.edu
Website: www.wvgs.wvnet.edu

Founded: 1897
Membership: 1–100
Scope: State, International
Description: Charged with the responsibility of examining all geological formations and physical features of the state with particular emphasis on their economic importance, utilization, and conservation and preparing reports and maps of the geology and natural resources of West Virginia.
Publication(s): Field trip guide, state park bulletins, educational series, county geologic reports, basic data reports, river basin bulletins, mineral resources series, environmental geology bulletins, coal-geology bulletins, reports of investigations.
Contact(s):
Larry Woodfork, Director and State Geologist; 304-594-2331; woodfork@geoserv.wvnet.edu
Katherine Avary, Program Manager for Oil and Gas
Mary Behling, Program Manager for Geologic Data
Nick Fedorko, Program Manager for Coal
Charles Gover, Program Manager for Publications and Graphics Section
Steven McClelland, Program Manager for Service
Gloria Rowan, Program Manager for Administration
Chuck Gover, Editor; 304-594-2331
John May, Deputy Director of Finance and Administration
Carl Smith, Associate State Geologist and Deputy Director; 304-594-2331

WEST VIRGINIA SOIL CONSERVATION AGENCY

1900 Kanawha Blvd. East
Charleston, WV 25305-0193 United States
Phone: 304-558-2204 Fax: 304-340-4839
Website: www.wvsca.org

Founded: N/A
Membership: 1–100
Scope: State
Description: This organization is dedicated in assisting landowners in implementing BMP's (Best Management Practices) and works hard with other State and Federal Agencies along with organized groups of citizens forming Watershed Associations in restoring and cleaning up West Virginia's watersheds.
Contact(s):
Lance Tabor, Executive Director; 304-558-2204; Fax: 304-340-4839; ltabor@wvsca.org

WEST VIRGINIA UNIVERSITY

EXTENSION SERVICE
West Virginia University
817 Knapp Hall
P.O. Box 6031
Morgantown, WV 26506 United States
Phone: 304-293-5691 Fax: 304-293-7163
E-mail: Larry.Cote@mail.wvu.edu
Website: www.wvu.edu/~exten/

Founded: N/A
Membership: 101–1,000
Scope: State
Description: Extension Service
Keyword(s): Agriculture/Farming, Forests/Forestry, Pollution (general), Reduce/Reuse/Recycle
Contact(s):
Ken Martin, Director, Center for Agricultural/Natural Resources Dev.; West Virginia University, 2080 Agricultural Sciences Bldg., P.O. Box 6108, Morgantown, WV 26506-6108; 304-293-6131, ext. 4206; Fax: 304-293-6954; Ken.Martin@mail.wvu.edu
Thomas Basden, Extension Specialist, Nutrient Management; West Virginia University, 1060 Agricultural Sciences Bldg., P.O. Box 6108, Morgantown, WV 26506-6108; 304-293-6131, ext. 4210; Fax: 304-293-6954; Tom.Basden@mail.wvu.edu
D. Bhumbla, Extension Specialist, Soil and Water Resources; West Virginia University, 1072 Agricultural Sciences Bldg., P.O. Box 6108, Morgantown, WV 26506-6108; 304-293-6131, ext. 4212; Devinder.Bhumbla@mail.wvu.edu
Lawrence Cote, Associate Provost for Extension and Public Service; West Virginia University, 817 Knapp Hall, P.O. Box 6031, Morgantown, WV 26506-6125; 304-293-5691; Larry.Cote@mail.wvu.edu
William Grafton, Extension Specialist, Wildlife; West Virginia University, 311-B Percival Hall, P.O Box 6125, Morgantown, WV 26506-6125; 304-293-4797, ext. 2493; Fax: 304-293-7553; Bill.Grafton@mail.wvu.edu
Jeffrey Skousen, Extension Specialist, Land Reclamation; West Virginia University, 1106 Agricultural Sciences Bldg., P.O. Box 6108, Morgantown, WV 26506-6108; 304-293-6131; Jeff.Skousen@mail.wvu.edu
Richard Zimmerman, Extension Specialist, Horticulture; West Virginia University, Tree Fruit Research & Ed. Ctr., P.O. Box 609, Kearneysville, WV 25430-0609; 304-876-6353; RKZimmerman@mail.wvu.edu

WILDLIFE RESOURCES AGENCY

P.O. Box 40747, Ellington Agricultural Center
Nashville, TN 37204 United States
Phone: 615-781-6500 Fax: 615-781-6654
Website: www.state.tn.us/twra

Founded: 1949
Scope: Regional
Description: Created to have full and exclusive jurisdiction of the duties and functions relating to wildlife and boating and to the management, protection, propagation, and conservation of wildlife, including hunting and fishing.
Publication(s): Tennessee Wildlife
Keyword(s): Recreation/Ecotourism, Wildlife & Species
Contact(s):
Gary Myers, Executive Director; 615-781-6552
Clarence Coffey, Regional Manager of Cumberland Plateau, Region III; 931-484-9571

State Government Agencies

Gary Cook, Regional Manager of West Tennessee, Region I; 901-423-5725
Richard Kirk, Manager of Nongame/Endangered Species; 615-781-6619
Steve Patrick, Regional Manager of Middle Tennessee, Region II; 615-781-6622
Bob Ripley, Regional Manager of East Tennessee, Region IV; 615-587-7037
Ed Carter, Chief of Boating Division; 615-781-6682
Jim Dillard, Chief of Personnel; 615-781-6594
Ron Fox, Assistant Director of Field Operations; 615-781-6557
Loy Fulford, Chief of Management Systems; 615-781-6528
L. Garland, General Counsel; 615-781-6606
Allen Gebhardt, Assistant Director of Staff Operations; 615-781-6555
John Gregory, Chief of Real Estate and Forestry Division; 615-781-6560
Les Haun, Chief of Engineering Division; 615-781-6545
Beverly Johnson, Commission Chairman; 931-363-7621; Fax: 931-363-9679
Larry Marcum, Chief of Wildlife Management Division; 615-781-6610
David McKinney, Chief of Environmental Division; 615-781-6643
Phil Neil, Education Supervisor; 615-781-6538; pneil@mail.state.tn.us
Bill Reeves, Chief of Fish Management Division; 615-781-6575
Sonny Richardson, Chief of Law Enforcement Division; 615-781-6580; srichard@mail.state.tn.us
Barry Summer, Chief of Planning and Federal Aid; 615-781-6599; bsummer@mail.state.tn.us
Ken Tarkington, Chief of Administrative Services Division; 615-781-6512
Gl Teague, Commission Vice Chairman; 731-847-0848; Fax: 731-847-0748
Dave Woodward, Editor; 615-781-6502
Dave Woodward, Chief of Information & Education; 615-781-6502

WISCONSIN CONSERVATION CORPS

30 W. Mifflin, Suite 406
Madison, WI 53703-2558 United States
Phone: 608-266-7730 Fax: 608-267-2733
E-mail: degolla@dwd.state.wi.us
Website: www.dwd.state.wi.us/wcc/

Founded: 1983
Membership: 101–1,000
Scope: State
Description: The WCC provides work experience and personal development opportunities to young adults ages 18-25, and valuable conservation and other services to Wisconsin communities. Approximately 200 corps members annually work at 3 dozen rotating project sites throughout the state. Government agencies and nonprofit organizations are eligible to apply for WCC assistance.
Keyword(s): Ecosystems (precious), Energy, Forests/Forestry, Public Lands/Greenspace, Recreation/Ecotourism, Wildlife & Species
Contact(s):
Laura Degolier, Executive Director; degolla@dwd.state.wi.us

WISCONSIN COOPERATIVE FISHERY RESEARCH UNIT USGS

College of Natural Resources, University of Wisconsin
Stevens Point, WI 54481 United States
Phone: 715-346-2178 Fax: 715-346-3624
E-mail: coopfish@uwsp.edu
Website: www.uwsp.edu/cnr/wicfru

Founded: N/A
Membership: 1–100
Scope: International
Description: Interagency organization on the federal, state, and university levels. It carries out research, training, and extension in biology and management of freshwater fishery resources.
Keyword(s): Recreation/Ecotourism, Water Habitats & Quality, Wildlife & Species
Contact(s):
Michael Bozek, Leader

WISCONSIN COOPERATIVE WILDLIFE RESEARCH UNIT (USDI)

USGS, Department of Wildlife Ecology
Room 204 Russell Laboratories, UW-Madison
1630 Linden Drive
Madison, WI 53706-1598 United States
Phone: 608-263-4519 Fax: 608-263-4519
E-mail: dlziebar@facstaff.wisc.edu
Website: www.wisc.edu/wildlife

Founded: 1972
Membership: 1–100
Scope: International
Description: Wildlife Research Unit
Keyword(s): Wildlife & Species
Contact(s):
Christine Ribic, Leader; caribic@facstaff.wisc.edu

WISCONSIN DEPARTMENT OF AGRICULTURE TRADE AND CONSUMER PROTECTION

LAND AND WATER RESOURCES BUREAU
2811 Agriculture Dr., P.O. Box 8911
Madison, WI 53708-8911 United States
Phone: 608-224-4620 Fax: 608-224-4615
Website: www.datcp.state.wi.us

Founded: N/A
Membership: 1–100
Scope: State
Description: Responsible for administering state soil and water conservation and farmland preservation programs.
Keyword(s): Land Issues, Sprawl/Urban Planning, Water Habitats & Quality
Contact(s):
David Jelinski, Bureau Director; 608-224-4621; Fax: 608-224-4615
James Harsdorf, Secretary

WISCONSIN DEPARTMENT OF NATURAL RESOURCES

101 South Webster St.
Madison, WI 53702 United States
Phone: 608-266-2121
Website: www.dnr.state.wi.us

Founded: N/A
Scope: State
Description: Responsibilities include: Fisheries, wildlife, forest, parks management, endangered resources protection, forest fire control, air and water pollution control, solid and hazardous waste management, mining regulation, enforcement of conservation and environmental laws, flood plain and shoreland zoning, water management and regulation, lake rehabilitation, and long-range planning in the broad fields of outdoor recreation and natural resources.
Publication(s): WI Natural Resources Magazine
Keyword(s): Air Quality/Atmosphere, Forests/Forestry, Land Issues, Recreation/Ecotourism, Reduce/Reuse/Recycle
Contact(s):
James Addis, Director of Bureau of Intergrated Science Services; 608-266-0837
Ruthe Badger, South Central Regional Director; 3911 Fish Hatchery Road, Madison, WI 53711; 608-275-3260

Suzanne Bangert, Director of Bureau of Waste Management; 608-266-0014
Susan Black, Director of Parks and Recreation; 608-266-2185
Kathryn Curtner, Director of Bureau of Community Financial Assistance; 608-266-0860
Paul Delong, Director of Bureau of Endangered Resources; 608-264-9224
Lloyd Eagan, Director of Bureau of Air Management; 608-266-0603
Gene Francisco, Director of Bureau of Forestry; 608-266-0842
Mark Giesfeldt, Director of Bureau of Remediation and Redevelopment; 608-267-7562
Thomas Harelson, Director of Bureau of Law Enforcement; 608-266-1115
Thomas Hauge, Director of Bureau of Wildlife Management; 608-266-2193
Scott Humrickhouse, West Central Regional Director; P.O. Box 4001, Eau Claire, WI 54702; 715-839-3711
Jill Jonas, Director of Bureau of Drinking Water and Ground Water; 608-267-7651
Ron Kazmierczak, Northeast Regional Director; P.O. Box 10448, Green Bay, WI 54307; 920-492-5815
Gloria McCutcheon, Southeast Regional Director; P.O. Box 12436, Milwaukee, WI 53212; 414-263-8510
Robert Roden, Director of Bureau of Facilities and Lands; 608-266-2197
William Smith, Northern Regional Director; 810 W. Maple Street, Spooner, WI 54801; 715-635-4010
Michael Staggs, Director of Bureau of Management and Habitat Protection; 608-267-0796
Laurel Steffes, Director of Bureau of Communication and Education; 608-266-8109
Bruce Baker, Deputy Administrator of Bureau of Water; 608-266-1902
Darrell Bazzell, Deputy Secretary; 608-266-2252
Jay Hochmuth, Administrator of Air and Waste Division; 608-267-9521
Mary Kopecky, Deputy Administrator of Air and Waste Division; 608-261-8448
Mark McDermid, Contact
David Meier, Administrator of Enforcement and Science Division; 608-266-0015
George Meyer, Secretary; 608-266-2121
Steven Miller, Administrator of Land Division; 608-266-5782
Allen Shea, Bureau of Watershed Management; 608-267-2759
Trygve Solberg, Natural Resources Board Chairman; 715-356-7711
Susan Sylvester, Administrator of Water Division; 608-266-1099

WISCONSIN DEPARTMENT OF PUBLIC INSTRUCTION

125 S. Webster St.
P. O. Box 7841
Madison, WI 53707-7841 United States
Phone: 800-441-4563 Fax: 608-267-1052
E-mail: barbara.ballweg@dpi.state.wi.us
Website: www.dpi.state.wi.us/

Founded: N/A

Scope: Local, State

Description: A state government agency that promotes environmental education in public schools and supervises teacher preparation programs. Conducts workshops, and provides consultant services to elementary and secondary schools, colleges and universities. Produces publications to aid in program development.

Publication(s): A Guide to Curriculum Planning in Environmental Education, "Wisconsin's Model Academic Standards for Environmental Education"

Contact(s):
Sue Grady, Environmental Education Consultant; 608-266-2364

WISCONSIN ENVIRONMENTAL EDUCATION BOARD (WEEB)

110B College of Natural Resources UW Stevens Point
Stevens Point, WI 54481 United States
Phone: 715-346-3805 Fax: 715-346-3025
E-mail: weeb@uwsp.edu
Website: www.uwsp.edu/cnr/weeb

Founded: 1990

Membership: N/A

Scope: State

Description: Grants board providing $200,000 annually to environmental education (EE) initiatives, $390,00 annually to forestry education initiatives and $180,000 annually to energy education initiatives to projects within the state of Wisconsin, with a maximum grant of $20,000 per project.

Publication(s): Annual Grant Recipients, Annual Report

Contact(s):
Ginny Carlton, Program Specialist
Rick Koziel, Chairperson

WISCONSIN GEOLOGICAL AND NATURAL HISTORY SURVEY

University of Wisconsin Extension, 3817 Mineral Point Rd.
Madison, WI 53705 United States
Phone: 608-262-1705 Fax: 608-262-8086
Website: www.uwex.edu/wgnhs

Founded: 1897

Scope: State

Description: Created by the legislature, with the responsibility to survey the state's geology, mineral, water, soil, plant, animal, and climate resources, and to coordinate topographic mapping.

Keyword(s): Land Issues

Contact(s):
James Robertson, State Geologist and Director; 608-263-7384
Ronald Hennings, Assistant Director; 608-263-7395

WISCONSIN STATE EXTENSION SERVICES

COMMUNITY NATURAL RESOURCE AND ECONOMIC DEVELOPMENT
University of Wisconsin Extension, 432 N. Lake St.
Madison, WI 53706 United States
Phone: 608-262-1748 Fax: 608-262-9166
Website: www.uwex.edu/ces/

Founded: N/A

Scope: State

Contact(s):
Carl Oconnor, Dean and Director of Cooperative Extension
Scott Craven, Wildlife Specialist; 8233 Russel Labs, 1630 Linden Dr., Madison, WI 53706; 608-263-6325; Fax: 608-262-6099; srcraven@facstaff.wisc.edu
Mark Rickenbach, Forest Ecology & Management Specialist; 608-262-0134; mrickenbach@cals.wisc.edu
Patrick Walsh, Statewide Program Leader; Community, Natural Resource and Economic Development, University of Wisconsin-Extension, Rm. 625, 432 N. Lake St., Madison, WI 53706; 608-262-1748; patrick.walsh@ces.uwex.edu

WYOMING COOPERATIVE EXTENSION SERVICES

University Station, Box 3354
Laramie, WY 82071 United States
Phone: 307-766-5124 Fax: 307-766-3998
Website: www.uwyo.edu/ces/ceshome.htm

Founded: N/A

Membership: 1–100
Scope: State
Publication(s): Journal Articles, Regional Publications, 4-H Publications, Bulletins, Research Journals, Science Monographs, Scientific Abstracts
Keyword(s): Agriculture/Farming, Development/Developing Countries
Contact(s):
Glen Whipple, Director and Associate Dean; glen@uwyo.edu
Barb Farmer, Manager of Communications & Technologies; 307-766-3702; barbaraa@uwyo.edu
Ruth Wilson, Associate Director; drruth@uwyo.edu

WYOMING COOPERATIVE FISH AND WILDLIFE RESEARCH UNIT (USDI)

University of Wyoming, Box 3166, Biological Sciences Bldg., Rm. 419
Box 3166, University Station
Laramie, WY 82071 United States
Phone: 307-766-5415 Fax: 307-766-5400

Founded: 1980
Membership: 1–100
Scope: National
Description: Conducts research under auspices of the USGS Biological Resources Division and Wyoming Game and Fish Department in the northern Rocky Mountain region.
Keyword(s): Wildlife & Species
Contact(s):
Stanley Anderson, Leader; anderson@uwyo.edu
Wayne Hubert, Assistant Leader of Fisheries; drhubert@uwyo.edu
Fred Lindzey, Assistant Leader of Wildlife; flindzey@uwyo.edu

WYOMING DEPARTMENT OF AGRICULTURE

2219 Carey Ave.
Cheyenne, WY 82002 United States
Phone: 307-777-7321 Fax: 307-777-6593
Website: www.wyagric.state.wy.us

Founded: N/A
Scope: State
Contact(s):
Ron Micheli, Director; 307-777-6569; Fax: 307-777-6593; rmiche@missc.state.wy.us
Grant Stumbough, Natural Resource and Policy Manager; 307-777-6579
Jim Schwartz, Deputy Director; 307-777-6591

WYOMING GAME AND FISH DEPARTMENT

5400 Bishop Blvd.
Cheyenne, WY 82006 United States
Phone: 307-777-4600 Fax: 307-777-4610
E-mail: wgf@state.wy.us
Website: wgf.state.wy.us/

Founded: 1939
Membership: 101–1,000
Scope: State
Description: To provide an adequate and flexible system for the control, propagation, management, protection, and regulation of Wyoming wildlife for the public interest.
Publication(s): Wyoming Wildlife News (2 months), Wyoming Wildlife (800-548-9453)
Keyword(s): Recreation/Ecotourism, Wildlife & Species
Contact(s):
Tom Thorne, Acting Director; 307-777-4501; Fax: 307-777-4699; Tom.Thorne@wgf.state.wy.us
Brent Knotts, Acting Services Division Chief; 307-777-4591; Fax: 307-777-4602
Green River Regional Office; 351 Astle, Green River, WY 82935; 307-857-3223; Fax: 307-875-3242
Jackson Regional Office; P.O. Box 67, 360 N. Cache, Jackson, WY 83001; 307-733-2321; Fax: 307-733-2276
Pinedale Regional Office; P.O. Box 850, 117 S. Sublette Avenue, Pinedale, WY 82941; 307-367-4353; Fax: 307-367-4403
Sheridan Regional Office; P.O. Box 6249, 700 Valley View, Sheridan, WY 82801; 307-672-7418; Fax: 307-672-0594
Laramie Regional Office; 528 S. Adams, Laramie, WY 82070; 307-745-4046; Fax: 307-745-8720
Lander Regional Office; 260 Buena Vista, Lander, WY 82520; 307-332-2688; Fax: 307-332-6669
Casper Regional Office; 3030 Energy Ln., Suite 100, Casper, WY 82604; 307-473-3400; Fax: 307-473-3433
Laramie Lab; Room 323, Biological Sciences Bldg., P.O. Box 3312 University Station, Laramie, WY 82071; 307-766-6313
Sybille Wildlife Research and Conservation Unit; 2362 Highway 34, Wheatland, WY 82201; 307-322-2571
Cody Regional Office; 2820 State Highway 120, Cody, WY 82414; 307-527-7125; Fax: 307-587-5430
Gregg Arthur, Deputy Director, Internal Programs
Lynda Cook, Assistant Attorney General; 307-777-4687
Larry Gabriele, Fiscal Division Chief; 307-777-4516; Fax: 307-777-4679; larry.gabriele@wgf.state.wy.us
Larry Kruckenberg, Special Assistant for Policy; 307-777-4539
Jay Lawson, Wildife Division Chief; 307-777-4579; Fax: 307-777-4650
Mike Stone, Fish Division Chief; 307-777-4559; Fax: 307-777-4611
Bill Wichers, Deputy Director, External Programs

WYOMING STATE BOARD OF LAND COMMISSIONERS

Herschler Building 3 W
Cheyenne, WY 82002 United States
Phone: 307-777-7331 Fax: 307-777-5400
E-mail: slfmail@state.wy.us
Website: www.state.wy.us

Founded: N/A
Scope: State
Keyword(s): Land Issues, Public Lands/Greenspace, Reduce/Reuse/Recycle
Contact(s):
Ron Arnold, Secretary
Jim Geringer, Chairman

WYOMING STATE GEOLOGICAL SURVEY

Box 3008
Laramie, WY 82071 United States
Phone: 307-766-2286 Fax: 307-766-2605
E-mail: wsgs@wsgs.uwyo.edu
Website: www.wsgsweb.uwyo.edu

Founded: 1933
Membership: 1–100
Scope: State
Description: Activities include surface and subsurface geologic mapping; mineral, rock, and fossil investigations; natural resource and natural hazards investigations; and assistance in resources development.
Publication(s): Maps, memoirs, list of publications sent on request, quarterly newsletter (Wyoming Geo-notes), public information circulars, reports of investigations, bulletins.
Keyword(s): Energy, Land Issues
Contact(s):
James Case, Geologic Hazards Geologist; 307-766-2286, ext. 225; jcase@wsgs.uwyo.edu
Lance Cook, State Geologist; lcook@wsgs.uwyo.edu
Rodney Debruin, Petroleum Geologist; 307-766-2286, ext. 226; rdebru@wsgs.uwyo.edu
Ray Harris, Industrial Minerals Geologist; 307-766-2286, ext. 228; rharri@wsgs.uwyo.edu

W. Hausel, Senior Economic Geologist of Metals and Precious Stones; 307-766-2286, ext. 229; dhause@wsgs.uwyo.edu
Joe Huss, Head of GIS; 307-766-2286, ext. 234; jhuss@wsgs.uwyo.edu
Richard Jones, Editor; 307-766-2286, ext. 238; rjones@wsgs.uwyo.edu
Robert Lyman, Coal Geologist; 307-766-2286, ext. 233; blyman@wsgs.uwyo.edu
Alan Verploeg, Geologic Mapping Geologist; 307-766-2286, ext. 230; averpl@wsgs.uwyo.edu

WYOMING STATE PARKS AND CULTURAL RESOURCES

DIVISION OF STATE PARKS AND HISTORIC SITES
1st Fl., Herschler Bldg. 1E
Cheyenne, WY 82002 United States
Phone: 307-777-6323 Fax: 307-777-6472
E-mail: sphs@state.wy.us
Website: www.wyobest.org

Founded: 1967
Membership: 1–100
Scope: Regional
Description: Responsible for administering the state parks, state recreation areas, historic sites, petroglyph site, archaeological site, markers and monuments, snowmobile program, and state trails program.
Keyword(s): Land Issues, Public Lands/Greenspace, Recreation/Ecotourism
Contact(s):
Bill Gentle, Director of Division of State Parks and Historic Sites

NON-GOVERNMENTAL NON-PROFIT ORGANIZATIONS

20/20 VISION
1828 Jefferson Pl., NW
Washington, DC 20036 United States
Phone: 202-833-2020 Fax: 202-833-5307
E-mail: vision@2020vision.org
Website: www.vision.org

Founded: 1986
Membership: 1,001–10,000
Scope: National
Description: 20/20 Vision is a nonprofit grassroots organization dedicated to protecting the environment and promoting peace through lobbying and citizen education and activism. 20/20 Vision empowers citizens to speak out for a clean environment and a world free of weapons of mass destruction. Each month we pick one issue that is critically important to the future of the planet, where your voice will make the most difference. Letters written in just 20 minutes a month can move political mountains.
Publication(s): Tools for Activists Fact Sheets, Action Alert Postcards, Viewpoint
Contact(s):
James Wyerman, Executive Director; jwyerman@2020vision.org
Chris Demers, Public Outreach Coordinator; chris@2020vision.org
Erik Olsen, Campaigns Coordinator; erik@2020vision.org

A

A CRITICAL DECISION
P.O. Box (Pending), Please Use EMail
Dayton, OH 45342 United States
Phone: 937-291-2066
E-mail: director@acriticaldecision.org
Website: www.acriticaldecision.org

Founded: 2001
Scope: International
Description: Please enjoy our nature gallery and thought-provoking prose. We encourage citizens to question the dangerous influences large corporations have over democracy, population, and the environment (our life-support system).
Keyword(s): Population, Reduce/Reuse/Recycle, Wildlife & Species

A.E. HOWELL WILDLIFE CONSERVATION CENTER INC.
HC#61 Box 6
Lycette Rd.
No. Amity, ME 04471-9601 United States
Phone: 207-532-6880, ext. 8357 Fax: 207-532-0910
E-mail: eagleman@mfx.net
Website: www.spruceacresrefuge.tripod.com

Founded: 1981
Membership: 101–1,000
Scope: Local, State, Regional, National
Description: The A.E.H.W.C.C., Inc. and Spruce Acres Refuge have combined to provide a 65+ acre Wildlife Rehabilitation Center for people from all over the world to enjoy. The center is a non-profit organization established for the purpose of preserving our natural resources and providing educational programs & tours to all people to encourage proper wildlife and natural resource management.
Keyword(s): Recreation/Ecotourism, Water Habitats & Quality, Wildlife & Species
Contact(s):
Penny Kern, VP; 207-764-7945; Fax: 207-769-6680; pkern@mfx.net
A. Eric Howell, Manager; 207-532-7981

ABUNDANT LIFE SEED FOUNDATION
5410 Grosvenor Lane, Suite 110
Bethesda, MD 98368 United States
Phone: 301-897-8616 Fax: 301-897-8096
E-mail: main@fisheries.org
Website: www.fisheries.org

Founded: 1975
Membership: 1,001–10,000
Scope: National
Description: Abundant Life Seed Foundation is a nonprofit, tax-exempt organization that propagates and preserves seeds of Northwest native plants and heritage (non-hybrid) vegetables, herbs, and flowers. The Foundation conducts the distribution of seeds (and related books) via a mail-order catalog. Also operates the World Seed Fund, donating seed internationally to those in need, both in the United States and internationally.
Publication(s): Seed Midden, Seed and Book Catalog
Keyword(s): Agriculture/Farming, Wildlife & Species
Contact(s):
Ken Beal, President
Kirsten Fzykitka, Outreach Coordinator
Gus Rassam, Executive Director; 301-897-8616

ACADEMY FOR EDUCATIONAL DEVELOPMENT
1825 Connecticut Ave.,Suite 800
Washington, DC 20009-8721 United States
Phone: 719-556-8318 Fax: 202-884-8997
E-mail: greencom@aed.org
Website: www.usaid.gov/environment/greencom

Founded: 1961
Scope: International
Description: A domestic and international development organization with a multi-million dollar environmental education, communication and environmental health population agenda working in over 25 countries.
Publication(s): Publication on website
Keyword(s): Agriculture/Farming, Air Quality/Atmosphere, Ethics/Environmental Justice, Recreation/Ecotourism, Reduce/Reuse/Recycle, Water Habitats & Quality, Wildlife & Species
Contact(s):
William Smith, Executive Vice President; 202-884-8750; Fax: 202-884-8752; bsmith@aed.org
Richard Bassi, Latin America Director; 202-884-8898; rbassi@aed.org
Brian Day, Director; 202-884-8897; bday@aed.org
Gregory Niblett, Senior Vice Presdent; niblett@aed.org

ACRES LAND TRUST
2000 N. Wells St.
Fort Wayne, IN 46808-2474 United States
Phone: 219-422-1004 Fax: 219-422-1004
E-mail: acreslt@fwi.com
Website: www.acres-land-trust.org

Founded: 1960
Scope: Regional
Description: A nonprofit organization dedicated to the acquisition and permanent preservation of natural areas in northeastern Indiana. Conducts a guided field-trip program for children and adults. Organizes canoe trips, concerts and festivals for the membership and the public. Administers 40 nature preserves totaling more than 2,600 acres.
Publication(s): Acres Quarterly, Field Guide, Acres Brochure
Keyword(s): Land Issues, Water Habitats & Quality, Wildlife & Species
Contact(s):
James Haddock, President
Theodore Heemstra, Vice President
Sam Schwartz, Vice President
Robert Weber, Vice President
Carolyn McNagny, Executive Director
Richard Walker, Treasurer

ACTION FOR NATURE, INC.

2269 Chestnut St., Suite 263
San Francisco, CA 94123 United States
Phone: 415-421-2640 Fax: 415-922-5717
E-mail: action@dnai.com
Website: www.actionfornature.org

Founded: 1983

Scope: National, International

Description: Action for Nature was organized to foster respect and affection for nature through personal action. AFN is a clearing-house and catalyst for personal environmental action projects and publicizes young people's successful environmental initiatives through a newsletter, website bulletin board and publication of a book of young people's environmental success stories from around the world. AFN has recently established a Nature Action Program for classrooms and children's groups.

Publication(s): Acting for Nature (book)

Contact(s):

Albert Baez, Science Educator, President, Vivamos Mejor
Evelyn De Ghetaldi, President
Huey Johnson, Founder, President, Renewal Resources Institute
Jean Barish, Attorney
Jerome Dodson, President, Parnassus Fund
Beryl Kay, Director Human Resources, California Academy of Science
B. Shimon Schwarzschild, Secretary; P.O. Box 1959, Sutter Creek, CA 95685; shimons@earthlink.net
Adrienne Scroggie, Retired Educator
Alan Scroggie, Retired Educator
Maria Cohen, Nature Council
Ruth Gottstein, Publisher, Volcano Press
Mary Griffin-Jones, Retired Physician
Sidney Holt, Bioligist, Marine Conservationist, Animal Protector
William Whalen, Consultant

ADIRONDACK COUNCIL, THE

P.O. Box D-2
2 Church Street
Elizabethtown, NY 12932 United States
Phone: 877-873-2240 Fax: 518-873-6675
E-mail: adkcouncil@aol.com
Website: www.adirondackcouncil.org

Founded: 1975

Membership: 10,001–100,000

Scope: Local, State, Regional, National

Description: A nonprofit environmental organization working for protection and preservation of the six million acre Adirondack Park in upstate New York. Programs include monitoring and influencing state programs in the Park, helping to promote understanding of the Park and the need to protect its very special character, and supporting and advancing positive programs to enhance the Park and benefit its people.

Publication(s): Adirondack Council Newsletter, State of the Park, Adirondack Wildguide: A Natural History, Acid Rain A Continuing National Tragedy

Keyword(s): Air Quality/Atmosphere, Development/Developing Countries, Land Issues, Public Lands/Greenspace

Contact(s):

Bernard Melewski, Executive Director
David Bronston, Vice Chairman
Edward Fowler, Treasurer
Barbara Glaser, Secretary
David Skovron, Chairman
Patricia Winterer, Vice Chairman

ADIRONDACK MOUNTAIN CLUB, INC., THE (ADK)

814 Goggins Rd.
Lake George, NY 12845-4117 United States
Phone: 518-668-4447 Fax: 518-668-3746
E-mail: adkinfo@adk.org
Website: www.adk.org

Founded: 1922

Membership: 10,001–100,000

Scope: State

Description: The Adirondack Mountain Club is dedicated to the protection and responsible recreational use of the New York State Forest Preserve, parks and other wild lands and waters. The Club is a member-directed organization committed to public service and stewardship. ADK employs a balanced approach to outdoor recreation, advocacy, environmental education and natural resource conservation. ADK has 26 chapters in NY and NJ.

Publication(s): Kids on the Trail!, Guidebook & Map to High Peaks Region, Views from on High: Fire Tower Trails, Adirondack Magazine, Annual Calendar, Adirondack cultural and literary history, Adirondack Canoe Waters, Guides and Maps to Adirondack

Keyword(s): Air Quality/Atmosphere, Forests/Forestry, Land Issues, Public Lands/Greenspace, Recreation/Ecotourism, Reduce/Reuse/Recycle, Transportation, Wildlife & Species

Contact(s):

Terry Sexton, President
Jo Benton, Executive Director; 518-668-4447
Jen Kretzer, Education Director
Greg Macdonald, Director of North Country Operations; P. O. Box 867, Lake Placid, NY 12946
Tim Tierney, Director of Field Programs; P. O. Box 867, Lake Placid, NY 12946
Neil Woodworth, Deputy Executive Director for Public and Legal Affairs; 518-449-3870; nwoodworth@nycap,rr,com
Neal Burdick, Editor; 35 Woods Dr., Canton, NY 13617

ADKINS ARBORETUM

P.O. Box 100
Ridgely, MD 21660 United States
Phone: 410-634-2847 Fax: 410-634-2878
E-mail: adkinsar@intercom.net
Website: www.adkinsarboretum.org

Founded: 1979

Membership: 101–1,000

Scope: Regional

Description: Adkins Arboretum is dedicated to the appreciation, understanding and stewardship of the indigenous, nontidal plant communities of the Central Delmarva Peninsula. It strives to maintain a divers and dynamic living collection that is authentic, engaging and a model for land management. As a significant cultural, education, scientific and recreational resource, the Arboretum fosters civic pride, encourages public dialogue and contributes to the economic vitality of the region.

Publication(s): Native Seed

Keyword(s): Land Issues, Reduce/Reuse/Recycle, Water Habitats & Quality, Wildlife & Species

Contact(s):

Lorie Staber, President of the Board
Kathy Carnean, Vice President
Ellie Altman, Executive Director; 410-634-2847; Fax: 410-634-2878; ealtman@intercom.net
Louise Barton, Secretary
Graham Donaldson, Treasurer

ADOPT-A-STREAM FOUNDATION, THE

600-128th St., SE
Everett, WA 98208-6353 United States
Phone: 425-316-8592 Fax: 425-338-1423
E-mail: aasf@streamkeeper.org
Website: www.streamkeeper.org

Founded: 1985
Membership: 101–1,000
Scope: National
Description: Adopt-A-Stream Foundation's mission is to empower people to become stewards of watersheds, wetlands and streams. The Foundation's long term goal is to ensure that all streams are adopted by watershed residents. The current focus is in the Pacific Northwest. The Foundation conducts "Streamkeeper" workshops that train volunteers and students of all ages how to conduct watershed inventories, monitor small streams and other educational programming.
Publication(s): Video: The Streamkeeper, The Streamkeeper (newsletter), A Streamkeeper's Field Guide, Adopting a Wetland: A Northwest Guide, Adopting a Stream: A Northwest Handbook
Keyword(s): Land Issues, Public Lands/Greenspace, Reduce/Reuse/Recycle, Water Habitats & Quality, Wildlife & Species
Contact(s):
Darryl Williams, Board President
Tom Murdoch, Executive Director
Dan Crouse, Secretary
Grant Woodfield, Treasurer

AFRICA VISION TRUST

P.B. Box 23389
Dar Es Salaam, Tanzania
Phone: 255-51-601497
E-mail: afrovisn@intafrica.com

Founded: 1998
Scope: National
Description: Production of media and communication materials for/and in support of environmental and conservation programs. Also educational and professional training.
Publication(s): New Kingo
Keyword(s): Development/Developing Countries, Oceans/ Coasts/ Beaches, Population, Recreation/Ecotourism, Sprawl/Urban Planning, Water Habitats & Quality, Wildlife & Species
Contact(s):
Vincent Shauri, Chairman; 255-51-121315; afrovisn@intafrica.com
S. Granger, Production Manager; 255-51-601497; afrovisn@intafrica.com
M. Macoun, Secretary; 255-51-601497; afrovisn@intafrica.com
D. Mmari, Treasurer/Administrator; 255-51-601497; afrovisn@intafrica.com

AFRICAN CONSERVATION FOUNDATION, THE

ACF

P.O. Box 44776
Linden, 2104 South Africa
Phone: 27-829391632 Fax: 27-117827352
E-mail: terry@africanconservation.org
Website: www.africanconservation.org

Founded: 2001
Membership: N/A
Scope: International
Description: Educational foundation and support group in terms of GIS, Remote Sensing, IT, Web databasing for all groups working in conservation in Africa. Features a massive directory of African NGOs.
Keyword(s): Development/Developing Countries, Ecosystems (precious), Forests/Forestry, Land Issues, Oceans/Coasts/ Beaches, Public Lands/Greenspace, Recreation/Ecotourism, Water Habitats & Quality, Wildlife & Species

AFRICAN WILDLIFE FOUNDATION

1400 16th St., NW
Washington, DC 20036 United States
Phone: 202-939-3333 Fax: 202-939-3332
E-mail: africanwildlife@awf.org
Website: www.awf.org

Founded: N/A
Membership: 101–1,000
Scope: International
Description: The African Wildlife Foundation recognizes that the wildlife and wild lands of Africa have no equal. We work with people—our supporters worldwide and our partners in Africa—to craft and deliver creative solutions for the long-term well-being of Africa's remarkable species, habitats, and the people who depend upon them.
Publication(s): African Wildlife News
Keyword(s): Development/Developing Countries, Reduce/Reuse/Recycle, Wildlife & Species
Contact(s):
Patrick Bergin, President of Africa Operations
R. Wright, President
Henry McIntosh, Treasurer
William Richards, Vice Chair of the Board
Stuart Saunders, Chairman of the Board

AIR AND WASTE MANAGEMENT ASSOCIATION

One Gateway Center, 3rd Fl.
420 Fort Duquense Blvd.
Pittsburgh, PA 15222 United States
Phone: 412-232-3444 Fax: 412-232-3450
E-mail: info@awma.org
Website: www.awma.org

Founded: 1907
Membership: 1,001–10,000
Scope: Local, State, Regional, National, International
Description: The Air & Waste Management Association is a nonprofit, technical, and environmental association that provides a neutral forum for discussing all sides of an environmental issue. The Association's membership includes engineers, scientists, researchers, health professionals and others from government, industry, academia, consulting, and other fields.
Publication(s): A&WMA News, quarterly newsletter, EM, other publications include proceedings, Journal of the Air & Waste Management Association
Keyword(s): Air Quality/Atmosphere, Climate Change, Reduce/Reuse/Recycle

Contact(s):
Robert Hall, 1st Vice President
Douglas Bisset, Treasurer

AIZA BIBY
P.O. Box 701
East Setauket, NY 11733 United States
Phone: 516-658-6871
E-mail: biby@biby.org
Website: www.biby.org

Founded: 1999
Membership: N/A
Scope: Local, State, Regional, National, International
Description: The purpose of the Aiza Biby charitable trust is to assist children, ages 3-18, in defining the future of conservation biology and to provide these youth with entertaining lessons in conservation education and hands-on experience in land stewardship across the world.
Keyword(s): Agriculture/Farming, Ecosystems (precious), Forests/Forestry, Recreation/Ecotourism, Wildlife & Species
Contact(s):
Rebecca Grella, President; 516-658-6871; becky@biby.org
Robert Meyer, CEO; 631-897-0442
Sarah Karpanty, Executive Director; 631-632-8600

ALABAMA ASSOCIATION OF SOIL AND WATER CONSERVATION DISTRICTS
Attn: Executive Director
P.O. Box 304800
Montgomery, AL 36130-4800 United States
Phone: 334-223-7257

Founded: N/A
Scope: State
Contact(s):
George Robertson, President; 2181 County Rd. 22, Waverly, AL 36879; 334-887-6070; Fax: 334-826-8219
Jake Harper, 1st Vice President; Rt. 1 Box 468, Camden, AL 36726; 334-682-4463
Terry Poague, 2nd Vice President; 3716 Clause Fleahop Rd., Tallahassee, AL 36078; 334-567-6183
Charles Holmes, Board Member; Rt. 1 Box 212, Marion, AL 36756; 334-683-6869; Fax: 334-583-6869
Charles Rittenour, Secretary/Treasurer; 1144 Meriwether Rd., Pike Road, AL 36064; 334-284-5320

ALABAMA B.A.S.S. CHAPTER FEDERATION
Attn: President, P.O. Box 190
Notasulga, AL 36866 United States
Phone: 334-257-1177 Fax: 334-257-4665
Website: www.albassfed.org

Founded: 1972
Membership: 1,001–10,000
Scope: Local, State, Regional, National
Description: An organization of Bassmaster chapters, affiliated with the Bass Anglers Sportsman Society, organized to fight pollution, assist state and national conservation agencies in their efforts, and teach the young people of our country good conservation practices. Dedicated to the realistic conservation of our water resources.
Contact(s):
Al Redding, President; P.O. Box 190, 209 Tallapoosa St. (shipping), Notasulga, AL 36866; 334-257-1177; Fax: 334-257-4665; alhred@prodigy.net
Jim Howard, Conservation Director; 501 Five Mile Rd., Eufaula, AL 36027; 334-616-6956; Fax: 334-616-7194; bassnbuddy@aol.com

ALABAMA ENVIRONMENTAL COUNCIL
2717 7th Ave., S., Suite 207
Birmingham, AL 35233 United States
Phone: 205-322-3126 Fax: 205-324-3784
E-mail: stateoffice@aeconline.ws
Website: www.aeconline.ws

Founded: 1967
Membership: 101–1,000
Scope: Local, State, Regional
Description: Dedicated to the preservation of Alabama's environment on all fronts: air, water, land and wildlife.
Publication(s): State News
Keyword(s): Agriculture/Farming, Air Quality/Atmosphere, Ecosystems (precious), Energy, Ethics/Environmental Justice, Forests/Forestry, Land Issues, Oceans/Coasts/Beaches, Pollution (general), Public Health, Public Lands/Greenspace, Recreation/Ecotourism
Contact(s):
Thomas Carruthers, President
Rachel Reinhart, Executive Director; 2717 7th Ave. S Suite 207, Birmingham, AL 35233; 205-322-3126; Fax: 205-324-3784; director@aeconline.ws
Jessica Robertson, Administrator; 205-322-3126; Fax: 205-324-3784; stateoffice@aeconline.ws

ALABAMA WATERFOWL ASSOCIATION (AWA)
1346 County Road 11
Scottsboro, AL 35768 United States
Phone: 256-259-2509
E-mail: awa@alabamawaterfowl.org
Website: www.alabamawaterfowl.org

Founded: 1987
Membership: 101–1,000
Scope: State
Description: Conserving Alabama's watersheds, wetlands and coastal regions. Enhancing waterfowl and protecting Alabama's hunting heritage
Keyword(s): Ecosystems (precious)
Contact(s):
Jerry Davis, CEO; 256-259-2509; Fax: 256-259-2509; jd@alabamawaterfowl.org

ALABAMA WATERFOWL ASSOCIATION, INC. (AWA)
P.O. Box 67
Guntersville, AL 35768 United States
Phone: 202-682-9400
E-mail: awa@alabamawaterfowl.org
Website: www.alabamawaterfowl.org

Founded: 1987
Scope: State
Description: To protect, enhance and create wetlands habitat for all wildlife species and other human values; and to enhance waterfowl population and protect our hunting heritage in Alabama.
Publication(s): Wetlands and Waterfowl News
Keyword(s): Recreation/Ecotourism, Water Habitats & Quality, Wildlife & Species
Contact(s):
Gary Benefield, Executive Director; P.O. Box 67, Guntersville, AL 35976; 205-593-7712
Roger Crouch, Executive Treasurer; P.O. Box 67, Guntersville, AL 35976
Jerry Davis, Chief Executive Officer; 1346 County Rd. 11, Scottsboro, AL 35768; 205-259-2509

ALABAMA WILDFLOWER SOCIETY, THE
606 India Rd.
Opelika, AL 36801 United States
Phone: 334-745-2494 Fax: 334-704-0455
Website: www.auburn.edu/~deancar

Founded: 1971
Membership: 101–1,000
Scope: State
Description: The society promotes knowledge, appreciation, use of native plants, preserves and propagates rare native plants, preserves areas of significant native flora and provides scholarships.
Publication(s): Wildflower Brochure, Newsletter of the Alabama Wildflower Society
Keyword(s): Reduce/Reuse/Recycle, Wildlife & Species
Contact(s):
George Wood, President/Editor; 205-339-2541
Shirley Fifield, Past President; 334-277-2070; rgfifi@aol.com
Caroline Dean, Board Member
Virginia Lusk, Past President; 205-988-0299; ginny1@bellsouth.net

ALABAMA WILDLIFE FEDERATION
46 Commerce St.
Montgomery, AL 36104 United States
Phone: 334-832-9453 Fax: 334-832-9454
E-mail: awf@mindspring.com
Website: www.alawild.org
Founded: 1935
Membership: 1,001–10,000
Scope: State
Description: A representative statewide organization affiliated with the National Wildlife Federation, dedicated to the protection and enhancement of wildlife and its habitat through public education and government interaction.
Publication(s): Managing Wildlife, Alabama Wildlife
Contact(s):
Robert Thornton, President
Tim Gothard, Executive Director, Alternate Representative and Editor
Clinton Berry, Treasurer
April Lupardus, Conservation Programs Specialist
Jeff McCollum, Education Programs Contact
Rebecca Prichett, Representative

ALASKA ASSOCIATION OF SOIL AND WATER CONSERVATION DISTRICTS
949 E. 36th Ave. Ste. 400
Anchorage, AK 99508 United States
Phone: 907-271-2424 Fax: 907-271-3951
E-mail: akdistrict@customcpu.com
Founded: N/A
Scope: State
Description: A representative statewide organiaztion affiliated with the National Wildlife Federation, dedicated to the protection and enhancement of wildlife and its habitat through public education and government interaction.
Contact(s):
Omar Stratman, President, Board Member; P.O. Box 2376, Kodiak, AK 99615; 907-486-5578; Fax: 907-486-5578
Meribeth Crick, 2nd Vice President; P.O. Box 56505, North Pole, AK 56505; 907-488-2215
Shirley Schollenberg, 1st Vice President; HC 67 Box 250, Anchor Point, AK 99556; 907-567-3467
Meg Burgett, Secretary-Treasurer; P.O. Box 874554, Wasilla, AK 99687; 907-373-0885
Mike Carlson, Alternate Board Member; P.O. Box 953, Delta Junction, AK 99737; 907-895-4819
Doug Witte, Project Coordinator; 351 W. Parks Hwy. #101, Wasilla, AK 99645; 907-373-7923; Fax: 907-373-7192

ALASKA CENTER FOR THE ENVIRONMENT
807 G Street, Suite 100
Anchorage, AK 99501 United States
Phone: 907-274-3621 Fax: 907-274-8733
E-mail: ace@akcenter.org
Website: www.akcenter.org
Founded: 1971
Membership: 1,001–10,000
Scope: State
Description: Nonprofit organization which functions as an advocacy and citizen organizing facility for Alaskan environmental activities. With a professional staff of twelve and a corps of volunteers, the center conducts policy analysis and encourages grassroots activism to conserve and protect Alaska's natural resources, particularly its wildlands.
Keyword(s): Ecosystems (precious), Forests/Forestry, Land Issues, Oceans/Coasts/Beaches, Pollution (general), Public Lands/Greenspace, Reduce/Reuse/Recycle, Sprawl/Urban Planning, Wildlife & Species
Contact(s):
Tom Burek, Director of Trailside Discovery Camp; trailside@akcenter.org
Dwayne Lee, Financial Director and Officer Manager; dwayne@akcenter.org
Randy Virgin, Executive Director; randy@akcenter.org
Andre Camara, Campaigner, Anchorage Quality of Life; andre@akcenter.org
Cliff Eames, Public Lands Director; cliff@akcenter.org
Joe Lebeau, Campaigner, Mat-Su Valley; 642 S. Alaska St., Suite 201, Palmer, AK 99645; 907-745-8223; Fax: 907-745-8223; joe@akcenter.org
Beth Porterfield, Director of Development and Membership; beth@akcenter.org
Theo Saner, Membership Assistant; theo@akcenter.org
Michelle Wilson, Campaigner, Prince William Sound; michelle@akcenter.org

ALASKA CONSERVATION ALLIANCE
750 West 2nd Ave., Suite 109
Anchorage, AK 99501 United States
Phone: 907-258-6171 Fax: 907-258-6177
E-mail: unite@akvoice.org
Website: www.akvoice.org
Founded: 1997
Scope: National
Description: An alliance dedicated to strengthening environmental organizations and empowering individuals to protect Alaska's environment through public education, training, advocacy, communication and strategy development, all with respect for communities and human dignity.
Publication(s): GIS
GIS Maps
Keyword(s): Air Quality/Atmosphere, Development/Developing Countries, Ecosystems (precious), Forests/Forestry, Land Issues, Pollution (general), Water Habitats & Quality, Wildlife & Species
Contact(s):
Tom Atkinson, Executive Director; tom@akvoice.org
Christy Garrett, Office Coordinator; christy@akvoice.org
Jason Geck, GIS Analyst; 907-258-6148; jason@akvoice.org
Sue Schrader, Conservation Advocate; sue@akvoice.org
Marlo Shedlock, Program Organizer; marlo@akvoice.org
Sandra Wright, Financial Officer; sandie@akvoice.org

ALASKA CONSERVATION FOUNDATION
441 W. 5th Ave., Suite 402
Anchorage, AK 99501-2340 United States
Phone: 907-276-1917 Fax: 907-274-4145
E-mail: acfinfo@akcf.org
Website: www.akcf.org
Founded: 1980

Membership: 1,001–10,000
Scope: State
Description: A public foundation providing grants for environmental conservation in Alaska. It is not a membership organization. It lists its donors as "Circle of Friends."
Publication(s): Alaska Conservation Directory, Grant Guidelines, Annual Report, Dispatch
Keyword(s): Climate Change, Ecosystems (precious), Forests/Forestry, Oceans/Coasts/Beaches, Water Habitats & Quality, Wildlife & Species
Contact(s):
Deborah Williams, Executive Director
Jimmy Carter, Honorary Chair
Ken Leghorn, Vice Chair of Alaska Trustees
Eric Myers, Chair
David Rockefeller, Advisor
Stacy Studebaker, Secretary
David Wigglesworth, Program Officer

ALASKA CONSERVATION VOTERS

750 West 2nd Ave., Suite 109
Anchorage, AK 99501 United States
Phone: 907-258-6171 Fax: 907-258-6177
E-mail: unite@akvoice.org
Website: www.akvoice.org

Founded: 1997
Membership: 1–100
Scope: State
Description: An organization dedicated to protecting Alaska's environment through public education and advocacy in the Alaska state legislature, Congress and other forums.
Publication(s): The Score Card, newsletter (end of year report)
Keyword(s): Air Quality/Atmosphere, Development/Developing Countries, Ecosystems (precious), Energy, Executive/Legislative/Judicial Reform, Forests/Forestry, Land Issues, Pollution (general), Water Habitats & Quality, Wildlife & Species
Contact(s):
Tom Atkinson, Director; 907-258-6174; tom@akvoice.org
Christy Garrett, Office Coordinator; christy@akvoice.org
Sandra Wright, Financial Officer; sandie@akvoice.org
Jason Geck, GIS Analyst; 907-258-6148; jason@akvoice.org
Sue Schrader, Lobbyist; 907-463-3366; sue@akvoice.org
Marlo Shedlock, Program Coordinator; 906-258-6181; marlo@akvoice.org

ALASKA NATURAL HISTORY ASSOCIATION

750 West Second Ave., Suite 100
Anchorage, AK 99501-2167 United States
Phone: 907-274-8440 Fax: 907-274-8343
E-mail: alaskanha@alaskanha.org
Website: www.alaskanha.org

Founded: 1959
Membership: 1,001–10,000
Scope: State
Description: The Alaska Natural History Association is dedicated to enhancing the understanding and conservation of Alaska's natural and cultural resources by providing educational materials and services.
Publication(s): Northern Migrations, Alaska Books Catalog, Online catalog
Keyword(s): Ecosystems (precious), Ethics/Environmental Justice
Contact(s):
Charles Money, Executive Director; charles-money@alaskanha.org

ALASKA NATURAL RESOURCE AND OUTDOOR EDUCATION ASSOCIATION

P.O. Box 110536
Anchorage, AK 99511-0536 United States
Phone: 907-456-0558 Fax: 253-498-2399
Website: www.anroe.org

Founded: 1983
Membership: 101–1,000
Scope: State
Description: ANROE is a statewide network of K-12 school teachers, state and federal agency staff, university faculty and staff, students and other concerned citizens united to promote the development, delivery and implementation of educational efforts that help people of all ages learn about and appreciate Alaska's natural resources.
Publication(s): Discovering Alaska's Salmon, Children's Activity Guide, Flyways, Pathways, and Waterways (newsletter), Targeting Excellence, ANROE Guide to Natural Resource Education Materials
Contact(s):
Janet Warburton, President

ALASKA RAINFOREST CAMPAIGN

201 Lincoln St., Suite 1
Sitka, AK 99835 United States
Phone: 907-747-8292 Fax: 907-747-8873
E-mail: info@akrain.org
Website: www.akrain.org

Founded: 1992
Scope: State, National
Description: Alaska Rainforest Campaign is a coalition of Alaska-based and national environmental organizations working to protect the coastal old-growth rainforests of Alaska, especially the Tongass and Chugach National Forests.
Keyword(s): Forests/Forestry
Contact(s):
Corrie Bosman, National Field Director
Brian McNitt, Campaign Manager

ALASKA WILDLIFE ALLIANCE, THE

P.O. Box 202022
Anchorage, AK 99520 United States
Phone: 907-277-0897 Fax: 907-277-7423
E-mail: awa@alaska.net
Website: www.akwildlife.org

Founded: 1978
Scope: State
Description: The Alliance is a nonprofit organization whose mission is the protection of Alaska's natural wildlife and habitat diversity for its intrinsic value as well as for the benefit of present and future generations.
Publication(s): The Spirit
Contact(s):
Paul Joslin, Executive Director
Karen Deatherage, Associate Director

ALBERTA FISH AND GAME ASSOCIATION

6924-104 St.
Edmonton, T6H 2L7 Alberta Canada
Phone: 780-437-2342 Fax: 780-438-6872
E-mail: office@afga.org
Website: www.afga.org

Founded: 1908
Membership: 10,001–100,000
Scope: Regional
Description: To promote through education, lobbying and programs the conservation and utilization of fish and wildlife and to protect and enhance the habitat they depend upon.
Publication(s): Outdoor Edge, The, Alberta Outdoorsman
Keyword(s): Wildlife & Species
Contact(s):
Rod Dyck, President

ALBERTA TRAPPERS ASSOCIATION

Commmunication Division, 9th floor
Petroleum Plaza, S. Tower, 9945-108 St.
Edmonton, T5K 2C6 Alberta Canada
Phone: 708-826-5026 Fax: 780-427-6247
E-mail: info@albertatrappers.com
Website: www.albertatrappers.com

Founded: 1974
Membership: 1,001–10,000
Scope: State
Description: Cooperates with all trappers associations and government agencies for a sensible conservation program.
Publication(s): Alberta Trapper, The
Contact(s):
Reed Gauthier, President; 780-826-5026
Gus Deisting, 1st Vice President
Ed Graham, 2nd Vice President
Bob Scott, Director; 780-427-6247

ALBERTA WILDERNESS ASSOCIATION

Box 6398, Station D
Calgary, T2P 2E1 Alberta Canada
Phone: 403-283-2025 Fax: 403-270-2743
E-mail: a.w.a@shaw.ca
Website: www.albertawilderness.ca

Founded: 1968
Membership: 1,001–10,000
Scope: Regional
Description: A province-wide, non-profit, charitable organization with a mission to be an advocate for wild Alberta through awareness and action and functioning on the values of eco-centredness, integrity, respectfulness, participation, tenacity and passion. The AWA promotes sound ideas and policies for wilderness conservation, fosters appreciation and enjoyment of wilderness, and works with government, industry, organizations and individuals to encourage careful management of Alberta's natural lands & water.
Publication(s): Wild Lands Advocate, Landscapes of Southern Alberta, Eastern Slopes Wildlands: Our Living Heritage
Keyword(s): Forests/Forestry, Land Issues, Public Lands/Greenspace, Reduce/Reuse/Recycle, Water Habitats & Quality, Wildlife & Species
Contact(s):
Cliff Wallis, President
A. Morasch, Finance & Operations Manager; 283-2025; Fax: 270-2743
Shirley Bray, Director, Wilderness Resource Centre; 270-2736; Fax: 270-2743; awa.wrc@shaw.ca
Christyann Olson, Executive Director; 283-2025; Fax: 270-2743

ALDO LEOPOLD FOUNDATION

P.O. Box 77
Baraboo, WI 53913-0077 United States
Phone: 608-355-0279 Fax: 608-356-7309
E-mail: mail@aldoleopold.org
Website: www.aldoleopold.org

Founded: 1982
Membership: 101–1,000
Scope: Local, Regional, National
Description: The Aldo Leopold Foundation, founded by the children of Aldo Leopold, keeps his legacy alive by promoting the "Land Ethic" he so eloquently defined. The Foundation actively integrates programs in Land Stewardship, Environmental Education, and Ecological Research to promote care of natural resources and foster an ethical relationship between people and land.
Publication(s): Leopold Outlook, The
Keyword(s): Ethics/Environmental Justice, Land Issues, Wildlife & Species
Contact(s):
Wellington Huffaker, Executive Director; buddy@aldoleopold.org
Sarah Lloyd, Membership Coordinator; sarah@aldoleopold.org
Estella Leopold, Chairman
Rob Nelson, Outreach Coordinator; rob@aldoleopold.org
Teresa Searock, Administrative Assistant; teresa@aldoleopold.org
Steve Swenson, Ecologist; steve@aldoleopold.org

ALLIANCE FOR THE CHESAPEAKE BAY

6600 York Road
Baltimore, MD 23236 United States
Phone: 410-377-6270 Fax: 410-377-7144
E-mail: mail@acb-online.org
Website: www.alliancechesbay.org

Founded: 1971
Membership: 101–1,000
Scope: Local, State, Regional
Description: To build, maintain and serve the partnership among the general public, the private sector and the government that is essential for establishing and sustaining policy, programs and the political will to preserve and restore the resources of the Chesapeake Bay.
Publication(s): Bay Journal, Watershed Watch
Keyword(s): Development/Developing Countries, Oceans/Coasts/Beaches, Pollution (general), Population, Water Habitats & Quality, Wildlife & Species
Contact(s):
Terry Harwood, Chairman; 410-377-6270
Charles Conklin, Vice Chairman, MD; 410-377-6270
David Cottingham, Vice Chairman, DC; 410-377-6270
Joseph Gartlan, Vice Chairman, Virginia; 410-377-6270
Marshall Kaiser, Vice Chairman, PA; 410-377-6270
David Bancroft, Executive Director; 6600 York Rd. Suite 100, Baltimore, MD 21212; 410-377-6270
Brigid Kenney, Secretary; 410-377-6270
Michael Marino, Treasurer; 410-377-6270

ALLIANCE FOR THE CHESAPEAKE BAY

HARRISBURG OFFICE
600 N. Second St., # 300B
Harrisburg, PA 17101 United States
Phone: 717-236-8825
E-mail: acbpa@acb-online.org
Website: www.acbpa.acb-online.org

Founded: 1971
Scope: Local, State, Regional
Description: The Alliance for the Chesapeake Bay is a regional, non-profit organization that builds consensus and fosters partnerships for the restoration of the Chesapeake Bay and its rivers.
Publication(s): Publications on website
Contact(s):
David Bancroft, Executive Director; dbancroft@acb-online.org

ALLIANCE FOR THE CHESAPEAKE BAY

RICHMOND, VA OFFICE
P.O. Box 1981
Richmond, VA 23218 United States
Phone: 804-775-0951 Fax: 804-775-0954
E-mail: ACBVA@yahoo.com
Website: AllianceChesBay.org

Founded: 1971
Membership: 1,001–10,000
Scope: Regional
Description: The Alliance is a coalition of educators, scientists, farmers, recreationists that builds and fosters partnerships to restore the Bay and its rivers. The Alliance has been a leader in facilitating these groups to come to consensus on positions

and programs that help to protect the Chesapeake Bay. In addition, the Alliance provides both the general public and decision-makers with information and opportunities to become involved in activities that help to restore the Bay watershed.

AMANAKAA AMAZON NETWORK

60 E. 13th St., 5th Fl.
New York, NY 10003 United States
Phone: 212-253-9502 Fax: 212-253-9507
E-mail: amanakaa@amanakaa.org
Website: www.amanakaa.org

Founded: 1990

Scope: National

Description: The Amanakaa's Amazon Network is a nonprofit environmental and social justice organization. Amanakaa serves as a liaison between the peoples of the Amazon and their allies in the U.S. We work to educate the American public about the Amazon Rainforest and its peoples and support grassroots organizations in the Amazon.

Publication(s): Amanakaa Update, series of booklets by people of the Amazon, Letters from the Amazon

Keyword(s): Development/Developing Countries, Ethics/Environmental Justice, Forests/Forestry

Contact(s):
Zeze Weiss, President
John Friede, Vice President
Christine Halvorson, Executive Director, Acting
Christine Halvorson, Secretary

AMERICA THE BEAUTIFUL FUND

1730 K St., NW, Suite 1002
Washington, DC 20006 United States
Phone: 202-638-1649 Fax: 202-204-0028
Website: www.freeseeds.org

Founded: 1965
Membership: 1,001–10,000
Scope: National

Description: America the Beautiful Fund gives recognition, technical support, small seed grants, gifts of free seeds and national recognition awards to volunteers and community groups to initiate new local action projects improving the quality of the environment, including design, land preservation, local food production, arts, historical and cultural preservation and horticultural therapy.

Publication(s): The Green Earth Guide, Better Times, Old Glory

Keyword(s): Agriculture/Farming, Ethics/Environmental Justice, Public Health, Reduce/Reuse/Recycle, Wildlife & Species

Contact(s):
Nanine Bilski, President; 1730 K St. Suite 1002, Washington, DC 20006
Jean Douglas, Vice President; 4733 Woodway Ln., NW, Washington, DC 20016
Kay Lautman, Vice President; 1730 Rhode Island Ave., NW, Suite 700, Washington, DC 20036
Susan Anderson, Treasurer; 235 Mason Dr., Manhasset, NY 11030
Thomas Farrell, Chairman of the Board; First Chicago, 153 W 51 St., New York, NY 10019
Daniel Schneider, Secretary; 31 Mill Hills Rd., Woodstock, NY 12498; 914-679-9868

AMERICAN ALLIANCE FOR HEALTH, PHYSICAL EDUCATION AND RECREATION AND DANCE

1900 Association Dr.
Reston, VA 22091-1502 United States
Phone: 703-476-3400 Fax: 703-476-9527
Website: www.aahperd.org

Founded: N/A
Membership: 1,001–10,000
Scope: State

Description: A voluntary professional organization for educators in the fields of physical education, sports and athletics, dance, health and safety, recreation and outdoor and environmental education. Its purpose is the improvement of education through such professional services as consultation, periodicals and special publications, conferences and workshops, leadership development, determination of standards and research.

Publication(s): Strategies, AAHPERD Update, Health Education, Research Quarterly for Exercise and Sport, Journal of Physical Education, Recreation and Dance

Contact(s):
Lucinda Adams, President of Board of Governors; Westfield State College, Westfield, MA 01086
Glenn Roswal, President Elect of Board of Governors

AMERICAN ASSOCIATION FOR LEISURE AND RECREATION - AALR

1900 Association Dr.
Reston, VA 20191 United States
Phone: 703-476-3472 Fax: 703-476-9527
E-mail: aalr@aahperd.org
Website: www.aahperd.org/aalr

Founded: 1978
Membership: 1,001–10,000
Scope: National

Description: Mission - The mission of the American Association for Leisure and Recreation (AALR) is to promote and support education, leisure, and recreation by: developing quality programming and professional training, providing leadership opportunities, disseminating guidelines and standards and enhancing public understanding of the importance of leisure and recreation in maintaining a creative and healthy lifestyle.

Publication(s): AAL Reporter, Leisure Today

Keyword(s): Ethics/Environmental Justice, Recreation/Ecotourism

Contact(s):
Marsha Carter, President; University of Northern Colorado, Greeley, CO
Gale Widow, Representative to the Board of Governors; University of South Dakota, Vermillion, SD 57069
Vicki Highstreet, Past President; University of Nebraska, Lincoln, NE 68588
Charles Killingsworth, President Elect; Pittsburg State University, Pittsburg, KS

AMERICAN ASSOCIATION FOR THE ADVANCEMENT OF SCIENCE

1200 New York Ave., NW
Washington, DC 20005 United States
Phone: 202-326-6400
E-mail: webmaster@aaas.org
Website: www.aaas.org

Founded: 1848

Scope: National

Description: Objectives are to further the work of scientists, to facilitate cooperation among them, to foster scientific freedom and responsibility, to improve the effectiveness of science in the promotion of human welfare and to increase public understanding and appreciation of the importance and promise of the methods of science in human progress.

Publication(s): Science Books and Films, Science's Next Wave

Keyword(s): Climate Change, Population, Wildlife & Species

Contact(s):
Mary Good, President
William Golden, Treasurer; 212-425-0333
Stephen Gould, Chairman of the Board
Donald Kennedy, Editor In Chief
Richard Nicholson, Executive Officer; 202-326-6639

AMERICAN ASSOCIATION OF BOTANICAL GARDENS AND ARBORETA, INC.

351 Longwood Rd.
Kennett Square, PA 19348 United States
Phone: 610-925-2500 Fax: 610-925-2700
E-mail: aabga@aabga.org
Website: www.aabga.org

Founded: 1940
Membership: 1,001–10,000
Scope: National
Description: AABGA is a nonprofit, membership organization serving North American botanical gardens, arboreta and their professional staffs.
Publication(s): AABGA Newsletter, Public Garden, The
Keyword(s): Agriculture/Farming, Wildlife & Species
Contact(s):
Mary Matheson, President
Carla Pastore, Executive Director
Mary Casey, Publications Manager; ext. 17; mjcasey887@aol.com
Gerald Donnelly, Past President; Executive Director of the Moton Arboretum, 4100 Illinois Rte. 53, Lisle, IL 60532-1293
Richard Piacentini, Treasurer; Executive Director of Phipps Conservatory and Botanical Gardens, One Schenley Park, Pittsburgh, PA 15213-3830
Kathleen Socolofsky, Secretary; Director of UC Davis Arboretum, One Shields Ave., Davis, CA 95616

AMERICAN ASSOCIATION OF ZOO KEEPERS, INC.

ADMINISTRATIVE OFFICES
3609 SW 29th St.
Topeka, KS 66614 United States
Phone: 785-273-9149 Fax: 785-273-1980
E-mail: akfeditor@kscable.com
Website: www.aazk.org

Founded: 1967
Membership: 1,001–10,000
Scope: National
Description: An international nonprofit organization of animal keepers and other persons interested in quality animal care and in promoting animal keeping as a profession. Chapters are active at zoos throughout North America. Promotes continuing education for keepers, national and international conservation projects, keeper-initiated zoo research, and educational publications.
Publication(s): Crisis Management Resource Notebook, Handbook of Zoonotic Diseases, Enrichment Notebook, second edition, Animal Keepers' Forum
Keyword(s): Reduce/Reuse/Recycle, Wildlife & Species
Contact(s):
Kevin Shelton, President; kshelton@flaquarium.org
Ed Hansen, Executive Director of the Board; 3601 SW 29th, Suite 133, Topeka, KS 66614; 785-273-9149
Jacque Blessington, Board of Directors; Kansas City Zoological Gardens, 6700 Zoo Dr., Kansas City, MO; 816-513-5700
Susan Chan, Editor
Bruce Elkins, Board of Directors; belkins@indyzoo.com
Bob Hayes, Board of Directors; bulletbobhayes@hotmail.com
Linda King, Board of Directors; lmking83@aol.com
Barbara Manspeaker, Administrative Secretary of Administrative Offices
Jan Reed-Smith, Board of Directors; John Ball Zoo, 1300 W. Fulton St., Grand Rapids, MI 49504; 616-336-4301
Denise Wagner, Board of Directors; dwagner@sandiegoz..org

AMERICAN B.A.S.S. ASSOCIATION OF EASTERN PENNSYLVANIA/ NEW JERSEY, THE

Attn: President, 7 Logan Dr
Summerville, NJ 08876 United States
Phone: 908-526-7721 Fax: 908-685-0970
Website: www.emterco.com

Founded: N/A
Scope: State
Contact(s):
Paul Rinaldo, President

AMERICAN BIRD CONSERVANCY

P.O. Box 249
The Plains, VA 20198 United States
Phone: 540-253-5780 Fax: 540-253-5782
E-mail: abc@abcbirds.org
Website: www.abcbirds.org

Founded: 1994
Membership: 1,001–10,000
Scope: International
Description: American Bird Conservancy (ABC) is a U.S. based, nonprofit, membership organization dedicated to the conservation of wild birds and their habitats throughout the Americas. The fundamental role of ABC is to build coalitions of conservation groups, scientists, and members of the public, to tackle key bird priorities using the best resources available. ABC produces the magazine Bird Conservation and the newsletter Bird Calls for its members.
Publication(s): Seabird Report, Tower Report, Recovering Paradise, All the Birds of North America, Bird Conservation Directory 2001, Annual Report, Bird Calls, Bird Conservation, Conservation of Land Birds of The US, Communication Towers: A Deadly Hazard to Birds
Keyword(s): Agriculture/Farming, Climate Change, Development/Developing Countries, Ecosystems (precious), Executive/Legislative/Judicial Reform, Land Issues, Oceans/Coasts/Beaches, Recreation/Ecotourism, Reduce/Reuse/ Recycle, Wildlife & Species
Contact(s):
George Fenwick, President; gfenwick@abcbirds.org
Merrie Morrison, Vice President for Operations; mmorr@abcbirds.org
Mike Parr, Vice President for Program Development; mparr@abcbirds.org
David Pashley, Vice President of Conservation; dpashley@abcbirds.org
Gerald Winegrad, Vice President for Policy; gww@abcbirds.org
Patricia Bright, Director of Pesticides and Birds Campaign; pbright@abcbirds.org
Robert Chipley, Director of Important Bird Areas; rchipley@abcbirds.org
Elizabeth Ennis, Director for Membership; eennis@abcbirds.org
Gavin Shire, Director of Communications Technology; gshire@abcbirds.org
Linda Winter, Director of Cats Indoors Campaign; lwinter@abcbirds.org
Howard Brokaw, Chairman

AMERICAN BIRDING ASSOCIATION (ABA)

P.O. Box 6599
Colorado Springs, CO 80934 United States
Phone: 719-578-9703 Fax: 719-578-1480
E-mail: member@aba.org
Website: www.americanbirding.org

Founded: 1969
Membership: 10,001–100,000
Scope: National
Description: The American Birding Association provides leadership to field birders by increasing their knowledge, skills

and enjoyment of birding. The ABA supports the interests of birders of all ages and experience and actively encourages the conservation of birds and their habitats.

Publication(s): Membership Directory, Volunteer Directory, ABA/Lane Series of Birdfinding Guides, ABA Checklist, North American Birds, Winging It, A Birds Eye View

Keyword(s): Recreation/Ecotourism, Wildlife & Species

Contact(s):

Paul Baicich, Director of Conservation and Public Policy; baicich@aba.org
Paul Green, Executive Director
Ted Floyd, Editor of the Magazine; tedfloyd@aba.org
Dennis Lacoss, Treasurer; dlacoss@mindspring.com
Richard Payne, Chairman of the Board; rhp@shsu.edu
Matt Pelikan, Editor of Newsletter; winging@aba.org
Ann Stone, Secretary; 104673.1143@compuserve.com

AMERICAN CAMPING ASSOCIATION, INC.

5000 State Rd. 67N
Martinsville, IN 46151 United States
Phone: 765-342-8456 Fax: 765-342-2065
E-mail: aca@acacamps.org
Website: www.acacamps.org

Founded: 1910

Scope: National

Description: The American Camping Association is a national community of camp professionals dedicated to enriching the lives of children and adults through camp experience. ACA recognizes the camp experience as a significant contributor to positive child and youth development. It is the only organization that accredits all types of camps based on 300 standards for health, safety and program quality.

Publication(s): Various camp-related publications, Guide to Accredited Camps, Camping Magazine

Keyword(s): Public Health, Recreation/Ecotourism

Contact(s):

Rodger Popkin, President
Terri Nicodemus, Director of Public Relations
Peg Smith, Executive Director

AMERICAN CANAL SOCIETY, INC.

840 Rinks Ln.
Savannah, TN 38372-6774 United States
Website: www.canals.com/ACS/acs.html

Founded: 1972

Scope: National

Description: A nonprofit organization dedicated to historic canal research, preservation and canal parks.

Publication(s): Best From American Canals #1, #2, #3, #4, American Canals (Quarterly Bulletin)

Keyword(s): Ethics/Environmental Justice

Contact(s):

Terry Woods, President; 6939 Eastham Circle, Canton, OH 44708
Charles Derr, Secretary and Treasurer; 117 Main St., Freemansburg, PA 18017; 610-691-0956
David Ross, Editor

AMERICAN CAVE CONSERVATION ASSOCIATION

119 E. Main St., P.O. Box 409
Horse Cave, KY 42749 United States
Phone: 270-786-1466 Fax: 270-786-1467
E-mail: debraheavers@cavern.org
Website: www.cavern.org

Founded: 1977

Membership: 101–1,000

Scope: National

Description: The ACCA is a national organization formed to conserve caves and karstlands and other resources associated with them. Primary objectives are to provide information, technical assistance, and public education and management training programs; and operation of the American Cave and Karst Center, a national environmental education center and museum.

Publication(s): American Caves Magazine

Keyword(s): Land Issues, Recreation/Ecotourism, Wildlife & Species

Contact(s):

David Foster, Executive Director; 270-786-1466; Fax: 270-786-1467
Debra Heavers, Associate Director; 270-786-1466; Fax: 270-786-1467; debraheavers@cavern.org

AMERICAN CETACEAN SOCIETY

San Pedro, CA 90733-0391 United States
Phone: 310-548-6279 Fax: 310-548-6950
E-mail: acs@pobox.com
Website: www.acsonline.org

Founded: 1967

Scope: National

Description: A nonprofit organization that works in the areas of conservation, education and research to protect marine mammals, especially whales, dolphins and porpoises and the oceans they live in.

Publication(s): Whalewatcher: Journal of the American Cetacen Society

Keyword(s): Water Habitats & Quality, Wildlife & Species

AMERICAN CHESTNUT FOUNDATION, THE

P.O. Box 4044
Bennington, VT 05201-4044 United States
Phone: 802-447-0110 Fax: 802-442-6855
E-mail: chestnut@acf.org
Website: www.acf.org

Founded: 1983

Membership: 1,001–10,000

Scope: National

Description: Funded by private contributions, the purpose of The American Chestnut Foundation is to promote the preservation and restoration of the American chestnut, an important wildlife and timber tree killed by a blight early in the Twentieth Century; to operate three research breeding farms in Meadowview, VA; to provide grants for cutting edge research; and to identify surviving trees and establish satellite research plantings.

Publication(s): Journal of The American Chestnut Foundation

Keyword(s): Forests/Forestry, Wildlife & Species

Contact(s):

Marshal Case, Executive Director
Ana Ronderos, Communications Director
Gerrie Rousseau, Membership Director
Phil Pritchard, Development Director; Southern Appalachian Regional Office, Asheville, NC 28801; 828-281-0047; Fax: 828-253-5373; pritchard@acf.org

AMERICAN CONSERVATION ASSOCIATION, INC.

1200 New York Ave., NW, Suite 400
Washington, DC 20005 United States
Phone: 202-289-2431 Fax: 202-289-1396

Founded: 1958

Scope: National

Description: A nonmembership, nonprofit, educational and scientific organization formed to advance knowledge and understanding of conservation and to preserve and develop natural resources for public use.

Keyword(s): Air Quality/Atmosphere, Oceans/Coasts/Beaches, Recreation/Ecotourism, Reduce/Reuse/Recycle

Contact(s):

Laurance Rockefeller, President
Charles Clusen, Executive Director

R. Greathead, Secretary
Carmen Reyes, Treasurer
Laurance Rockefeller, Founder, Honorary Trustee

AMERICAN CONSERVATION ASSOCIATION, INC.

NEW YORK OFFICE
30 Rockefeller Plaza, Rm. 5402
New York, NY 10112 United States
Phone: 212-649-5822
Website: www.synergos.org/globalphilanthropy/organizations/aca.htm

Founded: N/A

Scope: National

Contact(s):
Carmen Meyers, Main Contact

AMERICAN COUNCIL FOR AN ENERGY-EFFICIENT ECONOMY

1001 Connecticut Ave., NW, #801
Washington, DC 20036-5525 United States
Phone: 202-429-8873 Fax: 202-429-2248
E-mail: info@aceee.org
Website: www.aceee.org

Founded: 1980

Scope: National

Description: Advancing energy efficiency as a means of promoting both economic prosperity and environmental protection. ACEEE conducts technical and policy assessments; advises governments and utilities; publishes books, conference proceedings and reports; organizes conferences and workshops; and informs consumers.

Publication(s): Energy Innovations: A Prosperous Path, Using Consensus Building to Improve Utility Regulation, Transportation and Energy, Consumer Guide to Home Energy Savings

Keyword(s): Energy, Pollution (general), Transportation

Contact(s):
Carl Blumstein, President; 202-429-8873; Fax: 202-429-2248
Steve Nadel, Director; 202-429-8873; Fax: 202-429-2248

AMERICAN COUNCIL FOR THE UNITED NATIONS UNIVERSITY (ACUNU)

MILLENNIUM PROJECT
4421 Garrison Street, NW
Washington, DC 20016 United States
Phone: 202-0686-5179 Fax: 202-686-5179
E-mail: acunu@igc.org
Website: www.acunu.org

Founded: 1996

Membership: 101–1,000

Scope: Local, State, Regional, National, International

Description: The Millennium Project is a participatory think tank for global futures research with 1,200 futurists, scholars, business planners, policymakers who work for the United Nations, governments, corporations, NGOs, universities in 50 countries and produces the annual "State of the Future" reports. There are 15 Nodes (groups of institutions and individuals) around the world.

Keyword(s): Air Quality/Atmosphere, Climate Change, Development/Developing Countries, Energy, Ethics/Environmental Justice, Water Habitats & Quality

AMERICAN EAGLE FOUNDATION

P.O. Box 333
Pigeon Forge, TN 37868 United States
Phone: 865-429-0157 Fax: 865-429-4743
E-mail: eaglemail@eagles.org

Founded: 1985

Scope: National

Description: Dedicated to saving, restoring, and protecting America's endangered national symbol, the Bald Eagle, and preserving America's wildlife, waterways, forests, natural resources, ecosystems, and environment.

Publication(s): Eagle Extra, American Eagle News

Keyword(s): Ecosystems (precious), Wildlife & Species

Contact(s):
Al Cecere, President, CEO & Board Member; P.O. Box 333, Pigeon Forge, TN 37868; 865-429-0157; Fax: 865-429-4743; eaglemail@eagles.org
Bobby Halliburton, Vice President & Board Member
Steven Compton, Secretary & Board Member
Joseph Spivey, Treasurer & Board Member

AMERICAN FARMLAND TRUST

1200 18th St., NW
Washington, DC 20036 United States
Phone: 202-331-7300 Fax: 202-659-8339
E-mail: info@farmland.org
Website: www.farmland.org

Founded: 1980

Membership: 10,001–100,000

Scope: State, Regional, National

Description: AFT is a nationwide nonprofit organization working to stop the loss of productive farmland and to promote farming practices that lead to a healthy environment. Its programs include public education, technical assistance, policy development and direct farmland-protection projects.

Publication(s): Saving American Farmland: What Works, Sharing the Responsibility, Living on the Edge, Farming on the Edge II, Your Land Is Your Legacy

Keyword(s): Agriculture/Farming, Land Issues, Sprawl/Urban Planning, Water Habitats & Quality

Contact(s):
Ralph Grossi, President; rgrossi@farmland.org
Jimmy Daukas, Vice President for Marketing; jdaukas@farmland.org
Edward Thompson, Senior Vice President for Public Policy
Robert Wagner, Assistant Vice President of Field Programs
Tim Warman, Vice President for Programs; twarman@farmland.org
Dennis Bidwell, Director of Land Protection; dbidwell@farmland.org
Julia Freedgood, Director for Farmland Advisory Services; jfreedgood@farmland.org
Bryan Petrucci, Director of Farms
Bernadine Prince, Director of Public Education; bprince@farmland.org
Ann Sorensen, Director of Center for Agriculture In the Environment
Edward Harte, Vice Chairman of the Board
Sharon Phenneger, Controller
William Reilly, Chairman of the Board

AMERICAN FEDERATION OF MINERALOGICAL SOCIETIES (AFMS)

AFMS Central Office
2706 Lascassas Pike
Murfreesboro, TN 37130-1540 United States
Phone: 615-893-8270
E-mail: lfelrod@yahoo.com
Website: www.amfed.org/

Founded: 1945

Membership: 10,001–100,000

Scope: National

Description: To promote popular interest and education in the various earth sciences, in particular, the subjects of geology, mineralogy, paleontology, lapidary and other related subjects, and to sponsor and provide means of coordinating the work and efforts of all persons and groups interested therein; to sponsor and encourage the formation and international development of societies and regional federations, and by and through such means to strive toward greater international goodwill and fellowship.

Publication(s): AFMS Safety Manual, AFMS Uniform Rules booklets, American Federation Newsletter

Keyword(s): Land Issues, Public Lands/Greenspace

Contact(s):

Lewis F. Elrod, CFE, Administrator; 2699 Lascassas Pike, Murfreesboro, TN 37230

Dan McLennan, Secretary; P.O. Box 26523, Oklahoma City, OK 73126-0523

Mel Albright, Editor; Rt. 3 Box 8500, Bartlesville, OK 74003

Toby Cozens, Treasurer; 4401 SW Hill St., Seattle, WA 98116-1924

AMERICAN FISHERIES SOCIETY

5410 Grosvenor Ln. Suite 110
Bethesda, MD 20814 United States
Phone: 301-897-8616 Fax: 301-897-8096
E-mail: fisheriesmain@fisheries.org
Website: www.fisheries.org

Founded: N/A
Membership: 1–100
Scope: National

Description: Scientific society founded in 1870 dedicated to the conservation of fisheries resources and the professional growth of its members.

Contact(s):

Fred Harris, President
Gus Rassam, Executive Director

AMERICAN FISHERIES SOCIETY

AGRICULTURE ECONOMICS SECTION
University of Florida
Gainesville, FL 32611 United States
Phone: 352-392-4991 Fax: 352-392-3646
Website: www.fred.ifas.ufl.edu

Founded: N/A
Membership: 1–100
Scope: Regional

Contact(s):

Charles Adams, President; adams@fred.ifas.ufl.edu
Chris Andrew, Assistant Chairman
John Gordon, Chairman
Burl Long, Assistant Chairman

AMERICAN FISHERIES SOCIETY

ALABAMA CHAPTER
Alabama Chapter, 3355 Audubon Rd.
Montgomery, AL 36106-2404 United States
Phone: 334-353-7998

Founded: 1991
Scope: State

Contact(s):

Gregory Lein, President; 334-844-9318; glein@acesag.auburn.edu

AMERICAN FISHERIES SOCIETY

ALASKA CHAPTER
ASGS/Alaska Science Center
1011 East Tudor Road
Anchorage, AK 99703 United States
Website: www.fisheries.org/afs-ak/

Founded: 1973
Scope: State

Description: The American Fisheries Society is dedicated to the preservation and conservation of aquatic resources, and facilitating the information exchange between students, professionals, and the public regarding our knowledge of aquatic resources.

Contact(s):

Carol Ann Woody, President; 907-786-3314; Fax: 907-786-3636; carol_woody@usgs.gov

AMERICAN FISHERIES SOCIETY

ARIZONA-NEW MEXICO CHAPTER
2221 W. Green Rd.
Phoenix, AZ 85023 United States
Phone: 602-789-3258
Website: www.fisheries.org

Founded: 1967
Scope: International
Publication(s): AFS journals, online fisheries magazine

Contact(s):

Larry Riley, President; 602-789-3258

AMERICAN FISHERIES SOCIETY

ARKANSAS CHAPTER
Aquaculture & Fisheries Center UAPB
P.O. Box 4912
Pine Bluff, AR 71611 United States

Founded: 1986
Scope: State

Description: The American Fisheries Society is dedicated to the preservation and conservation of aquatic resources, and facilitating the information exchange between students, professionals, and the public regarding our knowledge of aquatic resources.

Contact(s):

Steve Lochmann, Member; 870-543-8165; slochmann@auex.edu

AMERICAN FISHERIES SOCIETY

ATLANTIC INTERNATIONAL CHAPTER
689 Farmington Rd
Strong, ME 04983 United States
Phone: 207-778-3322 Fax: 207-778-3323
Website: www.afs.org

Founded: 1975
Membership: 1–100
Scope: International
Publication(s): Atlantic International Chapter Newsletter

Contact(s):

Forrest Bonney, President; forrest.bonney@state.me.us

AMERICAN FISHERIES SOCIETY

AUBURN UNIVERSITY CHAPTER
Attn: President, 203 Swingle Hall
Auburn University, AL 36849 United States
Phone: 334-844-9318 Fax: 334-844-9208
E-mail: jollejc@acesag.auburn.edu
Website: www.ag.auburn.edu/faa/amerfishsoc/

Founded: 1973
Membership: 1–100
Scope: State

Description: Our membership draws from a diverse group, including students (undergraduate and graduate), fisheries professionals and university professors. Members encompass a wide variety of fisheries specializations including fisheries management, aquaculture, fish ecology, fish genetics, fish nutrition and fish diseases and seeks to influence and improve fisheries and aquaculture in Alabama through research and communication.

Contact(s):

Jeffrey Jolley; 334-844-9318; Fax: 334-844-9208; jollejc@acesag.auburn.edu

AMERICAN FISHERIES SOCIETY
BIOENGINEERING SECTION
1646 Jeannette Pl.
Bainbridge Island, WA 98110 United States
Phone: 508-829-6000 Fax: 206-842-8195
E-mail: dailydesign@bainbridge.net

Founded: N/A

Scope: National

Contact(s):
Ned Taft, President; 508-829-6000; ntaft@aldenlab.com
Wayne Daley, Past-President; wjd1163@aol.com

AMERICAN FISHERIES SOCIETY
BONNEVILLE CHAPTER
Attn: President, P.O. Box 305
Dutch John, UT 84023 United States
Phone: 801-789-3103

Founded: 1963

Scope: State

Publication(s): Quarterly newsletter, bulletins

Contact(s):
Scott Tollentino, President; 801-789-3103; nrdwr.stollent@state.ut.us

AMERICAN FISHERIES SOCIETY
CALIFORNIA-NEVADA CHAPTER
Trust for Public Land
116 New Montgomery Street, Suite 300
San Francisco, CA 94105 United States
Website: www.afs-calneva.org

Founded: 1963

Scope: Regional

Description: The American Fisheries Society is dedicated to the preservation and conservation of aquatic resources, and facilitating the information exchange between students, professionals, and the public regarding our knowledge of aquatic resources.

Contact(s):
Elise Holland, President; 415-495-5660; Fax: 415-495-0541; elise.holland@tpl.org

AMERICAN FISHERIES SOCIETY
CANADIAN AQUATIC RESOURCES SECTION
2204 Main Mall, Univ. BC
Vancouver, V6T 1Z4 British Columbia Canada
Phone: 604-222-6753 Fax: 604-660-1849
Website: www.fisheries.org/cars/index/htm

Founded: N/A

Scope: National

Contact(s):
Bruce Ward, President; bruce.ward@gems8.gov.bc.ca
Martin Castongue, President-Elect

AMERICAN FISHERIES SOCIETY
COLLEGE OF ENVIRONMENTAL SCIENCE AND FORESTRY CHAPTER
Syracuse, NY United States
Website: www.esf.edu/org/afs/

Founded: 1975

Scope: State

Description: The American Fisheries Society is dedicated to the preservation and conservation of aquatic resources, and facilitating the information exchange between students, professionals, and the public regarding our knowledge of aquatic resources.

Contact(s):
Stephen Coghlan, President; 315-472-0488; clapton18@hotmail.com

AMERICAN FISHERIES SOCIETY
COLORADO-WYOMING CHAPTER
Wyoming Game and Fish Department
P.O. Box 67
Jackson, WY 83001 United States
Phone: 307-733-2383, ext. 26
Website: www.fisheries.org/co-wy/

Founded: 1966

Scope: State

Description: The American Fisheries Society is dedicated to the preservation and conservation of aquatic resources, and facilitating the information exchange between students, professionals, and the public regarding our knowledge of aquatic resources.

Contact(s):
Rob Gipson, President; 307-733-2321; Fax: 307-733-2276; rgipso@state.wy.us

AMERICAN FISHERIES SOCIETY
COMPUTER USER SECTION
Dept. of Natural Sciences, MS Valley State Univ.
Itta Bena, MS 38941 United States
Phone: 601-254-3383 Fax: 601-254-3668
E-mail: cusfisheries@cus.org
Website: www.fisheries.org/cus

Founded: N/A

Scope: National

Contact(s):
Michael Porter, President; mdporter@cypress.mcsr.olemiss.edu

AMERICAN FISHERIES SOCIETY
DAKOTA CHAPTER
1200 Mossourri Ave. P.O. Box 5520
Bismarck, ND 58506 United States
Phone: 701-328-5210 Fax: 701-328-5200
Website: www.health.state.nd.us/ndhd/default.asp

Founded: 1964
Membership: 1–100
Scope: State
Publication(s): ARI News Bulletin

Contact(s):
Wade King, President
Scott Elstad, Environmental Scientist

AMERICAN FISHERIES SOCIETY
EARLY LIFE HISTORY
NOAA - National Marine Fisheries Service
The Beaufort Laboratory
101 Pivers Island Rd.
Beaufort, NC 28526 United States
Phone: 206-526-4108 Fax: 252-728-8747

Founded: N/A

Scope: National

Publication(s): Stages Newsletter

Contact(s):
Art Kendal, President; art.kendal@noaa.org

AMERICAN FISHERIES SOCIETY
EQUAL OPPORTUNITIES SECTION
Department of Fisheries and Wildlife-Michigan State University
13 Natural Resources
East Lansing, MI 48824-1222 United States
Phone: 517-432-8086 Fax: 517-432-1699
E-mail: habrong@msu.edu
Website: www.fisheries.org

Founded: N/A

Scope: National

Description: The Equal Opportunities Section works to encourage the exchange of information pertinent to the promotion of employment, education, scholarships, participation, professionalism, and recruitment for all individuals in the fisheries profession. Our goal is to increase the representation and involvement of diverse ethnic/racial groups and females in the American Fisheries Society.

Contact(s):
Gwen White, President; gwhite@dnr.state.in.us

AMERICAN FISHERIES SOCIETY
FISH CULTURE SECTION
3425 Settlers Rd
LaPorte, CO 80535 United States
Phone: 304-724-4457

Founded: N/A
Membership: 101–1,000
Scope: National
Publication(s): Quarterly Journal- North American Journal of Agriculture, Quarterly Newsletter
Contact(s):
Steve Flickinger, President; 970-484-4167; flick@worldnet.att.net

AMERICAN FISHERIES SOCIETY
FISH HEALTH SECTION
CA State Univ., Dept. of Biological Sciences
Hayward, CA 94542 United States
Phone: 541-737-1856 Fax: 541-737-0496
Website: www.fisheries.org/fhs/

Founded: N/A
Scope: National
Publication(s): Publications on website
Contact(s):
Jerri Bartholomew, President; baartholj@bcc.arst.edu

AMERICAN FISHERIES SOCIETY
FISHERIES ADMINISTRATORS SECTION
5410 Grosvenor Lane
Bethesda, MD 20814 United States
Phone: 301-897-8616 Fax: 301-897-8096
E-mail: main@fisheries.org
Website: www.fisheries.org

Founded: N/A
Scope: National
Contact(s):
Michael Staggs, President; 608-267-0796; Fax: 608-266-2244; staggm@dnr.state.wi.us

AMERICAN FISHERIES SOCIETY
FISHERIES HISTORY SECTION
2901 Channel Dr.
Stevens Point, WI 54481 United States
Phone: 715-344-0152 Fax: 715-346-3624
Website: www.fisheries.org

Founded: N/A
Membership: 101–1,000
Scope: International
Publication(s): Fisheries History Section Newsletter
Contact(s):
Daniel Coble, President

AMERICAN FISHERIES SOCIETY
FISHERIES MANAGEMENT SECTION
OK Fish Lab, 500 E. Constellation
Norman, OK 73072 United States
Phone: 405-325-7288 Fax: 405-325-7631

Founded: N/A
Scope: National
Contact(s):
Jeff Boxrucker, President; jboxrucker@aol.com

AMERICAN FISHERIES SOCIETY
FLORIDA CHAPTER
Website: nerps.nerdc.ufl.edu/~fafs/

Founded: 1981
Scope: State
Description: The American Fisheries Society is dedicated to the preservation and conservation of aquatic resources, and facilitating the information exchange between students, professionals, and the public regarding our knowledge of aquatic resources.
Contact(s):
Peter Hood, President; peter.hood@gulfcouncil.org

AMERICAN FISHERIES SOCIETY
GENETICS SECTION
4302 Underwood St.
University Park, MD 20782 United States
Phone: 301-864-2553
Website: www.fisheries.org

Founded: N/A
Scope: National
Contact(s):
John Epifanio, President; jepifan@atlas.vcu.edu

AMERICAN FISHERIES SOCIETY
GEORGIA CHAPTER
Attn: President, GA DNR Albany Fisheries, 2024 Newton Rd.
Albany, GA 31701-3576 United States
Phone: 229-430-4256 Fax: 229-430-5110

Founded: 1985
Membership: 1–100
Scope: State
Contact(s):
Matthew Thomas, Senior Biologist; 912-430-4256; Fax: 912-430-5110; matt_thomas@mail.dnr.state.ga.us

AMERICAN FISHERIES SOCIETY
GREATER PORTLAND, OR CHAPTER
Science Division, Mt. Hood Community College
26000 SE Stark Street
Gresham, OR 97030 United States

Founded: 1962
Scope: State
Publication(s): Audubon Warbler, Protecting a Vanishing Ecosystem, Familiar Birds of the Northwest, The Urban Naturalist
Contact(s):
Todd Hanna, President; 503-491-7163; Fax: 503-491-7481; hannat@mhcc.cc.or.us

AMERICAN FISHERIES SOCIETY
HAWAII CHAPTER
P.O. Box 22085
Honolulu, HI 96823 United States
Website: home.hawaii.rr.com/ikehara/afshi/index.html

Founded: 1982
Scope: State
Description: The American Fisheries Society is dedicated to the preservation and conservation of aquatic resources, and facilitating the information exchange between students, professionals, and the public regarding our knowledge of aquatic resources.
Contact(s):
Walter Ikehara, President; 808-587-0096; Fax: 808-587-0115; walter_n_ikehara@exec.state.hi.us

AMERICAN FISHERIES SOCIETY
HUMBOLDT CHAPTER
Arcata, CA 95521 United States
Founded: 1973
Scope: Local, Regional
Description: The American Fisheries Society is dedicated to the preservation and conservation of aquatic resources, and facilitating the information exchange between students, professionals, and the public regarding our knowledge of aquatic resources.
Contact(s):
Mary Knapp, President; mary_m_knapp@fws.gov

AMERICAN FISHERIES SOCIETY
IDAHO CHAPTER
Eagle, ID 83616 United States
Website: www.fisheries.org/idaho/
Founded: 1963
Scope: State
Description: The American Fisheries Society is dedicated to the preservation and conservation of aquatic resources, and facilitating the information exchange between students, professionals, and the public regarding our knowledge of aquatic resources.
Contact(s):
Steve Elle, President-Elect; selle@idfg.state.id.us

AMERICAN FISHERIES SOCIETY
ILLINOIS CHAPTER
IL Chapter of the Am. Fisheries Society
c/o IL Dept. of Natural Resource Division of Fisheries
One Natural Resources Way
Springfield, IL 62702-1271 United States
Phone: 217-784-4730 Fax: 217-784-8116
E-mail: glutterbie@dnrmail.state.il.us
Founded: 1963
Scope: Regional
Description: Professional organization
Contact(s):
R. Sallee, President; 309-582-5611

AMERICAN FISHERIES SOCIETY
INDIANA CHAPTER
Attn: President, Scott Shuler Aquatic Control, P.O. Box 100
Seymour, IN 47274 United States
Phone: 812-497-2410
Website: www.bsu.edu/csh/bio/inafs/
Founded: 1970
Scope: State
Contact(s):
Scott Shuler, President

AMERICAN FISHERIES SOCIETY
INTRODUCED FISH SECTION
1415 Green Road
Ann Arbor, MI 48105 United States
E-mail: jacqueline_savino@usgs.gov
Founded: N/A
Scope: National
Contact(s):
John Cassani, President; jcassani@peganet.com

AMERICAN FISHERIES SOCIETY
IOWA CHAPTER
110 Lake Darling Rd.
Brighton, IA 52540 United States
Founded: 1969
Scope: State
Contact(s):
Don Kline, President

AMERICAN FISHERIES SOCIETY
KANSAS CHAPTER
5800 A River Pond Rd.
Tuttle Creek Park
Manhattan, KS 66502 United States
Phone: 785-539-7941 Fax: 785-539-3183
Website: www.kdwp.state.ks.us
Founded: 1975
Membership: 1–100
Scope: State
Contact(s):
Chuck Bever, President

AMERICAN FISHERIES SOCIETY
KENTUCKY CHAPTER
Kentucky Department of Fish & Wildlife Resources
1 Game Farm Road
Frankfort, KY 40601 United States
Website: www.kfwis.state.ky.us/AFS/kyafs.htm
Founded: 1990
Scope: State
Description: The American Fisheries Society is dedicated to the preservation and conservation of aquatic resources, and facilitating the information exchange between students, professionals, and the public regarding our knowledge of aquatic resources.
Contact(s):
Kerry Prather, President; 502-564-5448; Fax: 502-564-4519; kprather@mail.state.ky.us

AMERICAN FISHERIES SOCIETY
LOUISIANA CHAPTER
Attn: President
LA Dept. of Wildlife and Fisheries
P.O. Box 98000
Baton Rouge, LA 70898 United States
Phone: 225-765-2375
Founded: 1979
Membership: 1–100
Scope: Local
Publication(s): Abstracts of Annual Technical Session
Contact(s):
Terry Tiersch, President

AMERICAN FISHERIES SOCIETY
MARINE FISHERIES SECTION
c/o Anne Richards
National Marine Fisheries Service
166 Water St.
Woods Hole, MA 97365 United States
Phone: 508-495-2305 Fax: 508-495-2393
Website: www.fisheries.org
Founded: N/A
Membership: 101–1,000
Scope: Regional, National, International
Description: The intent of the Marine Fisheries Section is to further the American Fisheries Society's objectives within marine fisheries science and practice. MFS members wish to attain further knowledge about marine fisheries, and to identify and publicize issues and problems related to development and management of marine fisheries. MFS also addresses research and education needs associated with biological, economic, social, and other aspects of marine fisheries.
Publication(s): www.fisheries.org/publications.html
Contact(s):
Anne Richards, President; Fax: 508-495-2393

AMERICAN FISHERIES SOCIETY
MICHIGAN CHAPTER
Attn: President, 484 Cherry Creek Rd.
Marquette, MI 49855 United States
Phone: 906-249-1611 Fax: 906-249-3190
Website: www.fw.msu.edu/orgf/mi_afs/afs.hdm

Founded: 1973

Scope: State

Contact(s):
Edgar Baker, President; 906-249-1611

AMERICAN FISHERIES SOCIETY
MID-ATLANTIC CHAPTER
P.O. Box 330
Little Creek, DE 19961 United States

Founded: 1983

Scope: State

Description: The American Fisheries Society is dedicated to the preservation and conservation of aquatic resources, and facilitating the information exchange between students, professionals, and the public regarding our knowledge of aquatic resources.

Contact(s):
Van Atkins, President; 2040 Church Creek Dr., Charleston, SC 29414; President@carolinabirdclub.org
Donna Bailey, SC Vice-President; 176 Ravens Place Winnsboro, SC 29180; dsbailey@conterra.com
John Wright, NC Vice-President; 1953-A Quail Ridge Rd. Greenville, NC 27858; jwright@skantech.net
Patricia Earnhardt Tyndall, Treasurer; 400 Kilmarnock Ct., Wake Forest, NC 27587; ptearn@aol.com
Sue Pulsipher, Secretary; 2441 Ramey Dr., Linden, NC 28356—9771; puls@infi.net

AMERICAN FISHERIES SOCIETY
MID-CANADA CHAPTER
Attn: President, 19 Acadia Bay
Winnipeg, R3T 3J1 Manitoba Canada
Phone: 204-945-7794

Founded: 1986

Scope: National

Contact(s):
Arthur Derksen, President; 204-945-7791; Fax: 204-948-2308; aderksen@nr.gov.mb.ca

AMERICAN FISHERIES SOCIETY
MINNESOTA CHAPTER
Attn: President, 5504 Hay Creek Rd.
Fort Ripley, MN 56449 United States
Phone: 218-828-2246 Fax: 218-828-6022
Website: www.fw.umn.edu/mnafs

Founded: 1967
Membership: 101–1,000
Scope: State
Description: The Minnesota Chapter of the American Fisheries Society is a professional organization of individuals interested in maintaining high standards for the fisheries profession and insuring conservation of Minnesota's fisheries.
Publication(s): Ryba (quarterly newsletter)
Keyword(s): Ecosystems (precious), Water Habitats & Quality
Contact(s):
Paul Radomski, President; 218-828-2246; Fax: 218-828-6022; paul.radomski@dnr.state.mn.us

AMERICAN FISHERIES SOCIETY
MISSISSIPPI CHAPTER
University MS United States
Website: www.cfr.msstate.edu/msafs/msafs.htm

Founded: 1975

Scope: State

Description: The American Fisheries Society is dedicated to the preservation and conservation of aquatic resources, and facilitating the information exchange between students, professionals, and the public regarding our knowledge of aquatic resources.

Contact(s):
Jim Franks, President; jim.franks@usm.edu

AMERICAN FISHERIES SOCIETY
MISSOURI CHAPTER
P.O. Box 10267
Columbia, MO 65205 United States
E-mail: moafs@tranquility.net
Website: www.moafs.org/

Founded: 1963

Scope: State

Description: The American Fisheries Society is dedicated to the preservation and conservation of aquatic resources, and facilitating the information exchange between students, professionals, and the public regarding our knowledge of aquatic resources.

Contact(s):
Bob DiStefano, President
Harold Kearns, President Elect

AMERICAN FISHERIES SOCIETY
MONTANA CHAPTER
Attn: President, MT Chapter AFS
P.O. Box 1336
Ennis, MT 59729 United States
Phone: 406-682-7807
E-mail: pcensfwp@3rivers.net
Website: www.fisheries.org/afsmontana

Founded: 1967
Membership: 101–1,000
Scope: State
Description: The American Fisheries Society is dedicated to the preservation and conservation of aquatic resources, and facilitating the information exchange between students, professionals, and the public regarding our knowledge of aquatic resources.
Contact(s):
Michael Enk, President; 406-791-7729; Fax: 406-761-1972; menk@fs.fed.us

AMERICAN FISHERIES SOCIETY
NATIVE PEOPLE FISHERIES SECTION
USFWS, 4401 N. Fairfax Dr., Suite 840
Arlington, VA 22203 United States
Phone: 703-358-1718 Fax: 703-358-2044

Founded: N/A

Scope: National

Contact(s):
Hannibal Bolton, President; hannibal_bolton@fws.gov

AMERICAN FISHERIES SOCIETY
NEBRASKA CHAPTER
Nebraska Game & Parks
2200 North 33rd Street
Lincoln, NE 68503 United States
Website: www.w.com/nebraskaAFS/

Founded: 1969
Membership: 1–100
Scope: State
Description: The American Fisheries Society is dedicated to the preservation and conservation of aquatic resources, and facilitating the information exchange between students, professionals, and the public regarding our knowledge of aquatic resources.

Contact(s):
Gerald Mestl, President; 402-471-5447; Fax: 402-471-5528; gmestl@ngpc.state.ne.us

AMERICAN FISHERIES SOCIETY
NEW MEXICO STATE UNIVERSITY STUDENT CHAPTER
1410 Durazno Drive
Las Cruces, NM 88001-4216 United States
Phone: 505-646-1707

Founded: 1972
Scope: State
Description: The American Fisheries Society is dedicated to the preservation and conservation of aquatic resources, and facilitating the information exchange between students, professionals, and the public regarding our knowledge of aquatic resources.
Contact(s):
Richard Saurez, President; 505-527-0172; rsaurez@nmsu.edu
Paul Turner, Research Biologist; 505-646-1707; paturner@nmsu.edu

AMERICAN FISHERIES SOCIETY
NEW YORK CHAPTER
Owego, NY United States

Founded: 1968
Scope: State
Description: The American Fisheries Society is dedicated to the preservation and conservation of aquatic resources, and facilitating the information exchange between students, professionals, and the public regarding our knowledge of aquatic resources.
Contact(s):
John Farrell, President; jmfarrel@mailbox.syr.edu

AMERICAN FISHERIES SOCIETY
NORTH CAROLINA CHAPTER
P.O. Box 129
Sedalia, NC 27342 United States
Phone: 336-449-7625
E-mail: bryants5@earthlink.net
Website: www.sdafs.org/ncafs

Founded: 1990
Membership: 101–1,000
Scope: State
Description: The American Fisheries Society is dedicated to the preservation and conservation of aquatic resources, and facilitating the information exchange between students, professionals, and the public regarding our knowledge of aquatic resources.
Publication(s): Quarterly Newsletter, Annual Meeting
Contact(s):
Shari Bryant, President; bryants5@earthlink.net
Tom Kwak, President Elect
Bob Curry, Past President

AMERICAN FISHERIES SOCIETY
NORTH PACIFIC INTERNATIONAL CHAPTER
Attn: President
King Cnty. Water & Land Resources, Div. 201
S. Jackson St., Suite 600
Seattle, WA 98104 United States
Phone: 360-902-2756

Founded: 1978
Scope: National
Contact(s):
Kurt Fresh, President; 360-902-2756; Fax: 360-902-2980; freshklf@dfw.wa.gov

AMERICAN FISHERIES SOCIETY
NORTHEASTERN DIVISION
Department of Environmental Protection
79 Elm Street
Hartford, CT 06106-5127 United States
Phone: 860-424-3482 Fax: 860-424-4070
E-mail: rick.jacobson@po.state.ct.us
Website: www.fisheries.org

Founded: 1951
Membership: 101–1,000
Scope: Regional, International
Description: The Northeastern Division (the Division or NED) is one of four geographic subdivisions of the American Fisheries Society (the Society or AFS) within North America. The mission of the Division is to (a) advance the conservation, development and wise use of fishery resources for optimum use and enjoyment by all, (b) gather and disseminate information on fisheries science and management, and (c) promote and evaluate the educational, scientific and technical aspects of the fisheries profession.
Contact(s):
Douglas Stang, President; 1156 Meadowdale Rd., Altamont, NY; 518-457-9435; Fax: 518-485-5827; dxstang@gw.bec.state.ny.us

AMERICAN FISHERIES SOCIETY
NORTHWESTERN ONTARIO CHAPTER
Thunder Bay, Ontario Canada

Founded: 1979
Scope: National
Description: The American Fisheries Society is dedicated to the preservation and conservation of aquatic resources, and facilitating the information exchange between students, professionals, and the public regarding our knowledge of aquatic resources.
Contact(s):
Rob Mackereth, President; rob.mackereth@mnr.gov.on.ca

AMERICAN FISHERIES SOCIETY
OHIO CHAPTER
1840 Belcher Dr., G-3
Columbus, OH 43224 United States
Phone: 614-265-6349 Fax: 614-262-1143
Website: www.community.cleveland.com/cc/ocafs

Founded: 1974
Scope: State
Publication(s): A Guide to Ohio Streams
Contact(s):
Debra Walters, President

AMERICAN FISHERIES SOCIETY
OREGON CHAPTER
Attn: President, 2910 NW Miller Ln.
Albany, OR 97321 United States
Phone: 54-175-3044

Founded: 1964
Scope: State
Contact(s):
Timothy Hardin, President; 541-926-2262; Fax: 541-926-1230; hardint@peak.org

AMERICAN FISHERIES SOCIETY
PENNSYLVANIA CHAPTER
1259 Edward St.
State College, PA 16801 United States
Phone: 814-353-2226

Founded: 1969
Scope: State

Contact(s):
Doug Nieman, President; 610-948-4700; dnieman@normandeau.com

AMERICAN FISHERIES SOCIETY
PHYSIOLOGY SECTION
Jay Nelson, President
Towson University Dept. of Biological Sciences
Towson, MD 21252-0001 United States
Phone: 410-704-3945 Fax: 410-704-2405
E-mail: jnelson@towson.edu
Website: www.fisheries.org/phs/

Founded: 1990
Membership: 101–1,000
Scope: International
Description: Although affiliated with the American Fisheries Society, this is a truly international organization for all individuals that work on, or are interested in, how fish work.
Contact(s):
George Iwama, President; giwama@unixg.ubc.ca

AMERICAN FISHERIES SOCIETY
POTOMAC CHAPTER
Attn: President
Dept. of Commerce NOAA, Rm. 6117
14th & Constitution Ave.
Washington, DC 20230 United States
Phone: 202-482-3260 Fax: 202-501-3024
Website: www.poyamac-afs.org

Founded: 1976
Membership: 101–1,000
Scope: Regional
Contact(s):
Lee Beneka, President

AMERICAN FISHERIES SOCIETY
SOUTH CAROLINA CHAPTER
South Carolina American Fisheries Society, P.O. Box 1040
Abbeville, SC 29620 United States
Phone: 864-223-2008 Fax: 864-223-0649
Website: www.inlet.geol.sc.edu/scafs

Founded: 1982
Membership: 101–1,000
Scope: State
Contact(s):
Wade Bales, President; 864-223-2008; Fax: 864-223-0649
Chris Thomason, President Elect; 803-259-5474

AMERICAN FISHERIES SOCIETY
SOUTH NEW ENGLAND CHAPTER
Attn: President, c/o NMFS NE Fish Center, 166 Water St.
Woods Hole, MA 02543-1097 United States
Phone: 508-495-2380 Fax: 508-495-2393
Website: www.nefsc.nmfs.gov/snecafs/index.html

Founded: 1967
Membership: 101–1,000
Scope: Regional
Contact(s):
Russ Brown, President

AMERICAN FISHERIES SOCIETY
SOUTHERN ONTARIO CHAPTER
Beak International, 14 Abacus Rd
Brampton, L6T 5B7 Ontario Canada
Phone: 905-794-2325 Fax: 905-794-2338
E-mail: bhendley@beak.com
Website: www.beak.com

Founded: 1988
Scope: National
Contact(s):
Cynthia Mitton-Walker, President; 416-235-5230; Fax: 416-235-4940; mitton@mto.gov.on.ca

AMERICAN FISHERIES SOCIETY
TEXAS A AND M CHAPTER
210 Nagle Hall- 2258 TAMU
College Station, TX 77843-2258 United States
Phone: 979-845-5777 Fax: 979-845-3786
Website: www.wfscnet.tamu.edu

Founded: 1969
Membership: 1–100
Scope: State
Description: This is a chapter of AFS at Texas A&M University for student participation.
Publication(s): Former Student Newsletter

AMERICAN FISHERIES SOCIETY
TIDEWATER CHAPTER
Attn: President James A. Morris
CCFHR, National Ocean Service, NOAA
101 Pivers Island Rd.
Beaufort, NC 28516 United States
Phone: 252-728-8782
E-mail: james.morris@noaa.gov
Website: www.sdafs.org/tidewater

Founded: 1986
Membership: 101–1,000
Scope: State, Regional
Description: The mission of the American Fisheries Society is to improve the conservation and sustainability of fishery resources and aquatic ecosystems by advancing fisheries and aquatic science and promoting the development of fisheries professionals. The Tidewater Chapter is composed of members of the fisheries community from Maryland, Virginia and North Carolina. The Tidewater Chapter membership is quite diverse with expertise ranging from inland to offshore fisheries.
Contact(s):
James Morris, President; 252-728-8782; james.morris@noaa.gov

AMERICAN FISHERIES SOCIETY
UNIVERSITY OF WYOMING STUDENT CHAPTER
Attn: President, P.O. Box 3166
Laramie, WY 82071-3166 United States
Phone: 307-766-2426
Website: www.fisheries.org/co-wy

Founded: N/A
Scope: State
Contact(s):
Seth Wite, President; oclark@uwyo.edu
Mark Smith, Vice President; masmith@uwyo.edu
Jason Burckhardt, Treasurer; jburck@uwyo.edu
Leisa Tooker, Secretary; leisatooker@hotmail.com

AMERICAN FISHERIES SOCIETY
VIRGINIA CHAPTER
4010 W. Broad St.
Richmond, VA 23230 United States
Phone: 804-367-8351
Website: fwie.fw.vt.edu/va-afs/index.htm

Founded: 1990
Membership: 101–1,000
Scope: State
Contact(s):
Becky Wajda, President
Charles Gowan, Past President

AMERICAN FISHERIES SOCIETY
VIRGINIA TECH CHAPTER
Attn: President, 101 Cheatham Hall
Blacksburg, VA 24061 United States
Phone: 540-231-3329 Fax: 540-231-7580
Website: filebox.vt.edu/org/vtafs

Founded: 1972

Scope: Regional

Publication(s): Lab Notes

Contact(s):
Anne Holloway, President
Jamie Roberts, Vice President
John Harris, Secretary
Louis Helfrich, Faculty Advisor; lhelfric@vt.edu
Ginnie Linthecum, Treasurer

AMERICAN FISHERIES SOCIETY
WATER QUALITY SECTION
5083 Veranda Terrace
Davis, CA 695616 United States
Phone: 541-754-4516 Fax: 916-278-3071

Founded: N/A
Membership: 1,001–10,000
Scope: National
Publication(s): Water Quality Matters

Contact(s):
Larry Brown, President
Robert Hughes, Past President
John Meldrum, Secretary- Treasurer

AMERICAN FISHERIES SOCIETY
WEST VIRGINIA
Elkins, WV 26241 United States
Phone: 304-637-0215 Fax: 304-637-0250

Founded: 1989

Scope: State

Contact(s):
Michael Shingleton, President; 304-637-0245, ext. 15; Fax: 304-637-0250; mshingleton@dnr.state.wv.us

AMERICAN FISHERIES SOCIETY
WESTERN DIVISION
Alaska Biological Science Center
1101 East Tubar Road
Anchorage, AK 99503 United States
Phone: 907-786-3842 Fax: 907-786-3636
Website: www.fisheries.org/wd

Founded: N/A

Scope: National

Contact(s):
Eric Knudsen, President; 907-786-3842; Fax: 907-786-3636; Eric_Knudsen@usga.gov

AMERICAN FISHERIES SOCIETY
WISCONSIN CHAPTER
University of Wisconsin, Eau Claire Biology Dept.
Eau Claire, WI United States
Phone: 715-836-3260
E-mail: lonzard@uwec.edu

Founded: 1972

Scope: State

Publication(s): Wisconsin Chapter American Fisheries Society Newsletter

Contact(s):
Dr. David Lonzarich, President

AMERICAN FOREST FOUNDATION
1111 19th St., NW, Suite 780
Washington, DC 20036 United States
Phone: 202-463-2462 Fax: 202-463-2461
Website: www.asfoundation.org

Founded: 1981
Membership: 1–100
Scope: National
Description: American Forest Foundation conducts charitable education and research programs. AFF supports American Tree Farm System — 71,000 private landowners managing 95 million acres of forests — and Project Learning Tree (PLT), award-winning pre K-12 environmental education curriculum and training program, active in U.S. and abroad. Nongrantmaking.
Publication(s): PLT Branch, Tree Farmer Magazine
Keyword(s): Forests/Forestry, Reduce/Reuse/Recycle
Contact(s):
Laurence Wiseman, President
Kathy Mcglauflin, Vice President of Project Learning Tree
Robert Simpson, Vice President of American Tree Farm System

AMERICAN FORESTS
P. O. Box 2000
Washington, DC 20013 United States
Phone: 202-955-4500 Fax: 202-955-4588
E-mail: member@amfor.org
Website: www.americanforests.org

Founded: 1875
Membership: 10,001–100,000
Scope: National
Description: (formerly American Forestry Association) Building on its rich history as the oldest national citizens' conservation organization in the U.S. and conservation movement pioneer, American Forests has several programs to address today's environmental challenges: Global ReLeaf 2000, the Urban Forest Center and the Forest Policy Center.
Publication(s): American Forests (quarterly magazine)
Keyword(s): Climate Change, Forests/Forestry, Public Lands/ Greenspace, Recreation/Ecotourism, Wildlife & Species
Contact(s):
Richard Crouse, Senior Vice President for Development; ext. 225; rcrouse@amfor.org
Gerald Gray, Vice President of Forest Policy Center; ext. 217; ggray@amfor.org
Gary Moll, Vice President of Urban Forest Center; ext. 220; gmoll@amfor.org
Christina Cromley, Director of Forest Policy; ext. 237; ccromley@amfor.org
Deborah Gangloff, Executive Director
Steve Westcott, Director of Communications
Doug Cowan, Board Chair
Doug Hall, Treasurer
Stacey Mandell, Southeast Region Coordinator; 305-372-6555
Jeff Meyer, Famous & Historic Tree Nursery; 904-765-0727; Fax: 904-768-4630; jmeyer@historictrees.org
Michelle Robbins, Editor; ext. 203; Fax: 202-887-1075; mrobbins@amfor.org
Bob Skiera, Field Representative
Zane Smith, Field Representative; 37899 Shenandoah Loop Rd., Springfield, OR 97478
Jane Westenberger, Field Representative; 7437 Saratoga Lane, Santa Fe, NM 87505

AMERICAN GEOGRAPHICAL SOCIETY
120 Wall St.
New York, NY 10005-3904 United States
Phone: 212-422-5456 Fax: 212-422-5480
E-mail: amgeosoc@earthlink.net
Website: www.amergeog.org

Founded: 1851
Membership: 1–100
Scope: National
Description: The AGS has sponsored research projects field work, and educational travel, held symposia and lectures, and published scientific and popular books, periodicals, and maps. Its publications bring accurate, up-to-date information on man and the land to more than 8,000 fellows and subscribers in over 100 countries.
Publication(s): Focus, Geographical Review, Ubique, Around the World Program
Keyword(s): Climate Change, Development/Developing Countries, Land Issues, Reduce/Reuse/Recycle
Contact(s):
William Doyle, President
Hilary Hopper, Editor, Focus and Around The World; Dept. of Geography, University of Kentucky, Lexington, KY 40506
Peter Lewis, Editor, Ubique
John Mccabe, Treasurer
Richard Nolte, Chair Emeritus
Paul Starrs, Editor; Geographical Review Dept. Geography, University of Nevada-Reno, Reno, NV 89557
John Wilford, Secretary

AMERICAN GEOLOGICAL INSTITUTE
4220 King St.
Alexandria, VA 22302-1502 United States
Phone: 703-379-2480 Fax: 703-379-7563
E-mail: agi@agiweb.org
Website: www.agiweb.org

Founded: 1948
Membership: 1–100
Scope: National
Description: AGI provides information services for earth scientists; works to be an advocate for the interests of the earth-science community; plays a major role in strengthening earth-science education; and increases public awareness of the role that earth sciences play in mankind's use of resources and interaction with the environment.
Publication(s): Bibliography and Index of Geology, Geotimes, Directory of Geoscience Departments, Glossary of Geology
Contact(s):
David Applegate, Director of Government Affairs
Christopher Keane, Director of Program Development and Communications
Marcus Milling, Executive Director
Michael Smith, Director of Education and Outreach
Sharon Tahirkheli, Director of Information Systems

AMERICAN GROUND WATER TRUST
P.O. Box 1796, 16 Centre St.
Concord, NH 03301 United States
Phone: 603-228-5444 Fax: 603-228-6557
E-mail: trustInfo@agwt.org
Website: www.agwt.org

Founded: 1987
Membership: 101–1,000
Scope: National
Description: The American Ground Water Trust is an independent nonprofit, membership organization which promotes public awareness of the environmental and economic importance of ground water through public education programs. The Trust promotes opportunity, cooperation and action among individuals, groups and organizations throughout America.
Publication(s): Ground Water and Wetlands in the United, Ground Water information pamphlets, Water Well Basics (video)
Keyword(s): Oceans/Coasts/Beaches, Water Habitats & Quality
Contact(s):
Andrew Stone, Executive Director
Mike Lally, Chairman
Richard Schramm, Treasurer
Scott Slater, Secretary

AMERICAN HIKING SOCIETY
1422 Fenwick Ln.
Silver Spring, MD 20910 United States
Phone: 301-565-6704 Fax: 301-565-6714
E-mail: info@americanhiking.org
Website: www.americanhiking.org

Founded: 1976
Membership: 10,001–100,000
Scope: National
Description: American Hiking Society (AHS) is a recreation-based conservation organization dedicated to establishing, protecting and maintaining foot trails in America. AHS is comprised of over 120 member trail clubs and 10,000 individual members, represents half a million outdoors people and serves as the voice of the American hiker. AHS effectively lobbies to encourage funding for trails and promotes volunteerism in trail building and maintenance.
Publication(s): Pathways Across America, American Hiker, Helping Out in the Outdoors, Volunteer Vacation
Keyword(s): Forests/Forestry, Land Issues, Public Lands/Greenspace, Recreation/Ecotourism
Contact(s):
Mary Margaret Sloan, President
Susan Crosby, Vice President and Development
Michael Hechter, Membership Coordinator

AMERICAN HORSE PROTECTION ASSOCIATION
1000 29th St., NW Suite T-100
Washington, DC 20007 United States
Phone: 202-965-0500 Fax: 202-965-9621
Website: www.americanhorseprotection.org

Founded: 1966
Scope: National
Description: A national nonprofit, tax-exempt organization dedicated entirely to the welfare of horses, both wild and domestic. Works for the enforcement of all humane legislation for both wild and domestic horses.
Publication(s): Special Bulletins, Newsletter
Keyword(s): Land Issues, Public Lands/Greenspace, Wildlife & Species
Contact(s):
Nancy Hargrave, President and Chairman of the Board of Directors
Robin Lohnes, Executive Director

AMERICAN HUMANE ASSOCIATION
63 Inverness Dr., E
Englewood, CO 80112 United States
Phone: 303-792-9900 Fax: 303-792-5333
E-mail: animal@americanhumane.org
Website: www.americanhumane.org

Founded: 1877
Membership: 1,001–10,000
Scope: National
Description: AHA provides training and resources to 6,500 animal care and control agencies in the U.S. and Canada; ensures the humane treatment of animals in movies and TV productions; serves as a national coordinator of emergency animal relief during natural disasters and works on legislation to protect animals.
Publication(s): Protecting Animals
Contact(s):
Tim O'Brien, President
Connie Howard, Director of Shelter Programs
Jack Sparks, Director of Communications
Lynn Anderson, Veterinarian; animal@americanhumane.org

AMERICAN INSTITUTE OF BIOLOGICAL SCIENCES

AIBS
1444 I St., NW
Suite 200
Washington, DC 20005 United States
Phone: 202-628-1500 Fax: 202-628-1509
E-mail: admin@aibs.org
Website: www.aibs.org

Founded: 1947
Membership: 1,001–10,000
Scope: National, International
Description: A national organization for biology and biologists, combining an individual membership organization with the federation principle. Operates educational, advisory, liaison, informational, publication and editorial programs to serve biologists, promote unity and effectiveness of effort and apply knowledge of biology to human welfare.
Publication(s): BioScience, Scientific Peer Review Services
Contact(s):

Gene Likens, 2002 President; Institute of Ecosystem Studies, Millbrook, NY 12545; 845-677-5343; Fax: 845-677-5976; likensg@ecostudies.org
Richard O'Grady, Executive Director; AIBS, 1444 I Street NW, Suite 200, Washington, DC 20005; 202-628-1500, ext. 258; Fax: 202-628-1509; rogrady@aibs.org
Adrienne Froelich, Public Policy Representative; AIBS, 1444 I Street NW, Suite 200, Washington, DC 20005; 202-628-1500, ext. 232; Fax: 202-628-1509; afroelich@aibs.org
Scott Glisson, Scientific Peer Review Services; AIBS, 107 Carpenter Drive, Suite 100, Sterling, VA 20164; 703-834-0812, ext. 202; Fax: 703-834-1160; sglisson@aibs.org
Matthew Greenstone, Science Editor, BioScience; AIBS, 1444 I Street NW, Suite 200, Washington, DC 20005; 405-607-0309; Fax: 405-607-0310; mgreenstone@aibs.org
Cathy Lundmark, Education Representative; AIBS, 1444 I Street NW, Suite 200, Washington, DC 20005; 202-628-1500, ext. 300; Fax: 202-628-1509; clundmark@aibs.org
Ellen Paul, Public Policy Representative; AIBS, 1444 I Street NW, Suite 200, Washington, DC 20005; 202-628-1500, ext. 250; Fax: 202-628-1509; epaul@aibs.org
Donna Royston, Communications Representative; AIBS, 1444 I Street NW, Suite 200, Washington, DC 20005; 202-628-1500, ext. 261; Fax: 202-628-1509; droyston@aibs.org

AMERICAN INSTITUTE OF FISHERY RESEARCH BIOLOGISTS

c/o National Marine Fisheries Science Center
SW Fisheries Science Center
P.O. Box 271
La Jolla, CA 92038 United States
Phone: 858-546-7177
Website: www.iattc.org/aifrb/default.htm

Founded: 1957
Scope: National
Description: The Institute was founded to advance the science of fishery biology and to promote conservation and proper use of fishery resources. It serves that goal primarily by being concerned with the professional development and performance of its members and recognition of their competence and achievement.
Publication(s): Briefs
Keyword(s): Reduce/Reuse/Recycle, Water Habitats & Quality, Wildlife & Species
Contact(s):

Gary Sakagawa, President; gary.sakagawa@noaa.gov
Gene Huntsman, Editor; 205 Blades Rd., Havelock, NC 28523; 704-274-7773
Alan Shimada, Treasurer; 7909 Sleaford Place, Bethesda, MD 20814
Barbara Warkentine, Secretary; SUNY-Maritime College, Science Dept., 6 Pennyfield Ave, Ft. Schuyler, Bronx, NY 10465-4198; 206-543-1101

AMERICAN LAND CONSERVANCY

1388 Sutter St.
San Francisco, CA 94109 United States
Phone: 415-749-3010 Fax: 415-749-3011
E-mail: mail@alcnet.org
Website: www.alcnet.org

Founded: 1990
Membership: 1–100
Scope: National
Description: To preserve land for this and future generations; in particular, to preserve its scientific, historic, educational, ecological, geological, recreational, agricultural and scenic features, and its native plant and animal life or biotic community.
Publication(s): Statement of Opportunity Brochure, American Land Conservancy Newsletter, Fifty Wildflowers of Bear Valley
Keyword(s): Forests/Forestry, Land Issues, Oceans/Coasts/Beaches, Public Lands/Greenspace, Wildlife & Species
Contact(s):

Harriet Burgess, President; mail@alcnet.org

AMERICAN LANDS

726 7th St., SE
Washington, DC 20003 United States
Phone: 202-547-9400 Fax: 202-547-9213
E-mail: wafcdc@americanlands.org
Website: www.americanlands.org

Founded: 1991
Scope: National
Description: (formerly Western Ancient Forest Campaign) The mission of American Lands is the protection and recovery of North American native forest, grassland, and aquatic ecosystems; the preservation of biological diversity; the restoration of watershed integrity; and the promotion of environmental justice in connection with these goals. This mission is accomplished by strengthening grassroots conservation networks; providing advocacy services and other assistance to local conservation groups.
Publication(s): Report from Washington
Keyword(s): Forests/Forestry, Public Lands/Greenspace, Water Habitats & Quality
Contact(s):

Randi Spivak, President; 310-458-8869
Jim Jontz, Executive Director; 202-547-9095
Steve Holmer, Campaign Coordinator; 202-547-9105
Christopher Peters, Treasurer; P.O. Box 4569, Arcata, CA 95518; 707-825-7640

AMERICAN LEAGUE OF ANGLERS AND BOATERS

1225 New York Ave., NW
Washington, DC 20005 United States
Phone: 202-682-9530 Fax: 202-682-9529
Website: www.funoutdoors.com

Founded: 1985
Membership: 1–100
Scope: National
Description: ALAB was formed to be a vigilant patron of the Sport Fishing and Boating Enhancement Act (PL 98-369) and the Aquatic Resources Trust Fund created by the Act. Composed of more than 30 organizations, ALAB is dedicated to this pioneering user-pays legislation which provides some $330 million annually in funding for U.S. Coast Guard recreational boating programs and in matching grants to the states for sportfish research and enhancement, as well as wetlands conservation, and boating safety.
Keyword(s): Recreation/Ecotourism, Wildlife & Species

Contact(s):
Derrick Crandall, Co-Chair; 301-897-8616
Veronica Floyd, Co-Chair; 703-960-2223
George Stewart, Treasurer; 302-678-9143

AMERICAN LITTORAL SOCIETY

Headquarters, Sandy Hook
Highlands, NJ 07732 United States
Phone: 732-291-0055
E-mail: als@netlabs.net
Website: www.alsnyc.org

Founded: 1961
Scope: National
Description: A national organization of professionals and amateurs interested in the study and conservation of coastal habitat, barrier beaches, wetlands, estuaries, and near-shore waters, and their fish, shellfish, bird, and mammal resources. Publishes scientific and popular material. Conducts field trips, dive and study expeditions, and a fish tag-and-release program. Special activities for scuba divers.
Publication(s): Coastal Reporter, Underwater Naturalist
Keyword(s): Oceans/Coasts/Beaches, Water Habitats & Quality, Wildlife & Species
Contact(s):
Michael Huber, President
Frank Steimle, Vice President
D. Bennett, Executive Director
Sheldon Abrams, Treasurer
Angela Cristini, Secretary

AMERICAN LITTORAL SOCIETY

DELAWARE RIVERKEEPER NETWORK
P.O. Box 326
Washington Crossing, PA 18977 United States
Phone: 215-369-1188 Fax: 215-369-1181
E-mail: drn@delawareriverkeeper.org
Website: www.delawareriverkeeper.org

Founded: N/A
Scope: Regional
Publication(s): Ten Case Studies, Stream Restoration In PA, Stormwater Runoff Community Asset
Contact(s):
Maya Van Rossum, Delaware Riverkeeper/Executive Director

AMERICAN LITTORAL SOCIETY

NORTHEAST CHAPTER
28 West 9th Rd.
Broad Channel, NY 11693 United States
Phone: 718-318-9344 Fax: 718-318-9345
E-mail: alsbeach@aol.com
Website: www.alsnyc.org

Founded: 1980
Membership: 1,001–10,000
Scope: Local, State, Regional, National
Description: The society is dedicated to the conservation and education of marine resources, wetland protection and habitat restoration.
Publication(s): Littorally Speaking (newsletter)
Contact(s):
Don Riepe, Director, Northeast Chapter; 718-634-6467; Fax: 718-318-9345; donriepe@aol.com
Barbara Cohen, New York State Beach Cleanup Coordinator; 718-471-2166; alsbeach@aol.com
Barbara Toborg, Editor; 718-474-1127; tobytoborg@aol.com

AMERICAN LIVESTOCK BREEDS CONSERVANCY

P.O. Box 477
Pittsboro, NC 27312 United States
Phone: 919-542-5704 Fax: 919-545-0022
E-mail: albc@albc-usa.org
Website: www.albc-usa.org

Founded: 1977
Membership: 1,001–10,000
Scope: National
Description: ALBC is a nonprofit membership organization working to protect genetic diversity in domestic animals through the conservation of nearly 100 rare breeds of livestock and poultry in America. ALBC does research on breed status and characteristics, operates a gene bank to preserve genetic materials for the future and provides technical support on conservation breeding and animal use in sustainable, diversified agriculture.
Publication(s): Taking Stock: The North American Livestock Census, Birds of A Feather: Saving Rare Turkeys, A Rare Breeds Album of American Livestock, A Conservation Breeding Handbook, Taking Stock of Water Fowl, ALBC News
Keyword(s): Agriculture/Farming, Development/Developing Countries, Wildlife & Species
Contact(s):
Donald Bixby, Executive Director
Marjorie Bender, Program Coordinator
Cindy Ehrman, Marketing Coordinator; cehrman@albc-usa.org
Phillip Sponenberg, Technical Coordinator

AMERICAN LUNG ASSOCIATION

1740 Broadway
New York, NY 10019-4374 United States
Phone: 212-315-8700 Fax: 212-265-5642
E-mail: info@lungusa.org
Website: www.lungusa.org

Founded: 1904
Membership: 1–100
Scope: National
Description: Formerly known as the National Tuberculosis and Respiratory Disease Association. The American Lung Association is a voluntary agency concerned with the conquest of lung disease and the promotion of lung health, which includes preventing and controlling air pollution. National Air Conservation Commission and local and state air conservation committees work with citizenry and other groups for effective air pollution control. Informational material available from national, state and local lung associations.
Publication(s): American Journal of Respiratory Cell, American Journal of Respiratory and Critical Care Medicine
Keyword(s): Air Quality/Atmosphere
Contact(s):
John Kirkwood, Chief Operating Officer

AMERICAN MUSEUM OF NATURAL HISTORY

COMMUNICATIONS
Central Park West at 79th St.
New York, NY 10024 United States
Phone: 212-769-5100 Fax: 212-769-5199
Website: www.amnh.org

Founded: 1869
Scope: National
Description: Conducts research in anthropology, astronomy, entomology, herpetology, ichthyology, invertebrates, mammalogy, earth and planetary sciences, ornithology and vertebrate and invertebrate paleontology using museum collections and field studies. Publishes scientific and popular material. Instructs the public, especially its over three million yearly visitors, in natural sciences, including living and extinct

animals, ecological relationships, evolution of earth and life, and development of human cultures.

Publication(s): Bulletin of the American Museum of Natural History, Curator, Micropaleontology Press, Anthropological Papers of the American Museum of Natural History

Keyword(s): Wildlife & Species

Contact(s):

Ellen Futter, President

AMERICAN NATURE STUDY SOCIETY

c/o PEEC, R.D. Box 1010
Dingmans Ferry, PA 18328 United States
Phone: 607-749-3655
Website: hometown.aol.com/anssonlne/

Founded: 1908

Scope: National

Description: Promotes environmental education and avocation by conducting meetings, workshops and field excursions, producing and distributing publications, and contributing to publications of other agencies; cooperates with organizations with allied interests, and, through membership in Alliance for Environmental Education, encourages members to contribute consultant services; assists in training nature lay leaders.

Publication(s): Nature Study, A Journal of Environmental Education and Interpretation, ANSS Newsletter

Keyword(s): Recreation/Ecotourism, Reduce/Reuse/Recycle

Contact(s):

Steve Melcher, President; 103 Kreag Rd., Fairport, NY 14450-363; 716-425-1059

Janet Hawkes, Editor; 1420 Tanghannock Blvd., Ithaca, NY 14850; 607-273-6260

Florence Mauro, Editor; PEEC, R.D. 2 Box 1010, Dingmans Ferry, PA 18328; 717-828-2319

Flo Mauro, Recording Secretary; PEEC, R.D. 2 Box 1010, Dingmans Ferry, PA 18328; 717-828-2319

Betty McKnight, Secretary; R.D. 3, Trumansburg, NY 14886

Paul Spector, Treasurer; Holden Arboretum, 9500 Sperry Rd., Mentor, OH 44094; 216-256-1110

AMERICAN OCEANS CAMPAIGN

WASHINGTON, DC OFFICE
600 Pennsylvania Ave., SE, Suite 210
Washington, DC 20003 United States
Phone: 202-544-3526 Fax: 202-544-5625
E-mail: info@americanoceans.org
Website: www.americanoceans.org

Founded: 1987

Scope: National

Description: The well-being and sustainability of the Earth is dependent upon healthy oceans. The mission of American Oceans Campaign is to safeguard the vitality of the oceans and our coastal waters. AOC is committed to scientific information in advocating for sound public policy. We are equally committed to developing partnerships with all entities interested in protecting the environment. AOC seeks to ensure healthy sources of food and coastal recreation as well as to protect the ocean's grandeur for future generations

Publication(s): Esturaries on the Edge, Drainage to the Oceans, Chemical Contaminant Release Into the Santa Monica Bay, Fish Briefs, Splash

Keyword(s): Oceans/Coasts/Beaches, Pollution (general), Public Health, Water Habitats & Quality, Wildlife & Species

Contact(s):

Ted Danson, Founding President

Annett Wolf, Vice President

Barbara Polo, Executive Director; bjpolo@americanoceans.org

Warner Chabot, Board Chair

Barbara Kohn, Treasurer

AMERICAN ORNITHOLOGISTS UNION

National Museum of Natural History
MRC-116
Smithsonian Institution
Washington, DC 20560-0116 United States
Phone: 202-357-2051 Fax: 202-633-8084
E-mail: aou@nmnh.si.edu

Founded: 1883

Scope: National

Description: Aims to advance ornithological science through its publications, annual meetings, committees and membership.

Publication(s): Ornithological Monographs, Ornithological Newsletter

Keyword(s): Wildlife & Species

Contact(s):

John Fitzpatrick, President; Laboratory of Ornithology at Cornell University, 159 Sap Sucker Woods Rd., Ithaca, NY 14850; 607-254-2410; Fax: 607-254-2415; jwf7@cornell.edu

Mary McDonald, Vice President; Lewis Science Center 129, University of Central Arkansas, Conway, AR 72035; 501-450-5924

Steven Beissinger, Chairman of the Conservation Committee; Director of Ecosystem Science, 151 Hilgard Hall, Suite 3110, University of California, Berkeley, CA 94720-3110; 313-763-5945

Jeff Brawn, Treasurer; Illinois Natural History Survey, 607 E. Peabody Drive, Champaign, IL 61820; 217-244-5937; Fax: 217-333-4949; j-brawn@uiuc.edu

M. Lein, Secretary; Dept. of Biology, University of Calgary, 2500 University Dr., NW, Calgary, Alberta T2N 1N4

Kimberly Smith, Editor; Department of Biological Sciences, University of Arkansas, Fayetteville, AR 72701; 501-575-3251; Fax: 501-575-4010; auk@comp.uark.edu

Cheryl Trine, Newsletter Editor; 3889 E. Valley View, Berrien Springs, MI 49103; 508-224-6521; ctrine@andrews.edu

David Wiedenfeld, Monographs Editor; Sutton Avian Research Center, P.O. Box 2007, Bartlesville, OK 74005

AMERICAN PIE (PUBLIC INFORMATION ON THE ENVIRONMENT)

P.O. Box 676
Northfield, MN 55057 United States
Phone: 800-320-2743 Fax: 507-645-5724
E-mail: info@americanpie.org
Website: www.americanpie.org

Founded: 1993

Membership: 101–1,000

Scope: National

Description: American PIE is a 501(c)3 nonprofit group serving the nation with an 800 Environmental Information Line. The organization offers action programs and uniquely accessible assistance to people who have environmental questions and concerns in a wide variety of subject areas ranging from drinking water safety to wetlands preservation. Trained staff answer the information line Monday-Friday, 8:30 - 5:00 central time.

Publication(s): American PIE

Keyword(s): Ethics/Environmental Justice, Pollution (general)

Contact(s):

Brad Easterson, President and Treasurer

Toni Easterson, Vice President and Secretary

Lawrence Bacon, Director; 36 Carriage Dr., Farmington, CT 06032; 860-674-8442

AMERICAN PLANNING ASSOCIATION

1776 Massachusetts Ave., NW, St. 400
Washington, DC 20036 United States
Phone: 202-872-0611 Fax: 202-872-0643
Website: www.planning.org

Founded: 1909

Membership: 1–100
Scope: National
Description: Provides informational services, education and research in city and regional planning. Includes the American Institute of Certified Planners which sets professional and ethical standards and participates in the accreditation of planning degree programs. Forty-six chapters include all of the states. Sixteen divisions address planning specialties and provide placement services and studies.
Publication(s): Journal of The American Planning Association, Environment and Development Newsletter, Land Use Law and Zoning Digest, Planning Magazine
Keyword(s): Land Issues, Reduce/Reuse/Recycle
Contact(s):
Eric Kelley, President
Frank So, Executive Director; 202-872-0611
Sam Casella, Immediate Past President
Sylvia Lewis, Editor
James Shelby, Secretary and Treasurer

AMERICAN RECREATION COALITION
1225 New York Ave., NW, Suite 450
Washington, DC 20005 United States
Phone: 202-682-9530 Fax: 202-682-9529
E-mail: arc@funoutdoors.com
Website: www.funoutdoors.com
Founded: 1979
Scope: National
Description: ARC is a national nonprofit, tax-exempt federation of more than 125 recreation-related trade associations, corporations and enthusiasts' organizations that provides a unified voice for American recreation interests to ensure their full participation in government policy-making on such issues as energy and public lands and waters management. ARC also initiates and supports partnerships between public and private recreation providers and conducts meetings, seminars and activities.
Contact(s):
Derrick Crandall, President
Catherine Ahern, Vice President of Member Services
David Humphreys, Chairman; RVIA, 1896 Preston White Dr., Reston, VA 22090; 703-620-6003

AMERICAN RESOURCES GROUP
374 Maple Ave. E., Suite 310
Vienna, VA 22180 United States
Phone: 703-255-2700 Fax: 703-281-9200
Website: www.nationalforestry.net
Founded: 1981
Membership: 1–100
Scope: National
Description: A conservation service organization engaged in education, monitoring, research, and related activities to promote the wise use of America's forest resources. Provides forestry, environmental inventory, conservation support services and land acquisition assistance to conservation organizations, public agencies and landowners. Programs include: Land Conservation Fund of America (land acquisition), National Forestry Network (referrals), National Historic Lookout Register, and American Woodlands.
Publication(s): Conservation News Digest, Woodland Report, National Woodlands Magazine
Keyword(s): Forests/Forestry, Public Lands/Greenspace, Reduce/Reuse/Recycle, Wildlife & Species
Contact(s):
Keith Argow, President/Editor
Loren Larson, Vice President of Forestry
David Edson, Green Tag Forestry Certification; 202-827-4456
Ray Kresek, Northwest Representative of National Historic Lookout Register; 509-466-9171
Bob Spear, Northeast Representative of National Historic Lookout Register; 973-209-7897

AMERICAN RIVERS
1025 Vermont Ave. NW 720
Washington, DC 20005 United States
Phone: 202-347-7550 Fax: 202-347-9240
E-mail: americanrivers@americanrivers.org
Website: www.americanrivers.org
Founded: N/A
Membership: 10,001–100,000
Scope: National
Description: (formerly American Rivers Conservation Council)
Publication(s): Available on website
Contact(s):
Rebecca Wodder, President; 202-347-7550

AMERICAN RIVERS
MONTANA FIELD OFFICE
215 Woodland Estates
Great Falls, MT 59404 United States
Phone: 406-454-2076 Fax: 406-454-2530
E-mail: malbers@amrivers.org
Website: www.americanrivers.org
Founded: N/A
Membership: 10,001–100,000
Scope: Regional
Description: (formerly American Rivers Conservation Council)
Publication(s): Available on website
Contact(s):
Mark Albers, Office Director

AMERICAN RIVERS
NEBRASKA FIELD OFFICE
650 J St.
Suite 400
Lincoln, NE 68508 United States
Phone: 402-477-7910 Fax: 402-477-2565
E-mail: csmith@amrivers.org
Website: www.SaveTheMissouri.org
Founded: 1998
Scope: Regional
Description: The focus of American Rivers' Nebraska Field Office is the organization's Missouri River Voyage of Recovery campaign.
Contact(s):
Chad Smith, Director; 402-477-7910; Fax: 402-477-2565; csmith@amrivers.org

AMERICAN RIVERS
NORTHWEST REGIONAL OFFICE
150 Nickerson St., Suite 311 Northwest Regional
Seattle, WA 98109 United States
Phone: 206-213-0330 Fax: 206-213-0334
E-mail: arnw@amrivers.org
Website: www.americanrivers.org
Founded: N/A
Scope: Regional
Description: American Rivers' Northwest Regional Office was founded in 1992 in order to restore the rivers of the Northwest and the region's once-magnificent Pacific salmon runs. Today, we're leading river restoration efforts throughout Idaho, Oregon, and Washington.
Keyword(s): Water Habitats & Quality, Wildlife & Species
Contact(s):
Rob Masonis, Director of Northwest Conservation Program; rmasonis@amrivers.org
Katherine Ransel, Senior Counsel; kransel@amrivers.org

AMERICAN RIVERS

VOYAGE OF RECOVERY
1025 Vermont Ave., NW
Suite 720
Washington, DC 20005 United States
Phone: 202-347-7550 Fax: 202-347-9240
E-mail: amrivers@americanrivers.org
Website: www.americanrivers.org

Founded: 1973
Membership: 10,001–100,000
Scope: National
Description: American Rivers is the leader of America's river conservation movement and is dedicated to preserving and restoring America's river systems and fostering a river stewardship ethic. Conservation goals include protecting wild rivers; restoring hometown rivers; repairing big rivers; removing dams that no longer make sense; reforming the operation of hydroelectric dams; and restoring portions of the rivers of Lewis & Clark to benefit people and wildlife.
Publication(s): River Monitor, America's Most Endangered Rivers, Voyage of Recovery, American Rivers Newsletter
Keyword(s): Ecosystems (precious), Energy, Recreation/Ecotourism, Reduce/Reuse/Recycle, Sprawl/Urban Planning, Transportation, Water Habitats & Quality, Wildlife & Species
Contact(s):

Rebecca Wodder, President
Pat Appel Cornell, Vice-President for Resource Development; ext. 3017; pappel@americanrivers.org
Peter Kelley, Vice President for Strategic Communications; ext. 3057; pkelley@americanrivers.org
Ann Mills, Vice-President for Conservation; ext. 3013; amills@americanrivers.org
Margaret Bowman, Deputy Vice President for Conservation; mbowman@americanrivers.org
Eric Eckl, Director of Media Affairs; 202-347-7550, ext. 3023; eeckl@americanrivers.org
Andrew Fahlund, Policy Director of Hydropower Programs; afahlund@americanrivers.org
Betsy Otto, Community Rivers Director; botto@americanrivers.org
Amy Souers, Managing Editor, American Rivers Online; asouers@americanrivers.org
Bea Keller, Manager, Membership Services; bkeller@americanrivers.org
Chad Smith, Missouri River Regional Representative; 402-477-7910; csmith@americanrivers.org

AMERICAN SOCIETY FOR ENVIRONMENTAL HISTORY

701 Vickers Ave.
Durham, NC 27701 United States
Phone: 919-682-9319 Fax: 919-682-2349
Website: www.h-net.msu.edu/~aseh

Founded: 1976
Scope: National
Description: A nonprofit international society that seeks understanding of human ecology through the perspectives of history and the humanities.
Publication(s): Newsletter, Environmental History
Keyword(s): Public Lands/Greenspace
Contact(s):

Carolyn Merchant, President
Lisa Mighetto, Secretary; Historical Research Associates, 119 Pine St., Suite 207, Seattle, WA 98101
Hal Rothman, Editor; Department of History, University of Nevada-Las Vegas, Las Vegas, NV 89154; 702-739-3349
Ed Russell, Book Review Editor
Jeffrey Stine, Past President; National Museum of American History, Smithsonian Institute, Washington, DC 20560; 202-357-2058

AMERICAN SOCIETY OF ICHTHYOLOGISTS AND HERPETOLOGISTS

Attn: Secretary College of Arts & Science Florida International University
Maureen Donnelly
Dept. of Biological Sciences
North Miami, FL 33181 United States
Phone: 305-919-5651 Fax: 305-919-5964
E-mail: donnelly@fiu.edu

Founded: 1913
Scope: International
Description: To advance the scientific study of fishes, amphibians and reptiles.
Publication(s): ASIH Special Publications, Copeia
Keyword(s): Water Habitats & Quality, Wildlife & Species
Contact(s):

Harry Greene, President
Brooks Burr, President-Elect
Maureen Donnelly, Secretary
Larry Page, Treasurer
Margaret Stewart, Historian

AMERICAN SOCIETY OF INTERNATIONAL LAW/WILDLIFE INTEREST GROUP

1702 Arlington Boulevard
El Cerrito, CA 94530 United States
Phone: 650-703-3280 Fax: 801-838-4710
E-mail: jiwlt@internationalwildlifelaw.org
Website: www.internationalwildlifelaw.org

Founded: 1984
Membership: 101–1,000
Scope: International
Description: The ASIL and WIG works to improve the effectiveness of international wildlife treaty regimes and national legislation that implements such regimes.
Publication(s): Journal of International Wildlife Law and Policy
Keyword(s): Finance/Banking/Trade, Wildlife & Species
Contact(s):

William Burns, Co-Chairman; jiwlt@internationalwildlifelaw.org

AMERICAN SOCIETY OF LANDSCAPE ARCHITECTS

636 Eye Street, NW
Washington, DC 20001-3736 United States
Phone: 202-898-2444 Fax: 202-898-1185
Website: www.asla.org

Founded: 1899
Membership: 10,001–100,000
Scope: National
Description: Founded in 1899, the American Society of Landscape Architects is the professional association representing landscape architects nationwide. Beginning with 11 original members, ASLA has grown to more than 13,500 members and 48 chapters, in all 50 states, the U.S. territories and 42 countries around the world. ASLA promotes the landscape architecture profession and advances the practice through advocacy, education, communication and networking.
Publication(s): Landscape Architecture
Keyword(s): Land Issues, Public Lands/Greenspace, Reduce/Reuse/Recycle, Sprawl/Urban Planning
Contact(s):

Nancy Somerville, Executive Vice President; nsomerville@asla.org
Marcia Argust, Director, Public and Government Affairs; margust@asla.org
Susan Cahill-Aylward, Managing Director, Information and Professional Practice; scahill@asla.org

AMERICAN SOCIETY OF LIMNOLOGY AND OCEANOGRAPHY

5400 Bosque Blvd., Suite 680
Waco, TX 76710-4446 United States
Phone: 254-399-9635 Fax: 254-776-3767
E-mail: business@aslo.org
Website: www.aslo.org/

Founded: 1936
Membership: 1,001–10,000
Scope: International
Description: To promote the advancement of the various aquatic science diciplines through scientific and technical symposia, colloquia and meetings; promotion of scientific research; discussion, publication and education; and conducting special programs in response to community interest.
Publication(s): Bulletin, Limnology and Oceanography
Keyword(s): Oceans/Coasts/Beaches, Water Habitats & Quality
Contact(s):
William Lewis, President
Jonathan Phinney, Executive Director; 1444 I St NW Ste. 200, Washington, DC 20005; jpinney@aslo.org
Denise Breitburg, Secretary
Everett Fee, Editor-In-Chief; 343 Lady MacDonald Crescent, Canmore, Alberta T1W 1H5; 403-609-2456; Fax: 403-609-2400; efee@telusplanet.net

AMERICAN SOCIETY OF MAMMALOGISTS

Phone: 805-892-2504
E-mail: asm@aibs.org
Website: www.mammalsociety.org

Founded: 1919
Scope: National
Description: Encourages research and learning in all phases of mammalogy and by holding annual meetings for presentation and discussion of the results of research dealing with mammals, through issuing periodicals and other publications and by giving advice on matters pertaining to mammals, particularly conservation issues.
Publication(s): Mammalian Species, Special Publications of American Society of Mammalogists, Journal of Mammalogy
Keyword(s): Wildlife & Species
Contact(s):
Tom Kunz, President; Dept. of Biology Boston University, 2 Cummington St., Boston, MA 02215
Sarah George, 2nd Vice President; Utah Museum of Natural History, University of Utah, Salt Lake City, UT 84112; 801-581-4889
Troy Best, Managing Editor; Department of Zoology, 331 Funchess Hall, Auburn University, AL 36849; 205-844-9260
John Hayning, Chairman of Committee on Marine Mammals; Natural History Museum of Los Angles CA, 900 Exposition Blvd., Los Angles, CA 90007; 213-746-2999
Gordon Kirkland, Chairman of Committee on Conservation of Land Mammals; The Vertebrate Museum, Shippensburg University, Shippensburg, PA 17257
Winston Smith, Chairman of Committee on Legislation and Regulations; Southern Forest Experimental Station, S. Hardwoods Laboratory, P.O. Box 227, Stoneville, MS 38776
H. Smith, Secretary and Treasurer; Department of Zoology, Brigham Young University, Provo, UT 84602; 801-378-2492

AMERICAN SPORTFISHING ASSOCIATION

1033 North Fairfax St., Suite 200
Alexandria, VA 22314 United States
Phone: 703-519-9691 Fax: 703-519-1872
E-mail: info@asafishing.org
Website: www.asafishing.org

Founded: 1994
Scope: National
Description: ASA is a nonprofit industry association working to ensure healthy and sustainable fisheries resources and increase sportfishing participation through education, conservation, promotion and marketing.
Publication(s): American Sportfishing
Contact(s):
Mike Hayden, President and CEO
Michael Nussman, Vice President
Norville Prosser, Vice President
Burt Steinberg, Chairman

AMERICAN SPORTFISHING ASSOCIATION

FISHAMERICA FOUNDATION
FUTURE FISHERMAN FOUNDATION
225 Reinekers Ln.
Alexandria, VA 22314 United States
Phone: 703-548-6338 Fax: 703-519-1872
E-mail: info@asafishing.org
Website: www.asafishing.org

Founded: N/A
Membership: 1–100
Scope: National
Description: FishAmerica Foundation is the conservation arm of the American Sportfishing Association. The Foundation is a nonprofit organization dedicated to enhancing the water quality and fish populations of North America.
Keyword(s): Oceans/Coasts/Beaches, Recreation/Ecotourism
Contact(s):
Mike Nussman, President/CEO; info@asafishing.org
Anne Glick, Executive Director; futurefisherman@asafishing.org
Tom Marshall, Managing Director; fishamerica@asafishing.org

AMERICAN WATER RESOURCES ASSOCIATION

4 West Federal St.
Middleburg, VA 20118-1626 United States
Phone: 540-687-8390 Fax: 540-687-8395
E-mail: info@awra.org
Website: www.awra.org

Founded: 1964
Membership: 1–100
Scope: International
Description: A nonprofit scientific organization which advances water resources research, planning, development and management; establishes a common meeting ground for engineers and physical, biological, and social scientists concerned with water resources; disseminates information in the field of water resources policy, science and technology through the publication of a scientific journal newsletter and symposium proceedings. Two specialty conferences/symposia and one Annual Conference on Water Resources.
Publication(s): Symposium Proceedings, Water Resources IMPACT, Journal of the American Water Resources Association
Keyword(s): Reduce/Reuse/Recycle, Water Habitats & Quality
Contact(s):
John Grounds, President
Kenneth Lanfear, President Elect
Kenneth Reid, Executive Vice President
D. Adams, Secretary and Treasurer
Christopher Lant, Editor of the Journal
N. Spangenberg, Editor of Water Resources Impact

AMERICAN WATER WORKS ASSOCIATION (AWWA)

6666 W. Quincy Ave.
Denver, CO 80235 United States
Phone: 303-794-7711 Fax: 303-795-1440
Website: www.awwa.org

Founded: 1881
Scope: International

Description: The AWWA advances the science, technology, consumer awareness management, government policies and water use efficiencies related to public drinking water.

Publication(s): AWWA Journal, WaterWiser, Opflow, Water Week, Mainstream

Keyword(s): Pollution (general), Public Health, Water Habitats & Quality

Contact(s):
Tom Curtis, Deputy Executive Director of Government Affairs Division; 202-628-8803
Jack Hoffbuhr, Executive Director
Robert Renner, Deputy Executive Director

AMERICAN WHITEWATER

1430 Fenwick Ln.
Silver Spring, MD 20910 United States
Phone: 301-589-9453 Fax: 301-589-6121
E-mail: nick@amwhitewater.org
Website: www.americanwhitewater.org

Founded: 1957
Membership: 1,001–10,000
Scope: National

Description: American Whitewater's mission is to conserve and restore America's whitewater resources and enhance opportunities to enjoy them safely. This is achieved by means of conservation, river access, education, safety and event programs.

Publication(s): Safety Code of American Whitewater, Inventory of Whitewater Rivers, American Whitewater Journal

Keyword(s): Recreation/Ecotourism, Water Habitats & Quality

Contact(s):
Jay Kenney, President; 303-534-5722; Fax: 303-534-5721; jaypkk@aol.com
Risa Shimoda, Executive Director; risa@amwhitewater.org
Nick Lipkowski, Executive Assistant; nick@amwhitewater.org

AMERICAN WILDERNESS COALITION

122 C Street NW
Suite 240
Washington, DC 20001 United States
Phone: 202-266-0455 Fax: 202-544-5197
E-mail: info@americanwilderness.org
Website: www.americanwilderness.org

Founded: 2000
Membership: 1–100
Scope: Local, State, Regional, National

Description: The American Wilderness Coalition seeks to expand and protect our National Wilderness Preservation System by providing additive resources and advocacy assistance to the many individuals and organizations involved in campaigns to protect additional Wilderness Areas today.

Keyword(s): Land Issues

Contact(s):
Melyssa Watson, Chair of the Board; P.O. Box 1620, Durango, CO 81302; 970-247-8788; Fax: 970-247-9020; mwatson@tws.org
Sara Shipley, Administrative Assistant; 202-266-0456; Fax: 202-544-5197; sara@americanwilderness.org

AMERICAN WILDLANDS

40 East Main #2
Bozeman, MT 59715 United States
Phone: 406-516-8175 Fax: 406-516-8242
E-mail: amwild@wildlands.org
Website: www.wildlands.org/

Founded: 1977
Scope: Regional

Description: A nonprofit conservation organization dedicated to ecologically sustainable use and protection of America's wildland resources in the Rocky Mountains West, including wilderness, wetlands, rangelands, free-flowing rivers, wildlife and fisheries and forests.

Publication(s): Forest Activist Green Papers, Policy Reports, On The Wild Side

Keyword(s): Forests/Forestry, Land Issues, Public Lands/Greenspace, Wildlife & Species

Contact(s):
Sally Ranney, President
Jeff Larmer, Executive Director
William Cunningham, Vice Chairman
Clifton Merritt, Executive Editor
Clifton Merritt, Secretary and Treasurer

AMERICAN WILDLIFE RESEARCH FOUNDATION, INC.

50 West High St.
Balton Spa, NY 12020 United States
E-mail: wms4@cornell.edu

Founded: 1911
Membership: 1–100
Scope: International

Description: AWRF uses the interest income of its funds to support research of wildlife and its habitats. Its mission is to enhance fish and wildlife resources and their habitats through research, education and conservation, ensuring that present and future generations can continue to use and enjoy them.

Publication(s): Newsletter

Contact(s):
Stuart Free, President; 518-861-5357; Fax: 518-452-6392
William Schwerd, Secretary; 518-885-8995; Fax: 518-885-9078

AMERICAN ZOO AND AQUARIUM ASSOCIATION (AZA)

8403 Colesville Rd., Suite 710
Silver Spring, MD 20910 United States
Phone: 301-562-0777 Fax: 301-562-0888
Website: www.aza.org

Founded: 1924
Membership: 101–1,000
Scope: National

Description: Dedicated to the improvement of modern, professionally-managed zoological parks and aquariums through conservation, public education, scientific research and membership services. Administers scientifically-managed captive breeding and field conservation programs for 134 threatened and endangered species through its Species Survival Plan Program.

Publication(s): AZA Membership Directory, Annual and Regional Conference Proceedings, Annual Report on Conservation and Science, COMMUNIQUE

Keyword(s): Oceans/Coasts/Beaches, Wildlife & Species

Contact(s):
Ted Beattie, President
Jane Ballentine, Director of Public Affairs; ext. 252
Laura Benson, Director of Finance and Administration; ext. 233
Sydney Butler, Executive Director
Bruce Carr, Director of Conservation Education; ext. 251
Michael Hutchins, Director of Conservation and Science
Linda Martin-MCormic, Director of Development and Marketing; ext. 243
Kristin Vehrs, Deputy Director and Director of Government Affairs

ANACOSTIA WATERSHED SOCIETY

4302 Baltimore Ave.
Bladensburg, MD 20710 United States
Phone: 301-699-6204 Fax: 301-699-3317
Website: www.anacostiaws.org

Founded: 1989
Membership: 1,001–10,000
Scope: Regional

Description: The Anacostia Watershed Society provides opportunities for volunteers to take part in local environmental restoration projects and provides advocacy for environmental equity issues in the Anacostia-Washington region.

Publication(s): Voice of the River

Keyword(s): Ecosystems (precious), Ethics/Environmental Justice, Pollution (general), Public Lands/Greenspace, Reduce/Reuse/Recycle, Sprawl/Urban Planning, Water Habitats & Quality

Contact(s):
Robert Boone, President; robert@anacostiaws.org
James Connolly, Executive Director; jim@anacostiaws.org
John Perhonis, Secretary; jperhoni@nsf.gov

ANCIENT FOREST INTERNATIONAL

P.O. Box 1850
Redway, CA 95560 United States
Phone: 707-923-3015 Fax: 707-923-4486
E-mail: afi@ancientforest.org
Website: www.ancientforest.org

Founded: 1989

Scope: International

Description: An alliance of conservationists dedicated to helping preserve, study and increase awareness of the Earth's few still-intact forest ecosystems, while providing habitat continuity through the creation of corridors. Old-growth forests of southern Chile, highland Mexico, Ecuador and the north Pacific coast are current projects. Work is also underway to document the distribution of ancient rainforests worldwide and to promote their preservation.

Publication(s): Chile's Native Forest: An Overview, News of Old Growth

Keyword(s): Forests/Forestry, Wildlife & Species

Contact(s):
Rick Klein, President
Suzelle Hunt, Secretary
Tim Metz, Treasurer

ANGLERS FOR CLEAN WATER

P.O. Box 17900
Montgomery, AL 36141-0900 United States
Phone: 334-272-9530 Fax: 334-270-8549

Founded: 1970

Scope: National

Description: A nonprofit organization dedicated to educating the American public on the status of America's natural resources, to provide education and information on conservation of aquatic resources and to serve as a strong advocate for sport-fishing.

Publication(s): Living Waters

Keyword(s): Pollution (general), Recreation/Ecotourism, Water Habitats & Quality, Wildlife & Species

Contact(s):
Bruce Shupp, Conservation Director
Matt Vincent, Editor

ANIMAL PROTECTION INSTITUTE

1122 S Street
Sacramento, CA 95814 United States
Phone: 916-447-3085 Fax: 916-447-3070
E-mail: info@api4animals.org
Website: www.apianimals.org

Founded: 1968

Membership: 1,001–10,000

Scope: National

Description: The Animal Protection Institute is a national animal advocacy nonprofit organization dedicated to protecting animals against abuse through enforcement and legislative actions, investigations, advocacy campaigns, crisis intervention, public awareness and education. Specific areas of concern are wildlife protection and habitat conservation, companion animals, marine mammals, domestic and farm animals, animals used in research and humane ecucation.

Publication(s): Animal Issues

Keyword(s): Public Lands/Greenspace, Recreation/Ecotourism, Wildlife & Species

Contact(s):
Alan Berger, Executive Director
Gil Lamont, Editor
Barbara Lawrie, Creative Services
Gary Pike, Chairman of the Board

ANIMAL WELFARE INSTITUTE

P.O. Box 3650
Washington, DC 20007 United States
Phone: 202-337-2332 Fax: 202-338-9478
E-mail: awi@awionline.org
Website: www.awionline.org

Founded: 1951

Membership: 10,001–100,000

Scope: National

Description: Active in improvement of conditions for laboratory animals and reducing the numbers used in research, protection of endangered species, Save the Whales campaign, ending use of steel jaw traps, stopping imports of wild birds for the pet trade and humane education. Albert Schweitzer award is presented for outstanding contributions to animal welfare.

Publication(s): Animals and Their Legal Rights, Alternative Traps, Endangered Species Handbook, Animal Welfare Institute Quarterly

Keyword(s): Wildlife & Species

Contact(s):
Christine Stevens, President; 202-337-2332
Cynthia Wilson, Vice President
Cathy Liss, Executive Director; 202-337-2332
Ava Armandarez, Publications Coordinator; 202-337-2332
Diane Halverson, Farm Animal Consultant
Lynne Hutchison, Executive Secretary
Fred Hutchison, Treasurer
Nell Naughton, Mail Order Secretary
Viktor Reinhardt, Laboratory Animal Consultant
Adam Roberts, Research Associate; 202-337-2332
Ben White, International Coordinator

ANIMALS ASIA FOUNDATION

P.O. Box 82
Sai Kung Post Office
Sai Kung
Kowloon, - Hong Kong
Phone: 852-2791-2225 Fax: 852-2791-2320
E-mail: info@animalsasia.org
Website: www.animalsasia.org

Founded: N/A

Membership: N/A

Scope: Regional

Description: The Animals Asia Foundation is devoted to the needs of wild, domesticated and endangered species throughout the Asia continent. Our mission is to end cruelty and promote an inherent respect for animals Asia wide. Animals Asia is currently undertaking the rescue of 500 farmed Moon Bears in China.

Publication(s): Campaigns of Animals Asia

Keyword(s): Executive/Legislative/Judicial Reform, Wildlife & Species

Contact(s):
Jill Robinson, Founder & CEO; 852-2791-2225; Fax: 852-2791-2320; jrobinson@animalsasia.org
Gail Cochrane, Veterinary Director; 852-2791-2225; Fax: 852-2791-2320; gcochrane@animalsasia.org
Annie Mather, Media Director; 852-2791-2225; Fax: 852-2791-2320; amather@animalsasia.org

Hanni Bevand, German Representative; Postfach 82 01 73, 81801, Munich; 894-277-5301; Fax: 894-277-5302; hbevand@animalsasia.org
David Neale, UK Representative; P.O. Box 5713,, Clacton on Sea, Essex C015 6QT; 0870-241-3723; Fax: 0870-225-6062; dneale@animalsasia.org
Ingrid Seymour, New Zealand Representative; P.O. Box 12440, Hamilton 2001; 07-829-4905; Fax: 07-829-4904; iseymour@animalsasia.org
Lyn White, Australia Representative; P.O. Box 1, Woodside, SA5244; 1800-666-004; Fax: 6188-389-7367; lwhite@animalsasia.org

ANTARCTICA PROJECT

P.O. Box 76920
Washington, DC 20013 United States
Phone: 202-234-2480 Fax: 202-387-4823
E-mail: antarctica@igc.org
Website: www.asoc.org

Founded: 1982
Scope: International
Description: Works to preserve Antarctica by monitoring all activities to ensure minimal environmental impact and consulting with key users of Antarctica, including scientists, tourists, governments. Conducts legal and policy research and analysis; produces educational materials; focuses international scientific community on globally-significant research. Secretariat to Antarctic and Southern Ocean Coalition (ASOC), composed of 240 conservation groups in 50 nations.
Publication(s): Antarctica Project
Keyword(s): Land Issues, Reduce/Reuse/Recycle, Wildlife & Species
Contact(s):
Beth Clark, Director
Scott Altmann, Coordinator of Protocol; scott.antarctica@igc.org
Jim Barnes, Counsel
Mark Stevens, Coordinator Fisheries Campaign; 202-238-8052; mark.antarctica@igc.org
Josh Stevens, Coordinator of Protocol Implementation Campaign; josh.antarctica@igc.org

APPALACHIAN MOUNTAIN CLUB

5 Joy St.
Boston, MA 02108 United States
Phone: 617-523-0636 Fax: 617-523-6617
E-mail: information@amcinfo.org
Website: www.outdoors.org

Founded: 1876
Membership: 10,001–100,000
Scope: Regional
Description: The AMC pursues a far-reaching conservation agenda while encouraging responsible recreation, based on the philosophy that successful, long-term conservation depends on firsthand experience and enjoyment of the natural environment. Areas of focus: Northern Forest, Sterling Forest, White Mountain N.F., NY and NJ Highlands, Berkshire and Taconics Region, Delaware Water Gap National Recreation Area, and Acadia National Park. Expertise: Conservation policy, advocacy; land, trail, river and greenways.
Publication(s): AMC Outdoors, AMC guidebooks and maps, Appalachia Journal
Keyword(s): Air Quality/Atmosphere, Public Lands/Greenspace, Recreation/Ecotourism, Water Habitats & Quality
Contact(s):
Laurie Burt, President
Eric Antebi, Director of Conservation Policy and Advocacy; 617-523-0655, ext. 353
Peg Brady, Director of Conservation Programs; 617-523-0655, ext. 383
Andrew Falender, Executive Director
Kenneth Kimball, Research Director; 603-466-2721
Walter Graff, Deputy Director; 603-466-2721

APPALACHIAN TRAIL CONFERENCE

P.O. Box 807
Harpers Ferry, WV 25425-0807 United States
Phone: 304-535-6331 Fax: 304-535-2667
E-mail: general@appalachiantrail.org
Website: www.appalachiantrail.org

Founded: 1925
Membership: 10,001–100,000
Scope: Regional
Description: Coordinates preservation and management of the Appalachian Trail, a 2,169-mile footpath and protective corridor generally following the crest of the Appalachian Mountains from Maine to Georgia. Prepares and distributes trail guidebooks and other user information.
Publication(s): Register, The, Trail Lands, Appalachian Trailway News
Keyword(s): Agriculture/Farming, Air Quality/Atmosphere, Ecosystems (precious), Forests/Forestry, Land Issues, Public Lands/Greenspace, Recreation/Ecotourism, Wildlife & Species
Contact(s):
Brian King, Director of Public Affairs; bking@atconf.org
David Startzell, Executive Director
Carl Demrow, Vice Chair; 202 Mason Rd., West Topsham, VT 05086
Kennard Honick, Treasurer; 1800 Second St., Suite 810, Sarasota, FL 34236; 941-366-3944
Terthema Martin, Sercretary
Maryanne Skwen, Vice Chair; 553 Forest Superior Ave., Decatur, GA 30033; 540-427-4536
Thyra Sperry, Vice Chair; 740 Oak Hill Dr., Boiling Springs, PA 17007-9624; 717-258-5261
Brian Fitzgerald, Chair; 55 Ward Hills Rd, S. Duxbury, VT 05660
Robert Rubin, Editor; rrubin@appalachiantrail.org

ARCHAEOLOGICAL CONSERVANCY

5301 Central Ave., NE, Suite 402
Albuquerque, NM 87108 United States
Phone: 505-266-1540 Fax: 505-266-0311
E-mail: archcons@nm.net
Website: www.americanarchaeology.org

Founded: 1979
Scope: National
Description: National nonprofit membership organization dedicated to the permanent preservation of the most significant archaeological sites in the United States, usually through acquisition. Cooperates with government, universities, museums, and private conservation organizations to acquire lands for permanent archaeological preserves.
Publication(s): American Archaeology
Keyword(s): Ethics/Environmental Justice, Wildlife & Species
Contact(s):
Mark Michel, President
Rob Crisell, Eastern Regional Director; 1307 S. Glebe Rd., Arlington, VA 22204; 703-979-4410
Lynn Dunbar, Western Regional Office Director; 1217 23rd St., Sacramento, CA 95816-4917; 916-448-1892
Paul Gardner, Midwest Regional Office Director; 295 Acton Rd., Columbus, OH 43214; 614-267-1100
Alan Gruber, Southeastern Regional Office Director; 5997 Cedar Crest Rd., Acworth, GA 30101; 770-975-4344
James Walker, Southwest Regional Office Director; 5301 Central Ave. NE, Suite 1218, Albuquerque, NM 87108; 505-266-1540
Earl Gadbery, Chairman of the Board

ARCHBOLD BIOLOGICAL STATION

P.O. Box 2057
Lake Placid, FL 33862-2057 United States
Phone: 863-465-2571 Fax: 863-699-1927
E-mail: archbold@archbold-station.org
Website: www.archbold-station.org

Founded: 1941
Membership: N/A
Scope: State
Description: The Station is an independent, nonprofit facility devoted to long-term ecological research and conservation. Primary focus is on organisms, including many endangered species, and environments of the unique Lake Wales Ridge and adjacent Florida.
Publication(s): Biennial Report
Keyword(s): Agriculture/Farming, Land Issues, Wildlife & Species
Contact(s):
Hilary Swain, Executive Director; 863-465-2571, ext. 251
Patrick Bolen, Assistant Director for Agro-Ecology; 863-699-0242
Nancy Deyrup, Education Coordinator; 863-465-2571, ext. 233
Tina Fleischer, Internship Coordinator; 863-465-2571, ext. 251
Fred Lohrer, Librarian; 863-465-2571, ext. 236

ARCHERY MANUFACTURERS AND MERCHANTS ORGANIZATION (AMO)

304 Brown St. East
Comfrey, MN 56019 United States
Phone: 703-242-8310 Fax: 507-877-2149
Website: www.amo-archery.org

Founded: 1953
Membership: 1,001–10,000
Scope: International
Keyword(s): Recreation/Ecotourism
Contact(s):
Jay McAninch, President and CEO
Kelly Kelly, Director of Operations and Membership Services; kelly@amoarchery.com

ARCTIC INSTITUTE OF NORTH AMERICA

University of Calgary
2500 University Drive NW
Calgary, T2N 1N4 Alberta Canada
Phone: 403-220-7515 Fax: 403-282-4609
Website: www.ucalgary.ca/aina

Founded: 1945
Membership: 1,001–10,000
Scope: Local, Regional, National, International
Description: A nonprofit research organization dedicated to acquisition, interpretation, and dissemination of knowledge of the polar regions. Sponsors research by its forty research associates.
Publication(s): Arctic, AINA Library
Keyword(s): Ecosystems (precious)
Contact(s):
Karla Jessen Williamson, Executive Director; 403-220-7515; wkjessen@ucalgary.ca
Ross Goodwin, Manager, ASTIS Database; 403-220-4036; rgoodwin@ucalgary.ca
Sonja Hogg, Business Manager; 403-220-7517; hogg@ucalgary.ca
Carl Benson, Chair of the U.S. Board of Governors
Karen McCullough, Editor; 403-220-4049; kmccullo@ucalgary.ca
Murray Todd, Chair of the Canadian Board of Directors

ARIZONA ASSOCIATION OF CONSERVATION DISTRICTS

Attn: Executive Director, 3003 N. Central Ave., Suite 800
Phoenix, AZ 85012 United States
Phone: 602-280-8803 Fax: 602-280-8779
E-mail: aacd@az.nrcs.usda.gov
Website: www.aacdonline.com

Founded: N/A
Scope: State
Contact(s):
Sharon Reid, President and Board Member; Rt. 1 Box 49-C, St. David, AZ 85630; 520-586-3347
Robert Ahkeah, Vice President; P.O. Box 550, Shiprock, NM 87420; 505-368-5430
Frank Martinez, 1st Vice President; Box 1152, Parker, AZ 85344; 520-669-8459
Marcareo Herrera, Executive Director; 602-280-8803; Fax: 602-280-8779
Johnny Lavin, Secretary/Treasurer; HC 1 Box 760, Benson, AZ 83602; 520-212-3211; Fax: 520-384-2735

ARIZONA B.A.S.S. CHAPTER FEDERATION

P.O. Box 577
Kearny, AZ 85237 United States
Phone: 520-363-5912

Founded: N/A
Membership: 101–1,000
Scope: State
Description: An organization of Bassmaster chapters, affiliated with the Bass Anglers Sportsman Society, organized to fight pollution, assist state and national conservation agencies in their efforts, and teach the young people of our country good conservation practices. Dedicated to the realistic conservation of our water resources.
Contact(s):
Mike Johnson, President
Dave Cohen, Conservation Director; 839 S. Westwood #266, Mesa, AZ 85210; 602-962-9009

ARIZONA WILDLIFE FEDERATION

644 N. Country Club Dr. - Suite E
Mesa, AZ 85201-4983 United States
Phone: 480-644-0077 Fax: 480-644-0078
E-mail: awf@azwildlife.org
Website: www.azwildlife.org

Founded: 1923
Membership: 1,001–10,000
Scope: State
Description: A representative statewide organization, affiliated with the National Wildlife Federation, dedicated to the protection and enhancement of wildlife and its habitat through public education and government interaction.
Publication(s): Arizona Wildlife News
Contact(s):
Jerry Thorson, President & Acting Treasurer
Randy Lamb, Vice-President
Mike Perkinson, Vice-President
Dave Gowdey, Executive Director; 644 N Country Club Dr.; Suite E, Mesa, AZ 85201; 480-644-0077; dgowdey@azwildlife.org
Ken Haefner, Publications / Volunteers Director; 644 N Country Club Dr., Suite E, Mesa, AZ 85201; 480-644-0077; Fax: 480-644-0078; haefner@azwildlife.org
Web Parton, Education / Outreach Coodinator
Don Farmer, Alternate Representative
Jack Simon, Representative

ARIZONA-SONORA DESERT MUSEUM
2021 North Kinney Road
Tucson, AZ 85743 United States
Phone: 520-883-1380 Fax: 520-883-2500
E-mail: rdaley@desertmuseum.org
Website: www.desertmuseum.org

Founded: 1952
Membership: 10,001–100,000
Scope: International
Description: The mission of the Arizona-Sonora Desert Museum is to inspire people to live in harmony with the natural world by fostering love, appreciation, and understanding of the Sonoran Desert.
Keyword(s): Development/Developing Countries, Ecosystems (precious), Forests/Forestry, Land Issues, Oceans/Coasts/Beaches, Public Lands/Greenspace, Recreation/Ecotourism, Sprawl/Urban Planning, Water Habitats & Quality, Wildlife & Species
Contact(s):
- Rick Daley, President/CEO; 520-883-3004; rdaley@desertmuseum.org
- Robert Edison, Vice President for Development; 520-883-3020; redison@desertmuseum.org
- Nancy Laney, Vice President for Administration; 520-883-3005; nlaney@desertmuseum.org
- Richard Brusca, Director of Conservation and Science; 520-883-3007; rbrusca@desertmuseum.org
- Mark Dimmitt, Director of Natural History; 520-883-3008; mdimmitt@desertmuseum.org
- Thomas VanDevender, Senior Scientist; 520-883-3029; tvandevender@desertmuseum.org
- Susan Williams, Director of Education; 520-883-3021; swilliams@desertmuseum.org
- Peter Siminski, Director of Collections; 520-883-3043; psiminski@desertmuseum.org

ARKANSAS ASSOCIATION OF CONSERVATION DISTRICTS
Attn: Exec. Vice President
101 E. Capital
Suite 350
Little Rock, AR 72201 United States
Phone: 501-643-3385

Founded: N/A
Scope: State
Contact(s):
- Bill Rainwater, President; P.O. Box 2245, Jonesboro, AR 72401; 870-935-1624
- Paul Mayfield, 1st Vice President; 783 Rio Vista Rd., Bald Knob, AR 72010; 501-724-5932; mayfield@IPA.Net
- Debbie Moreland, Executive Vice President; 20311 Lake Vista, Roland, AR 72135; 501-868-5294
- Roy Mahler, Secretary/Treasurer; Rt. 2 Box 130, Elkins, AR 72727; 501-643-3385

ARKANSAS B.A.S.S. CHAPTER FEDERATION
500 Coles Chapel Circle
Branch, AR 72928 United States
Phone: 501-635-5951
Website: www.arkansasbass.com

Founded: N/A
Membership: 101–1,000
Scope: National
Description: An organization of Bassmaster chapters, affiliated with the Bass Anglers Sportsman Society, organized to fight pollution, assist state and national conservation agencies in their efforts, and teach the young people of our country good conservation practices. Dedicated to the realistic conservation of our water resources.
Publication(s): Arkansas Bass Newsletter, available on website
Contact(s):
- Gene Carson, President
- Bobby Davenport, Conservation Director; 870-673-1799

ARKANSAS ENVIRONMENTAL EDUCATION ASSOCIATION
P.O. Box 488
Hackett, AR 72937 United States
Phone: 501-638-7151 Fax: 501-638-7151
E-mail: arkenved@aol.com

Founded: 1995
Membership: 1–100
Scope: Local, State, Regional, National
Description: The Association promotes environmental education and supports the work of environmental educators in Arkansas.
Publication(s): Membership Directory, EE Resource Directory
Contact(s):
- Frank Chandler, President-Elect
- Michelle Viney, President; 479-444-1860; Fax: 479-444-1880; mviney@tcswd.com
- Robert McAfee, Executive Director; 479-638-7151; Fax: 479-638-7151; arkenved@aol.com
- Suzanne Hirrel, President; 501-671-2288; Fax: 501-671-2110; shirrel@uaex.edu

ARKANSAS WILDLIFE FEDERATION
9700 Rodney Parham Road, Suite I-2
Little Rock, AR 72227-6212 United States
Phone: 501-224-9200 Fax: 501-224-9214
E-mail: arkwildlifefed@aristotle.net
Website: www.arkansaswildlifefederation.org

Founded: 1936
Membership: 1,001–10,000
Scope: State
Description: A representative statewide organization, affiliated with the National Wildlife Federation, dedicated to the protection and enhancement of wildlife and its habitat through public education and government interaction.
Publication(s): Arkansas Fish and Wildlife
Contact(s):
- Ducote Haynes, President
- Terry Horton, Executive Director & Education Programs Contact
- Bob Apple, Editor
- Steve Duzan, Alternate Representative
- Jim Wood, Representative & Treasurer

ARLINGTON OUTDOOR EDUCATION ASSOCIATION, INC. (AOEA)
PHOEBE HALL KNIPLING OUTDOOR LABORATORY
P.O. Box 5646
Arlington, VA 22205 United States
Phone: 540-347-2258 Fax: 540-349-3336
Website: CharityAdvantage.com/AOEA

Founded: 1967
Membership: 1,001–10,000
Scope: Local, Regional
Description: AOEA's Outdoor Lab annually provides approximately 9,000 northern Virginia school children, in grades kindergarten through twelve, with enriching environmental and educational opportunities in a natural setting. In addition to daily classes during the school year, the lab conducts camps during the summer and astronomical observatory sessions throughout the year.
Keyword(s): Land Issues, Water Habitats & Quality, Wildlife & Species
Contact(s):
- Terry Rusnak, President; 703-228-7650
- Lori Lowe, Vice President
- Neil Heinekamp, Lab Director

Maureen McManus, Treasurer
Anita Scott, Secretary

ASSOCIATION FOR CONSERVATION INFORMATION, INC.

Attn: President
New Hampshire Fish and Game Department
2 Hazen Dr.
Concord, NH 03301 United States
Website: www.aci-net.org

Founded: 1938

Scope: National

Description: Facilitates free exchange of ideas, materials, techniques, experiences, and procedures bearing on conservation information and education and establishes media furthering such exchange; promotes public understanding of basic conservation principles; informs states, territories, and provinces that do not have conservation education programs of their desirability and assists them in setting up conservation education, information and public relations programs.

Publication(s): Balance Wheel, The

Contact(s):

Judy Stokes, President; New Hampshire Fish & Game Department, 2 Hazen Drive, Concord, NH 03301; 603-271-3211

ASSOCIATION FOR NATURAL RESOURCES ENFORCEMENT TRAINING

Missouri Department of Conservation Box 180
Jefferson City, MO 65102 United States
Phone: 573-751-4115
E-mail: yamnil@mail.conservation.state.mo.us
Website: www.dirdid.com\anret

Founded: N/A

Scope: National

Description: The goal of the association is to promote and enhance professional standards of training in fish and wildlife enforcement. The objectives are: to promote officer safety and a safer working environment; exchange training information; promote law enforcement research and development; to encourage cost-effective training programs; to act as a repository for catalogue agency training personnel and materials; and to host annual workshop to facilitate the exchange of training information.

Contact(s):

Dave Windsor, Vice President; Indiana Department of Natural Resources, Law Enforcement Division 402W.Washington Street, Indianapolis, IN 46204; 317-232-4014; dwindsor@dnr.state.in.us

Fred Campbell, Treasurer; Natural Resources Conservation Authority, 10 Caledonia Ave, Kingston; 876-754-7567; fcampbell@nrca.org

Scottey Roxburgh, Secretary; Department of Fisheries and Oceans, 460-555 West Hasting St, Vancouver, British Columbia V6B 5G3; 604-666-0123; roxburgh@dfo/moo.ga.ca

ASSOCIATION FOR THE PROTECTION OF THE ADIRONDACKS, THE

Schenectady, NY 12301 United States
Phone: 518-377-1452 Fax: 518-377-1452
Website: www.protectadks.org

Founded: 1901

Membership: 1,001–10,000

Scope: International

Description: To protect the natural character of the state forest preserve lands in the Adirondacks and Catskills as water-holding and regulating forests which serve as a home for wildlife and as wilderness recreation areas, and to protect and enhance the natural resources of the Adirondack Park.

Publication(s): The Forest Preserve Magazine, The Association News Quarterly Newsletter

Keyword(s): Development/Developing Countries, Land Issues, Public Lands/Greenspace, Water Habitats & Quality, Wildlife & Species

Contact(s):

Abbey Verner, President
David Gibson, Executive Director

ASSOCIATION OF AMERICAN GEOGRAPHERS

1710 16th St., NW
Washington, DC 20009-3198 United States
Phone: 202-234-1450 Fax: 202-234-2744
E-mail: gaia@aag.org
Website: www.aag.org

Founded: 1904

Membership: 1,001–10,000

Scope: International

Description: To further professional investigations in geography and encourage the application of geographic findings in education, government, and business.

Publication(s): Professional Geographer, The, The Annals, AAG Newsletter

Keyword(s): Agriculture/Farming, Land Issues, Reduce/Reuse/Recycle

Contact(s):

Jan Monk, President
Duane Neelis, Vice President
Ronald Abler, Executive Director
Heather Baker, Editor of Newsletter
Susan Cutter, Past President
Robert Kent, Treasurer
Jennifier Wolch, Secretary
Amy Jo Woodruff, Managing Editor

ASSOCIATION OF AVIAN VETERINARIANS

Central Office, P.O. Box 811720
Boca Raton, FL 33481 United States
Phone: 561-393-8901 Fax: 561-393-8902
E-mail: aavctrlofc@aol.com
Website: www.aav.org/aav

Founded: 1980

Membership: 1,001–10,000

Scope: International

Description: The Association of Avian Veterinarians is a nonprofit international organization dedicated to advancing and promoting avian medicine and stewardship.

Publication(s): Journal of Avian Medicine and Surgery, The Proceedings the Assoc. of Avian Veterinarians

Keyword(s): Wildlife & Species

Contact(s):

Robert Groskin, Conservation Committee

ASSOCIATION OF CONSULTING FORESTERS OF AMERICA

732 North Washington St.,
Alexandria, VA 22314-1921 United States
Phone: 703-548-0990 Fax: 703-548-6395
E-mail: director@acf-foresters.com
Website: www.acf-foresters.com

Founded: 1948

Membership: 101–1,000

Scope: National

Description: The Association of Consulting Foresters of America, Inc. represents interests of private consulting foresters. Administers a continuing education program, enforces a code of ethics, and promotes use of private consulting foresters.

Publication(s): Membership Specialization Directory

Keyword(s): Forests/Forestry, Reduce/Reuse/Recycle

Contact(s):
David Parker, President
Glenn Dabney, Gulf Director
Michael Lewis, Southern Director
Richard Quarters, Western Director
William Steigerwaldt, Northern Director
Lynn Wilson, Executive Director
William Humphries Jr., Past President
J. Tobey Wright, President-Elect

ASSOCIATION OF FIELD ORNITHOLOGISTS

Attn: President, Inst. for Field Ornithology
Univ. of ME at Machias
9 O'Brien Ave.
Machias, ME 04654 United States
Website: www.afonet.org/

Founded: 1922
Scope: National
Description: To promote the study of birds in their natural habitats throughout the new world and dissemination of the information obtained from this study.
Publication(s): Journal of Field Ornithology
Keyword(s): Wildlife & Species
Contact(s):
Jerome Jackson, President; Whitaker Center, College of Arts & Sciences, Florida Gulf Coast University, 10501 FGCU Blvd. South, Fort Myers, FL 33965; jjackson@fgcu.edu
C. Chandler, Editor; Dept. of Bio., GA Southern Univ., Statesboro, GA 30460-8042; 912-681-5657; chandler@gasou.edu
Russ McClain, Secretary; Department of Biology, University of Memphis, Memphis, TN 38152; 901-678-2581; wrmcclain@msuvxi.memphis.edu
George Mock, Treasurer; P.O. Box 393, Mattapoisett, MA 02739; 508-758-4408; gmock@nyclubricants.com

ASSOCIATION OF GREAT LAKES OUTDOOR WRITERS (AGLOW)

P.O. Box 35
Benld, IL 62009 United States
Phone: 217-839-2490 Fax: 217-839-2490
E-mail: curthicken@aol.com
Website: www.greatlakeswriters.org

Founded: 1957
Membership: 101–1,000
Scope: Regional
Description: A nonprofit professional association of outdoor communicators dedicated to perpetuate the great outdoors through the judicious use of the written and spoken word.
Publication(s): AGLOW Horizons
Contact(s):
David Mull, President; pondermull@aol.com
Curt Hicken, Executive Director; 217-839-2490; Fax: 217-839-2490; curthicken@aol.com
Clayton Diskerud, Secretary
Dan Donarski, Vice President; 404 Golf Court, Sault Ste. Marie, MI 49783
P.J. Perea, Treasurer; 224 N. Shore Dr., Petersburg, IL 62675
Bob Schmidt, Editor; 5016 Argyle, Chicago, IL 60630; 773-283-7871
Mike Seeling, Chairman of the Board; 13608 Rt. 176, Woodstock, IL 60098

ASSOCIATION OF NEW JERSEY ENVIRONMENTAL COMMISSIONS (ANJEC)

P.O. Box 157
Mendham, NJ 07945 United States
Phone: 973-539-7547 Fax: 973-539-7713
E-mail: anjec@aol.com
Website: www.anjec.org

Founded: 1969
Membership: 1,001–10,000
Scope: State
Description: Private, nonprofit environmental organization serving the state's municipal environmental commissions, environmental organizations, and individual members by providing training programs, publications, research, reference, and liaison services.
Publication(s): ANJEC Report, Environmental Commission Handbook, Keeping Our Garden State Green, Environmental Manual for Municipal Officials
Keyword(s): Development/Developing Countries, Land Issues, Pollution (general), Public Lands/Greenspace, Sprawl/Urban Planning, Water Habitats & Quality
Contact(s):
Gary Szelc, President
Sandy Batty, Executive Director
Michelle Gaynor, Resource Center Director

ASSOCIATION OF PARTNERS FOR PUBLIC LANDS

8375 Jumpers Hole Rd. Suite 104
Millersville, MD 21108 United States
Phone: 410-647-9001 Fax: 410-647-9003
E-mail: appl@appl.org
Website: www.appl.org

Founded: 1977
Membership: 1–100
Scope: National
Description: CNPCA is the official umbrella organization for nonprofit interpretive associations that operate bookstores and sales areas in national parks and in other federal, state, and municipal vistor centers. The Associations are the single largest contributors of donated funds for the support of education, visitor services, and research activities in our nation's parks ($17 million per year).
Publication(s): Newswire, Cooperating Association Directory
Keyword(s): Public Lands/Greenspace, Recreation/Ecotourism
Contact(s):
Donna Asbury, Executive Director; 8375 Jumpers Hole Rd., Suite 104, Millersville, MD 21108; 410-647-9001

ASSOCIATION OF STATE AND TERRITORIAL HEALTH OFFICIALS

1275 K St., NW, Suite 800
Washington, DC 20005 United States
Phone: 202-371-9090 Fax: 202-371-9797
Website: www.astho.org

Founded: 1941
Scope: National
Description: ASTHO represents the directors of public health in each of the 50 states, the District of Columbia, and the U.S. Territories. Its purpose is to formulate and influence through collective action the establishment of sound national public health policy. ASTHO also assists and serves state health agencies in the development and implementation of state programs and policies in advancing the public health and prevention of disease.
Publication(s): Tobacco-Free Press, ASTHO Report, Environmental Health News
Keyword(s): Public Health
Contact(s):
George Hardy, Executive Director; 202-371-9090; Fax: 202-371-9797

ATLANTA AUDUBON SOCIETY

1447 Peachtree St. Suite 214
Atlanta, GA 30309 United States
Phone: 404-873-3034 Fax: 404-873-3135
Website: www.atlantaaudubon.org

Founded: 1975

Membership: 1,001–10,000
Scope: Local
Description: Atlanta Chapter of the National Audubon Society. Mission is to promote the enjoyment and understanding of birds and to protect and restore the ecosystems that support them.
Publication(s): Wingbars
Keyword(s): Ecosystems (precious), Forests/Forestry, Land Issues, Oceans/Coasts/Beaches, Pollution (general), Population, Public Lands/Greenspace, Reduce/Reuse/ Recycle, Sprawl/Urban Planning, Water Habitats & Quality, Wildlife & Species
Contact(s):
Jim Wilson, Iba Coordinator

ATLANTIC CENTER FOR THE ENVIRONMENT

NEW ENGLAND OFFICE
P.O. Box 217
Montpelier, VT 05602 United States
Phone: 802-229-0707 Fax: 802-223-3593
Website: www.qlf.org

Founded: N/A
Membership: 1–100
Scope: Regional
Publication(s): Compass
Contact(s):
Thomas Horn, Vice President

ATLANTIC CENTER FOR THE ENVIRONMENT

QUEBEC-LABRADOR FOUNDATION
55 S. Main St.
Ipswich, MA 01938-2396 United States
Phone: 978-356-0038 Fax: 978-356-7322
E-mail: atlantic@qlf.org
Website: www.qlf.org

Founded: N/A
Membership: N/A
Scope: Local, Regional, International
Description: A regional community-based conservation organization promoting public involvement in resource management. The mission of QLF Atlantic Center for the Environment is to: 1) Support the rural communities and environment of eastern Canada and New England with special emphasis on encouraging education and leadership in young people, and 2) Create models for stewardship of natural resources and cultural heritage that can be applied worldwide.
Publication(s): Compass
Keyword(s): Agriculture/Farming, Development/Developing Countries, Ecosystems (precious), Energy, Forests/Forestry, Land Issues, Oceans/Coasts/Beaches, Pollution (general), Public Lands/Greenspace, Recreation/Ecotourism, Reduce/Reuse/Recycle, Sprawl/Urban Planning
Contact(s):
Kathleen Blanchard, President of QLF Canada
Lawrence Morris, President
Jessica Brown, Vice President for International Programs
Thomas Horn, Vice President, New England/Maritimes Programs; P.O. Box 217, Montpelier, VT 05602; 802-229-0707; Fax: 802-223-3593
Brent Mitchell, Director, Stewardship; 978-356-0038, ext. 408; Fax: 978-356-7322; brentmitchell@qlf.org
Linda Mitton, Administrative Assistant

ATLANTIC CENTER FOR THE ENVIRONMENT

QUEBEC-LABRADOR FOUNDATION
CANADA OFFICE
1253 McGill College Ave., Suite 680
Montreal, H3B 2Y5 Quebec Canada
Phone: 514-395-6020 Fax: 514-395-4505
E-mail: montreal@qlf.org
Website: www.qlf.org

Founded: N/A
Membership: 1–100
Scope: International
Publication(s): Compass

ATLANTIC SALMON FEDERATION

International Headquarters, P.O. Box 5200
St. Andrews, E5B 3S8 New Brunswick Canada
Phone: 506-529-4581 Fax: 506-529-4438
E-mail: asf@nbnet.nb.ca
Website: www.asf.ca

Founded: 1982
Membership: 1,001–10,000
Scope: Local, State, Regional, National, International
Description: ASF, the largest international, nonprofit organization dedicated to conserving and managing the wild Atlantic salmon and its habitat, was established when two leading salmon groups, The Atlantic Salmon Association and The International Atlantic Salmon Foundation, consolidated. ASF programs are directed toward research, conservation, education, and international cooperation. ASF supports a network of 7 regional councils and 150 affiliates throughout the Atlantic salmon's North American range.
Publication(s): Atlantic Salmon Journal, The
Keyword(s): Agriculture/Farming, Climate Change, Ecosystems (precious), Forests/Forestry, Land Issues, Oceans/Coasts/Beaches, Pollution (general), Recreation/Ecotourism, Reduce/Reuse/Recycle, Water Habitats & Quality, Wildlife & Species
Contact(s):
Bill Taylor, President
Robert Beatty, Vice President of Development; 506-529-1031; rbeatty@nbnet.nb.ca
Frederick Whoriskey, Vice President-Research and Environment; 506-529-1039; asfres@nbnet.nb.ca
Charles Cusson, Director of Quebec Programs; Atlantic Salmon Federation 1253 Ave, McGill College, Bureau 680, Montreal, Quebec H3B 2Y5; 514-871-9660; fsa-asf-quebec@globetrotter.net
Andrew Goode, Director, U.S. Programs; 207-725-2833; goodeasf@blazenetme.net
Sue Scott, Executive Director of Communications; 506-529-1027; policy@nbnet.nb.ca
Jim Gourlay, Editor; P.O. Box 5200, St. Andrews, New Brunswick E5B 3S8; 506-529-4581; jgourlay@saltscapes.com
Bill Mallory, Controller; 506-529-1075; wmallory@nbnet.nb.ca
Donald O'Brien, Chairman of New York Office; Milbank, Tweed, Hadley, and McCloy, One Chase Manhattan Plaza, 54th Floor, New York, NY 10005-1413; 212-530-5818

ATLANTIC STATES LEGAL FOUNDATION

658 W. Onondaga St.
Syracuse, NY 13204-3757 United States
Phone: 315-475-1170 Fax: 315-475-6719
E-mail: atlantic.states@aslf.org
Website: www.aslf.org

Founded: 1982
Membership: 101–1,000
Scope: Local, State, Regional, National, International
Description: Atlantic States Legal Foundation, Inc., enforces environmental laws, engages in public education, conducts research and promotes environmental justice for the economically disadvantaged and people of color.
Publication(s): Superfund Review, Onondaga Lake Review, Quarterly newsletter
Keyword(s): Agriculture/Farming, Development/Developing Countries, Ecosystems (precious), Ethics/Environmental Justice, Land Issues, Oceans/Coasts/Beaches, Pollution (general), Public Health, Recreation/Ecotourism, Reduce/Reuse/Recycle, Water Habitats & Quality
Contact(s):
Samuel Sage, Senior Scientist

AUDUBON COUNCIL OF CONNECTICUT

c/o Audubon Center in Greenwich, 613 Riversville Rd.
Greenwich, CT 06831 United States
Phone: 203-629-1248

Founded: 1967

Scope: State

Description: The Audubon Council of Connecticut is a coalition of 16 chapters and affiliates of the National Audubon Society in Connecticut, representing close to 10,000 residents. The Council recognize humankind's dependence on the natural environment and appreciates the beauty and wondrous diversity of the natural world. The mission of the Council is, therefore, to protect and restore biodiversity in our state and on our planet.

Keyword(s): Wildlife & Species

AUDUBON COUNCIL OF ILLINOIS

434 N Charlotte
Palatine, IL 60067 United States
Phone: 847-797-7820

Founded: 1973

Membership: 10,001–100,000

Scope: State

Description: Composed of representatives of 13 National Audubon Society chapters in Illinois, the Council's purpose is to coordinate efforts of the chapters on statewide environmental issues.

Keyword(s): Land Issues, Water Habitats & Quality, Wildlife & Species

Contact(s):

Brian Herner, President; 434 N Charlotte, Palatine, IL 60067; 630-891-4879; brian_herner@premierinc.com
Marianne Hahn, Vice President; 18429 Gottschalk Ave., Homewood, IL 60430; 708-799-0249
Mary Blackmore, Treasurer; 9024 W. Grove Rd., Forreston, IL 61030; 815-938-3204
Bonnie John, Secretary; 824 S. Dunton, Arlington Heights, IL 60005; 847-259-5168; hayspella@aol.com

AUDUBON INTERNATIONAL

Headquarters, 46 Rarick Rd.
Selkirk, NY 12158 United States
Phone: 518-767-9051 Fax: 518-767-9076
E-mail: acss@audubonintl.org
Website: www.audubonintl.org

Founded: 1897

Membership: 1,001–10,000

Scope: International

Description: Audubon International is a nonprofit environmental organization that specializes in sustainable natural resource management. The mission of Audubon International is to improve the quality of life and the environment through research, education, and conservation assistance.

Publication(s): Stewardship News, Golf Course Design, A Guide to Environmental Stewardship on the Golf Course, Principles for Sustainable Resource Management, Landscape Restoration Handbook, Stewardship News, Managing Wildlife Habitat on Golf Courses, Guide to Environmental Stewardship for your business

Keyword(s): Development/Developing Countries, Land Issues, Reduce/Reuse/Recycle, Water Habitats & Quality, Wildlife & Species

Contact(s):

Ronald Dodson, President and CEO
Jean Mackay, Director of Environmental Education
Nancy Richardson, Director of Audubon Signature Program; 502-869-9419
Miles Smart, Director of Environmental Planning; 919-380-9640
Lawrence Woolbright, Director of Research; 518-783-2440
Paula Realbuto, Business Manager
Eric Dodson, MIS
Mary Jack, Executive Assistant

AUDUBON MISSOURI

1001 E. Walnut Ste. 200
Columbia, MO 65201 United States
Phone: 573-442-2139 Fax: 573-443-4378
Website: www.audubon.org/chapter/mo/

Founded: 1999

Membership: 1,001–10,000

Scope: State

Description: A statewide council composed of delegates from 14 National Audubon chapters and the Audubon Society of Missouri. Formed to coordinate efforts on various conservation and environmental issues in Missouri. Advised and assisted by the National Audubon Society.

Keyword(s): Water Habitats & Quality, Wildlife & Species

Contact(s):

Karen Uhlenhuth, Chairperson; 3714 E. Roanoke Dr., Kansas City, MO 64111; 816-561-1371

AUDUBON NATURALIST SOCIETY OF THE CENTRAL ATLANTIC STATES

8940 Jones Mill Rd.
Chevy Chase, MD 20815 United States
Phone: 301-652-9188 Fax: 301-951-7179
E-mail: hq@audubonnaturalist.org
Website: www.audubonnaturalist.org

Founded: 1897

Scope: Regional

Description: One of the original independent Audubon societies active in environmental education, conservation issues, sanctuaries, and natural science studies in the greater Washington metropolitan area for 100 years. The ANS is headquartered at Woodend, a 40-acre Nature Preserve in suburban Maryland.

Publication(s): Audubon Naturalist News, Environmental Education and Conservation Brochure

Keyword(s): Development/Developing Countries, Public Lands/Greenspace, Water Habitats & Quality, Wildlife & Species

Contact(s):

Neal Fitzpatrick, Director of Conservation
Mike Nelson, Executive Director
Muriel Robinson, Manager of Accounting
Leslie Cronin, Editor
Tara Fuad, Volunteer Coordinator
Regina Sakaria, Volunteer Coordinator

AUDUBON OF FLORIDA

444 Brickell Ave.
Suite 850
Miami, FL 33131 United States
Phone: 305-371-6399 Fax: 305-371-6398
E-mail: info@audubonofflorida.org
Website: www.audubonofflorida.org

Founded: 1900

Membership: 10,001–100,000

Scope: Local, State, Regional

Description: A statewide organization formed to promote public interest, understanding, and protection of Florida wildlife, and of the environment and habitats that support it.

Publication(s): Florida Naturalist, The

Keyword(s): Ecosystems (precious), Forests/Forestry, Land Issues, Oceans/Coasts/Beaches, Population, Public Lands/Greenspace, Reduce/Reuse/Recycle, Water Habitats & Quality, Wildlife & Species

Contact(s):

Stuart Strahl, President; 305-371-6399; Fax: 305-371-6398; sstrahl@audubon.org
Mark Kraus, Conservation Science Director; 305-371-6399; Fax: 305-371-6398; mkraus@audubon.org

AUDUBON OF FLORIDA

EVERGLADES CAMPAIGN OFFICE
444 Brickell Ave., Suite 850
Miami, FL 33131 United States
Phone: 305-371-6399 Fax: 305-371-6398
Website: www.audubonofflorida.org

Founded: N/A
Membership: 1–100
Scope: Regional
Publication(s): Everglades Report, Audubon Advocate, Florida Naturalist
Keyword(s): Ecosystems (precious)
Contact(s):
Stuart Strahl, President/CEO

AUDUBON OF KANSAS

P.O. Box 156
Manhattan, KS 66505-0156 United States
Phone: 785-537-4385
Website: www.audubonofkansas.org

Founded: 1974
Membership: 1,001–10,000
Scope: State
Description: (formerly Kansas Audubon Council) A statewide nonprofit organization working in partnership with eleven local Audubon chapters, a Board of Trustees and other members. Established in 1974, leadership was expanded in 1999 to establish Audubon of Kansas as a broad-based alliance to promote appreciation and stewardship of the natural ecosystems of Kansas, with special emphasis on conservation of prairies, grassland birds and other wildlife.
Publication(s): Prairie Wings
Keyword(s): Land Issues, Reduce/Reuse/Recycle, Wildlife & Species
Contact(s):
Ron Klataske, Executive Director
Carol Cumberland, Treasurer; 1106 Gretchen, Wichita, KS 67206
Patricia Marlett, Secretary; 4406 W. 11th, Wichita, KS 67212
Robert McElroy, Vice Chairman
Dick Seaton, Chairman of Board

AUDUBON PENNSYLVANIA

100 Wildwood Way
Harrisburg, PA 17110 United States
Phone: 717-213-6880 Fax: 717-213-6883
E-mail: painquiries@audubon.org
Website: www.audubon.org/chapter/pa/

Founded: 1987
Membership: 10,001–100,000
Scope: State
Description: The Pennsylvania Audubon Society promotes and encourages the conservation and protection of our natural resources through public education, communication with public officials, and sponsorship of programs to help children and adults become aware of their relationship to the environment.
Publication(s): Quarterly Newsletter, Wetlands Action Guide, Project Mayfly, Audubon Protecting Animals Through Habitat, Important Bird Areas of Pennsylvania Report, Pennsylvania Songbirds, Population & Habitat Newsletter
Keyword(s): Recreation/Ecotourism, Water Habitats & Quality, Wildlife & Species
Contact(s):
Carmen Santasania, President; 1410 Charles St., State College, PA 16801; 814-359-5760
Cindy Dunn, Executive Director
Leigh Altadonna, Treasurer; 161 Greenwood Ave., Wyncote, PA 15834; 215-886-0656
Marian Crossman, Secretary; 6 Tussey Circle, Pittsburgh, PA 15237; 412-366-3339

AUDUBON SOCIETY

850 Richards Street, #505
Honolulu, HI 96813-4709 United States
Phone: 212-979-3000 Fax: 808-537-5294
E-mail: hiaudsoc@pixi.com
Website: www.audubon.org#www.audubon.org#

Founded: 1939
Membership: 1,001–10,000
Scope: State
Description: for better understanding, appreciation, and conservation of Hawaii's native wildlife resources, especially its unique and endangered bird species and their associated ecosystems.
Publication(s): Elepaio (Journal), Map-Treasures of Oahu, field card checklist, checklists, Voice of Hawaii's Birds (cassette tapes), Hawaii's Birds
Keyword(s): Land Issues, Public Lands/Greenspace, Reduce/Reuse/Recycle, Water Habitats & Quality, Wildlife & Species
Contact(s):
Wendy Johnson, President
Sharon Reilly, Recording Secretary

AUDUBON SOCIETY OF MISSOURI

Attn: Susan Hazelwood, President
3005 Chapel Hill Rd.
Columbia, MO 65203 United States
Phone: 573-445-4925
E-mail: shazelwood@socket.net
Website: www.mobirds.org

Founded: 1901
Membership: 101–1,000
Scope: State
Description: A nonprofit statewide ornithological society dedicated to the preservation and protection of birds and all wildlife forms and habitat; to educate citizenry toward appreciation of the natural world; and to work for wise conservation practices related to people and wildlife.
Publication(s): Bluebird, The, Guide to the Birding Areas of Missouri,, Annotated Checklist of the Birds of Missouri
Keyword(s): Wildlife & Species
Contact(s):
Susan Hazelwood, President; 3005 Chapel Hill Rd., Columbia, MO 65203; 573-445-4925; shazelwood@socket.net
Jerry Wade, Vice President; 1221 Bradshaw Ave., Columbia, MO 65203; 573-445-6697; wadej@missouri.edu
Susan Dornfeld, Secretary; 700 S. Weller, Springfield, MO 65802; 417-831-9702; dornfelds@hotmail.com
Jean Graebner, Treasurer; 1800 S. Roby Farm Rd., Rocheport, MO 65279; 314-698-2855
Bonnie Heidy, Membership Chair; 501 Parkade, Columbia, MO 65202; 573-442-2191; bheidy@socket.net
Edge Wade, Bird Alert Compiler; 1221 Bradshaw Ave., Columbia, MO 65203-0807; 573-445-6697; edgew@socket.net

AUDUBON SOCIETY OF NEW HAMPSHIRE

3 Silk Farm Rd.
Concord, NH 03301-8200 United States
Phone: 603-224-9909 Fax: 603-226-0902
Website: www.nhaudubon.org

Founded: 1914
Membership: 1,001–10,000
Scope: State
Description: Independent statewide nonprofit organization dedicated to the preservation, understanding, and appreciation of New Hampshire's wildlife and other natural resources.
Publication(s): Newsletter, Bi-Monthly
Contact(s):
Richard Moore, President
Richard Cook, Vice President for Conservation

Scott Fitzpatrick, Director of Education
Kent Taylor, Director for Membership
Harry Vogel, Director of Loon Preservation Committee
Julian Zelazny, Director of Environmental Affairs
Sylvia Bates, Vice Chairperson; Rt. 1, Box 313, Ashland, NH 03217
Tupper Kinder, Chair of the Board of Trustees; Sheehan Phinney, Bas and Green, 1000 Elm St., Manchester, NH 03105-3701
Anita Maclean, Treasurer
Larry Sunderland, Secretary; RFD 1 Box 179, Hillsboro, NH 03244

AUDUBON SOCIETY OF OMAHA

11809 Old Maple Road
Omaha, NE 68164 United States
Phone: 402-493-0373 Fax: 402-493-0373

Founded: 1985
Membership: 1,001–10,000
Scope: Local
Description: A statewide council of representatives of the eight National Audubon Society chapters in Nebraska. The Council's purpose is to coordinate efforts of the chapters on statewide environmental issues and advocate protection, preservation, and wise use of our soil, water, plants, and wildlife.
Contact(s):
Ione Werthen, Contact

AUDUBON SOCIETY OF PORTLAND

5151 NW Cornell Rd.
Portland, OR 97210 United States
Phone: 503-292-6855 Fax: 503-292-1021
E-mail: general@audubonportland.org
Website: www.audubonportland.org

Founded: 1902
Membership: 1,001–10,000
Scope: Local, State, Regional, National
Description: The Audubon Society of Portland promotes the enjoyment, understanding and protection of native birds, other wildlife and their habitats, focusing on the local community and the Pacific Northwest.
Publication(s): Audubon Warbler
monthly newsletter
Keyword(s): Development/Developing Countries, Ecosystems (precious), Forests/Forestry, Land Issues, Oceans/Coasts/Beaches, Public Lands/Greenspace, Recreation/Ecotourism, Reduce/Reuse/Recycle, Sprawl/Urban Planning, Water Habitats & Quality, Wildlife & Species
Contact(s):
Jim Rapp, Board President
Sybil Ackerman, Director of Conservation
Dave Eshbaugh, Executive Director
Mitch Luckett, Sanctuary Director
Steve Robertson, Education Director
Bob Wilson, Nature Store Director
Scott Lukens, Secretary

AUDUBON SOCIETY OF RHODE ISLAND

12 Sanderson Rd.
Smithfield, RI 02917-2600 United States
Phone: 401-949-5454 Fax: 401-949-5788
Website: www.asri.org

Founded: 1897
Membership: 1,001–10,000
Scope: State
Description: To focus attention on critical natural resource problems, provide leadership when conservation action is necessary, carry out a broad program of public conservation education, and preserve examples of unique natural areas and native wildlife habitat.
Publication(s): Audubon Society of Rhode Island Report, Fields Notes of Rhode Island Birds, Checklist of Rhode Island Birds
Keyword(s): Air Quality/Atmosphere, Land Issues, Oceans/Coasts/Beaches, Public Lands/Greenspace, Reduce/Reuse/Recycle, Wildlife & Species
Contact(s):
Dickson Boenning, 2nd Vice President
A. Kohlenberg, 1st Vice President
Jeff Hall, Environmental Education Center Director; 401-245-7500; EEC@asri.org
Eugenia Marks, Research, Advocacy & Publications Director; 401-949-5454; emarks@asri.org
Lee Schisler, Executive Director; 401-949-5454
Lawrence Taft, Director of Properties and Acquistions; 401-949-5454; Fax: 401-949-5788; ltaft@asri.org
Sharon Cresci, Development Assistant
Joseph Dimase, Secretary
Frank Sciuto, Treasurer
Doris Thorpe, Membership Secretary
Ken Weber, Editor

AUDUBON SOCIETY OF WESTERN PENNSYLVANIA

BEECHWOOD FARMS NATURE RESERVE
TODD SANCTUARY
Beechwood Farms Nature Reserve
614 Dorseyville Road
Pittsburgh, PA 15238-1618 United States
Phone: 412-963-6100 Fax: 412-963-6761
E-mail: aswp@aswp.org
Website: www.aswp.org

Founded: 1916
Membership: 1,001–10,000
Scope: Local
Description: The mission of the Audubon Society of Western Pennsylvania is to inspire and educate the people of southwestern Pennsylvania to be respectful and responsible stewards of the natural world.
Publication(s): Bulletin, Teacher Guide, Seasoning
Keyword(s): Ecosystems (precious), Wildlife & Species
Contact(s):
Richard Adams, Executive Director
Roy Lenhardt, Director of Development
Trisha Harger, Director of Education

AUDUBON VERMONT

255 Sherman Hollow Rd.
Huntington, VT 05462 United States
Phone: 802-434-3068 Fax: 802-434-4686
E-mail: vermont@audubon.org
Website: www.audubon.org

Founded: 2000
Membership: 1,001–10,000
Scope: State
Description: National Audubon Society's Vermont State Office formed to protect birds, other wildlife and their habitats by promoting a culture of conservation through research, education and advocacy.
Keyword(s): Forests/Forestry, Water Habitats & Quality, Wildlife & Species
Contact(s):
Warren King, President; P.O. Box 77, Ripton, VT 05766
Seward Weber, Vice President; R.D. 2, Box 390, Plainfield, VT 05667
Suzanna Liepmann, Treasurer; P.O. Box 112, South Strafford, VT 05070

B

BACK COUNTRY LAND TRUST

338 West Lexington
Suite 204
El Cajon, CA 92020 United States
Phone: 619-590-2258 Fax: 619-590-2248
E-mail: noelle@bclt.org
Website: www.bclt.org

Founded: 1990
Membership: 101–1,000
Scope: Regional
Description: Conserving and managing rare habitat in eastern San Diego County.
Contact(s):
Don Hohimer, President; 619-590-2258; Fax: 619-590-2248; don@bclt.org
Noelle Collins, Executive Director; 619-590-2258; Fax: 619-590-2248; noelle@bclt.org

BAMA BACKPADDLERS ASSOCIATION

307 Madison Pl.
Trussville, AL 35173 United States
Phone: 205-592-2117
E-mail: backpaddlers@aol.com
Website: members.aol.com/backpaddlers/

Founded: 1978
Scope: State
Description: Dedicated to promoting recreation, conservation, education and safety on Alabama's waterways.
Publication(s): As the Eddy Turns
Keyword(s): Development/Developing Countries, Oceans/ Coasts/ Beaches, Recreation/Ecotourism, Reduce/Reuse/Recycle, Water Habitats & Quality
Contact(s):
Renee Clark, President
Nancy Cate, Treasurer
Betty Harrison, Newsletter; kayakbba@aol.com
Bob Shepard, Trip Coordinator
Jennifer Taylor, Conservation; 205-951-0320; cahabasierra@aol.com

BARRIER ISLAND TRUST, INC.

P.O. Box 37310
Tallahassee, FL 32315 United States
Phone: 850-933-2761 Fax: 203-629-2453
Website: www.bit.org

Founded: 1989
Scope: State
Description: To preserve the natural resources of Florida's barrier islands, initially focusing on Dog Island and Apalachicola Bay, hold and manage barrier island property to preserve it in its natural state, promote research on barrier island ecology and translate research into educational programs and effective policies for protection of barrier islands.
Keyword(s): Land Issues, Oceans/Coasts/Beaches
Contact(s):
Leroy Collins, Board of Trustee President; 16 Davis Blvd. Suite 12, Tampa, FL 33606; 813-259-9484
Dianne Mellon, Board of Trustee Vice President; 1515 Country Club, Tallahassee, FL 32301; 850-877-3942
Guy Smith, Board of Trustee Chair; 352 North St., Greenwich, CT 06830; 203-629-1264
Mitchell Smith, Board of Trustee Treasurer; P.O. Box 1912, Albany, GA 31702

BAT CONSERVATION INTERNATIONAL

P.O. Box 162603
Austin, TX 78716 United States
Phone: 512-327-9721 Fax: 512-327-9724
E-mail: batinfo@batcon.org
Website: www.batcon.org

Founded: 1982
Membership: 10,001–100,000
Scope: Local, State, Regional, National, International
Description: A nonprofit organization with 14,000 members in 72 countries. BCI's purpose is to document and publicize the values and conservation needs of bats, to promote bat conservation projects, and to assist with management initiatives worldwide.
Publication(s): Catalog of educational products, BATS Magazine
Keyword(s): Agriculture/Farming, Ecosystems (precious), Forests/Forestry, Public Health, Recreation/Ecotourism, Wildlife & Species
Contact(s):
Merlin Tuttle, Founder and President
Bob Benson, Public Information Manager and Bracken Campaign Manager; bbenson@batcon.org

BERKSHIRE-LITCHFIELD ENVIRONMENTAL COUNCIL, INC.

P.O. Box 552
Lakeville, CT 06039 United States
Phone: 203-435-2004

Founded: 1970
Scope: State
Description: Primarily concerned with energy, invasive transportation, and land use issues in the southern Berkshires and Litchfield Hills. Offers public programs and environmental education for all ages.
Publication(s): BLEC News
Keyword(s): Agriculture/Farming, Land Issues, Wildlife & Species
Contact(s):
Starling Childs, President; 203-542-5569
Nic Osborn, Vice President
Judy Thomas, Executive Director
Peter Dolan, Treasurer
William Morrill, Counsel; datibbetts@annapolis.net
Ellery Sinclair, Secretary

BEYOND PESTICIDES

NATIONAL COALITION AGAINST THE MISUSE OF PESTICIDES (NCAMP)
701 E St., SE, Suite 200
Washington, DC 20003 United States
Phone: 202-543-5450 Fax: 202-543-4791
E-mail: info@beyondpesticides.org
Website: www.beyondpesticides.org

Founded: 1981
Membership: 1,001–10,000
Scope: National
Description: Nonprofit membership organization committed to assisting individuals, organizations, and communities with useful information on pesticides and their alternatives. NCAMP's information clearinghouse provides material on a wide range of both agricultural and urban issues concerning protection of children, workers' safety, food safety, lawn care safety, groundwater problems, and alternatives to pesticides, as well as legislation.
Publication(s): Bi-monthly newsletter, Pesticides and You Newsletter (Quarterly), Safety at Home: A Guide to the Hazards of Lawn and Garden Pesticides and Safer Ways to Manage Pests, Poison Poles: Their Toxic Trial and the Safer Alternatives, Beyond Pesticides/NCAMPs Technical Report (Monthly)

Keyword(s): Agriculture/Farming, Air Quality/Atmosphere, Executive/Legislative/Judicial Reform, Pollution (general), Public Health, Wildlife & Species

Contact(s):
Jay Feldman, Executive Director; 202-453-5450; info@beyondpesticides.org
Becky Crouse, Information Coordinator; bcrouse@beyondpesticides.org
John Kepner, Program Associate; jkepner@beyondpesticides.org
Toni Nunes, Special Projects Director; tnunes@beyondpesticides.org
Kagan Owens, Program Director; 202-545-5450; Fax: 202-543-4791; kowens@beyondpesticides.org
Meghan Taylor, Public Education Associate; mtaylor@beyondpesticides.org

BIG BEND NATURAL HISTORY ASSOCIATION

P.O. Box 196
Big Bend National Park, TX 79834 United States
Phone: 915-477-2236
E-mail: bbnha@nps.gov
Website: www.bigbendbookstore.org

Founded: 1956
Membership: 101–1,000
Scope: National
Description: A private nonprofit organization whose main objectives are to facilitate popular interpretation of the scenic, scientific and historical values of Big Bend, and to encourage research related to those values. To accomplish these goals, the association is authorized by the National Park Service to publish, print, or otherwise provide books, maps, and illustrative material on the Big Bend region and to sponsor a Big Bend seminar program.
Publication(s): Big Bend Paisano
Keyword(s): Agriculture/Farming, Public Lands/Greenspace, Wildlife & Species
Contact(s):
Mike Boren, Executive Director
Rob Dunagan, Chairman; 915-336-5274
Thomas Vandenberg, Editor

BILLFISH FOUNDATION, THE

2161 E Commercial Blvd. 2nd Fl.
Ft. Lauderdale, FL 33308 United States
Phone: 954-938-0150 Fax: 954-938-5311
E-mail: tbf@billfish.org
Website: www.billfish.org

Founded: N/A
Membership: 10,001–100,000
Scope: International
Description: The Billfish Foundation is a nonprofit organization dedicated to the conservation of billfish worldwide through scientific research, education, and advocacy. Through scientific, economic and conservation decisions provided through research, TBF strives for sound and constructive measures to recover overfished stocks.
Publication(s): Billfish, Spearfish, TBF News, Tag & Brag - Quarterly Newsletter
Keyword(s): Recreation/Ecotourism, Wildlife & Species
Contact(s):
Ellen Peel, President
Paxson Offield, Treasurer of Trustees
Hal Prewitt, Vice Chairman
Winthrop Rockefeller, Chairman of Trustees
Ralph Vicente, Vice Chairman of Trustees

BIO-INTEGRAL RESOURCE CENTER

P.O. Box 7414
Berkeley, CA 94707 United States
Phone: 510-524-2567 Fax: 510-524-1758
E-mail: birc@igc.org
Website: www.birc.org

Founded: 1979
Membership: 1,001–10,000
Scope: International
Description: A nonprofit educational organization dedicated to providing information on least-toxic pest control.
Publication(s): Common Sense Pest Control Quarterly, Least-toxic Pest Management
Keyword(s): Agriculture/Farming, Pollution (general), Reduce/Reuse/Recycle, Wildlife & Species
Contact(s):
William Quarles, Executive Director, Managing Editor of Publications
Jennifer Bates, Business Manager

BIOMASS USERS NETWORK - CENTROAMERICA

573-2050 San Pedro Montes de Oca
San Jose, Costa Rica
Phone: 506-283-8835

Founded: 1985
Scope: International
Description: To advance rural economic development in Third World countries in an environmentally sound manner, through the innovative production and efficient use of biomass resources.
Publication(s): Network News
Keyword(s): Development/Developing Countries, Energy, Forests/Forestry, Land Issues, Wildlife & Species
Contact(s):
David Mazambani, Chairman

BIOSIS

2001 Market Street
Suite 700
Philadelphia, PA 19103 United States
Phone: 800-523-4806 Fax: 215-587-2016
E-mail: info@biosis.org
Website: www.biosis.org

Founded: N/A
Scope: Local, State, Regional, National, International
Description: Established in 1926, BIOSIS' mission is to facilitate understanding of the living world by helping researchers, educators, students and others to access information relevant to the life sciences. As the world's largest life sciences indexing and abstracting service, BIOSIS produces the BIOSIS Previews family of products, including Biological Abstracts, and jointly publishes Zoological Record with the Zoological Society of London.
Publication(s): Biosis Previews, Toxline
Keyword(s): Agriculture/Farming, Climate Change, Development/Developing Countries, Ecosystems (precious), Forests/Forestry, Oceans/Coasts/Beaches, Pollution (general), Population, Public Health, Water Habitats & Quality, Wildlife & Species
Contact(s):
Marisa Westcott, Director of Marketing; mwestcott@biosis.org

BIOSPHERE EXPEDITIONS

Sprat's Water
nr Carlton Colville
The Broads National Park
Suffolk, NR33 8BP United Kingdom
Phone: 0044-1502-583085 Fax: 0044-1502-587414
E-mail: info@biosphere-expeditions.org
Website: www.biosphere-expeditions.org

Founded: 1999
Membership: N/A
Scope: International
Description: Award-winning, non-profit wildlife conservation organisation with world-wide expeditions open to all. No special skills (biological or otherwise) required to join and no age limits whatsoever. You can join for anything from two weeks to several months and at least two-thirds of your expedition contribution will go directly into the conservation project. We always work with local scientists and people from the host country, teams are small and an expedition leader will be by your side.
Publication(s): Expedition reports
Keyword(s): Recreation/Ecotourism, Wildlife & Species
Contact(s):
Matthias Hammer, Dr.; 0044-1502-583085; Fax: 0044-1502-587414; info@biosphere-expeditions.org

BIRDLIFE INTERNATIONAL

Canada Nature Federation,1 Nicholas St., Ste. 606
Ottawa, KIN 7B7 Ontario Canada
Phone: 613-562-3447 Fax: 613-562-3371
E-mail: cnf@cnf.ca
Website: www.cnf.ca

Founded: N/A
Scope: National
Description: Protection of birds and their habitats in Canada, in their winter quarters in North and South America, and off Canada's coasts are among major concerns.
Publication(s): Nature Matters-Newsletter, Nature Canada
Keyword(s): Land Issues, Public Lands/Greenspace, Reduce/Reuse/Recycle, Wildlife & Species
Contact(s):
Michael Bradstreet, Contact; Bird Studies Canada, Box 160, Port Rowan, Ontario N0E 1M0; 519-586-3531; Fax: 519-586-3532
Caroline Schultz, Contact

BIRDS PROTECTION AND STUDY SOCIETY OF VOJVODINA

Drustvo za zastitu i proucavanje ptica Vojvodina
Radnicka 20, 21000 Novi Sad
Yugoslavia
21000 Novi Sad, 21000 Yugoslavia
Phone: 381-21-616344 Fax: 381-21-616252
E-mail: zzpsns@EUnet.yu

Founded: 1988
Membership: 1–100
Scope: Regional, National
Description: Birds Protection and Study Society of Vojvodina aims to conserve and protect birds and their habitats. With about 100 members, the society has conducted many research projects, one of the most recent being the survey of Serbian heronries in 1998 (when there were about 7,500 breeding pairs of herons and cormorants dispersed in about 60 heronries). Membership fee includes a free copy of annual journal Ciconia with papers and notes on birds and reports of rarities and interesting sightings.
Publication(s): Ciconia
Keyword(s): Wildlife & Species

BLUE GOOSE ALLIANCE

Blue Goose Alliance
2988 St. Johns Blvd.
Jacksonville Beach, FL 32250 United States
Phone: 904-241–1007
E-mail: nwf7cd@aol.com
Website: groups.yahoo.com/group/BGA-Bulletin

Founded: 2001
Scope: National
Description: The mission of the Blue Goose Alliance is to promote the establishment of the National Wildlife Refuge System as a separate agency within the Deparment of the Interior.

BLUEBIRDS ACROSS VERMONT PROJECT

255 Sherman Hollow Rd.
Huntington, VT 05462 United States
Phone: 802-434-3068

Founded: 1987
Scope: State
Description: A project of the Vermont Audubon Council and Green Mountain Audubon, Bluebirds Across Vermont (BAV) was formed to help restore native eastern bluebird populations. BAV promotes the proper placement of correctly-built nestboxes by informed citizens who monitor them throughout the nesting season and send the data to BAV for yearly compilation.
Contact(s):
Mark Labarr, Contact

BOONE AND CROCKETT CLUB

250 Station Dr.
Missoula, MT 59801 United States
Phone: 406-542-1888 Fax: 406-542-0784
E-mail: bcclub@boone-crockett.org
Website: www.boone-crockett.org

Founded: 1887
Membership: 101–1,000
Scope: National
Description: A 501 (c) (3) organization. Established by Theodore Roosevelt and other concerned sportsmen to promote hunting ethics, foster the concept of Fair Chase, and help establish wildlife conservation practices which led to the recovery of big game animals in North America. The Club documents the records of North American big game and exhibits its National Collection of Heads and Horns in Cody, WY.
Publication(s): Records of North American Big Game, Return of Royalty, Records of North American Whitetail Deer, An American Crusade for Wildlife, Records of North American Elk and Mule Deer
Keyword(s): Public Lands/Greenspace, Recreation/Ecotourism
Contact(s):
Earl Morgenorth, President
Robert Model, First Vice President
Thomas Price, Vice President
Jack Reneau, Director of North American Big Game Records; 406-542-1888
George Bettas, Executive Director; 406-542-1888
C. Byers, Records of North American Big Game Committee
Robert Hanson, Secretary
Joseph Ostervich, Treasurer

BOONE AND CROCKETT FOUNDATION

250 Station Dr.
Missoula, MT 59801 United States
Phone: 406-542-1888 Fax: 406-542-0784
E-mail: bcclub@boone-crockett.org
Website: www.boone-crockett.org

Founded: 1887
Scope: National
Description: The BCF owns and operates the 6,000 acre Theodore Roosevelt Memorial Ranch near Dupuyer, MT, as a working cattle ranch for research, education and demonstration. BCF supports natural resource conservation research, education, and demonstration primarily through the Boone and Crockett wildlife conservation program in conjunction with the University of Montana.
Publication(s): Fair Chase Magazine
Keyword(s): Development/Developing Countries, Recreation/Ecotourism, Reduce/Reuse/Recycle
Contact(s):
Earl Morgenroth, President

Lisa Flowers, Conservation Education Program Manager; 406-466-2078
John Rappold, TRMR Manager; 406-472-3380
Gilbert Adams, Secretary; 409-835-3000
George Bettas, Executive Director; 406-542-1888; bcclub@boone-crockett.org
Jack Thomas, Professor of Wildlife Conservation; 406-243-5566

BORDER ECOLOGY PROJECT (BEP)

Drawer CP
Bisbee, AZ 85603 United States
Phone: 520-432-7456 Fax: 520-432-7473
E-mail: bep@primenet.com
Website: www.borderep.org

Founded: 1983

Scope: National

Description: BEP advocates for solutions to environmental problems along the U.S. and Mexico border. Areas of focus include Right-to-Know, environmental pollution, international trade, mining, hazardous materials trucking, and bi-national environmental health issues including lupus.

Publication(s): Environmental Protection within the Mexican Mining Sector, Environmental and Health Conditions in the Interior of Mexico

Keyword(s): Air Quality/Atmosphere, Pollution (general), Reduce/Reuse/Recycle, Water Habitats & Quality

Contact(s):
Dick Kamp, Director
A. Hotaling, Coordinator

BOTANICAL CLUB OF WISCONSIN

c/o Wisconsin Academy of Science, Arts, and Letters,
1922 University Ave.
Madison, WI 53705 United States
Phone: 608-262-5489 Fax: 608-265-2993
Website: www.wisc.edu/botany/herbariun/dcwindex.html

Founded: 1969

Membership: 101–1,000

Scope: State, Regional

Description: Botanical Club of Wisconsin promotes preservation of Wisconsin's native plants and educates the public as to the value of plants. The Club also fosters research on plant biology and provides a means for fellowship and information exchange.

Publication(s): The Bulletin of the Botanical Club of Wisconsin, Wisconsin Flora

Keyword(s): Public Lands/Greenspace, Wildlife & Species

Contact(s):
Emmet Judziewicz, President; 715-346-4248; Emmet.Judziewicz@uwsp.edu
James Bennett, Vice President; 608-262-5489; Fax: 608-265-2993; jpbennet@facstaff.wisc.edu
Edward Glover, Treasurer; 608-437-4578; glover@oncology.wisc.edu

BOUNTY INFORMATION SERVICE

WILDLIFE BOUNTY INFORMATION SERVICE
4849 E. St. Charles Rd.
Columbia, MO 65201 United States
Phone: 573-474-6967
E-mail: Claun01@aol.com

Founded: 1966

Membership: 101–1,000

Scope: National, International

Description: Promotes the removal of bounties in North America by publishing Bounty News and studies of the bounty system and by coordinating activities and legal aspects.

Publication(s): A Guide to the Removal of Bounties, Bounty News, A History of Wildlife Bounties

Keyword(s): Wildlife & Species

Contact(s):
H. Laun, Director and Editor

BOY SCOUTS OF AMERICA

National Office, P.O. Box 152079
1325 West Walnut Hill Ln.
Irving, TX 75015-2079 United States
Phone: 972-580-2000 Fax: 972-580-2000
Website: www.bsa.scouting.org

Founded: 1910

Membership: 1,000,001 +

Scope: National

Description: Boy Scouts of America (BSA) was chartered by Congress in 1916 to provide an educational program for boys and young adults that builds character and develops responsibility, citizenship, and personal fitness. Community groups with goals compatible with BSA receive national charters to use the Scouting program as part of their own youth work.

Keyword(s): Recreation/Ecotourism

Contact(s):
Milton Ward, President
David Bates, Conservation Director
Raymond Blackwell, Regional Executive; P.O. Box 3085, Naperville, IL 60566-7085; 630-983-6730
Kenneth Connelly, Regional Executive of Northeast Region; P.O. Box 268, Jamesburg, NJ 08831-0268; 609-655-9600
John Cushman, Treasurer
Erik Nystrom, Regional Executive; P. O. Box 22019, Tempe, AZ 85285-2019
Francis Olmstead, Assistant Treasurer
Roy Williams, Chief Scout Executive

BRANDYWINE CONSERVANCY INC.

P.O. Box 141
Chadds Ford, PA 19317 United States
Phone: 610-388-2700 Fax: 610-388-1575
E-mail: enc@brandywine.org
Website: www.brandywineconservancy.org

Founded: 1967

Scope: Regional

Description: A nonprofit organization providing model land use and environmental regulations for Pennsylvania municipalities. Brandywine Conservancy provides land, water resources and historic site conservation and management assistance to landowners and conservation organizations, primarily in southeastern Pennsylvania and northern Delaware.

Publication(s): Catalyst, Environmental Management Handbook, Environmental Currents

Keyword(s): Land Issues, Pollution (general), Water Habitats & Quality

Contact(s):
James Duff, Executive Director
Kathryn Saterson, Director of Environmental Management Center
Wesley Horner, Associate Director of Municipal Assistance, Environmental Management
David Shields, Associate of Director of Land Stewardship, Environmental Management
John Snook, Associate Director of Design, Environmental Management Center
Halsey Spruance, Public Relations
George Weymouth, Chairman

BRITISH COLUMBIA FIELD ORNITHOLOGISTS

P.O. Box 8059
Victoria, V8W 3R7 British Columbia Canada
Website: birding.bc.ca/bcfo/

Founded: 1991

Scope: State

Description: To promote the study and enjoyment of birds in British Columbia; to disseminate knowledge and appreciation of birds by means of publications; to foster cooperation between amateur and professional ornithologists; and to promote conservation of birds and their habitats.

Publication(s): British Columbia Birds (journal), BC Birding (newsletter)

Keyword(s): Wildlife & Species

Contact(s):
Tony Greenfield, President; P.O. Box 319, Sechelt, British Columbia V0N 3A0; 250-885-5539
Bryan Gates, Vice President; 3085 Uplands Rd., Victoria, British Columbia V8R 6B3; 250-598-7789
Marilyn Buhler, Editor; 1132 Loenholm Rd., Victoria, British Columbia V8Z 2Z6; 250-744-2521
Andy Buhler, Editor; 1132 Loenholm Rd., Victoria, British Columbia V8Z 2Z6; 250-744-2521
Jim Fliczuck, Treasurer; 3614-1507 Queensbury Ave., Victoria, British Columbia V8P 5M5; 250-656-8066
Martin McNicholl, Editor; 4735 Canada Way, Burnaby, British Columbia V5G 1L3; 250-294-9333

BRITISH COLUMBIA WATERFOWL SOCIETY, THE

5191 Robertson Rd.
Delta, V4K 3N2 British Columbia Canada
Phone: 604-946-6980 Fax: 604-946-6980

Founded: N/A
Membership: 1,001–10,000
Scope: State

Description: The organization was set in 1963 on federal land leased for 30 years to be opened to the public as a bird viewing area at the mouth of the Fraser River, which supports one of the largest wintering populations of waterfowl in Canada. The organization attempts to promote awareness of all parts of the environment.

Publication(s): Marsh Notes, BirdCheck List

Contact(s):
Jack Bates, President
John Ireland, Manager
James Morrison, Treasurer

BROOKS BIRD CLUB INC., THE

P.O. Box 4077
Wheeling, WV 26003 United States
Phone: 304-233-3174
Website: www.brooksbirdclub.org

Founded: 1932
Scope: National

Description: A nonprofit organization formed to encourage the study and conservation of birds and other phases of natural history. Members in thirty-eight states, Canada, and eight foreign countries. Named in honor of A.B. Brooks, naturalist.

Publication(s): Mail Bag, The, Redstart, The

Keyword(s): Public Lands/Greenspace, Wildlife & Species

Contact(s):
Fred McCullough, President; P.O. Box 4077, Wheeling, WV 26003
Scott Emrick, Treasurer; P.O. Box 4077, Wheeling, WV 26003
Carl Slater, Administrator; P.O. Box 4077, Wheeling, WV 26003

BROTHERHOOD OF THE JUNGLE COCK, INC., THE

P.O. Box 576
Glen Burnie, MD 21061 United States
Phone: 410-761-7727 Fax: 410-553-0575

Founded: N/A
Membership: 1,001–10,000
Scope: National

Description: Seeks to teach youth the true meaning of conservation. Primary interest is the preservation of American game fishes, placing great emphasis on adult responsibility of personal instruction along those lines.

Keyword(s): Oceans/Coasts/Beaches, Wildlife & Species

Contact(s):
William Simms, President
Bosley Wright, Executive Vice President
M. Day, Treasurer; 706 Orchard Way, Silver Spring, MD 20904
Edward Little, Secretary; 6623 Kenwood Ave., Baltimore, MD 21237; 401-682-4631

C

C.A.S.T. FOR KIDS FOUNDATION

296 Southwest 43rd Street
Renton, WA 98055 United States
Phone: 425-251-3214 Fax: 425-251-3272
E-mail: castforkids@msn.com
Website: castforkids.org

Founded: 1991
Membership: N/A
Scope: National

Description: A national, non-profit organization that provides outdoor recreation opportunities and education to disabled and disadvantaged children through the sport of fishing.

Publication(s): Catch A Special Thrill

Newsletter

Keyword(s): Recreation/Ecotourism

Contact(s):
Patrick McBride, President; 1804 136th Place, N.E., #1, Redmond, WA 98005; 425-644-1446; Fax: 425-644-1921; office@gmsarch.com
Wayne Deason, Vice President; 786 Chimney Creek Road, Golden, CO 80401; 303-445-2781; Fax: 303-445-6464; wdeason@do.usbr.gov
Jim Owens, Executive Director; 425-251-3214; Fax: 425-251-3272; jowens@castforkids.org
Karen Megorden, Secretary/Treasurer; 4470 E. Columbia Road, Meridian, ID 83642; 208-378-5053; Fax: 208-378-5056; kmegorden@pn.usbr.gov

CADDO LAKE INSTITUTE, INC.

P.O. Box 2710
Aspen, CO 81612 United States
Phone: 970-925-2710 Fax: 970-923-4245
E-mail: dks@sopris.net
Website: www.caddolakeinstitute.org

Founded: 1993
Scope: Local

Description: A non-profit organization whose purpose is environmental awareness. The program director is based near Caddo Lake, Texas. The director will coordinate college programs. Students are paid a stipend to collect samples and return to the student's laboratory for analysis; will also give seminars at secondary schools, all to promote environmental awareness.

Publication(s): See publication website

Keyword(s): Water Habitats & Quality

Contact(s):
Dwight Shellman, President; dks@sopris.net
Sara Kneipp, Education Director; sjkneipp@aol.com

CALCASIEU PARISH ANIMAL CONTROL AND PROTECTION DEPARTMENT

5500A Swift Plant Rd.
Lake Charles, LA 70615 United States
Phone: 337-439-8879 Fax: 337-437-3343
Website: cpac.cppj.net

Founded: N/A
Scope: State

Description: Regional branch of Elsa Wild Animal Appeal; concerned with wildlife matters, educational programs, liaison with other wildlife and governmental groups for the betterment of natural environment and wildlife protection; establishes local volunteer corps to implement programs in conjunction with the Calcasieu Parish Animal Control and Protection Department; and participates in Wildlife Rehabilitation Programs with Heck Haven and Westlake Bird Sanctuary.

Keyword(s): Reduce/Reuse/Recycle, Wildlife & Species

Contact(s):
David Marcantel, Operations Supervisor

CALIFORNIA ACADEMY OF SCIENCES

Golden Gate Park
San Francisco, CA 94118 United States
Phone: 415-221-5100 Fax: 415-750-7346
Website: www.calacademy.org

Founded: 1853

Scope: State

Description: The Academy of Sciences' goal is the exploration and interpretation of natural history. Maintains research collections and operates a museum-aquarium-planetarium complex to which one and one-half million visitors come each year.

Publication(s): Academy Newsletter, Occasional Papers, Proceedings, California Wild

Keyword(s): Oceans/Coasts/Beaches, Public Lands/Greenspace, Wildlife & Species

Contact(s):
John Pearse, President
Patrick Kociolek, Director
W. Bingham, Board of Trustees Chairman
Lewis Coleman, Vice Chairman
John Larson, Vice Chairman
Sandra Linder, Secretary

CALIFORNIA ACADEMY OF SCIENCES LIBRARY

Golden Gate Park
San Francisco, CA 94118 United States
Phone: 415-750-7102 Fax: 415-750-7106
E-mail: biodiv@calacademy.org
Website: www.calacademy.org/research/library/

Founded: 1991

Membership: N/A

Scope: International

Description: Non-circulating, closed-stack collection open to the public. Reference requests accepted by mail, phone, fax or e-mail. Interlibrary loan requests accepted. Library holdings included in OCLC, University of CA MELVYL on-line catalog and CA Union List of Periodicals.

Contact(s):
Diane T. Sands, Coordinator

CALIFORNIA ASSOCIATION OF RESOURCE CONSERVATION DISTRICTS

3823 V Street
Suite 3
Sacramento, CA 95817 United States
Phone: 916-457-7904 Fax: 916-457-7934
E-mail: staff@carcd.org
Website: www.carcd.org

Founded: 1945

Membership: 101–1,000

Scope: State

Description: CARCD's mission is to enhance Resource Conservation Districts' effectiveness.

Publication(s): CARCD Newsline, Conservation Express, CCP News

Contact(s):
John Schramel, President; 681 Main St., Greenville, CA 95947; 530-284-7954; Fax: 530-284-6211
Nadine Scott, Vice President; 550 Hoover Street, Oceanside, CA 92054; 760-757-6685
Tom Wehri, Executive Director; 801 K St. Suite 1318, Sacramento, CA 95814; 916-447-7237; Fax: 916-447-2532; carcd@ns.net
Robert Beegle, Secretary-Treasurer; 3911 Yellowstone Ln., El Dorado, CA 95762; 916-852-6691; Fax: 916-852-6693
Donna Thomas, Past President; 760-377-4525; Fax: 760-377-4525

CALIFORNIA B.A.S.S. CHAPTER FEDERATION

President
21517 Appaloosa Court
Canyon Lake, CA 92587 United States
Phone: 909-244-6320
E-mail: fsh4bss@dellepro.com
Website: www.californiabass.org

Founded: 1989

Membership: 1,001–10,000

Scope: State

Description: An organization of Bassmaster chapters, affiliated with the Bass Anglers Sportsman Society, organized to fight pollution, assist state and national conservation agencies in their efforts, and teach the young people of our country good conservation practice. Dedicated to the realistic conservation of our water resources.

Contact(s):
Gary Bradford, President; 909-244-6320; fsh4bss@dellepro.com

CALIFORNIA INSTITUTE OF PUBLIC AFFAIRS

INTERENVIRONMENT
P.O. Box 189040
Sacramento, CA 95818 United States
Phone: 916-442-2472 Fax: 916-442-2478
E-mail: cipa@cipahq.org
Website: www.cipahq.org

Founded: 1969

Membership: N/A

Scope: State, National, International

Description: Works to improve policy-making on complex environmental issues in California and internationally through convening, research, publishing, and advice. Current major activities are the World Directory of Environmental Organizations, now online at www.InterEnvironment.org; and an international project on major cities and protected areas, both in cooperation with IUCN - The World Conservation Union.

Publication(s): California Environmental Directory

Contact(s):
Ted Trzyna, President
Michael Eaton, Senior Associate
Monty Hempel, Senior Associate
Daniel Mazmanian, Senior Associate
John Zierold, Senior Associate
Julie Didion, Program Coordinator

CALIFORNIA NATIVE PLANT SOCIETY, THE

1722 J St., Suite 17
Sacramento, CA 95814 United States
Phone: 916-447-2677 Fax: 916-447-2727
E-mail: cnps@cnps.org
Website: www.cnps.org

Founded: 1965

Membership: 1,001–10,000

Scope: State

Description: A statewide nonprofit organization of amateurs and professionals with a common interest in California's native plants. The society, working through its local chapters, seeks to increase understanding of California's native flora and to preserve the rich resource for future generations. Membership is open to all.

Publication(s): Fremontia, Plant Communities, Flora of San Bruno Mountain, Inventory of Rare and Endangered Vascula,

California's Changing Landscape, Terrestrial Vegetation of California, Conservation & Management of Rare and Endangered Plants

Keyword(s): Land Issues, Water Habitats & Quality, Wildlife & Species

Contact(s):

Sue Britting, President; 530-333-2679; Fax: 530-333-9178; britting@innercite.com
Jim Bishop, Vice President for Administration; 530-538-6761; cjbishop@cnc.net
Lorrae Fuentes, Vice President for Education; 909-625-8767; Fax: 909-626-7670; lorrae.fuentes@cgu.edu

CALIFORNIA TRAPPERS ASSOCIATION

Attn: Executive Secretary, 99 Poinsettia Gardens Dr.
Ventura, CA 93004 United States
Phone: 805-647-8903 Fax: 805-647-9970

Founded: 1969
Membership: 1,001–10,000
Scope: State

Description: Dedicated to the encouragement of conservation, enhancement, and scientific management of all our natural resources, especially furbearing mammals. Promotes state and federal wildlife projects through volunteer skilled labor and financial contributions. Gives $500 to $1,000 grants each year to college students studying furbearing mammals.

Publication(s): Fur Facts, Legislative Alerts

Keyword(s): Ethics/Environmental Justice, Land Issues, Reduce/Reuse/Recycle, Water Habitats & Quality, Wildlife & Species

Contact(s):

Keith Carly, President; P.O. Box 73, Elk Creek, CA 95939; 916-968-5038
John Clark, Vice President; 907 Holmes Flat Rd., Red Crest, CA 95569; 707-722-4259
Tom Laustalot, Treasurer; 18907 Indian Creek Rd., Fort Jones, CA 96032; 916-468-2228
Kathy Lynch, Lobbyist; 916-537-7169
Donald Stehsel, Executive Secretary

CALIFORNIA TROUT, INC.

870 Market St., Suite 1185
San Francisco, CA 94102 United States
Phone: 415-392-8887 Fax: 415-392-8895
E-mail: info@caltrout.org
Website: www.caltrout.org

Founded: 1970
Membership: 1,001–10,000
Scope: State

Description: Statewide organization of anglers dedicated to protection and restoration of wild trout, native steelhead, and their waters in California, and to the creation of high-quality angling adventures for the public to enjoy. Motto: "Keeper of the Streams."

Publication(s): Streamkeepers Log

Keyword(s): Energy, Forests/Forestry, Recreation/Ecotourism, Water Habitats & Quality, Wildlife & Species

Contact(s):

Mark Bergstrom, Executive Director; bergstrom@caltrout.org
Katrina Kuznick, Office Manager
Jeff Eshbaugh, Streamkeeper Coordinator

CALIFORNIA WATERFOWL ASSOCIATION

4630 Northgate Blvd., Suite 150
Sacramento, CA 95834 United States
Phone: 916-648-1406 Fax: 916-648-1665
Website: www.calwaterfowl.org

Founded: 1945
Membership: 10,001–100,000
Scope: State

Description: A statewide nonprofit, public benefit corporation, whose principal objectives are the conservation, protection, and enhancement of California's waterfowl resources and the waterfowling opportunities which they provide. The association directly represents the interests of over 13,000 sportsmen and conservationists throughout the state and indirectly represents the interests of other Californians who are concerned with and benefit from these unique resources.

Publication(s): California Waterfowl Magazine, Sprig Tales Newsletter

Keyword(s): Recreation/Ecotourism, Water Habitats & Quality, Wildlife & Species

Contact(s):

Robert McLandress, President; 916-648-1406; Fax: 916-648-1665; cwa@calwaterfowl.org
Mark Bergstrom, Director of Development; 916-648-1406; Fax: 916-648-1665; mark_bergstrom@calwaterfowl.org
Becky Easter, Director of Communications/Education; 916-648-1406; Fax: 916-648-1665; cwacomm@calwaterfowl.org
Bill Gaines, Director of Government Affairs; 916-648-1406; Fax: 916-648-1665; cwa_gov@calwaterfowl.org
Greg Yarris, Director of Waterfowl and Wetland Programs; 916-648-1406; Fax: 916-648-1665; cwawwp@calwaterfowl.org
Rob Plath, Chairman of the Board; 916-648-1406; Fax: 916-648-1665; cwa@calwaterfowl.org

CALIFORNIA WILD HERITAGE CAMPAIGN

915 20th Street
Sacramento, CA 95814 United States
Phone: 916-442-3155 Fax: 916-442-3396
E-mail: info@californiawild.org
Website: www.californiawild.org

Founded: 1997
Membership: 1,001–10,000
Scope: State

Description: The California Wild Heritage Campaign works to save California's last wild places.

Publication(s): Headwaters

Keyword(s): Ecosystems (precious), Forests/Forestry, Land Issues, Public Lands/Greenspace, Reduce/Reuse/Recycle, Water Habitats & Quality, Wildlife & Species

Contact(s):

Pamela Flick, Administrative Director; ext. 207
Jean Munoz, Communications Director; ext. 216
Traci Van Thull, Outreach Director; ext. 222
Craig Thomas, Forest Defense Coordinator; cthomas@innercite.com

CALIFORNIA WILDERNESS COALITION

2655 Portage Bay East #5
Davis, CA 95616 United States
Phone: 530-758-0380 Fax: 530-758-0382
E-mail: info@calwild.org
Website: www.calwild.org

Founded: 1976
Membership: 1,001–10,000
Scope: Local, State, Regional

Description: Our mission is to defend the landscapes that make California unique, provide a home to our wildlife, and preserve a place for spiritual renewal. We protect wilderness for its own sake, for ourselves, and for generations yet to come. We identify and protect the habitat necessary for the long-term survival of California's plants and animals. Since 1976, through advocacy and public education, we have enlisted the support of citizens and policy-makers in our efforts to preserve wildlands.

Publication(s): California's Last Wild Places, Missing Linkages, Off-Road to Ruin, Wilderness Record

Keyword(s): Agriculture/Farming, Ecosystems (precious), Forests/Forestry, Land Issues, Public Lands/Greenspace, Sprawl/Urban Planning, Wildlife & Species

CALIFORNIA WILDLIFE FEDERATION

P.O. Box 1527
Sacramento, CA 95812-1527 United States
Phone: 916-441-7563 Fax: 916-441-6490

Founded: 1952
Membership: 1,001–10,000
Scope: State
Description: A nonprofit statewide organization of councils, clubs, and individual members dedicated to promote the conservation, enhancement, scientific management, and wise use of all our natural resources.
Publication(s): California Wildlife
Keyword(s): Recreation/Ecotourism, Wildlife & Species
Contact(s):
Randy Walker, President; 4908 Sunset Dr., Fresno, CA 93704; 559-225-9003
Tim Leblanc, Vice President; P.O. Box 1343, Lake Arrowhead, CA 92352; 909-336-1048
Cheri Fuller, Editor; 916-441-7563; cheri_fuller@hotmail.com
C. Starr, Treasurer; 2105 Westhaven Ave., Bakersfield, CA 93304; 661-835-8337

CALIFORNIA, FOREST LANDOWNERS OF

980 9th St., Suite 1600
Sacramento, CA 95814 United States
Phone: 916-972-0273 Fax: 916-979-7892
Website: www.forestlandowners.org

Founded: 1974
Scope: Regional
Description: A statewide organization affiliated with the National Woodland Owners Association that provides educational programs, information services, and legislative representation to families who own forest land for long-term investment, recreational, and conservation reasons.
Publication(s): Forest Landowner
Keyword(s): Forests/Forestry
Contact(s):
Jim Little, President; 707-964-0690
Jim Chapin, 1st Vice President
John Williams, 2nd Vice President
Daniel Weldon, Executive Director and Editor
Ron Adams, Secretary

CALIFORNIANS FOR POPULATION STABILIZATION (CAPS)

1129 State Street
Suite 3-D
Santa Barbara, CA 93101 United States
Phone: 805-564-6626 Fax: 805-564-6636
E-mail: caps@cap-s.org
Website: www.cap-s.org

Founded: 1986
Membership: 1,001–10,000
Scope: State, National
Description: CAPS is a nonprofit membership organization dedicated to stabilizing population in California to protect and preserve the state's environment, ecology, and resources. CAPS believes overpopulation is the ultimate environmental threat. Activities include: public education, media campaigns, public policy research and advocacy, and grassroots organizing.
Publication(s): CAPS Data Reports, brochures and fact sheets, action alerts, CAPS Newsletters
Keyword(s): Air Quality/Atmosphere, Energy, Executive/Legislative/Judicial Reform, Land Issues, Population, Public Lands/Greenspace, Sprawl/Urban Planning
Contact(s):
Diana Hull, President of the Board
Jo Wideman, Director of Operations & Development; 805-564-6626; Fax: 805-564-6636; caps@cap-s.org

CAMP FIRE CLUB OF AMERICA

230 Campfire Rd.
Chappaqua, NY 10514 United States
Phone: 914-941-0199 Fax: 914-923-0977
E-mail: campfireclub@aol.com

Founded: 1897
Scope: National
Description: Works to preserve forests and woodland; to protect and conserve the wildlife of our country; and to sponsor and support all reasonable measures to the end that present and future generations may continue to enjoy advantages and benefits of life outdoors.
Publication(s): Backlog, The
Keyword(s): Forests/Forestry, Recreation/Ecotourism
Contact(s):
Lewis Jordan, President
David Petzal, Publications Chairman
Thomas Quirk, Secretary of Committee on Conservation of Forests and Wildlife
Leonard Vallender, Chairman of Committee on Conservation of Forests and Wildlife

CAMP FIRE CONSERVATION FUND

230 Campfire Rd.
Chappaqua, NY 10514 United States
Phone: 914-941-9681

Founded: 1977
Scope: National
Description: A tax-exempt membership organization, dedicated to the preservation of wildlife and its habitat to coordinate the efforts of sportsmen's and conservation organizations; to inform the general public and governmental agencies with regard to intelligent use of our natural resources; and to support and promote conservation research.
Keyword(s): Wildlife & Species
Contact(s):
George Lamb, President
Henry Ayres, Secretary
Mottell Peek, Treasurer

CAMP FIRE USA

4601 Madison Ave.
Kansas City, MO 64112-1278 United States
Phone: 816-756-1950 Fax: 816-756-0258
E-mail: info@campfire.usa.org
Website: www.campfireusa.org

Founded: 1910
Membership: 500,001–1,000,000
Scope: National
Description: Open to preschoolers to teens, without regard to race, creed, ethnic origin, sex, or income level. Provides a program of informal education that focuses on developing skills in interpersonal relationships, decision-making, leadership, creativity, citizenship, community service, and individual growth.
Keyword(s): Air Quality/Atmosphere, Public Health, Recreation/Ecotourism, Wildlife & Species
Contact(s):
Judy O'Connor, National President
Stewart Smith, National Executive Director and CEO

CANADA GOOSE PROJECT

11576 Morrison Street
Valley Village, CA 91601 United States
Phone: 818-769-1521, ext. 1
E-mail: canadagooseproj@aol.com
Website: canadagooseproject.org

Founded: 1989
Membership: 101–1,000
Scope: Local, State, Regional, National, International

Description: The Mission of the Canada Goose Project is to protect and conserve the Canada Geese and other migratory waterfowl using the Pacific Flyway, through habitat preservation, data collection, public education and through collaboration with other interested agencies and organizations.

Keyword(s): Ecosystems (precious), Land Issues, Public Lands/Greenspace, Sprawl/Urban Planning, Water Habitats & Quality, Wildlife & Species

CANADIAN ARCTIC RESOURCE COMMITTEE, INC.

7 Hinton Ave. N., Suite 200
Ottawa, K1Y 4P1 Ontario Canada
Phone: 613-759-4284 Fax: 613-722-3318
E-mail: info@carc.org
Website: www.carc.org

Founded: 1971
Membership: 1,001–10,000
Scope: International

Description: To ensure that important social, environmental, and economic ramifications of northern development are studied and analyzed before major decisions relating to northern Canada are made; to exchange information and viewpoints among the public, government, and industry; to develop better perspectives on options available; and to inform the public.

Publication(s): List of books on request, Northern Perspectives Member's Update, See publications on website

Keyword(s): Air Quality/Atmosphere, Ecosystems (precious), Reduce/Reuse/Recycle, Wildlife & Species

Contact(s):
Karen Wristen, Executive Director; kwristen@carc.org
Melissa Douglas, Information Officer; 613-759-4284, ext. 247; mdouglas@carc.org

CANADIAN COOPERATIVE WILDLIFE HEALTH CENTRE

Dept. of Veterinary Pathology, WCVM
Univ. of Saskatchewan
52 Campus Dr.
Saskatoon, S7N 5B4 Saskatchewan Canada
Phone: 306-966-5099 Fax: 306-966-7439
E-mail: ccwhc@sask.usask.ca

Founded: 1992
Scope: National

Description: The Canadian Cooperative Wildlife Health Centre is a national organization that provides diagnosis of disease, investigation of disease outbreaks, information, education, and consultation to wildlife managers, veterinarians, and members of the public on matters pertaining to the health of free-living wild animals in Canada.

Publication(s): Bulletin du Centre de la Sante de la Faune, Directory of Wildlife Health Expertise, Wildlife Disease Investigation Manual, Wildlife Health Centre Newsletter

Keyword(s): Wildlife & Species

Contact(s):
F. Leighton, Co-Director; 306-966-7281
G. Wobeser, Co-Director; 306-966-7310
I. Barker, Contact for Ontario Region; 519-823-8800
Trent Bollinger, Contact for West and North Region; 306-966-5099
Pierre Yves Daoust, Contact for Atlantic Region; 902-566-0667
Daniel Martineau, Contact for Quebec Region; 514-773-8521

CANADIAN ENVIRONMENTAL LAW ASSOCIATION

517 College St.
Suite 401
Toronto, M6G 4A2 Ontario Canada
Phone: 416-960-2284 Fax: 416-960-9392
E-mail: cela@web.ca
Website: www.cela.ca

Founded: 1970
Scope: National

Description: Nonprofit, independent, public-interest legal group formed to use current environmental laws to protect the environment, and to promote better environmental legislation throughout Canada.

Publication(s): Intervenor, The, Newsletter

Contact(s):
Paul Muldoon, Executive Director; mschanel@lao.on.ca
Michelle Swenarchuk, Director of International Programs; muldoonp@loa.on.ca
Kathy Cooper, Researcher; cela@web.ca
Richard Lindgren, Counsel; r.lindgren@sympatico.ca
Theresa Mclenaghan, Counsel; cela@web.ca
Lisa McShane, Librarian; r.lindgren@sympatico.ca
Sarah Miller, Coordinator; mcclenat@lao.on.ca
Ramani Nadarajah, Counsel; millers@lao.on.ca

CANADIAN FEDERATION OF HUMANE SOCIETIES

30 Concourse Gate, Suite 102
Nepean, K2E 7V7 Ontario Canada
Phone: 613-224-8072 Fax: 613-723-0252
E-mail: info@cfhs.ca
Website: www.cfhs.ca

Founded: 1957
Membership: 101–1,000
Scope: National

Description: CFHS is a national body comprised of animal welfare organizations and individuals whose purpose is to promote compassion and humane treatment for all animals.

Publication(s): Animal Welfare in Focus, The Humane Educator, Publications available on website

Keyword(s): Agriculture/Farming, Wildlife & Species

Contact(s):
J. Ripley, President
Robert Van Tongerloo, Executive Director
Shelagh MacDonald, Program Director; 613-224-8072; Fax: 613-723-0252; shelaghm@cfhs.ca

CANADIAN FORESTRY ASSOCIATION

185 Somerset St., W., Suite 203
Ottawa, K2P 0J2 Ontario Canada
Phone: 613-232-1815 Fax: 613-232-4210
E-mail: cfa@canadianforestry.com
Website: www.canadianforestry.com

Founded: 1900
Scope: National

Description: The Canadian Forestry Association is Canada's oldest conservation organization. It is nongovernmental and nonindustrial. Its purpose is to develop public understanding and cooperation in the wise use, conservation, and sustainable development of Canada's forests and related resources of land, water, and wildlife.

Publication(s): Smokey Bear Products Catalogue, Proceedings of National Forest Congress, Forest Forum, National Forest Week Teaching Guide, Proceedings: Canadian Urban Forests Conference, National Forest Education Resources Catalogue

Keyword(s): Forests/Forestry

Contact(s):
Barry Waito, President
David Lemkay, General Manager; 613-232-1815; Fax: 613-232-4210; lemkayd@canadianforestry.com
Sheila Rust, Office Administrator; 613-232-1815; Fax: 613-232-4210; rusts@canadianforestry.com
Susan Gesner, Immediate Past President

CANADIAN INSTITUTE FOR ENVIRONMENTAL LAW AND POLICY (CIELAP)

517 College St., Suite 400
Toronto, M6G 4A2 Ontario Canada
Phone: 416-923-3529 Fax: 416-923-5949
E-mail: cielap@cielap.org
Website: www.cielap.org

Founded: 1970
Scope: National
Description: CIELAP is an independent, not-for-profit research and education institute providing environmental law and policy analysis. CIELAP provides leadership in the development of environmental law and policy which promotes the public interest and the principles of sustainability, including the protection of the health and well-being of present and future generations, and of the natural environment.
Publication(s): A Carbon Dioxide Strategy for Ontario: A Discussion Paper, Environment on Trial: A Guide to Ontario Environmental Law and Policy, Hazardous Waste Management in Ontario: A Report and Recommendation, Ontario's Environment and the "Common Sense Revolution"
Contact(s):
David Powell, President
Anne Mitchell, Executive Director
Murray Klippenstein, Secretary and Treasurer

CANADIAN INSTITUTE OF FORESTRY / INSTITUTE FORESTIER DU CANADA

151 Slater St., Suite 606
Ottawa, K1P 5H3 Ontario Canada
Phone: 613-234-2242 Fax: 613-234-6181
E-mail: cif@cif-ifc.org
Website: www.cif-ifc.org

Founded: 1908
Membership: 1,001–10,000
Scope: Local, Regional, National
Description: Our mission is to advance the stewardship of Canada's forest resources through leadership, professional competence and public awareness. Our membership includes foresters, forest technicians, academics, scientists and others with a professional interest in Forestry. CIF/IFC represents the largest professional voice for forestry in Canada.
Publication(s): The Forestry Chronicle
Keyword(s): Forests/Forestry
Contact(s):
Roxanne Comeau, Executive Director; 151 Slater St., Suite 606, Ottawa, Ontario K1P 5H3; 613-234-2242; Fax: 613-234-6181; cif@cif-ifc.org

CANADIAN NATIONAL SPORTSMENS SHOWS

703 Evans Ave., Suite 202
Toronto, M9C 5E9 Ontario Canada
Phone: 416-695-0311 Fax: 416-695-0381
E-mail: info@sportshows.ca
Website: www.sportshows.ca

Founded: 1948
Membership: 1–100
Scope: National
Description: A national corporation presenting outdoor shows and events. Products relate to fishing, hiking, camping, boating, skiing, and the consumer shows are produced from Vancouver to Quebec City. All net proceeds are distributed to projects which encourage Canadians to appreciate, enjoy, and protect Canada's outdoor heritage.
Keyword(s): Recreation/Ecotourism
Contact(s):
Walter Oster, President; ext. 208
B. Meadows, Executive Assistant

CANADIAN NATURE FEDERATION

1 Nicholas St., Suite 606
Ottawa, K1N 7B7 Ontario Canada
Phone: 613-562-3447 Fax: 613-562-3371
Website: www.cnf.ca

Founded: 1971
Membership: 1–100
Scope: National
Description: Canada's national naturalists' organization promotes protection of nature, its diversity and the processes that sustain it. The Federation was formed from the Canadian Audubon Society, the CNF represents over 150 affiliated conservation groups and 40,000 individual supporters across the country.
Publication(s): Nature Canada Magazine, Nature Matters
Contact(s):
Jackie Krindle, President
Julie Gelfand, Executive Director; 613-562-3447
Caroline Schultz, Director of Conservation & Affiliate Development
Barbara Stevenson, Editor

CANADIAN PARKS AND WILDERNESS SOCIETY

880 Wellington St., Suite 506
Ottawa, K1R 6K7 Ontario Canada
Phone: 613-569-7226 Fax: 613-569-7098
E-mail: info@cpaws.org
Website: www.cpaws.org

Founded: 1963
Membership: 10,001–100,000
Scope: National
Description: A national, nonprofit advocacy organization dedicated to the protection of wilderness areas and the preservation and proper stewardship of Canada's national and provincial parks.
Publication(s): Wilderness Activist, The
Keyword(s): Land Issues, Public Lands/Greenspace
Contact(s):
David Thomson, President
Stephen Hazell, Executive Director; shazell@cpaws.org
Clayton Forrest, Manager of Membership Services

CANADIAN SOCIETY OF ENVIRONMENTAL BIOLOGISTS

P.O. Box 962, Station F
Toronto, M4Y 2N9 Ontario Canada
E-mail: cseb@freenet.edmonton.ab.ca
Website: freenet.edmonton.ab.ca

Founded: 1959
Scope: National
Description: A Canada-wide society of environmental biologists whose primary goals are: the conservation of the natural resources of Canada; the prudent management of these resources so as to minimize adverse environmental effects; the interchange of ideas among environmental biologists; and maintaining high professional standards in education, research, and management related to natural resources and the environment.
Publication(s): Canadian Society of Environmental Biologists
Keyword(s): Wildlife & Species
Contact(s):
Patrick Stewart, President; 902-798-4022; Fax: 902-798-4022; enviroco@ns.sympatico.ca

CANADIAN WILDLIFE FEDERATION

350 Michael Cowpland Dr.
Kanata, K2m 2W1 Ontario Canada
Phone: 613-721-2286 Fax: 613-271-9591
E-mail: info@cwf-fcf.org
Website: www.cwf-fcf.org

Founded: 1961

Membership: 100,001–500,000
Scope: National
Description: To foster understanding of natural processes so that people may live in harmony with the land and its resources for the long-term benefit and enrichment of society; to maintain a substantial program of information and education based on ecological principles; and to conduct or sponsor research and scientific investigation.
Publication(s): Canadian Wildlife, Wildlife Update, You Can Do It, Biosphere, Your Big Backyard, Wild Magazine
Contact(s):
Derek Stanley, President
Bob Barton, 1st Vice President
Pat Doyle, 3rd Vice President
Nicholas Laurin, 2nd Vice President
Colin Maxwell, Executive Vice President
Nestor Romaniuk, Past President

CANON ENVIROTHON
P.O. Box 855
408 E. Main
League City, TX 77574-0855 United States
Phone: 800-825-5547, ext. 16 Fax: 281-332-5259
E-mail: kay-asher@nacdnet.org
Website: www.envirothon.org
Founded: 1989
Membership: 1–100
Scope: Local, State, Regional, National, International
Description: Natural resource competition for high school students (grades 9-12). Core study areas are: aqautics, forestry, soils, wildlife and a fifth issue that comprises a current environmental issue that changes each year. Scholarship awards for 1st, 2nd and 3rd place winners at the international level.
Keyword(s): Agriculture/Farming, Forests/Forestry, Land Issues, Public Lands/Greenspace, Water Habitats & Quality, Wildlife & Species
Contact(s):
Clay Burns, Exec. Director; P.O. Box 23005, Jackson, MS 39225; 866-854-2898; Fax: 601-354-6628; clay-burns@nacdnet.org
Ellen Hutto, Manager; P.O. Box 855, 408 E. Main, League City, TX 77574; 800-825-5547, ext. 27; Fax: 281-332-5259; ellen-hutto@nacdnet.org
Kay Asher, Program Coordinator; P.O. Box 855, 408 E. Main, League City, TX 77574; 800-825-5547, ext. 16; Fax: 281-332-5259; kay-asher@nacdnet.org

CANVASBACK SOCIETY
P.O. Box 101
Gates Mills, OH 44040 United States
Founded: 1975
Scope: National
Description: A nonprofit, tax-exempt organization established to conserve, restore, and promote the increase of the canvasback species of duck on the North American continent.
Keyword(s): Reduce/Reuse/Recycle, Water Habitats & Quality, Wildlife & Species
Contact(s):
Oakley Andrews, President and Treasurer; 216-621-0200
Keith Russell, Chairman of the Board

CARIBBEAN CONSERVATION CORPORATION
4424 NW 13 St. Suite 8A1
Gainesville, FL 32609 United States
Phone: 352-373-6441 Fax: 352-375-2449
E-mail: ccc@cccturtle.org
Website: www.cccturtle.org
Founded: 1959
Membership: 1,001–10,000
Scope: International
Description: A nonprofit international membership organization founded in 1959 to support research and conservation of marine turtles in the Caribbean and throughout the world. In addition to conservation and education activities, CCC operates research programs in Tortuguero, Costa Rica—the site of the largest green turtle nesting colony in the Caribbean Sea.
Publication(s): Sea Turtle Educator's Guide
Keyword(s): Ecosystems (precious), Oceans/Coasts/Beaches, Pollution (general), Wildlife & Species
Contact(s):
Peggy Cavanaugh, President
David Godfrey, Executive Director
L. Clay, Chairman of the Board of Directors
Roger Stone, Secretary

CARIBBEAN NATURAL RESOURCES INSTITUTE
Fernandes Industrial Centre, Administration Building
Eastern Main Road
Laventille, W.I. Trinidad and Tobago
Phone: 868-626-6062 Fax: 868-626-1788
E-mail: canari@tstt.net.tt
Website: www.canari.org
Founded: 1986
Scope: Regional
Description: To create avenues for the equitable participation and effective collaboration of Caribbean communities and institutions in managing the use of natural resources critical to development.
Keyword(s): Development/Developing Countries, Forests/Forestry, Sprawl/Urban Planning, Water Habitats & Quality
Contact(s):
Vijay Krishnarayan, Managing Partner
Patricia Charles, Partnership Chairperson

CAROLINA BIRD CLUB, INC.
11 W. Jones St.
Raleigh, NC 27601-1029 United States
Phone: 919-733-7450, ext. 605 Fax: 919-715-6439
Website: www.carolinabirdclub.org
Founded: 1937
Scope: State
Description: A nonprofit, educational ornithological organization to promote bird study and conservation. Affiliated local chapters.
Publication(s): Chat, The, CBC Newsletter
Keyword(s): Wildlife & Species
Contact(s):
Len Pardue, President; 16th Circle, Asheville, NC 28801
Tullie Johnson, Headquarters Secretary; 919-733-7450
Judy Walker, Editor; 7639 Farm Gate Dr, Charlotte, NC 28215; jwalker@email.uncc.edu
Bob Wood, Editor; 2421 Owl Circle, West Columbia, NC 29169

CARRYING CAPACITY NETWORK
2000 P St., NW, Suite 310
Washington, DC 20036-5915 United States
Phone: 202-296-4548 Fax: 202-296-4609
E-mail: ccn@us.net
Website: www.carryingcapacity.org
Founded: 1989
Scope: National
Description: CCN is a nonprofit network which mobilizes many diverse individuals and groups to meet the critical challenges facing our nation with solid information and analysis, effective advocacy tools, and targeted solutions. CCN's action-oriented initiatives focus on achieving national revitalization, population stabilization, immigration limitation, resource conservation, and economic sustainability.

Publication(s): FOCUS, Network Bulletin
Keyword(s): Agriculture/Farming, Development/Developing Countries, Land Issues, Population, Reduce/Reuse/Recycle, Sprawl/Urban Planning
Contact(s):
David Durham, President of the Board
Virginia Abernethy, Vice President

CASCADIA RESEARCH

218 1/2 W. 4th Ave.
Olympia, WA 98501 United States
Website: www.cascadiaresearch.org

Founded: 1979
Scope: National
Description: A nonprofit, tax-exempt organization established to conduct scientific research and education related to marine mammals and birds. Primary funding for research projects comes from federal and state agencies and environmental groups.
Keyword(s): Oceans/Coasts/Beaches, Wildlife & Species
Contact(s):
Gretchen Steiger, President
James Cubbage, Vice President
John Calambokidis, Secretary and Treasurer

CATSKILL CENTER FOR CONSERVATION AND DEVELOPMENT, INC., THE

P. O. Box 504 Route 28
Arkville, NY 12406-0504 United States
Phone: 845-586-2611 Fax: 845-586-3044
E-mail: cccd@catskillcenter.org
Website: www.catskillcenter.org

Founded: 1969
Membership: 1,001–10,000
Scope: Regional
Description: The Catskill Center is a not-for-profit membership organization concerned with increasing public awareness of and involvement with issues affecting human communities and the natural environment of the Catskill Mountain Region. Its activities emphasize public education and regional planning advocacy, as well as development and support of programs relating to historic preservation, sustainable economic development and regional arts and culture in the Catskill Mountain Region of New York State.
Publication(s): Catskill Center News, Summary Guide to the Terms of the Waters, Successful Catskill Communities
Keyword(s): Agriculture/Farming, Development/Developing Countries, Land Issues, Recreation/Ecotourism, Sprawl/Urban Planning
Contact(s):
Geddy Sveikauskas, President
Philip Weinberg, Vice President
Helen Chase, Treasurer
H. Shostal, Secretary

CATSKILL FOREST ASSOCIATION

P.O. Box 336
Arkville, NY 12406 United States
Phone: 845-586-3054 Fax: 845-586-4071
E-mail: cfa@catskill.net
Website: www.catskillforest.org

Founded: 1982
Scope: Local
Description: Advocates of quality forest management practices to improve the health of the forest and prevent threats to the forest ecosystem. The Catskill Forest Association is an independent nonprofit regional organization that supports forest conservation efforts in New York's Catskill Mountains through the promotion of forest stewardship by landowners, foresters, timber harvesters, and the general public.
Publication(s): Tree Tubes & Forest Books, CFA News
Keyword(s): Development/Developing Countries, Energy, Forests/Forestry, Land Issues, Recreation/Ecotourism, Water Habitats & Quality, Wildlife & Species
Contact(s):
Joe Kraus, President
Robert Bishop, Vice President
Jim Waters, Executive Director
Tom Foulkrod, Natural Resource Specialist
Art Rotman, Secretary and Treasurer

CAVE RESEARCH FOUNDATION

Rick Toomey, President
Kartchner Caverns St Park
P.O. Box 1849
Benson, AZ 85602-1849 United States
Phone: 520-586-4138 Fax: 520-586-4113
E-mail: rtoomey@pr.state.az.us
Website: www.cave-research.org

Founded: 1957
Membership: 101–1,000
Scope: International
Description: The Foundation is a nonprofit organization that supports and promotes research, interpretation, and conservation activities in caves and karst areas. Permanent field operations are maintained within Mammoth Cave National Park, Carlsbad Caverns National Park, Sequoia and Kings Canyon National Parks, and Lava Beds National Monument. Approximately 800 joint-venturers participate in program.
Publication(s): CRF Newsletter, Annual Report, Cave Books
Keyword(s): Land Issues, Public Lands/Greenspace
Contact(s):
Pat Kambesis, President; P.O. Box 343, Winona, IL 61377-0343; 815-863-5184; kembesis@jun
Peter Bosted, Secretary; 2301 Sharon Rd, Menlo Park, CA 94025-680; 650-926-2319; bosted@slac.spanford.edu
Paul Cannaley, Treasurer; 317-862-5618
Paul Nelson, Editor; 2644 S Quarry Lane #D, Walnut, CA 91789-4067

CENTER FOR A NEW AMERICAN DREAM, THE

6930 Carroll Ave.#900
Takoma Park, MD 20912 United States
Phone: 301-891-3683 Fax: 301-891-3684
E-mail: newdream@newdream.org
Website: www.newdream.org

Founded: 1996
Scope: National
Description: The Center for a New American Dream helps individuals and institutions reduce and shift consumption to enhance quality of life and protect the natural environment.
Publication(s): Enough!, Simply the Holidays
Keyword(s): Climate Change, Energy, Forests/Forestry, Oceans/Coasts/Beaches, Population, Reduce/Reuse/Recycle, Transportation, Wildlife & Species
Contact(s):
Eric Brown, Communications Director; Eric@newdream.org
Nancy Smith, Director of Administration
Betsy Taylor, Executive Director; Betsy@newdream.org
Monique Tilford, Development Director; Monique@newdream.org
Sean Sheehan, National Outreach Manager; Sean@newdream.org

CENTER FOR A SUSTAINABLE COAST

221B Mallory St.
Saint Simons Island, GA 31522 United States
Phone: 912-638-3612 Fax: 912-638-3615
E-mail: susdev@gate.net
Website: www.sustainablecoast.com

Founded: 1997

Scope: Regional
Description: To promote sustainable use, protection, enhancement, and understanding of coastal Georgia's natural, economic, historic, and cultural resources through education, advocacy, technical assistance, and research.
Publication(s): Fisheries and Water Resource Permit Issues in the Lower Altamaha and Other Coastal Georgia Rivers, Surface Water Withdrawal and Coastal Economic Issues
Keyword(s): Water Habitats & Quality
Contact(s):
David Kyler, Executive Director

CENTER FOR BIOLOGICAL DIVERSITY

P.O. Box 710
Tucson, AZ 85702-0710 United States
Phone: 520-623-5252 Fax: 520-623-9797
E-mail: center@biologicaldiversity.org
Website: www.biologicaldiversity.org

Founded: 1989
Membership: 1,001–10,000
Scope: National
Description: The Center for Biological Diversity uses a combination of scientific research, public education, and strategic litigation to defend the forests, rivers and deserts of western North America.
Publication(s): White Papers, Biodiversity Activist
Keyword(s): Ecosystems (precious), Energy, Forests/Forestry, Land Issues, Oceans/Coasts/Beaches, Public Lands/Greenspace, Sprawl/Urban Planning, Water Habitats & Quality, Wildlife & Species
Contact(s):
Peter Galvin, Biologist; 510-841-0812
Todd Schulke, Ecosystem Restoration; 505-388-8799
Kieran Suckling, Executive Director; 520-623-5252, ext. 304; ksuckling@biologicaldiversity.org
David Hogan, Ecologist; 619-523-1498
Shane Jimerfield, IT; 520-623-5252, ext. 302
Monica Bond, Biologist; 909-659-6053, ext. 304
Curt Bradley, GIS; 520-623-5252, ext. 310
Brendan Cummings, Lawyer; 909-659-6053, ext. 301
Sonya Diehn, Office Manager; 520-623-5252, ext. 300
Michelle Harrington, Ecologist; 602-246-4170
Julie Miller, Membership; 520-623-5252, ext. 303
Jeff Miller, Watersheds; 510-841-0812
Brian Nowicki, Biologist; 928-774-6514
Daniel Patterson, Ecologist; 909-659-6053, ext. 306
Brent Plater, Lawyer; 510-841-0812
Michael Robinson, Wolf Campaign; 505-534-0360
Kassie Siegel, Lawyer; 909-659-6053
Tryg Sletteland, President; 520-623-5252, ext. 301
Martin Taylor, Research; 520-623-5252, ext. 307
Robin Silver, Conservation Chair; 602-246-4170; Fax: 602-249-2576; rsilver@biologicaldiversxity.org

CENTER FOR CHESAPEAKE COMMUNITIES

229 Hanover St. Suite 101
Annapolis, MD 21401 United States
Phone: 410-267-8595 Fax: 410-267-8597
E-mail: gallen@chesapeakecommunities.org
Website: www.chesapeakecommunities.org

Founded: 1997
Membership: N/A
Scope: Regional
Description: A nonprofit, independent organization dedicated to assisting local governments in the Chesapeake Bay watershed in their environmental restoration and protection initiatives.
Keyword(s): Air Quality/Atmosphere, Energy, Forests/Forestry, Land Issues, Pollution (general), Public Lands/Greenspace, Wildlife & Species
Contact(s):
Gary Allen, Executive Director

CENTER FOR ENVIRONMENT

1250 24th Street NW
Washington, DC 20037-1124 United States
Phone: 202-331-0664

Founded: 1985
Scope: National
Description: A nonprofit public interest organization dedicated to protecting the environment, enhancing the human ecology, and working to ensure the efficient use of natural resources. (CE)2's secondary mission is to provide opportunities for blacks and other minorities to participate in the environmental movement. Major areas of concern are: Air quality and pollution, water resources and pollution, energy, renewable resources, toxic substances, Africa and Third World environment, land use, and internships.
Publication(s): African American Environmentalist
Contact(s):
Norris McDonald, President; 202-879-3183
Jannie Pittman, Treasurer
Charles Stephenson, Chairman

CENTER FOR ENVIRONMENT AND POPULATION (CEP)

100 Market Street, Suite 204
Portsmouth, NH 03801 United States
Phone: 603-431-4066 Fax: 603-431-4063
E-mail: vmarkham@cepnet.org
Website: www.cepnet.org

Founded: 1999
Membership: N/A
Scope: Local, State, Regional, National, International
Description: The Center for Environment and Population (CEP) is a non-profit organization which works to strengthen the scientific basis of policies and public outreach on human population's environmental impacts in the United States and internationally.

CENTER FOR ENVIRONMENTAL EDUCATION

c/o Antioch New England, 40 Avon St.
Keene, NH 03431 United States
Phone: 603-355-3251 Fax: 603-357-0718
E-mail: cee@antiochne.edu
Website: www.schoolsgogreen.org

Founded: 1989
Membership: 1,001–10,000
Scope: National
Description: A nonprofit environmental education resource center housing one of the nation's most comprehensive collections of environmental education materials. The library has over 10,000 materials—books, videos, curricula and resources that can be accessed in person, by phone, fax, or through the website.
Publication(s): Grapevine Newsletter, Natures Course, Blueprint for a Green School
Contact(s):
David Sobel, Co-Executive Director
Cindy Thomashow, Co-Executive Director
Jayni Chase, Founder

CENTER FOR ENVIRONMENTAL HEALTH (CEH)

528 61st Street
Suite A
Oakland, CA 94609 United States
Phone: 510-594-9864 Fax: 510-594-9863
E-mail: ceh@cehca.org
Website: www.cehca.org

Founded: 1996
Membership: N/A
Scope: National
Description: CEH protects the public from environmental and consumer health hazards. We are committed to environmental

justice, reducing the use of toxic chemicals, supporting communities in their quest for a safer environment and corporate accountability. We change corporate behavior through education, litigation, and advocacy.

Keyword(s): Air Quality/Atmosphere, Ethics/Environmental Justice, Pollution (general), Public Health

Contact(s):

Michael Green, Executive Director; 510-594-9864, ext. 101; Fax: 510-594-9863; ceh@cehca.org
Alise Cappel, Research Director; 510-594-9864, ext. 102; Fax: 510-594-9863; ceh@cehca.org
Ignacio Gonzalez, Office Manager; 510-594-9864, ext. 103; Fax: 510-594-9863; ceh@cehca.org
Mamta Khanna, Health Care Without Harm Coordinator; 510-594-9864, ext. 109; Fax: 510-594-9863; ceh@cehca.org
Katherine Silberman, Public Policy Advocate; 510-594-9864, ext. 106; Fax: 510-594-9864; ceh@cehca.org

CENTER FOR ENVIRONMENTAL INFORMATION

55 St. Paul St.
Rochester, NY 14604-1314 United States
Phone: 716-262-2870 Fax: 716-262-4156
E-mail: ceiroch@aol.com
Website: www.rochesterenvironment.org

Founded: 1974
Membership: 101–1,000
Scope: National
Description: Provides on-call reference and referral and current awareness and educational services to scientists, educators, government agency staff, policymakers, business and industry managers and interested citizens. Sponsors conferences and seminars.
Publication(s): Proceedings of Annual Conferences
Keyword(s): Air Quality/Atmosphere, Climate Change, Energy

CENTER FOR ENVIRONMENTAL PHILOSOPHY

University of North Texas,
P.O. Box 310980
Denton, TX 76203-0980 United States
Phone: 940-565-2727 Fax: 940-565-4439
E-mail: ee@unt.edu
Website: www.cep.unt.edu

Founded: 1980
Membership: N/A
Scope: International
Description: A nonprofit, tax-deductible organization. The Center promotes research and instruction in environmental ethics and its application in environmental policy and decision-making. The Center works with governmental and environmental organizations on conferences, workshops, and other educational projects.
Publication(s): Environmental Ethics
Keyword(s): Ethics/Environmental Justice, Land Issues
Contact(s):

Eugene Hargrove, President, Editor and Publisher; Center for Environmental Philosophy, Univ. of North TX, P.O. Box 310980, Denton, TX 76203-0980; 940-565-2727; Fax: 940-565-4439; hargrove@unt.edu
J. Callicott, Vice President; Dept. of Philosophy, Univ. of North TX, P.O. Box 310920, Denton, TX 76203-0920; 940-565-2255; Fax: 940-565-4448; callicott@unt.edu
Jan Dickson, Executive Director; Center for Environmental Philosophy, Univ. of North TX, P.O. Box 310980, Denton, TX 76203-0980; 940-565-2727; Fax: 940-565-4439; jdickson@unt.edu
Max Oelschlaeger, Secretary and Treasurer; Dept. Humanities, Arts & Religion, Northern Arizona, P.O. Box 6031, Flagstaff, AZ 86011-6031; 520-523-0389; max.oelschlaeger@nau.edu

CENTER FOR ENVIRONMENTAL STUDY

528 Bridge St. NW, 1-C
Grand Rapids, MI 49504 United States
Phone: 616-988-2854 Fax: 616-988-2857
E-mail: ces1@cesmi.org
Website: www.cesmi.org

Founded: 1969
Membership: 101–1,000
Scope: Local, State, Regional
Description: The Center for Environmental Study, a 501C (3) organization, has served its community as an independent, science-based environmental education and research authority. It provides awareness programs on a variety of subjects ranging from water and air quality to tropical forest and Great Lakes issues.
Publication(s): Mahogany, The Great Lakes - An Interactive CD-ROM, Field Guide to Ecosystems and Habitats of the Great Lakes
Keyword(s): Air Quality/Atmosphere, Water Habitats & Quality
Contact(s):

Rick Sullivan, Executive Director
John Martin, Board Chair
Peter Wege, Founder

CENTER FOR HEALTH, ENVIRONMENT, AND JUSTICE

P.O. Box 6806
Falls Church, VA 22040-6806 United States
Phone: 703-237-2249 Fax: 703-237-8389
E-mail: chej@chej.org
Website: www.chej.org

Founded: 1981
Membership: 10,001–100,000
Scope: National
Description: CHEJ believes in the principle that people have the right to a clean and healthy environment regardless of their race or economic standing. The Center believes the most effective way to win environmental justice is from the bottom up through community organizing and empowerment. CHEJ seeks to help local citizens and organizations come together and take an organized, unified stand in order to hold industry and government accountable and work toward a healthy, environmentally sustainable future.
Publication(s): Dying from Dioxin, Everyone's Backyard, CHEJ's Catalog
Keyword(s): Ethics/Environmental Justice, Pollution (general), Population, Public Health
Contact(s):

Lois Gibbs, Executive Director
Jim Tramel, National Organizing Director; 703-237-2249, ext. 18; Fax: 703-237-8389; jttox@chej.org

CENTER FOR INDEPENDENT SOCIAL RESEARCH

Department of Environmental Sociology, 14 Vine
St. Petersburg, 197002 Russia
Phone: 812-234-50-18
E-mail: centre@indepsocres.org

Founded: 1994
Membership: 1–100
Scope: International
Description: Environmental nongovernmental management and accountability research collection of best sustainability practices in St. Petersburg region.
Contact(s):

Victor Voronkov, Director

CENTER FOR INTERNATIONAL ENVIRONMENTAL LAW (CIEL)

1367 Connecticut Ave., NW, Suite 300
Washington, DC 20036-1860 United States
Phone: 202-785-8700 Fax: 202-785-8701
E-mail: info@ciel.org
Website: www.ciel.org

Founded: 1989
Membership: 1–100
Scope: International
Description: The CIEL is a public interest environmental law organization founded to focus the energy and experience of the public interest environmental law movement on reforming international environmental law and institutions, and on forging stronger and more meaningful connection between the top down diplomatic approach of international law, and the bottom up participatory approach that has been the hallmark of the public interest environmental law movement.
Publication(s): International Environmental Law and Policy, Trade and the Environment, Biodiversity in the Seas
Keyword(s): Climate Change, Finance/Banking/Trade, Wildlife & Species
Contact(s):
Durwood Zaelke, President
David Hunter, Executive Director
Jeffrey Wanha, Director for Finance & Administration

CENTER FOR PLANT CONSERVATION

P.O. Box 299
St. Louis, MO 63166 United States
Phone: 314-577-9450 Fax: 314-577-9465
E-mail: cpc@mobot.org
Website: www.mobot.org/cpc

Founded: 1984
Membership: 1–100
Scope: National
Description: A national network of 33 botanical gardens and arboreta dedicated to the conservation and study of rare and endangered U.S. plants. The Center establishes conservation collections of endangered species in regional gardens and seed banks as a resource for conservation and research efforts: The National Collection of Endangered Plants.
Publication(s): Plant Conservation (newsletter), Guidelines for the Management of Orthodox Seeds, America's Vanishing Flora
Keyword(s): Land Issues, Wildlife & Species
Contact(s):
Kathryn Kennedy, Executive Director

CENTER FOR RESOURCE ECONOMICS/ISLAND PRESS

Island Press, 1718 Connecticut Ave., NW, Suite 300
Washington, DC 20009 United States
Phone: 202-232-7933 Fax: 202-234-1328
E-mail: info@islandpress.org
Website: www.islandpress.org

Founded: 1978
Membership: N/A
Scope: International
Description: The Center for Resource Economics, known as Island Press, is a nonprofit organization that develops, publishes, markets and disseminates books and other information products essential for solving local and global environmental problems.
Publication(s): Contact Island Press Book Distribution Center:
Keyword(s): Agriculture/Farming, Air Quality/Atmosphere, Climate Change, Development/Developing Countries, Ecosystems (precious), Energy, Ethics/Environmental Justice, Forests/Forestry, Land Issues, Oceans/Coasts/Beaches, Pollution (general), Public Lands/Greenspace
Contact(s):
Charles Savitt, President; 202-232-7933; csavitt@islandpress.org
Jan Curtis, VP for Development; 202-232-7933; jcurtis@islandpress.org
Kristy Manning, VP for Programs; 919-545-0286; kmanning@islandpress.org
Dan Sayre, VP and Publisher; 202-232-7933; dsayre@islandpress.org
Amelia Durand, Director of Communications; 202-232-7933, ext. 18; Fax: 202-234-1328; adurand@islandpress.org
Joanne Gibbs, Director of Operations; 800-828-1302; jgibbs@islandpress.org
Alphonse MacDonald, Director of New Media and IT; 202-232-7933; amacdonald@islandpress.org
Lani Hinman, Copyrights & Permissions Manager; 800-828-1302; lhinman@islandpress.org
Jonathan Cobb, Editor, Shearwater Books; 914-631-7088; jcobb@islandpress.org
Kenneth Hartzell, VP Finance and Administration, CFO; 202-232-7933; khartzell@islandpress.org

CENTER FOR SCIENCE IN THE PUBLIC INTEREST

1875 Connecticut Ave., NW, Suite 300
Washington, DC 20009 United States
Phone: 202-332-9110 Fax: 202-265-4954
E-mail: cspi@cspinet.org
Website: www.cspinet.org

Founded: 1971
Scope: National
Description: National consumer advocacy organization that focuses on health, nutrition, and alcohol issues. CSPI informs the public of its findings through a variety of publications, press releases, speeches, media appearances, and initiates legal actions.The Center has an intern program throughout the year.
Publication(s): Nutrition Action Healthletter, reports, posters, books, and video
Keyword(s): Agriculture/Farming, Pollution (general), Public Health
Contact(s):
Michael Jacobson, Executive Director

CENTER FOR SIERRA NEVADA CONSERVATION

P.O. Box 4057
Georgetown, CA 95634 United States
Phone: 530-333-1113 Fax: 530-333-1113
E-mail: csnc@innercite.com

Founded: 1986
Membership: 101–1,000
Scope: Local, State, Regional, National
Description: Grassroots group dedicated to preserving the wildlife and ecosystem values of the Sierra Nevada.
Keyword(s): Forests/Forestry, Recreation/Ecotourism

CENTER FOR THE STUDY OF TROPICAL BIRDS, INC.

ADMINISTRATIVE OFFICE
218 Conway Drive
San Antonio, TX 78209-1716 United States
Phone: 210-828-5306 Fax: 210-828-9732
E-mail: office@cstbinc.org
Website: www.cstbinc.org

Founded: 1987
Membership: N/A
Scope: International
Description: Non-profit organization devoted to tropical bird conservation issues. Current activities include research on Altamira Yellowthroat and Fuertes Oriole in N.E. Mexico, operation of a field station on the Rio Grande of Texas (Muscovy duck nestbox project, research on Red-billed

Pigeons, population dynamics of White-tipped Doves, status of Brown Jays) and publication of the proceedings of the Neotropical quail workshop held at the NOC in Monterrey, Mexico in 1999.

Publication(s): Publications available on website

Keyword(s): Water Habitats & Quality, Wildlife & Species

Contact(s):

Jack Eitniear, Director
Michael Gartside, Treasurer
Alvaro Tapia, Mexico Program Coordinator

CENTER FOR THE STUDY OF TROPICAL BIRDS, INC.

FIELD OFFICE
22 Cesar Lopez De Lara Y Carranza No. 553
Fovissste, Ciudad Victoria, C.P. 87020 Mexico
Phone: 5213160952

Founded: N/A

Scope: International

CENTER FOR WATERSHED PROTECTION

8391 Main St.
Ellicott City, MD 21043 United States
Phone: 410-461-8323 Fax: 410-461-8324
E-mail: center@cwp.org
Website: www.cwp.org

Founded: 1992

Membership: 1–100

Scope: National

Description: CWP is dedicated to new cooperative ways of protecting and restoring watersheds.

Publication(s): Environmental Indicators to Assess Stormwater Control Programs and Practices, Site Planning for Urban Stream Protection, Watershed Protection Techniques

Keyword(s): Land Issues, Reduce/Reuse/Recycle, Water Habitats & Quality

Contact(s):

Hye Kwon, Administrative Director; hyk@cwp.org
Thomas Schueler, Executive Director
Dan Oleary, Principal Engineer; djo@cwp.org

CENTER FOR WILDLIFE LAW

Institute of Public Law at
University of New Mexico School of Law
1117 Stanford NE
Albuquerque, NM 87131 United States
Phone: 505-277-5006 Fax: 505-277-5483
Website: ipl.unm.edu/cwl

Founded: 1990

Scope: National

Description: Through projects, publications, conferences, and training programs, the Center provides wildlife law and policy analysis and other educational information to legal and nonlegal communities. The Center also conducts a unique law-related wildlife education program. Staff have expertise in wildlife and environmental law and policy, biology, education, geographic information systems, publishing.

Publication(s): Wildlife Law News Quarterly, Wild News, The Status of Poaching in the U.S., Wild Friends: Kids Bringing People Together on Wildlife Issues, State Wildlife Laws Handbook, Federal Wildlife Laws Handbook

Contact(s):

Ruth Musgrave, Director

CENTRAL OHIO ANGLERS AND HUNTERS CLUB

P.O. Box 28224
Columbus, OH 43228 United States
Phone: 614-879-7757

Founded: N/A

Scope: Local

Description: Promotion of conservation and conservation education in all their phases, with a particular reference to land, air, and water; to promote good fellowship and good citizenship; to inculcate regard for the rights of others and respect for the obedience to law; to support a safe and effective conservation program for and by the state and nation.

Keyword(s): Recreation/Ecotourism, Reduce/Reuse/Recycle

Contact(s):

Doug Eakins, President; 767 Larri Ct., W. Jefferson, OH 43162; 614-879-7757
Kevin Burke, Secretary
Eric Obrein, Treasurer

CENTRO DE INFORMACION, INVESTIGACION Y EDUCACION SOCIAL (CIIES)

RR-9, Buzon 1722
San Juan, PR 00926-9736 United States
Phone: 787-292-0620 Fax: 787-760-0496
E-mail: sctinc@coqui.net

Founded: 1989

Scope: State

Description: CIIES was founded as a part of Servicios Cientificos y Tecnicos, a nonprofit organization dealing with natural resources, environmental health, and safety issues. It provides services in the form of seminars, workshops, and a resource center to students, teachers, journalists, communities, and workers.

Keyword(s): Ethics/Environmental Justice, Pollution (general), Wildlife & Species

Contact(s):

Neftali Martinez, Director
Jose Sepulveda, Secretary
Maria Vilches, Treasurer

CETACEAN SOCIETY INTERNATIONAL

P.O. Box 953
Georgetown, CT 06829 United States
Phone: 203-431-1606 Fax: 203-431-1606
E-mail: rossiter@csiwhalesalive.org
Website: www.csiwhalesalive.org

Founded: 1974

Membership: 101–1,000

Scope: State, Regional, National, International

Description: CSI is dedicated to the preservation and protection of all cetaceans (whales, dolphins, and porpoises) and the marine environment on a global basis. CSI is an all-volunteer, nonprofit conservation education and research organization with representatives in over 21 countries.

Publication(s): Whales Alive (newsletter), several education packages, Meet the Great Ones

Keyword(s): Climate Change, Development/Developing Countries, Ecosystems (precious), Oceans/Coasts/Beaches, Recreation/Ecotourism, Wildlife & Species

Contact(s):

William Rossiter, President; 16 Mountain Laurel Lane, Redding, CT 06896; 203-431-1606; Fax: 203-431-1606; rossiter@csiwhalesalive.org
Barbara Kilpatrick, Vice President; 15 Wood Pond Rd., West Hartford, CT 06107; 860-561-0187
Robbins Barstow, Director Emeritus; 190 Stillwold Dr., Wethersfield, CT 06109; 860-563-2565; robbinsb@aol.com
Martha Fitzgerald, Secretary; 120 Retreat Ave. C-3, Hartford, CT 06106; 860-246-3143
Robert Victor, Treasurer; 57 Crossroads Ln., Glastonbury, CT 06033; rfvictor@juno.com

CHARLES A. AND ANNE MORROW LINDBERGH FOUNDATION, THE

2150 Third Ave. N., Suite 310
Anoka, MN 55303-2200 United States
Phone: 763-576-1596 Fax: 763-576-1664
E-mail: info@lindberghfoundation.org
Website: www.lindberghfoundation.org

Founded: 1977
Membership: 1,001–10,000
Scope: International
Description: The Charles A. and Anne Morrow Lindbergh Foundation is a nonprofit organization, advancing Charles and Anne Morrow Lindbergh's vision of a balance between technological progress and environmental preservation by offering Lindbergh Grants to individuals for research and educational projects which will further this balance, presenting the Lindbergh Award for extraordinary contributions to the nature/technology balance, and sponsoring other projects and programs.
Publication(s): Newsletter
Contact(s):
Reeve Lindbergh, President
Clare Hallward, Vice President
Kristina Lindbergh, Vice President
Gene Bratsch, Secretary/Treasurer
Marlene White, Executive Director

CHAUTAUQUA WATERSHED CONSERVANCY

413 North Main Street
Jamestown, NY 14701 United States
Phone: 716-664-2166 Fax: 716-483-3524
E-mail: chautwsh@netsync.net
Website: chautauquawatershed.org

Founded: 1990
Membership: 101–1,000
Scope: Local
Description: The Chautauqua Watershed Conservancy is a county-wide organization with the mission to preserve and enhance the water quality, scenic beauty and ecological health of the lakes, streams and watersheds of the Chautauqua region.
Publication(s): The Shed Sheet
Contact(s):
John Jablonski, Executive Director; 413 N. Main Street, Jamestown, NY 14701; 716-664-2166; Fax: 716-483-3524; chautwsh@netsync.net
Lori Scott, Administrative Assistant; 413 N. Main Street, Jamestown, NY 14701; 716-664-2166; Fax: 716-483-3524; chautwsh2@netsync.net
Tracy Wilkin, Outreach Coordinator; 413 N. Main Street, Jamestown, NY 14701; 716-664-2166; Fax: 716-483-3524; chautwsh2@netsync.net

CHELONIA INSTITUTE

3330 Washington Blvd.
Arlington, VA 22201 United States
Phone: 703-516-2600 Fax: 703-522-1427
Website: www.truland.com

Founded: 1977
Membership: 101–1,000
Scope: National
Description: A private operating foundation with ecological concerns focused primarily on the conservation of marine turtles. The Institute undertakes a broad range of programs including technical publications, land acquisition, and so on, and works cooperatively with other organizations.
Contact(s):
Robert Truland, President
Mary Truland, Assistant Director

CHESAPEAKE BAY FOUNDATION, INC.

Philip Merrill Environmental Center
6 Herndon Avenue
Annapolis, MD 21403 United States
Phone: 410-268-8816 Fax: 410-268-6687
E-mail: chesapeake@cbf.org
Website: www.savethebay.cbf.org

Founded: 1966
Membership: 100,001–500,000
Scope: National
Description: A nonprofit membership organization established to promote the environmental protection and restoration of Chesapeake Bay and its full watershed. CBF operates programs in environmental education and environmental protection and restoration.
Publication(s): Save the Bay, Grassroots Bulletin, Megalops
Keyword(s): Water Habitats & Quality
Contact(s):
William Baker, President
Donald Baugh, Vice President for Education
Michael Shultz, Vice President for Public Affairs
Wayne Mills, Chairman

CHESAPEAKE BAY FOUNDATION, INC.

MARYLAND OFFICE
Philip Merrill Environmental Center
6 Herndon Avenue
Annapolis, MD 21403 United States
Phone: 410-268-8833 Fax: 410-280-3513
E-mail: chesapeake@cbf.org
Website: www.cbf.org

Founded: 1967
Membership: 100,001–500,000
Scope: Local, State, Regional
Description: The Chesapeake Bay Foundation's Maryland office conducts activities of the foundation specific to the state of Maryland and operates a field office on the Eastern Shore of Maryland as well as a farm (Clagett Farm) in Southern Maryland.
Publication(s): Save the Bay, Bay Savers Bulletin
Keyword(s): Agriculture/Farming, Ethics/Environmental Justice, Executive/Legislative/Judicial Reform, Forests/Forestry, Land Issues, Pollution (general), Reduce/Reuse/Recycle, Sprawl/Urban Planning, Transportation, Water Habitats & Quality
Contact(s):
Theresa Pierno, Executive Director; tpierno@savethebay.cbf.org
Kim Coble, Assistant Director/ Senior Scientist; 410-268-8833; Fax: 410-280-3513; kcoble@savethebay.cbf.org

CHESAPEAKE BAY FOUNDATION, INC.

PENNSYLVANIA OFFICE
The Old Waterworks Bldg., 614 N. Front St., Suite G
Harrisburg, PA 17101 United States
Phone: 717-234-5550 Fax: 717-234-9632
E-mail: chesapeake@savethebay.cbf.org
Website: www.savethebay.cbf.org

Founded: 1966
Membership: 10,001–100,000
Scope: State
Description: The Foundation conducts activities and programs specific to the Commonwealth of Pennsylvania.
Publication(s): Bay Beginnings - newsletter
Keyword(s): Air Quality/Atmosphere, Energy, Reduce/Reuse/Recycle, Transportation
Contact(s):
Jolene Chinchilli, Pennsylvania Executive Director

CHESAPEAKE BAY FOUNDATION, INC.

VIRGINIA OFFICE
1108 East Main St., Suite 1600
Richmond, VA 23219 United States
Phone: 804-780-1392 Fax: 804-648-4011
Website: www.savethebay.cbf.org

Founded: 1967

Scope: State

Description: The Chesapeake Bay Foundation conducts activities of the foundation in the Commonwealth of Virginia and operates field offices in Norfolk and Tappahannock, Virginia.

Keyword(s): Public Lands/Greenspace, Water Habitats & Quality, Wildlife & Species

Contact(s):
Joseph Maroon, Executive Director
Roy Hoagland, Assistant Director

CHESAPEAKE WILDLIFE HERITAGE (CWH)

P.O. Box 1745
Easton, MD 21601 United States
Phone: 410-822-5100 Fax: 410-822-4016
E-mail: info@cheswildlife.org
Website: www.cheswildlife.org

Founded: 1980

Membership: 101–1,000

Scope: State, Regional

Description: A private, nonprofit conservation group working with private and public landowners to restore and protect wildlife habitat in the Chesapeake Bay watershed. CWH constructs and manages wetlands, warm season grass and wildflower meadows, nesting structures, marshes, and woodlands. CWH advises on and carries out sustainable farming techniques in order to benefit the Chesapeake Bay and its wildlife. CWH also conducts ecological research on plants and migratory birds.

Publication(s): Annual Report, Habitat Works

Keyword(s): Agriculture/Farming, Ecosystems (precious), Water Habitats & Quality, Wildlife & Species

Contact(s):
Larry Albright, Board of Directors President
Susanna Engvall, Webmaster/PR
John Gerber, Habitat Ecologist
Michael Haggie, Habitat Ecologist
Chris Pupke, Development Director
Andi Pupke, Education Director

CHICAGO HERPETOLOGICAL SOCIETY

2060 N. Clark St.
Chicago, IL 60614 United States
Phone: 219-464-8514
E-mail: chris@graptemys.com
Website: www.chicagoherp.org

Founded: 1966

Membership: 1,001–10,000

Scope: State

Description: The Chicago Herpetological Society is a group of reptile and amphibian enthusiasts. Its goals are education, conservation, and the advancement of herpetology.

Publication(s): Bulletin of the Chicago Herpetological Society

Keyword(s): Wildlife & Species

Contact(s):
Jack Schoenfelder, President; c/o Ivy Tech College, 2401 Valley Dr., Valparaiso, IN 46383; 219-929-1525
Lori King, Vice President; 773-447-3645; loriguanid@aol.com
Greg Brim, Treasurer; 603-834-4446; gregbrim@mediaone.net

CHIHUAHUAN DESERT RESEARCH INSTITUTE

P.O. Box 905
Ft. Davis, TX 79734 United States
Phone: 915-364-2499 Fax: 915-364-2509
E-mail: manager@cdri.org
Website: www.cdri.org

Founded: 1974

Membership: 101–1,000

Scope: National

Description: Nonprofit organization formed to promote public awareness, appreciation, and concern for the natural diversity of the Chihuahuan Desert through research and education programs. Current studies include life history related studies, systematic zoology, systematic botany, desert ecology, anthropology, archeology, geology, and theoretical ecology.

Publication(s): Chihuahuan Desert Discovery

Keyword(s): Agriculture/Farming, Climate Change, Land Issues, Wildlife & Species

Contact(s):
Dr. John Barlow, Chairman
Dr. David Schmidly, Vice Chairman
Cathryn Hoyt, Executive Director; 915-364-2499; Fax: 915-364-2504; manager@cdri.org
Jennifer Bauer, Education Coordinator; 915-364-2499; education_cdri@overland.net
Debbie Pate, Business Manager; 915-364-2499
Thomas Brunner, Secretary
Larry Bryant, Treasurer

CHINA REGION LAKES ALLIANCE

RR 1, Box 970
South China, ME 04358 United States
Phone: 207-445-5021 Fax: 207-445-3208
E-mail: chiname@pivot.net

Founded: 1994

Membership: 1–100

Scope: Local

Description: To protect and improve water quality in 3 culturally eutrophic Maine lakes, (China Lake, Threemile Pond and Webber Pond) and to benefit our local economy through integrated watershed management.

Publication(s): Walk for a Rainy Day, Starting a Local Youth Conservation Corp, Vegetative Buffer Strips

Keyword(s): Oceans/Coasts/Beaches, Pollution (general), Water Habitats & Quality

Contact(s):
Daniel Dubord, President; 207-872-2743; Fax: 207-872-2962
Rebecca Manthey, Executive Director

CHLORINE-FREE PAPER CONSORTIUM

1411 Ellis Ave.
Northland College
Ashland, WI 54806 United States
Phone: 715-682-1847 Fax: 715-682-1308
E-mail: mail@clfree.org
Website: www.clfree.org

Founded: N/A

Scope: National

Description: The CPC aims to reduce the use of chlorinated substances in the paper-making process by informing people about the effects of chlorine by-products and facilitating communication between buyers and sellers of chlorine-free paper products. A project of Northland College and the National Wildlife Federation.

Publication(s): Brochure

Keyword(s): Finance/Banking/Trade, Pollution (general), Public Health, Water Habitats & Quality

Contact(s):
Jeffery Huxmann, Executive Coordinator; huxmann@clfree.org

CHRISTINA CONSERVANCY, INC.

P.O. Box 1680
Wilmington, DE 19899-1680 United States
Phone: 302-984-3801 Fax: 302-652-5379

Founded: N/A

Scope: Local

Description: The purpose of the Christina Conservancy, Inc. is to preserve, protect, and urge the wise use of the Christina River.

Keyword(s): Water Habitats & Quality

Contact(s):
Edward Cooch, President

CINCINNATI NATURE CENTER

ROWE WOODS, LONG BRANCH FARM, GORMAN HERITAGE FARM
4949 Tealtown Road
Milford, OH 45150-9752 United States
Phone: 513-831-1711 Fax: 513-831-8052
E-mail: cnc@cincynature.org
Website: www.cincynature.org

Founded: 1965
Membership: 1,001–10,000
Scope: Local, State

Description: A private, non-profit organization consisting of a nature preserve and two working farms which provide environmental, natural history and agricultural education for the Greater Cincinnati area.

Publication(s): Newsleaf (newsletter)

Keyword(s): Agriculture/Farming, Ecosystems (precious), Recreation/Ecotourism, Reduce/Reuse/Recycle, Wildlife & Species

Contact(s):
William Hopple, President/Executive Director; 513-965-4246; Fax: 513-831-8052; bhopple@cincynature.org
Connie Brockman, Education Director; 513-965-4891; Fax: 513-831-8052; cbrockman@cincynature.org
Ted Grannan, Operations Director; 513-965-4890; Fax: 513-831-8052; tgrannan@cincynature.org

CIRCUMPOLAR CONSERVATION UNION

600 Pennsylvania Avenue, SE
Suite 210
Washington, DC 20003 United States
Phone: 202-675-8370 Fax: 202-675-8373
E-mail: circumpolar@igc.org
Website: www.circumpolar.org

Founded: 1993
Membership: N/A
Scope: State, Regional, National, International

Description: Circumpolar Conservation Union is a public interest initiative dedicated to protecting the ecological and cultural integrity of the Arctic for present and future generations. CCU works nationally and internationally through policy advocacy, public education, and by building links among diverse constituencies, to achieve comprehensive legal protection for the Arctic.

Publication(s): Persistent Organic Pollutants in Alaska

Keyword(s): Climate Change, Development/Developing Countries, Ecosystems (precious), Ethics/Environmental Justice, Oceans/Coasts/Beaches, Pollution (general), Public Health

Contact(s):
Evelyn Hurwich, President
Pall Davidsson, Executive Director

CITIZENS ALLIANCE FOR SAVING THE ATMOSPHERE AND THE EARTH (CASA)

1-3-17-711 Tanimachi
Chuo-ku, Osaka, 540-0012 Japan
Phone: 8169413745 Fax: 8169415699
E-mail: casa@netplus.ne.jp
Website: www.netplus.ne.jp/-casa/

Founded: 1988

Scope: International

Description: CASA is committed to preserving both the local and global environment through solidarity with both Japanese and international environmental NGO's. CASA is composed of 50 NGO's and about 500 individuals, such as scientists, teachers, lawyers, farmers, grassroots activitists, artists, consumer group leaders, and others.

Contact(s):
Mitsutoshi Hayakawa, Managing Director
Yuji Nishi, Executive Director
Tsunetoshi Yamamura, Representative Director

CITIZENS FOR A SCENIC FLORIDA, INC.

4401 Emerson St., Suite 10
Jacksonville, FL 32207 United States
Phone: 904-396-0037 Fax: 904-398-4647
E-mail: scenicfl@scenicflorida.org
Website: www.scenicflorida.org

Founded: 1998

Scope: Regional

Description: Citizens for a Scenic Florida: Preserving Florida's Scenic Heritage.

Publication(s): Scenic Watch, Florida View Points

Keyword(s): Forests/Forestry, Land Issues, Sprawl/Urban Planning

Contact(s):
Lane Welch, Director

CITIZENS NATURAL RESOURCES ASSOCIATION OF WISCONSIN, INC.

Attn: President, 3805 Paunack St.
Madison, WI 53711 United States
Phone: 608-231-9721 Fax: 608-218-1647
E-mail: ekolink@aol.com

Founded: 1951

Scope: State

Description: To protect Wisconsin's natural resources through education, legislation, and the courts. The CNRA initiated and sponsored the action which resulted in the banning of DDT in Wisconsin and two years later in the United States. Recently, the CNRA has been concentrating on protecting and restoring native vegetation along Wisconsin's roads.

Publication(s): CNRA Report, The, Wisconsin Roadsides

Contact(s):
Kira Henschel, President
Jan Calpone, Vice President/ Editor; 2 Meminiee Dr., Oskosh, WI 54901
Louise Coumbe, Membership Chair; 1028 Elmwood Ave., Oshkosh, WI 54901
Zaiga Maassen, Secretary; 913 Honey Creek, Oshkosh, WI 54904
Charles Sturm, Treasurer; J-1233 Mayfair Rd. Suite 125, Milwaukee, WI 53226

CITIZENS' NUCLEAR INFORMATION CENTER

1-58-15-3F Higashi-Nakano
Nakano-ku, Tokyo, 164-0003 Japan
Phone: 81353309520 Fax: 81353309530

Founded: 1975

Scope: International

Description: A nonprofit organization to collect and provide the public a broad range of information on nuclear power issues, and cooperate with individuals and other organizations concerned with nuclear proliferation in Japan and around the world. Information includes the Japanese government policy of plutonium utilization, effects of radioactive contamination, nuclear power plant accidents, economics, and other impacts on the local communities caused by construction of nuclear power plants.

Keyword(s): Energy

Contact(s):
Hideyuki Ban, Co-Director
Gaia Hoerner, International Relations Officer

CLEAN OCEAN ACTION
MAIN OFFICE
P.O. Box 505
Sandy Hook, NJ 07732 United States
Phone: 732-872-0111 Fax: 732-872-8041
E-mail: sandyhook@cleanoceanaction.org
Website: www.cleanoceanaction.org

Founded: 1984

Scope: Local, State, Regional, National

Description: A broad-based coalition of 175 conservation, fishing, diving, boating, real estate, student, and civic groups; over 300 businesses; and thousands of citizens concerned with the degraded waters off the New York and New Jersey coasts. COA uses education, research, and citizen action to pressure public officials to enact and enforce protective laws for our marine resources. Programs include: storm drain stenciling; regulatory reviews; contaminated sediments; and non-point source pollution.

Publication(s): The Ocean is a Flush Away, Ocean Advocate, Annual Statewide Beach Sweep Report, Wasting Our Waters Away, Citizen Guide for Dredged Material Management

Keyword(s): Oceans/Coasts/Beaches, Pollution (general)

Contact(s):
Dery Bennett, President
William Decamp, Vice President
Cindy Zipf, Executive Director
Ben Forest, Treasurer
Pat Schneider, Secretary

CLEAN OCEAN ACTION
MID-COAST OFFICE
P.O. Box 1303
Tuckerton, NJ 08087 United States
Phone: 732-872-0111
E-mail: Tuckerton@cleanoceanaction.org
Website: www.cleanoceanaction.org

Founded: N/A

Scope: Local, State, Regional, National

Description: See COA Main Office.

Keyword(s): Oceans/Coasts/Beaches, Pollution (general)

Contact(s):
Currently Not Staffed

CLEAN OCEAN ACTION
SOUTH JERSEY OFFICE
P.O. Box 1098
Wildwood, NJ 08260 United States
Phone: 609-729-7262 Fax: 609-729-1091
E-mail: Wildwood@cleanoceanaction.org
Website: www.cleanoceanaction.org

Founded: N/A

Scope: Local, State, Regional, National

Description: See Main Office

Keyword(s): Oceans/Coasts/Beaches, Pollution (general)

Contact(s):
Anthony Totah, South Jersey Coordinator/ICE Coordinator; P.O. Box 1098, 3419 Pacific Avenue, Wildwood, NJ 08260; 609-729-9262; Fax: 609-729-1091; Wildwood@cleanoceanaction.org

CLEAN WATER ACTION
4455 Connecticut Ave., NW, Suite A300
Washington, DC 20008-2328 United States
Phone: 202-895-0420 Fax: 202-895-0438
E-mail: cwa@cleanwater.org
Website: www.cleanwateraction.org

Founded: N/A

Scope: National

Description: The national citizen's organization working full-time for clean safe water at an affordable cost, control of toxic chemicals, and protection of our natural resources.

Contact(s):
Jim Pierce, Development Associate

CLEAN WATER FUND
4455 Connecticut Ave., NW
Washington, DC 20008 United States
Phone: 202-895-0420 Fax: 202-895-0438
E-mail: cleanwater@essential.org
Website: www.cleanwaterfund.org

Founded: N/A

Scope: National

Description: Clean Water Fund is a 501 (3) research, training and educational organization that advances environmental and consumer protection with a special focus on water pollution, toxic hazards, solid waste management, and natural resources.

Publication(s): Water: Riches for Clean Up, Pennies for Prevention, 1993, Solid Waste: Expanding Rhode Island's Market with RI War on Waste, 1993

Contact(s):
Peter Van Lockwood, Board of Directors, President
David Zwick, Board of Directors, Executive Vice President; ext. 103; dzwick@cleanwater.org
Kathleen Aterno, Board of Directors, Treasurer; ext. 106; katerno@cleanwater.org
Jim Pierce, Development Associate; ext. 110; jpierce@cleanwater.org

CLEAN WATER NETWORK, THE
1200 New York Avenue, NW, Suite 400
Washington, DC 20005 United States
Phone: 202-289-2395 Fax: 202-289-1060
E-mail: cleanwaternt@igc.org
Website: www.cwn.org

Founded: 1992

Membership: 101–1,000

Scope: National

Description: The Clean Water Network is a national alliance of over 1,000 organizations representing environmentalists, commercial fishers, anglers, surfers, family farmers, environmental justice advocates, faith communities, civic associations, boaters, labor unions, and recreational enthusiasts working together for cleaner waters.

Publication(s): Prescription for Clean Water, Wetlands for Clean Water, America's Animal Factories, Spilling Swills, Spills and Kills

Keyword(s): Water Habitats & Quality

Contact(s):
Ami Grace, Grass Roots Director; 202-289-2421; agrace@nrdc.org
Merritt Frey, Policy Analyst/Idaho; 208-345-7776
Linda Young, Southeast Field Coordinator/Florida; 850-222-9188

CLEAR CREEK ENVIRONMENTAL FOUNDATION
507 Houston Avenue
League City, TX 77573 United States
Phone: 281-332-5822 Fax: 281-557-1302
E-mail: jol111@aol.com
Website: clearcreekcleanup.org

Founded: 2000

Membership: N/A

Scope: Local

Description: Caretaker of Clear Creek, Texas. Cleanup and trash pickup. Habitat restoration—Cordgrass planting.

Keyword(s): Ecosystems (precious)

CLEVELAND MUSEUM OF NATURAL HISTORY, THE

1 Wade Oval Drive
University Circle
Cleveland, OH 44106 United States
Phone: 216-231-4600, ext. 219 Fax: 216-231-5919
E-mail: botany@cmnh.org
Website: www.cmnh.org

Founded: 1920
Membership: 1,001–10,000
Scope: Regional
Description: To instill an understanding of and appreciation for nature and inspire responsibility for conservation and stewardship of natural diversity. The Museum program areas include exhibits, publications, education, collections, research, and natural areas. The Museum owns a system of 25 sanctuaries.
Publication(s): Explorer, Kirtlandia
Contact(s):
James Bissell, Coordinator of Natural Areas

CLIMATE INSTITUTE

333 1/2 Pennsylvania Ave., SE
Washington, DC 20003 United States
Phone: 202-547-0104 Fax: 202-547-0111
E-mail: info@climate.org
Website: www.climate.org

Founded: 1986
Scope: International
Description: Designed to serve as a catalyst for international response and cooperation to address the threats posed by climate change and depletion of the stratospheric ozone layer. The Climate Institute operates as a bridge between scientists and policymakers with the intent of expediting policy responses to the challenges posed by human-induced climate change.
Publication(s): Climate Alert, Environmental Exodus, Climate Change in Asia, Forests in a Changing Climate, Coping with Climate Change
Keyword(s): Development/Developing Countries, Energy, Forests/Forestry, Oceans/Coasts/Beaches
Contact(s):
John Topping, President; 202-547-0104, ext. 14; jtopping@climate.org

CLINTON RIVER WATERSHED COUNCIL (CRWC)

1970 East Auburn Rd.
Rochester Hills, MI 48307 United States
Phone: 248-853-9580 Fax: 248-853-0486
E-mail: contact@crwc.org
Website: www.crwc.org

Founded: 1972
Membership: 101–1,000
Scope: Local, State
Description: CRWC is a non-profit organization dedicated to preserving, enhancing, and celebrating the Clinton River, its watershed, and Lake St. Clair.
Publication(s): Clinton River Resource Center
Keyword(s): Ecosystems (precious), Land Issues, Pollution (general), Public Lands/Greenspace, Recreation/Ecotourism, Water Habitats & Quality, Wildlife & Species

COALITION FOR CLEAN AIR

10780 Santa Monica Blvd., # 210
Los Angeles, CA 90025 United States
Phone: 310-441-1544 Fax: 310-446-4362
Website: www.coalitionforcleanair.org

Founded: 1970
Membership: 1,001–10,000
Scope: State
Description: A nonprofit, tax-exempt organization dedicated to restoring clean, healthful air to Southern California residents through a combination of efforts including outreach and education, litigation, research, and policy advocacy.
Publication(s): Clearing the Air, publications available on website
Keyword(s): Air Quality/Atmosphere, Pollution (general)
Contact(s):
David Allgood, President
Wendy James, Vice President
Todd Campbell, Policy Director
Tim Carmichael, Executive Director
Abby Arnold, Treasurer

COALITION FOR EDUCATION IN THE OUTDOORS

E331 Park Center S.U.N.Y. at Cortland Box 2000
Cortland, NY 13045 United States
Phone: 607-753-4968 Fax: 607-753-5982
E-mail: yaplec@snycorva.cortland.edu
Website: www.outdooredcoalition.org

Founded: 1986
Scope: National
Description: The Coalition is composed of more than 100 businesses, institutions, organizations, associations, centers, agencies, and individuals affiliated in support of communicating and networking concerning education in, for and about the outdoors. The Coalition's magazine is a critically acclaimed education resource. The Coalition also conducts a biennial Outdoor Education Research Symposium.
Publication(s): Taproot, Outdoor Education Research Symposium Proceedings
Keyword(s): Ethics/Environmental Justice, Land Issues, Public Lands/Greenspace, Recreation/Ecotourism
Contact(s):
Charles Yaple, Executive Coordinator

COALITION FOR NATURAL STREAM VALLEYS, INC.

430 Orchard Rd.
Newark, DE 19711-5137 United States
Phone: 302-366-8059

Founded: N/A
Scope: Regional
Description: The purpose of the Coalition for Natural Stream Valleys, Inc. is to promote the wise use of, and the preservation of natural stream valleys.
Contact(s):
Dorothy Miller, Corresponding Secretary
Roland Roth, Chairman; 302-831-1300

COAST ALLIANCE

600 Pennsylvania Ave., SE
Suite 340
Washington, DC 20003 United States
Phone: 202-546-9554 Fax: 202-546-9609
E-mail: coast@coastalliance.org
Website: www.coastalliance.org

Founded: 1979
Membership: 101–1,000
Scope: National
Description: The Coast Alliance is a nonprofit public interest group dedicated to raising public awareness about our priceless coastal resources. Composed of concerned activists across the United States, the Coast Alliance provides information on activities affecting the nation's four coasts: the Atlantic, Pacific, Gulf of Mexico, and Great Lakes.
Publication(s): And Two If By Sea, Using Common Sense to Protect The Coasts, Mission Possible, Muddy Waters, Pointless Pollution, Storm on The Horizon
Keyword(s): Development/Developing Countries, Executive/

Legislative/Judicial Reform, Land Issues, Oceans/Coasts/Beaches, Pollution (general), Water Habitats & Quality

Contact(s):

Jacqueline Savitz, Executive Director; 202-546-9554; Fax: 202-546-9609; jsavitz@coastalliance.org
Diana Combs, Coastal Counsel; 202-546-9554; Fax: 202-546-9609; dcombs@coastalliance.org
Jaime Matera, Outreach Coordinator; 202-546-9554; Fax: 202-546-9609; jmatera@coastalliance.org
Dery Bennett, Chairperson of the Board; American Littoral Society,, Bldg. 18 Hartshorne Drive, Sandy Hook Highlands, NJ 07732; 732-872-8041
Todd Miller, Treasurer and Secretary; North Carolina Coastal Federation, 3609 Hwy. 24, Newport, NC 28570; 252-393-8185
David Miller, Vice Chairperson; National Audubon, 200 Trillium Lane, Albany, NY 12203; 518-869-9731

COASTAL AMERICA FOUNDATION

100 Muron Avenue
Bellingham, MA 02019 United States
Phone: 508-292-0251
E-mail: cstlamfnd@aol.com
Website: www.coastalamericafoundation.org

Founded: 1998
Membership: N/A
Scope: National, International
Description: The Coastal America Foundation is dedicated to supporting the restoration of our nation's wetlands and aquatic habitats.
Keyword(s): Ecosystems (precious), Energy, Ethics/Environmental Justice, Land Issues, Oceans/Coasts/Beaches, Pollution (general), Public Lands/Greenspace, Recreation/Ecotourism, Reduce/Reuse/Recycle, Sprawl/Urban Planning, Transportation, Water Habitats & Quality

COASTAL CONSERVATION ASSOCIATION

4801 Woodway, Suite 220 West
Houston, TX 77056 United States
Phone: 713-626-4234 Fax: 713-626-5852
E-mail: ntl@joincca.org
Website: www.joincca.org

Founded: 1977
Membership: 10,001–100,000
Scope: National
Description: A national nonprofit corporation organized exclusively for the purpose of promoting and advancing the conservation, and protection of the marine, animal, and plant life both onshore and offshore along the coastal areas of the United States for the benefit and enjoyment of the general public.
Publication(s): Tide
Keyword(s): Oceans/Coasts/Beaches, Recreation/Ecotourism, Water Habitats & Quality, Wildlife & Species

Contact(s):

David Cummins, President
Gus Schram, Vice President
Jeff Angers, Executive Director of Louisiana Regional Office; P.O. Box 373, Baton Rouge, LA 70821; 225-952-9200; Fax: 225-952-9204
Kevin Daniels, Executive Director of Texas Regional Office; 4801 Woodway, Suite 220W, Houston, TX 77056; 713-626-4222; Fax: 713-961-3801
David Dexter, Executive Director of Alabama Regional Office; 144 Florence Place, Mobile, AL 36607; 334-478-3474; Fax: 334-476-5214
Ted Forsgren, Executive Director of Florida Regional Office; 905 East Park Ave., Tallahassee, FL 32301-2646; 850-224-3474; Fax: 850-224-5199
Pat Keliher, Executive Director of Maine Regional Office; 40 Lafayette St., Yarmouth, ME 04096; 207-846-1015; Fax: 207-846-1168
Austin Ragsdale, Executive Director of North Carolina Regional Office; 3701 National Drive Suite 217, Raleigh, NC 27612; 919-781-3474; Fax: 919-781-3475
Richard Welton, Executive Director of Virginia Regional Office; 2100 Marina Shores Dr., Suite 108, Virginia Beach, VA 23451; 757-481-1226; Fax: 757-481-6910
Scott Whitaker, Executive Director of South Carolina Regional Office; P.O. Box 290640, Columbia, SC 29229; 803-865-4164; Fax: 803-865-5104
Walter Fondren, Chairman of the Board
Alex Jernigan, Vice Chairman
Will Ohmstede, Vice Chairman
Doug Pike, Editor

COASTAL CONSERVATION ASSOCIATION GEORGIA

515 Denmark St. Suite 300
Statesboro, GA 30458 United States
Phone: 800-266-0693 Fax: 912-764-6497
Website: www.ccaga.org

Founded: 1987
Membership: 1,001–10,000
Scope: State
Description: The CCAG promotes conservation through education—promoting, protecting and enhancing the availability of marine, animal, plant life and other coastal resources for the benefit and enjoyment of the general public.
Publication(s): Tide Magazine, Tidelines (newsletter)
Keyword(s): Oceans/Coasts/Beaches, Reduce/Reuse/Recycle, Water Habitats & Quality, Wildlife & Species

Contact(s):

Martin Nesmith, Chairman; 912-739-1744; Fax: 912-739-4889
William Phillips, Vice-Chairman; 912-764-6567; Fax: 912-764-6568; ringo@bulloch.com

COASTAL GEORGIA LAND TRUST INC.

428 Bull St., Suite 210
Savannah, GA 31401 United States
Phone: 912-231-0507 Fax: 912-231-1143
E-mail: cglt@bellsouth.net
Website: www.cglt.org

Founded: 1993
Membership: 101–1,000
Scope: Regional
Description: The mission of the Coastal Georgia Land Trust, Inc., a nonprofit organization, is to promote the responsible stewardship and preservation of land in coastal Georgia.
Publication(s): Coastal Georgia Land Trust Newsletter, Coastal Georgia Land Trust
Keyword(s): Development/Developing Countries, Forests/Forestry, Land Issues, Public Lands/Greenspace, Water Habitats & Quality, Wildlife & Species

Contact(s):

Rhett Mouchet, President of the Board of Directors
Alan Bailey, Vice President, Board of Directors; 912-925-3159; Fax: 912-927-9766; acbailey@worldnet.atf.net
Mary Elfner, Executive Director

COASTAL SOCIETY, THE

P.O. Box 25408
Alexandria, VA 22313-5408 United States
Phone: 703-768-1599 Fax: 703-768-1598
E-mail: coastal@aol.com
Website: www.coastalsociety.org

Founded: 1975
Membership: 101–1,000
Scope: International
Description: The Coastal Society is an organization of private sector, academic and governmental professionals and students dedicated to actively addressing emerging coastal issues, fostering dialog, forging partnerships and promoting communication and education.

Publication(s): Coastal Society, The Bulletin, conference proceedings

Keyword(s): Development/Developing Countries, Oceans/Coasts/Beaches, Water Habitats & Quality

Contact(s):

Walter Clark, President; University of Washington, Box 355060, Seattle, WA 98105-5060; 206-685-1108
Judy Tucker, Executive Director
Megan Bailiff, Past President; Nicholas School for the Environment, Duke University, 135 Duke Marine Lab Rd., Beaufort, NC 28516-9720
Robert Boyles, Secretary; University of Rhode Island, Kingston, RI; 301-713-3155
John Duff, President-Elect; University of Maine, Law School, 246 Deering, Portland, ME 04102-2898
William Hall, Treasurer; 3635 Fremont Ave. North, #307, Seattle, WA 98103; 406-442-4002

COEREBA SOCIETY

7336 16th Ave. SW
Seattle, WA 98106 United States
Phone: 206-768-8827
E-mail: info@coereba.org
Website: www.coereba.org

Founded: N/A

Scope: International

Description: Seattle-based environmental nonprofit education about nature and its conservation in Puerto Rico region and the greater Caribbean, especially through mass media channels and environmental interpretation.

Contact(s):

Jose Placer, Executive Director; jplacer@coereba.org

COLORADO ASSOCIATION OF SOIL CONSERVATION DISTRICTS

3000 Youngfield, #163
Lakewood, CO 80215 United States
Phone: 303-232-6246 Fax: 303-232-1624
E-mail: info@cascd.com
Website: www.cascd.com

Founded: N/A

Scope: National

Contact(s):

Robert Cordova, President, Alternate Board Member; 18105 Enoch Rd., Colorado Springs, CO 80930; 719-683-2126
Jim Rossi, Vice President; P.O. Box 247, Oak Creek, CO 80467; 970-638-4459
John Freziers, Board Member/Exec. Director; 1858 M Rd., Fruita, CO 81521; 970-858-7165
Lee Campbell, Secretary and Treasurer; 1603 Eastlawn Ave., Durango, CO 81301; 970-247-1496; Fax: 970-385-7910

COLORADO B.A.S.S. CHAPTER FEDERATION

Attn: President, 4485 Enchanted Circle N.
Colorado Springs, CO 80917 United States
Phone: 719-597-2304
Website: www.coloradobassfederation.org

Founded: N/A

Membership: 101–1,000

Scope: State

Description: An organization of Bassmaster chapters, affiliated with the Bass Anglers Sportsman Society, organized to fight pollution, assist state and national conservation agencies in their efforts, and teach the young people of our country good conservation practices. Dedicated to the realistic conservation of our water resources.

Contact(s):

John Bentz, President; 719-597-2304
Bernie Stein, Conservation Director; 1218 N 3rd St., Johnstown, CO 80534; 970-587-9163

COLORADO ENVIRONMENTAL COALITION

1536 Wynkoop #5C
Denver, CO 80202 United States
Phone: 303-534-7066 Fax: 303-534-7063
E-mail: infocec@cecenviro.org
Website: www.ourcolorado.org

Founded: 1965

Membership: 1,001–10,000

Scope: State

Description: The Colorado Environmental Coalition is the grass roots action arm of Colorado's environmental movement. The Coalition coordinates the conservation community and mobilizes citizen constituencies behind environmental campaigns to preserve wilderness, wildlife, and a sustainable way of life.

Publication(s): Conservationist's Wilderness Proposal for BLM Lands, Colorado Environmental Handbook-State of the State

Keyword(s): Land Issues, Public Lands/Greenspace

Contact(s):

John Powers, President
Elise Jones, Executive Director; ext. 204; sjtix@cecenviro.org
Monica Piergrossi, Front Range Field Director; ext. 207; monica@cecenviro.org
Carter Johnson, Circuit Rider; ext. 303; trey@cecenviro.org
Pete Kolbenschlag, West Slope Field Organizer; 1000 N 9th St., #29, Grand Junction, CO 81501; 970-243-0002; pete@cecenviro.org
Jeff Widen, Associate; 970-385-8509; widen@cecenviro.org

COLORADO FORESTRY ASSOCIATION

P.O. Box 270132
Ft. Collins, CO 80527 United States
Phone: 970-223-3255

Founded: 1982

Membership: 101–1,000

Scope: State

Description: A statewide organization affiliated with the National Woodland Owners Association, concerned with forest ecology and advocating a forest-perpetuating balance between preservation and harvest of Colorado forests.

Publication(s): Colorado Forestry

Keyword(s): Forests/Forestry

Contact(s):

Vincent Calderon, President; 38 Dartmouth Ave., Pueblo, CO 81005; 719-566-1648
Chris Crowley, Vice President; 10961 Stuart Ct., Westminister, CO 80031; 720-887-3052
Ken Ashley, Secretary; 5227 South County Rd. #7, Fort Collins, CO 80528; 970-223-3255
Edwin Olmsted, Treasurer; 1065 West 112th Ave. #B, Northglenn, CO 80234; 303-452-8643
John Oram, Editor; 303-477-0552

COLORADO NATURAL HERITAGE PROGRAM

254 General Services Bldg., Colorado State University
Ft. Collins, CO 80523 United States
Phone: 970-491-1309 Fax: 970-491-3349
E-mail: heritage@lamar.colostate.edu
Website: www.cnhp.colostate.edu

Founded: 1979

Scope: State

Description: The mission of the Colorado Natural Heritage Program is to preserve the natural diversity of life by contributing the scientific foundation that leads to lasting conservation of Colorado's biological wealth.

Publication(s): Rare and Imperiled Animals, Plants, and, Colorado Conservation Status Handbook, Colorado Rare Plant Guide

Keyword(s): Land Issues, Wildlife & Species

Contact(s):
Boyce Drummond, Director; 970-491-1309; Fax: 970-491-3349; heritage@lamar.colostate.edu

COLORADO TRAPPERS ASSOCIATION

0250 County Rd. 127
Glenwood Springs, CO 81601 United States
Phone: 970-945-7193 Fax: 970-945-0449

Founded: 1975
Membership: 101–1,000
Scope: Regional
Description: Associate of Fur Takers of America and National Trappers Association. Dedicated to the wise conservation and management of furbearing animals, the education of fur harvesters and public about furbearer management and the preservation of America's rich heritage in the harvest of wild furs.
Publication(s): Managing Rocky Mountain Furbearers, Fur Marketing and Trappers Supply Handbook
Keyword(s): Agriculture/Farming, Recreation/Ecotourism, Wildlife & Species
Contact(s):
Al Davidson, President; P.O. Box 625, Saguache, CO 81149; 719-655-2777
Marvin Miller, Vice President; 29156 Summit Ranch Dr., Golden, CO 80401; 303-526-9207
Maj. Boddicker, Director of Publications
Eddie Montoya, Metro Director
Maj. Boddicker, Editor
Kandy Herrman, Secretary; 0250 County Rd. 127, #19, Glenwood Springs, CO 81601; 970-945-7193; Fax: 970-945-0449
Darla Jackson, Treasurer; 719-643-5263

COLORADO WATER CONGRESS

1580 Logan St., Suite 400
Denver, CO 80203 United States
Phone: 303-837-0812 Fax: 303-837-1607
E-mail: macravey@cowatercongress.org
Website: www.cowatercongress.org

Founded: 1958
Scope: State
Description: To institute and advance programs for the conservation, development, protection, and efficient utilization of the water resources of Colorado.
Publication(s): Colorado Water Rights, Colorado Laws Enacted of Interest to Water Users, Water Quality News, Water Special Report, Water Research News, Water Legislative Report, Water Legal News, Water Intelligence Report, Colorado Water Almanac & Directory
Contact(s):
Rod Kuharich, President
Daniel Birch, Vice President
Richard Macravey, Executive Director

COLORADO WILDLIFE FEDERATION

445 Union Blvd., Suite 302
P.O. Box 280967
Lakewood, CO 80228-1243 United States
Phone: 303-987-0400 Fax: 303-987-0200
E-mail: cfw@coloradowildlife.org
Website: www.coloradowildlife.org

Founded: 1953
Membership: 1,001–10,000
Scope: State
Description: A representative statewide organization, affiliated with the National Wildlife Federation, dedicated to the protection and enhancement of wildlife and its habitat through public education and government interaction.
Publication(s): Colorado Wildlife
Contact(s):
Wayne East, Executive Director
Mike Brogan, Education Programs Contact
Dennis Buechler, Chair and Alternate Representative
Colleen Gadd, Representative
Jim Goddard, Treasurer
Suzanne O'Neill, Board Chair
Barbara Young, Editor

COLORADO WILDLIFE HERITAGE FOUNDATION

6060 Broadway
Denver, CO 80216 United States
Phone: 303-291-7212 Fax: 303-291-7416

Founded: 1989
Scope: State
Description: The Colorado Wildlife Heritage Foundation has been endorsed by four Colorado governors. The foundation's objectives are threefold: (1) environmental education, (2) habitat acquisition and management, and (3) wildlife research. Where appropriate, the foundation pursues projects with the support and expertise of the Colorado Division of Wildlife.
Publication(s): The Colorado Wildlife Viewing Guide
Keyword(s): Wildlife & Species
Contact(s):
Terry Combs, President; American Cargo Handling, P.O. Box 17594, Denver, CO 80217; 303-398-2416; Fax: 303-322-6142
Karen Ballard, Executive Director; Colorado Wildlife Heritage Foundation, 6060 Broadway, Denver, CO 80216; 303-291-7416
Charles Warren, Director; 333 Logan St., Denver, CO 80203; 303-778-7797; Fax: 303-698-5091
Bill Daley, Treasurer; Hutchison Western, P.O. Box 1158, Adams City, CO 80022; 303-287-2826; Fax: 303-289-3286
Ed Erickson, Secretary; 100 Dexter St., Denver, CO 80220; 303-388-8176
Linda Hamlin, Chairman; 378 S. Pontiac Way, Denver, CO 80224; 303-355-3957

COLUMBIA BASIN FISH AND WILDLIFE AUTHORITY

2501 SW 1st Ave. Suite 200
Portland, OR 97201 United States
Phone: 503-229-0191 Fax: 503-229-0443
Website: www.cbfwf.org

Founded: 1982
Scope: Regional
Description: A regional association of all the fish and wildlife agencies (two federal, five state) and Indian tribes (13 in the Columbia River Basin (Idaho, Montana, Oregon, and Washington). Established to coordinate planning and implementation of the fish and wildlife provisions of the Pacific Northwest Electric Power Planning and Conservation Act and for oversight of fish and wildlife resource management under the Fish and Wildlife Coordination Act and other authorities. Current charter: 1987.
Keyword(s): Wildlife & Species
Contact(s):
Jan Eckman, Staff

COLUMBIA ENVIRONMENTAL RESEARCH CENTER

USGS-BRD-ECRC, 4200 New Haven Rd.
Columbia, MO 65201-9634 United States
Phone: 573-875-5399 Fax: 573-876-1896

Founded: N/A
Membership: 101–1,000
Scope: National
Contact(s):
Pam Haverland, Past-President; pamela_haverland@usgs.gov

COMMITTEE FOR NATIONAL ARBOR DAY

Attn: National Chairman, 63 Fitzrandolph Rd.
West Orange, NJ 07052 United States

Founded: 1936

Scope: National

Description: To establish a unified national observance date on the last Friday in April.

Keyword(s): Wildlife & Species

Contact(s):

Harry Banker, National Chairman; 63 Fitzrandolph Rd., West Orange, NJ 07052; 973-731-3736

COMMUNITIES FOR A BETTER ENVIRONMENT

1611 Telegraph Ave. Suite 450
Oakland, CA 94612 United States
Phone: 510-302-0430 Fax: 510-302-0437
Website: www.cbecal.org

Founded: 1971

Membership: 10,001–100,000

Scope: State

Description: The CBE is a nonprofit, multiracial environmental health organization working to prevent public exposure to toxic chemical pollutants. CBE has over 19 years experience in the California environmental arena. CBE uses science-based research, legal tactics, and organizing strategies to prevent air and water pollution, to eliminate toxic hazards, and to improve the health of the people of California.

Publication(s): Environmental Review, Oil Rag

Keyword(s): Air Quality/Atmosphere, Ethics/Environmental Justice, Oceans/Coasts/Beaches

Contact(s):

Stephanie Pincetl, Board President
Richard Drury, Executive Director
Everett Delano, Secretary

COMMUNITY CONSERVATION CONSULTANTS/HOWLERS FOREVER, INC.

50542 One Quiet Lane
Gays Mills, WI 54631 United States
Phone: 608-735-4717 Fax: 608-735-4765
E-mail: ccc@mwt.net
Website: www.communityconservation.org

Founded: 1989

Membership: 1–100

Scope: International

Description: Specializing in catalyzing of community-based conservation initiatives and designing for their sustainability. Active in Wisconsin, Belize, and India. Coordination of volunteers for projects.

Publication(s): Check website for publication listings

Keyword(s): Reduce/Reuse/Recycle

Contact(s):

Rob Horwich, Director

COMMUNITY ENVIRONMENTAL COUNCIL (CEC)

930 Miramonte Dr.
Santa Barbara, CA 93109 United States
Phone: 805-963-0583 Fax: 805-962-9080
E-mail: cecadmin@cecmail.org
Website: www.communityenvironmentalcouncil.org

Founded: 1970

Membership: 1,001–10,000

Scope: Local

Description: Operating 6 centers and 10 programs, CEC's primary goal is to serve as a connecting institution linking government agencies, business and industry, universities and regulatory bodies, environmental organizations, and the community. Using Santa Barbara as its urban laboratory, CEC conducts research and develops local programs in recycling, hazardous waste, sustainable agriculture, and environmental education.

Publication(s): Gildea Review, A Question of Responsibility: Recycling, Manufacturing with Recyclables

Keyword(s): Agriculture/Farming, Development/Developing Countries, Land Issues, Pollution (general), Reduce/Reuse/Recycle

Contact(s):

Kim Kimbell, President
Sarita Vasquez, Vice President
Laurence Laurent, Executive Director

COMMUNITY RIGHTS COUNSEL

1726 M St., NW, Suite 703
Washington, DC 20036-4524 United States
Phone: 202-296-6889 Fax: 202-296-6895
E-mail: crc@communityrights.org
Website: www.communityrights.org

Founded: 1997

Membership: 1–100

Scope: National

Description: CRC is a public interest law firm defending laws that make our communities healthier, more livable, and socially just.

Publication(s): The Takings Project: Using Federal Courts to Attack Community and Environmental Protections, Hostile Environment: How Activist Federal Judges Threaten our Air, Water, Land, Nothing for Free: How Private Judicial Seminars are Undermining Environmental Protection and Breaking the Public's Trust

Keyword(s): Development/Developing Countries, Land Issues, Public Lands/Greenspace, Reduce/Reuse/Recycle, Water Habitats & Quality, Wildlife & Species

Contact(s):

Douglas Kendall, Executive Director; 202-296-6889; Fax: 202-296-6895; crc@communityrights.org
Leah Doney Neel, Research Associate; 202-296-6889; Fax: 202-296-6895; crc@communityrights.org
Timothy Dowling, Chief Counsel; 202-296-6889; Fax: 202-296-6895; crc@communityrights.org
Jason Rylander, Litigation and Policy Counsel; 202-296-6889; Fax: 202-296-6895; crc@communityrights.org

CONCERN, INC.

1794 Columbia Rd., NW
Washington, DC 20009 United States
Phone: 202-328-8160 Fax: 202-387-3378
E-mail: concern@igc.org
Website: www.sustainable.org

Founded: 1970

Membership: N/A

Scope: National

Description: A national nonprofit environmental education organization with a focus on sustainable communities. Its Sustainable Communities Program features initiatives that are environmentally sound, economically vital, and socially just. CONCERN offers resources and action steps. It facilitates the exchange of information on sustainability and smart growth through the Sustainable Communities Network website (www.sustainable.org) and the management of the Smart Growth Network website (www.smartgrowth.org).

Publication(s): Community Action Guides on Pesticides, Drinking Water, Farmland Waste, Household Waste, and Global Warming

Keyword(s): Development/Developing Countries, Pollution (general), Reduce/Reuse/Recycle

Contact(s):

Susan Boyd, Executive Director
Burks Lapham, Chair

CONFEDERATED SALISH AND KOOTENAI TRIBES

P.O. Box 278
Pablo, MT 59855 United States
Phone: 406-675-2700 Fax: 406-675-2739
E-mail: info@cskt.org
Website: www.cskt.org

Founded: N/A
Membership: 1,001–10,000
Scope: National
Description: The 1.25 million acre Flathead Indian Reservation was created in 1855 by the Treaty of the Hellgate as a homeland for the Salish, Kootenai, and Pend d'Oreille Tribes. The constitutional government of the Confederated Salish and Kootenai Tribes was formed in 1934 and approved by the Secretary of the Interior in 1935 to establish a more responsible organization, promote our general welfare, conserve and develop our land and resources, and secure to ourselves.
Publication(s): Char-Koosta News
Keyword(s): Ethics/Environmental Justice, Land Issues, Reduce/Reuse/Recycle
Contact(s):

Fred Matt, Tribal Chairman
Sandra Morigeau, Executive Secretary; ext. 1312
Gary Orr, Forestry Department Head; ext. 6028
Rhonda Swaney, Natural Resources Department Head; ext. 1263; rhondas@cskt.org

CONNECTICUT ASSOCIATION OF CONSERVATION DISTRICTS, INC.

106 Sherman Lee Dr.
Middletown, CT 06457 United States
Phone: 860-647-6379

Founded: N/A
Scope: State
Contact(s):

Ann Hadley, President
John Breakell, Vice President; 860-491-2243
Tony Inch, Secretary/Treasurer; 134 Heather Lane, Wilton, CT 06897; 203-762-9994

CONNECTICUT AUDUBON SOCIETY, INC.

2325 Burr Street
Fairfield, CT 06430 United States
Phone: 203-259-6305, ext. 103 Fax: 203-254-7673
E-mail: codonnell@ctaudubon.org
Website: www.ctaudubon.org

Founded: 1898
Membership: 10,001–100,000
Scope: State
Description: Connecticut Audubon is a statewide, non-profit membership organization dedicated to providing excellence in environmental education, encouraging the conservation of the state's natural resources and advocating for enlightened leadership on ecological matters.
Publication(s): The Connecticut Audubon News
Keyword(s): Air Quality/Atmosphere, Ecosystems (precious), Executive/Legislative/Judicial Reform, Land Issues, Oceans/Coasts/Beaches, Pollution (general), Public Lands/Greenspace, Recreation/Ecotourism, Reduce/Reuse/ Recycle, Water Habitats & Quality, Wildlife & Species
Contact(s):

Anne Harper, President; 2325 Burr St., Fairfield, CT 06430; 203-259-6305, ext. 101; Fax: 203-254-7673
Peter Kunkel, Vice President
W. Morehouse, Vice President of Legal
Judith Richardson, Vice President
Duffy Schade, Vice President
Milan Bull, Director; CT Audubon Coastal Center, 1 Milford Point Rd., Milford, CT 06460; 203-878-7440; Fax: 203-876-2813
Andrew Griswold, Director Eco Travel; 67 Main St., Essex, CT 06426; 860-767-0660; Fax: 860-767-9988
Ann Guion, Director of Pomfret Center; 189 Pomfret St., Pomfret Center, CT 06259; 860-928-4948
Judy Harper, Director of Glastonbury Center; 1361 Main St., Glastonbury, CT 06033; 860-633-8402; Fax: 860-659-9467
Patricia Kriss, Director of Development; 203-259-6305, ext. 102
Betty McLaughlan, Director of Environmental Affairs; 860-527-6750
Christopher Nevins, Director of Fairfield Region; 2325 Burr St., Fairfield, CT 06430; 203-259-6305, ext. 113
Christopher Nevins, Director of Birdcraft Museum; 314 Unquowa Rd., Fairfield, CT 06430; 203-259-0416; Fax: 203-259-1344
Kasha Breau, Teacher/Naturalist; 1361 Main St., Glastonbury, CT 06033; 860-633-8402
Debbie Dubitsky, Coordinator, Rolling Nature Center; 118 Oak St., Hartford, CT 06106; 860-246-6285
Ken Elkins, Coordinator, School Nature Area Program; 118 Oak St., Hartford, CT 06106; 860-246-6285
David Engelman, Chairman of the Board
Richard Julian, Teacher/Naturalist; 1 Milford Point Rd., Milford, CT 06460; 203-878-7440
Chris Krumperman, Teacher/Naturalist; 1361 Main St., Glastonbury, CT 06033
Cathy O'Donnell, Director Marketing Communications; 203-259-6305, ext. 103
Todd Russo, Teacher/Naturalist; 1361 Main St., Glastonbury, CT 06033; 860-633-8402; Fax: 860-659-9467
Jeff Weiler, Teacher/Naturalist; 189 Pomfret St., Pomfret Center, CT 06259; 860-928-4948

CONNECTICUT B.A.S.S. CHAPTER FEDERATION

Attn: President, 119 Straitsville Rd.
Prospect, CT 06712 United States
Phone: 203-758-0069
Website: www.geocities.com/Yosemite/Rapids/8723/

Founded: N/A
Scope: State
Description: An organization of Bassmaster chapters, affiliated with the Bass Anglers Sportsman Society, organized to fight pollution, assist state and national conservation agencies in their efforts, and teach the young people of our country good conservation practices. Dedicated to the realistic conservation of our water resources.
Contact(s):

Tom Reynolds, President; 309 Hamburg Road, Lyme, CT 06371; 863-434-7677
Ken Bell, Vice President; 21 Cloud Street, Enfield, CT 06082; 860-749-2044; gretafudge@earthlink.net
Lee Johnson, Conservation Director; 155 Candlewood Lake Rd. North, New Milford, CT 06776; 860-350-1368
Ron Murack, Tournament Director; P.O. Box 416, Granby, CT 06035; 860-653-6397
Jon Puhalski, Environmental Director; 53 Overlook Road, Winstead, CT 06098; 860-379-9387
Jim Marenzana, Secretary; 40 South Street Unit 17C, Bristol, CT 06010; J.Haren@snet.net
Joe Rackiewicz, Treasurer; 21 Birch Place, Milford, CT 06460; 203- 87-8909

CONNECTICUT BOTANICAL SOCIETY

CBS
New Haven, CT 06532 United States
Phone: 860-633-7557
Website: www.ct-botanical-society.org

Founded: 1903
Membership: 101–1,000
Scope: Local
Description: The Society increases knowledge of the state's flora accumulate and maintains specimens and records for a permanent botanical record. The Society also recommends

botanically significant areas for protection and supports scholarly botanical research.

Publication(s): The Vascular Flora of Southeastern Connecticut, Yearbook, Newsletter

Keyword(s): Public Lands/Greenspace, Reduce/Reuse/Recycle, Water Habitats & Quality, Wildlife & Species

Contact(s):

Casper Ultee, President; 860-633-7557; casperu@aol.com
Carol Lemmon, Vice President; 203-488-7813
Karen Sexton, Secretary; 860-228-4647
Paul Stetson, Treasurer

CONNECTICUT FOREST AND PARK ASSOCIATION

Middlefield, 16 Meriden Rd.
Rockfall, CT 06481-2961 United States
Phone: 860-346-2372 Fax: 860-347-7463
E-mail: info@ctwoodlands.org
Website: www.ctwoodlands.org

Founded: 1895
Membership: 1,001–10,000
Scope: State

Description: A representative statewide organization, affiliated with the National Wildlife Federation and the National Woodland Owners Association, dedicated to the protection and enhancement of wildlife and its habitat through public education and government interaction.

Contact(s):

Richard Whitehouse, President
Adam Moore, Executive Director
Ruth Cutler, Representative
Ron Manzi, Treasurer

CONNECTICUT FUND FOR THE ENVIRONMENT

205 Whitney Ave. 1st floor
New Haven, CT 06511 United States
Phone: 203-787-0646 Fax: 203-787-0246
E-mail: protect@cfenv.org
Website: www.cfenv.org

Founded: 1978
Membership: 1,001–10,000
Scope: State

Description: CFE is a nonprofit group dedicated to protecting Connecticut's natural resources through legal action, education and scientific investigation.

Publication(s): Newsletter, Annual Reports, Fact Sheets

Keyword(s): Air Quality/Atmosphere, Energy, Ethics/Environmental Justice, Land Issues, Oceans/Coasts/Beaches, Pollution (general), Public Lands/Greenspace, Sprawl/Urban Planning, Transportation, Water Habitats & Quality

Contact(s):

Michael Kashgarian, Vice-President
Donald Strait, Executive Director
Nancy Faesy, Secretary
Thomas Holloway, Treasurer

CONNECTICUT PUBLIC INTEREST RESEARCH GROUP (CONN PIRG)

198 Park Rd. 2 floor
W. Hartford, CT 06119 United States
Phone: 860-233-7554 Fax: 860-233-7574
Website: www.connpirg.org

Founded: 1972
Membership: 10,001–100,000
Scope: State

Description: Works for concrete solutions to improve and protect our environment. Engaged in public education, study, and legislative action in many areas of the environment, including water and air pollution and solid waste.

Publication(s): ConnPIRG Reports

Keyword(s): Air Quality/Atmosphere, Pollution (general), Reduce/Reuse/Recycle, Water Habitats & Quality, Wildlife & Species

CONNECTICUT RIVER WATERSHED COUNCIL INC.

15 Bank Row
Greenfield, MA 01301 United States
Phone: 413-772-2020 Fax: 413-772-2090
E-mail: crwc@crocker.com
Website: www.ctriver.org

Founded: 1952
Membership: 1,001–10,000
Scope: Regional

Description: A member-supported nonprofit organization, CRWC is a regional voice for improvement and protection of the Connecticut River and water resources throughout the 11,260 square-mile, four-state river basin of Vermont, New Hampshire, Massachusetts, and Connecticut. CRWC participates in relevant environmental and resource allocation issues through its land conservancy, water quality improvement, and watershed stewardship programs. Land conservancy revolving loan fund. Conservation education and research.

Publication(s): Currents and Eddies

Keyword(s): Land Issues, Oceans/Coasts/Beaches, Water Habitats & Quality

Contact(s):

Tom Miner, Executive Director
Erling Heistad, Vice Chair
Nancy Rogers, Secretary
Neil Sheridan, Chairman
Andy Wizner, Vice Chair

CONNECTICUT WATERFOWL ASSOCIATION, INC.

P.O. Box 74
Bozrah, CT 06334-0074 United States
Phone: 860-848-1879 Fax: 860-642-7964
E-mail: pcapotosto@snet.net
Website: www.geocities.com/ctwaterfowlersassociation

Founded: 1967
Membership: 101–1,000
Scope: State

Description: To preserve, reclaim, and enhance wetland and wildlife habitat in the state of Connecticut in a manner that promotes the wise use of our natural resources and the progress of our society.

Publication(s): Connecticut Waterfowl and Wetlands

Keyword(s): Water Habitats & Quality, Wildlife & Species

Contact(s):

Jack Harder, President; 203-227-9505, ext. 25; Jack.H@snet.net
Michael Ward, Vice President; 203-254-2600; WardMT@aol.com
Paul Capotosto, Treasurer
Chris Samor, Secretary; 203-888-0352; csamor16@aol.com

CONSERVANCY OF SOUTHWEST FLORIDA, THE

1450 Merrihue Dr.
Naples, FL 34102-3449 United States
Phone: 941-262-0304 Fax: 941-262-0672
E-mail: info@conservancy.org
Website: www.conservancy.org

Founded: 1964
Membership: 1,001–10,000
Scope: Local, Regional

Description: Leading the challenge to protect and sustain Southwest Florida's natural environment through environmental policy, science and education. The Conservancy manages two nature centers, offers learning adventures, rehabilitates injured wildlife, monitors sea turtles and acquires land.

Publication(s): Update, Learning Adventures, Yearbook, Eye on the Issues
Keyword(s): Land Issues, Wildlife & Species
Contact(s):
Kathy Prosser, President and CEO; kathyp@conservancy.org
Steve Bortone, Director, Environmental Science; steveb@conservancy.org
Tracy Zanpaglione, Director of Communications Marketing; tracyz @conservancy.org
E. Louise Taylor, School Programs Manager; 941-403-4239; Fax: 941-263-3019
Michael Simonik, VP, Environmental Policy; michaels@conservancy.org

CONSERVATION BIOLOGY INSTITUTE

260 Southwest Madison Avenue
Suite 106
Corvallis, OR 97333 United States
Phone: 541-757-0687 Fax: 541-757-0518
E-mail: stritt@consbio.org
Website: www.consbio.org

Founded: 1997
Membership: N/A
Scope: Local, State, Regional, National, International
Description: CBI is a non-profit research and planning institute. We work collaboratively to help conserve biodiversity through research, education, planning, and community service.

CONSERVATION COUNCIL FOR HAWAII

PMB-203, 111 E. Puainako St., Suite 585
Hilo, HI 96720 United States
Phone: 808-968-6360 Fax: 808-968-0896
E-mail: cch@aloha.net
Website: www.conservation-hawaii.org

Founded: N/A
Scope: State
Description: A representative statewide organization, affiliated with the National Wildlife Federation, dedicated to the protection and enhancement of wildlife and its habitat through public education and government interaction.
Publication(s): The Hawaii Conserver
Contact(s):
Steven Montgomery, President
Karen Blue, Executive Director and Editor
Janet Dellaria, Alternate Representative
Kate Schuerch, Representative & Treasurer

CONSERVATION COUNCIL OF NORTH CAROLINA

P.O. Box 12671
Raleigh, NC 27605 United States
Phone: 919-839-0006 Fax: 919-839-0767
E-mail: info@conservationcouncilnc.org
Website: www.conservationcouncilnc.org

Founded: 1968
Membership: 101–1,000
Scope: State
Description: A statewide lobbying group dedicated to protecting, preserving, and enhancing NC's natural environment through lobbying, educating and mobilizing citizens, making the environment a priority for legislators and the public, and holding legislators accountable for their environmental decisions.
Publication(s): Carolina Conservationist Newsletter, Legislative Scorecard
Keyword(s): Air Quality/Atmosphere, Energy, Forests/Forestry, Land Issues, Oceans/Coasts/Beaches, Pollution (general), Reduce/Reuse/Recycle, Sprawl/Urban Planning, Transportation, Water Habitats & Quality
Contact(s):
Nina Szlosberg, President
Laura Lauffer, Vice President
Dan Besse, Political Director
Carrie Oren, Executive Director; 919-839-0006
Steve Wall, Director of Governmental Relations; 919-839-0020; steve@conservationcouncilnc.org

CONSERVATION EDUCATION CENTER, THE

2473 160th Rd.
Guthrie Center, IA 50115 United States
Phone: 641-747-8383 Fax: 641-747-3951

Founded: 1958
Scope: State
Description: To encourage and lead the development and practice of a widespread and effective conservation education program in Iowa.
Contact(s):
Don Sievers, Training Officer; dsievers@pionet.net
A. Jay Winter, Training Officer; ajwinter@pionet.net

CONSERVATION FEDERATION OF MARYLAND/ F.A.R.M.

P.O. Box 455
Poolesville, MD 20837 United States
Phone: 301-916-3510 Fax: 301-349-5941
E-mail: f.a.r.m@erols.com
Website: www.darnet.com

Founded: N/A
Membership: 1,001–10,000
Scope: Regional
Description: The Conservation Federation of Maryland is devoted to the wise use, conservation, aesthetic appreciation, and restoration of wildlife and other natural resources. The Conservation Federation of Maryland was recently merged with for A Rural Maryland to help safeguard the dwindling supply of farmland and open space in the State of Maryland.
Publication(s): This Place We Call Home
Keyword(s): Agriculture/Farming, Development/Developing Countries, Ethics/Environmental Justice, Land Issues, Reduce/Reuse/Recycle
Contact(s):
Dolores Milmoe, President; 18801 River Rd., Poolesville, MD 20837
Caroline Taylor, Executive Director; 15711 Hughes Rd., Poolesville, MD 20837; 301-972-7866
Rudy Gole, Treasurer; 17105 Oxley Farm Rd., Poolesville, MD 20837
Cathy Hall, Secretary; 17826 Walling Rd., Poolesville, MD 20837

CONSERVATION FEDERATION OF MISSOURI

728 W. Main St.
Jefferson City, MO 65101-1159 United States
Phone: 573-634-2322 Fax: 573-634-8205
E-mail: confedmo@socket.net
Website: www.confedmo.com

Founded: 1935
Membership: 10,001–100,000
Scope: State
Description: A representative statewide organization, affiliated with the National Wildlife Federation, dedicated to the protection and enhancement of wildlife and its habitat through public education and government interaction.
Publication(s): Missouri Wildlife
Contact(s):
Ike Lovan, President and Alternate Representative
Denny Ballard, Executive Director; 573-634-2322; Fax: 573-634-5290; mofed@socket.net

Charles Davidson, Editor; cdfed@socket.net
Arnold Meysenburg, Secretary
Jennifer Mills, Education Programs Contact; 573-634-2322; Fax: 573-634-5290; confedmo@socket.net
Abe Phillips, Representative
Randy Washburn, Treasurer

CONSERVATION FORCE

3900 N. Causeway Blvd., Suite 1045
Metairie, LA 70002 United States
Phone: 504-837-1233 Fax: 504-837-1145
Website: www.conservationforce.org

Founded: 1997
Scope: International
Description: The force was formed to unify sportsmen's organizations, improve the profile of hunters and further the role and value of hunting in wildlife conservation as a force.
Publication(s): Conservation Force Supplement to the Hunting Report
Keyword(s): Ethics/Environmental Justice, Recreation/Ecotourism, Reduce/Reuse/Recycle, Wildlife & Species
Contact(s):
John Jackson, President; One Lakeway Center, 3900 N. Causeway Blvd., Suite 1045, Metairie, LA 70002; 504-837-1233; Fax: 504-837-1145; jjw-no@att.net
Bertrand Des Clers, International Vice President; 15 Rue de Teheran, 75008, Paris; 33-156-597755; Fax: 33-142-607763; igf@foundation-igf.fr
James Teer, Vice President; Texas A&M University, Department of Wildlife & Fisheries, College Station, TX 77845; 409-458-1359; Fax: 409-845-3786; jteer@tamu.edu
Don Lindsay, CF Board Member; P.O. Box, 1200 Nineteenth St.; 707-448-1902; Fax: 011-271-18843743; railwood@iafrica.com
Bart O'Gara, CF Board Member; 215 Red Fox Rd., Lolo, MN 59847; 406243-5372; Fax: 406243-6064; bogara@cellway.umt.edu

CONSERVATION FUND, THE

1800 North Kent St., Suite 1120
Arlington, VA 22209-2156 United States
Phone: 703-525-6300 Fax: 703-525-4610
E-mail: postmaster@conservationfund.org
Website: www.conservationfund.org

Founded: 1985
Membership: N/A
Scope: National
Description: The Conservation Fund forges partnerships to protect America's legacy of land and water resources. Through land acquisition, community initiatives, and leadership training, the Fund and its partners demonstrate sustainable conservation solutions emphasizing the integration of economic and environmental goals.
Publication(s): Common Ground
Keyword(s): Forests/Forestry, Land Issues, Public Lands/Greenspace, Sprawl/Urban Planning, Water Habitats & Quality, Wildlife & Species
Contact(s):
Patrick Noonan, Chairman
Lawrence Selzer, President & CEO
Richard Erdmann, Execuitve Vice President, General Counsel
Sydney Macy, Senior Vice President, Western Regional Office; 303-444-4369; Fax: 303-938-3763
David Sutherland, Senior Vice President, Real Estate
Rex Boner, Vice President, Georgia Office; 770-414-0211; Fax: 770-938-0585
Elizabeth Dowdle, Vice President, Florida Office; 561-832-7665; Fax: 561-832-8102
Pamela Gray, Vice President, Administration
Elizabeth Madison, Vice President, Development
Edward McMahon, Vice President, Director of Center for Conservation & Development
Jodi O'Day, Vice President, Regional General Counsel; 410-757-0370; Fax: 410-757-3791
David Phillips, Vice President & Chief Financial Officer
Mike McQueen, Editor, Common Ground; 804-973-7324

CONSERVATION INTERNATIONAL

1919 M St., NW, Suite 600
Washington, DC 20036 United States
Phone: 202-912-1000 Fax: 202-912-1045
Website: www.conservation.org

Founded: 1987
Scope: International
Description: Conservation International is a global, field-based environmental org. that works to protect biological diversity. CI focuses on the biodiversity hotspots, tropical wilderness areas and key marine ecosystems. The majority of CI staff work on the front lines where unique plant and animal species are most threatened. CI builds alliances with other NGOs, foreign governments, indigenous communities and industry, and works with communities living in biodiversity-rich areas.
Keyword(s): Forests/Forestry, Wildlife & Species
Contact(s):
Russell Mittermeier, President; 202-973-2212; Fax: 202-887-0192
Peter Seligmann, CEO and Chairman of the Board; 202-973-2275; p.seligmann.org

CONSERVATION LAW FOUNDATION, INC. (CLF)

120 Tillson Ave.
Rockland, ME 04841 United States
Phone: 207-594-8107 Fax: 207-596-7706
Website: www.clf.org

Founded: 1966
Membership: 1,001–10,000
Scope: Local, State, Regional
Description: CLF is a regional environmental advocacy organization with offices in Rhode Island, Massachusetts, Vermont, New Hampshire, and Maine.
Publication(s): Conservation Matters, The Wild Sea, City Routes City Rights, Effects of Fishing Gear on the Sea Floor of New England
Keyword(s): Agriculture/Farming, Air Quality/Atmosphere, Ecosystems (precious), Energy, Forests/Forestry, Land Issues, Oceans/Coasts/Beaches, Pollution (general), Public Health, Public Lands/Greenspace, Sprawl/Urban Planning, Transportation, Water Habitats & Quality,
Contact(s):
Peter Shelley, Center Director

CONSERVATION LAW FOUNDATION, INC. (CLF)

NEW ENGLAND REGION
62 Summer St.
Boston, MA 02110 United States
Phone: 617-350-0990 Fax: 617-350-4030
Website: www.clf.org

Founded: 1966
Membership: 1–100
Scope: Regional
Description: CLF is a nonprofit, member-supported environmental law organization dedicated to improving resource management, environmental protection, and public health in New England. Work includes: Energy and water conservation, environmental health, transportation planning, water resources protection, land preservation, and marine resources protection.
Publication(s): Take Back Your Streets, Troubled Waters, A Silent and Costly Epidemic, Power to Spare I&II
Keyword(s): Air Quality/Atmosphere, Energy, Forests/Forestry, Land Issues, Oceans/Coasts/Beaches, Pollution (general), Pub-

lic Health, Public Lands/Greenspace, Sprawl/Urban Planning, Transportation, Water Habitats & Quality

Contact(s):
Douglas Foy, President
Charles Cabot, Chairman of the Board
Eugene Clapp, Treasurer
Paula Gold, Vice Chairman of the Board
John Teal, Vice Chairman of the Board

CONSERVATION TECHNOLOGY INFORMATION CENTER

1220 Potter Dr.
West Lafayette, IN 47906-1383 United States
Phone: 765-494-9555 Fax: 765-494-5969
E-mail: ctic@ctic.purdue.edu
Website: www.ctic.purdue.edu

Founded: 1982
Membership: 1–100
Scope: National
Description: Conservation Technology Information Center (CTIC) is a nonprofit information and data transfer center. The national Center promotes environmentally and economically beneficial agricultural decision-making by: producing and circulating information, data, and contacts, coordinating national initiatives, and sponsoring interactive meetings and conferences. The Center is supported by members and participating governmental agencies.
Publication(s): CTIC Partners Newsletter, Watershed Management, Conservation Tillage
Keyword(s): Agriculture/Farming, Water Habitats & Quality
Contact(s):
John Hassell, Executive Director; hassell@ctic.purdue.edu
Ed Frye, Project Manager
Bruno Alesii, Chair, Board of Directors; 106 Pebble Creek, Boerne, TX 78006
Dan Towery, Natural Resources Specialist; towery@ctic.purdue.edu

CONSERVATION TREATY SUPPORT FUND

3705 Cardiff Rd.
Chevy Chase, MD 20815 United States
Phone: 301-654-3150 Fax: 301-652-6390
E-mail: ctsf@conservationtreaty.org
Website: www.conservationtreaty.org

Founded: 1986
Scope: International
Description: CTSF provides direct support to major inter-governmental treaties, including CITES (the endangered species treaty), the wetlands and the migratory species treaty, through fund-raising and education.
Publication(s): Bateman prints and posters, "Treasures of Wetlands" Poster, Caribbean Buyer Beware Poster, CITES Video, CITES Endangered Species Book
Keyword(s): Water Habitats & Quality, Wildlife & Species
Contact(s):
George Furness, President; 301-654-3150; Fax: 301-652-6390; ctsf@conservationtreaty.org
Frederick Morris, Vice President; 703-683-8512; Fax: 703-683-4622
Faith Campbell, Secretary; 202-547-9120; Fax: 202-547-9213
Lawrence Mason, Treasurer; 703-241-8896; Fax: 703-241-8896; lnmason@compuserve.com

CONSERVATION TRUST OF PUERTO RICO

P.O. Box 9023554
San Juan, 00902-3554 Puerto Rico
Phone: 787-722-5834 Fax: 787-722-5872
E-mail: fideicomiso@fideicomiso.org
Website: www.fideicomiso.org

Founded: 1970
Scope: State
Description: A private nonprofit institution created by the Governor of Puerto Rico and the U.S. Secretary of the Interior to preserve and enhance Puerto Rico's natural beauty and resources, primarily through land acquisition. Owns or manages over 16,000 acres representative of the island's major endangered habitats. It educates the public about environmental issues; manages a vast reforestation program; and finances conservation in Caribbean countries via debt-for-nature swaps.
Keyword(s): Land Issues
Contact(s):
Thomas Lovejoy, Chairman
Arleen Pabon, Trustee
Kate Romero, Trustee
Francisco Blanco, Executive Director
Blanca Santos, Administration Director

COOK INLET KEEPER

P.O. Box 3269
Homer, AK 99603 United States
Phone: 907-235-4068 Fax: 907-235-4069
E-mail: keeper@inletkeeper.org
Website: www.inletkeeper.org

Founded: 1995
Scope: Regional
Description: The mission of Cook Inlet Keeper is to protect the Cook Inlet Watershed and the life it sustains. Keeper relies on environmental monitoring, research, education, and advocacy to give citizens the tools they need to protect water quality.
Publication(s): Cook Inlet GIS Atlas on CD-ROM, Cook Inlet Watershed Directory, State of the Inlet Report
Keyword(s): Pollution (general), Water Habitats & Quality
Contact(s):
Bob Shavelson, Executive Director

COOPER ORNITHOLOGICAL SOCIETY

ORNITHOLOGICAL SOCIETIES OF NORTH AMERICA
P.O. Box 1897
Lawrence, KS 66044 United States
Phone: 800-627-0629, ext. 217 Fax: 208-378-5347
Website: www.cooper.org

Founded: 1893
Membership: 1,001–10,000
Scope: National, International
Description: Observation and cooperative study of birds; the spread of interest in bird study; the conservation of birds and wildlife in general; the publication of ornithological knowledge.
Publication(s): Condor, The, Studies in Avian Biology
Contact(s):
Terry Rich, President; Branch of Bird Conservation, Div. of Migratory Birds, U.S. FWS, 1387 S. Vinnell Way, Boise, ID 83709
Glenn Walfberg, President
Bonnie Bowen, President-Elect/Treasurer; Department of Animal Ecology 124 Science Hall II Iowa State Univ., Ames, IA 50011; 515-294-6391
David Dobkin, Editor, The Condor
Eileen Kirsch, Secretary; BRD/USGS, Upper Mississippi Science Center, P.O. Box 818, LaCrosse, WI 54602; 608-783-6451, ext. 226; eileen_kirsch@usgs.gov
John Rotenberry, Editor, Studies In Avian Biology; Department of Biology, University of California, Riverside, CA 92521; 909-787-3953; rote@citrus.ucr.edu

COOSA RIVER BASIN INITIATIVE

408 Broad St.
Rome, GA 30161 United States
Phone: 706-232-2724 Fax: 706-235-9066
E-mail: crbi@roman.net
Website: www.roman.net/~crbi

Founded: 1992

Membership: 101–1,000
Scope: Regional
Description: CRBI works to inform and empower citizens so they may become involved with the process of creating a cleaner, healthier, economically viable Coosa River Basin.
Publication(s): Main Stream, The
Keyword(s): Pollution (general), Water Habitats & Quality
Contact(s):
Ben Harrision, President; 706-295-0858; benhar@bellsouth.net
Joe Cook, Vice President; 706-235-117-; jmc@artfamily.com
Monica Cook, Publication Chair; 706-235-1170; jmc@artfamily.com
Bill Davin, Education Chair
Mitch Lawson, Coordinator; 706-232-2724

CORAL REEF ALLIANCE, THE (CORAL)

2014 Shattuck Ave
Berkeley, CA 94704 United States
Phone: 510-848-0110 Fax: 510-848-3720
E-mail: info@coral.org
Website: www.coralreefalliance.org/

Founded: 1994
Scope: International
Description: The Coral Reef Alliance is a nonprofit organization that works with diverse government conservation organizations, and others to promote coral reef conservation around the world. CORAL focuses primarily on helping local communities to establish their own marine protected area. CORAL also sponsors a number of educational programs and publications.
Publication(s): Coral News, Coral Reefs - The Vanishing Rainbow
Keyword(s): Oceans/Coasts/Beaches, Reduce/Reuse/Recycle
Contact(s):
Kalli De Meyer, Director Coral Parks Program; CORAL Bonaire Office, Kaya Madrid 3A, Sabana Bonaire; 599-717-3465; Fax: 599-717-3476; kdemeyer@coral.org
Ellen Horne, Director of Development; 510-848-0110; Fax: 510-848-3720; ehorne@coral.org
Brian Huse, Executive Director; 510-848-0110; Fax: 510-848-3720
Janine Kraus, Managing Director; 510-848-0110; Fax: 510-848-3720; jkraus@coral.org
Anita Daley, ICRIN Manager; 510-848-0110, ext. 313; Fax: 510-848-3720; adaley@coral.org

CORLANDS

25 E. Washington St.
Suite 1650
Chicago, IL 60602 United States
Phone: 312-427-4256 Fax: 312-427-6251
E-mail: info@corlands.org
Website: corlands.org

Founded: N/A
Scope: Local
Description: CorLands is a nonprofit organization that works with park and forest preserve districts, and other local governments and concerned citizens to save open space for public enjoyment.

CORNELL LAB OF ORNITHOLOGY

159 Sapsucker Woods Rd.
Ithaca, NY 14850 United States
Phone: 800-843-2473 Fax: 607-254-2415
E-mail: cornellbirds@cornell.edu
Website: www.birds.cornell.edu

Founded: 1917
Membership: 10,001–100,000
Scope: International
Description: The Lab is a membership institution interpreting and conserving the earth's biological diversity through research, education, and citizen science focused on birds.
Publication(s): Birdscope, Living Bird, News and Findings from the Lab
Keyword(s): Wildlife & Species
Contact(s):
Rick Bonney, Director of Education Program; 607-254-2440; birdeducation@cornell.edu
Christopher Clark, Director of Bioacoustics Research Program; 607-254-2405
John Fitzpatrick, Louis Agassiz Fuertes Director; 607-254-2410
Jennifer Smith, Communications Assistant; 607-254-2497
Gregory Budney, Curator of Library of Natural Sounds; 607-254-2406
Tim Gallagher, Living Bird Editor; 607-254-2443

COUNCIL FOR ENVIRONMENTAL EDUCATION

Executive Director c/o Josetta Hawthorne
5555 Morningside Dr.
Suite 212
Houston, TX 77005 United States
Phone: 713-520-1936 Fax: 713-520-8008
E-mail: info@c-e-e.org
Website: www.c-e-e.org

Founded: 1970
Scope: National
Description: The Council for Environmental Education is a nonprofit education organization creating a partnership and network between education and natural resource professionals. CEE co-sponsors balanced, non-biased environmental education programs such as Project WILD, Project WILD Aquatic, and WET in the City. In an effort to encourage more environmental education outreach to urban youth, CEE has launched WET in the City, a community-based water education initiative.
Publication(s): WET in The City Curriculum & Activity Guide, Project WILD Aquatic K-12 Curriculum & Activity Guide, Project WILD K-12 Curriculum & Activity Guide
Keyword(s): Reduce/Reuse/Recycle
Contact(s):
Bill Andrews, President; 916-657-5374
Josetta Hawthorne, Executive Director and Director, Wet In the City
Kathy Mcglauflin, Project Learning Tree Director; 1111 19TH St., NW, Suite 780, Washington, DC 20036; 202-436-2468

COUNCIL FOR PLANNING AND CONSERVATION

Box 228
Beverly Hills, CA 90213 United States
Phone: 310-276-2685
E-mail: esharris@earthlink.net
Website: www.beverlyhillscitizen.org

Founded: N/A
Scope: State
Description: Serves as a clearinghouse for information and gives inexperienced groups ready access to advice and assistance. Provides a center through which opportunities for southern California's environmental protection and enhancement may be communicated. Concerns include: air and water quality, water supply, energy options, waste management, land use, transportation, coastal conservation, urban planning and housing.
Keyword(s): Air Quality/Atmosphere, Energy, Forests/Forestry, Oceans/Coasts/Beaches, Reduce/Reuse/Recycle, Transportation
Contact(s):
Ellen Harris, President and Executive Director
Betty Harris, Vice President
Sam Weisz, Treasurer and Secretary

COUSTEAU SOCIETY, INC., THE

870 Greenbrier Cir.
Chesapeake, VA 23320 United States
Phone: 757-523-9335 Fax: 727-523-2747
E-mail: cousteau@infi.net
Website: www.cousteausociety.org

Founded: 1973
Membership: 100,001–500,000
Scope: International
Description: A nonprofit, membership-supported environmental education organization dedicated to the protection and improvement of the quality of life for present and future generations. Believing that an informed and alerted public can best make the choices that will sustain the water planet, it produces television films, research, books and other publications, exploring relationships between humans and ecosystems.
Publication(s): Calypso Log, Dolphin Log
Keyword(s): Oceans/Coasts/Beaches, Wildlife & Species
Contact(s):
Francine Cousteau, President
Robert Steele, Vice President Finance

COUSTEAU SOCIETY, INC., THE

FRANCE OFFICE
92 Avenue Kleber
Paris, 75116 France
Phone: 44340606

Founded: N/A
Scope: International

CRAIGHEAD ENVIRONMENTAL RESEARCH INSTITUTE

201 S. Wallace Avenue
Bozeman, MT 59715 United States
Phone: 406-585-8705 Fax: 406-585-8220
E-mail: ceri@avicom.net
Website: www.grizzlybear.org

Founded: 1955
Membership: 1–100
Scope: Regional, International
Description: A nonprofit professional organization of scientists, dedicated to exploring the cause-and-effect relationships of man and his environment. Activity includes research, education, and conservation, with emphasis on ecological studies and interdisciplinary approach. Originally the Outdoor Recreation Institute. Staff Members: 6.
Keyword(s): Water Habitats & Quality, Wildlife & Species
Contact(s):
Frank Craighead, President, Program Director
Charles Craighead, Media Director
April Craighead, Secretary

CRAIGHEAD WILDLIFE-WILDLANDS INSTITUTE

5200 Upper Miller Creek Rd.
Missoula, MT 59803 United States
Phone: 406-251-3867

Founded: 1977
Scope: National
Description: A nonprofit, multidisciplinary research center in the Northern Rockies devoted to field-based ecological discovery and scientific activism. The Institute's mission is to generate new ecological information and concepts, widely communicate these insights, and influence public policy and individual behavior in directions that preserve regional biodiversity.
Publication(s): The Grizzly Bears of Yellowstone: Their Ecology in the Yellowstone Ecosystem 1959-1992 (1995), Mapping Arctic Vegetation in Northwest Alaska Using Landsat MSS Imagery (1988), An Integrated Satellite Technique to Evaluate Grizzly Bear Habitat Use (1997)
Keyword(s): Wildlife & Species
Contact(s):
John Craighead, Chairman of the Board; 5125 Orchard Ln., Missoula, MT 59803; 406-251-3944

CRESTON VALLEY WILDLIFE MANAGEMENT AREA

Box 640
Creston, V0B 1G0 British Columbia Canada
Phone: 250-428-3260 Fax: 250-428-3276
E-mail: info@crestonwildlife.ca
Website: www.crestonwildlife.ca

Founded: 1968
Membership: 101–1,000
Scope: International
Description: Established in 1968, the Creston Valley Wildlife Management Area was the first and largest Management Area in the Province of British Columbia. Our mission is to manage the 17,000-acre (7,000-ha) wetland and upland area for conservation and natural species diversity. We do this through active habitat and wildlife management, research, education and public support.
Publication(s): Creston Valley Wildlife Management Area Annual
Contact(s):
Brian Stushnoff, Area Manager; 250-428-3260
Steve Bullock, Chairman of the Management Authority; 250-428-2214

CROSBY ARBORETUM, THE

MISSISSIPPI STATE UNIVERSITY
370 Ridge Rd.
Picayune, MS 39466 United States
Phone: 601-799-2311 Fax: 601-799-2372
E-mail: crosbyar@datastar.net
Website: www.msstate.edu/dept/crec/camain.html

Founded: 1980
Membership: 101–1,000
Scope: State
Description: The main activity of the Arboretum is to preserve, protect and display plants native to the Pearl River drainage basin. Additionally, we provide environmental and horticultural research opportunities and offer educational, scientific, and recreational programs.
Publication(s): Native Trees for Urban Landscapes
Keyword(s): Reduce/Reuse/Recycle, Wildlife & Species
Contact(s):
Stewart Gammill, President
Richard Clark, Vice President
Bob Brzuszek, Senior Curator; 601-799-2311; Fax: 601-799-2372; crosbyar@datastar.net
Jennifer McKay, Secretary
Norman Stevens, Treasurer

D

DAWES ARBORETUM, THE

7770 Jacksontown Rd., SE
Newark, OH 43056-9380 United States
Phone: 740-323-2355 Fax: 740-323-4058
Website: www.dawesarb.org

Founded: 1929
Membership: 1,001–10,000
Scope: State
Description: A not-for-profit organization that promotes the planting of forest and ornamental trees, and promotes increased love and knowledge of trees, shrubs, and related subjects. The 1,341-acre grounds are open daily from dawn to dusk, free of charge.
Publication(s): Dawes Arboretum Newsletter, The
Keyword(s): Wildlife & Species

Contact(s):
Luke Messinger, Director; lemessinger@ee.net
Michael Ecker, Horticulturist; meecker@ee.net
Laura Kaparoff, Public Relations Editor; lakaparoff@ee.net
Timothy Mason, Natural Resource Specialist; tamason@ee.net
Lori Totman, Naturalist and Educator; latotman@ee.net

DEEP-PORTAGE CONSERVATION RESERVE

2197 Nature Center Dr., NW
Hackensack, MN 56452-2431 United States
Phone: 218-682-2325 Fax: 218-682-3121
E-mail: portage@uslink.net
Website: www.deep-portage.org

Founded: 1975
Membership: 1–100
Scope: State
Description: Deep-Portage is a 6,100-acre demonstration working forest with a primary purpose of environmental education. The campus includes dormitories, classrooms, laboratory, theater, interpretive center, natural history museum, and thirty-seven miles of recreational trails. It is owned by Cass County and operated by the Deep-Portage Conservation Foundation, a nonprofit corporation.
Publication(s): Camp Brochures, Deep-Portage Log
Keyword(s): Forests/Forestry
Contact(s):
Bruce Steiner, President
Dale Yerger, Executive Director

DEFENDERS OF WILDLIFE

1101 14th Street, NW
Suite 1400
Washington, DC 20005 United States
Phone: 202-682-9400 Fax: 202-682-1331
E-mail: information@defenders.org
Website: www.defenders.org

Founded: 1947
Membership: 100,001–500,000
Scope: National
Description: Since 1947, Defenders of Wildlife has been one of the nation's most effective advocates for wildlife, endangered species, and habitat. Defenders works to protect and restore native species, habitats, ecosystems, and overall biological diversity. Defenders is a nonprofit, tax-exempt organization, supported by 430,000 members.
Publication(s): Defenders
Keyword(s): Land Issues, Oceans/Coasts/Beaches, Public Lands/Greenspace, Transportation, Wildlife & Species
Contact(s):
Rodger Schlickeisen, President
Robert Dewey, Vice President for Government Relations
Kate Mathews, Vice President of Membership
Charles Orasin, Senior Vice President for Operations
Philip Rabin, Vice President for Communications
Martha Schumacher, Vice President of Development
Mark Shaffer, Senior Vice President for Program
William Snape, Vice President for Law and Litigation
Sajjad Ahrabi, Director of Information Systems
Mary Beth Beetham, Director of Legistative Affairs
Maria Cecil, Director of Publications and Executive Editor
Kimberley Delfino, Director of California Programs; 926 J. St., Ste. 522, Sacramento, CA 95814
Nina Fascione, Director of Carnivore Conservation
Robert Jones, Director of Finance and Administration
Caroline Kennedy, Director of Special Projects, Species Conservation
Laurie MacDonald, Director of Florida Programs
Craig Miller, Southern Rockies Director; 302 S. Convent Ave., Tucson, AZ 85701
Michael Senatore, Director of Legal Department
Sara Vickerman, Director of West Coast; 1637 Laurel St., Lake Oswego, OR 97034; 503-697-3222
Laura Watchman, Director of Habitat Conservation Planning
Edward Asner, Secretary
Caroline Gabel, Vice Chairman
Winsome McIntosh, Chairman of the Board
Alan Steinberg, Treasurer

DELAWARE ASSOCIATION OF CONSERVATION DISTRICTS

President, P.O. Box 242
Dover, DE 19903-0242 United States
Phone: 302-739-4411 Fax: 302-739-6724

Founded: 1953
Membership: 1–100
Scope: Regional
Description: DACD is a voluntary nonprofit alliance that provides a forum for discussion and coordination among the Delaware Conservation Districts as they work to ensure the wise use and treatment of renewable resources.
Keyword(s): Agriculture/Farming, Land Issues, Reduce/Reuse/Recycle, Water Habitats & Quality
Contact(s):
Terry Pepper, President; 104 Captain Davis Dr., Campden-Wyoming, DE 19934; 302-697-6176; Fax: 303-736-2040; kentcol@aol.com
Ron Breeding, Vice President; Rt. 1, Box 345-B, Seaford, DE 19973; 302-629-3964; Fax: 302-739-6724
Martha Pileggi, Staff Assistant; P.O. Box 242, Dover, DE 19903-0242; 302-739-4411; Fax: 302-739-6724; mpilegg@state.de.us
Dariel Rakestraw, Past President, Board Member; 2138 Graves Rd., Hockessin, DE 19707; 302-239-2969

DELAWARE AUDUBON SOCIETY

P.O. Box 1713
Wilmington, DE 19899 United States
Phone: 302-428-3959
E-mail: mail@delawareaudubon.org
Website: www.delawareaudubon.org

Founded: 1977
Membership: 1,001–10,000
Scope: State
Description: The Delaware Audubon Society promotes an appreciation and understanding of nature to preserve and protect our natural environment and to affirm the necessity for clean air and water and the stewardship of our natural resources.
Publication(s): Delaware Audubon Journal
Keyword(s): Ecosystems (precious), Energy, Oceans/Coasts/Beaches, Pollution (general), Water Habitats & Quality, Wildlife & Species
Contact(s):
Matthew Delpizzo, Vice-President; mail@delawareaudubon.org
Leslie Savage, Vice President; mail@delawareaudubon.org

DELAWARE B.A.S.S. CHAPTER FEDERATION

Attn: President, 3700 South State St.
Camden, DE 19934 United States
Phone: 302-698-9257 Fax: 302-720-1230
Website: www.ezy.net/~delbass/

Founded: N/A
Membership: 101–1,000
Scope: State
Description: An organization of Bassmaster chapters, affiliated with the Bass Anglers Sportsman Society, organized to fight pollution, assist state and national conservation agencies in their efforts, and teach the young people of our country good conservation practices. Dedicated to the realistic conservation of our water resources.
Publication(s): Bassing on Delmarva

Contact(s):
Jim Fields, President; 302-698-9257
Roger Richardson, Conservation Director; 632 Fencepost Ln., Viola, DE 19979; 302-284-8383

DELAWARE GREENWAYS, INC.

P.O. Box 2095
Wilmington, DE 19899 United States
Phone: 302-655-7275 Fax: 302-655-7274
E-mail: greenwalks@aol.com
Website: www.delawaregreenways.org

Founded: 1989
Membership: 101–1,000
Scope: State
Description: Preserve, enhance, and connect the ecological, scenic, historical, cultural, and recreational resources in Delaware.
Publication(s): See publications on website
Keyword(s): Development/Developing Countries, Ethics/Environmental Justice, Land Issues, Transportation
Contact(s):
Tim Plemmons, Assistant Executive Director
Gail Van Gilder, Executive Director

DELAWARE MUSEUM OF NATURAL HISTORY

P.O. Box 3937
Wilmington, DE 19807 United States
Phone: 302-658-9111 Fax: 302-658-2610
Website: www.delmnh.org

Founded: 1957
Membership: 1,001–10,000
Scope: Regional
Description: The Delaware Museum of Natural History exists to excite and inform people about the natural world. The Museum's core purpose is to help develop a caring society which respects and values our planet. The major focus of the Museum is continued leadership in research and collections in malacology and ornithology and the ecology of the Delmarva Peninsula.
Publication(s): Nemouria, Musenews
Keyword(s): Ecosystems (precious), Wildlife & Species
Contact(s):
Geoff Halfpenny, Executive Director
Gene Hess, Collection Manager, Ornithology
Stephen Reynolds, Editor and Public Relations
Jean Woods, Curator of Birds

DELAWARE NATURE SOCIETY

P.O. Box 700
Hockessin, DE 19707-0700 United States
Phone: 302-239-2334 Fax: 302-239-2473
E-mail: webpage@dnsashland.org
Website: www.delawarenaturesociety.org

Founded: 1964
Membership: 1,001–10,000
Scope: Local, State, Regional, National, International
Description: A representative statewide organization, affiliated with the National Wildlife Federation, dedicated to the protection and enhancement of wildlife and its habitat through public education and government interaction. Operates two nature centers and manages four nature preserves.
Publication(s): Delaware Nature Society Voice
Keyword(s): Agriculture/Farming, Air Quality/Atmosphere, Development/Developing Countries, Ecosystems (precious), Executive/Legislative/Judicial Reform, Land Issues, Pollution (general), Recreation/Ecotourism, Sprawl/Urban Planning, Water Habitats & Quality, Wildlife
Contact(s):
Peter Flint, President
Mike Riska, Executive Director
Bernard Dempsey, Alternate Representative
Helen Fischel, Education Programs Contact
George Fisher, Treasurer
Richard Fleming, Representative
Janice Taylor, Editor, Delaware Nature Society VOICE
Linda Young, Communications Coordinator; 302-239-2334, ext. 10; Fax: 302-239-2473; webpage@dnsashland.org

DELAWARE WILD LANDS, INC.

P.O. Box 505
Odessa, DE 19730-0505 United States
Phone: 302-378-2736 Fax: 302-378-3629
E-mail: dwl@delanet.com

Founded: 1961
Scope: Local
Description: A nonprofit charitable land conservancy actively engaged in acquiring areas on the Delmarva Peninsula for their natural resource values and for educational purposes; presently owns and manages approximately 20,000 acres. Produced two films, "The Endangered Shore" and "Swamp," available on loan or for purchase.
Keyword(s): Land Issues, Oceans/Coasts/Beaches, Water Habitats & Quality, Wildlife & Species
Contact(s):
Holger Harvey, Executive Director
Susan Crawford, Administrative Assistant

DELMARVA ORNITHOLOGICAL SOCIETY

P.O. Box 4247
Greenville, DE 19807 United States

Founded: 1963
Scope: State
Description: The purpose of this society shall be the promotion of the study of birds, the advancement and diffusion of ornithological knowledge, and the conservation of birds and their environment.
Publication(s): Delmarva Ornithologist, DOS Flyer
Contact(s):
Jim White, President; 3507 Barley Mill Rd., Hockessin, DE 19707; 302-239-7065
Mike Smith, Vice President; msmith10@student.vill.edu
Irene Goverts; bbcdel@ezd.com

DELTA WATERFOWL FOUNDATION

R.R. 1 Box 1
Portage la Prairie, R1N 3A1 Manitoba Canada
Phone: 204-239-1900 Fax: 203-239-5950
E-mail: canada@deltawaterfowl.org
Website: www.deltawaterfowl.org

Founded: N/A
Scope: International
Description: Delta Waterfowl's primary mission is to support graduate student training and research on all aspects of waterfowl and wetlands ecology and management. Since 1938, Delta students have produced over 200 graduate theses and 600 scientific publications. In addition to graduate research, Delta is currently involved in several demonstration projects incuding Adopt-A-Pothole, a habitat easement program; Hen Houses, predator-resistant nesting structures, Voluntary Restraint, a hunter ethics program.
Publication(s): Publications on website
Keyword(s): Water Habitats & Quality, Wildlife & Species
Contact(s):
Jonathan Scarth, President
Lloyd Jones, Vice President
Donald Douglas, Vice Chair
Daniel Hughes, Chair
Thomas Hutchens, Treasurer
George Nolte, Secretary

DELTA WILDLIFE INC.
P.O. Box 276
433 Stoneville Road
Stoneville, MS 38776 United States
Phone: 662-686-3370 Fax: 662-686-3382
E-mail: info@deltawildlife.org
Website: deltawildlife.org

Founded: 1990
Membership: 1,001–10,000
Scope: Regional
Description: Delta Wildlife is committed to wildlife habitat enhancement, habitat restoration and conservation education in northwest Mississippi.
Publication(s): Delta Wildlife Magazine
Keyword(s): Agriculture/Farming, Ecosystems (precious), Forests/Forestry, Pollution (general), Public Lands/Greenspace, Water Habitats & Quality, Wildlife & Species
Contact(s):
Trey Cooke, Executive Director; 662-686-3370; teycoo@yahoo.com
Bill Kennedy, Chairman; 662-265-5828

DESCHUTES BASIN LAND TRUST, INC.
760 NW Harriman
Suite 100
Bend, OR 97701 United States
Phone: 541-330-0017 Fax: 541-330-0013
E-mail: info@deschuteslandtrust.org
Website: www.deschuteslandtrust.org

Founded: 1995
Membership: 101–1,000
Scope: Regional
Description: A regional land trust, based in Bend, Oregon, committed to conserving the special lands of the 6.8 million acre Deschutes Basin for present and future generations by working cooperatively with private landowners and local communities.
Keyword(s): Agriculture/Farming, Ecosystems (precious), Forests/Forestry, Land Issues, Public Lands/Greenspace, Water Habitats & Quality, Wildlife & Species

DESERT FISHES COUNCIL
P.O. Box 337
Bishop, CA 93515 United States
Phone: 760-872-8751 Fax: 760-872-8751
E-mail: phildesfish@telis.org
Website: www.desertfishes.org

Founded: 1969
Membership: 101–1,000
Scope: International
Description: A nationwide and international representation of state, federal, and university scientists and resource specialists and private conservation groups to provide for the exchange and transmittal of information on the status, protection, and management of the endemic fauna and flora of North American desert ecosystems.
Publication(s): Proceedings of the Desert Fishes Council
Keyword(s): Development/Developing Countries, Ecosystems (precious), Ethics/Environmental Justice, Land Issues, Reduce/Reuse/Recycle, Water Habitats & Quality, Wildlife & Species
Contact(s):
Paul Marsh, President; Box 871501, Tempe, AZ 85287; 480-965-2977; Fax: 480-965-2519; fish.dr@asu.edu
Dean Hendrickson, Editor of the Proceedings; 512-471-9774; Fax: 512-471-9775
Edwin Pister, Executive Secretary; Desert Fishes Council, P.O. Box 337, Bishop, CA 93515; 760-872-8751; phildesfish@telis.org

DESERT PROTECTIVE COUNCIL
P.O. Box 3635
San Diego, CA 92163 United States
Phone: 619-543-0757 Fax: 619-543-0757
E-mail: jtdesert@ixpres.com
Website: www.dpcinc.org

Founded: 1954
Membership: 101–1,000
Scope: Regional
Description: National desert oriented membership organization dedicated to educating the public about desert ecosystems and promoting wise and reverent enjoyment of desert lands.

DESERT RESEARCH FOUNDATION OF NAMIBIA, THE
7 Rossini Street
Windhoek, 9000 Namibia
Phone: 26461229855 Fax: 26461230172
E-mail: drfn@drfn.org.na
Website: www.drfn.org

Founded: 1963
Scope: Local, Regional, National, International
Description: The DRFN is a centre for arid land studies that conducts and facilitates appropriate, participatory and applied short- and long-term research on the environment. It is an independent, non-governmental organisation dedicated to sustainable use of Namibia's environment.
Keyword(s): Development/Developing Countries, Land Issues, Water Habitats & Quality, Wildlife & Species
Contact(s):
Mary Seely, Contact

DESERT TORTOISE COUNCIL
P.O. Box 3141
Wrightwood, CA 92397 United States
Phone: 619-431-8449
E-mail: info@deserttortoise.org
Website: www.deserttortoise.org

Founded: 1975
Scope: National
Description: Formed to assure the continued survival of viable populations of the desert tortoise, Gopherus agassizi, which is endemic to Arizona, California, Nevada, and Utah.
Keyword(s): Land Issues, Public Health, Public Lands/Greenspace, Reduce/Reuse/Recycle, Wildlife & Species
Contact(s):
Mike Coffeen, Treasurer
Tim Duck, Co-Chairman
Tracy Goodlett, Co-Chairman
Ed Larue, Secretary
Ed Larue, Recording Secretary

DESERT TORTOISE PRESERVE COMMITTEE, INC.
4067 Mission Inn Ave.
Riverside, CA 92501 United States
Phone: 909-683-3872 Fax: 909-683-6949
E-mail: dtpc@pacbell.net
Website: www.tortoise-tracks.org

Founded: 1974
Scope: Regional
Description: A nonprofit organization formed to promote the welfare of the desert tortoise in the southwestern United States and to manage and establish preserves in the Western Mojave Desert.
Publication(s): Tortoise Tracks
Keyword(s): Ecosystems (precious), Land Issues, Public Lands/Greenspace, Wildlife & Species

Contact(s):
Michael Connor, Executive Director; 909-683-3872; Fax: 909-638-6949; dtpc@pacbell.net

DISTRICT OF COLUMBIA SOIL AND WATER CONSERVATION - DISTRICT

Attn: Chair, 800 9th St. SW 3rd Fl.
Washington, DC 20024 United States
Phone: Fax: 202-442-8989
Website: www.obc.dc.gov

Founded: N/A
Scope: State
Contact(s):
Theodore Gordon, Chair; 202-442-8989

DRAGONFLY SOCIETY OF THE AMERICAS, THE

2091 Partridge Ln.
Binghamton, NY 13903 United States
Phone: 607-722-4939
E-mail: tdonnel@binghamton.edu

Founded: 1989
Membership: 101–1,000
Scope: International
Description: The organization is concerned with all factors relevant to the world species assemblage of Odonata (Insecta: Dragonflies). We study their systematics, biology, and taxonomy. The organization is also concerned with maintaining and improving the environmental conditions for Odonata through better water quality management, wetlands conservation, and aquatic habitat preservation.
Publication(s): ARGIA, Bulletin of American Odonatology
Keyword(s): Land Issues, Water Habitats & Quality, Wildlife & Species
Contact(s):
Roy Beckemeyer, President; 957 Perry, Wichita, KS 67203; royb@southwind.net
J.J. Daigle, Treasurer
T.W. Donnelly, Editor; 2091 Partridge Lane, Binghamton, NY 13903
S.W. Dunkle, Secretary; Biology Department, Collin County Community College, Plano, TX 75074

DUCKS UNLIMITED

QUEBEC OFFICE
Suite 260, 710 Bouvier St.
G2J 1C2 Quebec Canada
Phone: 418-623-1650 Fax: 418-623-0420
E-mail: du_quebec@ducks.ca
Website: www.ducks.ca

Founded: 1938
Membership: 100,001–500,000
Scope: International
Description: Ducks Unlimited Canada is an international, private, non-profit organization dedicated to the conservation of wetlands and associated habitats for the perpetuation of North America's waterfowl, which in turn provide healthy environments for wildlife and people.
Publication(s): Conservator, Conservationniste
Contact(s):
Patrick Plante, Director of Regional Operations
Paul St. George, Director of Fund Raising
Bernard Filion, Manager of Field Operations

DUCKS UNLIMITED

SASKATCHEWAN OFFICE
P.O. Box 4465, 1030 Winnipeg St.
Regina, S4P 3W7 Saskatchewan Canada
Phone: 306-569-0424 Fax: 306-565-3699
Website: www.ducks.ca

Founded: 1938
Scope: International
Description: A private, nonprofit, conservation organization dedicated to preserving waterfowl by creating and restoring breeding habitat in Canada. This organization is funded by sportsmen of United States and Canada.
Publication(s): Newsletter
Contact(s):
D. Chekay, Director of Public Policy
Tim Thiele, Manager of Field Operations
L. Moats, Agricultural Program Specialist

DUCKS UNLIMITED CANADA

ALBERTA OFFICE
#200, 10720 - 178 St.
Edmonton, T5S 1J3 Alberta Canada
Phone: 780-489-2002 Fax: 780-489-1856
E-mail: du_edmonton@ducks.ca
Website: www.ducks.ca

Founded: N/A
Scope: Regional
Description: Ducks Unlimited Canada is a private, nonprofit charitable organization dedicated to conserving wetlands for the benefit of North America's waterfowl, other wildlife and people.
Publication(s): Conservator
Keyword(s): Land Issues, Recreation/Ecotourism, Water Habitats & Quality, Wildlife & Species
Contact(s):
Gordon Edwards, Director of Regional Operations, Prairie Regions
Brett Calverley, Alberta NAWMP Coordinator
Gary Stewart, Conservation Programs Biologist, WBFI
Jim Wohl, Engineer

DUCKS UNLIMITED CANADA

MANITOBA OFFICE
1 Mallard Bay at Hwy. 220, P.O. Box 11660
Stonewall, R0C 2Z0 Manitoba Canada
Phone: 204-467-3000 Fax: 204-467-9028
E-mail: webfoot@ducks.ca
Website: www.ducks.ca

Founded: 1938
Membership: 101–1,000
Scope: National
Description: Ducks Unlimited Canada's mission is to conserve wetlands and associated habitats for the benefit of North America's waterfowl, which in turn provide healthy environments for wildlife and people.
Keyword(s): Water Habitats & Quality, Wildlife & Species
Contact(s):
Rod Fowler, Executive Vice President
Brian Gray, Director of Conservation Programs; 204-467-3349; Fax: 204-467-9028
Richard Walker, Director of Corporate Development and Major Gifts; 100-279 Midpark Way S.E., Calgary AB T2X IM2; 403-201-5577; Fax: 403-201-5580
Gary Goodwin, Human Resources Manager/Corporate Counsel
Robert Kindrachuk, Communications Manager
Rick Wishart, Manager of Education Program
L. Warren, Chief Financial Officer

DUCKS UNLIMITED CANADA

NOVA SCOTIA OFFICE
P.O. Box 430, #64 Highway 6
Amherst, B4H 3Z5 Nova Scotia Canada
Phone: 902-667-8726 Fax: 902-667-0916
Website: www.ducks.ca

Founded: 1938
Scope: Local, Regional, National, International

Description: Ducks Unlimited Canada is a private, nonprofit charitable organization dedicated to conserving wetlands for the benefit of North America's waterfowl, other wildlife and people

Contact(s):
Mark Gloutney, Manager of Conservation Programs-Atlantic Canada; m_gloutney@ducks.ca
Brian McCullough, Atlantic Engineer; b_mccullough@ducks.ca

DUCKS UNLIMITED CANADA
ONTARIO OFFICE
566 Welham Rd.
Barrie, L4N 8Z7 Ontario Canada
Phone: 705-721-4444 Fax: 705-721-4999
E-mail: du_barrie@ducks.ca
Website: www.ducks.ca

Founded: N/A
Membership: 10,001–100,000
Scope: Regional

Contact(s):
Bob Clay, Manager Western Ontario Field Office
Ron Maher, Manager Eastern Ontario Field Office

DUCKS UNLIMITED, INC.
One Waterfowl Way
Memphis, TN 38120 United States
Phone: 901-758-3825 Fax: 901-758-3850
E-mail: nhq@ducks.org

Founded: 1937
Membership: 500,001–1,000,000
Scope: National
Description: The mission of Ducks Unlimited is to fulfill the annual life cycle needs of North American waterfowl by protecting, enhancing, restoring, and managing important wetlands and associated uplands. Only those activities which contribute directly toward that end shall be undertaken by Ducks Unlimited, Inc.
Publication(s): Ducks Unlimited Magazine, Puddler Magazine

Contact(s):
L. Mayeux, President; P.O. Box 1529, Rue De Medecine, Marksville, LA 71351; 318-253-9643
D. Young, Executive Vice-President
Steve Adair, Director of Conservation Programs
Bruce Batt, Chief Biologist/Director, WWR
Montserrat Carbonell, Director of Latin American Program
Wayne Dierks, Director of Human Resources and Staff Development
Gary Goodpaster, National Director of Events & Membership Support
Eric Keszler, Director of Communications
Linda Schoenrock, National Director of Marketing & Communications
Dan Thiel, National Director of Major Gifts & Gift Planning
Jim Boyd, Group Manager Management Information Systems
James Ware, Group Manager Fundraising/Membership & Marketing
W. Wentz, Group Manager Conservation Programs
Dianne Legg, Executive Assistant
James Flood, General Counsel
Tom Fulgham, Magazine Editor-In-Chief
Randy Graves, Chief Financial Officer
W. Lewis, Treasurer; P.O. Box 1344, Natchez, MS 39120; 601-446-6621
Robert Mims, Controller
Stephen Reynolds, Secretary; 899 Madison Avenue, Memphis, TN 38146; 901-227-5117
Julius Wall, Chairman of the Board; 116 W. Jefferson, P.O. Box 226, Clinton, MO 64735; 660-885-2221
Bill Willsey, Executive Secretary

DUCKS UNLIMITED, INC.
WETLANDS AMERICA TRUST, INC. OFFICE
One Waterfowl Way
Memphis, TN 38120 United States
Phone: 901-758-3825 Fax: 901-758-3850
Website: www.ducks.org

Founded: N/A
Scope: Regional
Description: A nonprofit trust organized to operate exclusively for charitable, educational, scientific and conservation purposes. The Trust seeks to protect the natural balance of our continent's wetland ecosystems, ensuring the future viability of waterfowl and other wetland wildlife.
Keyword(s): Water Habitats & Quality, Wildlife & Species

Contact(s):
L. Mayeux, President
Bill Willsey, Assistant Secretary
D. Young, Chief Operating Officer

E

EAGLE NATURE FOUNDATION, LTD.
300 East Hickory
Apple River, IL 61001 United States
Phone: 815-594-2306 Fax: 815-594-2305
E-mail: eaglenature.tni@juno.com
Website: www.eaglenature.org

Founded: 1995
Membership: 101–1,000
Scope: Local, State, Regional, National, International
Description: ENF is a nonprofit international organization, which develops and implements habitat preservation strategies, conducts a wide variety of nature education and awareness programs, and engages in and supports bald eagle research.
Publication(s): Bald Eagle Bus Tours, Nature News, Bald Eagle News
Keyword(s): Agriculture/Farming, Air Quality/Atmosphere, Development/Developing Countries, Ecosystems (precious), Ethics/Environmental Justice, Forests/Forestry, Land Issues, Pollution (general), Population, Public Lands/Greenspace, Recreation/Ecotourism, Reduce/Reuse

Contact(s):
Terrence Ingram, President and Executive Director
Eugene Small, Vice President; 773-434-8328
Art Gorov, Director; 773-262-4662
Yvonne Johnson, Director; 815-895-4487
Joseph Lukascyk, Director; 708-430-0779
James Ronnerud, Director; 608-776-2755
David Smith, Director; 715-344-5084
Susan Ertmer, Treasurer; 815-845-2253
Juanita. Ray, Secretary; 708-447-1899

EARTH DAY NETWORK
1616 P St. NW
Suite 200
Washington, DC 20007 United States
Phone: 202-518-0044 Fax: 202-518-8794
E-mail: earthday@earthday.net
Website: earthday.net

Founded: N/A
Scope: International
Description: Founded by the organizers of Earth Day 1970, Earth Day Network's mission is to promote environmental awareness and stewardship by engaging grassroots organizations worldwide in environmental education, citizen action and organizing, capacity building, coordinated global campaigns, and annual Earth Day celebrations.

Contact(s):
Kathleen Rogers, President

EARTH DAY NEW YORK

201 E. 42nd St.
Suite 3200
New York, NY 10017 United States
Phone: 212-922-0048 Fax: 212-922-1936
E-mail: education@earthdayny.org
Website: www.earthdayny.org

Founded: 1989

Scope: Local, State, Regional, National

Description: Earth Day New York is a low-overhead, broadly educational nonprofit 501c(3) organization that promotes environmental awareness and solutions through a three-pronged program: 1) involving schools, teachers, and students through the Earth Day Education Program; 2) educating public and private policymakers through conferences; and 3) involving the general public in annual Earth Day events.

Publication(s): Lessons Learned, High Performance Buildings, Building the Sustainable Economy Conference I Proceedings

Keyword(s): Climate Change, Energy, Pollution (general), Sprawl/Urban Planning

Contact(s):

Fred Kent, President; 212-620-5660; Fax: 212-620-3821
Pamela Lippe, Executive Director and Vice President; 212-922-0048; Fax: 212-922-1936; plippe@aol.com
Myra Bresnahan, Deputy Director; 212-922-0048; Fax: 212-922-1936; myra@earthdayny.org
Douglas Durst, Chairman; 212-789-1155; Fax: 212-789-1199
Timon Malloy, Treasurer; 203-535-5326; Fax: 203-353-5329
Jim Tripp, Secretary; 212-505-2100; Fax: 212-505-2375

EARTH FORCE

1908 Mount Vernon Ave.
Alexandria, VA 22301 United States
Phone: 703-299-9400 Fax: 703-299-9485
E-mail: earthforce@earthforce.org
Website: www.earthforce.org

Founded: 1993

Membership: 1–100

Scope: National

Description: Earth Force is a national nonprofit environmental organization. Earth Force is dedicated to young people changing their communities and caring for our environment now, while developing life-long habits of active citizenship and environmental stewardship.

Publication(s): Free Campaign Materials for Kids and Educators

Contact(s):

Tom Martin, President and Director; 703-519-6867; Fax: 703-299-9485
Vince Meldrum, Vice President for National Programs
Donna Power, Vice President for Local Programs
Christine Bates, Board of Directors
F. Hagele, Secretary; 9th Flr., 1515 Market St., Philadelphia, PA 19102; 212-851-8640

EARTH FORCE

GREEN (GLOBAL RIVERS ENVIRONMENTAL EDUCATION NETWORK)
1908 Mt. Vernon Ave., Second Fl.
Alexandria, VA 22301 United States
Phone: 703-299-9400 Fax: 703-299-9485
E-mail: green@earthforce.org
Website: www.earthforce.org

Founded: 1989

Scope: Local, National

Description: Earth Force is youth for a change! Earth Force youth create long-term solutions to environmental issues in their communities. GREEN is program of Earth Force which seeks to improve education through a global network that promotes watershed stewardship.

Publication(s): Protecting Our Watersheds, Field Manual for Water Quality Monitoring, Sourcebook for Watershed Education, Investigating Streams and Rivers

Keyword(s): Land Issues, Oceans/Coasts/Beaches, Pollution (general), Reduce/Reuse/Recycle, Water Habitats & Quality, Wildlife & Species

Contact(s):

Thomas Martin, President; 703-519-6867
Chris Chopyak, Vice President of Development; 703-519-6862; cchopyak@earthforce.org
Vince Meldrum, Vice President of Programs; 703-519-6864

EARTH FOUNDATION

5401 Mitchelldale, Suite B4
Houston, TX 77092 United States
Phone: 713-686-9453
E-mail: sales@earthfound.com
Website: www.earthfound.com

Founded: 1990

Membership: 1–100

Scope: National

Description: The purpose of Earth Foundation is to empower educators and students to work towards a sustainable economy, just society, and healthy environment. Our focus is on education, fundraising for conservation, and cooperative programs with conservation groups and indigenous organizations working in the race to save the planet.

Publication(s): Rainforest Rescue Campaign Teacher Update

Keyword(s): Forests/Forestry, Land Issues, Wildlife & Species

Contact(s):

Cynthia Everage, President and Director; 5151 Mitchelldale B11, Houston, TX 77092

EARTH FRIENDS WILDLIFE FOUNDATION

P.O. Box 11217
Jackson, WY 83002-1217 United States
Phone: 307-734-5333 Fax: 307-739-0133
E-mail: lee@earthfriends.com
Website: www.earthfriends.com

Founded: 1995

Scope: Regional, National

Description: Earth Friends Wildlife Foundation is a charitable support organization committed to using its resources to support the work of conservation and wildlife protection groups. Our gifts are given as matching grants to make resources do more. We recognize the need for partnership among the concerns of business, wildlife interests and of those who will inherit the quality of life we create on this earth.

Publication(s): Yearly Annual Report

Keyword(s): Ecosystems (precious), Reduce/Reuse/Recycle, Wildlife & Species

EARTH ISLAND INSTITUTE

300 Broadway, Suite 28
San Francisco, CA 94133 United States
Phone: 415-788-3666 Fax: 415-788-7324
E-mail: earthisland@earthisland.org
Website: www.earthisland.org

Founded: 1982

Scope: National

Description: Through education and activism, Earth Island Institute counteracts threats to the biological and cultural diversity that sustains and enriches the global environment. The Institute develops and supports projects that promote the conservation, preservation, and restoration of the Earth. The Institute was founded by David Brower, veteran environmental leader.

Publication(s): Earth Island Journal, Ocean Alert, Paper Locator

Keyword(s): Development/Developing Countries, Reduce/Reuse/Recycle, Wildlife & Species

Contact(s):
Bob Wilkinson, President
John Knox, Executive Director
David Phillips, Executive Director
Maria Moyer-Angus, Secretary
Tim Rands, Treasurer

EARTH SHARE

3400 International Dr., NW, Suite 2K
Washington, DC 20008 United States
Phone: 202-537-7100 Fax: 202-537-7101
E-mail: robin@earthshare.org
Website: www.earthshare.org

Founded: 1988
Membership: 101–1,000
Scope: Local, State, Regional, National, International
Description: Earth Share is a nonprofit, federated fund-raising organization that represents nonprofit environmental and conservation organizations in workplace payroll deduction campaigns nationwide. Funds raised support these organizations' environmental and conservation programs and services. Earth Share also provides educational public service announcements about the environment.
Publication(s): Tips, Annual Newsletter
Contact(s):
Kalman Stein, President
Jay Feldman, Chairman; 701 E St. SE, Washington, DC 20003; 202-543-5450; Fax: 202-543-4791
Chuck Paquette, Secretary; 8925 Leesburg Pike, Vienna, VA 22184; 703-790-4016

EARTH SHARE OF GEORGIA

ENVIRONMENTAL FUND FOR GEORGIA
1447 Peachtree St
Suite 214
Atlanta, GA 30309 United States
Phone: 404-873-3173 Fax: 404-873-3135
E-mail: info@earthsharega.org
Website: www.earthsharega.org

Founded: 1992
Membership: N/A
Scope: Local, State, Regional, National, International
Description: Earth Share of Georgia is a nonprofit fund-raising organization that represents local and national nonprofit environmental and conservation organizations in workplace payroll deduction campaigns. Funds raised support these organizations' environmental and conservation programs and services. A state affiliate of Earth Share.
Contact(s):
Alice Rolls, Executive Director; 404-873-3173; Fax: 404-873-3135; alice@earthsharega.org
Elicia Fritsch, Campaign Coordinator; 404-873-3173; Fax: 404-873-3135; elicia@earthsharega.org

EARTHJUSTICE

BOZEMAN OFFICE
209 South Willson Avenue
Bozeman, MT 59715 United States
Phone: 406-586-9699 Fax: 406-586-9695
E-mail: eajusmt@earthjustice.org
Website: www.earthjustice.org

Founded: N/A
Scope: Regional
Description: Protects the rivers, streams, and wildlands of the Northern Rockies, the only place in the lower-48 states where grizzly bears, gray wolves, and bison still roam freely. Uses the power of the law to secure Endangered Species Act listings for imperiled species, challenge oil and gas development and mining operation on sensitive public lands, compel government agencies to restore Montana's water quality, and halt destructive logging and road building in national forests.
Contact(s):
Douglas Honnold, Managing Attorney
Abigail Dillen, Associate Attorney
Tim Preso, Staff Attorney

EARTHJUSTICE

DENVER OFFICE
1631 Glenarm Place
Suite 300
Denver, CO 80202 United States
Phone: 303-623-9466 Fax: 303-623-8083
E-mail: eajusco@earthjustice.org
Website: www.earthjustice.org

Founded: N/A
Scope: Regional
Description: Protects the raging rivers, inspiring land formations, and wide open spaces of the Four Corners states. Uses the power of the law to limit overgrazing on public lands, restore critical rivers and streams, prevent motor vehicle use and logging in roadless areas, and secure critical habitat for threatened and endangered species. Our office also works in conjunction with the Environmental Law Clinic at the University of Denver College of Law.
Contact(s):
Jim Angell, Staff Attorney
Keith Bauerle, Associate Attorney
Eric Huber, Project Attorney
Julie Teel, Associate Attorney
Susan Daggett, Managing Attorney

EARTHJUSTICE

ENVIRONMENTAL LAW CLINIC AT STANFORD UNIVERSITY
Owen House
553 Salvatierra Walk
Stanford, CA 94305 United States
Phone: 650-725-8571 Fax: 650-725-8509
E-mail: info@earthjustice.org
Website: www.earthjustice.org

Founded: N/A
Scope: Regional
Description: Environmental law clinic and regional litigation office.
Contact(s):
Debbie Sivas, Managing Attorney
Michael Lozeau, Staff Attorney

EARTHJUSTICE

ENVIRONMENTAL LAW CLINIC AT THE UNIVERSITY OF DENVER
University of Denver
Forbes House
1714 Poplar Street
Denver, CO 80220 United States
Phone: 303-871-6996 Fax: 303-871-6991
E-mail: info@earthjustice.org
Website: www.earthjustice.org

Founded: N/A
Scope: Regional
Description: Regional law clinic and litigation office of Earthjustice.
Publication(s): Publications on website
Contact(s):
Neil Levine, Staff Attorney
Jay Tutchton, Staff Attorney

EARTHJUSTICE
HEADQUARTERS
426 Seventeenth Street
Sixth Floor
Oakland, CA 94612 United States
Phone: 510-550-6700 Fax: 510-550-6740
E-mail: eajus@earthjustice.org
Website: www.earthjustice.org

Founded: 1971

Scope: National, International

Description: Non-profit public interest law firm dedicated to protecting the magnificent places, natural resources, and wildlife of this earth and to defending the right of all people to a healthy environment. We bring about far-reaching change by enforcing and strengthening environmental laws on behalf of hundreds of organizations and communities.

Publication(s): In Brief

Keyword(s): Air Quality/Atmosphere, Development/Developing Countries, Ecosystems (precious), Energy, Ethics/Environmental Justice, Executive/Legislative/Judicial Reform, Finance/Banking/Trade, Forests/Forestry, Land Issues, Oceans/Coasts/Beaches, Pollution (general)

Contact(s):
Buck Parker, Executive Director
Barbara Bosma, Vice President of Human Resources & Administration
Bill Curtiss, Vice President of Programs
Steve Katz, Vice President of Development
Bruce Neighbor, Vice President of Finance and Administration
Cara Pike, Vice President of Communications

EARTHJUSTICE
HONOLULU OFFICE
223 S. King Street #400
Honolulu, HI 96813-4501 United States
Phone: 808-599-2436 Fax: 808-521-6841
E-mail: eajushi@earthjustice.org
Website: www.earthjustice.org

Founded: 1971

Scope: Local, State, Regional

Description: Protects island and ocean ecosystems, native cultures, and endangered species in the mid-Pacific. Uses the power of the law to compel federal agencies to address the harmful effects of commercial fishing on marine ecosystems, restore contaminated inland waterways, secure endangered species, and support the islands' indigenous people and culture by safeguarding fragile ecosystems and water rights for local communities.

Publication(s): Hawaii Office Brochure

Contact(s):
Paul Achitoff, Managing Attorney
David Henkin, Staff Attorney
Kapua Sproat, Associate Attorney
Marjorie Ziegler, Resource Analyst

EARTHJUSTICE
INTERNATIONAL PROGRAM
426 Seventeenth Street
Seventh Floor
Oakland, CA 94612 United States
Phone: 510-550-6700 Fax: 510-550-6740
E-mail: eajusintl@earthjustice.org
Website: www.earthjustice.org

Founded: N/A

Scope: International

Description: Uses the power of the law to protect the environment and human health worldwide. Represents public interest and community groups in international tribunals and domestic courts to hold corporations and governments responsible for environmental harm, prevent trade rules from undermining public health and environmental protections, and create strong tools for citizens to defend the right to a healthy environment.

Contact(s):
Martin Wagner, Director
Anna Cederstav, Staff Scientist
Scott Pasternack, Associate Attorney

EARTHJUSTICE
JUNEAU OFFICE
325 4th Street
Juneau, AK 99801 United States
Phone: 907-586-2751 Fax: 907-463-5891
E-mail: eajusak@earthjustice.org
Website: www.earthjustice.org

Founded: N/A

Membership: N/A

Scope: Regional

Description: Protects Alaska's pristine wilderness, marine ecosystems, and wildlife. Uses the power of the law to safeguard Alaska's public lands and watersheds from the destructive effects of logging, road building, mining , and oil and gas drilling, and protect the sensitive North Pacific ecosystem from industrial trawl fishing.

Contact(s):
Dierdre McDonnell, Project Attorney
Janis Searles, Staff Attorney
Thomas Waldo, Staff Attorney
Chris Wilde, Associate Attorney
Eric Jorgensen, Managing Attorney

EARTHJUSTICE
NEW ORLEANS OFFICE
400 Magazine Street
Suite 401
New Orleans, LA 70130 United States
Phone: 504-522-1394 Fax: 504-566-7242
E-mail: eajus@earthjustice.org
Website: www.earthjustice.org

Founded: N/A

Scope: Regional

Description: Protects wetlands and coastal ecosystems and safeguards the health of communities in the southern United States. Uses the power of the law to secure critical habitat for threatened and endangered species, limit logging and development projects in key habitat areas, compel government agencies to enforce strict water quality standards, and defend poor communities and communities of color from the harmful effects of industrial pollution.

Contact(s):
Nathalie Walker, Managing Attorney
Esther Boykin, Staff Attorney
M. Mace, Associate Attorney
Monique Harden, Community Liaison Director

EARTHJUSTICE
OAKLAND OFFICE
426 Seventeenth Street
Fifth Floor
Oakland, CA 94612 United States
Phone: 510-550-6725 Fax: 510-550-6749
E-mail: eajusca@earthjustice.org
Website: www.earthjustice.org

Founded: N/A

Scope: Regional

Description: Protects ecosystems and communities, from the rolling hills of the San Francisco Bay Area through the rich agricultural lands of the central Valley to the ancient forests and high peaks of the Sierra. The campaign "Healthy Cities, Healthy Wildlands" uses the power of the law to promote smart growth, and limit destructive activities that threaten wildlands and endangered species.

Contact(s):
Greg Loarie, Associate Attorney
Deborah Reames Neighbor, Managing Attorney
Mike Sherwood, Staff Attorney

EARTHJUSTICE
POLICY AND LEGISLATION
1625 Massachussets Avenue, NW
Suite 702
Washington, DC 20036 United States
Phone: 202-667-4500 Fax: 202-667-2356
E-mail: eajusdc@earthjustice.org
Website: www.earthjustice.org

Founded: N/A
Scope: National
Description: Works to defend and strengthen the environmental laws that Earthjustice attorneys enforce in the courts and to block congressional attempts to override Earthjustice's legal victories.
Contact(s):
Joan Mulhern, Senior Legislative Counsel
Glen Sugameli, Senior Legislative Counsel
Marty Hayden, Vice President of Policy and Legislation
Susan Holmes, Legislative Representative
Sandra Schubert, Legislative Counsel
Maria Weidner, Policy Analyst

EARTHJUSTICE
SEATTLE OFFICE
705 Second Avenue
Suite 203
Seattle, WA 98104 United States
Phone: 206-343-7340 Fax: 206-343-1526
E-mail: eajuswa@earthjustice.org
Website: www.earthjustice.org

Founded: N/A
Membership: N/A
Scope: Regional
Description: Protects the cathedral forests, pristine waters, and wild salmon that are the heart and soul of the Pacific Northwest. A strategic campaign "Fish-Trees-Water" uses the power of the law to save endangered species from extinction, halt deforestation and road building on public lands, and restore streams and rivers impacted by hydroelectric dams, agriculture, mining, and other activities.
Contact(s):
Patti Goldman, Managing Attorney
Kristen Boyles, Staff Attorney
Steve Mashuda, Project Attorney
Mike Mayer, Associate Attorney
Todd True, Staff Attorney

EARTHJUSTICE
TALLAHASSEE OFFICE
111 S. Martin Luther King Jr. Blvd.
Tallahassee, FL 32301 United States
Phone: 850-681-0031 Fax: 850-681-0020
E-mail: eajusfl@earthjustice.org
Website: www.earthjustice.org

Founded: N/A
Membership: N/A
Scope: Regional
Description: Protects Florida's subtropical forests, wetlands, waterways, coastal ecosystems, and communities. Uses the power of the law to restore and maintain the state's surface and ground waters, defend public lakes and rivers against exploitation by mining, logging, and cattle interests, and safeguard marine species and ecosystems from environmentally unsound development, oil and gas drilling, and destructive industrial fishing practices.

Contact(s):
Allison Finn, Associate Attorney
Aliki Moncrief, Project Attorney
David Guest, Managing Attorney

EARTHJUSTICE
WASHINGTON, DC, OFFICE
1625 Massachusetts Avenue, NW
Suite 702
Washington, DC 20036 United States
Phone: 202-667-4500 Fax: 202-667-2356
E-mail: eajusdc@earthjustice.org
Website: www.earthjustice.org

Founded: N/A
Membership: N/A
Scope: Regional, National
Description: Protects water quality, public health, and ecosystems in Washington, DC, the mid-Atlantic region, and nationwide. Uses the power of the law to defend and strengthen federal Clean Air Act and Clean Water Act standards, ensure that federal, state, and municipal governments adopt and enforce these standards, and safeguard poor communities and communities of color from the harmful effects of toxic pollution and sewage discharges.
Keyword(s): Ethics/Environmental Justice
Contact(s):
Howard Fox, Managing Attorney
David Baron, Staff Attorney
Todd Hutchins, Associate Attorney
Jim Pew, Project Attorney

EARTHSCAN
120 Pentonville Rd.
London, N1 9JN United Kingdom
Phone: 2072780433 Fax: 2072781142
E-mail: earthinfo@earthscan.co.uk
Website: www.earthscan.co.uk

Founded: N/A
Scope: International
Description: A publishing house for books addressing environment and development issues in both industrialized countries and the developing world, taking as a starting point the inescapable link between poverty and environmental degradation. All aspects of sustainable development are covered, including international relations, environmental law and institutions, global environmental change, population growth, and the management of resources and economics, as well as social and cultural questions.
Keyword(s): Agriculture/Farming, Air Quality/Atmosphere, Climate Change, Development/Developing Countries, Ethics/Environmental Justice, Finance/Banking/Trade, Forests/Forestry, Land Issues, Oceans/Coasts/Beaches, Pollution (general), Population, Recreation/Ecotourism
Contact(s):
Jonathan Wilson, Publishing Director
Victoria Burrows, Desk Editor
Alan Leander, Editor
Frances MacDermott, Editor
Helen Rose, Marketing Executive

EARTHSTEWARDS NETWORK
P.O. Box 10697
Bainbridge Island, WA 98110 United States
Phone: 206-842-7986 Fax: 206-842-8918
E-mail: office@earthstewards.org
Website: www.earthstewards.org

Founded: 1980
Membership: 101–1,000
Scope: International
Description: Earthstewards is an international, multicultural network dedicated to inspiring and empowering ordinary

people to take bold action for conflict transformation and the creation of positive relationships bridging boundaries of gender, race, culture, nations, age and beliefs. Our projects include: PeaceTrees Vietnam and other projects involving people to people diplomacy, global networking and conflict resolution.

Publication(s): Essene Book of Meditations and Blessings, Essene Book of Days, Earthstewards Newsletter, Warriors of the Heart

Contact(s):
Chuck Meadows, Executive Director; 206-842-7986; chuckm@peacetreesvietnam.org
Lynn Ellis, Outreach Coordinator; RR5, Box 1, Augusta, ME 04330; 207-266-6095; outreach@earthstewards.org
Rosemary Jones, Publishing; 800-561-2909; healingpgs@aol.com

EARTHTRUST

25 Kaneohe Bay Dr.
Kailua, HI 96734 United States
Phone: 808-254-2866 Fax: 808-254-6409
E-mail: earthtrust@aloha.net
Website: www.earthtrust.org

Founded: 1976
Scope: International
Description: Earthtrust is an international nonprofit wildlife conservation organization. It involves small groups of highly capable people, involved with innovative investigations and projects, in partnership with private industry, governments and other environmental groups. Earthtrust is aimed at resolving wildlife crisis situations. Earthtrust's focus is to expose the poaching of endangered species and the sale of endangered whale meat in Asian markets through the use of DNA analysis.
Keyword(s): Wildlife & Species
Contact(s):
Donald White, President

EARTHWATCH INSTITUTE

CENTER FOR FIELD RESEARCH
EARTHWATCH GLOBAL CLASSROOM
3 Clocktower Place, Box 75
Maynard, MA 01754-0075 United States
Phone: 978-461-0081 Fax: 978-461-2332
E-mail: info@earthwatch.org
Website: www.earthwatch.org

Founded: 1971
Membership: 10,001–100,000
Scope: National, International
Description: Earthwatch is a nonprofit organization which sponsors scientific field research worldwide. It recruits paying volunteers to help field scientists with their research. Volunteers help on short term expeditions to 50 countries and 25 U.S. states.
Publication(s): Earthwatch Expedition Guide, Earthwatch Journal
Keyword(s): Climate Change, Development/Developing Countries, Ecosystems (precious), Ethics/Environmental Justice, Forests/Forestry, Wildlife & Species
Contact(s):
Roger Bergen, President; rbergen@earthwatch.org
Edward Wilson, Vice President; ewilson@earthwatch.org
Marie Studer, Chief Scientific Officer; mstuder@earthwatch.org
John Walker, Chief Financial Officer; jwalker@earthwatch.org

EAST CENTRAL ILLINOIS FUR TAKERS

853 E. 1000 N. Rd
Onarga, IL 60955 United States
Phone: 217-394-2577

Founded: 1974
Membership: 1–100
Scope: Local
Description: State chapter of Fur Takers of America. Helps monitor furbearing wildlife populations in the state and helps conserve this renewable resource.
Contact(s):
Louis Krumwiede, President; 217-394-2577

EASTERN SHORE LAND CONSERVANCY (ESLC)

P.O. Box 169
Queenstown, MD 21658 United States
Phone: 410-827-9756 Fax: 410-827-5765
E-mail: INFO@ESLC.ORG
Website: www.eslc.org

Founded: 1990
Membership: 101–1,000
Scope: Regional
Description: The Eastern Shore Land Conservancy preserves farms, forests and natural areas for future generations, utilizing a variety of voluntary land protection tools that are available to landowners.
Publication(s): Eastern Shore 2010: A Regional Vision, How to Hold on to the Family Farm, The Future Eastern Shore - Your Choice, Panorama, Fact Sheets, Preserving Land for Our Future
Keyword(s): Land Issues, Public Lands/Greenspace, Sprawl/Urban Planning
Contact(s):
Robert Etgen, Executive Director; 410-827-9756, ext. 166; Fax: 410-827-5765; retgen@eslc.org
Jennifer Nutt, Director of Development; 410-827-9756, ext. 155; Fax: 410-827-5765; jnutt@eslc.org
Amy Owsley, Director of Community Planning; 410-827-9756, ext. 168; Fax: 410-827-5765; aowsley@eslc.org
Nina White, Director of Administration; 410-827-9756, ext. 164; Fax: 410-827-5765; nwhite@eslc.org
Sandra Edwards, Land Protection Specialist; 410-827-9756, ext. 163; Fax: 410-827-5765; sedwards@eslc.org
Rex Linville, Land Protection Specialist; 410-827-9756, ext. 157; Fax: 410-827-5765; rlinville@eslc.org
Laurie Wilson, Administrative Assitant; 410-827-9756, ext. 162; Fax: 410-827-5765; lwilson@eslc.org

ECODEFENSE

Moskowsky pr. 120-34
Kaliningrad, 236006 Russia
Phone: 70112437286 Fax: 70112437286
E-mail: ecodefense@ecodef.koenig.su

Founded: N/A
Scope: Regional, International
Description: Ecodefense is a nongovernmental, nonprofit environmental organization that works to inform and involve more ordinary citizens to environment and social activity through the organizing of environmental events and spread of the information.
Keyword(s): Agriculture/Farming, Energy, Oceans/Coasts/Beaches, Public Lands/Greenspace, Recreation/Ecotourism
Contact(s):
Alexandra Korolera, Director of the Centre for Coordination of Education Project
Galina Ragouzina, Editor

ECOLOGICAL SOCIETY OF AMERICA, THE

1707 H St., NW, Suite 400
Washington, DC 20006 United States
Phone: 202-833-8773 Fax: 202-833-8775
E-mail: esahq@esa.org
Website: www.esa.org

Founded: 1915
Membership: 1,001–10,000
Scope: National
Description: The Ecological Society of America is the nation's premier professional society of ecologists. ESA promotes the responsible application of ecological principles to the solution

of environmental problems through ESA reports, journals, and expert testimony to Congress. Each summer, ESA convenes a conference featuring the latest findings in ecological research.

Publication(s): Ecology, Issues in Ecology, Bulletin of the Ecological Society of America, Ecological Monographs, Ecological Applications

Keyword(s): Ecosystems (precious), Wildlife & Species

Contact(s):
Pamela Matson, President
Nadine Lymn, Director for Public Affairs
Katherine McCarter, Executive Director

ECOLOGY CENTER

2530 San Pablo Ave.
Berkeley, CA 94702 United States
Phone: 510-548-2220 Fax: 510-548-2240
E-mail: info@ecologycenter.org
Website: www.ecologycenter.org

Founded: 1969
Membership: 1,001–10,000
Scope: Local, State, Regional

Description: A nonprofit organization working to develop a more responsible society by identifying environmentally destructive practices and demonstrating sound alternatives. Programs include an environmental information clearinghouse, library, classes, book and ecoproducts store, sponsorship of three weekly farmers' markets, and weekly residential curbside recycling service in the city of Berkeley, CA. Primary service area: Greater San Francisco Bay region.

Publication(s): Terrain

Keyword(s): Agriculture/Farming, Ethics/Environmental Justice, Forests/Forestry, Land Issues, Pollution (general), Public Lands/Greenspace, Reduce/Reuse/Recycle, Wildlife & Species

Contact(s):
Laird Townsend, Editor

EDUCATIONAL COMMUNICATIONS

P.O. Box 351419
Los Angeles, CA 90035 United States
Phone: 310-559-9160 Fax: 310-559-9160
E-mail: ecnp@aol.com
Website: www.ecoprojects.org

Founded: 1958
Scope: International

Description: EC creates and promotes educational and scientific projects and programs for the public, focusing on environmental concerns. It founded The Ecology Center of Southern California in 1972; since 1977 has sponsored the award-winning Environmental Directions, a weekly national and international radio series heard in 8 states and on shortwave and internet; and since 1984 has produced three-time Emmy-nominated ECONEWS, a weekly television series broadcast on over 100 cable and PBS outlets nationally.

Publication(s): The Compendium Newsletter: A Guide to Ecological Activism, Econews TV and Environmental Directions Radio

Keyword(s): Population, Recreation/Ecotourism

Contact(s):
Nancy Pearlman, Executive Producer and Director
Anna Harlowe, Associate Director
Leslie Lewis, Administrative Coordinator

ELM RESEARCH INSTITUTE

Elm St., P.O. Box 150
Westmoreland, NH 03467 United States
Phone: 603-358-6198 Fax: 603-358-6305
E-mail: libertyelm@webryders.com
Website: www.libertyelm.com

Founded: 1967
Membership: 1,001–10,000
Scope: National

Description: A nonprofit organization which has funded over $1,000,000 in research for the treatment of Dutch elm disease and development of the disease-resistant American Liberty Elm, supplies equipment and information pertaining to elm care and treatment of Dutch elm disease, propagates the American Liberty Elm and distributes it under the auspices of the Johnny Elmseed Project with the assistance of local Boy Scouts and other nonprofit groups. Over 750 nurseries have been established since 1984.

Publication(s): Specialized Elm Care Information, Data on Elm Injections, Elm Leaves

Keyword(s): Forests/Forestry, Wildlife & Species

Contact(s):
John Hansel, Executive Director
Yvonne Spalthoff, Assistant Director

ENDANGERED HABITATS LEAGUE

8424-A Santa Monica Boulevard, #592
Los Angeles, CA 90069-4267 United States
Phone: 323-654-1456

Founded: N/A
Scope: Regional

Description: The Endangered Habitats League is a Southern California organization dedicated to ecosystem protection, improved land use planning, and collaborative conflict resolution.

ENDANGERED SPECIES COALITION

1101 14th St., NW, Suite 1400
Washington, DC 20005 United States
Phone: 202-682-9400 Fax: 202-756-2804
E-mail: esc@stopextinction.org
Website: www.stopextinction.org

Founded: 1982
Scope: Local, State, Regional, National

Description: The goal of the Coalition is to broaden and mobilize public support for protecting endangered species.

Publication(s): Activist Tools, Newsletter

Keyword(s): Wildlife & Species

Contact(s):
Brock Evans, Executive Director

ENGENDERHEALTH

440 9th Ave.
New York, NY 10001 United States
Phone: 212-561-8000 Fax: 212-561-8067
E-mail: info@engenderhealth.org
Website: www.engenderhealth.org

Founded: 1943
Scope: International

Description: EngenderHealth is an international nonprofit agency that works worldwide to support and strengthen reproductive health services for women and men; providing technical assistance, training and information in the areas of family planning, maternity care, STIs/HIV/AIDS, quality improvement and reproductive health programs for men.

Publication(s): EngenderHealth News, see publications on website

Keyword(s): Population, Public Health

Contact(s):
Amy Pollack, M.D., M.P.H., President
Lynn Bakamjian, M.P.H., Senior Vice President of Programs
Jeanne Haws, M.P.A., Vice President for Operations
Terrence Jezowski, M.S., Vice President for Development
Maurice Middleberg, Executive Vice President
Rachael Pine, J.D., Vice President for Public Affairs
Lyman Brainerd, Board Chair

ENTOMOLOGICAL SOCIETY OF AMERICA

9301 Annapolis Rd.
Lanham, MD 20706-3115 United States
Phone: 301-731-4535 Fax: 301-731-4538
E-mail: esa@entsoc.org
Website: www.entsoc.org

Founded: 1889
Membership: 1,001–10,000
Scope: International
Description: To promote the scientific study of insects and related arthropods. Specialty sections include systematic behavior, toxicology, biogenetics, plant protection, medical and veterinary, regulatory and extension, and related scientific disciplines.
Publication(s): Annals of the Entomological Society of America, Arthropod Management Tests, ESA Newsletter, American Entomologist, Journal of Medical Entomology, Environmental Entomology, Journal of Economic Entomology
Keyword(s): Agriculture/Farming, Public Health, Wildlife & Species
Contact(s):
Jay McPherson, President; mcpherson@zoology.siu.edu
Paula Lettice, Executive Director; 301-731-4535, ext. 0; esa@entsoc.org
Larry Larson, Past President; llarson@dowagro.com

ENVIRONMENT AND NATURAL RESOURCES MANAGEMENT DIVISION

Capital Area
Prov. of Negros Oriental, Philippines, 2600
Phone: 352251601

Founded: N/A
Description: A Division of the Provl. Governor's Office of Negros Oriental in Central Philippines engaged in community-based resource management: near shore fisheries development; upland and agro forestry development.
Contact(s):
Josie Columna, Information Officer; 0352251691; Fax: 0352254835; jrcolumna@speed.com.ph
Mercy Teven, Division Chief; 0352251601; Fax: 0352254835

ENVIRONMENT COUNCIL OF RHODE ISLAND ECRI

P.O. Box 9061
Providence, RI 02940 United States
Phone: 401-621-8048 Fax: 401-331-5266
E-mail: environmentcouncil@earthlink.net
Website: www.environmentcouncilri.org

Founded: 1972
Membership: 101–1,000
Scope: Local, State, National
Description: A representative statewide organization, affiliated with the National Wildlife Federation, dedicated to the protection and enhancement of wildlife and its habitat through public education and government interaction.
Keyword(s): Agriculture/Farming, Air Quality/Atmosphere, Climate Change, Ecosystems (precious), Energy, Ethics/Environmental Justice, Executive/Legislative/Judicial Reform, Forests/Forestry, Land Issues, Oceans/Coasts/Beaches, Pollution (general), Population
Contact(s):
Alicia Karpick, President
Paul Beaudette, Representative
Kate Canada, Treasurer
Sheila Dormody, Editor
Jack Schemp, Alternate Representative

ENVIRONMENTAL ACTION FUND (EAF)

P.O. Box 22421
Nashville, TN 37202 United States
Phone: 615-385-4389
Website: www.civictrust.org.uk/eaf

Founded: 1976
Scope: State
Description: A nonprofit, nonpartisan union of citizen groups joined to preserve and protect Tennessee's natural resources and environmental health. EAF works for strong environmental legislative programs and policies.
Contact(s):
Mark Manner, President; 2424 Golf Club Ln., Nashville, TN 37215
Sandy Bivens, Secretary; 3504 General Bates Dr., Nashville, TN 37204
Paul Davis, Treasurer; 5462 Vanderbilt Rd., Old Hickory, TN 37138

ENVIRONMENTAL ADVOCATES OF NEW YORK

353 Hamilton St.
Albany, NY 12210 United States
Phone: 518-462-5526 Fax: 518-427-0381
E-mail: info@eany.org
Website: www.eany.org

Founded: 1969
Membership: 1,001–10,000
Scope: State
Description: A representative statewide organization, affiliated with the National Wildlife Federation, dedicated to the protection and enhancement of wildlife and its habitat through public education and government interaction.
Publication(s): Voters Guide, The Greensheet, Albany Report
Contact(s):
Oakes Ames, President
Val Washington, Executive Director & Education Programs Contact; ext. 228; vwash@eany.org
Steve Allinger, Representative
Jeff Jones, Editor; ext. 233; jjones@eany.org
Charles Kruzansky, Alternate Representative & Treasurer

ENVIRONMENTAL ALLIANCE FOR SENIOR INVOLVEMENT (EASI)

P.O. Box 250, 9292 Old Dumfries Rd
Catlett, VA 20119 United States
Phone: 540-788-3274 Fax: 540-788-9301
E-mail: easi@easi.org
Website: www.easi.org

Founded: 1990
Membership: N/A
Scope: Local, State, Regional, National, International
Description: EASI is the primary organization encouraging senior volunteers to use their expertise and leadership in restoring and sustaining communities while promoting intergenerational environmental stewardship, through an international network of Senior Environment Corps, wherever older citizens want to participate. EASI is the largest senior environmental action network in the world.
Contact(s):
Thomas (Tom) Benjamin, President; P.O. Box 250, 9292 Old Dumfries Road, Catlett, VA 20119-0250; 540-788-3274; Fax: 540-788-9301; tom@easi.org
Roy Geiger, VP-Administration; P.O. Box 250, 9292 Old Dumfries Road, Catlett, VA 20119-0250; 540-788-3274; Fax: 540-788-9301; rgeiger@swimmail.com
Peggy Knight, V.P. - Programs; 5616 North 26th St., Arlington, VA 22207-1407; 703-241-0019; Fax: 703-538-5504; mknighteco@aol.com
Karen Caron, Asst. to President; P.O. Box 250, 9292 Old Dumfries Road, Catlett, VA 20119-0250; 540-788-3274; Fax: 540-788-9301; karen@easi.org

ENVIRONMENTAL AND ENERGY STUDY INSTITUTE (EESI)

122 C St., NW
Washington, DC 20001 United States
Phone: 202-628-1400 Fax: 202-628-1825
E-mail: eesi@eesi.org
Website: www.eesi.org

Founded: 1985
Membership: 1–100
Scope: National
Description: The EESI is dedicated to promoting environmentally sustainable societies. EESI produces credible, timely information, and innovative public policy initiatives that lead to transitions to social and economic patterns that sustain people, the environment, and the natural resources upon which present and future generations depend.
Publication(s): Briefing Summaries, The ECO Newsletter
Keyword(s): Climate Change, Energy, Transportation
Contact(s):
Carol Werner, Director of Energy and Climate Change Program
Richard Ottinger, Chair

ENVIRONMENTAL CAREERS ORGANIZATION, INC., THE

179 South St., 3rd Fl.
Boston, MA 02111 United States
Phone: 617-426-4375 Fax: 617-423-0998
Website: www.eco.org

Founded: 1972
Scope: National
Description: ECO protects and enhances the environment through the development of professionals, the promotion of careers and the inspiration of individual action. This is accomplished through placement, career advisement, career products and research and consulting. ECO has three regional offices and an alumni network of over 6,500 individuals.
Publication(s): Complete Guide to Environmental Careers, Beyond the Green
Keyword(s): Ethics/Environmental Justice
Contact(s):
John Cook, President; ext. 125; jcook@eco.org

ENVIRONMENTAL CONCERN INC.

201 Boundary Lane
P.O. Box P
St. Michaels, MD 21663 United States
Phone: 410-745-9620 Fax: 410-745-3517
E-mail: order@wetland.org
Website: www.wetland.org

Founded: 1972
Membership: N/A
Scope: National
Description: Environmental Concern Inc., founded in 1972 as a not-for-profit corporation, is dedicated to promoting public understanding and stewardship of wetlands, through experiential learning, native species horticulture, and creation and restoration initiatives. Environmental Concern Inc. focuses on wetland creation and restoration, a wholesale native species nursery, and educator and professional trainings.
Publication(s): WOW! The Wonders of Wetlands, Do's and Don'ts of Wetland Construction, Educator Guide, Review of Wetland Assessment Procedures, Procedure for Assessing Wetland Function, Wetland Planting Guide: Northeastern US, Educator Guide
Keyword(s): Agriculture/Farming, Oceans/Coasts/Beaches, Water Habitats & Quality, Wildlife & Species
Contact(s):
Suzanne Pittenger-Slear, President
Edgar Garbisch, Vice President

ENVIRONMENTAL DEFENSE

ALLIANCE FOR ENVIRONMENTAL INNOVATION
6 North Market Bldg., Faneuil Hall Marketplace
Boston, MA 02109 United States
Phone: 617-723-2996 Fax: 617-723-2999
Website: www.envirnomentaldefense.org/alliance

Founded: N/A
Scope: Regional
Description: The Alliance for Environmental Innovation is a joint project of EDF and The Pew Charitable Trusts.
Contact(s):
Gwen Ruta, Director

ENVIRONMENTAL DEFENSE

CAPITAL OFFICE
1875 Connecticut Ave., NW Ste. 1016
Washington, DC 20009 United States
Phone: 202-387-3500 Fax: 202-234-6049
E-mail: members@enviromentaldefense.org
Website: www.environmentaldefense.org

Founded: N/A
Membership: 101–1,000
Scope: National
Contact(s):
Fred Krupp, Executive Director; 257 Park Ave. S, New York, NY 10010; 212-505-2100; fkrupp@enviromentaldefense.org

ENVIRONMENTAL DEFENSE

HEADQUARTERS
257 Park Ave. South
New York, NY 10010 United States
Phone: 212-505-2100 Fax: 212-505-2375
Website: www.enviromentaldefense.org

Founded: 1967
Scope: National
Description: Environmental Defense is an advocacy and research organization made up of scientists, economists, engineers, and attorneys who seek practical solutions to a broad range of environmental and human health problems.
Publication(s): EDF Letter
Keyword(s): Air Quality/Atmosphere, Energy, Pollution (general), Public Health, Transportation, Water Habitats & Quality, Wildlife & Species
Contact(s):
Steve Cochran, Strategic Communications Director
Fred Krupp, Executive Director; 212-505-2100
Elizabeth Thompson, Legislative Director
Marcia Aronoff, Deputy Director of Programs
Ed Bailey, Deputy Director of Operations
Annie Petsonk, International Counsel
Joel Plagenz, Editor; 212-505-2100
James Tripp, General Counsel
John Wilson, Chairman of the Board of Trustees

ENVIRONMENTAL DEFENSE

NORTH CAROLINA OFFICE
2500 Blue Ridge Rd., Suite 330
Raleigh, NC 27607 United States
Phone: 919-881-2601 Fax: 919-881-2607
Website: www.environmentaldefense.org

Founded: N/A
Membership: 101–1,000
Scope: Regional

ENVIRONMENTAL DEFENSE

ROCKY MOUNTAIN OFFICE
2334 N. Broadway
Boulder, CO 80304 United States
Phone: 303-440-4901 Fax: 303-440-8052
Website: www.environmentaldefense.org

Founded: 1967
Membership: 100,001–500,000
Scope: International
Description: Environmental Defense is a leading national nonprofit organization representing more than 300,000 members. Since 1967, we have linked science, economics and law to create innovative, equitable and cost-effective solutions to society's most urgent environmental problems.
Contact(s):
Fred Krupp, Regional Director; 257 Park Ave. S 17th Floor, New York, NY 10010; 212-505-2100

ENVIRONMENTAL DEFENSE
TEXAS OFFICE
44 East Ave.
Austin, TX 78701 United States
Phone: 512-478-5161 Fax: 512-478-8140
Website: www.enviromentaldefense.org

Founded: N/A
Membership: 100,001–500,000
Scope: Regional

ENVIRONMENTAL DEFENSE
WEST COAST OFFICE
5655 College Ave. Suite 304
Oakland, CA 94618 United States
Phone: 510-658-8008 Fax: 510-658-0630
Website: www.environmentaldefense.org

Founded: N/A
Membership: 1,000,001 +
Scope: International

ENVIRONMENTAL DEFENSE CENTER
906 Garden St.
Santa Barbara, CA 93101 United States
Phone: 805-963-1622 Fax: 805-962-3152
E-mail: edc@edcnet.org
Website: www.edcnet.org

Founded: 1977
Membership: 1,001–10,000
Scope: Regional
Description: A nonprofit, public-interest environmental law firm providing legal services to citizens' groups and environmental organizations on environmental issues facing California's central coast region since 1977. The Center focuses on a wide range of issues, including oil development, toxic wastes, air and water pollution, species and habitat protection, open space preservation, land use, and coastal access.
Keyword(s): Agriculture/Farming, Air Quality/Atmosphere, Ecosystems (precious), Ethics/Environmental Justice, Land Issues, Oceans/Coasts/Beaches, Pollution (general), Public Health, Public Lands/Greenspace, Recreation/Ecotourism, Sprawl/Urban Planning, Water Habitats

ENVIRONMENTAL EDUCATION ASSOCIATES
2929 Main Street
Buffalo, NY 14214 United States
Phone: 716-833-2929 Fax: 716-833-9292
E-mail: training@EnvironmentalEducation.com
Website: www.environmentaleducation.com/

Founded: 1994
Scope: State, National
Description: A non-profit organization working in public high schools to provide students with coursework in environmental law and policy with a focus on endangered species, environmental justice and water quality.
Publication(s): Environmental Justice: A Planning Commission Hearing to Approve/Deny a Household Hazardous Waste Facility Plan, Endangered Species Act: The Case of the Yellow-backed Rat Skunk
Keyword(s): Air Quality/Atmosphere, Ethics/Environmental Justice, Water Habitats & Quality, Wildlife & Species

ENVIRONMENTAL EDUCATION ASSOCIATION OF ILLINOIS
26893 Carol Ln.
Ingleside, IL 60041 United States
Phone: 847-740-2590
Website: web.stclair.k.il.us/eeai

Founded: 1970
Scope: State
Description: Environmental Education Association of Illinois is the only organization in Illinois that makes environmental literacy its primary goal as it strives to instill a sense of community between the native ecosystems and people.
Publication(s): Illinois Environmental Education Update
Keyword(s): Reduce/Reuse/Recycle, Water Habitats & Quality, Wildlife & Species
Contact(s):
Deb Chapman, President
Curt Carter, Membership; S.I.U.E. Mail Code 6888, Carbondale, IL 62901; 618-453-1121
Dave Guritz, Treasurer; 847-428-2240
Kim Petzing, Secretary; 217-384-4062
Karen Zuckerman, President-Elect; 309-697-1325

ENVIRONMENTAL EDUCATION ASSOCIATION OF INDIANA
Attn: Deb Messenger
2412 North Allison Drive
Indianapolis, IN 46224-5029 United States
Phone: 317-630-2044 Fax: 219-787-1341
E-mail: eeai@naaee.org
Website: www.eeai.org

Founded: 1969
Scope: State
Description: A statewide, nonprofit organization dedicated to the wise use and management of natural resources through environmental conservation education. Activities include an annual meeting, workshops, teaching materials, exhibits, and youth environmental summit.
Publication(s): CREED Newsletter
Contact(s):
Paul Steury, President Elect; P.O. BOX 263, Wolf Lake, IN 46796; 219-779-5869; paulds@goshen.edu
Deborah Messenger, Vice President; 402 W. Washington St. W-265, Indianapolis, IN 46204-2739; 317-233-3872; deborahmessenger@netzero.net
Doug Waldman, Treasurer; 11832 Kress Rd., Roanoke, IN 46783; 317-672-3842

ENVIRONMENTAL EDUCATION ASSOCIATION OF WASHINGTON
P.O. Box 4122
Bellingham, WA 98227 United States
Phone: 360-497-7131 Fax: 360-497-7132
E-mail: eeaw@eeaw.org
Website: www.eeaw.org

Founded: N/A
Scope: State
Description: The EEAW promotes and stimulates the development of effective environmental education in our state's schools and communities. The organization successfully creates an environmentally literate citizenry who practice care and respect for our state's natural environments. EEAW is a strong and vital organization that has successfully positioned environmental education as a resource to improve student learning and achievement, enhance business practices and support sustainable communities.
Publication(s): EEAW Newsletter

Keyword(s): Agriculture/Farming, Air Quality/Atmosphere, Climate Change, Development/Developing Countries, Ecosystems (precious), Energy, Ethics/Environmental Justice, Forests/Forestry, Land Issues, Oceans/Coasts/Beaches, Pollution (general), Population, Public Health

Contact(s):
Heather Moss, President; 206-615-1554; heather.moss@ci.seattle.wa.us
Robert Olson, Past-President; 509-624-4884; robert@arrowroot.net

ENVIRONMENTAL EDUCATION COUNCIL OF OHIO

P.O. Box 2911
Akron, OH 44309-2911 United States
Phone: 330-761-0855 Fax: 330-761-0856
E-mail: director@eeco-online.org
Website: www.eeco-online.org

Founded: 1967
Membership: 101–1,000
Scope: State
Description: EECO is a statewide organization whose purpose is to promote environmental education which nurtures knowledge, attitudes, and behaviors that foster global stewardship. EECO brings together educators from many settings to provide opportunities to share ideas, materials, and techniques. Members include classroom teachers, naturalists, camp staff, teacher educators, youth leaders, and agency personnel.
Publication(s): EECO Newsletter, Integrating Environmental Education and Science, Directory of Ohio Environmental Education Sites and Resources, Ohio Sampler: Outdoor and Environmental Education

Contact(s):
Dave Irvine, President; 330-668-8992; irvine@crownpt.org
Charles McClaugherty, Vice President; mcclauca@muc.edu
Teresa Mourad, Executive Director; 330-761-0855; director@eeco-online.org
Angela Manuszak, Treasurer; mnszk93@aol.com
Jeanne Russell, Secretary; 614-265-6682; jeanne.russell@dnr.state.oh.us

ENVIRONMENTAL EDUCATORS OF NORTH CAROLINA (EENC)

P.O. Box 4901
Chapel Hill, NC 27515-4901 United States
Phone: 919-250-1050
Website: www.eenc.org

Founded: 1990
Membership: 101–1,000
Scope: State
Description: EENC advocates and supports the development and implementation of quality education which promotes responsible environmental decision-making and actions. Sponsors workshops and an annual conference.
Publication(s): EENC Networking Directory, EENC Newsletter, EENC Brochure

Contact(s):
Aaryn Kay, President; 910-251-0191
Deborah Miller, Advisor; 919-541-5552

ENVIRONMENTAL ENTERPRISES ASSISTANCE FUND, INC.

1655 N. Fort Meyer Dr., Fifth Fl.
Arlington, VA 22209 United States
Phone: 703-522-5928 Fax: 703-522-6450
E-mail: eeaf@igc.org
Website: www.eeaf.org

Founded: 1990
Membership: 1–100
Scope: National
Description: EEAF is a non-profit organization that operates as a venture capital fund; it provides long term risk capital and management assistance to environmentally beneficial businesses in developing countries, where such capital is otherwise unavailable.
Keyword(s): Agriculture/Farming, Development/Developing Countries, Energy, Oceans/Coasts/Beaches, Pollution (general), Reduce/Reuse/Recycle, Wildlife & Species

Contact(s):
Brooks Browne, President
J. Doliner, Vice President
Marion Heckclay, Chief Financial Officer

ENVIRONMENTAL LAW ALLIANCE WORLDWIDE (E-LAW)

U.S. Office: 1877 Garden Ave.
Eugene, OR 97403 United States
Phone: 541-687-8454 Fax: 541-687-0535
E-mail: elawus@elaw.org
Website: www.elaw.org

Founded: 1989
Membership: N/A
Scope: International
Description: E-LAW is an international network of public-interest attorneys and scientists dedicated to using law to protect the environment. More than 200 E-LAW advocates in 60 countries around the world exchange vital legal and scientific information. Advocates are linked electronically and can call on E-LAW for information to support their environmental protection work.
Publication(s): E-LAW Advocate

Contact(s):
Bern Johnson, Executive Director

ENVIRONMENTAL LAW AND POLICY CENTER OF THE MIDWEST

35 East Wacker Dr., Suite 1300
Chicago, IL 60601-2208 United States
Phone: 312-673-6500 Fax: 312-795-3730
E-mail: elpc@elpc.org
Website: www.elpc.org

Founded: 1993
Membership: 1–100
Scope: Regional
Description: A nonprofit public interest environmental advocacy organization working to implement sustainable energy strategies, promote innovative transportation approaches, expand and develop green markets and develop sound environmental management practices in Illinois, Indiana, Michigan, Minnesota, Ohio and Wisconsin.
Publication(s): Repowering of the Midwest, Lake County at the Crossroads No. 2, Visions, Choosing a Future for Growing Communities
Keyword(s): Energy, Transportation

Contact(s):
Kevin Brubaker, Director of Operations; kbrubaker@elpc.org
Howard Learner, Executive Director; hlearner@elpc.org

ENVIRONMENTAL LAW INSTITUTE, THE

1616 P St., NW
Suite 200
Washington, DC 20036 United States
Phone: 202-939-3800 Fax: 202-939-3868
Website: www.eli.org

Founded: 1969
Scope: National, International
Description: The Environmental Law Institute advances environmental protection by improving law, policy and management. ELI researches pressing problems, educates professionals and citizens about the nature of these issues, and convenes all sectors in forging effective solutions.

Publication(s): Deskbooks & Monographs, ELR - Environmental Law Reporter, The, Environmental Forum, The, National Wetlands Newsletter

Keyword(s): Agriculture/Farming, Air Quality/Atmosphere, Development/Developing Countries, Land Issues, Pollution (general), Reduce/Reuse/Recycle, Sprawl/Urban Planning, Water Habitats & Quality, Wildlife & Species

Contact(s):
J. Futrell, President
Kim Goldberg, Director of Communications; 202-939-3833; goldberg@eli.org
Donald Stever, Chairman of the Board

ENVIRONMENTAL LEAGUE OF MASSACHUSETTS

14 Beacon St.
Boston, MA 02108 United States
Phone: 617-742-2553 Fax: 617-742-9656
E-mail: elm@environmentalleague.org
Website: www.environmentalleague.org

Founded: 1898

Scope: State

Description: Advocates for responsible environmental policy on the state level and the effective implementation of state programs dealing with issues such as land use, toxics use reduction, recycling, water resources protection and funding for environmental programs, in addition to educating the public about the environment and environmental issues.

Publication(s): ELM Bulletin, ELM Action Alerts

Keyword(s): Air Quality/Atmosphere, Development/Developing Countries, Land Issues, Oceans/Coasts/Beaches, Pollution (general), Public Lands/Greenspace, Water Habitats & Quality

Contact(s):
James Gomes, President
Pamela Dibona, Legislative Director
Nancy Goodman, Researcher Director
Jeremy Marin, Communications/ Mktg. Director
Jessica Champness, Business Manager
John Cronin, Treasurer
Lauren Stiller-Rikleen, Chairman

ENVIRONMENTAL MEDIA ASSOCIATION

10780 Santa Monica Blvd., Suite 210
Los Angeles, CA 90025 United States
Phone: 310-446-6244 Fax: 310-446-6255
E-mail: ema@ema-online.org
Website: www.ema-online.org

Founded: 1989

Scope: National

Description: EMA works to mobilize the entertainment community in a global effort to educate people about environmental problems, and inspire them to act on those problems now.

Publication(s): Green Light

Contact(s):
Debbie Levin, Executive Director; ext. 313
Patie Maloney, Director of Special Events & Public Relations; ext. 315
Jennifer Deperalta, Program & Events Manager; ext. 317

ENVIRONMENTAL PROTECTION ASSOCIATION OF GHANA

P.O. Box AS 32
Asawasi-Kumasi, Ghana
Phone: 23305129950 Fax: 2335122537

Founded: 1987

Membership: 101–1,000

Scope: International

Description: The Association was established with the major objective of promoting an environmentally clean society and ecologically sustainable development. Association activities have been concentrated on the following: tree planting, afforestation, education, awareness, seminars and workshops, health, women and development, income generation, and rural development.

Contact(s):
F. Jantuah, Director
John Owusu, Project Manager
Kwabena Antwi, First Deputy Director
F. Owusu, Second Deputy Director

ENVIRONMENTAL RESOURCE CENTER (ERC)

411 East Sixth St., P.O. Box 819
Ketchum, ID 83340 United States
Phone: 208-726-4333 Fax: 208-726-1531
E-mail: erc@ercsv.org
Website: www.ercsv.org

Founded: 1989

Membership: 101–1,000

Scope: Local, Regional

Description: The ERC is a nonprofit organization that provides resources and educational programs to the public about local, regional, and global environmental issues.

Publication(s): Local Dirt

Keyword(s): Energy

Contact(s):
Craig Barry, Executive Director

ENVIROSOUTH, INC.

P.O. Box 11468
Montgomery, AL 36111 United States
Phone: 334-277-7050 Fax: 205-277-7080
E-mail: scrc@mindspring.com

Founded: 1975

Scope: Regional

Description: A private nonprofit organization specializing in recycling information and related services for the Southeast Recycling Market Council, and the annual Southeast Recycling Conference and Trade Show.

Keyword(s): Reduce/Reuse/Recycle

Contact(s):
Martha McInnis, President

E-P EDUCATION SERVICES, INC.

15 Brittany Ct.
Cheshire, CT 06410 United States
Phone: 203-271-2756 Fax: 203-271-2756

Founded: 1972

Scope: State

Description: A nonprofit group formed to promote environmental and population education in Connecticut and committed to assisting educators in the task of providing quality environmental education for the citizens of our state.

Keyword(s): Land Issues, Pollution (general), Water Habitats & Quality

Contact(s):
Larry Schaefer, President and Executive Director
Michael Schaefer, Vice President
J. Bouchard, Treasurer
Lina Lawall, Secretary

EQUESTRIAN LAND CONSERVATION RESOURCE

P.O. Box 335
Galena, IL 61036 United States
Phone: 815-776-0150 Fax: 815-776-9420
E-mail: info@elcr.org
Website: www.elcr.org

Founded: 1997

Membership: 101–1,000

Scope: National

Description: National nonprofit organization dedicated to the preservation of access to and conservation of land for equestrian use. "Resource" is the operative word in our name as we assist individuals and groups to become effective land issue advocates.

Publication(s): Equestrian Economic Impact, Getting Organized, Equestrian Land Protection Guide

Contact(s):
Kandee Haertel, Executive Director

EUROPARC FEDERATION

Kroellstrasse 5
D - 94481 Grafenau, 94481 Germany
Phone: 49855296100
Fax: 4.9855296102e+011
E-mail: office@europarc.org
Website: www.europarc.org

Founded: 1973
Membership: 101–1,000
Scope: International

Description: The EUROPARC Federation (formally known as the Federation of Nature and National Parks of Europe) is a pan-European, not-for-profit, non-governmental organisation, which promotes and supports the full range of protected areas in Europe. EUROPARC aims to facilitate the exchange of technical and scientific expertise, information and personnel between parks and reserves. It organizes training and exchange programmes, and provides professional advice on the establishment and development of protected areas.

Keyword(s): Reduce/Reuse/Recycle

Contact(s):
Patrizia Rossi, President
Eva Pongratz, Director
Rachel Gray, Deputy Director

EUROPEAN ASSOCIATION FOR AQUATIC MAMMALS

P.O. Box 58, 3910AB
Rhenen, Netherlands
Phone: 31317612294

Founded: 1973
Membership: 101–1,000
Scope: National

Description: To promote the free exchange of knowledge and to further scientific progress pertaining to the treatment, management, and conservation of aquatic mammals; to provide an organization for the above individuals, to improve practical husbandry; and to advance, by continued study, the basis for maintaining aquatic mammals in captivity.

Keyword(s): Water Habitats & Quality, Wildlife & Species

Contact(s):
John Baker, President
Geraldine Lacave, President Elect
Frans Engelsma, Secretary and Treasurer

EUROPEAN CETACEAN SOCIETY

c/o Deutsches Meeresmuseum, Katharinenberg 14, 18439
Stralsund, Germany
Phone: 4.9383126502e+011
Fax: 4.9383126506e+011
Website: web.inter.NL.net/users/J.W.Broekema/ecs

Founded: 1987
Membership: 101–1,000
Scope: International

Description: The European Cetacean Society's main focus is to promote and coordinate scientific study and conservation of cetaceans and to gather and disseminate information to members and to the public.

Keyword(s): Land Issues, Wildlife & Species

Contact(s):
Peter Evans, Editor
Beatrice Jann, Secretary
Roland Lick, Treasurer; Rlick2059@aol.com
Christina Lockyer, Chairman

EVERGLADES COORDINATING COUNCIL (ECC)

22951 Southwest 190 Ave.
Miami, FL 33170 United States
Phone: 305-248-9924 Fax: 305-248-9924
E-mail: evcoord@aol.com

Founded: 1970
Membership: 1–100
Scope: State

Description: ECC is an umbrella organization of south Florida sportspersons and conservation organizations united in a desire to protect wildlife habitat, assure sound wildlife management practices, and provide for properly regulated outdoor recreational activities.

Publication(s): Newsletter

Keyword(s): Ecosystems (precious), Recreation/Ecotourism, Water Habitats & Quality

Contact(s):
Bishop Wright, President
Ralph Johnson, Director; 7901 W. 25th Ct., Hialeah, FL 33016; 305-825-4667; Fax: 305-362-7584; rj005@aol.com
Dave Charland, Treasurer; 3559 NW 52nd St., Ft. Lauderdale, FL 33309; 305-484-7777; Fax: 954-484-7834
Barbara Powell, Secretary; 22951 SW 190th Ave., Miami, FL 33170; barjnpwll@aol.com

F

FAIRFAX AUDUBON SOCIETY

4022 Hummer Rd.
Annandale, VA 22003-0128 United States
Phone: 703-256-6895 Fax: 703-256-2060
E-mail: fairfaxaud@erols.com
Website: www.fairfaxaudubon.org

Founded: 1980
Membership: 1,001–10,000
Scope: Local, State, Regional, National, International

Description: The Fairfax Audubon Society—a chapter of the National Audubon Society, is committed to the Audubon mission which is to conserve and restore natural ecosystems, focusing on birds and other wildlife, and their habitats.

Publication(s): Potomac Flier, Species Checklists

Keyword(s): Development/Developing Countries, Ecosystems (precious), Land Issues, Public Lands/Greenspace, Recreation/Ecotourism, Sprawl/Urban Planning, Water Habitats & Quality, Wildlife & Species

Contact(s):
Deblyn Flack, Executive Director
Christine Winslow, President

FEDERAL CARTRIDGE COMPANY

900 Ehlen Dr.
Anoka, MN 55303 United States
Phone: 612-323-3827 Fax: 612-323-2506
Website: www.federalcartridge.com

Founded: N/A
Scope: National
Keyword(s): Recreation/Ecotourism

Contact(s):
William Stevens, Conservation Manager

FEDERAL WILDLIFE OFFICERS ASSOCIATION

4094 Majestic Ln. PMB 214
Fairfax, VA 22033 United States
Phone: 603-433-0502
Website: www.fwoa.org

Founded: N/A

Scope: National

Description: The Federal Wildlife Officers Association is an organization dedicated to the protection of wildlife and plants, the enforcement of federal wildlife law, the fostering of cooperation and communication among federal wildlife officers and the perpetuation, enhancement and defense of the wildlife officer profession.

Publication(s): The Federal Wildlife Officer Newsletter

Keyword(s): Ethics/Environmental Justice, Pollution (general), Recreation/Ecotourism, Wildlife & Species

Contact(s):

Timothy Santel, President; 217-793-9554; Fax: 217-793-2835
Christopher Dowd, Vice President; 617-242-7874, ext. 1
James Gale, Secretary and Treasurer; 517-686-4578; Fax: 517-686-2837

FEDERATION OF ALBERTA NATURALISTS

Box 1472
Edmonton, T5J 2N5 Canada
Phone: 708-427-8124
Website: www.fanweb.ca

Founded: 1970

Scope: State

Description: To increase Albertans' knowledge of natural history; foster creation of new natural history groups; promote natural areas; and provide a forum for discussion and means of taking action on environmental problems of concern to naturalists.

Publication(s): Alberta Naturalist

Keyword(s): Public Lands/Greenspace, Wildlife & Species

Contact(s):

Derek Johnson, President
Glen Semenchuk, Executive Director
Pat Clayton, Treasurer
Brian Parker, Editor

FEDERATION OF ENVIRONMENTAL EDUCATION IN ST. PETERSBURG

Lomonosov St., 11
St. Petersburg, 191002 Russia
Phone: 8121106849 Fax: 8121106849
E-mail: fee@mail.spb.org
Website: spb.org.ru/fee

Founded: 1994

Scope: International

Description: The basic direction of the Federation is culture, education, enlightenment, public health, science, economics, business, and enterprise.

Keyword(s): Agriculture/Farming, Air Quality/Atmosphere, Development/Developing Countries, Recreation/Ecotourism

Contact(s):

Sergei Alexeev, President

FEDERATION OF FLY FISHERS

INTERNATIONAL FLY FISHING CENTER
P.O. Box 1595, 502 S. 19th, Suite 101
Bozeman, MT 59771 United States
Phone: 406-585-7592 Fax: 406-585-7596
E-mail: fffoffice@fedflyfishers.org
Website: www.fedflyfishers.org

Founded: 1965

Membership: 1,001–10,000

Scope: International

Description: To promote international fly fishing as a most enjoyable and sportsmanlike method of fishing and to preserve all species of fish in all classes of waters through local stream and fisher restoration projects, conservation grants, audiovisual programs, public education, and international committees.

Publication(s): Flyfisher, The, Clubwire, The, Osprey,The

Keyword(s): Land Issues, Recreation/Ecotourism, Water Habitats & Quality, Wildlife & Species

FEDERATION OF FLY FISHERS (NCCFFF)

NORTHERN CALIFORNIA COUNCIL
115 Wellfleet Court
Folsom, CA 95630 United States
Phone: 9163565913
E-mail: president@nccfff.org
Website: www.nccfff.org

Founded: 1965

Membership: 1,001–10,000

Scope: Local, State, Regional, National, International

Description: The NCCFFF, made up of Clubs and individual members, is dedicated to enhancing Fly Fishing through Education, Conservation, and Restoration in Northern California and Northern Nevada.

Publication(s): Flyfisher, The River Mouth

Keyword(s): Forests/Forestry, Land Issues, Oceans/Coasts/Beaches, Pollution (general), Public Lands/Greenspace, Recreation/Ecotourism, Reduce/Reuse/Recycle, Water Habitats & Quality, Wildlife & Species

FEDERATION OF NEW YORK STATE BIRD CLUBS, INC.

P.O. Box 440
Loch Sheldrake, NY 12759 United States
Website: birds.cornell.edu/fnysbc

Founded: 1947

Scope: State

Description: To further the study of birdlife in New York state and to disseminate knowlege thereof, to educate the public on the need for conserving natural resources and to document the ornithology of the state.

Publication(s): Kingbird, The, Checklist of the Birds of New York State, New York Birders

Keyword(s): Wildlife & Species

Contact(s):

Mary Koeneke, President; 362 Nine Mile Point Rd., Oswego, NY 13126; 315-342-3402

FEDERATION OF ONTARIO NATURALISTS

355 Lesmill Rd.
Don Mills, M3B 2W8 Ontario Canada
Phone: 416-444-8419 Fax: 416-444-9866
E-mail: info@ontarionature.org
Website: www.ontarionature.org

Founded: 1931

Scope: State

Description: Committed to protecting and increasing awareness of Ontario's natural areas and wildlife, and exerts influence to protect our natural environment. Eighty-three federated clubs across Ontario.

Publication(s): Seasons

Contact(s):

Mark Dorfman, President
Gregory Beck, Director of Conservation
Ric Stymmes, Executive Director
Nancy Clarke, Editor
Jean Labrecque, Chief Administrative Officer

FEDERATION OF WESTERN OUTDOOR CLUBS

512 Boylston Ave. E., #106
Seattle, WA 98102 United States
Phone: 206-322-3041

Founded: 1932

Scope: Regional

Description: Established for mutual service and for the promotion of the proper use, enjoyment and protection of America's scenic, wilderness, and outdoor recreation resources. Forty-three affiliated clubs in Alaska, British Columbia, and the western states.

Publication(s): Outdoors West

Keyword(s): Forests/Forestry, Land Issues, Recreation/Ecotourism

Contact(s):

Brock Evans, President; 5449 33rd Ave., NW, Washington, DC 20015

Winchell Hayward, Vice President; 208 Willard N., San Francisco, CA 94118

Martin Huebner, Treasurer; 1995 McKinzie Dr., Idaho Falls, ID 83404

Nancy Kroening, Secretary; 5615 40th Ave., W, Seattle, WA 98199

Hazel Wolf, Editor; 512 Boylston Ave., E, #106, Seattle, WA 98102

FISH FOREVER

1271 Quaker Hill Dr.
Alexandria, VA 22314 United States
Phone: 703-461-9201 Fax: 703-461-9290

Founded: N/A
Membership: 1,001–10,000
Scope: National

Contact(s):

David Allison, President; dallison@msn.com

FLINTSTEEL RESTORATION ASSOCIATION, INC.

610 Apache Drive
Wakefield, MI 49968 United States
Phone: 906-229-5074 Fax: 906-229-5074
E-mail: flintsteel@skyenet.net
Website: flintsteel.org

Founded: 1995
Membership: N/A
Scope: Regional

Description: Natural resource conservation organization.

Keyword(s): Ethics/Environmental Justice, Land Issues, Oceans/Coasts/Beaches, Public Lands/Greenspace, Water Habitats & Quality

FLORIDA ASSOCIATION OF SOIL AND WATER CONSERVATION DISTRICTS

Attn: President, 16806 NW 40th PL
Newberry, FL 32669 United States
Phone: 352-472-5462 Fax: 352-472-4473

Founded: N/A
Scope: State

Contact(s):

Tim Ford, President; 352-472-5462; Fax: 352-472-5435

FLORIDA B.A.S.S. CHAPTER FEDERATION

Attn: President
Cape Coral, FL 33915 United States
Phone: 863-763-9265
Website: www.floridabassfederation.com

Founded: N/A
Membership: 1,001–10,000
Scope: State

Description: An organization of Bassmaster chapters, affiliated with the Bass Anglers Sportsman Society, organized to fight pollution, assist state and national conservation agencies in their efforts, and teach young people of our good conservation practices. Dedicated to the realistic conservation of our water resources.

Publication(s): See website for publication listings

Contact(s):

Harvey Ford, President; 863-763-9265

Carroll Head, Conservation Director; 2252 SW 22nd Circle., Okeechobee, FL 34974; 863-763-3568

FLORIDA DEFENDERS OF THE ENVIRONMENT, INC.

HOME OFFICE
4424 NW 13 St., Suite C-8
Gainesville, FL 32609 United States
Phone: 352-378-8465 Fax: 352-377-0869
E-mail: fde@fladefenders.org
Website: www.fladefenders.org

Founded: N/A
Scope: State

Description: FDE promotes conservation, restoration, and sustainable use of Florida's natural resources by providing the public and private sector with objective information and analysis developed through a statewide network of volunteer specialists. Guided by the motto "FDE gets the facts," the organization achieves realistic goals by targeting a limited number of complex environmental issues and providing expert scientific analysis, sustained tracking, advocacy, and litigation when necessary.

Publication(s): Monitor, The

Keyword(s): Climate Change, Energy, Land Issues, Water Habitats & Quality, Wildlife & Species

Contact(s):

Richard Hamann, President; 352-392-2237; Fax: 352-392-1457

Joe Little, Vice President

Nick Williams, Interim Executive Director; 352-378-8465; Nick@fladefenders.org

David Bruderly, Secretary

Kristina Jackson, Ocklawaha Project Consultant; 352-378-8465; jackson@fladefenders.org

Steve Leitman, Coordinator of Apalachicola River

Frank Nordlie, Treasurer

Bob Simons, Coordinator of Suwannee River & Public Lands Committee

FLORIDA EXOTIC PEST PLANT COUNCIL

P.O. Box 24680
West Palm Beach, FL 33416 United States
Phone: 305-242-7846
E-mail: tony_ternas@nps.gov
Website: www.fleppc.org

Founded: 1984
Membership: 101–1,000
Scope: State

Description: FLEPPC goals are directed toward building public awareness about the serious threat invasive plants pose to native ecosystems, secure funding, and support for control and management of exotic plants, and developing integrated management and control methods.

Publication(s): Florida Exotic Pest Plant Council Newsletter, Wildland Weeds

Keyword(s): Land Issues, Reduce/Reuse/Recycle, Wildlife & Species

Contact(s):

Amy Ferriter, Editor; 561-682-6097; aferriter@sfwmd.gov

Ken Langeland, Chairperson; 305-242-7846; tony_pernas@nps.gov

Jackie Smith, Secretary; 561-791-4720

Dan Thayer, Treasurer; 561-682-6129; Fax: 561-681-6232

FLORIDA FEDERATION OF GARDEN CLUBS, INC.

1400 South Denning Drive
Winter Park, FL 32789-5662 United States
Phone: 407-647-1160 Fax: 407-647-5479
Website: www.ffgc.org

Founded: 1924
Membership: 10,001–100,000
Scope: Local, State, Regional, National

Description: Organized to further the education of the members and the public in the fields of gardening, horticulture, botany, environmental awareness through the conservation of natural resources, civic beautification, and nature studies. FFGC has an extensive youth activity program; provides for a six-week summer nature and environmental youth camp; college level scholarships; and an extensive youth activity program.

Publication(s): The Florida Gardener

Keyword(s): Air Quality/Atmosphere, Ecosystems (precious), Energy, Forests/Forestry, Land Issues, Oceans/Coasts/ Beaches, Pollution (general), Public Lands/Greenspace, Reduce/Reuse/Recycle, Water Habitats & Quality, Wildlife & Species

Contact(s):

Gloria Blake, President; 3616 N. Indian River Drive, Cocoa, FL 32926-8704; 321-636-1299; Fax: 321-633-6500

Joan Ochs, Second Vice President; 2813 Summerfield Road, Winter Park, FL 32792-5113; 407-671-4597; Fax: 407-678-9157; jnbochs@aol.com

Joan Pryor, First Vice President; P.O. Box 1465, Dade City, FL 33526-1465; 352-567-2109; Fax: 352-542-2211; pryor3498@aol.com

Marion Hilliard, Government/Agency Liaison; 2902 Greenridge Road, Orange Park, FL 32073-6412; 904-264-6619; Fax: 904-264-2440; marionh@bellsouth.net

FLORIDA FORESTRY ASSOCIATION

P.O. Box 1696
Tallahassee, FL 32302 United States
Phone: 850-222-5646 Fax: 850-222-6179
E-mail: info@forestfla.org
Website: www.floridaforest.org

Founded: 1923

Membership: 1,001–10,000

Scope: State

Description: Nonprofit, trade-supported organization of industries, businesses, and individuals who encourage the promotion, development and protection of forestry in Florida.

Publication(s): Pines and Needles, Florida Forests Magazine

Keyword(s): Forests/Forestry

Contact(s):

Doyle Majors, President
Jeff Doran, Executive Vice President and Editor
Charles Thompson, Secretary & Treasurer

FLORIDA NATIVE PLANT SOCIETY

P.O. Box 690278
Vero Beach, FL 32969-0278 United States
Phone: 561-562-1598
Website: www.fnps.org

Founded: 1980

Scope: State

Description: Promotes preservation, conservation, and restoration of native plants and native plant communities of Florida, and provides information through publications, conferences, workshops and a statewide membership organized by local chapters.

Publication(s): Palmetto, The, Big Trees: The Florida Register, Common Grasses of Florida and the Southeast, Butterfly Gardening with Florida's Native Plants, Planning and Planting Your Native Plant Yard, Florida's Incredible Wild Edibles

Keyword(s): Wildlife & Species

Contact(s):

Candace Weller, President; 1515 Country Club Rd. N., St. Petersburg, FL 33710; 727-345-4619

Don Spence, Vice President; P.O. Box 321, Roseland, FL 32957; 407-589-0319

Kim Zarillo, Vice President; 760 Cajeput Cir., Melbourne Village, FL 32904; 407-727-1713

Robert Bareiss, Treasurer; 10301 Bellwood Ave., New Port Richey, FL 34654; 727-842-3133

FLORIDA NATURAL AREAS INVENTORY

1018 Thomasville Rd., Suite 200-C
Tallahassee, FL 32303 United States
Phone: 850-224-8207 Fax: 850-681-9364
E-mail: joetting@fnai.org
Website: www.fnai.org

Founded: 1981

Membership: N/A

Scope: State

Description: Information is collected on the status and distribution of natural communities, rare and endangered species of plants and animals and other natural features, then analyzed through an integrated data management system.

Publication(s): Florida Conservation Lands 2001, Field Guides

Keyword(s): Ecosystems (precious), Land Issues, Public Lands/Greenspace, Wildlife & Species

FLORIDA ORNITHOLOGICAL SOCIETY

1503 Wekewa Nene c/o Peter Merritt
Hobe Sound, FL 33455 United States
Phone: 850-942-2489 Fax: 561-546-2781
Website: www.FOSbirds.org

Founded: 1072

Membership: 101–1,000

Scope: Regional

Description: To engage in pursuits that advance ornithology in Florida; to facilitate education about birds in the wild; to unite amateurs and professionals on the study of birds in the wild; and to publish a scientific journal and other publications, relevant to the members' common interests.

Publication(s): Florida Field Naturalist, Florida Ornithological Society Newsletter

Keyword(s): Wildlife & Species

Contact(s):

Peter Merritt, President

Ann Paul, Vice President; 7217 N. Ola, Tampa, FL 33604; 941-643-2249; Fax: 813-623-4086; aschnapf@audubon.org

Bob Henderson, Secretary

Jerry Jackson, Editor; Whitaker Center 10501 Fl. Coast University Blvd, Fort Myers, FL 33965-6565; 941-348-1468; Fax: 941-590-7200

Dean Jue, Treasurer; dsjue@earthlink.net

FLORIDA PANTHER PROJECT, INC., THE

P.O. Box 19866
Sarasota, FL 34276 United States
Phone: 941-379-2221
Website: www.atlantic.net/~oldfla/panther/panther.html

Founded: 1993

Scope: State

Description: To assist in the sensible and responsible recovery of the Florida Panther in Florida, by raising funds to purchase environmentally sensitive panther habitat across Florida. Guest Speakers Available

Keyword(s): Wildlife & Species

Contact(s):

William Samuels, President; P.O. Box 19866, Sarasota, FL 34276; 941-379-2221

Bob Mills, Executive Director; Gifts and Fundraising 4269 Hearthstone Pl., Sarasota, FL 34238; 941-966-7765

Judy Conda, Board of Directors; 6551 Gulfgate Pl., Sarasota, FL 34321; 941-921-7300

Tim Mallon, Advisory Board; 3715 Felda St., Cocoa, FL 32926; 407-633-4799

FLORIDA PANTHER SOCIETY, INC., THE

ROUTE 1, P.O. Box 1895
White Springs, FL 32096 United States
Phone: 386-397-2945 Fax: 386-397-2945
E-mail: oldflorida@atlantic.net
Website: www.atlantic.net/~oldfla/panther/panther.html

Founded: 1994
Membership: 101–1,000
Scope: Regional
Description: We are an environmental education and support organization. Our purpose is to provide a means of protection and support of Puma concolor coryi, the endangered Florida/Southeastern Panther.
Publication(s): Cat Track, Quarterly Newsletter
Keyword(s): Wildlife & Species
Contact(s):
Stephen Williams, President; Route 1, Box 1895, White Springs, FL 32096; oldfla@atlantic.net
Karen Hill, Vice President; 330 NE 4th Ave., High Springs, FL 32643; coolcat@atlantic.net

FLORIDA PUBLIC INTEREST RESEARCH GROUP (FLORIDA PIRG)

704 West Madison St.
Tallahassee, FL 32304 United States
Phone: 850-224-3321 Fax: 850-224-1310
E-mail: floridapirg@pirg.org
Website: www.pirg.org/floridapirg

Founded: 1981
Scope: State
Description: Florida PIRG is a nonprofit organization committed to researching, educating, organizing, and advocating programs to protect Florida's environment. These programs include preventing offshore drilling, promoting recycling, and other vital issues.
Publication(s): Citizen Agenda, Florida PIRG reports
Contact(s):
Mark Ferrulo, Executive Director

FLORIDA SPORTSMEN'S CONSERVATION ASSOCIATION

P.O. Box 20051
West Palm Beach, FL 33416-0051 United States
Phone: 561-478-5965

Founded: 1994
Scope: State
Description: The Florida Sportsmen's Conservation Association promotes conservation, preservation, and propagation of all forms of game wildlife species, nongame wildlife species, and marine life. The Association stimulates a greater interest in any and all legitimate outdoor recreational activities, assures sportsmen that they may continue to use areas for legitimate outdoor recreational activities, works towards the opening of all lands and waters for legitimate outdoor recreational activities.
Keyword(s): Land Issues, Public Lands/Greenspace, Recreation/Ecotourism
Contact(s):
Bishop Wright, President; 15439-94th St. N., West Palm Beach, FL 33412; 561-795-1375
Mark Dombroski, 2nd Vice President; 1842 Lynton Cir., Wellington, FL 33414; 561-793-7200
Robert Stossel, 1st Vice President; 14241-77th Pl. N., Loxahatchee, FL 33470; 561-753-7880
Bruce Britt, Publication Director; 7407 Southern Blvd., West Palm Beach, FL 33413; 561-688-2553
Richard Andrea, Treasurer; 12334-77th Pl. N., West Palm Beach, FL 33412; 561-795-1136
Kevin Smith, Secretary; 15856-93rd St. N., West Palm Beach, FL 33412; 561-795-4112

FLORIDA TRAIL ASSOCIATION, INC.

5415 SW 13th St.
Gainesville, FL 32608 United States
Phone: 877-445-3352 Fax: 352-378-4550
E-mail: fta@florida-trail.org
Website: www.florida-trail.org

Founded: 1964
Membership: 1,001–10,000
Scope: State
Description: This association was formed to instill in Floridians and in visitors to Florida an appreciation and a desire to conserve the natural beauty of Florida by all lawful means; to promote the creation of a hiking trail, to be called the Florida Trail, to run the length of the state; and to provide an opportunity for hiking and camping.
Publication(s): Footprint, The
Keyword(s): Recreation/Ecotourism, Transportation
Contact(s):
Deborah Stewart-Kent, President
Kevin Butler, 4th Vice President for Public Relations
Sylvia Dunnam, 2nd Vice President for Membership
Joan Hobson, 3rd Vice President for Trails
Eileen Wyand, 1st Vice President for Administration
Mary Anne Freyer, Secretary
Pam Hale, Treasurer

FLORIDA WILDLIFE FEDERATION

P.O. Box 6870
Tallahassee, FL 32314-6870 United States
Phone: 850-656-7113 Fax: 850-942-4431
E-mail: fwf@flawildlife.org
Website: www.flawildlife.org

Founded: 1937
Membership: 10,001–100,000
Scope: State
Description: A representative statewide organization, affiliated with the National Wildlife Federation, dedicated to the protection and enhancement of wildlife and its habitat through public education and government interaction.
Publication(s): Florida Fish and Wildlife News
Contact(s):
Manley Fuller, Executive Director/President
David White, President/Chair
Jenny Brock, NWF Representative
Richard Farren, Editor
Diane Hines, Education Programs Contact
Patricia Pearson, Backyard Wildlife Habitats Contact
Bob Reid, NWF Alternate Representative
Mike Webster, Treasurer & Vice Chair of Records

FOOD AND AGRICULTURE ORGANIZATION OF THE UNITED NATIONS

PLANT PRODUCTION AND PROTECTION DIVISION
Viale di Termi di Caracalla
Rome, 00 100 Italy
Phone: 39-06-57053643 Fax: 39-06-57056347
Website: www.fao.org

Founded: 1945
Membership: 101–1,000
Scope: International
Description: To raise levels of nutrition and standards of living, to improve the production and distribution of agricultural products, and to better the conditions of rural populations. FAO has adopted an overriding strategy of integrated sustainable development. All operations are geared to meet basic human needs without compromising those of future generations.
Keyword(s): Agriculture/Farming, Forests/Forestry, Public Health, Sprawl/Urban Planning, Wildlife & Species
Contact(s):
Jacques Diouf, Director-General
Christina Engfeldt, Director of Information Division
H. Carsalade, Contact for The Sustainable Development Department
D. Harcharik, Deputy Director-General
P. Wilson, Inspector-General

FOOD SUPPLY / HUMAN POPULATION EXPLOSION CONNECTION

1834 North Lakeshore Drive
Chapel Hill, NC 27514-6733 United States
Phone: 919-967-5764 Fax: 919-968-3331
E-mail: SESALMONY@aol.com

Founded: 2002
Membership: 1–100
Scope: International
Description: Develop viable strategies that protect Earth and all of its inhabitants. Promote consideration and discussion of unforeseen scientific facts of human overpopulation presumably in their correct relations. Thank those who discover ways to protect Earth and its inhabitants.
Publication(s): Human Population Numbers/Function/Food
Keyword(s): Agriculture/Farming, Air Quality/Atmosphere, Climate Change, Development/Developing Countries, Ecosystems (precious), Energy, Ethics/Environmental Justice, Executive/ Legislative/Judicial Reform, Finance/Banking/Trade, Forests/ Forestry, Land Issues, Oceans
Contact(s):
Steven Salmony, President; 919-967-5764; Fax: 919-968-3331; SESALMONY@aol.com

FOREST FIRE LOOKOUT ASSOCIATION

374 Maple Ave., E., Suite 210
Vienna, VA 22180 United States
Phone: 703-255-2700 Fax: 703-281-9200
Website: www.firelookout.org

Founded: 1990
Scope: National
Description: A national organization devoted to forest protection through the inventory, maintenance and volunteer staffing of forest fire lookouts and fire towers in the 49 states that have them and throughout the world. Maintains a data base of designs and available lookout parts and salvage. Organized into 21 states and regional chapters.
Publication(s): Lookout Network (quarterly)
Keyword(s): Forests/Forestry, Land Issues
Contact(s):
Keith Argow, Chairman of the Board; 703-255-2700
Nancy Gabriel, National Historic Lookout Register; 703-255-2700
Shirley Goodrich, Treasurer; 207-324-6537
Ray Grimes Jr., Secretary; 973-835-4487
Mark Haughwout, Eastern Deputy Chair; 802-476-8341
Joseph Higgins, Legal Counsel; 201-391-1091
Henry Isenberg, Restorations; 508-883-0834
Michael Pfeiffer, Historian; 501-967-4167
Gary Weber, Western Deputy Chair; 207-443-2465

FOREST HISTORY SOCIETY, INC.

701 William Vickers Ave
Durham, NC 27701 United States
Phone: 919-682-9319 Fax: 919-682-2349
Website: www.foresthistory.org

Founded: 1946
Membership: 1,001–10,000
Scope: National
Description: A nonprofit educational institution, the Forest History Society is dedicated to the advancement of historical understanding of human interaction with the forest environment—forest industries, forestry, conservation, and other forms of use and appreciation. A membership organization, it sponsors programs in research, publication, archives-library, and professional service.
Publication(s): Forest History Today, Environmental History, Forest Time Line Newsletter
Keyword(s): Forests/Forestry, Land Issues, Public Lands/Greenspace, Reduce/Reuse/Recycle
Contact(s):
Steve Anderson, President
William Bauthman, Chairman; 843-851-4653
Cheryl Oakes, Librarian
Adam Rome, Editor; Pennsylvania State University, University Park, PA; 814-863-0184; axr26@psu.edu

FOREST LANDOWNERS ASSOCIATION, INC.

3776 Lavista Rd. Suite 250
Tucker, GA 30084 United States
Phone: 404-325-2954 Fax: 404-325-2955
E-mail: snswton@forestland.org
Website: www.forestland.org

Founded: 1941
Membership: 10,001–100,000
Scope: National
Description: Nonprofit forestry organization of timberland owners large and small in 17 southern states seeking to give private timberland owners and related interests a greater voice in matters affecting their business.
Publication(s): Forest Landowner Magazine, Forest Landowner Manual
Keyword(s): Forests/Forestry, Reduce/Reuse/Recycle
Contact(s):
John Bowen, Regional Vice President; Box 159, Louisville, TN 37777
C. Bush, Regional Vice President; 6701 Carmel Road, Suite 404, Charlotte, NC 28226
Carroll Cochran, Regional Vice President
Guerry Doolittle, Regional Vice President; Champion International, 9485 Regency Sq. Blvd., Jacksonville, FL 32225-8155
L. Larson, Regional Vice President; P.O. Box 2143, Mobile, AL 36652
Steve Newton, Executive Vice President
Kirk Rodgers, Regional Vice President
Charles Tomlinson, Regional Vice President
Paige Cash, Editor
Otis Ingram, Government Affairs Chairman

FOREST MANAGEMENT TRUST

P.O. Box 110760
Gainesville, FL 32611 United States
Phone: 352-846-2240 Fax: 352-846-1332
E-mail: info@foresttrust.org
Website: www.foresttrust.org

Founded: 1997
Membership: N/A
Scope: Local, State, Regional, National, International
Description: Dedicated to maintaining forest cover and biological diversity through ecologically, economically, and socially sustainable management for timber and non-timber forest products and services.
Publication(s): Model forest workshops
Keyword(s): Development/Developing Countries, Ecosystems (precious), Forests/Forestry, Land Issues, Wildlife & Species
Contact(s):
Steve Taranto, Project Manager; 352-846-2240; staranto@foresttrust.org

FOREST SERVICE EMPLOYEES FOR ENVIRONMENTAL ETHICS (FSEEE)

P.O. Box 11615
Eugene, OR 97440 United States
Phone: 541-484-2692 Fax: 541-484-3004
E-mail: fseee@fseee.org
Website: www.fseee.org

Founded: 1989
Membership: 10,001–100,000
Scope: National, International

Description: A national nonprofit organization of Forest Service employees, retirees, other resource professionals, and concerned citizens working to change from within the Forest Service's basic management philosophy to a land ethic that ensures ecologically and economically sustainable management.

Publication(s): Forest Magazine, see publications on website

Keyword(s): Ecosystems (precious), Ethics/Environmental Justice, Executive/Legislative/Judicial Reform, Forests/Forestry, Land Issues, Public Lands/Greenspace, Wildlife & Species

Contact(s):

Dave Iverson, President

Andy Stahl, Executive Director; 541-484-2692; Fax: 541-484-3004; andy@fseee.org

Mark Blaine, Editor, Forest Magazine; 541-484-3170; Fax: 541-484-3004; mark@forestmag.org

Stephanie Detwiler, Dir. of Administration; 541-484-2692; Fax: 541-484-3004; stephanie@fseee.org

Martha Carlisle, Art Director; 541-484-3170; Fax: 541-484-3004; marthacarlisle@attbi.com

Kay Crider, Director of Development; 541-484-2692; Fax: 541-484-3004; kay@fseee.org

Bob Dale, Field Director; 541-484-2692; Fax: 541-484-3004; bobdale@fseee.org

Jamie Passaro, Asst. Editor, Forest Magazine; 541-484-3170; Fax: 541-484-3004; jamie@forestmag.org

Chuck Roth, Office Manager; 541-484-2692; Fax: 541-484-3004; chuck@fseee.org

FOREST SOCIETY OF MAINE

P.O. Box 775
115 Franklin Street
Bangor, ME 04402 United States
Phone: 207-945-9200 Fax: 207-945-9229
E-mail: info@fsmaine.org

Founded: 1984
Membership: N/A
Scope: State

Description: A statewide land trust working with landowners on forest land conservation projects that maintain the environmental, recreational and economic values of Maine's forests, primarily through conservation easements.

Keyword(s): Ecosystems (precious), Forests/Forestry, Land Issues, Reduce/Reuse/Recycle, Wildlife & Species

Contact(s):

Alan Hutchinson, Executive Director

FOREST STEWARDS GUILD

P.O. Box 8309
Santa Fe, NM 87504 United States
Phone: 505-983-3887 Fax: 505-986-0798
E-mail: info@foreststewardsguild.org
Website: www.foreststewardsguild.org

Founded: 1997
Membership: 101–1,000
Scope: Local, State, Regional, National, International

Description: The mission of the Guild is to promote ecologically responsible resource management that sustains the entire forest across the landscape. The Guild provides a forum and support system for practicing foresters and other resource management professionals working to advance this vision.

Publication(s): Resource Manager Certification Handbook, Distant Thunder

Keyword(s): Ethics/Environmental Justice, Forests/Forestry, Land Issues

Contact(s):

Mary Chapman, Director; 505-983-3887, ext. 37; Fax: 505-986-0798; mary@foreststewardsguild.org

FOREST STEWARDS GUILD

NORTHWEST REGIONAL CHAPTER (GUILDNW)
8400 Rocky Lane SE
Olympia, WA 98513 United States
Phone: 360-459-0946
E-mail: jeanforest@cco.net
Website: www.foreststewardsguild.org

Founded: 2000
Membership: 101–1,000
Scope: Local, State, Regional, National, International

Description: The Guild is a group of foresters and others committed to ecologically sustaining the entire forest across the landscape. The forum the NW Chapter provides to support this is hosting forest field trips, talks, producing a newsletter and running a moderated email listserve. Anyone can join the listserve by emailing jeanforest@cco.net, to talk, shop, teach, learn and network.

Publication(s): GuildNW Newsletter

Keyword(s): Forests/Forestry, Wildlife & Species

Contact(s):

Mary Chapman, Director; 505-983-8992, ext. 37; Fax: 509-986-0798; mary@foreststewardsguild.org

Steve Harrington, Coordinator; 505-983-8992, ext. 16; Fax: 505-986-0798; steve@foreststewardsguild.org

FOREST TRUST

P.O. Box 519
Santa Fe, NM 87504-0519 United States
Phone: 505-983-8992 Fax: 505-986-0798
E-mail: forest@theforesttrust.org
Website: www.theforesttrust.org

Founded: 1984
Scope: Regional, National

Description: A nonprofit organization dedicated to protecting the integrity of the forest ecosystem and improving the lives of people in rural communities. The Trust challenges conventional forest management philosophies and provides protection strategies to grassroots environmental organizations, rural communities, and public agencies. The Trust also provides land management services to owners of private lands with significant conservation values and serves as the institutional home for the Forest Stewards

Publication(s): Forest Trust Quarterly Report, Distant Thunder, Annual Report

Keyword(s): Development/Developing Countries, Forests/Forestry, Land Issues

Contact(s):

Henry Carey, Director
Ron Dryden, Accountant
Steven Harrington, Forest Stewards Guild
Shirl Harrington, National Forest Program
Laura McCarthy, Assistant Director

FOREST WATCH

10 Langdon St., Suite 1
Montpelier, VT 05602 United States
Phone: 802-223-3216 Fax: 802-223-1363
E-mail: forestwatch@forestwatch.org
Website: www.forestwatch.org

Founded: 1994
Membership: 1,001–10,000
Scope: Regional

Description: Forest Watch saves and recreates wild forests, reforms public land management, advocates ecological forestry and watches over the forests with a network of citizen volunteers.

Publication(s): State of the Forest Report, Visions, Quarterly

Keyword(s): Forests/Forestry, Public Lands/Greenspace, Wildlife & Species

Contact(s):
Jim Northup, Executive Director; jnorthup@forestwatch.org
Andrew Vota, Advocacy Director; avota@forestwatch.org
Sue Higby, Deputy Director; shigby@forestwatch.org

FOSSIL RIM WILDLIFE CENTER

P.O. Box 2189
Glen Rose, TX 76043 United States
Phone: 254-897-2960 Fax: 254-897-3785
E-mail: visitor-services@fossilrim.org
Website: www.fossilrim.org

Founded: 1987
Scope: National
Description: A 2,100-acre wildlife preserve dedicated to the preservation of endangered and rare species with the ultimate goal of returning these species to the wild. Sixty animal species are represented, and Fossil Rim participates in 12 Species Survival Plan programs. Programs include public education, research into the management and propagation of endangered species, training of conservation professionals, and support for the creation of similar efforts around the world.
Keyword(s): Wildlife & Species
Contact(s):
Bruce Williams, Vice President of Conservation; 254-897-2960, ext. 304
Yola Carlough, Director of Communications; 254-897-2960, ext. 206
M. Jurzykowski, Chairman of the Board
Jerry Millhon, Chief Operating Officer; 254-897-2960, ext. 202

FOUNDATION FOR NORTH AMERICAN BIG GAME

P.O. Box 2710
Woodbridge, VA 22193 United States
Phone: 703-878-2119 Fax: 703-878-2119

Founded: 1992
Membership: 101–1,000
Scope: National
Description: A nonprofit membership organization with major objectives of protection and encouragement of sport hunting in North America; education of the general public to the values of sport hunting, both direct and indirect; and the conservation and welfare of the big-game species of the continent.
Publication(s): North American Big Game
Keyword(s): Recreation/Ecotourism, Wildlife & Species
Contact(s):
Don Kirn, President; 816-761-4351; Fax: 816-761-8737
Warren Parker, Vice President; 816-229-8899; Fax: 816-229-5933
William Nesbitt, Executive Director; 703-590-4449; Fax: 703-878-2119
Don Morgan, Secretary; 352-473-2662; Fax: 352-473-2166
Edward Nannini, Board Member; 916-485-8111; Fax: 916-485-1709
E. Pocius, Treasurer; 215-536-9616; Fax: 215-536-5815

FOUNDATION FOR NORTH AMERICAN WILD SHEEP

720 Allen Ave.
Cody, WY 82414 United States
Phone: 307-527-6261 Fax: 307-527-7117
E-mail: fnaws@fnaws.org
Website: www.fnaws.org

Founded: 1977
Membership: 1,001–10,000
Scope: International
Description: A nonprofit organization whose purposes are to: promote the management of and safeguard against the extinction of all species of wild sheep native to the continent of North America; promote the protection of the remaining wild sheep populations and their habitat; and promote the re-establishment of wild sheep populations in suitable habitat. The Foundation funds wild sheep research, wildlife studies, improves habitat, finances sheep transplants, and supports hunting and game management policies
Publication(s): Wild Sheep
Keyword(s): Wildlife & Species
Contact(s):
Raymond Lee, Executive Director; 307-527-6261; Fax: 307-527-7117; rlee@fnaws.org

FRANKFURT ZOOLOGICAL SOCIETY—HELP FOR THREATENED WILDLIFE

Alfred-Brehm-Platz 16
Frankfurt, D-60316 Germany
Phone: 6994344644 Fax: 69439348
E-mail: info@zgf.de
Website: www.zgf.de

Founded: 1858
Membership: 1,001–10,000
Scope: International
Description: A private organization that supports wildlife/nature conservation and environmental/conservation education with international, national, and regional projects.
Contact(s):
Richard Faust, President
Ingrid Koberstein, Projects Officer and Executive Assistant to the President
Markus Borner, Regional Representative for Eastern Africa

FRIENDS OF ACADIA

43 Cottage Street
P.O. Box 45
Bar Harbor, ME 04609 United States
Phone: 207-288-3340 Fax: 207-288-8938
Website: www.friendsofacadia.org

Founded: 1986
Membership: 1,001–10,000
Scope: National
Description: Friends of Acadia is a nonprofit organization providing citizen support in partnership with the National Park Service to preserve and protect Acadia National Park and the communities that surround it.
Publication(s): Friends of Acadia Journal
Keyword(s): Air Quality/Atmosphere, Public Lands/Greenspace, Recreation/Ecotourism, Transportation
Contact(s):
W. Olson, President
Stephanie Clement, Conservation Director
Kelly Dickson, Director of Development
Marla Major, Stewardship Director
Diana McDowell, Director of Operations
H. Judd, Board of Directors Chairman

FRIENDS OF ANIMALS INC.

777 Post Rd., Suite 205
Darien, CT 06820 United States
Phone: 203-656-1522 Fax: 203-656-0267
E-mail: info@friendsofanimals.org
Website: www.friendsofanimals.org

Founded: 1957
Membership: 100,001–500,000
Scope: Local, State, Regional, National, International
Description: An international animal protection organization that works to protect animals from cruelty, abuse, and institutionalized exploitation. FOA's efforts protect and preserve animals and their habitats around the world.
Publication(s): ActionLine
Keyword(s): Agriculture/Farming, Development/Developing Countries, Recreation/Ecotourism, Wildlife & Species
Contact(s):
Priscilla Feral, President; 203-656-1522; Fax: 203-656-0267

FRIENDS OF DISCOVERY PARK

P.O. Box 99662
Seattle, WA 98199-0662 United States
Phone: 206-283-8643
E-mail: info@discoveryparkfriends.org
Website: www.discoveryparkfriends.org

Founded: 1974
Membership: 101–1,000
Scope: Regional
Description: To create and protect an open space of quiet and tranquility where the works of man are minimized. A place which emphasizes its natural environment and to promote the development of Discovery Park according to a master plan responsive to these goals.
Publication(s): Explorer - Quarterly Newsletter
Keyword(s): Land Issues, Public Lands/Greenspace, Water Habitats & Quality, Wildlife & Species
Contact(s):
Valerie Cholvin, President
Terry Mueller, Treasurer
John Wooten, Secretary

FRIENDS OF FAMOSA SLOUGH

FFS
P.O. Box 87280
San Diego, CA 92138-7280 United States
Phone: 619-224-4591
E-mail: famosa-slough@home.com
Website: groups.sdinsider.com/ffs

Founded: 1984
Membership: 101–1,000
Scope: Local
Description: Works to protect and restore Famosa Slough, an urban tidal wetland with lots of birdlife.
Keyword(s): Water Habitats & Quality, Wildlife & Species

FRIENDS OF MISSISQUOI NATIONAL WILDLIFE REFUGE, INC.

371 North River St.
Swanton, VT 05488 United States
Phone: 802-868-4781

Founded: 2001
Membership: 1–100
Scope: Local, National
Description: This non profit group is dedicated to the conservation and preservation of Missisquoi National Wildlife Refuge and to promoting public awareness and appreciation of the natural and cultural history of the refuge.

FRIENDS OF SUNKHAZE MEADOWS NATIONAL WILDLIFE REFUGE

1033 South Main Street
Old Town, ME 04468 United States
Phone: 207-827-6138 Fax: 207-827-6099
E-mail: info@sunkhaze.org
Website: www.sunkhaze.org

Founded: 1997
Membership: 1–100
Scope: Local
Description: Non profit organization formed to support the U.S. Department of the Interior, Fish and Wildlife Service, to protect Sunkhaze Meadows National Wildlife Refuge. Group sponsors community activities as well as engages in trail maintenance, fund raising, and community education.
Keyword(s): Ecosystems (precious), Land Issues, Recreation/Ecotourism, Water Habitats & Quality, Wildlife & Species

FRIENDS OF THE BOUNDARY WATERS WILDERNESS

401 North 3rd St., Suite 290
Minneapolis, MN 55401 United States
Phone: 612-332-9630 Fax: 612-332-9624
E-mail: info@friends-bwca.org
Website: www.friends-bwca.org

Founded: 1976
Membership: 1,001–10,000
Scope: International
Description: Established to protect, preserve, and restore the wilderness character of the Boundary Waters Canoe Area Wilderness (BWCAW) and the surrounding Quetico-Superior Ecosystem.
Publication(s): BWCA Wilderness News
Keyword(s): Air Quality/Atmosphere, Forests/Forestry, Land Issues, Water Habitats & Quality, Wildlife & Species
Contact(s):
Melissa Lindsay, Executive Director
Jeff Evans, Treasurer
Jon Nelson, Chairperson
Becky Rom, Vice-Chairperson
Elizabeth Schuniesing, Secretary

FRIENDS OF THE CARR REFUGE

P.O. Box 510988
Melbourne Beach, FL 32951 United States
Phone: 321-676-1701
E-mail: gheyes@aol.com
Website: www.nbbd.com/npr/fcr

Founded: 1998
Membership: 1–100
Scope: Local
Description: Support organization for the Archie Carr National Wildlife Refuge
Publication(s): Befriending a Refuge
Keyword(s): Ecosystems (precious), Oceans/Coasts/Beaches, Public Lands/Greenspace, Wildlife & Species

FRIENDS OF THE EARTH

The Global Bldg., 1025 Vermont Ave., NW, Suite 300
Washington, DC 20005 United States
Phone: 202-783-7400 Fax: 202-783-0444
E-mail: foe@foe.org
Website: www.foe.org

Founded: N/A
Scope: National, International
Description: A global environmental advocacy organization based in Washington, DC, with 70 international affiliates. Merged with Environmental Policy Institute and the Oceanic Society in 1990. Dedicated to protecting the planet from environmental disaster and preserving biological, cultural, and ethnic diversity. With strong ties to the grassroots in the U.S. and around the world, Friends of the Earth believes individuals and communities must have a voice in environmental policymaking that affects their lives.
Publication(s): Friends of the Earth Newsmagazine, Green Scissors Annual Report, Anatomy of a Deal
Keyword(s): Air Quality/Atmosphere, Pollution (general), Transportation, Water Habitats & Quality
Contact(s):
Brent Blackwelder, President; 202-783-7400, ext. 284
Norman Dean, Executive Director; 202-783-7400, ext. 193
Mark Helm, Director of Media Relations; 202-783-7400, ext. 102

FRIENDS OF THE LITTLE PEND OREILLE NATIONAL WILDLIFE REFUGE, THE

P.O. Box 215
Colville, WA 99114 United States
Phone: 509-684-8384
E-mail: twoods73@aol.com
Website: geocities.com/friendsofthelpo.com

Founded: 2001
Membership: 1–100
Scope: Local, State, Regional
Description: The Friends of the Little Pend Oreille NWR is an independent, nonprofit organization dedicated to promoting the conservation of native fish, wildlife, plants and their habitats on the Refuge, providing educational opportunities, and fostering understanding and appreciation of the Refuge.
Keyword(s): Wildlife & Species

FRIENDS OF THE REEDY RIVER

P.O. Box 9351
Greenville, SC 29604 United States
E-mail: reedyriver@aol.com
Website: www.reedyriver.org

Founded: 1993
Scope: Regional
Description: FORR is a nonprofit river advocacy group committed to watershed protection and restoration of the Reedy River in upstate South Carolina.
Publication(s): Padding Guide, NPS Brochure, Membership Brochure and Newsletter
Keyword(s): Forests/Forestry, Pollution (general), Public Lands/Greenspace, Water Habitats & Quality
Contact(s):
Dave Hargett, Executive Director; 864-297-3566; hargett@prodigy.net

FRIENDS OF THE RIVER

915 20th Street
Sacramento, CA 95814 United States
Phone: 916-442-3155 Fax: 916-442-3396
E-mail: info@friendsoftheriver.org
Website: www.friendsoftheriver.org

Founded: 1973
Description: Friends of the River was founded in 1973 during the struggle to save the Stanislaus River from New Melones Dam. Following that campaign, the organization grew to become California's statewide river conservation group. Friends of the River is dedicated to preserving, protecting, and restoring California's rivers, streams, and their watersheds.
Contact(s):
Meg Johnson
Julie Mitchell

FRIENDS OF THE SAN JUANS

P.O. Box 1344
Friday Harbor, WA 98250 United States
Phone: 360-378-2319 Fax: 360-378-2324
E-mail: friends@sanjuans.org
Website: www.sanjuans.org

Founded: 1979
Membership: 1,001–10,000
Scope: Regional
Description: To protect to the fullest extent possible the scenic, aesthetic, ecological and sociological qualities, and resources of the San Juan Islands and the Northwest straits marine ecosystem. Promoting long-range planning and monitoring development.
Publication(s): Friends of the San Juan Newsletter
Keyword(s): Development/Developing Countries, Forests/Forestry, Land Issues, Oceans/Coasts/Beaches, Water Habitats & Quality
Contact(s):
Stephanie Buffem, Executive Director

FRIENDS OF THE SEA OTTER

2150 Garden Rd., A3
Monterey, CA 93940 United States
Phone: 831-373-2747 Fax: 831-373-2749
E-mail: info@seaotters.org
Website: www.seaotters.org

Founded: 1968
Membership: 1,001–10,000
Scope: Local, State, Regional, National
Description: A nonprofit organization dedicated to the protection and maintenance of a healthy population of southern sea otters, a threatened species, as well as sea otters throughout their North Pacific range, and all sea otter habitat. Encourages research and public education to develop a sound conservation program.
Publication(s): Otter Raft, The
Keyword(s): Ecosystems (precious), Ethics/Environmental Justice, Executive/Legislative/Judicial Reform, Oceans/Coasts/Beaches, Pollution (general), Recreation/Ecotourism, Water Habitats & Quality, Wildlife & Species
Contact(s):
Tom Kieckhefer, Education Director; 831 373-2747; Fax: 831 373-2749; education@seaotters.org
Matt Rutishauser, Science Director; 831 373-2747; Fax: 831 373-2749; science@seaotters.org
Esther Trosow, Center Director; 381 Cannery Row, Suite Q, Monterey, CA; 831 642-9057; Fax: 831 642-9057; centerdirector@seaotters.org

FUND FOR ANIMALS

200 W. 57th St.
New York, NY 10019 United States
Phone: 888-405-3863 Fax: 212-246-2633
E-mail: fundinfo@fund.org
Website: www.fund.org

Founded: 1967
Membership: 100,001–500,000
Scope: National, International
Description: National nonprofit animal-protection organization whose purpose is to preserve wildlife and promote humane treatment for all animals. Primarily serves as an advocacy group and information and education agency to help domestic and wild animals. The Fund operates four hands-on facilities.
Keyword(s): Wildlife & Species
Contact(s):
Marian Probst, President; 212-246-2096; Fax: 212-246-2633
Michael Markarian, Executive Vice President; 8121 Georgia Ave., Silver Spring, MD 20190
Lia Albo, Field Officer, Manager of Have A Heart Clinic; 335 W. 52nd St., New York, NY 10019; 212-977-6877
Chris Byrne, Field Officer; Manager of Black Beauty Ranch, P.O. Box 367, Murchison, TX 75778; 903-469-3811
Doris Dixon, Field Officer; 2841 Colony Rd., Ann Arbor, MI 48104; 313-971-4632
Caroline Gilbert, Field Officer; Rt. 2 Box 559, Simponsville, SC 29681; 803-963-4389
Virginia Handley, Field Officer; Fort Mason Center, Rm. 3262, San Francisco, CA 94123; 415-474-4020
Andrea Reed, Field Officer; P.O. Box 11294, Jackson, WY; 307-859-8840
Laura Simon, Field Officer; 30 Mountainview Rd., Betany, CT 06524; 203-393-3669
Marion Stark, Field Officer; P.O. Box 9029, Albany, NY 12209
Kimberly Sturla, Field Officer; 808 Alamo Dr., Suite 306, Vacaville, CA 95688
Chuck Traisi, Field Officer; Manager of Animal Trust Sanctuary, 18740 Highland Valley Rd., Ramona, CA 92065; 760-789-2324

Edward Walsh, Legal Counsel; Vedder, Price, Kaufman, Kammholz, and Day, 805 3rd Ave., New York, NY 10022; 212-407-7740
Christine Wolf, Chief of Legislative Services; 8121 Georgia Ave., Silver Spring, MD 20910

FUNDACION NATURA - COLOMBIA

A. A. 55402
Santa Fe De Bogota, Colombia
Phone: 5.7134005693e+016 Fax: 5713400124

Founded: 1984

Scope: Regional

Description: Fundacion Natura is a Colombian nonprofit, non-governmental organization. It works with other national governmental and non-governmental organizations as well as international partners to attain the required knowledge to design viable conservation strategies which encompass biological, social, political, and economic variables.

Contact(s):
Elsa Angel, Executive Director

FUNDACION NATURA COLOMBIA

Calle 61 No. 4-26
Santa Fe De Bogaota, Colombia
Phone: 5712485820 Fax: 5713461382
E-mail: enatura@impsar.net.co
Website: www.natura.org.co

Founded: 1983

Keyword(s): Reduce/Reuse/Recycle, Wildlife & Species

Contact(s):
Elsa Escobar, Executive Director

FUTURE FISHERMAN FOUNDATION

225 Reinekers Lane Ste. 420
Alexandria, VA 22314 United States
Phone: 703-519-9691 Fax: 703-519-1872
E-mail: info@asafishing.org
Website: www.asafishing.org

Founded: N/A
Membership: 1–100
Scope: National

Description: The educational arm of the American Sportfishing Association, the Foundation is a nonprofit organization dedicated to promoting participation and education in fishing as well as enhancement and protection of aquatic resources. Develops and coordinates the national program "Hooked On Fishing - Not on Drugs". The Foundation is a national leader in recreational fishing and aquatic resource education and offers student and instructor educational materials.

Keyword(s): Oceans/Coasts/Beaches, Recreation/Ecotourism

Contact(s):
Anne Glick, Executive Director

FUTURE GENERATIONS

North Mountain
Franklin, WV 26807 United States
Phone: 304-358-2000 Fax: 304-358-3008
E-mail: info@future.org
Website: www.future.org

Founded: 1992
Membership: N/A
Scope: International

Description: Future Generations offers an inexpensive and systematic process for community-based change to realize the dual objectives of insuring sustainability on our planet and reducing the equity gap between rich and poor.

Publication(s): Just and Lasting Change

Keyword(s): Development/Developing Countries, Ecosystems (precious), Forests/Forestry, Public Health, Wildlife & Species

Contact(s):
Daniel Taylor-Ide, President

G

GALIANO CONSERVANCY ASSOCIATION

R.R. 1, Sturdies Bay Rd.
Galiano Island, V0N 1P0 British Columbia Canada
Phone: 250-539-2424 Fax: 250-539-2424
E-mail: galiano_conservancy@gulfislands.com

Founded: 1989

Scope: Local

Description: The Galiano Conservancy Association is a community-based, regionally-oriented conservation organization and land trust. Its purposes are to preserve, protect, and enhance the quality of the human and natural environment of the area through public education; management, and ownership of conservatrion land; and research and restoration projects.

Publication(s): Archipelago, Bulletin, Newsletter

Keyword(s): Forests/Forestry, Land Issues, Oceans/Coasts/Beaches, Pollution (general), Reduce/Reuse/Recycle, Water Habitats & Quality, Wildlife & Species

Contact(s):
Rose Longini, Secretary; 250-539-2424; Fax: 250-539-2424
Ken Millard, Coordinator; 250-539-2424; Fax: 250-539-2424
John Pritchard, Co-Coordinator; 250-539-2424

GAME AND PARKS COMMISSION-NEBRASKA

AK-SAR-BEN AQUARIUM
21502 W Hwy. 31
Gretna, NE 68028 United States
Phone: 402-332-3901 Fax: 402-332-5853
Website: www.ngpc.state.ne.us

Founded: N/A
Membership: 1–100
Scope: State

Contact(s):
Darrell Feit, Director; dfeit@ngpc.state.nd.us

GAME CONSERVANCY U.S.A.

P.O. Box 922
Darien, CT 06820-0922 United States
Phone: 203-662-0886 Fax: 203-662-9298
E-mail: cvm@gcusa.org
Website: www.gcusa.org

Founded: 1985
Membership: 101–1,000
Scope: National

Description: (formerly American Friends of the Game Conservancy) Game Conservancy USA's primary function is to raise funds to support the scientific research and educational activities of The Game Conservancy Trust in the U.K.

Publication(s): American Friends of the Game Conservancy

Contact(s):
F. Gillet, President; 159 Via del Lago, Palm Beach, FL 33480; 516-655-6789; Fax: 516-832-1762
Edward Shugrue, III, Vice President; 212-655-0225; Fax: 212-6550044
Christopher Van Munching, Executive Director; P.O. Box 922, Darien, CT 06820; 203-662-0886; Fax: 203-662-9298; cvm@gcusa.org

GAME CONSERVATION INTERNATIONAL (GAME COIN)

4600 Broad Ave.
Ft. Worth, TX 76107 United States
Phone: 817-738-5438 Fax: 817-737-2911

Founded: 1967

Scope: International

Description: A nonprofit organization dedicated to responsible sustainable use of fish and wildlife and preserving the hunting and fishing heritage for future generations. Supports strong educational programs for classrooms and sponsors the state and province Outstanding Hunter Education awards from Mexico to Canada. Its National Junior Wildlife Artist competition encourages high school youngsters to compete for thousands of dollars in prizes under the theme: Our Wildlife Heritage: Pass It On!

Keyword(s): Wildlife & Species

Contact(s):

Harry Tennison, President; 817-738-5438

GARDEN CLUB OF AMERICA, THE

14 East 60th St.
New York, NY 10022 United States
Phone: 212-753-8287 Fax: 212-753-0134
E-mail: hq@gcamerica.org
Website: www.gcamerica.org

Founded: 1913

Membership: 10,001–100,000

Scope: National

Description: A national nonprofit organization with member clubs from coast to coast and in Hawaii. Its purpose is to stimulate the knowledge and love of gardening, to share the advantages of association by means of educational meetings, conferences, correspondence and publications, and to restore, improve, and protect the quality of the environment through educational programs and action in the fields of conservation and civic improvement.

Keyword(s): Agriculture/Farming, Wildlife & Species

Contact(s):

Joseph Frierson, President
Peter Goedecke, Conservation Chairman
A. Gregg, Horticulture Chairman
John Murphy Jr., National Chairman
Daniel Will III, Corresponding Secretary

GENERAL FEDERATION OF WOMEN'S CLUBS

1734 N St., NW
Washington, DC 20036 United States
Phone: 202-347-3168 Fax: 202-835-0246
E-mail: gfwc@gfwc.org
Website: www.gfwc.org

Founded: 1890

Scope: National

Description: The General Foundation of Women's Clubs (GFWC) is an international organization of community-based volunteer women's clubs dedicated to community service since 1890. GFWC programs and projects encompass the major issues of our time including literacy, health, preservation of natural resources, abuse prevention, and solid waste management.

Publication(s): GFWC Clubwoman

Keyword(s): Energy, Land Issues, Public Lands/Greenspace, Reduce/Reuse/Recycle

Contact(s):

Shelby Hamlett, President
Judy Lutz, 1st Vice President
Ernie Shriner, 2nd Vice President
Pat Nolan, Program Director
Maryanne Potter, Director of Junior Clubs
Kelly Buckheit, Editor
Norma Chesney, Water Quality Program Chair; 1331 Jill Terrace, Homewood, IL 60430
Rose Ditto, Treasurer
Judy Lutz, President-Elect
Barbara Nunnari, Resource Conservation Program Chair; 13200 Ridge Dr., Rockville, MD 20850
Jacquelyn Pierce, Recording Secretary
Joyce Schaefer, Beautification Program Chair; Rt. #4 Box 32, Seaford, DE 19973
Terri Wogan, Conservation Department Coordinator; 5401 E. Marilyn Rd., Scottsdale, AZ 85254

GEORGE MIKSCH SUTTON AVIAN RESEARCH CENTER INC.

P.O. Box 2007
Bartlesville, OK 74005-2007 United States
Phone: 918-336-7778 Fax: 918-336-7783
E-mail: gmsarc@aol.com
Website: www.suttoncenter.org

Founded: 1983

Membership: 101–1,000

Scope: Local, State, Regional, National, International

Description: The Sutton Research Center is a non-profit, tax-exempt organization conducting scientific studies, conservation projects and educational programs regarding avian species worldwide. Topics of particular interest include raptor population surveys and studies, bald eagle population monitoring, avian captive breeding and reintroductions, ecological studies of grassland birds including songbirds and gamebirds, public education projects and cooperative wildlife conservation efforts with landowners.

Publication(s): The Sutton Newsletter

Keyword(s): Agriculture/Farming, Ecosystems (precious), Land Issues, Wildlife & Species

Contact(s):

Steve Sherrod, Executive Director; 918-336-7778; sksherrod@ou.edu
Stephen Adams, Board Chairman; Oklahoma Land & Cattle Co., 1437 S. Boulder Ave. Suite 930, Tulsa, OK 74119; 918-585-5411; sadams@adamsaff.com
Howard Burman, Treasurer

GEORGE WASHINGTON CARVER OUTDOOR SCHOOL, INC., THE

P.O. Box 60579
Washington, DC 20039 United States
Phone: 202-723-5437 Fax: 202-723-0411
E-mail: outdoorsch@aol.com
Website: www.gwcods.org

Founded: 1990

Membership: N/A

Scope: Local, State, Regional

Description: The GWC Outdoor School, Inc. is a year round, non-profit, 501(c)(3), tax-exempt, community based, health promotion and environmental awareness enrichment program for boys and girls, ages 7 - 17. Cultural adaptations and historical re-inactments are used in addition to nationally recognized curriculums to make learning more relevant for our youth. Our programs are safe, educational and fun. We provide cultural camping at its best.

Publication(s): Facilitators

Contact(s):

Jawara Kasimu-Graham, Founder & Director; 5702 Fourth Street, NW, Washington, DC 20011; 202-427-5437; Fax: 202-723-0411; outdoorsch@aol.com

GEORGE WRIGHT SOCIETY, THE

P.O. Box 65
Hancock, MI 49930 United States
Phone: 906-487-9722 Fax: 906-487-9405
E-mail: info@georgewright.org
Website: www.georgewright.org

Founded: 1980

Membership: 101–1,000

Scope: International

Description: The George Wright Society is organized for the purposes of promoting the application of knowledge, fostering communication, improving resource management, and providing information to improve public understanding and appreciation of the basic purposes of natural and cultural parks and equivalent reserves.

Publication(s): George Wright Forum, The
Keyword(s): Land Issues
Contact(s):
Bob Krumenaker, President; bob_krumenaker@nps.gov
David Harmon, Executive Director; Hancock Office,

GEORGIA ASSOCIATION OF CONSERVATION DISTRICT SUPERVISORS

P.O. Box 8024
Athens, GA 30603 United States
Phone: 706-542-9233
E-mail: info@gacds.org
Website: www.gacds.org

Founded: N/A
Scope: State

GEORGIA B.A.S.S. CHAPTER FEDERATION

Attn: President, 11575 Northgate Trail
Roswell, GA 30075 United States
Phone: 770-993-6597
Website: www.gabassfed.org

Founded: N/A
Scope: State
Description: An organization of Bassmaster chapters, affiliated with the Bass Anglers Sportsman Society, organized to fight pollution, assist state and national conservation agencies in their efforts, and teach young people of our country's good conservation practices. Dedicated to the realistic conservation of our water resources.
Publication(s): Georgia Federation Newsletter, Georgia Outdoor News
Contact(s):
Larry Lewis, President; 770-993-6597
Scott Hendricks, Conservation Director; 5131 Maner Rd., Smyrna, GA 30080; 404-799-2159

GEORGIA CONSERVANCY, INC., THE

1776 Peachtree Rd. NW, Suite 400, S.
Atlanta, GA 30309 United States
Phone: 404-876-2900 Fax: 404-872-9229
E-mail: mail@gaconservancy.org
Website: www.gaconservancy.org

Founded: 1967
Membership: 1,001–10,000
Scope: State
Description: The Georgia Conservancy works to protect Georgia's air, water and natural areas. Through environmental education and community outreach, the Conservancy teaches present and future leaders about responsible stewardship of Georgia's natural resources and works at the state level in support of thoughtful environmental policies. Serving as a resource to business and political leaders, planners and individual citizens, the Conservancy seeks to make Georgia a better place to live.
Publication(s): Teaching Conservation, Panorama, Wetlands: Georgia's Vanishing Treasure, The Hiking Trails of North Georgia, Highroad Guide to the Georgia Coast and Okefenokee
Keyword(s): Air Quality/Atmosphere, Forests/Forestry, Land Issues, Oceans/Coasts/Beaches, Pollution (general), Public Lands/Greenspace, Sprawl/Urban Planning, Transportation, Water Habitats & Quality
Contact(s):
John Sibley, President
Susan Kidd, Vice President for Education and Advocacy
Robert Smulian, Vice President for Planning and Development
Patricia McIntosh, Coastal Programs Director; 428 Bull St., Savannah, GA 31410; 912-447-5910; Fax: 912-447-0740
James Bostic, Treasurer
Joe Montgomery, Chairman of the Board

GEORGIA ENVIRONMENTAL COUNCIL, INC.

P.O. Box 997
Suwanee, GA 30024 United States
Phone: 706-546-7507 Fax: 770-614-0593
Website: www.gecweb.org

Founded: N/A
Membership: 1–100
Scope: State
Description: A statewide umbrella for organizations interested in environmental protection that seeks to facilitate the exchange of information among member organizations, to provide a forum for discussion of environmental issues of interest to the members, and to monitor state government legislative activities having to do with the environment.
Publication(s): Issues Forums, Legislative Monitor, Directory of Environmental Groups in Georgia
Contact(s):
Lucy Smethurst, President
Carol Hassell, Administrative Director
Patty McIntosh, Secretary
Hans Neuhauser, Treasurer

GEORGIA ENVIRONMENTAL ORGANIZATION, INC. (GEO)

3185 Center St.
Smyrna, GA 30080-7039 United States
Phone: 404-605-0000 Fax: 404-350-9997
E-mail: info@gaenv.org
Website: www.gaenv.org

Founded: 1991
Membership: 1–100
Scope: State
Description: GEO is a non-profit, citizen-oriented organization established to preserve and protect Georgia's environment through education, collaboration, research, planning, legislation, and grassroots organizing. The mission of GEO is to create an ecologically sound, sustainable society by developing and implementing cooperative, long-range policies, plans and programs and by carrying out hands-on projects within local communities.
Publication(s): Georgians on Sustainability
Keyword(s): Development/Developing Countries
Contact(s):
Trey Gibbs, Executive Director

GEORGIA ENVIRONMENTAL POLICY INSTITUTE

GEORGIA LAND TRUST SERVICE CENTER
380 Meigs St.
Athens, GA 30601 United States
Phone: 706-546-7507 Fax: 706-613-7775
E-mail: gepi@ix.netcom.com
Website: www.gepinstitute.com

Founded: 1993
Membership: N/A
Scope: Local, State, Regional, National, International
Description: GEPI helps communities develop proactive strategies for a healthy environment through technical and legal services. The organization's primary focus is on land conservation.
Publication(s): Right Whale News, A Summary of Takings Law, A Landowner's Guide
Keyword(s): Agriculture/Farming, Ecosystems (precious), Ethics/Environmental Justice, Forests/Forestry, Land Issues, Oceans/Coasts/Beaches, Public Lands/Greenspace, Reduce/Reuse/Recycle, Water Habitats & Quality, Wildlife & Species
Contact(s):
Hans Neuhauser, Executive Director; 706-546-7507; Fax: 706-613-7775; gepi@ix.netcom.com
Edwin Speir, Chair; 455 Riverview Road, Athens, GA 30606; 706-548-7943; Fax: 706-613-7775

GEORGIA FEDERATION OF FOREST OWNERS

2402 Manchester Drive
Waycross, GA 31501-7554 United States
Phone: 912-283-0871 Fax: 912-283-9141
E-mail: aemceuen@wayxcable.com

Founded: 1974

Scope: State

Description: A statewide organization affiliated with the National Woodland Owners Association to perpetuate good forest practices on private woodlands in Georgia including soil and water conservation, wildlife management, reforestation, and utilization of forest products.

Keyword(s): Forests/Forestry

Contact(s):

Patricia McCarthy, V P; 6043 Telmore-Dixie Union Rd., Millwood, GA 31552; 912-283-0075; mccarthy5@aol.com
Archie McEuen, Secretary; 2402 Manchester Dr., Waycross, GA 31501-7554; 912-283-0871; Fax: 912-283-0871; aemceuen@wayxcable.com

GEORGIA FORESTRY ASSOCIATION, INC.

505 Pinnacle Ct.
Norcross, GA 30071-3656 United States
Phone: 770-416-7621 Fax: 770-840-8961
E-mail: info@gfagrow.org
Website: www.gfagrow.org

Founded: 1907

Membership: 1,001–10,000

Scope: Regional

Publication(s): Tops, Legislative Bulletin, GFA News

Keyword(s): Forests/Forestry, Transportation

Contact(s):

Blake Sullivan, President
Paul Mott, Vice President
Dale Greene, Treasurer

GEORGIA TRAPPERS ASSOCIATION

P.O. Box 335
Doerun, GA 31744 United States
Phone: 912-782-5417
E-mail: tbehle@indy.tds.net
Website: www.geocities.com/yosemite/trails//GA-app.html

Founded: 1979

Scope: State

Description: An organization of Georgia trappers and friends of trappers, affiliated with Georgia Wildlife Federation and National Trappers Association, organized to protect the rights of trappers to trap, to coordinate a trappers education program with the Georgia Department of Natural Resources and to conserve and protect the natural resources of Georgia.

Contact(s):

Tom Ethridge, President; P.O. Box 335, Doerun, GA 31744
Ralph Goodson, NTA Director; P.O. Box 4398, Albany, GA 31706
Grace Conder, Secretary and Treasurer; P.O. Box 474, Brooklet, GA 30415
Tommy Key, General Organizer; Rt. 2, Newnan, GA 30623

GEORGIA TRUST FOR HISTORIC PRESERVATION

1516 Peachtree St., NW
Atlanta, GA 30309-2916 United States
Phone: 404-881-9980 Fax: 404-875-2205
E-mail: info@georgiatrust.org
Website: www.georgiatrust.org

Founded: 1973

Membership: 1,001–10,000

Scope: State

Description: The Georgia Trust for Historic Preservation promotes an appreciation of Georgia's diverse historic resources and provides for their protection and use to preserve, enhance and revitalize Georgia's communities.

Publication(s): The Rambler (bi-monthly newsletter)

Keyword(s): Development/Developing Countries, Ethics/Environmental Justice, Public Lands/Greenspace, Reduce/Reuse/Recycle, Sprawl/Urban Planning, Transportation

Contact(s):

Gregory Paxton, President and CEO; 404-885-7801; gpaxton@georgiatrust.org

GEORGIA WILDLIFE FEDERATION

11600 Hazelbrand Road
Covington, GA 30014 United States
Phone: 770-787-7887 Fax: 770-787-9229
E-mail: gwf@gwf.org
Website: www.gwf.org

Founded: 1936

Scope: State

Description: A representative statewide organization, affiliated with the National Wildlife Federation, dedicated to the protection and enhancement of wildlife and its habitat through public education and government interaction.

Publication(s): Georgia Wildlife Magazine

Contact(s):

Jerry McCollum, President and CEO and Alternate Representative
Laura Bryant, Education Programs Contact
David Haire, Representative
James Hayes, Treasurer
Charles Rabolli, Chair
James Wilson, Editor

GEORGIANS FOR CLEAN ENERGY

427 Moreland Ave., Suite 100
Atlanta, GA 30307 United States
Phone: 404-659-5675 Fax: 770-234-3909
E-mail: georgia@cleanenergy.ws
Website: www.cleanenergy.ws

Founded: 1983

Membership: 101–1,000

Scope: State

Description: Georgians for Clean Energy is a nonprofit statewide organization, protects the environment and improves the economy by changing the way energy is produced and consumed in Georgia through public education and advocacy.

Publication(s): Plugging In, Technical Reports

Keyword(s): Air Quality/Atmosphere, Development/Developing Countries, Energy

Contact(s):

Amy Macklin, President
Na`taki Osborne, Vice President
C. Copeland, Secretary
Miki Davis, Treasurer
Amy Macklin, Board Chair

GET AMERICA WORKING!

1700 North Moore Street
Arlington, VA 22209 United States
Phone: 703-527-8300 Fax: 703-527-8383
E-mail: wdrayton@ashoka.org
Website: www.getamericaworking.org

Founded: 1998

Membership: 1–100

Scope: National

Description: Get America Working! believes that a sustainable economy must reduce pollution and resource waste, while greatly expanding employment opportunities and improving the use of human capital. To this end, GAW! advocates a tax shift — reducing payroll taxes to encourage job creation, and instead taxing pollution, energy inefficiency, and resource waste. GAW! works with diverse constituencies including seniors, minorities, environmentalists, labor, women, and the disabled.

Publication(s): Key Questions & Answers, A Fresh Point of View, Job Creation Tax Options

Contact(s):
Susan Davis, Associate Chair
William Drayton, Chairman

GIRL SCOUTS OF THE USA

420 5th Ave.
New York, NY 10018-2798 United States
Phone: 212-852-8000 Fax: 212-852-6509
E-mail: wildlife@girlscouts.org
Website: www.girlscouts.org

Founded: 1912
Membership: 1,000,001 +
Scope: National

Description: The national organization offers an informal education and recreation program designed to help each girl develop her own values and sense of worth as an individual. It provides opportunities for girls to experience, to discover, and to share planned activities that meet their interests. These activities encourage personal development through a wide variety of projects in social action, environmental action, wildlife values education, youth leadership, career exploration and community service.

Publication(s): Outdoor Education in Girl Scouting, Fun and Easy Nature and Science Investigations, Fun and Easy Activities with Nature and Science, Investigaciones divertidas y faciles de la naturaleza y ciencia, Earth Matters

Keyword(s): Ethics/Environmental Justice, Recreation/Ecotourism, Reduce/Reuse/Recycle

Contact(s):
Connie Matsui, President; 212-852-5001; Fax: 212-852-6517; cmatsui@girlscouts.org
Marsha Evans, National Executive Director; 212-852-5000; mevans@girlscouts.org
Sharon Woods-Hussey, National Director of Membership and Program Cluster; 212-852-8150; Fax: 212-852-6515; shussey@girlscouts.org
Laverne Alexander, Washington Representative; 1025 Connecticut Ave. NW, Suite 309, Washington, DC 20036-5405; 202-659-3780; Fax: 202-331-8065

GLACIER INSTITUTE, THE

P.O. Box 7457
Kalispell, MT 59904 United States
Phone: 406-755-1211 Fax: 406-755-7154
E-mail: glacinst@digisys.net
Website: www.glacierinstitute.org

Founded: 1983
Membership: 101–1,000
Scope: International

Description: The Glacier Institute serves students of all ages as an educational leader in the Crown of the Continent Ecosystem, emphasizing hands-on, field-based experiences promoting a balanced understanding of the science of ecology and human interaction with the environment.

Publication(s): Annual Course Catalog

Keyword(s): Reduce/Reuse/Recycle, Water Habitats & Quality

Contact(s):
Bruce Hird, President
Doug Morehouse, Vice President
Jami Belt, Program Director
R. Devitt, Program Director
Alice Hutchison, Secretary

GLEN CANYON INSTITUTE

316 East Birch
Flagstaff, AZ 86001 United States
Phone: 928-556-9311 Fax: 928-779-3567
E-mail: info@glencanyon.org
Website: www.glencanyon.org

Founded: 1996
Membership: 1,001–10,000
Scope: Regional, National

Description: Dedicated to restoration of a free flowing Colorado River through Glen Canyon and Grand Canyon through decommissioning Glen Canyon Dam.

Publication(s): Report on Initial Studies, Hidden Passage

Keyword(s): Ecosystems (precious), Energy, Ethics/Environmental Justice, Pollution (general), Public Health, Public Lands/Greenspace, Recreation/Ecotourism, Water Habitats & Quality, Wildlife & Species

Contact(s):
Andrea Jaussi, Outreach Director; andrea@glencanyon.org
Jeri Ledbetter, Executive Director; jeri@glencanyon.org

GLOBAL CITIES PROJECT, THE

2962 Fillmore St.
San Francisco, CA 94123 United States
Phone: 415-775-0791 Fax: 415-775-4159
E-mail: epc@globalcities.org
Website: www.globalcities.org

Founded: 1989
Scope: National

Description: The Global Cities Project provides local governments, businesses, and citizens with comprehensive, up-to-date information on local environmental policies and programs, promoting the development of environmentally and economically sound policy at the local level.

Publication(s): Building Sustainable Communities

Keyword(s): Air Quality/Atmosphere, Development/Developing Countries, Energy, Forests/Forestry, Land Issues, Pollution (general), Public Lands/Greenspace, Reduce/Reuse/Recycle, Transportation, Water Habitats & Quality

Contact(s):
Walter McGuire, President
Colleen McCarty, Chief Financial Officer; 2962 Fillmore St., San Francisco, CA 94123; 415-775-0791

GLOBAL ENVIRONMENTAL MANAGEMENT INITIATIVE (GEMI)

1 Thomas Circle NW, 10th Fl.
Washington, DC 20005 United States
Phone: 202-296-7449 Fax: 202-296-7442
E-mail: gemi@worldweb.net
Website: www.gemi.org

Founded: 1990
Membership: 1–100
Scope: International

Description: The Global Environmental Management Initiative (GEMI), an industry-initiated coalition of domestic and multinational Fortune 500 companies, is dedicated to helping businesses achieve environmental, health, and safety excellence. Through the activities of its workgroups, it has generated and distributed concrete tools for industry use in a number of environmental management fields.

Publication(s): Fostering Environmental Prosperity Multinationals, Information Systems for Health, Safety & Environmental Management, New Paths to Business Value; Strategic Sourcing - Environment, Health & Safety

Keyword(s): Development/Developing Countries

Contact(s):
Steven Hellem, Executive Director
Amy Goldman, Contact
Richard Guimond, Chairman

GLOBAL INDUSTRIAL AND SOCIAL PROGRESS RESEARCH INSTITUTE (GISPRI)

3rd Fl., Skousenmitsui Bldg., 2-1-1 Toranomon
Minato-ku, Tokyo, 105-0001 Japan
Phone: 81355638800 Fax: 81355638810
E-mail: info@gispri.or.jp
Website: www.gispri.or.jp

Founded: 1988

Scope: International

Description: A nonprofit foundation established to conduct research and submit policy proposals in such areas as resource conservation, global environmental problems, and relationship between industry and economy.

Contact(s):
Gaishi Hiraiwa, President
Akinobu Yasumoto, Executive Director
Kiyoshi Kawamatsu, Secretary General

GLOBAL INFORMATION NETWORK

146 West 29th St., # 7E
New York, NY 10001 United States
Phone: 212-244-3123 Fax: 212-244-3522
E-mail: ipsgin@igc.org
Website: www.globalinfo.org

Founded: 1984

Membership: 101–1,000

Scope: International

Description: GIN is the distributor of Inter Press Service and other news wires from developing countries with unique coverage on the environment in those regions.

Contact(s):
Katherine Stapp

GOPHER TORTOISE COUNCIL

Florida Museum of Natural History
University of Florida
P.O. Box 117800
Gainesville, FL 32611 United States
Phone: 229-246-7374
Website: www.gophertortoisecouncil.org

Founded: 1978

Membership: 101–1,000

Scope: Regional

Description: A nonprofit organization formed to assure the continued survival of viable populations of the gopher tortoise, Gopherus polyphemus, and its associated upland habitat in the southeastern United States.

Publication(s): Tortoise Burrow, The Bulletin

Keyword(s): Wildlife & Species

Contact(s):
Mark Bailey, Editor/Web Manager
Matt Dinkins, Treasurer
Colleen Heise, Secretary
Sharon Hermann, Co-Chair
Lora L. Smith, Co-Chair

GRAND CANYON TRUST

2601 N. Fort Valley Rd
Flagstaff, AZ 86001 United States
Phone: 928-774-7488 Fax: 928-774-7570
E-mail: steele@grandcanyontrust.org
Website: www.grandcanyontrust.org

Founded: 1985

Membership: 1,001–10,000

Scope: Regional, National

Description: Regional Conservation Group working on the Colorado Plateau in Arizona and Utah.

Publication(s): www.grandcanyontrust.org, Colorado Plateau Advocate

Keyword(s): Air Quality/Atmosphere, Ecosystems (precious), Energy, Forests/Forestry, Land Issues, Public Lands/Greenspace, Sprawl/Urban Planning, Water Habitats & Quality

GRASSLAND HERITAGE FOUNDATION

P.O. Box 394
Shawnee Mission, KS 66201 United States
Phone: 913-262-3506
E-mail: grasslandheritage@grapevine.net
Website: www.grasslandheritage.org

Founded: 1976

Membership: 101–1,000

Scope: Local, Regional

Description: A tax-exempt, nonprofit organization dedicated to prairie preservation and education. We encourage the preservation of all remaining prairies and work to increase public awareness of our prairie heritage.

Publication(s): GHF News

Contact(s):
Sue Holcomb, Office Manager; 913-829-0037

GREAT BEAR FOUNDATION

P.O. Box 9383
Missoula, MT 59807 United States
Phone: 406-829-9378 Fax: 406-829-9379
E-mail: gbf@greatbear.org
Website: www.greatbear.org

Founded: 1982

Membership: 1,001–10,000

Scope: International

Description: A membership-based organization dedicated to protecting all eight species of bears and their habitat. Programs range from supporting scientific research to educational outreach in schools and through field courses.

Publication(s): Bear News, Biological Consulting

Keyword(s): Public Lands/Greenspace, Wildlife & Species

Contact(s):
Charles Jonkel, President
Patti Sowka, Assistant Director
Pam Uihlein, Education Outreach; 406-829-9638; pam@greatbear.org

GREAT LAKES SPORT FISHING COUNCIL

P.O. Box 297
Elmhurst, IL 60126 United States
Phone: 630-941-1351 Fax: 630-941-1196
E-mail: info@great-lakes.org
Website: www.great-lakes.org

Founded: 1973

Membership: 100,001–500,000

Scope: Regional, National

Description: A nonprofit confederation of organizations and individuals throughout the Great Lakes states and provinces whose members are concerned with the present and future of sport fishing in the Great Lakes and adjoining waters. The Council, which acts as a clearinghouse for the exchange of information among members, also seeks to protect the Great Lakes against pollution and exploitation by commercial, individual, or other interests.

Publication(s): Great Lakes Basin Report, Regional Government Reference Guide

Keyword(s): Recreation/Ecotourism, Water Habitats & Quality, Wildlife & Species

Contact(s):
Dan Thomas, President; P.O. Box 297, Elmhurst, IL 60126; 630-941-1351; Fax: 630-941-1196; dan@great-lakes.org
Robert Mitchell, Vice President; 6466 Parkview, Troy, MI 48098; 810-558-6547; Fax: 810-575-9713; bmitchel@cecom.com
Mel Both, Secretary; 4633 Ridgecrest Dr., Racine, WI 53403; 262-598-8802; rodnreel@wi.net

Tom Couston, Treasurer; 12 W. Schaumburg Rd., Schaumburg, IL 60194; 847-519-1711; tomdds@megsinet.net
R. James, Webmaster; webmaster@great-lakes.org
Bob Schmidt, Editor; 5016 West Argyle St., Chicago, IL 60630; 773-283-7871; editor@great-lakes.org

GREAT LAKES UNITED

Headquarters, Buffalo State College, Cassety Hall, 1300 Elmwood Ave.
Buffalo, NY 14222 United States
Phone: 716-886-0142 Fax: 716-886-0303
E-mail: glu@glu.org
Website: www.glu.org

Founded: 1982
Membership: 101–1,000
Scope: International
Description: An international coalition of environmental, conservation, sports, labor, business, and community organizations, and individuals throughout the eight Great Lakes states, two Canadian provinces. GLU is dedicated to the protection and restoration of the Great Lakes-St. Lawrence River Basin ecosystem.
Publication(s): Great Lakes News, occasional reports, Great Lakes: Habitat Watch, Sustainable Waters Watch, and Toxic Watch
Keyword(s): Ethics/Environmental Justice, Oceans/Coasts/Beaches, Pollution (general), Reduce/Reuse/Recycle, Water Habitats & Quality, Wildlife & Species
Contact(s):

Ed Michael, President, Trout Unlimited; 223 Barberry Rd., Highland Park, IL 60035; 847-831-4159; Fax: 847-831-1035; e1michael@cs.com
Lynda Lukasik, Vice President, Friends of Red Hill Valley; 148 Oakland Dr., Hamilton, Ontario L8E 1B6; 905-560-1177; lynda.lukasik@sympatico.ca
Margaret Wooster, Executive Director
Reg Gilbert, Senior Coordinator; reg@glu.org
Stephane Gingras, Coordinator, Quebec; 514-396-3333; Fax: 514-396-0297; sgingras@glu.org
John Jackson, Past President
Jim Mahon, Canadian Treasurer, Canadian Auto Workers, Local 1520; 120 Tufton Pl., London, Ontario N6C 4W9; 519-681-3680; Fax: 519-652-0586; jimahon@home.com
Robin McClellan, United States Treasurer, NYS Citizens Environmental Coalition; 2877 Gaines Basin Rd., Albion, NY 14411; 716-589-4695; robinm@eznet.net
Alexandra McPherson, Clean Production Coordinator; alex@glu.org
Jennifer Nalbone, Habitat and Biodiversity Coordinator; jen@glu.org
Patty O'Donnell, Secretary, Grand Traverse Band of Ottawa and Chippewa; 2605 NW Bay Shore Dr., Suttons Bay, MI 49682; 231-271-7368; Fax: 231-271-3576; patty@freeway.net

GREAT LAKES UNITED

CANADA OFFICE
4525 Derouen
Montreal, HiV IH1 Quebec Canada
Phone: 514-396-3333 Fax: 514-396-0297
Website: www.glu.org

Founded: N/A
Scope: National
Publication(s): Newsletter-Great Lakes
Contact(s):

Ed Michael, President
Liliane Cotnoir, Director; Front Common Quebecois pour une Gestion Ecologique des Dechets, 2025 A Masson #001, Montreal, Quebec H2H 2P7; 514-396-2286; Fax: 514-396-9041; cotnoirl@mlink.net
Daniel Green, Director; Societe pour Vaincre la Pollution; C.P. 65 Place D'Armes, Montreal, Quebec H2Y 3E9; 514-844-5477; Fax: 514-844-1446; greentox@total.net
Julian Holenstein, Director; Environment North; 427 Queen St., Thunder Bay, Ontario P7B 2K3; 807-345-7784; julian@tbaytel.net
Jim Mahon, Director; Canadian Auto Workers Local 1520; 120 Tufton Pl., London, Ontario N6C 4W9; 519-681-3680; Fax: 519-652-0586; jimahon@home.com
Jane Wilkins, Director; Sierra Club of Eastern Canada; 699 Bush St., Bel Fountain, Ontario L0N 1B0; 519-927-5924; Fax: 519-927-9828
Margaret Wooster, Executive Director

GREAT OUTDOORS CONSERVANCY, THE

4311 Manatee Ave., West, Suite 210
Bradenton, FL 34209-3948 United States
Phone: 941-708-3456 Fax: 941-708-3535
E-mail: conserve@TheGreatOutdoors.org
Website: www.thegreatoutdoors.org

Founded: 1998
Membership: 1,001–10,000
Scope: National
Description: The conservancy is a nonprofit national marketing, fundraising, and educational organization for land conservation and expands wild, natural, scenic and recreational areas in the United States by the acquisition of land for the benefit of wildlife and the public's enjoyment for generations to come.
Publication(s): Partnerships in Preservation
Keyword(s): Forests/Forestry, Land Issues, Public Lands/Greenspace, Water Habitats & Quality, Wildlife & Species
Contact(s):

Bill Lamee, President; BlaMee@TheGreatOutdoors.org

GREAT PLAINS NATIVE PLANT SOCIETY

P. O. Box 461
Hot Springs, SD 57747 United States
Phone: 605-745-3397 Fax: 605-745-3397
E-mail: cascade@gwtc.net

Founded: 1984
Membership: 101–1,000
Scope: Regional
Description: Promotes the protection and study of native plants of the Great Plains through the formation of a Botanic Garden, an annual seed exchange, field trips and newsletter.
Publication(s): Plains Plants
Keyword(s): Agriculture/Farming, Land Issues, Wildlife & Species
Contact(s):

Cynthia Reed, President
Ronald Weedon, Vice-President
Joe Lux, Secretary-Treasurer

GREAT SMOKY MOUNTAINS INSTITUTE AT TREMONT

9275 Tremont Rd.
Townsend, TN 37882 United States
Phone: 865-448-6709 Fax: 865-448-9250
E-mail: mail@gsmit.org
Website: www.gsmit.org

Founded: 1969
Membership: 1–100
Scope: State, National
Description: A residential environmental education center in the Great Smoky Mountains National Parks. Programs promote awareness, appreciation, and stewardship of national parks and are offered for children and adults.
Publication(s): Connecting People and Nature, Walker Valley Reflections (Newsletter)
Keyword(s): Public Lands/Greenspace
Contact(s):

Bill Cobble, President; 800-721-6064; Fax: 423-982-6583

Bill Oliphant, Vice President
Ken Voorhis, Executive Director; 423-448-6709; Fax: 423-448-9250; ken@smokiesnha.org
Herb Handly, Treasurer; 423-974-1755; Fax: 423-974-4631
Norma Ogle, Secretary; 803-635-3561; Fax: 803-635-3561

GREATER YELLOWSTONE COALITION

P.O. Box 1874, 13 S. Willson, Suite 2
Bozeman, MT 59771 United States
Phone: 406-586-1593 Fax: 406-586-0851
E-mail: gyc@greateryellowstone.org
Website: www.greateryellowstone.org

Founded: 1983
Membership: 1,001–10,000
Scope: Regional, National
Description: A nonprofit, tax-exempt organization to preserve and protect the Greater Yellowstone Ecosystem and its unique quality of life by enhancing the ecosystem concept, raising the national public consciousness about the Greater Yellowstone Ecosystem, and combining the political effectiveness of the coalition's 7,500 individual members and more than 120 national and regional member organizations.
Publication(s): Greater Yellowstone Report, EcoAction Alerts, Annual Report
Keyword(s): Ecosystems (precious), Forests/Forestry, Land Issues, Public Lands/Greenspace, Water Habitats & Quality, Wildlife & Species
Contact(s):
Stephanie Kessler, President
Stephen Unfried, Vice President
Michael Scott, Executive Director
Jon Catton, Communications Director
Farwell Smith, Secretary and Treasurer

GREEN GUIDES

SUSTAINABLE LANDSCAPES
P.O. Box 9043
Bend, OR 97708 United States
Phone: 541-948-0661 Fax: 541-318-1756
E-mail: sustainablelands@aol.com

Founded: 2002
Membership: N/A
Scope: Local, State
Description: A nonprofit organization working toward sustainable landscaping and land management practices throughout Oregon. Emphasis on conservation of native floral species ecotypes; water conservation practices in Oregon's High Desert; sustainable development; and creation of economic incentive for commercial and residential developers.
Keyword(s): Ecosystems (precious), Land Issues, Water Habitats & Quality
Contact(s):
Richard Martinson, President
Brandon Reese, Vice President
Karen Theodore, Secretary/Treasurer

GREEN MEDIA TOOLSHED

1320 18th Street, NW., Suite 200
Washington, DC 20036 United States
Phone: 202-223-2114 Fax: 202-463-6671
E-mail: info@greenmediatoolshed.org
Website: www.greenmediatoolshed.org

Founded: 2000
Membership: N/A
Scope: Local, State, Regional, National
Description: Effective communications takes people, training and tools. Green Media Toolshed provides the tools. Green Media Toolshed offers: * A media contact database * An image management system * A polling library * Training content * Online Press Rooms * Campaign coordination tools * Secure online campaign coordination area. * Enhancements to member web sites for managing calendars, press releases and images in real time by program staff.
Publication(s): Resources, tips, Opinion Research Library, Image Managemant System, Media Database, Calendar advice for the communications staff of environmental nonprofit organizations
Keyword(s): Agriculture/Farming, Air Quality/Atmosphere, Climate Change, Energy, Ethics/Environmental Justice, Executive/Legislative/Judicial Reform, Forests/Forestry, Land Issues, Oceans/Coasts/Beaches, Pollution (general), Population, Public Health, Public Lands
Contact(s):
Martin Kearns, Executive Director; 202-223-2114; kearns@greenmediatoolshed.org
Bobbi Russell, Director of Media Services and Marketing; 202-223-2114; bobbi@greenmediatooshed.org

GREEN MOUNTAIN CLUB INC., THE

4711 Waterbury-Stowe Rd.
Waterbury Center, VT 05677 United States
Phone: 802-244-7037 Fax: 802-244-5867
E-mail: gmc@greenmountainclub.org
Website: www.greenmountainclub.org

Founded: 1910
Membership: 1,001–10,000
Scope: National
Description: The mission of the GMC is to make Vermont mountains play a larger part in the life of the people by protecting and maintaining the Long Trail System and fostering, through education, the stewardship of Vermont's hiking trails and mountains. The Club operates field programs and publishes guidebooks, maps, and educational materials in its efforts to maintain and protect the 440-mile Long Trail system. It is the advocate group for hiking in Vermont.
Publication(s): Long Trail News, The Long Trail Guide, Green Mountain Adventure, Vermont's Long, Long Trail End-to-Ender's Guide, Day Hiker's Guide to Vermont
Keyword(s): Recreation/Ecotourism
Contact(s):
Marty Lawthers, President; 20 Birch St., Saranac Lake, NY 12983
Ben Rose, Executive Director
Walter Pomroy, Treasurer; Box 280, Johnson, VT 05606
Richard Windish, Secretary; 16 Forest St., Brattleboro, VT 05301

GREEN PARTNERS

P.O. Box 1551
Lakeland, FL 33802-1551 United States
Phone: 863-679-3932
E-mail: bfenton@greenpartners.org
Website: greenpartners.org

Founded: 1999
Membership: N/A
Scope: Local, State
Description: Green Partners is a partnership of businesses dedicated to protecting our environment.
Publication(s): Environmental Checklist
Keyword(s): Ethics/Environmental Justice, Pollution (general), Reduce/Reuse/Recycle

GREEN SEAL

1001 Connecticut Ave., NW, Suite 827
Washington, DC 20036 United States
Phone: 202-872-6400 Fax: 202-872-4324
E-mail: greenseal@greenseal.org
Website: www.greeenseal.org

Founded: 1989
Membership: 1–100
Scope: National
Description: Green Seal helps organizations and individuals make environmentally responsible choices in their purchases.

It develops environmental standards and tests products against these standards, identifing those products that are environmentally responsible through the award of an environmental "seal of approval.". The Environmental Partners Program helps businesses develop green procurement plans through buying guides and monthly reports on green products.

Publication(s): Environmental Criteria and Standards, Greening Your Property, Monthly Choose Green Reports, Office Green Buying Guide, Campus Green Buying Guide, Catalog of Green Seal-Certified Products

Keyword(s): Air Quality/Atmosphere, Development/Developing Countries, Energy, Reduce/Reuse/Recycle

Contact(s):
Arthur Weissman, President
Bryan Thomlison, Chair of the Board; 609-737-8841

GREEN SPHERE INC.

86-02 Park Lane South, Suite 6B5
Woodhaven, NY 11421 United States
Phone: 718-846-6243 Fax: 718-846-6243
E-mail: info@greensphere.org
Website: greensphere.org

Founded: 1987
Membership: N/A
Scope: Local, State, Regional, National, International

Description: Nonprofit grassroots media organization. Defending the rights of the people and the planet.

Keyword(s): Agriculture/Farming, Air Quality/Atmosphere, Climate Change, Development/Developing Countries, Ecosystems (precious), Energy, Ethics/Environmental Justice, Forests/Forestry, Land Issues, Oceans/Coasts/Beaches, Pollution (general), Population, Public Health

Contact(s):
Alvin Jones, President; 718-846-6243; Fax: 718-846-6243; info@greensphere.org
Betty Quick, Vice President
Frank Melli, Executive Director; 718-846-6243; Fax: 718-846-6243; info@greensphere.org
Glyn Emmerson, Secretary
Teresa Cristina Silva, Treasurer

GREEN TV

1125 Hayes St.
San Francisco, CA 94117 United States
Phone: 415-255-4797 Fax: 415-255-4664
E-mail: fgreen@greentv.org
Website: www.greentv.org

Founded: 1992
Scope: National

Description: A non-profit video production company specializing in television programming on subjects about human interaction with the natural world. Offers catalog of stock footage of California wildlife, endangered species habitats and the timber industry.

Contact(s):
Frank Green, Owner/President
Jeanne Jesse, Office Manager; 415-255-4797; jeanne@greentv.org

GREENPEACE, INC.

702 H St., NW. Suite 300
Washington, DC 20001 United States
Phone: 202-462-1177 Fax: 202-462-4507
E-mail: gp1@sharewest.com
Website: www.greenpeace.org

Founded: 1971
Scope: National

Description: A nonprofit organization dedicated to preserving the earth and the life it supports through nonviolent direct action, lobbying, public education, and research. Greenpeace seeks to protect biodiversity in all its forms; prevents pollution and abuse of the earth's ocean, land, air, and fresh water; end all nuclear threats; and promotes peace, global disarmament, and nonviolence.

Publication(s): Greenpeace Quarterly (magazine)

Keyword(s): Climate Change, Energy, Pollution (general), Wildlife & Species

Contact(s):
David Barre, Director of Communications
Julie Crudele, Director of Development
Lynn Thorp, National Campaigns Director
David Barre, Editor-In-Chief
Susan Sabella, Biodiversity and Ocean Ecology Campaign Coordinator

GROUNDWATER FOUNDATION, THE

P.O. Box 22558
Lincoln, NE 68542-2558 United States
Phone: 402-434-2740 Fax: 402-434-2742
E-mail: info@groundwater.org
Website: www.groundwater.org

Founded: 1985
Membership: 101–1,000
Scope: National

Description: The Groundwater Foundation is a nonprofit foundation dedicated to educating the public about conservation and management of groundwater. The Foundation is a clearinghouse for general groundwater information, sponsors the Nebraska Children's Groundwater Festival, and coordinates "Groundwater Guardian", a national community recognition program.

Publication(s): The Aquifer, The Groundwater Catalog

Keyword(s): Pollution (general), Water Habitats & Quality

Contact(s):
Susan Seacrest, President
Rachael Herpel, Groundwater Guardian Program Director

GULF OF MEXICO FISHERY MANAGEMENT COUNCIL

The Commons at Rivergate
Suite 1000
3018 U.S. Highway 301 North
Tampa, FL 33619-2266 United States
Phone: 813-228-2815 Fax: 813-225-7015
E-mail: gulfcouncil@gulfcouncil.org
Website: www.gulfcouncil.org

Founded: 1976
Membership: 1–100
Scope: Regional

Description: The Gulf Council is responsible for developing and monitoring fishery management plans to provide for the best use of the fishery resources in the federal waters of Gulf of Mexico.

Keyword(s): Wildlife & Species

Contact(s):
Wayne Swingle, Executive Director

GWINNETT OPEN LAND TRUST, INC.

3280 Westbrook Road
Suwanee, GA 30024 United States
Phone: 770-945-3111 Fax: 770-614-0593
E-mail: chassell@mindspring.com
Website: www.gwinnettlandtrust.org

Founded: 1998
Membership: 101–1,000
Scope: Local

Description: Land conservation membership organization committed to the preservation of open and greenspace in Gwinnett County and northern Georgia, and to education about the value of environmental conservation and protection.

Keyword(s): Land Issues

Contact(s):
Carol Hassell, President; 770-945-3111; Fax: 770-614-0593; chassell@mindspring.com
Joyce Nuszbaum, Vice President; 678-428-7849; Fax: 770-806-8111; joyce.nuszbaum@omnexus.com

H

H. JOHN HEINZ III CENTER FOR SCIENCE, ECONOMICS, AND THE ENVIRONMENT
1001 Pennsylvania Ave., NW, Suite 735, South
Washington, DC 20004 United States
Phone: 202-737-6307 Fax: 202-737-6410
E-mail: info@heinzctr.org
Website: www.heinzctr.org

Founded: 1995
Membership: 1–100
Scope: National
Description: The H. John Heinz III Center is a nonprofit institution dedicated to improving the scientific and economic foundation of environmental policy. The Center's mission is to collaboratively identify emerging environmental issues, conduct related scientific research and economic analyses, and create and disseminate nonpartisan policy options for solving environmental problems.
Keyword(s): Oceans/Coasts/Beaches, Wildlife & Species
Contact(s):
William Merrell, Senior Fellow and President
Robert Friedman, Senior Fellow and Vice President for Research
Mary Katsouros, Senior Fellow and Senior Vice President
G. William Miller, Board of Trustees Chair

HARBOR BRANCH OCEANOGRAPHIC INSTITUTION
5600 North U.S. 1
Fort Pierce, FL 34946 United States
Phone: 772-465-2400 Fax: 772-465-5957
E-mail: webmaster@hboi.edu
Website: www.hboi.edu

Founded: 1971
Membership: 1,001–10,000
Scope: Local, State, Regional, National, International
Description: Harbor Branch Oceanographic Institution is dedicated to exploring the world's oceans, integrating the science and technology of the sea with the needs of humankind. We are involved in a wide variety of research programs: to understand the life histories of marine species; to improve the health of threatened marine mammals; to establish environmentally responsible aquaculture techniques; and to discover novel marine compounds that may hold the cure to human diseases like cancer.
Keyword(s): Agriculture/Farming, Ecosystems (precious), Oceans/Coasts/Beaches, Water Habitats & Quality, Wildlife & Species

HARDWOOD FOREST FOUNDATION
P.O. Box 34518
Memphis, TN 38184-0518 United States
Phone: 901-377-1818, ext. 106 Fax: 901-382-6419
E-mail: c.allen@natlhardwood.org
Website: www.hardwoodforests.org

Founded: 1989
Membership: 1,001–10,000
Scope: National, International
Description: The Hardwood Forest Foundation is a nonprofit public foundation with the mission to give the public a new pair of eyes to see and understand the forest and the trees. The Foundation carries out its mission by supporting conservation, research, and educational programs designed to educate and reach the largest number of concerned citizens possible.
Keyword(s): Forests/Forestry, Land Issues, Reduce/Reuse/Recycle
Contact(s):
Christopher Allen, Director; 901-377-1818, ext. 106; Fax: 901-382-6419; c.allen@natlhardwood.org

HAWAII NATURE CENTER
INTERACTIVE NATURE MUSEUM, IAO VALLEY
2131 Makiki Heights Dr.
Honolulu, HI 96822 United States
Phone: 808-955-0100 Fax: 808-955-0116
E-mail: hawaiinaturecenter@hawaii.rr.com
Website: hawaiinaturecenter.org

Founded: 1981
Membership: N/A
Scope: State
Description: The Hawaii Nature Center promotes stewardship through environmental education for school children and the public. School programs are full-day, hands-on field adventures; community programs include adult interpretive hikes, family nature adventures and custom excursions for scouts, senior citizens and other special groups. The Iao Valley Interactive Nature Museum on Maui includes hands-on exhibits of native flora, fauna and streamlife for residents and visitors.
Publication(s): The Steward (Newsletter Quarterly)
Keyword(s): Forests/Forestry, Land Issues, Water Habitats & Quality, Wildlife & Species
Contact(s):
Diana King, Education Director

HAWAIIAN BOTANICAL SOCIETY
3190 Maile Way
Honolulu, HI 96822 United States
Phone: 808-956-8072 Fax: 808-956-3923

Founded: 1924
Scope: State
Description: Objectives of society are: to advance the science of botany in all of its applications; To encourage research in botany in all of its phases; to promote the botanical welfare of its members; and to develop the spirit of good fellowship and cooperation in botanical matters. The Society is particularly interested in the preservation of the Hawaiian flora.
Publication(s): Newsletter of the Hawaiian Botanical Society
Contact(s):
Mindy Wilkinson, President
Alvin Yoshinaga, Vice President
Leilani Durand, Secretary
Ron Fenstemacher, Treasurer
Clifford Morden, Editor

HAWK AND OWL TRUST, THE
c/o Zoological Society of London
Regent's Park, London, NW1 4RY United Kingdom
Phone: 1814500662 Fax: 1814500662

Founded: 1969
Scope: National
Description: The Hawk and Owl Trust works for the conservation and appreciation of wild birds of prey and their habitats through projects which involve practical research, creative conservation, and imaginative education. Current projects include: Barn Owl Conservation Network; Operation Raptor Link; Farmland, Riverside and Forestry Link Scheme; Habitat Link. Its National Conservation and Education Centre is situated in Buckinghamshire
Keyword(s): Wildlife & Species
Contact(s):
Colin Shawyer, Director of Conservation and Research
Barbara Hall, Press and Public Relations
Barbara Handley, Chairman
Robin Rees-Webbe, Vice Chairman

HAWK MIGRATION ASSOCIATION OF NORTH AMERICA

Attn: Treasurer,16 Thomas St.
High Bridge, NJ 08829 United States
Phone: 908-638-5616
E-mail: eagletotem@nac.net
Website: hmana.org

Founded: 1974
Membership: 101–1,000
Scope: National
Description: A nonprofit organization whose purpose is to advance the knowledge of bird-of-prey migration across the continent, to monitor raptor populations as an indicator of environmental health, to study further the behavior of raptors, and to contribute to greater public understanding of birds of prey.
Publication(s): Hawk Migration Studies
Keyword(s): Wildlife & Species
Contact(s):
Kirk Moulton, Chair; kirk.moulton@unisys.com
Will Weber, Vice-Chair; will@journeys-intl.com
Mark Blauer, Membership Secretary; 6595@email.msn.com
Eileen Halko, Treasurer; eagletotem@nac.net

HAWK MOUNTAIN SANCTUARY ASSOCIATION, VISITOR CENTER

1700 Hawk Mountain Rd.
Kempton, PA 19529 United States
Phone: 610-756-6961 Fax: 610-756-4468
Website: www.hawkmountain.org

Founded: 1934
Membership: 1,001–10,000
Scope: International
Description: The Association is a nonprofit organization devoted to the conservation of birds of prey worldwide and a greater understanding of the central Appalachian environment. A full-time staff assisted by interns and volunteers carries out coordinated programs in education, research, monitoring, and sanctuary management. A visitor center is open year-round, and the 2,400-acre Sanctuary is maintained as a high-quality natural area with trails open to the public.
Publication(s): Hawk Mountain News, Raptor Watch, Hawks Aloft, Mountain and the Migration, A Global Directory in Raptor Migration sites
Keyword(s): Land Issues, Wildlife & Species
Contact(s):
Keith Bildstein, Research Director
Cynthia Lenhart, Executive Director
Harry Cerino, Treasurer
Jeffrey Weil, Chairman

HAWKWATCH INTERNATIONAL, INC.

1800 South West Temple, No. 226
Salt Lake City, UT 84115 United States
Phone: 801-484-6808 Fax: 801-484-6810
E-mail: hwi@hawkwatch.org
Website: www.hawkwatch.org

Founded: 1986
Membership: 1,001–10,000
Scope: State, Regional, National, International
Description: HawkWatch International is a nonprofit organization that monitors and protects hawks, eagles, falcons, other birds of prey and their environments through research, education and conservation.
Publication(s): Raptorwatch
Keyword(s): Land Issues, Pollution (general), Public Lands/Greenspace, Wildlife & Species
Contact(s):
Howard Gross, Executive Director; 801-484-6502; hgross@hawkwatch.org
Jeff Smith, Science Director; 801-484-6758; jsmith@hawkwatch.org
Benita Pulins, Treasurer; C/O Pricewaterhouse Coopers LLP, 36 S. State St., Suite 1700, Salt Lake City, UT 84111; 801-537-5227; benita.r.pulins@us.pwcglobal.com
Dawn Sebesta, Chair; 2466 Meadows Dr., Park City, UT 84060-7032; 435-649-3024; stoney@pcfastnet.com

HEADLANDS INSTITUTE

Golden Gate National Recreation Area, Bldg. 1033
Sausalito, CA 94965 United States
Phone: 415-332-5771 Fax: 415-332-5784
E-mail: hi@yni.org
Website: www.yni.org

Founded: 1979
Membership: 1–100
Scope: National
Description: To create sustained global environmental stewardship through educational adventures in nature's classroom.
Keyword(s): Development/Developing Countries, Reduce/Reuse/Recycle
Contact(s):
Mike Lee, Executive Director

HEAL THE BAY

3220 Nebraska Avenue
Santa Monica, CA 90404 United States
Phone: 310-453-0395 Fax: 310-453-7927
E-mail: info@healthebay.org
Website: www.healthebay.org

Founded: 1985
Membership: 1,001–10,000
Scope: Local, State, Regional
Description: Heal the Bay is a non-profit environmental group dedicated to making Santa Monica Bay and Southern California coastal waters safe and healthy again for people and marine life.
Contact(s):
Mark Gold, Executive Director

HENRY A. WALLACE INSTITUTE FOR ALTERNATIVE AGRICULTURE (HAWIAA)

9200 Edmonston Rd., Suite 117
Greenbelt, MD 20770-1551 United States
Phone: 301-441-8777 Fax: 301-220-0164
E-mail: hawiaa@access.digex.net
Website: igc.apc.org

Founded: 1983
Scope: National
Description: HAWIAA is a nonprofit, membership research and education organization established to encourage and facilitate adoption of resource-conserving, low-cost, environmentally sound, and economically viable farming systems.
Keyword(s): Agriculture/Farming
Contact(s):
David Ervin, Policy Studies Program Director
Garth Youngberg, Executive Director

HENRY STIFEL SCHRADER ENVIRONMENTAL EDUCATION CENTER

Oglebay Institute, Burton Center
Wheeling, WV 26003 United States
Phone: 304-242-6855 Fax: 304-242-5197
Website: www.oionline.com

Founded: N/A
Scope: State
Description: Oglebay Institute operates a variety of programs: Resident nature summer camps for adults and children; Ecotourism Club; resident environmental education programs;

children's day camping; special workshops and weekends; exhibits; school programs; and also the A.B. Brooks Environmental Education Center and Speidel Observatory.

Keyword(s): Reduce/Reuse/Recycle, Water Habitats & Quality, Wildlife & Species

Contact(s):

Steve Gerkin, Director of Environmental Education; 304-242-6855; Fax: 304-242-5197; sgerkin@oionline.com
Cathy Gielty, Associate Director of Environmental Education
Lisa Mustico, Assistant Director; 304-242-6855; Fax: 304-242-5197; lmustico@oionline.com
Greg Park, Associate Director of Environmental Education

HERPDIGEST

67-87 Booth Street
Forest Hills, NY 11375 United States
Phone: 718-275-2190 Fax: 718-275-3307
E-mail: asalzberg@herpdigest.org
Website: www.herpdigest.org

Founded: 2000
Membership: 1,001–10,000
Scope: International
Description: The first and only free weekly newsletter to deliver the latest conservation and science news on reptiles and amphibians.
Publication(s): HerpDigest
Keyword(s): Wildlife & Species
Contact(s):

Allen Salzberg, Publisher/Editor; 718-275-2190; Fax: 718-275-3307; asalzberg@herpdigest.org

HIGH DESERT MUSEUM, THE

59800 S. Highway 97
Bend, OR 97702-7963 United States
Phone: 503-382-4754 Fax: 541-382-5256
E-mail: info@highdesertmuseum.org
Website: www.highdesertmuseum.org

Founded: 1974
Membership: 1,001–10,000
Scope: National
Description: Created to broaden the knowledge and understanding of the natural and cultural history and resources of the high desert country for the purpose of promoting thoughtful decision-making that will sustain the region's natural and cultural heritage. It is a "living," participation-oriented museum which focuses on the Intermountain West — portions of eight Western states and the Canadian province of British Columbia. Opened to the public in 1982.
Publication(s): High Desert Quarterly, Sagebrush Legacy
Keyword(s): Ethics/Environmental Justice, Land Issues
Contact(s):

Forrest Rodgers, President; Frodgers@highdesert.org
Kevin Britz, Vice President for Programs; Kbritz@highdesert.org
Becky Anderson, Zoological Manager; BAnderson@highdesert.org
Kristi Jacobs, Volunteer Program Manager; Kjacobs@highdesert.org
Sue McWilliams, Education Manager; SMcWilliams@highdesert.org
Sheila Timony, Exhibits Manager; Stimony@highdesert.org

HIGHLANDS CENTER FOR NATURAL HISTORY

P.O. Box 12828
Prescott, AZ 86304 United States
Phone: 928-776-9550 Fax: 928-776-9530
E-mail: highlands@cableone.net
Website: highlandscenter.org

Founded: 1973
Membership: 101–1,000
Scope: Local, Regional
Description: Provides: environmental-science programs to school children in Central Arizona, programs to prevent at-risk behavior, and adult programs.

HILTON POND CENTER FOR PIEDMONT NATURAL HISTORY

1432 DeVinney Road
York, SC 29745 United States
Phone: 803-684-5852
E-mail: education@hiltonpond.org
Website: www.hiltonpond.org

Founded: 1982
Membership: N/A
Scope: Local, State, Regional, National, International
Description: Mission is "to conserve animals, plants, habitats, and other natural components of the Piedmont Region of the eastern United States through observation, scientific study, and education for students of all ages." The Center is the most active bird banding site in the Carolinas. Its web-site includes text and photos of flora and fauna found in most habitats in the eastern U.S. There are descriptions of long-term bird banding research (including hummingbirds) and "This Week at Hilton Pond."
Keyword(s): Development/Developing Countries, Ecosystems (precious), Wildlife & Species
Contact(s):

Bill Hilton, Executive Director; 803-684-5852; education@hiltonpond.org

HIMALAYAN WILDLIFE FOUNDATION

Centre One, House 1, Street 15
Islamabad, F 7/2 Pakistan
Phone: 9251276113 Fax: 9251824484
E-mail: vzakaria@hbp.sdnpk.undp.org

Founded: 1993
Scope: International
Description: HWF is a nonprofit, nongovernmental organization dedicated to safeguarding the biodiversity of Pakistan's Northern areas. The efforts of HWF have included: involving local communities in the conservation process, coordinating protection and park management activities with the local administration and wildlife department.
Keyword(s): Ecosystems (precious), Public Lands/Greenspace, Wildlife & Species
Contact(s):

Mujahid Ahmad, Coordinator
Anis Rahman, Contact

HOLDEN ARBORETUM, THE

9500 Sperry Rd.
Kirtland, OH 44094-5172 United States
Phone: 440-946-4400 Fax: 440-602-3857
E-mail: holden@holdenarb.org
Website: www.holdenarb.org

Founded: 1931
Membership: 1,001–10,000
Scope: Local, State, Regional, National
Description: The Holden Arboretum connects people with nature for inspiration and enjoyment, fosters learning and promotes conservation.
Publication(s): Arboretum Leaves, The, The Arboretum Class Schedule
Keyword(s): Agriculture/Farming, Ecosystems (precious), Forests/Forestry, Land Issues, Public Lands/Greenspace, Reduce/Reuse/Recycle, Sprawl/Urban Planning, Water Habitats & Quality, Wildlife & Species
Contact(s):

Brian Parsons, Director of Conservation; 440-602-3841; Fax: 440-602-3857; bparsons@holdenarb.org

HOLLY SOCIETY OF AMERICA, INC.

4738 Hale Haven Dr.
Ellicott City, MD 21043-6669 United States
Phone: 410-730-0243
E-mail: SECRETARY@HOLLYSOCAM.ORG
Website: www.hollysocam.org

Founded: 1947
Membership: 101–1,000
Scope: National
Description: National nonprofit organization dedicated to bringing together persons interested in any phase of holly culture. Collects and disseminates information about holly; studies methods of conservatively cutting and marketing holly; promotes research and hybridization; publishes research papers; and popularizes the use of holly as a landscape material.
Publication(s): Holly Society Journal
Contact(s):
Daniel Turner, President
Michael Pontti, Executive Vice President; ponttim@gunet.georgetown.edu
Ronald Solt, Administrative Vice President; esolt79087@aol.com
Ruth Bradley, Treasurer
Rondalyn Reeser, Secretary
Nancy Smith, Editor

HOOSIER ENVIRONMENTAL COUNCIL

520 E. 12th St., Suite 14
Indianapolis, IN 46202 United States
Phone: 317-685-8800 Fax: 317-686-4794
E-mail: hec@hecweb.org
Website: www.hecweb.org

Founded: 1983
Membership: 10,001–100,000
Scope: State
Description: To encourage and promote more aggressive environmental regulation and enforcement in the State of Indiana. The Council objectives are as follows: Facilitation of communication between environmental groups and individuals; coordination of action on current environmental issues, educational programs and publications; and representation of the concerns of the membership before administrative officials and regulatory boards/agencies of the state and federal government.
Publication(s): Monitor, LDF Report, Boardwatch
Keyword(s): Air Quality/Atmosphere, Reduce/Reuse/Recycle, Water Habitats & Quality, Wildlife & Species
Contact(s):
Jack Miller, President; 520 E. 12th St., Suite 14, Indianapolis, IN 46202; 317-872-3516; Fax: 317-297-9271
Tim Maloney, Executive Director; 520 E 12th St. Ste. 14, Indianapolis, IN 46202; 317-685-8800; Fax: 317-686-4794
Denise Baker, Editor
Alice Schloss, Treasurer; 4525 N. Park Ave., Indianapolis, IN 46205
Dona Young, Secretary

HUDSONIA LIMITED

Bard College Field Station P.O Box 5000
Annandale, NY 12504-0500 United States
Phone: 845-758-7053 Fax: 914-758-7033
Website: www.hudsonia.org

Founded: 1981
Scope: Regional
Description: Hudsonia Limited is a nonprofit, nonadvocacy institute for research, education, and technical assistance in the environmental sciences, focusing on the Hudson River Valley. There are over 25 research associates and other technical personnel. Hudsonia conducts pure and applied research on natural and social-sciences aspects of the environment, produces educational publications, and offers programs for environmental decision makers and natural history courses for a broader audience.
Publication(s): News From Hudsonia (quarterly), Guide to Biodiversity in the Hudson River Valley
Keyword(s): Water Habitats & Quality, Wildlife & Species
Contact(s):
Erik Kiviat, Science Director; kiviat@bard.edu
Gretchen Stevens, Staff Botanist

HUMAN ECOLOGY ACTION LEAGUE, INC., THE (HEAL)

P.O. Box 29629
Atlanta, GA 30359-0629 United States
Phone: 404-248-1898 Fax: 404-248-0162
E-mail: healnatnl@aol.com
Website: www.members.aol.com/healnatnl/index.html

Founded: 1977
Scope: International
Description: A nonprofit volunteer organization of people affected by or concerned about environmental conditions that are hazardous to human health. It serves as an information clearinghouse on exposure-related illness; alerts the general public about the potential dangers of chemicals; and encourages healthy lifestyles that minimize potentially hazardous environmental exposures.
Publication(s): Resource List, Human Ecologist, The, Fragrance and Health, Environmental Consultant Directory, Travel Directory, Bibliographies
Keyword(s): Air Quality/Atmosphere, Pollution (general), Public Health, Reduce/Reuse/Recycle
Contact(s):
Muriel Dando, President
Donald Jones, Treasurer and Business Manager
Kenneth King, Secretary
Diane Thomas, Editor

HUMANE SOCIETY OF THE UNITED STATES, THE

2100 L St., NW
Washington, DC 20037 United States
Phone: 202-452-1100 Fax: 301-258-3077
Website: www.hsus.org

Founded: 1954
Membership: 1,000,001 +
Scope: Local, State, Regional, National, International
Description: A nonprofit organization dedicated to the protection of animals, both domestic and wild. Professional staff experienced in animal control, cruelty investigation, humane and environmental education, farm animals, federal and state legislative activities, wildlife and habitat protection, and laboratory animal welfare; offer resources to local organizations, government, media, and the general public.
Publication(s): All Animals, Animal Sheltering, Kind News, Kind Teacher
Keyword(s): Agriculture/Farming, Development/Developing Countries, Ecosystems (precious), Executive/Legislative/Judicial Reform, Finance/Banking/Trade, Oceans/Coasts/Beaches, Public Lands/Greenspace, Sprawl/Urban Planning, Water Habitats & Quality, Wildlife & Species
Contact(s):
Paul Irwin, President, Humane Society International
Paul Irwin, President, CEO
Paul Irwin, President of Earthvoice
Patricia Forkan, Executive Vice President
John Grandy, Senior Vice President of Wildlife
Roger Kindler, Vice President and General Counsel
Wayne Pacelle, Senior VP, Govt. Affairs & Communications; 202-452-1100
Richard Clugston, Director of the Center for Respect of Life and Environment

Sharon Geiger, Library Assistant; The Joyce Mertz Gilmore Library, HSUS Offices, 700 Professional Dr., Gaithersburg, MD 20879; 202-452-1100
Amy Lee, Secretary
G. Waite, CFO
David Wiebers, Vice Chairman
David Wiebers, Chairman of the Board

HUMBOLT FIELD RESEARCH INSTITUTE

P.O. Box 9
Steuben, ME 04680-0009 United States
Phone: 207-546-2821 Fax: 207-546-3042
E-mail: humboldt@nemaine.com
Website: www.maine.maine.edu/~taglehill

Founded: 1981

Scope: International

Description: A nonprofit educational and research organization providing advanced and professional training programs in all aspects of natural history (terrestrial, freshwater and marine) and encouraging similar pursuits. Classical natural history training programs are held in Maine and the American Tropics. Ecological restoration seminars are held in a number of cities across the United States and Canada.

Publication(s): Northeastern Naturalist

Keyword(s): Water Habitats & Quality, Wildlife & Species

Contact(s):
Joerg-Henner Lotze, Director

HUMMINGBIRD SOCIETY, THE

P.O. Box 394
Newark, DE 19715 United States
Phone: 302-369-3699 Fax: 302-369-1816
E-mail: info@hummingbird.org
Website: www.hummingbird.org

Founded: 1996
Membership: 1,001–10,000
Scope: National, International

Description: The Hummingbird Society is a nonprofit corporation dedicated solely to hummingbirds, through disseminating information, education, support of scientific research, and protection of habitat.

Publication(s): The Hummingbird Connection

Keyword(s): Wildlife & Species

Contact(s):
H. Hawkins, President; 302-369-3699; Fax: 302-369-1816; hummerman@hummingbird.org
Gary Griffith, Vice President; 410-392-4491; garygriffith@mris.com
Douglas Everett, Director; 610-469-0535
Robert Gell, Director; 410-287-2988
William Barry, Treasurer; 302-239-1797; billb@wserve.com

HUNTSMAN MARINE SCIENCE CENTRE

1 Lower Campus Rd.
St. Andrews, E5B 2L7 New Brunswick Canada
Phone: 506-529-1200 Fax: 506-529-1212
E-mail: huntsman@huntsmanmarine.ca
Website: www.huntsmanmarine.ca

Founded: 1969
Membership: 1–100
Scope: State, Regional, National, International

Description: The HMSC is a nonprofit organization with a reputation for excellence in coastal and marine science research and education. It is supported by universities, corporations, federal and provincial government agencies, and the public. Located on one of the most biologically active bodies of water in the world, it provides information, research, education, and training opportunities for students, investigators, industry, government and the public.

Publication(s): Huntsman Marine Science News, Atlantic Reference Centre Species Identfication Series, Sea Trek Bulletin, Seawords

Keyword(s): Agriculture/Farming, Air Quality/Atmosphere, Climate Change, Ecosystems (precious), Oceans/Coasts/Beaches, Pollution (general), Recreation/Ecotourism, Reduce/Reuse/Recycle, Water Habitats & Quality, Wildlife & Species

Contact(s):
Mark Costello, Executive Director; 506-529-1200; Fax: 506-529-1212; costello@huntsmanmarine.ca
Gerhard Pohle, Associate Director; Fax: 506-5291212; huntsman@huntsmanmarine.ca
Tracey Dean, Director of Education; Fax: 506-5291212; huntsman@huntsmanmarine.ca

I

IDAHO ASSOCIATION OF SOIL CONSERVATION DISTRICTS

P.O. Box 2637
Boise, ID 83701 United States
Phone: 208-338-5900 Fax: 208-338-9537
E-mail: kfoster@agri.state.id.us
Website: www.iascd.state.id.us

Founded: N/A

Scope: State

Contact(s):
Alice Wallace, President; 921 N. 5th Ave, Sandpoint, ID 83864; 208-263-0895; Fax: 208-265-8486
Kyle Hawley, Vice President; 1180 Lewis Rd., Moscow, ID 83843; 208-882-1290; Fax: 208-883-4239
Kent Foster, Executive Director; P.O. Box 2637, Boise, ID 83701; 208-338-5900; Fax: 208-338-9537
Kevin Koester, Director; 208-776-5382; Fax: 208-776-5043
Art Beal, Treasurer
David Ellsworth, Board Member
Roger Stutzman, Secretary; 1937-B E. 4100 N, Buhl, ID 83316; 208-543-6824; Fax: 208-543-6824

IDAHO CONSERVATION LEAGUE

P.O. Box 844
Boise, ID 83701 United States
Phone: 208-345-6933 Fax: 208-344-0344
E-mail: icl@wildidaho.org
Website: www.wildidaho.org

Founded: 1973
Membership: 1,001–10,000
Scope: State

Description: The Idaho Conservation League is Idaho's largest statewide conservation organization. for people who cherish Idaho's clean water, wildlands and wildlife, the Idaho Conservation League protects Wild Idaho for future generations.

Publication(s): Idaho Conservationist

Keyword(s): Forests/Forestry, Land Issues, Public Lands/Greenspace, Water Habitats & Quality, Wildlife & Species

Contact(s):
Justin Hayes, Program Director
Rick Johnson, Executive Director
John McCarthy, Policy Director
Suki Molina, Deputy Director
Mary Abbott, Office Manager
Andrea Bogle, Membership Assistant
Liz Edrich, Development Coordinator
Mary Beth Whitaker, Editor/Designer
Rachel Winer, Outreach Coordinator
Linn Kincannon, Central Idaho Director

IDAHO ENVIRONMENTAL COUNCIL

1568 Lola St.
Idaho Falls, ID 83402 United States
Phone: 208-523-6692

Founded: N/A

Scope: State

Description: Founded to coordinate and stimulate the creative ideas, manpower, and financial resources of conservation-minded individuals and organizations; and to provide an increased understanding of modern man's impact upon his environment. Action, the objective, is based on information and research.

Publication(s): IEC Newsletter

Contact(s):

Alan Hausrath, President; 208-336-4930
Dennis Baird, Vice President for Northern Idaho; 208-882-8289
Ralph Maughan, Vice President for Southeastern Idaho; 208-233-7091
Jerry Jayne, Editor; 208-523-6692

IDAHO STATE B.A.S.S. FEDERATION

16135 Gilenna Drive
Wilder, ID 83676 United States
Phone: 208-286-7138
Website: www.bassclubs.net/clubpages/idahofed

Founded: N/A

Scope: State

Description: An organization of Bassmaster chapters, affiliated with the Bass Anglers Sportsman Society, organized to fight pollution, assist state and national conservation agencies in their efforts, and teach the young people of our country good conservation practices. Dedicated to the realistic conservation of our water resources.

Contact(s):

Allan Chandler, President; 208-286-7138
James Raitter, Vice President, Communication
Steve Spicklemier, Conservation Director; 3766 S. Rush Creek Place, Boise, ID 83706; 208-342-5006
J. Worthen, Tournament Director
Steve Day, Secretary, Treasurer
Larry Raganit, Youth

IDAHO TROUT LIMITED

P.O. Box 72
Buhl, ID 83316-0072 United States
Phone: 208-543-6444 Fax: 208-543-8476
E-mail: info@idahotrout.com
Website: www.idahotrout.com

Founded: N/A

Membership: 1,001–10,000

Scope: State

Description: A statewide council with eight active chapters dedicated to the protection and enhancement of the coldwater fishery resource.

Contact(s):

Robert Dunnagan, President; 57 Maxie Ln., Sandpoint, ID 83864; 208-263-4433; Fax: 815-346-1400; rdunnagan@nidlink.com

IDAHO WILDLIFE FEDERATION

P.O. Box 6426
Boise, ID 83707-6426 United States
Phone: 208-342-7055 Fax: 208-342-7097
E-mail: iwfboise@micron.net

Founded: N/A

Scope: Regional

Description: A representative statewide organization, affiliated with the National Wildlife Federation, dedicated to the protection and enhancement of wildlife and its habitat through public education and government interaction.

Publication(s): Idaho Wildlife News

Contact(s):

Jack Fisher, President and Representative
Corrine Fisher, Alternate Representative
Bill Goodnight, Editor

ILLINOIS ASSOCIATION OF CONSERVATION DISTRICTS

9313 Bull Valley Rd.
Woodstock, IL 60098 United States
Phone: 815-338-7664 Fax: 815-338-2773
E-mail: ohanas@aol.com

Founded: 1972

Membership: 1–100

Scope: State

Description: To promote the objectives and activities of the Conservation District of Illinois as set forth in the Illinois Conservation District Act and to cooperate with county, state, federal, and private agencies in resource management.

Keyword(s): Ethics/Environmental Justice, Land Issues, Wildlife & Species

Contact(s):

Kathy Merner, President; 3939 Nearing Lane, Decatur, IL 62521; 217-423-7708; Fax: 217-423-2837; MCCD@fgi.net
Ken Konsis, Vice President; 217-442-1691; Fax: 217-442-1695; vccd@soltec.net
Ken Fiske, Assistant Secretary and Treasurer; 815-338-7664; Fax: 815-338-2773; ohanas@aol.com
Dan Kane, Secretary/Treasurer; 603 Appleton Road, Belvidere, IL 61008; 815-547-7935; Fax: 815-547-7939; CONSDIST1@AOL.COM

ILLINOIS ASSOCIATION OF SOIL AND WATER CONSERVATION DISTRICTS

2520 Main St. State Fairgrounds, Emerson Bldg.
Springfield, IL 62702 United States
Phone: 217-744-3414 Fax: 217-744-3420
E-mail: aiswcdcs@aol.com
Website: www.aiswcd.org.com

Founded: N/A

Membership: 1–100

Scope: State

Contact(s):

Mark Besse, President; 7341 Sand Rd., Erie, IL 61250; 309-659-7716; Fax: 309-659-7716
Jerry Snodgrass, Vice President; 13501 N.1700th Ave., Geneseo, IL 61254; 309-944-2869; Fax: 309-937-2171; jerrypam@netexpress.net
Chris Stone, Executive Director; 217-744-3414; Fax: 217-744-3420
Terry Bogner, Board Member; Rte. 1 Box 186, Henry, IL 61537; 309-364-3478; Fax: 309-364-3802
Virginia Hayter, Treasurer; 2020 Hassell Rd. Apt. 101, Hoffman, IL 60195; 847-882-9100; Fax: 847-882-2621; virginia.hayter@hoffmanestate.org
Kim Pate, Administrative Coordinator

ILLINOIS AUDUBON SOCIETY

425 B N. Gilbert St., P.O. Box 2418
Danville, IL 61834 United States
Phone: 217-446-5085 Fax: 217-446-6375
Website: www.illinoisaudubon.org

Founded: 1897

Membership: 1,001–10,000

Scope: State

Description: The Society is dedicated to the preservation and enjoyment of wildlife and their habitats.

Publication(s): Illinois Audubon, Cardinal News, The

Keyword(s): Land Issues, Wildlife & Species

Contact(s):

David Miller, President; 813 N Cntr., McHenry, IL 60050
Mary Hoeffliger, Vice President; 6752 E 2000th Ave., Shumway, IL 62461
Marilyn Campbell, Executive Director and Editor, Cardinal News
Susan Shaw, Sanctuary Director; Adams Wildlife Sanctuary, P.O. Box 20106, Springfield, IL 62708; 217-544-5781

Debbie Newman, Editor, Illinois Audubon

ILLINOIS B.A.S.S. CHAPTER FEDERATION

Attn: President, 2425 Huntington Rd.
Springfield, IL 62703 United States
Phone: 217-529-8341
Website: www.ilbassfed.com

Founded: N/A

Scope: State

Description: An organization of Bassmaster chapters, affiliated with the Bass Anglers Sportsman Society, organized to fight pollution, assist state and national conservation agencies in their efforts, and to teach the young people of our country good conservation practices. Dedicated to the realistic conservation of our water resources.

Publication(s): Illinois B.A.S.S. Federation Newsletter

Contact(s):
Stan Leigh, President; Sleach183@aol.com

ILLINOIS ENVIRONMENTAL COUNCIL

107 W. Cook St., Suite E
Springfield, IL 62704 United States
Phone: 217-544-5954 Fax: 217-544-5958
E-mail: iec@ilenviro.org
Website: www.ilenviro.org

Founded: 1975

Scope: State

Description: Statewide coalition committed to advocating for Illinois laws and policies that promote a healthful environment and conservation of resources. The Illinois Environmental Council Education Fund administers programs of education and outreach for the coalition.

Publication(s): IEC Bulletin, Environmental Voting Record, Action Alerts

Keyword(s): Agriculture/Farming, Air Quality/Atmosphere, Energy, Land Issues, Pollution (general), Public Health, Public Lands/Greenspace, Sprawl/Urban Planning, Transportation, Water Habitats & Quality

Contact(s):
Jonathan Goldman, Executive Director

ILLINOIS NATIVE PLANT SOCIETY

Forest Glen Preserve, 20301 E. 900 N. Rd.
Westville, IL 61883 United States
Phone: 217-662-2142
E-mail: ilnps@aol.com
Website: www.vccd.org

Founded: 1982
Membership: 101–1,000
Scope: State

Description: Dedicated to the preservation, conservation, and study of the native plants and vegetation of Illinois.

Publication(s): Erigenia, Harbinger

Keyword(s): Land Issues, Reduce/Reuse/Recycle, Water Habitats & Quality, Wildlife & Species

Contact(s):
Ken Konsis, Executive Board

ILLINOIS PRAIRIE PATH

P.O. Box 1086
Wheaton, IL 60189 United States
Phone: 630-752-0120
Website: www.ipp.org

Founded: 1963

Scope: State

Description: To preserve natural areas and establish footpaths and other protected areas to be used for scientific, educational, and recreational purposes by the public. Adds trail amenities and promotes development of a 61-mile trail for bicyclists, hikers, and joggers on a former railroad right-of-way spanning DuPage County, extended Jan. 1972 into Kane County to the Fox River, and extended Dec. 1979 4 1/2 miles into Cook County. Incorporated 1965, in 1971 designated part of National Trails System.

Publication(s): Newsletter, Trail Map, Illinois Prairie Path, The

Keyword(s): Land Issues, Public Lands/Greenspace, Recreation/Ecotourism, Transportation

Contact(s):
David Tate, President
Nancy Becker, Secretary
Jean Mooring, Editor; 295 Abbotsford Ct., Glen Ellyn, IL 60137; 630-469-4289
Paul Mooring, Treasurer

ILLINOIS RAPTOR CENTER

5695 W. Hill Road
Decatur, IL 62522 United States
Phone: 963-6909, ext. 217
E-mail: barnowl@illinoisraptorcenter.org
Website: www.illinoisraptorcenter.org

Founded: 1991
Membership: 101–1,000
Scope: State

Description: The Illinois Raptor Center provides wildlife and environmental education to Illinois through its "Education on the Wing" Presentations.

Publication(s): Wildlife Intervention Services, Nuzzo Raptor Equipment at IRC, Illinois Raptor Center publications

Keyword(s): Wildlife & Species

Contact(s):
Jacques Nuzzo, Program Director; 963-6909, ext. 217; nuzzoraptorequipment@juno.com
Jane Seitz, Executive Director; 963-6909, ext. 217; barnowl@illinoisraptorcenter.org

ILLINOIS STUDENT ENVIRONMENTAL NETWORK

ISEN
110 S. Race St., Suite 202
Urbana, IL 61801 United States
Phone: 217-384-0830 Fax: 217-278-2105
E-mail: isen@isenonline.org
Website: www.isenonline.org

Founded: 1996
Membership: 1,001–10,000
Scope: State

Description: Through educational programs such as email alerts, conferences, trainings, capacity building workshops, and how-to manuals, ISEN keeps 3,500 students in 117 student groups on 90 Illinois college campuses updated on critical environmental issues.

Publication(s): Resource Library and Action Center, Advocating for Campus Waste Reduction, Tips for the Environmental Job Search

Keyword(s): Agriculture/Farming, Air Quality/Atmosphere, Climate Change, Energy, Forests/Forestry, Public Lands/Greenspace, Reduce/Reuse/Recycle, Sprawl/Urban Planning, Transportation, Water Habitats & Quality, Wildlife & Species

Contact(s):
Laura Huth, Executive Director; 217-384-0830; Fax: 217-278-2105; isen@isenonline.org
Lindsay Robinson, Networking Coordinator; 217-384-0830; Fax: 217-278-2105; lindsay@isenonline.org
Orion Weill, Member Services Coordinator; 217-384-0830; Fax: 217-278-2105; orion@isenonline.org

ILLINOIS WALNUT COUNCIL

Forest Glen Preserve, 20301 E. 900 N. Rd.
Westville, IL 61883 United States
Phone: 217-442-1691 Fax: 217-442-1695
E-mail: vccd@soltec.net
Website: www.vccd.org

Founded: N/A
Scope: Regional
Description: To promote the growth and use of the black walnut (Juglans nigra), and the education of good forestry practices with concerns toward wildlife and soil erosion.
Publication(s): Walnut Council Bulletin, Juglans
Keyword(s): Development/Developing Countries, Forests/Forestry, Land Issues, Pollution (general), Reduce/Reuse/Recycle, Water Habitats & Quality, Wildlife & Species
Contact(s):
Doug Bleichner, President; 2290 Knox Road 1000 N, Yates City, IL 61572
John Katzke, Vice President; 2619 North Woodhaven, Peoria, IL 61604
Steve Felt, Secretary; 522 Roberts Ln., Sherrard, IL 61281

INDIAN CREEK NATURE CENTER

6665 Otis Rd., SE
Cedar Rapids, IA 52403 United States
Phone: 319-362-0664 Fax: 319-362-2876
E-mail: naturecenter@aol.com
Website: www.indiancreeknaturecenter.org

Founded: 1973
Membership: 101–1,000
Scope: State
Description: The Indian Creek Nature Center is dedicated to fostering an appreciation of nature through environmental education and providing a natural facility for education and non-obtrusive recreation.
Publication(s): Indian Creek Currents
Contact(s):
Leslie Smith, President; lsmith@berthel.com
Rich Patterson, Director
Dennis Redmond, Past President; 319-366-2163; Fax: 319-366-7710; dredmond@rbjcpas.com

INDIANA ASSOCIATION OF SOIL AND WATER CONSERVATION DISTRICTS, INC.

225 S. East St., Suite 740
Indianapolis, IN 46202 United States
Phone: 317-692-7374 Fax: 317-692-7363
E-mail: iaswcd@iaswcd.org
Website: www.iaswcd.org

Founded: 1968
Scope: State
Description: We represent Indiana's 92 soil and water conservation districts. We support the districts in their efforts to combat non-point source pollution.
Contact(s):
Steve Graber, President; 3850 Greenhurst Court, Auburn, IN 46706; 219-925-0676
Sherman Bryant, Vice-President; 7343 N 650 E., N. Webster, IN 46555-9332; 219-834-2496

INDIANA AUDUBON SOCIETY, INC.

Mary Gray Bird Sanctuary, R.R. 6 Box 163
Connersville, IN 47331 United States
Phone: 765-825-9788
Website: www.indianaaudubon.org

Founded: 1898
Scope: State
Description: Works for the conservation of wildlife, especially birds.
Keyword(s): Reduce/Reuse/Recycle, Wildlife & Species
Contact(s):
Jane Miller, President; 4020 S. Rural, Independence, IN 46227-3865
Larry Carter, Vice President; 7496 N. Co. Rd. 2005, Ridgeville, IN 47380-9546
Deanna Barricklow, Resident Agent and Manager of Sanctuary Management; 3499 S. Bird Sanctuary Rd., Connersville, IN 47331-8721; 317-825-9788
Mary Gough, Editor; 901 Maplewood Dr., New Castle, IN 47362; 317-529-5225
Charles Keller, Editor; 2505 E. Maynard Dr., Indianapolis, IN 46226; 317-786-5822
Dan Leach, Secretary; 2313 S. 30th St., Bedford, IN 47421-5415
Clare Oskay, Treasurer; 551 Teton Trail, Indianapolis, IN 46217-3927

INDIANA B.A.S.S. CHAPTER FEDERATION

Attn: President, 1415 Cherokee Rd.
Ft. Wayne, IN 46808 United States
Phone: 219-483-0525
Website: www.indianabass.com/ibf/index.html

Founded: N/A
Scope: State
Description: An organization of Bassmaster chapters, affiliated with the Bass Anglers Sportsman Society, organized to fight pollution, assist state and national conservation agencies in their efforts, and teach the young people of our country good conservation practices. Dedicated to the realistic conservation of our water resources.
Contact(s):
Paul Hollabaugh, President; 1415 Cherokee Rd., Ft. Wayne, IN 46808; 219-483-0525
Dan Pardue, Conservation Director; 7244 Holmestead Rd., Morgantown, IN 46160; 812-988-8763

INDIANA FORESTRY AND WOODLAND OWNERS ASSOCIATION

5578 South 500 W.
Atlanta, IN 46031-9363 United States
Phone: 317-758-4735

Founded: 1977
Scope: State
Description: A statewide organization affiliated with the National Woodland Owners Association, providing leadership and programs to advance forestry in Indiana.
Publication(s): Leaves and Limbs
Keyword(s): Forests/Forestry
Contact(s):
Robert Koenig, President
Alan Bolenbaugh, 2nd Vice President
Thomas Moehl, 1st Vice President
Warren Baird, Treasurer
Pete Halstead, Forestry Educational Foundation
Jan Myers, Editor; 317-583-2422
William Sigman, Secretary

INDIANA NATIVE PLANT AND WILDFLOWER SOCIETY

6106 Kingsley Dr.
Indianapolis, IN 46220 United States
Phone: 317-253-3863
E-mail: rai38@aol.com
Website: www.inpaws.org

Founded: 1993
Scope: State
Description: To promote the appreciation, preservation, conservation, utilization and scientific study of the flora native to Indiana; and to educate the public about the values, beauty,

diversity, and environmental importance of indigenous vegetation.

Publication(s): Indiana Native Plant and Wildflower Society News

Keyword(s): Land Issues, Public Lands/Greenspace, Wildlife & Species

Contact(s):

Carolyn Bryson, President; quinnell@iquest.net
Ken Collins, Vice President; 317-891-9804

INDIANA STATE TRAPPERS ASSOCIATION, INC.

20941 Fir Road
Tippecanoe, IN 46570 United States
Phone: 219-498-6354
Website: www.krause.com/outdoors/tr/associations

Founded: 1961

Scope: State

Description: A statewide organization dedicated to the conservation, restoration, and wise use of wildlife and other renewable natural resources. Provides public education concerning the role of trapping in the management of wildlife.

Contact(s):

Doyle Flory, President; 219-498-6354
Richard McOlvanine, Vice President; 812-834-5514

INDIANA WILDLIFE FEDERATION

950 N. Rangeline Rd.,Suite A
Carmel, IN 46032-1315 United States
Phone: 317-571-1220 Fax: 317-571-1223
E-mail: iwf@indy.net
Website: www.indianawildlife.org

Founded: 1939

Membership: 1,001–10,000

Scope: State, Regional, National

Description: A representative statewide organization, affiliated with the National Wildlife Federation, dedicated to the protection and enhancement of wildlife and its habitat through public education and government interaction.

Publication(s): Hoosier Conservation

Contact(s):

Dale Back, President; back@indianawilfide.org
Paula Yeager, Executive Director; 317-571-1220; yeager@indianawildlife.org
Jack Dold, Editor and Alternate Representative; dold@indianawildlife.org
Becky Scheibelhut, Education Programs Contact
George Vargo, Treasurer

INDO-PACIFIC CONSERVATION ALLIANCE

1620-D Belmont St., NW
Washington, DC 20009 United States
Phone: 202-939-9773 Fax: 202-265-1169
E-mail: info@indopacific.org
Website: www.indopacific.org

Founded: 1998

Membership: N/A

Scope: International

Description: IPCA is a science-oriented conservation organization dedicated to the study and conservation of the native ecosystems of the tropical Indo-Pacific region (Indonesia, Melanesia, Micronesia, and Polynesia), and support for traditional peoples in their stewardship of these globally significant natural resources. Our activities include environmental education, local NGO capacity-building, community resource mapping, natural resource monitoring, ecotourism support, and biodiversity surveys.

Keyword(s): Development/Developing Countries, Ecosystems (precious), Forests/Forestry, Oceans/Coasts/Beaches, Recreation/Ecotourism, Wildlife & Species

INFORM, INC.

120 Wall St., 16th Fl.
New York, NY 10005 United States
Phone: 212-361-2400 Fax: 212-361-2412
E-mail: brown@informinc.org
Website: www.informinc.org

Founded: 1973

Scope: National

Description: A nonprofit tax-exempt environmental research and education organization that identifies and reports on practical solutions for problems in municipal solid waste, chemical hazards, air quality, and alternative vehicle fuels, with an emphasis on pollution prevention and waste reduction.

Publication(s): INFORM Reports (Newsletter), Rethinking Resources, Tracking Toxic Chemicals, Building for the Future, Gearing up for Hydrogen, China at the Crossroads

Keyword(s): Air Quality/Atmosphere, Energy, Pollution (general), Reduce/Reuse/Recycle, Transportation

Contact(s):

Joanna Underwood, President; ext. 222; underwood@informinc.org
Samuel Arnoff, Director of Operation; ext. 238; arnoff@informinc.org
Joanna Underwood, Director of Research
Stephen Land, Chairman of the Board; 212-424-9018; sbland@linklaters.com

INITIATIVE FOR SOCIAL ACTION AND RENEWAL IN EURASIA

ISAR
1601 Connecticut Ave., NW, Suite 301
Washington, DC 20009 United States
Phone: 202-387-3034 Fax: 202-667-3291
E-mail: postmaster@isar.org
Website: www.isar.org

Founded: 1983

Membership: 101–1,000

Scope: International

Description: ISAR promotes citizens participation and the development of the NGO sector in the former Soviet Union by supporting community activists and grassroots groups.

Publication(s): ISAR in Focus, Give and Take

Keyword(s): Energy, Ethics/Environmental Justice, Oceans/Coasts/Beaches, Public Health, Water Habitats & Quality

Contact(s):

Eliza Klose, Executive Director; eliza@isar.org
Kathleen Watters, Deputy Director; kwatters@isar.org

INLAND BIRD BANDING ASSOCIATION

P.O. Box 832
Tiffin, OH 44883 United States
E-mail: MCGREEN@AOL.COM
Website: www.aves.net/inlandbba/ibbamain.htm

Founded: 1922

Scope: National

Description: Promotes cooperation among its members and other organizations, with state, federal, or other officials or individuals engaged in bird banding or other scientific work with birds; informs the public of the purposes and results secured by banding.

Publication(s): North American Bird Bander, Inland Bird Banding Newsletter

Contact(s):

Ruth Green, President
Dan Kramer, Editor; 3451 Co. Rd. 256, Victory, OH 43464
Wiletta Lueshen, Editor; R. 2 Box 26, Wisner, NE 68791
Carol Rudy, Secretary; W. 3866 Hwy. H, Chilton, WI 53084
C. Smith, Treasurer; 6305 Cumberland Rd. SW, Sherrodsville, OH 44675

Al Valentine, Membership Secretary; 17403 Oakington Ct., Dallas, TX 75252

INSTITUTE FOR CIVIC INITIATIVES SUPPORT

Chayanova St., 4-13
Moscow, Russia
Phone: 70952517617 Fax: 70952517617
E-mail: clearh@glasnet.ru

Founded: 1993

Scope: International

Description: The Institute supports civic initiatives through information, publications, training, grant-making programs, and environmental education projects.

Contact(s):
Bogdan Mila, Director

INSTITUTE FOR CONSERVATION LEADERSHIP

EASTERN OFFICE
6930 Carroll Ave. Suite 420
Takoma Park, MD 20912 United States
Phone: 301-270-2900 Fax: 301-270-0610
E-mail: icl@icl.org
Website: www.icl.org

Founded: 1990

Membership: N/A

Scope: National

Description: The mission of the Institute is to train and empower volunteer leaders and to build volunteer institutions that protect and conserve the earth's environment. Services offered include training and technical assistance for nonprofit organizations and leaders in organizational development, fundraising, board development, volunteer recruitment, strategic planning, and related topics. Services also include meeting facilitation, coalition development, and network building.

Publication(s): Benchmarking Workbook, The Network

Contact(s):
Dianne Russell, Executive Director; dianne@icl.org
Baird Straughan, Associate Director; baird@icl.org
Chiquita Edwards, Office Manager; chiquita@icl.org
Peter Lane, Program Associate; peter@icl.org
Grant LaRouche, Development & Outreach Associate; grant@icl.org
Brian Lewis, Administrative Assistant; 13 South Willson Ave., Suite 9, Bozeman, MT 59715; 406-582-1838; Fax: 406-582-0323; brian@icl.org
Barbara Rusmore, Senior Program Associate; 13 South Willson Ave., Suite 9, Bozeman, MT 59715; 406-582-1838; Fax: 406-582-0323; barbara@icl.org
Brad Webb, Program Associate; 13 South Willson Ave., Suite 9, Bozeman, MT 59715; 406-582-1838; Fax: 406-582-0323; brad@icl.org

INSTITUTE FOR EARTH EDUCATION, THE

Cedar Cove
P.O. Box 115
Greenville, WV 24945 United States
Phone: 304-832-6404 Fax: 304-832-6077
E-mail: iee1@aol.com
Website: www.eartheducation.org

Founded: 1974

Scope: International

Description: The Institute for Earth Education develops and disseminates focused educational programs to promote an understanding of, appreciation for, and harmony with the earth's natural systems and communities. The Institute conducts workshops, provides a seasonal journal, hosts an international conference, supports local and international branches, and publishes numerous books and program materials.

Publication(s): Talking Leaves Journal, Sunship III, Earth Speaks, The, Earthkeepers, Earth Education: A New Beginning, Earth Education Sourcebook, Sunship Earth

Contact(s):
Bill Weiler, Executive Staff Chair
Fran Bires, International Internship Coordinator
Laurie Farber, International Membership Services Coordinator
Bruce Johnson, International Program Coordinator
Mike Mayer, International Training Coordinator
Steve Van Matre, Chair

INSTITUTE FOR TROPICAL ECOLOGY AND CONSERVATION (ITEC)

1023 SW 2nd Avenue
Gainesville, FL 32601 United States
Phone: 352-337-0223
E-mail: ITEC@ITEC-edu.org
Website: itec-edu.org

Founded: 1997

Membership: N/A

Scope: International

Description: Dedicated to conservation and education in the neotropics. Offers college level field courses, marine turtle research, forest restoration, local education and conservation programs, internships, volunteering opportunities. Scientific research projects are on-going, and more are welcome.

Keyword(s): Agriculture/Farming, Climate Change, Development/Developing Countries, Ecosystems (precious), Forests/Forestry, Land Issues, Oceans/Coasts/Beaches, Recreation/Ecotourism, Reduce/Reuse/Recycle, Water Habitats & Quality, Wildlife & Species

INSTITUTE OF ECOSYSTEM STUDIES

Mary Flagler Cary Arboretum, Box AB
Millbrook, NY 12545-0129 United States
Phone: 845-677-5343 Fax: 845-677-5976
Website: www.ecostudies.org

Founded: N/A

Scope: International

Description: Devoted to the understanding of ecosystem structure and function. The program focus is on disturbance and recovery of northern temperate ecosystems. Education and research interests include wildlife management, biogeochemistry, landscape ecology, aquatic ecology, plant-animal interactions, microbial ecology, forest ecology, chemical ecology, and air and water quality.

Publication(s): Newsletter, occasional publications, scientific journals

Keyword(s): Air Quality/Atmosphere

Contact(s):
Gene Likens, Director
Alan Berkowitz, Head of Education; 845-677-5359
Charles Canham, Forest Ecologist
Nina Caraco, Biogeochemist
Jonathan Cole, Aquatic Microbiologist
Stuart Findlay, Aquatic Ecologist
Peter Groffman, Microbial Ecologist
Clive Jones, Ecologist
Chloe Keefer, Librarian
Gary Lovett, Plant Ecologist
Richard Ostfeld, Animal Ecologist
Michael Pace, Aquatic Ecologist
Steward Pickett, Plant Ecologist
David Strayer, Freshwater Ecologist
Joseph Warner, Administrator
Kathleen Weathers, Forest Ecologist
Raymond Winchcombe, Wildlife Biologist and Field Research Facilities; 845-677-9818

INSTITUTO BRASIL DE EDUCACAO AMBIENTAL

Rua Visconde De Piraja 547 Sala 710
Ipanema CEP, Rio De Janeiro,
22410-003 Brazil
Phone: 55-21-294-1231 Fax: 55-21-294-1231
E-mail: instbrasil@openlink.com.br

Founded: N/A

Description: Instituto Brasil is an environmental institution throughout Brazil among education NGOs that works with teachers and community leaders in their capacity. Its network is currently 60 partner city councils, universities, other NGOs and 2000 teachers and members. Implementation of local projects building through courses.

Contact(s):

Vera Rodrigues, Executive Director

INTERFAITH COUNCIL FOR THE PROTECTION OF ANIMALS AND NATURE INC. (ICPAN)

3691 Tuxedo Rd., NW
Atlanta, GA 30305 United States
Phone: 404-814-1371 Fax: 404-814-0440

Founded: 1980
Membership: 1,001–10,000
Scope: National

Description: Composed of people of all faiths, ICPAN works to promote conservation and environmental and humane education, mainly within the religious community. We try to make religious leaders, institutions, and the general public aware of our moral spiritual obligations, as emphasized in the Bible, to protect animals and the natural environment.

Publication(s): Replenish the Earth, Losing Paradise, Cleaning up America the Poisoned

Keyword(s): Development/Developing Countries, Wildlife & Species

Contact(s):

Lewis Regenstein, President; 3691 Tuxedo Rd. NW, Atlanta, GA 30327; 404-814-1371
Paul Irwin, Director; 2100 L St. NW, Washington, DC 20037; 202-452-1100
John Hoyt, Chairman; 2100 L St. NW, Washington, DC 20037; 202-452-1100

INTERNATIONAL ASSOCIATION FOR BEAR RESEARCH AND MANAGEMENT

UNIVERSITY OF TENNESEE
274 Ellington PSB
Knoxville, TN 37901-1071 United States
Phone: 865-974-4790 Fax: 865-974-3555
E-mail: jclark1@utk.edu
Website: www.bearbiology.com

Founded: 1968
Membership: 101–1,000
Scope: International

Description: A professional organization of biologists, animal or land managers, and private citizens with an interest or involvement in bear research and management. The Association encourages and reports research and management by various agencies or university research groups, sponsors the triannual International Conference on Bear Research and Management, publishes the proceedings of the conference, and sponsors or aids a world network of regional bear workshops, groups, and committees, and the IUCN Bear

Publication(s): Ursus, formerly Bears, International Bear News

Keyword(s): Land Issues, Public Lands/Greenspace, Wildlife & Species

Contact(s):

Harry Reynolds, President; 1300 College Rd., Fairbanks, AK 99701; 907-459-7238
Sterling Miller, Vice President; 240 N Higgins Ste. 2, Missoula, MT 59802; 406-721-6705
Joe Clark, Secretary; 274 Ellington PSB, University of Tennessee, Knoxville, TN 37996; 865-974-4790
Frank van Manen, Treasurer; 274 Ellington PSB, Knoxville, TN 37996; 865-974-0200

INTERNATIONAL ASSOCIATION FOR ENVIRONMENTAL HYDROLOGY (IAEH)

P.O. Box 35324
San Antonio, TX 78235 United States
Phone: 210-344-5418 Fax: 210-344-9941
E-mail: hydroweb@mail.org
Website: www.hydroweb.com

Founded: 1991
Scope: International

Description: IAEH works to foster a global interchange of ideas, approaches, and technologies for environmental cleanup and protection of fresh water resources and pollution prevention; to place special focus on approaches to cleanup, prevention, and protection that are practical in less affluent countries; to further the development of environmentally sound solutions that are realistic from the economic standpoint; to seek solutions to cleanup, pollution prevention, and environmental protection.

Publication(s): Journal of Environmental Hydrology, Environmental Hydrology Report

Keyword(s): Development/Developing Countries, Oceans/Coasts/Beaches, Pollution (general)

Contact(s):

Roger Peebles, President; 308 Montfort Dr., San Antonio, TX 78216; 210-344-5418

INTERNATIONAL ASSOCIATION OF FISH AND WILDLIFE AGENCIES

444 North Capitol St., NW Suite 544
Washington, DC 20001 United States
Phone: 202-624-7890 Fax: 202-624-7891
E-mail: iafwa@sso.org
Website: www.iafwa.org

Founded: 1902
Membership: 101–1,000
Scope: International

Description: Association of states or territories of the United States, provinces of Canada, the Commonwealth of Puerto Rico, the United States Government, the Dominion Government of Canada, and governments of countries located in the western hemisphere, as well as individual associate members whose principal objective is conservation, protection, and management of wildlife and related natural resources.

Publication(s): Newsletter, Annual Proceedings

Keyword(s): Agriculture/Farming, Air Quality/Atmosphere, Forests/Forestry, Land Issues, Public Lands/Greenspace, Recreation/Ecotourism, Water Habitats & Quality, Wildlife & Species

Contact(s):

Robert McDowell, President; Director, New Jersey Division of Fish and Wildlife, P.O. Box 400, Trenton, NJ 08625; 609-292-9410; Fax: 609-292-8207; dzook@dep.state.nj.us
Allan Egbert, Vice President; Florida Fish & Wildlife Conservation Commission, 620 S. Meridian Street, Tallahassee, FL 32399-1600; 850-488-2975; Fax: 850-921-5786
R. Peterson, Executive Vice President; 202-624-7890; Fax: 202-624-7891; iafwa@sso.org
John Baughman, Chair, Executive Committee; Director, Wyoming Game and Fish Department, 5400 Bishop Boulevard, Cheyenne, WY 82006; 307-777-4600
C. Thomas Bennett, Executive Committee Member; Kentucky Department of Fish and Wildlife Resources, One Game Farm Rd., Frankfort, KY 40601; 502-564-3400
Michael Budzik, Executive Committee Member, Past President; Ohio Division of Wildlife, 1840 Belcher Drive, Columbus, OH 43224-1329; 614-265-6300; Fax: 614-262-1143
Cameron Mack, Executive Committee; Director, Fish and Wildlife Branch, Ontario Ministry of Natural Resources, 300 Water Street, 5th Floor, P.O. Box 7000, Peterborough, Ontario K9J 8M5; 705-755-1909

G. Manning, Vice Chair, Executive Committee; Illinois Department of Natural Resources, 524 South Second Street, Springfield, IL 62701-1787; 217-785-0075
Edward Parker, Executive Committee Member; 860-424-3010; Fax: 860-424-4078
M.N. "Corky" Pugh, Secretary/Treasurer; Alabama Division of Freshwater Fisheres, 64 N. Union Street, Montgomery, AL 36130; 334-242-3849; Fax: 334-242-3032
Ron Regan, Executive Committee Member; Vermont Department of Fish & Wildlife, 103 S. Main Street, 10 South, Waterbury, VT 05671-0501; 802-241-3730; Fax: 802-241-3295
Rodney Sando, Executive Committee Member; Director, Idaho Fish and Game Department, Box 25, 600 South Walnut, Boise, ID 83707
David Waller, Past President; Georgia Wildlife Resources Division, 2070 U.S. Highway 278, SE, Social Circle, GA 30025; 770-918-6401; Fax: 706-557-3030
Naomi Edelson, Wildlife Diversity Director
Donald MacLauchlan, International Resource Director
Bob Miles, Resource Director
Gary Taylor, Legislative Director
Len Ugarenko, NAWMP Coordinator
Paul Lenzini, Legal Counsel; 703-684-4450; Fax: 703-684-4428
Wm. Nesbitt, Annual Proceedings Editor; 703-590-4449; Fax: 703-878-2119
Samara Trusso, Fur Resources Committee Project Coordinator

INTERNATIONAL ASSOCIATION OF FISH AND WILDLIFE AGENCIES

NORTHEAST ASSOCIATION OF FISH AND WILDLIFE RESOURCE AGENCIES
c/o Maine Department of Inland Fisheries and Wildlife
Attention: Lee Perry
284 State Street - Station 41
Augusta, ME 04333 United States
Phone: 207-287-5202 Fax: 207-287-6395
E-mail: lee.perry@state.me.us

Founded: N/A
Membership: 1–100
Scope: State, Regional, National, International
Description: State and Canadian provincial agencies protecting fish and wildlife resources in the northeast U.S. and eastern Canada.
Publication(s): Northeast Fish and Wildlife Conference
Contact(s):
Gerry Barnhart, President; 518-402-8924; Fax: 518-402-8925
Lee Perry, Secretary/Treasurer; 207-287-5202; Fax: 207-287-6395; lee.perry@state.me.us

INTERNATIONAL ASSOCIATION OF NATURAL RESOURCE PILOTS

IANRP
9740 Briarwood Drive
Plain City, OH 43064 United States
Phone: 614-873-4163 Fax: 614-873-4860
E-mail: info@ianrp.org
Website: ianrp.org

Founded: 1972
Membership: 101–1,000
Scope: International
Description: Performs aviation and aircrew conservation-related responsibilities for federal and state game and fish divisions and departments of natural resources throughout the U.S. and for their counterparts in the Canadian provinces. Additional membership includes a variety of aviation-oriented corporations and advanced technological suppliers of equipment used in the performance of the aviation missions.
Publication(s): Conservation Aviation
Keyword(s): Air Quality/Atmosphere, Forests/Forestry, Land Issues, Pollution (general), Recreation/Ecotourism, Reduce/Reuse/Recycle, Transportation, Water Habitats & Quality, Wildlife & Species
Contact(s):
George Peachee, President; 330 BJ Boulevard, Bedford, IN 47421; 812-279-0075; peachee@hpcisp.com
Joseph Barber, Treasurer; Ohio Div. of Wildlife, 1840 Belcher Dr. Bldg. C, Columbus, OH 43224; 614-265-6328; Fax: 614-262-1143; jabarber@earthlink.net
John Clem, Librarian; Ohio Division of Wildlife, 9740 Briarwood Dr., Plain City, OH 43064; 614-873-4163; Fax: 614-873-4860; john@clem.ws
Michael Jeffries, Secretary; Technical Representative AOS, 2741 Airport Hwy., Boise, ID 83705; 208-334-9310; Fax: 208-334-9303; michael_jefferies@oas.gov
Val Judkins, Newsletter Editor; Washington Fish and Wildlife, 600 Capital Way North, Olympia, WA 98501; 360-753-4717; Fax: 360-586-4374; valjudkins@hotmail.com
Francis Satterlee, Public Affairs Officer; 200 Patrick St., SW, Vienna, VA 22180; 703-560-1271

INTERNATIONAL ASSOCIATION OF WILDLAND FIRE

E. 8109 Bratt Rd.
Fairfield, WA 99012 United States
Phone: 509-523-4003 Fax: 509-523-5001
E-mail: greenlee@cet.com
Website: www.wildfiremagazine.com

Founded: 1991
Membership: 1,001–10,000
Scope: International
Description: (formerly Fire Research Institute) The International Association of Wildland Fire was organized to promote a fuller understanding of wildland fire. The Association is built on the belief that an understanding of this dynamic natural force is vital for natural resource management, firefighter safety, and harmonious interactions between people and their environment.
Publication(s): International Directory of Wildland Fire, Current Titles in Wildland Fire, Wildfire Magazine, International Journal of Wildland Fire, International Bibliography of Wildland Fire
Keyword(s): Forests/Forestry, Land Issues, Wildlife & Species
Contact(s):
Mike Degrosky, President; 307-543-0949
Jason Greenlee, Executive Director; 509-283-2397
Mike Weber, Editor; 403-435-7210

INTERNATIONAL BICYCLE FUND

4887 Columbia Dr. S.
Seattle, WA 98108-1919 United States
Phone: 206-767-0848
E-mail: ibike@ibike.org
Website: www.ibike.org

Founded: 1983
Membership: N/A
Scope: International
Description: The International Bicycle Fund's programs fall into the areas of transportation planning, sustainable economic development, safety education and promoting international understanding. Within these programs we address issues of the environment, energy policy, public health, appropriate technology, land use patterns, sustainable systems, resource conservation and employment generation. IBF coordinates and cooperates with organizations and individuals worldwide. IBF is a nonprofit organization.
Publication(s): See publications on website, IBF News
Keyword(s): Development/Developing Countries, Land Issues, Transportation
Contact(s):
David Mozer, President; ibike@ibike.org

INTERNATIONAL CENTER FOR EARTH CONCERNS

2162 Baldwin Rd.
Ojai, CA 93023 United States
Phone: 805-649-3535 Fax: 805-649-1757
E-mail: information@earthconcerns.org
Website: www.earthconcerns.org

Founded: 1994
Membership: 101–1,000
Scope: Local
Description: The ICEC involves people with nature by fostering their appreciation of the natural world through environmental education and training.
Publication(s): Brochure, Annual Newsletters
Contact(s):
Paul Irwin, President
Melody Taft, Executive Director
John Taft, Chairman

INTERNATIONAL CENTER FOR GIBBON STUDIES

P.O. Box 800249
Santa Clarita, CA 91380 United States
Phone: 661-296-2737 Fax: 661-296-1237
E-mail: gibboncntr@aol.com
Website: www.gibboncenter.org

Founded: 1977
Scope: International
Description: The International Center for Gibbon Studies ensures the preservation and propagation and a safe haven for all gibbon species living in the wild and in captivity; supports ongoing field conservation projects; and educates the public about the importance of this species and saving their natural habitat.
Publication(s): Brochures, The Gibbon's Voice - yearly newletters
Contact(s):
Alan Mootnick, Board of Directors President, Facility Director, and Chairman; P.O. Box 800249, Santa Clarita, CA 91380; 661-296-2737
Geril-Ann Galanti, Board of Directors Vice President; 2906 Ocean Ave., Venice, CA 90291; 310-827-0937
Bjorn Merker, Acting Director of Research; Institute for Biomusicology, Mid Sweden, Ostersund S-83125
Lori Sheeran, Director of Education and Conservation; California State University at Fullerton; 714-773-2765
Elaine Baker, Assistant Director of Research; Department of Psychology, Marshall University, Huntington, WV 25755

INTERNATIONAL CENTER FOR TROPICAL ECOLOGY

The University of Missouri at St. Louis
R224 Research Bldg.
8001 Natural Bridge Rd.
St. Louis, MO 63121-4499 United States
Phone: 314-516-5219 Fax: 314-516-6233
E-mail: icte@umsl.edu
Website: icte.umsl.edu

Founded: 1990
Membership: 101–1,000
Scope: International
Description: The ICTE is one of the premier institutes in the United States for the study of tropical biology and conservation. The Center's three primary missions include the training of graduate students in the vital areas of tropical ecology and conservation, the education of undergraduates about the importance of these areas, and involvement of the community in educational actvities with respect to issues related to conservation and biodiversity.
Keyword(s): Development/Developing Countries, Ecosystems (precious), Wildlife & Species
Contact(s):
Bette Loiselle, Director; 314-516-6224; Fax: 314-516-6233; loiselle@umsl.edu
Patrick Osborne, Executive Director; 314-516-5219; Fax: 314-516-6233; posborne@jinx.umsl.edu

INTERNATIONAL CENTRE FOR CONSERVATION EDUCATION

Greenfield House
Guiting Power, Cheltenham, GL54 5TZ United Kingdom
Phone: 1.4412426748e+012
Fax: 1.4412426748e+012
E-mail: maikcec@aol.com

Founded: 1984
Scope: International
Description: ICCE works to promote a greater understanding of global environmental issues and sustainable development.
Keyword(s): Development/Developing Countries, Wildlife & Species
Contact(s):
Mark Boulton, Director; Greenfield House Guiting Power, Cheltenham GL5 45TZ; 1441242674

INTERNATIONAL COUNCIL OF ENVIRONMENTAL LAW

COUNSEIL INTERNATIONAL DU DROIT DE L'ENVIRONNMENT
ICEL/CIDE
Godesberger Allee 108-112
Bonn, D-53175 Germany
Phone: 4.9228269224e+011
Fax: 4.9228269225e+011
E-mail: icel@intlawpol.org
Website: www.i-c-e-l.org

Founded: 1969
Membership: 101–1,000
Scope: Regional, International
Description: A nonprofit, nongovernmental international organization with elected membership, structured in ten regions worldwide, for the purpose of exchange of information on international environmental law, policy, and administration and mutual assistance among members.
Publication(s): Conservation in Sustainable Development, International Environmental Soft Law, International Environmental Law, Environmental Policy and Law
Contact(s):
Wolfgang Burhenne, Executive Governor
Amado Tolentino, Executive Governor; Embassy of the Philippines, Doha

INTERNATIONAL CRANE FOUNDATION

E-11376 Shady Ln. Rd., P.O. Box 447
Baraboo, WI 53913-0447 United States
Phone: 608-356-9462 Fax: 608-356-9465
E-mail: cranes@savingcranes.org
Website: www.savingcranes.org

Founded: 1973
Membership: 1–100
Scope: International
Description: Preservation of cranes through research, conservation, captive propagation, restocking, field ecology, and public education.
Publication(s): ICF Bugle, The (Quarterly Magazine), Reflections: The Story of Cranes, Proceedings of the 7th N. American Crane Workshop
Keyword(s): Water Habitats & Quality, Wildlife & Species
Contact(s):
Peter Murray, Vice President of Finance and Administration; 608-356-9462, ext. 153; pmurray@savingcranes.org

Kate Fitzwilliams, Director of Public Relations and Marketing; 608-356-9462, ext. 147; kate@savingcranes.org
C Dietrich Schaaf, Director of Education; 608-356-9462, ext. 152; cdschaaf@savingcranes.org
David Chesky, Site Manager; 608-356-9462, ext. 120; dchesky@savingcranes.org
Susan Finn, Assistant to the President; 608-356-9462, ext. 118; sfinn@savingcranes.org
George Archibald, Co-Founder; george@savingcranes.org
Jeb Barzen, Field Ecologist; 608-356-9462, ext. 125; jeb@savingcranes.org
Betsy Didrickson, Librarian; The Ron Sauey Memorial Library for Bird Conservation, Baraboo, WI 53913-0447; 608-356-9462, ext. 124; betsy@savingcranes.org
Robert Hallam, Development; 608-356-9462, ext. 119; bhallam@savingcranes.org
James Harris, Pesident; 608-356-9462, ext. 129; harris@savingcranes.org
Claire Mirande, Conservation Coordinator; 608-356-9462, ext. 122; mirande@savingcranes.com
Mike Putnam, Curator of Birds; ext. 159

INTERNATIONAL ECOLOGY SOCIETY (IES)

1471 Barclay St.
St. Paul, MN 55106-1405 United States
Phone: 612-579-7008

Founded: 1975
Membership: N/A
Scope: International
Description: Volunteer-staffed, nonprofit organization dedicated to the protection of the environment and the encouragement of better understanding of all life forms.
Publication(s): Eco-Humane Letter, Action Alerts, Sunrise (neighborhood news)
Keyword(s): Wildlife & Species
Contact(s):
R. Kramer, President and Publisher
George Johnson, Vice President
Bina Robinson, North East Representative; Box 26, Swain, NY 14884-0026

INTERNATIONAL ECOTOURISM SOCIETY, THE

P.O. Box 668
Burlington, VT 05402-0668 United States
Phone: 802-651-9818 Fax: 802-651-9819
E-mail: ecomail@ecotourism.org
Website: www.ecotourism.org

Founded: 1990
Membership: 1,001–10,000
Scope: Local, State, Regional, National, International
Description: The Ecotourism Society is an international nonprofit membership organization dedicated to finding the resources and building the expertise to make tourism a viable tool for conservation and sustainable development.
Publication(s): Flagship Species: Case Studies in Wildlife Tourism Management, The Business of Ecolodges, by Edward Sanders and Elizabeth Halpenny, Ecotourism: Principles, Practices and Policies for Sustainability - by Megan Epler Wood, Ecotourism: A Guide for Planners and Managers Volume I&II, Ecolodge Sourcebook for Planners and Developers, Ecotourism Guidelines for Nature Tour Operators
Keyword(s): Development/Developing Countries, Ecosystems (precious), Land Issues, Oceans/Coasts/Beaches, Population, Recreation/Ecotourism, Wildlife & Species
Contact(s):
Megan Wood, President; P.O. Box 668, Burlington, VT 05402; 802-651-9818; Fax: 802-651-9819; ecomail@ecotourism.org
Jeremy Garrett, Membership and Publications Director; 802-651-9818; Fax: 802-651-9819; jeremy@ecotuorism.org
Fergus Maclaren, Director, International Year of Ecotourism; 802-651-9818; Fax: 802-651-9819; fergus@ecotourism.org
Patricia Carrington, Media Relations Manager; 802-651-9818; Fax: 8002-651-9819; patricia@ecotourism.org
Anjanette DeCarlo, Information and Education Specialist; 802-651-9818; Fax: 802-651-9819; anjanette@ecotourism.org
Jessica Staats, Assistant to the President; 802-651-9818; Fax: 802-651-9819; jessica@ecotourism.org

INTERNATIONAL EROSION CONTROL ASSOCIATION (IECA)

P.O. Box 774904
Steamboat Springs, CO 80477 United States
Phone: 970-879-3010 Fax: 970-879-8563
E-mail: ecinfo@ieca.org
Website: www.ieca.org

Founded: 1972
Membership: 1,001–10,000
Scope: International
Description: To provide opportunities for the worldwide exchange of information and economic methods of erosion control.
Publication(s): Proceedings of Annual Conference, Products and Services Directory, Membership Directory
Keyword(s): Land Issues, Oceans/Coasts/Beaches
Contact(s):
Ben Northcutt, Executive Director

INTERNATIONAL FUND FOR ANIMAL WELFARE

411 Main St.
Yarmouth Port, MA 02675 United States
Phone: 508-362-4944 Fax: 508-744-2009
E-mail: info@ifaw.org
Website: www.ifaw.org

Founded: 1969
Membership: 100,001–500,000
Scope: International
Description: An international nonprofit, tax-exempt organization in the U.S. dedicated to the protection of wild and domestic animals and their habitats. IFAW's goals are pursued through a strategic plan consisting of three distinct program areas: Commercial Expoitation and Trade of Wild Animals, Animals in Crisis and Distress, and Habitat for Animals.
Contact(s):
Aczedine Downes, Contact
Fred O'Regan, Chief Executive Officer

INTERNATIONAL FUND FOR ANIMAL WELFARE

ASIA/PACIFIC
8-10 Belmore Street
Surry Hills, NSW 2010 Australia
Phone: 612 9288 4900 Fax: 292884901
Website: www.ifaw.org

Founded: N/A
Scope: International
Contact(s):
Sally Wilson, Contact

INTERNATIONAL FUND FOR ANIMAL WELFARE

EUROPEAN UNION
13 Rue Boduognat B-1000
Brussels, Belgium
Phone: 322 230 9717 Fax: 322 231 0402
Website: www.ifaw.org

Founded: N/A
Scope: International
Contact(s):
Stanley Johnson, Contact

INTERNATIONAL FUND FOR ANIMAL WELFARE
FRENCH OFFICE
BP 78 51170
Fismes, France
Phone: 33 326 480 548 Fax: 33 326 481 435
Website: www.ifaw.org

Founded: N/A
Scope: International
Contact(s):
Chantal Derty, Contact

INTERNATIONAL FUND FOR ANIMAL WELFARE
GERMAN OFFICE
Postfach 10 46 23 20032
Hamburg, Germany
Phone: 040 866 5000 Fax: 040 866 500 22

Founded: N/A
Scope: International
Contact(s):
Tom Martens, Contact

INTERNATIONAL FUND FOR ANIMAL WELFARE
HOLLAND OFFICE
Sterrenweg 3B, 2651 HZ Berkel en Rodenrijs
Holland, Netherlands

Founded: N/A
Scope: International
Contact(s):
Jetty Tak, Office Manager

INTERNATIONAL FUND FOR ANIMAL WELFARE
HONG KONG OFFICE
P.O. Box 82 Sai Kung PO
Kowloon, Hong Kong

Founded: N/A
Scope: International
Contact(s):
Jill Robinson, Contact

INTERNATIONAL FUND FOR ANIMAL WELFARE
ITALIAN OFFICE
Via Bocca di Leone 36-Int 4
Rome, 187 Italy

Founded: N/A
Scope: International
Contact(s):
Walter Caporale, Contact

INTERNATIONAL FUND FOR ANIMAL WELFARE
PHILIPPINES OFFICE
14 East Maya
Phil-Am Homes, Quezon City, 1100 Philippines

Founded: N/A
Scope: International
Contact(s):
Mel Alipio, Contact

INTERNATIONAL FUND FOR ANIMAL WELFARE
RUSSIAN OFFICE
Apt. 84
Protochniy Pereulok 11, Moscow, 21099 Russia

Founded: N/A
Scope: International
Contact(s):
Masha Vorontsova, Contact

INTERNATIONAL FUND FOR ANIMAL WELFARE
SOUTH AFRICAN OFFICE
P.O. Box 2587
Rivonia, 2128 South Africa

Founded: N/A
Scope: International
Contact(s):
David Barritt, Contact

INTERNATIONAL FUND FOR ANIMAL WELFARE
UNITED KINGDOM
Warren Court Park Rd.
Crownborough, E. Sussex, TN6 2QH United Kingdom

Founded: N/A
Scope: International
Contact(s):
Cindy Milburn, Director

INTERNATIONAL GAME FISH ASSOCIATION
300 Gulf Stream Way
Dania Beach, FL 33004 United States
Phone: 954-927-2628 Fax: 954-924-4299
E-mail: igfahq@aol.com
Website: www.igfa.org

Founded: 1939
Scope: International
Description: Nonprofit, tax-deductible organization which maintains and promotes ethical international angling regulations and compiles world game fish records for saltwater, freshwater, and fly fishing. Also represents and informs recreational fishermen regarding research, conservation, and legislative developments related to the sport. Encourages and supports game fish tagging programs and other scientific data collection efforts. More than 250 IGFA international representatives worldwide.
Publication(s): World Record Game Fishes, Rule Book for Freshwater, Saltwater and Fly Fishing, International Angler
Keyword(s): Recreation/Ecotourism, Wildlife & Species
Contact(s):
Michael Leech, President
John Anderson, Vice Chairman
Pamela Basco, Treasurer
Michael Levitt, Chairman
Roy Naftzger, Secretary

INTERNATIONAL HUNTER EDUCATION ASSOCIATION
P.O. Box 490
Wellington, CO 80549 United States
Phone: 970-568-7954 Fax: 970-568-7955
E-mail: ihea@frii.com
Website: www.ihea.com

Founded: N/A
Scope: International
Description: To provide leadership and establish standards in the development of hunters to be safe, responsible, knowledgeable, and involved.
Publication(s): Hunter Education Journal, Hunter Education Student Guide
Keyword(s): Recreation/Ecotourism
Contact(s):
Mac Lang, President-Elect
Tim Lawhern, President
David Knotts, IHEA Executive Vice President
Helen McCracken, Vice President of Zone 2
Robert Paddon, Vice President of Zone 1
Keith Snyder, Vice President of Zone 3
Mark Birkhauser, Secretary
Bill Blackwell, Instructor Board Representative

Joe Huggins, Treasurer
Jan Morris, Instructor Board Representative of Zone 3
John Panio, Instructor Board Member
Albert Ross, IHEA Legal Counsel
Christopher Tymeson, Instructor Board Representative of Zone 2

INTERNATIONAL INSTITUTE FOR ENERGY CONSERVATION

CERF/IIEC
2131 K Street, NW, Suite 700
Washington, DC 20002 United States
Phone: 202-785-6420 Fax: 202-785-2604
Website: www.cerf.org

Founded: 1984

Scope: International

Description: A nonprofit organization established to accelerate the global adoption of energy-efficiency policies, technologies, and practices to enable econimically and ecologically sustainable development.

Publication(s): Global Energy Efficiency Initiative Sustainable Energy Guide, Integrated Transport Management and Development, Opportunities for the U.S. Energy Efficiency Industry in Chile, E-Notes

Keyword(s): Climate Change, Development/Developing Countries, Energy, Transportation

Contact(s):
Russell Sturm, Executive Director and President
Stewart Boyle, Director
Steve Hall, Director
Terry Oliver, Director
John Fox, Chairman of the Board

INTERNATIONAL MARINE MAMMAL PROJECT, THE

EARTH ISLAND INSTITUTE
300 Broadway
Suite 28
San Francisco, CA 94133 United States
Phone: 415-788-3666 Fax: 415-788-7324
Website: www.earthisland.org

Founded: 1982

Scope: International

Description: IMMP is a nonprofit research, education, and monitoring project of Earth Island Institute. IMMP is committed to ending dolphin mortality caused by the U.S. and international tuna industries, stopping the use of driftnets, and promoting sustainable fishing practices. In addition, IMMP aims to halt commercial whaling worldwide and ban live capture and display of marine mammals.

Publication(s): Earth Island Journal, Ocean Alert

Keyword(s): Oceans/Coasts/Beaches, Public Lands/Greenspace, Water Habitats & Quality, Wildlife & Species

Contact(s):
David Phillips, Executive Director

INTERNATIONAL MARITIME ORGANIZATION

4 Albert Embankment
London, SE1 7SR United Kingdom
Phone: 1717357611 Fax: 7178573210
E-mail: info@imo.org
Website: www.imo.org

Founded: 1959

Membership: 101–1,000

Scope: International

Description: To improve maritime safety and to prevent marine pollution from ships, through the adoption of international conventions, protocols, codes, and recommendations.

Keyword(s): Climate Change, Development/Developing Countries, Transportation, Water Habitats & Quality

Contact(s):
William O'neil, Secretary-General

INTERNATIONAL OCEANOGRAPHIC FOUNDATION

University of Miami
Rosenstiel School of Marine & Atmosphere Science
4600 Rickenbacker Causeway Virginia Key
Miami, FL 33149 United States
Phone: 305-361-4061 Fax: 305-361-4931
Website: www.rsmas.miami.edu/iof/

Founded: 1953

Scope: International

Description: Nonprofit foundation organized to encourage the extension of human knowledge by scientific study and exploration of the oceans in all their aspects and to acquaint and educate the general public concerning the vital role of the oceans to all life on this planet.

Keyword(s): Oceans/Coasts/Beaches, Recreation/Ecotourism, Wildlife & Species

Contact(s):
Edward Foote, President
Otis Brown, Vice President
Luis Glaser, Vice President
David Lieberman, Vice President
Diane Cook, Treasurer
Lourdes Lapaz, Secretary; 400 SE 2nd Ave., 4th Fl., Miami, FL 33131; 305-375-8498; Fax: 305-375-9188

INTERNATIONAL OSPREY FOUNDATION INC., THE

P.O. Box 250
Sanibel, FL 33957 United States
Phone: 941-472-1862

Founded: 1981

Scope: International

Description: A nonprofit organization dedicated to studying the problem of restoring osprey numbers to a stable population, making recommendations to enhance the continued survival of the osprey and initiating educational programs. Yearly grant of up to $1000.00 given for graduate work. Work relating to all raptors is acceptable, but osprey study is given priority.

Publication(s): TIOF Newsletter

Keyword(s): Wildlife & Species

Contact(s):
David Loveland, President
Anne Mitchell, Vice President
Inge Glissman, Secretary and Treasurer

INTERNATIONAL PLANT PROPAGATORS SOCIETY, INC.

Washington Park Arboretum, 2300 Arboretum Dr.
Seattle, WA 98112 United States
Phone: 206-543-8602 Fax: 206-325-8893
E-mail: ippsint@aol.com
Website: www.ipps.org

Founded: 1950

Membership: 1,001–10,000

Scope: International

Description: The Society was founded to seek and share information on plant propagation. The Sociey has nine regional chapters, three in USA and Canada, Australia, New Zealand, Great Britain and Ireland, Scandinavia, Japan and Southern Africa and holds area meetings in Latin America.

Publication(s): Annual Proceedings of all regional meetings and papers, regional newsletters of meetings for members

Keyword(s): Agriculture/Farming, Forests/Forestry, Reduce/Reuse/Recycle, Wildlife & Species

Contact(s):
John Wott, Executive Secretary and Treasurer

INTERNATIONAL PRIMATE PROTECTION LEAGUE

P.O. Box 766
Summerville, SC 29484 United States
Phone: 843-871-2280 Fax: 843-871-7988
E-mail: ippl@awod.com
Website: www.ippl.org/

Founded: 1973
Membership: 10,001–100,000
Scope: International
Description: A nonprofit international organization devoted to the conservation and protection of nonhuman primates. There are branches in the United States and United Kingdom, and field representatives in 32 countries.
Publication(s): International Primate Protection League News
Keyword(s): Forests/Forestry, Wildlife & Species
Contact(s):
Shirley McGreal, Chairwoman
Marjorie Doggett, Secretary
Diane Walters, Treasurer

INTERNATIONAL RIVERS NETWORK (IRN)

1847 Berkeley Way
Berkeley, CA 94703 United States
Phone: 510-848-1155 Fax: 510-848-1008
E-mail: irn@irn.org
Website: www.irn.org

Founded: 1986
Scope: International
Description: IRN supports local communities working to protect their rivers and watersheds. We work to halt destructive river development projects and encourage equitable and sustainable methods of meeting needs for water, energy and flood management. Members include environmentalists, engineers, hydrologists, human rights activists, and academics who are committed to the study and defense of rivers and riverine communities.
Publication(s): World Rivers Review, working papers, action alerts, special briefings
Keyword(s): Development/Developing Countries, Water Habitats & Quality
Contact(s):
Annie Ducmanis, Assistant to Executive Director; ext. 329; annie@irn.org
Juliette Majot, Executive Director; ext. 305; juliette@irn.org
Patrick McCully, Campaign Director; ext. 309; patrick@irn.org
Yvonne Cuellar, Library Coordinator
Lori Pottinger, Africa Campaigns & Editor; ext. 306; lori@irn.org
Glenn Switkes, South America Campaigns; glenn@altanet.com.br

INTERNATIONAL SNOW LEOPARD TRUST

4649 Sunnyside Ave., N., Suite 325
Seattle, WA 98103 United States
Phone: 206-632-2421 Fax: 206-632-3967
E-mail: info@snowleopard.org
Website: www.snowleopard.org

Founded: 1981
Membership: 1,001–10,000
Scope: International
Description: A nonprofit organization dedicated to the conservation of the endangered snow leopard and its mountain habitat through a balanced approach that considers the needs of the local people and the environment; and provides workshops, field training, equipment, publications, conservation education programs, and a centralized database for organizing and disseminating information.
Publication(s): Snow Leopard News
Keyword(s): Wildlife & Species
Contact(s):
Charlie Morse, President
Lewis Macfarlane, Vice President
Tom McCarthy, Conservation Director; tmccarthy@snowleopard.org
Brad Rutherford, Executive Director; brad@snowleopard.org
Peter Graham, Intern; 206-632-2421; peter@snowleopard.org
Owen Rogers, Program Assistant; 206-632-2421; owen@snowleopard.org
Pricilla Allen, Conservation Program Officer; 206-632-2421; priscilla@snowleopard.org
Helen Freeman, Founder
Steven Kearsley, Treasurer

INTERNATIONAL SOCIETY FOR ECOLOGICAL ECONOMICS (ISEE)

1313 Dolley Madison Blvd., Suite 402
McLean, VA 22101 United States
Phone: 703-790-1745 Fax: 703-790-2672
E-mail: isee@igc.com
Website: www.ecologicaleconomics.org

Founded: 1988
Scope: International
Description: ISEE actively encourages the integration of the study and the management of ecology and economics in order to achieve an ecologically and economically sustainable world.
Publication(s): Ecological Economics
Keyword(s): Development/Developing Countries, Wildlife & Species
Contact(s):
Richard Norgarrd, President of Board of Directors

INTERNATIONAL SOCIETY FOR ENDANGERED CATS (ISEC)

3070 Riverside Dr., Suite 160
Columbus, OH 43221 United States
Phone: 614-487-8760 Fax: 614-487-8769
E-mail: eduacation@isec.org
Website: www.isec.org

Founded: 1988
Scope: International
Description: ISEC's purpose is to raise awareness of the plight of endangered wild cats, and thereby prevent their extinction. ISEC offers conservation education programs, collects and disseminates information about wild cats, and supports specific conservation projects around the world.
Publication(s): Cat Tales
Keyword(s): Wildlife & Species
Contact(s):
Bill Simpson, President; 3070 Riverside Dr., Suite 160, Columbus, OH 43221
Patricia Currie, Executive Director; 196 W. Central, Delaware, OH 43015; 740-369-9794

INTERNATIONAL SOCIETY FOR ENVIRONMENTAL ETHICS

Department of Philosophy, University of Windsor
Windsor, N9B 3P4 Ontario Canada
Phone: 519-253-3000 Fax: 519-971-3610
E-mail: philos@uwindsor.ca
Website: www.cep.unt.edu/isEE.html

Founded: 1990
Scope: International
Description: The International Society for Environmental Ethics' main purpose is to promote the critical analysis of ethical issues related to the natural environment, to further and support philosophical and scientific meetings and conferences nationally and internationally, and to provide material and media aids suitable for teaching environmental philosophy and environmental ethics.

Publication(s): International Society for Environmental Ethics Newsletter

Contact(s):
Mark Sagoff, President; Director of Institute for Philosophy and Public Policy, University of Maryland, Baltimore, MD 20742
J. Callicott, Vice President; Philosophy Department, University of Wisconsin at Stevens Point, Stevens Point, WI 54481
Edward Hettinger, Treasurer; College of Charleston, Charleston, SC 29424
Laura Westra, Secretary; University of Windsor, Windsor, Ontario N9B 3P4; 519-253-4232

INTERNATIONAL SOCIETY FOR THE PRESERVATION OF THE TROPICAL RAINFOREST, THE

3931 Camino De La Cumbre
Sherman Oaks, CA 91423 United States
Phone: 818-788-2002 Fax: 818-990-3333
E-mail: forest@nwc.net

Founded: 1984
Membership: 1,001–10,000
Scope: International
Description: The International Society for the Preservation of the Tropical Rainforest is dedicated to the global conservation of tropical forest resources through the promotion of park implementation, sustainable agriculture, and timber harvesting.
Publication(s): Tropical Rainforest Our Most Valuable and Endangered Habitat With A Blueprint for Its Survival Into The Third Millennium
Keyword(s): Climate Change, Ethics/Environmental Justice, Land Issues, Wildlife & Species

Contact(s):
Edward Asner, Co-Director; 3931 Camino De La Cumbre, Sherman Oaks, CA 91423; 818-788-2002
Roxanne Kremer, Co-Director; 3931 Camino De La Cumbre, Sherman Oaks, CA 91423; 626-572-0233; Fax: 6265729521
Arnold Newman, Co-Director; 3931 Camino De La Cumbre, Sherman Oaks, CA 91423; 818-788-2002

INTERNATIONAL SOCIETY OF ARBORICULTURE

P.O. Box 3129
Champaign, IL 61826-3129 United States
Phone: 217-355-9411 Fax: 217-355-9516
Website: www.isa-arbor.com

Founded: 1924
Membership: 10,001–100,000
Scope: International
Description: Through research, technology, and education promote the professional practice of arboriculture and foster a greater public awareness of the benefits of trees.
Publication(s): Publication listings to include "A Photographic Guide for Evaluation of Hazard Trees in Urban Areas", Valuation of Landscape Trees, Shrubs, and Other Plants

Contact(s):
Kim Coder, President
Michael Neal, President-Elect
Harvey Holt, Vice President
Melinda Jones, Vice President
Lauren Lanphear, Vice President
Paul Harter, Executive Director
Peggy Currid, Managing Editor
Bailey Hudson, President-Elect
Robert Miller, Editor

INTERNATIONAL SOCIETY OF TROPICAL FORESTERS, INC.

5400 Grosvenor Ln.
Bethesda, MD 20814 United States
Phone: 301-897-8720 Fax: 301-897-3690
E-mail: istf.bethesda@verizon.net
Website: www.cof.orst.edu/org/istf

Founded: 1950
Membership: 1,001–10,000
Scope: International
Description: A nonprofit organization founded with the objective of providing an information exchange for members involved in the management, protection, and wise use of tropical forests.
Publication(s): ISTF News, ISTF Notices (Spanish)
Keyword(s): Forests/Forestry, Reduce/Reuse/Recycle, Wildlife & Species

Contact(s):
Warren Doolittle, President; USA
Napoleon Vergara, Vice President & Director of Asia & Philippines
Jeffery Burley, Director At Large; United Kingdom
John Fox, Director At Large; Australia
Chun K. Lai, Director At Large; Philippines
Rodolfo Salazar, Director of Latin America; Costa Rica
B. Taal, Director of Africa; Gambia
Napoleon Vergara, Director of Asia; Philippines
Patricia Heaton Holmgren, Office Manager
Frank Wadsworth, Editor

INTERNATIONAL SONORAN DESERT ALLIANCE

P.O. Box 687
Ajo, AZ 85321 United States
Phone: 520-387-6823 Fax: 520-387-5626
E-mail: isda@tabletoptelephone.com
Website: www.isdanet.org

Founded: 1992
Membership: 1,001–10,000
Scope: International
Description: The purpose of the International Sonoran Desert Alliance is to promote environmentally sustainable and culturally sound economic development while protecting the natural and tri-cultural heritage of the western Sonoran Desert.
Keyword(s): Development/Developing Countries, Ethics/Environmental Justice, Land Issues

Contact(s):
Carlos Nagel, President; closfree@aol.com
Manuel Gonzalez, Vice President
Reynaldo Cantu, Executive Director
Isabel Granillo, Secretary; isabel@laruta.org
Sue Tout, Treasurer

INTERNATIONAL UNION FOR CONSERVATION OF NATURE

Rue Mauvemey 28 1196
Gland, Switzerland
Phone: 41 22 999 0001
Website: www.ucn.org

Founded: N/A

Contact(s):
Achim Steiner, Director; achimsteiner@iucn.org

INTERNATIONAL UNION FOR CONSERVATION OF NATURE

REGIONAL OFFICE CENTRAL AMERICA
B.P. 5506 c/o IUCN Project Office DHA
Yacunde, Cameroon
Phone: 237-216-497 Fax: 237-216-497
E-mail: roca.iucn@camnet.cm
Website: www.iucn.org

Founded: N/A

Contact(s):
Daniel Ngantou, Regional Director

INTERNATIONAL UNION FOR CONSERVATION OF NATURE
REGIONAL OFFICE FOR MESO AMERICA
Phone: 5062362733 Fax: 5062409934
E-mail: correo@orma.iucn.org
Website: www.iucn.org

Founded: 1988

Contact(s):
Enrique Lahmann, Regional Director

INTERNATIONAL UNION FOR CONSERVATION OF NATURE AND NATURAL RESOURCES (IUCN)
Rue Mauverney 28 CH-1196
Gland, Switzerland
Phone: 41 22 999 001
E-mail: mail@hq.iucn.ch
Website: www.iucn.org

Founded: N/A

Contact(s):
Martha Koch-Weser, Director General

INTERNATIONAL UNION FOR CONSERVATION OF NATURE AND NATURAL RESOURCES (IUCN) THE WORLD CONSERVATION UNION
Headquarters, Rue Mauverney 28, CH-1196
Gland, Switzerland
Phone: 229990001
Website: www.iucn.org

Founded: 1948

Scope: International

Description: An independent body to promote scientifically-based action for the conservation of nature and to ensure that development is sustainable and provides a lasting improvement in the quality of life for people all over the world. Eight hundred eighty voting members in 138 countries; 73 states, 107 government agencies, and 623 non-governmental organizations. Also 35 non-voting affiliate members. Maintains a global network of more than 6,000 scientists and professionals organized into six commissions

Keyword(s): Development/Developing Countries, Reduce/Reuse/Recycle

Contact(s):
Yolanda Kakabadse, President
Patrick Dugan, Director of Global Programme, Switzerland
Maria Iuri, Director of Finance
Marietta Koch-Weser, Director General, Germany
Jeffrey McNeely, Director of Biodiversity Policy Coordination Division
David Brackett, Chairman for Species Survival Commission
Tariq Bunuri, Chairman of Commission on Environmental Economic and Social Justice
Claes De Dardel, Treasurer
Fritz Hesselink, Chairman of Commission on Education and Communication
Sra Kakabadse, Chairman of the Bureau, Eduador
Edward Maltby, Chairman of Commission on Ecosystem Management, United Kingdom
Adrian Phillips, Chairman of Commission on Protected Areas
Nicholas Robinson, Chairman of Commission on Environmental Law

INTERNATIONAL UNION FOR CONSERVATION OF NATURE AND NATURAL RESOURCES (IUCN) THE WORLD CONSERVATION UNION
P.O. Box 11536
Hatfield, Pretoria, 28 South Africa
Phone: 27 12 420 4116 Fax: 27 12 420 3917

Founded: N/A

Scope: International

Contact(s):
Saliem Fakir

INTERNATIONAL UNION FOR CONSERVATION OF NATURE AND NATURAL RESOURCES (IUCN) THE WORLD CONSERVATION UNION
BANGLADESH COUNTRY OFFICE
House #3 A, Road 15, Dhanmondi, RIA 1205
Dhaka, 1207 Bangladesh
Phone: 880 2 8122577 Fax: 880 2 8126209
E-mail: IUCNBD@CITECHCO.NET

Founded: N/A

Scope: International

Contact(s):
Anwarul Islam, Head

INTERNATIONAL UNION FOR CONSERVATION OF NATURE AND NATURAL RESOURCES (IUCN) THE WORLD CONSERVATION UNION
BOTSWANA COUNTRY OFFICE
Plot 2403 Hospital Way, Extension 9 Private Bag 00300
Gaborone, Botswana
Phone: 267 371 584 Fax: 267 371 584
E-mail: iucn@iucnbot.bw

Founded: N/A

Scope: International

Contact(s):
Ruud Jansen, Country Representative

INTERNATIONAL UNION FOR CONSERVATION OF NATURE AND NATURAL RESOURCES (IUCN) THE WORLD CONSERVATION UNION
BURKINA COUNTRY FASSO OFFICE
01 BP 3133, 515 Rue Agostino Neto, Ouagadougou 01
01 BP 1618
Ouagadougou, 1 Burkina Faso
Phone: 226-307-047 Fax: 226-308-580
E-mail: uicnbrao@fasonet.bf

Founded: N/A

Scope: International

Contact(s):
Michel Kouda, Country Representative

INTERNATIONAL UNION FOR CONSERVATION OF NATURE AND NATURAL RESOURCES (IUCN) THE WORLD CONSERVATION UNION
CANADA OFFICE
555 René-Lévesque Blvd. W., Office 500
Montréal, Québec, H2Y 3X7, H2Z 1B1 Quebec Canada
Phone: 514-287-9704, ext. 357 Fax: 514-287-9687
E-mail: poste@iucn.ca
Website: www.iucn.ca

Founded: 1948

Membership: 101–1,000

Scope: International

Description: Canada Office of IUCN - The World Conservation Union

Keyword(s): Agriculture/Farming, Climate Change, Development/Developing Countries, Ecosystems (precious), Forests/Forestry, Land Issues, Oceans/Coasts/Beaches, Water Habitats & Quality

Contact(s):
Andrew Deutz, Head; 287-9704, ext. 355; Fax: 287-9687; adeutz@iucn.ca
Micheline Legault-Alaurent, Office Manager; 287-9704, ext. 353; Fax: 287-9687; mil@iucn.ca

Therese Beaudet, Programme Officer; 287-9704, ext. 354; Fax: 287-9687; beaudet@iucn.ca
Danielle Cantin, Project Officer; 287-9704, ext. 358; Fax: 287-9687; dcantin@iucn.ca
Chris Morry, Programme Officer; 287-9704, ext. 357; Fax: 287-9687; cmorry@iucn.ca
Elizabeth Pelletier, Project Assistant; 287-9704, ext. 356; Fax: 287-9687; epelletier@iucn.ca

INTERNATIONAL UNION FOR CONSERVATION OF NATURE AND NATURAL RESOURCES (IUCN) THE WORLD CONSERVATION UNION

ENVIRONMENTAL LAW CENTRE
Godesbergerallee 108-112
Bonn, 53175 Germany
Phone: 49-228-2692-231 Fax: 49-228-2692-250
E-mail: secretariat@elc.iucn.org

Founded: N/A

Scope: International

Contact(s):
John Scanlon, Head

INTERNATIONAL UNION FOR CONSERVATION OF NATURE AND NATURAL RESOURCES (IUCN) THE WORLD CONSERVATION UNION

GUINEA-BISSAU COUNTRY OFFICE
Apartado 23, 1031
Bissau, Guinea Bissau
Phone: 245 201 230/245 203 264 Fax: 245 201 168
E-mail: uicn.bi@sol.gtelecom.gw

Founded: N/A

Scope: International

Contact(s):
Nelson Dias, Chef De Mission

INTERNATIONAL UNION FOR CONSERVATION OF NATURE AND NATURAL RESOURCES (IUCN) THE WORLD CONSERVATION UNION

IUCN BEIRA PROJECT OFFICE
MOZAMBIQUE COUNTRY OFFICE
635 Eduardo Mondlane Ave.
P.O. Box 4770 - Maputo
Beira, Mozambique
Phone: 258 3323 807 Fax: 258 3322 957
E-mail: uicn@sortmoz.com

Founded: N/A

Scope: International

Contact(s):
Ebenizario Chonguica, Country Representative

INTERNATIONAL UNION FOR CONSERVATION OF NATURE AND NATURAL RESOURCES (IUCN) THE WORLD CONSERVATION UNION

LAO PEOPLE'S DEMOCRATIC REPUBLIC COUNTRY OFFICE
P.O. Box 4340, 15 Fa Ngum Rd.
Vientiane, Laos
Phone: 856 21 216 401 Fax: 856 21 216 127
E-mail: iucnlao@loxinfo.co.th

Founded: N/A

Scope: International

Contact(s):
Stuart Chape, Country Representative

INTERNATIONAL UNION FOR CONSERVATION OF NATURE AND NATURAL RESOURCES (IUCN) THE WORLD CONSERVATION UNION

MALI COUNTRY OFFICE
BP 1567
Bamako, Mali
Phone: 223 227 572 Fax: 223 230 092
E-mail: uicn@spider.toolnet.org

Founded: N/A

Scope: International

Contact(s):
Moctar Traore, Chef de Mission

INTERNATIONAL UNION FOR CONSERVATION OF NATURE AND NATURAL RESOURCES (IUCN) THE WORLD CONSERVATION UNION

NEPAL COUNTRY OFFICE
P.O. Box 3923, Lalitpur
Kathmandu, Nepal
Phone: 977-1 52876 Fax: 977- 536786
E-mail: info@iucn.org.np
Website: www.iucn.org/places/Nepal

Founded: 1948

Scope: International

Description: The main purpose for IUCN's activities in Nepal is to strengthen institutional capacity for conservation and sustainable use of natural resources in Nepal. IUCN will use its comparative advantage to transfer to Nepalese organizations relevant information management tools, and essential skills to strengthen their capacity to manage natural resources. This is in line with IUCN's overall mission.

Contact(s):
Ambika Adhikari, Country Representative

INTERNATIONAL UNION FOR CONSERVATION OF NATURE AND NATURAL RESOURCES (IUCN) THE WORLD CONSERVATION UNION

NIGER COUNTRY OFFICE
BP 10933
Niamey, Niger
Phone: 227 724 028 Fax: 227 724 005
E-mail: iucn@intnet.ne

Founded: N/A

Scope: International

Contact(s):
M. Mamane, Country Representative

INTERNATIONAL UNION FOR CONSERVATION OF NATURE AND NATURAL RESOURCES (IUCN) THE WORLD CONSERVATION UNION

PAKISTAN COUNTRY OFFICE
1 Bath Island Rd.
Karachi, 75530 Pakistan
Phone: 92 21 586 1543 Fax: 92 21 587 0287
E-mail: amk@iucn.khi.sdnpk.undp.org

Founded: N/A

Scope: International

Contact(s):
Aban Kabraji, Country Representative

INTERNATIONAL UNION FOR CONSERVATION OF NATURE AND NATURAL RESOURCES (IUCN) THE WORLD CONSERVATION UNION

REGIONAL OFFICE FOR CENTRAL AFRICA
B.P. 5506, c/o IUCN Project Office DHA
Yaounde, Cameroon
Phone: 237-221-6496 Fax: 237-221-6497
E-mail: pwl@iccnet.com

Founded: N/A
Scope: International
Contact(s):
Assitou Ndinga, Coordinator for Central Africa

INTERNATIONAL UNION FOR CONSERVATION OF NATURE AND NATURAL RESOURCES (IUCN) THE WORLD CONSERVATION UNION
REGIONAL OFFICE FOR EASTERN AFRICA
P.O. Box 68200, Mukoma Rd.
Langata, Nairobi, Kenya
Phone: 254 2890 605 Fax: 254 2890 615
E-mail: emt@iucrearo.org
Founded: N/A
Scope: International
Contact(s):
Eldad Tukahirwa, Regional Representative

INTERNATIONAL UNION FOR CONSERVATION OF NATURE AND NATURAL RESOURCES (IUCN) THE WORLD CONSERVATION UNION
REGIONAL OFFICE FOR EUROPE
Rue Vergot, 15
Brussels, 1030 Belgium
Phone: 0032-2-7328299 Fax: 0032-2-7329499
E-mail: europe@iucn.org
Website: www.iucn-ero.nl
Founded: N/A
Membership: 101–1,000
Scope: International
Description: To contribute to a sustainable Europe by influencing policy development and implementation for biodiversity and landscape conservation, restoration and sustainable use inside and outside Europe.
Keyword(s): Agriculture/Farming, Ecosystems (precious), Forests/Forestry, Wildlife & Species
Contact(s):
Tamas Marghescu, Regional Director
Edina Biro, Project Operations Officer
Pien Zalen, Office Manager
Jean-Claude Jacques, Senior Officer

INTERNATIONAL UNION FOR CONSERVATION OF NATURE AND NATURAL RESOURCES (IUCN) THE WORLD CONSERVATION UNION
REGIONAL OFFICE FOR MESO AMERICA
Apartado 0146-2150
Moravia, San Jose, 2150 Costa Rica
Phone: 001 506 2410101 Fax: 1506240994
E-mail: correo@orma.incn.org
Website: www.iucn.org//placeslorma
Founded: 1989
Membership: 1–100
Scope: International
Description: Conservation and Sustainable Development
Contact(s):
Enrique Lahmann, Regional Director

INTERNATIONAL UNION FOR CONSERVATION OF NATURE AND NATURAL RESOURCES (IUCN) THE WORLD CONSERVATION UNION
REGIONAL OFFICE FOR SOUTH AMERICA
Casilla Postal 17-17-626
Avenida Atahualpa 955
y Republica Edificio Digicom Piso 4
Quito, Ecuador
Phone: 593 2466 622/623 Fax: 593 2466 624
E-mail: samerica@iucnsur.satnet.net
Founded: N/A
Scope: International
Contact(s):
Roberto Franco, Regional Representative

INTERNATIONAL UNION FOR CONSERVATION OF NATURE AND NATURAL RESOURCES (IUCN) THE WORLD CONSERVATION UNION
REGIONAL OFFICE FOR SOUTHERN AFRICA (ROSA)
P.O. Box 745
Harare, Zimbabwe
Phone: 263 4728 266 Fax: 263 4720 738
E-mail: postmaster@iucnrosa.org.zw
Founded: N/A
Scope: International
Contact(s):
Yemi Katerere, Regional Representative

INTERNATIONAL UNION FOR CONSERVATION OF NATURE AND NATURAL RESOURCES (IUCN) THE WORLD CONSERVATION UNION
REGIONAL OFFICE FOR WEST AFRICA
BP 1618
Ouagadougou, 1 Burkina Faso
Phone: 226 307 047 Fax: 226 307 561
Founded: N/A
Scope: International
Contact(s):
Ibrahim Thiaw, Regional Representative

INTERNATIONAL UNION FOR CONSERVATION OF NATURE AND NATURAL RESOURCES (IUCN) THE WORLD CONSERVATION UNION
REGIONAL OFFICE OF SOUTH AND SOUTHEAST ASIA
P.O. Box 4, 302 Outreach Bldg., AIT
Klong Luang, Pathumthani, 12120 Thailand
Phone: 662-524-6745 Fax: 662-524-5392
Founded: N/A
Scope: International
Contact(s):
Mohammed Hussain, Head

INTERNATIONAL UNION FOR CONSERVATION OF NATURE AND NATURAL RESOURCES (IUCN) THE WORLD CONSERVATION UNION
SENEGAL COUNTRY OFFICE
BP 3215 Ave. Bourguiba x rue 3
Castors, Dakar, Senegal
Phone: 221 824 0545 Fax: 221 824 9246
Founded: N/A
Scope: International
Contact(s):
Abdoulaye Kane, Chef de Mission

INTERNATIONAL UNION FOR CONSERVATION OF NATURE AND NATURAL RESOURCES (IUCN) THE WORLD CONSERVATION UNION
SRI LANKA COUNTRY OFFICE
48 Vajira Ln.
Colombo, 5 Sri Lanka
Phone: 941 580 202 Fax: 941 580 202
E-mail: twcus@sri.lanka.net
Founded: N/A
Scope: International
Contact(s):
Shiranee Yasaratne, Country Representative

INTERNATIONAL UNION FOR CONSERVATION OF NATURE AND NATURAL RESOURCES (IUCN) THE WORLD CONSERVATION UNION
SUBREGIONAL OFFICE FOR CENTRAL EUROPE
U1 Narbutta 40/21
Warsaw, 02-541 Poland
Phone: 48 22 881 0552 (53) Fax: 48 22 881 0554
E-mail: iucr@iucr-ce.org.pl

Founded: N/A

Scope: International

Contact(s):
Zenon Tederko, Head

INTERNATIONAL UNION FOR CONSERVATION OF NATURE AND NATURAL RESOURCES (IUCN) THE WORLD CONSERVATION UNION
SUBREGIONAL OFFICE FOR THE COMMONWEALTH OF INDEPENDENT STATES
P.O. Box 265
Moscow, 1254755 Russia
Phone: 7095 190 7077 Fax: 7095 490 5878

Founded: N/A

Scope: International

Contact(s):
Vladimir Moshkalo, Head

INTERNATIONAL UNION FOR CONSERVATION OF NATURE AND NATURAL RESOURCES (IUCN) THE WORLD CONSERVATION UNION
UGANDA COUNTRY OFFICE
P.O. Box 10950, Plot 39 Acacia Ave.
Kampala, Uganda
Phone: 256 41 344 508 Fax: 256 41 342 298

Founded: N/A

Contact(s):
Alex Muhweezi, Country Representative

INTERNATIONAL UNION FOR CONSERVATION OF NATURE AND NATURAL RESOURCES (IUCN) THE WORLD CONSERVATION UNION
UNITED STATES OFFICE, WASHINGTON, DC
1630 Connecticut Ave., NW
Washington, DC 20009 United States
Phone: 202-387-4826 Fax: 202-387-4823
E-mail: postmaster@iucnus.org
Website: www.iucn.org

Founded: N/A
Membership: 1–100
Scope: International
Publication(s): Amman 2000, Life At The Edge, Tooth & Law-newsletter

INTERNATIONAL UNION FOR CONSERVATION OF NATURE AND NATURAL RESOURCES (IUCN) THE WORLD CONSERVATION UNION
VIETNAM COUNTRY OFFICE
P.O. Box 60, International Post Office, 13, Tran Hung Dao
8 Chuong Duong Do
Hanoi, Vietnam
Phone: 844 9320 970 Fax: 844 9320 996
E-mail: ntfp.project@hn.vnn.vn

Founded: N/A

Scope: International

Contact(s):
Nguyen Thong, Country Representative

INTERNATIONAL UNION FOR CONSERVATION OF NATURE AND NATURAL RESOURCES (IUCN) THE WORLD CONSERVATION UNION
ZAMBIA COUNTRY OFFICE
Asco Bldg., Private Bag W, 356 Luanshya Rd., Plot No 5116
Lusaka, Zambia
Phone: 260 1231 866 Fax: 260 1231 867

Founded: N/A

Scope: International

Contact(s):
Sally Mulala, Country Representative

INTERNATIONAL WILD WATERFOWL ASSOCIATION
5614 River Styx Rd.
10114 54th Place N.E., Everett WA 98205
Medina, OH 44256 United States
Website: www.greatnorthern.net

Founded: 1958

Scope: International

Description: Works toward protection, conservation, and reproduction of any species of wild waterfowl considered in danger of eventual extinction; encourages breeding of well known and rare species in captivity. Established Avicultural Hall of Fame. Sponsors annual conference and gives grants in field.

Publication(s): IWWA Newsletter
Keyword(s): Wildlife & Species
Contact(s):
Walter Sturgeon, President; 7 James Farm, Durham, NH 03824; 603-659-5442
Edward Asper, 1st Vice President; Vice President of Sea World, 7007 Sea World Dr., Orlando, FL 32821; 407-351-3600
Paul Dye, 2nd Vice President; 10114 54th Pl. NE, Everett, WA 98205; 425-334-8223; Fax: 425-397-8136; dye@greatnorthern.net
Nancy Collins, Secretary; 5614 River Styx Rd., Medina, OH 44256; 330-725-8782
William Lowe, Treasurer; 3010 Shady Ln., Billings, MT 59102; 406-245-6119

INTERNATIONAL WILDLIFE COALITION (IWC) AND THE WHALE ADOPTION PROJECT
70 E. Falmouth Highway
E. Falmouth, MA 02536 United States
Phone: 508-548-8328 Fax: 508-548-8542
Website: www.iwc.org

Founded: 1984

Scope: International

Description: IWC is a nonprofit, tax-exempt organization dedicated to preserving wildlife and their habitats. As an internationally recognized non-governmental organization, IWC's achievements have been accomplished through grassroots advocacy, activism, research, and education efforts. IWC's Whale Adoption Project protects and researches marine mammals.

Publication(s): WhaleWatch, Wildlife and You and What You Can Do To Help, Whales of the World Teacher's Kit, Wildlife Watch
Keyword(s): Wildlife & Species
Contact(s):
Daniel Morast, President; 70 E. Falmouth Highway, E. Falmouth, MA 02536; 508-548-8328; Fax: 508-548-8542; dmorast@iwc.org
Ronald Orenstein, Canada Project Director; 130 Adelaide St. West, Suite 1940, Toronto, Ontario M5H 3P5; 905-820-7886; Fax: 905-569-0116; ornstn@inforamp.net
Charles Wartenberg, United Kingdom Director; 141A, High St., Edenbridge, Kent TN8 5AX

Jose Palazzo, Brazil Project Coordinator; P.O. Box 5087, Florianopolis, SC 88040; brazilian_wildlife@zaz.com.br

INTERNATIONAL WILDLIFE REHABILITATION COUNCIL (IWRC)

IWRC
4437 Central Pl., Suite B-4
Fairfield, CA 94534-1633 United States
Phone: 707-864-1761 Fax: 707-864-3106
E-mail: iwrc@inreach.com
Website: www.iwrc-online.org

Founded: 1972
Membership: 1,001–10,000
Scope: International
Description: An organization dedicated to conserving and protecting wildlife and habitat through wildlife rehabilitation
Publication(s): Journal of Wildlife Rehabilitation, IWRC Literature Catalog, other publications and catalogs available, Minimum Standards and Accreditation, Basic Wildlife Rehabilitation
Keyword(s): Wildlife & Species
Contact(s):

Edward Clark, President
Penny Elliston, Vice President
Lee Theisen-Watt, Secretary
Dody Wyman, Treasurer

INTERNATIONAL WOLF CENTER

1396 Highway 169
Ely, MN 55731 United States
Phone: 218-365-4695 Fax: 218-365-3318
E-mail: wolfinfo@wolf.org
Website: www.wolf.org

Founded: 1985
Membership: 1,001–10,000
Scope: International
Description: The International Wolf Center supports the survival of the wolf around the world by teaching about its life, its associations with other species and its dynamic relationship to humans.
Publication(s): International Wolf Magazine, various educational pamphlets, Guidelines for Gray Wolf Management
Keyword(s): Wildlife & Species
Contact(s):

Walter Medwid, Executive Director; 763-560-7374; Fax: 763-560-7368; wmedwid@wolf.org

INTERNATIONAL WOLF CENTER

ADMINISTRATIVE OFFICES
3300 Bass Lake Road
Suite 202
Minneapolis, MN 55429 United States
Phone: 763-560-7374 Fax: 763-560-7368
E-mail: wolfinfo@wolf.org
Website: www.wolf.org

Founded: 1985
Membership: 1–100
Scope: International
Description: The International Wolf Center supports the survival of the wolf around the world by teaching about its life, its associations with other species and its dynamic relationship to humans.
Publication(s): International Wolf
Contact(s):

George Knotek, Development Director; 3300 Bass Lake Rd, Suite 202, Minneapolis, MN 55429; 763-560-7374; Fax: 763-560-7368; develop@wolf.org

Walter Medwid, Executive Director; 3300 Bass Lake Rd, Suite 202, Minneapolis, MN 55429; 763-560-7374; Fax: 763-560-7368

Mary Ortiz, Marketing & Communications Director; 3300 Bass Lake Road, Suite 202, Minneapolis, MN 55429; 763-560-7374; Fax: 763-560-7368; comdir@wolf.org

INTERPRETATION CANADA

c/o Kerry Wood Nature Centre, 6300-45 Ave.
Red Deer, T4N 3M4 Alberta Canada
Phone: 403-346-2010 Fax: 403-347-2590
E-mail: webmaster@interpcan.ca
Website: www.interpcan.ca

Founded: 1973
Membership: 101–1,000
Scope: National
Description: Interpretation Canada is dedicated to raising public awareness, understanding, and appreciation for Canada's natural and cultural heritage, provides training, networking, and advocacy for interpretors, and promotes the role of interpretation in fields such as conservation, education, recreation, and tourism.
Publication(s): Interpscan - national journal, annual membership directory, regional newsletters

INTERTRIBAL BISON COOPERATIVE (ITBC)

1560 Concourse Drive
Rapid City, SD 57703 United States
Phone: 605-394-9730 Fax: 605-394-7742
E-mail: itbc@enetis.net
Website: intertribalbison.org

Founded: 1992
Membership: 1–100
Scope: National
Description: Native American Cooperative made up of federally recognized tribes, whose mission is to restore bison to Native lands.
Publication(s): Buffalo Tracks
Keyword(s): Development/Developing Countries, Ecosystems (precious), Wildlife & Species

IOWA ACADEMY OF SCIENCE

University of Northern Iowa 175 Baker Hall
Cedar Falls, IA 50614-0508 United States
Phone: 319-273-2021 Fax: 319-273-2807
Website: www.iren.net/ias/ias_2.htm

Founded: 1875
Membership: 101–1,000
Scope: State
Description: To further the work of scientists, facilitate cooperation among them, and increase public understanding and appreciation of the importance and promise of the methods of science in human progress. A conservation section meets each year as part of an annual convention submitting papers dealing with all conservation happenings.
Publication(s): IAS Bulletin, Journal of the Iowa Academy of Science, Iowa Science Teachers Newsletter
Contact(s):

Raymond Anderson, President Elect; 319-335-1575; Fax: 319-335-2754; randerson@igsb.uiowa.edu

Lynn Brant, President; 319-273-6160; Fax: 319-273-7124; lynnbrant@uni.edu

David McCalley, Executive Director; 319-273-2021; Fax: 319-273-2807; davidmccalley@uni.edu

Charlie Martinson, Past President; 515-294-1062; Fax: 515-294-9420; cmartins@iastate.edu

IOWA ASSOCIATION OF NATURALISTS

CONSERVATION EDUCATION CENTER
2473 160th Rd.
Guthrie Center, IA 50115 United States
Phone: 641-747-8383 Fax: 641-747-3951
E-mail: ajay.winter@dnr.state.ia.us
Website: www.ianpage.20m.com

Founded: 1978
Membership: 101–1,000
Scope: State
Description: Organization of persons interested in promoting the development of skills and education within the art of interpreting the natural and cultural environment. Members representing county, state, federal, and private conservation education agencies, organizations, and facilities.

IOWA B.A.S.S. CHAPTER FEDERATION

Attn: President, 3282 Midway
Marion, IA 52302 United States
Phone: 319-393-1481
E-mail: tbowler1@go.com

Founded: N/A
Scope: State
Description: An organization of Bassmaster chapters, affiliated with the Bass Anglers Sportsman Society, organized to fight pollution, assist state and national conservation agencies in their efforts, and teach the young people of our country good conservation practices. Dedicated to the realistic conservation of our water resources.
Contact(s):
Tom Bowler, President; 319-393-1481
Russell Engelbart, Conservation Director; 12565 Amber Rd., Highway X44, Anamosa, IA 52205; engelbartbass101@uswest.net

IOWA ENVIRONMENTAL COUNCIL

711 E. Locust St.
Des Moines, IA 50309 United States
Phone: 515-244-1194 Fax: 515-244-7856
E-mail: iecmail@earthweshare.org
Website: www.earthweshare.org

Founded: 1994
Membership: 101–1,000
Scope: State
Description: The Iowa Environmental Council is an alliance of diverse organizations and individuals working with all Iowans to protect our natural environment. We seek a sustainable future through shaping public policy, research and education, coalition-building, and advocacy.
Publication(s): Legislative Action, News Bulletin, Iowa Environmental Quarterly
Keyword(s): Agriculture/Farming, Pollution (general), Public Health, Water Habitats & Quality, Wildlife & Species
Contact(s):
David Hurd, President
Debbie Neustadt, Vice President
Elizabeth Plasket, Executive Director; 515-244-1194, ext. 11; Fax: 515-244-7856; plasket@earthweshare.org
Mark Ackelson, Treasurer
Ray Heinicke, Secretary

IOWA NATIVE PLANT SOCIETY

Botany Department
341A Bessey Hall
Iowa State University
Ames, IA 50011-1020 United States
Phone: 515-294-9499 Fax: 515-294-1337
E-mail: dlewis@iastate.edu
Website:
www.public.iastate.edu/~herbarium/inps/inpshome.htm

Founded: 1995
Membership: 101–1,000
Scope: State
Description: Iowa Native Plant Society is an organization of amateurs and professionals who are interested in the scientific, educational, cultural aspects, preservation, and conservation of Iowa's native plants.
Publication(s): Iowa Native Plant Society Newsletter
Keyword(s): Land Issues, Reduce/Reuse/Recycle, Water Habitats & Quality, Wildlife & Species
Contact(s):
Tom Rosburg, President; Drake University, Olin Hall, Des Moines, IA 50311; 515-377-2930; thomas.rosburg@drake.edu
Connie Mutel, Vice President; 2345 Sugar Bottom Road, Solon, IA 52333
Diana Horton, Treasurer; 720 Sandusky Drive, Iowa City, IA 52240; 319-337-5430; diana-horton@uiowa.edu
Linda Scarth, Secretary; 1630 Wildwood Drive NE, Cedar Rapids, IA 52402

IOWA NATURAL HERITAGE FOUNDATION

Attn: Comm. Coordinator
Insurance Exchange Bldg.
Suite 444, 505 Fifth Ave.
Des Moines, IA 50309 United States
Phone: 515-288-1846 Fax: 515-288-0137
E-mail: info@inhf.org
Website: www.inhf.org

Founded: 1979
Membership: 1,001–10,000
Scope: State
Description: An independent, statewide, nonprofit organization that protects Iowa's land, water and wildlife "for those who follow." Program emphasis on land protection, landowner education, resource planning, wetland restoration and rail-trail development in Iowa.
Publication(s): Enjoy Iowa's Recreation Trails Guidebook, Iowa Natural Heritage, The Landowner's Options
Keyword(s): Development/Developing Countries, Ecosystems (precious), Land Issues, Public Lands/Greenspace, Recreation/Ecotourism, Reduce/Reuse/Recycle, Sprawl/Urban Planning, Water Habitats & Quality, Wildlife & Species
Contact(s):
Mark Ackelson, President
Anita O'Gara, VP, Director of Development and Communications
Judy Frazier, Director of Administration
Lisa Hein, Director of Trails and Greenways
Joe McGovern, Director of Land Stewardship
Bruce Mountain, Director of Land Projects
Perry Thostenson, Land Protection Program Director
Laura McVay, Finance Manager
Cathy Engstrom, Communications Coordinator
Cheri Grauer, Gift Planner
Mike Lamair, Board Chairman

IOWA PRAIRIE NETWORK

IPN
1308 160 th Ave
Knoxville, IA 50138 United States
Phone: 402-571-6230
E-mail: webmaster@iowaprairienetwork.org
Website: www.IowaPrairieNetwork.org

Founded: 1990
Scope: State
Description: The Iowa Prairie Network is dedicated to protecting Iowa prairie heritage.
Publication(s): A Prairie Bioliography, Native Prairie Management Guide, IPN News
Keyword(s): Land Issues
Contact(s):
Glenn Pollock, President
Cindy Hildebrand, Vice President
David Hansen, Director; 515-357-3665
Carole Kern, Treasurer; 319-273-2813

IOWA TRAILS COUNCIL

P.O. Box 131
Center Point, IA 52213-0131 United States
Phone: 319-849-1844 Fax: 319-849-1844

Founded: 1983
Membership: 1,001–10,000
Scope: National
Description: A membership nonprofit organization primarily active in the Midwest, but with membership in over one-half the states and in several foreign countries. Primary purpose is to acquire and convert former railroad rights-of-way into recreational trails.
Publication(s): Trails Advocate (bi-monthly mini magazin, Bicycle Trails of Iowa
Keyword(s): Land Issues, Public Lands/Greenspace, Recreation/Ecotourism, Transportation
Contact(s):
Tom Neenan, Secretary/Treasurer and Executive Director; P.O. Box 131, Center Point, IA 52213-0131; 319-849-1844; tomneenan1@aol.com
Eldon Colton, Chairman; 1008 Bowler St., Hiawatha, IA 52233; 319-378-8971; Fax: 319-294-1914
David Lyon, Vice Chairman; 116 10th Ave., S., Mt. Vernon, IA 52314; 319-895-8240

IOWA TRAPPERS ASSOCIATION, INC.

c/o Anna Marie Scalf, 123 N. Madison Ave.
Ottumwa, IA 52501 United States
Phone: 641-682-3937 Fax: 641-682-9092
E-mail: iantadtr@lisco.com

Founded: 1950
Scope: State
Description: A nonprofit organization that works to continue the wise use and harvest of Iowa's renewable resource of furbearing animals. Cooperates with all recognized conservation agencies, law enforcement agencies, and legislative committees, and provides input on the benefits and necessity of trapping.
Publication(s): Trapper and Predator Caller, The
Keyword(s): Recreation/Ecotourism
Contact(s):
Tom Walters, President; 1723 20th St., Bettendorf, IA 52722-3829; 319-359-6949
James Stauffer, Vice President; 29602 202nd St., Clarksville, IA 50619-9801; 319-278-4004
Chris Grillot, Secretary; 2769 110th Ave., Wheatland, IA 52777; 319-374-1074
Anna Scalf, Treasurer; 123 N. Madison Ave., Ottumwa, IA 52501; 515-682-3937
Paul Wait, Editor; 700 E. State St., Iola, WI 54990; 715-445-2214

IOWA WILDLIFE FEDERATION

P.O. Box 3332
Des Moines, IA 50316-0332 United States
Phone: 319-624-3107 Fax: 319-644-3213

Founded: N/A
Scope: State
Description: A representative statewide organization, affiliated with the National Wildlife Federation, dedicated to the protection and enhancement of wildlife and its habitat through public education and government interaction.
Contact(s):
Joe Wilkinson, President and Education Program Contact
Mike Hodges, Editor
Kevin Thomasson, Treasurer
Doug Thompson, Representative
John Zietlow, Alternate Representative

IOWA WILDLIFE REHABILITATORS ASSOCIATION

1005 Harken Hill Dr., P.O. Box 217
Osceola, IA 50213 United States
Phone: 641-342-2783

Founded: 1986
Membership: 1–100
Scope: State
Description: A nonprofit organization established to disseminate information pertaining to wildlife rehabilitation and medicine to veterinarians, rehabilitators, naturalists and others; to communicate and cooperate with environmental/conservation organizations; and to encourage the public to become more aware of the earth and its wild creatures. This is done through newsletters, educational material, state and regional conferences, and presentations.
Publication(s): Newsletters, educational materials
Contact(s):
Marlene Ehresman, President; 515-296-2995
Heather Blevins, Vice President; 641-277-7745
Beth Brown, Treasurer; 641-342-2783
Wendy Dewalle, Secretary; 641-964-9592

IOWA WOMEN IN NATURAL RESOURCES

P.O. Box 20083
Des Moines, IA 50320-0083 United States
Phone: 515-795-2354
E-mail: KShannon@aol.com
Website: www.hometown.aol.com

Founded: 1988
Membership: 1–100
Scope: State
Description: A nonprofit organiaztion dedicated to providing professional development to individuals interested in all natural resource careers by promoting communication among professionals, encouraging girls and women to consider natural resource careers, conducting outdoor skills workshops, providing networking and support systems for women working in natural resources and providing career enhancement training.
Publication(s): IWINR News, IWINR Membership Directory
Keyword(s): Ethics/Environmental Justice
Contact(s):
Kathy Shannon, President; 515-795-2354; KShannon@aol.com
Theresa Blackburn, Education Chair; 563-872-5495; Fax: 563-872-5659; theresa_blackburn@usgs.gov
Theresa Minaya, Treasurer; 712-258-0838

ISLAND CONSERVATION EFFORT

90 Edgewater Dr. #901
Coral Gables, FL 33133 United States
Phone: 305-666-5381 Fax: 305-663-9941
E-mail: tropbird@unspoiledqueen.com

Founded: 1988
Scope: International
Description: Island Conservation Effort is dedicated to the preservation of island natural resources, fauna, and habitats on which their preservation depends. We promote conservation, education, and research to obtain necessary data to support conservation measures.
Keyword(s): Wildlife & Species
Contact(s):
Martha Walsh-McGehee, President; 90 Edgewater Dr., Suite 901, Coral Gables, FL 33133; 305-666-5381; tropbird@gate.net
Michelle Pugh, Vice President; P.O. Box 4254, Christiansted, St. Croix, VI 00820; 340-773-7030; divexp@viaccess.net
Rosemarie Gnam, Secretary and Treasurer; 1872 Stanhope St., Ridgewood, NY 11385

ISLAND INSTITUTE, THE

P.O. Box 648
Rockland, ME 04841 United States
Phone: 207-594-9209 Fax: 207-594-9314
E-mail: inquiry@islandinstitute.org
Website: www.islandinstitute.org

Founded: 1983

Scope: National

Description: Private, nonprofit organization dedicated to sustaining island and coastal communities through community initiatives, publications, resource management, science and marine research.

Publication(s): Island Journal, Islands in Time, Gulf of Maine Environmental Atlas, Working Waterfront

Keyword(s): Development/Developing Countries, Ecosystems (precious), Ethics/Environmental Justice, Oceans/Coasts/ Beaches, Sprawl/Urban Planning, Water Habitats & Quality

Contact(s):

Philip Conkling, President; 207-594-9209
Peter Ralston, Vice President for Development; 207-594-9209
Josee Shelley, Vice President for Finance and Operations; 207-594-9209
Sandra Thomas, Vice President for Programs; 207-594-9209
David Platt, Managing Editor; 207-594-9209

ISLAND RESOURCES FOUNDATION

6292 Estate Nazareth, #100
St. Thomas, VI 00802 United States
Phone: 340-775-6225 Fax: 340-779-2022
E-mail: irrf@irf.org
Website: www.irf.org

Founded: 1972

Membership: 101–1,000

Scope: State, Regional, National, International

Description: A 30-year old international NGO devoted to solving the problems of sustainable development in small tropical islands

Publication(s): E-mail groups, publications on website

Keyword(s): Climate Change, Development/Developing Countries, Ecosystems (precious), Ethics/Environmental Justice, Land Issues, Oceans/Coasts/Beaches, Pollution (general), Recreation/Ecotourism, Water Habitats & Quality, Wildlife & Species

Contact(s):

Bruce Potter, President; bpotter@irf.org
Jean Pierre Bacle, Cartographer; 1718 P Street NW, Suite T-4, Washington, DC 20036; 202-265-9712; Fax: 202-232-0748; jpbacle@irf.org
Charles Consolvo, Secretary
Edward Towle, Chairman; etowle@irf.org
Judith Towle, Treasurer; jtowle@irf.org
Henry Wheatley, Vice Chairman

ISLAND RESOURCES FOUNDATION

EASTERN CARIBBEAN BIODIVERSITY PROGRAM OFFICE
P.O. Box 2103
St. Johns, Antigua Barbuda
Phone: 2684637740 Fax: 2684637740
E-mail: klindsay@irf.org

Founded: N/A

Scope: Regional

ISSAQUAH ALPS TRAILS CLUB (I.A.T.C.)

P.O. Box 351
Issaquah, WA 98027 United States
Phone: 206-328-0480
E-mail: LATCDrew@aol.com
Website: www.issaquahalps.org

Founded: 1979

Scope: Local

Description: A nonprofit membership organization established to preserve and promote trails and open space in the area east of Seattle along the I-90 highway corridor from Lake Washington to the Cascades, primarily in the area known as the "Issaquah Alps."

Publication(s): Washington State Public Port Districts, Speaking of Ground Water, Targeting Tomorrow

Keyword(s): Air Quality/Atmosphere, Energy, Reduce/Reuse/ Recycle, Water Habitats & Quality

Contact(s):

Steve Drew, President
Barbara Johnson, Vice President of Operations
Steve Drew, Treasurer-Acting
Kitty Gross, Secretary
Harvey Manning, Founder

IZAAK WALTON LEAGUE OF AMERICA ENDOWMENT

3185 Dubuque St., NE
Iowa City, IA 52240 United States
Phone: 319-351-7037 Fax: 319-351-7037
Website: www.iwla.org

Founded: 1943

Scope: National

Description: Organized to help rebuild Outdoor America by the acquisition for governmental agencies of unique natural areas for the use of future generations. Members of the Izaak Walton League of America.

Keyword(s): Air Quality/Atmosphere, Recreation/Ecotourism, Wildlife & Species

Contact(s):

Wendell Haley, President; 1840 NE 92nd Ave., Portland, OR 97220; 503-253-9749
Larry Smith, Vice President; 1611 Alderman Dr., Greensboro, NC 27408; 336-834-0018
Charles Eldridge, Secretary; 2008 74th St., Des Moines, IA 50322; 515-244-0932
Robert Russell, Executive Secretary
William Weber, Treasurer; 6357 W. Encantado Ct., Rockford, MI 49341; 616-456-8691; Fax: 616-456-1915
Howard White, Honorary President; P.O. Box 527, Havana, IL 62644; 309-543-4391

IZAAK WALTON LEAGUE OF AMERICA, INC., THE

Headquarters, 707 Conservation Ln.
Gaithersburg, MD 20878-2983 United States
Phone: 301-548-0150, ext. 222 Fax: 301-548-0146
Website: www.iwla.org

Founded: 1922

Membership: 10,001–100,000

Scope: National

Description: Promotes means and opportunities for educating the public to conserve, maintain, protect, and restore the soil, forest, water, air, and other natural resources of the U.S. and promotes the enjoyment and wholesome utilization of those resources.

Publication(s): Outdoor America

Keyword(s): Air Quality/Atmosphere, Ethics/Environmental Justice, Public Lands/Greenspace, Recreation/Ecotourism, Water Habitats & Quality

Contact(s):

Stan Adams, National President
Chuck Clayton, National Vice President
Paul Hansen, Executive Director
Jason McGarvey, Editor
Jim Mosher, Conservation Director
Georgia Townsend, Secretary
William West, Treasurer

IZAAK WALTON LEAGUE OF AMERICA, INC., THE

ALASKA DIVISION
P.O. Box 670650
Chugiak, AK 99567 United States
Phone: 907-333-0243

Founded: N/A

Scope: State

Contact(s):

Thomas Carter, President; 907-333-0243

IZAAK WALTON LEAGUE OF AMERICA, INC., THE

CALIFORNIA DIVISION
504 E. Oakmont Avenue
Orange, CA 92867 United States
Phone: 714-516-9483

Founded: 1938

Scope: State

Contact(s):

Peter Hillebrecht, President; 310-791-0793

IZAAK WALTON LEAGUE OF AMERICA, INC., THE

COLORADO DIVISION
12175 West Ohio Place
Lakewood, CO 80228-3319 United States
Phone: 303-986-1747
Website: www.iwla.org

Founded: N/A

Membership: 101–1,000

Scope: State

Publication(s): Outdoor America-Magazine

Contact(s):

Leah Whellan, President
Nelson Burton, National Director; 719-473-0700
Amy Miller, Secretary and National Director; 513 Strachan Dr., Fort Collins, CO 80525-2130; 970-223-5379

IZAAK WALTON LEAGUE OF AMERICA, INC., THE

FLORIDA DIVISION
P.O. Box 97
Estero, FL 33928 United States
Phone: 941-992-2184 Fax: 941-495-0201
E-mail: koreshanfound@mindspring.com
Website: www.iwla.org

Founded: N/A

Membership: 1–100

Scope: Regional

Contact(s):

Charles Dauray, President
Michael Chenoweth, National Director; P. O. Box 236, Homestead, FL 33090-0236; 305-451-0993; Fax: 305-451-3627; michael.chenoweth@mail.com
Sarah Bergquist, Secretary

IZAAK WALTON LEAGUE OF AMERICA, INC., THE

ILLINOIS DIVISION
Attn: President, 314 Townhall Rd., RR-2
Metamora, IL 61548 United States
Phone: 309-383-4203

Founded: N/A

Scope: State

Publication(s): Illini Ike (Newsletter)

Contact(s):

Jim Tyas, President; 309-383-4203
Marsha Johnson, Secretary; 1512 45th St., Moline, IL 61265-3544; 309-797-8255

IZAAK WALTON LEAGUE OF AMERICA, INC., THE

INDIANA DIVISION
Attn: President, 2173 Pennsylvania St.
Portage, IN 46368-2444 United States
Phone: 219-762-4876
Website: www.in-iwla.org

Founded: 1922

Membership: 1,001–10,000

Scope: Local, State, National

Description: Grassroots organization mission: To conserve, maintain, protect and restore the soil, forest, water and other natural resources of the United States and other lands; to promote means and opportunities for the education of the public with respect to such resources and their enjoyment and wholesome utilization.

Publication(s): Hoosier Waltonian, The

Contact(s):

Charles Siar, President; 219-762-4876
Ed Bohle, Secretary; 206 Greenwood Ave., Michigan City, IN 46360; 219-879-8020
James Daniels, Editor/Vice Pres.; 1808 Ravenswood Dr., Evansville, IN 47717; 812-477-7250; jimdaniels3@juno.com
Emil Garcia, Treasurer; 3420 W 40Th Pl., Gary, IN 46408; 219-980-2612; elgarcia@earthlink.net

IZAAK WALTON LEAGUE OF AMERICA, INC., THE

IOWA DIVISION
321 East Walnut Street
Suite 130
Des Moines, IA 50309-2048 United States
Phone: 515-883-2358 Fax: 515-883-2362
E-mail: iowaikes@mcleodusa.net
Website: www.iowaikes.net

Founded: 1922

Scope: State

Description: Non-Profit Conservation Organization

Contact(s):

Doyle Adams, President; 707 N. 7th St., Indianola, IA 50125-1430; 515-961-6004

IZAAK WALTON LEAGUE OF AMERICA, INC., THE

MARYLAND DIVISION
703 Conservation Lane
Gaithersburg, MD 20871 United States
Phone: 301-972-1627

Founded: N/A

Membership: 1,001–10,000

Scope: Local, Regional

Contact(s):

Georgia Townsend, President; 406 Leighton Ave., Silver Spring, MD 20901; 301-588-8335
Bill Gorman, Executive Secretary

IZAAK WALTON LEAGUE OF AMERICA, INC., THE

MICHIGAN DIVISION
c/o President, 6260 Blythefield NE
Rockford, MI 49341 United States
Phone: 616-866-8475
E-mail: jtrimber@earthlink.net
Website: www.mich-iwla.org

Founded: 1927

Membership: 101–1,000

Scope: State, National
Description: Conservation organization with a mission to conserve, maintain, protect and restore our natural resources and educate the public on their wise use.
Keyword(s): Agriculture/Farming, Air Quality/Atmosphere, Development/Developing Countries, Ecosystems (precious), Energy, Ethics/Environmental Justice, Executive/Legislative/Judicial Reform, Forests/Forestry, Land Issues, Oceans/Coasts/Beaches, Pollution (general)
Contact(s):
E. John Trimberger, President; 6260 Blythefield NE, Rockford, MI 49341; 616-866-8475; jtrimber@earthlink.net
Robert Stegmier, Secretary; 5285 Windmill Dr. NE, Rockford, MI 49341-9311; 616-866-4769

IZAAK WALTON LEAGUE OF AMERICA, INC., THE
MINNESOTA DIVISION
555 Park St., Suite140
St. Paul, MN 55103 United States
Phone: 651-221-0215 Fax: 651-221-0215
E-mail: mn-ikes@mtn.org
Website: www.mtn.org/~mn-ikes
Founded: N/A
Membership: 1,001–10,000
Scope: State
Publication(s): Avaliable on website
Contact(s):
Lee Barthel, President

IZAAK WALTON LEAGUE OF AMERICA, INC., THE
NEBRASKA DIVISION
Attn: President, 3017 Midway Rd.
Grand Island, NE 68803-2436 United States
Phone: 308-384-0656
Founded: N/A
Scope: State
Contact(s):
Roger Mettenbrink, President; 308-384-0656
Lurlie Campbell, Secretary; 17125 Sodtown Rd., Ravenna, NE 68869; 308-452-3800

IZAAK WALTON LEAGUE OF AMERICA, INC., THE
NEW YORK STATE DIVISION
c/o President, 3826 Lane Rd.
Cazenovia, NY 13035 United States
Phone: 315-655-3375
E-mail: cheneyweb@aol.com
Founded: N/A
Membership: 101–1,000
Scope: Regional
Description: New York State Division of IWLA
Publication(s): Periodical Outdoor America
Contact(s):
Matt Webber, President; 315-655-3375
Les Monostory, Secretary; 315-435-6600; hllmomo@health.ongov.net

IZAAK WALTON LEAGUE OF AMERICA, INC., THE
OHIO DIVISION
Attn: Secretary, 953 Greenwood Ave.
Hamilton, OH 45011-1817 United States
Phone: 513-697-6100
E-mail: kflowers@fuse.net
Website: www.iwla.org
Founded: 1922
Membership: 1,001–10,000
Scope: State
Publication(s): Quarterly magazine - Outdoor America, Tri-annual newsletter - Buckeye Ike Line
Contact(s):
Bill Ashbaugh, President
Kevin Flowers, Environmental Director; 6793 Midnight Sun Dr., Mainville, OH 45039; 513-697-6100
Yvonne Hayes, Secretary; 513-863-8018

IZAAK WALTON LEAGUE OF AMERICA, INC., THE
OREGON DIVISON
15056 Quall Rd.
Silverton, OR 97381 United States
Phone: 503-873-2681
E-mail: olsondaw@juno.com
Founded: 1930
Scope: State
Description: To protect, perpetuate, and strive for renewal of Oregon's natural resources, including the air, soil, woods, waters, and wildlife; to promote means and opportunities for education of the public in respect to such resources and the enjoyment and utilization thereof.
Contact(s):
Jeanne Norton, President; 503-235-7634
Coral Torley, Secretary; 1820 NW Woodland Dr., Corvallis, OR 97330-1019; 541-752-0114

IZAAK WALTON LEAGUE OF AMERICA, INC., THE
OWATONNA MINNESOTA CHAPTER
c/o Cherry Schwartz, President
100 Shady Avenue
Owatonna, MN 55060 United States
Phone: 507-451-6676 Fax: 507-444-8999
E-mail: ikepres@hotmail.com
Founded: 1926
Membership: 101–1,000
Scope: Local
Description: This 100+ member environmental organization advocates for land, water, air and wildlife. Major projects include the Game and Fish Building at the Steele County Free Fair (mid-August) and the restoration of an Oak Savanna on a 23 acre parcel south of Owatonna, MN. The Ikes chapterhouse is in these woods and can be rented by members of the public. It seats 100, has a full kitchen, gas grills and is completely handicapped accessible.
Publication(s): Izaak Walton League, Owatonna Chapter
Keyword(s): Agriculture/Farming, Ecosystems (precious), Ethics/Environmental Justice, Executive/Legislative/Judicial Reform, Forests/Forestry, Land Issues, Oceans/Coasts/Beaches, Pollution (general), Public Lands/Greenspace, Recreation/Ecotourism, Reduce/Reuse/Recycle

IZAAK WALTON LEAGUE OF AMERICA, INC., THE
PENNSYLVANIA DIVISION
460 New Salem Rd.
Uniontown, PA 17313 United States
Website: www.iwla.org
Founded: N/A
Scope: State
Keyword(s): Land Issues, Wildlife & Species
Contact(s):
Raymond Kossler, President; 460 New Salem Rd., Uniontown, PA 15401-9013; 724-437-5356
Martha Shaffer, Secretary; P.O. Box 35, Loganville, PA 17342-0035; 717-428-2883

IZAAK WALTON LEAGUE OF AMERICA, INC., THE

SOUTH DAKOTA DIVISION
Attn: President, 798 11th St., SW
Watertown, SD 57350-3060 United States
Phone: 605-352-2598
E-mail: clayton@santel.net
Website: itc-web.com/sdikes#

Founded: N/A

Scope: State

Contact(s):
Charles Clayton, President; 605-352-2598

IZAAK WALTON LEAGUE OF AMERICA, INC., THE

VIRGINIA DIVISION
Attn: President, 5235 Richardson Dr.
Fairfax, VA 22032-3930 United States
Phone: 703-361-5729

Founded: N/A

Scope: State

Publication(s): PEC Newsreporter, periodic books and special reports.

Contact(s):
Birtrun Kidwell, President; 703-232-6563
Jeanne Kling, Secretary; 6110 Occoquan Forest Drive, Manassas, VA 20112-3018

IZAAK WALTON LEAGUE OF AMERICA, INC., THE

WASHINGTON DIVISION
Attn: Bruce McGlenn, 2031 Franklin Ave. E, # 304
Seattle, WA 98102 United States
Phone: 425-455-1986 Fax: 425-453-9629
Website: www.seattleikes.org

Founded: N/A

Scope: State

Contact(s):
Ronni McGlenn, President, Washington State Division; ronnimc@juno.com

IZAAK WALTON LEAGUE OF AMERICA, INC., THE

WEST VIRGINIA DIVISION
79 E. Main Street
Richwood, WV 26261 United States
Phone: 304-846-6818
Website: www.izaakwaltonleague.com

Founded: N/A

Scope: State

Contact(s):
Don McClung, President; 304-876-2457

IZAAK WALTON LEAGUE OF AMERICA, INC., THE

WISCONSIN DIVISION
Attn: President, 5316 Forest Cir., N
Stevens Point, WI 54481-5605 United States
Phone: 715-344-1803
E-mail: bob_elliker@usa.net
Website: www.iwla.org

Founded: 1922

Membership: 1,001–10,000

Scope: State

Description: Wisconsin Division of the Izaak Walton League of America, a national Conservation Organization whose goal is to protect, manage, and use America's natural resources in such a way as to assure long term quality of life.

Publication(s): Wisconsin Waltonian Newsletter

Keyword(s): Water Habitats & Quality

Contact(s):
Robert Elliker, President; 715-344-1803; bob_elliker@usa.net
Gerald Ernst, Secretary; 811 4th St., Plover, WI 54467-2253; 715-344-4668

IZAAK WALTON LEAGUE OF AMERICA, INC., THE

WYOMING DIVISION
Attn: President, 1072 Empinado
Laramie, WY 82070 United States
Phone: 307-742-2785
E-mail: quot@uwyo.edu

Founded: N/A

Scope: State

Keyword(s): Agriculture/Farming, Energy, Reduce/Reuse/Recycle

Contact(s):
Raymond Jacquot, President; 307-742-2785

IZAAK WALTON LEAGUE OF AMERICA, INC., THE

YORK CHAPTER #57
Attn: William Shaffer P.O. Box 35
Loganville, PA 17342 United States
Phone: 717-428-2883
E-mail: reg6govike@aol.com
Website: www.iwla.org

Founded: 1926

Description: The strive for the purity of water, the clarity of air, the wise stewardship of the land and its resources; to know the beauty and understanding of nature and the value of wildlife, woodlands, and open space; to the preservation of this heritage and to man's sharing in it. Mission Statement: We're a diverse group of 50,000 men and women dedicated to protecting our nation's soil, air, woods, waters and wildlife.

Publication(s): Outdoor America, Waltonian News Monthly

Contact(s):
William Shaffer, Corresponding Secretary; P.O. Box 35, Loganville, PA 17342

J

J.N. (DING) DARLING FOUNDATION

785 Crandon Blvd., Suite 1206
Key Biscayne, FL 33149 United States
Phone: 305-361-9788 Fax: 305-361-9789
E-mail: kipkoss@hotmail.com
Website: www.dingdarling.org

Founded: 1962

Membership: 1–100

Scope: National

Description: A nonprofit organization formed to continue the ideals and work of pioneer conservationist "Ding" Darling, with an emphasis on conservation education. The Foundation has no paid staff. With all services, including legal and accounting, provided by its trustees, the Foundation is able to funnel 100% of contributed funds into selected projects.

Publication(s): "Ding", The Life of Jay N. Darling, "Ding" Darling's Conservation Cartoons

Keyword(s): Agriculture/Farming, Climate Change, Ecosystems (precious), Energy, Ethics/Environmental Justice, Finance/Banking/Trade, Forests/Forestry, Land Issues, Pollution (general), Population, Public Health, Public Lands/Greenspace, Transportation, Water Habitats

Contact(s):
Christopher Koss, President of Board of Trustees and Chairman of Executive Committee; 305-361-9788; Fax: 305-361-9789; kipkoss@hotmail.com

Kristie Anders, Executive Director; P.O. Box 482, Sanibel, FL 33957; 941-472-2329; Fax: 941-472-6421; kanders@sccf.org

JACK H. BERRYMAN INSTITUTE FOR WILDLIFE DAMAGE MANAGEMENT

DEPT. OF FISHERIES AND WILDLIFE
Utah State University
Logan, UT 84322-5210 United States
Phone: 435-797-2436 Fax: 435-797-1871
Website: www.berrymaninstitute.org

Founded: N/A
Membership: 1–100
Scope: National
Description: The Jack H. Berryman Institute is a national non-profit organization which is centered at Utah State University. It engages in research, education, and extension activities aimed at resolving human and wildlife conflicts, enhancing the positive aspects of wildlife, and increasing human tolerance of wildlife problems.

JACK MINER MIGRATORY BIRD FOUNDATION, INC.

P.O. Box 39
Kingsville, N9Y 2E8 Ontario Canada
Phone: 519-733-4034
E-mail: info@jackminer.com
Website: www.jackminer.com

Founded: 1904
Scope: International
Description: A nonprofit (501(c)3) foundation in both the U.S. and Canada. This sanctuary and its founder, Jack Miner, have become internationally known as one of the earliest efforts in waterfowl conservation. Often referred to as "The Father of Conservation", Jack Miner pioneered the tagging of waterfowl in 1909. The sanctuary is open year round to the public with no admission fee.
Keyword(s): Wildlife & Species
Contact(s):
Kirk Miner, President and Treasurer
Edna Miner, Vice President
Marilyn Hageniers, Secretary

JACKSON HOLE CONSERVATION ALLIANCE

P.O. Box 2728
Jackson, WY 83001 United States
Phone: 307-733-9417 Fax: 307-733-9008
E-mail: jhca@wyoming.com
Website: www.jhalliance.org

Founded: 1979
Membership: 1,001–10,000
Scope: Local, Regional
Description: The Alliance is a nonprofit organization dedicated to responsible land stewardship in Jackson Hole, Wyoming, to ensure that human activities are in harmony with the area's irreplaceable wildlife, scenic and other natural resources.
Publication(s): Welcome to the Neighborhood, Mosquito Abatement Program in Teton County, Fiscal Impacts of Growth in Teton County, Alliance News, The
Keyword(s): Forests/Forestry, Land Issues, Public Lands/Greenspace, Reduce/Reuse/Recycle, Wildlife & Species
Contact(s):
Marcia Kunstel, President
Julius Muschaweck, Co-Vice President
Becky Woods-Bloom, Co-Vice President
Franz Camenzind, Executive Director; franz@jhalliance.com
Pamela Lichtman, Program Director; pam@jhalliance.com
Jean Barash, Secretary; 307-739-8669; Fax: 307-739-9691; jbarash@wyoming.com
John Carney, Treasurer

JACKSON HOLE LAND TRUST

P.O. Box 2897
Jackson, WY 83001 United States
Phone: 307-733-4707 Fax: 307-733-4144
E-mail: info@jhlandtrust.org
Website: www.jhlandtrust.org

Founded: 1980
Membership: N/A
Scope: Local
Description: A private, nonprofit land conservation organization which works to preserve open space and the scenic, ranching, and wildlife values of Jackson Hole by assisting landowners who wish to protect their land in perpetuity. Not a membership organization.
Publication(s): Land Trust Newsletter
Keyword(s): Agriculture/Farming, Land Issues, Public Lands/Greenspace, Wildlife & Species
Contact(s):
Scott Pierson, President
Michael Caruso, Second Vice President
Leslie Mattson, Executive Director
Mia Jensen, Treasurer
Richard Vangyeek, Secretary

JACKSON HOLE PRESERVE, INC.

30 Rockefeller Plaza, Rm. 5600
New York, NY 10112 United States
Phone: 212-649-5819 Fax: 212-649-5729

Founded: 1940
Scope: National
Description: Nonprofit, charitable, and educational organization, established to conserve areas of outstanding primitive grandeur and natural beauty and to provide facilities for their use and enjoyment by the public.
Contact(s):
C.W. Frye, Chairman of the Board
Antonia Grumbach, Secretary
Carmen Reyes, Treasurer

JANE GOODALL INSTITUTE, THE

P.O. Box 14890
Silver Spring, MD 20911 United States
Phone: 301-565-0086 Fax: 301-565-3188
E-mail: jgiinformation@janegoodall.org
Website: www.janegoodall.org

Founded: 1977
Membership: 1–100
Scope: International
Description: The Jane Goodall Institute is an international organization dedicated to the conservation and understanding of wildlife, particularly chimpanzees, and to promoting environmental education, reforestation, and humanitarianism worldwide.
Publication(s): ChimpanZOO Newsletter, Semi-annual Roots and Shoots Network, Annual JGI World Report
Keyword(s): Forests/Forestry, Wildlife & Species
Contact(s):
Jeanne McCarty, Director of Roots and Shoots; j.mccarty@janegoodall.org
Gary North, Deputy Director of Merchandise; gwnjhu@aol.com

JAPAN WILDLIFE RESEARCH CENTER (JWRC)

Shitaya 3-10-10
Taito-ku, Tokyo, 110-8676 Japan
Phone: 81-3-5824-0966 Fax: 81-3-5824-0968
E-mail: mkomoda@jwrc.or.jp
Website: www.jwrc.or.jp/

Founded: 1978
Scope: Local, National, International

Description: JWRC has carried out research works and has accumulated data on nature of Japan and developed techniques for research and management of wildlife and its habitat. JWRC is also trying to contribute to the conservation of nature through fact finding and accumulation of basic data.

Keyword(s): Recreation/Ecotourism, Wildlife & Species

Contact(s):
Yasuyuki Oshima, President
Kazuhiro Yamase, Executive Director

JOHN INSKEEP ENVIRONMENTAL LEARNING CENTER

19600 S. Molalla Ave.
Oregon City, OR 97045 United States
Phone: 503-657-6958, ext. 2351 Fax: 503-650-6669
E-mail: elc@clackamas.cc.or.us
Website: www.clackamas.cc.or.us

Founded: 1972

Scope: State

Description: A source of teacher training and community education on environmental education topics, focusing on urban watershed issues. Located on a restored industrial site featuring buildings made from salvaged and recycled materials.

Keyword(s): Reduce/Reuse/Recycle, Water Habitats & Quality

Contact(s):
John Lecavalier, Director

JOURNALISM TO RAISE ENVIRONMENTAL AWARENESS

San Francisco de los Viveros 701, E2-104
Fracc. Ojocaliente
Aguascalientes, 20190 Mexico
Phone: 449-970-1593 Fax: 449-970-1593
E-mail: jaguar@infosel.net.mx

Founded: 1994

Scope: Local, State, Regional, National, International

Description: Improve environmental education in the mass media.

K

KANSAS ACADEMY OF SCIENCE

c/o Brenda Oppert
USDA ARS GMPRC
1515 College Ave.
Manhattan, KS 66502 United States
Phone: 785-776-2780 Fax: 785-537-5584
E-mail: bso@ksu.edu
Website: www.washburn.edu/kas

Founded: 1868

Membership: 101–1,000

Scope: State

Description: The purposes of the Academy are to encourage education in the sciences and dissemination of scientific information through the facilities of the Academy, and to achieve closer cooperation and understanding between scientists and nonscientists, so that they may work together in a common cause of furthering science.

Publication(s): Transactions of the Kansas Academy of Science

Keyword(s): Agriculture/Farming, Ecosystems (precious), Water Habitats & Quality, Wildlife & Species

Contact(s):
Brenda Oppert, President; USDA ARS GMPRC, 1515 College Ave., Manhattan,, KS 66502; 785-776-2780; Fax: 785-537-5584; bso@ksu.edu
Pieter Berendsen, Secretary; Kansas Geological Survey University of Kansas, Lawrence, KS 66047; 785-864-4991
Dan Merriam, Editor; Kansas Geological Survey University of Kansas, Lawrence, KS 66047; 913-864-4991

KANSAS ASSOCIATION FOR CONSERVATION AND ENVIRONMENTAL EDUCATION

2610 Claflin Rd.
Manhattan, KS 66502-2743 United States
Phone: 785-532-3322 Fax: 785-532-3305
E-mail: ldowney@oznet.ksu.edu
Website: www.kacee.org

Founded: 1969

Membership: 101–1,000

Scope: State

Description: Kansas Association for Conservation and Environmenal Education was organized to promote and support effective conservation and environmental education in Kansas. The Association is made up of over 200 public and private organizations and 280 individuals.

Publication(s): Strategic Plan, Workshop Brochure, Annual Report, KACEE NEWS

Keyword(s): Air Quality/Atmosphere, Energy, Forests/Forestry, Land Issues, Pollution (general), Public Health, Reduce/Reuse/Recycle, Sprawl/Urban Planning, Water Habitats & Quality, Wildlife & Species

Contact(s):
Brad Loveless, President; 785-575-8115; Fax: 785-575-8039; brad_loveless@wstnres.com
Kate Grover, Vice President; 785-368-3801; Fax: 785-368-3806; kgover@topeka.org
Laura Downey, Executive Director; 785-532-3322; Fax: 785-532-3305; ldowney@oznet.ksu.edu
Clark Duffy, Treasurer; 785-296-3185; Fax: 785-296-0878

KANSAS ASSOCIATION FOR CONSERVATION AND ENVIRONMENTAL EDUCATION

KACEE
Executive Director
2610 Claflin Rd
Manhattan, KS 66612-2743 United States
Phone: 785-532-3322 Fax: 785-532-3305
E-mail: ldowney@oznet.ksu.edu
Website: www.kacee.org

Founded: 1969

Membership: 10,001–100,000

Scope: State

Description: Organized to promote and support effective environmental education in order to enhance awareness, knowledge, and concern about the environment among the citizens of Kansas. The association is made up of representatives of over 400 public and private organizations, institutions, business organizations, and individuals.

Publication(s): KACEE News

Contact(s):
Clark Duffy, President and Council Member; 1005 Merchants Tower, Topeka, KS 66612; 913-234-0589
Carol Williamson, Vice President; 1209 Willow Dr., Olathe, KS 66061; 913-764-6036
Connie Elders, Secretary; 455 N. Main 11th Fl., Wichita, KS 67202; 316-264-8323
Ruth Gennrich, Treasurer; Museum of Natural History University of Kansas, Lawrence, KS 66045-2454; 913-864-4173

KANSAS ASSOCIATION OF CONSERVATION DISTRICTS

Attn: President, Rt. 1 Box 110
Glen Elder, KS 67446 United States
Phone: 785-475-2342 Fax: 785-475-3886

Founded: N/A

Scope: State

Contact(s):
Carl Jordan, President, Alternate Board Member; 785-545-3361; Fax: 785-545-3659

Sandra Jones, Vice President; 5160 E Rd. 17, Johnson, KS 67855; 316-492-6495; Fax: 316-492-2772
Richard Jones, Executive Director; 522 Winn Rd., Salina, KS 67401-3668; 785-827-5847; Fax: 785-827-7784
Don Paxson, Board Member; P.O. Box 487, Penokee, KS 67659; 785-421-2480; Fax: 785-421-5662
Don Rezac, Secretary-Treasurer; 12350 Ranch Rd., Emmett, KS 66422; 785-535-2961; Fax: 785-457-2868

KANSAS B.A.S.S. CHAPTER FEDERATION

Attn: President, P.O. Box 330
Alba, MO 64830 United States
Phone: 417-525-4940
E-mail: onemorefish@ckt.net
Website: www.kbcf.com

Founded: N/A

Scope: State

Description: An organization of Bassmaster chapters, affiliated with the Bass Anglers Sportsman Society, organized to fight pollution, assist state and national conservation agencies in their efforts, and teach the young people of our country good conservation practices. Dedicated to the realistic conservation of our water resources.

Publication(s): KBCF News and Views

Contact(s):

Jon Stewart, President; 417-525-4940
Greg Clark, Conservation Director; 9320 E. Osie Apt. #2104, Wichita, KS 67207; 316-681-1887

KANSAS DEPARTMENT OF WILDLIFE AND PARKS

MIDWEST ASSOCIATION OF FISH AND WILDLIFE AGENCIES
512 Southeast 25th Avenue
Pratt, KS 67124 United States
Phone: 620-672-5911 Fax: 620-672-2972
E-mail: joek@wp.state.ks.us

Founded: 1934

Membership: N/A

Scope: State, Regional, National

Description: State agencies/Canadian provinces protecting wildlife resources on public and private lands; scrutinize state and federal wildlife legislation; clearinghouse for the exchange of ideas concerning wildlife management, research techniques, wildlife law enforcement, hunting and outdoor safety, and information and education; assist sportsmen's and conservationists' organizations in the protection, preservation, restoration and management of our fish and wildlife resources.

Publication(s): Proceedings of the MAFWA

Keyword(s): Agriculture/Farming, Ecosystems (precious), Executive/Legislative/Judicial Reform, Forests/Forestry, Land Issues, Pollution (general), Public Lands/Greenspace, Recreation/Ecotourism, Water Habitats & Quality, Wildlife & Species

Contact(s):

Jerry Conley, President; Missouri Department of Conservation, P.O. Box 180, Jefferson City, MO 65102; 573-751-4115, ext. 3212; Fax: 573-751-4467; conlej@mail.conservation.state.mo.us
Joe Kramer, Secretary/Treasurer; 620-672-5911, ext. 190; Fax: 620-672-2972; joek@wp.state.ks.us

KANSAS HERPETOLOGICAL SOCIETY

University of Kansas Natural History Museum, Dyche Hall
Lawrence, KS 66045 United States

Founded: 1974

Scope: State

Description: The Kansas Herpetological Society is a nonprofit organization designed to encourage education and dissemination of scientific information through the facilities of the Society; and to encourage conservation of wildlife in general and of amphibians and reptiles in Kansas in particular.

Publication(s): Kansas Herpetological Society Newsletter

Keyword(s): Wildlife & Species

Contact(s):

Eric Rundquist, Editor; Animal Care Unit, B054 Malott, University of Kansas, Lawrence, KS 66045
Karen Toepfer, Treasurer; 303 W. 39th St., Hays, KS 67601; 785-628-1437

KANSAS NATURAL RESOURCE COUNCIL

Topeka, KS 66601 United States
Phone: 785-746-8885
Website: www.knrc.ws

Founded: 1981

Membership: 101–1,000

Scope: State

Description: Environmental advocacy including public education, lobbying, and litigation.

Publication(s): KNRC Journal, Weekly Legislative Updates

Keyword(s): Agriculture/Farming, Energy, Land Issues, Water Habitats & Quality

Contact(s):

Joan Vibert, President; 1981 Indiana, Ottawa, KS 66067; 785-746-8885; joan@windwalker-farm.com
John Barnes, Executive Director

KANSAS ORNITHOLOGICAL SOCIETY

14207 Robin Rd.
Leavenworth, KS 66048 United States
Phone: 913-651-2565
Website: ksbirds.org/kos

Founded: 1949

Scope: State

Description: Formed to promote the study of ornithology, to advance the members in ornithological science, to promote conservation, and the appreciation of birds by the general public.

Publication(s): K.O.S. Bulletin, Horned Lark, The

Keyword(s): Wildlife & Species

Contact(s):

John Schukman, President; schuksaya@aol.com
Gene Young, Vice President; P.O. Box 1147 Natural Science Dept, Cowley County Community College, Arkansas City, KS 67005; youngg@cowley.cc.ks.us

KANSAS WILDFLOWER SOCIETY

R.L. McGregor Herbarium, 2045 Constant Ave.
Lawrence, KS 66047-3729 United States
Phone: 785-864-3453 Fax: 785-864-5093

Founded: 1978

Scope: State

Description: The Society provides educational materials and sponsors activities to promote the conservation and cultivation of the native plants of Kansas.

Publication(s): KWS Newsletter

Keyword(s): Land Issues, Reduce/Reuse/Recycle, Wildlife & Species

Contact(s):

Dwight Platt, President; 316-283-2500; Fax: 316-284-5286
Cynthia Ford, Secretary; 316-235-4726
Craig Freeman, Agent
Patricia Stanley, Treasurer; 316-689-4070; wichitacsj@feist.com

KANSAS WILDLIFE FEDERATION

P.O. Box 8237
Wichita, KS 67208-0237 United States
Phone: 785-526-7466 Fax: 785-658-2466

Founded: N/A

Scope: State
Description: A representative statewide organization, affiliated with the National Wildlife Federation, dedicated to the protection and enhancement of wildlife and its habitat through public education and government interaction.
Publication(s): Kansas Wildlife Federation: The Voice of Outdoor Kansas (Newsletter)
Contact(s):
Tommie Berger, President & Representative; 785-658-2465
Roger Brooner, Treasurer; 316-768-3827
Velma Miller, Alternate Representative & Editor
Steve Montgomery, Education Programs Contact

KANSAS WILDSCAPE FOUNDATION

1 Riverfront Plaza
Suite 123
Lawrence, KS 66044 United States
Phone: 785-843-9453 Fax: 785-843-6379
E-mail: kansaswildscape@aol.com
Website: kansaswildscape.com

Founded: 1991
Membership: 1,001–10,000
Scope: State
Description: The Kansas Wildscape Foundation is dedicated to conserving and perpetuating the land, wild species, and the rich beauty of Kansas for the use and enjoyment of all. Wildscape is a public/private partnership with the Kansas Department of Wildlife and Parks.
Keyword(s): Land Issues, Recreation/Ecotourism, Water Habitats & Quality, Wildlife & Species
Contact(s):
Gene Argo, Chairman
Rachael Humphrey, Director of Administration/Member Services; 1 Riverfront Plaza, Suite 123, Lawrence, KS 66044; 785-843-9453; Fax: 785-843-6379; kansaswildscape@aol.com
Harland Priddle, Executive Director
Robert Beachy, Past Chairman
Charlie Becker, Treasurer

KEEP AMERICA BEAUTIFUL, INC.

1010 Washington Blvd., 7th Fl.
Stamford, CT 06901 United States
Phone: 203-323-8987 Fax: 203-325-9199
Website: www.kab.org

Founded: 1953
Scope: National
Description: A national nonprofit public education organization dedicated to litter prevention and improved waste handling practices in American communities. Keep America Beautiful trains and certifies communities into the Keep America Beautiful System, a behavior-based approach to improved waste handling.
Publication(s): Network News
Keyword(s): Land Issues, Public Lands/Greenspace, Reduce/Reuse/Recycle
Contact(s):
G. Empson, President
Susanne Woods, Senior Vice President of Development and Environmental Programs
John Bard, Vice Chairman of the Board
Thomas Tomoney, Chairman of the Board

KEEP FLORIDA BEAUTIFUL, INC.

201 East Park Avenue
Tallahassee, FL 32302 United States
Phone: 850-385-1528 Fax: 850-385-4020
Website: www.keepfloridabeautiful.org

Founded: 1991
Membership: 1–100
Scope: State
Description: KFB's mission is to empower individuals to take greater responsibility for their community environment.
Keyword(s): Land Issues, Reduce/Reuse/Recycle, Water Habitats & Quality
Contact(s):
Shane McIntosh, Chairman, Board of Directors

KEEPING TRACK, INC

P.O. Box 444
Huntington, VT 05462 United States
Phone: 802-434-7000 Fax: 802-434-5383
E-mail: info@keepingtrackinc.org
Website: www.keepingtrackinc.org

Founded: 1994
Membership: 1,001–10,000
Scope: Local, State, Regional, National
Description: Keeping Track teaches adults and children to observe, interpret, record, and monitor evidence of wildlife, especially wide-ranging carnivores, in their communities, and support citizens' use of monitoring data in local and regional conservation planning. The Keeping Track Youth Program focuses on educating youth in grades K - 12 about tracking as a monitoring tool, wildlife ecology, and habitat conservation.
Publication(s): Guide to Photographing Tracks & Signs, Project and Data Management Protocol, Keeping Track quarterly newsletter
Keyword(s): Sprawl/Urban Planning, Wildlife & Species
Contact(s):
Lars Botzojorns, Executive Director; lars@keepingtrackinc.org
Susan Morse, Program and Research Director
Sean Lawson, Youth Program Coordinator; sean@keepingtrackinc.org
Monica Mac, Office Manager; monica@keepingtrackinc.org
Jim Siriano, Technical Support Coordinator; jim@keepingtrackinc.org

KENTUCKY ACADEMY OF SCIENCE

Attn: Dr. Jerry W. Warner, President
Department of Biological Sciences
Northern Kentucky University
Highland Heights, KY 41099 United States
Phone: 859-572-5277 Fax: 859-572-5639
E-mail: warner@nku.edu
Website: kas.wku.edu/kas/

Founded: 1914
Membership: 101–1,000
Scope: Regional
Description: To encourage scientific research, promote the diffusion of scientific knowledge, and unify the scientific interests of Kentucky.
Publication(s): Newsletter of KY Academy of Science, Journal of the Kentucky Academy of Science
Contact(s):
Jerry Warner, President; Department of Biological Sciences, Northern Kentucky University, Nunn Drive, Highland Heights, KY 41099; 859-572-5277; Fax: 859-572-5639; warner@nku.edu
Robert Kingsolver, Vice President; Department of Biology, Kentucky Wesleyan College, Owensboro, KY 42302; 270-852-3161; Fax: 270-926-3196; kingsol@kwc.edu
Robert Barney, President Elect; Atwood Research Facility, Kentucky State University, Frankfort, KY 40601; 502-597-6178; rbarney@gwmail.kysu.edu
Kenneth Crawford, Treasurer; Dept. of Biology, Western Kentucky University, Bowling Green, KY 42101; 270-745-6005; Fax: 270-745-6856; kenneth.crawford@wku.edu
Stephanie Dew, Secretary; Dept. of Biology, Centre College, 600 West Walnut Street, Danville, KY 40422; 859-238-5316; dews@centre.edu

Claire Rinehart, Webpage Editor; Department of Biology, Western Kentucky University, Bowling Green, KY 42101; 270-745-6006; Fax: 270-745-6856; claire.rinehart@wku.edu

Ron Rosen, Past President; Dept. of Biology, Berea College, Berea, KY 40404; 859-985-3345; Fax: 859-985-3303; ron_rosen@berea.edu

Raymond Sicard, Editor; School of Osteopathic Medicine, Pikeville College, 147 Sycamore Street, Pikeville, KY 41501; 606-218-5426; Fax: 606-218-5442; rsicard@pc.edu

Elizabeth Sutton, Director, Jr. Academy of Science; Department of Chemistry, Campbellville University, 1 University Drive, Campbellsville, KY 42718; 270-789-5327; eksutton@campbellsvil.edu

Susan Templeton, Newsletter Editor; 130 Atwood Research Faciltiy, Kentucky State University, Frankfort, KY 40601; 502-597-6030; Fax: 502-597-6381; stempleton@gwmail.kysu.edu

KENTUCKY ASSOCIATION FOR ENVIRONMENTAL EDUCATION (KAEE)

P.O. Box 176055
Covington, KY 41017 United States
Phone: 859-578-3012
Website: www.kaee.org

Founded: N/A

Scope: State

Description: Organized to promote and support formal and nonformal environmental education programs throughout the state. Promotes information sharing, research, and development of EE programs and activities. Annually sponsors a three-day conference.

Publication(s): Newsletter, Earth Day Handbook, E.E. Resource Guide

Contact(s):

Joe Baust, President; Center for Environmental Education, Murray State University, Murray, KY 42071; 270-762-2595; joe.baust@coe.murraystate.edu

Karen Reagor, Executive Director; P.O. Box 176055, Covington, KY 41017; 606-578-0312; KPReagor@aol.com

KENTUCKY ASSOCIATION OF CONSERVATION DISTRICTS

Attn: President, 1299 Lillies Ferry Rd.
Winchester, KY 40391 United States
Phone: 786-836-2272

Founded: N/A

Scope: State

Contact(s):

John Chism, President, Alternate Board Member; 606-744-8909; Fax: 502-564-9195

Patrick Henderson, Vice President; Rt. 1 Box 146, Irvington, KY 40146; 502-547-6206; Fax: 502-564-9195

Kevin Jeffries, Secretary-Treasurer; 1503 E. Hwy. 22, Crestwood, KY 40014; 502-222-9877; Fax: 502-222-0046

James Lacy, Board Member; 300 Sanfield Rd., Campton, KY 41301; 606-662-4161; Fax: 606-668-7033

KENTUCKY B.A.S.S. CHAPTER FEDERATION

P.O. Box 71
4058 U.S. 42 W
Warsaw, KY 41095 United States
Phone: 859-567-2885
E-mail: donkee311@earthlink.net
Website: www.kybassfed.com

Founded: N/A

Scope: State

Description: An organization of Bassmaster chapters, affiliated with the Bass Anglers Sportsman Society, organized to fight pollution, assist state and national conservation agencies in their efforts, and teach the young people of our country good conservation practices. Dedicated to the realistic conservation of our water resources.

Contact(s):

Donnie Keeton, President; P.O. Box 71, 4058 U.S. 42 West, Warsaw, KY; 859-567-2885; donkee311@earthlink.net

John Romans, Conservation Director; 209 Park Ave., Carrollton, KY 41008; john.romans@dowcorning.com

KENTUCKY NATURAL LANDS TRUST

433 Chestnut Street
Berea, KY 40403 United States
Phone: 1-877-367-5658 Fax: 1-859-986-1299
E-mail: info@blantonforest.org
Website: www.blantonforest.org

Founded: 1995

Membership: N/A

Scope: State

Description: Kentucky Natural Lands Trust is a statewide land trust working with the Kentucky State Nature Preserves Commission and other organizations to secure funds for the protection of natural land and its long-term stewardship and to serve as a resource and partner to other land trusts and conservation groups.

Publication(s): Blanton Forest Journal

Keyword(s): Forests/Forestry, Land Issues, Public Lands/Greenspace, Wildlife & Species

Contact(s):

Donna Alexander, Development Assistant; 1-877-367-5658, ext. 228; dalexander@blantonforest.org

KENTUCKY RESOURCES COUNCIL

P.O. Box 1070
Frankfort, KY 40602-1070 United States
Phone: 502-875-2428 Fax: 502-875-2845
E-mail: fitzkrc@aol.com
Website: www.kyrc.org

Founded: N/A

Scope: State

Description: The KRC is a nonprofit, membership-based statewide organization dedicated to the conservation and prudent use of Kentucky's natural resources. The membership shares a common concern with the impact of mineral extraction, natural resource development, and economic development on our homes, health, and quality of life. The Council provides legal assistance to individuals and groups, without charge, on air, waste, water and mining issues in the state.

Keyword(s): Pollution (general), Water Habitats & Quality

Contact(s):

Tom FitzGerald, Director

KENTUCKY WOODLAND OWNERS ASSOCIATION

433 Chestnut St.
Berea, KY 40403 United States
Phone: 859-986-2373 Fax: 859-986-1299
E-mail: kstratton@maced.org

Founded: 1991

Membership: 1–100

Scope: State

Description: A statewide nonprofit organization, affiliated with the National Woodland Owners Association, organized to promote good forest stewardship, circulate information on timber marketing, and encourage private property responsibility among woodland owners throughout the Commonwealth of Kentucky.

Publication(s): Kentucky Woodlands

Keyword(s): Forests/Forestry

Contact(s):

Joe Ball, President

Herb Loyd, Vice-President
Bill Green, Secretary
Pete McNeill, Treasurer

KEYSTONE CENTER, THE

1628 Saints John Rd.
Keystone, CO 80435 United States
Phone: 970-513-5800 Fax: 970-262-0152
E-mail: tkcspp@keystone.org
Website: www.keystone.org

Founded: 1975
Membership: 1–100
Scope: National
Description: A nonprofit center for environmental dispute resolution, mediation, and facilitation. Conducts national policy dialogues on environmental, energy, natural resources, health, and science/technology issues; assists in environmental decisionmaking and regulatory negotiations; provides environmental mediation services; provides training and organizational development services in environmental conflict resolution.
Publication(s): Consensus, Discovery
Keyword(s): Energy, Public Health
Contact(s):
Tom Grumbly, President

KIDS FOR SAVING EARTH WORLDWIDE

P.O. Box 421118
Minneapolis, MN 55442 United States
Phone: 763-559-1234 Fax: 763-559-6980
E-mail: kseww@aol.com
Website: www.kidsforsavingearth.org/

Founded: 1989
Membership: 1,001–10,000
Scope: National
Description: KSEW's mission is to educate and empower children to help to protect the Earth's environment by providing free educational materials to kids, schools, and organizations through the KSE Network. Curriculum guides are also available.
Publication(s): The Earth is a Gift Poster, So What's a Toxic Waste Site, Travel the Earth Book, A Trip to a Forest, Toxic Waste Site Poster. List available upon request. Free Membership, KSE News, Rock the World Concert Kit, KSE Action Guide
Keyword(s): Air Quality/Atmosphere, Energy, Land Issues, Pollution (general), Public Lands/Greenspace, Reduce/Reuse/Recycle, Water Habitats & Quality, Wildlife & Species
Contact(s):
Tessa Hill, President and Director
Steve Henningsgaard, Webmaster
Jacob Taintor, Educational Support Services

KODIAK BROWN BEAR TRUST

11930 Circle Dr.
Anchorage, AK 99516 United States
Phone: 907-345-2939 Fax: 907-348-0450

Founded: 1981
Scope: National
Description: The Kodiak Brown Bear Trust is an Alaska-based nonprofit wildlife conservation trust whose mission is to support conservation of the majestic Kodiak brown bear through funding of habitat protection, research and public education.
Publication(s): Exxon Valdez conservation saga
Keyword(s): Wildlife & Species
Contact(s):
Tim Richardson, Executive Director; 6707 Old Stage Rd., North Bethesda, MD 20852-4329; 301-770-6496
Dave Cline, Chairman

L

LA JOLLA FRIENDS OF THE SEALS (LJFS)

P.O. Box 2016
La Jolla, CA 92038 United States
Phone: 619-687-3588
E-mail: phoca@lajollaseals.org
Website: www.lajollaseals.org

Founded: 1999
Membership: 101–1,000
Scope: Local
Description: La Jolla Friends of the Seals is an independent nonprofit organization that was established in 1999 to protect the La Jolla Harbor seal colony and promote safe viewing of the seals by way of education and respect through its naturalist-docent program. In addition to educating the public, docents gather valuable data about the seals.
Keyword(s): Ecosystems (precious), Oceans/Coasts/Beaches, Recreation/Ecotourism, Water Habitats & Quality, Wildlife & Species
Contact(s):
Patrick Hord, Executive Director; patrick@lajollaseals.org

LADY BIRD JOHNSON WILDFLOWER CENTER

4801 La Crosse Ave.
Austin, TX 78739 United States
Phone: 512-292-4200 Fax: 512-292-4627
Website: www.wildflower.org

Founded: 1982
Scope: National
Description: The Lady Bird Johnson Wildflower Center's purpose is to educate people about the environmental necessity, economic value, and natural beauty of native plants. The Wildflower Center, a nonprofit organization, serves North America by promoting the preservation and use of native plants through education programs, information dissemination, and by example.
Publication(s): Native Plants magazine, Wild Ideas, The Store Catalog
Keyword(s): Land Issues, Wildlife & Species
Contact(s):
Robert Breunig, Executive Director
Denise Delaney, Director of Horticulture
Flo Oxley, Acting Director of Education/Senior Botanist
Karen Stevenson, Communications Director
Helen Hayes, Co-Founder
Lady Bird Johnson, Co-Founder
Leslie Lewis, Contact

LAKE ERIE CLEAN-UP COMMITTEE, INC.

Attn: President, 29789 Fort Rd.
Rockwood, MI 48173 United States
Phone: 313-379-3891

Founded: 1959
Scope: National
Description: The LECC's mission is to stop pollution of Lake Erie and of all freshwater lakes and streams; to inform the public of the need for greater pollution controls; to prevent the return to the methods of the past; and to encourage industry to do more research. Our Great Lakes are a fragile part of our ecosystem and we must continue to protect them. Membership includes representatives of Michigan and Ohio citizen groups.
Keyword(s): Oceans/Coasts/Beaches, Water Habitats & Quality, Wildlife & Species
Contact(s):
Leonard Mannausa, President; 29789 Fort Rd., Rockwood, MI 48173; 313-379-3891
Jerome Falwell, Treasurer; 30251 Worth, Gibraltar, MI 48173
Richard Micka, Secretary; 47 E. Elm, Monroe, MI 48162; 313-242-0909

LAKE HOPATCONG PROTECTIVE ASSOCIATION

P.O. Box 443
Lake Hopatcong, NJ 07849 United States
Phone: 973-398-2511 Fax: 973-398-2511
E-mail: lakehse8@yahoo.com

Founded: 1955
Membership: 101–1,000
Scope: Regional
Description: Preserve and protect Lake Hopatcong
Contact(s):
Clifford Lundin, President; 973-398-2511; Fax: 973-398-2511; lakehse8@yahoo.com

LAKE MICHIGAN FEDERATION

220 S. State St., Suite 1900
Chicago, IL 60604 United States
Phone: 312-939-0838 Fax: 312-939-2708
E-mail: Info@lakemichigan.org
Website: www.lakemichigan.org

Founded: 1970
Membership: 101–1,000
Scope: Regional
Description: A coalition of citizens and citizen organizations in Wisconsin, Illinois, Indiana, and Michigan dedicated to protecting Lake Michigan through community action and research. Supported by foundation and corporate grants, membership and contributions.
Publication(s): Lake Michigan Monitor, Wetlands and Water Quality, A Citizen's Guide to Cleaning Up Contaminated Sediments, A Citizen's Action Guide
Keyword(s): Oceans/Coasts/Beaches, Pollution (general), Water Habitats & Quality
Contact(s):
Cameron Owens, Executive Director
Sophia Twichell, Board of Directors

LAKE SUPERIOR GREENS

P.O. Box 1144
Superior, WI 54880 United States
Phone: 715-392-5782

Founded: 1991
Membership: 1–100
Scope: National
Description: Lake Superior Greens is a grassroots group joined to other Green groups in our dedication to a more sustainable lifestyle and a healthy planet. We are active locally as well as on a state, national, and international basis, recognizing that all issues are interrelated.
Publication(s): Monthly newsletter
Keyword(s): Pollution (general), Water Habitats & Quality
Contact(s):
Bob Browne, Contact; 422 Fisher Ogden, Superior, WI 54880; 715-394-6235
Jan Conley, Steering Committee; 2406 Hughitt, Superior, WI 54880; 715-392-5782
John Schraufnagel, Contact; 1506 N. 19th, Superior, WI 54880; 715-394-6660
Rosie Seymour, Contact; 1606 N. 18th St., Superior, WI 54880; 715-395-0494

LAND AND WATER FUND OF THE ROCKIES

2260 Baseline Rd., Suite 200
Boulder, CO 80302 United States
Phone: 303-444-1188 Fax: 303-786-8054
E-mail: landwater@lawfund.org
Website: www.lawfund.org

Founded: 1991
Scope: Regional
Description: Founded in 1991, the Land and Water Fund of the Rockies (LAW Fund) is an environmental law and policy center serving the Interior West. The LAW Fund uses law, economics, and policy analysis to protect land and water resources, protect essential habitats for plants and animals, and assure that energy demands are met in environmentally sound and sustainable ways.
Keyword(s): Air Quality/Atmosphere, Ecosystems (precious), Energy, Forests/Forestry, Water Habitats & Quality, Wildlife & Species

LAND BETWEEN THE LAKES ASSOCIATION

Golden Pond, KY 42211-9001 United States
Phone: 270-924-2000 Fax: 270-924-2119
Website: www.lbl.org

Founded: 1983
Membership: 1,001–10,000
Scope: National
Description: A private nonprofit membership organization supporting and promoting Tennessee Valley Authority's Land Between The Lakes, a 170,000-acre national demonstration in natural resource management, environmental education, and recreation.
Keyword(s): Ethics/Environmental Justice, Land Issues, Public Lands/Greenspace, Water Habitats & Quality
Contact(s):
Loran Wagoner, President
Gaye Lueber, Director
Ramay Winchester, Chairman

LAND CONSERVANCY OF WEST MICHIGAN

1345 Monroe Avenue NW
Suite 324
Grand Rapids, MI 49505 United States
Phone: 616-451-9476
E-mail: lcwm@naturenearby.org
Website: www.naturenearby.org

Founded: 1976
Scope: Local
Description: Local land conservancy that works to protect lands that contribute to the scenic and natural heritage of central west Michigan, including Oceana, Muskegon, Newaygo, Ottawa, Kent, northern Allegan, and southern Lake counties.
Keyword(s): Agriculture/Farming, Ecosystems (precious), Land Issues, Oceans/Coasts/Beaches, Public Lands/Greenspace, Recreation/Ecotourism, Water Habitats & Quality, Wildlife & Species
Contact(s):
Nora Callow, Membership and Business Coordinator; 616-451-9476; lcwm@naturenearby.org
Douglas Powless, Science and Stewardship Coordinator; 616-451-9476, ext. 6; doug@naturenearby.org
April Scholtz, Land Protection Director; 616-451-9476; lcwm@naturenearby.org
Julie Stoneman, Executive Director; 616-451-9476; lcwm@naturenearby.org
Danielle Tassin, Program Assistant; 616-451-9476; lcwm@naturenearby.org

LAND TRUST ALLIANCE, THE

1331 H St., NW, 4th Fl.
Washington, DC 20005 United States
Phone: 202-638-4725 Fax: 202-638-4730
E-mail: lta@lta.org
Website: www.lta.org

Founded: 1982
Scope: National
Description: Provides training, technical assistance and publications for local and regional land trusts to increase their skills and strengthen the land trust movement; fosters public policies that further land trusts' goals; sponsors the National Land Trust Rally; and builds awareness among a broad constituency of the

consequences of diminishing land resources and the role of land trusts in saving land.

Publication(s): Exchange, Conservation Easement Stewardship Guide, National Directory of Conservation Land Trusts, Starting a Land Trust, Federal Tax Law of Conservation Easement, Appraising Easements, Conservation Easement Handbook

Keyword(s): Forests/Forestry, Land Issues, Wildlife & Species

Contact(s):
Jean Hocker, President
John Chappell, Vice President of Development
Phil Jones, Vice President of Operations
Andrew Zepp, Vice President for Programs
Constance Best, Secretary
James Espy, Chairman
David Hartwell, Treasurer
John Turner, Vice Chair

LANDOWNER PLANNING CENTER

P.O. Box 2242
Boston, MA 02101 United States

Founded: N/A

Publication(s): Preserving Family Lands, Book 2, Preserving Family Land, Book 1

Contact(s):
Connie Small

LANDWATCH MONTEREY COUNTY

LANDWATCH
MONTEREY COUNTY LANDWATCH
Box 1876
Salinas, CA 93902 United States
Phone: 831-422-9390 Fax: 831-422-9391
E-mail: landwatch@mclw.org
Website: www.landwatch.org

Founded: 1997

Membership: 1,001–10,000

Scope: Regional

Description: Land Watch is committed to fundamental land use reform and works to build public support for better land use policies at the local, regional, and state level.

Publication(s): Update, State of Monterey County

Keyword(s): Agriculture/Farming, Ethics/Environmental Justice, Land Issues, Public Lands/Greenspace, Sprawl/Urban Planning, Transportation, Wildlife & Species

Contact(s):
Gary Patton, Executive Director; 831-422-9390, ext. 10; Fax: 831-422-9391; gapatton@mclw.org
Lupe Garcia, Community Action Advocate; 831-422-9390, ext. 13; Fax: 831-422-9391; lygarcia@mclw.org
Arianne Tucker, Administrative Director; 831-422-9390, ext. 11; Fax: 831-422-9391; atucker@mclw.org
Chris Fitz, Deputy Director; 831-422-9390, ext. 12; Fax: 831-422-9391; cfitz@mclw.org

LEAGUE OF CONSERVATION VOTERS

1920 L St., NW, Suite 800
Washington, DC 20036 United States
Phone: 202-785-8683 Fax: 202-835-0491
E-mail: lcv@lcv.org
Website: www.lcv.org

Founded: 1970

Membership: 1–100

Scope: National

Description: The LCV is the national, bipartisan political action arm of the environmental movement. LCV works to elect pro-environment candidates to Congress; publishes the National Environmental Scorecard, which rates members of Congress on key environmental votes; raises funds for campaigns through its Political Action Committee and Earthlist; and is governed by a Board of Directors made up of leaders from major national environmental organizations.

Publication(s): National Environmental Scorecard, LCV Insider Newsletter., Presidential Scorecard

Keyword(s): Reduce/Reuse/Recycle

Contact(s):
Deb Callahan, President
Beth Sullivan, Executive Director, Educational Fund
Wade Greene, Secretary
Winsome McIntosh, Treasurer
Theodore Roosevelt, Chair
Anne Saer, Chief Financial Officer

LEAGUE OF ENVIRONMENTAL JOURNALISTS

P.O. Box 2062
Accra, na Ghana
Phone: 233-21-236806 Fax: 233-21-310028
E-mail: lejcec@ghana.com

Founded: 1992

Membership: 1–100

Scope: National, International

Description: To mobilize journalists and the mass media for the effective and meaningful coverage of the environment and development issues.

Keyword(s): Development/Developing Countries, Energy, Finance/Banking/Trade, Reduce/Reuse/Recycle, Water Habitats & Quality, Wildlife & Species

Contact(s):
Mike Anane, President; 233-21-236806; Fax: 233-21-310028; lejcec@ghana.com
Isabella Gyan, Vice President
Elliot Ansah, Treasurer

LEAGUE OF KENTUCKY SPORTSMEN, INC.

P.O. Box 8527
Lexington, KY 40533 United States
Phone: 859-276-3518
E-mail: office@kentuckysportsmen.com
Website: kentuckysportsmen.com

Founded: 1935

Scope: State

Description: A representative statewide organization, affiliated with the National Wildlife Federation, dedicated to the protection and enhancement of wildlife and its habitat through public education and government interaction.

Publication(s): Kentucky Sportsman, The

Contact(s):
Rowland Beers, President and Education Programs Contact
Ben Hall, Editor
Linda Saunders, Representative
Jim Thompson, Alternate Representative
Don York, Treasurer

LEAGUE OF OHIO SPORTSMEN

3953 Indianola Ave.
Columbus, OH 43214 United States
Phone: 614-268-9924 Fax: 614-268-9924
E-mail: info@leagueofohiosportsmen.org
Website: www.leagueofohiosportsmen.org

Founded: N/A

Scope: State

Description: A representative statewide organization, affiliated with the National Wildlife Federation, dedicated to the protection and enhancement of wildlife and its habitat through public education and government interaction.

Publication(s): Ohio Out of Doors Magazine

Contact(s):
Larry Mitchell, President & Representative
Larry Mitchell, Editor & Executive Director
Pat Agner, Secretary

Marilyn Lieb, Alternate Representative, Treasurer & Education Programs
George Lynch, Alternate Representative

LEAGUE OF WOMEN VOTERS OF IOWA

P.O. Box 93775
Des Moines, IA 50393-3775 United States
Phone: 641-777-9739
E-mail: vote@iwvia.org
Website: www.lwvia.org/

Founded: 1920
Membership: 101–1,000
Scope: State
Description: A nonpartisan organization of local chapters and members-at-large, affiliated with the League of Women Voters of the U.S., whose purpose is to promote political responsibility through informed and active participation of citizens in government and to act on selected governmental issues. We promote and support management, preservation, and conservation of our natural resources.
Publication(s): Iowa Voter, Legislative Newsletter
Keyword(s): Air Quality/Atmosphere, Energy, Land Issues, Pollution (general), Reduce/Reuse/Recycle, Water Habitats & Quality
Contact(s):
Jan McNelly, President
Cheryl Kieffer, Vice President
Judie Hoffman, Environmental Coordinator; 515-292-2660

LEAGUE OF WOMEN VOTERS OF THE U.S.

1730 M St., NW
Washington, DC 20036 United States
Phone: 202-429-1965 Fax: 202-429-0854
E-mail: lwv@lwv.org
Website: www.lwv.org

Founded: 1920
Scope: National
Description: Nonpartisan organization of 100,000 members located in all 50 states, the District of Columbia, Hong Kong, and the Virgin Islands, working to promote political responsibility through informed and active participation of citizens in government. Takes political action on water and air quality, solid and hazardous waste management, land use, and energy. The League of Women Voters Education Fund carries out educational projects, publishes materials, and arranges conferences on water and energy issue
Publication(s): National Voter, The
Keyword(s): Energy
Contact(s):
Carolyn Jenkins, President
Nancy Tate, Executive Director
Bob Adams, Editor

LEAGUE OF WOMEN VOTERS OF WASHINGTON

4710 University Way NE
#214
Seattle, WA 98105 United States
Phone: 206-622-8961 Fax: 206-622-4908
E-mail: lwvwa@lwvwa.org
Website: www.lwvwa.org

Founded: 1920
Membership: 1,001–10,000
Scope: State
Description: The League of Women Voters is a nonpartisan political organization that encourages the informed and active participation of citizens in government and influences public policy through education and advocacy. Any citizen over 18 may become a voting member.
Publication(s): The State We're In: Washington, Gun Control in Washington, Higher Education in Washington State, Public Assistance as Social Policy, Washington State Public Port Districts, Speaking of Ground Water, Washington's Dynamic Forest 1&2, Evaluation of Major Election Methods & Selected Laws
Keyword(s): Climate Change, Energy, Forests/Forestry, Land Issues, Public Lands/Greenspace, Transportation, Water Habitats & Quality
Contact(s):
Judy Hedden, President; 206-622-8961; Fax: 206-622-4908; lwvwa@lwvwa.org
Elizabeth Davis, Second Vice President
Jean Wells, First Vice President
Betsy Greene, Secretary
Myra Howrey, Treasurer

LEAGUE TO SAVE LAKE TAHOE

955 Emerald Bay Rd.
South Lake Tahoe, CA 96150 United States
Phone: 530-541-5388 Fax: 530-541-5454
E-mail: info@keeptahoeblue.org
Website: www.keeptahoeblue.org

Founded: 1957
Membership: 1,001–10,000
Scope: Regional
Description: A private, nonprofit corporation dedicated to preserving the environmental balance, scenic beauty, and recreational opportunities of the Lake Tahoe Basin.
Publication(s): Keep Tahoe Blue
Keyword(s): Ecosystems (precious), Forests/Forestry, Land Issues, Public Lands/Greenspace, Recreation/Ecotourism, Sprawl/Urban Planning, Transportation, Water Habitats & Quality, Wildlife & Species
Contact(s):
Rochelle Nason, Executive Director

LEARNING FOR ENVIRONMENTAL ACTION PROGRAMME (LEAP)

University of Victoria, Faculty of Education
MacLaurin Building
Victoria, V8W 3N4 British Columbia Canada
Phone: 250-721-7784 Fax: 250-721-6190
E-mail: clover@uvic.ca

Founded: 1990
Scope: International
Description: Book by LEAP: The Nature of Transformation: Environmental Adult Education. The book contains theory but also more than 50 hands-on activities that stimulate critical and creative thinking, teach about place, weave environmental, cultural, economic, political and social issues, and examine a diversity of local and global issues. To purchase a copy make cheque or money order payable to Darlene E. Clover and post to her at the University of Victoria.
Publication(s): Convergence on Environmental Adult Education, 2000, The Nature of Transformation: Environmental Adult Education, second ediition
Keyword(s): Ethics/Environmental Justice, Reduce/Reuse/Recycle
Contact(s):
Darlene Clover, International Coordinator; 250-721-7785; Fax: 250-721-6190; clover@uvic.ca

LEGACY INTERNATIONAL

GLOBAL YOUTH VILLAGE
1020 Legacy Drive
Bedford, VA 24523 United States
Phone: 540-297-5982 Fax: 540-297-1860
E-mail: mail@legacyintl.org
Website: www.legacyintl.org

Founded: 1979
Membership: 1,001–10,000
Scope: Local, National, International
Description: Mission: Creating environments to address

community & global needs while developing effective responses to change. The Global Youth Village challenges teens to turn cross-cultural theory into action while living with others from 20+ cultures. Workshops address issues concerning youth: prejudice, conflict, & more. Cooperative living help participants respect differences & discover similarities that transcend cultural, religious & political barriers. (Summer staff openings - visit website.)

Publication(s): Organization Brochure, Global Youth Village

Keyword(s): Development/Developing Countries

Contact(s):

Mary Helmig, Director; 1020 Legacy Drive, Bedford, VA 24523; 703-297-5982

LEGACY LAND TRUST

236 Linden Street
Fort Collins, CO 80524 United States
Phone: 970-266-1711 Fax: 970-407-1356
E-mail: llt@frii.com
Website: www.legacylandtrust.org

Founded: 1993

Membership: 101–1,000

Scope: Regional

Description: We are a regional land trust serving northern Colorado. Working with private landowners and local governments, we have helped protect over 11,000 acres of natural areas, agricultural lands, and open space.

Keyword(s): Agriculture/Farming, Ecosystems (precious), Forests/Forestry, Land Issues

LEGAL ENVIRONMENTAL ASSISTANCE FOUNDATION INC. (LEAF)

1114 Thomasville Rd., Suite E
Tallahassee, FL 32303-6290 United States
Phone: 850-681-2591 Fax: 850-224-1275
Website: www.leaf-envirolaw.org

Founded: 1979

Scope: Regional

Description: LEAF is a charitable public-interest environmental law firm that protects human health from pollution. We provide legal and technical assistance to citizens and grassroots organizations in Florida, Georgia, and Alabama. LEAF is a membership organization and provides assistance and services free of charge.

Publication(s): LEAF BRIEFS quarterly newsletter, various educational documents.

Keyword(s): Energy, Ethics/Environmental Justice, Oceans/Coasts/Beaches, Pollution (general), Water Habitats & Quality

Contact(s):

B. Ruhl, President
Larry Thompson, Vice President; lthompson@leaf-enviro-law.org
Cynthia Valencic, Vice President; cvalencic@leaf-enviro-law.org
Aliki Moncrief, Staff Attorney; amoncrief@leaf-enviro-law.org
Jeanne Zokovitch, Staff Attorney; jzokovitch@leaf-enviro-law.org
David Ludder, General Counsel; dludder@leaf-enviro-law.org
Jim Presswood, Energy Program; jpresswood@leaf-enviro-law.org
Deb Swim, Energy Program Attorney; dswim@leaf-enviro-law.org

LIFE OF THE LAND

76 North King St., Suite 203
Honolulu, HI 96817 United States
Phone: 808-533-3454 Fax: 808-533-0993
E-mail: life_of_the_land@hotmail.com
Website: www.lifeoftheland.orf

Founded: 1970

Membership: 101–1,000

Scope: Local, State

Description: To preserve and protect the life of the land through sustainable land use and energy policies and to promote open government through research, education, advocacy and, when necessary, litigation.

Publication(s): Ka Uila News, Life of the Land Newsletter

Keyword(s): Agriculture/Farming, Air Quality/Atmosphere, Climate Change, Ecosystems (precious), Energy, Ethics/Environmental Justice, Executive/Legislative/Judicial Reform, Forests/Forestry, Land Issues, Oceans/Coasts/Beaches, Pollution (general), Recreation/Ecotourism

Contact(s):

Kapua Sproat, President
Kat Brady, Asst. Executive Director; 808-533-3454; katbrady@hotmail.com
Henry Curtis, Executive Director; 808-533-3454; life_of_the_land@hotmail.com

LIGHTHAWK

P.O. Box 653
Lander, WY 82520 United States
Phone: 307-332-3242 Fax: 307-332-1641
E-mail: info@lighthawk.org
Website: www.lighthawk.org

Founded: 1979

Scope: International

Description: LightHawk's Mission is to champion environmental protection utilizing the unique perspective of flight. LightHawk's all-volunteer pilot corps conducts aerial missions with key decision-makers, media representatives, community leaders and conservation groups, illuminating critical environmental concerns by flying over and into lands otherwise inaccessible. LightHawk operates regional programs in the Pacific Northwest, British Columbia, California, the Rocky Mountains, and Mesoamerica

Publication(s): Lighthawk Newsletter

Keyword(s): Forests/Forestry, Land Issues, Oceans/Coasts/Beaches, Reduce/Reuse/Recycle, Water Habitats & Quality, Wildlife & Species

Contact(s):

Michael Azeez, President
Marty Fujita, Executive Director
Patricia Farrar, Treasurer
Blaine Townsend, Secretary

LIGHTHAWK

NORTHERN ROCKY MOUNTAIN FIELD OFFICE
31845 Frontage Rd.
Bozeman, MT 59715 United States
Phone: 406-586-8572 Fax: 406-585-7835
E-mail: sarahd@lighthawk.org

Founded: N/A

Scope: Regional

Contact(s):

Sarah Deopscine, Program Coordinator

LIGHTHAWK

NORTHWEST FIELD OFFICE
2915 E. Madison St., Suite 306
Seattle, WA 98112 United States
Phone: 360-344-3550 Fax: 360-301-4253
E-mail: susen@lighthawk.org
Website: www.lighthawk.org

Founded: N/A

Scope: Regional

Contact(s):

Susen Seth, Program Manager; susen@lighthawk.org

LIGHTHAWK

SOUTHERN ROCKY MOUNTAIN FIELD OFFICE
404 Hutton Avenue
Rifle, CO 81650 United States
Phone: 970-625-8809
E-mail: micheleg@lighthawk.org
Website: www.lighthawk.org

Founded: 1979
Membership: 101–1,000
Scope: International
Description: LightHawk mission is to; "Champion environmental protection utilizing the unique perspective of flight."

LITTLE JUNIATA RIVER CHAPTER

(LJRC)
RD5 Box 210B
Tyrone, PA 16686 United States
Phone: 814-684-4274
E-mail: webmaster@littlejuniata.org
Website: www.littlejuniata.org

Founded: 2002
Membership: 1–100
Scope: Local
Description: Working to promote fly fishing, watershed restoration and conservation in Central Pennsylvania through educational programs and volunteer activities.

LIVING RIVERS

UTAH OFFICE
ARIZONA OFFICE
GLEN CANYON ACTION NETWORK
P.O. Box 466
21 North Main Street
Moab, UT 84532 United States
Phone: 435-259-1063 Fax: 435-259-7612
E-mail: info@livingrivers.net
Website: www.livingrivers.net

Founded: 2000
Scope: Local, State, Regional, National, International
Description: Living Rivers promotes large-scale river restoration through broad-based mobilization. People putting rivers first, reviving their natural habitat and spirit by undoing the extensive damage brought on by dams, diversions, and unmitigated pollution. Whether investigation, litigation or demonstration, Living Rivers is on the front lines articulating the conservation and alternative management strategies necessary to bring rivers back to life.
Publication(s): Living Rivers Currents
Keyword(s): Agriculture/Farming, Ecosystems (precious), Energy, Ethics/Environmental Justice, Executive/Legislative/Judicial Reform, Forests/Forestry, Land Issues, Oceans/Coasts/Beaches, Public Health, Public Lands/Greenspace, Recreation/Ecotourism, Water Habitats
Contact(s):
Lisa Force, Program Director; P.O. Box 1589, Scottsdale, AZ 85252; 480-990-7839; Fax: 480-990-2662; lforce@livingrivers.net
Owen Lammers, Executive Director; 435-259-1063; Fax: 435-259-7612; owen@livingrivers.net
David Orr, Director of Field Programs; 435-259-1063; Fax: 435-259-7612; david@livingrivers.net
John Weisheit, Conservation Director; 435-259-1063; Fax: 435-259-7612; john@livingrivers.net

LONG LIVE THE KINGS

1305 4th Ave.Suite 810
Woodinville, WA 98101 United States
Phone: 206-382-9555
Website: www.longlivethekings.org/home.html

Founded: 1985
Scope: Regional
Description: To rebuild wild salmon populations in specific Northwest Rivers and to enhance their habitat. We are supported by foundations, corporations, individuals, Indian tribes, and fishing and environmental organizations. We are not a membership group.
Publication(s): Long Live the Kings Newsletter
Keyword(s): Water Habitats & Quality, Wildlife & Species
Contact(s):
John Sayre, Executive Director
Jim Youngren, Chairman of the Board

LOS ANGELES AND SAN GABRIEL RIVERS WATERSHED COUNCIL, THE

111 North Hope Street, Suite 627
Los Angeles, CA 90012 United States
Phone: 213-367-4111 Fax: 213-367-4138
E-mail: info@lasgrwc.org
Website: www.lasgrwc.org

Founded: 1996
Membership: 1,001–10,000
Scope: Local, Regional
Description: The Watershed Council is an organization of community groups, government agencies, business and academia working cooperatively to solve problems in the watershed.
Publication(s): Beneficial Uses of the LA & San Gabriel, Stormwater: Asset Not Liability, WatershedWise

LOUISIANA ASSOCIATION OF CONSERVATION DISTRICTS

Attn: President, 663 Holmes Rd.
Keatchie, LA 71046 United States
Phone: 318-933-5375

Founded: N/A
Scope: State
Contact(s):
Jerry Holmes, President; 663 Holmes Rd., Keatchie, LA 71046; 318-933-5375; Fax: 318-872-3178
John Woodward, Vice President, Board Member; 1902 Savanne Rd., Houma, LA 70360; 504-879-3528; Fax: 504-876-5267
John Compton, Board Member; 6267 Moss Side Ln., Baton Rouge, LA 70808; 225-766-7979
Charles Dupuy, Secretary/Treasurer and Board Member; 313 N. Monroe St, Ste. #4, Marksville, LA 71351; 318-253-7603; Fax: 318-253-8890

LOUISIANA B.A.S.S. CHAPTER FEDERATION

Attn: President, 603 Terri Dr.
Luling, LA 70070 United States
Phone: 504-785-9069
E-mail: kevgobear@aol.com

Founded: N/A
Scope: State
Description: An organization of Bassmaster chapters, affiliated with the Bass Anglers Sportsman Society, organized to fight pollution, assist state and national conservation agencies in their efforts, and teach the young people of our country good conservation practices. Dedicated to the realistic conservation of our water resources.
Contact(s):
Kevin Gaubert, President; 504-785-9069
Will Courtney, Conservation Director; 4548 Chelsea Dr., Baton Rouge, LA 70809; 225-923-1908

LOUISIANA FORESTRY ASSOCIATION

P.O. Drawer 5067
Alexandria, LA 71307 United States
Phone: 318-443-2558 Fax: 318-443-1713
E-mail: lfa@laforestry.com
Website: www.laforestry.com

Founded: 1947
Membership: 1,001–10,000
Scope: State
Description: Non-profit trade association whose mission is to promote the health and productivity of Louisiana's forests for present and future generations through the practice of sustainable forestry.
Publication(s): Forests and People, Louisana Logger
Keyword(s): Forests/Forestry
Contact(s):
Charles Vandersteen, Executive Director
Clyde Todd, Staff Forester

LOUISIANA WILDLIFE FEDERATION, INC.

P.O. Box 65239
Baton Rouge, LA 70896-5239 United States
Phone: 225-344-6762 Fax: 225-344-6707
E-mail: lawildfed@aol.com

Founded: 1940
Membership: 10,001–100,000
Scope: State
Description: A representative statewide organization, affiliated with the National Wildlife Federation, dedicated to the protection and enhancement of wildlife and its habitat through public education and government interaction.
Publication(s): Louisiana Wildlife Federation magazine
Keyword(s): Oceans/Coasts/Beaches, Recreation/Ecotourism, Water Habitats & Quality, Wildlife & Species
Contact(s):
Randy Lanctot, Executive Director and Editor; 225-344-6762; Fax: 225-344-6707; lawildfed@aol.com
Jodie Singer, Office Manager; 225-344-6762; Fax: 225-344-6707

LOWER MISSISSIPPI RIVER CONSERVATION COMMITTEE

2524 S. Frontage Rd., Suite C
Vicksburg, MS 39180-5269 United States
Phone: 601-629-6602 Fax: 601-636-9541
Website: www.lmrcc.org

Founded: N/A
Scope: Regional
Description: The Committee provides an organizational structure and forum for coordinating and facilitating cooperative activities involving the natural resources of the Lower Mississippi River. Also encourages sustainable use of Lower Mississippi River natural resources for long-term environmental, social, and economic benefits.
Publication(s): LMRCC Newsletter, The
Keyword(s): Land Issues, Water Habitats & Quality, Wildlife & Species
Contact(s):
Ron Nassar, Coordinator; 2524 S. Frontage Rd., Ste. C, Vicksburg, MS 39180-5269; 601-629-6602
Dugan Sabins, Chairman; P.O. Box 82178, Baton Rouge, LA 70884; 225-765-0246; Fax: 225-765-0617; dugans@deq.state.la.us

LVIV REGIONAL INSTITUTE OF EDUCATION

18A Ohiyenko St.
Lviv, 79007 Ukraine
Phone: 3.8032272475e+011 Fax:3.8032272807e+011
E-mail: lonmio@lonmio.lviv.ua

Founded: 1992
Scope: Regional
Description: Provides updated scientific and methodological information on different disciplines to the schools of Lviv region as well as postgraduate training for school teachers.
Keyword(s): Ethics/Environmental Justice, Water Habitats & Quality
Contact(s):
Oleh Harasewych, Senior Researcher; oharasew@lonmio.lviv.ua

M

MACBRIDE RAPTOR PROJECT

W.H., KCC, 6301 Kirkwood Blvd., SW
Cedar Rapids, IA 52406 United States
Phone: 319-398-5495 Fax: 319-398-5611
E-mail: iaraptor@avalon.net
Website: www.ai-design.com/stargig/raptor/ai/main.html

Founded: 1985
Membership: 101–1,000
Scope: State
Description: The Macbride Raptor Project is devoted to the preservation of Iowa's birds of prey and their natural habitats through rehabilitation of sick or injured raptors, education of the public to the role of raptors in our environment, and research on various aspects of raptor biology.
Publication(s): Raptor Review
Keyword(s): Wildlife & Species
Contact(s):
Jodeane Cancilla, Director
Eric Burrough, Veterinarian; 319-398-4979
Gail Dawson, Assistant Director; 319-398-5495
Mary Ebert, Veterinarian; 319-398-5495

MACOMB LAND CONSERVANCY

P.O. Box 332
Romeo, MI 48065 United States
Phone: 5867845848 Fax: 5867845848
E-mail: info@savingplaces.org
Website: www.savingplaces.org

Founded: 2000
Membership: 101–1,000
Scope: Local, Regional
Description: A public land trust dedicated to the preservation of forests, wetlands, wildlife habitats, farmland, rivers and streams of Macomb County
Keyword(s): Agriculture/Farming, Ecosystems (precious), Forests/Forestry, Land Issues, Oceans/Coasts/Beaches, Public Health, Public Lands/Greenspace, Sprawl/Urban Planning, Water Habitats & Quality, Wildlife & Species

MAGIC

P.O. Box 15894
Stanford, CA 94309 United States
Phone: 650-323-7333 Fax: 650-323-4233
E-mail: magic@ecomagic.org
Website: www.ecomagic.org

Founded: 1979
Scope: Regional
Description: Magic's programs apply methods and principles of ecology to clarify values, improve health, increase cooperation, and steward the environment. Activities include lectures and seminars about the nature of value; life-planning workshops, swim, run, and hatha yoga instruction; mentoring, community organizing, habitat enhancement, water and land, resource planning; neighborhood design and publishing.
Publication(s): Human Ecology, A Science for Living Well, Oak Regeneration on Stanford Lands, Liveable City
Keyword(s): Public Health, Reduce/Reuse/Recycle

Contact(s):
Robin Bayer, President; robin@ecomagic.org
David Schrom, Treasurer; david@ecomagic.org

MAINE ASSOCIATION OF CONSERVATION COMMISSIONS (MACC)

P.O. Box 702
Bath, ME 04330 United States
Phone: 207-443-2925 Fax: 207-443-6913
E-mail: macc@clinic.net

Founded: 1969
Membership: 1–100
Scope: State
Description: A membership organization whose objectives are twofold: to assist Maine municipalities in establishing conservation commissions; to assist the existing 200+ conservation commissions through technical assistance and educational programs.
Publication(s): Grass Roots
Keyword(s): Reduce/Reuse/Recycle
Contact(s):
Mike Cline, President
Bob Cummings, Executive Director

MAINE ASSOCIATION OF CONSERVATION DISTRICTS

Attn: President, 2467 Exeter Rd.
Exeter, ME 04435-3107 United States
Phone: 207-622-7589

Founded: N/A
Scope: State
Contact(s):
Neil Crane, President, Alternate Board Member; 207-379-2641; Fax: 207-379-2644
John Hemond, President; 46 N. Verreill Rd., Minot, ME 04258; 207-345-5333
Bruce Roope, Vice President
William Bell, Executive Director; P.O. Box 228, Augusta, ME 04330; 207-622-4443; Fax: 207-623-3748; newengag@mint.net
Fred Hardy, Treasurer; 879 Weeks Mill Rd., New Sharon, ME 04955; 207-778-4320
Raymond Harris, Board Member; Rt. 1 Box 8396, Washburn, ME 04786; 207-764-3217
Larry Macdonald, Secretary; Box 1187, Greenville, ME 04441; 207-695-2639

MAINE B.A.S.S. CHAPTER FEDERATION

Heath Morris
15 Blue Rock Road Lot 12
Monmouth, ME 04259 United States
Phone: 207-933-5978

Founded: N/A
Membership: 101–1,000
Scope: State
Description: An organization of Bassmaster chapters, affiliated with the Bass Anglers Sportsman Society, organized to fight pollution, assist state and national conservation agencies in their efforts, and teach young people of our country good conservation practices. Dedicated to the realistic conservation of our water resources.
Publication(s): Federation Guide
Contact(s):
Norm Moulton, President; 207-266-6914

MAINE COAST HERITAGE TRUST

1 Main St.
Topsham, ME 04086 United States
Phone: 207-729-7366 Fax: 207-729-6863
E-mail: info@mcht.org
Website: www.mcht.org

Founded: 1970
Membership: 1–100
Scope: State
Description: To protect land that is essential to the character of Maine, in particular its coastline and islands. Provides free advisory services on open-space protection to landowners, town officials, state and federal agencies, land trusts, and other private conservation organizations.
Publication(s): Technical Bulletins, Maine Heritage, Annual Report, Conservation Options, A Guide for Maine Landowners, Directory of Maine Land Conservation Trusts
Keyword(s): Land Issues, Oceans/Coasts/Beaches, Public Lands/Greenspace
Contact(s):
James Espy, President; jespy.mcht.org
Chris Hamilton, Editor; chamiltion@mcht.org
John Robinson, Treasurer
Harold Woodsum, Chairman

MAINE ENVIRONMENTAL EDUCATION ASSOCIATION

485 Chewonki Neck Rd.
Wiscasset, ME 04578 United States
Phone: 207-882-7323 Fax: 207-882-4074

Founded: 1981
Membership: 101–1,000
Scope: State
Description: The Maine Environmental Education Association (MEEA) facilitates and promotes environmental education in Maine through the sharing of ideas, resources, information and cooperative programs among educators, organizations and concerned individuals. MEEA offers a newsletter, annual conference, Environmental Educator of the Year award and Teacher Mine Grants.
Publication(s): New England Journal of Environmental Education, Connections
Contact(s):
Dot Lamson, President; 207-882-7323; dlamson@chewonki.org

MANASOTA-88

P.O. Box 14119
Bradenton, FL 34280 United States
Phone: 941-966-6256

Founded: 1968
Scope: State
Keyword(s): Energy, Pollution (general), Wildlife & Species
Contact(s):
Rebecca Eger, Director; 941-366-1765
Laurence Quy, Director; 1619 Palma Sola Blvd., Bradenton, FL 34209; 941-792-5509
Glenn Compton, Editor
Glenn Compton, Chairman; 419 Reubens Drive, Nokomis, FL 34275; 941-966-6256

MANITOBA NATURALISTS SOCIETY

401-63 Albert St.
Winnipeg, R3B 1G4 Manitoba Canada
Phone: 204-943-9029 Fax: 204-943-9029
E-mail: mns@escape.ca
Website: www.manitobanature.ca

Founded: 1920
Membership: 1,001–10,000
Scope: Regional
Description: Fosters an awareness and appreciation of the natural environment and an understanding of humanity's place therein; and sponsors lectures, workshops, field trips on natural history topics, and recreational outings that are environmentally friendly.
Publication(s): The Wild Plants of the Great Plains, The Wild Plants of Birds Hill Park, Wings Along Winnipeg, The Birds of

Southeastern Manitoba, Bulletin, Manitoba's Tall Grass Prairie
Keyword(s): Recreation/Ecotourism
Contact(s):
Larry De March, President; 204-943-9029
Gordon Fardoe, Executive Director; 204-943-9029

MANITOBA WILDLIFE FEDERATION

70 Stevenson Rd.
Winnipeg, R3H 0W7 Manitoba Canada
Phone: 204-633-5967 Fax: 204-632-5200
E-mail: mwf@mb.sympatico.ca
Website: www.mwf.mb.ca

Founded: 1944
Scope: State
Description: Promotes conservation, safety, and good sportsmanship. Manages the Habitat Trust Fund which secures critical land to ensure habitat for wildlife. Protects the interests of anglers and hunters.
Publication(s): Wildlife Crusader/Outdoor Edge
Contact(s):
Lloyd Lintott, President
Darlene Garnham, Secretary
Randy Walker, Past President

MANOMET CENTER FOR CONSERVATION SCIENCES

P.O. Box 1770
Manomet, MA 02345-1770 United States
Phone: 508-224-6521 Fax: 508-224-9220
E-mail: info@manomet.org
Website: www.manomet.org

Founded: 1969
Scope: International
Description: Manomet is a non-profit conservation research institute dedicated to promoting informed conservation policy and natural resource management through applied research. At study sites throughout the Americas, Manomet scientists and volunteers monitor migrant songbird and shorebird populations, identify critical wetlands habitats, design fisheries conservation and management strategies, and develop plans for sustainable management of temperate and tropical forest ecosystems.
Publication(s): Various articles and books, Conservation Sciences
Keyword(s): Forests/Forestry, Land Issues, Oceans/Coasts/Beaches, Pollution (general), Wildlife & Species
Contact(s):
Linda Leddy, President and Director; lleddy@manomet.org
Jennie Robbins, Office Manager; jrobbins@manomet.org
Jeptha Wade, Chair

MANTA MEXICO

105 Rose Ave
Venice, CA 90291 United States
Phone: 310-314-6875
E-mail: paul@mantamexico.org
Website: www.mantamexico.org

Founded: 2001
Membership: N/A
Scope: Regional
Description: Research, public education leading to greater understanding and conservation of the Giant Manta Ray in the Sea of Cortez, Mexico
Publication(s): Manta Mexico Photo catalog
Keyword(s): Ecosystems (precious), Oceans/Coasts/Beaches, Pollution (general), Recreation/Ecotourism, Wildlife & Species

MARIE SELBY BOTANICAL GARDENS, THE

811 South Palm Ave.
Sarasota, FL 34236-7726 United States
Phone: 941-366-5731 Fax: 941-366-9807
E-mail: contactus@selby.org
Website: www.selby.org

Founded: 1975
Membership: 1,001–10,000
Scope: International
Description: A 13-acre bayfront botanical garden whose mission is to passionately pursue knowledge about tropical plants and their habitats and apply that expertise to advance their conservation and display.
Publication(s): Selbyana Bulletin-Newsletter, Selbyana-Journal
Contact(s):
Margaret Lowman, Executive Director; mlowman@selby.org
Wesley Higgins, Director, Systematics; whiggins@selby.org
Bruce Holst, Director, Plant Collections; bholst@selby.org
Harry Luther, Director, Bromeliad Identification Center; hluther@selby.org
H. Bruce Rinker, Director of Canopy Ecology; brinker@selby.org
John Beckner, Curator, Orchid Identification Center; jbeckner@selby.org
Barry Walsh, Staff Editor; 941-955-7553, ext. 10; bwalsh@selby.org

MARIN CONSERVATION LEAGUE

1623A Fifth Avenue
San Rafael, CA 94901 United States
Phone: 415-485-6257 Fax: 415-485-1409
E-mail: mcl@conservationleague.org
Website: www.conservationleague.org

Founded: 1934
Scope: State
Description: The Marin Conservation League has worked to preserve and protect the natural assets of Marin County. The league works on all issues affecting the county environment, seeking partnerships with diverse groups to influence public policy and educate citizens and decisionmakers in understanding critical issues and options.
Publication(s): MCL News
Keyword(s): Agriculture/Farming, Land Issues, Public Lands/Greenspace
Contact(s):
Kathy Lowrey, President
Jana Haehl, 1st Vice President
Charles McGlashan, 2nd Vice President
Kenneth Drexler, Treasurer
Tim Duane, Secretary

MARINE CONSERVATION BIOLOGY INSTITUTE

15806 NE 47th Ct.
Redmond, WA 98052-5208 United States
Phone: 425-883-8914 Fax: 425-883-3017
Website: www.mcbi.org

Founded: 1996
Membership: 1–100
Scope: National
Description: MCBI is a nonprofit, non-partisan, tax-exampt organization dedicated to advancing the multidisciplinary science of marine conservation biology. MCBI helps scientists to generate information that arms people with knowledge crucial for informed decision-making.
Keyword(s): Oceans/Coasts/Beaches, Wildlife & Species
Contact(s):
Elliott Norse, President; 425-883-8914; elliott@mcbi.org
William Chandler, Vice President; 702-465-5959; bill@mcbi.org

MARINE ENVIRONMENTAL RESEARCH INSTITUTE (MERI)

772 W. End Ave.
New York, NY 10025 United States
Phone: 212-864-6285 Fax: 212-864-1470
E-mail: meri@downeast.net
Website: www.merireserch.org

Founded: 1990
Membership: 101–1,000
Scope: National
Description: MERI is a nonprofit organization dedicated to protecting the health and biodiversity of the marine environment. MERI's programs are international in scope and include direct field research, environmental and conservation education, training, and collaboration with the world's scientific community. MERI strives to address the problems of global marine pollution, endangered species and habitat degradation, and environmental emergencies affecting marine life.
Publication(s): MERI News, research publications, MERI Resource Center News
Keyword(s): Wildlife & Species
Contact(s):
Susan Shaw, President; P.O. Box 179, Brooklin, ME 04616
Suzanne Hopkins, Vice President; 15200 Old York Road, Monkton, MD 21111
Elizabeth Petterson, Resource Center Director; MERI Resource Center, Main St., P.O. Box 300, Brooklin, ME 04616; 207-359-8078; Fax: 207-359-8079; meri@downeast.net
Lemuel Evans, Chairman; 3536 Paintwater Pl., Las Vegas, NV 89129-7338
Joan Koven, Secretary; Astrolabe Inc., 4812 V St. NW, Washington, DC 20007
Pamela Stacey, Treasurer

MARINE FISH CONSERVATION NETWORK

660 Pennsylvania Ave., SE, Suite 302B
Washington, DC 20003 United States
Phone: 202-543-5509 Fax: 204-543-5774
E-mail: network@conservefish.org
Website: www.conservefish.org

Founded: N/A
Membership: 101–1,000
Scope: National
Description: The Marine Fish Conservation Network is a coalition of national and regional environmental organizations, commerical and recreational fishing associations, aquariums, and marine science groups dedicated to promoting the long-term sustainability of marine fisheries.
Publication(s): Network News
Keyword(s): Ecosystems (precious), Oceans/Coasts/Beaches, Water Habitats & Quality, Wildlife & Species
Contact(s):
Lee Crockett, Executive Director

MARINE MAMMAL CENTER, THE

Marin Headlands
1065 Fort Cronkhite
Sausalito, CA 94965 United States
Phone: 415-289-7325 Fax: 415-289-7333
E-mail: com@tmmc.org
Website: www.marinemammalcenter.org

Founded: 1975
Membership: 10,001–100,000
Scope: Local, State, National, International
Description: The Marine Mammal Center is a nonprofit organization dedicated to the rescue and rehabilitation of sick, injured, and orphaned marine mammals that strand along 600 miles of northern and central California coast. Information derived from routine medical treatment is shared with scientists worldwide. Through education and communication programs, the Center promotes public awareness of the ocean environment among over 100,000 visitors annually.
Publication(s): Release, various scientific papers., Annual Report
Keyword(s): Oceans/Coasts/Beaches
Contact(s):
B.J. Griffin, Executive Director
Dennis Di Domenico, Chairman of the Board
Sheldon Wolfe, Treasurer

MARINE SCIENCE INSTITUTE

500 Discovery Parkway
Redwood City, CA 94063 United States
Phone: 650-364-2760 Fax: 650-364-0416
E-mail: info@sfbaymsi.org
Website: www.sfbaymsi.org

Founded: 1970
Membership: 101–1,000
Scope: Local, State, Regional
Description: The Marine Science Institute is a non-profit organization that provides interdisciplinary science programs, using a marine biology theme, to help students develop a responsibility for the natural environment and our human communities.
Keyword(s): Oceans/Coasts/Beaches, Recreation/Ecotourism, Water Habitats & Quality, Wildlife & Species
Contact(s):
Jeff Rutherford, President; 650-364-2760, ext. 13; Fax: 650-364-0416; Jeff@sfbaymsi.org

MARINE TECHNOLOGY SOCIETY

5565 Sterrett Place
Suite 108
Columbia, MD 21044 United States
Phone: 410-884-5330 Fax: 410-884-9060
E-mail: mtspubs@aol.com
Website: www.mtsociety.org

Founded: 1963
Scope: International
Description: An ocean-oriented, multidisciplinary, international professional society, formed to encourage the development of the technology, education, operational expertise, and public awareness needed to advance man's capability to work effectively in all ocean areas and depths.
Publication(s): Marine Technology Society Journal, various proceedings, MTS Newsletter Currents
Keyword(s): Oceans/Coasts/Beaches
Contact(s):
Judith Krauthamer, Executive Director

MARYLAND ASSOCIATION OF CONSERVATION DISTRICTS

53 Slama Rd
Edgewater, MD 21037 United States
Phone: 410-956-5771 Fax: 410-956-0161

Founded: N/A
Membership: 1–100
Scope: Local
Contact(s):
Robert Wilson, President and Alternative Board Member
Robert Fitzgerald, Vice President; 27570 Fitzgerald Rd., Princess Anne, MD 21853; 410-651-3701
Lynne Hoot, Executive Director; 53 Slama Rd., Edgewater, MD 21037; 410-956-5771; Fax: 410-956-0161
Sharon Mariaca, Secretary
Donald Spickler, Treasurer and Council Member; 14854 Hicksville Rd., Clear Spring, MD 21722; 301-842-2534; Fax: 301-842-2534; dspick@erols.com

MARYLAND ASSOCIATION OF SOIL CONSERVATION DISTRICTS (MASCD)

53 Slama Road
Edgewater, MD 21037 United States
Phone: 410-956-5771 Fax: 410-956-0161
E-mail: lynnehoot@aol.com

Founded: N/A

Scope: State

Description: The mission of MASCD is to promote practical and effective soil, water, and related natural resource programs to all citizens through individual conservation districts on a voluntary basis through leadership, education, cooperation, and local direction.

Keyword(s): Agriculture/Farming

MARYLAND B.A.S.S. CHAPTER FEDERATION

Attn: President, 1106 West Washington St.
Hagerstown, MD 21740 United States
Phone: 301-791-3724
Website: www.mdbass.com

Founded: N/A

Scope: State

Description: An organization of Bassmaster chapters, affiliated with the Bass Anglers Sportsman Society, organized to fight pollution, assist state and national conservation agencies in their efforts, and teach the young people of our country good conservation practices. Dedicated to the realistic conservation of our water resources.

Publication(s): Maryland State Federation Update

Contact(s):
- Jim Kline, Conservation Rep. - Western; 301-791-3724
- Ken Penrod, Conservation Director; 4708 Sellman Rd, Beltsville, MD 20705; 301-937-0010

MARYLAND FORESTS ASSOCIATION

P.O. Box 599
Grantsville, MD 21536 United States
Phone: 301-895-5369 Fax: 301-895-5369
E-mail: mfa@hereintown.net
Website: www.mdforests.org

Founded: N/A

Membership: 101–1,000

Scope: State

Description: A nonprofit 501c (3) citizens organization for people interested in trees, forests, related natural resources, and forestry. To promote the maintenance of a healthy and productive forestland base to enhance the economic, environmental, and social well-being of all who live in the state.

Publication(s): Crosscut, The, MFA Legislative Update

Keyword(s): Forests/Forestry, Reduce/Reuse/Recycle

Contact(s):
- Peter Alexander, President
- Tony Dipaolo, Vice President
- Kevin Simpson, Vice President
- Karin Miller, Executive Director
- Richard Stanfield, Secretary and Treasurer

MARYLAND NATIVE PLANT SOCIETY

P.O. Box 4877
Silver Spring, MD 20914 United States
Phone: 410-286-2928
Website: www.mdflora.org/index.html

Founded: 1990

Scope: State, National

Description: MNPS is a nonprofit organization that uses education, research, and community service to foster awareness and appreciation for Maryland's native flora and habitats, leading to their conservation.

Publication(s): Marilandica (Journal/Newsletter)

Keyword(s): Wildlife & Species

Contact(s):
- Karyn Molinas, President
- Louis Aronica, Vice President; 202-722-1081
- Roderick Simmons, Vice President
- Marc Imlay, Director; 301-283-0808
- Samuel Jones, Secretary; 410-838-7950
- Joseph Metzger Jr., Treasurer

MARYLAND ORNITHOLOGICAL SOCIETY, INC.

Cylburn Mansion, 4915 Greenspring Ave.
Baltimore, MD 21209 United States
Phone: 800-823-0050
Website: www.mdbirds.org

Founded: 1945

Membership: 1,001–10,000

Scope: State

Description: Nonprofit statewide organization of 16 chapters. Aims to promote the knowledge, protection, and conservation of wildlife and natural resources; to foster appreciation of the natural environment; to establish educational and scientific projects to inform and enrich the public; and to record, evaluate, and publish observations of birdlife in Maryland.

Publication(s): Maryland Birdlife, Maryland Yellowthroat, The

Keyword(s): Wildlife & Species

Contact(s):
- Robert Rineer, President; 8326 Philadelphia Rd., Baltimore, MD 21237; 410-391-8499
- Norm Saunders, Vice President; 1261 Cavendish Rd., Colesville, MD 20905; 301-989-9035
- Jeff Metter, Treasurer; 1301 N. Rolling Rd., Catonsville, MD 21228; 410-788-4877
- Chandler Robbins, Editor; Patuxent Wildlife Research Center, Laurel, MD 20811; 301-498-0281
- Sybil Williams, Secretary; 2000 Baltimore Rd. #A24, Rockville, MD 20851; 301-762-0560

MASSACHUSETTS ASSOCIATION OF CONSERVATION COMMISSIONS (MACC)

10 Juniper Rd.
Belmont, MA 02478 United States
Phone: 617-489-3930 Fax: 617-489-3935
E-mail: staff@maccweb.org
Website: www.maccweb.org

Founded: 1961

Membership: 1,001–10,000

Scope: Local, State

Description: Protects wetlands and open space through education and advocacy.

Publication(s): Newsletter of the Association for members of conservation commissions, government agencies, educational institutions, Envir. Handbook for MA Cons. Comm. 2002

Keyword(s): Land Issues, Public Lands/Greenspace, Water Habitats & Quality, Wildlife & Species

Contact(s):
- George Hall, President
- Patrick Garner, V.P. for Advocacy
- Ingeborg Hegemann, President Elect; ingeborg@maccweb.org
- Sally Zielinski, Executive Director; sally@maccweb.org
- Helen Bethell, Treasurer; helen@maccweb.org

MASSACHUSETTS ASSOCIATION OF CONSERVATION DISTRICTS

Attn: President, 25 Shore Rd.
Bourne, MA 02532 United States
Phone: 508-759-4363 Fax: 508-759-4363

Founded: N/A

Scope: State

Contact(s):
Peggy Pacheco, President, Alternate Board Member; 25 Shore Rd., Bourne, MA 02532; 508-759-4363; Fax: 508-759-4363
Ed Himlan, Vice President; P.O. Box 577, Leominister, MA 01453; 978-534-0379; Fax: 978-534-1329
Donald Lambert, Treasurer; 178 Moulton Hill Rd, Monson, MA 01057; 413-267-4837
Anne Merriam, Secretary; 157 State Rd. E, Westminster, MA 01473; 978-874-2432
Thomas Quink, Board Member; 67 Church St., Gilbertville, MA 01031-9864; 413-477-8870; Fax: 413-477-8870

MASSACHUSETTS B.A.S.S. CHAPTER FEDERATION
Attn: President, 15A Bolton St.
Waltham, MA 02453 United States
Phone: 781-647-5288
Website: www.massbass.com

Founded: N/A
Scope: State
Description: An organization of Bassmaster chapters, affiliated with the Bass Anglers Sportsman Society, organized to fight pollution, assist state and national conservation agencies in their efforts, and teach young people of our country good conservation practices. Dedicated to the realistic conservation of our water resources.
Contact(s):
Joe Mckinnon, President; 781-647-5288
Dean Percival, Conservation Director; 396 Green St., Northboro, MA 01532; 508-366-2030; mail@whiznet.com

MASSACHUSETTS FORESTRY ASSOCIATION
P.O. Box 1096
Belchertown, MA 01007-1096 United States
Phone: 413-323-7326 Fax: 413-339-5526
Website: massforests.org

Founded: 1970
Membership: 1,001–10,000
Scope: State
Description: A voluntary nonprofit association, affiliated with the National Woodland Owners Association; dedicated to conservation, stewardship, and advocacy of the forestland of Massachusetts. An educational organization offering information, workshops, conferences, publications, and professional assistance. Begun in 1970 as the Massachusetts Land League, changed to present name in 1986.
Publication(s): Woodland Steward, The
Keyword(s): Forests/Forestry
Contact(s):
Mary Lees, President
Hugh Putnam, Vice President
Gregory Cox, Executive Director, Editor
Tim Fowler, Secretary and Treasurer

MASSACHUSETTS TRAPPERS ASSOCIATION, INC.
741 Pulaski Blvd.
Bellingham, MA 02019 United States
Phone: 508-883-4214

Founded: 1950
Scope: State
Description: Objectives are to develop leadership for the advancement of the interests of the trapper and the fur industry, and to promote sound management for the conservation of furbearing animals.
Publication(s): Fur Ever
Keyword(s): Water Habitats & Quality, Wildlife & Species
Contact(s):
David Black, President; 741 Pulaski Blvd., Bellingham, MA 02019; 508-883-4214
Frederick Frazier, Vice President East; 111 Newport Rd., Hull, MA 02045; 781-925-5841
Debra Benedetto, Treasurer; P.O. Box 60, Wakefield, MA 01880; 781-246-2136
Irene Hayes, Secretary; 155 Williams Rd., Concord, MA 01742; 978-369-5065
Tom Hayes, Public Relations; 155 Williams Rd., Concord, MA 01742; 508-369-5065

MATTS (MID-ATLANTIC TURTLE AND TORTOISE SOCIETY, INC.)
2914 E. Joppa Rd.
Baltimore, MD 21234-3031 United States
Phone: 410-882-2769 Fax: 410-882-0839
Website: matts.herptiles.com/

Founded: 1997
Scope: National
Description: A nonprofit organization dedicated to promoting the study of Mid-Atlantic chelonian natural history, responsible herpetoculture, and conservation of habitat.
Publication(s): Terrapin Tales, The
Keyword(s): Reduce/Reuse/Recycle, Wildlife & Species
Contact(s):
Gregory Pokrywka, President
Brian McLaren, Vice President; 301-384-7444; briancrcc@aol.com
Donald Keefer, Secretary; 410-561-1668; keefercham@aol.com

MAX MCGRAW WILDLIFE FOUNDATION
P.O. Box 9
Dundee, IL 60118 United States
Phone: 847-741-8000 Fax: 847-741-8157
E-mail: info@mcgrawwildlife.org

Founded: 1962
Scope: National
Description: Conducts wildlife and fisheries research and management and conservation education projects; cooperates with other conservation agencies and institutions.
Publication(s): Descriptive brochure, Annual Research Report, Wildlife Management Notes Series
Keyword(s): Land Issues, Public Lands/Greenspace, Recreation/Ecotourism, Wildlife & Species
Contact(s):
John Thompson, Director of Research

MERCK FOREST AND FARMLAND CENTER
P.O. Box 86
Rte. 315
Rupert, VT 05768 United States
Phone: 802-394-7836 Fax: 802-394-2519
E-mail: merck@vermontel.net
Website: www.merckforest.org

Founded: 1950
Membership: 101–1,000
Scope: Local, State
Description: Over 3,100 acres of field, farm, and forest open year-round to the public in the heart of the Taconic range in southwestern Vermont. Outdoor and environmental education experiences for individuals, families, and organized groups. Over 28 miles of trails, 65-acre organic demonstration farm, camping cabins and sites, a solar-powered visitor center and sustainable forestry information.
Publication(s): Ridgeline-newsletter
Keyword(s): Agriculture/Farming, Energy, Forests/Forestry
Contact(s):
Alan Calfee, President
Ken Smith, Director

MICHIGAN ASSOCIATION OF CONSERVATION DISTRICTS

Attn: President, 14302, OP Ave. E.
Climax, MI 49034 United States
Phone: 231-876-0348 Fax: 231-871-0372

Founded: N/A

Scope: State

Contact(s):

Larry Leach, President and Board Member; 616-746-4648; Fax: 616-746-4393
Joe Slater, Vice President; 6780 Brunswick Rd, Holton, MI 49425; 616-821-2843
Marilyn Shy, Executive Director; 101 S. Main P.O. Box 539, Lake City, MI 49651; 616-839-3360; Fax: 616-839-3361; mdistricts@aol.com
Carol Bogard, Administrative Assistant; 101 S. Main, P.O. Box 539, Lake City, MI 49651; 616-839-3360; Fax: 616-839-3361
Rodney Dragicevich, Secretary and Treasurer, Alternate Board Member; 29396 Heritage Lane, Paw Paw, MI 49079; 616-375-3005

MICHIGAN B.A.S.S. CHAPTER FEDERATION

Attn: President, 41970 Jason Drive
Clinton Township, MI 48038 United States
Phone: 810-286-3523 Fax: 810-286-3588
Website: www.michiganbass.org

Founded: 1974

Membership: 101–1,000

Scope: State

Description: An organization of Bassmaster chapters, affiliated with the Bass Anglers Sportsman Society, organized to fight pollution, assist state and national conservation agencies in their efforts, and teach the young people of our country good conservation practice. Dedicated to the realistic conservation of our water resources.

Publication(s): Bass Lines

Contact(s):

Dennis Beltz, President; 810-286-3523
Ron Spitler, Conservation Director; 2710 Browning Dr., Lake Orion, MI 48360; 248-391-4393

MICHIGAN ENVIRONMENTAL COUNCIL

119 Pere Marquette
Ste. 2A
Lansing, MI 48912 United States
Phone: 517-487-9539 Fax: 917-487-9541
E-mail: mec@voyager.net
Website: www.mecprotects.org

Founded: 1980

Membership: N/A

Scope: State

Description: A statewide coalition of more than 50 environmental, public health and faith-based organizations with a collective membership of over 175,000 residents. In addition to serving as a clearinghouse of environmental information, MEC develops public policy, educates state officials and the public, and provides technical assistance and support to member organizations.

Publication(s): Michigan Environmental Report, Groundwater at Risk: A Citizen's Guide, Land: Michigan's Promise, Michigan's Future

Keyword(s): Energy, Land Issues, Pollution (general), Reduce/Reuse/Recycle

Contact(s):

Lana Pollack, President; 517-487-9539
Carol Misseldine, Executive Director
Alice Austin, Vice Chair; 517-663-2400
Elizabeth Harris, Chairman; E. Michigan Environmental Action Council 21220 W. 14 Mile Rd., Bloomfield Township, MI 48301-4000; 313-258-5188
Alison Horton, Vice Chair
Brian Imus, Secretary; 734-662-6597

MICHIGAN FORESTS ASSOCIATION

1558 Barrington St.
Ann Arbor, MI 48103-5603 United States
Phone: 734-665-8279 Fax: 734-913-9167
E-mail: mfa@i-star.com
Website: www.mfa.nu

Founded: 1951

Membership: 101–1,000

Scope: State

Description: A statewide organization affiliated with the National Woodland Owners Association, with concern for the full spectrum of forest activity, enterprise, development, and conservation in Michigan.

Publication(s): Green Gold: Michigan Forrest History, Leaves - Newsletter, Michigan Forests

Keyword(s): Forests/Forestry

Contact(s):

Gordon Terry, President
Collin Burnett, Vice President
McClain Smith, Executive Director
Don Ingle, Editor; P.O. Box 78, Baldwin, MI 49304-0078
Allan Kerton, Treasurer

MICHIGAN LAND USE INSTITUTE

P.O. Box 228
Benzonia, MI 49016 United States
Phone: 231-882-4723 Fax: 213-882-7350
Website: www.mlui.org

Founded: 1995

Membership: 1,001–10,000

Scope: State

Description: Michigan Land Use Institute is a nonprofit environmental economic policy research organization focused on reforming land use policy and curbing sprawl.

Publication(s): Rivers at Risk, Great Lakes Bulletin, Benzie County Wetlands - A Resource Worth Protecting

Contact(s):

Keith Schneider, Program Director
Hans Voss, Executive Director
Richard Hitchingham, Treasurer

MICHIGAN NATURAL AREAS COUNCIL

University of Michigan
Botanical Gardens
1800 N. Dixboro Rd.
Ann Arbor, MI 48105 United States
Phone: 313-461-9390
E-mail: mnac@cyberspace.org
Website: www.cyberspace.org

Founded: 1947

Scope: State

Description: The Michigan Natural Areas Council promotes the preservation of outstanding natural areas, prepares reports based on field investigations, and serves as an informed-citizens advisory on such matters.

Publication(s): Michigan Natural Areas News and Views

Keyword(s): Land Issues, Public Lands/Greenspace, Wildlife & Species

Contact(s):

Christopher Graham, Treasurer; 725 Peninsula Ct., Ann Arbor, MI 48105; kfdh64@prodigy.com
Robert Grese, Editor
Robert Grese, Vice Chair; 1512 Carlton, Ann Arbor, MI 48103; bgrese@umich.edu
Sylvia Taylor, Chair; 10353 Judd Rd., Willis, MI 48191; 313-461-9390; smtaylot@umich.edu

MICHIGAN NATURE ASSOCIATION

326 E. Grand River Ave.
Williamston, MI 48895 United States
Phone: 517-655-5655 Fax: 517-655-5506
E-mail: mna@greatlakes.net

Founded: 1952
Membership: 101–1,000
Scope: State
Description: Purpose is to acquire and maintain nature sanctuaries that contain examples of Michigan's original flora and fauna. Has 160 nature sanctuaries and preserves totaling over 8,000 acres in 54 counties of Michigan. MNA lands contain 206 of Michigan's endangered, threatened, and of special concern species. Available to public for nature education and appreciation.
Publication(s): Members' Newsletter, In Our Trust (1990-91, 30-minute Wildlife Video), Walking Paths in Keweenaw, MNA—In Retrospect, MNA Nature Sanctuary Guidebook 7th edition
Keyword(s): Ecosystems (precious), Ethics/Environmental Justice, Forests/Forestry, Land Issues, Oceans/Coasts/Beaches, Public Lands/Greenspace, Sprawl/Urban Planning, Water Habitats & Quality, Wildlife & Species
Contact(s):
Karen Weingarden, President; 248-546-5429
Jeremy Emmi, Executive Director; 326 E. Grand River Ave., Williamston, MI 48895; 517-655-5655
Bertha Daubendiek, Founder and Trustee; 810-324-2626

MICHIGAN STATE UNIVERSITY

DEPARTMENT OF FISHERIES AND WILDLIFE
EDUCATION SECTION
13 Natural Resources Bldg.
East Lansing, MI 48824 United States
Phone: 517-353-3373 Fax: 517-432-1699
E-mail: WEBMASTER@PERM3.FW.MSU.EDU
Website: www.fw.msu.edu

Founded: N/A
Membership: 1,001–10,000
Scope: State
Publication(s): Publications on website
Contact(s):
Thomas Coon, Dept. Chairperson; coontg@msu.edu

MICHIGAN UNITED CONSERVATION CLUBS, INC.

2101 Wood St.
Lansing, MI 48912-3728 United States
Phone: 517-371-1041 Fax: 517-371-1505
E-mail: mucc@mucc.org
Website: www.mucc.org

Founded: 1937
Membership: 10,001–100,000
Scope: State
Description: A representative statewide organization, affiliated with the National Wildlife Federation, dedicated to the protection and enhancement of wildlife and its habitat through public education and government interaction.
Publication(s): Michingan Out-of-Doors Magazine
Contact(s):
Dan Delisle, President
Jim Goodheart, Executive Director
James Campbell, Representative
Kevin Frailey, Education Programs Contact
Dennis Knickerbocker, Editor
Michael Leach, Treasurer
William Whippen, Alternate Representative

MICHIGAN WILDLIFE HABITAT FOUNDATION

6380 Drumheller Road, P.O. Box 393
Bath, MI 48808 United States
Phone: 517-641-7677 Fax: 517-641-7877
E-mail: wildlife@mwhf.org
Website: www.mwhf.org

Founded: 1982
Membership: 1,001–10,000
Scope: State
Description: The Michigan Wildlife Habitat Foundation is a nonprofit membership organization, which restores and improves wildlife habitat through cost-effective projects. We want future generations to enjoy the same world of natural experiences we do today.
Publication(s): Wildlife Volunteer, The
Keyword(s): Land Issues, Reduce/Reuse/Recycle, Water Habitats & Quality
Contact(s):
Keith Groty, President
Dennis Fijalkowski, Executive Director
Michael Depolo, Chairman

MID-ATLANTIC COUNCIL OF WATERSHED ASSOCIATIONS

12 Morris Rd.
Ambler, PA 19002 United States
Phone: 215-372-3916

Founded: N/A
Scope: National
Description: Promotes exchange of ideas on citizen watershed association activities and advises any group wishing to start a new watershed association.
Keyword(s): Land Issues, Oceans/Coasts/Beaches, Water Habitats & Quality

MID-ATLANTIC FISHERY MANAGEMENT COUNCIL

300 S. New St., Rm. 2115
Dover, DE 19904 United States
Phone: 302-674-2331 Fax: 302-674-5399
Website: www.mafmc.org

Founded: 1976
Membership: 1–100
Scope: National
Description: Mid-Atlantic Fishery Management Council is one of eight regional fishery management councils established to carry out provisions of Magnuson-Stevens Fishery Conservation and Management Act. The Council is charged with responsibility to prepare fishery management plans and amendments to such plans for implementation by the Secretary of Commerce.
Publication(s): Newsletter
Keyword(s): Oceans/Coasts/Beaches, Water Habitats & Quality, Wildlife & Species
Contact(s):
Daniel Furlong, Executive Director; dfurlong@mafmc.org
Marla Trollan, Public Affairs; mtrollan@mafmc.org

MINERAL POLICY CENTER

1612 K St., NW, Suite 808
Washington, DC 20006 United States
Phone: 202-887-1872 Fax: 202-887-1875
E-mail: mpc@mineralpolicy.org
Website: www.mineralpolicy.org

Founded: 1988
Membership: 1,001–10,000
Scope: International
Description: MPC is a national environmental membership organization. The Center is a research, education, and advocacy organization dedicated to cleaning up and preventing pollution

from mining. The Center works for common sense environmental reform of mineral policy. The Center produces educational materials on mining impact, offers training for and works closely with citizens groups affected by mining damage.

Publication(s): MPC News, Golden Dreams, Poison Streams, Mine Wire, Canary Calls / not on web

Keyword(s): Land Issues, Oceans/Coasts/Beaches, Pollution (general), Public Lands/Greenspace, Reduce/Reuse/Recycle

Contact(s):

Alan Septoff, Research Director; ext. 205

MINNESOTA ASSOCIATION OF SOIL AND WATER CONSERVATION DISTRICTS

790 Cleveland Ave. S.
Ste. 216
St. Paul, MN 55116 United States
Phone: 651-690-9028 Fax: 651-690-9065
E-mail: maswcd@maswcd.org
Website: www.maswcd.org

Founded: 1952

Scope: State

Description: MASWCD is a nonprofit organization which exists to provide a common voice for Minnesota's soil and water conservation districts and to maintain a positive, results-oriented relationship with rule making agencies, partners and legislators; expanding education opportunities to the districts so they may carry out effective conservation programs.

Contact(s):

Richard Zupp, President; 417 136th St., Pipestone, MN 56164; 507-825-3024; Fax: 507-825-2855; rlzupp@svtv.com
Scott Hoese, Vice President; 5520 Polk Ave., Mayer, MN 55360; 952-657-2223; sfhoese@aol.com
LeAnn Buck, Executive Director; 790 Cleveland Ave. S., Ste. 216, St. Paul, MN 55116; 651-690-9028; Fax: 651-690-9065; lbuck@pioneerplanet.infi.net

MINNESOTA B.A.S.S. CHAPTER FEDERATION

Attn: President, P.O. Box 225
Howard Lake, MN 55349 United States
Phone: 612-339-5609
Website: www.mnbf.org

Founded: N/A

Membership: 101–1,000

Scope: Regional

Description: An organization of Bassmaster chapters, affiliated with the Bass Anglers Sportsman Society, organized to fight pollution, assist state and national conservation agencies in their efforts, and teach the young people of our country good conservation practices. Dedicated to the realistic conservation of our water resources.

Contact(s):

Jay Green, President; 612-339-5609

MINNESOTA CENTER FOR ENVIRONMENTAL ADVOCACY (MCEA)

26 E. Exchange St., Suite 206
St. Paul, MN 55101-2264 United States
Phone: 651-223-5969 Fax: 651-223-5967
E-mail: mcea@mncenter.org
Website: www.mncenter.org

Founded: 1974

Membership: 1,001–10,000

Scope: State

Description: The Minnesota Center for Environmental Advocacy is a nonprofit organization that uses law, science, and research to protect Minnesota's natural resources, wildlife, and the health of its people.

Publication(s): Advocacy Update

Keyword(s): Air Quality/Atmosphere, Pollution (general), Water Habitats & Quality

Contact(s):

Peter Bachman, Executive Director
Steven Thorne, Chair

MINNESOTA CONSERVATION FEDERATION

551 S. Snelling Avenue South, Suite B
St. Paul, MN 55116-1525 United States
Phone: 651-690-3077
E-mail: mncf@mtn.org
Website: www.mncf.org

Founded: 1935

Membership: 1,001–10,000

Scope: State

Description: A representative statewide organization, affiliated with the National Wildlife Federation, dedicated to the protection and enhancement of wildlife and its habitat through public education and government interaction.

Publication(s): Walk-on-the-Wildside, Minnesota-Out-of-Doors

Keyword(s): Public Lands/Greenspace, Water Habitats & Quality

Contact(s):

Kenneth Hiemenz, President; kenny406@juno.com
Gordy Meyer, Past President; gmeyer9330@aol.com
Leigh Currie, Editor and Office Manager; 651-690-3077; Fax: 651-690-3077; mncf@mtn.org
Joan Moore, Treasurer
Barb Prindle, Education Programs Contact; bprindle@msn.com
Chris Vokaty, Secretary; chrisvokaty@cmgate.com

MINNESOTA FORESTRY ASSOCIATION

P.O. Box 496
Grand Rapids, MN 55744 United States
Phone: 218-326-3000 Fax: 218-326-3224
E-mail: info@mnforest.com
Website: www.mnforest.com

Founded: 1876

Membership: 101–1,000

Scope: State

Description: A nonprofit organization, affiliated with the National Woodland Owners Association, dedicated to promoting the high potential advantages of intensive scientific management of forests, woodlots, and other renewable resources.

Publication(s): Minnesota Better Forests, Minnesota Forest newsletter.

Keyword(s): Forests/Forestry

Contact(s):

James Lemmerman, President; 6316 Nashua St., Duluth, MN 55807; 218-624-3847
Culver Adams, Vice President; 612-823-2618
Stephanie Kessler, Executive Director; 218-326-3000; mfakessler@yahoo.com
Richard Holter, Treasurer; 218-328-5173

MINNESOTA GROUND WATER ASSOCIATION

4779 126th St., N.
White Bear Lake, MN 55110-5910 United States
Phone: 651-296-7822 Fax: 651-297-8676

Founded: 1981

Membership: 101–1,000

Scope: State

Description: MGWA's mission is to advocate the wise use and protection of gound water, and to provide education to the users of Minnesota's ground water.

Publication(s): Minnesota Ground Water Association Newsletter, Minnesota Ground Water Association Directory

Keyword(s): Land Issues, Water Habitats & Quality

Contact(s):

James Lundy, President; 651-296-7822; Fax: 651-297-8676; jm.lundy@pca.state.mn.us

Leigh Harrod, Advertising Manager; 651-474-8678; mn_homebase@worldnet.att.net
Jeanette Leete, Business Manager; 651-426-6122; Fax: 651-426-5449
Tom Clark, Editor; 651-296-8580; Fax: 651-297-7709; tom.p.clark@pca.state.mn.us
Jan Falteisek, Secretary and Membership; 651-296-3877; Fax: 651-296-0445; jan.falteisek@dnr.state.mn.us
James Piegat, Past President; 612-470-6075
Lee Trotta, Treasurer; 651-638-3160; Fax: 651-638-3226; trottaLC@usfilter.com

MINNESOTA HERPETOLOGICAL SOCIETY

JAMES FORD BELL MUSEUM OF NATURAL HISTORY
10 Church St., SE, University of Minnesota
Minneapolis, MN 55455-0104 United States
Phone: 612-624-7065

Founded: 1981
Scope: State
Description: A nonprofit organization chartered for the conservation and preservation of reptiles and amphibians, through the education of members and the public.
Publication(s): MHS Newsletter
Keyword(s): Public Lands/Greenspace, Wildlife & Species
Contact(s):
Bill Moss, President; mngatorguy@qwest.net

MINNESOTA LAND TRUST

2356 University Ave. West
Suite 240
Saint Paul, MN 55114 United States
Phone: 651-647-9590 Fax: 651-647-9769
E-mail: mnland@mnland.org
Website: www.mnland.org

Founded: 1991
Membership: 101–1,000
Scope: State
Description: The Minnesota Land Trust protects the land and water resources that define our communities and enrich our quality of life.
Publication(s): Landowner Options Book
Keyword(s): Land Issues, Water Habitats & Quality

MINNESOTA NATIVE PLANT SOCIETY

220 Biological Sciences Center
1445 Gortner Ave.
University of Minnesota
St. Paul, MN 55108 United States
Phone: 507-867-4692
E-mail: mnps@HotPOP.com
Website: www.stolaf.edu/depts/biology/mnps

Founded: 1982
Membership: 101–1,000
Scope: State
Description: A nonprofit organization dedicated to education about native Minnesota flora and to its preservation and conservation. Activities include monthly meetings, summer field trips, sponsorship of symposia and publication of a regular newsletter.
Publication(s): Minnesota Plant Press
Keyword(s): Land Issues, Wildlife & Species

MINNESOTA ORNITHOLOGISTS' UNION

James Ford Bell Museum of Natural History
10 Church St. SE
University of Minnesota
Minneapolis, MN 55455 United States
Phone: 763-780-8890
E-mail: mou@biosci.umn.edu

Founded: 1937
Membership: 1,001–10,000
Scope: State
Description: Statewide organization contributing to scientific knowledge through bird observations; stimulating public interest in birds; and working to preserve bird life and bird habitat.
Publication(s): Loon, The, Minnesota Birder
Keyword(s): Wildlife & Species
Contact(s):
Ann Kessen, President; 31145 Genesis Ave., Stacy, MN 55079
Al Batt, Recording Secretary; RR 1, Box 56A, Hartland, MN 56042
Elizabeth Bell, Membership Secretary; 5868 Pioneer Rd., St. Paul Park, MN 55071
Mark Citsay, Treasurer; 210 Mariner Way, Bayport, MN 55003
Anthony Hertzel, Editor; 8461 Pleasant View Dr., Mounds View, MN 55112
Jim Williams, Editor; 5239 Cranberry Lane, Webster, WI 54893

MINNESOTA WILDLIFE HERITAGE FOUNDATION, INC.

5701 Normandale Rd., Suite 325
Minneapolis, MN 55424 United States
Phone: 952-925-1923 Fax: 952-925-3487

Founded: N/A
Membership: 101–1,000
Scope: State
Description: Formed to promote the idea of charitable giving for conservation purposes and to assist people in making charitable donations of property for wildlife habitat.
Contact(s):
James Mady, President; 7338 Frontier Trail, Chanhassen, MN 55317
Hugh Price, Vice President and Director; 5707 Knox Ave.S, Minneapolis, MN 55419; 612-925-2486
Laurence Koll, Secretary and Legal Counsel; 633 Sunset Ln., Mendota Heights, MN 55118; 612-291-9155

MINNESOTA WINGS SOCIETY, INC.

P.O. Box 11323
Minneapolis, MN 55411 United States
Phone: 612-588-2966

Founded: 1978
Scope: State
Description: To present a program to high school students called "Sight and Save Wildlife Management." This program helps students and enables them to improve wildlife habitat around some of the species they see every day.
Publication(s): Wings (newsletter)
Keyword(s): Land Issues, Wildlife & Species
Contact(s):
Thurman Tucker, President; 1321 N. Irving Ave., Minneapolis, MN 55411; 612-588-2466
David Donna, Vice President; 4200 IDS Center, 80 S. 8th St., Minneapolis, MN 55402; 612-371-3211
Martin Hanson, Secretary; 1530 Quinlan Ave., So., St. Croix Beach, MN 55043; 612-436-8242
Jim McLellan, Treasurer; 10273 Yellow Cir. Dr., Minnetonka, MN 55343; 612-933-2263

MISSISSIPPI ASSOCIATION OF CONSERVATION DISTRICTS, INC.

P.O. Box 23005
Jackson, MS 39225-3005 United States

Founded: N/A
Scope: State
Contact(s):
Benny Goff, President; 228-769-3070; Fax: 228-769-3005

Marc Curtis, 1st Vice President; P.O. Box 958, Leland, MS 38756; 601-686-2321
Jack Winstead, 2nd Vice President; 5337 Lawrence Rd., Lawrence, MS 39336
Daryl Burney, Board Member; P.O. Box 603, Coffeeville, MS 38922; 601-675-2703; Fax: 601-675-2786
Gale Martin, Secretary and Treasurer; P.O. Box 23005, Jackson, MS 39225-3005; 601-354-7645; Fax: 601-354-6628

MISSISSIPPI B.A.S.S. CHAPTER FEDERATION

295 Country Rd. 4701
Meridian, MS 39301 United States
Website: www.msbass.com

Founded: N/A

Scope: State

Description: An organization of Bassmaster chapters, affiliated with the Bass Anglers Sportsman Society, organized to fight pollution, assist state and national conservation agencies in their efforts, and teach the young people of our country good conservation practices. Dedicated to the realistic conservation of our water resources.

Contact(s):
John Hamilton, Conservation Director; 404 Meadow Lane, Aberdeen, MS 39730; 662-369-8290

MISSISSIPPI INTERSTATE COOPERATIVE RESOURCE ASSOCIATION

P.O. Box 774
Bettendorf, IA 52722-0774 United States
Phone: 309-793-5811
Website: wwwaux.cerc.cr.usgs.gov/MICRA/

Founded: 1989
Membership: 101–1,000
Scope: Regional
Description: An interstate organization of 28 state departments of conservation and natural resources working in collaboration with federal agencies, Native American tribes, and other interests to improve the conservation, development, management, and utilization of interjurisdictional fishery resources in the Mississippi River basin through improved coordination and communication among the responsible management entities.
Publication(s): River Crossings, Other Periodic Reports
Keyword(s): Recreation/Ecotourism, Water Habitats & Quality, Wildlife & Species

Contact(s):
Norm Stucky, Chairman; 573-781-4115; Fax: 573-526-4047; stuckyn@mail.conservation.state.mo.us
Bill Reeves, Past Chairman; 615-781-6575; Fax: 615-781-6667; breeves@mail.state.tn.us

MISSISSIPPI NATIVE PLANT SOCIETY

c/o Crosby Arboretum, P.O. Box 190
Picayune, MS 39466 United States
Phone: 601-799-2311, ext. 22 Fax: 601-799-2372
E-mail: crosbyar@datastar.net
Website: msstate.edu/dept/crec/camain.html

Founded: 1981
Membership: 101–1,000
Scope: Local, State
Description: The Mississippi Native Plant Society promotes the study and use of native and naturalized species of Mississippi, their use in landscaping, the appreciation of natural ecological communities of the state, and the conservation or preservation of these species, habitats and plant associations, using the principles of conservation biology and ecosystem management.
Publication(s): Mississippi Native Plants
Keyword(s): Land Issues, Wildlife & Species

Contact(s):
Debora Mann, Secretary and Treasurer; Millsaps College 1701 North State St., Jackson, MS 39210; 601-974-1415; Fax: 601-974-1401; manndl@millsap.edu

MISSISSIPPI RIVER BASIN ALLIANCE

708 N. First St. Ste. 238
Minneapolis, MN 55401 United States
Phone: 612-334-9460 Fax: 612-340-1632
E-mail: mrbaoffice@mrba.org
Website: www.mrba.org

Founded: 1992
Membership: 101–1,000
Scope: Regional
Description: To protect and restore the ecological, economic, cultural, historical, and recreational resources in the Basin, and to eliminate barriers of race, class, and economic status which divide U.S. in the quest to achieve these purposes.
Publication(s): Alliance Newsletter, Mississippi River Basin Directory
Keyword(s): Ethics/Environmental Justice, Public Lands/Greenspace, Water Habitats & Quality
Contact(s):
James Falvey, Assistant Director
Tim Sullivan, Executive Director; ext. 111

MISSISSIPPI WILDLIFE FEDERATION

855 South Pear Orchard Road, Suite 500
Ridgeland, MS 39157-5138 United States
Phone: 601-206-5703 Fax: 601-206-5705
E-mail: cshropshire@mswf.org
Website: www.mswildlife.org

Founded: 1946
Membership: 1,001–10,000
Scope: State
Description: A representative statewide organization, affiliated with the National Wildlife Federation, dedicated to the protection and enhancement of wildlife and its habitat through public education and government interaction.
Publication(s): Mississippi Wildlife Magazine
Contact(s):
Marty Brunson, President
Cathy Shropshire, Executive Director
Melanie Starnes, Office Manager
Jimmy Bullock, Representative
Bob Fairbank, Alternate Representative
Johnny McArthur, Treasurer
Cathy Shropshire, Education Programs Contact

MISSOURI ASSOCIATION OF SOIL AND WATER CONSERVATION DISTRICTS

19050 State Hwy. O
Tarkio, MO 64491 United States
Phone: 660-736-4368

Founded: N/A

Scope: State

Contact(s):
Steve Hopper, President and Board Member; 660-639-2575
David Dix, Treasurer; P.O. Box 756, Eminence, MO 65466; 573-226-3787
Peggy Lemons, Executive Secretary; 1209 Biscayne Dr., Jefferson City, MO 65109; 573-893-5188; Fax: 573-893-7328; peggy@mojefferso.fsc.usda.gov

MISSOURI B.A.S.S. CHAPTER FEDERATION

Attn: President, 220 W. 6th Street
Sedalia, MO 65301 United States
Phone: 660-826-5251
Website: www.mobass.com

Founded: N/A

Scope: State
Description: An organization of Bassmaster chapters, affiliated with the Bass Anglers Sportsman Society, organized to fight pollution, assist state and national conservation agencies in their efforts, and teach the young people of our country good conservation practices. Dedicated to the realistic conservation of our water resources.

MISSOURI FOREST PRODUCTS ASSOCIATION

611 E. Capitol Ave., Suite One
Jefferson City, MO 65101 United States
Phone: 573-634-3252 Fax: 573-636-2591
E-mail: moforest@moforest.org
Website: www.moforest.org

Founded: 1970
Membership: 101–1,000
Scope: State
Description: The Missouri Forest Products Association is a nonprofit organization committed to promoting closer working relationships among the wood products industry and the conservation and wise use of natural resources.
Publication(s): Professional Timber Harvester, MFPA News
Keyword(s): Agriculture/Farming, Air Quality/Atmosphere, Ethics/Environmental Justice, Executive/Legislative/Judicial Reform, Forests/Forestry, Reduce/Reuse/Recycle, Wildlife & Species
Contact(s):
Cory Ridenhour, Executive Director; 573-634-3252; Fax: 573-636-2591; cory@moforest.org

MISSOURI NATIVE PLANT SOCIETY

P.O. Box 20073
St. Louis, MO 63144-0073 United States
Phone: 314-894-9021
Website: www.missouri.edu/~umo_herb/monps

Founded: 1979
Scope: State
Description: To promote the enjoyment, preservation, conservation, restoration, and study of the flora native to Missouri; to educate the public about the values of the beauty, diversity and environmental importance of indigenous vegetation; and to publish related information.
Publication(s): Missouriensis, Petal Pusher
Keyword(s): Agriculture/Farming, Forests/Forestry, Land Issues, Public Lands/Greenspace, Wildlife & Species
Contact(s):
Jack Harris, President
Sue Hollis, Vice President; 816-561-9419; serngro@worldnet.att.net
Pat Harris, Editor; 314-894-9021; pharris@stlnet.com
Donna Kennedy, Treasurer; 636-256-7578; fishn2@primary.net
George Yatskievych, Editor; 314-577-9522; gyatskievych@rschctr.mobot.org

MISSOURI PRAIRIE FOUNDATION

P.O. Box 200
Columbia, MO 65205 United States
Phone: 888-843-6739 Fax: 573-442-0260
E-mail: gfreeman@coin.org
Website: www.moprairie.org

Founded: 1966
Membership: 1,001–10,000
Scope: State
Description: A nonprofit citizens' group organized to ensure the preservation of native prairie along with associated plant and animal life by acquisition, management protection, control, and perpetuation of the prairie; to carry on educational programs; and to provide scientific research relative to native prairie.
Publication(s): Missouri Prairie Journal
Keyword(s): Ecosystems (precious), Land Issues, Public Lands/Greenspace, Recreation/Ecotourism, Reduce/Reuse/Recycle, Wildlife & Species
Contact(s):
Robert Elworth, President; 417-742-2775; bobelworth@aol.com
Wayne Morton, Vice President; 417-646-2450; wayne2946@yahoo.com
John Cline, Treasurer; 314-581-6566; jrc01@socket.net
Carol Davit, Editor; 573-751-4115, ext. 874; davitleahy@earthlink.net
Gary Freeman, Membership Coordinator; 888-843-6739; Fax: 573-442-0260; gfreeman@coin.org
Warren Lammert, Secretary; 314-961-8768; wlamm01@earthlink.com

MONITOR INTERNATIONAL

300 State St.
Annapolis, MD 21403 United States
Phone: 410-268-5155 Fax: 410-268-8788
E-mail: info@monitorinternational.org
Website: www.monitorinternational.org

Founded: 1978
Membership: N/A
Scope: National, International
Description: Monitor International, a nonprofit organization, conserves biological diversity and cultural heritage, and promotes environmentally sustainable development of marine and freshwater ecosystems throughout the world.
Publication(s): LakeNet Report Series, Success Stories, Sustainable Development.
Keyword(s): Development/Developing Countries, Ecosystems (precious), Land Issues, Oceans/Coasts/Beaches, Pollution (general), Public Health, Recreation/Ecotourism, Water Habitats & Quality, Wildlife & Species
Contact(s):
David Barker, President; 410-268-5155; Fax: 410-268-8788; drbarker@monitorinternational.org
Lisa Borre, Vice President; 410-268-5155; Fax: 410-268-8788; lborre@monitorinternational.org
Laurie Duker, LakeNet Conservation Director; 410-268-5155; Fax: 410-268-8788; lduker@worldlakes.org
John Dolan, Secretary
Jan Hartke, Board of Trustees Chairman
Richard Tobin, Treasurer

MONO LAKE COMMITTEE

P.O. Box 29
Lee Vining, CA 93541 United States
Phone: 760-647-6595 Fax: 760-647-6377
E-mail: info@monolake.org
Website: www.monolake.org

Founded: 1978
Membership: 10,001–100,000
Scope: Local, State, Regional, International
Description: The Mono Lake Committee is a nonprofit citizens' group dedicated to protecting and restoring the Mono Basin ecosystem; educating the public about Mono Lake and the impacts on the environment of excessive water use; and promoting cooperative solutions that protect Mono Lake and meet real water needs without transferring environmental problems to other areas.
Publication(s): Geology of the Mono Basin, Plants of the Mono Basin, Mono Lake Guidebook, South Tufa: A Self-guided Walking Tour, Mono Lake Newsletter.
Keyword(s): Air Quality/Atmosphere, Climate Change, Development/Developing Countries, Ecosystems (precious), Energy, Land Issues, Pollution (general), Recreation/Ecotourism, Reduce/Reuse/Recycle, Transportation, Water Habitats & Quality, Wildlife & Species

Contact(s):
Geoffrey McQuilkin, Executive Director-Operations
Francis Spivy-Weber, Executive Director-Policy; 310-316-0041
Lisa Cutting, Acting E.S. Policy Director
Arya Degenhardt, Communications Director
Bartshe Miller, Education Director

MONTANA ASSOCIATION OF CONSERVATION DISTRICTS

501 N. Sanders, Suite 2
Helena, MT 59601 United States
Phone: 406-443-5711 Fax: 406-443-0174
E-mail: mail@macdnet.org
Website: www.macdnet.org

Founded: N/A
Membership: 1–100
Scope: State
Publication(s): Conservation Conversation - Monthly Newsletter
Contact(s):
Mike Wendland, President
Bob Fossum, Vice President
Jan Fontaine, Administrative Assistant; 501 N. Sanders, Suite 2, Helena, MT 59601; 406-443-5711; Fax: 406-443-0174
Dale Marxer, Treasurer

MONTANA B.A.S.S. CHAPTER FEDERATION

Attention: President, P.O. Box 4952
Missoula, MT 59808 United States
Phone: 406-549-1303
E-mail: riska@montana.com

Founded: N/A
Scope: State, Regional
Description: An organization of Bassmaster chapters, affiliated with the Bass Anglers Sportsman Society, organized to fight pollution, assist state and national conservation agencies in their efforts, and teach the young people of our country good conservation practice. Dedicated to the realistic conservation of our water resources.
Contact(s):
Mike Riska, President; 406-549-1303
Tony Quinnell, Conservation Director; 1535 Trumbel Creek Rd., Kallispell, MT 59901; 406-755-7867

MONTANA ENVIRONMENTAL INFORMATION CENTER

P.O. Box 1184
Helena, MT 59624 United States
Phone: 406-443-2520 Fax: 406-443-2507
E-mail: meic@meic.org
Website: www.meic.org

Founded: 1973
Membership: 1,001–10,000
Scope: State
Description: Overall purpose is to protect and restore Montana's natural environment. Educates and mobilizes citizens on Montana environmental issues to press for wise decisions at local, state, and federal levels. Priority issues include: Water quality, solid waste, hardrock mining, hazardous waste, environmental policy, air quality, land use planning, toxic chemicals, and energy conservation.
Publication(s): Down to Earth, Capitol Monitor, Montana Environment
Keyword(s): Air Quality/Atmosphere, Climate Change, Energy, Forests/Forestry, Land Issues, Pollution (general), Reduce/Reuse/Recycle, Sprawl/Urban Planning, Transportation, Water Habitats & Quality
Contact(s):
Jim Jensen, Executive Director; jjensen@meic.org
Anne Hedges, Program Director; ahedges@meic.org
Adam McLane, Business Manager; mclane@meic.org

MONTANA FOREST OWNERS ASSOCIATION

17975 Ryan's Ln.
Evaro, MT 59808 United States
Phone: 406-726-3787 Fax: 406-549-2287
E-mail: info@forestsmontana.com
Website: www.forestsmontana.com/index.html

Founded: N/A
Scope: State
Description: A statewide organization affiliated with the National Woodland Owners Association, dedicated to the careful use and active enjoyment of private forest lands in Montana. Goals are achieved through active forestry education programs, public communications, networking, and political advocacy.
Publication(s): Big Sky NIPF-TY Notes
Keyword(s): Forests/Forestry
Contact(s):
Thorn Liechty, President
Tom Castles, Vice President
Peter Kolb, Vice President
Jim Haviland, Treasurer
Karen Liechty, Secretary

MONTANA LAND RELIANCE

P.O. Box 355
Helena, MT 59624-0355 United States
Phone: 406-443-7027 Fax: 406-443-7061
Website: www.mtlandreliance.org

Founded: 1978
Membership: N/A
Scope: State
Description: A private nonprofit land trust protecting and conserving ecologically and agriculturally significant land in Montana, as well as sharing knowledge of voluntary, private-sector land conservation techniques. Pioneering ways to assure a legacy of responsibly managed private land.
Publication(s): Better Trout Habitat, Annual Report, Montana Spaces
Keyword(s): Agriculture/Farming, Forests/Forestry, Land Issues, Public Lands/Greenspace, Water Habitats & Quality, Wildlife & Species
Contact(s):
Roy O'Connor, President; 5015 Larch Ave., Missoula, MT 59802; rsocmt@bigsky.net
Jerry Townsend, Vice President; Elk Run Ranch, Highwood, MT; elkrun@3rivers.net
Christopher Montague, Eastern Manager; P.O. Box 171, Billings, MT 59103-0171; 406-259-1382; mlr@mcn.net
Amy Eaton, Glacier/Flathead Regional Office; P.O. Box 460, Bigfork, MT 59911-0460; 406-837-2178; mlrnw@digisys.net
George Olsen, Secretary and Treasurer; Galusha, Higgens & Galusha, Box 1699, Helena, MT 59624-1699

MONTANA WILDERNESS ASSOCIATION

P.O. Box 635
Helena, MT 59624 United States
Phone: 406-443-7350 Fax: 406-443-0750
E-mail: mwa@wildmontana.org
Website: www.wildmontana.org

Founded: 1958
Membership: 1,001–10,000
Scope: Local, State, Regional
Description: A nonprofit membership organization dedicated to the preservation and proper management of Montana's wild lands, including designated and de facto wilderness areas, national parks, national forests, wildlife refuges, and BLM lands in Montana. The Montana Wilderness Association has five chapter affiliates and four field offices.
Publication(s): Wild Montana, Wilderness Walks Program
Keyword(s): Air Quality/Atmosphere, Ecosystems (precious),

Forests/Forestry, Land Issues, Public Lands/Greenspace, Water Habitats & Quality, Wildlife & Species

Contact(s):

Ross Rogers, President
Gerry Jennings, Vice President
Bob Decker, Executive Director
John Gatchell, Conservation Director; 406-443-7350; Fax: 406-443-0750; jgatchell@wildmontana.org
Karole Lee, Administrative Director; 406-443-7350; Fax: 406-443-0750; klee@wildmontana.org
Susan Miles, Director of Membership Services

MONTANA WILDLIFE FEDERATION

P.O. Box 1175
Helena, MT 59624-1175 United States
Phone: 406-458-0227 Fax: 406-458-0373
E-mail: mwf@mtwf.org
Website: www.montanawildlife.com

Founded: 1935

Scope: State

Description: A representative statewide organization, affiliated with the National Wildlife Federation, dedicated to the protection and enhancement of wildlife and its habitat through public education and government interaction.

Publication(s): Montana Wildlife

Contact(s):

John Gibson, President; jcgibson@imt.net
Craig Sharpe, Editor & Executive Director
Stan Frasier, Alternate Representative
Kathy Hadley, Representative; khadley@ncat.org
Brian Logan, Education Programs Contact
Bill Orsello, Treasurer

MOTE MARINE LABORATORY

MOTE ENVIRONMENTAL SERVICES, INC.
1600 Ken Thompson Parkway
Sarasota, FL 34236 United States
Phone: 941-388-4441 Fax: 941-388-4312
E-mail: info@mote.org
Website: www.mote.org

Founded: 1955

Membership: 1,001–10,000

Scope: Local, State, Regional, National, International

Description: MML is an independent, nonprofit research organization dedicated to excellence in marine and environmental sciences. Since its inception, the laboratory's primary mission has been the pursuit of excellence in scientific research and the dissemination of information to the scientific community as well to the general public. MML specializes in fifteen research programs, the Arthur Vining Davis Library, marine science education and distance learning programs, and operates the public Mote Aquarium.

Publication(s): Mote Technical Reports, 2000 Annual Report, Mote Marine Laboratory Collected Papers, Mote News.

Keyword(s): Agriculture/Farming, Ecosystems (precious), Oceans/Coasts/Beaches, Public Health, Wildlife & Species

Contact(s):

Kumar Mahadevan, Executive Director; 941-388-4441; Fax: 941-388-4007; info@mote.org
Daniel Bebak, Director, Aquarium and Special Projects Division; 941-388-4441; Fax: 941-388-4312; danbebak@mote.org
Howard Crowell, Vice-President, Development Division; 941-388-4441; Fax: 941-388-4312; howard@mote.org
Ernest Estevez, Director, Center for Coastal Ecology; 941-388-4441; Fax: 941-388-4312; estevez@mote.org
Don Hayward, Director, Information Systems Division; 941-388-4441; Fax: 941-388-4312; don@mote.org
Robert Hueter, Director, Center for Shark Research; 941-388-4441; Fax: 941-388-4007; rhueter@mote.org
Peter Hull, Director, Marine Operations Division; 941-388-4441; Fax: 941-388-4312; pete@mote.org
Kenneth Leber, Director, Center for Fisheries Enhancement; 941-388-4441; Fax: 941-388-6461; kleber@mote.org
Steve LeGore, President, Mote Environmental Services, Inc.; 941-388-4441; Fax: 941-388-4312; slegore@mote.org
Kevan Main, Director, Center for Aquaculture Research and Development; 941-388-4441; Fax: 941-388-4312; kmain@mote.org
Erich Mueller, Director, Center for Tropical Research; 305-745-2729; Fax: 305-745-2730; emueller@mote.org
Richard Pierce, Director, Center for Eco-Toxicology; 941-388-4441; Fax: 941-388-4312; rich@mote.org
Dena Smith, Director, Administration Division; 941-388-4441; Fax: 941-388-4312; dena@mote.org
Derek Templeton, Director, Facilities Division; 941-388-4441; Fax: 941-388-4007; temple@mote.org
Randall Wells, Director, Center for Marine Mammal and Sea Turtle Research; 941-388-4441; Fax: 941-388-4317; rwells@mote.org
Nelio Barros, Manager, Marine Mammal Stranding Program; 941-388-4441; Fax: 941-388-4317; nbarros@mote.org
John Buck, Manager, Marine Microbiology Program; 941-388-4441; Fax: 941-388-4312; jbuck@mote.org
Karen Burns, Manager, Fisheries Biology Program; 941-388-4441; Fax: 941-388-4312; kburns@mote.org
James Culter, Manager, Benthic Ecology Program; 941-388-4441; Fax: 941-388-4312; jculter@mote.org
L. Dixon, Manager, Chemical Ecology Program; 941-388-4441; Fax: 941-388-4312; lkdixon@mote.org
Jerris Foote, Manager, Sea Turtle Research Program; 941-388-4441; Fax: 941-388-4317; jerris@mote.org
Jay Gorzelany, Manager, Waterways Management Program; 941-388-4441; Fax: 941-388-4317
Robert Griffin, Manager, Offshore Cetacean Ecology Program; 941-388-4441; Fax: 941-388-4312; bgriffin@mote.org
Michael Henry, Manager, Chemical Fate and Effects Program; 941-388-4441; Fax: 941-388-4312; mhenry@mote.org
Barbara Kirkpatrick, Manager, Environmental Health Program; 941-388-4441; Fax: 941-388-4312; bkirkpat@mote.org
Gary Kirkpatrick, Manager, Phytoplankton Ecology Program; 941-388-4441; Fax: 941-388-4312; gkirkpat@mote.org
Carl Luer, Manager, Biomedical Research Program; 941-388-4441; Fax: 941-388-4312; caluer@mote.org
John Miller, Manager, Fisheries Habitat Program; 941-388-4441; Fax: 941-388-6461; jmiller@mote.org
John Reynolds, Manager, Manatee Research Program; 941-388-4441; Fax: 941-388-4317; reynolds@mote.org
Brad Robbins, Manager, Landscape Ecology Program; 941-388-4441; Fax: 941-388-4312; robbins@mote.org
William Tavolga, Manager, Sensory Biology and Behavior Program; 941-388-4441; Fax: 941-388-4312; tavolga@mote.org
Dana Wetzel, Manager, Aquatic Toxicology Program; 941-388-4441; Fax: 941-388-4312; dana@mote.org
Eugenie Clark, Mote Eminent Scientist; 941-388-4441; Fax: 941-388-4312; yoppe@mote.org

MOUNT GRACE LAND CONSERVATION TRUST

1461 Old Keene Road
Athol, MA 01331 United States
Phone: 978-248-2043 Fax: 978-248-2053
E-mail: landtrust@mountgrace.org
Website: www.mountgrace.org

Founded: 1986

Membership: 101–1,000

Scope: Regional

Description: Mount Grace Land Conservation Trust is dedicated to the protection of forests, agricultural land, and other open space in North Central Massachusetts. In 16 years, Mount Grace Land Conservation Trust has permanently protected 13,500 acres in 145 separate projects.

Publication(s): Views From Mount Grace Quarterly

Keyword(s): Agriculture/Farming, Ecosystems (precious), Forests/Forestry, Land Issues

Contact(s):
Leigh Youngblood, Director of Land Protection
Pam Kimball-Smith, Development Administrator
Chuck Levin, Land Protection Specialist
Alain Peteroy, Stewardhip Coordinator

MOUNTAIN CONSERVATION TRUST OF GEORGIA, INC.

104 N. Main St., Suite B3
Jasper, GA 30143 United States
Phone: 706-692-4077 Fax: 706-692-4077
E-mail: mctg@mindspring.com

Founded: 1994
Membership: 101–1,000
Scope: Local, Regional
Description: Dedicated to the permanent conservation of the natural resources and scenic beauty of the mountains and foothills of north Georgia through land protection, partnerships and education.
Keyword(s): Land Issues, Water Habitats & Quality
Contact(s):
Gary Reece, President; 706-692-2424
Barbara Decker, Executive Director

MOUNTAIN DEFENSE LEAGUE

434 Creelman Lane
Ramona, CA 92065 United States
Phone: 760-789-8134 Fax: 760-789-8134
E-mail: PandoraRose_farm@hotmail.com
Website: mountaindefenseleague.org

Founded: 1973
Membership: 101–1,000
Scope: Local, Regional
Description: Mountain Defense League is a grassroots organization dedicated to the protection of the local and regional mountains, wildlands, and rural communities through wise land-use planning.
Contact(s):
Pandora Rose, Assistant Director; 760-789-8134; PandoraRose_farm@hotmail.com
Byron Lindsley, Director; P.O. Box #19852, San Diego, CA 92159; 619-298-3738; Fax: 619-465-4442; MDL1973-2000@webtv.net

MOUNTAIN LION FOUNDATION

P.O. Box 1896
Sacramento, CA 95812 United States
Phone: 916-442-2666 Fax: 916-442-2871
E-mail: mlf@mountainlion.org
Website: www.mountainlion.org

Founded: 1986
Membership: 1,001–10,000
Scope: State
Description: The Mountain Lion Foundation is a nonprofit conservation and education organization dedicated to protecting wildlife and their habitat throughout California.
Publication(s): Crimes Against the Wild: Poaching in California, Preserving Cougar Country, Mountain Lion Update, Cougar: The American Lion.
Keyword(s): Land Issues, Recreation/Ecotourism, Reduce/Reuse/Recycle, Wildlife & Species
Contact(s):
Kathy Fletcher, President
Joseph Hurwitz, Vice President
Michelle Cullens, Director of Conservation Pograms
Lynn Sadler, Executive Director; 916-442-2666
Sharon Cavallo, Secretary
Toby Cooper, Treasurer

MOUNTAINEERS, THE

CONSERVATION DIVISION
300 3rd Ave., W.
Seattle, WA 98119 United States
Phone: 206-284-6310 Fax: 206-284-4977
E-mail: clubmail@mountaineers.org
Website: www.mountaineers.org

Founded: 1906
Membership: 10,001–100,000
Scope: Regional
Description: The Mountaineers provides opportunities for outdoor recreation and training to its members and strives to protect the environment through community outreach, education, and political action.
Publication(s): Numerous titles published by Mountaineer Books, see publications on website
Keyword(s): Forests/Forestry, Land Issues, Oceans/Coasts/Beaches, Public Lands/Greenspace, Recreation/Ecotourism, Water Habitats & Quality, Wildlife & Species
Contact(s):
Ed Henderson, President
Steve Costie, Executive Director
Kelly McCaffrey, Public Policy Assistant

MRFC FISH CONSERVATION

PITTSBURGH OFFICE
1058 Larchdale Drive
Pittsburgh, PA 15243 United States
Phone: 412-279-0793 Fax: 412-279-4753
E-mail: serval05@aol.com

Founded: 1997
Membership: 1–100
Scope: Local, State
Description: A volunteer service born out of Pittsburgh, Pennsylvania in 1997. The group focuses on preventing housing/building development on state park lands and sport fishing lakes, streams, etc. Ensuring the survival and welfare of all species of gamefish has been the top priority since the introduction of the MRFC. Everyone who loves the outdoors knows it worth conserving for future generations.
Keyword(s): Water Habitats & Quality, Wildlife & Species
Contact(s):
Matt Kiswardy, President; 1058 Larchdale Drive, Pittsburgh, PA 15243; 412-279-0793; Fax: 412-279-4753; serval05@aol.com
Robert Truesdell, Vice President; 412-302-8749; rjtrues@aol.com

MULE DEER FOUNDATION

1005 Terminal Way, Suite 170
Reno, NV 89502 United States
Phone: 775-322-6558 Fax: 775-322-3421
E-mail: tmdfreno@aol.com
Website: www.muledeer.org

Founded: 1988
Membership: 10,001–100,000
Scope: National
Description: The Mule Deer Foundation's mission is to ensure the conservation of mule and blacktail deer and their habitats.
Publication(s): Mule Deer Magazine, Mule Deer Chronicle
Keyword(s): Recreation/Ecotourism
Contact(s):
Ron Knapp, Regional Director for WA,OR,ID; 706 F and S Grade Road, Sedro-Wooley, WA 98284; 360-856-2188; Fax: 360-856-4047; knapprh@aol.com
Rich Gordon, VP of Field Operations; 775-322-6558; Fax: 775-322-3421; rgordon@muledeer.org
Rick Bulloch, Regional Director for CA; 629 Fair Street, Petaluma, CA 94952; 707-763-4567; Fax: 707-763-6035; rbulltrcamdf@attibi.com

Ken Kortan, Merchandise Director; 21362 Twin Peaks Lane, Morrison, CO 80467; 303-697-3829; Fax: 303-697-2691; mdfmerchandise@muledeer.org

Bob Meulengracht, Regional Director for CO,SD,KS,NE and all states East; 13995 Berry Road, Golden`, CO 80401; 303-384-0103; Fax: 303-384-0104; rhmeul@aol.com

Tom Mortensen, Regional Director for NV; 313 Egles Way, Sparks, NV 89431; 775-359-6255; Fax: 775-356-1828; mortou312@aol.com

Todd Rathner, Regional Director for AZ,NM,TX & OK; 1173 N. Thunder Ridge, Tucson, AZ 85745; 520-903-1666; Fax: 520-388-9857; trathner@aol.com

Bob Wharff, Regional Director for WY,ND,MT,ID,UT; 137 Shady Lane, Evanston, WY 82930; 307-789-4093; rwharff@allwest.net

Debra Richards, Membership Manager; 775-322-6558; Fax: 775-322-3421

Linda Williams, Office Manager; 775-322-6558; Fax: 775-322-3421; tmdfreno@aol.com

MUSKIES, INC.

P.O. Box 120870
New Brighton, MN 58112 United States
Phone: 1-888-710-8286
E-mail: info@muskiesinc.org
Website: www.muskiesinc.org

Founded: 1966
Membership: 1,001–10,000
Scope: National
Description: A nonprofit organization dedicated to establishing hatcheries and introducing the Muskellunge into suitable waters, abating water pollution, promoting a high quality muskellunge sport fishery, supporting selected conservation practices, promoting muskellunge research, disseminating muskellunge information, maintaining records of habits, growth, and range, and promoting good fellowship and sportsmanship.
Publication(s): Muskie
Keyword(s): Recreation/Ecotourism, Water Habitats & Quality

N

NATIONAL 4-H COUNCIL

7100 Connecticut Ave.
Chevy Chase, MD 20815-4999 United States
Phone: 301-961-2800 Fax: 301-961-2894
Website: www.fourhcouncil.edu

Founded: 1976
Scope: Local, State, Regional, National
Description: The mission statement of National 4-H Council is "To advance the 4-H youth development movement, building a world in which youth and adults learn, grow and work together as catalysts for positive change." The Environmental Stewardship program engages youth and adults to work as partners in developing creative, community-based solutions to environmental challenges. We also provide science-based educational materials that promote critical thinking skills and youth action grants.
Publication(s): Monthly e-mail update, environmental education materials on biotechnology, energy, transportation, food issues, endangered species and water quality.
Keyword(s): Development/Developing Countries, Energy, Pollution (general), Public Health, Reduce/Reuse/Recycle, Transportation
Contact(s):

Kashyap Choksi, Project Director; Fax: 301-961-2894; choksi@fourhcouncil.edu

David Carrier, Project Coordinator; Fax: 301-961-2894; carrier@fourhcouncil.edu

NATIONAL ANTI-VIVISECTION SOCIETY

53 W. Jackson Boulevard
Suite 1552
Chicago, IL 60604 United States
Phone: 1-800-888-6287 Fax: 312-427-6524
E-mail: navs@navs.org
Website: www.navs.org

Founded: 1929
Scope: State, National, International
Description: The National Anti-Vivisection Society is a national, not-for-profit educational organization incorporated in the State of Illinois. NAVS promotes greater compassion, respect and justice for animals through educational programs based on respected ethical and scientific theory and supported by extensive documentation of the cruelty and waste of vivisection.
Contact(s):

Peggy Cunniff, Executive Director

NATIONAL ARBOR DAY FOUNDATION

100 Arbor Ave.
Nebraska City, NE 68410 United States
Phone: 402-474-5655 Fax: 402-474-0820
E-mail: info@arborday.org
Website: www.arborday.org

Founded: 1971
Membership: 1,000,001 +
Scope: National
Description: A nonprofit, membership organization, sponsors Trees for America, Arbor Day, Tree City USA, Conservation Trees and Rain Forest Rescue educational programs. The Foundation publishes "Arbor Day National Poster Contest" and other instructional units for grade schools.
Publication(s): Arbor Day, all publications on website, Library of Trees, Celebrate Arbor Day (booklet), Conservation Trees (booklet), Tree City USA Bulletin
Keyword(s): Forests/Forestry, Land Issues, Wildlife & Species
Contact(s):

John Rosenow, President
Gary Brienzo, Information Director
Mary Yager, Program Director; 211 N. 12th St., Lincoln, NE 68508
Preston Cole, Vice Chair; 211 N. 12th St., Lincoln, NE 68508
Tony Dorrell, Chair
James Fazio, Editor
Stewart Udall, Honorary Trustee and Chairman

NATIONAL ASSOCIATION FOR INTERPRETATION

P.O. Box 2246
Fort Collins, CO 80522 United States
Phone: 970-484-8283 Fax: 970-484-8179
E-mail: membership@interpnet.com
Website: www.interpnet.com

Founded: 1954
Membership: 1,001–10,000
Scope: National, International
Description: A nonprofit professional organization, employed by agencies and organizations concerned with natural and cultural resources, conservation, management and with the interpretation of the natural and historical environment.
Publication(s): Legacy, El Interpretacion and Investigaciones en Interpretacion, Journal of Interpretation Research, Jobs in Interpretation, Interp News, Centers Directory, The
Contact(s):

Sarah Blodgett, President; 978-369-5655; Fax: 978-369-6241; sdblodge@earthlink.net

Tim Merriman, Executive Director; P.O. Box 2246, Fort Collins, CO 80522; 970-484-8283; Fax: 970-484-8179; naiexec@aol.com

Heather Manier, Membership Manager
Nancy Nichols, Editor; Communication Director of NAI, P.O. Box 2246, Fort Collins, CO 80522; 970-484-8283; naicom@aol.com

NATIONAL ASSOCIATION OF BIOLOGY TEACHERS

11250 Roger Bacon Dr., #19
Reston, VA 20190-5202 United States
Phone: 703-471-1134 Fax: 703-435-5582
E-mail: nabter@aol.com
Website: www.nabt.org

Founded: 1938
Membership: 1,001–10,000
Scope: National
Description: The only national association specifically organized to assist teachers in the improvement of biology/life science teaching. NABT offers teachers an opportunity to develop professionally through its journal, annual convention, summer workshops, and other publication programs.
Publication(s): American Biology Teacher, The, The Monograph Series, News and Views
Keyword(s): Public Health, Wildlife & Species
Contact(s):
Richard Storey, President; Chair, Dept. of Biology, The Colorado College, Colorado Springs, CO 80903; 719-389-6406; rstorey@coloradocollege.edu
Wayne Carley, Executive Director; NABT, 11250 Roger Bacon Drive, #19, Reston, VA 20190-5202; 703-471-1134; nabt31@bellatlantic.net
Christine Chantry, Managing Editor; NABT, 11250 Roger Bacon Drive, #19, Reston, VA 20190-5202; 703-471-1134
Randy Moore, Editor; College of Arts & Sciences, University of Louisville, Louisville, KY 40292; 502-852-6490; r0moor01@homer.louisville.edu
Vivian Ward, Past President; Access Excellence-Genentech, Inc., Mail Stop 16B, 460 Point San Bruno Blvd., South San Francisco, CA 94080; 650-225-8750; vlward@gene.com
Catherine Wilcoxson, Secretary and Treasurer; 2833 Douglas Dr., Fremont, NE 68025; catherine.wilcoxson@nau.edu

NATIONAL ASSOCIATION OF CONSERVATION DISTRICTS

509 Capitol Ct., NE
Washington, DC 20002 United States
Phone: 202-547-6223 Fax: 202-547-6450
E-mail: info@nacdnet.org
Website: www.nacdnet.org

Founded: 1946
Membership: 1,001–10,000
Scope: National
Description: A nonprofit organization serving as the national instrument of its membership - 3,000 local districts and 54 state and territorial associations. Conservation districts, local subdivisions of state government, work to promote the conservation, wise use and orderly development of land, water, forests, wildlife, and related natural resources.
Publication(s): Buffer Notes, Forestry Notes, Environmental Film Service Catalogue, Guide to Conservation Careers, America's Conservation Districts, District Leader, The, Tuesday Letter
Keyword(s): Agriculture/Farming, Land Issues, Oceans/Coasts/Beaches, Reduce/Reuse/Recycle
Contact(s):
J. Smith, President; 11751 Lancaster Rd., St. John, WA 99171-9723; 509-648-3922; Fax: 509-648-3293; read-smith@nacdnet.org
Gary Mast, 2nd Vice President; 6055 CR 203 Rte. 4, Millersburg, OH 44654; 330-674-6278; Fax: 330-674-3690
Billy Wilson, Second Vice President; 918-768-3542; bwilson@cwis.net
Debra Bogar, Director of Leadership Services, North; 9150 W. Jewell Ave. Ste. 111, Lakewood, CO 80232-6469; 303-988-1893; Fax: 303-988-1896
Robert Doucette, Director of Operations; bob-doucette@nacdnet.org
Ron Francis, Director of Public Affairs; 408 East Main Street, League City, TX 77574; 281-332-3402, ext. 28; Fax: 281-332-5259; ron-francis@nacdnet.org
David Gagner, Director of Government Affairs; david-gagner@nacdnet.org
Bill Horvath, Director of North Central Program Office; 1052 Main St. Ste. 204, Stevens Point, WI 54481-2895; 715-341-1022; Fax: 715-341-1023
Eugene Lamb, Director of Programs; eugene-lamb@nacdnet.org
Ray Ledgerwood, Director of Leadership Services, West; NE 1615 Eastgate Blvd., Suite B, Pullman, WA 99163; 509-334-1823; Fax: 509-334-3453
Robert Toole, Director of Leadership Services, South; 4617 Cahaan Creek Rd., Edmond, OK 73034; 405-359-9011; Fax: 405-359-9047
Linda Neel, Meeting Services Manager; 9150 W. Jewell Ave. Suite 102, Lakewood, CO 80232-6469; 303-988-1810; Fax: 303-988-1896
Laura McNichol, Government Affairs/Communications Specialist; laura-mcnichol@nacdnet.org
Tim Reich, Secretary/Treasurer; 1007 Kingsbury St., Belle Fourche, SD 57717; 605-892-4366
Ernest Shea, Chief Executive Officer; 202-547-6223; Fax: 202-547-6450; ernie-shea@nacdnet.org
Donna Smith, Administrative Assistant; donna-smith@nacdnet.org

NATIONAL ASSOCIATION OF CONSERVATION DISTRICTS

LEAGUE CITY OFFICE
P.O. Box 855
League City, TX 77574 United States
Phone: 281-332-3402 Fax: 281-332-5259
Website: www.nacd.net.org

Founded: N/A
Membership: 1,001–10,000
Scope: National
Publication(s): NACD News & Views - newsletter
Contact(s):
Ronald Francis, Office of Public Affairs Director; ext. 27; ron-francis@nacdnet.org
Maxine Mathis, Service Center Production Manager; ext. 32; maxine-mathis@nacdnet.org

NATIONAL ASSOCIATION OF ENVIRONMENTAL PROFESSIONALS, THE

NATIONAL OFFICE
P.O. Box 2086
Bowie, MD 20718 United States
Phone: 888-251-9902 Fax: 301-860-1141
E-mail: office@naep.org
Website: www.naep.org

Founded: 1975
Membership: 1,001–10,000
Scope: National
Description: NAEP is the professional association of the environmental professions, dedicated to the promotion of ethical practice, technical competency, and professional standards in the environmental field and recognition of the environmental profession since 1975.
Keyword(s): Air Quality/Atmosphere, Energy, Reduce/Reuse/Recycle

NATIONAL ASSOCIATION OF RECREATION RESOURCE PLANNERS

c/o Tim Hogsett
Treasurer, Texas Parks & Wildlife Dept.
4200 Smith School Rd.
Austin, TX 78744-3291 United States
Phone: 512-912-7109 Fax: 512-707-2742
E-mail: rec.grants@tpwd.state.tx.us
Website: www.tpwd.state.tx.us/park/grants

Founded: N/A
Membership: 1–100
Scope: State
Description: A nonprofit organization involved in the exchange of recreation resource planning information among fedreal, state and regional agencies. Participates in national recreation concerns, promotes improvements in the state-of-the-art of recreation planning and professionalism among its members and acts as an advocate for conservation and recreation opportunities for the future.
Publication(s): NARRP Newsletter
Keyword(s): Land Issues, Public Lands/Greenspace, Recreation/Ecotourism
Contact(s):
Gordon Kimball, President; Minnesota,
Robert Sammon, Vice President; New Hampshire,

NATIONAL ASSOCIATION OF SERVICE AND CONSERVATION CORPS (NASCC)

666 11th St., NW, Suite 1000
Washington, DC 20001 United States
Phone: 202-737-6272 Fax: 202-737-6277
E-mail: nascc@nascc.org
Website: www.nascc.org

Founded: 1985
Membership: 101–1,000
Scope: Local, State, National
Description: NASCC unites and supports youth corps as a preminent strategy for achieving the nation's youth development, community service, and environmental restoration goals. NASCC serves as an advocate, central reference point, and source of assistance for the growing number of state and local youth corps around the country.
Publication(s): Youth Corps Profiles, Urban Waterways Restoration Training Manual, Corpsmember Wellness Guide, Youth Corps Resource Book
Keyword(s): Agriculture/Farming, Air Quality/Atmosphere, Climate Change, Development/Developing Countries, Energy, Ethics/Environmental Justice, Forests/Forestry, Oceans/Coasts/Beaches, Public Lands/Greenspace, Recreation/Ecotourism, Reduce/Reuse/Recycle, Transportation
Contact(s):
Harry Bruell, Vice President, Field Services; ext. 103; hbruell@nascc.org
Andrew Moore, Vice President, Government Relations and Public Affairs; ext. 107; amoore@nascc.org
Leslie Wilkoff, Director for Member Services; ext. 101; lwilkoff@nascc.org

NATIONAL ASSOCIATION OF STATE DEPARTMENTS OF AGRICULTURE

1156 15th St., NW, Suite 1020
Washington, DC 20005 United States
Phone: 202-296-9680 Fax: 202-296-9686
E-mail: nasda@patriot.net
Website: www.nasda-hq.org

Founded: N/A
Scope: National
Description: The National Association of State Departments of Agriculture (NASDA) is a nonprofit, nonpartisan association of public officials comprised of the executive heads of the fifty State Departments of Agriculture and those from territories of Puerto Rico, Guam, American Samoa, and the Virgin Islands. NASDA's mission is to support and promote the American agriculture industry, while protecting consumers and the environment, through the development, implementation, and communication of sound policy.
Publication(s): NASDA News (weekly), Ag In Perspective (quarterly)
Keyword(s): Agriculture/Farming, Oceans/Coasts/Beaches, Pollution (general), Public Health, Public Lands/Greenspace, Reduce/Reuse/Recycle, Sprawl/Urban Planning, Water Habitats & Quality
Contact(s):
Richard Kirchhoff, Chief Executive Officer; ext. 209; rick@nasda-hq.org

NATIONAL ASSOCIATION OF STATE FORESTERS

NASF
444 N. Capitol St., NW, Suite 540
Washington, DC 20001 United States
Phone: 202-624-5415 Fax: 202-624-5407
E-mail: nasf@sso.org
Website: www.stateforesters.org

Founded: 1920
Membership: 1–100
Scope: State, Regional, National, International
Description: Members are state foresters or equivalent officials whose agencies are the legally-constituted authorities for public forestry work within the states. In cooperation with federal agencies, private organizations, and individuals, NASF promotes sound forest management on public and private lands.
Keyword(s): Forests/Forestry
Contact(s):
Anne Heissenbuttel, Executive Director; Hall of States, 444 North Capitol Street, NW, Suite 540, Washington, DC 20001; 202-624-5415; Fax: 202-624-5407; nasf@sso.org

NATIONAL ASSOCIATION OF STATE PARK DIRECTORS

9894 E. Holden Pl.
Tucson, AZ 85748 United States
Phone: 520-298-4924 Fax: 520-298-6515
Website: www.naspd.org

Founded: 1962
Membership: 1–100
Scope: National
Description: Works to unite the states on a common ground for the development of park systems to meet the intensive public demand for out-of-doors recreational opportunities; to promote the exchange of ideas regarding the development of state park systems; to encourage and develop professional leadership; and to expand and improve park policies and practices.
Publication(s): NASPD, The Directory, NASPD, Annual Information Exchange
Keyword(s): Land Issues, Public Lands/Greenspace, Recreation/Ecotourism, Wildlife & Species
Contact(s):
Phil Mcknelly, President
Glen Alexander, Executive Director; 9894 E. Holden Pl., Tucson, AZ 85748

NATIONAL ASSOCIATION OF UNIVERSITY FISHERIES AND WILDLIFE PROGRAMS

President
Department of Animal Ecology
Iowa State University
Ames, IA 50011-3221 United States
Phone: 515-294-6148 Fax: 515-294-7874
Website: www.naufwp.iastate.edu

Founded: 1991
Membership: 1–100
Scope: National
Description: Meets annually at the North American Wildlife and Natural Resources Conference. The purpose is to foster improved communications among members and between other agencies, organizations, and the general public in order to provide a unified voice for academic fisheries and wildlife programs.
Keyword(s): Wildlife & Species
Contact(s):
Bruce Menzel, President and Chair; Department of Animal Ecology, Iowa State University, Ames, IA 50011-3221; 515-294-7419
Erik Fritzell, Secretary and Treasurer; Department of Fisheries and Wildlife, Oregon State University, Corvallis, OR 97331; 541-737-5906
Daniel Pletscher, President-Elect; Wildlife Biology Program, School of Forestry at the University of Montana, Missoula, MT 59812; 406-243-6364

NATIONAL AUDUBON SOCIETY
Headquarters, 700 Broadway
New York, NY 10003-9501 United States
Phone: 212-979-3000 Fax: 212-979-3188
Website: www.audubon.org

Founded: 1905
Membership: 500,001–1,000,000
Scope: National
Description: Solid science, policy research, lobbying, citizen science and action, and education — these are the tools used by the Audubon Society to protect the land and habitat that are critical to our health and the health of the planet. With the support of 550,000 members (in addition to the 500,000 elementary school students in the Audubon Adventures Program) and an extensive chapter network in the United States and Latin America, Audubon draws on the enthusiasm and power of the grassroots to save our planet.
Publication(s): Audubon, Audubon Adventures, Audubon Field Notes
Keyword(s): Wildlife & Species
Contact(s):
John Flicker, President and CEO
Alan Bayersdorfer, Vice President of Membership
James Cunningham, Senior Vice President of Operations
Patrick Downes, Vice President of Publishing
Frank Gill, Senior Vice President of Science
Carol May, Senior Vice President of Development
Carole McNamara, Vice President/Controller
Glenn Olson, Senior Vice President of Field Operations and Sanctuaries
Daniel Beard, Chief Operating Officer
Donal O'Brien, Chairman of the Board; Fax: 212-353-0377
David Seideman, Editor-In-Chief Audubon Magazine

NATIONAL AUDUBON SOCIETY
ALASKA CHAPTER
308 G St., Suite 217
Anchorage, AK 99501 United States
Phone: 907-276-7034 Fax: 907-276-5069
Website: www.audubon.org/chapter/ak/ak

Founded: 1977
Membership: 1,001–10,000
Scope: State, National, International
Description: Audubon Alaska applies sound science and common sense to protect birds, other wildlife and their habitats in Alaska. The staff works in cooperation with five local chapters to foster an environmental ethic that supports a healthy, sustainable economy and a quality of life in harmony with Alaska's natural environment.
Publication(s): Alaska Audubon News
Keyword(s): Ecosystems (precious), Forests/Forestry, Public Lands/Greenspace, Wildlife & Species
Contact(s):
Stanley Senner, Executive Director
Catherine Dennerlein, Education Specialist
Rebecca Downey, Office Manager
John Schoen, Senior Scientist

NATIONAL AUDUBON SOCIETY
AUDUBON OHIO
692 N High St Ste. 208
Columbus, OH 43215-1585 United States
Phone: 614-224-3303
E-mail: ohio@audubon.org
Website: oh.audubon.org

Founded: N/A
Scope: State
Description: The mission of Audubon Ohio is to conserve and restore ecosystems, focusing on birds and other wildlife through advocacy, education, stewardship and chapter support for the benefit of Ohio citizens of today and tomorrow.

NATIONAL AUDUBON SOCIETY
AUDUBON VERMONT
255 Sherman Hollow Rd.
Huntington, VT 05462 United States
Phone: 802-434-3068 Fax: 802-434-4686
E-mail: vermont@audubon.org
Website: www.audubon.org

Founded: 1962
Membership: 1,001–10,000
Scope: Local, State
Description: Audubon Vermont is a program of the National Audubon Society. We protect birds, other wildlife and their habitat by creating a culture of conservation through education, research and advocacy. We educate focusing on site-based learning at the Green Mountain Audubon Center and the High Pond camps. Our conservation programs focus on citizen science intiatives that indentify and protect Important Bird Areas. Audubon advocates for ecosystem management of our state's natural communities.
Contact(s):
Shirley Johnson, Board President

NATIONAL AUDUBON SOCIETY
DAVIESS COUNTY AUDUBON SOCIETY
11201 Fields Road South
Utica, KY 42376 United States
Phone: 270-275-4250
E-mail: mikesherry@email.msn.com
Website: audubon.wku.edu/daviess/

Founded: 1967
Membership: 101–1,000
Scope: Local
Description: A local chapter of the National Audubon Society dedicated to nature conservation and education based in Daviess County, KY.

NATIONAL AUDUBON SOCIETY
IOWA AUDUBON
P.O. Box 71174
Grinnell, IA 50325 United States
Phone: 515-727-4271
E-mail: p2eph@audubon.org

Founded: N/A
Scope: State
Description: The state office of the National Audubon Society supporting the 12 Audubon groups in Iowa. Iowa Audubon's mission is to promote the enjoyment, protection and restoration of Iowa's natural ecosystems with a focus on birds, other wildlife and their habitats.

Keyword(s): Wildlife & Species
Contact(s):
Paul Zeph, Executive Director

NATIONAL AUDUBON SOCIETY
KENTUCKY AUDUBON COUNCIL
Attn: President, 306 Hoover Hill Rd.
Hartford, KY 42347 United States
Phone: 270-298-4237
E-mail: xlavian@starband.net
Website: www.audubon.wku.edu

Founded: 1971
Membership: 1,001–10,000
Scope: Regional
Description: A statewide Audubon Council for the seven key chapters of the National Audubon Society. Works to promote, foster, and encourage the conservation and preservation of all wildlife, plants, soils, water, air, and other natural resources for the benefit of all people.
Publication(s): Kentucky's Cause
Contact(s):
George W. (Bill) Little, President; 270-298-4237
Jeff Frank, Past-President; 16509 Bradbe Rd., Fisherville, KY 40023; 502-266-7181
Maggie Selvidge, Secretary; 904 North Dr., Hopkinsville, KY 42240; 502-886-8078
Bertha Timmel, Treasurer; 3604 Graham Rd., Louisville, KY 40207; 502-893-5601

NATIONAL AUDUBON SOCIETY
LIVING OCEANS PROGRAM
550 South Bay Ave.
Islip, NY 11751 United States
E-mail: livingoceans@audubon.org
Website: www.audubon.org/campaign/lo

Founded: 1993
Scope: National
Description: Living Oceans is the marine conservation program of National Audubon Society. The program is dedicated to reversing the mismanagement of marine fisheries which has led to the depletion of marine wildlife, and to restore the health of our marine environment and coastal habitats.
Publication(s): Audubon Guide to Seafood, Living Oceans News
Keyword(s): Oceans/Coasts/Beaches
Contact(s):
Carl Safina, Director
Merry Camhi, Staff Scientist; 516-581-2927
Mercedes Lee, Assistant Director; 516-224-3669

NATIONAL AUDUBON SOCIETY
LOUISIANA AUDUBON COUNCIL
355 Napoleon St.
Baton Rouge, LA 70802-5955 United States
Phone: 225-346-8761 Fax: 225-338-9806

Founded: 1989
Membership: 1–100
Scope: State
Description: To implement the Audubon cause in Louisiana on issues of statewide concern; coordinate activities among the Audubon chapters in Louisiana; and advocate on behalf of birds, wildlife and their habitat.
Keyword(s): Water Habitats & Quality, Wildlife & Species
Contact(s):
Doris Falkenheiner, President
Donna Lafleur, Vice President
Esther Boykin, Secretary
Clyde Mattison, Treasurer

NATIONAL AUDUBON SOCIETY
MAINE AUDUBON
20 Gilsland Farm Rd.
Falmouth, ME 04105 United States
Phone: 207-781-2330 Fax: 207-781-6185
E-mail: info@maineaudubon.org
Website: www.maineaudubon.org

Founded: 1843
Scope: State
Description: Dedicated to the protection, conservation, and enhancement of Maine's ecosystems through the promotion of individual understanding and actions. Programs focusing on forest conservation, endangered and threatened species protection, wildlife and wildlife habitats, grassroots activism, environmental education, and school curriculum enhancement. Nature day camp, field trip and world tour program, store, and 13 sanctuaries.
Publication(s): Habitat: Journal of the Maine Audubon Society.
Keyword(s): Forests/Forestry, Oceans/Coasts/Beaches, Wildlife & Species
Contact(s):
Carol Hammond, Editor; chammond@maineaudubon.org

NATIONAL AUDUBON SOCIETY
MASSACHUSETTS AUDUBON SOCIETY, INC.
208 S. Great Rd.
Lincoln, MA 01773 United States
Phone: 781-259-9500 Fax: 781-259-8899
E-mail: info@massaudubon.org
Website: www.massaudubon.org

Founded: 1896
Membership: 10,001–100,000
Scope: State
Description: A nonprofit organization committed to the protection of the environment for people and wildlife. One of the oldest conservation organizations in the world and the largest in New England. Owns and protects 28,000 acres with 40 wildlife sanctuaries across Massachusetts. Programming priorities: conservation, education and advocacy.
Publication(s): Sanctuary
Keyword(s): Air Quality/Atmosphere, Ecosystems (precious), Land Issues, Wildlife & Species
Contact(s):
Laura Johnson, President; ext. 7100; ljohnson@massaudubon.org
John Mitchell, Editor; ext. 7550; jmitchell@massaudubon.org
Eleanor Pansar, Secretary; ext. 7101; epansar@massaudubon.org

NATIONAL AUDUBON SOCIETY
MICHIGAN AUDUBON SOCIETY
6011 W. St. Joseph, Suite 403, P.O. Box 80527
Lansing, MI 48908-0527 United States
Phone: 517-886-9144 Fax: 517-886-9466
E-mail: mas@michiganaudubon.org
Website: www.mas.mi.audubon.org

Founded: 1904
Membership: 1,001–10,000
Scope: State
Description: The Michigan Audubon Society works to protect the Great Lakes ecosystem for people and wildlife. The society conducts scientific research, educates, and advocates for the protection of species and habitats through five major centers, three affiliate organizations, forty-six chapters, and sanctuaries totalling over 5,000 acres of land.
Publication(s): Jack-Pine Warbler, Michigan Birds & Natural History
Keyword(s): Land Issues, Wildlife & Species

Contact(s):
Gary Siegrist, President; 11772 Trist Rd., Grass Lake, MI 49240
Loretta Gold, 1st Vice President; 143 Lillie Ave., Battle Creek, MI 49015
Harold Prowse, 2nd Vice President; P.O. Box 336, Metamora, MI 48455
Eileen Scamehorn, Business Manager
Julie Craves, Editor-In-Chief
Charles Macdonald, Treasurer; 945 Tihart, Okemos, MI 48864
Larry Uhrie, Secretary; 19057 12 Mile Rd., Battle Creek, MI 49014
David Worthington, Editor-In-Chief

NATIONAL AUDUBON SOCIETY
MONTANA AUDUBON
P.O. Box 595
Helena, MT 59624 United States
Phone: 406-443-3949 Fax: 406-443-7144
E-mail: mtaudubon@montana.com
Website: www.mtaudubon.org

Founded: 1976
Membership: 1,001–10,000
Scope: State
Description: Montana Audubon works with people to identify and conserve vital ecological systems for birds and other wildlife. We use the best available science to identify the threats to systems such as riparian zones, grasslands and forests. Our programs are designed to be applicable to diverse audiences, local interests, concerns and needs. It is a focused, community-based program to assist people in attaining the inspiration, knowledge and desire to take action to conserve these vital systems.
Publication(s): Montana Bird Distribution
Keyword(s): Agriculture/Farming, Ecosystems (precious), Energy, Forests/Forestry, Land Issues, Recreation/Ecotourism, Water Habitats & Quality, Wildlife & Species
Contact(s):
Dorothy Poulsen, President; 406-727-7516
Ray Johnson, Executive Director
Bill Ballard, Treasurer; 5120 Larch Ave., Missoula, MT 59802; 406-549-5097
Chuck Carlson, Secretary; P.O. Box 227, Ft. Peck, MT 59223; 406-526-3245

NATIONAL AUDUBON SOCIETY
NEW JERSEY CHAPTER
P.O. Box 126
9 Hardscrabble Road
Bernardsville, NJ 07924 United States
Phone: 908-204-8998 Fax: 908-204-8960
E-mail: hq@njaudubon.org
Website: www.njaudubon.org

Founded: 1897
Membership: 10,001–100,000
Scope: State
Description: Fosters environmental awareness and a conservation ethic among New Jersey citizens; protects New Jersey's birds, mammals, other animals, and plants, especially endangered and threatened species; and promotes preservation of New Jersey's valuable natural habitats.
Publication(s): Bridges to the Natural World, Birds of New Jersey, Records of New Jersey Birds, New Jersey Audubon
Keyword(s): Land Issues
Contact(s):
Thomas Gilmore, President and CEO; 908-204-8998; Fax: 908-204-8960
John Carno, Vice President for Development; 908-204-8998; jcarno@njaudubon.org
Peter Dunne, Vice President of Natural History Information; Cape May Bird Observatory, Center for Research and Education, 600 Rt. 47 N., Cape May Court House, NJ 08210; 609-861-0700
Dale Rosselet, Vice President for Education; Cape May Bird Observatory, Center for Research & Education, 600 Route 47 North, Cape May, NJ 08210; 609-861-0700
Eric Stiles, Vice President for Conservation; Scherman—Hoffman Sanctuaries, P.O. Box 693, Bernardsville, NJ 07924; 908-766-5787
Karl Anderson, Director of Rancocas Nature Center; 794 Rancocas Rd., Mt. Holly, NJ 08060; 609-261-2495
Pete Bacinski, Director of Sandy Hook Bird Observatory; Sandy Hook Bird Observatory, 2 Hart Shoren Drive, P. O. Box 446, Fort Hancock, NJ 07732; 732-780-7007
Gretchen Ferrante, Director of Nature Center of Cape May; 1600 Delaware Ave., Cape May, NJ 08204; 609-898-8848
Karla Risdon, Director of Weis Ecology Center; 150 Snake Den Rd., Ringwood, NJ 07456; 973-835-2160
Gordon Schultze, Director of Lorrimer Sanctuary; P.O. Box 125, 790 Ewing Ave., Franklin Lakes, NJ 07417; 201-891-2185
Brian Vernachio, Director of Plainsboro Preserve; Plainsboro Preserve, P.O. Box 446, Plainsboro, NJ 08536; 609-897-9400
Jean Clark, Board Chairperson

NATIONAL AUDUBON SOCIETY
PROJECT PUFFIN
159 Sapsucker Woods Rd.
Ithaca, NY 14850 United States
Phone: 212-979-3000 Fax: 212-979-3188

Founded: N/A
Scope: Regional
Contact(s):
Stephen Kress, Director

NATIONAL AUDUBON SOCIETY
PUBLIC POLICY OFFICE
GRASSROOTS DEPARTMENT
1901 Pennsylvania Ave.
Suite 1100
Washington, DC 20006 United States
Phone: 1-800-659-2622 Fax: 202-861-4290
E-mail: audubonaction@audubon.org
Website: www.audubon.org

Founded: N/A
Scope: National
Description: Enhance & expand Audubon's grassroots constituency and capabilities to promote effective conservation policies that will conserve and restore natural ecosytems for birds and other wildlife that will benefit humanity and the earth's biological diversity.
Keyword(s): Agriculture/Farming, Ecosystems (precious), Forests/Forestry, Land Issues, Oceans/Coasts/Beaches, Population, Public Lands/Greenspace, Water Habitats & Quality, Wildlife & Species
Contact(s):
Kristen Berry, Grassroots Coordinator - IN, MT, WA, OR, ID, WY, IL; 202-861-2242; Fax: 202-861-4290; kberry@audubon.org
Emily Byram, Grassroots Coordinator - AL, AR, LA, MS, KY, TN, OK, TX; 202-861-2242; Fax: 202-861-4290; ebyram@audubon.org
Janine Clifford, Grassroots Coordinator - NJ, PA, AZ, CO, NV, NM, UT; 202-861-2242; Fax: 202-861-4290; jclifford@audubon.org
Judd Klement, Grassroots Coordinator - CA, AK, HI; 415-222-9246; Fax: 415-947-0332; jklement@audubon.org

Jason Kneeland, Grassroots Coordinator - ME, VT, NH, MA, CT, RI, NY, DE; 202-861-2242; Fax: 202-861-4290; jkneeland@audubon.org

Desiree Sorenson Groves, Grassroots Coordinator - IA, KS, MN, MO, NE, WI, SD, ND; 202-861-2242; Fax: 202-861-4290; dgroves@audubon.org

Corry Westbrook, Grassroots Coordinator - OH, MD, WV, VA, SC, NC, GA, FL; 202-861-2242; Fax: 202-861-4290; cwestbrook@audubon.org

NATIONAL AUDUBON SOCIETY

SAN DIEGO CHAPTER
2321 Morena Boulevard, Suite D
San Diego, CA 92110 United States
Phone: 619-275-0557
E-mail: sdaudubon@aol.com

Founded: 1916
Membership: 101–1,000
Scope: Local, State, Regional, National
Description: The mission of the San Diego Audubon Society is to foster the protection and appreciation of birds, other wildlife and their habitats through study and education and advocate for a cleaner, healthier environment.
Keyword(s): Ecosystems (precious), Land Issues, Oceans/Coasts/Beaches, Public Lands/Greenspace, Recreation/Ecotourism, Sprawl/Urban Planning, Transportation, Water Habitats & Quality, Wildlife & Species

NATIONAL AUDUBON SOCIETY

SCULLY SCIENCE CENTER
National Audubon Society 700 Broadway
New York, NY 10003 United States
Phone: 212-979-3000 Fax: 212-979-3188
E-mail: education@audubon.org
Website: www.audubon.org

Founded: N/A
Scope: Regional
Contact(s):
Carl Safina, Director

NATIONAL AUDUBON SOCIETY

SEATTLE AUDUBON SOCIETY
8050 35th Avenue NE
Seattle, WA 98115 United States
Phone: 206-523-4483 Fax: 206-528-7779
E-mail: info@seattleaudubon.org
Website: www.seattleaudubon.org

Founded: 1916
Membership: 1,001–10,000
Scope: Local, Regional
Description: Protecting birds and nature by involving volunteers and the community in education, advocacy, preservation, science and enjoyment.
Publication(s): Nature publications, Internships, Volunteer opportunities, Nature-related merchandise
Keyword(s): Ecosystems (precious), Forests/Forestry, Land Issues, Oceans/Coasts/Beaches, Public Lands/Greenspace, Recreation/Ecotourism, Sprawl/Urban Planning, Water Habitats & Quality, Wildlife & Species
Contact(s):
Christina Peterson, Executive Director; 206-523-8243; Fax: 206-528-7779; info@seattleaudubon.org

NATIONAL AUDUBON SOCIETY

TAVERNIER SCIENCE CENTER
115 Indian Mound Tr.
Tavernier, FL 33070 United States
Phone: 305-852-5318 Fax: 305-852-8012

Founded: N/A
Membership: 1–100
Scope: Regional
Contact(s):
Jerry Lorenz, Director of Reserch

NATIONAL AUDUBON SOCIETY

TUCSON AUDUBON SOCIETY
300 E. University Blvd. #120
Tucson, AZ 85716 United States
Phone: 520-622-5622 Fax: 520-623-3476
E-mail: tucsonaudubonso1@qwest.net
Website: www.tucsonaudubon.org

Founded: 1946
Membership: 1,001–10,000
Scope: Local
Description: Tucson Audubon Society is dedicated to improving the quality of the environment by providing education, conservation, and recreation programs, as well as environmental leadership and information.

NATIONAL AUDUBON SOCIETY

WASHINGTON, D.C. OFFICE
P.O. Box 15726
Suite 1100
Washington, DC 20006 United States
Phone: 202-861-2242 Fax: 202-861-4290
E-mail: judyschaefer@attglobal.net
Website: www.dcaudubon.org

Founded: N/A
Scope: National
Publication(s): Audubon Magazine
Contact(s):
Dan Beard, Senior Vice President; dbeard@audubon.org

NATIONAL AVIARY

Allegheny Commons West
Pittsburgh, PA 15212-5248 United States
Phone: 412-323-7235 Fax: 412-321-4364
E-mail: info@aviary.org
Website: www.aviary.org

Founded: 1952
Membership: 1,001–10,000
Scope: National
Description: The National Aviary works to inspire respect for nature through the appreciation of birds. Travel the world at the National Aviary and visit over 500 exotic and endangered birds in natural habitats.
Publication(s): Bird Calls
Keyword(s): Reduce/Reuse/Recycle, Wildlife & Species
Contact(s):
Dayton Baker, Executive Director; ext. 217; dayton.baker@aviary.org

NATIONAL BIRD-FEEDING SOCIETY

P.O. Box 23
Northbrook, IL 60065-0023 United States
Phone: 847-272-0135 Fax: 773-404-0923
E-mail: feedbirds@aol.com
Website: www.birdfeeding.org

Founded: 1989
Membership: 10,001–100,000
Scope: National
Description: The Society's goal is to help people create good bird habitat — one backyard at a time. Without breeding birds there will be no feeding birds. Society resources help people learn more ways to attract and care for birds, to experience the environment where it's closest and easiest to do — right outside their doors.Bird feeding may be the only opportunity for many people to connect with nature. Sponsors support research and development to further enhance positive backyard experiences.

Publication(s): The Bird -Eye reView
Keyword(s): Reduce/Reuse/Recycle, Wildlife & Species
Contact(s):
Sue Wells, Executive Director
Donald Stokes, Chairman Emeritus

NATIONAL BISON ASSOCIATION

4701 Marion St.,
Denver, CO 80216 United States
Phone: 303-292-2833 Fax: 303-292-2564
E-mail: info@bisoncentral.com
Website: www.bisoncentral.com

Founded: N/A
Membership: 1,001–10,000
Scope: National
Description: The National Bison Association represents public and private bison herds through educational programs, public education and scholarships.
Publication(s): Bison World (quarterly)

NATIONAL BOATING FEDERATION

P.O. Box 4111
Annapolis, MD 21403 United States

Founded: 1966
Scope: National
Description: National, all-volunteer, non-profit boating organization consisting principally of regional or special interest boating organizations and yacht clubs. Activities include monitoring federal legislation and rule-making as they affect recreational boating. The NBF promotes the interests of those who use boats for cruising, water skiing, fishing, and other water sports.
Publication(s): The LOOKOUT, Recreational Boating News and Legislative Issues.
Keyword(s): Oceans/Coasts/Beaches, Recreation/Ecotourism, Water Habitats & Quality
Contact(s):
Robert David, President; 70 Garfield Lane, West Dennis, MA 02670-2321; 508-394-5670; Fax: 508-394-7236
Roger Brown, Vice-President; 111 S. View Court, Shore Acres, NJ 08723-7520; 732-236-3516; Fax: 732-477-0071
Jill Andrick, Public Relations and Editor; P.O. Box 211, Salem, OR 97308-0211; 503-580-0769
William Heider, Secretary and Treasurer; 1114 Appletree Lane, Erie, PA 16509-3917; 814-825-3011; Fax: 814-825-5284
William Mitchelson, Past President; 9483 N. Fairway Cr., Milwaukee, WI 53217-1316; 414-352-0967

NATIONAL CAUCUS OF ENVIRONMENTAL LEGISLATORS (NCEL)

1625 K Street, NW
Suite 790
Washington, DC 20006 United States
Phone: 202-293-7800 Fax: 202-293-7808
E-mail: adam@ncel.net
Website: www.ncel.net

Founded: 1996
Membership: 101–1,000
Scope: National
Description: The National Caucus of Environmental Legislators (NCEL) was organized for the purpose of providing environmentally progressive legislators with an opportunity to coordinate their activities with respect to national legislative organizations, and to share ideas both on affirmative and negative environmental issues.

NATIONAL CENTER FOR APPROPRIATE TECHNOLOGY

P.O. Box 3838
Butte, MT 59702 United States
Phone: 406-494-4572 Fax: 406-494-2905
E-mail: info@ncat.org
Website: www.ncat.org

Founded: 1976
Membership: N/A
Scope: Local, State, Regional, National
Description: Provide technical assistance to people in sustainable energy, housing, agriculture areas, with a special emphasis on assisting low income people
Keyword(s): Agriculture/Farming, Energy, Land Issues
Contact(s):
Kathleen Hadley, Executive Director; 406-494-4572; Fax: 406-494-2905; kathyh@ncat.org

NATIONAL COALITION FOR MARINE CONSERVATION

3 N. King St.
Leesburg, VA 20176 United States
Phone: 703-777-0037 Fax: 703-777-1107
E-mail: christine@savethefish.org
Website: www.savethefish.org

Founded: 1973
Membership: 1,001–10,000
Scope: National
Description: A nonprofit, privately-supported organization devoted exclusively to the conservation of ocean fish and the protection of their environment. Promotes public awareness of marine conservation issues and stimulates the formulation of responsible public policy.
Publication(s): Marine Bulletin.
Keyword(s): Oceans/Coasts/Beaches, Recreation/Ecotourism, Water Habitats & Quality, Wildlife & Species
Contact(s):
Ken Hinman, President and Editor
Tim Hobbs, Fisheries Project Director
Christine Snovell, Director of Communications and Development

NATIONAL COUNCIL FOR GEOGRAPHIC EDUCATION

16A Leonard Hall, Indiana University of Pennsylvania
Indiana, PA 15705 United States
Phone: 412-357-6290
Website: www.oneonta.edu

Founded: 1915
Membership: 1,001–10,000
Scope: National
Description: To promote and advance geographic and environmental education in the public schools and colleges of the U.S. and Canada.
Publication(s): Journal of Geography, list of other publications available upon request, Water In the Global Environment
Contact(s):
James Peterson, President
Robert Bednarz, Vice President of Curriculum and Instruction
Gary Elbow, Vice President of Publications and Products
Celeste Fraser, Vice President of Finance
Ruth Shirey, Executive Director
Jonathan Leib, Editor; Department of Geography, Florida State University, Tallahassee, FL 32306-4016
Sandra Mather, Secretary

NATIONAL COUNCIL FOR SCIENCE AND THE ENVIRONMENT, THE

1707 H Street NW
Suite 200
Washington, DC 20006 United States
Phone: 202-530-5810 Fax: 202-628-4311
E-mail: rob@NCSEonline.org
Website: www.NCSEonline.org

Founded: 1990
Membership: N/A
Scope: National, International
Description: NCSE works to improve the scientific basis for environmental decisionmaking. With the support by nearly 500 academic, scientific, environmental, business and governmental organizations, NCSE promotes a new crosscutting approach to environmental science that integrates interdisciplinary research; scientific assessment; communication of science-based information to decisionmakers and the general public; and environmental education.
Publication(s): Over 800 Congressional Service Reports and many other resources available through on-line library. Federal Environmental Research and Development Programs
Keyword(s): Development/Developing Countries
Contact(s):
Richard Benedick, President
Peter Saundry, Executive Director
A. Ahmed, Secretary and Treasurer; President, Global Children's Health and Environmental Fund; 202-789-1201; Fax: 202-789-1206
Stephen Hubbell, Chair; Professor of Botany, University of Georgia, Dpt. of Botany, Athens, GA 30602; 706-583-0393; Fax: 706-542-1805

NATIONAL EDUCATION ASSOCIATION

1201 16th St., NW
Washington, DC 20036 United States
Phone: 202-833-4000
Website: www.nea.org

Founded: 1857
Membership: 1,000,001 +
Scope: National
Description: Works to elevate the character and advance the interests of the teaching profession and to promote the cause of education in the U.S.
Publication(s): Newsletter- NEA Today, newsletter- NEA Now
Contact(s):
Robert Chase, President
Reg Weaver, Vice President
John Wilson, Executive Director
Dennis Roekel, Secretary and Treasurer

NATIONAL ENVIRONMENTAL EDUCATION AND TRAINING FOUNDATION

THE ENVIRONMENTORS PROJECT
NATIONAL PUBLIC LANDS DAY
1707 H Street, NW
Suite 900
Washington, DC 20006 United States
Phone: 202-833-2933 Fax: 202-261-6464
E-mail: info@neetf.org
Website: neetf.org

Founded: 1990
Membership: N/A
Scope: National
Description: A 501(c)(3) non-profit established by Congress, NEETF strives to help America meet critical challenges by connecting environmental learning to subjects of national concern including education, health care, and economic growth.
Publication(s): The National Report Card (Environmental Attitudes and Knowledge Survey).
Keyword(s): Energy, Pollution (general), Public Lands/Greenspace, Sprawl/Urban Planning, Water Habitats & Quality
Contact(s):
Kevin Coyle, President; coyle@neetf.org
Deborah Sliter, Vice President for Programs; sliter@neetf.org

NATIONAL ENVIRONMENTAL HEALTH ASSOCIATION

720 S. Colorado Blvd., S. Tower, Suite 970
Denver, CO 80246-1925 United States
Phone: 303-756-9090 Fax: 303-691-9490
E-mail: staff@neha.org
Website: www.neha.org

Founded: 1937
Membership: 1,001–10,000
Scope: National
Description: NEHA is a member nonprofit organization that offers a wide variety of educational credentialing and advancement opportunities for people involved or interested in environmental health issues. It is the largest society of environmental health practitioners in the nation today, numbering almost 5,000 members and growing.
Publication(s): Journal of Environmental Health, various books, manuals, etc., Self Paced Learning Modules
Keyword(s): Air Quality/Atmosphere, Oceans/Coasts/Beaches, Pollution (general), Public Health, Reduce/Reuse/Recycle
Contact(s):
Nelson Fabian, Executive Director; ext. 300

NATIONAL FARMERS UNION

11900 E. Cornell Ave.
Aurora, CO 80014-3194 United States
Phone: 303-337-5500 Fax: 303-368-1390
Website: www.nfu.org

Founded: 1902
Scope: National
Description: Believes that the soil, water, forest and other natural resources of the nation should be used and conserved in a manner to pass these resources on undiminished to future generations and that publicly and privately owned land and resources should be administered in the interest of all the public.
Publication(s): National Farmers Union News
Keyword(s): Agriculture/Farming, Land Issues, Public Health, Reduce/Reuse/Recycle
Contact(s):
David Frederickson, President
Tom Buis, Vice President of Legislative Services; 400 Virginia Ave. SW, Suite 710, Washington, DC 20024
Clay Pederson, Vice President
David Carter, Treasurer/Secretary
Rae Price, Editor; 11900 E. Cornell Ave., Aurora, CO 80014-3194; 303-337-5500

NATIONAL FFA ORGANIZATION

P.O. Box 68960, 6060 FFA Drive
Indianapolis, IN 46268-0960 United States
Phone: 317-802-6060 Fax: 317-802-6061
E-mail: info@ffa.org
Website: www.ffa.org

Founded: 1928
Membership: 100,001–500,000
Scope: National
Description: The FFA is a national organization of high school agriculture students in public secondary schools. Congress granted the organization a federal charter in 1950, making it an integral part of the high school agriculture program. Major aims are to provide activities that will stimulate students to higher achievement in the study of production agriculture, agriscience, agribusiness, and agrimarketing, and give them opportunities

through student-planned programs for leadership and self-development.

Publication(s): FFA New Horizons Magazine, The, Update Newsletter, FFA Advisor Publication

Keyword(s): Agriculture/Farming, Public Health, Reduce/Reuse/Recycle

Contact(s):

Larry Case, National FFA Advisor and CEO; 1410 King Street, Ste. 400, Alexandria, VA 22314; 703-838-5889; Fax: 703-838-5888; lcase@ffa.org

C. Harris, Executive Secretary; 1410 King Street, Ste. 400, Alexandria, VA 22314; 703-838-5889; Fax: 703-838-5888; charris@ffa.org

NATIONAL FIELD ARCHERY ASSOCIATION

31407 Outer I-10
Redlands, CA 92373 United States
Phone: 909-794-2133 Fax: 909-794-8512
E-mail: nfaarchery@aol.com
Website: www.nfaa-archery.org

Founded: N/A
Membership: 10,001–100,000
Scope: National
Description: A nonprofit national membership headquarters for all archers.
Publication(s): Archery Magazine
Keyword(s): Recreation/Ecotourism
Contact(s):

Walter Rueger, President; 122 Stanton Ave., Ripon, WI 54971
Tim Atwood, Bowhunting Committee Chairman; 3175 Racine, Riverside, CA 92503
Marihelen Rogers, Executive Secretary
Marihelen Rogers, Editor

NATIONAL FISH AND WILDLIFE FOUNDATION

1120 Connecticut Ave., NW, Suite 900
Washington, DC 20036 United States
Phone: 202-857-0166 Fax: 202-857-0162
E-mail: info@nfwf.org
Website: www.nfwf.org

Founded: 1984
Scope: National
Description: A national nonprofit grant-making and grant-seeking organization dedicated to the conservation of natural resources — fish, wildlife, and plants. NFWF was established by Congress to leverage federally appropriated funds by forging public and private partnerships which result in conservation activities that pinpoint and solve root causes of environmental problems.
Keyword(s): Wildlife & Species
Contact(s):

John Berry, Executive Director; berry@nfwf.org
Gary Guinn, Director of Development and Marketing; guinn@nfwf.org
Lorraine Howerton, Director of Conservation Policy
Gary Kania, Director of Wildlife and Habitat Initiative
Tom Kelsch, Director of Conservation Education Initiative
Peter Stangel, Regional Director of Southeast; stangel@nfwf.org
Whitney Tilt, Director of Conservation Programs
Jerry Clark, Deputy Director Regional Programs; clark@nfwf.org
Alex Echols, Special Assistant
Steve Peet, Chairman of the Board
Ginette Ring, Chief Financial Officer

NATIONAL FLYWAY COUNCIL

South Dakota Game Fish and Parks, 523 E. Capitol
Pierre, SD 57501 United States
Phone: 605-773-4192 Fax: 605-773-6245
E-mail: george.vandel@state.sd.us

Founded: N/A
Membership: N/A
Scope: National
Description: The National Flyway Council contains one appointed representative from each of the four Flyway Councils, Atlantic, Mississippi, Central and Pacific. The purpose of the NFC is to coordinate and facilitate resolving migratory game bird regulatory issues that cross flyway boundaries. Meetings are held in conjunction with the North American Fish and Wildlife Conference and the Service Regulations Committee meetings.
Contact(s):

George Vandel, Chairman; South Dakota Game, Fish, and Parks Department, 523 E. Capitol, Pierre, SD 57501

NATIONAL FLYWAY COUNCIL

ATLANTIC FLYWAY OFFICE
Forest, Wildlife and Heritage Admin.
Tawes State Office Building
580 Taylor Ave.
Annapolis, MD 21401 United States
Phone: 410-260-8534 Fax: 410-260-8595
Website: www.dec.state.ny.us

Founded: N/A
Scope: National
Contact(s):

Gerald Barnhart, Chairman

NATIONAL FLYWAY COUNCIL

CENTRAL FLYWAY OFFICE
WY Game & Fish Dept.
5400 Bishop Blvd.
Cheyenne, WY 82006 United States
Phone: 307-777-4501
E-mail: bwiche@missc.state.wy.us

Founded: N/A
Scope: National
Contact(s):

William Wichers, Chairman

NATIONAL FLYWAY COUNCIL

MISSISSIPPI FLYWAY OFFICE
IA DEPARTMENT OF NATURAL RESOURCES
Wallace State Office Bldg. 502 E-9th St.
Des Moines, IA 50036 United States
E-mail: rbishop@max.state.ia.us

Founded: N/A
Scope: National
Contact(s):

Richard Bishop, Chairman

NATIONAL FOREST FOUNDATION

2715 M St., NW
Suite 410
Washington, DC 20007 United States
Phone: 202-298-6740 Fax: 202-298-6758
Website: www.natlforests.org

Founded: 1993
Membership: 1,001–10,000
Scope: National
Description: As the independent, not-for-profit partner organization of the U.S. Forest Service, the NFF seeks to build relationships that result in measurable improvements in the health, productivity, and diversity of our National Forests and Grasslands for present and future generations.
Publication(s): Mosaic
Keyword(s): Forests/Forestry, Public Lands/Greenspace, Recreation/Ecotourism, Water Habitats & Quality, Wildlife & Species

Contact(s):
William Possiel, President
Doug Crandall, Vice President
Mary Mitsos, Director of Conservation Programs
Cindy Pandini, Director of Marketing and Communications
Maria Ferrio, Office Services Coordinator
Alexandra Kenny, Conservation Programs Officer
Jennifer McConnell, Program Development Officer
Mathew Esserman, Program Development Officer

NATIONAL FOREST FOUNDATION
MONTANA OFFICE
Building 27, Suite 3
Missoula, MT 59804 United States
Phone: 406-542-2805 Fax: 406-542-2810
Website: www.natlforests.org/donate.html

Founded: N/A

Scope: National

Description: As the independent, not-for-profit partner organization of the U.S. Forest Service, the NFF seeks to build relationships that result in measurable improvements in the health, productivity, and diversity of our National Forests and Grasslands for present and future generations.

NATIONAL GARDEN CLUBS INC
4401 Magnolia Ave.
St. Louis, MO 63110 United States
Phone: 314-776-7574 Fax: 314-776-5108
E-mail: headquarters@gardenclub.org
Website: www.gardenclub.org

Founded: 1929
Membership: 100,001–500,000
Scope: International
Description: Coordinates and furthers the interests and activities of the State Federations of Garden Clubs and aids in the protection and conservation of natural resources; protects civic beauty and encourages the improvement of roadsides and parks; encourages and assists in establishing and maintaining botanical gardens and horticultural centers; and advances the arts of gardening and landscape design, and study of horticulture.
Publication(s): National Gardener, The
Keyword(s): Agriculture/Farming
Contact(s):
Lois Shuster, President; 77 Water Wheel Drive, Champion, PA 15622; 814-352-7777, ext. 7514; lois@shalkl.com
June Wood, 1st Vice President; 7000 Seminole Rd., NE, Albuquerque, NM 87110-2739
Fran Mantler, Executive Director
Jan Blair, Conservation/Natural Resources Wildlife/Endangered Species; Louis Rd., Irvington, NY; 914-591-6959; envirojb@aol.com
Susan Davidson, Editor; 102 S. Elm St., St. Louis, MO 63119; Fax: 314-968-1664; susand4@juno.com
Susan Slivken, Treasurer; 4613 37th Ave., Rock Island, IL 61201-7108
Katrina Vollmer, Corresponding Secretary; 3134 N Greenbriar, Nashville, IN 47448; 812-988-0063; katrina@bigfoot.com

NATIONAL GARDENING ASSOCIATION
1100 Dorset St.
South Burlington, VT 05403 United States
Phone: 800-538-7476 Fax: 802-864-6889
Website: www.kidsgardening.com

Founded: 1972
Membership: 1–100
Scope: National
Description: The mission of the National Gardening Association is to sustain the essential values of life and community, renewing the fundamental links between people, plants, and the earth. Through gardening, we promote environmental responsibility, advance multidisciplinary learning and scientific literacy, and create partnerships that restore and enhance communities.
Publication(s): Ruth Page's Gardening Journal, GrowLab: A Complete Guide to Gardening in the Classroom, Gardening Video Series, Gardening, National Gardening Survey, Community Garden Book, The, Guide to Kids Gardening.
Keyword(s): Agriculture/Farming, Wildlife & Species
Contact(s):
Valerie Kelsey, President; valeriek@kidsgardening.com
Larry Sommers, Director of Advertising; 180 Flynn Ave., Burlington, VT 05401; 802-863-1308; Fax: 802-863-5962; l.sommers@nationalgardening.com
Bruce Butterfield, Market Research; ext. 113; bruceb@gardenresearch.com
Amy Gifford, Administratve Coordinator of Growlab
Charlie Nardozzi, Horticulturist; 180 Flynn Ave., Burlington, VT; 802-863-1308; Fax: 802-863-5962; c.nardozzi.nationalgardening.com
Eve Pranis, Associate Director of Education; evep@kidsgardening.com
William Vandeventer, Assistant Treasurer and CFO; billv@kidsgardening.com

NATIONAL GEOGRAPHIC SOCIETY
1145 17th St., NW
Washington, DC 20036 United States
Phone: 800-647-5463
E-mail: askngs@nationalgeographic.com
Website: www.nationalgeographic.com

Founded: 1888

Scope: International

Description: for the increase and diffusion of geographic knowledge.

Publication(s): National Geographic, National Geographic Channel, National Geographic Adventure Magazine, Classroom Materials, Documentary Films, Filmstrips, Globes, Books/Maps/Atlases, National Geographic Traveler, National Geographic World Magazine (for children).

Keyword(s): Oceans/Coasts/Beaches, Public Lands/Greenspace

NATIONAL GRANGE, THE
1616 H St., NW
Washington, DC 20006-4999 United States
Phone: 202-628-3507 Fax: 202-347-1091
Website: www.nationalgrange.org

Founded: 1867

Scope: National

Description: Rural family service organization with special interests in community service and agriculture.

Publication(s): View From The Hill, Grange Today
Keyword(s): Agriculture/Farming, Land Issues, Transportation
Contact(s):
Leroy Watson, Legislative Director; Washington D.C. Office; ext. 114
Robert Clark, Executive Committee Chairman; 360-683-4431
A. Henninger, Executive Committee Secretary; 815-544-4522
Shirley Lawson, Secretary; 120 Wilson Ave., Rumford, RI 02916; 401-434-1491; Fax: 401-434-6772
Kermit Richardson, Master; Washington DC Office,

NATIONAL GROUND WATER ASSOCIATION, THE
601 Dempsey Rd.
Westerville, OH 43081 United States
Phone: 614-898-7791 Fax: 614-898-7786
E-mail: ngwa@ngwa.org
Website: www.ngwa.org

Founded: 1948
Membership: 10,001–100,000
Scope: International
Description: The NGWA is the world's leading organization committed to the study of the occurrence, development, and

protection of ground water. The Association annually sponsors educational programs dealing with a wide variety of water issues, including toxic substances, solid waste, and water pollution. Operates on-line data bases at web site.

Publication(s): Water Well Journal, Journal of Ground Water, Ground Water Monitoring and Remediation

Keyword(s): Oceans/Coasts/Beaches

Contact(s):

Kevin McCray, Executive Director; ext. 503

Sandy Masters, Information; National Ground Water Information Center, 601 Dempsey Dr., Westerville, OH 43081, ext. 502

NATIONAL HUNTERS ASSOCIATION, INC.

P.O. Box 820
Knightdale, NC 27545 United States
Phone: 919-365-7157 Fax: 919-366-2142
E-mail: nhadvs@worldnet.att.net
Website: www.nationalhunters.com

Founded: 1976

Scope: National

Description: The National Hunters Association, Inc. was incorporated under the laws of NC to protect your hunting rights in the U.S. and around the world. Dedicated to hunter safety, the preservation of the rights of the individual sportsman to pursue the sport of hunting and the preservation of an adequate supply of game for the sportsman to hunt — now and in the future.

Publication(s): NHA Newsletter

Keyword(s): Recreation/Ecotourism

NATIONAL MILITARY FISH AND WILDLIFE ASSOCIATION

12428 Pinecrest Ln.
Newburg, MD 20664 United States
Phone: 845-691-6878 Fax: 619-545-5225
E-mail: nmfwa@nmfwa.org
Website: www.nmfwa.org

Founded: 1983

Membership: 101–1,000

Scope: National

Description: A nonprofit organization established to promote professional natural resources management on over 25.5 million acres of United States Department of Defense lands worldwide. Membership is comprised primarily of professional Department of Defense natural resources personnel.

Publication(s): Fish and Wildlife News (FAWN).

Keyword(s): Ecosystems (precious), Forests/Forestry, Land Issues, Public Lands/Greenspace, Water Habitats & Quality, Wildlife & Species

Contact(s):

James Beemer, President; 20 Roxanne Boulevard, Highland, NY 12528; 845-691-6878; Fax: 845-938-2324; ravenwindrider@earthlink.net

Chester Martin, President-Elect; 113 Estelle Drive, Vicksburg, MS 39180; martinc@wes.army.mil

Jim Bailey, Vice President; 93 Windmill Road, Conowingo, MD 21918; jim.bailey@usag.apg.army.mil

Coralie Cobb, Regional Director-West; 10954 Creekbridge Place, San Diego, CA 92131; 858-748-1719; CobbCH@efdsw.navfac.navy.mil

Jim Copeland, At-Large Director; Jim.Copeland@cnet.navy.mil

Rhys Evans, At-Large Director; 760-; ext. 234; Fax: 760-; evansrm@29palms.usmc.mil

Hildy Reiser, Regional Director - West; Hildy.Reiser@holloman.af.mil

Scott Smith, Regional Director-East; Dare County AF Range, P.O. Box 2480, Mantelo, NC 27954; 919-722-1011; Fax: 919-722-0494; scott.smith@seymourjohnson.af.mil

Tammy Conkle, Treasurer; Natural Resources Office, P.O. Box 357088 (Code N4515TC), NAS North Island (Bldg.3), San Diego, CA 92135-7088; 619-545-3703; Fax: 619-545-3489; conkle.tamara@ni.cnrsw.navy.mil

Julie Eliason, Secretary; julie.eliason@ca.ngb.army.mil

Mike Passmore, Newsletter Editor; Environmental Laboratory, U.S. Army Engineer Research & Development Center, 3909 Halls Ferry Rd., ATTN: CEERD-EN-S, Vicksburg, MS 39180-6199; 601-634-4862; Fax: 601-634-3726; passmom@wes.army.mil

Carl Petrick, Regional Director-East; carl.petrick@eglin.af.mil

Don Pitts, Immediate Past President; ATTN:CEERD-CD-N, P.O. Box 9005, Champaign, IL 61825-9005; Fax: 217-373-7266; donald.pitts@erdc.usace.army.mil

NATIONAL NETWORK OF FOREST PRACTITIONERS

305 S Main St.
Providence, RI 02903 United States
Phone: 401-273-6507 Fax: 401-273-6508
E-mail: info@nnfp.org
Website: www.nnfp.org

Founded: 1990

Membership: 101–1,000

Scope: National

Description: The National Network of Forest Practitioners is a grassroots alliance of rural people, organizations and businesses finding practical ways to integrate economic development, environmental protection and social justice.

Publication(s): Engaging Communities in the Research Process, Directory, Practitioner (newsletter)

Keyword(s): Development/Developing Countries, Ethics/Environmental Justice, Forests/Forestry, Sprawl/Urban Planning

Contact(s):

Thomas Bendler, Executive Director; 29 Temple Pl., 2nd Fl., Boston, MA 02111; 617-338-7821; Fax: 617-422-0881; tbendler@igc.org

NATIONAL ORGANIZATION FOR RIVERS (NORS)

212 W. Cheyenne MT Blvd.
Colorado Springs, CO 80906 United States
Phone: 719-579-8759 Fax: 719-576-6238
E-mail: nors@rml.net
Website: www.nationalriver.org

Founded: 1979

Scope: National

Description: A nonprofit organization dedicated to education about whitewater river sports, including kayaking, rafting, and canoeing; to preserving rivers; and to protecting river access rights of the general public.

Publication(s): Currents

Contact(s):

Gary Lacy, President

Ben Harding, Vice President

Eric Leaper, Secretary, Treasurer, and Executive Director

Fletcher Anderson, Board Member

Earl Perry, Board Member

NATIONAL PARK FOUNDATION

NPF
11 Dupont Circle, N.W.
6th Floor
Washington, DC 20036 United States
Phone: 202-238-4200 Fax: 202-234-3103
Website: www.nationalparks.org

Founded: 1967

Scope: National

Description: The National Park Foundation, chartered by Congress, strengthens the enduring connection between the American people and their National Parks by raising private funds, making strategic grants, creating innovative partnerships and increasing public awareness.

Publication(s): Complete Guide to America's National Parks, The

Keyword(s): Ethics/Environmental Justice, Public Lands/Greenspace, Recreation/Ecotourism

Contact(s):

James Maddy, President
Jill Nicoll, Executive Vice President
Claudia Schechter, Treasurer
Robert Stanton, Secretary
B. West, Vice Chairman

NATIONAL PARK TRUST

415 2nd St., NE, Suite 210
Washington, DC 20002 United States
Phone: 202-548-0500 Fax: 202-548-0595
E-mail: legacy@parktrust.org
Website: www.parktrust.org

Founded: 1983
Membership: 10,001–100,000
Scope: National

Description: The private nonprofit land conservancy dedicated exclusively to protecting resources within and around parklands and other natural and historic properties. The Trust is the only private citizen group recognized by Congress to own and manage, in cooperation with the National Park Service, a unit of the National Park System, the Tallgrass Prairie National Preserve. Established in 1996. The Trust has acquired land in over 40 other parks units and finished 4 parks.

Publication(s): Park Education Resource Center, Parkland News, NPT Legacy News, Legacy Report

Keyword(s): Land Issues, Public Lands/Greenspace, Wildlife & Species

Contact(s):

Paul Pritchard, President; paul@parktrust.org
Davinder Khanna, Senior Vice President; 202-548-0500, ext. 15; Fax: 202-548-0595; davinder@parktrust.org
William Brownell, Secretary
Paul Duffendack, Vice Chairman of the Board of Trustees
Stephan Miller, Chairman of the Board of Trustees
Barry Schimel, Treasurer

NATIONAL PARKS CONSERVATION ASSOCIATION (NPCA)

1300 19th St. NW
Suite 300
Washington, DC 20036 United States
Phone: 800-628-7275
E-mail: npca@npca.org
Website: www.npca.org

Founded: 1919
Scope: National

Description: A private nonprofit citizen organization, dedicated solely to preserving, protecting, and enhancing the U.S. National Park System. As a watchdog group, NPCA has been an advocate as well as a constructive critic of the National Park Service. NPCA concerns itself with the health of the entire system and specific sites, programs, the processes of planning, management, and evaluation.

Publication(s): National Parks, Park Lines.

Keyword(s): Ecosystems (precious), Ethics/Environmental Justice, Land Issues, Public Lands/Greenspace, Wildlife & Species

NATIONAL PARKS CONSERVATION ASSOCIATION (NPCA)

ALASKA REGIONAL OFFICE
750 West 2nd Ave.
Anchorage, AK 99501 United States
Phone: 907-277-6722 Fax: 907-277-6723
E-mail: AKRO@NPCA.ORG
Website: www.eparks.org

Founded: N/A
Membership: 100,001–500,000
Scope: Regional
Publication(s): National Parks Magazine

Contact(s):

Chip Dennerlein, Director

NATIONAL PARKS CONSERVATION ASSOCIATION (NPCA)

HEARTLAND REGIONAL OFFICE
P.O. Box 25354
Woodbury, MN 55125-5354 United States
Phone: 612-735-8008
E-mail: npca@npca.org
Website: www.npca.org

Founded: N/A
Scope: Regional

Contact(s):

Lori Nelson, Director

NATIONAL PARKS CONSERVATION ASSOCIATION (NPCA)

NORTHEAST REGIONAL OFFICE
41 Winter Street, Suite 403
Boston, MA 02108 United States
Phone: 617-338-0126 Fax: 617-338-0232
E-mail: northeast@npca.org
Website: www.npca.org

Founded: N/A
Scope: Regional

Contact(s):

Eileen Woodford, Director

NATIONAL PARKS CONSERVATION ASSOCIATION (NPCA)

PACIFIC REGIONAL OFFICE
P.O. Box 1289
Oakland, CA 94604 United States
Phone: 510-839-9922 Fax: 510-839-9926
E-mail: pacific@npca.org
Website: www.npca.org

Founded: N/A
Membership: 1–100
Scope: Regional

Description: Regional office that serves as a watchdog of units of the National Park System in California, Oregon, Washington, Hawaii, American Samoa and Guam.

Contact(s):

Courtney Cuff, Regional Director
Michelle Jesperson, Associate Regional Director
Elizabeth North, Regional Director of Development
Alan Baker, Office Coordinator

NATIONAL PARKS CONSERVATION ASSOCIATION (NPCA)

SOUTHEAST REGIONAL OFFICE
101 South Main Street, Suite 322
Clinton, TN 37716 United States
Phone: 865-457-7775 Fax: 865-457-6499
E-mail: southeast@npca.org
Website: www.npca.org/

Founded: N/A
Scope: Regional

Contact(s):

Don Barger, Director

NATIONAL PARKS CONSERVATION ASSOCIATION (NPCA)

SOUTHWEST REGIONAL OFFICE
823 Gold Ave., SW
Albuquerque, NM 87102 United States
Phone: 505-247-1221 Fax: 505-247-1222
E-mail: southwest@npca.org
Website: www.npca.org

Founded: N/A
Membership: N/A
Scope: Regional
Description: Regional office that serves as watchdog of units of the National Park System in Arizona, New Mexico, Texas, and Oklahoma.
Publication(s): Guide to National Parks Pacific Region, Guide to National Parks North East Region, Guide to National Parks Heartland Region, Guide to National Parks South East Region, Guide to National Parks Rocky Mountain Region, Guide to National Parks Pacific Northwest Region, National Park Activist Guide, A Manual for Citizen Action, NPCA Policy Papers, Defending the Desert.
Contact(s):
David Simon, Director

NATIONAL PARKS CONSERVATION ASSOCIATION (NPCA)

STATE OF THE PARKS PROGRAM OFFICE
P.O. Box 737
Fort Collins, CO 80521 United States
Phone: 970-493-2545 Fax: 970-493-9164
E-mail: stateoftheparks@npca.org
Website: www.npca.org

Founded: 1919
Membership: 100,001–500,000
Scope: National
Description: Since 1919, the National Parks Conservation Association has been the sole voice of the American people in the fight to safeguard the scenic beauty, wildlife, and historical and cultural treasures of the largest and most diverse park system in the world.
Contact(s):
Mark Peterson, Director for State of the Parks Program

NATIONAL RECREATION AND PARK ASSOCIATION

22377 Belmont Ridge Rd.
Ashburn, VA 20148 United States
Phone: 703-858-0784 Fax: 703-858-0794
Website: www.nrpa.org

Founded: N/A
Membership: 10,001–100,000
Scope: National
Description: A national nonprofit service, education, and research organization dedicated to the improvement of park and recreation leadership, programs, and facilities. The Association attempts to build public understanding that leisure programs and environments are indispensable to the well-being of a nation and its citizens.
Publication(s): Parks and Recreation Magazine, Dateline, Recreation and Parks Law Reporter, Therapeutic Recreation Journal, Journal of Leisure Research
Contact(s):
Alice Conkey, President; aconkey@nrpa.org
Pamela Earle, Pacific Regional Director; 350 S. 333rd St., #103, Federal Way, WA 98003; 206-661-2265; pearle@nrpa.org
Kathy Spangler, National Programs Director; Recreation and Park Assoc., 22377 Belmont Ridge Road, Ashburn, VA 20148; 703-858-0784; kspangler@nrpa.org
Maria Stamats, Western Regional Director; 719-632-7031; mstamats@nrpa.org
Barry Tindall, Director of Public Policy; btindall@nrpa.org
Larry Zehnder, Southeast Regional Director; 1285 Parker Rd., Conyers, GA 30207; 404-760-1668; lzehnder@nrpa.org
T. Jarvis, Contact; tjarvis@nrpa.org
Suzanne Mathis, Trustee Liaison & Coordinator of Friends of Parks and Rec.; smathis@nrpa.org
Rip Wilkenson, Chairman; rwillkenson@nrpa.org

NATIONAL RESEARCH COUNCIL

2101 Constitution Ave., NW
Washington, DC 20418 United States
Phone: 202-334-2000
Website: www.nas.edu

Founded: 1916
Scope: National
Description: An independent advisor to the federal government on scientific and technical questions of national importance. Jointly administered by the National Academies of Sciences and Engineering and the Institute of Medicine.
Publication(s): Catalogue available upon request.
Contact(s):
Susan Vines, Director of Office of News and Public Information
Bruce Alberts, Chairman
Suzanne Woolsey, Chief Operating Officer

NATIONAL RIFLE ASSOCIATION OF AMERICA

11250 Waples Mill Rd.
Fairfax, VA 22030 United States
Phone: 703-267-1000 Fax: 703-267-3909
E-mail: nra.contact@nra.org
Website: www.nra.org

Founded: 1871
Scope: National
Description: A nonprofit organization dedicated to protect and defend the Constitution of the United States, especially the right to possess and use firearms for recreation and personal protection; to promote public safety, law and order, and the national defense; and to train members of law enforcement agencies, the military, and private citizens of good repute in marksmanship and the safe handling and efficient use of small arms.
Publication(s): American Rifleman, America's First Freedom, Insights, American Hunter
Keyword(s): Recreation/Ecotourism
Contact(s):
Charlton Heston, President
Sandra Froman, 2nd Vice President
Wayne Lapierre, Executive Vice President
Kayne Robinson, 1st Vice President
Susan Lamson, Director of Conservation, Wildlife and Natural Resources Division; 703-267-1541
William Poole, Director of Education and Training Division; 703-267-1414
Craig Sandler, Executive Director of General Operations
Robert Davis, Manager of Hunter Services; 703-267-1522
Charles Mitchell, Manager for Training; 703-267-1431
Matthew Szramoski, Manager for Youth Programs; 703-267-1596
Montey Embrey, Program Assistant of Hunter Services; 703-267-1503
Britt Ford, Program Coordinator of Hunter Services; 703-267-1516
Edward Land, Secretary
Howard Moody, Instructor and Coach Trainer for Training; 703-267-1401
Wilson Phillips, Treasurer
Janice Taylor, Assistant Manager of Hunter Services; 703-267-1523

Billy Templeton, Wildlife Management Specialist of Hunter Services, ECHO; 703-267-1501

NATIONAL RIFLE ASSOCIATION WEST VIRGINIA

WHITE HORSE FIREARMS AND OUTDOOR EDUCATION CENTER, INC.
P.O. Box 4538
Bridgeport, WV 26330 United States
Phone: 304-472-1449 Fax: 304-472-9489
E-mail: nrdc@westvirginia.net
Website: www.wvsrpa.org/news/education.htm

Founded: 1983
Membership: N/A
Scope: Local, State, Regional
Description: Outdoor Education
Keyword(s): Recreation/Ecotourism, Wildlife & Species

NATIONAL SCIENCE TEACHERS ASSOCIATION

1840 Wilson Blvd.
Arlington, VA 22201 United States
Phone: 703-243-7100 Fax: 703-243-7177
Website: www.nsta.org

Founded: 1944
Membership: 10,001–100,000
Scope: National
Description: NSTA is the world's largest organization committed to improving science education at all levels - preschool through college. NSTA's membership includes science teachers, science supervisors, administrators, scientists, business and industry representatives, and others involved in science education.
Publication(s): Science and Children, Quantum, NSTA Reports!, Journal of College Science Teaching, The Science Teacher, Science Scope
Contact(s):
Gerald Wheeler, Executive Director; 703-312-9254; gwheeler@nsta.org
Shelley Carey, Editor; 703-312-9238; scarey@nsta.org

NATIONAL SHOOTING SPORTS FOUNDATION, INC.

Flintlock Ridge Office Center, 11 Mile Hill Rd.
Newtown, CT 06470-2359 United States
Phone: 203-426-1320 Fax: 203-426-1087
E-mail: info@nssf.org
Website: www.nssf.org

Founded: 1960
Membership: 1–100
Scope: National
Description: Nonprofit educational, trade-supported association sponsors a wide variety of programs to create a better understanding of and a more active participation in the shooting sports and in practical conservation.
Keyword(s): Recreation/Ecotourism, Reduce/Reuse/Recycle
Contact(s):
Robert Delfay, President and CEO
Nancy Coburn, Vice President of Finance and Administration
Bill Brassard, Editorial Director
Larry Ference, Director of Research and Information Services
Douglas Painter, Executive Director
Jodi DiCamillo, National Coordinator of Step Outside

NATIONAL SPELEOLOGICAL SOCIETY, INC.

2813 Cave Ave.
Huntsville, AL 35810-4431 United States
Phone: 256-852-1300 Fax: 256-851-9241
E-mail: nss@caves.org
Website: www.caves.org

Founded: 1941
Membership: 10,001–100,000
Scope: National
Description: A nonprofit membership organization dedicated to the exploration, study, and conservation of America's caves and caverns, related features, and the ecology of caves.
Publication(s): NSS News, publishers of speleological books, Journal of Cave and Karst Studies
Keyword(s): Wildlife & Species
Contact(s):
Michael Hood, President
David Jagnow, Conservation Chairman; 1300 Iris St., Apt. 103, Los Alamos, NM 87544-3140; 505-662-0553; djagnow@roadrunner.com
John Moses, International Secretary; 15807 River Roads Dr., Houston, TX 77079-5041; 281-597-1494

NATIONAL TRAPPERS ASSOCIATION, INC.

P.O. Box 632018
Nacogdoches, TX 75963-2018 United States
Phone: 304-455-2656 Fax: 309-829-7615
E-mail: trappers@aol.com
Website: www.nationaltrappers.com

Founded: 1959
Scope: National, International
Description: A national trappers organization dedicated to promoting sound conservation legislation; to conserving the nation's natural resources; to helping implement environmental education programs; and to promoting a continued annual furbearer harvest as a necessary wildlife management tool.
Publication(s): American Trapper
Keyword(s): Development/Developing Countries, Reduce/Reuse/Recycle
Contact(s):
Dave Sollman, President; RR 1, Box 391-1, Heltonsville, IN 47436; 812-834-5334; Fax: 812-834-5334
Steve Fitzwater, Vice President; P.O. Box 106, Dubois, ID 83423-0106; 208-374-5479; dubois5@yahoo.com
Robert Colona, Conservation Director; 5539 Sharptown Rd., Rhodesdale, MD 21659; 410-883-2607; Fax: 410-376-3916
Scott Hartman, Director of National and International Affairs; 304-455-4865; Fax: 304-455-5735
Tom Krause, Editor and Advertising Manager; P.O. Box 513, Riverton, WY 82501; 307-856-3830; Fax: 307-857-2993; tkrause@wyoming.com
Royl Schoonover, General Organizer; P.O. Box 308, Westminster, VT 05158-0308; 802-722-9062; Fax: 802-722-9062

NATIONAL TREE TRUST

1120 G St., NW, Suite 770
Washington, DC 20005 United States
Phone: 202-628-8733 Fax: 202-628-8735
E-mail: info@nationaltreetrust.org
Website: www.nationaltreetrust.org

Founded: 1990
Membership: N/A
Scope: National
Description: The National Tree Trust serves as a catalyst for local volunteer and community service groups in growing, planting, and maintaining trees in rural communities, urban areas, and along the nation's highways. NTT mobilizes volunteer groups, promotes public awareness, provides educational and tree planting grants, and unites civic and corporate institutions in support of public land tree plantings.
Publication(s): National Tree Trust News, The
Keyword(s): Forests/Forestry, Public Lands/Greenspace
Contact(s):
George Cates, Executive Director; Major General, USMC (Ret.),
Cindy Zimar, Assistant Executive Director

NATIONAL TRUST FOR HISTORIC PRESERVATION

1785 Massachusetts Ave., NW
Washington, DC 20036 United States
Phone: 202-588-6000 Fax: 202-588-6038
E-mail: feedback@nthp.org
Website: www.nthp.org

Founded: 1949
Membership: 100,001–500,000
Scope: National
Description: Private nonprofit membership organization chartered by Congress to encourage the public to participate in the preservation of America's historic and cultural heritage through advocacy, education, technical assistance, financial aid to nonprofit groups, and demonstration programs.
Publication(s): Historic Preservation Forum, Preservation Law Reporter, Preservation Magazine
Keyword(s): Land Issues, Reduce/Reuse/Recycle
Contact(s):
Richard Moe, President; 202-588-6000

NATIONAL TRUST FOR HISTORIC PRESERVATION

MID ATLANTIC
One Penn Center at Suburban Station
Suite 1520
1617 John F. Kennedy Blvd.
Philadelphia, PA 19144 United States
Phone: 215-568-8162

Founded: N/A
Scope: Regional
Contact(s):
Patricia Wilson, Director

NATIONAL TRUST FOR HISTORIC PRESERVATION

MIDWEST OFFICE
53 W. Jackson Blvd., Suite 350
Chicago, IL 60604 United States
Phone: 312-939-5547 Fax: 312-939-5651

Founded: N/A
Scope: Regional
Publication(s): Preservation Magazine
Contact(s):
James Mann, Director

NATIONAL TRUST FOR HISTORIC PRESERVATION

MOUNTAINS - PLAINS OFFICE
910 16th St., Ste. 1100
Denver, CO 80202 United States
Phone: 303-623-1504 Fax: 303-623-1508
E-mail: mpro@nthp.org
Website: www.nthp.org

Founded: N/A
Scope: Regional
Contact(s):
Barbara Pahl, Director

NATIONAL TRUST FOR HISTORIC PRESERVATION

NORTHEAST OFFICE
7 Faneuil Hall Marketplace, 4th Fl.
Boston, MA 02109 United States
Phone: 617-523-0885 Fax: 617-523-1199
E-mail: nero@nthp.org
Website: www.nationaltrust.org

Founded: N/A
Membership: 10,001–100,000
Scope: National
Contact(s):
Wendy Nicholas, Director
Tina White, Admistrative Assistant; 7 Faneuil Hall Marketplace, Boston, MA 02109

NATIONAL TRUST FOR HISTORIC PRESERVATION

SOUTHERN OFFICE
456 King St.
Charleston, SC 29403 United States
Phone: 803-722-8552 Fax: 843-722-8652
E-mail: soro@hthp.org
Website: www.nationaltrust.org

Founded: 1949
Scope: Regional
Contact(s):
John Hildreth, Director

NATIONAL TRUST FOR HISTORIC PRESERVATION

SOUTHWEST OFFICE
500 Main St., Suite 1030
Fort Worth, TX 76102 United States
Phone: 817-332-4398 Fax: 817-332-4512
E-mail: swo@nthp.org
Website: www.nthp.org

Founded: N/A
Scope: Regional
Contact(s):
Daniel Carey, Director

NATIONAL TRUST FOR HISTORIC PRESERVATION

WESTERN
8 California Street
Suite 400
San Francisco, CA 94111-4828 United States
Phone: 415-956-0610 Fax: 415-956-0837
E-mail: wro@nthp.org

Founded: N/A
Scope: Regional
Description: The National Trust for Historic Preservation, the country's largest private nonprofit preservation organization, is dedicated to protecting the irreplaceable. With more than a quarter million members nationwide, it provides leadership, education and advocacy to save America's diverse historic places and revitalize communities. It has six regional offices and 20 historic sites and works with thousands of local community groups in all 50 states.
Contact(s):
Holly Fiala, Director

NATIONAL WATER RESOURCES ASSOCIATION

3800 N. Fairfax Dr., Suite 4
Arlington, VA 22203 United States
Phone: 703-524-1544 Fax: 703-524-1548
E-mail: nwra@nwra.org
Website: www.nwra.org

Founded: N/A
Membership: 1,001–10,000
Scope: National
Description: Promotes development, conservation and management of the water resources of 17 western state associations, including cities, counties, conservation districts, and individual members.
Publication(s): National Waterline, Water Report

Keyword(s): Agriculture/Farming, Oceans/Coasts/Beaches, Pollution (general), Water Habitats & Quality, Wildlife & Species

Contact(s):
David Sprynczynatyk, President
Thomas Donnelly, Executive Vice President

NATIONAL WATERSHED COALITION

9304 Lundy Ct.
Burke, VA 22015-3431 United States
Phone: 703-455-4387 Fax: 703-455-6888
E-mail: jwpeterson@erols.com
Website: www.watershedcoalition.org

Founded: 1989
Membership: 1,001–10,000
Scope: National

Description: The NWC is a nonprofit coalition made up of national, regional, state, and local organizations, associations, and individuals, that advocate dealing with natural resources problems and issues using the watershed as the planning and implementation unit.

Publication(s): Congressional Testimony, Watershed News, Watershed Newsletter & Conference Proceedings

Keyword(s): Agriculture/Farming, Development/Developing Countries, Ecosystems (precious), Forests/Forestry, Land Issues, Oceans/Coasts/Beaches, Pollution (general), Public Lands/Greenspace, Recreation/Ecotourism, Water Habitats & Quality, Wildlife & Species

Contact(s):
John Peterson, Executive Director; 703-455-4387; Fax: 703-455-6888; jwpeterson@erols.com
Tammy Sawatzky, Accountant
Dan Lowrance, Vice Chair
Dan Sebert, Secretary, Treasurer
Larry Smith, Chair

NATIONAL WATERWAYS CONFERENCE INC.

1130 17th St., NW
Washington, DC 20036-4676 United States
Phone: 202-296-4415 Fax: 202-835-3861
E-mail: information@waterways.org
Website: www.waterways.org

Founded: 1960
Scope: National

Description: To promote a better understanding of the public value of water resource and water transportation programs and to show their importance to the total environment.

Publication(s): Washington Watch

Keyword(s): Energy, Oceans/Coasts/Beaches, Water Habitats & Quality

Contact(s):
Harry Cook, President and Editor
Fred Raskin, Vice Chairman; Pres. and CEO of Eastern Enterprises, Inc., 9 Riverside Rd., Weston, MA 02493-2214; 781-647-2300
Scott Robinson, Treasurer; Port Director of Muskogee City-County Port Authority, 4901 Harold Scoggins Dr., Muskogee, OK 74403; 918-682-7886
Michael Toohey, Secretary; Director of Federal Government Relations, Ashland, Inc., 601 Pennsylvania Ave., NW, #540-N, Washington, DC 20004; 202-223-8290

NATIONAL WHISTLEBLOWER CENTER

Legal Defense and Education Fund
3238 P St., NW
Washington, DC 20007 United States
Phone: 202-342-1902 Fax: 202-342-1904
E-mail: whistle@whistleblowers.org
Website: www.whistleblowers.org

Founded: 1988
Scope: National

Description: The Fund is the only public interest law firm dedicated to enforcing and enhancing the legal protections of employees who blow the whistle on significant violations of law, environmental protection, nuclear safety, and first amendment rights. The Fund provides legal advice, resources, and referrals for counsel to whistleblowers nationwide and conducts seminars and other outreach activities.

Publication(s): Whistleblower News, Law Reporter

Keyword(s): Ethics/Environmental Justice

Contact(s):
Stephen Kohn, Chairperson; 202-342-6980

NATIONAL WILD TURKEY FEDERATION, CANADA, INC., THE

c/o Kevin Townsend, Regional Director
75 Mill Street
Wroxeter, N0G 2X0 Ontario Canada
Phone: 519-335-6893 Fax: 519-335-6050
E-mail: ontrdkt@wcl.on.ca

Founded: 1998
Scope: International

Description: A nonprofit organization dedicated to the conservation and management of the North American wild turkey and the preservation of the hunting tradition. The organization supports an annual research grants program.

Keyword(s): Recreation/Ecotourism, Wildlife & Species

Contact(s):
Russ Davies, President
Rob Keck, CEO
James Kennamer, Vice President of Conservation Programs
Randy Roloson, Vice President
Jack Playne, Secretary-Treasurer

NATIONAL WILD TURKEY FEDERATION, INC., THE

770 Augusta Rd., P.O. Box 530
Edgefield, SC 29824-0530 United States
Phone: 803-637-3106 Fax: 803-637-0034
E-mail: nwtf@nwtf.net
Website: www.nwtf.org

Founded: 1973
Membership: 100,001–500,000
Scope: International

Description: A nonprofit organization dedicated to the conservation of the wild turkey and the preservation of the hunting tradition. Comprised of 2,000 state and local chapters. The organization supports an annual research grants program.

Publication(s): Wheelin' Sportsmen Magazine, Turkey Call Magazine, Women in the Outdoors Magazine, JAKES Magazine, The Caller

Keyword(s): Forests/Forestry, Public Lands/Greenspace, Recreation/Ecotourism, Wildlife & Species

Contact(s):
Rob Keck, Chief Executive Officer
Tammy Bristow, Vice President of Communications
Carl Brown, Chief Operating Officer
James Kennamer, Sr. Vice President of Conservation Programs
Dick Rosenlieb, Vice President of Sales & Marketing
James Sparks, Chief Financial Officer
Donna Leggett, Director of Development

NATIONAL WILDLIFE FEDERATION

ALASKA PROJECT OFFICE
750 W. Second Ave.
Anchorage, AK 99501 United States
Phone: 907-258-8480 Fax: 907-258-4811
Website: www.nwf.org

Founded: N/A
Membership: N/A
Scope: Regional

Description: National Wildlife Federation's Alaska office was established in 1988 and specializes in wetlands issues. Our work ranges from educational programs in public schools to federal court lawsuits designed to influence national wetlands policy. Increasingly, the office builds and leads conservation coalitions. NWF currently coordinates the Cooper River Delta Coalition and Prince William Sound Alliance. We also manage Alaska Women's Environmental Network and Alaska Youth for Environmental Action.

Contact(s):
Tony Turrini, Director; Turrini@nwf.org

NATIONAL WILDLIFE FEDERATION
GREAT LAKES NATURAL RESOURCE CENTER
213 W. Liberty, Suite 200
Ann Arbor, MI 48104-1398 United States
Phone: 734-769-3351 Fax: 734-769-1449
E-mail: greatlakes@nwf.org
Website: www.nwf.org

Founded: 1982
Membership: N/A
Scope: Regional
Description: The National Wildlife Federation's Great Lakes Natural Resource Center unites people throughout the eight-state Great Lakes region, the U.S. and Canada to protect the world's greatest freshwater seas and the surrounding ecosystem. The Center's staff of scientists, educators, lawyers, and organizers work with citizens and activists to end the toxic pollution and habitat destruction that threaten the health of wildlife, fish, and people in the Great Lakes region.

Contact(s):
Andrew Buchsbaum, Director; 734-769-3351, ext. 35; Fax: 734-769-1449; buchsbaum@nwf.org
Tim Eder, Director Water Resources; 734-769-3351, ext. 25; eder@nwf.org
Guy O. Williams, Senior Director of Community Programs; 734-769-3351, ext. 19; Fax: 734-769-1449; williamsg@nwf.org

NATIONAL WILDLIFE FEDERATION
GULF STATES NATURAL RESOURCE CENTER
44 East Ave., Suite 200
Austin, TX 78701 United States
Phone: 512-476-9805 Fax: 512-476-9810
Website: www.nwf.org

Founded: N/A
Membership: N/A
Scope: Regional
Description: The Gulf States Natural Resource Center is working to protect threatened rivers and important wetlands in the region and to restore polluted watersheds. The Center also promotes NWF's educational programs by working with schools and other organizations.
Publication(s): Publication on website

Contact(s):
Susan Kaderka, Director; 512-476-9818; Fax: 512-476-9810; kaderka@nwf.org

NATIONAL WILDLIFE FEDERATION
HEADQUARTERS
11100 Wildlife Center Drive.
Reston, VA 20190-5362 United States
Phone: 703-438-6000 Fax: 703-442-7332
E-mail: info@nwf.org
Website: www.nwf.org/

Founded: 1936
Membership: 1,000,001 +
Scope: Local, State, Regional, National, International
Description: A non-profit organization whose mission is to educate, inspire, and assist individuals and organizations of diverse cultures to conserve wildlife and other natural resources and to protect the Earth's environment in order to achieve a peaceful, equitable, and sustainable future. NOTE. Any correspondence for a member of the Board of Directors of the National Wildlife Federation should be directed to the National Wildlife Federation mailing address or fax number.
Publication(s): NatureScope, Conservation Directory, National Wildlife, Wild Animal Baby, EarthSavers, EnviroAction, Your Big Backyard, Ranger Rick, International Wildlife, National Wildlife Week
Keyword(s): Agriculture/Farming, Climate Change, Development/Developing Countries, Ecosystems (precious), Executive/Legislative/Judicial Reform, Finance/Banking/Trade, Forests/Forestry, Land Issues, Population, Public Lands/Greenspace, Recreation/Ecotourism, Sprawl/Urban Planning.

Contact(s):
Mark Van Putten, President and Chief Executive Officer; vanputten@nwf.org
Lawrence Amon, Senior Vice President for Finance and Administration & CFO; amon@nwf.org
Jessie Brinkley, Vice President of Development; brinkley@nwf.org
Dan Chu, Vice President of Affiliate Relations; chu@nwf.org
Jamie Clark, Senior Vice President for Conservation Programs; clark@nwf.org
Robert Ertter, Vice President of Human Resources; ertter@nwf.org
R. Fischer, Policy Director; 802-229-0650; fischer@nwf.org
Carole Fox, Vice President of Operations, Winchester Facility; fox@nwf.org
Philip Kavits, Vice President of Communications; kavits@nwf.org
Jaime Matyas, Vice President of Internet and Cause Related Marketing; matyas@nwf.org
Thomas McGuire, Vice President of Membership; mcguire@nwf.org
Christopher Palmer, President and CEO of National Wildlife Productions; 703-438-6077; palmer@nwf.org
James Stofan, Senior Vice President of Education; stofan@nwf.org
Natalie Waugh, Senior Vice President of Constituent Programs; 703-438-6010; waugh@nwf.org
Susan Rieff, Policy Director; 512-476-9805; rieff@nwf.org
Wayne Schmidt, Staff Director; schmidt@nwf.org
Edward Clark, Board of Directors, Vice Chair
Tom Dougherty, Senior Advisor; dougherty@nwf.org
Doug Inkley, Senior Advisor; inkley@nwf.org
Eileen Johnson, General Counsel; johnsone@nwf.org
Bryan Pritchett, Board of Directors, Chair
Rebecca Scheibelhut, Board of Directors, Vice Chair
William Street, Sr. Director of Education, Editor of Conservation Directory; street@nwf.org

NATIONAL WILDLIFE FEDERATION
INTERNATIONAL AFFAIRS
1400 16th St., NW, Suite 501
Washington, DC 20036 United States
Phone: 202-797-6800
Website: www.nwf.org

Founded: N/A
Membership: N/A
Scope: Regional
Description: The international affairs team, also based in Washington D.C. office, works to advance the conservation agenda, recognizing the borderless reality of ecosystems and migratory species in North America and beyond. Staff members work with state affiliates and field offices to educate and to build a constituency for U.S. leadership on key international conservation issues and with other stakeholders and like-minded organizations, domestic and foreign, to address international conservation priorities.

Contact(s):
Paul Joffe, Senior Director, International Affairs; Joffe@nwf.org

NATIONAL WILDLIFE FEDERATION
NORTHEAST NATURAL RESOURCE CENTER
58 State St., Suite 1
Montpelier, VT 05602 United States
Phone: 802-229-0650 Fax: 802-229-4532
Website: www.nwf.org

Founded: N/A
Membership: N/A
Scope: Regional
Description: The Northeast Natural Resource Center of the National Wildlife Federation works on a range of conservation and natural resource issues across the six-state New England region and often in close coordination with our state-based affiliate conservation groups. We also collaborate with a variety of other like-minded organizations to focus on the protection and restoration of our unique "woods, water, and wildlife" across with the region.
Contact(s):
Eric Palola, Director; palola@nwf.org

NATIONAL WILDLIFE FEDERATION
NORTHERN ROCKIES PROJECT OFFICE
240 N. Higgins, Suite 2
Missoula, MT 59802 United States
Phone: 406-721-6705 Fax: 406-721-6714
Website: www.nwf.org

Founded: N/A
Membership: N/A
Scope: Regional
Description: The Northern Rockies Project Office focuses on endangered species recovery as a key to protecting not only the species themselves, but many other fish and wildlife populations as well. Projects include work on wolf, grizzly bear, sage grouse, and black-tailed prairie dog recovery. The Northern Rockies office works at a landscape level to ensure the conservation of these species across millions of acres of important wildlife habitat.
Keyword(s): Ethics/Environmental Justice, Executive/Legislative/Judicial Reform, Land Issues, Wildlife & Species
Contact(s):
Thomas France, Director & Legal Counsel; 406-721-6705; Fax: 406-721-6714; france@nwf.org
Ben Deeble, Sage Grouse Project Coordinator
Hank Fischer, Wildlife Conflict Resolution Coordinator
Sterling Miller, Senior Wildlife Biologist
Susan Scaggs, Staff Assistant

NATIONAL WILDLIFE FEDERATION
NORTHWESTERN NATURAL RESOURCE CENTER
418 First Ave. West
Seattle, WA 98119 United States
Phone: 206-285-8707 Fax: 206-285-8698
E-mail: salmon@nwf.org
Website: www.nwf.org

Founded: N/A
Membership: N/A
Scope: Regional
Description: Located in Seattle, Washington, the Northwestern Natural Resource Center focuses on the issues critical to this region, such as wild salmon, water quality, smart growth, and wolf recovery. NWF provides the tools, the expertise, and the grassroots clout to make a difference for wildlife and wild places in the Northwest, the nation, and the world.
Contact(s):
Paula Del Giudice, Director; 206-285-8707; delgiudice@nwf.org

NATIONAL WILDLIFE FEDERATION
OFFICE OF CONGRESSIONAL AND FEDERAL AFFAIRS
1400 16th St., NW, Suite 501
Washington, DC 20036 United States
Phone: 202-797-6800 Fax: 202-797-6646
Website: www.nwf.org

Founded: N/A
Membership: N/A
Scope: Regional, National
Description: Advocates NWF's position on conservation issues of national importance. It provides technical, scientific, and legal support to state affiliates and field offices on selected issues. Advocates NWF's position before all three branches of government and works cooperatively with the private sector to achieve mutually desired goals.
Contact(s):
Jim Lyon, Senior Director for Congressional and Federal Affairs; Lyon@nwf.org

NATIONAL WILDLIFE FEDERATION
ROCKY MOUNTAIN NATURAL RESOURCE CENTER
2260 Baseline Rd., Suite 100
Boulder, CO 80302 United States
Phone: 303-786-8001 Fax: 303-786-8911
Website: www.nwf.org

Founded: N/A
Membership: N/A
Scope: Regional
Description: The Rocky Mountain Natural Resource Center is dedicated to the conservation of wildlife and natural resources on public, private, and tribal lands throughout the Rocky Mountains and Plains States. Center staff are working to restore biological diversity on millions of acres of native grasslands, to promote the restoration of water quality in our streams and rivers, and to promote the restoration of bison populations residing in Yellowstone National Park to lands throughout their historic range.
Keyword(s): Land Issues, Public Lands/Greenspace, Sprawl/Urban Planning, Wildlife & Species
Contact(s):
Stephen Torbit, Director; torbit@nwf.org

NATIONAL WILDLIFE FEDERATION
SOUTHEASTERN NATIONAL RESOURCE CENTER
1330 West Peachtree St., Suite 475
Atlanta, GA 30309 United States
Phone: 404-876-8733 Fax: 404-892-1744
Website: www.nwf.org

Founded: N/A
Membership: N/A
Scope: Regional
Description: The Southeastern Natural Resource Center in Atlanta forges links between people and the environment, promoting sustainable practices to enhance the quality of life in our communities for people and wildlife. The SE Natural Resource Center was established in 1986 to address the water issues that affect both people and animals in the southeastern United States. In fact, the southeastern states are home to some of the highest levels of freshwater and upland diversity in the world.
Contact(s):
Andrew Schock, Director; schock@nwf.org

NATIONAL WILDLIFE FEDERATION

WESTERN NATURAL RESOURCE CENTER
3500 5th Avenue
Suite 101
San Diego, CA 92103 United States
Phone: 619-296-8353 Fax: 619-296-8355
E-mail: wnrc@nwf.org
Website: www.nwf.org/western

Founded: 2000
Membership: N/A
Scope: Local, State, Regional, National
Description: The mission of the Western Natural Resource Center of National Wildlife Federation is to educate, inspire and empower people from all walks of life to conserve wildlife and other natural resources throughout California, Nevada, and within the Mexico/U.S. border region.
Keyword(s): Ecosystems (precious), Land Issues, Sprawl/Urban Planning, Transportation, Wildlife & Species
Contact(s):
Kevin Doyle, Director, Habitat Conservation Programs; 619-296-8353, ext. 208; Fax: 619-296-8355; doyle@nwf.org
David Younkman, Center Director; 619-296-8353, ext. 210; Fax: 619-296-8355; younkman@nwf.org
Robert Opliger, Sr. Education Coordinator; 619-296-8353, ext. 204; Fax: 619-296-8355; opliger@nwf.org

NATIONAL WILDLIFE FEDERATION ENDOWMENT, INC.

11100 Wildlife Center Drive
Reston, VA 20190-5362 United States
Phone: 703-438-6000 Fax: 703-438-6060

Founded: N/A
Membership: N/A
Scope: Regional
Description: Established to support the conservation education and resource management programs of the National Wildlife Federation. Gifts and bequests are invested, and income is transferred to the National Wildlife Federation.
Contact(s):
Lawrence Amon, Treasurer
Raymond Golden, Board of Trustee
Allen Guisinger, Board of Trustee Vice Chair
Mary Harris, Board of Trustee
Eileen Johnson, Secretary
John Rainey, Chairman and Trustee

NATIONAL WILDLIFE PRODUCTIONS, INC.

11100 Wildlife Center Drive
Reston, VA 20190-5362 United States
Phone: 703-438-6077 Fax: 703-438-6076
E-mail: palmer@nwf.org
Website: www.nwf.org

Founded: 1994
Membership: N/A
Scope: National, International
Description: National Wildlife Productions is the television, film, and multimedia arm of the National Wildlife Federation (NWF). The goal of NWP is to fulfill NWF's conservation mission by creating and producing television and mass-media projects, including children's television programs, documentaries, large format films for IMAX theaters, feature films, TV movies, and interactive multimedia programs.
Publication(s): India - Kingdom of the Tiger, Bears Educator's Guide, Dolphins, Wolves, Bears
Contact(s):
Christopher Palmer, President and Chief Executive Officer; 703-438-6077; palmer@nwf.org
Ed Capelle, Distribution Chief Executive; National Wildlife Productions, Inc., 3210 Kinsrow Avenue, Suite 261, Eugene, OR 97401; 541-345-5171; Fax: 541-345-5179; ecapelle@attbi.com

NATIONAL WILDLIFE REFUGE ASSOCIATION

1010 Wisconsin Avenue NW, Suite 200
Washington, DC 20007 United States
Phone: 202-333-9075 Fax: 202-333-9077
E-mail: nwra@refugenet.org
Website: www.refugenet.org

Founded: 1975
Scope: Local, Regional, National
Description: The mission of the NWRA is to protect, enhance and expand the National Wildlife Refuge System, lands set aside by the American people to protect our country's diverse wildlife heritage. NWRA is the only national membership organization dedicated solely to protecting the Refuge System.
Publication(s): Shortchanging America's Wildlife, Building Your Nest Egg, Taking Flight, Blue Goose Flyer
Keyword(s): Land Issues, Public Lands/Greenspace, Water Habitats & Quality, Wildlife & Species
Contact(s):
Evan Hirsche, President; 202-333-9075; Fax: 202-333-9077; ehirsche@refugenet.org
Debbie Harwood, Office Manager; dharwood@refugenet.org
Gretchen Muller, Project Manager; gmuller@refugenet.org

NATIONAL WILDLIFE REHABILITATORS ASSOCIATION

14 N. 7th Ave.
St. Cloud, MN 56303 United States
Phone: 320-259-4086
E-mail: nwra@nwrawildlife.org
Website: www.nwrawildlife.org

Founded: 1982
Membership: 1,001–10,000
Scope: International
Description: A nonprofit membership organization committed to promoting and improving the integrity and professionalism of wildlife rehabilitation and contributing to the preservation of natural ecoystems. The organization disseminates information, provides training, and encourages networking through a quarterly journal, an annual membership directory, reviewed publications, annual symposia, and active committees for standards, wildlife medicine, education, awards, and grants.
Publication(s): Wildlife Rehabilitation annual volumes, Minimum Standards for Wildlife Rehabilitation, Training Opportunities in Wildlife Rehabilitation, NWRA Quick Reference Guide, Principles of Wildlife Rehabilitation, Wildlife Rehabilitation Bulletin.
Keyword(s): Wildlife & Species
Contact(s):
Elaine Thrune, President; 320-255-4911
Curtiss Clumpner, Vice President
Diane Nickerson, Vice President; 609-883-6606
Florina Tseng, Vice President
John Huckabee, Treasurer; 425-787-2500
Daneil Ludwig, Editor; P.O. Box 2339, Glen Ellyn, IL 60138
Erica Miller, Secretary

NATIONAL WOODLAND OWNERS ASSOCIATION

374 Maple Ave., E., Suite 310
Vienna, VA 22180 United States
Phone: 703-255-2700 Fax: 703-281-9200
E-mail: info@woodlandowners.org
Website: www.woodlandowners.org

Founded: 1983
Membership: 10,001–100,000
Scope: National
Description: A nationwide organization made up of non-industrial private woodland owners. Membership includes landowners in all 50 states and Canada and also includes affiliations with 32 state and 287 county woodland owner associations throughout the United States. Programs and benefits include the National Woodlands Magazine, Woodland Report Newsletter, represen-

tation in Washington, DC, professional forester referrals, and the Green Tag Forest Certification Program.

Publication(s): Woodland Report, National Woodlands Magazine, Green Tag Certification Program, Professional Forester Referrals.

Keyword(s): Agriculture/Farming, Ecosystems (precious), Ethics/Environmental Justice, Executive/Legislative/Judicial Reform, Forests/Forestry, Land Issues, Public Lands/Greenspace, Reduce/Reuse/Recycle, Sprawl/Urban Planning, Water Habitats & Quality, Wildlife & Species.

Contact(s):

Keith Argow, President; 703-255-2700; Fax: 703-281-9200; argow@woodlandowners.org
Courtney Murrill, Director of Forestry; 12105-A Pine Forest Cir., Fairfax, VA 22030; 571-217-5612; cam@aloha.net
Linda Martin, Member Services; 703-255-2700; Fax: 703-281-9200; lmartin@woodlandowners.org
Eric Johnson, Editor National Woodlands Magazine; P.O. Box 332, Old Forge, NY 13420; 315-369-3078; nela@telenet.net

NATIVE AMERICAN FISH AND WILDLIFE SOCIETY (NAFWS)

750 Burbank St.
Broomfield, CO 80020 United States
Phone: 303-466-1725 Fax: 303-466-5414
Website: www.nafws.org

Founded: 1982
Membership: 1,001–10,000
Scope: National

Description: The Native American Fish and Wildlife Society is a nonprofit organization serving the needs of fish, wildlife, and natural resources on Tribal lands across the United States, including Alaska. The Society membership is comprised of approximately 1,500 professional and technical personnel associated with Native American natural resource programs. Two hundred sixteen federally-recognized tribes represent the Society, and many federal agencies rely on the Society's expertise and established network

Publication(s): From the Eagles Nest

Keyword(s): Ethics/Environmental Justice, Forests/Forestry, Wildlife & Species

Contact(s):

Matthew Vanderhoop, President; 508-645-9265; natres@vineyard.net
Teresa Harris, Vice President; 803-366-4792; harristeresa@yahoo.com
Mike Fox, Technical Services Director
Ira New Breast, Director; 303-466-1725
Ken Poynter, Executive Director; 303-466-1725
Faith McGruther, Secretary and Treasurer; 906-632-0043; cotfma@up.net

NATIVE PLANT SOCIETY OF NORTHEASTERN OHIO

640 Cherry Park Oval
Aurora, OH 44202 United States
Phone: 330-562-4053
E-mail: bjroche@aol.com
Website: npsohio@hotmail.com

Founded: 1982
Membership: 101–1,000
Scope: Local, State, Regional

Description: The Native Plant Society of Northeastern Ohio promotes education about and conservation of native plants, encourages research, publication of the information and cooperation with other programs and organizations concerned with conservation of natural resources.

Publication(s): On the Fringe

Keyword(s): Forests/Forestry, Land Issues, Public Lands/Greenspace, Reduce/Reuse/Recycle, Water Habitats & Quality, Wildlife & Species

Contact(s):

Jean Roche, President; 640 Cherry Park Oval, Aurora, OH 44202; 330-562-4053; bjroche@aol.com
George Wilder, Vice President; 216-932-3351
Judy Bradt-Barnhart, Treasurer; 440-548-2414
Brian Gilbert, Secretary; 216-486-8765
Tom Sampliner, Board Member; 216-371-4454

NATIVE PLANT SOCIETY OF OREGON

P.O. Box 902
Eugene, OR 97440 United States
Phone: 541-343-2364 Fax: 541-341-1752
Website: www.npsoregon.org/

Founded: 1961
Scope: State

Description: The Native Plant Society of Oregon is a nonprofit statewide organization. The Society is dedicated to the enjoyment, conservation, and study of Oregon's native vegetation.

Publication(s): Bulletin of the Native Plant Society of Oregon, KALMIOPSIS: Journal of the Native Plant Society of Oregon, Proceedings from a Conference of the Native Plant Society of Oregon, Atlas of Oregon Carex, Conservation and Management of Native Plants and Fungi, Biography of Louis F. Henderson.

Keyword(s): Reduce/Reuse/Recycle, Wildlife & Species

Contact(s):

Bruce Newhouse, President; 541-343-2364
Michael McKeag, Vice-President; 503-642-3965; vice_president@npsoregon.org
Candice Guth, Treasurer
Kelli Van Norman, Secretary

NATIVE PLANT SOCIETY OF TEXAS

P.O. Box 891
Georgetown, TX 78627 United States
Phone: 512-868-8799 Fax: 512-931-1166
E-mail: dtucker@io.com
Website: www.npsot.org

Founded: 1980
Membership: 1,001–10,000
Scope: State

Description: A nonprofit organization dedicated to the education and promotion of conservation, preservation, and utilization of the native plants and the plant habitats of Texas.

Publication(s): Native Plant Society of Texas News

Keyword(s): Wildlife & Species

NATIVE PRAIRIES ASSOCIATION OF TEXAS

P.O. Box 210
Georgetown, TX 78627 United States
Phone: 512-339-0618
E-mail: prairie65@aol.com
Website: www.texasprairie.org

Founded: 1986
Membership: 101–1,000
Scope: State

Description: Native Prairies Association of Texas is dedicated to conservation and restoration of native prairies, through education, research, public awareness, agency cooperation, management, restoration, and acquisitions.

Publication(s): Prairie Dog, The

Keyword(s): Forests/Forestry, Land Issues

Contact(s):

Gene Heinemann, President
Clint Josey, Vice President
Lee Stone; 512-581-9822

NATURAL LAND INSTITUTE

320 S. 3rd St.
Rockford, IL 61104 United States
Phone: 815-964-6666 Fax: 815-964-6661
E-mail: nli@aol.com
Website: www.naturalland.org

Founded: 1982
Membership: 101–1,000
Scope: Regional
Description: A nonprofit organization to protect Illinois's native flora and fauna, and to encourage wise stewardship of the natural resources that affect them.
Publication(s): Pecatonica River Watershed, Flora of Winnebago County, Land and Nature (Quarterly Newsletter)
Keyword(s): Land Issues, Wildlife & Species
Contact(s):
Randall Vincent, President
Gary McIntyre, Vice President
Jerry Paulson, Executive Director
Jill Kennay, Assistant Director
Rebecca Olson, Land Preservation Specialist

NATURAL AREAS ASSOCIATION

Bend, OR 97709 United States
Phone: 541-317-0199 Fax: 541-317-0140
E-mail: naa@natareas.org
Website: www.natareas.org

Founded: 1980
Membership: 1,001–10,000
Scope: International
Description: A nonprofit organization of professional and active volunteers in natural area identification, preservation, protection, management, and research. Provides a medium of exchange and coordination to advance the understanding and appreciation of natural areas and natural diversity.
Publication(s): Natural Areas Journal, Natural Area News
Keyword(s): Land Issues, Public Lands/Greenspace, Reduce/Reuse/Recycle, Wildlife & Species
Contact(s):
Harry Tyler, President; Maine State Planning Office, 184 State St., State House Station 38, Augusta, ME 04333; 207-287-1489; Fax: 207-287-7379; hank.tyler@state.me.us
Carl Becker, Vice President; Natural Heritage Division, Illinois Dept. of Natural Resources, 524 Second St., Springfield, IL 62701-1787; 217-785-8774; Fax: 217-785-8277; cbecker@dnrmail.state.il.us
Reid Schuller, Executive Director; P.O. Box 1504, Bend, OR 97709; 541-317-0199; Fax: 541-317-0140; naa@natareas.org
Peg Kohring, Secretary; P.O. Box 506, Sawyer, MI 49125; 312-913-9459; Fax: 312-913-9523; Pkohring@aol.com
Sam Pearsall, Treasurer; 1307 Chaney Rd., Raleigh, NC 27606; 919-403-8558; Fax: 919-403-0379; spearsall@tnc.org
Chuck Williams, Journal Editor; Biology Dept., Clarion University, Clarion, PA 16214; 814-226-1936; Fax: 814-226-2731; cwilliams@mail.clarion.edu

NATURAL HISTORY SOCIETY OF MARYLAND, INC., THE

2643 N. Charles St.
Baltimore, MD 21218-4590 United States
Phone: 410-235-6116
E-mail: membership@naturalhistory.org
Website: www.naturalhistory.org

Founded: 1929
Membership: 101–1,000
Scope: Local, State
Description: A nonprofit membership organization formed to promote the appreciation of natural history through education, research, and publication—thereby fostering stewardship of natural and cultural resources. The Society bestows the Edmund B. Fladung Award to recognize persons exemplifying the society's goals.
Publication(s): Bulletin of the Maryland Herpetological Society, News and Views, The Maryland Naturalist
Keyword(s): Wildlife & Species
Contact(s):
Joe McSharry, President; jmcsharry@naturalhistory.org
Charles Davis, Chairman of the Board

NATURAL LAND INSTITUTE

320 S. 3rd St.
Rockford, IL 61104 United States
Phone: 815-964-6666 Fax: 815-964-6661
E-mail: nli@aol.com
Website: www.naturalland.org

Founded: 1958
Membership: 101–1,000
Scope: State
Description: A nonprofit organization dedicated to preserving natural areas and biological diversity through a comprehensive program of land protection, stewardship, research, education, and advocacy.
Publication(s): Flora of Winnebago County, Land and Nature, Boone and Winnebago Regional Greenways Plan.
Keyword(s): Ecosystems (precious), Land Issues, Reduce/Reuse/Recycle, Water Habitats & Quality, Wildlife & Species
Contact(s):
Jill Kennay, Assistant Director; 815-964-6666; Fax: 815-964-6661; nli@aol.com
Jerry Paulson, Executive Director; 815-964-6666; Fax: 815-964-6661; paulsonjerry@aol.com

NATURAL LANDS TRUST

Hildacy Farm, 1031 Palmers Mill Rd.
Media, PA 19063 United States
Phone: 610-353-5587 Fax: 610-353-0517
E-mail: info@natlands.org
Website: www.natlands.org

Founded: 1953
Membership: 1,001–10,000
Scope: Regional
Description: Natural Lands Trust is a regional land trust working to protect the most critical remaining open lands in the extended Philadelphia area. Primary programs include: permanently protecting land through acquisition and easements; providing conservation planning services to communities, institutions and landowners; and, managing the group's 45 nature preserves in southeastern Pennsylvania and southern New Jersey.
Publication(s): Native Trees and Plants, Controlling Invasive Plants, Environmentally Friendly Lawn, Growing Greener.
Keyword(s): Forests/Forestry, Land Issues, Public Lands/Greenspace, Sprawl/Urban Planning, Water Habitats & Quality, Wildlife & Species

NATURAL RESOURCES COUNCIL OF AMERICA

1025 Thomas Jefferson St., NW, Suite 109
Washington, DC 20007-5291 United States
Phone: 202-333-0411 Fax: 202-333-0412
E-mail: nrca@naturalresourcescouncil.org
Website: www.naturalresourcescouncil.org

Founded: 1946
Scope: National
Description: An association of nonprofit environmental and conservation organizations dedicated to the protection, conservation, and responsible management of the nation's natural resources. The Council coordinates cooperative efforts between its members, government agencies, private citizens, and businesses. The Council also administers the Conservation Round Table Luncheon series, an annual

Conservation Community Banquet and Awards program, and publishes a bimonthly newsletter.

Publication(s): NEP, The Conservation Voice

Contact(s):
Andrea Yank, Executive Director; andrea@nationalresourcescouncil.org
Melissa Bondi, Assistant Director; melissa@nationalresourcescouncil.org

NATURAL RESOURCES COUNCIL OF MAINE

3 Wade St.
Augusta, ME 04330-6351 United States
Phone: 207-622-3101 Fax: 207-622-4343
E-mail: nrcm@nrcm.org
Website: maineenvironment.org

Founded: N/A
Membership: 1–100
Scope: State
Description: A representative statewide organization, affiliated with the National Wildlife Federation, dedicated to the protection and enhancement of wildlife and its habitat through public education and government interaction.
Publication(s): Maine Environment, other available on website
Contact(s):
Ellen Baum, President
Brownie Carson, Executive Director and Alternate Representative
Mac Deford, Treasurer
Paul Liebow, Representative
Patty Renaud, Editor & Education Programs Contact

NATURAL RESOURCES DEFENSE COUNCIL, INC.

6310 San Vicente Blvd.
Suite 250
Los Angeles, CA 90048 United States
Phone: 323-934-6900 Fax: 323-934-1210
Website: www.nrdc.org

Founded: N/A
Membership: 100,001–500,000
Scope: National
Description: The Natural Resources Defense Council is a national non-profit environmental advocacy organization. The NRDC is a membership organization dedicated to protecting the environment and improving the quality of public health. NRDC has more than 500,000 members and contributors in the U.S. and abroad.
Contact(s):
Gayle Petersen, Office Manager

NATURAL RESOURCES DEFENSE COUNCIL, INC.

NATURAL RESOURCES DEFENSE COUNCIL
Headquarters, 40 W. 20th St.
New York, NY 10011 United States
Phone: 212-727-2700 Fax: 212-727-1773
E-mail: nrdcinfo@nrdc.org
Website: www.nrdc.org

Founded: 1970
Membership: 500,001–1,000,000
Scope: National
Description: Nonprofit membership organization dedicated to protecting America's endangered natural resources and to improving the quality of the human environment. Combines interdisciplinary legal and scientific approach in crafting innovative solutions, monitoring government agencies, bringing legal action, and disseminating citizen information. Areas of concentration: air and water pollution, global warming, nuclear safety, land use, urban environment, pollution prevention, ecosystem management.
Publication(s): OnEarth Magazine, books & reports are available upon request
Contact(s):
John Adams, President; 212-727-2700
Frances Beinecke, Executive Director
Kathrin Lassila, Editor
Frederick Schwarz, Chairman of the Board; 212-727-2700

NATURAL RESOURCES DEFENSE COUNCIL, INC.

NEW YORK, NY
40 West 20th Street
New York, NY 10011 United States
Phone: 212-727-2700 Fax: 212-727-1773
E-mail: nrdcinfo@nrdc.org
Website: www.nrdc.org

Founded: 1970
Membership: 500,001–1,000,000
Scope: International
Description: The Natural Resources Defense Council is a national non-profit environmental advocacy organization. The NRDC is a membership organization dedicated to protecting the environment and improving the quality of public health. NRDC has more than 500,000 members and contributors in the U.S. and abroad.
Publication(s): See website for publications, The Amicus Journal
Contact(s):
John Adams, President

NATURAL RESOURCES DEFENSE COUNCIL, INC.

SAN FRANCISCO, CALIFORNIA OFFICE
71 Stevenson St., # 1825
San Francisco, CA 94105 United States
Phone: 415-777-0220 Fax: 415-495-5996
Website: www.nrdc.org

Founded: N/A
Scope: National
Contact(s):
Kai-Lukas Barlow, Office Manager
Linda Ward, Staff
Gwen Thomas, Clerical Assistant

NATURAL RESOURCES INFORMATION COUNCIL

Anne Hedrich Science & Technology Library, 3100 Old Main Hill
Logan, UT 84322-3100 United States
Phone: 435-797-2165 Fax: 435-797-7475
E-mail: annhed@cc.usu.edu
Website: www.quinneylibrary.usu.edu/NRIC/Index.htm

Founded: 1991
Scope: International
Description: Federal, state, provincal, academic, and special research librarians and information specialists from U.S. and Canada who facilitate the exchange of information on sustainable natural resources. Goals are to build a network of resource people to collect and disseminate information on sustainable natural resources and to provide continuing education.
Publication(s): Annual Newsletter (Yearly), Fish and Game Natural Resource Library Survey.
Keyword(s): Reduce/Reuse/Recycle
Contact(s):
Anne Hedrich, Membership; 435-797-2165; Fax: 435-797-7475; annhed@cc.usu.edu
Barbara Voeltz, Treasurer; bvoeltz@ngpc.state.ne.us

NATURAL SCIENCE FOR YOUTH FOUNDATION

130 Azalea Dr.
Roswell, GA 30075 United States
Phone: 770-594-9367 Fax: 770-594-7738

Founded: 1952

Scope: National

Description: Provides counseling to community groups in the planning and development of environmental and natural science centers, museums, and native animal parks which are designed particularly to meet the needs and interests of children and young people. Conducts an annual conference as part of its widespread effort to promote professional excellence in environmental and natural science centers and museums.

Publication(s): Directory of Natural Science Centers

Keyword(s): Recreation/Ecotourism

Contact(s):
John Forbes, Founder and President Emeritus
Joe Witley, President
Owen Winters, Publications Director
John Hammaker, Treasurer
Georgine Pindar, Secretary

NATURE AND NATURAL RESOURCES (IUCN)

PISO 4
QUITO, Ecuador
Phone: 593-2-466-622 Fax: 593-2-466-624
E-mail: SAMERICA@SUR.IUCN.ORG
Website: www.iucn.org

Founded: N/A

Contact(s):
Roberto Franco, Regional Representative

NATURE CONSERVANCY, THE

4245 North Fairfax Dr.
Arlington, VA 22208 United States
Phone: 703-841-5300 Fax: 703-841-1283
Website: www.nature.org

Founded: 1951

Membership: 1,000,001 +

Scope: International

Description: International nonprofit membership organization committed to preserving biological diversity by protecting natural lands, and the life they harbor; cooperates with educational institutions, public and private conservation agencies. Works with states through "natural heritage programs" to identify ecologically significant natural areas. Manages a system of over 1,600 nature sanctuaries nationwide.

Publication(s): The Nature Conservancy Magazine

Keyword(s): Wildlife & Species

Contact(s):
Steve McCormick, President; 703-841-5300
Donna Cherel, Membership; 703-841-5300
Maggie Coon, Government Relations; 703-841-5300; mcoon@tnc.org
Ray Culter, Administration; 703-841-5300
Mike Dennis, General Counsel; 703-841-5300
Joy Gaddy, Human Resources Field Services; 703-841-5300
Ron Geatz, Editor-in-Chief; 703-841-5300
Diane Gosting, Human Resources Business Services; 703-841-5300
Steve Howell, Chief Operations Officer; 703-841-5300
Deborah Jensen, Conservation Science; 703-841-5300
Bob Reynolds, Chairman of the Board; 703-841-5300
Greg Row, Domestic Conservation; 703-841-5300
Grace Vance, Development and Marketing; 703-841-5300
Alexander Watson, International Conservation; 703-841-5300
Bill Weeks, Chief Conservation Officer; 703-841-5300
David Williamson, Communications; 703-841-5300

NATURE CONSERVANCY, THE

4245 North Fairfax Drive, Suite 100
Arlington, VA 22203-1606 United States
Phone: 703-841-5300 Fax: 703-841-1283
Website: www.nature.org

Founded: 1951

Membership: 1,000,001 +

Scope: International

Description: The mission of The Nature Conservancy is to preserve the plants, animals and natural communities that represent the diversity of life on Earth by protecting the lands and waters they need to survive.

Keyword(s): Development/Developing Countries, Ecosystems (precious), Forests/Forestry, Land Issues, Oceans/Coasts/Beaches, Public Lands/Greenspace, Recreation/Ecotourism, Water Habitats & Quality, Wildlife & Species

Contact(s):
Steven McCormick, President and CEO

NATURE CONSERVANCY, THE

ADIRONDACK CHAPTER
P.O. Box 65
Keene Valley, NY 12943 United States
Phone: 518-576-2082
E-mail: cprickett@tnc.org
Website: www.nature.org/adirondacks

Founded: 1971

Membership: 1,001–10,000

Scope: Local

Description: The Adirondack Nature Conservancy and Adirondack Land Trust are separate land conservation organizations that have acted in partnership since 1988, coordinating programs and staff. The Adirondack Nature Conservancy protects the plants, animals, and natural communities that represent the diversity of life in the Adirondacks by protecting the lands and waters they need to survive.

Publication(s): Developing a Land Conservation Strategy: A Handbook for Land Trusts (1987)

Keyword(s): Agriculture/Farming, Development/Developing Countries, Forests/Forestry, Land Issues, Public Lands/Greenspace

Contact(s):
Timothy Barnett, Vice President; 518-576-2082; Fax: 518-576-4203; tbarnett@tnc.org
Michael Carr, Executive Director; 518-576-2082; Fax: 518-576-4203; mcarr@tnc.org
Todd Dunham, Director of Land Protection; 518-576-2082; Fax: 518-576-4203; tdunham@tnc.org
Francisca Irwin, Secretary; Rt. 1 Box 80, Essex, NY 12936
Edward McNeil, Chairman; 108 Burlingame Rd., Syracuse, NY 13202-1604
Meredith Prime, Treasurer; Heather Hill, Lake Placid, NY 12946

NATURE CONSERVANCY, THE

ALABAMA CHAPTER
NATURAL HERITAGE PROGRAM
Alabama Natural Heritage Program
Huntingdon College
1500 E. Fairview Ave.
Montgomery, AL 36106 United States
Phone: 334-834-4519 Fax: 334-834-5439
E-mail: bstinson@alnhp.org
Website: www.natureserve.org/nhp/us/al/

Founded: 1989

Membership: 1–100

Scope: State, Regional

Description: The mission of the Alabama Natural Heritage program is to provide the best available scientific information on the biological diversity of Alabama, guide conservation action and promote sound stewardship practices within the state and throughout the Southeast.

Publication(s): Natural Heritage News, Inventory List of Rare Threatened and Endangered Plants, Animals, and Natural Communities of Alabama

Keyword(s): Land Issues, Public Lands/Greenspace, Reduce/Reuse/Recycle, Wildlife & Species

Contact(s):
Robert Hastings, Director, Heritage Program; 334-834-4519, ext. 21; bhastings@alnhp.org

NATURE CONSERVANCY, THE
ALABAMA OPERATING UNIT
2821 2nd Avenue S, Suite C
Birmingham, AL 35233 United States
Phone: 205-251-1155 Fax: 205-251-4444
E-mail: cwilborn@tnc.org
Website: www.nature.org

Founded: 1989
Membership: 1,001–10,000
Scope: State
Description: The mission of The Nature Conservancy is to preserve the plants, animals, and natural communities that represent the diversity of life on Earth by protecting the lands and waters they need to survive.
Keyword(s): Agriculture/Farming, Executive/Legislative/Judicial Reform, Forests/Forestry, Land Issues, Oceans/Coasts/Beaches, Public Lands/Greenspace, Recreation/Ecotourism, Water Habitats & Quality, Wildlife & Species
Contact(s):
Kathy Stiles Freeland, State Director

NATURE CONSERVANCY, THE
ALASKA CHAPTER
421 W. First Ave., Suite 200
Anchorage, AK 99501 United States
Phone: 907-276-3133 Fax: 907-276-2584
E-mail: alaska@tnc.org
Website: www.nature.org

Founded: 1988
Membership: 1,001–10,000
Scope: State
Description: The mission of The Nature Conservancy is to preserve the plants, animals, and natural communities that represent the diversity of life on Earth by protecting the lands and waters they need to survive.
Publication(s): Nature Conservancy of Alaska
Keyword(s): Ecosystems (precious), Land Issues
Contact(s):
David Banks, State Director; 907-276-3133; alaska@tnc.org
Erin Dovichin, Director of Communications; alaska@tnc.org

NATURE CONSERVANCY, THE
ARKANSAS FIELD OFFICE
601 N. University Ave.
Little Rock, AR 72205 United States
Phone: 501-663-6699 Fax: 501-663-8332

Founded: N/A
Scope: State
Contact(s):
Nancy Delamar, State Director; cbornemeier@tnc.org

NATURE CONSERVANCY, THE
ASIA/PACIFIC PROGRAM
1116 Smith St., #201
Honolulu, HI 96817 United States
Phone: 808-537-4508

Founded: N/A
Scope: International

NATURE CONSERVANCY, THE
CALIFORNIA CHAPTER
201 Mission St., 4th Fl.
San Francisco, CA 94105 United States
Phone: 415-777-0487 Fax: 415-777-0244
Website: www.tnccalifornia.org

Founded: 1951
Membership: 500,001–1,000,000
Scope: State, Regional, International
Description: The mission of The Nature Conservancy is to preserve plants, animals, and natural communities that represent the diversity of life on Earth by protecting the lands and waters they need to survive.
Contact(s):
Williams Jody, Program Manager

NATURE CONSERVANCY, THE
CANADA CHAPTER
110 Eglinton Ave. W., Suite 400
Toronto, M4R 1A3 Ontario Canada
Phone: 416-932-3202 Fax: 416-932-3208
E-mail: nature@natureconservancy.ca
Website: www.natureconservancy.ca

Founded: 1962
Scope: National
Description: The Nature Conservancy of Canada is the only national charity dedicated to preserving ecologically significant areas, places of special beauty and education interest through outright purchase, donations and conservation agreements.
Publication(s): Annual Report, The Ark
Keyword(s): Land Issues, Wildlife & Species
Contact(s):
Lynn Gran, Director of Development; lynn.gran@natureconservancy.ca
John Lounds, Executive Director
Ted Boswell, Chairman

NATURE CONSERVANCY, THE
COLORADO CHAPTER
2424 Spruce Street
Boulder, CO 80302 United States
Phone: 303-444-2950 Fax: 303-444-2986
E-mail: gbailey@tnc.org
Website: www.nature.org /colorado

Founded: N/A
Membership: 1,000,001 +
Scope: State
Description: The Nature Conservancy is a private, international, non-profit organization that preserves plants, animals and natural communities representing the diversity of life on Earth by protecting the lands and waters they need to survive. To date, the Conservancy and its more than one million members have been responsible for the protection of more than 12 million acres in the U.S. and have helped preserve more than 80 million acres in Latin America, the Caribbean, Asia and the Pacific.
Publication(s): Land Mark, The
Keyword(s): Ecosystems (precious), Ethics/Environmental Justice, Forests/Forestry, Land Issues, Pollution (general), Public Lands/Greenspace, Recreation/Ecotourism, Water Habitats & Quality, Wildlife & Species
Contact(s):
Mark Burget, State Director; 303-444-2950, ext. 1010; Fax: 303-444-2986; mburget@tnc.org
Geneva Bailey, Office Co-ordinator; 303-444-2950
Charles Bedford, Associate Director; 303-444-2950, ext. 1232; Fax: 303-444-2968; cbedford@tnc.org

NATURE CONSERVANCY, THE
CONNECTICUT CHAPTER
55 High Street
Middletown, CT 06457 United States
Phone: 860-344-0716
E-mail: ct@tnc.org
Website: nature.org/connecticut

Founded: 1960

Scope: International

Description: The mission of The Nature Conservancy is to preserve the plants, animals and natural communities that represent the diversity of life on Earth by protecting the lands and waters they need to survive.

Contact(s):
Dennis McGrath, State Director

NATURE CONSERVANCY, THE
DELAWARE CHAPTER
100 W. 10th St. #1107
Wilmington, DE 19801 United States
Phone: 302-654-4707 Fax: 302-654-4708
E-mail: delaware@tnc.org
Website: www.nature.org

Founded: 1989
Membership: 1,001–10,000
Scope: State, Regional
Description: The mission of The Nature Conservancy is to preserve the plants, animals and natural communities that represent the diversity of life on Earth by protecting the lands and waters they need to survive.
Keyword(s): Land Issues, Public Lands/Greenspace, Water Habitats & Quality, Wildlife & Species
Contact(s):
Jennifer Burns, Director of Development & Communications; 302-654-4707, ext. 125; jburns@tnc.org
Roger Jones, State Director

NATURE CONSERVANCY, THE
EASTERN NEW YORK CHAPTER
19 North Moger Avenue
Mount Kisco, NY 10549 United States
Phone: 914-244-3271 Fax: 914-244-3275
Website: www.nature.org

Founded: 1951
Membership: 10,001–100,000
Scope: Local, State, Regional, National, International
Description: The mission of The Nature Conservancy is to protect the plants, animals, & natural communities that represent the diversity of life on Earth by protecting the lands and waters they need to survive.
Publication(s): Preserve Guide, avaliable on website.
Keyword(s): Ecosystems (precious), Forests/Forestry, Land Issues, Recreation/Ecotourism, Water Habitats & Quality, Wildlife & Species
Contact(s):
Kathy Moser, Executive Director

NATURE CONSERVANCY, THE
FLORIDA CHAPTER
222 S. Westmonte Dr. Suite 300
Altamonte Springs, FL 32714 United States
Phone: 407-682-3664 Fax: 407-682-3077
E-mail: mcantillo@tnc.org
Website: nature.org/

Founded: N/A

Scope: State

NATURE CONSERVANCY, THE
GEORGIA CHAPTER
1330 W. Peachtree St., Ste. 410
Atlanta, GA 30309-2904 United States
Phone: 404-873-6946 Fax: 404-873-6984
Website: www.nature.org

Founded: 1987
Membership: 10,001–100,000
Scope: State
Publication(s): Quarterly newsletter
Contact(s):
Tavia McCuean, Vice President and State Director

NATURE CONSERVANCY, THE
GREAT PLAINS DIVISION
1313 5th St., SE, Suite 320
Minneapolis, MN 55414 United States
Phone: 612-331-0750 Fax: 612-331-0770
Website: www.nature.org

Founded: 1951

Scope: Local, State, Regional, International

Description: The mission of The Nature Conservancy is to protect plants, animals and natural communities that represent the diversity of life on Earth by protecting the land and water they need to survive. The Great Plains Division includes the programs in 7 states: Iowa, Kansas, Minnesota, Missouri, Nebraska, North Dakota and South Dakota and concentrates on the protection of Great Plains ecoregions including Tallgrass Prairie.

Publication(s): National Magazine, Newsletter, Annual Report

Contact(s):
Robert McKim, Division Director

NATURE CONSERVANCY, THE
HAWAII CHAPTER
923 Nu'uanu Avenue
Honolulu, HI 96817 United States
Phone: 808-537-4508 Fax: 808-545-2019
E-mail: mwaits@tnc.org
Website: nature.org

Founded: N/A

Scope: State

NATURE CONSERVANCY, THE
IDAHO CHAPTER
Sun Valley, ID 83353 United States
Phone: 208-726-3007 Fax: 208-726-1258
Website: www.nature.org

Founded: N/A

Scope: State

Contact(s):
Geoff Pampush, State Director

NATURE CONSERVANCY, THE
ILLINOIS CHAPTER
8 S. Michigan Ave.
Suite 900
Chicago, IL 60603 United States
Phone: 312-580-2100 Fax: 312-346-5600

Founded: N/A

Scope: State

Contact(s):
Bruce Boyd, State Director

NATURE CONSERVANCY, THE
INDIANA CHAPTER
1505 N. Delaware St.
Suite 200
Indianapolis, IN 46202 United States
Phone: 317-951-8818 Fax: 317-917-2478
E-mail: csutton@tnc.org
Website: www.nature.org/indiana

Founded: 1959
Membership: 10,001–100,000
Scope: Regional
Description: Not-for-profit land conservation organization.
Publication(s): Preserve Guide, Chapter Newsletter (twice yearly)
Keyword(s): Ecosystems (precious), Forests/Forestry, Water Habitats & Quality, Wildlife & Species
Contact(s):
Mary McConnell, State Director; 317-951-8818; Fax: 317-917-2478; mmcconnell@tnc.org

NATURE CONSERVANCY, THE
IOWA CHAPTER
108 3rd St.,
Des Moines, IA 50309-4758 United States
Phone: 515-244-5044 Fax: 515-244-8890
E-mail: iowa@tnc.org
Website: www.nature.org/iowa

Founded: N/A
Membership: 1,001–10,000
Scope: State
Publication(s): Nature Conservancy, Iowa Field Notes
Contact(s):
Dave Degeus, Director of Protection
Ann Robinson, Director of Development

NATURE CONSERVANCY, THE
KANSAS CHAPTER
700 SW Jackson St., Suite 804
Topeka, KS 66603 United States
Phone: 785-233-4400 Fax: 785-233-2022
E-mail: rpalmer@tnc.org
Website: nature.org/kansas

Founded: 1989
Membership: 1,001–10,000
Scope: State
Description: The mission of The Nature Conservancy is to preserve plants, animals, and natural communities that represent the diversity of life on Earth by protecting the lands and waters they need to survive.
Contact(s):
Alan Pollom, Vice President

NATURE CONSERVANCY, THE
KENTUCKY CHAPTER
642 W. Main St.
Lexington, KY 40508 United States
Phone: 859-259-9655 Fax: 859-259-9678
E-mail: nature@mis.net
Website: www.nature.org

Founded: N/A
Membership: 10,001–100,000
Scope: Regional
Contact(s):
James Aldrich, State Director

NATURE CONSERVANCY, THE
LOUISIANA CHAPTER
P.O. Box 4125
Baton Rouge, LA 70821 United States
Phone: 225-338-1040 Fax: 225-338-0103
E-mail: lafo@tnc.org
Website: www.louisiananature.org

Founded: N/A
Membership: 1,001–10,000
Scope: State
Contact(s):
Keith Ouchley, State Director

NATURE CONSERVANCY, THE
MAINE CHAPTER
14 Maine St., #401
Brunswick, ME 04011 United States
Phone: 207-729-5181
E-mail: naturemaine@tnc.org
Website: nature.org

Founded: N/A
Scope: Local, State, Regional, National, International
Description: The Maine Chapter is an operating unit, located in Maine, of The Nature Conservancy nationwide.

NATURE CONSERVANCY, THE
MARYLAND/DISTRICT OF COLUMBIA CHAPTER
5410 Grosvenor Lane
Suite 100
Bethesda, MD 20814 United States
Phone: 301-897-8570 Fax: 301-897-0858
E-mail: ndeane@tnc.org
Website: nature.org/marylanddc

Founded: N/A
Scope: Local, State, Regional, National, International
Description: The Nature Conservancy's mission is to preserve the plants, animals and natural communities that represent the diversity of life on Earth by protecting the lands and waters they need to survive.
Contact(s):
Nat Williams, State Director & Vice President

NATURE CONSERVANCY, THE
MASSACHUSETTS CHAPTER
70 Milk St.
Suite 300
Boston, MA 02109 United States
Phone: 617-227-7017 Fax: 617-227-7688
E-mail: mmail@tnc.org
Website: www.nature.org

Founded: N/A
Scope: State

NATURE CONSERVANCY, THE
MICHIGAN CHAPTER
2840 E. Grand River Ave., Suite 5
East Lansing, MI 48823 United States
Phone: 517-332-1741 Fax: 517-332-8382

Founded: N/A
Scope: State
Contact(s):
Helen Taylor, State Director

NATURE CONSERVANCY, THE
MID-ATLANTIC DIVISION OFFICE
4705 University Dr., Suite 290
Durham, NC 27707 United States
Phone: 919-403-8558 Fax: 919-403-0379

Founded: N/A
Scope: Regional
Contact(s):
Katherine Skinner, Vice President

NATURE CONSERVANCY, THE
MINNESOTA CHAPTER
1313 Fifth St., SE, #320
Minneapolis, MN 55414 United States
Phone: 612-331-0750 Fax: 612-331-0770
Founded: N/A
Scope: State
Contact(s):
Rob McKim, State Director

NATURE CONSERVANCY, THE
MISSISSIPPI CHAPTER
6400 Lakeover Rd., Suite C
Jackson, MS 39213 United States
Phone: 601-713-3355 Fax: 601-982-9499
Website: www.nature.org/Mississippi
Founded: N/A
Scope: National, International
Description: Private non-profit whose mission is to preserve plants, animals and natural communities by protecting the lands and water they need to survive.
Contact(s):
Robbie Fisher, State Director

NATURE CONSERVANCY, THE
MISSOURI CHAPTER
2800 S. Brentwood Blvd.
St. Louis, MO 63144 United States
Phone: 314-968-1105 Fax: 314-968-3659
E-mail: missouri@tnc.org
Website: nature.org
Founded: N/A
Membership: 1–100
Scope: State

NATURE CONSERVANCY, THE
MONTANA CHAPTER
32 South Ewing Street
Suite 215
Helena, MT 59601 United States
Phone: 406-443-0303 Fax: 406-443-8311
E-mail: ktrepanier@tnc.org
Website: www.nature.org
Founded: 1950
Membership: 1,001–10,000
Scope: State
Description: The mission of The Nature Conservancy is to preserve the plants, animals, and natural communities that represent the diversity of life on Earth by protecting the lands and waters they need to survive.
Contact(s):
Jamie Williams, State Director

NATURE CONSERVANCY, THE
NEBRASKA CHAPTER
1019 Leaveniworth St.
Omaha, NE 68102 United States
Phone: 402-342-0282 Fax: 402-342-0474
E-mail: nebraska@tnc.org
Website: www.nature.org
Founded: 1951
Membership: 1,000,001 +
Scope: International
Description: Private, non-profit conservation organization.
Contact(s):
Vince Shay, State Director

NATURE CONSERVANCY, THE
NEVADA CHAPTER
1771 E. Flamingo,
Las Vegas, NV 89119 United States
Phone: 702-737-8744 Fax: 702-737-5787
E-mail: swainscott@tnc.org
Website: www.nature.org
Founded: N/A
Membership: 1,001–10,000
Scope: State
Contact(s):
Ame Hellman, State Director

NATURE CONSERVANCY, THE
NEW HAMPSHIRE CHAPTER
22 Bridge 4th floor
Concord, NH 03301 United States
Phone: 603-224-5853 Fax: 603-228-2459
Website: nature.org/newhampshire
Founded: N/A
Membership: 1,001–10,000
Scope: State
Description: The Nature Conservancy is a private, non-profit organization whose mission is to preserve the plants, animals and natural communities that represent the diversity of life on Earth by protecting the lands and waters they need to survive.
Contact(s):
Daryl Burtnett, State Director; 603-224-5853; dburtnett@tnc.org

NATURE CONSERVANCY, THE
NEW JERSEY CHAPTER
200 Pottersville Rd.
Chester, NJ 07930 United States
Phone: 908-879-7262 Fax: 908-879-2172
Website: www.nature.org
Founded: 1988
Membership: 10,001–100,000
Scope: Local
Description: The Nature Conservancy (est. 1951) is an international, non-profit organization dedicated to preserving the plants, animals and natural communities that represent the diversity of life on Earth by protecting the lands and waters they need to survive. Active in the Garden State since 1955, the New Jersey Chapter was established in 1988. Through more than 300 conservation transactions with the help of corporate sponsors, foundations and 33,000 members we have protected more than 54,000 acres.
Publication(s): Oak Leaf Quarterly Newsletter
Contact(s):
Michael Catania, State Director

NATURE CONSERVANCY, THE
NEW MEXICO CHAPTER
212 E. Marcy, #200
Santa Fe, NM 87501 United States
Phone: 505-988-3867
E-mail: smacfarland@tnc.org
Website: www.nature.org
Founded: N/A
Scope: State
Contact(s):
Bill Waldman, State Director

NATURE CONSERVANCY, THE
NEW YORK ADIRONDACK CHAPTER
Route 73
Keene Valley, NY 12943 United States
Phone: 518-576-2082 Fax: 518-576-4203

Founded: N/A
Membership: 1–100
Scope: Local, Regional
Contact(s):
Michael Carr, Director

NATURE CONSERVANCY, THE
NEW YORK CENTRAL/WESTERN CHAPTER
339 East Ave.
Rochester, NY 14604 United States
Phone: 716-546-8030 Fax: 706-546-7825
Website: www.nature.org

Founded: N/A
Membership: 1–100
Scope: Local, Regional
Publication(s): Quarterly newsletter

NATURE CONSERVANCY, THE
NEW YORK CITY CHAPTER
570 Seventh Ave.,
New York, NY 10018 United States
Phone: 212-997-1880 Fax: 212-997-8451
Website: www.nature.org

Founded: N/A
Scope: International
Publication(s): Nature Conservancy of New York

NATURE CONSERVANCY, THE
NEW YORK LONG ISLAND CHAPTER
250 Lawrence Hill Rd.
Cold Spring Harbor, NY 11724 United States
Phone: 631-367-3225 Fax: 631-367-4775
E-mail: cgordon@tnc.org
Website: nature.org/

Founded: 1951
Scope: Local, State, Regional, National, International
Description: Works cooperatively with other conservation groups, businesses and many levels of government. Two conservancy chapters on Long Island have protected 40,000 acres and own approximately 5,000 acres in preserves.
Keyword(s): Ecosystems (precious), Forests/Forestry, Land Issues, Oceans/Coasts/Beaches, Public Lands/Greenspace, Water Habitats & Quality, Wildlife & Species
Contact(s):
Paul Rabinovitch, Executive Director
John Turner, Director of Conservation

NATURE CONSERVANCY, THE
NEW YORK SOUTH FORK/ SHELTER ISLAND CHAPTER
P.O. Box 5125
E. Hampton, NY 11937 United States
Phone: 631-329-7689 Fax: 631-329-0215

Founded: N/A
Scope: Local, Regional
Contact(s):
Nancy Kelley, Director

NATURE CONSERVANCY, THE
NORTH CAROLINA CHAPTER
4705 Univeristy Dr., #290
Durham, NC 27707 United States
Phone: 919-403-8558 Fax: 919-403-0379

Founded: N/A
Scope: State
Contact(s):
Katherine Skinner, Executive Director

NATURE CONSERVANCY, THE
NORTH DAKOTA CHAPTER
1256 N. Parkview Dr.
Bismarck, ND 58501 United States
Phone: 701-222-8464 Fax: 701-222-8061
Website: www.nature.org

Founded: N/A
Membership: 1,001–10,000
Scope: State
Description: The mission of The Nature Conservancy is to preserve the plants, animals, and natural communities that represent the diversity of life on Earth by protecting the lands and waters they need to survive.
Contact(s):
Gerald Reichert, Field Representative; 1256 North Parkview Dr., Bismarck, ND 58501; 701-222-8464; Fax: 701-222-8061; greichert@tnc.org
Eric Rosenquist, Preserve Manager; 1401 River Road, Center, ND 58530-9445; 701-794-8741; Fax: 701-794-3544; erosenquist@tnc.org

NATURE CONSERVANCY, THE
NORTHEAST/ CARIBBEAN DIVISION OFFICE
159 Waterman St.
Providence, RI 02906 United States
Phone: 401-751-2521 Fax: 401-751-7596
Website: www.tnc.org

Founded: N/A
Scope: International
Description: Mission is to preserve the plants, animals and natural communities that represent the diversity of life on Earth by protecting the lands and waters they need to survive.
Publication(s): Nature Conservancy - Bi-monthly magazine
Contact(s):
John Cook, Vice President
Jennifer Bristol, Sr. Exec. Assistant; 401-751-2521

NATURE CONSERVANCY, THE
NORTHWEST AND HAWAII DIVISION OFFICE
217 Pine St., Suite 1100
Seattle, WA 98101 United States
Phone: 206-343-4344

Founded: N/A
Scope: Regional
Contact(s):
Elliot Marks, Vice President

NATURE CONSERVANCY, THE
OHIO CHAPTER
6375 Riverside Dr.
Dublin, OH 43017 United States
Phone: 614-717-2770 Fax: 614-717-2777
Website: www.nature.org

Founded: 1951
Membership: 10,001–100,000
Scope: State, National
Description: The mission of The Nature Conservancy is to preserve the plants, animals and natural communities that represent the diversity of life on Earth by protecting the lands and waters they need to survive.
Keyword(s): Agriculture/Farming, Development/Developing Countries, Ecosystems (precious), Forests/Forestry, Land Issues, Public Lands/Greenspace, Sprawl/Urban Planning, Water Habitats & Quality, Wildlife & Species
Contact(s):
Rich Shank, State Director

NATURE CONSERVANCY, THE
OKLAHOMA CHAPTER
2727 East 21st
Tulsa, OK 74114 United States
Phone: 918-585-1117 Fax: 918-585-2383
Website: www.nature.org
Founded: N/A
Scope: State
Contact(s):
Mary Collins, State Director

NATURE CONSERVANCY, THE
OREGON CHAPTER
821 SE 14th Ave.
Portland, OR 97214 United States
Phone: 503-230-1221 Fax: 503-230-9639
Website: www.nature.org
Founded: 1961
Membership: 10,001–100,000
Scope: Local, State, Regional, National, International
Description: The Nature Conservancy's mission is to preserve the plants, animals and natural communities representing the diversity of life on Earth by protecting the lands and waters they need to survive. The Conservancy has projects in every state and 29 countries.
Publication(s): Newsletter, Annual Report
Contact(s):
Russell Hoeflich, State Director

NATURE CONSERVANCY, THE
PENNSYLVANIA CHAPTER
1100 E. Hector St.
Suite 470
Conshohocken, PA 19428 United States
Phone: 610-834-1323 Fax: 610-834-6533
Website: www.nature.org
Founded: 1981
Membership: 10,001–100,000
Scope: State
Description: Biodiversity Conservation
Publication(s): Penns Woods-Bi-annually
Keyword(s): Development/Developing Countries, Ecosystems (precious), Forests/Forestry, Land Issues, Water Habitats & Quality, Wildlife & Species
Contact(s):
P. Gray, State Director
Scott Anderson, Director of Development & Communications; 610-834-1323, ext. 119
Nels Johnson, Director of Conservation Programs; 717-232-6001, ext. 108
Ron Ramsey, Director of Government Relations; 717-232-6001, ext. 106

NATURE CONSERVANCY, THE
RHODE ISLAND CHAPTER
159 Waterman Street
Providence, RI 02906 United States
Phone: 401-331-7110 Fax: 401-273-4902
Website: nature.org
Founded: N/A
Scope: Local, State, Regional, National, International
Description: Saving biodiversity
Keyword(s): Climate Change, Development/Developing Countries, Ecosystems (precious), Forests/Forestry, Land Issues, Oceans/Coasts/Beaches, Water Habitats & Quality, Wildlife & Species
Contact(s):
Terry Sullivan, State Director

NATURE CONSERVANCY, THE
ROCKY MOUNTAIN DIVISION OFFICE
117 E. Mountain Ave.
Fort Collins, CO 80524 United States
Phone: 970-484-2886 Fax: 970-498-0225
Website: www.nature.org
Founded: N/A
Scope: National
Contact(s):
Bruce Runnels, Vice President

NATURE CONSERVANCY, THE
SOUTH CAROLINA CHAPTER
P.O. Box 5475
Columbia, SC 29250 United States
Phone: 803-254-9049 Fax: 803-252-7134
Founded: N/A
Scope: State
Contact(s):
Mark Robertson, State Director

NATURE CONSERVANCY, THE
SOUTHEAST DIVISION OFFICE
222 S. Westmonte Dr., Suite 300
Altamonte Springs, FL 32714 United States
Phone: 407-682-3664 Fax: 407-682-3077
Founded: N/A
Scope: Regional
Contact(s):
Robert Benedick, Vice-President

NATURE CONSERVANCY, THE
TENNESSEE CHAPTER
2021 21st. Ave. S.
Nashville, TN 37212 United States
Phone: 615-383-9909 Fax: 615-383-9717
Website: www.nature.org/tennessee
Founded: N/A
Membership: 10,001–100,000
Scope: State
Publication(s): Newsletter - bi-annual
Contact(s):
Scott Davis, State Director

NATURE CONSERVANCY, THE
TEXAS CHAPTER
P.O. Box 1440
San Antonio, TX 78295-1440 United States
Phone: 210-224-8774 Fax: 210-228-9805
Founded: N/A
Scope: State
Contact(s):
Robert Potts, State Director

NATURE CONSERVANCY, THE
UTAH CHAPTER
559 E. South Temple
Salt Lake City, UT 84102 United States
Phone: 801-531-0999 Fax: 801-531–1003
Website: www.nature.org
Founded: 1995
Membership: 1,001–10,000
Scope: Local, State, Regional, National, International
Description: Our mission is to preserve the plants, animals and natural communities in Utah by protecting the lands & waters they need to survive.
Keyword(s): Agriculture/Farming, Development/Developing Countries, Ecosystems (precious), Executive/Legislative/ Judicial

Reform, Land Issues, Population, Public Lands/Greenspace, Recreation/Ecotourism, Sprawl/Urban Planning, Transportation, Water Habitats & Quality,

Contact(s):
David Livermore, State Director; 801-531-0999; Fax: 801-531–1003; dlivermore@tnc.org
Larisa Barry, Communications Manager; 801-531-0999, ext. 21; Fax: 801-531–1003; lbarry@tnc.org
Libby Ellis, Director of Development; 801-531-0999, ext. 17; Fax: 801-531–1003; lellis@tnc.org
Jill Lehmann, Executive Assistant; 801-531-0999; Fax: 801-531–1003; jlehmann@tnc.org
Chris Montague, Director of Conservation Programs; 801-531-0999, ext. 13; Fax: 801-531–1003; cmontague@tnc.org
Elaine York, Director of Volunteer & Education Programs; 801-531-0999, ext. 20; Fax: 801-531–1003; eyork@tnc.org

NATURE CONSERVANCY, THE
VERMONT CHAPTER
27 State. St.
Montpelier, VT 05602 United States
Phone: 802-229-4425 Fax: 802-229-1347

Founded: N/A
Scope: State
Contact(s):
Robert Klein, State Director

NATURE CONSERVANCY, THE
VIRGIN ISLANDS CHAPTER
14B Norre Gade, 2nd Fl.
Charlotte Amalie, VI 00802 United States
Phone: 340-774-7633 Fax: 340-774-7736
E-mail: c.philyaw@att.net
Website: www.nature.org

Founded: N/A
Scope: State
Publication(s): Available on web
Contact(s):
Robert Weary, Director

NATURE CONSERVANCY, THE
VIRGINIA CHAPTER
490 Westfield Rd.
Charlottesville, VA 22901 United States
Phone: 434-295-6106 Fax: 434-979-0370
E-mail: dwhite@tnc.org
Website: nature.org/virginia

Founded: 1960
Membership: 10,001–100,000
Scope: State, Regional
Description: The Nature Conservancy seeks to protect the diversity of life on Earth by protecting land and water habitats.
Publication(s): Virginia News
Contact(s):
Michael Lipford, Executive Director

NATURE CONSERVANCY, THE
WASHINGTON CHAPTER
217 Pine St., #1100
Seattle, WA 98101 United States
Phone: 206-343-4344 Fax: 206-343-5608

Founded: N/A
Membership: 10,001–100,000
Scope: State
Contact(s):
David Weekes, State Director

NATURE CONSERVANCY, THE
WEST VIRGINIA CHAPTER
723 Kanawha Blvd. East, #500
Charleston, WV 25301 United States
Phone: 304-345-4350 Fax: 304-345-4351
Website: www.nature.org

Founded: N/A
Membership: 1,001–10,000
Scope: State
Contact(s):
Paul Trianosky, State Director

NATURE CONSERVANCY, THE
WISCONSIN CHAPTER
633 W. Main St.
Madison, WI 53703 United States
Phone: 608-251-8140 Fax: 608-251-8535
E-mail: wmail@tnc.org
Website: nature.org/wisconsin

Founded: 1960
Membership: 10,001–100,000
Scope: State
Description: Preserves habitat for native plants and animals.
Publication(s): The Places We Save; A Guide to Conservancy Preserves in WI
Keyword(s): Ecosystems (precious), Water Habitats & Quality, Wildlife & Species
Contact(s):
Cate Harrington, Director of Communications/Media; 608-251-8140

NATURE CONSERVANCY, THE
WYOMING CHAPTER
258 Main St., #200
Lander, WY 82520 United States
Phone: 307-332-2971 Fax: 307-332-2974
E-mail: wyoming@tnc.org
Website: tncwyoming.org

Founded: N/A
Scope: State
Description: The Nature Conservancy is a private, non-profit, 501(c)(3) international membership organization whose mission is to preserve the plants, animals and natural communities that represent the diversity of life on earth by protecting the lands and waters they need to survive.

NATURE CONSERVATION SOCIETY OF JAPAN, THE (NACS-J)
Yamaji Sanbancho Bldg. 3F,
5-24 Sanbancho
Chiyoda-Ku, Tokyo, 102-0075 Japan
Phone: 81332650521 Fax: 81332650527
E-mail: nature@nacsj.or.jp
Website: www.nacsj.or.jp

Founded: 1951
Membership: 10,001–100,000
Scope: National
Description: A nonprofit, membership conservation organization devoted to promoting conservation, research, and education concerning the natural areas and wildlife in Japan, and also a recently launched international project to support biodiversity in developing countries.
Contact(s):
Masahito Yoshida, Executive Director; 81332650523; Fax: 81332650527; myoshida@nacsj.or.jp

NATURE SASKATCHEWAN

206, 1860 Lorne St
Regina, S4P 2L7 Saskatchewan Canada
Phone: 306-780-9273 Fax: 306-780-9263
E-mail: info@naturesask.com
Website: www.naturesask.com

Founded: 1947
Membership: 1,001–10,000
Scope: Regional
Description: Nature Saskatchewan is the largest non-profit nature organization in the province, committed to preserving our natural environment. We operate a nature bookshop, offer ecological tours, own nature sanctuaries, and support conservation and research activities and nature education.
Publication(s): Blue Jay, special publication, Nature Views
Keyword(s): Land Issues, Reduce/Reuse/Recycle, Water Habitats & Quality, Wildlife & Species

NATURESERVE

1101 Wilson Blvd.
15th floor
Arlington, VA 22209 United States
Phone: 703-908-1800 Fax: 703-908-1917
E-mail: laura_jarrell@natureserve.org
Website: www.natureserve.org

Founded: 1994
Scope: Regional
Description: NatureServe is a non-profit organization dedicated to providing knowledge to protect natural heritage programs and conservation data centers, NatureServe is a leading source for scientific information on rare and endandered species and threatened ecosystems. NatureServe and its member programs operate in the United States, Canada, Latin America, and the Caribbean providing essential information for conservation action.
Contact(s):
Mark Schaefer, President and CEO
Joy Gaddy, Vice President for Operations
Dennis Grossman, Vice President for Science
Mary Klein, Vice President for Natural Heritage Network Operations
Bruce Stein, Vice President for Programs
Larry Sugarbaker, Chief Information Officer

NCAT CENTER FOR RESOURCEFUL BUILDING TECHNOLOGY

P.O. Box 100
Missoula, MT 59806 United States
Phone: 406-549-7678 Fax: 406-549-4100
E-mail: crbt@ncat.org
Website: www.crbt.org

Founded: 1991
Membership: N/A
Scope: National
Description: NCAT's Center for Resourceful Building Technology (CRBT) is dedicated to promoting environmentally responsible practices in construction. It serves as both catalyst and facilitator in encouraging building technologies which realize a sustainable and efficient use of resources.
Publication(s): Building Our Children's Future, ReCraft 90 Handbook
Keyword(s): Development/Developing Countries, Energy, Reduce/Reuse/Recycle
Contact(s):
Tracy Mumma, Research Director
Steve Loken, Founder; P.O. Box 9317, Missoula, MT 59807; 406-543-1931

NEBRASKA ASSOCIATION OF RESOURCE DISTRICTS

601 South 12th St.
Lincoln, NE 68508 United States
Phone: 402-471-7670 Fax: 402-471-7677
E-mail: nard@nrd.net.org
Website: www.nrd.net.org

Founded: N/A
Membership: 1–100
Scope: Regional
Contact(s):
Orval Gigstad, President; Rt. 1, Box 54, Syracuse, NE 68446; 402-269-3267
Dave Nelson, Vice President; 402-756-0724
Dean Edson, Executive Director; 601 S. 12th St., Suite 201, Lincoln, NE 68508; 402-471-7674; Fax: 402-471-7677

NEBRASKA B.A.S.S. CHAPTER FEDERATION

Attn: President, 1518 Kozy Dr.
Columbus, NE 68601 United States
Phone: 402-563-2297
E-mail: jlcitta@nppd.com

Founded: N/A
Scope: State
Description: An organization of Bassmaster chapters, affiliated with the Bass Anglers Sportsman Society, organized to fight pollution, assist state and national conservation agencies in their efforts, and teach the young people of our country good conservation practices. Dedicated to the realistic conservation of our water resources.
Contact(s):
Joe Citta, President; 402-563-2297
Tom Boyd, Conservation Director; 1610 S. Blaine, Grand Island, NE 68803; 308-382-8357

NEBRASKA ORNITHOLOGISTS UNION, INC.

W436 Nebraska Hall
Lincoln, NE 68588-0514 United States
Phone: 402-472-8366

Founded: 1899
Scope: State
Description: To promote the study of ornithology in Nebraska by both professionals and amateurs; to publish the results of independent studies; and to promote the passage and enforcement of judicious laws for bird protection.
Publication(s): Nebraska Bird Review, The
Keyword(s): Wildlife & Species
Contact(s):
Clem Klaphake, President
Janice Paseka, Vice President
Mark Brogie, Director; 508 Seeley, Box 316, Creighton, NE 68729; 402-358-5675
Mitzi Fox, Secretary
Mary Pritchard, Librarian; 6325 O St. #515, Lincoln, NE 68510-2246
Jan Uttecht, Board of Directors

NEBRASKA WILDLIFE FEDERATION, INC.

P.O. Box 81437
Lincoln, NE 68501-1437 United States
Phone: 402-994-2001 Fax: 402-994-2021
E-mail: nebraskawildlife@alltel.net
Website: www.omaha.org/newf

Founded: 1970
Membership: 101–1,000
Scope: State
Description: A representative statewide organization, affiliated with the National Wildlife Federation, dedicated to the conservation of wildlife and its habitat through environmental

education, fish and wildlife conservation, and common sense public policy.

Publication(s): Prairie Blade, Stream Conservation - quarterly newsletter.

Keyword(s): Agriculture/Farming, Ecosystems (precious), Energy, Executive/Legislative/Judicial Reform, Finance/Banking/Trade, Land Issues, Population, Public Lands/Greenspace, Sprawl/Urban Planning, Water Habitats & Quality, Wildlife & Species

Contact(s):
Gene Oglesby, President
Duane Hovorka, Editor & Executive Director
Mike Coe, Education Programs Contact
David Koukol, Representative
Galen Wray, Alternate Representative & Treasurer

NEGATIVE POPULATION GROWTH (NPG)

1717 Massachusetts Avenue, NW
Suite 101
Washington, DC 20036 United States
Phone: 202-667-8950 Fax: 202-667-8953
E-mail: npg@npg.org
Website: www.npg.org

Founded: 1972
Membership: 10,001–100,000
Scope: Local, State, Regional, National, International

Description: NPG is a national nonprofit organization founded in 1972 to educate the American public and political leaders about the detrimental effects of overpopulation on our environment, resources, and quality of life.

Publication(s): Forum Series, state population reports, Population and Resource Outlook

Keyword(s): Air Quality/Atmosphere, Ecosystems (precious), Forests/Forestry, Land Issues, Oceans/Coasts/Beaches, Pollution (general), Population, Public Lands/Greenspace, Sprawl/Urban Planning, Water Habitats & Quality, Wildlife & Species

NEVADA ASSOCIATION OF CONSERVATION DISTRICTS

Attn: President
2002 Idaho St.
Elko, NV 89810 United States
Phone: 775-738-8431, ext. 11 Fax: 775-738-7229

Founded: N/A
Membership: 101–1,000
Scope: Local

Contact(s):
Patsy Tomera, President, Alternative Board Member; Attn: President, HC 65 Box 11, Carlin, NV 89822-9701; 775-754-2333
Eleanor O'Donnell, Executive Director; 775-738-8431; Fax: 775-738-7229
Joe Sicking, Board Member; 1550 Cushman Rd., Fallon, NV 89406; 775-423-5216; Fax: 775-738-7229

NEVADA WILDLIFE FEDERATION, INC.

P.O. Box 71238
Reno, NV 89570 United States
Phone: 775-677-0927 Fax: 775-677-0927
E-mail: weaver@gbis.com
Website: www.nvwf.org

Founded: N/A
Scope: State

Description: A representative statewide organization, affiliated with the National Wildlife Federation, dedicated to the protection and enhancement of wildlife and its habitat through public education and government interaction.

Publication(s): Nevada Wildlife

NEVIS HISTORICAL AND CONSERVATION SOCIETY

P.O. Box 563
Charlestown, 99999 St. Kitts and Nevis
Phone: 8694695786 Fax: 8694690274
E-mail: nhcs@caribsurf.com
Website: www.nevis-nhcs.org

Founded: 1980
Membership: 101–1,000
Scope: National

Description: To foster the conservation of the natural, historic, and cultural aspects of Nevis and its surrounding waters by educational programs, publishing projects, and other awareness endeavors.

Keyword(s): Development/Developing Countries, Ethics/Environmental Justice, Oceans/Coasts/Beaches, Public Lands/Greenspace, Recreation/Ecotourism, Reduce/Reuse/Recycle

Contact(s):
David Robinson, President; 869-469-2117; Fax: 469-0274; drobinson@nevis-nhcs.org
Clara Walters, Vice President; 869-469-2289
Suzanne Gordon, Secretary; 869-469-1093; limehill@caribsurf.com
Kay Loomis, Treasurer; 869-469-5752

NEW BRUNSWICK WILDLIFE FEDERATION

P.O. Box 20211
Fredericton, E3B 7A2 New Brunswick Canada
Phone: 888-272-6411 Fax: 506-458-9941
E-mail: nbwf1@nbnet.nb.ca
Website: www.wildlife.nb.ca/

Founded: 1924
Membership: 1,001–10,000
Scope: State

Description: Promotes the wise use of renewable natural resources, with prime emphasis on education of the young. Affiliated with the Canadian Wildlife Federation.

Keyword(s): Forests/Forestry, Wildlife & Species

Contact(s):
Sharon Kingston Eldridge, President; 1-88-272-6411; nbwf1@nbnet.nb.ca

NEW ENGLAND ASSOCIATION OF ENVIRONMENTAL BIOLOGISTS (NEAEB)

60 Westview St.
Lexington, MA 02173 United States
Phone: 617-860-4300

Founded: 1976
Scope: Regional

Description: A professional society of environmental scientists, engineers and planners from industry and state and federal agencies in the northeast, working to coordinate and enhance environmental programs in each state. The organization advances technical information on environmental research, planning and management and evaluates the effectiveness of environmental regulations for protection of water quality.

Contact(s):
David McDonald, Information Officer; EPA 60 Westview St., Lexington, MA 02421; 781-860-4609
Ernest Pizzuto, Executive Committee

NEW ENGLAND COALITION FOR SUSTAINABLE POPULATION (NECSP)

P.O. Box 194
Sullivan, NH 03445 United States
Phone: 603-847-9798
E-mail: d9cat@cheshire.net
Website: cheshire.net/~dcat/necsp.html

Founded: 1996
Scope: Regional

Description: NECSP is a network of organizations and individuals committed to achieving a sustainable human population at the local, state, regional, national and global levels.
Publication(s): NECSP News (quarterly newsletter)
Keyword(s): Population, Reduce/Reuse/Recycle
Contact(s):
Annie Faulkner, Coordinator

NEW ENGLAND NATURAL RESOURCES CENTER

Box 44
Wayland, MA 01778 United States
Phone: 508-358-2261 Fax: 508-358-2261
E-mail: hagenstein@aol.com

Founded: 1970
Membership: 1–100
Scope: Regional
Description: A nonprofit trust organized to provide a focal point for discussion and resolution of regional natural resource and environmental issues.
Keyword(s): Reduce/Reuse/Recycle
Contact(s):
Russell Brenneman, Vice Chairman; Murtha, Cullina, Richter & Pinney, 101 Pearl St., Hartford, CT 06102
Robert Eisenmenger, Treasurer
Perry Hagenstein, Chairman; Box 44, Wayland, MA 01778

NEW ENGLAND WILD FLOWER SOCIETY, INC.

180 Hemeway Rd.
Framingham, MA 01701-2699 United States
Phone: 508-877-7630 Fax: 508-877-3658
E-mail: newfs@newfs.org
Website: www.newfs.org

Founded: 1900
Scope: National
Description: The New England Wild Flower Society is a nonprofit organization that promotes the conservation of temperate North American plants through conservation and research, education, horticulture and habitat preservation.
Publication(s): Garden in the Woods Trail Guide, Annual Seed and Book Catalogue, Botanical Clubs and Native Plant Societies of the U.S., New England Wild Flower - Conservation Notes of New England Wild Flower Society, New England Wild Flower - Journal and Program Events
Keyword(s): Agriculture/Farming, Reduce/Reuse/Recycle, Wildlife & Species

NEW HAMPSHIRE ASSOCIATION OF CONSERVATION COMMISSIONS

54 Portsmouth St.
Concord, NH 03301 United States
Phone: 603-224-7867 Fax: 603-228-0423
E-mail: info@nhacc.org
Website: www.nhacc.org

Founded: 1970
Scope: State
Description: A nonprofit organization of municipal conservation commissions whose purpose is to foster conservation and appropriate use of NH's natural resources by providing assistance to conservation commissions, facilitating communication and cooperation among commissions, and helping to create a climate in which commissions can be successful.
Publication(s): Handbook for New Hampshire Conservation Commission, New Hampshire Commission News, Conservation News Bulletin.
Keyword(s): Forests/Forestry, Land Issues, Public Lands/Greenspace, Sprawl/Urban Planning, Water Habitats & Quality, Wildlife & Species
Contact(s):
Marjory Swope, Executive Director; 603-224-7867; Fax: 603-228-0423; info@nhacc.org

NEW HAMPSHIRE ASSOCIATION OF CONSERVATION DISTRICTS

NHACD
P.O. Box 2311
Concord, NH 03302-2311 United States
Phone: 603-796-2615 Fax: 603-796-2600
E-mail: mtrembla@tds.net
Website: nhacd.org

Founded: 1946
Scope: State, National
Description: Since 1946, the New Hampshire Association of Conservation Districts has provided statewide coordination, representation, and leadership for Conservation Districts to conserve, protect, and promote responsible use of New Hampshire's natural resources.
Keyword(s): Agriculture/Farming, Forests/Forestry, Land Issues, Oceans/Coasts/Beaches, Pollution (general), Public Lands/Greenspace, Recreation/Ecotourism, Sprawl/Urban Planning, Water Habitats & Quality, Wildlife & Species
Contact(s):
Calvin Perkins, President; 68 Isaac Perkins Rd., Lyme, NH 03768
Robert Goodrich, 1st Vice President; 321 Portsmouth Av, Stratham, NH 03885
Stanley Grimes, 2nd Vice President; 529 Buck St., Pembroke, NH 03275
Michele Tremblay, Executive Director; P.O. Box 3019, Boscawen, NH 03303; 603-796-2615; Fax: 603-796-2600
Stanely Grimes, Secretary and Treasurer; 529 Buck St., Pembroke, NH 03275; 603-485-9326; Fax: 603-233-6030
John Hodsdon, Board Member; 85 Daniel Webster Hwy., Meredith, NH 03253; 603-279-6126; Fax: 603-528-8783
Joan Richardson, Administrator; 73 Main St., P.O. Box 533, Conway, NH 03818-0533; 603-447-2771; Fax: 603-447-8945

NEW HAMPSHIRE B.A.S.S. CHAPTER FEDERATION

Attn: President, P.O. Box 282
Wolfeboro, NH 03894 United States
Phone: 603-569-6035
Website: www.nhbassfederation.com

Founded: N/A
Scope: State
Description: An organization of Bassmaster chapters, affiliated with the Bass Anglers Sportsman Society, organized to fight pollution, assist state and national conservation agencies in their efforts, and teach the young people of our country good conservation practices. Dedicated to the realistic conservation of our water resources.
Contact(s):
Doug Plasencia, President; 603-569-6035
A. Disilva, Conservation Director; P.O. Box 923, North Conway, NH 03860; 603-356-2220

NEW HAMPSHIRE LAKES ASSOCIATION

5 South State St.
Concord, NH 03301 United States
Phone: 603-226-0299 Fax: 603-224-9442
E-mail: info@nhlakes.org
Website: www.nhlakes.org

Founded: 1992
Membership: 101–1,000
Scope: Local
Description: The New Hampshire Lakes Association is a nonprofit education and advocacy organization dedicated to protecting and preserving New Hampshire's lakes for the responsible and

equitable enjoyment of everyone. The NHLA provides assistance to individuals and lake associations throughout New Hampshire.

Publication(s): Lakeside (quarterly magazine), Educational Brochures

Keyword(s): Land Issues, Public Lands/Greenspace, Recreation/Ecotourism, Water Habitats & Quality

Contact(s):

Nancy Christie, Executive Director; nchristie@nhlakes.org

NEW HAMPSHIRE TIMBERLAND OWNERS ASSOCIATION

54 Portsmouth St.
Concord, NH 03301 United States
Phone: 603-224-9699 Fax: 603-225-5898
E-mail: info@nhtoa.org
Website: www.nhtoa.org

Founded: 1911
Membership: 1,001–10,000
Scope: Local, National
Description: A statewide organization dedicated to the promotion of wise forest management and the protection of forestry interests in New Hampshire.
Publication(s): The Forest Bulletin, The Forest Fax, The Timber Crier.
Keyword(s): Forests/Forestry
Contact(s):

Bruce Jacobs, President
Hunter Carbee, Program Director; hcarbee@nhtoa.org
Jasen Stock, Executive Director; 603-224-9699; Fax: 603-225-5898; jstock@nhtoa.org
Eric Darbe, Communications Director; edarbe@nhtoa.org
Tim Frizzell, Treasurer
Don Winsor, Secretary

NEW HAMPSHIRE WILDLIFE FEDERATION

54 Portsmouth St.
Concord, NH 03301 United States
Phone: 603-228-0423
E-mail: nhwf@aol.com
Website: www.nhwf.org

Founded: N/A
Membership: 1,001–10,000
Scope: State
Description: A representative statewide organization, affiliated with the National Wildlife Federation, dedicated to the protection and enhancement of wildlife and its habitat through public education and government interaction.
Publication(s): New Hampshire Wildlife
Contact(s):

Sharon Guaraldi, President
Mary Brown, Executive Director
Russ Kott, Alternate Representative
Margaret Lane, Editor
John Monson, Representative

NEW JERSEY AGRICULTURAL SOCIETY

Trenton, NJ 08625 United States
Phone: 609-394-7766 Fax: 609-292-3978
Website: www.state.nj.us/agriculture/agsociety

Founded: 1781
Membership: 101–1,000
Scope: Regional
Description: The Society has continually worked to educate the public and promote agriculture in New Jersey. The Society is charitable, nonprofit, and conducts numerous educational programs about agriculture's vital role in the economy of New Jersey.
Publication(s): Harbinger, Garden View
Keyword(s): Agriculture/Farming
Contact(s):

Pam Mount, President
Richard Nieuwenhuis, Vice President
Arthur Brown, Secretary and Treasurer
Joni Elliott, Editor
Terry Haaf, Assistant Secretary and Treasurer

NEW JERSEY ASSOCIATION OF CONSERVATION DISTRICTS

P.O. Box 330
Trenton, NJ 08625 United States
Phone: 973-398-2511 Fax: 973-398-2511
E-mail: clifford-lundin@nj.nacdnet.org

Founded: 1955
Membership: 1–100
Scope: State
Description: Represents New Jersey's 16 Soil Conservation Districts and 80 soil conservation supervisors
Keyword(s): Agriculture/Farming, Development/Developing Countries, Executive/Legislative/Judicial Reform, Forests/Forestry, Land Issues
Contact(s):

Clifford Lundin, President; 8 Skytop Rd., Andover, NJ 07821; 973-398-2511
Kenneth Marsh, 1st Vice President; 534 Hanford Place, Westfield, NJ 07909; 908-233-4528
Allen Carter, Treasurer; P.O. Box 403, Tuckahoe, NJ 08250; 609-628-2466
Edward Dipolvere, Secretary, Alternative Board Member; 53 Cubberly Rd., Trenton, NJ 08690; 609-586-2684
Jay Kandle, Past President; 609-589-7916
Kenneth Roehrich, Board Member; 451 Schooley's Mountain Rd., Hackettstown, NJ 07840; 908-852-5787

NEW JERSEY B.A.S.S. CHAPTER FEDERATION

Attn: President, 77 Kenvil Ave.
Succasunna, NJ 07876 United States
Phone: 973-584-9387
E-mail: amgolng@bellatlantic.net
Website: www.njbassfed.org

Founded: N/A
Membership: 101–1,000
Scope: International
Description: An organization of Bassmaster chapters, affiliated with the Bass Anglers Sportsman Society, organized to fight pollution, assist state and national conservation agencies in their efforts, and teach the young people of our country good conservation practices. Dedicated to the realistic conservation of our water resources.
Publication(s): Reel to Reel, Fishing Line
Contact(s):

Tony Going, President; 973-584-9387
John Carlone, Conservation Director; 402 Ames Rd., Highland Lakes, NJ 07422; 973-764-9723

NEW JERSEY CONSERVATION FOUNDATION

170 Longview Rd.
Far Hills, NJ 07931 United States
Phone: 908-234-1225 Fax: 908-234-1189
E-mail: info@njconservation.org
Website: www.njconservation.org

Founded: 1960
Membership: 1,001–10,000
Scope: Local, State, Regional
Description: A nonprofit membership organization founded in 1960 dedicated to protecting New Jersey's land, water and natural resources through acquisition and development of sound land use policies. Provides support and technical assistance to local groups and works in partnership with fellow

non-profits and the State to insure permanent protection of New Jersey's remaining open spaces.

Publication(s): Charting a Course for the Delaware Bay Watershed, Greenways to the Arthurkill, New Jersey Conservation, New Jersey Highlands, The: Treasures at Risk.

Keyword(s): Agriculture/Farming, Development/Developing Countries, Forests/Forestry, Land Issues, Public Lands/Greenspace, Reduce/Reuse/Recycle, Sprawl/Urban Planning, Water Habitats & Quality, Wildlife & Species

Contact(s):
Samuel Lambert, President of Board of Trustees

NEW JERSEY ENVIRONMENTAL LOBBY

204 W. State St.
Trenton, NJ 08608 United States
Phone: 609-396-3774 Fax: 609-396-4521
Website: www.njenvironment.org

Founded: 1969
Scope: State
Description: To advocate for legislation and regulation that is protective and preservative of both the natural and the built environment with a view, always, of protecting human health for all citizens and future generations. Conversely, we oppose those laws and regulations that are detrimental to the above.
Publication(s): NJ Environmental Lobby News, periodic special reports
Keyword(s): Air Quality/Atmosphere, Development/Developing Countries, Energy, Land Issues, Transportation
Contact(s):
Anne Poole, President; 43 Four Mile Rd., Pemberton, NJ 08068; 609-894-4113; newpoole@bellatlantic.net
Eileen Hogan, Vice President; 96 Briarcliff Rd., Mountain Lakes, NJ 07046; 973-267-6100
Mark Herzberg, Treasurer; 24 Clinton Pl., Metuchen, NJ 08840; 908-494-4883; mherzb8468@aol.com

NEW JERSEY FORESTRY ASSOCIATION

1628 Prospect St.
Trenton, NJ 08638 United States
Phone: 609-771-8301
Website: loki.stockton.edu/~forestry/

Founded: 1975
Scope: State
Description: A statewide organization affiliated with the National Woodland Owners Association. Formed to encourage the scientific management and perpetuation of woodlands in New Jersey.
Publication(s): New Jersey Woodlands
Keyword(s): Forests/Forestry
Contact(s):
Thomas Bullock, President; 609-696-5300
George Pierson, Vice President; 609-737-0489
Ron Sheay, Executive Secretary and Editor
Richard West, Editor

NEW MEXICO ASSOCIATION OF CONSERVATION DISTRICTS

163 Trail Canyon Rd.
Carlsbad, NM 88220 United States
Phone: 505-981-2400 Fax: 505-981-2422
E-mail: nmacd@dellcity.com
Website: www.nm.nacdnet.org

Founded: N/A
Membership: 1–100
Scope: State
Contact(s):
Brian Greene, President; Rt. 1 Box 22, Mountainair, NM 87036; 505-849-1080; Fax: 505-847-0615
Leedrue Hyatt, Vice President; 8410 Flying U Rd., NE, Deming, NM 88030; 505-546-9694; Fax: 505-546-3265
Debbie Hughes, Executive Director; 163 Trail Canyon Rd., Carlsbad, NM 88220; 505-981-2400; Fax: 505-981-2422
Eddie Vigil, Secretary Treasurer

NEW MEXICO ENVIRONMENTAL LAW CENTER

1405 Luisa St., Suite 5
Santa Fe, NM 87505 United States
Phone: 505-989-9022 Fax: 505-989-3769
E-mail: nmelc@nmelc.org

Founded: 1987
Membership: 101–1,000
Scope: State
Description: The New Mexico Environmental Law Center is a nonprofit, public interest law firm. The Law Center is the only New Mexico organization that provides free and at-cost legal services for the preservation of the state's natural resources and protection of citizens against environmental hazards. The Law Center represents grassroots organizations, individuals, and environmental groups in site-specific efforts; participates in statewide and federal legislative advocacy; and provides public education.
Publication(s): The Green Fire Report
Contact(s):
Douglas Meiklejohn, Executive Director

NEW YORK ASSOCIATION OF CONSERVATION DISTRICTS, INC.

Attn: President,104 Edwards Ave.
Calberton, NY 11933 United States
Phone: 631-727-3777 Fax: 631-727-3721
Website:
www.agmkt.state.ny.us/soilwater/intro.asp#www.agmkt.stats.ny.us/soilwater/intro.asp

Founded: N/A
Scope: State
Contact(s):
Joe Gerdela, President; P.O. Box 341, Center Moriches, NY 11934; 631-727-3777
Anita Cartin, Executive Vice President; 1 Winners Cir., Albany, NY 12235; 518-457-7229; Fax: 518-457-2716
William Chamberlain, Treasurer; Box 487, Henderson Harbor, NY 13651; 315-938-7106
Carl Seymour, Secretary; 242 Grange Hall Rd., Schuylerville, NY 12871; 518-695-9249

NEW YORK B.A.S.S. CHAPTER FEDERATION

Attn: President, 177 Barmore Rd.
LaGrangeville, NY 12540 United States
Phone: 845-902-1204
Website: www.nybassfed.com

Founded: N/A
Scope: State
Description: An organization of Bassmaster chapters, affiliated with the Bass Anglers Sportsman Society, organized to fight pollution, assist state and national conservation agencies in their efforts, and teach the young people of our country good conservation practices. Dedicated to the realistic conservation of our water resources.
Publication(s): Fishlines
Contact(s):
Wayne Tomassi, President; wayne@nybassfed.com
Bernie Haney, Conservation Director; 826 C Tamarack Dr., West Carthage, NY 13619; 315-493-2356; bernie@nybassfed.com

NEW YORK FOREST OWNERS ASSOCIATION, INC.

P.O. Box 180
Fairport, NY 14450 United States
Phone: 585-377-6060 Fax: 585-388-7592
E-mail: nyfoainc@hotmail.com
Website: www.nyfoa.org

Founded: 1962
Membership: 1,001–10,000
Scope: State
Description: A statewide organization organized to unite the 500,000 owners of 11 million acres of forest land in New York in encouraging the wise management of private woodland resources in New York State by promoting, protecting, representing, and serving the interests of woodland owners.
Publication(s): Forest Owner
Keyword(s): Forests/Forestry
Contact(s):
Ronald Pederson, President; 518-785-6061
Deborah Gill, Administrator; 716-377-6060
Mary Malmsheimer, Editor; Desktop Solutions, 34 Lincklaen St., Cazenovia, NY 13035; 315-655-4110; Fax: 315-655-9694
Jerry Michael, Treasurer; 315-733-7391

NEW YORK PUBLIC INTEREST RESEARCH GROUP (NYPIRG)

NYPIRG
Main Office, 9 Murray St.,
3rd Fl.
New York, NY 10007 United States
Phone: 212-349-6460 Fax: 212-349-7474
E-mail: nypirg@nypirg.org
Website: www.nypirg.org

Founded: 1973
Membership: 10,001–100,000
Scope: Local, State
Description: The NYPIRG is a nonprofit, nonpartisan research group established and directed by New York state college students. Staff lawyers, researchers, and advocates work with students and other citizens developing citizenship skills and shaping public policy on environmental preservation, good government, and consumer issues.
Publication(s): Get the Lead Out, NYC CouncilWatch, NYPIRG Agenda
Keyword(s): Ethics/Environmental Justice, Pollution (general), Reduce/Reuse/Recycle, Transportation

NEW YORK TURTLE AND TORTOISE SOCIETY

P.O. Box 878
Orange, NJ 07051-0878 United States
Phone: 212-459-4803
E-mail: info@nytts.org
Website: www.nytts.org/

Founded: 1970
Scope: National
Description: The Society is dedicated to the conservation and preservation of habitat, and the promotion of proper husbandry and captive propagation of turtles. Education of members and the public is a key goal. Events held in the NYC area include a seminar, field trips, and show.
Publication(s): Plastron Papers, NewsNotes, NYTTS, Journal of the New York Turtle and Tortoise Society.
Keyword(s): Wildlife & Species
Contact(s):
Suzanne Dohm, President
Allen Foust, Vice President
Lori Craner, Treasurer of Wildlife Rehabilitation
Rita Devine, Secretary
Joan Frumkies, Membership
Jim Van Abbemg, Editor of Proceedings

NEW YORK-NEW JERSEY TRAIL CONFERENCE INC.

156 RamaP.O.Valley Road
Mahurah, NJ 07430 United States
Phone: 212-685-9699 Fax: 212-779-8102
E-mail: office@nynjtc.org
Website: www.nynjtc.org

Founded: 1920
Scope: Regional
Description: A nonprofit organization which coordinates the efforts of hiking and outdoor groups in New York and New Jersey to build and maintain over 1,300 miles of foot trails and whose purpose is to protect and conserve open space, wildlife, and places of natural beauty and interest.
Publication(s): Trail Walker, Delaware Water Gap National Recreation Area Hiking, Iron Mine Trails, Hiking the Catskills, Catskill Trails Map Set, Guide to the Long Path, Guide to the Appalachian Trail in New York and New Jersey, New Jersey Walk Book, New York Walk Book
Keyword(s): Land Issues, Public Lands/Greenspace, Recreation/Ecotourism
Contact(s):
Gary Haugland, President
Jane Daniels, Vice President
Daniel Chazin, Secretary
Gary Haughland, Chairman of Trails Council

NEWFOUNDLAND LABRADOR WILDLIFE FEDERATION

Attn: President, 67 Commonwealth Ave
Mount Pearl, A1N 1W7 Newfoundland Canada
Phone: 709-364-8415 Fax: 709-753-4709

Founded: N/A
Membership: 10,001–100,000
Scope: International
Keyword(s): Air Quality/Atmosphere, Ethics/Environmental Justice, Forests/Forestry, Reduce/Reuse/Recycle, Water Habitats & Quality, Wildlife & Species
Contact(s):
Gordon Cooper, Vice President; 67 Commonwealth Ave., Mount Pearl, Newfoundland A1N 1W7; 709-368-6180
Clifford Head, Secretary; 49 Harnum Crescent, Mt. Pearl, Newfoundland A1N 1W7; 709-335-2226

NIPPON ECOLOGY NETWORK

Ecology Center Bldg., 3 Fukuromachi
Shinjukku-ku, Tokyo, 162 Japan
Phone: 81352283344 Fax: 81352286040
Website: www.venture-web.or.jp/ecoland

Founded: N/A
Scope: International
Description: NEN is currently involved in many aspects of environment, agriculture, and food safety issues. Among NEN operations are: Radish boya, an organic and natural food home delivery system servicing over 55,000 homes; the Japan Ecology Center, an information center; Atopikko Chikyu no ko, a network of medical advisors and the allergy afflicted; and the Tree Free Club, an organization that promotes the use of alternatives to tree-based papers and manages the Tree Free Fund.
Contact(s):
Michiaki Tokue, Chairman

NO LONGER EXISTENT RIVER FEDERATION

United States

Founded: 1981
Scope: National
Publication(s): Institutional Frameworks for Watershed Management Programs (1994), River Conservation Directory (1990), River Federation Newsletter, Profiles in River Management

Keyword(s): Land Issues, Recreation/Ecotourism, Water Habitats & Quality

Contact(s):

Douglas Carter, President; Michigan Department of Natural Resources; 517-373-1172; Fax: 517-373-9965
Edward Fite, Vice President; Oklahoma Scenic Rivers Commission; 918-456-3281; Fax: 918-456-3281
Robert Hoffman, Executive Director; 301-589-9454; Fax: 301-589-6121; riverfed1@aol.com
Molly Macgregor, Secretary and Treasurer; Mississippi Headwaters Board; 218-547-3300; Fax: 218-547-2440

NORTH AMERICAN ASSOCIATION FOR ENVIRONMENTAL EDUCATION

410 Tarvin Rd.
Rock Spring, GA 30739 United States
Phone: 706-764-2926 Fax: 706-764-2094
E-mail: email@naaee.org
Website: www.naaee.org

Founded: 1971

Scope: National

Description: NAAEE is dedicated to promoting environmental education and supporting the work of environmental educators in North America and around the world. NAAEE is made up of students and professionals who have thought seriously about how individuals become literate concerning environmental issues and about how to prepare people to work together towards resolving environmental problems.

Publication(s): NAAEE Directory of Environmental Educators, Annual Conference Proceedings, Environmental Communicator

Keyword(s): Reduce/Reuse/Recycle

Contact(s):

Judy Braus, President
Bonnie Shelton, Executive Director
James Elder, Treasurer

NORTH AMERICAN ASSOCIATION FOR ENVIRONMENTAL EDUCATION

CONFERENCE, PUBLICATIONS AND MEMBERSHIP OFFICE
410 Tarvin Rd.
Rock Spring, GA 30739 United States
Phone: 706-764-2926 Fax: 706-764-2094
Website: www.naaee.org

Founded: N/A

Membership: 1,001–10,000

Scope: International

Description: NAAEE is a network of people who practice and support environmental education. Our mission is to provide environmental educators with quality resources, training, publications, and networking opportunities to enable them to spread environmental knowledge.

Contact(s):

Barbara Eager, Acting Deputy Director
Connie Smith, Membership Development Services Manager
Sarah Gray, Conference & Publications Administrative Assistant

NORTH AMERICAN BEAR FEDERATION

3503 Hwy. 89
South Livingston, MT 59047 United States
Phone: 406-333-4414 Fax: 406-333-9733
E-mail: nabear@nabear.org
Website: www.nabear.org

Founded: N/A

Membership: 1,001–10,000

Scope: National

Publication(s): Bear Bulletin - every other month, The Bear Facts - magazine

Contact(s):

Carl Brooke, President, Co-Founder; 406-333-4414

NORTH AMERICAN BENTHOLOGICAL SOCIETY

c/o Allen Marketing and Management, P.O. Box 1897
Lawrence, KS 66044-8897 United States
Website: www.benthos.org

Founded: 1953

Scope: National

Description: The Society is an international scientific organization whose purpose is to promote better understanding of the biotic communities of lake and stream bottoms and their role in aquatic ecosystems. The Society provides media for disseminating results of scientific investigations and other information to aquatic biologists and to the scientific community at large.

Publication(s): Current and Selected Bibliography of Benthic Biology, Bulletin of the North American Benthological Society, Journal of the North American Benthological Society

Keyword(s): Water Habitats & Quality, Wildlife & Species

Contact(s):

Nancy Grimm, President; 602-965-4735
Steve Canton, Editor; Chadwick and Associates Inc., 5575 S. Sycamore St., Suite 101, Littleton, CO 80120
Donna Giberson, Secretary; 902-566-0797
Kim Haag, Treasurer; 813-243-5800
David Rosenberg, Editor; Freshwater Institute, 501 University Crescent, Winnipeg, Manitoba R3T 2N6
Donald Webb, Editor; Illinois Natural History Survey, 607 E. Peabody St., Champaign, IL 61820

NORTH AMERICAN BLUEBIRD SOCIETY

The Wilderness Center
P.O. Box 244
Wilmot, OH 44689-0244 United States
Phone: 330-359-5511 Fax: 330-359-5455
E-mail: info@nabluebirdsociety.org
Website: www.nabluebirdsociety.org

Founded: 1978

Membership: 1,001–10,000

Scope: Local, State, Regional, National, International

Description: The North American Bluebird Society, a non-profit conservation, education and research organization, promotes the recovery of bluebirds and other native, cavity-nesting species. On-going research, educational material development, outreach initiatives through the NABS Speakers Bureau and a comprehensive website on bluebirding, address issues related to bluebirds and other native cavity-nesting bird species.

Publication(s): Bluebird Educators Packet, Bluebird Magazine (formerly Sialia), Transcontinental Bluebird Trail Program (network of bluebird trails across North America), Educational Bluebird posters and Educational Slide Program, Stokes Bluebird Basics "10 Minute Introductory Video"

Keyword(s): Wildlife & Species

Contact(s):

Doug LeVasseur, President; emdlev@clover.net
Joan Harmet, Vice President; joandick@aeroinc.net
Arlene Ripley, Webmaster; webmaster@nabluebirdsociety.org
Bob Martin, Treasurer
Darlene Sillick, Secretary; azuretrails@columbus.rr.com
Jim Williams, Editor

NORTH AMERICAN BUTTERFLY ASSOCIATION

4 Delaware Rd.
Morristown, NJ 07960 United States
Phone: 973-285-0907 Fax: 973-285-0936
E-mail: naba@naba.org
Website: www.naba.org

Founded: 1993

Membership: 1,001–10,000

Scope: International

Description: NABA promotes public enjoyment and conservation of butterflies, encouraging non-consumption activities such as butterfly watching, gardening and photography.

Publication(s): NABA 4th of July Butterfly Count Report, Butterfly Gardener, American Butterflies, NABA Checklist and English Names of North America Butterflies

Keyword(s): Agriculture/Farming, Recreation/Ecotourism, Reduce/Reuse/Recycle, Wildlife & Species

Contact(s):

Jeffrey Glassberg, President
Ann Swengel, Vice-President
Jim Springer, Webmaster; springer@naba.org

NORTH AMERICAN COALITION ON RELIGION AND ECOLOGY (NACRE)

5 Thomas Cir., NW
Washington, DC 20005 United States
Phone: 202-462-2591 Fax: 202-462-6534
E-mail: nacre@earthlink.net
Website: www.caringforcreation.net

Founded: 1989

Membership: 1,001–10,000

Scope: National

Description: NACRE is an ecumenical and interfaith environmental organization designed to help the North American religious community enter into the environmental movement in the 1990s and to help environmental organizations and the wider society become aware and act upon these same ethical values.

Publication(s): ECO-Letter

Keyword(s): Reduce/Reuse/Recycle, Wildlife & Species

Contact(s):

Donald Conroy, President and CEO
Bruce Anderson, Chairman of the Board
Carolyn Gutowski, Secretary and Treasurer

NORTH AMERICAN CRANE WORKING GROUP

341 W. Olympic Pl. Suite 300
Seattle, WA 98119-3719 United States
Phone: 206-286-8607
E-mail: thoffmann@hoffmanns.com
Website: www.portup.com/~nacwg

Founded: 1988

Membership: 101–1,000

Scope: National

Description: An organization of professional biologists, aviculturists, land managers, and other interested individuals dedicated to the conservation of cranes and their habitats in North America.

Publication(s): Wookshop Proceedings, Unison Call, The

Keyword(s): Water Habitats & Quality, Wildlife & Species

Contact(s):

Scott Hereford, President; Mississippi Crane Refuge, 7200 Crane Ln., Gauthier, MS 39553
Wendy Brown, Vice President; 1208 Claire Ct. NW, Albuquerque, NM 87104
Thomas Hoffmann, Treasurer; 206-286-8607; thoffmann@hoffmanns.com
Stephen Nesbitt, Secretary; 4005 S. Main St., Gainesville, FL 32601
Jane Nicolich, Editor; R.R. 2 Box 264A, Laurel, MD 20708

NORTH AMERICAN FALCONERS ASSOCIATION

559 Fuller Road
Chicopee, MA 01020 United States
Phone: 4135925696
Website: www.n-a-f-a.org

Founded: 1962

Scope: International

Description: A nonprofit fraternal organization with the following purposes: improve and encourage competency in the practice of falconry; urge recognition of falconry as a legal field sport; and promote scientific study, conservation, and welfare of birds of prey with an appreciation of their value in nature.

Publication(s): Journal (annual), Hawk Chalk (quarterly)

Keyword(s): Recreation/Ecotourism, Reduce/Reuse/Recycle, Wildlife & Species

NORTH AMERICAN GAMEBIRD ASSOCIATION, INC.

1214 Brooks Ave.
Raleigh, NC 27607 United States
Phone: 919-782-6758 Fax: 919-515-7070
E-mail: gamebird@naga.org
Website: www.naga.org

Founded: 1932

Scope: National

Description: To promote educational work and develop interest in game bird breeding and hunting preserves (nonprofit); to afford a means of cooperation with the federal and state governments in all matters of concern to the industry; and to encourage study of the sciences connected with the live production, preparation for markets, and marketing of game bird eggs and game birds.

Publication(s): Membership Directory, Wildlife Harvest Magazine, List of Hunting Resort Members, Game Bird Propagation Book

Keyword(s): Recreation/Ecotourism, Wildlife & Species

Contact(s):

Royd Hatt, President; Box 134, Green River, UT 84525; 801-564-3224
Gary Davis, Executive Director; 1214 Brooks Ave., Raleigh, NC 27607; 919-782-6758

NORTH AMERICAN LOON FUND

6 Lily Pond Rd.
Gilford, NH 03246 United States
Phone: 989-772-9611
Website: facstaff.uww.edu/wentzl/nalf/aNALFhomepage.html

Founded: 1979

Scope: National

Description: A nonprofit organization established to sponsor loon conservation, public education, and scientific research projects across the U.S. and Canada. Sponsors annual grant program, and organizes annual research conference.

Publication(s):, Loon Call Newsletter, Annotated Bibliography of the Loons, Gaviidae, Educational poster and resource directory

Keyword(s): Water Habitats & Quality, Wildlife & Species

Contact(s):

Linda Obara, Executive Director
Ellen Barth, Treasurer
Jordan Prouty, Chairman
Guy Swenson, Clerk

NORTH AMERICAN MEMBERSHIP GROUP

12301 Whitewater Dr.
Minnetonka, MN 55343 United States
Phone: 952-936-9333 Fax: 952-936-9755
Website: www.naog.com

Founded: 1978

Membership: 1,000,001 +

Scope: International

Description: The North American Fishing Club is a membership organization dedicated to enhancing the fishing skills and enjoyment of anglers. The NAFC is the largest association of multi-species anglers in North America.

Publication(s): North American Fisherman

Keyword(s): Recreation/Ecotourism, Water Habitats & Quality, Wildlife & Species

Contact(s):

Nancy Evensen, President
Steve Pennaz, Executive Director

NORTH AMERICAN NATIVE FISHES ASSOCIATION

123 W. Mt. Airy Ave.
Philadelphia, PA 19119 United States
E-mail: nanfa@att.net
Website: www.nanfa.org

Founded: 1972

Scope: National

Description: Membership includes ichthyologists, students, sportsmen, amateur naturalists, and aquarists who seek to promote the study, research, and conservation of North American native fishes. Goals are to promote the restoration and protection of habitat and to distribute information about native fishes.

Publication(s): American Currents Magazine

Keyword(s): Water Habitats & Quality, Wildlife & Species

Contact(s):

Bruce Stallsmith, President; 801 Wells Ave., Huntsville, IL 35801; 256-519-2099; fundulus@hotmail.com
Mark Binkley, Vice President; 21 Orchard Dr., Worthington, OH 43085; 614-844-6042; mbinkley@columbus.rr.com
Stephanie Brough, Treasurer; 1107 Argonne Dr., Baltimore, MD 21218; 410-243-9050; ichthos@charm.net
D. Martin Moore, Secretary; 155 David Henderson Rd., Penahatchie, MS 39145; 601-546-2320; archimed@netdoor.com

NORTH AMERICAN WILDLIFE PARK FOUNDATION, INC.

WOLF PARK
4004 E 800 N.
Battle Ground, IN 47920 United States
Phone: 765-567-2265 Fax: 765-567-4299
E-mail: wolfpark@wolfpark.org
Website: www.wolfpark.org

Founded: 1972

Membership: 1,001–10,000

Scope: International

Description: A nonprofit organization which features socialized wolves, coyote, foxes and bison; provides continuous behavior research programs; offers lectures and a teaching program, as well as four Wolf Behavior seminars per year; monitors legislation on predators; and provides research opportunities for scientists and students.

Publication(s): Wolf ! Magazine, Wolf Park News

Keyword(s): Wildlife & Species

Contact(s):

Erich Klinghammer, Director

NORTH AMERICAN WOLF ASSOCIATION

23214 Tree Bright Lane
Spring, TX 77373 United States
Phone: 281-821-4439 Fax: 281-821-4417
E-mail: nawa@nawa.org
Website: www.nawa.org

Founded: 1993

Membership: 10,001–100,000

Scope: Local, State, Regional, National, International

Description: NAWA is a nonprofit organization dedicated to natural wolf recovery, rescue, preservation and education. Produces educational materials/programs (all age levels), an electronic newsletter (includes news of wolves and wolf-related issues internationally), lectures in universities, colleges & schools in addition to comprehensive workshops, wolf ambassador programs and an Adopt-A-Wolf program. NAWA is highly focused on the plight of captive wolves and the epidemic of wolfdog breeding.

Publication(s): Yearly summaries, publications on web, NAWA News (newsletter)

Keyword(s): Ecosystems (precious), Ethics/Environmental Justice, Wildlife & Species

Contact(s):

Rae Evening Earth Ott, Director; 281-821-4439; Fax: 281-821-4417; nawa@nawa.org
Tina Hart, Assistant Director; 281-821-4439; Fax: 281-821-4417; tina@nawa.org
Eric Schweig, International Celebrity Spokesperson

NORTH ATLANTIC SALMON CONSERVATION ORGANIZATION

11 Rutland Square
Edinburgh, EH1 2AS United Kingdom
Phone: 1312282551 Fax: 1312284384
E-mail: hq@nasco.int
Website: www.nasco.int

Founded: 1984

Membership: N/A

Scope: International

Description: NASCO is an intergovernmental treaty organization established to contribute to the conservation, restoration, enhancement, and rational management of salmon stocks in the North Atlantic Ocean through international cooperation. The member parties are: Canada, Denmark (in respect to the Faroe Islands and Greenland), the European Union, Iceland, Norway, the Russian Federation, and the USA.

Keyword(s): Air Quality/Atmosphere, Climate Change, Wildlife & Species

Contact(s):

M.I. Windsor, Secretary

NORTH CAROLINA ASSOCIATION OF SOIL AND WATER CONSERVATION DISTRICTS

512 N. Salisbury St.
1614 Mail Service Center, Raleigh, NC 27699
Raleigh, NC 27604 United States
Phone: 919-733-2302 Fax: 919-715-3559
Website: www.enr.state.nc.us

Founded: N/A

Scope: State

Contact(s):

David Vogel, Director; 919-715-6097; david.vogel@ncmail.net

NORTH CAROLINA B.A.S.S. CHAPTER FEDERATION

Attn: President, 403 Red Wood Ct.
Lenoir, NC 28645 United States
Phone: 828-728-8550 Fax: 828-728-8549

Founded: N/A

Membership: 1,001–10,000

Scope: State

Description: An organization of Bassmaster chapters, affiliated with the Bass Anglers Sportsman Society, organized to fight pollution, assist state and national conservation agencies in their efforts and teach the young people of our country good conservation practices. Dedicated to the realistic conservation of our water resources.

Contact(s):

Ed Cannon, President; 828-728-8550
Randy Lee, Conservation Director; 1730 Allens Crossroads Road, Four Oaks, NC 27524; SmTrp19@aol.com

NORTH CAROLINA BEACH BUGGY ASSOCIATION, INC.

Box 940
Manteo, NC 27954 United States
Phone: 252-473-4880
Website: www.ncbba.org

Founded: N/A

Scope: National

Description: NCBBA is an organization dedicated to preserving natural resources and coastal areas of North Carolina. Its purpose is to unite in an organization all persons interested in the natural beach resources of the Outer Banks of North Carolina and elsewhere, and establish a Code of Ethics of beach behavior to which each member must subscribe to uphold.

Publication(s): NCBBA News, The

Keyword(s): Oceans/Coasts/Beaches, Recreation/Ecotourism, Wildlife & Species

Contact(s):

W. Keene, President; 23134 Homestead Lane, Franklin, VA 23851; 757-562-2554

Tom Burke, Vice President; 2512 S. Virginia Dare Trl., Nags Head, NC 27959

John Newbold, Editor

Sharon Newbold, Secretary; 600 S. Memorial Drive, Kill Devil Hills, NC 27948; 252-480-2453

Brenda Outlaw, Treasurer; P.O. Box 940, Manteo, NC 27954; 252-473-4880; brendaoutlaw@hotmail.com

NORTH CAROLINA COASTAL FEDERATION, INC.

Attn: Alicia Kramer 3609 Highway 24 (Ocean)
Newport, NC 28570 United States
Phone: 252-393-8185 Fax: 252-393-7508
Website: www.nccoast.org

Founded: 1982

Membership: 1,001–10,000

Scope: Regional

Description: The Coastal Federation focuses on the twenty coastal counties in North Carolina, with citizens working together for a healthy coast..

Publication(s): Coastal Review, alternative to shoreline erosion control, Magazine Sound Advice, State of Coast Report

Keyword(s): Land Issues, Water Habitats & Quality

Contact(s):

Jessica Kester, Director of Education; ext. 32

Todd Miller, Executive Director; toddm@nccoast.org

Sally Steele, Director of Development; ext. 28; sallys@nccoast.org

NORTH CAROLINA CONSERVATION NETWORK

112 South Blunt Street
Raleigh, NC 27601 United States
Phone: 919-857-4773
E-mail: info@ncconnet.org
Website: www.ncconnet.org

Founded: 1999

Membership: 101–1,000

Scope: State

Description: NC ConNet is an environmental nonprofit that deals primarily with strengthening and uniting other grassroots organizations within the state through a variety of services and tools.

Contact(s):

Brian Buzby, Executive Director

Mindy Hiteshue, Administrative Associate

Grady McCallie, Environmental Liaison

Heather Yandow, Outreach Coordinator

NORTH CAROLINA FORESTRY ASSOCIATION (NCFA)

1600 Glenwood Ave
Suite I
Raleigh, NC 27608 United States
Phone: 919-834-3943 Fax: 919-832-6188
E-mail: cbrown@ncforestry.org
Website: www.ncforestry.org

Founded: 1911

Membership: 1,001–10,000

Scope: State

Description: The NCFA is North Carolina's oldest forest conservation group. The NCFA is a private, non-profit organization comprised of over 2,700 forest managers, landowners, mill operators, loggers, furniture manufacturers and educators.

Keyword(s): Forests/Forestry

Contact(s):

Chris Brown, Director of Communications; 919-834-3943; Fax: 919-832-6188; cbrown@ncforestry.org

Bob Slocum, Executive Vice President; 919-834-3943; Fax: 919-832-6188; rwslocum@ncforestry.org

NORTH CAROLINA MUSEUM OF NATURAL SCIENCES

11 W. Jones
Raleigh, NC United States
Phone: 877-462-8724
Website: www.naturalsciences.org

Founded: 1978

Scope: State

Description: A nonprofit group formed to promote an interest in and to educate members and the general public concerning the ecological importance and conservation of reptiles and amphibians.

Publication(s): NC HERPS

Keyword(s): Wildlife & Species

Contact(s):

Tom Thorp, President; 804-261-8230; tt-threelakes@juno.com

Dan Lockwood, Vice President; 112 E. Skyhawk Dr., Cary, NC 27513; 919-460-3504; ddlockwood@email.msn.com

Jeff Beane, Editor; 4433 Graham Newton Rd., Raleigh, NC 27606; 919-733-7450, ext. 754; jeff_beane@mail.enr.state.nc.us

Alvin Braswell, Advisor; 1208 Buffaloe Rd., Garner, NC 27529; 919-733-7450, ext. 751; alvin_braswell@mail.enr.state.nc.us

Dan Dombrowski, Treasurer; NC State Museum of Natural Sciences, P.O. Box 29555, Raleigh, NC 27626-0555; 919-733-7450, ext. 504; dan_dombrowski@mail.enr.state.nc.us

Joe Zawadowski, Secretary; 503 Valley Dr., Durham, NC 27704; 919-684-6062; Joe_Zawadowski@bba.mc.duke.edu

NORTH CAROLINA RECREATION AND PARK SOCIETY, INC.

883 Washington St.
Raleigh, NC 27605 United States
Phone: 919-832-5868 Fax: 919-832-3323
E-mail: ncrps@bellsouth.net
Website: www.ncrps.org

Founded: 1944

Scope: State

Description: A nonprofit organization formed to promote the wise use of leisure and intelligent development of the state's recreation resources. An affiliate of The National Recreation and Park Association.

Publication(s): North Carolina Recreation and Park Review, NCRPS News

Keyword(s): Land Issues, Public Lands/Greenspace, Recreation/Ecotourism

Contact(s):

Phil Rea, President; NC State University, P.O. Box 8004, Raleigh, NC 27695; 919-515-3675; Fax: 919-515-3687; phil_rea@ncsu.edu

Mike Waters, Executive Director; 883 Washington St., Raleigh, NC 27605

Paul Herbert, Editor; Cornelius Park Recreation, P.O. Box 399, Cornelius, NC 28031; 704-892-6031; Fax: 704-892-2462; pherbert@cornelius.org

NORTH CAROLINA WATERSHED COALITION, INC.

P.O. Box 337
Colfax, NC 27035 United States
Phone: 336-992-8734
E-mail: newcom@ynet.net
Website: www.ncwatershedcoalition.org

Founded: 1998

Scope: State

Description: The coalition promotes conservation, protection and enhancement of watersheds and rivers; encourages founding and growth of local organizations devoted to those ends through information sharing and cooperation.

Keyword(s): Air Quality/Atmosphere, Oceans/Coasts/Beaches, Pollution (general), Reduce/Reuse/Recycle, Water Habitats & Quality

NORTH CAROLINA WILD FLOWER PRESERVATION SOCIETY

NC NATIVE PLANT SOCIETY
c/o NC Botanical Garden, CB #3375, Totten Center, UNC-CH
Chapel Hill, NC 27599-3375 United States
Phone: 919-834-4172 Fax: 336-370-8172
E-mail: alice@ncwildflower.org
Website: www.ncwildflower.org

Founded: 1951

Membership: 101–1,000

Scope: State

Description: A non-profit organization dedicated to the enjoyment and conservation of native plants and their habitats through education, protection and propagation.

Publication(s): NC Native Plant Propagation Handbook, NC Wild Flower Preservation Society Newsletter.

Keyword(s): Agriculture/Farming, Wildlife & Species

Contact(s):

Ken Bridle, President; 336-591-5882; Fax: 336-591-5882; bridle@netunlimited.net
Alice Zawadzki, Vice-President; 919-834-4172; alice@ncwildflower.org
Ginny Bacik, Treasurer; ginny@ncwildflower.org
Marlene Kinney, Corresponding Secretary; marlenek@ncwildflower.org
Zack Murrell, Recording Secretary; murrellze@appstate.edu
Ed Tokas, Editor; eteditor@ncwildflower.org

NORTH CAROLINA WILDLIFE FEDERATION

P.O. Box 10626
Raleigh, NC 27605 United States
Phone: 919-833-1923 Fax: 919-829-1192
E-mail: ncwf_chuck@mindspring.com
Website: www.ncwf.org

Founded: 1945

Membership: 1,001–10,000

Scope: State

Description: A representative statewide organization, affiliated with the National Wildlife Federation, dedicated to the protection and enhancement of wildlife and its habitat through public education and government interaction.

Publication(s): Friend of Wildlife Magazine

Contact(s):

Gary Shull, President and Alternate Representative
Chuck Rice, Executive Director
Richard Mode, Representative
Eddie Nickens, Editor
Stan Warlen, Treasurer
Lisa West, Education Programs Contact

NORTH CASCADES CONSERVATION COUNCIL

P.O. Box 95980
Seattle, WA 98145-2980 United States
Phone: 206-282-1644 Fax: 206-684-1379
Website: www.northcascade.org

Founded: 1957

Membership: 101–1,000

Scope: Regional

Description: The Council seeks to protect and perserve the North Cascades' scenic, scientific, recreational, educational, wildlife, and wilderness values from the Columbia River to the U.S.-Canadian border in the State of Washington.

Publication(s): Wild Cascades, The

Keyword(s): Forests/Forestry, Land Issues, Public Lands/Greenspace, Recreation/Ecotourism, Reduce/Reuse/Recycle, Water Habitats & Quality, Wildlife & Species

Contact(s):

Marc Bardsley, President; steveb@premier1.net
Charles Ehlert, Vice President
Thomas Brucker, Treasurer
Patrick Goldsworthy, Chairman; 206-282-1644
Phil Zalesky, Secretary

NORTH DAKOTA ASSOCIATION OF SOIL CONSERVATION DISTRICTS

P.O. Box 1601
Bismarck, ND 58502 United States
Phone: 701-223-8518 Fax: 701-223-1291
E-mail: lincoln@tic.bisman.com
Website: www.lincolnoakes.com

Founded: N/A

Membership: 101–1,000

Scope: State

Contact(s):

Rodney Hickle, President; 1631 28th Ave., SW, Center, ND 58530; 701-794-3342
Gary Puppe, Executive Vice President; P.O. Box 1601, 3310 University Dr., Bismarck, ND 58502-1601; 701-223-8518; Fax: 701-223-1291
Dale Tinjum, Vice President

NORTH DAKOTA NATURAL SCIENCE SOCIETY

Dept. of Biological Sciences
600 Park Street
Fort Hays State University
Hays, KS 67601-4099 United States
Phone: 785-628-4214 Fax: 785-628-4153
E-mail: efinck@fhsu.edu
Website: www.npwrc.usgs.gov/ndnss/

Founded: 1967

Scope: Regional

Description: Dedicated to the observation, recording, study, and preservation of all aspects of the natural history of the Great Plains.

Publication(s): Prairie Naturalist, The

Keyword(s): Land Issues, Wildlife & Species

Contact(s):

Jane Austin, President; Northern Prairie Wildlife Research Center, Jamestown, ND 58401
Elmer Finck, Editor; Div. of Biological Sciences, Box 4050, Emporia, KS 66801

NORTH DAKOTA WILDLIFE FEDERATION

P.O. Box 7248
Bismarck, ND 58507-7248 United States
Phone: 701-222-2557 Fax: 701-222-0334
E-mail: ndwf@gcentral.com
Website: www.ndwf.org

Founded: 1935

Membership: 1,001–10,000
Scope: State
Description: A representative statewide organization, affiliated with the National Wildlife Federation, dedicated to the protection and enhancement of wildlife and its habitat through public education and government interaction.
Publication(s): Flickertales, NDWF's official newsletter
Contact(s):
John Kopp, President
Dick McCabe, Vice-President
James Boley, NWF Representative
Conrad Carlson, Treasurer
Paula Mielke, Education Programs
Cameo Skager, Office Manager

NORTHCOAST ENVIRONMENTAL CENTER

575 H Street
Arcata, CA 95521 United States
Phone: 707-822-6918 Fax: 707-822-0827
E-mail: nec@igc.org
Website: www.necandeconews.to
Founded: 1971
Membership: 1,001–10,000
Scope: Regional
Description: A tax-exempt educational organization dedicated to illuminating the relationships between humankind and the biosphere. The Center provides environmental information and referral services for northwestern California and southwestern Oregon and operates a library open to the public.
Publication(s): Econews
Keyword(s): Forests/Forestry, Land Issues, Public Lands/Greenspace, Water Habitats & Quality, Wildlife & Species
Contact(s):
Tim McKay, Director
Connie Stewart, Office Manager
Sid Dominitz, Editor
Gail Sellstrom, Librarian

NORTHEAST CONSERVATION LAW ENFORCEMENT CHIEFS' ASSOCIATION (CLECA)

Attn: Secretary
RI Dept. of Environmental Management
83 Park St.
Providence, RI 02908 United States
Phone: 401-277-2284
Founded: N/A
Scope: Regional
Contact(s):
Ronald Alie, President; Chief, New Hampshire Fish and Game Dept., Law Enforcement Division, 2 Hazen Dr., Concord, NH 033301; 603-271-3127; Fax: 603-271-1438
Thomas Kamerzel, Vice President; Dir., Bureau of Law Enforcement, Pennsylvania Fish and Boat Commission, P.O. Box 67000, Harrisburg, PA 17106-7000; 717-567-4542; Fax: 717-657-4033
Thomas Greene, Secretary and Treasurer

NORTHEAST SUSTAINABLE ENERGY ASSOCIATION

50 Miles St.
Greenfield, MA 01301 United States
Phone: 413-774-6051 Fax: 413-774-6053
E-mail: nesea@nesea.org
Website: www.nesea.org
Founded: 1974
Membership: 1,001–10,000
Scope: Regional
Description: The Northeast Sustainable Energy Association (NESEA) aims to strengthen the economy and lessen our impact on the environment by bringing sustainable energy into everyday use. Through its programs and activities, NESEA offers an alternative vision of responsible energy use and works with policymakers, industry, educators, students, and the general public to make this vision a reality.
Publication(s): Northeast Sun, Totally Tree-mendous Activities, Getting Around Without Gasoline
Keyword(s): Energy, Sprawl/Urban Planning, Transportation
Contact(s):
Nancy Hazard, Director of Transportation Programs; nhazard@nesea.org
Warren Leon, Executive Director; wleon@nesea.org
Chris Mason, Director of Education; cmason@nesea.org
Sandy Thomas, Director of Energy Park; sthomas@nesea.org
Jonathon Tauer, Manager of Building Program; jtauer@nesea.org
Nancy Hazard, Associate Director; nhazard@nesea.org
Peter Taggert, Board of Directors Chair
Michael Tennis, Secretary

NORTHERN ALASKA ENVIRONMENTAL CENTER

830 College Rd
Fairbanks, AK 99701-2806 United States
Phone: 907-452-5021 Fax: 907-452-3100
E-mail: info@northern.org
Website: www.northern.org
Founded: 1971
Membership: 1,001–10,000
Scope: Local, State, Regional, National, International
Description: The Northern Alaska Environmental Center works to protect some of the wildest country left in North America — the vast Interior and Arctic regions of Alaska — through education, advocacy, grassroots organizing, and sheer perseverance. The Northern Center's priorities are to protect Alaska's Arctic from oil drilling; promote ecologically sound, sustainable management of Alaska's boreal forests; defend wild rivers from mining pollution and roads; and encourage better environmental understanding,
Publication(s): Mining Memos - email list, Northern Line, The, Conservation Abstracts, Boreal Briefs, Arctic Action, Camp Habitat-email list
Keyword(s): Air Quality/Atmosphere, Ecosystems (precious), Forests/Forestry, Land Issues, Public Lands/Greenspace, Water Habitats & Quality
Contact(s):
Arthur Hussey, Executive Director; arthur@northern.org
Mara Bacsujlaky, Assistant Director and Mining Coordinator; mara@northern.org
Sara Elzey, Bookkeeper; sara@northern.org
Paul Ollig, Membership and Communications Director; paul@northern.org
Linda Paganelli, Denali Watch Coordinator
Leah Sansone, Camp Habitat Director; leah@northern.org
Nancy Fresco, Boreal Forest Campaign Coordinator; nancy@northern.org
Deb Moore, Arctic Coordinator; deb@northern.org

NORTHERN PLAINS RESOURCE COUNCIL

2401 Montana Ave., Suite 200
Billings, MT 59101-2336 United States
Phone: 406-248-1154 Fax: 406-248-2110
E-mail: info@nprcmt.org
Website: www.nprcmt.org
Founded: 1972
Scope: National
Description: NPRC is a grassroots citizens' organization of farmers, ranchers, townspeople, and other conservationists. NPRC works on natural resource and agricultural issues to promote sustainable economic development, and to maintain Montana's unique rural quality of life. NPRC is dedicated to family agriculture and to stewardship of air, land, and water.

Publication(s): Plains Truth, The, Legislative Bulletin, Reclaiming the Wealth (A Citizens' Guide to Hard Rock Mining in Montana)
Keyword(s): Agriculture/Farming, Air Quality/Atmosphere, Energy, Land Issues, Reduce/Reuse/Recycle, Water Habitats & Quality
Contact(s):
Teresa Erickson, Staff Director
Jeanie Alderson, Secretary
Mary Fitzpatrick, Vice Chair
Amy Frykman, Research Coordinator
Denna Hoff, Chair
Dan Teigen, Treasurer

NORTHERN WINGS

22 Rittenhouse Rd.
Broomall, PA 19008 United States
Phone: 610-353-1535 Fax: 610-356-5814
Founded: 1989
Scope: National
Description: A nonprofit membership organization dedicated to providing free aviation services to environmental and conservation groups worldwide. These services are provided through a network of member pilots and include aerial surveys and photography, flying essential observers, etc.
Publication(s): Despatches
Keyword(s): Land Issues
Contact(s):
Alan Brecher, Executive Director

NORTHWEST ATLANTIC FISHERIES ORGANIZATION (NAFO)

Dartmouth, B2Y 3Y9 Nova Scotia Canada
Phone: 902-468-5590 Fax: 902-468-5538
E-mail: info@nafo.ca
Website: www.nafo.ca
Founded: 1979
Membership: 1–100
Scope: International
Description: Works for the optimum utilization, rational management, and conservation of the fishery resources of the convention area in the Northwest Atlantic. Contracting Parties: Bulgaria, Canada, Cuba, Denmark for the Faroes and Greenland, Estonia, European Union, France (for St. Pierre and Miquelon), Iceland, Japan, Korea, Latvia, Lithuania, Norway, Poland, Romania, Russia and the USA.
Publication(s): Annual Report, Index of Meeting Documents, Sampling Yearbook, Scientific Council Studies, Statistical Bulletin, Journal of Northwest Atlantic Fishery Science, all publications available on web
Keyword(s): Oceans/Coasts/Beaches, Wildlife & Species
Contact(s):
E. Otuski, President of NAFO and Chairman of General Council
T. Amaratunga, Assistant Executive Secretary
W. Brodie, Scientific Council Chairman
P. Chamut, General Council, Vice Chairman
Leonard Chepel, Executive Secretary
P. Gullestad, Fisheries Commission Chairman
R. Mayo, Scientific Council Vice Chairman
D. Swanson, Fisheries Commission Vice Chairman

NORTHWEST COALITION FOR ALTERNATIVES TO PESTICIDES

P.O. Box 1393
Eugene, OR 97440 United States
Phone: 541-344-5044 Fax: 541-344-6923
E-mail: info@pesticide.org
Website: www.pesticide.org
Founded: 1977
Membership: 1,001–10,000
Scope: Regional
Description: The Northwest Coalition for Alternatives to Pesticides works to protect people and the environment by advancing healthy solutions to pest problems.
Publication(s): Farmer Exhange, The, Journal of Pesticide Reform
Keyword(s): Agriculture/Farming, Pollution (general), Public Health, Water Habitats & Quality
Contact(s):
Norma Grier, Executive Director
Becky Long, Development Director
Caroline Cox, Editor/Staff Scientist
Aimee Code, Right-To-Know Coordinator
Megan Kemple, Public Education Coordinator; info@pesticide.org
Pollyanna Lind, Salmon and Water Quality
Kay Rumsey, Librarian
Edward Winter, Office Coordinator/ Financial Coordinator

NORTHWEST ECOSYSTEM ALLIANCE

THE CASCADES CONSERVATION PARTNERSHIP
1421 Cornwall Ave., Suite 201
Bellingham, WA 98225 United States
Phone: 360-671-9950 Fax: 360-671-8429
E-mail: nwea@ecosystem.org
Website: www.ecosystem.org
Founded: 1989
Membership: 10,001–100,000
Scope: Regional
Description: Northwest Ecosystem Alliance protects and restores wildlands in the Pacific Northwest and supports such efforts in British Columbia. The Alliance bridges science and advocacy, working with activists, policymakers, and the public to conserve our natural heritage.
Publication(s): Northwest Conservation
Keyword(s): Ecosystems (precious), Forests/Forestry, Public Lands/Greenspace, Wildlife & Species
Contact(s):
Mary Humphries, Business Manager and Development Director; meh@ecosystem.org
Lisa McShane, Community Outreach Director; lmcshane@ecosystem.org
Fred Munson, Deputy Director; 206-675-9747, ext. 202; fmunson@ecosystem.org
Hudson Dodd, Volunteer Coordinator; 360-671-9950, ext. 26; hdodd@ecosystem.org

NORTHWEST ENVIRONMENT WATCH

1402 3rd Ave., Suite 500
Seattle, WA 98101 United States
Phone: 206-447-1880 Fax: 206-447-2270
E-mail: new@northwestwatch.org
Website: www.northwestwatch.org
Founded: 1993
Membership: 1,001–10,000
Scope: Regional
Description: NEW's mission is to foster sustainability in the Pacific Northwest. NEW provides citizens with intelligence reports on the latest findings from the natural and social sciences, and guides them in creating a sustainable economy.
Publication(s): State of the Northwest, Stuff, Misplaced Blame, The Car and The City, Tax Shift, Green Collared Jobs, Hazardous Handouts, This Place on Earth, Over our Heads
Keyword(s): Development/Developing Countries, Population, Sprawl/Urban Planning, Transportation
Contact(s):
Alan Durning, Executive Director; ext. 103
Clark Williams Derry, Research Director; 447-1880, ext. 106

NORTHWEST INTERPRETIVE ASSOCIATION

909 1st Ave., Suite 630
Seattle, WA 98104-3627 United States
Phone: 206-220-4140 Fax: 206-220-4143
Website: www.nwpubliclands.com

Founded: 1974

Scope: Regional

Description: The Association supports interpretation and education on public lands administered by the National Park Service, U.S. Forest Service, and other agencies in the Pacific Northwest. Proceeds from the sale of interpretive publications are donated to these agencies to educate visitors in the area's natural and cultural history.

Keyword(s): Ethics/Environmental Justice, Land Issues, Recreation/Ecotourism

Contact(s):
Mary Quackenbush, Executive Director
Tom Scribner, Vice Chairman
Jim Torrence, Chairman of the Board

NORTHWEST RESOURCE INFORMATION CENTER

P.O. Box 427
Eagle, ID 83616 United States
Phone: 208-939-0714 Fax: 208-939-0714
E-mail: edchaney@nwric.org
Website: www.nwric.org

Founded: 1976
Membership: 1–100
Scope: State, Regional, National, International

Description: NRIC promotes through research, public education, technology transfer, and litigation the concept that ecological diversity and environmental quality are synonymous with long-term economic productivity and quality of life.

Keyword(s): Development/Developing Countries, Ecosystems (precious), Energy, Ethics/Environmental Justice, Executive/Legislative/Judicial Reform, Water Habitats & Quality, Wildlife & Species

Contact(s):
Ed Chaney, Executive Director; 2811 W. State St., Eagle, ID 83616; 208-939-8731

NOVA SCOTIA FEDERATION OF ANGLERS AND HUNTERS

NOVA SCOTIA WILDLIFE FEDERATION
P.O. Box 654
Halifax, B3J 2T3 Nova Scotia Canada
Phone: 902-477-8898 Fax: 902-477-8898
E-mail: tr.NSWF@chebucto.ns.ca

Founded: 1930
Membership: 1,001–10,000
Scope: State, National

Description: Affiliated with the Canadian Wildlife Federation and the National Coalition of Provincial and Territorial Wildlife Federations. Aims to unite all conservation organizations in Nova Scotia, fosters appreciation of wildlife and habitat, promotes fish and game management, seeks enactment and enforcement of laws necessary for environmental controls as well as conservation of wildlife resources.

Publication(s): Nova Outdoors.

Keyword(s): Ecosystems (precious), Ethics/Environmental Justice, Executive/Legislative/Judicial Reform, Forests/Forestry, Land Issues, Oceans/Coasts/Beaches, Pollution (general), Recreation/Ecotourism, Water Habitats & Quality, Wildlife & Species

Contact(s):
Bob Bancroft, President
A.J. (Tony) Rodgers, Executive Director; tony.rodgers@3web.net

NOVA SCOTIA FORESTRY ASSOCIATION

P.O. Box 1113
Truro, B2N 5G9 Nova Scotia Canada
Phone: 902-893-4653 Fax: 902-893-1197
Website: www.nsfa.ca

Founded: 1959

Scope: International

Description: The Nova Scotia Forestry Association is a nonprofit, charitable organization dedicated to promoting the wise use and management of our forest resources through education programs for youth. Programs emphasize the importance of being good stewards of our natural resources.

Publication(s): Annual Teachers Guide for National Forest Week.

Keyword(s): Forests/Forestry, Pollution (general)

Contact(s):
Russ Waycott, President
Debbie Totten, Executive Director

NW ENERGY COALITION

219 First Ave., S.
#100
Seattle, WA 98104 United States
Phone: 206-621-0094 Fax: 206-621-0097
E-mail: nwec@nwenergy.org
Website: www.nwenergy.org

Founded: 1981
Membership: 101–1,000
Scope: State, Regional, National

Description: The NW Energy Coalition is a regionwide alliance of progressive utilities, consumer advocates, and green businesses. The Coalition advocates cost-effective energy conservation, renewable energy resources, low-income/consumer protection and the restoration of fish and wildlife.

Publication(s): NW Energy Coalition Report, Plugging People into Power, Energy Activist

Keyword(s): Energy, Reduce/Reuse/Recycle, Wildlife & Species

Contact(s):
Rob Gala, Outreach Director
Mark Glyde, Communications Director
Nancy Hirsh, Policy Director
Sara Patton, Director

O

OCEAN CONSERVANCY, THE

1725 DeSales St., NW, Suite 600
Washington, DC 20036 United States
Phone: 202-429-5609 Fax: 202-872-0619
Website: www.oceanconservancy.org

Founded: 1972
Membership: 100,001–500,000
Scope: National

Description: A nonprofit, scientific organization dedicated to protecting marine wildlife and its habitats, and to conserving coastal and ocean resources. The center's programs are conducted in five major areas: Fisheries and Wildlife Conservation, Ecosystem Protection, Biodiversity Conservation, International Initiatives, Citizen Monitoring, and Outreach. Program efforts focus on research, policy analysis, education, and public information and involvement.

Publication(s): list of additional publications on request, International Coastal Cleanup Report, Coastal Connection, Blue Planet Quarterly

Keyword(s): Oceans/Coasts/Beaches, Pollution (general), Reduce/Reuse/Recycle, Water Habitats & Quality, Wildlife & Species

Contact(s):
Roger Rufe, President; 202-429-5609
Warner Chabot, Vice President for Regions; 580 Market St., Suite 550, San Francisco, CA 94104; 415-391-6204

Stephanie Drea, Vice President for Communications and Marketing; 202-429-5609
Elliot Gruber, Vice President for Development and Membership; 202-429-5609
David Guggenheim, Vice President for Conservation Policy; 202-429-5609
David Hoskins, Vice President for Government Affairs and General Counsel; 202-429-5609
Peter Jones, Vice President for Finance and Administration
Kris Balliet, Director of the Alaska Region; 425 G. St., Anchorage, AK; 907-258-9922
David Dixon, Director of Constituency Development; 202-429-5609
Linda Sheehan, Director of the Pacific Coast Region; 580 Market St., Suite 550, San Francisco, CA 94104; 415-391-6204
Jack Sobel, Director of Ecosystem Programs; 202-429-5609
David White, Director of the Southeast Atlantic & Gulf of Mexico Region; One Beach Dr. SE, #304, St. Petersburg, FL 33701; 727-895-2188
Nina Young, Director of Marine Conservation Wildlife; 202-429-5609; Fax: 202-872-0619
Nicole Sandberg, International Coastal Cleanup Manager; 202-429-5609; Fax: 202-872-0619
John Bierwirth, Chairman of the Board

OCEAN PROJECT, THE

102 Waterman Street
Suite 16
Providence, RI 02906 United States
Phone: 401-272-8822 Fax: 401-272-8877
E-mail: info@theoceanproject.org
Website: www.theoceanproject.org

Founded: 1998
Membership: N/A
Scope: Local, State, Regional, National, International
Description: The Ocean Project is an unprecedented collaboration of more than 160 aquariums, zoos, science, technology and natural history museums, and other educational institutions that collectively reach 140 million visitors annually. Together, we have formed a relatively new initiative that intends to create an educated public with a lasting, measurable, top-of-mind awareness of and concern for the importance, value and sensitivity of the oceans.
Keyword(s): Oceans/Coasts/Beaches, Water Habitats & Quality
Contact(s):
Bill Mott, Director; 401-272-8822; Fax: 401-272-8877; bmott@theoceanproject.org

OCEAN VOICE INTERNATIONAL

3332 McCarthy Rd.
Ottawa, K1V 0W0 Ontario Canada
Phone: 613-721-4541 Fax: 613-721-4562
E-mail: oceans@superaje.com
Website: www.ovi.ca

Founded: 1987
Membership: 101–1,000
Scope: National
Description: To conserve the diversity of marine life, protect and restore marine ecosystems and ecological services, enhance the quality of life and equity of benefits for coastal peoples, and promote ecologically sustainable harvest of marine resources.
Publication(s): Sea Wind, Striving for the Integrity of Freshwater Ecosystems, Global Freshwater Biodiversity, Green School Biodiversity Booklet, The Status of the World Ocean and its Biodiversity, How Green is Your School?, Save Our Coral Reefs
Keyword(s): Development/Developing Countries, Water Habitats & Quality, Wildlife & Species
Contact(s):
Jaime Baquero, President; 819-243-1334

OCEANIC SOCIETY

Fort Mason Center, Building E
San Francisco, CA 94123 United States
Phone: 415-441-1106 Fax: 415-474-3395
E-mail: director@oceanic-society.org
Website: www.oceanic-society.org

Founded: 1969
Membership: 101–1,000
Scope: International
Description: Founded in 1969, The Oceanic Society is a non-profit marine conservation organization whose mission is to protect marine wildlife through an integrated program of scientific research, environmental education, and volunteerism.
Keyword(s): Ecosystems (precious), Ethics/Environmental Justice, Oceans/Coasts/Beaches, Recreation/Ecotourism, Wildlife & Species

OFFICE OF PROTECTIVE RESOURCES (NATIONAL MARINE FISHERIES SVC)

NOAA/NMFS F/HP4 Off., Hab. Prot., 1315 East-West Highway
Silver Spring, MD 20910-3282 United States
Phone: 301-713-2319 Fax: 301-713-0376
Website: www.noaa.gov

Founded: N/A
Membership: 1–100
Scope: National
Contact(s):
Don Knowles, Director; don.knowles@noaa.org

OFFICE OF THE SECRETARY OF DEFENSE

INSTALLATIONS
3E1074 Defense Pentagon
Washington, DC 20321 United States
Phone: 703-697-8080

Founded: N/A
Description: The Installations office of Acquisition and Technology in the Office of the Secretary of Defense is responsible for U.S. and worldwide policy and services coordination regarding land management, energy policy and energy purchasing policy, and base closure issues.

OHIO ACADEMY OF SCIENCE, THE

1500 W. 3rd Ave., Suite 223
Columbus, OH 43212-2817 United States
Phone: 614-488-2228 Fax: 614-488-7629
E-mail: oas@iwaynet.net
Website: www.ohiosci.org

Founded: 1891
Membership: 1,001–10,000
Scope: Regional
Description: A nonprofit organization designed to stimulate interest in the sciences, to promote research, to improve instruction in the sciences, to disseminate scientific knowledge, and to recognize high achievement in attaining these objectives.
Publication(s): Ohio Journal of Science, The, Ohio Academy of Science Newsletter
Keyword(s): Public Health
Contact(s):
Lynn Elfner, Executive Officer

OHIO ALLIANCE FOR THE ENVIRONMENT

1500 West Third Ave.
Columbus, OH 43212 United States
Phone: 614-487-9957 Fax: 614-487-9957
E-mail: probasco@ohioalliance.org
Website: www.ohioalliance.org

Founded: 1977
Membership: 101–1,000

Scope: State

Description: The Ohio Alliance for the Environment is a statewide nonprofit organization which promotes education, communication and interaction on environmental issues among diverse groups including representatives from government, education, business and environmental organizations. We accomplish this through conferences, seminars, publications, and roundtable discussions.

Publication(s): Focus on the Issue, OAE Newsletter

Contact(s):

Lisa Novosat-Gradert, President; Environmental Attorney, Brouse McDowell, 500 First National Tower, Akron, OH 44308-1471; 330-535-5711, ext. 316; Fax: 330-253-8601; lngradert@brouse.com

Mike Parkes, President Elect; Community Relations Manager, Waste Technologies Industries, 1250 St. George Street, East Liverpool, OH 43920; 330-385-7337; Fax: 330-650-1853; mparkes@vonrollwti.com

Irene Probasco, Executive Director; 1500 West Third Ave., Suite 30, Columbus, OH 43212; 614-487-9957; Fax: 614-487-9957; probasco@ohioalliance.org

Jane Haynes, Newsletter Editor; 614-885-3735; Fax: 614-885-3735; sjhaynes@juno.com

OHIO B.A.S.S. CHAPTER FEDERATION

Attn: President, 376 N. Dorset
Troy, OH 45373 United States
E-mail: dbecker@erinet.com
Website: www.ohiobass.org

Founded: N/A

Scope: State

Description: An organization of Bassmaster chapters, affiliated with the Bass Anglers Sportsman Society, organized to fight pollution, assist state and national conservation agencies in their efforts, and teach the young people of our country good conservation practices. Dedicated to the realistic conservation of our water resources.

Contact(s):

Dennis Becker, President; 376 North Dorset, Troy, OH 45373; 937-335-2078; dbecker@erinet.com

Jim Doss, Conservation Director; 43 Portsmouth Rd., Gallipolis, OH 45631; 740-446-9810; JSDoss@zoomnet.net

OHIO BIOLOGICAL SURVEY

1315 Kinnear Rd.
Columbus, OH 43212-1192 United States
Phone: 614-292-9645 Fax: 614-688-4322
E-mail: obsinfo01@postbox.acs.ohio-state.edu
Website: www.biosci.ohio-state.edu/~ohbiol/

Founded: 1912

Membership: 101–1,000

Scope: Regional

Description: An inter-institutional organization of 106 colleges, universities, museums and other organizations in Ohio, ten other states and the province of Ontario. Produces and disseminates scientific and technical information concerning the flora and fauna of the Ohio environment, and larger areas of which Ohio is an integral part.

Publication(s): Bulletins, In Ohio's Backyard Series, Informative Publications, Notes, Miscellaneous Publications, publications available on website

Keyword(s): Public Lands/Greenspace, Wildlife & Species

Contact(s):

Brian Armitage, Executive Director; armitage.7@osu.edu

Terry Keiser, Chairman of the Advisory Board; Ohio Northern University,

OHIO ENERGY PROJECT

OHIO NEED PROJECT
640 Enterprise Dr.
Suite A
Lewis Center, OH 43035 United States
Phone: 614-785-1717 Fax: 614-785-1731
E-mail: oep@ohioenergy.org
Website: www.ohioenergy.org

Founded: 1984

Membership: 10,001–100,000

Scope: State

Description: A nonprofit organization promoting energy education, efficiency and conservation and youth leadership development, using a fun hands-on, inter-disciplinary approach and the "kids teaching kids" philosophy.

Publication(s): Curriculum Materials

Keyword(s): Energy

Contact(s):

Shauni Nix, Executive Director
Rich Smith, Director
Annie Rasor, Programs Manager
Melissa Fu, Education Coordinator
Mary McCarron, Statewide Coordinator
Mike Stranges, Education Coordinator

OHIO ENVIRONMENTAL COUNCIL, INC.

1207 Grandview Ave.
Suite 201
Columbus, OH 43212 United States
Phone: 614-487-7506 Fax: 614-487-7510
E-mail: oec@theoec.org
Website: www.theoec.org

Founded: 1969

Membership: 1,001–10,000

Scope: State

Description: The Ohio Environmental Council is a statewide organization providing resources for local environmental organizations across Ohio. The OEC promotes improved environmental quality in the state through advocacy, research, education and collaborative efforts.

Publication(s): Ohio Environmental Report Newsletter, Green Pages, publications available on web.

Keyword(s): Agriculture/Farming, Air Quality/Atmosphere, Development/Developing Countries, Energy, Ethics/Environmental Justice, Pollution (general), Water Habitats & Quality

Contact(s):

Daniel Binder, Board President; 817 S. Remmington Rd., Bexle, OH
Vicki Deisner, Executive Director
Keith Dimoff, Water Program Manager
Sarah Hovanec, Development and Program Coordinator
Peter Johnsen, Business and Technology Manager
Jack Shaner, Public Affairs Manager
Susan Studer King, Community Outreach and Development Manger
Kurt Waltzer, Clean Air Program Manager
Lindy Black, Membership and Administrative Assistant
Heidi Ehret, Power Plant Campaign Coordinator
Alice Woerner, Outreach Coordinator

OHIO FEDERATION OF SOIL AND WATER CONSERVATION DISTRICTS

4383 Fountain Sq. Ct. Building B-3
Columbus, OH 43224 United States
Phone: 614-265-6610
Website: www.dnr.state.oh.us/odnr/soil+water

Founded: N/A

Scope: State

Description: To provide leadership and services that enable Ohioans to conserve, protect and enhance soil, water and land resources

Contact(s):
Brad Ross, Administrator; 614-265-6616

OHIO FEDERATION OF SOIL AND WATER CONSERVATION DISTRICTS

OFSWCD
P.O. Box 24518
Columbus, OH 43224 United States
Phone: 6147841900 Fax: 6147849180
E-mail: alicia-connelly@oh.nacdnet.org

Founded: 1943
Membership: 101–1,000
Scope: Local, State
Description: Statewide federation representing 88 Soil & Water Conservation Districts and their 440 publicly elected board members. SWCDs assist local land users with information and technical assistance in making land use decisions on private working lands.
Keyword(s): Agriculture/Farming, Forests/Forestry, Pollution (general), Sprawl/Urban Planning, Water Habitats & Quality

OHIO FORESTRY ASSOCIATION, INC., THE

Grove City, OH 43123 United States
Phone: 614-497-9580 Fax: 614-497-9581
E-mail: nichoel@ohioforest.org
Website: www.ohioforest.org

Founded: 1903
Membership: 101–1,000
Scope: Regional
Description: A statewide organization, affiliated with the National Woodland Owners Association, organized to promote the welfare of the people and private enterprise of Ohio by improving, through education, the wise management of Ohio's forest resource. Sponsors annual forestry camp for youths 14-19; assists schools' conservation activities and education; and coordinates American Tree Farm Program in Ohio.
Publication(s): Ohio Woodlands, Bark and Bunk
Keyword(s): Forests/Forestry, Recreation/Ecotourism
Contact(s):
Melvin Yoder, President
Jim Doll, 2nd Vice President
C. Wayne Lashbrook, 1st Vice President
Roy Palmer, 3rd Vice President
Robert B. Redett, Treasurer
Karl Gebhardt

OHIO NATIVE PLANT SOCIETY

6 Louise Dr.
Chagrin Falls, OH 44022 United States
Phone: 440-338-6622
Website: dir.gardenweb.com/directory/onps#

Founded: 1982
Membership: 101–1,000
Scope: Local, State, Regional
Description: The Ohio Native Plant Society is dedicated to preservation, conservation and education concerning all native plants of Ohio.
Keyword(s): Ecosystems (precious), Ethics/Environmental Justice, Land Issues, Wildlife & Species
Contact(s):
A. Malmquist, Executive Secretary

OKLAHOMA ACADEMY OF SCIENCE

P.O. Box 701915
Tulsa, OK 74170-1915 United States
Phone: 918-495-6944
Website: bmb-fs.biochem.okstate.edu/OAS/

Founded: 1909
Membership: 101–1,000
Scope: State
Description: To stimulate scientific research; to promote fraternal relationship among those engaged in scientific work in Oklahoma; to diffuse among the citizens of the state a knowledge of the various departments of science; and to investigate and make known the material, education, and other resources of the state.
Publication(s): Proceedings-Oklahoma Academy of Science, CAS Newsletter, Transactions-Oklahoma Junior Academy of Science.

OKLAHOMA ASSOCIATION OF CONSERVATION DISTRICTS

Attn: President, P.O. Box 107
Chelsea, OK 74016-0107 United States
Phone: 918-696-7612

Founded: N/A
Scope: State
Keyword(s): Reduce/Reuse/Recycle
Contact(s):
Carol Gaunt, President, Alternate Board Member; Rt. 5 Box 244, Weatherford, OK 73096-8815; 405-772-5107
Matt Gard, Vice President; Rt. 1, Box 16, Fairview, OK 73737-9621; 580-438-2320
Rick Jeans, Vice President; Rt. 1 Box 184, Tonkawa, OK 74653; 405-628-2223
Mark Moehle, Vice President; 1601 Shadow Court, Edmond, OK 73013-2683; 405-340-8884; Fax: 405-842-8744
George Fraley, Past President; P.O. Box 107, Chelsea, OK 74016-0107; 918-789-2511; Fax: 918-789-2835
Christy Kimble, Secretary; Oklahoma County CD, 1120 NW 63rd Ste. G101, Oklahoma City, OK 73116; 405-848-1933; Fax: 405-842-8744
Wayne Smith, Treasurer; 506 N. Pennsylvania, Mangum, OK 73554-3036; 405-782-3575; Fax: 405-782-3581
Billy Wilson, Board Member; P.O. Box 208, Kinta, OK 74552-0208; 918-768-3542; bwilson@cwis.net

OKLAHOMA AUDUBON COUNCIL

P.O. Box 2476
Tulsa, OK 74101 United States
Phone: 918-592-1614
E-mail: info@tulsaaudubon.org

Founded: 1987
Membership: 1,001–10,000
Scope: State
Description: A statewide council of representatives of the eight National Audubon Society chapters in Oklahoma. The council coordinates the efforts of the chapters on statewide environmental issues, and advocates protection, preservation, and wise use of soil, water, plants, and wildlife.

OKLAHOMA B.A.S.S. CHAPTER FEDERATION

Attn: President, 2300 E. Coleman Rd.
Ponca City, OK 74604 United States
Phone: 580-765-0165
E-mail: bigc@ponca.net
Website: www.okbass.org

Founded: N/A
Scope: State
Description: An organization of Bassmaster chapters, affiliated the with Bass Anglers Sportsman Society, organized to fight pollution, assist state and national conservation agencies in their efforts, and teach the young people of our country good conservation practices. Dedicated to the realistic conservation of our water resources.
Publication(s): Scissortail, The, Oklahoma B.A.S.S. Federation Newsletter.
Contact(s):
Robert Cartlidge, President; 2300 E. Coleman Road, Ponca City, OK 74604; 580-765-0165

Don Linder, Conservation Director; 2409 Cardinal, Ponca City, OK 74604; 580- 76-3301; dlinder@horizon.hit.net
James Hardage, Treasurer; 1352 Bridle Path Lane, Lindale, TX 75771; 903-882-8652
R. Kitterman, Secretary, Editor; 411 W. 6th, Dewey, OK 74029; 918-534-1720

OKLAHOMA DEPARTMENT OF WILDLIFE AND CONSERVATION

75-B Rte. 1
Porter, OK 74454 United States
Phone: 918-683-1031 Fax: 918-683-9406
E-mail: trodwc@oknet1.net
Website: www.wildlifedepartment.com

Founded: 1968
Membership: 1–100
Scope: State
Contact(s):
Paul Balkenbush, Regional Supervisor

OKLAHOMA NATIVE PLANT SOCIETY

c/o Tulsa Garden Center, 2435 S. Peoria
Tulsa, OK 74114 United States
Phone: 405-872-9652 Fax: 405-872-8361
E-mail: cox.chadwick@worldnet.http.net
Website: www.telepath.com/chadcox/onps.html

Founded: 1986
Membership: 101–1,000
Scope: State
Description: Oklahoma Native Plant Society encourages the study, protection, propagation, appreciation, and use of Oklahoma's native plants.
Publication(s): Gaillardia, The, Native Plant Selection Guide for Oklahoma Woody Plants.
Keyword(s): Land Issues, Public Lands/Greenspace, Reduce/Reuse/Recycle, Sprawl/Urban Planning, Water Habitats & Quality, Wildlife & Species
Contact(s):
Patricia Folley, President; 405-872-8361; pfolley7@juno.com
Chad Cox, Vice President; 405-598-6742
Mary Korthase, Treasurer; 918-743-2743; mkorthase@webzone.net
Maurita Nations, Secretary; nationsokc@juno.com

OKLAHOMA ORNITHOLOGICAL SOCIETY

Attn: Business Manager, 1701 W. Will Rogers
Claremore, OK 74017 United States
Phone: 918-343-7706 Fax: 918-343-7563
E-mail: kwmartin@rsu.edu

Founded: 1950
Membership: 101–1,000
Scope: State
Description: Affiliated with National Audubon Society and the Oklahoma Wildlife Federation. Dedicated to the observation, study, and conservation of birds in Oklahoma.
Publication(s): Bulletin of the Oklahoma Ornithological Society.
Contact(s):
Keith Martin, President
Jo Loyd, Business Manager; 6736 E. 28th St., Tulsa, OK 74129; 918-835-2946
Michael Bay, Secretary; Dept. Biology, East Central State Univ., Ada, OK 74820
Charles Brown, Editor; Biology Dept. University of Tulsa, Tulsa, OK 74104; 918-631-3943
Marty Kamp, Treasurer; 6422 S. Indianapolis Pl., Tulsa, OK 74136
Richard Stewart, Editor; birdbander@aol.com

OKLAHOMA WILDLIFE FEDERATION

P.O. Box 60126
Oklahoma City, OK 73146-0126 United States
Phone: 405-524-7009 Fax: 405-521-9270
E-mail: owf@nstar.net
Website: www.okwildlife.org

Founded: 1963
Scope: State
Description: A representative statewide organization, affiliated with the National Wildlife Federation, dedicated to the protection and enhancement of wildlife and its habitat through public education and government interaction.
Publication(s): Outdoor News, Urban Landscaping
Contact(s):
Royce Meek, President and Representative
Margaret Ruff, Education Programs Contact & Executive Director
Mich Entz, Alternate Representative
Dick Gunn, Secretary
Lance Meek, Editor
James Menzer, Treasurer

OKLAHOMA WOODLAND OWNERS ASSOCIATION

2657 S. Trenton
Tulsa, OK 74114-2727 United States
Phone: 918-569-4287 Fax: 918-743-6941

Founded: N/A
Scope: State
Description: A statewide organization affiliated with the National Woodland Owners Association to advance forest management skills of Oklahoma woodland owners. Other objectives are to promote education and networking, provide timber marketing, and to monitor and act upon legislation.
Publication(s): OWOA Bulletin
Keyword(s): Forests/Forestry
Contact(s):
Patt Nelson, President and Editor
John Ahern, 1st Vice President
Rick Hutchinson, Board Member
Tom Kee, Secretary
Miles Schulze, Board Member

OLYMPIC PARK ASSOCIATES

168 Lost Mountain Lane
Sequim, WA 98362-9292 United States
Phone: 360-681-2480 Fax: 360-681-2480
E-mail: mcmorgan@olypen.com
Website: www.drizzle.com/~rdpayne/opa.htmo

Founded: 1948
Membership: 101–1,000
Scope: Local, State, Regional, National
Description: Dedicated to preserving the wilderness and integrity of Olympic National Park and the surrounding Olympic ecosystem, as well as supporting wild land and wildlife habitat protection elsewhere in the nation. Currently working on restoration of the Elwha River ecosystem, reintroduction of extirpated species like the wolf, and elimination of exotic species from Olympic National Park. We also promote restoration and protection of native salmon stocks in Olympic Peninsula waters.
Publication(s): Voice of the Wild Olympics
Keyword(s): Ecosystems (precious), Forests/Forestry, Land Issues, Public Lands/Greenspace, Wildlife & Species
Contact(s):
Polly Dyer, President; 206-364-3933
Tim McNulty, Vice President; 360-681-2480
John Anderson, Treasurer; 206-523-5043

Sally Soest, Editor; 206-860-2865
Philip Zalesky, Secretary; 425-337-2479

OLYMPIC PARK INSTITUTE

111 Barnes Point Rd.
Port Angeles, WA 98363 United States
Phone: 360-928-3720 Fax: 360-928-3046
E-mail: opi@yni.org
Website: www.yni.org/opi

Founded: 1987

Scope: National

Description: Mission is to inspire personal connection to the natural world and responsible actions to sustain it. OPI provides residential field science programs in Olympic National Park for adults, families and K-12 classrooms. Elderhostel and field seminar programs are also available. Programs introduce themes of ecology, sustainability and stewardship.

Publication(s): Publications on website

Keyword(s): Energy, Ethics/Environmental Justice, Forests/Forestry, Oceans/Coasts/Beaches, Public Lands/Greenspace, Reduce/Reuse/Recycle, Wildlife & Species

ONTARIO FEDERATION OF ANGLERS AND HUNTERS

Box 2800
Peterborough, K9J 8L5 Ontario Canada
Phone: 705-748-6324 Fax: 705-748-9577
E-mail: ofah@ofah.org
Website: www.ofah.org

Founded: 1928

Membership: 10,001–100,000

Scope: Local, State, Regional, National

Description: Canada's largest Provincial conservation organization with over 83,000 members and 630 affiliated Member Clubs. Nonprofit, nongovernment agency respresenting hunting and angling interests related to natural resources managment in the Province of Ontario.

Publication(s): Call of the Loon, Angler & Hunter Hotline

Keyword(s): Agriculture/Farming, Air Quality/Atmosphere, Climate Change, Ecosystems (precious), Executive/Legislative/Judicial Reform, Forests/Forestry, Land Issues, Pollution (general), Public Lands/Greenspace, Recreation/Ecotourism, Water Habitats & Quality, Wildlife & Species.

Contact(s):

Michael Reader, Executive Director; 705-748-6324; Fax: 705-748-9577; mike_reader@ofah.org
Greg Farrant, Government Relations Manager; 705-748-6324; Fax: 705-748-9577; greg_farrant@ofah.org
Terry Quinney, Prov. Mgr., Fish & Wildlife; 705-748-6324; Fax: 705-755-1757; terry_quinney@ofah.org
Mark Holmes, Communications Specialist; 705-748-6324; Fax: 705-748-9577; mark_holmes@ofah.org

ONTARIO FORESTRY ASSOCIATION

307—200 Consumers Rd.
Toronto, M2J 4R4 Ontario Canada
Phone: 416-493-4565 Fax: 416-493-4608
E-mail: forestry@oforest.on.ca
Website: www.oforest.on.ca

Founded: 1949

Scope: International

Description: Ontario Forestry Association works to raise awareness and understanding of all aspects of Ontario's forests and to develop commitment to stewardship of forest ecosystems. Programs include: Envirothon, Community Woodland Steward Initiative, Consultant Registry, land use and forest management, forestry publicity and historical data.

Publication(s): Ontario Forest Products Marketing Bulletin, Re:View

Keyword(s): Forests/Forestry

Contact(s):

Anne Koven, President
James Farrell, 2nd Vice President
Alex Rigsby, 1st Vice President
Erik Turk, Executive Director

OPENLANDS PROJECT

25 E. Washington St., Suite 1650
Chicago, IL 60602 United States
Phone: 312-427-4256 Fax: 312-427-6251
E-mail: info@openlands.org
Website: www.openlands.org

Founded: 1963

Membership: 101–1,000

Scope: Local, State, Regional

Description: A private, nonprofit organization, Openlands Project was founded in 1963 to provide a healthy environment and a more livable place for all people of the region. Openlands preserves, protects, enhances, and expands open space through land acquisition, greenways, watershed planning and restoration, urban greening initiatives, advocacy and technical assistance.

Publication(s): Openlander, Under Pressure: Land Consumption in the Chicago Region, Annual Report

Keyword(s): Land Issues, Reduce/Reuse/Recycle, Water Habitats & Quality, Wildlife & Species

Contact(s):

Tony Dean, President
Gerald Adelmann, Executive Director
Ders Anderson, Greenways Director
Glenda Daniel, Urban Greening Director
J. Ritchie, Treasurer
Charles Saltzman, Secretary

OPERATION MIGRATION

2731 Durham Road 19
Blackstock, L0B 1B0 Ontario Canada
Phone: 800-675-2618 Fax: 905-986-0780
E-mail: opmig@durham.net
Website: www.operationmigration.org

Founded: 1994

Membership: 101–1,000

Scope: International

Description: Dedicated to the restoration of migration routes for endangered or threatened species of birds through the use of ultralight aircraft

Keyword(s): Wildlife & Species

ORANGUTAN FOUNDATION INTERNATIONAL

822 S. Wellesley Avenue
Los Angeles, CA 90049 United States
Phone: 310-207-1655 Fax: 310-207-1556
E-mail: ofi@orangutan.org
Website: www.orangutan.org

Founded: 1986

Membership: 1,001–10,000

Scope: National, International

Description: Orangutan Foundation International's mission is to support the conservation of the orangutan and its habitat. Probably no more than 15,000 orangutans survive in the wild. Illegal mining and logging and the conversion of land into palm oil plantations pose the most serious threats. Some conservationists estimate that if illegal logging continues at its current rate, the rain forests in Indonesia could be gone in five to ten years, leading to the extinction of the orangutan in the wild.

Publication(s): Reflections of Eden, Orangutan Odyssey.

Keyword(s): Development/Developing Countries, Ecosystems (precious), Forests/Forestry, Land Issues, Recreation/Ecotourism, Water Habitats & Quality, Wildlife & Species

OREGON B.A.S.S. CHAPTER FEDERATION

Attn: President, 1601 S. Dogwood St.
Cornelius, OR 97113 United States
Phone: 503-357-4798
Website: orbass.oregonbass.net

Founded: N/A

Scope: State

Description: An organization of Bassmaster chapters, affiliated with Bass Anglers Sportsman Society, organized to fight pollution, assist state and national conservation agencies in their efforts, and teach the young people of our country good conservation practices. Dedicated to the realistic conservation of our water resources.

Publication(s): EarthWatch Oregon

Keyword(s): Air Quality/Atmosphere, Land Issues, Transportation, Water Habitats & Quality

Contact(s):

Orville Alleman, President
Chuck Lang, Conservation Director; 4775 Gardner Rd., SE, Salem, OR 97302; 503-588-1920; charleslang@home.com

OREGON ENVIRONMENTAL COUNCIL

520 SW 6th Ave
Suite 940
Portland, OR 97204-1535 United States
Phone: 503-222-1963 Fax: 503-222-1405
E-mail: oec@orcouncil.org
Website: www.orcouncil.org

Founded: 1968

Membership: 1,001–10,000

Scope: State

Description: Oregon Environmental Council is a nonprofit organization whose mission is to restore and protect Oregon's clean water and air now and for future generations. OEC brings Oregonians together to create and promote socially just and economically sound environmental policies.

Publication(s): EarthWatch Oregon.

Keyword(s): Air Quality/Atmosphere, Climate Change, Ethics/Environmental Justice, Pollution (general), Public Health, Transportation, Water Habitats & Quality

Contact(s):

James Whitty, Vice President
Jeff Allen, Executive Director
Carl Lamb, Treasurer
Jesse Reeder, President
Dorothy Fisher-Atwood, Secretary

OREGON NATURAL RESOURCES COUNCIL

5825 N. Greeley Avenue
Portland, OR 97217 United States
Phone: 503-283-6343 Fax: 503-283-0756
E-mail: sr@onrc.org
Website: www.onrc.org

Founded: 1972

Membership: 1,001–10,000

Scope: State

Description: A nonprofit, state-wide organization working to aggressively protect and restore Oregon's wildlands, wildlife, and waters as an enduring legacy.

Publication(s): Wild Oregon.

Keyword(s): Forests/Forestry, Land Issues, Public Lands/Greenspace, Reduce/Reuse/Recycle, Water Habitats & Quality, Wildlife & Species

Contact(s):

Pat Clancy, President
Tim Lillebo, Advocacy Director; 16 NW Kansas, Bend, OR 97701; 541-382-2616; Fax: 503-385-3370; tl@onrc.org
Regna Merritt, Executive Director; rm@onrc.org
Jacki Richey, Director of Finance
David Wilkins, Director of Development; dw@onrc.org
Brad Aaron, Development Assistant; ba@onrc.org
Alex Brown, Grassroots Coordinator; ab@onrc.org
Doug Heiken, Western Oregon Field Rep.; P.O. Box 11648, Eugene, OR 97440; 541-344-0675; Fax: 541-343-0996; onrcdoug@efn.org
Wendell Wood, Southern Oregon Field Rep.; 541-885-4886; Fax: 541-885-4887; ww@onrc.org

OREGON SMALL WOODLANDS ASSOCIATION

1775 32nd Place, NE, Suite C
Salem, OR 97303 United States
Phone: 503-588-1813 Fax: 503-588-1970
E-mail: oswa@oswa.org
Website: www.oswa.org

Founded: 1967

Membership: 1,001–10,000

Scope: State

Description: A statewide organization affiliated with the National Woodland Owners Association, dedicated to the protection, management, use and enhancement of Oregon's forest resources.

Publication(s): Northwest Woodlands, The Update

Keyword(s): Forests/Forestry, Reduce/Reuse/Recycle

Contact(s):

John Poppino, President; 541-447-1342
Bill Arsenault, 1st Vice-President; 541-584-2272
Ken Faulk, 2nd Vice-President; 541-447-6762
Denny Miles, Executive Director
Lori Rasor, Editor; 503-228-3624

OREGON TROUT

117 SW Naito Parkway
Portland, OR 97204-3595 United States
Phone: 503-222-9091 Fax: 503-222-9187
E-mail: info@ortrout.org
Website: www.ortrout.org

Founded: N/A

Membership: 1,001–10,000

Scope: Regional

Description: An Oregon-based organization focused on the protection and restoration of native fish and their ecosystems.

Publication(s): Riverkeeper

Contact(s):

Jim Myron, Conservation Director
Joe Whitworth, Executive Director

OREGON WILDLIFE HERITAGE FOUNDATION

P.O. Box 30406
Portland, OR 97294-3406 United States
Phone: 503-255-6059 Fax: 503-255-6467
E-mail: owhf@aol.com
Website: www.owhf.org

Founded: 1981

Membership: 101–1,000

Scope: State

Description: The Oregon Wildlife Heritage Foundation is a nonprofit, tax-exempt foundation incorporated under the laws of the state of Oregon. It has a 501(c)3 determination under the I.R.S. code. It receives grants and contributions to be used to fund selected projects beneficial to the fish and wildlife resources of Oregon and the people who enjoy them.

Contact(s):

E. Kimbark MacColl, President
Marcia Hartman, Vice President
Rod Brobeck, Executive Director
Charles Lilley, Secretary
Nelson Rutherford, Treasurer

ORGANIZATION FOR BAT CONSERVATION

1553 Haslett Rd.
Haslett, MI 48840 United States
Phone: 517-339-5200 Fax: 517-339-5618
E-mail: obcbats@aol.com
Website: www.batconservation.org

Founded: 1990

Scope: International

Description: One of the only international non-profit organizations dedicated to bat conservation. This mission is fulfilled through education and habitat preservation.

Publication(s): Stokes Guide to Bat Identification, Simple Guide to Bat House Designs, Understanding Bats

Keyword(s): Reduce/Reuse/Recycle, Wildlife & Species

Contact(s):

Rob Mies, Director; 517-339-5200, ext. 9; Fax: 517-339-5619; obcbats@aol.com

Kim Williams, Executive Director; 517-339-5200, ext. 9; Fax: 517-339-5618; obcbats@aol.com

ORGANIZATION OF WILDLIFE PLANNERS

1900 Kanawha Blvd., East
Charleston, WV 25305 United States
Phone: 304-558-2771 Fax: 304-558-3147
E-mail: wildlife@dnr.state.wv.us
Website: www.dnr.state.wv.us

Founded: 1978

Membership: 1–100

Scope: State

Description: A nonprofit, tax-exempt organization comprised of professional state and federal fish and wildlife resource planners, natural resources educators, professional conservationists, and associated interests dedicated to improving, through education and training, the quality of state-level resources management and planning. The focus of the organization is on developing the necessary tools and skills to conduct effective planned management systems.

Publication(s): Tomorrow's Management, Newsletter

Contact(s):

Paul Johansen, Assistant Chief, Game Management

ORION SOCIETY, THE

187 Main St
Great Barrington, MA 01230 United States
Phone: 413-528-4422 Fax: 413-528-0676
E-mail: orion@orionsociety.org
Website: www.oriononline.org

Founded: N/A

Membership: 1,001–10,000

Scope: National, International

Description: The Orion Society is an award-winning publisher, an environmental eduation organization, and a communication support network for grassroots environmental and community organizations across North America. It is a nonprofit member organization with 8000 members, individual and organization representing all fifty states and thirty-one countries.

Publication(s): Orion Afield magazine, Orion magazine, The Orion Grassroots Network.

ORNITHOLOGICAL COUNCIL

1707 H St., N.W., Suite 200
Washington, DC 20006 United States
Phone: 301-986-8568 Fax: 301-986-5205
Website: nmnh.si.edu/BIRDNET

Founded: 1992

Scope: International

Description: The Council provides impartial scientific information about birds for sound decisions, policies, or management actions; links the scientific community with public and private decision-makers; informs ornithologists of actions that affect birds or the study of birds; and speaks for scientific ornithology when the study of birds might be affected. Website contains links to ornithological scientific societies.

Keyword(s): Wildlife & Species

Contact(s):

David Blockstein, Chairman; 1707 H St., N.W., Suite 200, Washington, DC 20006; 202-530-5810; Fax: 202-628-4311

Ellen Paul, Executive Director; 301-986-8568; Fax: 301-986-5205; epaul@concentric.net

OUTDOOR CIRCLE, THE

1314 S. King, Suite 306
Honolulu, HI 96814 United States
Phone: 808-593-0300 Fax: 808-593-0525
E-mail: mail@outdoorcircle.org
Website: www.outdoorcircle.org

Founded: 1912

Membership: 1,001–10,000

Scope: Local, State

Description: A nonprofit organization whose purpose is to work for and develop a more beautiful state, freeing it from disfigurement, conserving and developing its natural beauty, and cooperating in educational and other efforts towards preservation of open spaces, parklands, recycling, and antilitter.

Publication(s): Our Familiar Island Trees, Trees and Flowers of the Hawaiian Island, Majesty II, Majesty: Exceptional Trees of Hawaii, Pua Nani: Hawaii is a Garden, The Greenleaf Newsletter, Keep Hawaii Green, Exceptional Trees of Hawaii, The

Keyword(s): Forests/Forestry, Land Issues, Public Lands/Greenspace, Wildlife & Species

Contact(s):

Mary Steiner, Chief Executive Officer; mary@outdoorcircle.org

Eileen Helmstetter, Landscape and Planting Project Manager; eileen@outdoorcircle.org

Kimberly Hillebrand, Membership Manager; kimberly@outdoorcircle.org

Aldrina Ventura, Administrator; aldrina@outdoorcircle.org

OUTDOOR RECREATION COUNCIL OF BRITISH COLUMBIA

334 - 1367 W. Broadway
Vancouver, V6H 4A9 British Columbia Canada
Phone: 604-737-3058 Fax: 604-737-3666
E-mail: orc@intergate.ca
Website: www.orcbc.ca

Founded: 1976

Scope: State

Description: The ORC of BC is a nonprofit society formed to serve as a mechanism independent from government, through which the interests and activities of groups organized on a provincial basis concerned with outdoor recreation, education, and conservation can be coordinated and represented to government, industry, and the public.

Publication(s): Reference library on outdoor recreation, Outdoor Report

Keyword(s): Land Issues, Public Lands/Greenspace, Recreation/Ecotourism, Reduce/Reuse/Recycle, Water Habitats & Quality

OUTDOOR WRITERS ASSOCIATION OF AMERICA, INC.

121 Hickory St., Suite 1
Missoula, MT 59801 United States
Phone: 406-728-7434 Fax: 406-728-7445
E-mail: owaa@montana.com
Website: www.owaa.org

Founded: 1927

Membership: 1,001–10,000

Scope: National

Description: We strive to improve ourselves in the art and media of our craft and to increase our knowledge and understanding in supporting the conservation of our natural resources. To this end we pledge ourselves to maintain the highest ethical standards in the exercise of our craft.

Publication(s): OWAA Directory, Outdoors Unlimited.

Keyword(s): Ethics/Environmental Justice, Recreation/Ecotourism

Contact(s):

William Geer, Executive Director; 406-728-7434; Fax: 406-728-7445; owaa@montana.com

Lisa Carter, Membership Services Manager; 406-728-7434; Fax: 406-728-7445; members@montana.com

Kevin Rhoades, Editor; 406-728-7434; Fax: 406-728-7445; oueditor@montana.com

OZARK SOCIETY, THE

P.O. Box 2914
Little Rock, AR 72203 United States
Phone: 501-666-2989 Fax: 501-666-2989
E-mail: steward810@aol.com
Website: www.ozarksociety.net

Founded: 1962

Membership: 101–1,000

Scope: State

Description: To promote the knowledge and enjoyment of the scenic and scientific resources, particularly free-flowing streams, wilderness areas, and unique natural areas of the Ozark-Ouachita mountain region, and to help protect those resources for present and future generations.

Publication(s): Pack and Paddle, The

Keyword(s): Land Issues

Contact(s):

Stewart Noland, President; 5210 Sherwood Rd., Little Rock, AR 72207; 501-666-2989; Bosshq@aol.com

OZARKS RESOURCE CENTER

P.O. Box 3
Brixey, MO 65618 United States
Phone: 417-679-4773
E-mail: jlorrain@goin.missouri.org

Founded: 1978

Membership: 1,001–10,000

Scope: National

Description: The Center provides research, education, technical assistance, and dissemination of information on renewable resources-based technology, sustainable agriculture, environmentally responsible practices, sustainable community economic development, and self-reliance for the family, farm, community, Ozarks, and other bio-regions.

Publication(s): Broadcaster, The (newsletter), Talking Oak Leaves (newsletter)

Keyword(s): Development/Developing Countries, Ethics/Environmental Justice, Land Issues, Sprawl/Urban Planning

Contact(s):

Donna Jones, President; RR 1 Box 68A-1, Dora, MO 65637; 417-261-2518

Corliss Schaffer, Vice President; HCR 64 Box 221, West Plains, MO 65775; 417-257-0670

Janice Lorrain, Executive Director; Rt. 1 Box 393, Ava, MO 65608; 417-683-5049

Kathi Trantham, Secretary; 7969 County Rd. 3010, West Plains, MO 65775; 417-256-6518

Denise Vaughn, Treasurer; Rt. 3 Box 200, Mtn. View, MO 65548; 417-256-6518

OZONE ACTION

1700 Connecticut Ave., NW, 3rd Fl.
Washington, DC 20009 United States
Phone: 202-265-6738 Fax: 202-986-6041
E-mail: ozone_action@ozone.org

Founded: 1992

Scope: National

Description: Ozone Action educates the public about threats from ozone depletion and human-induced climate change. Ozone Action investigates and publicizes attempts to weaken our global environmental protections and exposes attempts by industry to distort public debate.

Publication(s): Ozone Action News, Climate Change Current Effects Summaries, Black Market CFC Reports, Ties That Blind

Keyword(s): Air Quality/Atmosphere, Climate Change

Contact(s):

Kevin Sweeney, Board Chair

P

PA CLEANWAYS

VENANGO COUNTY
406 Oakland Ave
Grove City, PA 16127 United States
Phone: 724-458-0391
E-mail: amy0731@pgh.net
Website: www.pacleanways.org

Founded: 1999

Membership: 1–100

Scope: Local

Description: PA CleanWays has helped people and their communities clean up mountains of trash from PA lands and waters. If you're offended by litter and trash in your community, PA CleanWays, a nonprofit environmental organization, can help you.

PACIFIC BASIN ASSOCIATION OF SOIL AND WATER CONSERVATION DISTRICTS

Attn: President, P.O. Box 12596
Tamuning, GU 96931 United States

Founded: N/A

Scope: State

Contact(s):

Felix Quan, President; 671-632-7114; Fax: 671-632-7114

Patrick Calvo, Vice President; P.O. Box 2795, Saipan, MP 96950; 670-234-6120; Fax: 670-235-6122

Estanislao Hocog, Secretary-Treasurer; P.O. Box 12, Tinian MP, GU 96952; 670-433-0690; Fax: 670-433-3152

PACIFIC FISHERY MANAGEMENT COUNCIL

2130 SW 5th Ave., Suite 224
Portland, OR 97201 United States
Phone: 503-820-2280 Fax: 503-326-6831
Website: www.pcouncil.org

Founded: N/A

Scope: National

Description: Nonprofit organization established by the Magnuson-Stevens Fishery Conservation and Management Act of 1976. Develops management plans for fisheries off the coasts of Washington, Oregon, and California. Fourteen voting and five nonvoting members, of which nine are appointed by the Secretary of Commerce. Members include state and federal fishery agency managers, knowledgable citizens, and a tribal representative.

Keyword(s): Recreation/Ecotourism, Reduce/Reuse/Recycle, Water Habitats & Quality, Wildlife & Species

Contact(s):

Donald McIsaac, Executive Director

John Coon, Fishery Management Coordinator, Salmon

James Glock, Fishery Management Coordinator, Marine

James Seger, Economic Analysis Coordinator

PACIFIC INSTITUTE FOR STUDIES IN DEVELOPMENT, ENVIRONMENT, AND SECURITY

654 13th St.
Oakland, CA 94612 United States
Phone: 510-251-1600 Fax: 510-251-2203
E-mail: pistaff@pacinst.org
Website: www.pacinst.org

Founded: 1987
Membership: N/A
Scope: Local, State, Regional, National, International
Description: The institute is a policy research organization that focuses on the interface of security, development, and environmental protection issues. Areas of focus include climate change and water.
Publication(s): Global Change, Pacific Institute Reports.
Keyword(s): Air Quality/Atmosphere, Climate Change, Development/Developing Countries, Reduce/Reuse/Recycle, Water Habitats & Quality
Contact(s):
Nick Cain, Director of Communications; ncain@pacinst.org
Peter Gleick, Executive Director; pgleick@pipeline.com

PACIFIC NORTHWEST TRAIL ASSOCIATION

13595 Avon Allen Rd.
Mount Vernon, WA 98273 United States
Phone: 306-424-0407
E-mail: JDMEL@NWLINK.COM
Website: www.pnt.org

Founded: 1977
Membership: 101–1,000
Scope: National
Description: The PNTA was formed to promote the development of a continuous foot and horse trail from the Continental Divide at Glacier National Park to the Pacific Ocean at Olympic National Park. The PNTA encourages land use and conservation education through exposure to the historic and natural diversity of the Pacific Northwest.
Publication(s): Nor'wester, Blanchard Hill and Chuckanut Mountain Map, Pacific Northwest Trail, The.
Keyword(s): Public Lands/Greenspace, Recreation/Ecotourism, Transportation
Contact(s):
Duane Melcher, Chair; 306-424-0407

PACIFIC RIVERS COUNCIL

P.O. Box 10798
Eugene, OR 97440 United States
Phone: 541-345-0119 Fax: 541-345-0710
E-mail: info@pacrivers.org
Website: www.pacrivers.org

Founded: 1987
Membership: 1,001–10,000
Scope: National
Description: The Pacific Rivers Council's mission is to protect and restore rivers, their watersheds and the native aquatic species that depend on them.
Publication(s): Entering the Watershed, various briefing books and reports, Freeflow
Keyword(s): Agriculture/Farming, Ecosystems (precious), Executive/Legislative/Judicial Reform, Forests/Forestry, Land Issues, Pollution (general), Public Lands/Greenspace, Water Habitats & Quality, Wildlife & Species
Contact(s):
David Bayles, Executive Director (Acting)

PACIFIC SEABIRD GROUP, UNIVERSITY OF VICTORIA BIOLOGY DEPARTMENT

UNIVERSITY OF VICTORIA BIOLOGY DEPARTMENT
Box 179, 4505 University Way, NE
Seattle, WA 98105 United States
Website: www.nmnh.sl.edu/BIRDNET/PacBirds/

Founded: 1972
Scope: International
Description: An international organization to promote the knowledge, study and conservation of Pacific seabirds.
Publication(s): Pacific Seabird Group Bulletin
Keyword(s): Wildlife & Species
Contact(s):
Lisa Ballance, Chair-Elect; Noah, MNFS Southwest Fisheries Science Center, 8604 La Jolla Shores Dr., La Jolla, CA 92037; 858-546-7173; Fax: 858-546-7003; lisa@caliban.ucsd.edu
Lora Leschner, Secretary; Washington Dept. of Fish & Wildlife, 16018 Mill Creek Blvd., Mill Creek, WA 98102; 425-776-1311, ext. 421; Fax: 425-338-1066; leschlll@dfw.wa.gov
Vivian Mendenhall, Editor; 4600 Rabbit Creek Rd., Anchorage, AK 99516; 907-345-7124; Fax: 907-345-0686; fasgadair@worldnet.att.net
Bill Sydeman, Chair; Point Reyes Bird Observatory 4990 Shoreline Hwy, Stinson, CA 94970; 415-868-1221; Fax: 415-868-1946; wjsydeman@prbo.org
Breck Tyler, Treasurer; Long Marine Laboratory 100 Shaffer Rd., Santa Cruz, CA 95060; 831-426-5740; ospr@cats.ucsc.edu

PACIFIC WHALE FOUNDATION

101 N. Kihei Rd.
Kihei, HI 96753 United States
Phone: 808-879-8860 Fax: 808-879-2615
E-mail: info@pacificwhale.org
Website: www.pacificwhale.org

Founded: 1980
Scope: Local, Regional, National
Description: A nonprofit tax-exempt 501(c)(3) organization dedicated to saving whales, dolphins and their ocean habitats through marine research, public education and marine conservation. Pacific Whale Foundation actively studies whales, dolphins and coral reef communities throughout the Pacific to ensure their survival and recovery. The award-winning Ocean Outreach Program educates people about marine conservation through research internships, school programs, an Adopt-a-Whale program, and an Adopt-a-Dolphin program.
Publication(s): Fin and Fluke, Maui Outdoor Adventure, Whalewatch News, Soundings
Keyword(s): Water Habitats & Quality, Wildlife & Species
Contact(s):
Gregory Kaufman, President
Paul Forestell, Vice President
Dixie Bongolan, Secretary and Treasurer
Anne Rillero, Editor

PANOS INSTITUTE, THE

1701 K St., NW, 11th Fl.
Washington, DC 20006 United States
Phone: 202-223-7949 Fax: 202-223-7947
E-mail: panos@cais.com
Website: www.panosinst.org

Founded: 1986
Scope: International
Description: The Panos Institute consists of three autonomous nonprofit, nongovernmental organizations located in London, Paris, and Washington, DC, working to raise public understanding of sustainable development issues. The Washington,

DC institute focuses its work on Latin America, the Caribbean, and the United States.

Publication(s): We Speak for Ourselves, From Information to Education, Eco-Reports, SIDAmerica

Keyword(s): Development/Developing Countries, Population

Contact(s):

Gretchen Maynes, Executive Director/ Secretary
John Kramer, Acting Chairman
Michael McDowell, Vice Chairman
George Woodring, Treasurer

PARKS AND TRAILS COUNCIL OF MINNESOTA

275 E. 4th St. #642
St. Paul, MN 55101 United States
Phone: 651-726-2457 Fax: 651-726-2458
E-mail: info@parksandtrails.org
Website: www.parksandtrails

Founded: 1954
Membership: 1,001–10,000
Scope: State

Description: The mission of the Council is to further the establishment, development, and enhancement of parks and trails within the state of Minnesota, and to encourage their prudent use and protection.

Publication(s): Newsletter

Keyword(s): Land Issues, Public Lands/Greenspace, Recreation/Ecotourism, Wildlife & Species

Contact(s):

Jeffrey Olson, President
Barbara Burgum, Vice President
David Hartwell, Vice President
Greg Murray, Vice President
Dorian Grilley, Executive Director
Howard Olson, Secretary
Michael Prichard, Treasurer

PARTNERS IN AMPHIBIAN AND REPTILE CONSERVATION (PARC)

P.O.Drawer E
Aiken, SC 29802 United States
Phone: 803-725-2473 Fax: 803-725-3309
E-mail: forrest@srel.edu
Website: www.parcplace.org

Founded: 1998
Scope: National, International

Description: PARC is an international organization and a multi-sector partnership dedicated to the conservation of the herpetofauna (amphibians and reptiles) and their habitats.

Keyword(s): Ecosystems (precious), Land Issues, Water Habitats & Quality, Wildlife & Species

PARTNERS IN PARKS

P.O. Box 130
205 E. 3rd St
Paonia, CO 81428 United States
Phone: 970-527-6691 Fax: 970-527-7297
E-mail: partpark@mindspring.com
Website: www.partnersinparks.org

Founded: 1988
Membership: N/A
Scope: National

Description: A nonprofit organization that encourages, promotes, and establishes professional level partnerships between national park and other public land managers and those who would contribute their time and skills to studying, protecting, and interpreting natural and cultural features.

Keyword(s): Ecosystems (precious), Land Issues, Public Lands/Greenspace, Water Habitats & Quality, Wildlife & Species

Contact(s):

Sarah Bishop, President

PARTNERSHIP FOR SUSTAINABLE FORESTRY

229 Hanover Street
Suite 101
Annapolis, MD 21401 United States
Phone: 410-267-8595 Fax: 410-267-8597
E-mail: gallenbay@aol.com
Website: psf.biz

Founded: 2001
Membership: N/A
Scope: State

Description: An alliance of business and civic organizations dedicated to sustainable forestry practices in rural and urban Maryland.

Keyword(s): Forests/Forestry, Public Lands/Greenspace

Contact(s):

Gary Allen, Co-Director

PENNSYLVANIA ASSOCIATION OF CONSERVATION DISTRICTS, INC.

4999 Jonestown Rd.
Suite 203
Harrisburg, PA 17109 United States
Phone: 717-545-8878 Fax: 717-545-8850
E-mail: pacd@pacd.org
Website: www.pacd.org

Founded: N/A
Membership: 101–1,000
Scope: State

Description: The Pennsylvania Association of Conservation Districts, Inc. (PACD) was organized in 1950 to serve as a collective voice of Pennsylvania's conservation districts. PACD provides districts with education and information to help them in their work in land and water conservation. Over the years, the Association has been an integral part of the shaping of the modern conservation district.

Contact(s):

Ron Rohall, President; 534 Kennedy Rd., Airville, PA 17032; 717-862-3486; Fax: 717-862-3486
Susan Fox, Executive Director; 4999 Jonestown Road, Suite 203, Harrisburg, PA 17109; 717-545-8878, ext. 14; Fax: 717-545-8850; susan-fox@pacd.org

PENNSYLVANIA CENTER FOR ENVIRONMENTAL EDUCATION (PCEE)

010 Eisenberg
Slippery Rock University
Slippery Rock, PA 16057 United States
Phone: 724-738-4555 Fax: 724-738-4502
E-mail: pcee@sru.edu
Website: pcee.org

Founded: 1997
Membership: N/A
Scope: State

Description: The PCEE is a cooperative partnership of 13 Pennsylvania organizations formed to maximize statewide environmental education resources and efforts and to ensure continued access to high quality environmental education for all commonwealth citizens.

Contact(s):

Paulette Johnson, Executive Director; 724-738-4555; Fax: 724-738-4502; paulette.johnson@sru.edu
Rita Hawrot, Project Manager; 724-738-4527; Fax: 724-738-4502; rita.hawrot@sru.edu
Richard Knight, Project Manager; 724-738-4528; Fax: 724-738-4502; richard.knight@sru.edu
Lisa Theodorson, Secretary; 724-738-4555; Fax: 724-738-4502; lisa.theodorson@sru.edu

PENNSYLVANIA CITIZENS ADVISORY COUNCIL TO DEPARTMENT OF ENVIRONMENTAL PROTECTION

Rachel Carson State Office Building, Floor 13
P.O. Box 8459
Harrisburg, PA 17105-8459 United States
Phone: 717-787-4527 Fax: 717-787-2878
E-mail: suswilson@state.pa.us
Website: www.cacdep.state.pa.us

Founded: N/A
Membership: 1–100
Scope: Regional
Description: Created by Act 275 of the PA General Assembly, 1971.
Publication(s): Advisory, Regional Report, Annual Report
Keyword(s): Air Quality/Atmosphere, Reduce/Reuse/Recycle
Contact(s):
Susan Wilson, Executive Director
Stephanie Mioff, Administrative Assistant
Dave Strong, Chairperson

PENNSYLVANIA ENVIRONMENTAL COUNCIL, INC. (PEC)

117 S. 17th St., 23rd Fl.
Philadelphia, PA 19103-5022 United States
Phone: 215-563-0250 Fax: 215-563-0528
Website: www.pecpa.org

Founded: 1969
Scope: State
Description: Private nonprofit statewide membership organization devoted to the protection and improvement of Pennsylvania's environment through education, advocacy and consensus-building. PEC brings together nonprofits, government agencies, businesses and citizens to develop environmental policy, take action on environmental issues and work for effective environmental legislation, regulation and enforcement.
Publication(s): Environmental Forum Newsletter, Urban Vacant Land Handbook, Transit-Oriented Development Handbook, Environmental Advisory Council Handbook, Building Better Communities and Preserving our Countryside, Guiding Growth, Pennsylvania Legislative Updates.
Keyword(s): Development/Developing Countries, Public Lands/Greenspace, Water Habitats & Quality
Contact(s):
Andrew McElwaine, President and CEO
Brian Hill, Vice President and Director of French Creek Project
Ellen Alaimo, Regional Director of Northeastern PA Office
Anna Brienich, Regional Director of Community Planning Western PA Office
Patrick Starr, Regional Director of Southeastern Office
Davitt Woodwell, Regional Director of Western PA Office

PENNSYLVANIA FEDERATION OF SPORTSMENS CLUBS

2426 N. Second St.
Harrisburg, PA 17110 United States
Phone: 717-232-3480 Fax: 717-231-3524
E-mail: info@pfsc.org
Website: www.pfsc.org

Founded: 1932
Membership: 10,001–100,000
Scope: State
Description: A representative statewide organization, affiliated with the National Wildlife Federation, dedicated to the protection and enhancement of wildlife and its habitat, and preserving, promoting, and protecting our Outdoor Heritage through public education and government interaction.
Publication(s): On Target
Contact(s):
Pete Dalby, President
Melody Zullinger, Executive Director
Mark Henry, Representative
Ray Martin, Treasurer
Linda Steiner, Editor
Ed Zygmut, Alternate Representative

PENNSYLVANIA FORESTRY ASSOCIATION, THE

56 E. Main St.
Mechanicsburg, PA 17055 United States
Phone: 717-766-5371
E-mail: thepfa@juno.com
Website: www.pfa.cas.psu.edu

Founded: 1886
Membership: 1,001–10,000
Scope: State
Description: An independent nonprofit conservation organization, affiliated with the National Woodland Owners Association dedicated to environmental improvement and wise use of natural resources in Pennsylvania. Membership includes a cross section of all groups and individuals interested in true conservation.
Publication(s): Pennsylvania Forest Magazine - Quarterly
Keyword(s): Forests/Forestry, Public Lands/Greenspace, Recreation/Ecotourism
Contact(s):
Roy Seifert, President; 717-225-4711
Lloyd Casey, Vice-President
William Cook, Treasurer; 717-787-2039
William Corlett, Secretary; 717-737-7118
Jan Zinn, Editor; 717-632-1648

PENNSYLVANIA ORGANIZATION FOR WATERSHEDS AND RIVERS (POWR)

P. O. Box 765
Harrisburg, PA 17108-0765 United States
Phone: 717-234-7910 Fax: 717-234-7929
E-mail: info@pawatersheds.org
Website: www.pawatersheds.org

Founded: 1993
Membership: 101–1,000
Scope: Local, State
Description: POWR is dedicated to the protection, sound management and enhancement of Pennsylvania's rivers and watersheds and to the empowerment of local organizations with the same commitment. This is done through advocacy, publications, educational activities, public and open conferences/workshops, leadership training and through direct assistance.
Publication(s): Pennsylvania's Watersheds Map, River Sojourn Organizers Manual, Fact Packs, Main Stream newsletter, Monitoring Matters newsletter, Watershed Weekly newsletter
Keyword(s): Ecosystems (precious), Executive/Legislative/Judicial Reform, Forests/Forestry, Land Issues, Pollution (general), Public Lands/Greenspace, Recreation/Ecotourism, Water Habitats & Quality
Contact(s):
Walt Pomeroy, Executive Director; wpomeroy@pawatersheds.org
Sue Brockman, Environmental Monitoring Project Coordinator; sbrockman@pawatersheds.org
Lisa Daly, Office Manager; sdaly@pawatersheds.org
Susan Parry, Watershed Programs Coordinator; sparry@pawatersheds.org
John Coutts, Director of Information Technology; jcoutts@pawatersheds.org
Bonnie Swinehart, Editor/Writer; bswinehart@pawatersheds.org

PENNSYLVANIA RECREATION AND PARK SOCIETY, INC.

1315 W. College Ave., Suite 200
State College, PA 16801-2776 United States
Phone: 814-234-4272 Fax: 814-234-5276
E-mail: prps@vicon.net
Website: www.prps.org

Founded: 1935
Membership: 1,001–10,000
Scope: State
Description: To promote quality recreation and park opportunities for all the citizens of the Commonwealth of Pennsylvania by actively involving professionals and citizens in recreation, park, and conservation programs, by fostering and maintaining high standards of professional qualifications and ethics, and by providing quality educational opportunities.
Publication(s): The PRPS Update (Monthly), Pennsylvania Recreation and Parks
Keyword(s): Forests/Forestry, Land Issues, Pollution (general), Public Health, Public Lands/Greenspace, Recreation/Ecotourism
Contact(s):
Robert Griffith, Executive Director
Steven Landes, Secretary
R. Mcfate, President; Park Manager, Caledonia State Park, 40 Rocky Mtn. Rd., Fayetteville, PA 17222-9610; 717-352-2161
William Rosevear, Treasurer; Park Manager, PA Bureau of State Parks, 1100 Pine Grove Rd., Gardners, PA 17324-7174; 717-486-7174; Fax: 717-486-4961
Vanyla Tierney, Editor; Recreation Planner, DCNR-Bureau of State Parks, P.O. Box 1519, Mechanicsburg, PA 17055-9019; 717-783-2654

PENNSYLVANIA RESOURCES COUNCIL, INC.,

3606 Providence Rd.
Newtown Square, PA 19073 United States
Phone: 610-353-1555 Fax: 610-353-6257
Website: www.prc.org

Founded: 1939
Scope: Regional
Description: (formerly PA Roadside Council) The Pennsylvania Resources Council (PRC) is recognized nationally for its expertise in recycling, waste reduction, and litter control. PRC produces educational materials, as well as seminars and conferences for citizens, municipalities, civic groups and corporations. PRC also sponsors the nation's only environmental shopping hotline (1-800-Go-To-PRC). Open to the public, PRC's environmental living center has exhibits and workshops.
Publication(s): Environmental Living Magazine, Recyclers Roundup
Keyword(s): Pollution (general), Public Health, Recreation/Ecotourism, Reduce/Reuse/Recycle
Contact(s):
Howard Wein, President
David Mazza, Regional Director Pittsburgh Area; 412-488-7490
Marcia Weller, Regional Director Philadelphia Area

PEOPLE FOR PUGET SOUND

911 Western Ave.
Suite 580
Seattle, WA 98104 United States
Phone: 206-382-7007 Fax: 206-382-7006
E-mail: people@pugetsound.org
Website: www.pugetsound.org

Founded: 1991
Membership: 1,001–10,000
Scope: Regional
Description: People for Puget Sound works to protect and restore the imperiled marine and estuarine ecosystems of Puget Sound and the Northwest Straits.
Publication(s): Toxics in the Puget Sound Food Web, KidSound, Sound & Straits
Keyword(s): Oceans/Coasts/Beaches, Pollution (general), Water Habitats & Quality, Wildlife & Species
Contact(s):
Christopher Townsend, President of the Board of Directors
Kathy Fletcher, Executive Director; 206-382-7007; Fax: 206-382-7006; kfletcher@pugetsound.org
Pam Johnson, Field Director; 206-382-7007; Fax: 206-382-7006; pjohnson@pugetsound.org
Jacques White, Habitat Director; 206-382-7007; Fax: 206-382-7006; jwhite@pugetsound.org
Stephanie Raymond, Education Coordinator; 206-382-7007; Fax: 206-382-7006; sraymond@pugetsound.org

PEOPLE FOR PUGET SOUND

NORTH SOUND OFFICE
407 Main St. Ste. 201
Mt. Vernon, WA 98273 United States
Phone: 306-336-1931 Fax: 360-336-5422
E-mail: northsound@pugetsound.org
Website: www.pugetsound.org

Founded: N/A
Scope: Local, Regional
Contact(s):
Mike Sato, Director

PEOPLE FOR PUGET SOUND

SOUTH SOUND OFFICE
1063 Capitol Way S., Suite 206
Olympia, WA 98501 United States
Phone: 360-754-9177 Fax: 360-534-9371
E-mail: southsound@pugetsound.org
Website: www.pugetsound.org

Founded: 1991
Membership: 1,001–10,000
Scope: Regional
Description: People for Puget Sound works to protect and restore the imperiled marine and estuarine ecosystems of Puget Sound and the Northwest Straits.
Publication(s): Sound and Straits
Keyword(s): Oceans/Coasts/Beaches, Pollution (general), Water Habitats & Quality, Wildlife & Species
Contact(s):
Bruce Wishart, Director; bwishart@pugetsound.org
Lisa Noble, Outreach Coordinator; lnoble@pugetsound.org

PEOPLE'S FORUM 2001, JAPAN

Maruko Bldg. 3F, 1-20-6 Higashiueno
Taitou-ku, Tokyo, 110-0015 Japan
Phone: 81338342436 Fax: 81338342406
E-mail: pf2001jp@jca.ax.apc.org

Founded: N/A
Scope: International
Description: People's Forum 2001, Japan is an NGO network of national environmental NGO's, CBO's, and individuals being active to bring about sustainable society. The Forum's task is to serve as a clearinghouse as well as to provide a framework of activities for the members. The Forum's activities include research, education, publication, and policy dialogues with different sectors to alter current economic and political systems to be ecologically and socially sustainable.
Contact(s):
Tomoko Sakuma, Director

PEREGRINE FUND, THE

5668 W. Flying Hawk Ln.
Boise, ID 83709 United States
Phone: 208-362-3716 Fax: 208-362-2376
E-mail: tpf@peregrinefund.org
Website: www.peregrinefund.org

Founded: 1970
Membership: 1,001–10,000
Scope: National, International
Description: The Peregrine Fund works nationally and internationally to conserve biological diversity and enhance environmental health by working with birds of prey through management and conservation of species and their habitat, and through education and scientific investigation. Although best known nationally for species restoration, they have assisted on conservation projects in over 40 countries.
Publication(s): The Peregrine Fund Newsletter, progress reports, Operation Report, Annual Report
Keyword(s): Wildlife & Species
Contact(s):
William Burnham, President and CEO
Jeffrey Cilek, Vice President
J. Jenny, Vice President
Karen Hixon, Treasurer
D. Nelson, Chairman of Board
Paxson Offield, Vice Chairman of the Board
Ronald Yanke, Secretary

PHEASANTS FOREVER, INC.

1783 Buerkle Circle
St. Paul, MN 55110 United States
Phone: 651-773-2000 Fax: 651-773-5500
E-mail: pf@pheasantsforever.org
Website: www.pheasantsforever.org

Founded: 1982
Membership: 10,001–100,000
Scope: National
Description: Pheasants Forever, Inc. is a nonprofit conservation organization formed in response to the continued decline of ring-necked pheasants. The mission of Pheasants Forever is to protect and to enhance pheasant and other wildlife populations throughout North America through public awareness and education, habitat restoration, development and maintenance, and improvements in land and water management policies.
Publication(s): Pheasants Forever
Keyword(s): Agriculture/Farming, Recreation/Ecotourism, Wildlife & Species
Contact(s):
Joseph Duggan, Vice President of Development and Public Affairs; 651-773-2000; jduggan@pheasantsforever.org
David Nomsen, Vice President of Governmental Affairs; 2101 Ridgewood Dr., Alexandria, MN 56308; 320-763-6103; pfnomsen@rea-alp.com
Rick Young, Vice President of Field Operations; 651-773-2000; ryoung@pheasantsforever.org
Peter Berthelsen, Director of Conservation-Nebraska; 1101 Alexander Ave., Elba, NE 68835; 308-754-5339; phasianus@aol.com
Walt Bodie, Regional Representative; 2909 Navajo Drive, Nampa, ID 83686; 208-461-7350; wbodie@pheasantsforever.org
Keith Brus, Regional Representative; 5995 W. Little Portage Rd., Pt. Clinton, OH 43452; 419-732-7149; kbrus@cros.net
Barth Crouch, Regional Representative; 1625 E. Beloit Ave., Salina, KS 67401; 785-823-0240; vcrouch@juno.com
Jeff Gaska, Regional Represenative; W. 9947 Ghost Hill Rd., Beaver Dam, WI 53916; 920-927-3579; jgaska@pheasantsforever.org
Dan Hare, Regional Representative; 315 Tucson Ave, Bismarck, ND 58504; 701-250-9921; danhare@home.com
Mark Heckenlaible, Regional Representative; 2103 County Rd., 23 Lyons, NE 68038; 402-687-2004; mh52934@navix.net
Eric Henning, Regional Representative; 29570 Camp Adair Rd., Monmouth, OR 97361; 541-745-5363; henning_erk@hotmail.com
Bruce Hertzke, Treasurer
Mark Herwig, Editor; 651-773-2000; herwig@pheasantsforever.org
Matthew Holland, Regional Representative; 679 W. River Dr., New London, MN 56273; 320-354-4377; ringneck@tds.net
Thomas Kirschenmann, Regional Representative; 600 W. Beck St., Worthing, SD 57077; 605-372-2037; tkirschenmann@pheasantsforever.org
Robert Larson, Secretary
Aaron McCormick, Regional Representative; P.O. Box 537408 S. Said St., Cairo, NE 68824; 308-485-0154; pfbiologist@nebi.com
Matthew O'Connor, Regional Field Representative; 2880 Thunder Rd., Hopkinton, IA 52237; 319-926-2357; niapfmatt@n-connect.net
Mike Parker, Regional Reptresentative; 117 Wilson St., De Witt, MI 48820; 517-668-1033; mparkerpf@aol.com
Mike Pruss, Regional Representative; HC 67 Box 104A, Mifflin, PA 17058; 717-436-0005; mpruss@pheasantsforever.org
Tom Schwartz, Regional Representative; 40 Crater Lake Dr., Springfield, IL 62707; 214-498-7558; tschwartz@pheasantsforever.org
Howard Vincent, Chief Executive Officer; 651-773-2000; hvincent@pheasantsforever.org
George Wilson, Chairman
James Wooley, Senior Regional Wildlife Biologist; 1205 Ilion Ave., Chariton, IA 50049; 641-774-2238; jwooley@pheasantsforever.org

PHYSICIANS FOR SOCIAL RESPONSIBILITY

1875 Connecticut Avenue NW, Suite 1012
Washington, DC 20009 United States
Phone: 202-667-4260 Fax: 202-667-4201
E-mail: psrnatl@psr.org
Website: www.psr.org

Founded: 1961
Scope: National
Description: Promotes arms reduction, international cooperation to protect the environment, and education and programs aimed at reducing violence.
Publication(s): Monitor, PSR Reports
Keyword(s): Energy, Pollution (general)
Contact(s):
Peter Wilk, President
Robert Musil, Executive Director

PICKERING CREEK AUDUBON CENTER

11450 Audubon Lane
Easton, MD 21601 United States
Phone: 410-822-4903 Fax: 410-822-5104
E-mail: pcec@pickeringcreek.org
Website: www.pickeringcreek.org

Founded: N/A
Scope: Local, State, Regional
Description: Environmental Education
Publication(s): Views
Newsletter
Contact(s):
Rick Leader, Executive Director; 410-822-4903; rleader@audubon.org
Mark Scallion, Assistant Director; 410-822-4903; mscallion@pickeringcreek.org

PIEDMONT ENVIRONMENTAL COUNCIL

P.O. Box 460
Warrenton, VA 20188 United States
Phone: 540-347-2334 Fax: 540-349-9003
E-mail: pec@pecva.org
Website: pec@pecva.org

Founded: 1972
Membership: 1,001–10,000

Scope: Local, State, Regional

Description: Established in 1972 to promote and protect the rural economy, natural resources, history and beauty of the Piedmont.

Keyword(s): Air Quality/Atmosphere, Energy, Land Issues, Sprawl/Urban Planning, Transportation, Water Habitats & Quality

Contact(s):

Christopher Miller, President; 540-347-2334, ext. 13; Fax: 540-349-9003; cmiller@pecva.org

PINCHOT INSTITUTE FOR CONSERVATION

1616 P St., NW, Suite 100
Washington, DC 20036 United States
Phone: 202-797-6580 Fax: 202-797-6583
E-mail: pinchot@pinchot.org
Website: www.pinchot.org

Founded: 1963
Membership: 1,001–10,000
Scope: National

Description: The Pinchot Institute for Conservation is an independent nonprofit organization established to advance forest conservation thought, policy, and action. Serves as a bridge between the scientific and policymaking communities, providing timely, objective policy research, facilitation, leadership, training, and environmental education on issues relating to the protection and sustainable management of forests.

Publication(s): The Pinchot Letter, numerous policy reports, discussion papers and lecture series, Grey Towers Press books.

Keyword(s): Forests/Forestry, Public Lands/Greenspace

Contact(s):

V. Sample, President; 202-797-6580; Fax: 202-797-6583; alsample@pinchot.org
Edgar Brannon, Director of Grey Towers National Historic Landmark; P.O. Box 188, Milford, PA 18337; 570-296-9630; Fax: 570-296-9675
Peter Pinchot, Chair; Milford Experimental Forest, 123 Moon Valley Road, Milford, PA 18337; 570-296-7940; Fax: 570-296-9313; peterpin@aol.com
Denise Cooke, Secretary; Delaware Gap National Recreation Area, Milford, PA 18337; 570-296-6952, ext. 16; Fax: 570-296-4706; denise_cooke@pikeonline.net
James Grace, Vice Chair; Pennsylvania Bureau of Forestry, P.O. Box 8552, Harrisburg, PA 17105-8552; 717-787-2703; Fax: 717-783-5109; jagrace@state.pa.us
Richard Snyder, Treasurer; P.O. Box 927, Milford, PA 18337; 570-296-6249; Fax: 570-296-8006; snyder@pikeonline.net

PITTSBURGH HERPETOLOGICAL SOCIETY, THE

c/o The Pittsburgh Zoo & Aquarium, One Wild Pl.
Pittsburgh, PA 15206 United States
Phone: 412-361-0835 Fax: 412-361-2718
E-mail: phs14@lycos.com
Website: www.trfn.clpgh.org/phs

Founded: 1993
Membership: 101–1,000
Scope: National, International

Description: The society is dedicated to fostering an appreciation of all reptiles and amphibians through husbandry, conservation, and education.

Publication(s): Pittsburgh Herpetological Society Newsletter, The.

Keyword(s): Reduce/Reuse/Recycle, Water Habitats & Quality, Wildlife & Species

Contact(s):

Dolly Ellerbrock, Co-Founder; diguana@bellatlantic.net

PLANNED PARENTHOOD FEDERATION OF AMERICA, INC.

810 Seventh Ave.
New York, NY 10019 United States
Phone: 212-541-7800 Fax: 212-245-1845
E-mail: communications@ppfa.org
Website: www.plannedparenthood.org

Founded: 1916
Membership: 101–1,000
Scope: National

Description: Planned Parenthood Federation of America (PPFA) is a federation of 132 not-for-profit affiliates operating nearly 900 medically-supervised health centers nationwide. Planned Parenthood centers provide a wide range of services—including family planning counseling, contraception, prenatal care, adoption referrals, abortion services, cancer screening, testing and treatment for HIV/AIDS, and other sexually transmitted infections, and sexuality education—to nearly 5 million men and women each year.

Keyword(s): Population, Public Health

Contact(s):

Gloria Feldt, President
Susan Pichler, Librarian; Katherine Dexter McCormick Library, 810 Seventh Ave., New York, NY 10019; 212-261-4637
Alfred Poindexter, Secretary
John Romo, Chief Operating Officer
Mary Shallenberger, Chairperson
Barbara Singhaus, Treasurer
Alfredo Vigil, Vice Chairperson

PLANNING AND CONSERVATION LEAGUE

926 J St., Suite 612
Sacramento, CA 95814 United States
Phone: 916-444-8726 Fax: 916-448-1789
E-mail: pclmail@pcl.org
Website: www.pcl.org

Founded: 1965
Membership: 10,001–100,000
Scope: Local, State, Regional

Description: A representative statewide organization, affiliated with the National Wildlife Federation, dedicated to the protection and enhancement of wildlife and its habitat through public education and government interaction.

Publication(s): Central Valley Grassroots Guide, Merging Currents, Cost Saving Solutions to Save Energy, Community Guide to Urban Parks, Citizens Guide to the General Plan, Community Guide to CEQA, Guide to Local Growth Control Initiative, California Today.

Keyword(s): Agriculture/Farming, Air Quality/Atmosphere, Climate Change, Energy, Ethics/Environmental Justice, Forests/Forestry, Land Issues, Oceans/Coasts/Beaches, Public Health, Public Lands/Greenspace, Sprawl/Urban Planning, Transportation, Water Habitats & Quality

Contact(s):

Sage Sweetwood, President
Karen Douglas, Natural Resources Director; 916-313-4512; Fax: 916-448-1789; kdouglas@pcl.org
Gerald Meral, Executive Director, Editor and Alternate Representative; 916-313-4514; Fax: 916-448-1789; jmeral@pcl.org
Sandra Spelliscy, General Counsel; 916-313-4513; Fax: 916-448-1789; sas@pcl.org
Dan Frost, Representative
William Yeates, Treasurer

PLAYA LAKES JOINT VENTURE

103 E. Simpson
Suite 200
Lafayette, CO 80026 United States
Phone: 303-926-0777 Fax: 303-926-8102

Founded: 1989
Membership: N/A
Scope: Regional
Description: Playa Lakes Joint Venture is a partnership-based conservation organization operating in Colorado, Kansas, New Mexico, Oklahoma and Texas. PLJV's mission is to create partnerships that work toward sustainable landscapes for the benefit of birds, other wildlife and humans. PLJV's primary interest is in Playa Lakes habitat and associated uplands for the benefit of wintering, migrating and breeding birds. PLJV awards grants on a semi-annual basis for research, projects and outreach efforts.
Keyword(s): Agriculture/Farming, Ecosystems (precious), Land Issues, Recreation/Ecotourism, Sprawl/Urban Planning, Water Habitats & Quality, Wildlife & Species
Contact(s):
Michael Carter, Coordinator; mike.carter@pljv.org
Christopher Rustay, Shortgrass BCR Coordinator; chrustay@aol.com
Debbie Slobe, Communications Team Leader; debbie.slobe@pljv.org
Brian Sullivan, Biological Team Leader; brian.sullivan@pljv.org

POCONO ENVIRONMENTAL EDUCATION CENTER

R.R. 2 Box 1010
Dingmans Ferry, PA 18328 United States
Phone: 570-828-2319 Fax: 570-828-9695
E-mail: peec@ptd.net
Website: www.peec.org

Founded: 1986
Scope: State, National, International
Description: The Pocono Environmental Education Center (PEEC) advances environmental awareness, knowledge, and skills through education, in order that those who inhabit and will inherit the planet may better understand the complexities of natural and human-designed environments.
Contact(s):
James Rienhardt, Executive Director/CEO; jimpeec@aol.com
Florence Mauro, Director of Education; fmauro@peec.org
Thomas Shimalla, Director of Operations; shimalla@peec.org

POLLUTION PROBE

625 Church St., Suite 402
Toronto, M4Y 2G1 Ontario Canada
Phone: 416-926-1907 Fax: 416-926-1601
E-mail: pprobe@pollutionprobe.org
Website: www.pollutionprobe.org

Founded: 1969
Scope: National
Description: Pollution Probe is a Canadian nonprofit organization that exists to define environmental problems through research; to promote understanding through education; and to press for practical solutions through advocacy.
Publication(s): See publications on website
Contact(s):
Ken Ogilvie, Executive Director; 416-926-1907, ext. 231; kogilvie@pollutionprobe.org

POPE AND YOUNG CLUB

273 Mill Creek Rd, P.O. Box 548
Chatfield, MN 55923 United States
Phone: 507-867-4144 Fax: 507-867-4144
E-mail: pyclub@isl.net
Website: www.pope-young.org

Founded: 1961
Scope: National
Description: A North American bowhunting and wildlife conservation organization dedicated to the promotion and protection of our bowhunting heritage and North America's wildlife.
Publication(s): Bow Hunting Record Book "Bow Hunting Big Game Records of North America".
Contact(s):
G. Asbell, President
C. Randall Byers, First Vice President
Kevin Hisey, Executive Secretary
Donald Morgan, Treasurer

POPULATION ACTION INTERNATIONAL

1300 19th St., NW, 2nd Fl.
Washington, DC 20036 United States
Phone: 202-557-3400 Fax: 202-728-4177
E-mail: pai@popact.org
Website: www.populationaction.org

Founded: 1965
Membership: 1–100
Scope: International
Description: Develops worldwide support for international population and voluntary family planning programs through public education, policy analysis, and liaison with international leaders and organizations.
Publication(s): Population & reproductive health, studies of population-environment linkages, annual report of activities, legislative and policy updates.
Keyword(s): Development/Developing Countries, Population, Public Health, Reduce/Reuse/Recycle
Contact(s):
Amy Coen, President
Terri Bartlett, Vice President, Public Policy
Robert Engelman, Vice President, Research
Sally Ethelston, Vice President, Communications
Carol Wall, Vice President, Development
Phyllis Piotrow, Secretary
Scott Spangler, Treasurer

POPULATION COMMUNICATIONS INTERNATIONAL

777 United Nations Plaza 5th Fl.
New York, NY 10017 United States
Phone: 212-687-3366 Fax: 212-661-4188
E-mail: pciny@population.org
Website: www.population.org

Founded: 1985
Scope: International
Description: PCI works through mass media and nongovernmental organizations to promote elevation of women's status, use of family planning, and small family norms. PCI's social-content soap operas in developing countries are locally researched and produced and weave social themes into long-term script development for radio and television dramas. In the United States PCI also works with broadcasters and NGOs. Currently PCI is collaborating with NWF to develop an environmental/human sexuality soap opera.
Publication(s): On Air (quarterly newsletter), Global Intersections (Monthly Electronic Newsletter), see publications on website.
Keyword(s): Population, Public Health
Contact(s):
David Andrews, President

POPULATION INSTITUTE, THE

107 Second St., NE
Washington, DC 20002 United States
Phone: 202-544-3300 Fax: 202-544-0068
E-mail: web@populationinstitute.org
Website: www.populationinstitute.org

Founded: 1969
Membership: 10,001–100,000
Scope: International
Description: To enlist and motivate key leadership groups to participate in the effort to bring population growth into balance

with resources by means consistent with human dignity and freedom. Works in communications and with mass membership organizations, educational leaders, and policy leaders.

Publication(s): POPLINE - World Population News Service, Towards The 21st Century (Monograph Series), Annual Report.

Keyword(s): Development/Developing Countries, Population

Contact(s):

Werner Fornos, President; 202-544-3300, ext. 104

POPULATION REFERENCE BUREAU, INC.

1875 Connecticut Ave., NW, Suite 520
Washington, DC 20009 United States
Phone: 202-483-1100 Fax: 202-328-3937
E-mail: popref@prb.org
Website: www.prb.org

Founded: 1929

Scope: National

Description: PRB is a nonprofit educational organization which provides timely and objective information on U.S. and international population trends and their implications.

Publication(s): Population Bulletin, list available on request., World and U.S. Population Data Sheets, teaching kits on population topics, Population Today, PRB Reports on America

Keyword(s): Development/Developing Countries, Population

Contact(s):

Peter Donaldson, President
Ellen Carnevale, Director of Communications
Michael Bentzmen, Chair of the Board
Carl Haub, Senior Demographer
Zuali Malsawma, Librarian

POPULATION-ENVIRONMENT BALANCE, INC.

2000 P St., NW, Suite 600
Washington, DC 20036-5915 United States
Phone: 202-955-5700 Fax: 202-955-6161
E-mail: uspop@us.net
Website: www.balance.org

Founded: 1973

Membership: 10,001–100,000

Scope: National

Description: Population-Environment Balance is a grassroots membership organization dedicated to public education regarding the adverse effects of population growth on the environment. "BALANCE" advocates measures that would encourage population stabilization in the U.S.; encourages a responsible immigration policy for the U.S.; and promotes increased funding for contraceptive research and availability. Activities include public education, advocacy, media campaigns, and publications.

Publication(s): Balance Activist, Action Alerts, Balance Data

Keyword(s): Air Quality/Atmosphere, Energy, Forests/Forestry, Land Issues, Pollution (general), Population, Reduce/Reuse/Recycle, Sprawl/Urban Planning, Transportation, Water Habitats & Quality

Contact(s):

Virginia Abernethy, Chairman of the Board

POTOMAC APPALACHIAN TRAIL CLUB

118 Park St., SE
Vienna, VA 22180 United States
Phone: 703-242-0693 Fax: 703-242-0968
Website: www.patc.net

Founded: 1927

Membership: 1,001–10,000

Scope: Regional

Description: Maintains 240 miles of the Appalachian Trail from Rock Fish Gap in Virginia to Pine Grove Furnace State Park in Pennsylvania. Also maintains an additional 750 miles of trails. Activities include publication of maps and guidebooks, outdoor recreation leadership, construction and maintenance of shelters and cabins and conservation of trail lands through purchase or easements.

Publication(s): Newsletter Monthly-The Potomac Appalachian

Keyword(s): Recreation/Ecotourism

Contact(s):

Walter Smith, President
Wilson Riley, Director of Administration
Gerhard Salinger, Treasurer
Linda Shannon-Beaver, Chief Editor; PA@patc.net
Warren Sharp, General Secretary
Kerry Snow, Supervisor of Trails

POULSBO MARINE SCIENCE CENTER

18743 Front St., NE, P.O. Box 2079
Poulsbo, WA 98370 United States
Phone: 360-779-5549 Fax: 360-779-8960
E-mail: info@poulsbomsc.org
Website: www.poulsbomsc.org

Founded: 1968

Scope: Regional

Description: The Marine Science Center works to meet the science education needs of public citizens and of students and teachers nationally, regionally, and locally. Hands-on environmental education is at the heart of its mission and is reflected in direct instruction from its facility on Washington's State's Liberty Bay, part of the Puget Sound.

Keyword(s): Oceans/Coasts/Beaches

Contact(s):

Cindy Rathbone, Marine Society of the Pacific Northwest, President
Michelle Benedict, Director

POWDER RIVER BASIN RESOURCE COUNCIL

P.O. Box 1178
Douglas, WY 82633 United States
Phone: 307-358-5002 Fax: 307-358-6771
E-mail: doprbrc@coffey.com
Website: powderriverbasin.org/prbrc

Founded: 1973

Membership: 101–1,000

Scope: State

Description: Nonprofit grassroots organization whose major purpose is to help Wyoming people work to prevent and alleviate environmental and rural problems. Major issues include: Coal mining, water development, toxics, wastes, energy conservation, agriculture, and accountable government.

Publication(s): The Powder River Breaks - quarterly newsletter

Keyword(s): Agriculture/Farming, Air Quality/Atmosphere, Energy, Land Issues, Pollution (general), Reduce/Reuse/Recycle

Contact(s):

Kevin Lind, Director; 23 N. Scott, Sheridan, WY 82801; 307-672-5809; Fax: 307-672-5800; klind@powderriverbasin.org
Vickie Goodwin, Organizer; P.O. Box 1178, Douglas, WY 82633; 307-358-5002; Fax: 307-358-6771; doprbrc@coffey.com
Jill Morrison, Organizer; 307-672-5809; jillm@powderriverbasin.org
Cheryl Phinney, Organizer; 307-672-5809; cheyrlp@powderriverbasin.org

PRAIRIE CLUB, THE

533 W. North Ave.Suite 10
Elmhurst, IL 60626 United States
Phone: 630-516-1277 Fax: 630-516-1278
E-mail: prairieclb@aol.com
Website: www.prairieclb.org

Founded: 1911

Membership: 101–1,000

Scope: National

Description: Organized for the promotion of outdoor recreation in the form of walks, outings, camping, and canoeing; the establishment and maintenance of permanent and temporary camps; and the encouragement of the love of nature.
Publication(s): The Bulletin
Keyword(s): Land Issues, Recreation/Ecotourism, Wildlife & Species
Contact(s):
Lloyd Anderson, President
Linda Mullikin, 2nd Vice President
Leo Nelson, 1st Vice President
Loretta Davies, Executive Director
Milt Davies, Chairman of Conservation Committee
Glenn Krus, Secretary
Susan Messer, Editor
Tom Meyers, Treasurer

PRAIRIE GROUSE TECHNICAL COUNCIL
WILDLIFE AND FISHERIES SCIENCES DEPT
Wildlife and Fisheries Sciences Department 2258 TAMU
College Station, TX 77843-2258 United States
Phone: 979-845-5777 Fax: 979-845-3786
Website: wfscnet.tamu.edu
Founded: N/A
Scope: National
Description: Comprises federal, state, and private agency biologists or administrators concerned with the status, research, and management of the prairie-chicken and sharp-tailed grouse in North America.
Publication(s): Newsletter and Proceedings
Keyword(s): Land Issues, Wildlife & Species
Contact(s):
Kenneth Giesen, Executive Committee; 317 W. Prospect, Ft. Collins, CO 80526

PRAIRIE RIVERS NETWORK
809 S. Fifth St.
Champaign, IL 61820 United States
Phone: 217-344-2371 Fax: 217-344-2381
E-mail: info@prairierivers.org
Website: www.prairierivers.org
Founded: 1968
Scope: State
Description: (Formerly Central States Education Center) A statewide river conservation organization working to protect the rivers and streams of illinois. Organizational and technical assistance is provided to persons and organizations in related activities.
Publication(s): Dirty Water, Dirty Business, NPDES Permit Handbook, Rivers Directory
Keyword(s): Water Habitats & Quality
Contact(s):
Bruce Hannon, President; 217-352-3646
Robert Moore, Executive Director; robmoore@prairierivers.org
John McNussen, Treasurer; 217-398-8531
Marc Miller, Watershed Organizer; 217-344-2371; mmiller@prairierivers.org

PREDATOR CONSERVATION ALLIANCE
PREVIOUSLY KNOWN AS PREDATOR PROJECT
P.O. Box 6733
Bozeman, MT 59771-6733 United States
Phone: 406-587-3389 Fax: 406-587-3178
E-mail: pca@predatorconservation.org
Website: www.predatorconservation.org
Founded: 1991
Membership: 1,001–10,000
Scope: National
Description: Predator Conservation Alliance (PCA) is dedicated to conserving, protecting and restoring native predators and their habitats in the Northern Rockies and Northern Plains. In short, we are saving a place for America's predators. This place is on the ground where we work to protect predators and the places they live. This place is also within the human heart and mind where we strive to increase public awareness about the important ecological role predators play.
Publication(s): The Wolf and its Place in the N. Rockies, Roaded Lands, Eroded Habitat, The Wild Bunch, Restoring the Prairie Dog Ecosystem, The Home Range (quarterly newsletter)
Keyword(s): Ecosystems (precious), Land Issues, Public Lands/Greenspace, Transportation, Wildlife & Species
Contact(s):
David Engel, Board President; dengel@san.rr.com
Thomas Skeele, Executive Director; 406-587-3389; Fax: 406-587-3178; tom@predatorconservation.org
Sara Folger, Conservation Director; 406-587-3389; Fax: 406-587-3178; sara@predatorconservation.org

PRESERVATION SOCIETY FOR SPRING CREEK FOREST
Preservation Society for Spring Creek Forest
P.O. Box 450176
Garland, TX 75054-0176 United States
Phone: 972-272-2094
E-mail: jfdanahy@juno.com
Website: springcreekforest.virtualave.net
Founded: 1985
Membership: 1–100
Scope: Local
Description: To promote preservation and protection and educational and scientific pursuits at Spring Creek Forest and Preserve.
Contact(s):
Jack Hill, Board of Directors; 1511 Baltimore Drive, Richardson, TX 75081; 214-665-6497; hill.jack@epa.gov

PRIORITIES INSTITUTE, THE
1565 California St. #511
Denver, CO 80202 United States
Phone: 303-777-5511 Fax: 303-777-5511
E-mail: logan@priorities.org
Website: www.priorities.org
Founded: 1996
Membership: N/A
Scope: State, Regional, National, International
Description: Non-partisan, non-profit research organization focusing on sustainable land use planning, designing car-free eco-cities, international communities, holistic indexing and moral evolution.
Publication(s): Perspectives and Priorities, Livable Cities
Keyword(s): Development/Developing Countries, Land Issues, Reduce/Reuse/Recycle, Transportation
Contact(s):
Logan Perkins, Director/Founder; logan@priorities.org
Melissa Moon, Assistant

PRO PENINSULA
P.O. Box 7175
San Diego, CA 92167 United States
Phone: 619-226-4277
E-mail: ksdean@ucsd.edu
Founded: 2001
Membership: 101–1,000
Scope: Regional, International
Description: Pro Peninsula is devoted to improving the effectiveness of environmental organizations on the Baja California Peninsula through identification of needs and transfer of resources to these organizations. This ranges from funding to technical and legal resources, as well as organizational development. Pro Peninsula can serve both as an intermediary

and as a consulting organization to perform needs assessments and best-fit evaluations for foundations and other parties.

Publication(s): Pro Peninsula News/Noticias de Pro Peninsula, (Quarterly Newsletter).

Contact(s):
Kama Dean, Co-Executive Director; 619-226-4277; ksdean@ucsd.edu
Chris Pesenti, Co-Executive Director; 858-551-4231; cpesenti@ucsd.edu

PROFESSIONAL BOWHUNTERS SOCIETY

P.O. Box 246
Terrell, NC 28682 United States
Phone: 704-664-2534 Fax: 704-664-7471
E-mail: bowhunters@worldnet.att.net
Website: www.bowsite.com/pbs

Founded: 1963
Membership: 1,001–10,000
Scope: National
Description: Created as an organization of dedicated bowhunters interested in promoting a high level of ethics in the taking of wild game with bow and arrow. To provide training for others in safety, shooting skill, and hunting techniques. To practice and promote the wise use of our natural resources and conservation of wildlife.
Publication(s): Professional Bowhunter Magazine, The
Contact(s):
Wayne Capp, President
Larry Fischer, Vice President
Louie Adams, Senior Councilman
Brenda Kisner, PBS Office; 704-664-2534; Fax: 704-664-7471
Jack Smith, Secretary and Treasurer; P.O. Box 246, Terrell, NC 28682; 704-664-2534; Fax: 704-664-7471
Jack Smith, Editor

PROGRESSIVE ANIMAL WELFARE SOCIETY

PAWS WILDLIFE DEPARTMENT
LYNNWOOD WILDLIFE CENTER
15305 44th Ave. West
Lynnwood, WA 98037 United States
Phone: 425-787-2500, ext. 817 Fax: 425-742-5711
E-mail: info@paws.org
Website: www.paws.org

Founded: 1981
Scope: State, National, International
Description: PAWS is a nonprofit, tax-exempt organization that advocates for animals through education, legislation, and direct care. We operate a wildlife rehabilitation center dedicated to the care of sick, injured, and orphaned wildlife in Lynnwood, north of Seattle, Washington.
Publication(s): PAWS News, PAWS Lynnwood Wildlife Center.
Keyword(s): Land Issues, Pollution (general), Recreation/Ecotourism, Reduce/Reuse/Recycle, Sprawl/Urban Planning, Wildlife & Species
Contact(s):
Kip Parker, Wildlife Director; 425-787-2500, ext. 815; Fax: 425-742-5711; kparker@paws.org
Kevin Mack, Naturalist; 425-787-2500, ext. 854; Fax: 425-742-5711; kmack@paws.org

PROVINCE OF QUEBEC SOCIETY FOR THE PROTECTION OF BIRDS, INC.

Station B
Montreal, H2B 3J5 Quebec Canada
Phone: 514-637-2141
Website: www.minet.ca/~pqspb

Founded: 1917
Membership: 101–1,000
Scope: Regional
Publication(s): Tchebec (Annual Review), The Song Sparrow (monthly newsletter), Birdfinding in the Montreal Area, Field Check List of Birds in the Montreal Area.
Keyword(s): Wildlife & Species
Contact(s):
Bess Muhlstock, President; 4807 Jeanne Mance, Montreal, Quebec H2V 4J6; 514-274-3810
Betsy McFarlane, Vice President
Sheila Arthur, Editor; 3804 Royal Ave., Montreal, Quebec H4E 1P1; 514-487-4047
Kyra Emo, Hon. Secretary; 140 Irvine Ave., Westmount, Quebec H3Z 2K2; 514-939-9666
Kenneth Thorpe, Hon. Treasurer; 5615 Eldridge, Cote St-Luc, Quebec H4W 2C9; 514-483-5031

PTARMIGANS, THE

P.O. Box 1821
Vancouver, WA 98668 United States
Phone: 360-834-4520
Website: www.ptarmigans.org

Founded: 1960
Membership: 1–100
Scope: State
Description: The Ptarmigans were established for the purpose of conducting mountaineering activities in the northwest and in promoting the preservation of the northwest forests, wilderness lands, and mountain scenery. The only membership requirement is a love of the outdoors. Offer a variety of outdoor activities led in an ecologically-minded manner. Help maintain several local trail systems and conduct an annual Basic Climbing School. Visit and observe changes proposed in our northwest forests and mountains
Keyword(s): Land Issues, Wildlife & Species
Contact(s):
Ruth Rowland, President
Jon Bell, 1st Vice President
Linda Lebard, Treasurer
Don Spencer, Secretary

PUBLIC EMPLOYEES FOR ENVIRONMENTAL RESPONSIBILITY (PEER)

PEER
2001 S St., NW, Suite 570
Washington, DC 20009 United States
Phone: 202-265-7337 Fax: 202-265-4192
E-mail: info@peer.org
Website: www.peer.org

Founded: 1993
Membership: 1,001–10,000
Scope: Local, State, National
Description: PEER is an alliance of land managers, scientists, biologists, law enforcement officials, and other government professionals dedicated to the protection of the nation's environment. PEER advocates the responsible management of natural resources and promotes environmental ethics, professional integrity and accountability within local, state and federal agencies.
Publication(s): PEEReview, various employee-authored white papers
Keyword(s): Air Quality/Atmosphere, Ecosystems (precious), Ethics/Environmental Justice, Forests/Forestry, Land Issues, Oceans/Coasts/Beaches, Public Lands/Greenspace, Recreation/Ecotourism, Water Habitats & Quality, Wildlife & Species
Contact(s):
Amanda Carufel, Communications Director
Danielle Lawson, Administrative Director
Dennis McKinney, Development Director
Jeffrey Ruch, Executive Director
Eric Wingerter, National Field Director
Mark Davis, Outreach Membership Coordinator
Dan Meyer, General Counsel
Howard Wilshire, Board Chair

PUBLIC EMPLOYEES FOR ENVIRONMENTAL RESPONSIBILITY (PEER)

WEST COAST OFFICE
P.O. Box 30
Hood River, OR 97031 United States
Phone: 530-333-1106 Fax: 541-387-4783
Website: www.peer.org

Founded: 1992

Scope: National

Description: Organize a broad base of support among employees within local, state, and federal resource management agencies. Monitor natural resource management agencies by serving as a "watch dog" for the public interest. Inform the administration, the media and the public about substantive environmental issues of concern to public employees who speak out about issues concerning natural resource management and environmental protection. Provide free legal assistance if and when necessary.

PUBLIC LANDS FOUNDATION

P.O. Box 7226
Arlington, VA 22207 United States
Phone: 703-790-1988 Fax: 703-821-3490
E-mail: leaplf@erols.com
Website: www.publicland.org

Founded: 1987
Membership: 101–1,000
Scope: National

Description: A national, nonprofit, independent advocate to keep the public lands public and for the proper use and protection of the public lands administered by the Bureau of Land Management; implementation of the Federal Land Policy and Management Act (FLPMA); and for professional land management by professional employees.

Publication(s): Public Lands Monitor, The

Keyword(s): Land Issues, Public Lands/Greenspace, Reduce/Reuse/Recycle

Contact(s):
George Lea, President/ Editor; 703-790-1988
Bill Leavell, Vice President; 301-881-0964

PUERTO RICO ASSOCIATION OF SOIL AND WATER CONSERVATION DISTRICTS

Attn: President, P.O. Box 91
Orocovis, PR 00720 United States

Founded: N/A

Scope: State

Publication(s): Puerto Rican Parrot Teacher's Kit, Pablo y Marisol van a la Playa, Puerto Rico Conservation Directory, Verde Luz Newsletter, Puerto Rico Environmental Laws.

Keyword(s): Oceans/Coasts/Beaches, Water Habitats & Quality, Wildlife & Species

Contact(s):
Pedro Fuentes, President; P.O. Box 91, Orocovis, PR 00720; 787-867-4707
Carlos Mantras, Vice President, Board Member; 1722 Pastemark St., Urb Purple Tree, San Juan, PR 00926; 787-761-6247
Hilda Bonilla, Secretary; HC 1 Box 8162, Luquillo, PR 00773; 787-860-0045
Norberto Colon, Treasurer; P.O. Box 175, Barranquitas, PR 00794; 787-857-7965
Migdalia Rodriguez, Administrative Secretary; P.O. Box 1225, Casguas, PR 00726; 787-258-0490; Fax: 787-258-0490

PUERTO RICO CONSERVATION FOUNDATION, THE (PRCF)

527 Avenue Andalucia, Suite 75
San Juan, PR 00920-4131 United States
Phone: 787-763-9875 Fax: 787-772-4645
E-mail: fconserv@tld.net
Website: www.prcf.org

Founded: 1987
Membership: 1–100
Scope: Local

Description: The PRCF is a private nonprofit tax-exempt 501(c)3 organization, dedicated to protecting Puerto Rico's biological biodiversity, focusing on the conservation of threatened and endangered species and other keystone and lesser known species.

Publication(s): Sea Turtle Kit and various brochures, Pablo y Marisol van Playa, Puerto Rican Parrot Teacher's Kit, Puerto Rico NGOs Directory, Verde Luz Newsletter

Keyword(s): Reduce/Reuse/Recycle, Wildlife & Species

Contact(s):
Roberto Biaggi, President
Miguel Iturregui, Director
Esther Rojas, Executive Director
Jose Dueno, Treasurer
Juan Ricart, Secretary

PUGET SOUNDKEEPER ALLIANCE

4401 Leary Way NW
Seattle, WA 98107 United States
Phone: 206-297-7002 Fax: 206-297-0409
E-mail: psa@pugetsoundkeeper.org
Website: www.pugetsoundkeeper.org

Founded: 1984
Membership: 101–1,000
Scope: Regional

Description: A nonprofit organization whose mission is to protect and preserve Puget Sound by stopping the discharge of pollution into the waters of the Sound.

Publication(s): Sounder

Keyword(s): Pollution (general), Recreation/Ecotourism, Water Habitats & Quality

Contact(s):
Tom Diller, President
Sue Joerger, Executive Director / Soundkeeper

PURPLE MARTIN CONSERVATION ASSOCIATION

Edinboro University of Pennsylvania
Edinboro, PA 16444 United States
Phone: 814-734-4420 Fax: 814-734-5803
E-mail: pmca@edinboro.edu
Website: www.purplemartin.org

Founded: 1987
Membership: 1,001–10,000
Scope: Local, State, Regional, National, International

Description: An international tax-exempt, nonprofit organization dedicated to the conservation of the Purple Martin (Progne subis) species of bird through scientific research, state-of-the-art wildlife management techniques, and public education. The PMCA's scientific staff conducts research on all aspects of martin biology throughout the bird's North, South, and Middle American breeding, wintering, and migratory ranges.The organization functions as a centralized data-gathering/information source on martins.

Publication(s): Purple Martin Update.

Keyword(s): Agriculture/Farming, Air Quality/Atmosphere, Climate Change, Ecosystems (precious), Ethics/Environmental Justice, Land Issues, Pollution (general), Population, Public Lands/Greenspace, Recreation/Ecotourism, Sprawl/Urban Planning, Water Habitats & Quality

Contact(s):
James Hill, Director and Editor; 814-734-4420; Fax: 814-734-5803; jhill@edinboro.edu

Q

QUAIL UNLIMITED, INC.

31 Quail Run, P.O. Box 610
Edgefield, SC 29824-0610 United States
Phone: 803-637-5731 Fax: 803-637-0037
E-mail: national@qu.org
Website: www.qu.org

Founded: 1981

Scope: National

Description: A national nonprofit conservation organization dedicated to improving quail and upland game bird populations through habitat management and research. Organized to re-establish and manage suitable upland game habitat, both public and private lands across the country, and to educate the public to the needs for wildlife habitat management.

Publication(s): Quail Unlimited Magazine Bi-Monthly

Keyword(s): Wildlife & Species

Contact(s):

Steve Mcghee, President; 100 Patterson Circle, Oliver Springs, TN 37840; 423-574-3685
Jerry Allen, Administrative Vice President; 1884 Highway 23 West, Edgefield, SC 29824; 803-637-5877; national@qu.org
Joseph Evans, Executive Vice President; 3012 Sussex Rd., Augusta, GA 30909; 706-738-0692; national@qu.org
Harvey Bray, Rocky Mountain Regional Director; 13 Archway Lane, Pueblo, CO 81005; 719-561-3825; Fax: 719-561-8977
Tommy Dean, Director of Chapter Development; 815 Shawnee Dr., N. Augusta, SC 29841; 803-637-5731; chapterdev@qu.org
Randy Guthrie, South Central Regional Director; 2061 Crow Mt. Rd., Russellville, AR 72801; 501-967-2200; Fax: 501-767-2716; rguthrie@cswnet.com
Dick Haldeman, Western Regional Director; 39455 Black Oak Rd., Temecula, CA 92592; 909-767-3435; Fax: 909-767-2716; quwest@pe.net
Jeff Hodges, Great Plains Regional Director; 382 NW Hwy. 18, Clinton, MO 64735; 660-885-7057; Fax: 660-885-7152
David Howell, Director of Agricultural Wildlife Services; 10364 S. 950 E., Stendal, IN 47585; 812-536-2272; dhowell@psci.net
Yale Leiden, Southeast Regional Director
Chip Martin, Southwest Regional Director; 3320 FM 3326, Anson, TX 79501; 915-823-3347; Fax: 915-823-3340
Mike Newell, Oklahoma Regional Director; 2607 NW Columbia, Lawton, OK 73505; Fax: 580-357-0619; mnewell@qu.org
Wade Teague, Mid-Atlantic Regional Director; 271 Stevens Church Rd., Goldsboro, NC 27530; 919-689-3884; Fax: 919-689-2726; wadequ@earthlink.net
Chris Wolkonowski, Midwest Regional Director; HCR 76 Box 645 Hwy. 108, Gruetli-Laager, TN 37339; 931-779-4868; Fax: 812-536-2272; cwolk@qu.org
D. Kogon, Editor; qumag@qu.org
Roger Wells, National Habitat Coordinator; 868 Road 290, Americus, KS; 316-443-5834; rwells@americusks.net

QUALITY DEER MANAGEMENT ASSOCIATION

P.O. Box 227
Watknisville, GA 30677 United States
Phone: 800-209-3337 Fax: 706-769-3464
E-mail: qdma@charter.net
Website: www.qdma.com

Founded: 1988

Membership: 10,001–100,000

Scope: State, National, International

Description: National nonprofit wildlife conservation organization dedicated to promoting sustainable, high-quality white-tailed deer populations, wildlife habitats and ethical hunting experiences through education, research and management in partnership with hunters, landowners, natural resource professionals and the public.

Publication(s): Educational Resources, Quality Whitetails journal

Keyword(s): Wildlife & Species

Contact(s):

Brian Murphy, Executive Director; 800-209-3337; Fax: 706-769-3464; bmurphy-qdma@charter.net

QUEBEC WILDLIFE FEDERATION

6780 1st Ave., Bureau 109
Charlesbourg, G1H 2W8 Quebec Canada
Phone: 418-626-6858 Fax: 418-622-6168
E-mail: fede@fqf.qc.ca
Website: www.fqf.qc.ca

Founded: 1945

Scope: Regional

Publication(s): INFO-FQF

Keyword(s): Development/Developing Countries, Public Lands/Greenspace, Recreation/Ecotourism, Reduce/Reuse/Recycle, Wildlife & Species

Contact(s):

Aurele Blais, President
Alain Bisson, Vice President and Secretary
Alain Gagnon, Vice President
Rodolphe Lasalle, Vice President
Michel Savard, Vice President
Alain Cossette, General Director
Patrick Filiatrault, Forest Engineer
Annie Guertin, Communication Coordinator
Bruno Paradis, Treasurer
Gaetan Roy, Biologist

R

RACHEL CARSON COUNCIL, INC.

8940 Jones Mill Rd.
Chevy Chase, MD 20815 United States
Phone: 301-652-1877 Fax: 301-587-3863
E-mail: rccouncil@aol.com
Website: members.aol.com/rccouncil/ourpage

Founded: 1965

Membership: N/A

Scope: National

Description: (Formerly: Rachel Carson Trust for the Living Environment Inc.) An international clearinghouse for information on toxic substances, particularly pesticides, for both scientists and laymen. Information is distributed by means of publications, workshops, conferences, and responses to specific questions. Rachel Carson Council is devoted to fostering a sense of wonder and respect toward nature and to helping society realize Rachel Carson's vision of a healthy and diverse environment.

Publication(s): Basic Guide to Pesticides, list of current publications available on request, books, pamphlets and sheets on specific alternative pest control methods and on pesticides effects, Rachel Carson Council News.

Keyword(s): Agriculture/Farming, Land Issues, Pollution (general), Public Health, Water Habitats & Quality, Wildlife & Species

Contact(s):

Martha Talbot, Vice President
Diana Post, Executive Director and Secretary
Aaron Blair, Liaison to the Board
David McGarth, Treasurer

RAINBOW PUSH COALITION

1002 Wisconsin Ave., NW
Washington, DC 20007 United States
Phone: 202-333-5270 Fax: 202-728-1192
E-mail: info@rainbowpush.org
Website: www.rainbowpush.org

Founded: 1984
Scope: International
Description: RPC is a national progressive membership organization committed to public education, empowerment, economic and social justice, and gender and racial equality. The Rainbow Push Coalition has state chapters and a national membership base. The Rainbow Push Coalition addresses such issues as education, voter registration, economic justice, civil rights, environment, labor, and working people's rights.
Publication(s): Rainbow Newsletter, Rainbow Push Magazine or The Rainbow JaxFax, various issue papers, speeches, and briefings.
Keyword(s): Development/Developing Countries, Pollution (general), Reduce/Reuse/Recycle
Contact(s):
Jesse Jackson, President and Founder
Willie Barrow, Co-Chairman of the Board
Dennis Rivera, Co-Chairman of the Board

RAINFOREST ACTION NETWORK
221 Pine St.,
San Francisco, CA 94104 United States
Phone: 415-398-4404 Fax: 415-398-2732
E-mail: rainforest@ran.org
Website: www.ran.org
Founded: 1985
Scope: National
Description: RAN works nationally and internationally on major campaigns to protect rainforests and defend the rights of indigenous people, using non-violent direct action such as: letter-writing campaigns, boycotts, and demonstrations against corporations and lending agencies contributing to rainforest destruction. RAN also produces educational materials, a teachers' packet, and fact sheets for community organizers.
Publication(s): World Rainforest Week Organizers Manual, Action Alert
Keyword(s): Forests/Forestry, Wildlife & Species
Contact(s):
Randall Hayes, Board Secretary, President
Christopher Hatch, Executive Director
Sara Riggs, Communications Director
Laura Fauth, Publications Editor
Jim Gollin, Board Chair
Scott Price, Board Treasurer

RAINFOREST ALLIANCE
65 Bleecker St.
New York, NY 10012 United States
Phone: 212-677-1900 Fax: 212-677-2187
E-mail: canopy@ra.org
Founded: 1986
Scope: International
Description: The Rainforest Alliance is an international nonprofit organization dedicated to the conservation of tropical forests for the benefit of the global community. Its primary mission is to develop and promote economically viable and socially desirable alternatives to the destruction of tropical forests.
Publication(s): CANOPY, The, Catfish Connection, The, So Fruitful a Fish, Tales from the Jungle, Floods of Fortune
Keyword(s): Development/Developing Countries, Forests/Forestry, Wildlife & Species
Contact(s):
Tensie Whealan, President
Daniel Katz, Executive Director
Karin Kreider, Associate Director

RAINFOREST RELIEF
P.O. Box 150566
Brooklyn, NY 11215 United States
Phone: 718-398-3760 Fax: 718-398-3760
E-mail: relief@igc.org
Website: www.enviroweb.org/rainrelief
Founded: 1989
Membership: 101–1,000
Scope: National
Description: Rainforest Relief, a nonprofit 501(c)3 organization, works through education and non-violent direct action to end the loss of tropical and temperate rain forests by reducing the demand for products and materials for which rainforests are destroyed. These materials include tropical hardwoods, paper, oil, metals and agricultural products such as bananas, beef, coffee and chocolate.
Publication(s): Roots, Rainforest Relief Reports, Raindrops
Keyword(s): Ethics/Environmental Justice, Forests/Forestry, Reduce/Reuse/Recycle, Wildlife & Species
Contact(s):
Tim Keating, President and Director
Jeffrey Lockwood, Vice President and Portland Oregon Chapter, Director; P.O. Box 14232, Portland, OR 97293; 503-236-3031; rainrelief@hotmail.com

RAINFOREST TRUST
SAVE THE JAGUAR
6001 SW 63rd Avenue
Miami, FL 33143 United States
Phone: 305-669-2115 Fax: 305-665-0691
E-mail: rft@rainforesttrust.com
Website: www.rainforesttrust.com
Founded: 1995
Membership: 1–100
Scope: International
Description: The Rainforest Trust supports and maintains a Jaguar sanctuary and Rainforest preserve in Belize. It also promotes eco-tourism and sustainable agriculture as economically viable alternatives to deforestation, and actively promotes educational programmes to teach farmers and school children about conservation, fragile eco-systems, organic agriculture, and wildlife preservation. The Trust has also recently established a second Wildlife sanctuary and Rainforest preserve in Jamaica.
Keyword(s): Agriculture/Farming, Ecosystems (precious), Forests/Forestry, Recreation/Ecotourism, Reduce/Reuse/Recycle, Wildlife & Species
Contact(s):
Brett Ashmeade-Hawkins, President; The Rainforest Trust, San Ignacio P.O.; 305-669-2115; Fax: 305-665-0691; rft@rainforesttrust.com
Mark Ashmeade-Hawkins, Secretary and Treasurer; 305-669-2115; Fax: 305-665-0691; rft@rainforesttrust.com
T. Hawkins, Chairman; 305-666-2158

RAPTOR EDUCATION FOUNDATION, INC.
P.O. Box 200400
Denver, CO 80220 United States
Phone: 303-680-8500 Fax: 303-680-8502
E-mail: raptor2@usaref.org
Website: www.usaref.org
Founded: 1980
Membership: 1,001–10,000
Scope: National
Description: A nonprofit, charitable educational organization utilizing nonreleasable raptors to promote environmental literacy. Lecturers travel nationwide.
Publication(s): Talon, Castings (volunteer newsletter), Talon Supplement
Keyword(s): Ecosystems (precious), Ethics/Environmental Justice, Land Issues, Wildlife & Species

Contact(s):
Peter Reshetniak, President and Editor
Patrick Duran, Executive Director
Shellie Sage, Mews Manager
Anne Price, Secretary
Anne Price, Curator of Raptors

RAPTOR RESEARCH FOUNDATION, INC.

USGS Forest and Rangeland
Ecosystem Science Center
Snake River Field Station, 970 Lusk St.
Boise, ID 83706 United States
Phone: 208-426-5201
Website: biology.boisestate.edu/raptor

Founded: 1966
Scope: National
Description: A nonprofit corporation formed to stimulate and coordinate the dissemination of information on the biology and management of birds of prey and their habitats. Areas of particular interest include: raptor banding, behavior, captive breeding, conservation, ecology, research techniques, management, migration, population monitoring, pathology, and rehabilitation.
Publication(s): Journal of Raptor Research, Wingspan
Keyword(s): Wildlife & Species
Contact(s):
Michael Kochert, President; 208-426-5201; Fax: 208-426-5210; mkochert@eagle.idbsu.edu
Keith Bildstein, Vice President; Hawk Mountain Sanctuary, Route 2, Box 191, Kempton, PA 19529; 910-756-6961; bildstein@hawkmountain.org
James Bednarz, Editor-In-Chief; Department of Biology, Boise State University,
Jim Fitzpatrick, Treasurer and Membership Information; Carpenter, St. Croix Valley Nature Center, 12805 St. Croix Tr., Hastings, MN 55033; 651-437-4359; jim@cncstcroix.com
Patricia Hall, Secretary; 436 David Dr. E, Flagstaff, AZ 86001; 520-526-6222; pah@alpine.for.nau.edu

RARE CENTER FOR TROPICAL CONSERVATION

1840 Wilson Blvd., Ste. 402
Arlington, VA 22201 United States
Phone: 703-522-5070 Fax: 703-522-5027
E-mail: rare@rarecenter.org
Website: www.rarecenter.org

Founded: 1973
Membership: 1,001–10,000
Scope: International
Description: RARE Center's mission is to protect wildlands of globally significant biological diversity by enabling local people to benefit from their protection. Focusing on education and economic opportunities, we pursue this mission by working in partnership with local communities, non-governmental organizations (NGOs) and other stakeholders to develop and replicate locally managed conservation strategies.
Publication(s): Nature Guide Training, Nature Trails, Conservation Education, Radio Dramas
Keyword(s): Ecosystems (precious), Population, Public Lands/Greenspace, Recreation/Ecotourism, Wildlife & Species
Contact(s):
Brett Jenks, President/CEO

REEF RELIEF

P.O. Box 430
201 William Street
Key West, FL 33041 United States
Phone: 305-294-3100 Fax: 305-293-9515
E-mail: reef@bellsouth.net
Website: www.reefrelief.org

Founded: 1989
Membership: 1,001–10,000
Scope: Local, Regional, International
Description: Reef Relief is a nonprofit membership organization dedicated to preserve and protect Living Coral Reef Ecosystems through local, regional, and global efforts.
Publication(s): Reef Line Newsletter, Coral Reefs brochure
Keyword(s): Ecosystems (precious), Oceans/Coasts/Beaches, Pollution (general), Water Habitats & Quality, Wildlife & Species
Contact(s):
Paul Johnson, Special Projects
Deevon Quirolo, Executive Director
Craig Quirolo, Founder and Director of Marine Projects
Joel Biddle, Educational Coordinator
Michael Blades, Project Coordinator

REEFKEEPER INTERNATIONAL

2809 Bird Ave., PMB 162
Miami, FL 33133 United States
Phone: 305-358-4600 Fax: 305-358-3030
E-mail: reefkeeper@reefkeeper.org
Website: www.reefkeeper.org

Founded: N/A
Scope: International
Publication(s): Reef Monitor Update, Reef Dispatch, Reef Alert, ReefKeeper Report
Contact(s):
Alexander Stone, Director

RENEW THE EARTH

1200 18th St., NW, Suite 1100
Washington, DC 20036 United States
Phone: 202-721-1545 Fax: 202-467-5780
E-mail: renew@renewtheearth.org
Website: www.renewtheearth.org

Founded: 1978
Membership: N/A
Scope: International
Description: Renew the Earth, formerly Renew America, identifies, links and awards sustainable environmental programs from civil society, all levels of government and the private sector worldwide. We have created an internet-based international Success Index to list and disseminate information about verified, solution-oriented programs; a global network of practitioners and an annual Awards Program to recognize environmental achievement
Publication(s): Environmental Ambassador Index
Contact(s):
Katy Moran, Executive Director; 202-721-1545; katymoran@renewtheearth.org

RENEWABLE ENERGY POLICY PROJECT (REPP)

1612 K St., NW, Suite 202
Washington, DC 20006 United States
Phone: 202-293-2898 Fax: 202-293-5857
Website: www.repp.org

Founded: 1995
Scope: International
Description: The Renewable Energy Policy Project (REPP) investigates the emerging relationships among policies, markets and public demand for renewable energy technologies. REPP's mission is to accelerate growth of the renewable energy industry and maximize deployment of renewable energy technology, by providing credible information, insightful analysis and innovative strategies.
Publication(s): Wind Clusters: Expanding the Market Appeal of Wind Energy Systems (Nov. 1996), Natural Gas: Bridge to a Renewable Energy Future (May 1997), Clean Government: Options for Governments to Buy Renewable Energy (May 1999), Renewable Energy Policy Outside the United States

(Oct. 1999), Federal Energy Subsidaries: Not all Technologies are Created Equal (July 2000), Rural Electrification with Solar Energy as a Climate Protection Strategy (Jan. 2000)
Keyword(s): Energy, Reduce/Reuse/Recycle
Contact(s):
Mary Campbell, Internet and Publications Director
Virinder Singh, Research Director
Fred Beck, Research Manager
Karl Rabago, Chairman of the Board of Directors

RENEWABLE NATURAL RESOURCES FOUNDATION

RNRF
5430 Grosvenor Ln.
Bethesda, MD 20814-2193 United States
Phone: 301-493-9101 Fax: 301-493-6148
E-mail: info@rnrf.org
Website: www.rnrf.org
Founded: 1972
Membership: 1–100
Scope: National
Description: A public, nonprofit, operating foundation. Members are 15 professional, scientific and educational organizations. Conducts meetings on public policy issues. Publisher of Renewable Resources Journal. Developer of the 35-acre Renewable Natural Resources Center, an office complex for natural resource organizations.
Publication(s): Renewable Resources Journal
Keyword(s): Agriculture/Farming, Air Quality/Atmosphere, Climate Change, Ecosystems (precious), Forests/Forestry, Land Issues, Oceans/Coasts/Beaches, Pollution (general), Population, Public Lands/Greenspace, Recreation/Ecotourism, Reduce/Reuse/Recycle, Sprawl/Urban Planning.
Contact(s):
Robert Day, Executive Director
Albert Grant, Vice Chairman of the Board
David Moody, Chairman of Board of Directors
Ryan Colker, Director of Programs
Chandru Krishna, Director of Administration and Finance

REP AMERICA/REPUBLICANS FOR ENVIRONMENTAL PROTECTION

Deerfield, IL 60015 United States
Phone: 847-940-0320 Fax: 847-940-0320
Website: www.repamerica.org
Founded: 1995
Scope: National
Description: REP aims to resurrect the GOP's conservation tradition and restore natural resource conservation and sound environmental protection as fundamental elements of the Republican Party.
Publication(s): The Green Elephant
Keyword(s): Ethics/Environmental Justice, Forests/Forestry, Pollution (general), Reduce/Reuse/Recycle, Wildlife & Species
Contact(s):
Martha Marks, President; martha@repamerica.org
Aurie Kryzuda, Vice-President
Jim Scarantino, Executive Director
Anthony Cobb, Treasurer
Vince Williams, Secretary

RESOURCE CENTER FOR ENVIRONMENTAL EDUCATION, THE

Okeanskill Prospect
Vladivostok, 690106 Russia
Phone: 4.2322505662e+015 Fax: 4232225763
E-mail: liliko@mail.primorye.ru
Founded: 1997
Scope: International
Description: The RCEE is the only center in the Russian Far East, dedicated to promoting experiential learning in the fields of environmental education, science, and art for students and teachers.
Keyword(s): Oceans/Coasts/Beaches, Recreation/Ecotourism
Contact(s):
Lilia Kondrashova, Director; 742-324-2801; Fax: 423-222-5763; liliko@mail.primorye.ru

RESOURCE RENEWAL INSTITUTE, THE

Fort Mason Center Building A
San Francisco, CA 94123 United States
Phone: 415-928-3774 Fax: 415-928-6529
E-mail: info@rri.org
Website: www.rri.org
Founded: 1983
Scope: National, International
Description: The RRI is a national, nonprofit organization advocating state and national comprehensive, integrated environmental strategies (known as Green Plans), modeled on those of the Netherlands and New Zealand. RRI has set up a Global Green Plan Center to act as a clearinghouse for information on Green Plans. for more information, use RRI's e-mail address.
Publication(s): Saving Cities, Saving Money, Green Plans: Greenprint for Sustainability, The International Green Planner.
Keyword(s): Development/Developing Countries, Executive/Legislative/Judicial Reform
Contact(s):
Huey Johnson, President
Allison Lengauer, Acting Executive Director; 415-928-3774

RESOURCES FOR THE FUTURE

1616 P St., NW
Washington, DC 20036 United States
Phone: 202-328-5000 Fax: 202-939-3460
Website: www.rff.org
Founded: 1952
Scope: National
Description: An independent nonprofit organization that works to advance research and education in the development, conservation, and use of environmental and natural resources. Staff is comprised primarily of economists and policy analysts who research a variety of environmental and natural resource issues.
Publication(s): Resources
Keyword(s): Air Quality/Atmosphere, Development/Developing Countries, Energy, Forests/Forestry, Land Issues, Reduce/Reuse/Recycle, Transportation, Wildlife & Species
Contact(s):
Paul Portney, President; 202-328-5000; portney@rff.org.com
Edward Hand, Vice President of Finance and Administration; 202-328-5029; hand@rff.org.com
Lesli Creedon, Director of Development; creedon@rff.org.com
J. Davies, Center for Risk Management Director; 202-328-5093; davies@rff.org.com
Alan Krupnick, Quality of the Environment Division Director; 202-328-5059; krupnick@rff.org.com
Michael Toman, Energy and Natural Resources Division Director; 202-328-5091; toman@rff.org.com
Dan Quinn, Manager of Public Affairs; 202-328-5019; quinn@rff.org.com
Christopher Clotworthy, Librarian; 202-328-5089; clotworthy@rff.org.com

RESPONSIVE MANAGEMENT

130 Franklin St.
Harrisonburg, VA 22801 United States
Phone: 540-432-1888 Fax: 540-432-1892
Website: www.responsivemanagement.com
Founded: 1986

Scope: State, Regional, National, International
Description: Developed to help fish and wildlife organizations understand and work with their constituents. Responsive Management conducts focus group research, telephone and mail surveys, public opinion and attitude research, literature reviews, demographic analysis, and workshops in public opinion polling, marketing, change, communications, dispute resolution, and human dimensions of natural resource management.
Publication(s): Responsive Management Report
Contact(s):
Mark Duda, Executive Director; 540-432-1888

RESTORE HETCH HETCHY

P.O. Box 289
Yosemite, CA 95389-0289 United States
Phone: 209-372-8660
E-mail: info@hetchhetchy.org
Website: www.hetchhetchy.org

Founded: 1999
Membership: 10,001–100,000
Scope: National
Description: The mission of Restore Hetch Hetchy is to restore the Hetch Hetchy Valley in Yosemite Valley, currently inundated by the O'Shaughnessy Dam. Our goal is to accomplish a "win-win" outcome for Hetch Hetchy Valley, and for the cities of the Bay Area and the Turlock and Modesto Irrigation Districts that rely on Hetch Hetchy water and power — drop for drop, kilowatt for kilowatt, and dollar for dollar — to the extent that is technically feasible.
Keyword(s): Finance/Banking/Trade, Public Lands/Greenspace, Water Habitats & Quality
Contact(s):
Ron Good, Executive Director; 209-372-8660; info@hetchhetchy.org

RETURNED PEACE CORPS VOLUNTEERS FOR ENVIRONMENT AND DEVELOPMENT (RPCV-ED)

P.O. Box 102
Iowa City, IA 52240-0102 United States
Phone: 319-351-3375
E-mail: kwhansen@ia.net
Website: www.cboss.com/rpcv-eandd/

Founded: 1991
Membership: 101–1,000
Scope: National
Description: The RPCVs-ED was formed to serve as a focal point for action on environment and development issues by Peace Corps alumni and friends.
Publication(s): Under the Village Tree.
Keyword(s): Climate Change, Development/Developing Countries
Contact(s):
Katy Hansen, Chair; kwhansen@ia.net
Susan Singh, Editor; 918-749-7004; sukising@aol.com

RHODE ISLAND B.A.S.S. CHAPTER FEDERATION

10 Ridgeway Drive
Warren, RI 02885 United States
Phone: 401-245-6264
E-mail: ribassfed@aol.com
Website: www.edgenet.net/ebbm/state/main.html

Founded: N/A
Scope: State
Description: An organization of Bassmaster chapters, affiliated with the Bass Anglers Sportsman Society, organized to fight pollution, assist state and national conservation agencies in their efforts, and teach the young people of our country good conservation practices. Dedicated to the realistic conservation of our water resources.
Publication(s): Forest Conservationist, The
Keyword(s): Forests/Forestry
Contact(s):
Roger Pray, President
Bill Weikert, Conservation Director; 156 Ridgewood Rd., Middletown, RI 02842; 401-846-0512; riscnrdbil@aol.com

RHODE ISLAND FOREST CONSERVATOR'S ORGANIZATION, INC.

P.O. Box 53
No. Scituate, RI 02857 United States
Phone: 401-568-3421
Website: www.rifco.org/resources.htm

Founded: 1989
Membership: 1–100
Scope: State
Description: A statewide organization affiliated with the National Woodland Owners Association organized to promote stewardship of Rhode Island's wooded lands and watersheds and protect their heritage for future generations.
Publication(s): Newsletter
Keyword(s): Agriculture/Farming, Forests/Forestry, Land Issues
Contact(s):
Milton Schumacher, President
Marc Tremblay, Outreach Coordinator & Editor
Milton Schumacher, Secretary
Virginia Warrender, Treasurer

RHODE ISLAND STATE CONSERVATION COMMITTEE

Chair, Sosnowski Farm, P.O. Box 722
W. Kingston, RI 02892 United States

Founded: N/A
Contact(s):
Susan Sosnowski, Chair; Sosnowski Farm, P.O. Box 722, W. Kingston, RI 02892; 401-783-7704; senmike@uriacc.uri.edu

RHODE ISLAND WILD PLANT SOCIETY

Box 114
Peace Dale, RI 02883-0114 United States
Phone: 410-783-5895
Website: www.riwps.org/

Founded: 1987
Membership: 101–1,000
Scope: State
Description: The Rhode Island Wild Plant Society is a nonprofit conservation organization dedicated to the preservation and protection of Rhode Island's native plants and their habitats. Activities include talks, inventories of local flora, native plant restoration projects and a spring flower show and garden exhibit.
Publication(s): RIWPS Newsletter (biannual newsletter)
Keyword(s): Land Issues, Wildlife & Species
Contact(s):
Jules Cohen, President; 85 Scrabbletown Rd., N. Kingston, RI 02852
Deborah Poor, Executive Director

RIVER ALLIANCE OF WISCONSIN

306 East Wilson, Suite 2W
Madison, WI 53703 United States
Phone: 608-257-2424 Fax: 608-260-9799
E-mail: wisrivers@wisconsinrivers.org
Website: www.wisconsinrivers.org

Founded: 1993
Membership: 1,001–10,000
Scope: State
Description: The River Alliance is a nonprofit, nonpartisan citizen advocacy organization for rivers. Our mission is to lead the

growing statewide effort to protect, enhance and restore Wisconsin's rivers and watersheds for their ecological, recreational, aesthetic, and cultural values. Recent program work includes education and information about the impacts of dams on river system health, minimizing ecosystem damage through federal relicensing of hydro dams, and advocacy for selective removal of uneconomic

Publication(s): Small Groups Building Tool Kit, Local Groups Directory for Wisconsin, Dam Removal, Canoe (e-mail newsletter), News Bulletins and Fact Sheets, Wisconsin Rivers (Quarterly), Periodic Action Alerts.

Keyword(s): Energy, Oceans/Coasts/Beaches, Water Habitats & Quality, Wildlife & Species

Contact(s):
Todd Ambs, Executive Director

RIVER NETWORK

520 SW 6th Ave., Suite 1130
Portland, OR 97204-1511 United States
Phone: 503-241-3506 Fax: 503-241-9256
E-mail: info@rivernetwork.org
Website: www.rivernetwork.org

Founded: 1988

Scope: Local, State, Regional, National

Description: River Network supports river advocates at the grassroots, state and regional levels; helps them build effective organizations; and links them together in a national movement to protect and restore America's rivers and watersheds.

Publication(s): River Talk! Communicate Watershed Message, Clean Water Act: An Owner's Manual, Starting Up: A Handbook for New Organizations, Living Waters, How to Save a River, The Volunteer Monitor, River Fundraising Alert, River Voices, River Network Poster

Keyword(s): Water Habitats & Quality

Contact(s):
Ken Margolis, President
Don Elder, Vice President for Program Development
Susan Schwartz, Director of Finance & Administration
Thalia Zepatos, Director of Communications
David Borden, Chairman of Board of Directors

RIVER NETWORK

EASTERN OFFICE
4000 Albemarle St., NW, Suite 303
Washington, DC 20016 United States
Phone: 202-364-2550 Fax: 202-364-2520
E-mail: dc@rivernetwork.org
Website: www.rivernetwork.org

Founded: N/A

Membership: 101–1,000

Scope: National

Description: River Network is a national non-profit organization dedicated to helping people save rivers.

Publication(s): Fundraising Alert, River Voices, How to Save a River, The Clean Water Act Owners Manual

RIVER NETWORK

NORTHERN ROCKIES OFFICE: RIVER CONSERVANCY FIELD OFFICE
44 North Last Chance Gulch, # 4
Helena, MT 59601 United States
Phone: 406-442-4777 Fax: 406-442-8883
E-mail: montanazac@aol.com
Website: www.rivernetwork.org

Founded: N/A

Scope: National

Contact(s):
Hugh Zackheim, Contact

RIVER OTTER ALLIANCE, THE

6733 S. Locust Ct.
Englewood, CO 80112 United States
Phone: 303-773-2749
Website: www.otternet.com/ROA

Founded: 1990

Membership: 101–1,000

Scope: National

Description: The River Otter Alliance promotes the survival of the North American River Otter through education, research, and habitat protection. We support current research and reintroduction programs, monitor abundance and distribution in the United States, and educate through our newsletter on the need to restore and sustain river otter populations.

Publication(s): River Otter Journal, The

Keyword(s): Water Habitats & Quality, Wildlife & Species

Contact(s):
Tracy Johnston, President
Carol Peterson, Vice President
John Mulvihill, Treasurer; 6733 S. Locust Ct., Englewood, CO 80112-1007

RIVER PROJECT, THE

11950 Ventura Boulevard, #7
Studio City, CA 91604 United States
Phone: 818-980-9660 Fax: 818-980-0700
E-mail: winter@theriverproject.org
Website: www.theriverproject.org

Founded: 2001

Membership: N/A

Scope: Local, Regional

Description: A 501(c)(3) non-profit organization engaged in outreach, education, scientific study, habitat restoration and multi-use open space projects along the rivers and streams of Los Angeles County.

Keyword(s): Ecosystems (precious), Ethics/Environmental Justice, Land Issues, Oceans/Coasts/Beaches, Pollution (general), Public Health, Public Lands/Greenspace, Recreation/Ecotourism, Reduce/Reuse/Recycle, Sprawl/Urban Planning, Water Habitats & Quality, Wildlife & Species.

RIVERS COUNCIL OF WASHINGTON

509 10th Ave., East, Suite 200
Seattle, WA 98102 United States
Phone: 206-568-1380 Fax: 206-568-1381
E-mail: riverswa@brigadoon.com
Website: www.riverscouncilofwa.org

Founded: 1984

Scope: State

Description: (formerly Northwest Rivers Council) The mission of the Rivers Council of Washington is to lead an expanding grassroots effort to preserve, enhance, and restore rivers and their watersheds in Washington state for their natural, recreational, and cultural values, and support compatible efforts of other organizations in the Pacific Northwest.

Publication(s): Washington Rivers

Keyword(s): Recreation/Ecotourism, Water Habitats & Quality

Contact(s):
Doug North, President and Chair of Trustees
Kate Sullivan, Vice President
Scott Andrews, Executive Director
Andy Held, Secretary
Matt Scobel, Treasurer

ROBERT ROADS ILLINOIS DEPARTMENT OF NATURAL RESOURCES

524 S. Second St
Springfield, IL 62701 United States
Phone: 217-782-1329 Fax: 217-782-9599
E-mail: BROADS@DNRMAIL.IL.STATE.US
Website: www.conservation.state.mo.us/engineering/ace/

Founded: 1961
Scope: National
Description: To encourage and broaden the educational, social, and economic interests of conservation engineering practices; to promote recognition of the importance of sound engineering practices in fish, wildlife, and recreation development; to enable each member to take advantage of the experience of other states.
Publication(s): Membership Directory, A.C.E. Newsletter, Informational Brochure, Conference Proceedings, Handbook
Keyword(s): Recreation/Ecotourism
Contact(s):
Robert Roads, President; 217-782-2605
Norval Olson, Secretary and Treasurer

ROCK RIVER HEADWATERS, INC.

(RRHI)
P.O. Box 151
Horicon, WI 53032 United States
Phone: 920-485-3019
E-mail: lynn_hanson@lycos.com

Founded: 2000
Membership: 101–1,000
Scope: Regional
Description: Builds collaboration between citizens, organizations and governments in the Upper Rock River Basin of Wisconsin
Publication(s): Finding the Common Ground (report describing collaboration process).
Keyword(s): Land Issues, Water Habitats & Quality
Contact(s):
Lynn Hanson, Director; P.O. Box 75, Horicon, WI 53032; 920-485-3019; Fax: 920-485-3028; lynn_hanson@lycos.com

ROCKY MOUNTAIN BIGHORN SOCIETY

P.O. Box 8320
Denver, CO 80201 United States
Phone: 303-697-4896 Fax: 303-697-2921
Website: www.bighornsheep.org

Founded: 1975
Membership: 1,001–10,000
Scope: National
Description: The purpose of the Society is to support the sound management of the Rocky Mountain bighorn sheep and its habitat and to promote the advancement and knowledge of the bighorn.
Publication(s): The Bighorn
Keyword(s): Recreation/Ecotourism
Contact(s):
Dennis Gardner, President; 19114 Silver Ranch Rd., Conifer, CO 80433; 303-697-4896
Victor Lauer, Vice President; P. O. Box 1811, Woodland, CO 80866
Todd Brickell, Secretary; 8181 Cooper River Dr., Colorado Springs, CO 80920
Kevin Wilson, Treasurer; P.O. Box 485, Conifer, CO 80433

ROCKY MOUNTAIN BIRD OBSERVATORY

14500 Lark Bunting Lane
Brighton, CO 80601 United States
Phone: 303-659-4348 Fax: 303-654-0791
E-mail: george.wallace@rmbo.org
Website: www.rmbo.org

Founded: 1988
Membership: 101–1,000
Scope: Local, State, Regional, National, International
Description: A non-profit NGO dedicated to the conservation of Rocky Mountains and Great Plains birds and their habitats through research, monitoring, education, and outreach.
Keyword(s): Agriculture/Farming, Ecosystems (precious), Forests/Forestry, Land Issues, Wildlife & Species
Contact(s):
George Wallace, Executive Director; 303-659-4348; Fax: 303-654-0791; george.wallace@rmbo.org
Alison Banks, Wetlands Program Coordinator; 1510 South College Avenue, Fort Collins, CO 80524; 970-482-1707; Fax: 970-407-9996; alison.banks@rmbo.org
Scott Gillihan, Forested Ecosystems Program Coordinator; 1510 South College Ave., Fort Collins, CO 80524; 970-482-1707; Fax: 970-407-9996; scott.gillihan@rmbo.org
Tony Leukering, Monitoring Program Coordinator; 303-659-4348; Fax: 303-654-0791; tony.leukering@rmbo.org
Shelly Morrell, Education Program Coordinator; 1510 S. College Ave., Fort Collins, CO 80524; 970-482-1707; Fax: 970-407-9996; shelly.morrell@rmbo.org
Ted Toombs, Prairie Partners Program Coordinator; 1510 South College Avenue, Fort Collins, CO 80524; 970-482-1707; Fax: 970-407-9996; ted.toombs@rmbo.org

ROCKY MOUNTAIN ELK FOUNDATION

2291 W. Broadway
P.O. Box 8249
Missoula, MT 59808 United States
Phone: 406-523-4500 Fax: 406-523-4581
E-mail: info@elkfoundation.org
Website: www.elkfoundation.org

Founded: 1984
Scope: Regional
Description: The Foundation's mission is to ensure the future of elk, other wildlife and their habitat. Projects funded by RMEF include: land protection, habitat enhancement, management, research, conservation education, and hunting heritage.
Contact(s):
Mike Carter, Regional VP - Southwest Region; 406-523-3452
Dave Messics, Regional VP - Northeast Region; 814-353-1667
Dave Torrell, Regional VP - Northwest Region; 406-523-4516
Ron White, Regional VP - Southeast Region; 615-370-0370

ROCKY MOUNTAIN ELK FOUNDATION

INTERMOUNTAIN REGION OFFICE
P.O. Box 290
Coaldale, CO 81222 United States
Phone: 719-547-8212 Fax: 719-942-5505
Website: www.elkfoundation.org

Founded: N/A
Membership: 1–100
Scope: Regional
Contact(s):
Tom Brown, Intermountain Regional Dev. Director; 303-279-7974; tjbrown@rmi.net
Bill Christensen, Regional Director of UT.; 801-254-1922
Blake Henning, Regional Director WY; 307-634-4099
Marty Holmes, Director of Field Operations; 719-547-8212
Lance Schul, Regional Director CO.; 303-984-4456
Joe Coker, Reg. Dir. of Kentucky & Tennessee
Doug Robinson, Southern Rockies Regional Lands Mngr.; 303-216-1953; drobinson@rmef.org

ROCKY MOUNTAIN ELK FOUNDATION

INTERNATIONAL HEADQUARTERS
2291 W. Broadway
P.O. Box 8249
Missoula, MT 59807 United States
E-mail: info@elkfoundation.org

Founded: N/A
Scope: Regional
Contact(s):
Dakota Livesay, Regional Director; 520-286-1833
Lyle Button, Contact for AZ; 520-714-1774
Mike Ford, Contact for Northern CA; 530-842-2021
Bill Harris, Contact for Southern CA; 619-486-5601
Tony Kavalok, Contact for NV; 775-971-9000

ROCKY MOUNTAIN ELK FOUNDATION
NORTH-CENTRAL REGION OFFICE
1320 Canal St.
Custer, SD 57730 United States
Phone: 605-673-2396

Founded: N/A

Scope: Regional

Contact(s):
- Mike Mueller, Regional Director; 605-673-2396
- Larry Baesler, Contact for ND; 605-673-2396
- Ralph Cinfio, Contact for MN and IA; 320-203-0932
- Bill Hunyadi, Contact for WI; 715-769-3559
- Mike Mueller, Contact for SD; 605-644-2396

ROCKY MOUNTAIN ELK FOUNDATION
NORTHEAST REGION OFFICE
198 Bennett Rd.
Julian, PA 16844 United States
Phone: 814-353-1667 Fax: 814-353-2963

Founded: N/A

Scope: Regional, International

Publication(s): Bugle

Contact(s):
- David Kelner, Regional Director for NY, CT, RI, MA, VT, NH, ME; 315-633-0308
- Dennis McGraw, Regional Director Western PA & OH; 814-357-3799
- Dave Messics, Director of Notheast Field Operations; 814-353-1667
- Dave Ragantesi, Regional Director of Eastern PA, NJ, MD, DE; 570-756-3867
- Bruce Wojcik, Michigan Regional Director; 517-668-0613

ROCKY MOUNTAIN ELK FOUNDATION
NORTHWEST REGION OFFICE
10400 Duck Ln.
Nampa, ID 83686 United States
Phone: 208-882-5689
Website: www.atalsmarema.org

Founded: N/A

Membership: 100,001–500,000

Scope: Regional

Publication(s): Wapiti-Newsletter, Bugle-Magazine

Contact(s):
- Ted Beach, Regional Director; 208-882-5689; tbeach@moscow.com
- Todd Bastain, Contact for OR
- Kevin Brown, Contact for Eastern WA
- Pat Cudmore, Contact for SW, MT and Eastern ID
- Lloran Johnson, Contact for AK, and Western WA; 253-539-7651
- Kirk Murphy, Contact for MT; 406-883-1147

ROCKY MOUNTAIN ELK FOUNDATION
SOUTH-CENTRAL REGION OFFICE
1480 8th NE, 186th St.
Holt, MO 64048 United States
Phone: 816-320-2681 Fax: 816-320-2682
E-mail: tcloutier@rmef.org
Website: www.rmef.org

Founded: N/A

Membership: 100,001–500,000

Scope: Regional

Publication(s): Bugle Magazine, WOW Magazine

Contact(s):
- Wayne Bivans, Regional Director for Indiana; 4541 Greenthread Ct., Zionsville, IN 46077; 317-769-2163; wbivans@rmef.org
- Don Blakely, Regional Director for IL; 618-893-4142
- Terry Cloutier, Director of South Central Operations; 816-320-2681
- Dale Miller, Regional Director for MO; 311 Salt Lake Circle, Napoleon, MO 64074; 816-240-2846; dmiller@rmef.org
- Randy Porterfield, Regional Director for OK and East TX; 903-677-5740

ROCKY MOUNTAIN ELK FOUNDATION
SOUTHEAST REGION OFFICE
320 Fallen Oak Cir.
Seymour, TN 37865 United States
Phone: 865-609-9593 Fax: 865-609-9190
E-mail: jmechler@rmef.org
Website: www.rmef.org

Founded: 1984

Scope: State, Regional

Description: International non-profit wildlife conservation organization, whose mission is to ensure the future of elk, other wildlife and their habitat.

Contact(s):
- Kevin Brown, Regional Director AL, AR, LA, MS; 877-286-3016
- Tom Jones, Regional Director VA, WV, NC, SC; 540-382-0022
- John Mechler, Regional Director KY, TN; 865-609-9593
- Dale Nolan, Regional Director GA, FL; 828-389-1692

ROGER TORY PETERSON INSTITUTE OF NATURAL HISTORY
311 Curtis St.
Jamestown, NY 14701 United States
Phone: 716-665-2473 Fax: 716-665-3794
E-mail: webmaster@rtpi.org
Website: www.rtpi.org

Founded: 1984

Membership: 1,001–10,000

Scope: National

Description: The mission of the Roger Tory Peterson Institute is to create a passion for and knowledge of the natural world in the hearts and minds of children by guiding and inspiring the study of nature in our schools and communities.

Publication(s): Quarterly publication for members

Keyword(s): Reduce/Reuse/Recycle

Contact(s):
- Jim Berry, President; 716-665-2473; Fax: 716-665-3794; jim@rtpi.org
- Mark Baldwin, Director of Education; 716-665-2473; Fax: 716-665-3794; mark@rtpi.org
- Mike Lyons, Director of Development; 716-665-2473; Fax: 716-665-3794; mike@rtpi.org

RUFFED GROUSE SOCIETY, THE
451 McCormick Rd.
Coraopolis, PA 15108 United States
Phone: 412-262-4044 Fax: 412-262-9207
E-mail: rgs@ruffedgrousesociety.org
Website: www.ruffedgrousesociety.org

Founded: 1961

Membership: 10,001–100,000

Scope: National

Description: Nonprofit conservation organization dedicated to improving the environment for ruffed grouse, woodcock, and other forest wildlife through maintenance, improvement, and expansion of their habitat. Assists private, industrial, county, state, and federal landholders in forest wildlife habitat improvement programs.

Publication(s): RGS Magazine.

Keyword(s): Forests/Forestry, Wildlife & Species

Contact(s):
- Edwin Gott, President

Robert Patterson, Interim Executive Director Ph.D.; 412-262-4044, ext. 11; Fax: 412-262-9207; BobP@ruffedgrousesociety.org
James Jurries, Secretary
S. Mellon, Executive Vice President
Stephen Quill, Vice President
David Sandstrom, Treasurer
Ronald Burkert, Group Director, Administration and Information Systems; RonB@ruffedgrousesociety.org
Paul Carson, Group Director, Publications and Communications; PaulC@ruffedgrousesociety.org
Dan Dessecker, Sr. Biologist; P.O. Box 2, Rice Lake, WI 54868; 715-234-8302; rgsdess@chibardun.net
Louis George, Regional Director Supervisor; 964 Milson Ct, LaCrosse, WI 54601; 608-788-1786; GeorgeLou@msn.com
William Goudy, Group Director, Field Services; 5633 Route 654 Hwy., Williamsport, PA 17702; 570-745-7313
Brenda Osborn, Group Director, Headquarters Services; BrendaO@ruffedgrousesociety.org
Thomas Word, Financial Development Director; 1405 Northgate Square #31C, Reston, VA 20190; 703-471-0721; tscottwordiii@earthlink.net
Mark Banker, Regional Biologist, Mid-Atlantic; P.O. Box 1171, Lemont, PA 16851-1171; 616-829-4797; rgsbank@lazerink.com
C. Bump, Regional Biologist, Eastern Great Lakes; 300 W. Hibbard Rd., Owosso, MI 48867; 989-729-9378; rgsbump@onemain.com
Mark Fouts, Regional Director, MN, ND; 8154 S. Dowling Lake Rd. W, Superior, WI 54880; 715-399-2270; mfouts@lbdata2.net
Rick Horton, Regional Biologist, MN; P.O. Box 657, Grand Rapids, MN 55744; 218-697-2820; rgshort@uslink.net
Paul Karczmarczyk, Regional Biologist, New England; P.O. Box 2504, West Brattleboro, VT 05303; 802-325-2114; rgskarz@prodigy.net
William Klein, Regional Director, Mid-Atlantic, Southeast; P.O. Box 243, Roscoe, PA 15477; 724-938-3705; billklein_rgs@yahoo.com
Walt Noa, Regional Director, Mid-West/MI,WI; 10175 H 5 Ln., Cornell, MI 49818; 906-384-6366; wnoa@uplogon.com
Gary Zimmer, Regional Biologist, Western Great Lakes; P.O. Box 116, Laona, WI 54541; 715-674-7505; rgszimm@newnorth.net
Owen Nisbett, RGS-Canada Executive Director; RR 2, 2006 County Road 44, Lakefield, Ontario K0L 2H0; 705-877-8274; onisbett.rgs@on.aibn.com

RUFFNER MOUNTAIN NATURE COALITION, INC.

1214 81st Street South
Birmingham, AL 35206 United States
Phone: 205-833-8264
Website: www.ruffnermountain.org

Founded: 1978
Membership: 1,001–10,000
Scope: Local
Description: Ruffner Mountain is a 1,000-acre nature preserve in eastern Birmingham that provides outdoor education and recreation opportunities to the surrounding communities. The protected forest, ridges and valleys provide a sanctuary for a wide variety of native plants and wildlife in the center of Alabama's largest urban area. With the addition of 416 acres in 2000, Ruffner Mountain is now the second largest urban nature preserve in the country and is larger than New York's Central Park.
Keyword(s): Forests/Forestry, Public Lands/Greenspace, Recreation/Ecotourism, Wildlife & Species

S

SACRED PASSAGE AND THE WAY OF NATURE

Nature Fellowship
Drawer CZ
Bisbee, AZ 85603 United States
Phone: 877-818-1881
Website: www.sacredpassage.com

Founded: 1972
Scope: International
Description: An international center seeking to improve mankind's understanding of and relationship to the environment at five levels: Individual and home, neighborhood, city, bioregion, national, and international. Projects involve environmental research, case studies, planning, education, communication, conferencing, and demonstration activities. Primary focus is on wilderness retreats, vision quests, and awareness training in nature.
Keyword(s): Land Issues
Contact(s):
John Milton, Spiritual Director; 877-818-1881; officemanager@sacredpassage.com
Sarah Sher, Visual Arts Director and Media Consultant
Jennifer Lennon, Editor and Office Manager
Vasken Kalayjian, Graphic Design Angel
Bud Wilson, Director of Public Relations and Senior Guide

SAFARI CLUB INTERNATIONAL

4800 W. Gates Pass Rd.
Tucson, AZ 85745 United States
Phone: 520-620-1220 Fax: 520-622-1205
Website: www.safariclub.org

Founded: 1971
Membership: 10,001–100,000
Scope: International
Description: A world-wide charitable organization of hunter-conservationists dedicated to the conservation of wildlife, education of people, service to people in need and the protection of hunters' rights. Sponsors wildlife management research, field projects and works with national and international agencies and governments to promote conservation programs worldwide. Operates two education facilities: the International Wildlife Museum at headquarters and the American Wilderness Leadership School.
Publication(s): Safari Magazine, Record Book of Trophy Animals, Worldwide Hunting Annual, Safari Club, Safari Times
Keyword(s): Recreation/Ecotourism, Wildlife & Species
Contact(s):
Gary Bogner, President
Peter Dart, Executive Director
James Brown, Public Relations Director
Donald Brown, Education Director
Steve Comus, Publications Director
Richard Parsons, Director of Governmental and Conservation Affairs
Tom Stevenson, Conventions Director
Barbara Strawberry, Corporate Secretary

SAFARI CLUB INTERNATIONAL

INTERNATIONAL HEADQUARTERS
4800 West Gates Pass Rd.
Tucson, AZ 85745 United States
Phone: 520-620-1220 Fax: 520-622-1205
Website: www.safariclub.org

Founded: 1973
Membership: 101–1,000
Scope: State
Description: Goals are to educate the public, especially children, in the realm of conservation as it relates to the hunter. Especially concerned with environmental respect and the preservation of any endangered species.

Contact(s):
Gary Bogner, President; 616-669-1610
Denny Anastor, Secretary and Treasurer; 616-942-8877
Betty Dykstra, Education; 616-676-9704
Lance Norris, Program; 616-798-3410
Len Vining, President-Elect; 616-698-7440

SAFARI CLUB INTERNATIONAL
SOUTH AFRICA OFFICE
P.O. Box 10362
Centurion, 46 South Africa
Phone: 27126638073 Fax: 27126638075

Founded: N/A
Scope: National

SAFARI CLUB INTERNATIONAL
WASHINGTON, DC OFFICE
501 2nd St., NE
Washington, DC 20007 United States
Phone: 703-709-2293 Fax: 703-709-2296
Website: www.sci-dc.org

Founded: N/A
Scope: International
Publication(s): Safari Magazine, Safari Times

SAFE ENERGY COMMUNICATION COUNCIL
1717 Massachusetts Ave., NW, Suite 106
Washington, DC 20036 United States
Phone: 202-483-8491 Fax: 202-234-9194
E-mail: safeenergy@erols.com
Website: www.safeenergy.org

Founded: 1980
Scope: National
Description: A coalition of 10 national environmental, safe energy, and public interest media groups. SECC produces broadcast and print ads, studies, commentaries, and graphic editorial services to promote sustainable energy policies and respond to nuclear industry and utility campaigns and helps groups develop media skills.
Publication(s): Power Boosters, polls and various energy reports, Enfacts, Viewpoint, MYTHBusters Series
Keyword(s): Energy, Reduce/Reuse/Recycle
Contact(s):
Andrew Schwartzman, President
Scott Denman, Executive Director; ext. 14; sdenman@erols.com
Linda Gunter, Communications Director; ext. 13; lcpentz@erols.com
Amy Ringold, Administrative Director; ext. 11; aringold@erols.com
Christopher Sherry, Research Director; ext. 12; csherry@erols.com

SALMON-SAFE
805 SE 32nd Avenue
Portland, OR 97214 United States
Phone: 503-232-3750 Fax: 503-232-3791
E-mail: info@salmonsafe.org
Website: salmonsafe.org

Founded: 2001
Membership: N/A
Scope: Regional
Description: Salmon-Safe works to restore West Coast agricultural and urban watersheds and the species that inhabit them through certification and other market-based incentives.
Contact(s):
Dan Kent, Managing Director

SAN DIEGO NATURAL HISTORY MUSEUM
P.O. Box 121390
San Diego, CA 92111 United States
Phone: 619-232-3821 Fax: 619-232-0248
E-mail: mhager@sdnhm.org
Website: www.sdnhm.org

Founded: 1874
Membership: 1,001–10,000
Scope: Local
Description: Binational natural history museum.
Keyword(s): Ecosystems (precious), Recreation/Ecotourism, Wildlife & Species

SAN ELIJO LAGOON CONSERVANCY
P. O. Box 230634
Encinitas, CA 92023-0634 United States
Phone: 760-436-3944 Fax: 760-944-9606
E-mail: info@sanelijo.org
Website: sanelijo.org

Founded: 1987
Membership: 1,001–10,000
Scope: Local
Description: A 401 (c) (3) non-profit organization dedicated to the preservation, protection, and enhancement of the 1000-acre San Elijo Lagoon Ecological Reserve, a coastal wetland in northern San Diego County.
Keyword(s): Ecosystems (precious), Land Issues, Oceans/Coasts/Beaches, Pollution (general), Recreation/Ecotourism, Wildlife & Species
Contact(s):
Andrew Mauro, President
Doug Gibson, Executive Director
Maryanne Bache, Administrative Officer

SAN JUAN PRESERVATION TRUST, THE
P.O. Box 327
Lopez Island, WA 98261 United States
Phone: 360-468-3202 Fax: 360-468-3509
E-mail: sjpt@sjpt.org
Website: www.sjpt.org

Founded: 1979
Scope: Regional
Description: The trust is supported by voluntary contributions from members who support the preservation of wildlife, scenery, and natural heritage of the San Juan Islands of Washington state.
Publication(s): Mom's Marsh and Other Fine Places (video), Landowner's Guide, Preserve Farmlands, A Place in the Islands.
Contact(s):
Alan Davidson, President
Karin Agosta, Vice President
David Ashbaugh, Treasurer
Anne Hay, Secretary

SANIBEL-CAPTIVA CONSERVATION FOUNDATION, INC.
P.O. Box 839, 3333 Sanibel-Captiva Rd.
Sanibel, FL 33957 United States
Phone: 941-472-2329 Fax: 941-472-6421
E-mail: sccf@sccf.org
Website: www.sccf.org

Founded: 1967
Membership: 1,001–10,000
Scope: Regional
Description: The Sanibel-Captiva Conservation Foundation is a not-for-profit organization dedicated to the preservation of natural resources and wildlife habitat on and around Sanibel and Captiva Islands. Community programs include: Land acquisition, habitat management, landscaping for wildlife,

research (estuarine marine research laboratory), education, and sea turtle conservation program. The Foundation utilizes the time and talent of over 250 dedicated volunteers.

Publication(s): Stewardship Update, Growing Native, Conservation Update, Bighorn, The, Walk in the Wetlands

Keyword(s): Land Issues, Water Habitats & Quality

Contact(s):
Kristie Anders, Education Director
Erick Lindblad, Executive Director
Kathy Boone, Native Plant Nursery Manager
Jean Laswell, Business Manager
David Ceilley, Restoration Ecologist

SASKATCHEWAN WILDLIFE FEDERATION

444 River St., W.
Moose Jaw, S6H 6J6 Saskatchewan Canada
Phone: 306-692-8812 Fax: 306-692-4370
E-mail: sask.wildlife@sk.sympatico.ca
Website: www.swf.sk.ca

Founded: 1929
Membership: 10,001–100,000
Scope: State

Description: Affiliated with the Canadian Wildlife Federation. A nonprofit, citizens' conservation group established for the protection and enhancement of fish and wildlife habitat. One hundred and thirty-seven local branches representing 32,000 members. Includes the Habitat Trust Fund holding title to 15,000 purchased and donated acres, and the Wildlife Tomorrow Program with 400,000 acres under free easement.

Publication(s): Outdoor Edge

Contact(s):
Joe Schemenauer, President
Sandra Dewald, Office Manager; 444 River St. W., Moose Jaw, Saskatchewan S6H 6J6; 306-692-8812
James Kroshus, Land Coordinator; 444 River St. W., Moose Jaw, Saskatchewan S6H 6J6; 306-693-9022

SAVE AMERICAS FORESTS

4 Library Ct., SE
Washington, DC 20003 United States
Phone: 202-544-9219
E-mail: info@saveamericasforest.org
Website: www.saveamericasforests.org

Founded: 1990
Membership: 1,001–10,000
Scope: National

Description: A nationwide coalition of grassroots regional and national environmental groups, public interest groups, responsible businesses, and individuals working together to pass strong forest protection legislation in the U.S. Congress.

Keyword(s): Development/Developing Countries, Forests/Forestry, Public Lands/Greenspace, Wildlife & Species

Contact(s):
Carl Ross, Director

SAVE OUR RIVERS, INC.

P.O. Box 122
Franklin, NC 28744 United States
Phone: 828-369-7877 Fax: 828-369-7877
E-mail: rivers@dnet.net

Founded: 1990

Scope: State

Description: Committed to facilitating active public involvement in decisions concerning our rivers by providing information, initiating programs, encouraging public awareness, promoting coordination of services, activities, resources and opportunities.

Publication(s): The Current

Keyword(s): Ethics/Environmental Justice, Oceans/Coasts/Beaches, Pollution (general), Reduce/Reuse/Recycle, Water Habitats & Quality

Contact(s):
Peg Jones, President

SAVE SAN FRANCISCO BAY ASSOCIATION

SAVE THE BAY
1600 Broadway
Suite 300
Oakland, CA 94612 United States
Phone: 510-452-9261 Fax: 510-452-9266
E-mail: savebay@savesfbay.org
Website: www.savesfbay.org

Founded: 1961
Membership: 10,001–100,000
Scope: Regional

Description: Member-supported, non-profit environmental organization dedicated to restoring and protecting San Francisco Bay. We work for the improvement of water quality, adequate fresh water inflow and protection of the Bay's plant, wildlife, fish and human populations and their habitats. Our efforts are focused on public education, collaboration with other organizations, coalition-building, litigation, the monitoring of regulatory agencies and input into the legislative process.

Publication(s): Protecting Local Wetlands, Volunteer Opportunities, Watershed, information fact sheets

Keyword(s): Ecosystems (precious), Ethics/Environmental Justice, Oceans/Coasts/Beaches, Pollution (general), Public Health, Recreation/Ecotourism, Reduce/Reuse/Recycle, Sprawl/Urban Planning, Transportation, Water Habitats & Quality, Wildlife & Species

Contact(s):
Ralph Benson, President
Joe Engbeck, Vice President
David Lewis, Executive Director
Dirk Manskopf, Grassroots Coordinator; dirk@savesfbay.org
Paul Revier, Outreach and Communications Director

SAVE THE BAY - PEOPLE FOR NARRAGANSETT BAY

434 Smith St.
Providence, RI 02908-3770 United States
Phone: 401-272-3540 Fax: 401-273-7153
E-mail: savebay@savebay.org
Website: www.savebay.org

Founded: 1970
Membership: 10,001–100,000
Scope: Local, State, Regional

Description: Save the Bay is dedicated to protecting, restoring and exploring Narragansett Bay—a designated estuary of national significance. As a nonprofit, member-supported environmental organization, Save the Bay works to ensure that the environmental quality of Narragansett Bay and its watershed is restored and protected from the harmful effects of human activity.

Publication(s): Coastal Property and Landscape Management Guidebook, The Uncommon Guide to Common Life of Narragansett Bay, Backyards on the Bay: A Yard Care Guide for the Coastal Home Owner.

Keyword(s): Ecosystems (precious), Land Issues, Oceans/Coasts/Beaches, Pollution (general), Public Lands/Greenspace, Recreation/Ecotourism, Sprawl/Urban Planning, Water Habitats & Quality

Contact(s):
H. Spalding, Executive Director

SAVE THE DUNES CONSERVATION FUND

444 Barker Rd.
Michigan City, IN 46360 United States
Phone: 219-879-3564 Fax: 219-872-4875
Website: www.savedunes.org

Founded: 1994
Membership: 101–1,000

Scope: Local, Regional

Description: The Mission of Save the Dunes Conservation Fund is to preserve, protect, and restore the Indiana Dunes and all natural resources in Northwest Indiana's Lake Michigan Watershed for an enhanced quality of life. This Mission is pursued ethically with perserverance, credibility, nonpartisanship, informed positions, and a holistic approach.

Publication(s): Save the Dunes (newsletter)

Keyword(s): Ecosystems (precious), Water Habitats & Quality, Wildlife & Species

Contact(s):

Thomas Anderson, Executive Director
Sandra Wilmore, Fund Director

SAVE THE DUNES COUNCIL

444 Barker Rd.
Michigan City, IN 46360 United States
Phone: 219-879-3937 Fax: 219-872-4875
E-mail: std@savedunes.org
Website: www.savedunes.org

Founded: 1952

Membership: 101–1,000

Scope: National

Description: Dedicated to the preservation of the Indiana Dunes National Lakeshore for public use and enjoyment. Concerned with protecting the ecological values of the dunes region, preserving Lake Michigan, and combating air, water, and hazardous waste pollution. Established by Dorothy Buell.

Publication(s): Newsletter

Keyword(s): Air Quality/Atmosphere, Land Issues, Oceans/Coasts/Beaches, Public Lands/Greenspace, Recreation/Ecotourism

Contact(s):

Thomas Serynek, President; 1000 N. Warrick, Gary, IN 46403; 219-938-5410
Dorothy Potucek, 1st Vice President; 1608 Parkview Ave., Whiting, IN 46394
Thomas Anderson, Executive Director
Sandra Wilmore, Program Director
Christine Livingston, Administrative Assistant
Mark Mihalo, Treasurer; 8 Diana Road, Ogden Dunes, Portage, IN 46368; 219-763-4871
Charlotte Read, Assistant Director

SAVE THE HARBOR/SAVE THE BAY

59 Temple Pl., Suite 304
Boston, MA 02111 United States
Phone: 617-451-2860 Fax: 617-451-0496
E-mail: wolfe@savetheharbor.org
Website: www.savetheharbor.org

Founded: 1986

Membership: 1,001–10,000

Scope: State

Description: Save the Harbor/Save the Bay is a nonprofit organization whose mission is to foster a positive vision of Boston Harbor and Massachusetts Bay, and to build a broad-based constituency to promote the restoration and protection of these valuable resources. Services include narrated boat tours of Boston Harbor, discussions of harbor pollution, cleanup projects, history, celebratory events, summer youth program, and a Baywatch Program.

Publication(s): Splash (newsletter)

Keyword(s): Oceans/Coasts/Beaches, Water Habitats & Quality

Contact(s):

Bruce Berman, Baywatch & Communications Director
Patricia Foley, Exec. Director
Lisa Mantoni, Program Coordinator; ext. 102; mantoni@savetheharbor.org
Beth Nicholson, Chairperson & President
Matt Wolfe, Events Coordinator

SAVE THE MANATEE CLUB

500 N. Maitland Ave.
Maitland, FL 32751 United States
Phone: 407-539-0990 Fax: 407-539-0871
E-mail: education@savethemanatee.org
Website: www.savethemanatee.org

Founded: 1981

Membership: 10,001–100,000

Scope: International

Description: A national nonprofit organization founded by Governor Bob Graham and singer and songwriter Jimmy Buffett. Objectives are public awareness and education; funding research, rescue, rehabilitation and advocacy and appropriate legal action for the endangered West Indian manatee and its habitat. Funded primarily by the club's Adopt-A-Manatee program.

Keyword(s): Wildlife & Species

Contact(s):

Nancy Sadusky, Communications Director
Judith Vallee, Executive Director
Jimmy Buffett, Co-Chairman
Helen Spivey, Co-Chairman

SAVE-THE-REDWOODS LEAGUE

114 Sansome St., Suite 1200
San Francisco, CA 94104 United States
Phone: 415-362-2352 Fax: 415-362-7017
E-mail: info@savetheredwoods.org
Website: www.savetheredwoods.org

Founded: 1918

Membership: 10,001–100,000

Scope: State

Description: The League purchases redwood forest and associated lands for inclusion in State and Federal parks and reserves. The League also sponsors research and education through a grants program. Please visit www.savetheredwoods.org for more information.

Publication(s): California Redwood Parks and Preserves, Redwoods of the Past, The Redwood Forest, Trees, Shrubs and Flowers of the Redwood, Bulletin.

Keyword(s): Ecosystems (precious), Forests/Forestry, Public Lands/Greenspace, Wildlife & Species

Contact(s):

Richard Otter, President of the Board
Kate Anderton, Secretary and Executive Director
Bruce Howard, Chairman of the Board
Frank Westworth, Treasurer; P.O. Box 44614, San Francisco, CA 94144-0001

SAVE THE SOUND, INC.

20 Marshall Street
South Norwalk, CT 06854 United States
Phone: 203-354-0036 Fax: 203-354-0041
E-mail: savethesound@savethesound.org
Website: www.savethesound.org

Founded: 1972

Membership: 1,001–10,000

Scope: Local, State, Regional, National

Description: Save the Sound, Inc. is devoted to protecting, restoring, and appreciating Long Island Sound and its watershed. With a staff of nine full-time employees and additional seasonal employees, STS operates year-round programs in education, research, and advocacy, including Sea Camp, Soundshore Ecology, water quality monitoring, habitat restoration, beach cleanups, and an extensive library.

Publication(s): Annual Water Quality Report, SoundBites, Long Island Sound Municipal Report Cards, Water Quality Monitoring: A Guide for Concerned Citizens.

Keyword(s): Ecosystems (precious), Executive/Legislative/Judicial Reform, Pollution (general), Public Lands/Greenspace, Sprawl/Urban Planning, Water Habitats & Quality

Contact(s):
John Atkin, President; 203-354-0036; Fax: 203-354-0041; jatkin@savethesound.org
John Brooks, Vice President, Marketing & Development; 203-354-0036; Fax: 203-354-0041; jbrooks@savethesound.org
Bridgett Byrnes, Director of Education; 203-354-0036; Fax: 203-354-0041; bbyrnes@savethesound.org
Leah Lopez, Staff Attorney; 203-354-0036; Fax: 203-354-0041; llopez@savethesound.org
William Shadel, Director of Research and Restoration; 203-354-0036; Fax: 203-354-0041; wshadel@savethesound.org

SAVE THE SOUND, INC.

GARVIES POINT MUSEUM
50 Barry Dr.
Glen Cove, NY 11542 United States
Phone: 516-759-2165 Fax: 516-759-0644
E-mail: savethesound@savethesound.org
Website: www.savethesound,org

Founded: 1972
Membership: 1,001–10,000
Scope: Local, State, Regional, National
Description: Save the Sound is dedicated to protecting and restoring Long Island Sound and its watershed through advocacy, education and research.
Publication(s): Long Island Sound Conservation Blueprint, SoundBites.
Keyword(s): Ecosystems (precious), Executive/Legislative/Judicial Reform, Pollution (general), Public Lands/Greenspace, Sprawl/Urban Planning, Water Habitats & Quality
Contact(s):
John Atkin, President; 516-759-2165; Fax: 203-354-0041; jatkin@savethesound.org
John Brooks, Vice President, Marketing and Development; 516-759-2165; Fax: 203-354-0041; jbrooks@savethesound.org
Bridgett Byrnes, Director of Education; 516-759-2165; Fax: 203-354-0041; bbyrnes@savethesound.org

SAVE WETLANDS AND BAYS

24353 Thorneby Trace
Millsboro, DE 19966 United States
Phone: 302-945-1317 Fax: 302-945-1317

Founded: 1989
Membership: 101–1,000
Scope: Local
Description: To protect Delaware's inland bays and fringing marshes from perceived threats.
Contact(s):
Til Purnell, Executive Director; purnell@ce.net

SCENIC AMERICA

801 Pennsylvania Ave., SE, Suite 300
Washington, DC 20003 United States
Phone: 202-543-6200 Fax: 202-543-9130
E-mail: scenic@scenic.org
Website: www.scenic.org

Founded: 1978
Membership: 1,001–10,000
Scope: National
Description: National membership organization dedicated to preserving and enhancing the scenic character of America's communities and countryside. Provides information and technical assistance on billboard and sign control, scenic byways, tree preservation, highway design, cellular tower siting, and other scenic conservation issues.
Publication(s): Scenic News, Viewpoints, series of videos and technical bulletins, Fighting Billboard Blight: An Action Guide for Citizens and Elected Officials
Keyword(s): Land Issues, Reduce/Reuse/Recycle
Contact(s):
Meg Maguire, President
Kathryn Whitmire, Chairman

SCENIC AMERICA

SCENIC CALIFORNIA
c/o LSA Associates, 2215 Fifth Street
Berkeley, CA 94710 United States
Phone: 510-540-7331
E-mail: sceniccalifornia@earthlink.net
Website: www.sceniccalifornia.org

Founded: 1998
Scope: State
Description: Scenic California is dedicated to protecting natural beauty in the environment, preserving and enhancing landscapes and streetscapes, protecting historical and cultural resources, promoting the enhancement of scenic approaches and settings of cities and towns, improving community appearance and fostering the establishment and preservation of scenic roads and viewsheds.
Contact(s):
Sheila Brady, Manager

SCENIC AMERICA

SCENIC HUDSON, INC.
9 Vassar St.
Poughkeepsie, NY 12601 United States
Phone: 845-473-4440
E-mail: info@scenichudson.org
Website: www.scenichudson.org

Founded: 1963
Membership: N/A
Scope: Local, State, Regional
Description: A nonprofit conservation and environmental organization dedicated to protecting and enhancing the scenic, natural, recreational and historic treasures of the Hudson River Valley. Speakers' Bureau available to the public.
Publication(s): Scenic Hudson News, Adventure Guide
Keyword(s): Agriculture/Farming, Air Quality/Atmosphere, Land Issues, Pollution (general), Public Lands/Greenspace, Sprawl/Urban Planning, Water Habitats & Quality
Contact(s):
Ned Sullivan, President
Jay Burgess, Communications & Public Outreach Program Director
Deborah DeWan, Riverfront Communities Program Director
Alix Gerosa, Environmental Quality Program Director
Warren Reiss, General Counsel
Erin Riley-West, Development Director
Steve Rosenberg, Executive Director, The Scenic Hudson Land Trust, Inc.
Theresa Vanyo, Human Resources Director
Marjorie Hart, Chairman
Joseph Kazlauskas, CFO & COO

SCENIC AMERICA

SCENIC MICHIGAN
445 E. Mitchell St.
Petoskey, MI 49770 United States
Phone: 231-347-1171 Fax: 231-347-1185
E-mail: info@scenicmichigan.org
Website: www.scenicmichigan.org

Founded: N/A
Scope: State
Description: Scenic Michigan started under the aegis of Michigan United Conservation Clubs, the largest nonprofit conservation organization in the United States, as a billboard control task force in 1989. The mission of Scenic Michigan is to protect and enhance the appearance and scenic character of Michigan's communities and countryside.

Publication(s): Recommended Elements of a Sign Ordinance
Contact(s):
Debbie Rohe, President
Julie Metty, Vice President
Rick Barber, Admin. Asst.; 231-347-1171; Fax: 231-347-1185; rick@scenicmichigan.org
Bethany Goodman, Secretary
Mary Tanton, Treasurer

SCENIC AMERICA
SCENIC MISSOURI
5650-A S. Sinclair Rd.
Columbia, MO 65203-8611 United States
Phone: 573-446-3129 Fax: 573-443-3748
E-mail: scenicmo@tranquility.net
Website: www.scenicmissouri.org

Founded: 1993
Membership: 101–1,000
Scope: State
Description: Scenic Missouri was founded because of a growing concern about the loss of Missouri's scenic heritage. Its mission is to preserve and enhance the scenic beauty of Missouri.
Publication(s): Model Ordinance, Scenic Views, Scenic Missouri web site.
Keyword(s): Public Lands/Greenspace, Sprawl/Urban Planning, Transportation
Contact(s):
Karl Kruse, Executive Director; 573-446-3129; Fax: 573-443-3748; scenicmo@tranquility.net
Amelia Miner Cottle, Membership Director; 573-446-3120; Fax: 573-443-3748; scenicmo@tranquility.net

SCENIC AMERICA
SCENIC NORTH CAROLINA INC.
P.O. Box 628
Raleigh, NC 27602 United States
Phone: 919-832-3687 Fax: 919-832-3299
E-mail: scenic.nc@worldnet.att.net
Website: www.scenicnc.org

Founded: N/A
Scope: State
Description: Our sense of identity as North Carolinians is tied to special places and buildings and views. Each type of landscape has its own kind of beauty, character and uniqueness. Scenic North Carolina is dedicated to preserving and enhancing scenic resources and community appearance in North Carolina.
Publication(s): Scenic North Carolina News
Contact(s):
Dale McKeel, Executive Director

SCENIC AMERICA
SCENIC TEXAS
3015 Richmond Suite 220
Houston, TX 77098 United States
Phone: 713-629-0481 Fax: 713-629-0485
E-mail: scenic@scenictexas.org
Website: www.scenictexas.org

Founded: N/A
Membership: 1,001–10,000
Scope: State
Description: The mission of Scenic Texas is to preserve and enhance the scenic character of the visual environment. Scenic Texas has chapters in Houston, Austin, San Antonio, Fort Worth, and Galveston.
Publication(s): Scenic Views
Contact(s):
Cece Fowler, Executive Director

SCIENTISTS CENTER FOR ANIMAL WELFARE
7833 Walker Drive, Suite 410
Greenbelt, MD 20770 United States
Phone: 301-345-3500 Fax: 301-345-3503
E-mail: info@scaw.com
Website: www.scaw.com

Founded: 1978
Membership: 1,001–10,000
Scope: National, International
Description: A nonprofit educational organization that promotes the belief that high standards of animal welfare complement the quality of scientific results. SCAW publishes educational material about current issues of animal use in research, testing, and teaching.
Publication(s): SCAW (Newsletter), see publications on website
Keyword(s): Oceans/Coasts/Beaches, Public Health, Wildlife & Species
Contact(s):
Lee Krulisch, Executive Director

SEA SHEPHERD CONSERVATION SOCIETY
22774 Pacific Coast Hwy.
Malibu, CA 90265 United States
Phone: 310-456-1141 Fax: 310-456-2488
Website: www.seashepherd.com

Founded: 1977
Scope: International
Description: An international direct action marine mammal conservation organization involved in stopping marine mammal slaughters. Special projects include: campaigns against drift net fishing, whaling, the Faeroese pilot whale slaughter, and sealing. The Society owns and operates three ships, the Ocean Warrior, the submarine Mirage and the Edward Abbey.
Publication(s): Sea Shepherd Log Quarterly
Keyword(s): Wildlife & Species
Contact(s):
Andrew Christie, Information Director; andrew@seashepherd.org
Paul Watson, Editor
Paul Watson, Founder

SEA SHEPHERD CONSERVATION SOCIETY
AUSTRALIA OFFICE
P.O. Box A2330
Sydney South, NSW 1235 Australia
E-mail: seashepherd@chili.net.au

Founded: N/A
Scope: National
Description: Sea Shepherd is dedicated to the protection of marine ecosystems and biodiversity. The Sea Shepherd Conservation Organization Society was founded by Paul Watson in 1977 as a non-profit "direct action" organization, and for 24 years, we have been in the forefront of marine wildlife conservation. Sea Shepherd is known for aggressive confrontation and the use of media to bring attention to illegal and hidden practices.

SEA SHEPHERD CONSERVATION SOCIETY
CANADA OFFICE
P.O. Box 2670
Malibu, V7X 1A2 Canada
Phone: 310-456-1141 Fax: 310-456-2248
E-mail: seashepherd@cshepherd.org
Website: www.seashepherd.org

Founded: N/A
Membership: 10,001–100,000
Scope: International
Publication(s): Ocean Warrior, Annual Report, Captain Log, Earth Force

Contact(s):
Pepper Fernandez, Executive Director

SEA SHEPHERD CONSERVATION SOCIETY

EUROPEAN COMMUNITY
Liendense Singel 30
Lienden, 4033 KJ Netherlands
Phone: 31-344-604-130
E-mail: seashepherd@seashepherd.org
Website: seashepherd.org

Founded: 1977

Scope: International

Description: Sea Shepherd is dedicated to the protection of marine ecosystems and biodiversity. The Sea Shepherd Conservation Organization Society was founded by Paul Watson in 1977 as a non-profit "direct action" organization, and for 24 years, we have been in the forefront of marine wildlife conservation. Sea Shepherd is known for aggressive confrontation and the use of media to bring attention to illegal and hidden practices.

Keyword(s): Ecosystems (precious), Oceans/Coasts/Beaches, Wildlife & Species

Contact(s):
Ivor Verbon, Volunteer; Liendense Singel 30, Lienden 4033 KJ; wizzard@xs4al.nl

SEA SHEPHERD CONSERVATION SOCIETY

GREAT BRITAIN OFFICE
35 Vicarage Grove
London, SE5 7LY United Kingdom
Website: www.seashepherd.nl/index

Founded: N/A

Scope: National

SEA SHEPHERD CONSERVATION SOCIETY

NETHERLANDS OFFICE
P.O. Box 97702
2509 GC The Hague, Netherlands

Founded: N/A

Scope: National

SEA SHEPHERD CONSERVATION SOCIETY

USA OFFICE
22774 Pacific Coast Highway
Malibu, CA 90265 United States
Phone: 310-456-1141 Fax: 310-456-2488
E-mail: seashepherd@seashepherd.org
Website: www.seashepherd.org

Founded: 1979
Membership: 1,001–10,000
Scope: National, International

Description: The Sea Shepherd Conservation Society has been actively engaged in marine wildlife conservation for over 20 years. A non-profit organization SSCS is involved with the investigation and documentation of violations of international laws, regulations and treaties that maintain global biodiversity through the protection of marine wildlife species, and utilizes many innovative approaches to marine conservation. Sea Shepherd publishes a quarterly newsletter which contains reports and updates of SSCS

Publication(s): The Log

Contact(s):
Capt. Paul Watson, Founder and President
Andrew Christie, Information Director
Jose Fernandez, Executive Director
Angela Navarro, Accounts Manager

SEA TURTLE PRESERVATION SOCIETY

P.O. Box 910588
Melbourne Beach, FL 32951 United States
Phone: 321-676-1701
Website: SeaTurtleSpaceCoast.org

Founded: 1982
Membership: 101–1,000
Scope: Local

Description: Nonprofit conservation group located in Brevard County working for preservation of sea turtles along Florida's East Coast. Largest turtle rescue & recovery program in state. Conducting educational presentations and walks to over 5000 visitors each year under Florida Fish & Wildlife Conservation Commission (FFWCC) permits.

Publication(s): STPS Newsletter.

Keyword(s): Ecosystems (precious), Oceans/Coasts/Beaches, Water Habitats & Quality, Wildlife & Species

Contact(s):
Richard Winn, Chairman; 321-984-2960; Fax: 321-951-0701; rjpjotb@Juno.com
Christin Stewart, Managing Director; 321-676-1701

SEACAMP ASSOCIATION, INC.

1300 Big Pine Ave.
Big Pine Key, FL 33043-3336 United States
Phone: 305-872-2331 Fax: 305-872-2555
E-mail: info@seacamp.org
Website: www.seacamp.org

Founded: 1964

Scope: International

Description: Non-profit organization encompassing two marine education organizations in the Florida Keys, a summer camp and the school program Newfound Harbor Marine Institute (NHMI). Strong international program with Russia. Member NAAEE.

Keyword(s): Oceans/Coasts/Beaches, Recreation/Ecotourism, Water Habitats & Quality

Contact(s):
Russel Bachert, Director of Special Projects
John Booker, Program Director
Chuck Brand, Institute Director, NHMI
Mary Hensel, Development Director
Irene Hooper, Executive Director
Elena Istoma, Director of International Programs
Grace Upshaw, Camp Director

SEACOAST ANTI-POLLUTION LEAGUE

P.O. Box 1136
Portsmouth, NH 03802 United States
Phone: 603-431-5089
Website: www.sapl.org

Founded: 1969

Scope: State

Description: To promote the wise use of natural resources of the seacoast region, and to alert and educate the community and relevant government agencies of threats to the environment. SAPL works to prevent ecological, economic and public health damage from the Seabrook nuclear reactor, the Portsmouth Naval Shipyard and over-development.

Keyword(s): Development/Developing Countries, Energy

Contact(s):
Davie Hills, President
Mary Metcalf, Vice President
Steve Haberman, Executive Director
Jim Horrigan, Treasurer
Johanna Lyons, Secretary
Peter Vandermark, Tag Coordinator

SEAPLANE PILOTS ASSOCIATION

4315 Highland Park Blvd. Suite C
Lakeland, FL 33813 United States
Phone: 301-695-2083
Website: www.seaplanes.org

Founded: 1972
Membership: 1,001–10,000
Scope: National
Description: A unit formed to provide seaplane services to agencies and environmental groups involved in forest fire detection, search and rescue, wildlife surveys, pollution patrols, and other related environmental and ecological projects.
Publication(s): Water Flying, Water Landing Directory, Water Flying Annual
Keyword(s): Oceans/Coasts/Beaches, Recreation/Ecotourism, Water Habitats & Quality
Contact(s):
J. Frey, President
Walter Windus, Vice President
Michael Volk, Executive Director
Jerry Potter, Secretary

SEAWEB

1731 Connecticut Ave., 4th Floor
Washington, DC 20009 United States
Phone: 202-483-9570 Fax: 202-483-9354
E-mail: seaweb@seaweb.org
Website: www.seaweb.org

Founded: 1996
Scope: National, International
Description: SeaWeb was launched in 1996 to raise awareness about the growing threat to the ocean and its living resources. SeaWeb's goal is to make ocean protection a high environmental priority in the U.S. and around the world. SeaWeb provides science-based information from a variety of sources to a variety of media outlets. With the help of scientists, educators, researchers and communications specialists, SeaWeb has become a respected independent resource for journalists, and government officials.
Keyword(s): Oceans/Coasts/Beaches
Contact(s):
Jessica Brown

SHEEPSCOT VALLEY CONSERVATION ASSOCIATION, THE

P.O. Box 125
Alna, ME 04535 United States
Phone: 207-586-5616 Fax: 207-586-6442
E-mail: svca@lincoln.midcoast.com
Website: www.lincoln.midcoast.com/~svca

Founded: 1970
Membership: 101–1,000
Scope: Local, State, Regional
Description: Our mission is to conserve and restore the natural and historic heritage of the Sheepscot Watershed.
Contact(s):
Sam Merrill, Executive Director

SHELBURNE FARMS

1611 Harbor Rd.
Shelburne, VT 05482 United States
Phone: 802-985-8686 Fax: 802-985-8123
Website: www.shelburnefarms.org/

Founded: N/A
Membership: 1,001–10,000
Scope: Local, State, Regional, National, International
Description: Shelburne Farms is a 1,400 acre working farm, National Historic Landmark and non-profit environmental education center. Our mission is to cultivate a conservation ethic by teaching and demonstrating stewardship of our natural and agricultural resources.
Publication(s): This Lake Alive, Project Seasons
Keyword(s): Agriculture/Farming, Forests/Forestry, Land Issues, Recreation/Ecotourism, Water Habitats & Quality
Contact(s):
Alexander Webb, President; ext. 16; awebb@shelburnefarms.org
Megan Camp, VP and Program Director; ext. 14; mcamp@shelburnefarms.org
Linda Wellings, School Programs Director; ext. 27; jelson@shelburnefarms.org

SIERRA CLUB

85 2nd St.
San Francisco, CA 94105-3459 United States
Phone: 415-977-5500 Fax: 415-977-5799
E-mail: information@sierraclub.org
Website: www.sierraclub.org/

Founded: 1892
Membership: 500,001–1,000,000
Scope: National
Description: To explore, enjoy, and protect the wild places of the earth; to practice and promote the responsible use of the earth's ecosystems and resources; to educate and enlist humanity to protect and restore the quality of the natural and human environment; and to use all lawful means to carry out these objectives. With 65 chapters and 396 groups in North America, the Club's nonprofit program work includes legislation, litigation, public information, publishing, wilderness outings, and conferences.
Publication(s): Sierra, chapter and group newsletters, Planet, The
Keyword(s): Air Quality/Atmosphere, Energy, Pollution (general), Public Lands/Greenspace
Contact(s):
Jennifer Ferenstein, President; jennifer.ferenstein@sierraclub.org
Charlie Ogle, Vice President
Bob Bingaman, Director of Conservation Field Services
Gene Coan, Senior Advisor to the Executive Director
Kim Haddow, Communication Director
Bruce Hamilton, Associate Executive Director of Conservation and Communication.
Carl Pope, Executive Director
Joan Hamilton, Editor-In-Chief of Sierra
Helen Sweetland, Publisher of Books

SIERRA CLUB

2906 Medical Arts St.
Austin, TX 78705 United States
Phone: 512-472-9094 Fax: 512-472-8710
E-mail: txar@earthlink.net
Website: www.sierraclub.org

Founded: 1892
Membership: 500,001–1,000,000
Scope: Local, Regional, National
Description: National representatives of the Sierra Club. Assisting volunteers in the planning and implimentation of grassroots based conservation campaigns.
Contact(s):
Alejandro Queral, Border Representative
Larry Freilich, Representative
Ayelet Hines, End Commercial Logging on Public Land Organizer
Nicole Holt, Global Warming & Energy Program Organizer

SIERRA CLUB

1330 21st Way South, Suite 110
Birmingham, AL 35205 United States
Phone: 205-972-0252
Website: alabama.sierraclub.org/

Founded: N/A
Scope: State

Contact(s):
Jay Hudson, Chair; 205-972-0252; jayhudson@mindspring.com

SIERRA CLUB
13114 W. 125th Terrace
Overland Park, KS 66213-2463 United States
Phone: 913-402-9244 Fax: 913-402-7244
E-mail: wildlife1@aol.com
Website: www.kssierra.org/

Founded: N/A

Scope: State

Contact(s):
Scott Smith, Chair; 9844 Georgia Avenue, Kansas City, KS 66109; 785-539-1973; wizard1@kscable.com

SIERRA CLUB
921 N. Congress St.
Jackson, MS 39202-2554 United States
Phone: 601-352-1026
Website: mississippi.sierraclub.org/

Founded: N/A

Scope: State

SIERRA CLUB
ALASKA CHAPTER
P.O. Box 103441
Anchorage, AK 99501-3441 United States
Phone: 907-276-4048 Fax: 907-276-4048
E-mail: nw-ak.field@sierraclub.org
Website: www.sierraclub.org/chapters/ak/

Founded: N/A

Scope: State

SIERRA CLUB
ALASKA OFFICE
201 Barrow St.
Suite 101
Anchorage, AK 99501-2429 United States
Phone: 907-276-4068 Fax: 907-258-6807
E-mail: nw-ak.field@sierraclub.org
Website: www.sierraclubalaska.org

Founded: 1892
Membership: 1,001–10,000
Scope: Regional
Description: Purpose is to explore, enjoy and protect the wild places of the earth; practice and promote responsible use of earth's ecosystems/resources.

Contact(s):
Maryellen Oman, Program Assistant; 907-276-4068; Fax: 907-258-6807; maryellen@sierraclubalaska.org
Sara Callaghan-Chapell, Regional Representative; 907-276-4088; Fax: 907-258-6807; sara@sierraclubalaska.org
Jack Hession, Senior Regional Representative; 907-276-4078; Fax: 907-258-6807; jack@sierraclubalaska.org

SIERRA CLUB
ANGELES CHAPTER
3435 Wiltshire Blvd., Suite 320
Los Angeles, CA 90010-1904 United States
Phone: 213-387-4287 Fax: 213-387-5383
E-mail: info@angeleschapter.org
Website: www.angeleschapter.sierraclub.org

Founded: N/A

Scope: Local, Regional

Publication(s): The Southern Sierran, The Schedule of Activities (quarterly)

Contact(s):
Bill Corcoran, Public Lands Coordinator
Martin Schlageter, Conservation Coordinator

SIERRA CLUB
APPALACHIAN FIELD OFFICE
200 N. Glebe Rd., Suite 905
Arlington, VA 22203-3728 United States
Phone: 703-312-0533 Fax: 703-312-0508
E-mail: ap-va.field@sierraclub.org
Website: www.sierraclub.org

Founded: N/A

Scope: Regional

Description: DC, DE, GA, MD, NC, SC, TN, VA, WV

Contact(s):
Joy Oakes, Appalachian Field Director

SIERRA CLUB
ATLANTIC CHAPTER
116 John St.
New York, NY 10038-3401 United States
Phone: 212-791-2400 Fax: 212-791-0839
E-mail: atlantic.chapter@sierraclub.org
Website: www.atlantic.sierraclub.org

Founded: N/A
Membership: 10,001–100,000
Scope: State
Publication(s): Sierra Atlantic

SIERRA CLUB
ATLANTIC COAST OFFICE
P.O. Box 160
Nassau, DE 19969 United States
Phone: 902-422-5091 Fax: 302-644-9712
Website: www.sierraclub.org

Founded: N/A

Scope: Regional

SIERRA CLUB
BAY AREA FIELD OFFICE
827 Broadway, Suite 310
Oakland, CA 94607 United States
Phone: 510-622-0290 Fax: 510-622-0278
E-mail: ca-oa.field@sierraclub.org
Website: www.sierraclub.org/ca

Founded: 1892

Scope: Regional

Description: Regional Field Office for National Sierra Club priorities, ranging from Wilderness Preservation to Energy Action Network

SIERRA CLUB
BRITISH COLUMBIA CHAPTER
576 Johnson St.
Victoria, V8W 1M3 British Columbia Canada
Phone: 250-386-5255 Fax: 250-386-4453
E-mail: info@sierraclubbc.org
Website: www.sierraclub.ca/bc/

Founded: N/A

Scope: Regional

Publication(s): The Sierra Report - magazine

Contact(s):
Bill Warham, Executive Director

SIERRA CLUB
CALIFORNIA/NEVADA/HAWAII OFFICE AND CALIFORNIA LEGISLATIVE OFFICE
1414 K St., Suite 300
Sacramento, CA 95814-3929 United States
Phone: 916-557-1100 Fax: 916-557-9669

Founded: N/A
Membership: 101–1,000
Scope: Regional
Contact(s):
Barbara Boyle, Staff Director
Bill Craven, State Director

SIERRA CLUB
CASCADE CHAPTER
8511 15th Ave. NE, Rm. 201
Seattle, WA 98115-3101 United States
Phone: 206-523-2147
E-mail: cascade.chapter@sierraclub.org
Website: www.cascade.sierraclub.org/

Founded: N/A
Membership: 10,001–100,000
Scope: Local, State
Description: Representing more than 25,000 Sierra Club members in Western and Central Washington State.
Publication(s): The Cascade Crest.
Contact(s):
Roy Goodman, Chapter Coordinator

SIERRA CLUB
CLEVELAND OFFICE
2460 Fairmont Blvd., Suite C
Cleveland, OH 44106-3125 United States
Phone: 216-791-9110 Fax: 216-791-9138
E-mail: mw-oh.field@sierraclub.org
Website: www.sierraclub.org

Founded: N/A
Membership: 500,001–1,000,000
Scope: National
Contact(s):
Glenn Landers, Clean Air Specialist

SIERRA CLUB
COLORADO FIELD OFFICE
2260 Baseline Rd., Suite 105
Boulder, CO 80302-7737 United States
Phone: 303-449-5595 Fax: 303-449-6520
E-mail: sw-co.field@sierraclub.org
Website: www.sierraclub.org

Founded: N/A
Membership: 10,001–100,000
Scope: Regional

SIERRA CLUB
COLUMBIA BASIN OFFICE
85 Second St., Second Floor
San Francisco, CA 94105 United States
Phone: 415-977-5500 Fax: 415-977-7579
E-mail: nw-cb.field@sierraclub.org
Website: www.sierraclub.org

Founded: N/A
Scope: Regional

SIERRA CLUB
CONNECTICUT CHAPTER
118 Oak St.
Hartford, CT 06106-1514 United States
Phone: 860-525-2500
Website: www.sierraclub.org/chapters/ct/

Founded: N/A
Scope: State

SIERRA CLUB
CUMBERLAND CHAPTER
259 W. Short St.
Lexington, KY 40507-1226 United States
Phone: 806-299-4410
Website: www.sierraclub.org/chapters/ky/

Founded: 1968
Scope: State

SIERRA CLUB
DACOTAH CHAPTER
311 E. Thayer #113
Bismarck, ND 58501 United States
Phone: 701-530-9288 Fax: 701-530-9290
Website: www.sierraclub.org/chapters/nd/

Founded: N/A
Membership: 101–1,000
Scope: Local, State
Description: Grassroots environmental organization
Publication(s): Dakota Prairie, newsletter
Keyword(s): Agriculture/Farming, Air Quality/Atmosphere, Climate Change, Ecosystems (precious), Energy, Ethics/Environmental Justice, Land Issues, Pollution (general), Public Health, Public Lands/Greenspace, Recreation/Ecotourism, Reduce/Reuse/Recycle, Sprawl/Urban Planning
Contact(s):
Jonathan Bry, Conservation Organizer; 701-530-9288; Fax: 701-530-9290; jonathan.bry@sierraclub.org

SIERRA CLUB
DELAWARE CHAPTER
1304 N. Rodney St.
Wilmington, DE 19806 United States
Phone: 302-425-4911
E-mail: delaware.chapter@sierraclub.org
Website: delaware.sierraclub.org

Founded: N/A
Scope: State
Description: Delaware Sierra Club
Publication(s): Chapter Newsletter.
Contact(s):
Matt Urban, Chapter Chair; 302-661-2050; mattsierra@yepatata.com
Shiray Shipley, Chapter Coordinator; 302-425-4911; shiray.shipley@sierraclub.org

SIERRA CLUB
DELTA CHAPTER
P.O. Box 19469
New Orleans, LA 70179-0469 United States
Phone: 504-836-3062
E-mail: delta.chapter@sierraclub.org
Website: www.sierraclub.org/chapters/la/

Founded: N/A
Scope: State

SIERRA CLUB
EASTERN CANADA CHAPTER
24 Mercer St., Suite 102
Toronto, M5V 1H3 Ontario Canada
Phone: 416-960-9606 Fax: 416-960-0020
E-mail: eastern.canada.chapter@sierraclub.org
Website: eastern.sierraclub.ca

Founded: N/A
Membership: 101–1,000
Scope: Regional

Description: The Sierra Club Eastern Canada Chapter is a regional entity of the Sierra Club of Canada, a registered not-for-profit corporation. Our mandate is to protect and restore the health of the natural environment, including human communities in Ontario and Quebec, by empowering the membership through education, advocacy and outdoor adventures.

Publication(s): Newsletters

Contact(s):
Kim Neill, Chapter Coordinator; 416-960-9606

SIERRA CLUB
FLORIDA CHAPTER
475 Central Ave., Suite M1
St. Petersburg, FL 33701-3817 United States
Phone: 813-824-8813 Fax: 813-824-0936
E-mail: geraldine.swormstead@sierraclub.org
Website: florida.sierraclub.org

Founded: N/A
Scope: State
Contact(s):
Geraldine Swormstead, Chair

SIERRA CLUB
FLORIDA FIELD OFFICE
475 Central Ave., Suite M-1 (Florida Field Office)
St. Petersburg, FL 33701 United States
Phone: 727-824-8813 Fax: 727-824-0936
Website: www.sierraclub.org

Founded: N/A
Membership: 100,001–500,000
Scope: Regional

SIERRA CLUB
FLORIDA-MIAMI FIELD OFFICE
2700 SW 3rd Ave., Suite 2F
Miami, FL 33129 United States
Phone: 305-860-9888 Fax: 305-860-9862
E-mail: information@sierraclub.org
Website: www.sierraclub.org

Founded: N/A
Membership: 500,001–1,000,000
Scope: Local, Regional, National

SIERRA CLUB
GEORGIA CHAPTER
1447 Peachtree St., NE,
Atlanta, GA 30309-3034 United States
Phone: 404-607-1262 Fax: 404-876-5260
E-mail: georgia.chapter@sierraclub.org
Website: www.georgia.sierraclub.org

Founded: N/A
Membership: 10,001–100,000
Scope: State
Description: Environmentalist
Publication(s): Georgia Sierran (newsletter)
Contact(s):
Karen Austin, Chapter Coordinator; ext. 221
Bryan Hager, Conservation Organizer; ext. 226

SIERRA CLUB
GEORGIA FIELD OFFICE/LOUISIANA AND ALABAMA FIELD OFFICE
1447 Peachtree St., NE, Suite 305
Atlanta, GA 30309-3034 United States
Phone: 404-888-9778 Fax: 404-876-5260
E-mail: ap-ga.field@sierraclub.org

Founded: N/A
Scope: Regional

SIERRA CLUB
GRAND CANYON CHAPTER
202 East McDowell Road
Suite 277
Phoenix, AZ 85004 United States
Phone: 602-253-8633 Fax: 602-258-6533
E-mail: grand.canyon.chapter@sierraclub.org
Website: www.arizona.sierraclub.org/

Founded: N/A
Membership: 10,001–100,000
Scope: State
Publication(s): Canyon Echo - monthy newsletter

SIERRA CLUB
HAWAII CHAPTER
P.O. Box 2577
Honolulu, HI 96803-2577 United States
Phone: 808-538-6616 Fax: 808-537-9019
Website: hawaii.sierraclub.org/

Founded: N/A
Scope: State

SIERRA CLUB
HOOSIER CHAPTER
6224 N. College Ave
Indianapolis, IN 46220 United States
Phone: 317-466-9992
E-mail: sierra@netdirect.net
Website: hoosier.sierraclub.org/

Founded: N/A
Scope: State

SIERRA CLUB
ILLINOIS CHAPTER
200 N. Michigan Ave., Suite 505
Chicago, IL 60601-5908 United States
Phone: 312-251-1680 Fax: 312-251-1780
E-mail: illinois.chapter@sierraclub.org
Website: www.sierraclub.org/chapters/il

Founded: N/A
Membership: 10,001–100,000
Scope: State
Publication(s): Lake and Prairie
Contact(s):
Jack Darin, Contact

SIERRA CLUB
IOWA CHAPTER
Thoreau Center, 3500 Kingman Blvd.
Des Moines, IA 50311-3798 United States
Phone: 515-277-8868
E-mail: iowa.chapter@sierraclub.org
Website: iowa.sierraclub.org

Founded: N/A
Scope: State
Contact(s):
Charlie Winterwood, Chair; 319-588-2783

SIERRA CLUB
JOHN MUIR CHAPTER
222 S. Hamilton St., Suite 1
Madison, WI 53703-3201 United States
Phone: 608-256-0565 Fax: 608-256-4562
E-mail: john.muir.chapter@sierraclub.org
Website: www.sierraclub.org/chapters/wi/

Founded: N/A
Membership: 10,001–100,000
Scope: Regional
Publication(s): The Muir View

SIERRA CLUB
KERN-KAWEAH CHAPTER
P.O. Box 3357
Bakersfield, CA 93385-3357 United States
Phone: 661-323-5569
E-mail: kern-kaweah.chapter@sierraclub.org
Website: www.sierraclub.org/chapters/kernkaweah/

Founded: N/A
Membership: 1,001–10,000
Scope: Local, Regional
Publication(s): The Road Runner
Contact(s):
Lorraine Unger, Executive Officer

SIERRA CLUB
LOMA PRIETA CHAPTER
3921 E. Bayshore Rd., Suite. 204
Palo Alto, CA 94303-4303 United States
Phone: 650-390-8411 Fax: 650-390-8497
E-mail: loma.prieta.chapter@sierraclub.org
Website: lomaprieta.sierraclub.org

Founded: N/A
Membership: 10,001–100,000
Scope: Local, Regional
Publication(s): Loma Prietan
Contact(s):
Dan Kalb, Director; loma.prieta.director@sierraclub.org

SIERRA CLUB
LONE STAR CHAPTER
P.O. Box 1931
Austin, TX 78767 United States
Phone: 512-477-1729 Fax: 512-477-8526
E-mail: lonestar.chapter@sierraclub.org
Website: www.texas.sierraclub.org

Founded: N/A
Membership: 10,001–100,000
Scope: State
Publication(s): The Lone Star Sierran, State Capitol Report
Contact(s):
Tracy Arambula, Environmental Justice Director; tracy.arambula@sierraclub.org
Neil Carman, Clean Air Program Director
Ken Kramer, Chapter Director
Fred Richardson, Communications Director; fred.richardsom@sierraclub.org
Erin Rogers, Grass Roots Coordinator; erin.rogers@sierraclub.org
Brian Sybert, Natural Resources
Jennifer Walker, Adminstrative Assistant

SIERRA CLUB
LOS PADRES CHAPTER
P.O. Box 90924
Santa Barbara, CA 93190-0924 United States
Phone: 805-966-6622
Website: lospadres.sierraclub.org/

Founded: N/A
Scope: State
Contact(s):
Rick Skillin, Chapter Chair; 805-735-4190; rick.skillin@sierraclub.org

SIERRA CLUB
MACKINAC CHAPTER
109 E. Grand River
Lansing, MI 48906 United States
Phone: 517-484-2372 Fax: 517-484-3108
E-mail: mackinac.chapter@sierraclub.org
Website: www.michigan.sierraclub.org

Founded: N/A
Membership: 10,001–100,000
Scope: State
Publication(s): Mackinac, The, quarterly
Contact(s):
Anne Woiwode, Director

SIERRA CLUB
MAINE CHAPTER
One Pleasant St.
Portland, ME 04101-3936 United States
Phone: 207-761-5616 Fax: 207-773-6690
E-mail: maine.sierra@prodigy.net
Website: www.sierraclub.org/chapters/me/

Founded: 1992
Membership: 1,001–10,000
Scope: State
Description: for over a century the Sierra Club has been devoted to the conservation of our forests, mountains, rivers, coasts and other natural areas. The Maine Chapter, a volunteer-run grassroots organization, is working to restore the natural and human communities of the North Woods, halt global warming, protect Maine's clean water and coastline, and support pro-environmental candidates for public office.
Publication(s): Mainely Sierran Bimonthly Newsletter
Keyword(s): Air Quality/Atmosphere, Climate Change, Ecosystems (precious), Energy, Forests/Forestry, Oceans/Coasts/Beaches, Pollution (general), Population, Public Lands/Greenspace, Recreation/Ecotourism, Sprawl/Urban Planning, Water Habitats & Quality, Wildlife & Species
Contact(s):
Karen Woodsum, Maine Woods Regional; 207-791-2821; maine.woods@prodigy.net

SIERRA CLUB
MARYLAND CHAPTER
7338 Baltimore Ave., Suite 101A
College Park, MD 20740-3211 United States
Phone: 301-277-7111 Fax: 301-277-6699
Website: www.sierraclub.org/chapters/md/

Founded: N/A
Membership: 1,001–10,000
Scope: State, National, International
Publication(s): See publication web site
Contact(s):
Jon Robinson, Chapter Chairman

SIERRA CLUB
MASSACHUSETTS CHAPTER
100 Boylston St., Suite 760
Boston, MA 02116-4610 United States
Phone: 617-423-5775 Fax: 617-423-5858
E-mail: office@sierraclubmass.org
Website: www.sierraclubmass.org

Founded: N/A
Membership: 10,001–100,000
Scope: State
Description: Environmental
Publication(s): Massachusetts Sierran
Keyword(s): Air Quality/Atmosphere, Ecosystems (precious), Forests/Forestry, Land Issues, Oceans/Coasts/Beaches, Pollution (general), Population, Public Lands/Greenspace, Reduce/Reuse/Recycle, Sprawl/Urban Planning, Transportation, Water Habitats & Quality, Wildlife
Contact(s):
James McCaffrey, Director; director@sierraclubmass.org
Lorraine Foster, Office Administrator; 617-423-5775; Fax: 617-423-5885; office@sierraclubmass.org

SIERRA CLUB
MIDWEST OFFICE
214 N. Henry St., Suite 203
Madison, WI 53703 United States
Phone: 608-257-4994 Fax: 608-257-3513
E-mail: mw-wi.field@sierraclub.org
Website: www.sierraclub.org

Founded: 1892
Membership: 500,001–1,000,000
Scope: Regional
Description: IA, IL, IN, KY, MI, MN, MO, OH, WI
Publication(s): Mississippi Times
Contact(s):
Emily Green, Great Lakes Program Director; emily.green@sierraclub.org
Brett Hulsey, Senior Regional Representative; brett.hulsey@sierraclub.org
Jennifer Feyerherm, Great Lakes Toxins Specialist; jennifer.feyerherm@sierraclub.org
Eric Uram, Midwest Regional Representative; eric.uram@sierraclub.org
Bill Redding, Midwest Regional Representative; bill.redding@sierraclub.org

SIERRA CLUB
MIDWEST OFFICE
TRAVERSE CITY, MI
229 Lake Avenue, Suite 4
Traverse City, MI 49684 United States
Phone: 231-922-2201 Fax: 231-922-2909
Website: sierraclub.org

Founded: 1892
Membership: 500,001–1,000,000
Scope: Local, State, Regional, National, International
Description: Regional Field Office for National Sierra Club: IA, IL, IN, KY, MI, MN, MO, OH, WI
Contact(s):
Alison Horton, Midwest Regional Staff Director; alison.horton@sierraclub.org

SIERRA CLUB
MONTANA CHAPTER
P. O. Box 7312
Missoula, MT 59807 United States
Phone: 406-549-6031
E-mail: accipiter4@juno.com
Website: www.sierraclub.org

Founded: N/A
Scope: Regional
Publication(s): Big Sky Sierran
Contact(s):
Kathryn Hohmann, Associate Field Rep.; kathryn.holmann@sierraclub.org
Christine Phillips, Contact; 406-582-1281; magpie@mcn.net

SIERRA CLUB
MONTANA FIELD OFFICE
P.O. Box 1290
Bozeman, MT 59771 United States
Phone: 406-582-8365, ext. 3002 Fax: 406-582-9417
E-mail: katie.craig@sierraclub.org
Website: www.sierraclub.org

Founded: 1892
Membership: 500,001–1,000,000
Scope: Local, State, Regional, National, International
Description: Largest and oldest grassroots conservation organization in the U.S.
Publication(s): Newsletter
Contact(s):
Kathryn Hohmann, Sr. Regional Representative

SIERRA CLUB
MOTHER LODE CHAPTER
1414 K St., Suite 300
Sacramento, CA 95814-3929 United States
Phone: 916-557-1100, ext. 108 Fax: 916-557-9669
E-mail: motherload@mcsweb1.com
Website: www.motherload.sierraclub.org

Founded: N/A
Scope: Regional
Publication(s): The Bonanza, bimonthly newsletter
Contact(s):
Julie Parker, Administrative Assistant; ext. 119

SIERRA CLUB
NEBRASKA CHAPTER
5106 Western Ave.
Omaha, NE 68132 United States
Phone: 402-556-1830
E-mail: nebraska.chapter@sierraclub.org
Website: www.sierraclub.org/chapters/ne/

Founded: N/A
Membership: 1–100
Scope: State
Publication(s): The Nebraska Sierran (newsletter)
Contact(s):
Mary Green, Chair.
Pat Knapp, State Coordinator; 1614 N. 31st. St., Lincoln, NE 68503; 402-464-8537; patanap@alltel.net

SIERRA CLUB
NEW COLUMBIA CHAPTER
1416 33rd St., NW
Washington, DC 20007 United States
Phone: 202-333-5424 Fax: 202-965-3769
Website: newcolumbia.sierraclub.org

Founded: N/A
Scope: State
Contact(s):
Danilo Pelletiere, Conservation Chair; 202-543-7791; dpelleti@gmu.edu
Mark Wenzler, Vice Chair; 202-547-3410

SIERRA CLUB
NEW HAMPSHIRE CHAPTER
Three Bicentennial Sq.
Concord, NH 03301-4058 United States
Phone: 603-224-8222 Fax: 603-224-4719
Website: www.sierraclub.org/chapters/nh/

Founded: N/A
Scope: State
Description: This is the NH chapter of the Sierra Club, the nation's oldest and largest grassroots environmental organization. We have roughly 5000 members in NH.
Publication(s): The New Hampshire Sierran
Keyword(s): Agriculture/Farming, Air Quality/Atmosphere, Climate Change, Energy, Executive/Legislative/Judicial Reform, Forests/Forestry, Pollution (general), Public Lands/Greenspace, Sprawl/Urban Planning, Transportation
Contact(s):
Cathy Corkery, Legislative Advocate; 603-224-8222; Fax: 603-224-4719; catherine.corkery@sierraclub.org

SIERRA CLUB
NEW JERSEY CHAPTER
57 Mountain Ave.
Princeton, NJ 08540-2611 United States
Phone: 609-924-3141 Fax: 609-924-8799
Website: www.sierraactivist.org

Founded: 1970

Membership: 10,001–100,000
Scope: Local, State
Description: Grassroots Environmental Organization
Publication(s): The Sierran
Contact(s):
Jeff Tittel, Director; 609-924-3141; Jefft1@voicenet.com
Lori Herpen, Chapter Coordinator; 609-924-3141; lori.herpen@sierraclub.org
Bill Wolfe, Policy Director; 609-924-3141; bill.wolfe@sierraclub.org

SIERRA CLUB
NEW YORK CITY OFFICE
116 John St., 31st Fl.
New York, NY 10038 United States
Phone: 212-791-9291 Fax: 212-791-0839
E-mail: ne-nyc.field@sierraclub.org
Website: www.sierraclub.org
Founded: N/A
Scope: Regional
Contact(s):
Emma McGregor, Administrative Assistant

SIERRA CLUB
NORTH CAROLINA CHAPTER
112 S. Blount St.
Raleigh, NC 27601 United States
Phone: 919-833-8467 Fax: 919-833-8460
E-mail: info@sierraclub-nc.org
Website: www.sierraclub-nc.org
Founded: N/A
Membership: 10,001–100,000
Scope: State
Publication(s): Footnotes
Contact(s):
Molly Diggins, State Director
John Hudson, Resources Development Coordinator
David Knight, Lobbyist

SIERRA CLUB
NORTH STAR CHAPTER (MINNESOTA)
1313 5th St., SE, Suite 323
Minneapolis, MN 55414-4504 United States
Phone: 612-379-3853 Fax: 612-379-3855
E-mail: north.star.chapter@sierraclub.org
Website: www.northstar.sierraclub.org/
Founded: N/A
Membership: 10,001–100,000
Scope: Regional
Publication(s): The North Star Journal - bimonthly newsletter.
Contact(s):
Scott Elkins, State Director; selkins@igc.org

SIERRA CLUB
NORTHEAST REGION OFFICE
85 Washington St.
Saratoga Springs, NY 12866 United States
Phone: 518-587-9166 Fax: 518-583-9062
E-mail: ne-ny.field@sierraclub.org
Website: www.sierraclub.org
Founded: N/A
Membership: 500,001–1,000,000
Scope: Regional
Description: CT, MA, ME, NH, NJ, NY, PA, RI, VT
Publication(s): Magazine- Sierra
Contact(s):
Mark Bettinger, Staff Director
Baret Pinyoun, Associate Regional Representative

SIERRA CLUB
NORTHERN PLAINS REGION
23 N. Scott St., Suite 27
Sheridan, WY 82801 United States
Phone: 307-672-0425 Fax: 307-674-6187
E-mail: np-wy.field@sierraclub.org
Website: www.sierraclub.org
Founded: N/A
Membership: 1,001–10,000
Scope: Regional
Description: KS, MT, NE, ND, SD, WY
Publication(s): National Sierra newsletter
Contact(s):
Steve Thomas, Deputy Field Director; larry.mehlhaff@sierra.org
Liz Howell, Conservation Organizer
Kirk Koepsel, Regional Rep; kirk.koepsel@sierra.org

SIERRA CLUB
NORTHERN ROCKIES CHAPTER (IDAHO/WASHINGTON)
P.O. Box 552
Boise, ID 83701-0552 United States
Phone: 208-384-1023 Fax: 208-384-0239
E-mail: northern.rockies.chapter@sierraclub.org
Website: www.sierraclub.org/chapters/id/
Founded: N/A
Membership: 1,001–10,000
Scope: Regional
Contact(s):
Roger Singer, Chapter Director; roger.singer@sierraclub.org

SIERRA CLUB
NORTHWEST OFFICE
180 Nickerson Ave. Suite 207
Seattle, WA 98109 United States
Phone: 206-378-0114 Fax: 206-378-0034
E-mail: nw-wa.field@sierraclub.org
Website: www.sierraclub.org
Founded: N/A
Membership: 100,001–500,000
Scope: Regional
Description: AK, ID, OR, WA
Publication(s): Sierra Magazine
Keyword(s): Agriculture/Farming, Air Quality/Atmosphere, Climate Change, Ecosystems (precious), Energy, Ethics/Environmental Justice, Finance/Banking/Trade, Forests/Forestry, Land Issues, Oceans/Coasts/Beaches, Pollution (general), Population, Public Lands/Greenspace
Contact(s):
Bill Arthur, Staff Director
Jim Young, Associate Representative

SIERRA CLUB
OHIO CHAPTER
36 W. Gayn St., Suite 314
Columbus, OH 43215-3006 United States
Phone: 606-255-1946 Fax: 606-233-4099
E-mail: ogeralds@lexkylaw.com
Website: kentucky.sierraclub.com
Founded: N/A
Scope: State
Publication(s): Ohio Sierran Chapter Newsletter
Contact(s):
Marc Conte, Legislative Coordinator
Shannon Harps, Transportation Policy Specialist

SIERRA CLUB
OKLAHOMA CHAPTER
P.O. Box 60644
Oklahoma City, OK 73146-0644 United States
Phone: 415-977-5500 Fax: 415-977-5799
E-mail: oklahoma.chapter@sierraclub.org
Website: www.sierraclub.org/chapters/ok/

Founded: 1892
Scope: State

SIERRA CLUB
OREGON CHAPTER
2950 SE Stark St., Suite 110
Portland, OR 97214 United States
Phone: 503-238-0442 Fax: 503-238-6281
E-mail: oregon.chapter@sierraclub.org
Website: www.oregon.sierraclub.org

Founded: N/A
Membership: 10,001–100,000
Scope: State
Publication(s): The Conifer — Bi-Monthly Newsletter
Contact(s):
Mari Margil, Conservation Coordinator; 503-232-1723; mari.margil@sierraclub.org

SIERRA CLUB
OZARK CHAPTER (MISSOURI)
1007 North College Ave., Suite 1
Columbia, MO 65201-4725 United States
Phone: 573-815-9250 Fax: 573-442-7051
E-mail: ozark.chapter@sierraclub.org
Website: missouri.sierraclub.org

Founded: N/A
Membership: 10,001–100,000
Scope: State
Description: Grassroots advocacy to protect the environment.
Publication(s): Ozark Sierran
Keyword(s): Agriculture/Farming, Air Quality/Atmosphere, Climate Change, Ecosystems (precious), Energy, Ethics/Environmental Justice, Forests/Forestry, Land Issues, Recreation/Ecotourism, Sprawl/Urban Planning, Transportation, Water Habitats & Quality, Wildlife & Species.
Contact(s):
Carla Klein, Director; 573-815-9250; ozark.chapter@sierraclub.org
Keet Kopecky, Chair; 816-966-9544; kkopecky@kc.rr.com

SIERRA CLUB
PENNSYLVANIA CHAPTER
P.O. Box 663
Harrisburg, PA 17108 United States
Phone: 717-232-0101 Fax: 717-238-6330
E-mail: sierraclub.pa@paonline.com
Website: pennsylvania.sierraclub.org/

Founded: N/A
Membership: 10,001–100,000
Scope: Local, State
Description: Non-profit environmental advocacy organization.
Publication(s): Sierra Club Chapter Newsletter, The Sylvanian
Keyword(s): Agriculture/Farming, Air Quality/Atmosphere, Energy, Forests/Forestry, Land Issues, Pollution (general), Public Health, Reduce/Reuse/Recycle, Sprawl/Urban Planning, Transportation, Water Habitats & Quality, Wildlife & Species
Contact(s):
Jeff Schmidt, Senior Chapter Director; 717-232-0101; Fax: 717-238-6330; sierraclub.pa@paonline.com
M. Willett, Administrative Assistant; 717-232-0101; Fax: 717-238-6330; sierraclub.pa@paonline.com

SIERRA CLUB
PRAIRIE CHAPTER (AB, MB, SK)
10511 Saskatchewan Dr.
Edmonton, T6E 4S1 Alberta Canada
Phone: 780-439-1160 Fax: 780-437-3932
E-mail: sierraclub@connect.ab.ca
Website: www.sierraclub.ca/prairie

Founded: N/A
Scope: Regional

SIERRA CLUB
REDWOOD CHAPTER (NORTHERN CALIFORNIA)
P. O. Box 466
Santa Rosa, CA 95402 United States
Phone: 707-544-7651 Fax: 707-544-9861
E-mail: heyneedles@aol.com
Website: redwood.sierraclub.org

Founded: N/A
Scope: State
Publication(s): Redwood Needles
Contact(s):
Margaret Pennington, Chapter Chair; penningt@sonic.net

SIERRA CLUB
RHODE ISLAND CHAPTER
21 Meeting St. Garden Entrance
Providence, RI 02903-1000 United States
Phone: 401-521-4734 Fax: 401-521-4001
E-mail: contactus@sierraclubri.org
Website: www.sierraclubri.org

Founded: N/A
Membership: 1,001–10,000
Scope: State
Publication(s): Transportation Reform Alliance, Coastlines (newsletter), Transit Users Survey 2000, Nasty Nine Sprawl Report

SIERRA CLUB
RIO GRANDE CHAPTER (NEW MEXICO/WEST TEXAS)
207 Ricardo Road
Santa Fe, NM 87501 United States
Phone: 505-988-5760
E-mail: jhanna505@aol.com
Website: riogrande.sierraclub.org/

Founded: N/A
Scope: Regional
Contact(s):
Jennifer De Garmo, Staff Member; 202 Central Avenue SE, Albuquerque, NM 87102; 505-243-7767; nmex.field1@prodigy.net

SIERRA CLUB
ROCKY MOUNTAIN CHAPTER (COLORADO)
1410 Grant St., Suite B303
Denver, CO 80203-1848 United States
Phone: 303-861-8819 Fax: 303-861-2436
Website: www.rmc.sierraclub.org/

Founded: N/A
Membership: 10,001–100,000
Scope: State
Publication(s): The Sierra - bimonthly magazine, The Peak & Prairie - bi-monthly newsletter.
Contact(s):
Susan Lefever, Program Director; slefever@rmi.net

SIERRA CLUB
SAN DIEGO CHAPTER (SOUTHERN CALIFORNIA)
3820 Ray St.
San Diego, CA 92104-3623 United States
Phone: 619-299-1743 Fax: 619-299-1742
E-mail: san-diego.chapter@sierraclub.org
Website: sandiego.sierraclub.org/home/index.asp

Founded: 1948

Scope: Local, Regional

Contact(s):
Cheryl Reiff, Office Administrator

SIERRA CLUB
SAN FRANCISCO BAY CHAPTER
2530 San Pablo Ave., Suite 1
Berkeley, CA 94702-2000 United States
Phone: 510-848-0800 Fax: 510-848-3383
E-mail: info@sfasc.org
Website:
www.sierraclub.org/chapters/sanfranciscobay/nindex.html

Founded: N/A

Scope: Local

Publication(s): SF Bay chapter schedule of activities.

Contact(s):
Michael Bornstein, Chapter Director; michael.bornstein@sierraclub.org

SIERRA CLUB
SAN GORGONIO CHAPTER (SOUTHERN CALIFORNIA)
4079 Mission Inn Ave.
Riverside, CA 92501-3204 United States
Phone: 909-684-6203, ext. 2 Fax: 909-684-6172
Website: sangorgonio.sierraclub.org/

Founded: N/A

Scope: Local, Regional

SIERRA CLUB
SANTA LUCIA CHAPTER
P.O. Box 15755
San Luis Obispo, CA 93406-5755 United States
Phone: Fax: 805-543-8727
E-mail: gfelsman@thegrid.net
Website: santalucia.sierraclub.org/

Founded: N/A

Scope: Local, Regional

SIERRA CLUB
SOUTH CAROLINA CHAPTER
P.O. Box 2388, 1314 Lincoln St., Suite 211
Columbia, SC 29202 United States
Phone: 803-256-8487 Fax: 803-256-8448
E-mail: scsierra@conterra.com
Website: www.sierraclub.org/chapters/sc/

Founded: 1978
Membership: 1,001–10,000
Scope: State
Publication(s): The Congaree Chronicle - bi monthy newsletter.

Contact(s):
Dell Isham, Chapter Director; 803-256-8487; scsierra@conterra.com

SIERRA CLUB
SOUTH DAKOTA CHAPTER
P.O. Box 1624
Rapid City, SD 57709-1624 United States
Phone: 605-348-1345 Fax: 605-348-1344
E-mail: brademey@rapidnet.com
Website: www.sierraclub.org/chapters/sd/

Founded: N/A
Membership: 1,000,001 +
Scope: Local, Regional, National
Publication(s): Newsletter Quarterly, Sierra Magazine, Pines & Prairie

Contact(s):
Sam Clauson, S. D. Chapter Chair
Heather Morijah, Conservation Organizer; 1101 E. Phildelphia St., Rapid City, SD 57701; 605-342-2244; Fax: 605-342-2255; heather.morijah@sierraclub.org

SIERRA CLUB
SOUTHEAST OFFICE
1330 21st Way South, Suite 100
Birmingham, AL 35205 United States
Phone: 205-933-9111 Fax: 205-939-1020
E-mail: jim.price@sierraclub.org
Website: www.sierraclub.org

Founded: N/A

Scope: National

Description: AL, AR, FL, LA, MS, TX

Contact(s):
Jim Price, Senior Regional Staff Director; jimprice@sierraclub.org

SIERRA CLUB
SOUTHERN CALIFORNIA/NEVADA FIELD OFFICE
3435 Wilshire Blvd., Suite #320
Los Angeles, CA 90010 United States
Phone: 213-387-6528 Fax: 213-387-5383
E-mail: ca-sc.field@sierraclub.org
Website: www.sierraclub.org/field/southerncal/

Founded: N/A

Scope: Regional

Publication(s): Publications on website

Contact(s):
Jim Blomquist, Sr. Regional Representative

SIERRA CLUB
SOUTHWEST OFFICE
202 East McDowell Road
Suite 277
Phoenix, AZ 85004 United States
Phone: 602-254-9330 Fax: 602-258-6533
E-mail: sw.field@sierraclub.org
Website: www.sierraclub.org

Founded: N/A
Membership: 10,001–100,000
Scope: Regional
Description: AZ, CO, NM, OK, UT

Contact(s):
Rob Smith, Staff Director
Philip Church, Administrative Coordinator, Southwest Region

SIERRA CLUB
TEHIPITE CHAPTER (NORTHERN CALIFORNIA)
P.O. Box 5396
Fresno, CA 93755-5396 United States
Phone: 559-271-0652
E-mail: Tehipite.Chapter@sierraclub.org
Website: tehipite.sierraclub.org/

Founded: N/A

Scope: Local, Regional

SIERRA CLUB
TENNESSEE CHAPTER
4641 Villa Green Dr.
Nashville, TN 37215-4331 United States
Phone: 615-665-1010
E-mail: tennessee.chapter@sierraclub.org
Website: www.sierraclub.org/chapters/tn/

Founded: N/A
Scope: State

SIERRA CLUB
TOIYABE CHAPTER (NEVADA/EASTERN CALIFORNIA)
P.O. Box 8096
Reno, NV 89507-8096 United States
Phone: 775-323-3162
Website: nevada.sierraclub.org/

Founded: N/A
Scope: State

SIERRA CLUB
UTAH CHAPTER
2120 South 1300 East, Ste. 204
Salt Lake City, UT 84106-3785 United States
Phone: 801-467-9297
E-mail: utah.chapter@sierraclub.org
Website: utah.sierraclub.org/

Founded: 1962
Scope: State
Description: We work within the state of Utah to advance the goals and policies of the National Sierra Club and of Utah volunteers.
Keyword(s): Ecosystems (precious), Land Issues, Sprawl/Urban Planning
Contact(s):
Nina Dougherty, Chapter Chair
Tony Guay, Vice-Chair; tpguay@hotmail.com
Dan Schroeder, Secretary/Treasurer; dschroeder@weber.edu

SIERRA CLUB
UTAH FIELD OFFICE
2273 S. Highland Dr., Suite 2-D
Salt Lake City, UT 84106-2832 United States
Phone: 801-467-9294 Fax: 801-467-9296
E-mail: sw-ut.field@sierraclub.org
Website: www.sierraclub.org

Founded: N/A
Membership: 1,001–10,000
Scope: Regional

SIERRA CLUB
VENTANA CHAPTER (NORTHERN CALIFORNIA)
P.O. Box 5667
Carmel, CA 93921-5667 United States
Phone: 831-624-8032
E-mail: ventana@mbay.net
Website: www.ventana.org/

Founded: N/A
Scope: Local, Regional

SIERRA CLUB
VERMONT CHAPTER
P.O. Box 3154
Burlington, VT 05401-0031 United States
Phone: 802-651-0169 Fax: 888-729-4109
Website: vermont.sierraclub.org/

Founded: N/A
Membership: 1,001–10,000
Scope: State
Description: Vermont state chapter of the national Sierra Club
Publication(s): Vermont Sierran (quarterly newsletter)

SIERRA CLUB
VIRGINIA CHAPTER
Six N. 6th St., Suite 401
Richmond, VA 23219-2419 United States
Phone: 804-225-9113 Fax: 804-225-9114
Website: www.sierraclubva.org

Founded: N/A
Membership: 10,001–100,000
Scope: State
Publication(s): Old Dominion Sierran
Contact(s):
Pat Dezern, Conservation Organizer

SIERRA CLUB
WASHINGTON, DC OFFICE
408 C St., NE
Washington, DC 20002 United States
Phone: 202-547-1141 Fax: 202-547-6009
Website: www.sierraclub.org

Founded: 1892
Membership: 500,001–1,000,000
Scope: National
Description: The Sierra Club is a non-profit, 501(c)(4), member-supported, public interest organization that promotes conservation of the natural environment by influencing public policy decisions: legislative, administrative, legal and electoral.
Publication(s): Sierra Magazine
Keyword(s): Agriculture/Farming, Air Quality/Atmosphere, Climate Change, Energy, Ethics/Environmental Justice, Forests/Forestry, Land Issues, Pollution (general), Population, Public Lands/Greenspace, Sprawl/Urban Planning, Water Habitats & Quality, Wildlife & Species
Contact(s):
Bob Bingaman, Field Director
Debbie Sease, Legislative Director

SIERRA CLUB
WEST VIRGINIA CHAPTER
P.O. Box 4142
Morgantown, WV 26504-4142 United States
Phone: 304-279-6975

Founded: N/A
Membership: 1,001–10,000
Scope: State
Description: West Virginia chaper contains 1600+ members that work on Mountaintop Removal, wilderness, and other environmental issues.
Publication(s): Chapter Newsletter - Mountain State Sierran.
Contact(s):
Paul Potter, Chapter Chair; 304-363-4006; paul_wilson@fws.gov

SIERRA CLUB
WYOMING CHAPTER
23 N. Scott, #27
Sheridan, WY 82801 United States
Phone: 307-672-0425 Fax: 307-674-6187
E-mail: wyoming.chapter@sierraclub.org
Website: www.sierraclub.org/chapters/wy/

Founded: N/A
Membership: 1,001–10,000
Scope: State
Description: Protecting Wyoming's Wild Places for our families and for our future.
Publication(s): Wyoming Sierran Newsletter.
Keyword(s): Air Quality/Atmosphere, Forests/Forestry, Public Lands/Greenspace, Water Habitats & Quality, Wildlife & Species

Contact(s):
Liz Howell, Wyoming Chapter Staff; 307-672-0425; liz.howell@sierraclub.org

SIERRA CLUB FOUNDATION, THE

85 Second Street
Suite 750
San Francisco, CA 94105 United States
Phone: 415-995-1780 Fax: 415-995-1791
E-mail: sierraclub.foundation@sierraclub.org
Website: www.tscf.org

Founded: 1960
Membership: N/A
Scope: National
Description: A nonprofit, tax-deductible, public foundation established to finance the educational, literary, and scientific projects of citizen-based groups working on national and international environmental problems. Manages assets in excess of $70 million and over 600 regional or special interest funds principally for charitable conservation purposes. Also manages charitable remainder unitrusts and a pooled income fund with assets over $7.5 million.
Publication(s): Annual Report.
Keyword(s): Agriculture/Farming, Air Quality/Atmosphere, Ecosystems (precious), Energy, Ethics/Environmental Justice, Forests/Forestry, Land Issues, Oceans/Coasts/Beaches, Pollution (general), Population, Public Health, Public Lands/Greenspace, Reduce/Reuse/Recycle
Contact(s):
Michael Loeb, President; sierraclub.foundation@sierraclub.org
John DeCock, Executive Director; sierraclub.foundation@sierraclub.org

SIERRA CLUB OF CANADA

#1 Nicholas St., Suite 412
Ottawa, K1N 7B7 Ontario Canada
Phone: 613-241-4611 Fax: 613-241-2292
Website: www.sierraclub.ca/national

Founded: N/A
Scope: International
Publication(s): SCAN, Sierra Magazine
Contact(s):
Elizabeth May, Executive Director

SIERRA STUDENT COALITION

P.O. Box 2402
Providence, RI 02906-0402 United States
Phone: 401-861-6012 Fax: 401-861-6241
Website: www.ssc.org

Founded: N/A
Membership: 1–100
Scope: National
Publication(s): Generation E
Contact(s):
Myke Bybee, Director

SINAPU

2260 Baseline Rd., Suite 212
Boulder, CO 80302 United States
Phone: 303-447-8655 Fax: 303-447-8612
E-mail: sinapu@sinapu.org
Website: www.sinapu.org

Founded: 1991
Membership: 101–1,000
Scope: Regional
Description: Sinapu, named after the Ute word for wolves, is dedicated to the recovery of native carnivores in the Southern Rocky Mountains and to the restoration of the wild habitat in which all species flourish.
Publication(s): Wild Again
Keyword(s): Forests/Forestry, Land Issues, Public Lands/Greenspace, Wildlife & Species
Contact(s):
Rob Edward, Program Director
Kimberly Riggs, Executive Director; kim@sinapu.org
Wendy Keefover-Ring, Program Staff; wendy@sinapu.org

SISKIYOU PROJECT

9335 Takilma Rd.
Cave Junction, OR 97523 United States
Phone: 541-592-4459

Founded: N/A
Description: We believe in the power of place and of biological cycles, and in modeling our lives, actions, and community on the ideals of wholeness and being-of-a-place. For us the ultimate model is the wild, and we are reaching for the wild inside ourselves as well as "out there". We see all life forms as interconnected and inseparable, and realizing that we are in a time of crisis, we feel urgency in effecting change in the way human industrial culture deals with nature.
Contact(s):
David Johns, President
Dave Willis, Vice President
Romain Cooper, Program Director
Steve Marsden, Executive Director
Jennifer Marsden, SFI Director
Jim McBride, Finance Director
Barbara Ulliam, Conservation Director
Kelpie Wilson, Development Director
Kindi Fahrnkopf, Office Manager
Lori Cooper, Staff Attorney
Tom Dimitre, East Siskiyou Conservation Coordinator
Lou Gold, Storyteller Emeritus
Steven Jessup, Secretary
Erik Jules, Treasurer
Julie Norman, Video Project Coordinator
Marjorie Reynolds, Mail and Data Processor
Vicky Rummel, SFI Admin. Coordinator
Linda Serrano, Network Coordinator
Barry Snitkin, Community Outreach

SMALL WOODLAND OWNERS ASSOCIATION OF MAINE

153 Hospital St., P.O. Box 836
Augusta, ME 04332 United States
Phone: 207-626-0005 Fax: 207-626-7992
E-mail: swoam@mint.net
Website: www.swoam.com

Founded: 1975
Scope: State
Description: A statewide nonprofit organization, affiliated with the National Woodland Owners Association, which pursues better understandings, skills, and directions in small woodland ownership/management under integrated use objectives.
Publication(s): SWOAM News
Keyword(s): Forests/Forestry

SMITHSONIAN INSTITUTION

1000 Jefferson Dr., SW
Washington, DC 20560 United States
Phone: 202-357-2700
Website: www.si.edu

Founded: 1846
Scope: National
Description: An education, museum, and research complex as well as an independent trust instrumentality of the United States, established for the increase and diffusion of knowledge. Mission accomplished by: field investigations; national collections development in arts, history, and science, and their preservation for study, reference, and exhibition; scientific research and publications; programs of national and interna-

tional cooperative research, conservation, education, and training; answering inquiries

Publication(s): Smithsonian Institution Press, The Smithsonian Magazine

Keyword(s): Agriculture/Farming, Ethics/Environmental Justice, Forests/Forestry, Water Habitats & Quality, Wildlife & Species

Contact(s):
J. O'Connor, Under Secretary of Science
Lawrence Small, Secretary

SMITHSONIAN INSTITUTION

NATIONAL MUSEUM OF NATURAL HISTORY
10th St. and Constitution Ave., NW
Washington, DC 20560 United States
Phone: 202-357-2700 Fax: 202-357-1729
E-mail: info@infor.si.edu
Website: www.si.edu

Founded: N/A

Scope: National

Description: A center for the study of humans, plants, animals, fossil organisms, terrestrial and extraterrestrial rocks, and minerals as well as other fields of scientific investigation.

Contact(s):
Robert Fri, Director
David Correll, Chief Scientist of Environmental Research Center; Smithsonian Environmental Research Center, P.O. Box 28, Edgewater, MD 21037; 301-261-4190

SMITHSONIAN INSTITUTION

OFFICE OF FELLOWSHIPS
Victor Bldg., 750 9th St. N. W.
Suite 9300
Washington, DC 20560 United States
Phone: 202-275-0655 Fax: 202-275-0489
E-mail: siofg@si.edu
Website: www.si.edu/research+study

Founded: N/A
Membership: 1–100
Scope: International

Description: Oversees all Smithsonian fellowships and supports a wide range of research activities. It also provides program and administrative assistance for cooperative teaching arrangements between the Institution and local universities in American history, museum studies, and other areas.

Contact(s):
Roberta Rubinoff, Director

SMITHSONIAN INSTITUTION

OFFICE OF INTERNATIONAL RELATIONS
Smithsonian Institution, 1100 Jefferson Dr., SW,
Washington, DC 20560 United States
Phone: 202-357-4795 Fax: 202-786-2557
Website: www.prism.edu

Founded: N/A
Membership: 1–100
Scope: National

Description: The Foreign Currency Program supports the research activities of American institutions of higher learning through grants in U.S.-owned local currencies.

Contact(s):
Francine Berkowitz, Director

SMITHSONIAN INSTITUTION

SMITHSONIAN PRESS/SMITHSONIAN PRODUCTIONS
470 L'Enfant Plaza, Suite 7100
Washington, DC 20560 United States
Phone: 202-287-3738
Website: www.si.edu/sipress/

Founded: N/A

Scope: National

Description: Information on history, art, and science research is presented in non-technical style in Smithsonian Institution Research Reports issued four times a year by the Office of Public Affairs (202-357-2627). Smithsonian, the official magazine of the Institution, presents general interest feature articles each month in every subject area of the Smithsonian museums: art, culture, history, science, and technology.

Publication(s): Research in various fields is reported in a continuing series of publications by the Smithsonian Institution Press.

Contact(s):
Daniel Goodwin, Director
David Umansky, Director of Communications; Arts and Industries Bldg., 900 Jefferson Dr. SW, Rm. 4210, Washington, DC 20560; 202-357-2627
Don Moser, Editor; Smithsonian Magazine, Arts and Industries, Bldg. 900 Jefferson Dr. SW, Rm. 1310C, Washington, DC 20560

SMITHSONIAN INSTITUTION

SMITHSONIAN TROPICAL RESEARCH INSTITUTE
AP.O.AA, FL 34002-0948 United States
Phone: 202-357-2700

Founded: N/A

Scope: National

SMITHSONIAN INSTITUTION NATIONAL ZOOLOGICAL PARK

3001 Connecticut Ave. NW
Washington, DC 20008 United States
Phone: 202-673-4717
Website: www.nationalzoologicalpark.com

Founded: 1889
Membership: 10,001–100,000
Scope: Local, Regional, National, International

Description: Research concentrates on a better understanding of animal behavior and health, particularly endangered species. Through the operation of the zoo's Conservation and Research Center in Front Royal, VA, the NZP is developing a program of animal propagation which will aid in the survival of threatened and endangered species. Undertakes a number of programs overseas to develop new methodology and increase knowledge of species in the wild. The Migratory Bird Center is located at the zoo.

Contact(s):
Lucy Spelman, Director; 202-673-4721

SMITHSONIAN MARINE STATION AT FORT PIERCE

701 Seaway Dr.
Fort Pierce, FL 34949 United States
Phone: 772-465-6630 Fax: 772-461-8154
Website: www.sms.si.edu

Founded: N/A

Scope: International

Description: Marine studies aim at understanding the ecological function of inland waterways and their relationship to land use policy.

Contact(s):
Mary Rice, Director; ext. 142; rice@sms.si.edu

SOCIEDAD AMBIENTE MARINO

Sociedad Ambiente Marino
P.O. Box 22158
San Juan, PR 00931 United States
Phone: 787-485-2896
E-mail: sambientemarino@aol.com

Founded: 2001
Membership: 101–1,000
Scope: Regional

Description: Censos de corales y peces, limpiezas de playa, trasplante de coral. Educacion en Ambiente Marino.

Keyword(s): Ecosystems (precious), Oceans/Coasts/Beaches, Recreation/Ecotourism, Water Habitats & Quality

Contact(s):

Samuel Suleiman, President; 787-485-2896; buzo@coqui.net

SOCIETY FOR ANIMAL PROTECTIVE LEGISLATION

P.O. Box 3719, Georgetown Station
Washington, DC 20007 United States
Phone: 202-337-2334 Fax: 202-338-9478
E-mail: sapl@saplonline.org
Website: www.saplonline.org

Founded: 1955

Scope: National

Description: Nonprofit organization which keeps its 7,000 correspondents apprised of current developments in legislation for the protection of animals. Has been instrumental in obtaining enactment of 14 federal laws.

Keyword(s): Wildlife & Species

Contact(s):

John Kullberg, President
John Gleiber, Executive Secretary; 202-337-2334
Christine Stevens, Secretary; 202-337-2334

SOCIETY FOR CONSERVATION BIOLOGY

4245 North Fairfax Dr.
Arlington, VA 22203 United States
Phone: 703-276-2384 Fax: 703-995-4633
E-mail: information@conbio.org
Website: www.conservationbiology.org

Founded: 1985

Membership: 1,001–10,000

Scope: National, International

Description: A professional society dedicated to providing the scientific information and expertise required to protect the world's biological diversity. Incorporated as a tax-exempt scientific organization, the Society has a board composed of scholars, government personnel, and members of both national and international scientific and conservation organizations.

Publication(s): Conservation Biology bi-monthly scientific journal, Society for Conservation Biology - quarterly newsletter, Conservation Biology In Practice - quarterly magazine

Keyword(s): Development/Developing Countries, Wildlife & Species

Contact(s):

Malcolm Hunter, President; Dept. of Wildlife Ecology, University of Maine, Orono, ME 04469; 207-581-2865; Fax: 207-581-2858
Alan Thornhill, Executive Director; 703-276-2384, ext. 102; Fax: 703-995-4633; athornhill@conbio.org
Stephen Humphrey, Treasurer; 352-392-9230; Fax: 352-392-9748; humphrey@ufl.edu
Kathy Kohm, Editor of Conservation Biology in Practice; 206-685-4724; Fax: 206-221-7839; kkohm@u.washington.edu
Gary Meffe, Editor of Conservation Biology; 352-846-0557; Fax: 352-846-2823; conbio@gnv.ifas.ufl.edu
Elizabeth Parish, Operations Manager; 703-276-2384; Fax: 703-995-4633; membership@conbio.org

SOCIETY FOR ECOLOGICAL RESTORATION

1955 W. Grant Rd. #150
Tucson, AZ 85745 United States
Phone: 520-622-5485
E-mail: info@ser.org
Website: www.ser.org

Founded: 1989

Membership: 1,001–10,000

Scope: International

Description: Created to promote the development of ecological restoration both as a discipline and as a model for a healthy relationship with nature, and to raise awareness of the value and limitations of restoration as a conservation strategy.

Publication(s): Ecological Restoration, Proceedings from the Seventh SER Conference, 1995, Restoration Ecology, SER News

Keyword(s): Reduce/Reuse/Recycle

Contact(s):

Donald Falk, Executive Director; 520-626-7201
George Gann, Vice Chair; 305-245-6547
William Halvorson, Treasurer; 520-670-6885
Eric Higgs, Secretary; 403-492-5469
William Niering, Editor; 203-447-1911
Edith Read, Chair; 714-751-7373

SOCIETY FOR INTEGRATIVE AND COMPARATIVE BIOLOGY

1313 Dolley Madison Blvd. Ste. 402
McLean, VA 22101 United States
Phone: 703-790-1745 Fax: 703-790-2672
E-mail: sicb@burkinc.com
Website: www.sicb.org

Founded: 1890

Membership: 1,001–10,000

Scope: National

Description: (formerly AMERICAN SOCIETY OF ZOOLOGISTS) The Society for Integrative and Comparative Biology (SICB) is one of the largest and most prestigious professional associations of its kind. SICB is dedicated to promoting the pursuit and public dissemination of important information relating to comparative biology.

Publication(s): American Zoologist, The

Keyword(s): Wildlife & Species

Contact(s):

Albert Bennett, President; School of Biological Sciences, University of California+I365, Irvine, CA 92717; 714-856-6930; Fax: 714-725-2181
Marquesa Mills, Business Manager; 104 Sirius Cir., Thousand Oaks, CA 91360; 805-492-3585; Fax: 805-492-0370
Mary Adams-Wiley, Executive Officer; 104 Sirius Cir., Thousand Oaks, CA 91360; 805-492-3585; Fax: 805-492-0370
Milton Fingerman, Managing Editor; Department of Biology, Tulane University, New Orleans, LA 70118; 504-865-5546
Mary Ottinger, Secretary; Department of Poultry Science, University of Maryland, College Park, MD 20742; 301-405-5780; Fax: 301-314-9557
Marjorie Reaka, Treasurer; Department of Zoology, University of Maryland, College Park, MD 20742; 301-454-0259

SOCIETY FOR MARINE MAMMALOGY, THE

BIOLOGICAL SCIENCES AND CENTER FOR MARINE SCIENCE RESEARCH
CORPORATE ZOOLOGICAL OPERATIONS
SEAWORLD, INC.
7007 Busch Entertainment Corporation, Moon Seaworld Dr.
Wilmington, NC 28403 United States
Phone: 407-363-2662 Fax: 407-345-5397
E-mail: dan.odell@seaworld.com

Founded: 1981

Scope: National

Description: To promote the educational, scientific, and managerial advancement of marine mammal science; gather and disseminate scientific, technical, and management information, through publications and meetings to members of the society, the public, and public and private institutions; and promote the wise conservation and management of marine mammal resources.

Publication(s): Marine Mammal Science

Keyword(s): Wildlife & Species

Contact(s):

Carol Fairfield, Awards & Scholarship Committee; NOAA/NMFS/SEFSC, 1002 Forest Dr., Arnold, MD 21012; 410-757-7224; carol.fairfield@noaa.gov

Edward Keith, Education Committee; Oceanographic Center, Nova Southeastern University, 8000 N. Ocean Dr., Dania, FL 33004; 954-262-8322; Fax: 954-921-7764; edwardok@hpd.nova.edu

Paul Nachtigall, Scientific Program Committee; Marine Mammal Research Program, Hawaii Institute of Marine Science, University of Hawaii, P.O. Box 1106, Kailua, HI 96734; 808-247-5297; Fax: 808-247-5831; nachtiga@hawaii.edu

Daniel Odell, President-Elect; Sea World, Inc., 7007 Sea World Dr., Orlando, FL 32821-8097

D. Pabst, Secretary; 910-962-7266; Fax: 910-962-4066; pbasta@uncwil.edu

William Perrin, Editor; Southwest Fisheries Science Center, NMFS, P.O. Box 271, LaJolla, CA 92109; 619-546-7093; Fax: 619-546-7003; wperrin@ucsd.edu

Steven Swartz, Committee of Scientific Advisors; National Marine Fisheries Service, 75 Virginia Beach Dr., Miami, FL 33149; 305-361-4487; Fax: 305-361-4478; Steven.Swartz@noaa.gov

Glenn Vanblaricom, Membership Committee; WA Cooperative Fish & Wildlife Research Unit, Box 357980, University of Washington, Seattle, WA 98195; 206-543-6475; Fax: 206-616-9012

SOCIETY FOR RANGE MANAGEMENT

445 Union Blvd.
Suite 230
Lakewood, CO 80228 United States
Phone: 303-986-3309 Fax: 303-986-3892
E-mail: sam_albrecht@rangelands.org
Website: www.rangelands.org

Founded: 1948
Membership: 1,001–10,000
Scope: International
Description: Professional society which promotes understanding of rangeland ecosystems and their management and use for tangible products and intangible values; reports new findings and techniques in range science; promotes public appreciation of rangelands and benefits derived from them; promotes professional development of members.
Publication(s): Journal of Range Management, Rangelands, Trail Boss News
Keyword(s): Agriculture/Farming, Ecosystems (precious), Forests/Forestry, Land Issues, Public Lands/Greenspace, Reduce/Reuse/Recycle, Water Habitats & Quality, Wildlife & Species

Contact(s):

Samuel Albrecht, Executive Vice-President; 303-986-3309; Fax: 303-986-3892; sam_albrecht@ix.netcom.com

Aaron Barr, Memberships Services Manager; 303-986-3309; Fax: 303-986-3892; acbarr@rangelands.org

Natalie Bolleurs, Office Services Assistant; 303-986-3309; Fax: 303-986-3892; nbolleurs@rangelands.org

Ann Harris, Director of Administration/Programs; 303-986-3309; Fax: 303-986-3892; amharris@rangelands.org

Leonard Jolley, Rangeland Management Specialist; 303-986-3309; Fax: 303-986-3892; ljolley@rangelands.org

Patty Rich, Production Editor; 3059A Hwy. 92, Hotchkiss, CO 81419; 970-872-5932; Fax: 970-872-5962; prich@starband.net

Kirsten Tardy, Manager of Accounting/Sales; 303-986-3309; Fax: 303-986-3892; ktardy@rangelands.org

SOCIETY FOR THE PRESERVATION OF BIRDS OF PREY

P.O. Box 66070
Mar Vista Station
Los Angeles, CA 90066-0070 United States
Phone: 310-840-2322

Founded: 1966
Scope: National
Description: A private charity, nonmembership, national association advocating the strictest protection for birds of prey; educates about the role of raptors in the ecosystem; opposes lenient harvesting practices & the sale of birds of prey for profit; endorses captive raptor breeding as a conservation technique; & supports the largest collection of literature on birds of prey at any public university. The Society is the oldest organization emphasizing birds of prey occuring naturally in the wild.
Publication(s): Leaflet series, Raptor Report
Keyword(s): Ecosystems (precious), Wildlife & Species

Contact(s):

Richard Hilton, President and Editor; 310-319-9417

SOCIETY FOR THE PROTECTION OF NEW HAMPSHIRE FORESTS

THE FOREST SOCIETY
54 Portsmouth St.
Concord, NH 03301-5400 United States
Phone: 603-224-9945 Fax: 603-228-0423
E-mail: info@spnhf.org
Website: www.spnhf.org

Founded: 1901
Membership: 1,001–10,000
Scope: Regional
Description: A voluntary nonprofit organization promoting balanced conservation of New Hampshire's renewable natural resources through land protection, education, advocacy, and forestry.
Publication(s): Forest Notes
Keyword(s): Forests/Forestry, Wildlife & Species

Contact(s):

Jane Difley, President/ Forester

Paul Doscher, Senior Director of Land Conservation

SOCIETY OF AMERICAN FORESTERS

5400 Grosvenor Ln.
Bethesda, MD 20814 United States
Phone: 301-897-8720 Fax: 301-897-3690
E-mail: safweb@safnet.org
Website: www.safnet.org

Founded: 1900
Membership: 1,000,001 +
Scope: National
Description: The national organization representing all segments of the forestry profession and the accreditation authority for professional forestry education in the U.S. Objectives are to advance the science, technology, education, and practice of professional forestry and to use the knowledge and skills of the profession to benefit society.
Publication(s): Forestry Source, The, Western Journal of Applied Forestry, Northern Journal of Applied Forestry, Southern Journal of Applied Forestry, Forest Science, Journal of Forestry
Keyword(s): Forests/Forestry, Public Lands/Greenspace, Reduce/Reuse/Recycle

Contact(s):

Karl Wenger, President

William Banzhaf, Executive Vice President

James Coufal, Vice President

Lori Gardner, Director of Communications and Marketing Services

Lawrence Hill, Director of Resource Policy

Charles Jackson, Director of Finance and Administration

Diane Perl, Director of Conventions and Meetings
P. Smith, Director of Science and Education
Rebecca Staebler, Editorial Director and Director of Publications
Robert Bosworth, Past President
Harry Wiant, Past President

SOCIETY OF AMERICAN FORESTERS

NORTHWEST OFFICE
4033 SW Canyon Rd.
Portland, OR 97221 United States
Phone: 503-224-8046 Fax: 503-226-2515
Website: www.forestry.org

Founded: 1900
Membership: 1,001–10,000
Scope: Regional
Description: The mission of the society is to advance the science, education, technology, and practice of forestry; enhance its members' competency and professionalism; and use the knowledge and skills of the profession to benefit society.
Publication(s): Western Forester
Contact(s):
Lori Rasor, Manager and Editor; 4033 SW Canyon Rd., Portland, OR 97221; 503-224-8046

SOCIETY OF AMERICAN FORESTERS

UNIVERSITY OF KENTUCKY
DEPARTMENT OF FORESTRY
UK Thomas Poe Cooper Bldg
Lexington, KY 40546-0073 United States
Phone: 859-257-5994 Fax: 859-323-1031
Website: www.uky.edu-agriculture-forestry-forestry.html

Founded: N/A
Membership: 1–100
Scope: Regional, National
Description: K-T SAF is the Kentucky-Tennessee section of the Society of American Foresters, and carries out the policies and programs of SAF within these two states. See the Society of American Foresters listing for more information.
Keyword(s): Forests/Forestry, Reduce/Reuse/Recycle
Contact(s):
Jim Ringe, Director of Undergraduate Studies; 859-257-7594; jringe@uky.edu
Jeff Stringer, Extension Coordinator; Dept. of Forestry, Universtity of Ky., Lexington, KY 40546-0073; 859-257-5994

SOCIETY OF TYMPANUCHUS CUPIDO PINNATUS LTD.

Stone Ridge II, Suite 280, N 14 W23777 Stone Ridge Dr.
Waukesha, WI 53188-1188 United States
E-mail: mihal@execpc.com

Founded: 1961
Scope: National
Description: Nonprofit organization dedicated to the preservation of the prairie chicken for all future generations in Wisconsin and all threatened and endangered species native to the State of Wisconsin.
Publication(s): Boom
Keyword(s): Land Issues, Wildlife & Species
Contact(s):
Russell Schallert, President
Lawrence Deleers, Jr., Vice President; 4665 Highway Y, Saukville, WI 53080; 773-373-3366
William Emory, Vice President; Klug and Smith Company, 4425 W. Mitchell, Milwaukee, WI 53214
Gregory Septon, Vice President; Milwaukee Public Museum; 800 W. Wells Street, Milwaukee, WI 53233
Glenn Goergen, Treasurer; Deloitte and Touche, 250 E. Wisconsin Ave., Milwaukee, WI 53202
Kurt Remus, Jr., Secretary; 3860 N. Port Washington Rd., Milwaukee, WI 53217

SOCIETY OF WETLAND SCIENTISTS

P.O. Box 7060
Lawrence, KS 66044-7060 United States
Phone: 785-843-1235 Fax: 785-843-1274
E-mail: sws@allenpress.com
Website: www.sws.org

Founded: 1979
Membership: 1,001–10,000
Scope: International
Description: International nonprofit education and charitable society of persons interested in wetland science, technology, and related fields. Encourages educational, scientific, and technological development and advancement in all fields of wetland science. Encourages protection, restoration, and stewardship of wetlands. Student memberships and scholarships.
Publication(s): Wetlands, SWS Bulletin
Keyword(s): Water Habitats & Quality
Contact(s):
Barry Warner, President
Virginia Carter, Past President
Glenn Guntenspergen, Secretary; 301-497-5523
Mary Kentula, Treasurer; 541-754-4478, ext. 5682

SOIL AND WATER CONSERVATION SOCIETY

Attn: Deb Happe-Von Arb, 7515 NE Ankeny Rd.
Ankeny, IA 50021-9764 United States
Phone: 515-289-2331 Fax: 515-289-1227
E-mail: swcs@swcs.org
Website: www.swcs.org

Founded: 1945
Membership: 1,001–10,000
Scope: National, International
Description: (formerly Soil Conservation Society of America) The Soil and Water Conservation Society is a multidisciplinary membership organization advocating protection, enhancement, and wise use of soil, water, and related natural resources. SWCS programs emphasize the interdependence of natural resources through education, publications, and a network of local chapters throughout the U.S. and Canada. SWCS also manages the World Association of Soil and Water Conservation.
Publication(s): Journal of Soil and Water Conservation
Keyword(s): Agriculture/Farming, Climate Change, Ecosystems (precious), Ethics/Environmental Justice, Forests/Forestry, Land Issues, Oceans/Coasts/Beaches, Recreation/Ecotourism, Sprawl/Urban Planning, Water Habitats & Quality, Wildlife & Species
Contact(s):
Craig Cox, Executive Director; 7515 NE Ankeny Road, Ankeny, IA 50021; 515-289-2331, ext. 13; Fax: 515-289-1227; craigcox@swcs.org
Bob Eddleman, President; 8729 Chapel Glen Drive, Indianapolis, IN 46234; 317-271-4413; Fax: 317-290-3225; RLEddleman@aol.com
Deb Happe-Von Arb, Communications Director/Editor; 7515 NE Ankeny Road, Ankeny, IA 50021; 515-289-2331, ext. 26; Fax: 515-289-1227; deb@swcs.org
Norman Berg, Washington, DC Representative; 202-659-5668; Fax: 202-659-8339; nberg46738@aol.com
James Bruce, Ottawa, Canada Representative; 613-731-5929; Fax: 613-731-3509; jpbruce@sympatico.ca

SONORAN INSTITUTE

7630 E. Broadway Blvd., Suite 203
Tucson, AZ 85710 United States
Phone: 520-290-0828 Fax: 520-290-0969
E-mail: sonoran@sonoran.org
Website: www.sonoran.org

Founded: 1990

Scope: National

Description: The mission of the Sonoran Institute is to promote community-based conservation strategies that preserve the ecological integrity of protected lands and at the same time meet the economic aspirations of adjoining landowners and communities. Underlying this mission is the conviction that locally-driven and inclusive approaches to conservation produce the most effective results.

Keyword(s): Development/Developing Countries, Land Issues, Public Lands/Greenspace, Water Habitats & Quality

Contact(s):

Mark Briggs, Director of Research
Steve Cornelius, Director of Borderlands Program
Lee Nellis, Director of Land Use Policy
Luther Propst, Executive Director
Lara Schmit, Director of Communications
Fred Bosselman, Vice Chair
Susan Culp, Research Associate
Frank Gregg, Chairman
Jake Kittle, Secretary/Treasurer
Joaquin Murriet, Associate Director of Borderlands Program
Josh Schachter, Program Associate
John Shepard, Associate Director

SONORAN INSTITUTE

NORTHWEST OFFICE
201 South Wallace Avenue
Bozeman, MT 59715 United States
Phone: 406-587-7331 Fax: 406-587-2027
E-mail: sonoran@sonoran.org
Website: www.sonoran.org

Founded: 1990

Scope: Local, State, Regional, International

Description: The Sonoran Institute works with communities to conserve and restore important natural landscapes in Western North America, including the wildlife and cultural values of these lands. The Sonoran Institute's community stewardship work creates lasting benefits including healthy landscapes and vibrant, livable communities that embrace conservation as an integral element of their economies and quality of life.

Keyword(s): Agriculture/Farming, Development/Developing Countries, Ecosystems (precious), Land Issues, Public Lands/Greenspace, Recreation/Ecotourism, Reduce/Reuse/Recycle, Sprawl/Urban Planning, Water Habitats & Quality

Contact(s):

John Shepard, Associate Director; 520-290-0828; Fax: 520-290-0969; john@sonoran.org
Luther Propst, Executive Director; luther@sonoran.org
Nancy Laney, Chairman of the Board

SOUND EXPERIENCE

HISTORIC SCHOONER ADVENTURESS
2310 Washington St.
Port Townsend, WA 98368 United States
Phone: 360-379-0438 Fax: 360-379-0439
E-mail: soundexp@olypen.com
Website: www.soundexp.org

Founded: 1989

Scope: National

Description: Sound Experience involves participants in exploration of Puget Sound from the decks of a traditional sailing ship (the 101' Schooner Adventuress). Our mission is protecting Puget Sound through education.

Publication(s): Publications available on website

Keyword(s): Recreation/Ecotourism

Contact(s):

Nick Worden, President
Jenell DeMatteo, Executive Director; 360-379-0438; Fax: 360-379-0439; soundexp@olypen.com
Dani Turissini, Communications Manager; 360-379-0438; Fax: 360-379-0439; soundexp@olypen.com
Kelley Watson, Education Director; 360-379-0438; Fax: 360-379-0439; soundexp@olypen.com

SOUTH CAROLINA ASSOCIATION OF CONSERVATION DISTRICTS

1835 Assembly St., Rm. 950 Strom Thurmond Federal Building
Columbia, SC 29201 United States
Phone: 803-755-0319 Fax: 803-253-3670

Founded: N/A

Membership: 101–1,000

Scope: State

Contact(s):

Larry Nates, President; 112 Luther Dr., Gaston, SC 29053; 803-755-0319
Ed McAllister, Vice President
Linda Tansill, Executive Director
Amanda Bauknight, Secretary; 1967 Burles Ridge Rd., Easley, SC 23640
Diane Edwins, Treasurer; 4169 State Rd., Ridgeville, SC 29472; 843-688-5461

SOUTH CAROLINA B.A.S.S. CHAPTER FEDERATION

Attn: President, 1469 Schurlknight Rd.
St. Stephen, SC 29479-3627 United States
Phone: 803-567-4680
E-mail: tonybennett@dycon.com
Website: www.scbass.com

Founded: N/A

Scope: State

Description: An organization of Bassmaster chapters, affiliated with the Bass Anglers Sportsman Society, organized to fight pollution, assist state and national conservation agencies in their efforts, and teach the young people of our country good conservation practices. Dedicated to the realistic conservation of our water resources.

Publication(s): South Carolina Forestry Journal, South Carolina B.A.S.S. Federation, Inc. Newsletter.

Keyword(s): Forests/Forestry, Land Issues, Transportation, Water Habitats & Quality

Contact(s):

Tony Bennett, President; 803-567-4680
Tom Hueble, Conservation Director; 446 Baker Rd., Whitmire, SC 29178; 803-694-3602; hueblefamily@mindsprings.com

SOUTH CAROLINA COASTAL CONSERVATION LEAGUE

P.O. Box 1765
Charleston, SC 29402 United States
Phone: 843-723-8035 Fax: 843-723-8308
E-mail: scccl@charleston.net
Website: www.scccl.org

Founded: 1989

Scope: Local

Description: SCCCL works to protect our state's coastal resources through programs in land use, forestry, water quality and public education.

Publication(s): Conservation League Newsletter

Keyword(s): Land Issues, Oceans/Coasts/Beaches, Pollution (general), Public Lands/Greenspace, Reduce/Reuse/Recycle, Water Habitats & Quality, Wildlife & Species

Contact(s):

Dana Beach, Executive Director; danabeach@scccl.org
Jane Lareau, Contact for Forestry; janel@sccoast.net
Sam Passmore, Contact for Land Use; samp@scccl.org
Nancy Vinson, Contact for H2O; nancyv@scccl.org

SOUTH CAROLINA ENVIRONMENTAL LAW PROJECT

P.O. Box 1380
Pawleys Island, SC 29585 United States
Phone: 843-527-0078 Fax: 843-527-0540
Website: www.scelp.org

Founded: 1987
Membership: N/A
Scope: Regional
Description: SCELP is a nonprofit organization whose mission is to protect the natural environment of South Carolina by providing legal services and advice to environmental organizations and concerned citizens, and by improving the state's system of environmental regulation.
Publication(s): Mountains and Marshes
Keyword(s): Land Issues, Water Habitats & Quality
Contact(s):
James Chandler, President and General Counsel

SOUTH CAROLINA FORESTRY ASSOCIATION

4901 Broad River Rd., P.O. Box 21303
Columbia, SC 29221 United States
Phone: 803-798-4170 Fax: 803-798-2340
E-mail: scfa@scforestry.org
Website: www.scforestry.org

Founded: 1968
Scope: State
Description: A nonprofit educational organization with a membership of timberland owners, wood dealers, wood-using industries, equipment suppliers, and individuals interested in forest conservation and wise use of natural resources.
Contact(s):
Robert Scott, President
Sam Coker, Chairman of the Board; SC Pole at Piling Company P.O. Box 3309, Leesville, SC 29070; 803-532-5806

SOUTH CAROLINA NATIVE PLANT SOCIETY

P.O. Box 759
Pickens, SC 29671 United States
Phone: 864-868-7798
Website: www.clemson.edu/scnativeplants

Founded: 1996
Scope: State
Description: Promotes native plants and plant communities through an education-based agenda. The Society sponsors field trips, symposiums, workshops and lectures. The Society also works with government agencies to assist in seed collection and management.
Publication(s): Newsletter, Brochure
Keyword(s): Wildlife & Species
Contact(s):
Rick Huffman, President; 864-868-7798; rhuffman@innova.net
Bill Stringer, Vice-President; 864-656-3527

SOUTH CAROLINA WILDLIFE FEDERATION

2711 Middleburg Dr.
Suite 104
Columbia, SC 29204 United States
Phone: 803-256-0670 Fax: 803-256-0690
E-mail: mail@scwf.org
Website: www.scwf.org

Founded: 1931
Membership: 1,001–10,000
Scope: State
Description: South Carolina Wildlife Federation is a nonprofit citizens' conservation organization that advocates environmental stewardship by promoting wildlife habitat enhancement and natural resources conservation. SCWF is active in promoting sound stewardship of SC's natural treasures through educational and public awareness programs. Drawing strength from a committed membership and unique partnerships, SCWF establishes policies that protect and enhance the natural systems which give life to us all.
Publication(s): Out of Doors
Keyword(s): Ethics/Environmental Justice, Forests/Forestry, Land Issues, Oceans/Coasts/Beaches, Public Lands/Greenspace, Reduce/Reuse/Recycle, Water Habitats & Quality, Wildlife & Species
Contact(s):
Andy Brack, President
Angela Viney, Executive Director
Robert Barber, Lobbyist
Sara Green, Director of Education
Katie Myers, Development Coordinator
Rose Thielke, Membership Administrative Assistant

SOUTH DAKOTA ASSOCIATION OF CONSERVATION DISTRICTS

SDACD
P.O. Box 275
116 N Euclid
Pierre, SD 57501 United States
Phone: 695-895-4099 Fax: 605-895-9424
E-mail: info@sdconservation.org
Website: sdconservation.org

Founded: 1942
Membership: 1–100
Scope: State
Description: Our mission is to assist, lead, and coordinate conservation districts (local units of government) in their efforts to promote sensible, voluntary, self-governed conservation management and development of South Dakota's natural resources for ourselves and our posterity.
Keyword(s): Agriculture/Farming, Air Quality/Atmosphere, Climate Change, Ecosystems (precious), Forests/Forestry, Land Issues, Pollution (general), Public Lands/Greenspace, Recreation/Ecotourism, Reduce/Reuse/Recycle, Water Habitats & Quality, Wildlife & Species
Contact(s):
Lynn Denke, President; 19580 224th St., Creighton, SD 57729-9747; 605-279-2633; ldenke@gwtc.net
Angela Ehlers, Executive Director; 116 N. Euclid, P.O. Box 275, Pierre, SD 57501-0275; 605-895-4099; Fax: 605-895-9424; info@sdconservation.org
Dean Colling, Nutrient Mgt. Technical Assistance Team; 1820 N. Kimball #4, Mitchell, SD 57301-1114; 605-996-1564, ext. 5; Fax: 605-996-4708; Dean-Colling@sd.nacdnet.org
Justin (Judge) Jessop, Grasslands Mgt. Technical Assistance Team; 24690 299th Avenue, Presho, SD 57568; 605-280-0127; Justin-Jessop@sd.nacdnet.org
Eric Muller, Buffer Technical Assistance Team; 44644 164th Street, Florence, SD 57235-5606; 605-690-2655; Eric-Muller@sd.nacdnet.org

SOUTH DAKOTA B.A.S.S. CHAPTER FEDERATION

Attn: President, P.O. Box 377
Brandon, SD 57005 United States
Phone: 605-582-2309 Fax: 605-582-2309
Website: www.sdbassfederation.com

Founded: N/A
Membership: 101–1,000
Scope: State
Description: An organization of Bassmaster chapters, affiliated with the Bass Anglers Sportsman Society, organized to fight pollution, assist state and national conservation agencies in their efforts, and teach young people of our country good con-

servation practices. Dedicated to the realistic conservation of our water resources.

Publication(s): South Dakota Bird Notes, Birds of South Dakota, 1991, B.A.S.S. Federation Newsletter "Dakota Bassin", The South Dakota Breeding Bird Atlas, 1995.

Keyword(s): Wildlife & Species

Contact(s):
Chuck Doom, President
Phillip Risnes, Conservation Director; 26643 461st. Ave., Hartford, SD 57033; 605-526-4339; philrisnes@aol.com

SOUTH DAKOTA ORNITHOLOGISTS UNION

Dept. of Biology, University of South Dakota
Vermillion, SD 57069 United States
Phone: 605-677-6175 Fax: 605-677-6557

Founded: 1949
Membership: 101–1,000
Scope: State

Description: To encourage the study of birds in South Dakota and to promote the study of ornithology by more closely uniting the students of this branch of natural science.

Publication(s): South Dakota Bird Notes, South Dakota Breeding Bird Atlas, The (1995), Birds of South Dakota (1991).

Keyword(s): Agriculture/Farming, Air Quality/Atmosphere, Energy, Reduce/Reuse/Recycle

Contact(s):
Robb Schenck, President; 422 N. Linwood Ct., Sioux Falls, SD 57103
Nelda Holden, Treasurer; 1620 Elmwood Dr., Brookings, SD 57006; 605-692-8278
Jeffrey Palmer, Past President; 821 NW Fifth St., Madison, SD 57041; 605-256-9745
David Swanson, Secretary; Biology Department, University of South Dakota, Vermillion, SD 57069; 605-624-0203
Dan Tallman, Editor; Box 740, Northern State University, Aberdeen, SD 57401; 605-226-2255

SOUTH DAKOTA RESOURCES COALITION

P.O. Box 66
Brookings, SD 57006 United States
Phone: 605-697-6675 Fax: 605-697-6675
E-mail: sdrc@brookings.net
Website: www.geocities.com/sdrc/

Founded: 1972
Membership: 101–1,000
Scope: State

Description: Seeks to promote the survival and integrity of water, energy, land, wildlife, and air resources, along with justice in their allocation.

Publication(s): ECO FORUM.

Keyword(s): Agriculture/Farming, Energy, Executive/Legislative/Judicial Reform, Pollution (general), Water Habitats & Quality

Contact(s):
Luanne Napton, President; 605-693-4893
Lawrence Novotny, Board Secretary; 605-688-6171
Sue Grant, Staff Assistant; 605-697-6675; Fax: 605-697-6675; sdrc@brookings.net

SOUTH DAKOTA WILDLIFE FEDERATION

P.O. Box 7075
Pierre, SD 57501-7075 United States
Phone: 605-224-7524 Fax: 605-224-7524
E-mail: sdwf@sbtc.net
Website: www.sdwf.org

Founded: 1945
Membership: 1,001–10,000
Scope: National

Description: A representative statewide organization, affiliated with the National Wildlife Federation, dedicated to the protection and enhancement of wildlife and its habitat through public education and government interaction.

Publication(s): Out of Doors

Keyword(s): Reduce/Reuse/Recycle, Water Habitats & Quality, Wildlife & Species

Contact(s):
Mike Larsen, President and Representative
Chris Hesla, Executive Director and Editor. Education Programs Contact
Chuck Clayton, Alternate Representative
Robert Jacobson, Treasurer

SOUTH OAHU SOIL AND WATER CONSERVATION DISTRICT

938 Kamiloniu Place,
Honolulu, HI 96825 United States
E-mail: swcd@soswcd.org
Website: sos.wcd.org

Founded: 1939
Membership: 1,001–10,000
Scope: State

Description: for better understanding, appreciation, and conservation of Hawaii's native wildlife resources, especially its unique and endangered bird species and their associated ecosystems.

Contact(s):
David Norbriga, President; 808-244-7951; Fax: 808-244-4108
Joloyce Kaia, 1st Vice President; P.O. Box 404, Hana, HI 96713; 808-248-7725
Mike Tulang, Executive Director; 919 Ala Moana Blvd. Rm. 309, Honolulu, HI 96814; 808-586-4389; Fax: 808-586-4300
Ted Inouye, Alternate Board Member; P.O. Box 278, Hanamaulu, HI 96715; 808-245-3027
Valerie Mendes, Alternate Board Member; 1100 Alakea St. #1200, Honolulu, HI 96813; 808-531-8181

SOUTHEAST ALASKA CONSERVATION COUNCIL (SEACC)

419 6th St., Suite 200
Juneau, AK 99801 United States
Phone: 907-586-6942 Fax: 907-463-3312
E-mail: info@seacc.org
Website: www.seacc.org

Founded: 1969
Membership: 1,001–10,000
Scope: Regional

Description: SEACC is a coalition of 18 local conservation groups, dedicated to preserving the integrity of Southeast Alaska's magnificent natural environment. SEACC works to protect the region's pristine coastal rainforest, abundant fish and wildlife, and outstanding scenery. SEACC helps foster a sustainable approach to economic stability, subsistence use areas, recreational opportunities, and Southeast Alaska's unique way of life.

Publication(s): RAVENCALL, Action Alerts

Keyword(s): Development/Developing Countries, Forests/Forestry, Land Issues, Oceans/Coasts/Beaches, Pollution (general), Public Lands/Greenspace, Recreation/Ecotourism, Reduce/Reuse/Recycle, Transportation, Water Habitats & Quality, Wildlife & Species

Contact(s):
Wayne Weihing, President; P.O. Box 1193, Ward Cove, AK 99928
John Wisenbaugh, Vice President; P.O. Box 512, Tenakee Springs, AK 99841
Katya Kirsch, Executive Director
Buck Lindekugel, Conservation Director and Staff Attorney
Bart Koehler, Associate Director; 432 Country Rd. 312, Ignacio, CO 81137
Dana Owen, Treasurer; 949 Goldbelt, Juneau, AK 99801

Sue Schrader, Secretary; 10780 Mendenhall Loop Rd, Juneau, AK 99801

SOUTHEASTERN ASSOCIATION OF FISH AND WILDLIFE AGENCIES

8005 Freshwater Farms Rd.
Tallahassee, FL 32309 United States
Phone: 850-893-1204 Fax: 850-893-6204
E-mail: seafwa@aol.com
Website: www.seafwa.org

Founded: 1938
Membership: N/A
Scope: State, Regional, National
Description: Members are state agencies with responsibility for management and protection of fish and wildlife resources in 16 states, Puerto Rico, and the U. S. Virgin Islands; reviews state and federal legislation and regulations and consults with and makes suggestions to federal agencies in order that programs are in the best interest of states; serves as clearinghouse for exchange of ideas concerning wildlife and fisheries management, research techniques, law enforcement, and information and education
Publication(s): Proceedings of the SEAFWA.
Keyword(s): Agriculture/Farming, Ecosystems (precious), Executive/Legislative/Judicial Reform, Forests/Forestry, Land Issues, Oceans/Coasts/Beaches, Pollution (general), Public Lands/Greenspace, Recreation/Ecotourism, Water Habitats & Quality, Wildlife & Species
Contact(s):

Robert Brantly, Executive Secretary; 8005 Freshwater Farms Rd., Tallahassee, FL 32309; 850-893-1204; Fax: 850-893-6204; seafwa@aol.com
James Jenkins, Vice President; Secretary, Department of Wildlife and Fisheries, P. O. Box 98000, Baton Rouge, LA 70898-9000; 225-765-2623
Paul Sandifer, President; Department of Natural Resources, Rembert C. Dennis Building, P. O. Box 167, Columbia, SC 29202; 803-734-4007

SOUTHEASTERN COOPERATIVE WILDLIFE DISEASE STUDY

College of Veterinary Medicine, University of Georgia
Athens, GA 30602 United States
Phone: 706-542-1741 Fax: 706-542-5865
Website: www.scwds.org

Founded: 1957
Membership: 1–100
Scope: Regional, National
Description: The first regional diagnostic and research service in the U.S. for the specific purpose of investigating wildlife diseases. This joint-state organization currently is sponsored by the Southeastern Association of Fish and Wildlife Agencies; Veterinary Services of APHIS, USDA; and the Biological Resources Division of USDI. Participating states: AL, AR, FL, GA, KY, LA, MD, MO, MS, NC, PR, SC, TN, VA, WV.
Publication(s): SCWDS BRIEFS Newsletter
Keyword(s): Agriculture/Farming, Public Health
Contact(s):

John Fischer, Director

SOUTHEASTERN FISHES COUNCIL

c/o Stephen T. Ross
Dept. of Biological Studies
University of Southern Mississippi
Hattiesburg, MS 39406-5018 United States
E-mail: STEPHENROSS@USM.EDU
Website: flmnh.ufl.edu/fish/organization

Founded: N/A
Scope: National
Description: Objectives are to provide for the pursuit and transmittal of information on the status and protection of southeastern fishes and their habitats, and to promote the perpetuation of rich natural assemblages of fishes and their habitats, as well as the localized unique forms and their habitats.
Publication(s): Proceedings of the Southeastern Fishes Council
Keyword(s): Reduce/Reuse/Recycle, Water Habitats & Quality, Wildlife & Species
Contact(s):

Gerry Dinkins, Secretary; 3D International Environmental Group, 7039 Maynardville Highway, Knoxville, TN 37830-7976
Frank Pezold, Editor; Department of Biology, Northeast Louisiana State University, Monroe, LA 71209
Stephen Ross, Chair
Peggy Shute, Treasurer; Tennessee Valley Authority, Natural Heritage Program, Norris, TN 37820
Melvin Warren, Past Chair

SOUTHERN AFRICAN INSTITUTE OF FORESTRY

Postnet, Suite 329, P/Bag X4
Menlo Park, Pretoria, 102 South Africa
Phone: 27123481745

Founded: 1967
Membership: 101–1,000
Scope: International
Description: Represents professional forestry science at all levels in silviculture, forestry conservation, and timber processing, and disseminates information about forestry inside and outside of the profession.
Keyword(s): Forests/Forestry
Contact(s):

W. Olivier, President
P. Kime, Vice President
D. Van der Zel, Publicity Officer; P.O. Box 1673, Pretoria 0001; 271-254-5926
C. Viljoen, Secretary

SOUTHERN APPALACHIAN BOTANICAL SOCIETY

Biology Department, 2100 College St., Newberry College
Newberry, SC 29108 United States
Phone: 803-321-5257 Fax: 803-321-5636

Founded: 1936
Membership: 101–1,000
Scope: Regional
Description: A nonprofit organization to disseminate information on the native plants of eastern North America through meetings and publications.
Publication(s): Castanea (journal), Chinquapin (newsletter).
Keyword(s): Ecosystems (precious), Forests/Forestry, Public Lands/Greenspace, Wildlife & Species
Contact(s):

Zack Murrell, President; Biology Department, Appalachian State University, Boone, NC 28608; 828-262-2674; murrellze@appstate.edu
Patricia Cox, Membership Secretary; Botany Department, University of Tennessee, Knoxville, TN 37996; 865-974-6225; pcox@utk.edu
Charles Horn, Treasurer; 803-321-5257; Fax: 803-321-5636; chorn@newberry.edu

SOUTHERN ENVIRONMENTAL LAW CENTER

201 W. Main St., Suite 14
Charlottesville, VA 22902-5065 United States
Phone: 434-977-4090 Fax: 434-977-1483
E-mail: selcva@selcva.org
Website: www.SouthernEnvironment.org

Founded: 1986
Membership: N/A
Scope: Local, State, Regional, National
Description: A regional nonprofit advocacy organization committed to protecting the natural resources of the Southeast

through regulatory reform and the judicial process; through partnerships with more than 100 federal, state and local organizations; and through providing regional leadership on key Southeastern environmental issues. SELC works in Alabama, Georgia, North Carolina, South Carolina, Tennessee and Virignia.

Publication(s): Beyond Asphalt, Power That Pollutes, Where Are We Growing?, Smart Growth in the Southeast, Southern Resources, Phil Reed Writing Award

Keyword(s): Agriculture/Farming, Air Quality/Atmosphere, Executive/Legislative/Judicial Reform, Forests/Forestry, Oceans/Coasts/Beaches, Pollution (general), Sprawl/Urban Planning, Transportation, Water Habitats & Quality, Wildlife & Species

Contact(s):

Lark Hayes, Carolinas Office; 200 West Franklin Street, Suite 330, Chapel Hill, NC 27516; 919-967-1450

Frederick Middleton, Executive Director; 434-977-4090

Wes Woolf, Deep South Office; 127 Peachtree Street, Suite 605, Atlanta, GA 30303; 404-521-9900

Cathryn McCue, Media Director; 434-977-4090

Deaderick Montague, Board Chairman

SOUTHERN ENVIRONMENTAL LAW CENTER

NORTH CAROLINA OFFICE
200 W. Franklin St., Suite 330
Chapel Hill, NC 27516-2559 United States
Phone: 919-967-1450 Fax: 919-929-9421
E-mail: selcnc@selcnc.org
Website: www.southernenviroment.org

Founded: N/A
Membership: 1–100
Scope: Regional
Description: Environmental Law Center
Publication(s): Southern Resources

SOUTHERN NEW ENGLAND FOREST CONSORTIUM, INC. (SNEFCI)

P.O. Box 760
Chepachet, RI 02816 United States
Phone: 401-568-1610 Fax: 401-568-7874
E-mail: sneforest@efortress.com

Founded: 1985
Membership: 1–100
Scope: Regional

Description: SNEFCI promotes wise conservation practices in Southern New England. Our goals are to reduce forest fragmentation, promote stewardship of forest resources, and enhance urban and community forest resources.

Publication(s): Preferential Property Tax Treatment of Open Space Land in New England, Forest Land Conversion, Fragmentation, and Partialization, Threatened and Endangered Species Field Guide in New England, Land Conservation Development and Property Taxes in Rhode Island, Cost of Community Services in Southern New England, Your Family Lands: Legacy or Memory: Commonly Asked Questions

Keyword(s): Forests/Forestry

Contact(s):

Thomas Dupree, President; 401-277-1414; Fax: 401-647-3590; riforestry@edgenet.net

Donald Smith, Vice President; 860-424-3630; Fax: 860-424-4070; don.smith@po.state.ct.us

Christopher Modisette, Executive Director

Hans Bergey, Treasurer; 401-821-8746; Fax: 401-821-8746; hberg16@aol.com

SOUTHERN RHODE ISLAND STATE ASSOCIATION OF CONSERVATION DISTRICTS

60 Quaker Ln., Suite 46
Warwick, RI 02866-0114 United States
Phone: 401-822-8832 Fax: 401-828-0433
Website: ri.nacdnet.org/sricd_web/index.htm

Founded: N/A
Scope: State

Publication(s): Cultivation Notes 1-16, Bi-Annual Newsletter, Wild Plants! (some basic information, other resources and fact sheets).

Keyword(s): Land Issues, Public Lands/Greenspace, Wildlife & Species

Contact(s):

Jesse Carpenter, President, Board Member; 401-762-7346; Fahma1@aol.com

Emerson Wildes, Vice President; Whimshaw Farm, Shaw Rd., Little Compton, RI 02837; 401-635-2935

John Devany, Treasurer

Robert Swanson, Chair; 39 Shannock Hill Rd., Carolina, RI 02812; 401-364-4069

SOUTHERN UTAH WILDERNESS ALLIANCE

Headquarters, 1471 S. 1100 E.
Salt Lake City, UT 84105-2423 United States
Phone: 801-486-3161 Fax: 801-486-4233
E-mail: suwa@suwa.org
Website: www.suwa.org

Founded: 1983
Membership: 10,001–100,000
Scope: International

Description: SUWA advocates wilderness preservation for qualifying federal public lands in Utah's incomparable canyon country. Through the allied efforts of SUWA's staff, Utah activists, and concerned citizens across the United States, SUWA seeks to give its members and the general public a voice in deciding the fate of America's redrock wilderness.

Publication(s): America's Redrock Wilderness - quarterly newsletter, bulletins

Contact(s):

Larry Young, Executive Director

Greg Miner, Secretary

Mark Ristow, Treasurer

Ted Wilson, Vice Chairman

Hansjorg Wyss, Chairman

SOUTHERN UTAH WILDERNESS ALLIANCE

MOAB OFFICE
P.O. Box 968
Moab, UT 84532-0968 United States
Phone: 435-259-5440 Fax: 435-259-9151
E-mail: suwa@suwa.org
Website: www.suwa.org

Founded: N/A
Scope: State

SOUTHERN UTAH WILDERNESS ALLIANCE

ST. GEORGE OFFICE
P.O. Box 1726
Cedar City, UT 84721 United States
Phone: 801-486-3161

Founded: N/A
Scope: State

SOUTHERN UTAH WILDERNESS ALLIANCE

WASHINGTON, DC OFFICE
122 C St., NW
Washington, DC 20001 United States
Phone: 202-546-2215 Fax: 202-544-5197
Website: www.suwa.org

Founded: N/A
Scope: State
Publication(s): Redrock Wilderness (Quarterly Newsletter).

Contact(s):

Keith Hammond

SOUTHFACE ENERGY INSTITUTE

SOUTHFACE ENERGY AND ENVIRONMENTAL RESOURCE CENTER
241 Pine St.
Atlanta, GA 30308 United States
Phone: 404-872-3549 Fax: 404-872-5009
E-mail: info@southface.org
Website: www.southface.org

Founded: 1978
Membership: 101–1,000
Scope: International
Description: The Southface is a nonprofit organization that promotes the use of sustainable energy and environmental technologies and policies in the building sciences through education, research, and technical assistance.
Publication(s): The Southface Journal of Sustainable Building, A Builder's Guide to Energy Efficient Homes in Georgia, Sustainable Design, Construction & Land Development Guidelines for the Southeast
Keyword(s): Development/Developing Countries, Energy
Contact(s):
David Dimling, President
Dennis Creech, Executive Director; ext. 110; dcreech@southface.org
Aziza Cooper, Outreach Coordinator; aziza@southface.org

SOUTHWEST RESEARCH AND INFORMATION CENTER

105 Standford SE
P.O Box 4524
Albuquerque, NM 87106 United States
Phone: 505-262-1862 Fax: 505-262-1864
E-mail: sricdon@earthlink.net
Website: www.sric.org

Founded: 1971
Membership: N/A
Scope: Regional, National
Description: SRIC is a nonprofit organization founded to provide timely, accurate information to the public on a broad range of issues related to the environment, human, and natural resources. SRIC's twin objectives are to promote citizen participation and environmental justice, and to protect natural resources.
Publication(s): Voices from the Earth, Workbook, The
Keyword(s): Ethics/Environmental Justice, Land Issues, Pollution (general), Public Health, Sprawl/Urban Planning
Contact(s):
Anne Albrink, Vice President
Lalora Charles, Secretary
Don Hancock, Administrator
Wilfred Rael, Treasurer

SOUTHWESTERN HERPETOLOGISTS SOCIETY

P.O. Box 7469
Van Nuys, CA 91409 United States
Phone: 818-503-2052
E-mail: SWHS@SWHS.org
Website: www.swhs.org

Founded: 1954
Membership: 101–1,000
Scope: Local, State, Regional, National, International
Description: A California non profit corporation dedicated to the education of its members and the public concerning the roles of reptiles and amphibians in the natural world, the conservation of all wildlife, in particular reptiles and amphibians, and the cooperation between amateur and professional herpetologists, the hobbyist and the academician, for the promotion of the study of lizards, snakes, turtles, tortoises, geckos, skinks, monitors, frogs, toads, and all other reptiles and amphibians.
Publication(s): Herpetology, SWHS Newsletter.
Contact(s):
Jay McAusland, President
Tim Haub, Vice President
Curt Steindler, Secretary

SPORTSMAN'S NETWORK, INC.

501 S. Kentucky Ave., P.O. Box 427
Corbin, KY 40702-0427 United States
Phone: 606-528-9353 Fax: 606-528-2287
E-mail: sportsman@sportsmansnetwork.org
Website: www.sportsmansnetwork.org

Founded: 1991
Membership: 1,000,001 +
Scope: Regional
Description: An incorporated 501(c)(3) nonprofit organization, the Sportsman's Network, Inc., is dedicated to raising the public awareness of wildlife conservation issues through programs which promote controlled hunting, fishing, trapping and other related activities. It produces the "Moment in Conservation" radio program and operates and maintains a wildlife refuge and wildlife animal rehabilitation center and conducts research for restoration of endangered wildlife.
Keyword(s): Wildlife & Species
Contact(s):
Peter Samples, State Chairman; 1681 Knoxville-Gardnersville Road, Williamstown, KY 41097; 859-824-7585; Fax: 859-824-0556; pos1944@hotmail.com
Elmer Chavies, Jr., Executive Director; 606-528-9353; Fax: 606-528-2287; sportsman@sportsmansnetwork.org
Paul Cookendorfer, 1st Vice President
Kenneth Hale, Treasurer
Dean Russell, Secretary
Stacy Suter, 2nd Vice President

SPORTSMANS ALLIANCE OF MAINE

R.R. 12 , Church Hill Rd.
Augusta, ME 04330-9749 United States
Phone: 207-622-5503 Fax: 207-622-5596
Website: www.samcef.org

Founded: 1975
Membership: 1,001–10,000
Scope: State
Description: SAM is a statewide nonprofit organization of sportsmen and women dedicated to hunting, fishing, trapping, protection of wildlife habitat, and conservation. Lobbies and works with state agencies on behalf of Maine sportsmen.
Publication(s): SAM News
Contact(s):
Edye Cronk, President
Robert Cram, 2nd Vice President
James Hilly, 1st Vice President
George Smith, Executive Director and Editor
Herbert Morse, Secretary and Clerk
Richard Paradis, Treasurer

SPORTSMEN'S NATIONAL LAND TRUST, THE

NATIONAL HEADQUARTERS
4311 Manatee Avenue West
Suite 210
Bradenton, FL 34209 United States
Phone: 941-708-3456 Fax: 941-708-3535
E-mail: BillLaMee@TheSportsmens.org
Website: TheSportsmens.org

Founded: 1998
Membership: N/A
Scope: National
Description: THE SPORTSMEN'S saves land for hunters.
Keyword(s): Land Issues, Public Lands/Greenspace, Recreation/Ecotourism, Sprawl/Urban Planning, Wildlife & Species

Contact(s):
Bill LaMee, President; 941-708-3456; Fax: 941-708-3535; BillLaMee@TheSportsmens.org
Terry Steele, Vice President - National Programs Director; 14 Boxelder Court, Homosassa, FL 34446; 941-708-3456; Fax: 941-708-3535; bigt2@mindspring.com

ST. CROIX INTERNATIONAL WATERWAY COMMISSION

Box 610
Calais, ME 04619 United States
Phone: 506-466-7550 Fax: 506-466-7551
E-mail: staff@stcroix.org

Founded: 1989
Membership: 1–100
Scope: International
Description: A commission of the State of Maine and province of New Brunswick to help implement a cooperative international management plan for the St. Croix River boundary corridor, which forms 110 miles of the US/Canada border.
Publication(s): St. Croix Heritage Brochure, Annual Report, Management Plan for the St. Croix International Waterway.
Contact(s):
Lee Sochasky, Executive Director
Don Carson, Co-Chairman
Ken Gordon, Co-Chairman

ST. FRANCIS WILDLIFE ASSOCIATION

P.O. Box 38160
Tallahassee, FL 32315 United States
Phone: 850-386-6296
E-mail: ellen@stfranciswildlife.org
Website: www.stfranciswildlife.org

Founded: 1978
Membership: 1,001–10,000
Scope: Regional
Description: Providing humane wildlife care, rehabilitation, and environmental education to promote responsible relationships with our natural wildlife resources.
Keyword(s): Wildlife & Species
Contact(s):
Ellen Eichorn, Development Director; 850-893-7577; Fax: 850-893-7135; ellen@stfranciswildlife.org
Jon Johnson, Executive Director; 850-386-6296; jon@stfranciswildlife.org

ST. REGIS MOHAWK TRIBE

Environment Division 412 State Rt. 37
Akwesasne, NY 13655 United States
Phone: 518-358-5937 Fax: 518-358-6252
E-mail: earth@northnet.org
Website: www.northnet.org/earth

Founded: N/A
Membership: 1–100
Scope: Local, State, Regional, National
Description: To monitor, maintain, and protect the environment of the St. Regis Mohawk Tribe for the prevention of disease and injury to body, mind, and spirit. Participation in hazardous waste remediation, Superfund site cleanups, reservation environmental protection, and air and water quality.
Publication(s): Iroquois Environmental Newsletter
Contact(s):
Ken Jock, Director of Environment Division; ext. 16
Les Benedict, Assistant Director of Environment Division; ext. 18; earth-lbenedic@northnet.org

STANFORD ENVIRONMENTAL LAW SOCIETY

Stanford Law School-559 Nathan Abbott Way
Stanford, CA 94305-8610 United States
Phone: 650-723-4421 Fax: 650-723-0501
Website: www.els.stanford.edu

Founded: 1969
Scope: Local
Description: The Stanford Environmental Law Society is the oldest student organization of its kind in the United States. Its primary function is sponsorship of original research in developing areas of environmental law. The Society relies on contributions, grants, and proceeds from the sale of publications.
Publication(s): Stanford Environmental Law Journal, Who Runs the Rivers?, Hazardous Waste Disposal Sites, Endangered Species Act, Handbook, Strategies for Environmental Law Enforcement.
Contact(s):
Janelle Smith, Co-President
Katherine Wannamaker, Co-President
Louise Warren, Business Manager

STATE AND TERRITORIAL AIR POLLUTION PROGRAM ADMINISTRATORS AND THE ASSOCIATION OF LOCAL AIR POLLUTION

STAPPA/ALAPCO
444 N. Capitol St., NW, Suite 307
Washington, DC 20001 United States
Phone: 202-624-7864 Fax: 202-624-7863
E-mail: 4clnair@sso.org
Website: www.cleanairworld.org

Founded: 1980
Membership: 101–1,000
Scope: National
Description: The national associations of air pollution control agencies in the states, territories, and major metropolitan areas. The associations' members have primary responsibility for ensuring healthy air quality and represent the technical expertise behind the implementation of our nation's air pollution control laws and regulations.
Publication(s): Meeting the 15% Rate of Progress Requirement Under The Clean Air Act: A Menu of Options (1993), Controlling Particulate Matter Under The Clean Air Act: A Menu of Options (1995), Controlling Nitrogen Oxides Under The Clean Air Act: A Menu of Options (1994)
Keyword(s): Air Quality/Atmosphere, Climate Change, Pollution (general)
Contact(s):
S. Becker, Executive Director; 202-624-7864; Fax: 202-624-7863; bbecker@sso.org

STATE ENVIRONMENTAL RESOURCE CENTER (SERC)

106 East Doty Street, #200
Madison, WI 53703 United States
Phone: 608-252-9800

Founded: N/A
Scope: State
Description: The State Environmental Resource Center is working state by state to promote positive state legislation, while combating the harmful legislation currently so prevalent at the state level. Working directly with a nationwide network of pro-environmental state legislators, SERC is the first — and only — project of its kind.
Keyword(s): Agriculture/Farming, Air Quality/Atmosphere, Ecosystems (precious), Energy, Ethics/Environmental Justice, Forests/Forestry, Land Issues, Pollution (general), Public Health, Public Lands/Greenspace, Reduce/Reuse/Recycle, Sprawl/Urban Planning, Transportation.

STATE IOWA WOODLANDS ASSOCIATIONS

2735 14th Ave.
Marion, IA 52302-1848 United States
Phone: 515-233-1161

Founded: 1987
Scope: State

Description: A statewide organization affiliated with the National Woodland Owners Association, organized to advance good forestry on the 1.5 million acres of timberland owned by 28,000 nonindustrial private landowners in Iowa.

Publication(s): Timber Talk

Keyword(s): Forests/Forestry

Contact(s):

Al Manning, President
Tom Woodruff, Vice President
E. Frye, Secretary and Editor; 319-377-2540
Joanne Mensinger, Treasurer; 319-259-1160

STATEWIDE PROGRAM OF ACTION TO CONSERVE OUR ENVIRONMENT (SPACE)

N.H. Current Use Coalition, 54 Portsmouth St.
Concord, NH 03301 United States
Phone: 603-224-3306 Fax: 603-228-0423
E-mail: space@conknet.com
Website: www.nhspace.org

Founded: 1966

Scope: State

Description: A private, not-for-profit advocacy coalition of groups dedicated to conserving open space land. S.P.A.C.E.'s work includes advocacy, education, supporting research and working with the state, towns, and individuals on the administration and monitoring of the current use program.

Publication(s): SPACE Newsletter

Keyword(s): Land Issues

STEAMBOATERS, THE

P.O. Box 176
Idleyld Park, OR 97447 United States
Website: www.steamboaters.org

Founded: 1966
Membership: 101–1,000
Scope: National

Description: Formed to preserve, promote, and restore the natural production of wild fish populations, the habitat which sustains them, and the unique aesthetic values of the North Umpqua River for present and future generations.

Keyword(s): Wildlife & Species

Contact(s):

Jim Watson, President; 541-496-3512; samnjim@rosenet.net
Len Janssen, Vice President; 541-440-9375
Paul Moore, Treasurer
Charlie Spooner, Secretary

STOP

230-651 Notre Dame West
Montreal, H3C 1H9 Quebec Canada
Phone: 514-393-9559 Fax: 514-393-9588

Founded: 1970

Scope: State

Description: Devoted to preserving and improving the quality of the physical and human environment, and to promoting rational utilization of natural resources.

Publication(s): Stop Press

Keyword(s): Air Quality/Atmosphere, Oceans/Coasts/Beaches, Pollution (general), Reduce/Reuse/Recycle, Transportation

STROUD WATER RESEARCH CENTER

970 Spencer Rd.
Avondale, PA 19311 United States
Phone: 610-268-2153 Fax: 610-268-0490
E-mail: webmaster@stroudcenter.org
Website: www.stroudcenter.org

Founded: 1967
Membership: 101–1,000
Scope: International

Description: The mission of the Stroud Center is to advance the knowledge of river and stream ecosystems through research and education.

Publication(s): Upstream (newsletter)

Keyword(s): Climate Change, Ecosystems (precious), Land Issues, Water Habitats & Quality, Wildlife & Species

Contact(s):

Claire Birney, Development Director; clairebirney@stroudcenter.org
James Mcgonigle, Education Director; jmcgonigle@stroudcenter.org
Bernard Sweeney, Director; sweeney@stroudcenter.org

STUDENT CONSERVATION ASSOCIATION, INC.

689 River Rd.
Charlestown, NH 03603 United States
Phone: 603-543-1700 Fax: 603-543-1828
Website: www.sca-inc.org

Founded: 1957

Scope: National

Description: SCA's mission is "To build the next generation of conservation leaders and inspire lifelong stewardship of our environment and communities by engaging young people in hands-on service to the land."

Keyword(s): Ecosystems (precious), Forests/Forestry, Land Issues, Oceans/Coasts/Beaches, Pollution (general), Public Lands/Greenspace, Recreation/Ecotourism, Reduce/Reuse/Recycle, Water Habitats & Quality, Wildlife & Species

Contact(s):

Dale Penny, President
Elizabeth Titus, Founding President
Robert Holley, Vice President of Development
Scott Weaver, Vice President of Programs
Edmund Bartlett, Chair of the Board
Mark Bodin, Chief Financial Officer
Kevin Hamilton, Communications

STUDENT CONSERVATION ASSOCIATION, INC.

CALIFORNIA SOUTHWEST REGIONAL OFFICE
655 13th St., Suite 304
Oakland, CA 94612 United States
Phone: 510-832-1966 Fax: 510-832-4726
Website: www.sca-inc.org

Founded: N/A

Scope: Regional, National

Publication(s): The Volunteer - newsletter

Contact(s):

Bob Coates, Regional Vice President
Rick Covington, Director of Regional Programs; ext. 306; rick@sca-inc.org

STUDENT CONSERVATION ASSOCIATION, INC.

NORTHWEST OFFICE
1265 S. Main St., Suite 210
Seattle, WA 98144 United States
Phone: 206-324-4649 Fax: 206-324-4998
E-mail: susan@sca-inc.org
Website: www.sca-inc.org

Founded: 1957

Scope: Regional, National, International

Description: SCA's mission statement: To build the next generation of conservation leaders and inspire lifelong stewardship of our environment and communities by engaging young people in hands-on service to the land.

Publication(s): The Volunteer - quarterly newletters

Contact(s):

Jay Satz, Vice President National Field Operations NW Regional Officer; ext. 11

STUDENT CONSERVATION ASSOCIATION, INC.

OFFICE OF THE NATIONAL CAPITAL REGION
MID-ATLANTIC/SOUTHEAST REGIONAL OFFICE
1800 N. Kent St.
Suite 102
Arlington, VA 22209 United States
Phone: 703-524-2441 Fax: 703-524-2451
E-mail: info@sca-inc.org
Website: www.sca-inc.org

Founded: N/A

Scope: Local, Regional, National

Description: Our mission is to help build the next generation of conservation leaders in the 16 state Mid-Atlantic/ Southeast region which includes Alabama, Arkansas, Delaware, DC, Florida, Georgia, Kentucky, Louisiana, Maryland, Mississippi, North Carolina, Oklahoma, South Carolina, Tennessee, Texas and Virginia.

Contact(s):
R. Flip Hagood, Vice President; 703-524-2441, ext. 18; Fax: 703-524-2451; flip@sca-inc.org
Karen Blaney, Director of College Program; 703-524-2441, ext. 22; Fax: 703-524-2451; karen@sca-inc.org
Gary King, Director of Regional Programs; 703-524-2441, ext. 12; Fax: 703-524-2451; gary@sca-inc.org
Nadine Morrison, Administrative Coordinator; 703-524-2441, ext. 10; Fax: 703-524-2451; nadine@sca-inc.org
Nancy Oswald, Regional Program Manager; 703-524-2441, ext. 13; Fax: 703-524-2451; nancyo@sca-inc.org
Leib Kaminsky, Regional Development Officer; 703-524-2441, ext. 19; Fax: 703-524-2451; leib@sca-inc.org

STUDENT ENVIRONMENTAL ACTION COALITION (SEAC)

P.O. Box 31909
Philadelphia, PA 19104-0609 United States
Phone: 215-222-4711 Fax: 215-222-2896
E-mail: seac@seac.org
Website: www.seac.org

Founded: 1988

Membership: 101–1,000

Scope: Local, State, Regional, National, International

Description: SEAC is a student and youth run national network of progressive organizations and individuals whose aim is to uproot environmental injustices through action and education. We define the environment to include the physical, economic, political, and cultural conditions in which we live. By challenging the power structure which threatens these environmental conditions, SEAC works to create progressive social change on both the local and global levels.

Publication(s): Resource Materials, Student Environmental Organizing Guide, Threshold, Internships.

Keyword(s): Climate Change, Development/Developing Countries, Ethics/Environmental Justice, Forests/Forestry, Land Issues, Pollution (general), Reduce/Reuse/Recycle

Contact(s):
Jason Fults, National Council Coordinator; 215-222-4711; ncc@seac.org

STUDENT PUGWASH USA

2029 P St. NW
Suite 301
Washington, DC 20036 United States
Phone: 202-429-8900 Fax: 202-429-8905
E-mail: spusa@spusa.org
Website: www.spusa.org

Founded: N/A

Scope: National

Description: The mission of Student Pugwash USA is to promote the socially-responsible application of science and technology in the 21st century. As a student organization, Student Pugwash USA encourages young people to examine the ethical, social, and global implications of science and technology, and to make these concerns a guiding focus of their academic and professional endeavors.

Publication(s): Global Issues Guidebook, Pugwatch, Jobs You Can Live With: Working at the Crossroads of Science, Technology, and Society, Mindfull: a brainsnack for future leaders with ethical appetites.

Keyword(s): Energy, Public Health

Contact(s):
Susan Veres, Executive Director
Eric Roberts, Executive Committee Chairman

STUDENTS PARTNERSHIP WORLDWIDE

Lazimpat, near Hotel Radisson, P.O. Box 4892
Kathmandu, Nepal
Phone: 9771435107 Fax: 9771434645
E-mail: spwnepal@mos.com.np
Website: www.spw.org

Founded: 1986

Membership: 1,001–10,000

Scope: International

Description: Youth focus development programme, working in the field of formal and non-formal education and environmental education in rural government, school of Nepal, and form Green Club school student group to conserve environment in their own surroundings.

Keyword(s): Development/Developing Countries, Ecosystems (precious), Ethics/Environmental Justice, Forests/Forestry, Oceans/Coasts/Beaches, Reduce/Reuse/Recycle, Sprawl/ Urban Planning

Contact(s):
Bishnu Bhalta, Extension Coordinator
Gaurab Rene, Administrative Coordinator

STURGEON FOR TOMORROW

BLACK LAKE CHAPTER
1604 N. Black River Road
Cheboygan, MI 49721 United States
Phone: 231-625-2776 Fax: 231-625-2775
E-mail: brenda@sturgeonfortomorrow.org
Website: sturgeonfortomorrow.org

Founded: 1999

Membership: 101–1,000

Scope: Local, State, Regional, National, International

Description: Lake sturgeon conservation, public relations/ education, research and funding

Keyword(s): Ecosystems (precious), Water Habitats & Quality, Wildlife & Species

SUDBURY VALLEY TRUSTEES

Two Clock Tower Place
Maynaro, MA 01754 United States
Phone: 978-897-5500 Fax: 978-461-0322
E-mail: svt@sudburyvalleytrustees.org
Website: www.sudburyvalleytrustees.org

Founded: 1953

Scope: Local, Regional

Description: Sudbury Valley Trustees was founded in 1953, committed to protecting wildlife habitat and the ecological integrity of the Sudbury, Assabet and Concord Rivers for the benefit of present and future generations. SVT carries out its mission through land acquisition and stewardship, advocacy and education.

SUNCOAST SEABIRD SANCTUARY INC.

18328 Gulf Blvd.
Indian Shores, FL 33785 United States
Phone: 727-391-6211 Fax: 727-399-2923
E-mail: seabird@seabirdsanctuary.org
Website: www.seabirdsanctuary.org

Founded: 1972
Membership: 10,001–100,000
Scope: Local, State, Regional, National, International
Description: A private, nonprofit, membership organization dedicated to the rescue, repair, rehabilitation, and release of healed sick and injured wild birds. Considered the largest wild bird center in the United States, the Sanctuary treats over 10,500 birds each year. It provides a safe home for over 600 permanently injured avian species and sends others to wildlife zoos and parks worldwide. The Sanctuary is open FREE for visitation daily from 9:00 a.m. till dusk. Guided tours available - free admission.
Publication(s): Suncoast Seabird Sanctuary Newsletter, If You Find A Baby Bird Book, S.S.S. Brochure (Blue)
Keyword(s): Oceans/Coasts/Beaches, Wildlife & Species
Contact(s):
Ralph Heath Jr., Founder and Director; 18323 Sunset Blvd., Redington Shores, FL 33708; 727-391-6211; Fax: 727-399-2923; seabird@seabirdsanctuary.org
Suzanne Sakal, Marketing/PR Director; 18328 Gulf Blvd., Indian Shores, FL 33785; 727-392-4291; Fax: 727-399-2923; Suzanne@webcoast.com
Barbara Suto, Hospital Supervisor; 18328 Gulf Blvd., Indian Shores, FL 33785; 727-391-6211; Fax: 727-399-2923; seabird@ij.net

SUSTAIN
THE ENVIRONMENTAL INFORMATION GROUP
920 N. Franklin St. #301
Chicago, IL 60610 United States
Phone: 312-951-8999, ext. 101 Fax: 312-951-5696
E-mail: info@sustainusa.org
Website: www.sustainusa.org

Founded: 1996
Membership: N/A
Scope: Local, State, Regional, National, International
Description: Sustain is a full-service non-profit advertising and public relations agency which partners with regional and national organizations to promote a healthy, sustainable environment. Sustain has played a key role in many national and regional environmental victories. The leading graphic arts publication in the country, Communication Arts, recently raved, "In an eye catching, direct style with an emotional appeal, Sustain aims to make people see things in a way that they might not have before."
Publication(s): The Power of Images.
Keyword(s): Agriculture/Farming, Air Quality/Atmosphere, Climate Change, Ecosystems (precious), Energy, Ethics/Environmental Justice, Executive/Legislative/Judicial Reform, Finance/Banking/Trade, Forests/Forestry, Land Issues, Oceans/Coasts/Beaches, Pollution.
Contact(s):
John Beske, Creative Director; 312-951-8999, ext. 103; Fax: 312-951-5696; john@sustainusa.org
Jim Slama, Executive Director; 312-951-8999, ext. 107; Fax: 312-951-5696; jim@sustainusa.org
Ilsa Flanagan, Associate Director; 312-951-8999, ext. 105; Fax: 312-951-5696; ilsa@sustainusa.org
James Bell, Program Director; 312-951-8999, ext. 101; Fax: 312-951-5696; jamesbell@sustainusa.org

SUSTAINABLE ENERGY INSTITUTE
P.O. Box 4347
Arcata, CA 95518-4347 United States
Phone: 707-826-7775
E-mail: info@culturechange.org
Website: www.culturechange.org

Founded: 1988
Description: As the founder of the Alliance for a Paving Moratorium, Fossil Fuels Action directs road-fighting and education to address loss of farmland, wilderness, and community. APM unites over 150 groups and businesses in a call for an end to new road construction while promoting alternative transportation and the car-free lifestyle. We envision sustainability, embracing nature and sharing, rejecting the technofix designed to perpetuate status quo economics.
Publication(s): Culture Change
Keyword(s): Air Quality/Atmosphere, Development/Developing Countries, Energy, Finance/Banking/Trade, Land Issues, Population, Reduce/Reuse/Recycle, Transportation, Water Habitats & Quality
Contact(s):
Jan Lundberg, Board of Directors President
Eve Gilmore, Vice President, Board Member and Secretary
Pincas Jawetz, Board Member
Debbie Lukas, Board of Directors Member
Lonnie Maxfield, Board of Directors Member
Richard Register, Board of Directors Member

SUSTAINABLE ENERGY INSTITUTE
CULTURE CHANGE MAGAZINE
P.O. Box 4347
Arcata, CA 95518 United States
Phone: 707-826-7775
E-mail: info@culturechange.org
Website: www.culturechange.org

Founded: 1988
Membership: 1,001–10,000
Scope: Local, State, Regional, National, International
Description: We assist people in defining sustainability, mainly through discussing petroleum dependence and solutions such as human-powered transport and local economics. As reforms and regulations have only fed the status quo, we promote cultural change to deal with the ecological crisis.
Publication(s): Sail Transport Network.
Keyword(s): Agriculture/Farming, Air Quality/Atmosphere, Climate Change, Energy, Oceans/Coasts/Beaches, Population, Sprawl/Urban Planning, Transportation
Contact(s):
Raul Riutor, South American Correspondent

T

TALL TIMBERS RESEARCH STATION
13093 Henry Beadel Dr.
Tallahassee, FL 32312-9712 United States
Phone: 850-893-4153 Fax: 850-668-7781
Website: www.talltimbers.org

Founded: 1958
Membership: 1,001–10,000
Scope: International
Description: A nonprofit, tax-exempt scientific and educational organization with a focus on land management, conservation, ecological research, and fire ecology. Information is exchanged in print and on the Internet. Tall Timbers provides publications, seminars, conferences and training programs for land owners and managers, scholars, research scientists, students and concerned citizens.
Publication(s): Newsletters, annual reports, proceedings, technical reports, and informational bulletins.
Keyword(s): Wildlife & Species
Contact(s):
Leonard Brennan, Research Director
Lane Green, Executive Director
Ann Bruce, Librarian; Tall Timbers Library; Fax: 850-668-7781
Kate Ireland, Chairman
Lawton Langford, Treasurer
Walter Sedgwick, Vice Chairperson

TALLAHASSEE MUSEUM OF HISTORY AND NATURAL SCIENCE

3945 Museum Dr.
Tallahassee, FL 32310 United States
Phone: 850-575-8684 Fax: 850-574-8243
Website: www.tallahasseemuseum.org

Founded: 1957
Membership: 1,001–10,000
Scope: Local, State, Regional
Description: To educate residents of and visitors to Tallahassee and the Big Bend area about the region's natural and cultural history, from the beginning of the 19th-century until the present. for this purpose, the museum collects, preserves, and exhibits artifacts and historic buildings, maintains native animals in natural habitats, and operates a 19th century farmstead.
Publication(s): The Newsletter of The Tallahassee Museum of History and Natural Science
Keyword(s): Recreation/Ecotourism, Wildlife & Species
Contact(s):
Russell Daws, Executive Director/CEO; daws@tallhasseemuseum.org
Jennifer Golden, Director of Education
Paula Moyer, Director of Institutional Advancement
Linda Deaton, Curator of Collections and Exhibits
Mike Jones, Curator of Animals

TEENS FOR RECREATION AND ENVIRONMENTAL CONSERVATION (TREC)

Seattle Department of Parks and Recreation, 100 Dexter Ave., N.
Seattle, WA 98109-5199 United States
Phone: 206-684-7097 Fax: 206-684-7025
Website: www.seattletrec.org

Founded: 1992
Scope: State
Description: TREC is an outdoor expedition-level program designed to expose multi-ethnic teens to environmental education, urban conservation, and stewardship, while creating an environment for community leadership and empowerment.
Contact(s):
Robert Warner, Contact; 360-705-1903; robert.warner@ci.seattle.wa.us

TENNESSEE ASSOCIATION OF CONSERVATION DISTRICTS

Attn: President, 2205 Armour Dr., Rte. 2, Box 3712
Somerville, TN 38068 United States
Phone: 731-465-9684

Founded: N/A
Scope: State
Contact(s):
Harris Armour, President; 731-465-9684; Fax: 731-465-5608
Roy Gills, Vice President; 419 Nofattie Rd., Limestone, TN 37615; 423-257-2305
Phil Cherry, Executive Director; 144 Southeast Parkway, Suite 210, Franklin, TN 37064; 615-595-9978, ext. 110; Fax: 615-595-9982
Barry Lake, Secretary-Treasurer; P.O. Box 107, Hickory Valley, TN 38042; 731-764-2909
John Wilson, Board Member; 560 Orr Rd., Arlington, TN 38002; 731-867-8289

TENNESSEE B.A.S.S. CHAPTER FEDERATION

2597 Ogden Rd.
McEwen, TN 37101 United States
Phone: 931-296-4428
Website: www.tnbass.com

Founded: N/A
Scope: State
Description: An organization of Bassmaster chapters, affiliated with the Bass Anglers Sportsman Society, organized to fight pollution, assist state and national conservation agencies in their efforts, and teach the young people of our country good conservation practices. Dedicated to the realistic conservation of our water resources.
Publication(s): Chapter Newsletter
Keyword(s): Water Habitats & Quality, Wildlife & Species
Contact(s):
Charles Mitchell, President; 931-296-4428
Chuck Harger, Conservation Director; 731 Oakland Dr., New Johnsonville, TN 37134; 931-535-2209

TENNESSEE CITIZENS FOR WILDERNESS PLANNING

130 Tabor Rd.
Oak Ridge, TN 37830 United States
Phone: 865-481-0286
E-mail: tcwp@korrnet.org
Website: www.korrnet.org/tcwp/

Founded: 1966
Membership: 101–1,000
Scope: Local, State, Regional, National
Description: Dedicated to achieving and perpetuating protection of natural lands and waters by means of public ownership, legislation, or cooperation with the private sector. Our first focus is the Cumberland and Appalachian regions of East Tennessee, but efforts may extend to the rest of the state and the nation.
Publication(s): TCWP Newsletter
Keyword(s): Forests/Forestry, Land Issues, Public Lands/Greenspace, Water Habitats & Quality, Wildlife & Species
Contact(s):
Jimmy Groton, President; 87 Outer Dr., Oak Ridge, TN 37830; 423-482-5799
Eric Hirst, Vice President; 106 Capital Cir., Oak Ridge, TN 37830; 423-483-1289
Mary Lynn Dobson, Secretary; 209 Cove Point Road, Rockwood, TN 37854; 423-354-4924

TENNESSEE CONSERVATION LEAGUE

300 Orlando Ave.
Nashville, TN 37209-3257 United States
Phone: 615-353-1133 Fax: 615-353-0083
E-mail: tcl@conservetn.com
Website: www.conservetn.com

Founded: 1946
Membership: 1,001–10,000
Scope: State
Description: A representative statewide organization, affiliated with the National Wildlife Federation, dedicated to the protection and enhancement of wildlife and its habitat through public education and government interaction.
Publication(s): Tennessee Out-of-Doors
Contact(s):
Monty Halcomb, President
Phil Craig, Vice-President
Marty Marina, Executive Director, Alternate Representative
Rick Murphree, Treasurer
Bruce Newport, Director of Development and Communications

TENNESSEE ENVIRONMENTAL COUNCIL

One Vantage Way, Suite D-105
Nashville, TN 37228 United States
Phone: 615-248-6500 Fax: 615-248-6545
E-mail: tec@tectn.org
Website: www.tectn.org/tectnhome.html

Founded: 1970
Membership: 1,001–10,000

Scope: State

Description: A nonprofit coalition working to protect and improve Tennessee's public health, quality of life, and natural heritage. TEC is a 28-year-old organization, focused on carrying out the state's environmental policies and regulations on behalf of Tennessee citizens.

Publication(s): ProTECt

Keyword(s): Air Quality/Atmosphere, Development/Developing Countries, Ethics/Environmental Justice, Forests/Forestry, Oceans/Coasts/Beaches, Pollution (general), Public Health, Reduce/Reuse/Recycle

Contact(s):
Robert Diehl, President
Will Callaway, Executive Director; will@tectn.org
Sandi Kurtz, Secretary; 423-892-4403
William Miller, Treasurer; 931-486-9504

TENNESSEE FORESTRY ASSOCIATION

P.O. Box 290693
Nashville, TN 37229 United States
Phone: 615-883-3832 Fax: 615-883-0515
E-mail: info@tnforestry.com
Website: www.tnforestry.com

Founded: 1951
Membership: 1,001–10,000
Scope: State, National

Description: A nonprofit conservation group of over 2,000 woodland owners, public and private foresters, educators, and wood using companies, as well as individual citizens and allied businesses, encouraging the development and wise use of Tennessee's forest resources.

Publication(s): Treeline Newsletter, TN Sustainable Forestry Initiative.

Keyword(s): Forests/Forestry

Contact(s):
Candace Dinwiddie, Executive Director; 615-883-3832; Fax: 615-883-0515; cdinwiddie@tnforestry.com
Tracy O'Neill, Communications & Government Affairs; 615-883-3832; Fax: 615-883-0515; toneill@tnforestry.com

TENNESSEE WOODLAND OWNERS ASSOCIATION

P.O. Box 1400
Crossville, TN 38557 United States
Phone: 615-484-5535

Founded: 1976
Membership: 1–100
Scope: State

Description: A statewide organization affiliated with the National Woodland Owners Association to focus on the special needs and concerns of non-industrial private forest owners throughout Tennessee and to promote responsible resource stewardship.

Keyword(s): Forests/Forestry

Contact(s):
Robert Harrison, Secretary/Treasurer

TERRA PENINSULAR

Belgrado 101
Colonia Ampliacion Moderna
Ensenada, 22879 Mexico
Phone: 52-646-174-5397 Fax: 52-646-174-5397
Website: www.terrapeninsular.org

Founded: 2000

Scope: Regional

Description: Terra Peninsular is a land conservation organization dedicated to protecting the landscapes of the Baja California peninsula.

Keyword(s): Development/Developing Countries, Land Issues, Public Lands/Greenspace, Recreation/Ecotourism, Sprawl/Urban Planning

Contact(s):
Alberto Carreto, General Director; 52-646-174-5397; Fax: 52-646-174-5397; albertocarreto@hotmail.com
Rosi Bustamante, Institutional Development Director; 3560 24th Street #5, San Francisco, CA 94110; 415-821-2495; Fax: 415-821-2495; rosibustamante@yahoo.com
Oscar Rivera, Community Coordinator; 52-646-174-5397; Fax: 52-646-174-5397

TERRENE INSTITUTE, THE

4 Herbert St.
Alexandria, VA 22305 United States
Phone: 703-548-5473 Fax: 703-548-6299
E-mail: terrinst@aol.com
Website: www.terrene.org

Founded: 1990

Scope: National

Description: The Terrene Institute is a nonprofit organization that works with corporate, environmental, and government partners to promote innovative and economical solutions for improving environmental quality. Terrene is an environmental education organization that develops conferences, issues forums, and publications that serve both corporate and nonprofit audiences. Terrene's principal work is water issues, including the coordination of American Wetlands Month activities.

Keyword(s): Pollution (general), Water Habitats & Quality

Contact(s):
Judy Taggart, Executive Vice President; 4 Herbert St., Alexandria, VA 22305; 703-548-5473

TEXAS ASSOCIATION OF SOIL AND WATER CONSERVATION DISTRICTS

Attn: President P.O. Box 13
Temple, TX 77653 United States
Phone: 254-778-8741 Fax: 254-773-3311

Founded: N/A

Scope: State

Publication(s): Big Bend Paisano, The, Big Bend seminars and sales catalog available on request, Official Park Newspaper

Contact(s):
Jose Dodier, President; P.O. Box 13, Zapata, TX 78076; 956-936-2007
Aubrey Russell, Vice President
Dayton Elam, Secretary-Treasurer; 600 SW 21st St., Seminole, TX 79360; 915-758-3504
Beatrice White, Secretary; P.O. Box 658, Temple, TX 76503; 254-778-8741; Fax: 254-773-3311

TEXAS B.A.S.S. CHAPTER FEDERATION

Attn: President, 2221 Apache Dr.
Harker Heights, TX 76548 United States
Phone: 254-698-2015
Website: www.texas-bass.com

Founded: N/A

Scope: State

Description: An organization of Bassmaster chapters, affiliated with the Bass Anglers Sportsman Society, organized to fight pollution, assist state and national conservation agencies in their efforts, and teach the young people of our country good conservation practices. Dedicated to the realistic conservation of our water resources.

Publication(s): SCOT Sportsmen Conservation of Texas, Texas Tightline Magazine

Keyword(s): Forests/Forestry, Land Issues, Water Habitats & Quality

Contact(s):
Stacy Twiggs, President
Alan Allen, Conservation Director; 807 Brazos, Suite 311, Austin, TX 78701; 512-472-2267; AlanAllen-SCOT@att.net

TEXAS COMMITTEE ON NATURAL RESOURCES

1301 South IH-35, Suite 301
Austin, TX 78741 United States
Phone: 512-441-1122 Fax: 512-441-3300
E-mail: tconr@texas.net
Website: tconr.home.texas.net

Founded: 1968
Membership: 1,001–10,000
Scope: Regional
Description: A representative statewide organization, affiliated with the National Wildlife Federation, dedicated to the protection and enhancement of wildlife and its habitat through public education and government interaction.
Publication(s): Conservation Progress
Keyword(s): Ecosystems (precious)
Contact(s):
David Gray, Chair/President
Richard Donovan, Vice Chair
Susan Petersen, NWF Representative
Janice Bezanson, Executive Director, Alternate Representative
Claude Albritton III, Treasurer
Edward Fritz, Editor

TEXAS DISCOVERY GARDENS

CATERPILLARS EXHIBIT
ALL-AMERICAN SELECTIONS
BENNY J. SIMPSON PLANT COLLECTIONS
P.O. Box 152537
Dallas, TX 75315 United States
Phone: 214-428-7476 Fax: 214-428-5338
E-mail: edu@texasdiscoverygardens.org
Website: www.texasdiscoverygardens.org

Founded: 1936
Membership: 101–1,000
Scope: Local, State, Regional
Description: Commmitted to teaching people ways to conserve, restore and preserve the urban environment using native and adapted plants that illustrate the interrelationships of butterflies, bugs and botany.
Keyword(s): Public Lands/Greenspace, Reduce/Reuse/Recycle, Sprawl/Urban Planning, Wildlife & Species

TEXAS FORESTRY ASSOCIATION

P.O. 1488
Lufkin, TX 75902-1488 United States
Phone: 936-632-8733 Fax: 936-632-9461
E-mail: tfa@lcc.net
Website: www.texasforestry.org

Founded: 1914
Scope: State
Description: Private nonprofit statewide organization promoting the conservation, fullest economic development, and utilization of forest and related resources.
Publication(s): Texas Forestry
Keyword(s): Forests/Forestry, Wildlife & Species
Contact(s):
Eric Watson, President
Ronald Hufford, Executive Vice President

TEXAS ORGANIZATION FOR ENDANGERED SPECIES

P.O. Box 12773
Austin, TX 78711-2773 United States
Website: www.rice.edu

Founded: 1972
Membership: 101–1,000
Scope: State
Description: A nonprofit statewide organization dedicated to the conservation of endangered, threatened, or rare species and biotic communities of Texas.
Publication(s): TOES News & Notes
Keyword(s): Development/Developing Countries, Recreation/Ecotourism
Contact(s):
Gary Valentine, President; 254-297-1291
Deborah Holle, Secretary; 512-482-5700
Peggy Homer, Chair of Natural Resources; 512-912-7047
David Lemke, Editor; 512-245-2178
Lee Ann Linam, Past-President; 512-847-9480
Bob Murphy, Education Chairman
C. Sherrod, Treasurer; 512-328-2430
Jason Singhurst, Chair of Conservation Committee; 512-912-7011

TEXAS PARKS AND WILDLIFE

TEXAS CHAPTER
Attn: Executive Director
c/o Texas Parks and Wildlife Division
4200 Smith School Rd.
Austin, TX 78744 United States
Phone: 512-389-4800
Website: www.tpwd.state.tx.us

Founded: 1976
Membership: 101–1,000
Scope: State
Description: An organization that has approximately 3,000 employees including Law Enforcement for Game Laws. To manage and conserve the natural and cultural resources of Texas for the use and enjoyment of present and future generations.
Contact(s):
Robert Cook, Executive Director
Paul Hammerschmidt, Coastal Fisheries Regulations Manager; 512-389-4650; Fax: 512-389-4388; paul.hammerschmidt@tpwd.state.tx.us

TEXAS WILDLIFE ASSOCIATION

401 Isom Rd. Ste. 237
San Antonio, TX 78216 United States
Phone: 210-826-2904 Fax: 210-826-4933
E-mail: twa@texas-wildlife.org
Website: www.texas-wildlife.org

Founded: 1985
Scope: State
Description: Texas Wildlife Association is a nonprofit corporation, formed to protect and promote the rights of Texas' wildlife managers, land owners, sportsmen, and the state's wildlife resources—especially on private lands.
Publication(s): Texas Wildlife

THE ROCKY MOUNTAIN BIOLOGICAL LABORATORY

P.O. Box 519
Crested Butte, CO 81224 United States
Phone: 970-349-7231
E-mail: info@rmbl.org
Website: www.rmbl.org

Founded: 1928
Membership: 10,001–100,000
Scope: International
Description: We are a private, non-profit corporation providing facilities for research and education in the biological sciences in the Rocky Mountains.
Keyword(s): Climate Change, Wildlife & Species
Contact(s):
Ian Billick, Director; ibillick@rmbl.org

THEODORE ROOSEVELT CONSERVATION ALLIANCE

27 Ft. Missoula Rd.
Suite 4
Missoula, MT 59804 United States
Phone: 406-549-0101 Fax: 406-549-7402
E-mail: info@trca.org
Website: www.trca.org

Founded: 1999
Membership: 10,001–100,000
Scope: National
Description: The Alliance's mission is to inform and engage Americans to foster our conservation legacy while working to nurture, enhance and protect our fish, wildlife and habitat resources on America's Public Lands.
Publication(s): Square Dealer-quarterly newsletter
Keyword(s): Forests/Forestry, Public Lands/Greenspace
Contact(s):
Kristen Wagner, Office Manager/Executive Assistant; 406-549-0101; Fax: 406-549-7402; kwagner@trca.org

THORNE ECOLOGICAL INSTITUTE

P.O Box 19107
Boulder, CO 80308-2107 United States
Phone: 303-447-1769 Fax: 303-499-8340
E-mail: info@thorne-eco.org
Website: www.thorne-eco.org

Founded: 1954
Scope: State
Description: A nonprofit educational institute creating inovative outdoor learning experiences and other educational opportunities that teach stewardship of the earth to children and adults. The Institute offers a variety of environmental education classes to children from the Boulder, Denver area with science-based activities and exciting hands-on lessons.
Keyword(s): Recreation/Ecotourism, Water Habitats & Quality
Contact(s):
Susan Peterson, Chairman; susankae@aol.com
Oakleigh Thorne, Founder and Honorary President

THREE CIRCLES CENTER FOR MULTICULTURAL ENVIRONMENTAL EDUCATION

P.O. Box 1946
Sausalito, CA 94965 United States
Phone: 415-331-4540
E-mail: circlecenter@igc.apc.org

Founded: 1990
Scope: National
Description: Three Circles Center introduces, encourages, and cultivates multicultural perspectives and values in environmental and outdoor education, recreation, and interpretation.
Publication(s): Journal of Multicultural Environmental Education, Research Papers, Monographs, Perspectives
Keyword(s): Ethics/Environmental Justice
Contact(s):
Running-Grass, Executive Director; P.O. Box 1946, Sausalito, CA 94965; 415-331-4540

TOGETHER FOUNDATION, THE

113 East 64th Street
2nd Floor
NYC, NY 10021 United States
Phone: 212-879-9334 Fax: 212-879-9440
E-mail: info@together.org
Website: www.sustainabledevelopment.org

Founded: 1989
Scope: Local, State, Regional, National, International
Description: To facilitate positive global change by establishing communications and information systems that inventory and integrate the resources and needs of people, projects, and organizations working on environment, sustainable development, and human rights.
Keyword(s): Development/Developing Countries
Contact(s):
Ella Cisneros, President; 212-879-9334; Fax: 212-879-9440; info@together.org
Martha Vargas, Executive Director; 212-879-9334; Fax: 212-879-9440; info@together.org
Carol Simon, Information Manager; 212-879-9334; Fax: 212-879-9440; info@together.org
Rafael Oliveira, System Administrator; 212-879-9334; Fax: 212-879-9440; info@together.org

TRAFFIC NORTH AMERICA

c/o World Wildlife Fund
1250 24th Street NW
Washington, DC 20037 United States
Phone: 202-293-4800 Fax: 202-775-8287
E-mail: tna@wwfus.org
Website: www.traffic.org

Founded: N/A
Scope: National, International
Description: Trade Records Analysis of Flora and Fauna in Commerce is a scientific, information-gathering program that monitors the trade in wild animals and plants and the products made from them. It is a program of World Wildlife Fund and IUCN and is a part of an international network of TRAFFIC offices.
Publication(s): Traffic North America, Special Reports
Keyword(s): Wildlife & Species
Contact(s):
Simon Habel, Director; simon.habel@wwfus.org
Craig Hoover, Senior Program Officer; craig.hoover@wwfus.org
Holly Reed, Program Assistant; holly.reed@wwfus.org
Chris Robbins, Program Officer; chris.robbins@wwfus.org

TREAD LIGHTLY! INC

298 24th St., Suite 325
Ogden, UT 84401 United States
Phone: 801-627-0077 Fax: 801-621-8633
E-mail: tlinc@xmission.org
Website: www.treadlightly.org

Founded: 1990
Membership: 1–100
Scope: National
Description: Tread Lightly!, Inc. is a nonprofit organization that is an ethical and educational force among outdoor enthusiasts and the industries that serve them. Tread Lightly annually carries out programs designed to instill a proactive, low impact message among enthusiasts, manufacturers, advertising agencies, the media and children of all ages.
Publication(s): Tread Lightly! Trails Newsletter, Guide to Responsible Personal Watercraft Use, Guide to Responsible Mountain Biking, Guide to Responsible ATV Riding, Guide to Responsible Trail Biking, Guide To Responsible Snowmobiling, Guide to Responsible Four-Wheeling
Keyword(s): Land Issues, Recreation/Ecotourism
Contact(s):
Lori Davis, Executive Director; lori@treadlightly.org
Andrew Clurman, Secretary and Treasurer; 929 Pearl St., Suite 200, Boulder, CO 80302; aclurman@skinet.com
Scott Heath, Vice Chairman; 9 Calle Catrina, Rancho Santa Margarita, CA 92688; 949-713-6574; Fax: 949-713-6579; scottheath4@home.com
Philip Milburn, Chairman; 1 Olympic Plaza, Colorado Springs, CO 80909; pmilburn@usacycling.org

TREEPEOPLE

12601 Mulholland Dr.
Beverly Hills, CA 90210 United States
Phone: 818-753-4600 Fax: 818-753-4635
E-mail: info@treepeople.org
Website: www.treepeople.org

Founded: 1973

Scope: Regional

Description: Andy Lipkis and his teenage friends became known as the "TreePeople" when they began planting trees to restore a dying forest. Through innovative education and training programs, TreePeople has involved thousands of students and volunteers in neighborhood renewal and community service throughout southern California. Today, TreePeople is at the forefront of the urban forestry movement, offering sustainable solutions for the urban ecosystem.

Publication(s): Seedling News (member newsletter), The Simple Act of Planting a Tree, Second Nature: Adapting L.A.'s Landscape for Sustainable Living, Healing Your Neighborhood, Your City and Your World

Keyword(s): Forests/Forestry, Reduce/Reuse/Recycle, Wildlife & Species

Contact(s):
Andy Lipkis, President
Jeff Hohensee, Director of Education Program
Jim Summers, Director of Forestry Programs

TREES ATLANTA

96 Poplar St., NW
Atlanta, GA 30303 United States
Phone: 404-522-4097 Fax: 404-522-6855
E-mail: info@treesatlanta.org
Website: www.treesatlanta.org

Founded: 1984
Membership: 1,001–10,000
Scope: Local, Regional

Description: Trees Atlanta is a citizens group that plants, maintains, and conserves trees in metro Atlanta area and educates the public about the importance of trees.

Publication(s): Tree Walk Brochure, Atlanta Treebune

Keyword(s): Climate Change, Ecosystems (precious), Forests/Forestry, Pollution (general), Public Health, Sprawl/ Urban Planning, Wildlife & Species

Contact(s):
Marcia Bansley, Executive Director
Cheryl Bramblett, Director of Communications
Andrew Kramb, NeighborWoods Coordinator; 404-522-4097
Greg Levine, Volunteer Coordinator

TREES FOR THE FUTURE, INC.

9000 16th St., P.O. Box 7027
Silver Spring, MD 20907 United States
Phone: 301-565-0630 Fax: 301-565-5012
E-mail: info@treesftf.org
Website: www.treesftf.org

Founded: 1989
Membership: 1,001–10,000
Scope: International

Description: Trees for the Future offers multi-purpose tree seeds, training materials, and technical assistance for requesting communities, institutions and individuals throughout the developing regions of the world. In addition, Trees for the Future creates awareness of the potential threat of Global Climatic Change and the simple, cost-effective solutions of tree-planting to counter the "Global Warming" effect.

Publication(s): Johnny Appleseed News, Technical Papers

Keyword(s): Agriculture/Farming, Air Quality/Atmosphere, Climate Change, Development/Developing Countries, Energy, Land Issues, Pollution (general), Reduce/Reuse/Recycle, Sprawl/ Urban Planning, Wildlife & Species

Contact(s):
Dave Deppner, President Emeritus
Bill Ligon, Executive Director
Julio Navarro-Monzo, Executive Director
Joseph Permetti, Director of Development
Amy Martin Burns, Office Manager
Patricia Aiken, Secretary
Scott Bode, Africa Program Coordinator
Celso Maatac, Treasurer
John Moore, Chairman

TREES FOR TOMORROW, NATURAL RESOURCES EDUCATION CENTER

P.O. Box 609
519 Sheridan St.
Eagle River, WI 54521 United States
Phone: 800-838-9472 Fax: 715-479-2318
E-mail: trees@nnex.net
Website: www.treesfortomorrow.com

Founded: 1944
Membership: 101–1,000
Scope: Regional

Description: An accredited specialty school which conducts multi-day workshops with natural resource themes for middle and high school students and others from WI, MI and IL. Most topics taught outdoors. Call for free brochure. Also sells tree seedlings.

Publication(s): Tree Tips - biweekly newsletter, Northbound-natural resources journal

Keyword(s): Energy, Forests/Forestry, Land Issues, Public Lands/Greenspace, Recreation/Ecotourism, Reduce/Reuse/ Recycle, Water Habitats & Quality, Wildlife & Species

Contact(s):
Lee Jackson, President; 800-838-9472; Fax: 715-479-2318; trees@nnex.net
Jim Holperin, Director

TREES, WATER, AND PEOPLE

633 S. College Ave.
Fort Collins, CO 80524 United States
Phone: 970-484-3678 Fax: 970-224-0126
E-mail: twp@treeswaterpeople.org
Website: www.treeswaterpeople.org

Founded: 1998
Membership: 1,001–10,000
Scope: Local, Regional, International

Description: Trees, Water, and People is a nonprofit conservation organization established in 1998 with the mission of working collaboratively with communities to establish sustainable forests and watersheds while improving people's lives. We currently have programs in four countries in Central America, and in Colorado, and Wyoming in the U.S.

Publication(s): Forests Forever, Watershed Currents

Contact(s):
Tempra Board, Director of Development; tempra@treeswaterpeople.org
Stuart Conway, International Director; stuart@treeswaterpeople.org
Richard Fox, National Director; twp@treeswaterpeople.org

TRIANGLE RAILS-TO-TRAILS CONSERVANCY

P.O. Box 61091
Durham, NC 27715 United States
Phone: 919-545-9104 Fax: 919-851-0531
E-mail: billbus@gte.net
Website: www.ncrail-trails.org/trtc/index.htm

Founded: 1992
Membership: 101–1,000
Scope: Regional

Description: The mission of the Triangle Rails-to-Trails Conservancy is to work with local and state government officials to preserve local abandoned railroad corridors for future transportation and other interim uses such as recreational trails. TRTC works within the Triangle J Council of Governments service area of Durham, Orange, Wake, Chatham, Johnston, and Lee counties of North Carolina.

Publication(s): TRTC T-shirt

Keyword(s): Land Issues, Recreation/Ecotourism, Sprawl/Urban Planning, Transportation

Contact(s):

Bill Bussey, President; 919-233-8444; Fax: 919-851-0531; billbus@gte.net

TRI-STATE BIRD RESCUE AND RESEARCH, INC.

110 Possum Hollow Rd.
Newark, DE 19711 United States
Phone: 302-737-9543 Fax: 302-737-9562
Website: www.tristatebird.org

Founded: 1976

Scope: International

Description: To study and promote healthy populations of native wildlife by rehabilitation of oiled birds; rehabilitation of injured, diseased, and orphaned birds for release back into the wild; conducting training and education programs for colleagues, peers, and the general public; and conducting medical and biological research consistent with goals of providing for the general well-being of native wildlife.

Publication(s): Effects of Oil on Wildlife, The, Wildlife and Oil Spills Bulletin, Oiled Bird Rehabilitation, Medical Notes for Rehabilitators, Wildlife and Oil Spills: Rehabilitation, Research, and Contingency Planning.

Keyword(s): Pollution (general), Wildlife & Species

Contact(s):

David Mooberry, President; 106 Spottswood Ln., Kennett Square, PA 19348; 610-444-5495
John Frink, Vice President; 400 Milton Dr., Wilmington, DE 19802
Chris Motoyoshi, Executive Director, Contact for Human Resources
Barbara Druding, Secretary; 110 Possum Hollow Rd., Newark, DE 19711; 302-737-9543
Cindy Peterson, Treasurer

TROUT UNLIMITED

National Headquarters, 1500 Wilson Blvd., #310
Arlington, VA 22209-2404 United States
Phone: 703-522-0200 Fax: 703-284-9400
E-mail: trout@tu.org
Website: www.tu.org

Founded: 1959

Membership: 100,001–500,000

Scope: National

Description: A nonprofit, tax-deductible international coldwater fisheries organization dedicated to the conservation, protection, and restoration of coldwater fisheries and their watersheds. Affiliates in Canada, New Zealand, and Australia.

Publication(s): Trout Magazine, Lines To Leaders

Keyword(s): Air Quality/Atmosphere, Water Habitats & Quality, Wildlife & Species

Contact(s):

Charles Gauvin, President and Chief Executive Officer
Lorine Albright, Regional Vice President of Northern Rockies; P.O. Box 1525, Great Falls, MT 59403-1525; 406-454-1384; Fax: 406-761-2610; evenson@mch.net
David Bowie, Regional Vice President of New England; 540 Duck Pond Rd., Westbrook, ME 04092-2510; 207-854-9978; Fax: 207-770-1211; usunmz6m@ibmmail.com
Mike Brock, Regional Vice President of Great Lakes; 23410 Beech Rd., Southfield, MI 48034-3482; 248-356-8195; Fax: 810-592-6098; mikebrock@medidone.net
Stan Griffin, Regional Vice President of Southwest; 27 Dorset Ln., Mill Valley, CA 94941-5203; 510-528-5390; Fax: 510-528-7880; tucalif@ziplink.net
K. Johnson, Regional Vice President of Pacific Northwest; 14727 SE 145th Pl., Renton, WA 98059-7336; 425-865-2201; Fax: 425-271-6378; kbob@halcyon.com
Paul Maciejewski, Regional Vice President of Northeast; 47 Flintlock Dr., Long Valley, NJ 07835-0320; 973-765-6673; Fax: 973-705-5974; 72077.1327@compuserve.com
Steven Moyer, Vice President of Conservation Programs
Kirk Otey, Regional Vice President of Southeast; 1308 Lexington Ave., Charlotte, NC 28203-4837; 704-334-3060; Fax: 704-334-0768; kskotey@mindspring.com
Fred Rasmussen, Regional Vice President of Southern Rockies; 225 County Road 516, Ignacio, CO 81137-9728; 790-563-6517; Fax: 970-563-9599; engelbj@compuserve.com
Lou Schmidt, Regional Vice President of Mid-Atlantic; Rt. 1 Box 109-A, Bristol, WV 26332-9801; 304-367-2724; Fax: 304-367-2727; lschmidt@lolina.net
Ray Smith, Regional Vice President of Midwest; 70 N. College Ave., Suite 11, Fayetteville, AR 72701-5337; 501-521-7011; Fax: 501-443-4333; rsmith7011@aol.com
Whit Fosburgh, Director of Development
Sarah Johnson, Director, National Volunteer Operations; 608-250-2757; Fax: 608-255-1326; johnson@tu.org
Joseph Mcgurrin, Director of Resources
David Nickum, Regional Director of Southern Rockies; 1900 13th St., Ste. 101, Boulder, CO 80302; 303-440-2937; Fax: 303-440-7933
Wendy Reed, Manager of Membership Services
Christine Arena, Editor
Stephen Born, Chairman of National Resource Board; 424 Washburn Pl., Madison, WI 53403; 608-257-6625
Kathy Buchner, Wyoming TU Office Administrator; P.O. Box 4069, Jackson, WY 83001; 307-733-6991; Fax: 307-733-9678; kbuchner@wyoming.com
Don Duff, Coordinator of TU and FS
Kenneth Mendez, Chief Operating and Financial Officer
Oakleigh Thorne, Chairman of the Board

TROUT UNLIMITED

1500 Wilson Blvd.
Suite 310
Arlington, VA 22209-2404 United States
Phone: 703-522-0200
Website: www.tu.org

Founded: N/A

Membership: 100,001–500,000

Scope: Local, State, Regional, National

Description: A national organization with a membership of 125,000 dedicated to the conservation, protection and restoration of trout and salmon and their watersheds.

Publication(s): Trout Magazine, see publications on website

Keyword(s): Energy, Forests/Forestry, Land Issues, Water Habitats & Quality, Wildlife & Species

TROUT UNLIMITED

1966 13th St., Suite LL60
Boulder, CO 80302 United States
Phone: 303-440-2937 Fax: 303-440-7933
E-mail: dnickum@tu.org
Website: www.cotrout.org

Founded: N/A

Scope: State

Description: A statewide council with 28 active chapters working for the protection and enhancement of coldwater fishery resources.

Publication(s): Currents, Rocky Mountain Streamside

Contact(s):

David Nickum, Executive Director
Tom Krol, State Chairman

TROUT UNLIMITED
820 Old Crystal Bay Rd.
Wayzata, MN 55391-9365 United States
Phone: 612-341-9360 Fax: 612-341-9363

Founded: N/A
Scope: State
Description: A statewide council with nine active chapters working for the protection and enhancement of coldwater fishery resources.
Contact(s):
George Hust, Chairman; 952-475-2054

TROUT UNLIMITED
ALASKA COUNCIL
P.O. Box 876675, Wasilla, AK 99687-6675
Homer, AK 99603-3324 United States
Phone: 907-376-1666 Fax: 907-376-1666
E-mail: tuakcoun@alaska.net

Founded: 1988
Membership: 101–1,000
Scope: State
Description: A statewide council with ten active chapters dedicated to the protection and enhancement of the cold water fishery resource.
Contact(s):
Jack Willis, Chairman; 907-235-3860

TROUT UNLIMITED
ARIZONA COUNCIL
Trout Unlimited, Arizona Council
519 East Thomas Road
Phoenix, AZ 85012 United States
Phone: 602-264-5840 Fax: 602-230-7579
E-mail: carm.moehle@azbar.org

Founded: 1989
Membership: 1,001–10,000
Scope: State
Description: A statewide council with four active chapters working for the protection and enhancement of coldwater fishery resources.
Keyword(s): Ecosystems (precious), Forests/Forestry, Recreation/ Ecotourism, Water Habitats & Quality, Wildlife & Species
Contact(s):
Craig Hegel, Treasurer; 830 E. Seldon Lane, Phoenix, AZ 85020; 602-437-5030; Fax: 602-944-9193; craig.h@ix.netcom.com
Carm Moehle, Chairman; 602-264-5840; Fax: 602-230-7579; carm.moehle@azbar.org

TROUT UNLIMITED
CALIFORNIA COUNCIL
State Office, 828 San Pablo Ave.,
Suite 208
Albany, CA 94706 United States
Phone: 510-528-5390 Fax: 510-528-7880
E-mail: tucalif@earthlink.net
Website: californiatu.org

Founded: 1984
Membership: 1,001–10,000
Scope: State
Description: A statewide council with ten active chapters working for the protection and enhancement of coldwater fishery resources.
Keyword(s): Water Habitats & Quality
Contact(s):
Stan Griffin, Office Director

TROUT UNLIMITED
CONNECTICUT COUNCIL
654 Cyprus Rd.
Newington, CT 06111-5612 United States
Phone: 860-667-2515
E-mail: fraa@fraa.org

Founded: N/A
Scope: State
Description: A statewide council with nine active chapters working for the protection and enhancement of coldwater fishery resources.
Contact(s):
Steve Lewis, Chairman

TROUT UNLIMITED
GEORGIA COUNCIL
4450 Oklahoma Way
Kennesaw, GA 30152 United States
Phone: 404-584-7057
E-mail: lvflyfish@mindspring.com

Founded: 1980
Scope: State
Description: A statewide council with 14 active chapters working for the protection and enhancement of coldwater fishery resources.

TROUT UNLIMITED
ILLINOIS COUNCIL
Attn: Chairman, P.O. Box 1280
Oak Brook, IL 60522-1280 United States
Phone: 312-751-4730 Fax: 219-756-7735
E-mail: wjbock1@attbi.com
Website: www.tu.org

Founded: N/A
Membership: 1,001–10,000
Scope: Regional
Description: A statewide council with four active chapters working for the protection and enhancement of coldwater fishery resources.
Contact(s):
Walter Bock, Chairman; wjbock1@home.com

TROUT UNLIMITED
MARYLAND COUNCIL, MID-ATLANTIC
Attn: President, 3509 Pleasant Plains Dr.
Reisterstown, MD 21136-4417 United States
Phone: 410-239-8468 Fax: 410-374-5719
E-mail: tedgodfrey@erols.com
Website: www.tu.org

Founded: N/A
Scope: State
Description: A statewide council with seven active chapters working for the protection and enhancement of coldwater fishery resources.
Contact(s):
Ted Godfrey, Chairman

TROUT UNLIMITED
MICHIGAN COUNCIL
7 Trowbridge NE
Grand Rapids, MI 49503 United States
Phone: 616-460-0477
Website: www.montanatu.org/

Founded: N/A
Scope: State
Description: A statewide council with 21 active chapters working for the protection and enhancement of coldwater fishery resources.

Contact(s):
Richard Rowman, Executive Director

TROUT UNLIMITED
MONTANA COUNCIL
P.O. Box 7186
Missoula, MT 59807 United States
Phone: 406-543-0054 Fax: 406-543-0054
E-mail: montrout@montana.com
Website: www.montanatu.org

Founded: N/A
Membership: 1,001–10,000
Scope: State
Description: A statewide council with 12 chapters working for the protection and enhancement of coldwater fishery resources.
Contact(s):
Bruce Farling, Executive Director

TROUT UNLIMITED
NEVADA COUNCIL
474 South Blakeland Drive
Spring Creek, NV 89815 United States
Phone: 775-778-3159 Fax: 775-778-8199
E-mail: nvtu@rabbitbrush.com
Website: www.rabbitbrush.com/nvtu/

Founded: N/A
Scope: State
Description: A statewide council with three active chapters, dedicated to the protection and enhancement of coldwater fishing resources.
Contact(s):
Matt Holford, Executive Director

TROUT UNLIMITED
NEW HAMPSHIRE COUNCIL
Attn: Chairman, 9 Sirod Rd.
Windham, NH 03087-1401 United States
Phone: 603-896-2236

Founded: N/A
Scope: State
Description: A statewide council with six active chapters working for the protection and enhancement of coldwater fishery resources.
Contact(s):
James Norton, Chairman

TROUT UNLIMITED
NEW YORK COUNCIL
Attn: Chairman, 111 High Point Mountain Rd.
West Shokan, NY 12494-5337 United States
Phone: 914-892-8630
E-mail: karwac@ibm.org
Website: nyscounciltu.homestead.com/HOME.html

Founded: N/A
Scope: State
Description: A statewide council with 37 active chapters working for the protection and enhancement of coldwater fishery resources.
Publication(s): Long Casts
Contact(s):
Chester Karwatowski, Chairman

TROUT UNLIMITED
NORTH CAROLINA
Attn: Chairman, 438 Armfield St.
Statesville, NC 28677-5702 United States
Phone: 704-878-3560 Fax: 704-878-3464
E-mail: davidstewart@usiway.net

Founded: N/A
Scope: State
Description: Dedicated to the protection and enhancement of coldwater fishing resources.
Contact(s):
David Stewart, Chairman

TROUT UNLIMITED
NORTH CAROLINA COUNCIL
Attn: Chairman, 135 Tacoma Cir.
Asheville, NC 28801-1625 United States
Phone: 704-684-5178 Fax: 704-687-1689
E-mail: grant@vnet.net
Website: www.nctu.org

Founded: N/A
Scope: State
Description: A statewide council with 18 active chapters working for the protection and enhancement of coldwater fishery resource.
Contact(s):
Kirk Otey, Chairman; 1308 Lexington Ave., Charlotte, NC 28203; 800-432-6268; Fax: 704-375-6425; kskotey@mindspring.com

TROUT UNLIMITED
OHIO COUNCIL
Attn: Chairman, 1487 New Way Dr.
Beaver Creek, OH 45434-6925 United States
Phone: 937-426-5757
E-mail: mark.blauvelt@stdreg.com

Founded: N/A
Scope: State
Description: Dedicated to the protection and enhancement of the coldwater fishery resource.
Contact(s):
Mark Blauvelt, President

TROUT UNLIMITED
OREGON COUNCIL
213 SW Ashe, Ste. 205
Portland, OR 97024 United States
Phone: 503-827-5700 Fax: 503-827-5672
Website: www.teleport.com/~tuwest

Founded: N/A
Scope: State
Description: A statewide council with seven active chapters working for the protection and enhancement of the coldwater fishery resource.
Contact(s):
Jeff Curtis, Western Conservation Director; jcurtis@tu.org
Alan Moore, Western Communications Coordinator; dmoore@tu.org
Scott Yates, Western Legal and Policy Coordinator; syates@tu.org

TROUT UNLIMITED
OZARKS COUNCIL, MISSOURI
2010 Daisy Ln.
Jefferson, MO 65109-1810 United States
Phone: 573-751-1039 Fax: 573-634-3096
Website: www.agron.missouri.edu/lyfishing/mmtu.html

Founded: N/A
Membership: 1,001–10,000
Scope: State
Description: A statewide council with four active chapters working for the protection and enhancement of coldwater fishery resources.
Contact(s):
John Wenzlick, Chairman

TROUT UNLIMITED
PENNSYLVANIA COUNCIL
RD4 Box 140 AA
Greensburg, PA 15601 United States
Phone: 814-863-7585 Fax: 814-865-9131
Website: www.patrout.org

Founded: N/A
Membership: 10,001–100,000
Scope: Regional
Description: A statewide council with 56 active chapters working for the protection and enhancement of the coldwater fishery resource.
Publication(s): Pennsylvania Trout
Keyword(s): Land Issues, Water Habitats & Quality
Contact(s):
Ken Undercoffer, Chairman

TROUT UNLIMITED
SOUTH CAROLINA COUNCIL
115 Conrad Cir.
Columbia, SC 29212-2619 United States
Phone: 803-777-7652 Fax: 803-777-4760
E-mail: malcolml@gwm.sc.edu
Website: www.tu.org

Founded: 1983
Membership: 1,001–10,000
Scope: State
Description: A statewide council with four active chapters working for the protection and enhancement of coldwater fishery resources.
Publication(s): Web page
www.tu.org
Keyword(s): Agriculture/Farming, Ecosystems (precious), Ethics/Environmental Justice, Forests/Forestry, Land Issues, Public Health, Public Lands/Greenspace, Recreation/Ecotourism, Sprawl/Urban Planning, Water Habitats & Quality
Contact(s):
Malcolm Leaphart, Chairman

TROUT UNLIMITED
TENNESSEE COUNCIL
Attn: Chairman, 1326 Lipscomb Dr.
Brentwood, TN 37027 United States
Phone: 615-371-9211
E-mail: johns@bwood.com

Founded: N/A
Scope: State
Description: A statewide council with 10 active chapters working for the protection and enhancement of the coldwater fishery resource.
Contact(s):
John Smitherman, Chairman

TROUT UNLIMITED
UTAH COUNCIL
Attn: Chairman, 1471 E. Canyon Dr.
South Weber, UT 84405-9629 United States
Phone: 801-538-7353 Fax: 801-538-7278

Founded: N/A
Scope: State
Description: Dedicated to the protection and enhancement of the coldwater fishery resource.
Contact(s):
Wes Johnson, Chairman

TROUT UNLIMITED
VIRGINIA COUNCIL
Attn: Chairman, 202 Deerfield Ln.
Lynchburg, VA 24502-3122 United States
Phone: 804-239-1017
E-mail: dorffly@aol.com

Founded: N/A
Scope: State
Description: A statewide organization with 16 active chapters working for the protection and enhancement of the coldwater fishery resource.
Contact(s):
Thomas Reisdorf, Chairman

TROUT UNLIMITED
WASHINGTON COUNCIL
Attn: Chairman, 2701 NE 148th Ave.
Vancouver, WA 98684-7877 United States
Phone: 360-896-6967
E-mail: ohio12@uswest.net

Founded: N/A
Scope: State
Description: A statewide council with 31 active chapters working for the protection and enhancement of coldwater fishery resources.
Publication(s): Trout and Salmon Leader
Contact(s):
James Derry, Chairman

TROUT UNLIMITED
WEST VIRGINIA COUNCIL
Attn. Dave Bott, 124 Ohio Ave
Westover, WV 26501 United States
Phone: 304-937-2214
E-mail: dwbott@wstdm1.westco.net
Website: www.tu.org

Founded: N/A
Membership: 1,001–10,000
Scope: State
Description: A statewide council with 8 active chapters working for the protection and enhancement of coldwater fishery resources.
Contact(s):
Dave Bott, Chairman of West Virginia Council

TROUT UNLIMITED
WYOMING COUNCIL
Attn: Chairman, P.O. Box 1022
Jackson, WY 83001 United States
Phone: 307-733-4944 Fax: 413-383-1125

Founded: N/A
Scope: State
Description: A statewide council with 16 active chapters dedicated to the protection and enhancement of the coldwater fishery resource.
Contact(s):
Kathy Buchner, Director; kbuchner@wyoming.com
Jay Buchner, Chairman

TRUMPETER SWAN SOCIETY, THE
3800 County Rd. 24
Maple Plain, MN 55359 United States
Phone: 763-476-4663, ext. 113 Fax: 763-476-1514
E-mail: ttss@hennepinparks.org
Website: www.taiga.net/swans/index.html

Founded: 1968
Membership: 101–1,000
Scope: International

Description: International scientific and educational organization dedicated to assuring the vitality and welfare of wild Trumpeter Swan populations in North America, and to restoring the species to its original range. The Society promotes research into Trumpeter ecology and management, and provides a framework for exchange of knowledge about the species.

Publication(s): Proceedings and Papers of the 17th Trump, North American Swans, Bulletin of the Trumpeter Swan Society, Proceedings and Papers of the 16th Trumpeter Swan Society Conference, Proceedings and Papers of the 15th Trumpeter Swan Society Conference, Proceedings and Papers of the 14th Trumpeter Swan Society Conference

Keyword(s): Water Habitats & Quality, Wildlife & Species

Contact(s):

Harvey Nelson, President and Editor; 10515 Kell Ave., Bloomington, MN 55437
Gary Ivey, Vice President; ivey@oregonvos.net
Ruth Shea, Executive Director; 3346 East 200 N., Rigby, ID 83442
Madeleine Linck, Editor

TRUST FOR PUBLIC LAND, THE

Headquarters, National Office
Attn: Public Affairs Assistant, 4th Fl.
116 New Montgomery St.
San Francisco, CA 94105 United States
Phone: 415-495-4014 Fax: 415-495-4103
E-mail: info@tpl.org
Website: www.tpl.org

Founded: 1972

Scope: Local, State, Regional, National

Description: Since its founding in 1972, TPL has worked with public agencies, landowners and citizen groups to protect more than 1.2 million acres in 45 states nationwide and has recently launched its Greenprint for Growth campaign to help sprawl-threatened communities protect land as a way to guide development and sustain a healthy economy and a high quality of life.

Publication(s): Land and People, Regional newsletters

Keyword(s): Land Issues, Public Lands/Greenspace, Recreation/Ecotourism, Reduce/Reuse/Recycle, Sprawl/Urban Planning, Water Habitats & Quality, Wildlife & Species

Contact(s):

Will Rogers, President
W. Allen, Senior Vice President & Regional Director; 306 N. Monroe St., Tallahassee, FL 32301-7635; 904-222-7911
Kathy Blaha, Senior Vice President & Green Cities Initiative Program Director; 666 Pennsylvania Ave. SE, Washington, DC 20003; 202-543-7552
Bowen Blair, Senior Vice President & National Director of Projects; 1211 SW Sixth Ave., Portland, OR 97204-1001; 503-228-6620
Laura Brehm, V.P. & Director of Development
Ernest Cook, Senior Vice President; 33 Union St., 4th Fl., Boston, MA 02108; 617-367-6200
Tod Dobratz, V.P. & Asst. CFO
Alan Front, Senior Vice President & Director of Federal Affairs
Rose Harvey, Senior Vice President & Mid-Atlantic Regional Director; 666 Broadway, New York, NY 10012; 212-677-7171
Whitney Hatch, Vice President & New England Regional Director; 33 Union St., 4th Fl., Boston, MA 02108; 617-367-6200
Reed Holderman, V.P. & Western Regional Director; 116 New Montgomery, 3rd Fl., San Francisco, CA 94105; 415-495-5660
Susan Ives, V.P./Director of Public Affairs and Editor of Land & People
Lesley Kane-Synal, V.P. & Director Federal Legislative Office; 666 Pennsylvania Ave. SE Suite 401, Washington, DC 20003-4334; 202-543-7552
Nelson Lee, Senior Vice President and General Counsel
Felicia Marcus, Executive Vice President
Robert McIntyre, Senior Vice President and CFO
Stephen Thompson, Senior Vice President; 418 Montezuma, Santa Fe, NM 87501; 505-988-5922
Cynthia Whiteford, V.P. & Regional Director; 2610 University Ave. #300,
Becky Mitchell, Director of External Affairs

TRUST FOR WILDLIFE, INC.

127 Ehrich Rd.
Shaftsbury, VT 05262 United States
Phone: 802-447-0746 Fax: 802-447-0746
E-mail: trustforwildlife@net0.net
Website: www.neotropicalbirds.net

Founded: 1983

Membership: 1–100

Scope: International

Description: Dedicated to wildlife conservation and education with a focus on wildlife habitats, international partnerships with a focus on Russia, and wildlife rehabilitation with an emphasis on public education.

Keyword(s): Land Issues, Public Lands/Greenspace, Wildlife & Species

Contact(s):

Marshal Case, President
Les Line, Director; P.O. Box 323, Amenia, NY 12501; 914-373-9135
Ed Metcalfe, Director; 6373 Vermont Rt. 100, Whitingham, VT 05361; 802-464-0048
Gregory Sharp, Secretary; 225 Reeds Gap Rd., East Northford, CT 06472; 203-240-6046

TRUSTEES FOR ALASKA

1026 West 4th Ave., Suite 201
Anchorage, AK 99501-2101 United States
Phone: 907-276-4244 Fax: 907-276-7110
E-mail: ecolaw@trustees.org
Website: www.trustees.org

Founded: 1974

Scope: State

Description: Trustees for Alaska is a public interest law firm whose mission is to provide legal counsel to protect and sustain Alaska's natural environment. We represent local and national environmental groups, Alaska Native villages and nonprofit organizations, community groups, hunters, fishers and others where the outcome of our advocacy could benefit Alaska's environment.

Publication(s): Under The Influence, The Environmental Advocate.

Contact(s):

Ann Rothe, Executive Director; ext. 111
Peter van Tuyn, Litigation Director; ext. 110
Michael Frank, Staff Attorney; ext. 116
Joanna Parker, Legal Support Staff; ext. 109
Mary Mcburney, Vice Chair
Ken Robertson, Chair
Chris Rose, Secretary
Lisa Taylor, Treasurer

TRUSTEES OF RESERVATIONS, THE

572 Essex St.
Beverly, MA 01915-1530 United States
Phone: 978-921-1944 Fax: 978-921-1948
E-mail: information@ttor.org
Website: www.thetrustees.org

Founded: 1891

Membership: 10,001–100,000

Scope: Local, State

Description: The Trustees of Reservations has been conserving the Massachusetts landscape since 1891. Our mission is to preserve, for public use and enjoyment, properties of exceptional scenic, historic and ecological value in Massachusetts.

Publication(s): Conserving our Commonwealth: A Vision for the Massachusetts Landscape, Reservations Guidebook, Newsletter, Land Conservation Options: A Guide for Massachusetts Landowners, Annual Report, Land of the Commonwealth

Keyword(s): Agriculture/Farming, Land Issues, Public Lands/Greenspace

Contact(s):

Janice Hunt, President
John Bradley, Director of Membership
Sarah Carothers, Director of Planned Giving
Andy Kendall, Executive Director
John McCrae, Director of Finance and Administration
Ann Powell, Director of Development
Michael Triff, Director of Communications and Marketing
Wesley Ward, Director of Land Conservation
Charles Kane, Treasurer
F. Smithers, Secretary
Elliot Surkin, Chairman

TUG HILL TOMORROW LAND TRUST

P.O. Box 6063
Watertown, NY 13601 United States
Phone: 315-785-2382 Fax: 315-785-2574
E-mail: thtomorr@northnet.org
Website: www.tughilltomorrowlandtrust.org

Founded: 1990
Membership: 1–100
Scope: State

Description: Tug Hill Tomorrow is a private nonprofit corporation that works to help retain the forests, farms, recreational, and wild lands of the Tug Hill region through education, research, and voluntary land protection.

Publication(s): Greenings, Tug Hill Natural History Field Guide, Tug Hill Resource Guide to Educational Programs, Tug Hill Working Lands, Tug Hill Recreation Guide: A Guide to Cross-Country Skiing, Hiking, Biking, and Fishing

Keyword(s): Forests/Forestry, Land Issues, Public Lands/Greenspace

Contact(s):

Robert Boice, Chair

TUMAINI ENVIRONMENTAL CONSERVATION GROUP

P.O. Box 1353 Tanga Tanzania
Tanga, none Tanzania
Phone: 0255-2647366 Fax: 0255-2646114
E-mail: victormassawe@hotmail.com
Website: www.nwf.org/conservationdirectory

Founded: 1997
Scope: Local, Regional

Description: Engaged in forestation and sensitization of communties in rationally exploiting natural resources available in the area.

Publication(s): NIL

Contact(s):

N. Kiariro, Secretary; 0272643117
V. Massawe, Executive Chairman; 0811 60826; tccia.tanga@cats-net.com

TURTLE CREEK WATERSHED ASSOCIATION, INC.

325 Commerce Street, Suite 204
Wilmerding, PA 15148 United States
Phone: 412-829-2817
E-mail: GOODFISH@helicon.net
Website: trfn.clpgh.org/tcwa/

Founded: 1969
Membership: 101–1,000
Scope: Local, Regional

Description: The objective of the Turtle Creek Watershed Association, Inc. is to preserve and protect natural resources; educate the community about important environmental issues; monitor and improve water quality; and work with responsible agencies to encourage wise land use planning in the Turtle Creek Watershed.

Publication(s): TCWA Report, Business Associate Conserve

Keyword(s): Agriculture/Farming, Ecosystems (precious), Energy, Ethics/Environmental Justice, Executive/Legislative/Judicial Reform, Forests/Forestry, Land Issues, Pollution (general), Public Lands/Greenspace, Recreation/Ecotourism, Reduce/Reuse/Recycle, Water Habitats & Quality

Contact(s):

Steve Wiedemer, President
James Brucker, Vice President; ftma@westol.com
Edward Fischer, Executive Director, Acting; 412-829-2817; Fax: 412-829-2817; goodfish@helicon.net
James Tempero, Director Emeritus
Chris Droste, Secretary
Edward Fischer, Treasurer; 412-824-3376; goodfish@helicon.net

U

UNEP WORLD CONSERVATION MONITORING CENTRE

219 Huntingdon Rd.
Cambridge, CB3 0DL United Kingdom
Phone: 123277314 Fax: 1223277136
E-mail: info@unep-wcmc.org
Website: www.unep-wcmc.org

Founded: 1979
Membership: N/A
Scope: International

Description: The World Conservation Monitoring Centre is UNEP's resource centre for assessment and sustainable use of the living world. It provides specialised services that include ecosystem assessments, capacity building for implementation of conventions, regional and global biodiversity information support, research on threats to ecosystems and species and development of future scenarios for the living world.

Keyword(s): Development/Developing Countries, Forests/Forestry, Land Issues, Oceans/Coasts/Beaches, Reduce/Reuse/Recycle, Water Habitats & Quality, Wildlife & Species

Contact(s):

Mark Collins, Chief Executive

UNION OF CONCERNED SCIENTISTS

Two Brattle Square
Cambridge, MA 02238 United States
Phone: 617-547-5552 Fax: 617-864-9405
E-mail: ucs@ucsusa.org
Website: www.ucsusa.org

Founded: 1969
Membership: 10,001–100,000
Scope: National

Description: The Union of Concerned Scientists is a national non-profit alliance working for a cleaner environment and a safer world. UCS is working to encourage preservation of life-sustaining resources, promote energy technologies that are renewable, safe, and cost-effective, promote advanced transportation technologies, encourage sustainable agriculture, and curtail weapons proliferation.

Publication(s): Newsletter: NUCLEUS, Earthwise, Now or Never: Serious New Plans to Save a Natural Pest Control, Powerful Solutions: Seven Ways to Switch America to Renewable Electricity, The Consumer's Guide to Effective Environmental Choices

Keyword(s): Agriculture/Farming, Climate Change, Development/Developing Countries, Ecosystems (precious), Energy, Forests/

Forestry, Public Health, Reduce/Reuse/Recycle, Transportation, Wildlife & Species

Contact(s):
Howard Ris, President
Kurt Gottfried, Chairman

UNITED NATIONS ENVIRONMENT PROGRAMME

P.O. Box 30552
Nairobi, Kenya
Phone: 2542623089 Fax: 2542623692
E-mail: ipainfo@unep.org
Website: www.unep.org

Founded: 1972

Scope: International

Description: The United Nations Environment Programme (UNEP) was established by the U.N. General Assembly to be the environmental conscience of the U.N. system. It assesses the state of the world's environment; environmental management capacity of developing countries; and raises environmental considerations for the social and economic policies and programmes of UN agencies. UNEP provides a unique forum to bring countries to the table for negotiations, to build consensus and forge international agreements.

Keyword(s): Air Quality/Atmosphere, Ethics/Environmental Justice, Oceans/Coasts/Beaches, Pollution (general), Public Health, Reduce/Reuse/Recycle, Wildlife & Species

Contact(s):
Shafqat Kakakhel, Deputy Executive Director
Klaus Toepfer, Under Secretary General of the United Nations and Executive

UNITED NATIONS ENVIRONMENT PROGRAMME

LATIN AMERICAN AND CARIBBEAN
Boulevard de Los Virreyes 155 Lomas de Virreyes
Mexico D.F., Mexico
Phone: 52-5-202-6394 Fax: 52-5-202-0950
E-mail: ROLAC@ROLAC.UNE.P.MX
Website: WWW.ROLAC.UNEP.ORG

Founded: N/A

Contact(s):
Ricardo Sosa, Director
Rody Zuniga, Information

UNITED NATIONS ENVIRONMENT PROGRAMME

LATIN AMERICA AND CARIBBEAN REGION
UNEP-ROLAC
(United Nations Environment Programme) Apdo.
Postal 10.793
D.F., 11000 Mexico
Phone: 5252024841 Fax: 5252020950
E-mail: rolac@rolac.unep.mx
Website: www.rolac.unep.mx

Founded: N/A

Scope: International

UNITED NATIONS ENVIRONMENT PROGRAMME

NEW YORK OFFICE
2 United Nations Plaza
Room DC-2-803
New York, NY 10017 United States
Phone: 212-963-8210 Fax: 212-963-7341
E-mail: info@nyo.unep.org
Website: www.nyo.unep.org

Founded: 1972

Membership: 101–1,000

Scope: International

Description: UNEP's mission is to provide leadership and encourage partnerships in caring for the environment by inspiring, informing and enabling nations and peoples to improve their quality of life without compromising that of future generations.

Publication(s): The Global Environment Outlook, Our Planet

Contact(s):
Adnan Amin, Director; 1-212-963-8138; adnan.amin@nyo.unep.org
James Sniffen, Information Officer; 1-212-963-8094; sniffenj@nyo.unep.org

UNITED STATES CHAMBER OF COMMERCE

ENVIRONMENT, TECHNOLOGY AND REGULATORY AFFAIRS
1615 H St., NW
Washington, DC 20062 United States
Phone: 202-463-5533 Fax: 202-887-3445
E-mail: environment@uschamber.com
Website: www.uschamber.com

Founded: 1912

Membership: 1,000,001 +

Scope: Local, State, Regional, National, International

Description: The U.S. Chamber of Commerce is the world's largest business federation, representing more than three million businesses and organizations of every size, sector, and region. Positions on national issues are developed by a cross-section of Chamber members serving on committees, subcommittees, and task forces. Currently, some 1,800 business people participate in this process.

Keyword(s): Agriculture/Farming, Air Quality/Atmosphere, Climate Change, Energy, Ethics/Environmental Justice, Executive/Legislative/Judicial Reform, Finance/Banking/Trade, Forests/Forestry, Land Issues, Oceans/Coasts/Beaches, Pollution (general), Public Lands/Greens

Contact(s):
William Kovacs, Vice President

UNITED STATES COMMITTEE FOR THE UNITED NATIONS ENVIRONMENT PROGRAMME, THE (U.S. AND UNEP)

2013 Q St., NW
Washington, DC 20009 United States
Phone: 202-234-3600 Fax: 202-332-3221

Founded: N/A

Scope: National

Description: A nonprofit support group for the U.N. Environment Programme, U.S. and UNEP generates public awareness of global environmental issues, including ozone layer depletion, the greenhouse effect, and the transport of hazardous chemicals, and UNEP's response to these issues. The organization links UNEP to environmental groups across the U.S.

Publication(s): U.S. - UNEP NEWS

Keyword(s): Agriculture/Farming, Climate Change, Wildlife & Species

Contact(s):
Richard Hellman, President

UNITED STATES PUBLIC INTEREST RESEARCH GROUP

UNITED STATES PIRG
218 D St., SE
Washington, DC 20003 United States
Phone: 202-546-9707 Fax: 202-546-2461
E-mail: uspirg@pirg.org
Website: www.uspirg.org

Founded: 1983

Membership: 500,001–1,000,000

Scope: State, National

Description: U.S. PIRG is the national lobbying office for state PIRGs around the country, representing more than one million members. We conduct independent research and lobby for national environmental and consumer protections.

Publication(s): Citizen Agenda - newsletter, Various Reports

Keyword(s): Air Quality/Atmosphere, Climate Change, Ecosystems (precious), Energy, Finance/Banking/Trade, Forests/Forestry,

Land Issues, Oceans/Coasts/Beaches, Pollution (general), Public Health, Public Lands/Greenspace, Water Habitats & Quality, Wildlife & Species,

UNITED STATES SPORTSMEN'S ALLIANCE AND UNITED STATES SPORTSMEN'S ALLIANCE FOUNDATION

801 Kingsmill Parkway
Columbus, OH 43229-1137 United States
Phone: 614-888-4868 Fax: 614-888-0326
E-mail: info@ussportsmen.org
Website: www.ussportsmen.org

Founded: 1978

Scope: National

Description: Companion nonprofit organizations established to protect America's hunting, trapping and fishing heritage, and the scientific wildlife management practices that support it. The U.S. Sportsmen's Alliance is the legislative arm. The U.S. Sportsmen's Alliance Foundation is the legal defense, public education and research arm.

Publication(s): On Target, Update

Keyword(s): Recreation/Ecotourism

Contact(s):
Walter Pidgeon, President & CEO
Rick Story, Vice President
William Horn, Director of Federal Affairs
Doug Jeanneret, Director of Communcations
William McKinley, Membership Director
Robert Sexton, Manager of Government Affairs
Richard Cabela, Chairman of the Board
Gilbert Humphrey, Treasurer
Mason Lampton, Finance Chairman
C. Wood, Vice Chairman

UNITED STATES TOURIST COUNCIL

Drawer 1875
Washington, DC 20013-1875 United States

Founded: N/A

Scope: National

Description: A nonprofit association of conservation-concerned individuals, industries, and institutions who travel or cater to the traveler. Emphasis is on historic and scenic preservation, wilderness and roadside development, ecology through sound planning and education, and support of scientific studies of natural wilderness.

Keyword(s): Forests/Forestry, Water Habitats & Quality

Contact(s):
Stanford West, Chairman of Board of Trustees and Executive Director

UPPER CHATTAHOOCHEE RIVERKEEPER

1900 Emery St., Suite 450
Atlanta, GA 30318 United States
Phone: 404-352-9828 Fax: 404-352-8676
E-mail: bbolton@usriverkeeper.org
Website: www.chattahoochee.org

Founded: 1994

Membership: 1,001–10,000

Scope: Regional

Description: To advocate snd secure the protection and stewardship of the Chattahoochee River, its tributaries and watershed using education, research, communication, cooperation, monitoring and legal actions.

Publication(s): Stream Chat, River Chat

Keyword(s): Water Habitats & Quality

Contact(s):
Sally Bethea, Executive Director; ext. 11; sbethea@mindspring.com
Darcie Doden, Director of Headwater Conservation
Matt Kales, Program Manager for River Basin Protection; mkrinverkeeper@mindspring.com
Alice Chamipagne, Watershed Protection Specialist
Michelle Fried, General Counsel; mfriverkeeper@mindspring.com

UPPER MISSISSIPPI RIVER CONSERVATION COMMITTEE

4469 - 48th Avenue Ct.
Rock Island, IL 61201 United States
Phone: 309-793-5800, ext. 522 Fax: 309-739-5804
E-mail: umrcc@mississippi-river.com
Website: www.mississippi-river.com/umrcc

Founded: 1943

Membership: 101–1,000

Scope: Regional

Description: Promotes preservation, development, and wise use of the natural and recreational resources of the Upper Mississippi River and formulates policies, plans, and programs for conducting cooperative studies. Members: state conservation departments of Illinois, Iowa, Minnesota, Missouri, and Wisconsin.

Publication(s): Annual Proceedings, and miscellaneous technical reports, Newsletter

Keyword(s): Development/Developing Countries, Water Habitats & Quality, Wildlife & Species

Contact(s):
Ken Brummett, Secretary and Treasurer; Missouri Dept. of Conservation, 653 Clinic Rd., Hannibal, MO 63401; 309-582-5611
Jon Duyvejonck, Coordinator; 309-793-5800

URBAN HABITAT PROGRAM

P.O. Box 29908, Presidio Station
San Francisco, CA 94129 United States
Phone: 415-561-3333 Fax: 415-561-3334
E-mail: contact@urbanhabitatprogram.org
Website: www.urbanhabitatproram.org

Founded: 1989

Scope: National

Description: The Urban Habitat Program is a project of Tides Center. Its mission is to build multi-cultural urban environmental leadership for socially-just and sustainable communities in the San Francisco Bay area. Our project areas include transportation, regional land use and social justice, land recycling and brown fields, leadership institute for sustainability and justice, and the goal of ecological literacy, all from an ecological and social justice perspective.

Publication(s): Race, Poverty & the Environment

Keyword(s): Ethics/Environmental Justice, Land Issues, Reduce/Reuse/Recycle, Transportation

Contact(s):
Carl Anthony, Director

URBAN WILDLIFE RESOURCES

5130 W. Running Brook Rd.
Columbia, MD 21044 United States
Phone: 410-997-7161 Fax: 410-997-6849
Website: www.erols.com/urbanwildlife

Founded: 1995

Scope: International

Description: Urban Wildlife Resources works to facilitate interaction and cooperation among land managers and planners, biologists, landscape architects, and others in achieving better management of natural resources in urban and urbanizing areas.

Publication(s): Urban Open Space Manager, The

Keyword(s): Forests/Forestry, Public Lands/Greenspace, Reduce/Reuse/Recycle

Contact(s):
Lowell Adams, President

UTAH ASSOCIATION OF CONSERVATION DISTRICTS

1860 N.100 East
Logan, UT 84341 United States
Phone: 435-753-6029 Fax: 435-755-2117
Website: www.uacd.org

Founded: N/A
Membership: 101–1,000
Scope: State
Publication(s): book - Study on Low Impact Street Design, book - Citizen Planners Guide to Sub Division Development, newsletter - The Leader
Contact(s):
Randy Greenhalgh, President; 435-623-0845; Fax: 435-623-0845
Larry Johnson, Vice President /Board Member; P.O. Box 177, Randolph, UT 84064; 435-793-5625; Fax: 435-793-5625
Gordon Younker, Executive Vice President; 1860 N. 100 E., North Logan, UT 84341-2215; 435-753-6029; Fax: 435-755-2117; gordon-younker@ut.nacdnet.org
William Rigby, Past President
Richard Saunders, Secretary and Treasurer; 4083 W. 12680 S., Payson, UT 84651; 801-465-2777

UTAH B.A.S.S. CHAPTER FEDERATION

Attn: President, 3460 Scott Cir.
Salt Lake City, UT 84115 United States
Phone: 801-487-8711
E-mail: gjlables@aol.com
Website: www.utahbassfederation.org

Founded: N/A
Scope: State
Description: An organization of Bassmaster chapters, affiliated with the Bass Anglers Sportsman Society, organized to fight pollution, assist state and national conservation agencies in their efforts, and teach young people of our country good conservation practices. Dedicated to the realistic conservation of our water resources.
Publication(s): Nature News Notes
Keyword(s): Public Lands/Greenspace, Wildlife & Species
Contact(s):
George Sommer, President; 801-487-8711
Walter Maldonado, Conservation Director; P.O. Box 482, Green River, UT 84525-0482; 435-564-8147; viper@etv.net

UTAH NATIVE PLANT SOCIETY

P.O. Box 520041
Salt Lake City, UT 84152-0041 United States
Phone: 801-272-3275
E-mail: unps@xmission.com
Website: www.unps.org

Founded: 1978
Membership: 101–1,000
Scope: Local
Description: Our organization is a charitable, non-profit dedicated to the understanding, preservation, enjoyment, and responsible use of the Utah native plants. We wish to foster public recognition of the diverse flora of the state.
Publication(s): Sego Lily, UNPS.org website, Heritage Garden Native Plant Propagation Workshop booklet
Contact(s):
Mindy Wheeler, Salt Lake Chapter President; 801-561-0779; mindywheeler@usa.net
Susan Meyer, Chairman; smeyer@sisna.com
Therese Meyer, Secretary; 801-272-3275; tmeyer@xmission.com
Janett Warner, Central Utah Chapter; janettw@hubwest.com

UTAH NATURE STUDY SOCIETY

Attn: President Utah Nature Study Society, 2853 S. 23rd East
Salt Lake City, UT 84109 United States
Phone: 801-484-2366

Founded: 1954
Scope: State
Description: Promotes conservation and nature education through workshops and field trips for members; publicizes conservation problems and issues through meetings and its newsletter. Member of Utah Associated Garden Clubs.
Publication(s): UWA Review
Keyword(s): Land Issues, Public Lands/Greenspace, Wildlife & Species
Contact(s):
Dorothy Platt, President; 2853 S. 23rd East, Salt Lake City, UT 84109
Maria Dickerson, Secretary; 323 S. 2nd W., Tooele, UT 84074
Catherine Quinn, Editor; 1383 S. 300 East, Salt Lake City, UT 84115
Jean White, Executive Secretary; 377 E. 5300 S., Murray, UT 84107-6019

UTAH WILDERNESS COALITION

P.O. Box 520974
Salt Lake City, UT 84152-0974 United States
Phone: 801-486-2872 Fax: 801-485-5572
E-mail: wildutah@xmission.com
Website: www.uwcoalition.org

Founded: 1985
Scope: National
Description: Promote and coordinate the preservation of U.S. BLM wildlands in southern and western Utah through public education and the passage of America's Redrock Wilderness Act. The goal includes protection of the remaining wilderness quality public lands under the National Wilderness Preservation System.
Keyword(s): Land Issues, Public Lands/Greenspace, Recreation/Ecotourism

UTAH WILDLIFE FEDERATION

P.O. Box 526367
Salt Lake City, UT 84152-6367 United States
Phone: 801-487-1946 Fax: 801-773-0412
E-mail: uwfhal@xmission.com

Founded: N/A
Scope: State
Description: A representative statewide organization, affiliated with the National Wildlife Federation, dedicated to the protection and enhancement of wildlife and its habitat through public education and government interaction.
Publication(s): Utah Wildlife News

UTAH WOODLAND OWNERS COUNCIL

2829 Sleep Hollow Dr.
Salt Lake City, UT 84117 United States
Phone: 801-277-1615

Founded: 1997
Membership: 1–100
Scope: State
Description: A statewide organization affiliated with the National Woodland Owners Association and associated with Utah Farms Bureau, that is working for good forest management practices on the private forest and ranch land in Utah.
Keyword(s): Forests/Forestry
Contact(s):
Richard Oldroyd, Chairman

V

VENICE AREA BEAUTIFICATION, INC

VENETIAN WATERWAY PARK
Venice Area Beautification Inc.
333 South Tamiami Trail, Suite 225
Venice, FL 34285 United States
Phone: 941-486-8756 Fax: 941-486-8795
E-mail: knight.marketing@verizon.net
Website: www.vabi.org

Founded: 1993
Membership: 1–100
Scope: Local, State
Description: Venice Area Beautification, Inc (VABI) is the non-profit organization constructing and maintaining the Venetian Waterway Park (VWP). This linear trail upon completion will run along both sides of the Intracoastal Waterway in Venice, FL. To date, 2.5 of the planned 10-mile trail are complete. The trail is promoting a clean environment, stressing the importance of protecting natural habitats and encouraging daily outdoor exercise.

VERMONT ASSOCIATION OF CONSERVATION DISTRICTS

487 Rowell Hill Rd.
Berlin, VT 05602 United States
Phone: 802-229-9250

Founded: N/A
Scope: State
Publication(s): Annual Reports
Contact(s):
Claire Ayer, Vice President; 802-545-2142
Rita Visson, Treasurer; 240 Vermont Rt. 100, Orange, VT 05641; 802-479-9538

VERMONT B.A.S.S. CHAPTER FEDERATION

Attn: President, 19 Pinewood Rd.
Montpelier, VT 05602 United States
Phone: 802-223-7793
E-mail: nsk1@together.net
Website: www.vermontbass.com

Founded: 1991
Membership: 101–1,000
Scope: State
Description: An organization of Bassmaster chapters, affiliated with the Bass Anglers Sportman Society, organized to fight pollution, assist state and national conservation agencies in their efforts, and teach the young people of our country good conservation practices. Dedicated to the realistic conservation of our water resources.
Keyword(s): Pollution (general), Recreation/Ecotourism, Water Habitats & Quality, Wildlife & Species
Contact(s):
David Derner, Conservation Director; 46 Cooper Rd., Milton, VT 05468-4013; 802-893-1386; docbass@sover.net

VERMONT INSTITUTE OF NATURAL SCIENCE

27023 Church Hill Rd.
Woodstock, VT 05091 United States
Phone: 802-457-2779 Fax: 802-457-1053
E-mail: info@vinsweb.org
Website: www.vinsweb.org

Founded: 1972
Scope: State
Description: The mission of VINS is to protect Vermont's natural heritage through environmental education and research. VINS Raptor Center, Living Museum of birds of prey, on VINS nature preserve.
Publication(s): Hands on Nature, Records of Vermont Birds, Vermont Institute of Natural Science
Keyword(s): Agriculture/Farming, Forests/Forestry, Land Issues
Contact(s):
Deborah Granquist, President Board of Directors
Jenepher Linglebach, Vice President
Sherman Kent, Executive Director
Christopher Rimmer, Research Director
Marsha Whitney, Education Director

VERMONT LAND TRUST

8 Bailey Ave.
Montpelier, VT 05602 United States
Phone: 802-223-5234 Fax: 802-223-4223
E-mail: info@vlt.org
Website: www.vlt.org

Founded: 1977
Membership: 1,001–10,000
Scope: Regional
Description: Conserving the productive, recreational, and scenic lands that help give Vermont and its communities their distinctive rural character.
Publication(s): Tri-annual newsletters, Annual Report
Keyword(s): Land Issues
Contact(s):
Darby Bradley, President; 8 Bailey Ave., Montpelier, VT 05602; 802-223-5234; darby@vlt.org
Gil Livingston, Vice President for Land Conservation; 8 Bailey Ave., Montpelier, VT 05602; 802-223-5234
Barbara Wagner, Vice President of Operations; 8 Bailey Ave., Montpelier, VT 05602; 802-223-5234

VERMONT NATURAL RESOURCES COUNCIL

VNRC
9 Bailey Ave.
Montpelier, VT 05602 United States
Phone: 802-223-2328, ext. 110 Fax: 802-223-0287
E-mail: info@vnrc.org
Website: www.vnrc.org

Founded: 1963
Membership: 1,001–10,000
Scope: Local, State, Regional, National
Description: The Vermont Natural Resources Council is Vermont's leading environmental education, policy, & advocacy organization since 1963. VNRC maintains strong programs in forests, land use and water quality. VNRC uses a 4 point strategy in its conservation programs: 1) research, 2) policy development 3) passage, implementation and/or enforcement of the environmental laws; 4) citizen education and grassroots action. VNRC contributes to statewide and national environmental policy development
Publication(s): Vermont Environmental Report, The Legislative Bulletin, Vermont Environmental Directory
Contact(s):
Elizabeth Courtney, Executive Director
Kelly Lowry, General Counsel/Water Program Director
Patrick Berry, Communication Director
Matteo Burani, Outreach Coordinator
Steve Holmes, Sustainable Communities Director
Stephanie Mueller, Editor/Development Director
Mark Naud, Board Chair
Leonard Wilson, Representative

VERMONT STATE-WIDE ENVIRONMENTAL EDUCATION PROGRAMS (SWEEP)

c/o Vermont Natural Resources Council,
9 Bailey Avenue
Montpelier, VT 05602 United States
Phone: 802-985-8686

Founded: 1973
Membership: 1–100
Scope: State

Description: SWEEP is a coalition of individuals and organizations promoting environmental education in Vermont. SWEEP's purpose is to foster environmental appreciation and understanding in order to enable Vermonters to make responsible decisions affecting the environment.

Publication(s): SWEEP Newsletter

Contact(s):

Steve Hagenbuch, Co Chair; Audubon Vermont, 255 Sherman Hollow Rd., Huntington, VT 05462; 802-434-3068

Linda Wellings, Co Chair; Shelburne Farms, 1611 Harbor Rd., Shelburne, VT 05482; 802-985-8686

VERMONT WOODLANDS ASSOCIATION

664 North County Rd.
Groton, VT 05046 United States
Phone: 802-584-3333
E-mail: vtwoods@together.net

Founded: N/A

Scope: State

Description: A statewide organization, affiliated with the National Woodland Owners Association, organized to promote sound forest management throughout Vermont.

Publication(s): Vermont Woodlands, forestry and caring for Vermont forests.

Keyword(s): Forests/Forestry

Contact(s):

Putnam W. Blodgett, President; putblodgett@valley.net

John Hemenway, Vice President; 802-765-4324; jthemenway@aol.com

Stanley James, Vice President; 822 Lemon Fair Rd., Weybridge VT, 05753,

Harry Chandler, Executive Director

Robert Darrow, Immediate Past President; 802-773-7144

VERNAL POOL SOCIETY, THE

P.O. Box 2154
Ramona, CA 92065 United States
Phone: 760-789-4085 Fax: 760-789-4566
E-mail: maryanne@pentis.com
Website: www.pentis.com

Founded: 1999

Membership: N/A

Scope: Local, State

Description: The Vernal Pool Society is dedicated to the preservation of the few remaining Vernal Pools by maintaining a voice for this precious and unique biome. We are creating an awareness and understanding of the environmental problems facing these isolated wetlands through education and advocacy. We develop and promote effective management and monitoring practices which will ensure survival of the entire Vernal Pool ecosystem.

Publication(s): The Magic of Vernal Pools, Vernal Pool Consulting

Keyword(s): Ecosystems (precious), Ethics/Environmental Justice, Land Issues, Public Lands/Greenspace, Recreation/Ecotourism, Sprawl/Urban Planning, Water Habitats & Quality, Wildlife & Species

Contact(s):

Mary Anne Pentis, President/CEO; 760-789-4085; Fax: 760-789-4566; maryanne@pentis.com

Alisha Leigh, Director; 760-789-4085; Fax: 760-789-40566; moonbeam@adnc.com

Al Pentis, Wetland Biologist; 760-789-4085; Fax: 760-789-40566; al@pentis.com

VIRGIN ISLANDS CONSERVATION DISTRICT

Attn: President, P.O. Box 1576
Frederiksted, VI 00841 United States

Founded: N/A

Scope: State

Publication(s): Federation Record, The

Contact(s):

Hans Lawaetz, President and Board Member; P.O. Box 1576, Fredericksted, VI 00841; 340-788-2229; Fax: 340-778-0270

Joseph Samuel, Vice President; P.O. Box 241, Fredericksted, St. Croix, VI 00841; 340-772-3168

Enrico Gasperi, Secretary and Treasurer; P.O. Box 895, Christiansted, VI 00824; 340-773-2386

Cedrick Lewis, Alternate Board Member; P.O. Box 303142, St. Thomas, VI 00803; 340-775-7393

VIRGIN ISLANDS CONSERVATION SOCIETY, INC.

Arawak Bldg., Suite 3, Gallows Bay
Christiansted, VI 00820 United States
Phone: 340-773-1989 Fax: 340-773-7545
E-mail: sea@viaccess.net

Founded: 1968

Membership: 101–1,000

Scope: Regional

Description: A representative statewide organization, affiliated with the National Wildlife Federation, dedicated to the protection and enhancement of wildlife and its habitat through public education and government interaction.

Keyword(s): Agriculture/Farming, Land Issues, Pollution (general)

Contact(s):

Carlos Tesitor, President

Carla Joseph, Representative

Tysha Jules, Education Programs Contact

Stevie Ketcham, Treasurer

Emy Thomas, Editor; fhenry@vvi.edu

VIRGINIA ASSOCIATION FOR PARKS

5616 Bloomfield Drive #103
Alexandria, VA 22312 United States
Phone: 703-941-1350 Fax: 202-548-0595
E-mail: info@virginiaparks.org
Website: www.virginiaparks.org

Founded: 1997

Membership: 1–100

Scope: State

Description: Assisting park friends organizations where they exist and helping to organize them in parks without a support group.

Keyword(s): Land Issues, Public Lands/Greenspace, Recreation/Ecotourism, Wildlife & Species

Contact(s):

Davinder Khanna, Treasurer; davinder@parksonline.org

Robert Williams, Co-Chairman; 540-972-9954; robwilliams@erols.com

VIRGINIA ASSOCIATION OF CONSERVATION DISTRICTS

7293 Hanover Green Dr., Suite B-101
Mechanicsville, VA 23111 United States
Phone: 804-559-0324

Founded: N/A

Scope: State

Contact(s):

Daphne Jamison, President; 540-721-2361; rjam229@aol.com

Greg Evans, 2nd Vice President; 8400 Oakford Dr., Springfield, VA 22152; 703-644-1227; soilandh2o@aol.com

Jay Gilliam, 1st Vice President; 540-377-6179; strmiwla@cfw.com

Stephanie Martin, Executive Director; 7293 Hanover Green Dr., Suite B101, Mechanicsville, VA 23111; 804-559-0324; Fax: 804-559-0325

James Byrne, Secretary/Treasurer; Rt. 1 Box 351, Reva, VA 22735; 540-547-2932; tohisplace1@juno.com

John Dixon, Past President; 1228 Rendezous Ln., Bedford, VA 24523; 540-586-8969

VIRGINIA B.A.S.S. CHAPTER FEDERATION

Attn: President, 28447 Cabin Point Rd.
Disputanta, VA 23842 United States
Phone: 757-428-4280 Fax: 804-834-8198
Website: www.vabass.com

Founded: N/A
Membership: 1,001–10,000
Scope: State
Description: An organization of Bassmaster chapters, affiliated with the Bass Anglers Sportsman Society, organized to fight pollution, assist state and national conservation agencies in their efforts, and teach the young people of our country good conservation practices. Dedicated to the realistic conservation of our water resources.
Publication(s): Virginia B.A.S.S. Federation Newsletter
Keyword(s): Air Quality/Atmosphere, Land Issues, Water Habitats & Quality
Contact(s):
Roger Fitchett, President
Mitchell Perkins, Acting Conservation Director; 12003 Bourne Road, Glen Allen, VA 23059; 804-264-1124; HUNTNBASS1@aol.com

VIRGINIA CONSERVATION NETWORK

1001 E. Broad St., Suite LL 35-C
Richmond, VA 23219 United States
Phone: 804-644-0283 Fax: 804-644-0286
E-mail: ellenshepard@yahoo.com
Website: www.vcnva.org

Founded: 1969
Scope: State
Description: The Virginia Conservation Network is a network of 100 organizations. VCN's mission is to protect the Commonwealth's air, lands, and waters for the benefit of the people, as guaranteed by the Virginia Constitution.
Publication(s): 1999 Voting Summary
Contact(s):
Chris Miller, President; cmiller@pecva.org
Anne Marshall, Vice President; aamvirginia@hotmail.com
Jo Ann Spevacek, Secretary
Martha Wingfield, Treasurer; marlridge@aol.com

VIRGINIA FORESTRY ASSOCIATION

8810B Patterson Ave.
Richmond, VA 23229 United States
Phone: 804-741-0836 Fax: 804-741-0838
E-mail: vafa@erols.com
Website: www.vaforestry.org

Founded: 1943
Scope: State
Description: An association of landowners and forest industry that promotes stewardship and wise use of forest resources for the economic and environmental benefits of all Virginians.
Publication(s): Bulletin, invasive alien plant list, brochure, fact sheets, nursery source list, checklists, wildflower conservation guidelines, chapter newsletters, News and Notes - newsletter, Virginia Forest Magazine, all publications on web
Keyword(s): Agriculture/Farming, Wildlife & Species
Contact(s):
Paul Howe, Executive Vice President & Editor
Dave Froggatt, Treasurer

VIRGINIA NATIVE PLANT SOCIETY

Blandy Experimental Farm, 400 Blandy Farm Lane—Unit 2
Unit 2
Boyce, VA 22620 United States
Phone: 540-837-1600 Fax: 540-837-1523
E-mail: vnpsofc@shentel.net
Website: www.vnps.org

Founded: 1982
Membership: 1,001–10,000
Scope: State
Description: The VNPS and ten chapters throughout Virginia seek further appreciation and conservation of Virginia's wild plants and habitats. Programs emphasize public education, protection of endangered species, habitat preservation, control of invasive alien plants and encouragement of appropriate landscape use of native plants. Includes both amateurs and professionals.
Publication(s): Bulletin, Chapter Newsletters, List of Recommended Native Plants, Factsheets on Invasive Alien Plants, List of Invasive Alien Plants, Nursery Sources to Native Plants, Virginia Wildflower of the Year.
Keyword(s): Forests/Forestry, Land Issues, Public Lands/Greenspace, Reduce/Reuse/Recycle, Water Habitats & Quality, Wildlife & Species
Contact(s):
Julie Alexander, Blue Ridge Wildflower Society Chapter President; 628 Walnut Avenue, Roanoke, VA 24014; 540-427-0117; jalexa7266@aol.com
Carol Gardner, Shenandoah President; 3858 Wayfarers Trail, Bridgewater, VA 22812; w-cgardner@rica.net
Jocelyn Slayden & Mary Anne Gibbons, Piedmont Co-Presidents; P.O. Box 677, The Plains, VA 20198; 540-349-3248; jocelyna@erols.com
Marianne Mooney, Potowmack President; 1112 N. Powhatan St., Arlington, VA 22205; e-mail-moosfy@webtv.net
Richard Moss, Pocahontas President; 12565 Brook Lane, Chester, VA 23831; rmoss@richmond.infi.net
Karen Renda, South Hampton Roads President; 4433 Revere Drive, Virginia Beach, VA 23456; karenrenda@hotmail.com
Michael Sawyer, John Clayton Chapter President; P.O. Box 369, Toano, VA 23168-0369; 804-262-9887; Waterborne@aol.com
Nicky Staunton, President; 8815 Fort Drive, Manassas, VA 20110; 703-368-9803; nstaunton@earthlink.net
Anita Tuttle, Fredericksburg Area President; 7286 Sherwood Forest Dr., King George, VA 22485; 540-775-4188; amtuttle@crosslink.net
Nancy Vehrs, Prince William Wildflower Society President; 8318 Highland St., Manassas, VA 20110-3671; nvehrs@attglobal.net
Pat Willis, Jefferson Chapter President; 1611 Hamilton Rd., Louisa, VA 23093; 757-967-1776; pdwillis@nexet.net
Shirely Gay, 2nd Vice President; 210 South Abington St., Arlington, VA 22204; cgay1153@aol.com
Michael Swayer, 1st Vice President; P.O. Box 677, Yorktown, VA 23690; 804-262-9887, ext. 333; waterborne@aol.com
Pat Baldwin, Director; 430 Yale Dr., Hampton, VA 23666; 757-874-0892; Fax: 757-874-3037
Allen Bellden, Director; 1202 W. 45th St., Richmond, VA 23225; 804-786-7951; ajb@dcr.state.va.us
Jim Bruce, Director; 20042 Sterling Creek Ln., Rockville, VA 23146; 804-749-4304; jgbruce@erols.com
Cole Burrell, Director; P.O. Box 76, Free Union, VA 22940; 804-975-2859; nldr@aol.com
Faith Campbell, Director; 8208 Dabney Ave., Springfield, VA 22152; phytodoer@aol.com
Boleyn Dale, Director of Registry; P.O. Box 85, Rt. 1006, Moon, VA 23119; bkd@visi.net
Deanne Eversmyer, Director of Horticulture; 1918 Leonard Road, Falls Church, VA 22043; d.eversmeyer@prodigy.net
Carol Gardner, Director of Publicity; 3858 Wayfarers Trail, Bridgewater, VA 22812; w-cgardner@rica.net
Nancy Hugo, Director; 11208 Gwathmey Church Rd., Ashland, VA 23005; nancyhugo@aol.com
Mary Painter, Director of Membership Chair; P.O. Box D, Hume, VA 22639; vanatvs@erols.com
Stanwyn Shetler, Director of Botany; 142 E. Meadowland Lane, Sterling, VA 20164-1144; 202-786-2996; Fax: 202-786-2563; shetler.stanwyn@nmnh.si.edu

Charles Smith, Director of Fund Raising; 8407 Sunset Dr., Manassas, VA 201112; chrissmith@juno.com
Jessica Strother, Director of Conservation; 6004 Windward Dr., Burke, VA 22015; 703-324-1795; sylvantica9@juno.com
Pam Weiringo, Director of Publication; 2740 Derwent Dr., SW, Roanoke, VA 24015; 540-772-3660
Sally Anderson, Co-Recording Secretary; 112 Old Forest Circle, Winchester, VA 22602; 540-722-3072; rccsca@visuallink.com
John Magee, Corresponding Secretary; 2716 West Ox Road, Herndon, VA 20171; euphorbia@aol.com
Mary Pockman, Co-Recording Secretary; 7301 Hooking Road, McLean, VA 22101
Roma Sherman, Treasurer; 658 Federal St, Paris, VA 20130; roma@ashbyinn.com

VIRGINIA RESOURCE-USE EDUCATION COUNCIL

P.O. Box 11104
Richmond, VA 23230 United States
Phone: 804-698-4442 Fax: 804-698-4533
E-mail: amregn@deq.state.va.us
Website: www.vanaturally.com

Founded: 1952
Membership: 1–100
Scope: State
Description: A volunteer, nonprofit organization, composed of members of the state and federal government, colleges, and private industry, working to promote the broad principle of environmental education. The Council offers conservation education workshops for educators across Virginia, and is staff to the Commonwealth's EE network and statewide education program, Virginia Naturally (www.vanaturally.com).
Publication(s): The Virginia Natural Resources Education Guide
Contact(s):
Dawn Shank, Chairman; Dept. of Conservation & Recreation, 203 Governor Street, Richmond, VA 23219; 804-692-0903; dshank@dcr.state.va.us
Susan Gilley, Secretary; Department of Game and Inland Fisheries, Box 11104, Richmond, VA 23230; 804-367-1000
Ann Regn, Treasurer; Department of Environmental Quality, P.O. Box 10009, Richmond, VA 23240-0009; 804-698-4442; Fax: 804-698-4453; amregn@deq.state.va.us

VIRGINIA SOCIETY OF ORNITHOLOGY

7451 Little River Turnpike, #202
Annandale, VA 22003 United States
Phone: 703-305-7381

Founded: 1929
Scope: State
Description: Dedicated to all aspects of the birds of Virginia, including conservation, field research, education of any interested person or group, and dissemination of all types of information. The VSO coordinates with state agencies and with other private organizations in this mission.
Publication(s): Raven, The, VSO Newsletter
Keyword(s): Wildlife & Species
Contact(s):
Larry Lynch, President
Larry Lynch, Vice President; 9430 Tuxford Rd., Richmond, VA 23236; 804-272-8582
Lauren Scott, Secretary
Barbara Thrasher, Treasurer; 120 Woodbine Dr., Lynchburg, VA 24502; 804-239-5850

W

WARREN COUNTY CONSERVATION BOARD

ANNETT NATURE CENTER
1555 118th Avenue
Indianola, IA 50125 United States
Phone: 515-961-6169 Fax: 515-961-7100
E-mail: wccb@mindspring.com
Website: www.mindspring.com/~wccb

Founded: N/A
Membership: 1,001–10,000
Scope: Local, State
Description: Located in central Iowa, the Warren County Conservation Board provides environmental and outdoor education for all ages for nearly all environmental concerns. County parks include points of interest such as biking trails, public hunting, and historical landmarks.
Publication(s): Three Rivers Journal.
Keyword(s): Air Quality/Atmosphere, Climate Change, Ecosystems (precious), Energy, Ethics/Environmental Justice, Forests/Forestry, Land Issues, Pollution (general), Public Lands/Greenspace, Recreation/Ecotourism, Reduce/Reuse/Recycle, Sprawl/Urban Planning, Water Habitats & Quality
Contact(s):
Laura Surber, Naturalist
Joel Van Roeckel, Naturalist

WASHINGTON ASSOCIATION OF CONSERVATION DISTRICTS

Attn: Executive Director
3911 South K Street
Tacoma, WA 98418 United States
Phone: 253-473-4999 Fax: 253-473-7246
E-mail: patmcgregor@juno.com
Website: www.wacd.org

Founded: 1942
Membership: 101–1,000
Scope: State
Description: Association of Conservation District supervisors
Contact(s):
Colin Bennett, President; 185 Beebe Rd., Goldendale, WA 98620; 509-773-5065; Fax: 509-773-5600; cbennett@gorge.net
Wade Troutman, Vice President; 509-686-2061
Bob Haberman, National Director; 771 Hungry Junction Rd., Ellensburg, WA 98926; 509-925-1713; Fax: 509-925-7730; bobhaber@eburg.net
Pat McGregor, Executive Director; 3911 S. K St., Tacoma, WA 98418; 253-473-4999; Fax: 253-473-7246
Monte Marti, Secretary and Treasurer; 11605 33rd Ct., NE, Lake Stevens, WA 98258; 425-261-6678; Fax: 425-258-4839

WASHINGTON B.A.S.S. CHAPTER FEDERATION

1721 South Methow St.
Wenatchee, WA 98801 United States
Phone: 425-251-3214
E-mail: joe.arballo@wabass.org
Website: www.wabass.org

Founded: N/A
Membership: 101–1,000
Scope: State
Description: An organization of Bassmaster chapters, affiliated with the Bass Anglers Sportsman Society, organized to fight pollution, assist state and national conservation agencies in their efforts, and teach the young people of our country good conservation practices. Dedicated to the realistic conservation of our water resources.
Publication(s): The Washington State B.A.S.S (Quarterly Newsletter).
Keyword(s): Energy, Land Issues, Reduce/Reuse/Recycle

Contact(s):
Joe Arballo, President
Martin Bixby, Conservation Director; 427 West 18th Ave., Kennewick, WA 99337; 509-582-7239; martin.bixby@wabass.org

WASHINGTON ENVIRONMENTAL COUNCIL

615 2nd Avenue, Suite 380
Seattle, WA 98104 United States
Phone: 206-622-8103 Fax: 206-622-8113
E-mail: wec@wecprotects.org
Website: www.wecprotects.org

Founded: 1967
Membership: 1,001–10,000
Scope: State
Description: The Washington Environmental Council protects Washington's environment & natural heritage for this and future generations by educating key state decision-makers and advocating for the improvement and enforcement of environmental laws.
Publication(s): WEC Voices, State Legislative Briefing Book
Keyword(s): Development/Developing Countries, Forests/Forestry, Oceans/Coasts/Beaches, Water Habitats & Quality, Wildlife & Species
Contact(s):
Jay Manning, President
Josh Baldi, Policy Director
Joan Crooks, Executive Director
Tom Geiger, Editor

WASHINGTON FARM FORESTRY ASSOCIATION

Olympia, WA 98507 United States
Phone: 360-459-0984 Fax: 360-570-1537
Website: www.wafarmforestry.com

Founded: 1944
Membership: 1,001–10,000
Scope: State
Description: A statewide organization affiliated with the National Woodland Owners Association, founded to help small woodland owners acquire information on better management of small timber tracts.
Publication(s): Northwest Woodlands, Landowner News
Keyword(s): Forests/Forestry
Contact(s):
Sherry Fox, President; 360-978-6448; tmp@i-link-2.net
Nels Hanson, Executive Director and Editor, Landowner News; 360-943-3875; nelswh@home.com
Norma Green, Treasurer; nfgreen@reachone.com
Lori Rasor, Editor, Northwest Woodlands; 4033 SW Canyon Rd., Portland, OR 97221; 502-228-1367
Bill Woods, Secretary
Erin Woods, Secretary

WASHINGTON FOUNDATION FOR THE ENVIRONMENT

P.O. Box 2123
Seattle, WA 98111 United States
Phone: 253-838-3466
E-mail: info@wffe.org
Website: www.wffe.org

Founded: 1979
Scope: State
Description: Dedicated to preserving and enhancing the environmental heritage of Washington state by making small grants to support educational and innovative projects in both the public and private sectors. for grant guidelines, send a message to JudyTurpin@aol.com

WASHINGTON NATIVE PLANT SOCIETY

7400 Sand Point Way NE
Seattle, WA 98115 United States
Phone: 206-527-3210
E-mail: wnps@wnps.org
Website: www.wnps.org

Founded: 1976
Membership: 1,001–10,000
Scope: State
Description: To promote the appreciation and conservation of Washington's native plants and their habitats through study, education, and advocacy.
Publication(s): Syllabus
Keyword(s): Forests/Forestry, Public Lands/Greenspace, Recreation/Ecotourism, Water Habitats & Quality, Wildlife & Species
Contact(s):
Joan Frazee, President; P.O. Box 1082, Leavenworth, WA 98826; 509-548-2166
Richard Robohm, Vice President; 963 N. Motor Pl. #4, Seattle, WA 98103; 206-545-1823
Richard Easterly, Treasurer; P.O. Box 4027, Tenino, WA 98589; 360-264-5644
Tom Johnson, Secretary; 7742 32nd Ave., Seattle, WA 98115; 206-525-3176
Dottie Knecht, Past President; P.O. Box 48, Peshatin, WA 98847; 509-548-7393

WASHINGTON RECREATION AND PARK ASSOCIATION

350 S. 333rd St., Suite 103
Federal Way, WA 98003 United States
Phone: 253-874-1283 Fax: 253-661-3929
E-mail: wrpa@wrpatoday.org
Website: www.wrpatoday.org

Founded: 1947
Membership: 1,001–10,000
Scope: State
Description: Dedicated to enhanching and promoting parks, recreation, and leisure pursuits in Washington state, and plays a vital role in promoting public support for parks and recreation.
Publication(s): Syllabus
Keyword(s): Recreation/Ecotourism
Contact(s):
Daryl Faber, President
Mike Dobb, Vice President
Brit Kramer, Executive Director

WASHINGTON SOCIETY OF AMERICAN FORESTERS

NORTHWEST
4033 SW Canyon Rd.
Portland, OR 97221 United States
Phone: 503-224-8046 Fax: 503-226-2515

Founded: 1900
Scope: State
Description: Represents the forestry profession in advancing the science, technology, education, and practice of forestry for the benefit of forests, forest managers, and the public.
Contact(s):
Lori Rasor, Manager/Editor; 4033 SW Canyon Rd., Portland, OR 97221
Art Schick, Chair-Elect; 2585 NE Ortis Rd., Poulsbo, WA 98370

WASHINGTON TOXICS COALITION

4649 Sunnyside Ave., N.
Suite 540
Seattle, WA 98103 United States
Phone: 206-632-1545 Fax: 206-632-8661
E-mail: info@watoxics.org
Website: www.watoxics.org

Founded: 1981
Membership: 1,001–10,000
Scope: State
Description: Works to reduce society's reliance on toxic chemicals through research, education, advocacy, organizing and litigation.
Publication(s): Alternatives, Fact Sheets, Home Safe Home (fact sheets), No Place for Poisons: Reducing Pesticides in School, Trubbling Bubbles: The Case for Replacing Alkylphenol Ethoxylate Surfacants, Grow Smart, Grow Safe: A Consumer Guide to Lawn and Garden Products
Keyword(s): Ethics/Environmental Justice, Pollution (general), Public Lands/Greenspace, Recreation/Ecotourism, Transportation
Contact(s):
David Stitzhal, President
Gregg Small, Executive Director
Don Bollinger, Treasurer
Dave Coffman, Secretary
Martha Dale, Secretary

WASHINGTON TRAILS ASSOCIATION

1305 4th Ave., Suite 512
Seattle, WA 98101-2401 United States
Phone: 206-625-1367 Fax: 206-625-9249
Website: www.wta.org

Founded: 1973
Membership: 1,001–10,000
Scope: State
Description: Washington Trails Association works to protect and enhance hiking opportunities in Washington state through education, volunteer trail maintenance, advocacy and cooperation with other trail users.
Publication(s): Washington Trails - Monthly Magazine
Keyword(s): Public Lands/Greenspace, Recreation/Ecotourism
Contact(s):
Elizabeth Lunney, Executive Director; elunney@wta.org

WASHINGTON WILDERNESS COALITION

4649 Sunnyside Ave., N., Suite 520
Seattle, WA 98103 United States
Phone: 206-633-1992 Fax: 206-633-1996
E-mail: info@wawild.org
Website: www.wawild.org

Founded: 1979
Membership: 10,001–100,000
Scope: State
Description: WWC is a statewide organization of individuals and groups dedicated to preserving wilderness and biodiversity for the benefit of future generations. WWC works to protect and restore wildlands and waters in Washington State through outreach, public education, organizing, and support of grassroots conservation groups.
Publication(s): Washington Wildfire
Keyword(s): Land Issues, Wildlife & Species
Contact(s):
Martin Loesch, President
Mike Peterson, Vice President
John Leary, Executive Director
Jon Owen, Campaign Director
Kristen Tremoulet, Canvass Director
Michelle Kinsch, Treasurer
Cyndi Lewis, Secretary

WASHINGTON WILDLIFE AND RECREATION COALITION

811 First Avenue, Suite 262
Seattle, WA 98104 United States
Phone: 206-748-0082 Fax: 206-748-0580
E-mail: info@WildlifeRecreation.org
Website: www.WildlifeRecreation.org

Founded: 1989
Scope: State
Description: A diverse group of more than 120 environmental, business, labor, sporting, and community organizations dedicated to advocating for the permanent protection of parks and habitat in Washington State. The Coalition works to secure funding for the Washington Wildlife and Recreation Program, a competitive state grant program that enables local and state agencies to acquire and develop land for neighborhood parks and wildlife habitat areas.
Publication(s): E-newsletter, Land News
Keyword(s): Public Lands/Greenspace, Recreation/Ecotourism, Wildlife & Species
Contact(s):
Peter Scholes, President
Joanna Grist, Executive Director; 206-748-0082; joanna@WildlifeRecreation.org
Shamra Harrison, Outreach Director; 206-748-0082; shamra@WildlifeRecreation.org

WASHINGTON WILDLIFE FEDERATION

P.O. Box 1966
Olympia, WA 98507-1966 United States
Phone: 360-705-1903
Website: www.washingtonwildlife.org

Founded: N/A
Scope: State
Description: A representative statewide organization, affiliated with the National Wildlife Federation, dedicated to the protection and enhancement of wildlife and its habitat through public education and government interaction.
Publication(s): Washington Wildlife News
Keyword(s): Land Issues, Water Habitats & Quality, Wildlife & Species
Contact(s):
Ed Forslof, President
Kyle Winton, Executive Director; 360-951-1727

WATER EDUCATION FOUNDATION

717 K Street
Suite 317
Sacramento, CA 95814 United States
Phone: 916-444-6240 Fax: 916-448-7699
E-mail: feedback@watereducation.org
Website: www.watereducation.org

Founded: 1977
Membership: 1–100
Scope: Local, State, Regional, National
Description: for more than 25 years, the Water Education Foundation has provided in-depth, unbiased information about water resource issues through its publications, school programs, conferences, tours, maps and videos. The Foundation's mission is to develop and implement education programs leading to a broader understanding of water issues and to resolution of water problems.
Contact(s):
Christine Schmidt, Development Director; 916-444-6240; Fax: 916-448-7699; cschmidt@watereducation.org

WATER ENVIRONMENT FEDERATION

601 Wythe St.
Alexandria, VA 22314-1994 United States
Phone: 703-684-2400 Fax: 703-684-2492
Website: www.wef.org

Founded: 1928
Membership: 10,001–100,000
Scope: International
Description: A nonprofit technical and educational organization with the mission to preserve and enhance the global water environment. Federation members are water quality specialists from around the world, including environmental, civil and chemical engineers, biologists, government officials, treatment plant managers and operators, laboratory technicians, college professors, students, and equipment manufacturers and distributors.
Publication(s): Water Environment Research, other titles available on request, Watershed and Wet Weather Technical Bulletin, WEF Industrial Wastewater, Water Environment Regulation Watch, WEF Highlights, Water Environment and Technology
Keyword(s): Pollution (general), Water Habitats & Quality
Contact(s):
James Clark, President
William Bertera, Executive Director

WATER RESOURCES ASSOCIATION OF THE DELAWARE RIVER BASIN

P.O. Box 867
Valley Forge, PA 19482-0867 United States
Phone: 610-917-0090 Fax: 610-917-0091
E-mail: wradrb@aol.com
Website: www.wrabrb.org

Founded: 1959
Scope: Regional
Description: Nonprofit federation of businesses, industries, academia, government, environmental, and citizen organizations which serves to advise of and advocate the need for adequate water supplies through the orderly conservation, development, and equitable use and reuse of the water and related land resources of the Delaware River Basin.
Publication(s): Newsletter
Keyword(s): Oceans/Coasts/Beaches, Water Habitats & Quality
Contact(s):
William Palmer, Executive Director
William McElroy, Chair

WATERLOO-WELLINGTON WILDFLOWER SOCIETY

c/o Botany Dept., University of Guelph
Guelph, N1G 2W1 Ontario Canada
Phone: 519-821-7766 Fax: 519-767-1991
E-mail: bhallett@juliet.albedo.net
Website: www.uoguelph.ca/~botcal/

Founded: 1990
Membership: 1–100
Scope: Local, Regional
Description: (Formerly the Dogtooth Group) A non-profit organization based in Guelph, Ontario dedicated to the use and protection of native plants in parks, gardens and other open spaces.
Publication(s): Dogtooth, annual native plant sale
Keyword(s): Agriculture/Farming, Ecosystems (precious), Public Lands/Greenspace, Wildlife & Species
Contact(s):
Barbara Hallett, President; bhallett@juliet.albedo.net

WATERSHED MANAGEMENT COUNCIL

P.O. Box 1090
Mammoth Lakes, CA 93546 United States
E-mail: WMC@watershed.org
Website: www.watershed.org/

Founded: 1986
Scope: Regional
Description: The Watershed Management Council is a nonprofit, educational organization dedicated to advancing the art and science of watershed management, with an emphasis on the Western region.
Publication(s): Proceedings, Networker, The
Keyword(s): Land Issues, Pollution (general), Water Habitats & Quality

WELDER WILDLIFE FOUNDATION

P.O. Box 1400
Sinton, TX 78387 United States
Phone: 361-364-2643 Fax: 361-364-2650
E-mail: welderwf@aol.com
Website:
www.hometown.aol.com/welderwf/welderweb.html

Founded: 1954
Scope: National
Description: Established by the will of the late Rob Welder, the Foundation is dedicated to the cause of conservation through research and education in wildlife ecology and management and closely related fields. Operates through a small staff, with research fellowships to graduate students only.
Keyword(s): Wildlife & Species
Contact(s):
D. Drawe, Director
Terry Blankenship, Assistant Director/Wildlife Biologist
Selma Glasscock, Assistant Director/Conservation Educator

WEST MICHIGAN ENVIRONMENTAL ACTION COUNCIL

1514 Wealthy SE, Suite 280
Grand Rapids, MI 49506-2755 United States
Phone: 616-451-3051 Fax: 616-451-3054
Website: www.wmeac.org

Founded: 1968
Scope: Local
Description: Provide leadership in environmental protection and preservation in west Michigan and throughout Michigan on issues such as water quality, land use planning and sustainable business. Through the involvement of concerned volunteers, WMEAC has helped landmark environmental legislation and assured application of existing laws.
Publication(s): Action Issue, see publications on website
Keyword(s): Air Quality/Atmosphere, Land Issues, Reduce/Reuse/Recycle
Contact(s):
Karel Rogers, President
Tom Leonard, Executive Director

WEST VIRGINIA ASSOCIATION OF CONSERVATION DISTRICT SUPERVISORS ASSOCIATION, INC.

Attn: President, P.O. Box 711
Gallipolis Ferry, WV 25515 United States

Founded: N/A
Scope: State

WEST VIRGINIA B.A.S.S. CHAPTER FEDERATION

Attn: President
John Burdette
P. O. Box 418
Buckhannon, WV 26201 United States
Phone: 304-472-3600 Fax: 304-472-3601
E-mail: jburdette@neumedia.net
Website: www.wvbass.com

Founded: 1973
Membership: 101–1,000
Scope: State
Description: An organization of Bassmaster chapters, affiliated with the Bass Anglers Sportsman Society, organized to fight pollution, assist state and national conservation agencies in their efforts, and teach the young people of our country good conservation practices. Dedicated to the realistic conservation of our water resources.
Publication(s): Monongahela National Forest Hiking Guide, Highlands Voice, The
Keyword(s): Forests/Forestry, Land Issues, Public Lands/ Greenspace, Water Habitats & Quality
Contact(s):
John Burdette, President; 304-472-3600; Fax: 304-472-3601; jburdette@neumedia.net
Jim Summers, Conservation Director; Rte. 1 Box 205, Worthington, WV 26591; 304-287-7700; JSummers8@compuserve.com

WEST VIRGINIA HIGHLANDS CONSERVANCY

P.O. Box 306
Charleston, WV 25321 United States

Founded: 1967
Membership: 101–1,000
Scope: State
Description: An organization devoted to the conservation and wise management of West Virginia's natural and historic resources. Active in wilderness preservation, river conservation, public lands management, forestry, mining, air and water quality, water resources management and a wide variety of other environmental and conservation issues.
Publication(s): The Highlands Voice, The Monongahela National Forest Hiking Guide
Keyword(s): Forests/Forestry, Land Issues
Contact(s):
Frank Young, President; Rt. 1 Box 108, Ripley, WV 25271; 304-372-9329
Judy Rodd, Senior Vice President; Rt. 1, Box 178, Moatsville, WV 26405; 304-265-0018
Norm Steenstra, Vice President of State Affairs; 1001 Valley Rd., Charleston, WV 25302; 304-346-5891
Jacqueline Hallinan, Treasurer; 1120 Swan Rd., Charleston, WV 25314; 304-345-3718
Andrew Maier, Secretary; Rt. 1 Box 27, Hinton, WV 25952; 304-466-3864
Bill Reed, Editor; 350 Bucks Branch, Beckley, WV 25801; 304-934-5828
Dave Saville, Membership Secretary; P.O. Box 569, Morgantown, WV 26507; 304-284-9548

WEST VIRGINIA RAPTOR REHABILITATION CENTER

P.O. Box 333
Morgantown, WV 26505 United States
Phone: 304-366-9286
E-mail: raptor@wvrrc.org
Website: www.wvrrc.org

Founded: 1983
Membership: 101–1,000
Scope: Regional
Description: The WVRRC, established in 1983, is a non-profit volunteer based organization dedicated to the rehabilitation and ultimate release of injured, sick and orphaned wild birds of prey while providing environmental education to the general public, schools and other organizations.
Publication(s): The Falcon (Newsletter).
Keyword(s): Air Quality/Atmosphere, Ecosystems (precious), Pollution (general), Water Habitats & Quality, Wildlife & Species
Contact(s):
Natasha Diamond, Executive Director; 304-366-2867; raptor@wvrrc.org

WEST VIRGINIA WILDLIFE FEDERATION, INC.

P.O. Box 275
Paden City, WV 26159 United States
Phone: 304-782-3685
E-mail: pleinbach@aol.com
Website: www.wvwf.org

Founded: N/A
Scope: State
Description: A representative statewide organization, affiliated with the National Wildlife Federation, dedicated to the protection and enhancement of wildlife and its habitat through public education and government interaction.
Publication(s): West Virginia Wildlife Notes
Contact(s):
William Mullins, President and Alternate Representative

WEST VIRGINIA, WOODLAND OWNERS ASSOCIATION OF

P.O. Box 13695
Sissonville, WV 25360 United States
Phone: 304-594-3648 Fax: 304-594-3648

Founded: 1991
Scope: State
Description: A statewide organization affiliated with the National Woodland Owners Association that promotes good forestry and sustainable management by non-industrial private owners in West Virginia.
Publication(s): West Virginia Woods
Keyword(s): Forests/Forestry
Contact(s):
Mark Burke, President; dadobourke@aol.com
Russ Richardson, Vice-President; P.O. Box 206, Weston, WV 26452; 304-269-3862; Fax: 304-269-3964; forestruss@aol.com
Mark Metz, Treasurer; 1017 Mt. Vernon Circle, Barboursville, WV 25504; 304-733-1043; themetzs@gateway.net
Edward Murriner, Secretary; Rt. 3. Box 186D, Hurricane, WV 25526; 304-727-5591; Fax: 304-558-0143; emmurin@gwmail.state.wv.us
Clay Smith, Editor; HC 64 Box 50, Parsons, WV 26287-9709; 304-478-2104
Bob Whipkey, Forestry Advisor; 304-558-2788

WESTERN ASSOCIATION OF FISH AND WILDLIFE AGENCIES

5400 Bishop Blvd.
Cheyenne, WY 82006 United States
Phone: 307-777-4569 Fax: 307-777-4699
Website: www.wafwa.org

Founded: N/A
Scope: Regional, National
Description: A regional organization including 18 fish and wildlife agencies of 15 states and three Canadian provinces. Meets annually to consider mutual problems and provide a forum for the exchange of information at both administrative and technical levels.
Publication(s): Western Proceedings

Keyword(s): Wildlife & Species

Contact(s):
Jeff Koenings, President
Ken Ambrock, 2nd Vice President
Steven Huffaker, 1st Vice President
Dean Hildebrand, Secretary and Treasurer; 307-777-4569

WESTERN ENVIRONMENTAL LAW CENTER

1216 Lincoln Street
Eugene, OR 97401 United States
Phone: 541-485-2471 Fax: 541-485-2457
E-mail: eugene@westernlaw.org
Website: www.westernlaw.org

Founded: 1993
Membership: 1,001–10,000
Scope: Regional
Description: The Western Environmental Law Center is a nonprofit public interest law firm with offices in Eugene, Oregon; Ketchum, Idaho; and Taos, New Mexico. The Center represents activists, conservation groups, Indian tribes, and local governments that seek to protect and restore the forests, rivers, deserts, grasslands, wildlife, and human communities in the West.
Publication(s): Biannual Report, Defending the West
Keyword(s): Air Quality/Atmosphere, Ethics/Environmental Justice, Forests/Forestry, Land Issues, Pollution (general), Water Habitats & Quality

Contact(s):
Corrie Yackulic, President; yackulic@schroeter-goldmark.com
Mary Wood, Vice President, Secretary and Treasurer; mwood@law.uoregon.edu
Michael Axline, Litigation Director
Grove Burnett, Director of Taos Office; 505-751-0351; Fax: 505-751-1775; law@welctaos.org
Peter Frost, Executive Director

WESTERN FORESTRY AND CONSERVATION ASSOCIATION

4033 SW Canyon Rd.
Portland, OR 97221 United States
Phone: 503-226-4562 Fax: 503-226-2515
Website: www.westernforestry.org

Founded: 1909
Scope: Regional
Description: The mission of the WFCA is to promote forest stewardship in western North America. The Association's objectives are to promote the science and practice of forestry, promote the dissemination of forestry research and technical information, and foster cooperation between federal, state, provincial, and private forest agencies.
Keyword(s): Forests/Forestry

Contact(s):
Richard Zabel, President
Blair Holman, Treasurer

WESTERN HEMISPHERE SHOREBIRD RESERVE NETWORK (WHSRN)

c/o Manomet Center for Conservation Svcs.
81 Stage Point Rd.
P.O. Box 1770
Manomet, MA 02345 United States
Phone: 508-224-6521 Fax: 508-224-9220
E-mail: jmcorven@manomet.org
Website: www.manomet.org/WHSRN.htm

Founded: 1985
Membership: 101–1,000
Scope: Local, State, Regional, National, International
Description: WHSRN is a voluntary nonregulatory network of over 225 partner organizations at 54 critical wetland sites in seven countries of South and North America that have joined together to study, manage, and promote the sustainable conservation of shorebirds and their habitats for the benefit of the ecosystems and people. WHSRN's strategy promotes a multiple species ecosystem approach to protection of over twenty million acres of habitats that are critical staging, nesting, and nonbreeding sites.
Publication(s): Shorebirds Across the Americas, Conservation Sciences-Quarterly, Save Our Migratory Shorebirds (curriculum guide), Shorebird Atlas, Important Shorebird Staging Sites Meeting WHSRN Criteria in the U.S., Shorebird Migrations: Fundamentals for Land Managers
Keyword(s): Ecosystems (precious), Oceans/Coasts/Beaches, Public Lands/Greenspace, Recreation/Ecotourism, Water Habitats & Quality, Wildlife & Species

Contact(s):
Jim Corven, Director; 508-224-6521, ext. 227; Fax: 508-224-9220; jmcorven@manomet.org
Brian Harrington, Senior Scientist; 508-224-6521, ext. 241; Fax: 508-224-9220; BHarr@manomet.org
Heidi Luquer, Education/Outreach Coordinator; 802-436-1999; Fax: 802-436-1998; HLuquer@manomet.org

WESTERN PENNSYLVANIA CONSERVANCY

209 4th Ave.
Pittsburgh, PA 15222 United States
Phone: 412-288-2777 Fax: 412-281-1792
E-mail: wpc@paconserve.org
Website: www.paconserve.org/

Founded: 1932
Membership: 10,001–100,000
Scope: Local, State, Regional, National
Description: The Western Pennsylvania Conservancy, working together to save the places we care about, protects natural lands, promotes healthy and attractive communities and preserves Frank Lloyd Wright's masterwork Fallingwater. The Conservancy fosters the integration of ecological protection with economic and social needs while building on the core values of the community and has protected more than 200,000 acres of natural lands in Pennsylvania.
Publication(s): Conserve, Annual Calendar
Keyword(s): Agriculture/Farming, Forests/Forestry, Land Issues, Public Lands/Greenspace, Reduce/Reuse/Recycle, Wildlife & Species

Contact(s):
Larry Schweiger, President and CEO
Jacquelyn Bonomo, Vice President of Conservation Programs
Cynthia Carrow, Executive Vice President and COO
Lynda Waggoner, Vice President and Director of Fallingwater
Mike Boyle, Chairman
Julie Lalo, Vice President of Public Affairs

WESTERN WATERSHEDS PROJECT

P.O. Box 1770
Hailey, ID 83333 United States
Phone: 208-788-2290 Fax: 208-788-2298
E-mail: wwp@westernwatersheds.org
Website: www.westernwatersheds.org

Founded: 1993
Membership: 101–1,000
Scope: Local, State, Regional, National
Description: The mission of Western Watersheds Project is to protect and restore watersheds in the West by retiring livestock grazing from public lands through monitoring, advocacy, education, litigation and restoration. WWP works in partnership with several regional conservation groups, including the Oregon Natural Desert Association, Forest Guardians, the Center for Biological Diversity, the Committee for Idaho's High Desert and American Lands Alliance.
Publication(s): Welfare Ranching, Watersheds Messenger
Keyword(s): Ecosystems (precious), Ethics/Environmental Justice, Land Issues, Public Lands/Greenspace, Water Habitats & Quality, Wildlife & Species

Contact(s):
Jon Marvel, Executive Director; 208-788-2290; Fax: 208-788-2298; jon@westernwatersheds.org
John Carter, Utah Director; WWP/Utah, P.O. Box 280, Mendon, UT 84325; 435-753-2701; utah@westernwatersheds.org
Stew Churchwell, Central Idaho Director; East Fork, HC67 Box 2096, Challis, ID 83226; 208-838-2374; Fax: 208-838-2374; stew@westernwatersheds.org
Judy Hall, Director of Fund Development; 208-788-2290; Fax: 208-788-2298; judy@westernwatersheds.org
Keith Raether, Director of Public Information; WWP/Montana, 2220 Landusky Ct., Missoula, MT 59801; 406-543-3030; Fax: 406-543-3769; kraether@westernwatersheds.org
Teri Stewart, Office Administrator; 208-788-2290; Fax: 208-788-2298; teri@westernwatersheds.org

WETLAND HABITAT ALLIANCE OF TEXAS

118 E. Hospital, Suite 208
Nacogdoches, TX 75961 United States
Phone: 936-569-9428 Fax: 936-569-6349
E-mail: whatduck@txucom.net
Website: www.whatduck.org

Founded: 1984
Membership: 1,001–10,000
Scope: State, Regional
Description: A nonprofit organization of conservationists, dedicated to preserving, reclaiming, and enhancing Texas wetland habitat, that promotes the wise use of our natural resources and the progress of our society. Constructs habitat improvement projects on public and private lands, promotes educational programs, performs priority wetland research, and supports legislative conservation efforts.
Publication(s): Texas Wetlands
Keyword(s): Water Habitats & Quality
Contact(s):
John Gardere, Vice President
John Frasier, Executive Director
Neal Jenkins, Treasurer
Bruce Klingman, Chairman

WETLANDS ACTION NETWORK

P.O. Box 1145
Malibu, CA 90265 United States
Phone: 310-456-5604 Fax: 310-456-5612
E-mail: wetlandact@earthlink.net
Website: www.wetlandsactionnetwork.org

Founded: 1995
Membership: 1,001–10,000
Scope: Local, State, Regional, International
Description: We work to protect and restore wetlands along the Pacific Migratory Pathways, serving as a resource and network for wetlands activists in ten western states, Canada, Mexico and Central America. A primary focus area is Southern California, where more than 95% of historical wetlands have been destroyed in the heart of the Pacific Flyway. Los Angeles' Ballona Wetlands is a prominent campaign to recover wetlands in the Pacific bioregion.
Publication(s): Great Blue Heron Report.
Keyword(s): Ecosystems (precious), Ethics/Environmental Justice, Executive/Legislative/Judicial Reform, Land Issues, Oceans/Coasts/Beaches, Water Habitats & Quality, Wildlife & Species
Contact(s):
Robert Roy van de Hoek, Director of Research and Restoration; 310-456-5604; Fax: 310-456-5612; rjvandehoek@yahoo.com

WHALE AND DOLPHIN CONSERVATION SOCIETY

Brookfield House
38 St. Paul Street
Chippenham, SN15 1LY United Kingdom
Phone: 1249449500 Fax: 12494495017
E-mail: campaign@wdcs.org
Website: www.wdcs.org

Founded: 1987
Membership: 10,001–100,000
Scope: International
Description: WDCS is dedicated to the conservation, welfare, and appreciation of all species of whale, dolphins and porpoises and their environment.
Keyword(s): Oceans/Coasts/Beaches, Recreation/Ecotourism, Wildlife & Species
Contact(s):
S. Davis-Hilton, Director of Finance
Mark Simmonds, Director of Science
Chris Vick, Marketing & Communications Director
Alison Wood, Director of Conservation
Victoria Reinthal, Communications Officer; vreinthal@wdcs.org
Chris Stroud, Chief Executive

WHITE CLAY WATERSHED ASSOCIATION

760 Chambers Rock Rd.
Landenberg, PA 19350 United States
Phone: 610-274-8499
Website: home.ccil.org/~wcwa/

Founded: 1965
Scope: Regional
Description: The White Clay Watershed Association is a nonprofit organization devoted to protection and improvement of the environmental quality of the White Clay Creek and valley. The Association works to improve water quality in local streams, conserve open space, woodlands, wetlands and geological features; aid in the preservation of cultural, historical and archaeological sites; increase outdoor recreation opportunities; and conduct educational programs relating to the environment.
Keyword(s): Ethics/Environmental Justice, Public Lands/Greenspace, Water Habitats & Quality
Contact(s):
John Murray, President
Robert Stark, Vice President
Donna Bush, Treasurer
Carol Catanese, Secretary

WHITETAILS UNLIMITED, INC.

P.O. Box 720, 1715 Rhode Island St.
Sturgeon Bay, WI 54235 United States
Phone: 920-743-6777 Fax: 920-743-4658
E-mail: wtu@itol.com
Website: www.whitetailsunlimited.com

Founded: 1982
Membership: 1–100
Scope: National
Description: Whitetails Unlimited is a national, nonprofit conservation organization. Its purpose is to raise funds in support of education, habitat enhancement, and the preservation of the hunting tradition for the direct benefit of the white-tailed deer and other wildlife species.
Publication(s): Whitetails Unlimited Magazine
Keyword(s): Recreation/Ecotourism
Contact(s):
Jeffrey Schinkten, President
William Gerl, Executive Vice President
David Hawkey, Vice President of Field Operations
Peter Gerl, Executive Director and Production Manager
Eric Carper, Manager of Merchandise and Advertising

Kevin Devault, Manager of Conservation Funding
Janet Gerl, Office Manager
Kim McKinney, Event Program Manager
Denise Dubick, Production/Design
Kevin Naze, Field Editor
Arlene Peterson, Inventory Shipment Coordinator
Peter Schoonmaker, Field Editor
Cheryl Uecker, Membership Services Coordinator

WHOOPING CRANE CONSERVATION ASSOCIATION INC.

1393 Henderson Highway
Breaux Bridge, LA 70517 United States
Phone: 337-228-7563 Fax: 337-228-7424
E-mail: wcca@excelonline.com
Website: www.whoopingcrane.com

Founded: 1961
Scope: National, International
Description: A scientific and educational organization, international in scope, working to prevent the extinction of the whooping crane and save wetland habitats.
Publication(s): Grus Americana, The Whooping Crane, North America's Symbol of Conservation by Jerome J. Pratt
Keyword(s): Water Habitats & Quality, Wildlife & Species
Contact(s):
Mary Courville, Secretary and Treasurer
Marie Maltese, Editor
Jerome Pratt, Past Editor & Communication Coordinator

WILD CANID SURVIVAL AND RESEARCH CENTER

P.O. Box 760
Eureka, MO 63025 United States
Phone: 636-938-5900 Fax: 636-938-6490
E-mail: edu@wolfsantuary.org
Website: www.wolfsanctuary.org

Founded: 1971
Membership: 101–1,000
Scope: National
Description: A nonprofit, conservation organization dedicated to the preservation of wolves and other wild canids through education, research, and captive breeding.
Publication(s): Wild Canid Center Review, Wolf Pack Press
Keyword(s): Wildlife & Species
Contact(s):
Sue Lindsey, Executive Director
Patricia Biggerstaff, Treasurer
Margaret Ratz, Vice-Chair
William Sadler, Chairman

WILD DOG FOUNDATION, THE

P.O. Box 1603
Mineola, NY 11501-0901 United States
Phone: 516-746-0005 Fax: 516-746-0005
E-mail: savewilddogs@hotmail.com
Website: www.wilddog.org

Founded: 1996
Membership: 1–100
Scope: International
Description: The foundation is a conservation and educational group. The foundation promotes wolf restoration to the Adirondack State Park in New York and the Northeast, and deals with less popular predators, mostly wild canines and hyenas. Its flagship species are the african Wild Dog, and coyote.
Publication(s): Wild, The
Keyword(s): Reduce/Reuse/Recycle, Wildlife & Species
Contact(s):
Frank Vincenti, President; 516-746-0005; savewilddogs@hotmail.com
Robert Berghaier, Vice President
Hope Ryden, Vice President
Pat Traub, Vice President
Peggy Weinberg, Vice President
Lew Egol, Vice Presdent

WILD FOUNDATION, THE

(INTERNATIONAL WILDERNESS LEADERSHIP FOUNDATION)
P.O. Box 1380
Ojai, CA 93024 United States
Phone: 805-640-0390 Fax: 805-640-0230
E-mail: info@wild.org
Website: www.wild.org

Founded: 1974
Membership: N/A
Scope: National, International
Description: Working for wilderness, wildife and people. The WILD Foundation protects and promotes the sustainability of wilderness and wildlands worldwide, and provides environmental information, education, experience and training.
Publication(s): Wilderness and Human Communities, Wilderness and Humanity - A Global Issue, Wilderness, Arctic Wilderness, Wilderness, the Way Ahead, for the Conservation of Earth, Wilderness Management, International Journal of Wilderness, Leaf Newsletter, The
Keyword(s): Development/Developing Countries, Ecosystems (precious), Forests/Forestry, Land Issues, Recreation/Ecotourism, Wildlife & Species
Contact(s):
Vance Martin, President; 805-640-0390
John Hendee, Editor in Chief, International Journal of Wilderness; hendeejo@uidaho.edu
Michael Sweatman, Chairman, Treasurer; michael@gmtcap.com

WILD HORSE ORGANIZED ASSISTANCE, INC. (WHOA)

P.O. Box 555
Reno, NV 89504 United States
Phone: 702-851-4817
Website: www.ipt.com/htmlpub/jpi/whoa.htm

Founded: 1971
Membership: 10,001–100,000
Scope: National
Description: Directs efforts toward the welfare of wild horses and burros; implementation of federal efforts in carrying out terms of the management, protection, and control program for their welfare; student projects pertaining to all phases of our heritage.
Keyword(s): Wildlife & Species
Contact(s):
Dawn Lappin, Executive Director and Chairman of the Board; 702-851-4817
Leslie Johnson, Treasurer; 702-851-4817
Russell Johnson, Vice Chairman; 702-786-7600
Bert Lappin, Secretary; 702-851-4817

WILD ONES NATURAL LANDSCAPERS, LTD

WILD ONES
Headquarters
P.O. Box 1274
Appleton, WI 54912-1274 United States
Phone: 877-394-9453 Fax: 920-730-8654
E-mail: woresource@aol.com
Website: www.for-wild.org

Founded: 1977
Membership: 1,001–10,000
Scope: Local, National
Description: Wild Ones is a nonprofit organization seeking to educate and inform members and the public at the plants-roots

level and to promote biodiversity and environmental sound practices, thru natural landscaping using native species in developing plant communities.

Publication(s): Wild Ones Journal, Wild Ones Handbook

Keyword(s): Agriculture/Farming, Ecosystems (precious), Ethics/Environmental Justice, Forests/Forestry, Land Issues, Public Lands/Greenspace, Reduce/Reuse/Recycle, Water Habitats & Quality, Wildlife & Species

Contact(s):

Joe Powelka, President; President@for-wild.org
Mariette Nowak, Vice President; VicePresident@for-wild.org
Steve Maassen, SFE Director; SFEdirector@for-wild.org
Donna VanBuecken, Executive Director; ExecDirector@for-wild.org
Portia Brown, Secretary; Secretary@for-wild.org
Klaus Wisiol, Treasurer; Treasurer@for-wild.org

WILDCOAST

757 Emory Street
P.O. Box 161
Imperial Beach, CA 91932 United States
Phone: 619-423-8665 Fax: 619-423-8488
E-mail: info@wildcoast.net
Website: www.wildcoast.net

Founded: 1999
Membership: N/A
Scope: Local, State, Regional, National, International

Description: WiLDCOAST is a partnership-based international conservation team preserving the endangered marine species and coastal wildlands of the Calfornias. Our projects include: — Sea turtle recovery program of the Eastern Pacific—halting the slaughter of 30,000 sea turtles annually in Baja California — Developing three protected areas totalling 1.3 million-acres in the Baja California Peninsula.

Keyword(s): Ecosystems (precious), Land Issues, Oceans/Coasts/Beaches

WILDERNESS EDUCATION ASSOCIATION

900 East 7th Street
Bloomington, IN 47405 United States
Phone: 812-855-4095 Fax: 812-855-8697
E-mail: wea@indiana.edu
Website: www.ebl.org/wea/

Founded: 1977
Membership: 1,001–10,000
Scope: National

Description: WEA is a nonprofit membership organization. It promotes national wilderness education and preservation programs by providing for-credit, expedition-based wilderness leadership training programs, developing and publishing state-of-the-art wilderness education publications and training manuals, promoting scholarly research programs, establishing and maintaining national outdoor leadership certification standards, and providing support to wildland management agencies to promote wilderness education.

Publication(s): WEA Legend, Wilderness Educator, New Wilderness Handbook, WEA Affiliate Handbook, The Backcountry Classroom, Trustees and Affiliates Briefing System (TABS).

Keyword(s): Land Issues, Recreation/Ecotourism

Contact(s):

David Cockrell, President; Department of Human Performance and Leisure Studies, University of Southern Colorado, 2200 Bonforte Blvd., Pueblo, CO 81001-4901; 719-549-2775; Fax: 719-549-2732
Mitchell Sakofs, Vice President; Outward Bound USA, Rt. 9, R. D. 2, Box 280, Garrison, NY 10524-9757; 914-424-4000
Darla Deruiter, Executive Director; WEA Department of Natural Resource Recreation and Tourism, Colorado State University, Fort Collins, CO 80523; 970-223-6252; Fax: 970-223-6252
William Forgey, Treasurer; One Tower Plaza, 109 E. 89th Ave., Merrillville, IN 46410; 219-769-6055; Fax: 219-769-6035
W. Norton, Publisher
Jeff Olson, Secretary; Confidence Learning Center, 6260 Mary Fawcett Memorial Dr., Brainerd, MN 56401; 218-828-2344

WILDERNESS LAND TRUST, THE

4060 Post Canyon Dr.
Hood River, OR 97031 United States
Phone: 541-386-9546 Fax: 541-386-9547
Website: www.wildernesstrust.org

Founded: 1992
Scope: Regional

Description: To facilitate public acquisition of private lands (inholdings) within units of the National Wilderness Preservation System to fulfill the promise of Congress made in The Wilderness Act of 1964 that all generations of Americans will enjoy an enduring resource of wilderness.

Publication(s): Wilderness Heritage Newsletter

Keyword(s): Land Issues, Reduce/Reuse/Recycle, Wildlife & Species

Contact(s):

Jon Mulford, President
John Fielder, Chairman; P.O. Box 1261, Englewood, CO 80150; 303-935-0900
Andy Wiessner, Secretary and Treasurer; 811 Potato Patch Dr., Vail, CO 81657; 303-715-3570

WILDERNESS SOCIETY, THE

1615 M Street, NW
Washington, DC 20036 United States
Phone: 202-833-2300 Fax: 202-429-3958
Website: www.wilderness.org

Founded: 1935
Membership: 100,001–500,000
Scope: Regional, National

Description: A nonprofit membership organization devoted to preserving wilderness and wildlife, protecting America's prime forests, parks, rivers, and shorelands, and fostering an American land ethic. The Society welcomes membership inquiries, contributions and requests.

Publication(s): Annual Report, Quarterly Newsletter, Wilderness Magazine

Keyword(s): Ecosystems (precious), Energy, Forests/Forestry, Land Issues, Oceans/Coasts/Beaches, Public Lands/Greenspace, Sprawl/Urban Planning, Water Habitats & Quality, Wildlife & Species

Contact(s):

Burt Fingerhut, Chair
William Meadows, President
G. Bancroft, Vice President of Ecology and Economic Research
Donald Barry, Executive Vice President
Elizabeth Coit, Vice President of Membership and Development
Jerry Greenberg, Vice President of Regional Conservation
Fran Hunt, Deputy Vice President of Regional Conservation
Linda Lance, Vice President of Public Policy
Barrington McFarlane, Vice President of Finance and Administration
Gaylord Nelson, Counselor
Dave Alberswerth, Director of BIM Program
William Clay, Acting Regional Director (SE); 1447 Peachtree Street NE, Suite 812, Atlanta, GA 30309
Pamela Eaton, Regional Director (Four Corners); 7475 Dakin St., Suite 410, Denver, CO 80221
Robert Ekey, Regional Director (Montana); 105 West Main St., Suite E, Bozeman, MT 59715
Michael Francis, Director of National Forest Program

Robert Freimark, Regional Director; 1424 Fourth Ave., Suite 816, Seattle, WA 98101; 206-624-6430
Bonnie Galvin, Director of Budget and Appropriations
Craig Gehrke, Regional Director; 2600 Rose Hill, Suite 201, Boise, ID 83705; 208-343-8153
Sue Gunn, Director of National Parks Program
Eleanor Huffines, Alaska Regional Director; 430 West 7th Avenue, Suite 210, Anchorage, AK 99501
Bart Kohler, Regional Director (Wilderness Support Center); 835 East 2nd Ave., Suite 440, Durango, CO 81301
Jim Waltman, Director of Alaska and National Wildlife Refuge
Jay Watson, Regional Director (CA/NV); Presidio Building 1016, P.O. Box 29241, San Francisco, CA 94129
Julie Wormser, Regional Director; 45 Bromfield Street, Suite 1109, Boston, MA 02108; 817-350-8866

WILDERNESS WATCH

P.O. Box 9175
Missoula, MT 59807 United States
Phone: 406-542-2048 Fax: 406-542-7714
E-mail: wild@wildernesswatch.org
Website: www.wildernesswatch.org

Founded: 1989
Membership: 1,001–10,000
Scope: National
Description: Wilderness Watch is a national, nonprofit, citizen organization dedicated solely to the protection and proper stewardship of lands within the National Wilderness Preservation System and Wild and Scenic Rivers System. We achieve our goals through the efforts of citizen activists, local chapters, wilderness "adopters", and by working with other local organizations concerned about wilderness and wild river issues.
Publication(s): Wilderness Watcher, Wilderness Guardian
Keyword(s): Ecosystems (precious), Land Issues, Oceans/Coasts/Beaches, Public Lands/Greenspace, Water Habitats & Quality, Wildlife & Species
Contact(s):
George Nickas, Executive Director

WILDFLOWER ASSOCIATION OF MICHIGAN

c/o Marji Fuller
3853 Farrell Road
Hastings, MI 49058 United States
Phone: 269-948-2496 Fax: 269-948-2957
E-mail: wam@iserv.net
Website: www.wildflowersmich.org

Founded: 1986
Membership: 101–1,000
Scope: State
Description: The Wildflower Association of Michigan promotes, coordinates, and participates in education, enjoyment, science, and stewardship of native wildflowers and their habitats.
Publication(s): Wildflowers (quarterly newsletter).
Keyword(s): Land Issues, Reduce/Reuse/Recycle, Wildlife & Species
Contact(s):
Stephan Keto, President; 616-343-1669; Fax: 616-343-0768
Marilyn Case, Membership Coordinator; 15232 24 Mile Road, Albion, MI 49224; 269-630-8546; mcase15300@aol.com
Marji Fuller, Managing Editor; 269-948-2496; Fax: 269-948-2957; marjif@iserv.net
Kathryn Johnson, Editor; 11155 Hastings Pte Road, Middleville, MI 49333; 269-795-9691; Fax: 269-795-8730; kathyj@voyager.net
Valerie Reed, Secretary; 269-964-0477; vfrrabbit@aol.com

WILDFOWL TRUST OF NORTH AMERICA, INC., THE

P.O. Box 519, Discovery Ln.
Grasonville, MD 21638 United States
Phone: 410-827-6694 Fax: 410-827-6713
E-mail: horsehead@wildfowltrust.org
Website: www.wildfowltrust.org

Founded: 1979
Membership: 101–1,000
Scope: International
Description: A nonprofit, tax-exempt organization dedicated to the preservation of wildlife and wetlands through education, conservation, and research. The Trust operates The Horsehead Wetlands Center on its 500-acre wetland refuge on the Chesapeake Bay's Eastern Shore. The Center provides environmental education programs, a collection of resident waterfowl and raptors in natural habitat settings, a Visitor's Center, trails, and observation blinds and towers. Canoes are available for rental.
Publication(s): On The Wing-Newsletter
Keyword(s): Water Habitats & Quality, Wildlife & Species
Contact(s):
Torrey Brown, President
William Stott, Vice President
Edward Delaney, Executive Director

WILDFUTURES

353 Wallace Way, NE
Suite 12
Bainbridge Island, WA 98110 United States
Phone: 206-780-9718 Fax: 206-780-9718
E-mail: snegri@igc.org
Website: www.earthisland.org/wildfutures

Founded: 1994
Scope: National
Description: WildFutures provides essential tools and training to groups working to protect wildlife and habitat. WildFutures also works to bridge the gap between science and conservation, finding collaborative ways to develop and implement effective conservation strategies.
Keyword(s): Wildlife & Species

WILDLANDS CONSERVANCY

3701 Orchid Pl.
Emmaus, PA 18049-1637 United States
Phone: 610-965-4397 Fax: 610-965-7223
E-mail: wildlands@aol.com
Website: www.wildlandspa.org

Founded: 1973
Membership: 1,001–10,000
Scope: Local
Description: A nonprofit, member-supported organization serving eastern Pennsylvania, involved in land and river preservation and environmental education. Wildlands has preserved over 30,000 acres of open space, much of it in cooperation with the Pennsylvania Game Commission. Some of the activities involve the operation of nature preserves and sanctuaries; developing and implementing plans for river conservation and other preservation projects; and the creation of a curriculum (K-College).
Publication(s): Wildlands quarterly newsletter
Keyword(s): Land Issues, Water Habitats & Quality
Contact(s):
David Kepler, Chairman; 702 Hamilton Mall, Allentown, PA 18101

WILDLANDS PROJECT

WILD EARTH SOCIETY, INC.
P.O. Box 455
Richmond, VT 05477 United States
Phone: 802-434-4077 Fax: 802-434-5980
E-mail: info@wildlandsproject.org
Website: www.wildlandsproject.org

Founded: 1992
Membership: 1,001–10,000
Scope: International
Description: The Wildlands Project is working to restore and protect the natural heritage of North America. Through advocacy, education, scientific consultation, and cooperation with partners, we are designing and helping create systems of interconnected wilderness areas that can sustain the diversity of life.
Publication(s): Wild Earth - special edition, Wildlands Project, The: First Thousand Days of the Next Thousand Years.
Keyword(s): Land Issues, Reduce/Reuse/Recycle, Wildlife & Species
Contact(s):
Bob Howard, President
Leanne Klyza Linck, Executive Director
Dave Foreman, Chairman
David Johns, Secretary and Treasurer

WILDLIFE ACTION, INC.

P.O. Box 866
Mullins, SC 29574 United States
Phone: 843-464-8473 Fax: 843-464-8859
E-mail: info@wildlifeaction.com
Website: www.wildlifeaction.com

Founded: 1977
Membership: 10,001–100,000
Scope: Local, State, Regional, National
Description: Wildlife Action is a private nonprofit 501(c)3 tax-exempt organization dedicated to the appreciation and enjoyment of our wildlife heritage and to educating the public in the value of protection, restoration, enhancement, and wise use of our natural resources.
Publication(s): Wildlife Pride, Wild Things - Our Resource Education Center
Keyword(s): Air Quality/Atmosphere, Development/Developing Countries, Ecosystems (precious), Energy, Ethics/Environmental Justice, Executive/Legislative/Judicial Reform, Forests/Forestry, Land Issues, Oceans/Coasts/Beaches, Pollution (general), Population, Public Health
Contact(s):
M. Beeson, President and CEO; P.O. Box 866, Mullins, SC 29574; 843-464-8473; Fax: 843-464-8859; info@wildlifeaction.com
Tommy Simpson, Vice President
Sandra Bane, Secretary
Ted Williams, Treasurer

WILDLIFE CENTER OF VIRGINIA, THE

P.O. Box 1557
Waynesboro, VA 22980-1414 United States
Phone: 540-942-9453 Fax: 540-943-9453
E-mail: wildlife@wildlifecenter.org
Website: www.wildlifecenter.org

Founded: 1982
Membership: 1–100
Scope: International
Description: A nonprofit organization that operates the nation's largest professionally-staffed veterinary teaching and research hospital for native wildlife. Study and documentation of environmental factors that cause injuries, especially pesticide poisoning, are used to monitor environmental and wildlife health trends and support public policy positions. The Center also trains students and professionals from the fields of veterinary medicine, wildlife management and wildlife rehabilitation.
Publication(s): Handbook of Wildlife Medicine, Annual and Mid-year reports, The Wildlife Center Teacher's Packet
Keyword(s): Wildlife & Species
Contact(s):
Edward Clark, President; eclark@wildlifecenter.org
Lisa Briskey, Vice President
Lisa Briskey, Director of Environmental Education; briskey@wildlifecenter.org
Jonathan Sleeman, Director of Veterinary Services
Erwin Bohmfalk, Chairman of the Board

WILDLIFE CONSERVATION SOCIETY

BRONX ZOO
NEW YORK AQUARIUM
CENTRAL PARK ZOO
2300 Southern Blvd.
Bronx, NY 10460-1099 United States
Phone: 718-220-5100 Fax: 718-220-2685
E-mail: feedback@wcs.org
Website: www.wcs.org

Founded: 1895
Membership: 100,001–500,000
Scope: Local, State, Regional, National, International
Description: WCS operates an international conservation program with a full-time staff of wildlife biologists conducting field research and training programs around the world. Headquartered in New York City, the Society operates the Bronx Zoo, New York Aquarium, Central Park Zoo, Queens Zoo, Prospect Park Zoo, and St. Catherines Wildlife Survival Center off the coast of Georgia. Their award-winning education programs are used in all 50 U.S. states.
Publication(s): Wildlife Conservation, Annual Report
Keyword(s): Oceans/Coasts/Beaches, Wildlife & Species
Contact(s):
Steven Sanderson, President and CEO
Annette Berkovits, Senior Vice-President of Education; 718-220-5131; aberkovits@wcs.org
Robert Cook, Vice-President for Wildlife Health Science
Louis Garibaldi, Vice-President, Dir. of Aquarium Science
John Hoare, Vice-President—Financial Services
John Hoare, Vice-President & Comptroller
Richard Lattis, Senior Vice-President for Zoos and Aquariums
W. McKeown, Vice-President—General Counsel
John Robinson, Senior Vice-President of International Conservation
George Amato, Director of Science Resource Center
Joan Downs, Editor-In-Chief; 718-220-5897; Fax: 718-584-2625; jdowns@wcs.org
Jennifer Herring, Public Affairs and Development
Steve Johnson, Librarian; 718-220-6874
David Schiff, Chairman

WILDLIFE DAMAGE REVIEW (WDR)

P.O. Box 85218
Tucson, AZ 85754 United States
E-mail: wdr@azstarnet.com
Website: www.Azstarnet.com/~WDR

Founded: 1991
Membership: 1,001–10,000
Scope: National
Description: Wildlife Damage Review's mission is to bring much needed public attention to the USDA's Animal Damage Control (ADC) program, renamed Wildlife Services in 1997. This taxpayer supported program traps, snares, poisons, and aerial guns 1-2 million of America's wildlife yearly for private interests. WDR's ultimate goal is to place wildlife management into the hands of those agencies whose vested interest is protection of native diversity and banish management guided by predator prejudice.

Publication(s): The War on Wildlife (audio CD), Wildlife Damage Review, Investigating J.F.K. International Airport Gull Hazard Reduction, Audit of the USDA Animal Damage Control Program, Waste, Fraud, Abuse in the U.S. Animal Damage Control Program

Keyword(s): Agriculture/Farming, Pollution (general), Wildlife & Species

Contact(s):
Nancy Zierenberg, Executive Director

WILDLIFE DISEASE ASSOCIATION

6006 Shroeder Road
Madison, WI 53711 United States
Phone: 785-843-1221 Fax: 785-843-1274
Website: www.wildlifedisease.org

Founded: 1951
Membership: 1,001–10,000
Scope: International

Description: An international nonprofit organization of scientists interested in advancing knowledge of the effects of infectious, parasitic, toxic, genetic, and physiologic diseases and environmental factors upon the health and survival of free-living and captive wild animals, and upon their relationships to humans.

Publication(s): Journal of Wildlife Diseases, Newsletter

Keyword(s): Public Health, Wildlife & Species

Contact(s):
Robert McLean, President
Irwin Polls, Business Manager
Elizabeth Howerth, Secretary
Daniel Pence, Editor
Leslie Uhazy, Treasurer

WILDLIFE EDUCATION PROGRAM AND DESIGN

44781 Bittner Point Rd
Bovey, MN 55709 United States
Phone: 218-245-3049

Founded: N/A
Membership: 1–100
Scope: International

Description: A non-profit education organization with slide lectures, Wolf Display, education programs and teachers workshops with "Wolves and Humans" curriculum and a Wolf and Wetland Learning Stations box of environmental education materials. Nationwide programs available. No jobs available.

Contact(s):
Karlyn Berg, Director; karlyn@uslink.net

WILDLIFE FEDERATION OF ALASKA

1120 E. Huffman Road, #216
Anchorage, AK 99515-3516 United States
Phone: 907-274-3388 Fax: 907-258-4811
E-mail: wfa@micronet.net
Website: www.micronet/users/~wfa/default.html

Founded: 1985
Scope: State

Description: A representative statewide organization, affiliated with the National Wildlife Federation, dedicated to the protection and enhancement of wildlife ands its habitat through public education and government interaction.

Publication(s): Tracks

Contact(s):
Tracy Shafer, President and Representative
Laurie Fairchild, Editor & Alternate Representative
Rosa Meehan, Education Programs Contact & Treasurer

WILDLIFE FOREVER

10365 West 70th St.
Eden Prairie, MN 55344 United States
Phone: 952-833-1522 Fax: 952-833-0804
E-mail: info@wildlifeforever.org
Website: www.wildlifeforever.org

Founded: 1987
Membership: 10,001–100,000
Scope: National

Description: Wildlife Forever is a non-profit conservation organization dedicated to preserving America's wildlife heritage through conservation education, the preservation of habitat, and the management of fish and wildlife.

Publication(s): Cry of the Wild, Annual Report, Wildlife Forever Fish, Wildlife Forever Critter Pocket Guide Series, Wildlife Forever CD-ROM Curriculum, Sports Fish Pocket Guide Series

Keyword(s): Public Lands/Greenspace, Recreation/Ecotourism, Water Habitats & Quality, Wildlife & Species

Contact(s):
Douglas Grann, President, CEO
Ann McCarthy, Director of Education
Pete Wuebker, Director of Marketing
Mark Petersen, Merchandise Manager
David Fredrick, Grants Coordinator
James Gallagher, Accountant

WILDLIFE FOUNDATION OF FLORIDA, INC.

Tallahassee, FL 32302 United States
Phone: 850-487-3796 Fax: 850-488-6988
Website: www.wildlifefoundationofflorida.com

Founded: 1994
Membership: 1–100
Scope: State

Description: The mission of the Wildlife Foundation of Florida, Inc. is to provide assistance, funding, and promotional support for the Florida Game and Wildlife Conservation Commission, and in so doing, contribute to the health and well-being of Florida's fish and wildlife resources and their habitats.

Keyword(s): Recreation/Ecotourism, Wildlife & Species

Contact(s):
William Blake, Board of Directors
William Bostick, Board of Directors
Robert Brantly, Board of Directors
Linda Bremer, Board of Directors
Allan Egbert, Board of Directors
George Matthews, Board of Directors
C. Rainey, Board of Directors

WILDLIFE HABITAT CANADA

7 Hinton Ave., North
Suite 200
Ottawa, K1Y 4P1 Ontario Canada
Phone: 613-722-2090 Fax: 613-722-3318
E-mail: reception@whc.org
Website: www.whc.org

Founded: 1984
Scope: National, International

Description: Wildlife Habitat Canada is a national non-profit organization dedicated to working with private citizens, governments, non-government organizations, and industry to conserve the great variety of wildlife habitats across Canada. The organization develops and implements its own conservation initiatives, such as the Forest Biodiversity Program, but also provides grants for conservation, research, communication and education projects and has a graduate scholarship program.

Publication(s): Investors in Habitat Report, Stewardship Programs Annual Reports, State of Wildlife Habitat in Canada, Annual Reports.

Keyword(s): Agriculture/Farming, Forests/Forestry, Water Habitats & Quality, Wildlife & Species

Contact(s):
Jean Cinq-Mars, Executive Director
Doug Wolthausen, Director of Programs

WILDLIFE HABITAT COUNCIL

PITTSBURGH REGIONAL OFFICE
GREAT LAKES REGIONAL OFFICE
SOUTHWEST REGIONAL OFFICE
1010 Wayne Ave., Suite 920
Silver Spring, MD 20910 United States
Phone: 301-588-8994 Fax: 301-588-4629
E-mail: Whc@wildlifehc.org
Website: www.wildlifehc.org

Founded: 1988
Membership: 101–1,000
Scope: Local, State, Regional, National, International
Description: The Wildlife Habitat Council is a nonprofit, nonlobbying group of corporations, conservation organizations and individuals dedicated to enhancing and restoring wildlife habitat. Created in 1988, WHC helps large landowners, particularly companies, manage their unused lands in an ecologically sensitive manner for the benefit of wildlife. More than 1.2 million acres in 46 states, Puerto Rico and twelve other countries are managed for wildlife through WHC-assisted projects.
Publication(s): Habitat Management Leaflets, Registry of Certified Sites, Corporate Homes for Wildlife Calendar, Wildlife Habitat, Nest Monitoring Brochure
Keyword(s): Development/Developing Countries, Ecosystems (precious), Forests/Forestry, Land Issues, Wildlife & Species
Contact(s):
William Howard, President
Robert Johnson, Executive Vice President
Mandy Chesnutt, Dir. of Membership & Development
Laurie Coran, Controller
Vanessa Kauffman, Dir. of Marketing & Communications
Rob Pauline, Dir. of Field Programs
Hugh Dillingham, III, Past-Chairman
Stephen Elbert, Board of Directors Secretary/Treasurer
Robert A. Fenech, Chairman of the Board
Lawrence A. Selzer, Board of Directors Secretary/Treasurer Vice Chairman

WILDLIFE HERITAGE FOUNDATION OF WYOMING (WHFW)

P.O. Box 20088
Cheyenne, WY 82003-7002 United States
Phone: 307-777-4693 Fax: 307-777-4699
E-mail: wildlifeheritage@wyoming.com

Founded: 2000
Membership: N/A
Scope: State
Description: The Wildlife Heritage Foundation of Wyoming was established in April 2000 as an independent, 501(c)(3) nonprofit corporation. The purpose of the foundation is to provide financial support, through philanthropy, to the critical conservation efforts of the Wyoming Game and Fish Department and its many partners. Its mission is to create an enduring natural legacy for future generations through stewardship of all Wyoming's wildlife.
Keyword(s): Wildlife & Species
Contact(s):
Marlene Brown, Executive Director; 307-777-4693; Fax: 307-777-4699; wildlifeheritage@wyoming.com

WILDLIFE INFORMATION CENTER, INC.

P.O. Box 198
Slatington, PA 18080 United States
Phone: 610-760-8889 Fax: 610-760-8889
E-mail: wildlife@fast.net
Website: www.wildlifeinfo.org

Founded: 1986
Membership: 101–1,000
Scope: Local, State, Regional, National
Description: A nonprofit, member-supported organization whose mission is to preserve wildlife and habitat through education, research, and conservation for the benefit of the earth and all its inhabitants. Programs include: The Kittatinny Raptor Corridor Project and long-term hawk migration field studies at Bake Oven Knob, PA.; public education; maintaining a wildlife library; and advocating preservation of wildlife habitat and biodiversity.
Publication(s): Wildlife Conservation Reports, American Hawkwatcher, Wildlife Activist
Keyword(s): Ecosystems (precious), Land Issues, Recreation/Ecotourism, Wildlife & Species
Contact(s):
Dan Kunkle, President
Robert Hoopes, Treasurer; 610-760-8889; Fax: 610-760-8889
Dan Kunkle, Editor
Kathie Romano, Secretary

WILDLIFE MANAGEMENT INSTITUTE

1101 14th St., NW
Washington, DC 20005 United States
Phone: 202-371-1808 Fax: 202-408-5059
Website: www.wildlifemgt.org/wmi

Founded: N/A
Membership: 1–100
Scope: National
Description: International nonprofit scientific and educational private membership organization, supported by industries, groups, and individuals, promoting improved professional management of wildlife and other natural resources for the benefit of those resources and North American, including its people.
Publication(s): Outdoor News Bulletin, books and booklets, Transactions North American Wildlife and Natural Resources Conference.
Contact(s):
Rollin Sparrowe, President
Richard McCabe, Vice President
Robert Byrne, Wildlife Program Coordinator
Ronald Helinski, Conservation Policy Specialist
Terry Riley, Director of Conservation
Carol Peddicord, Finance Manager
Kathryn Reis, Partners Network Coordinator
James Woehr, Senior Scientist
Len Carpenter, Southwest Field Representative; 4015 Cheney Dr., Fort Collins, CO 80526; 970-223-1099; Fax: 970-204-9198; lenc@verinet.com
Robert Davison, Northwestern Field Representative; 20325 Sturgeon Road, Bend, OR 97701; 541-330-9045; Fax: 541-382-9372; wmibd@aol.com
Yolanda Finney, Secretary/Receptionist
Rob Manes, Midwest Field Representative; 10201 South Highway 281, Pratt, KS 67124; 620-672-5650; Fax: 620-672-5650; wmimanes@prattusa.com
Donald McKenzie, Southeast Field Representative; 2388 Cocklebur Road, Ward, AR 72176; 501-941-7994; Fax: 501-941-7995; wmidm@ipa.net
Bette McKown, Administrative/Conference Secretary
Jennifer Rahm, Publications Assistant/Transactions Editor
Scot Williamson, Northeast Field Representative; R.R. 1, Box 587, Spur Rd., North Stratford, NH 03590; 603-636-9846; Fax: 603-636-9853; wmisw@together.net

WILDLIFE SOCIETY

5410 Grosvenor Ln.
Bethesda, MD 20814 United States
Phone: 301-897-9770 Fax: 301-530-2471
E-mail: tws@wildlife.org
Website: www.wildlife.org

Founded: 1937
Membership: 1,001–10,000
Scope: National

Description: International scientific and educational organization of professionals and students engaged in wildlife research, management, education, and administration. Dedicated to sound stewardship of wildlife resources and the environments upon which wildlife and humans depend; undertakes an active role in preventing human-induced environmental degradation; increases awareness and appreciation of wildlife values; and seeks the highest standards in all activities of the wildlife profession.

Publication(s): The Journal of Wildlife Management, The Wildlifer, Wildlife Society Bulletin, Wildlife Monographs

Keyword(s): Reduce/Reuse/Recycle, Wildlife & Species

Contact(s):

Diana Hallett, President; MO Dept. of Conservation, 1110 College Ave., Columbia, MO 65201; 573-882-9880; halled@mail.conservation.state.mo.us

Robert Warren, President Elect; Warnell School of Forest Resources, University of Georgia, Athens, GA 30602; 706-542-6474; warren@smokey.forestry.uga.edu

Daniel Decker, Vice President; Cornell Univ. Agricultural Experiment Station, 245 Roberts Hall, Ithaca, NY 14853; 607-255-2559; djd6@cornell.edu

Thomas Franklin, Wildlife Policy Director; The Wildlife Society, 5410 Grosvenor Lane, Bethesda, MD 20814; 301-897-9770; tom@wildlife.org

Harry Hodgdon, Executive Director; The Wildlife Society, 5410 Grosvenor Lane, Bethesda, MD 20814; 301-897-9770; harry@wildlife.org

Sandra Staples-Bortner, Program Director; 18214 NE 125th Way, Brush Prairie, WA 98606; 360-253-4611; sstaplesbortner@msn.com

Robert Brown, Southwest Section Representative; Dept. of Wildlife & Fisheries Sciences, 210 Nagle Hall, Texas A&M University, College Station, TX 77843; 979-845-1261; rdbrown@tamu.edu

Len Carpenter, Past President; Wildllife Management Institute, 4015 Cheney Dr., Fort Collins, CO 80526; 970-223-1099; lenc@verinet.com

Winifred Kessler, Northwest Section Representative; USDA Forest Service, P.O. Box 21628, Juneau, AK 99802; 907-586-7916; wkessler@fs.fed.us

Marti Kie, Western Section Representative; CALFED Bay-Delta Program, 1416 Ninth St., Suite 630, Sacramento, CA 95814; 916-653-6059; mkie@water.ca.gov

Gerald Kobriger, Central Mountains & Plains Section Representative; 225 30th Ave., SW, Dickinson, ND 58601; 701-227-7431; gkobrige@state.nd.us

Richard Lancia, Southeast Section Representative; Forestry Dept. Box 8002, North Carolina State University, Raleigh, NC 27695; 919-515-7578; lancia@unity.ncsu.edu

John Organ, Northeast Section Representative; U.S. Fish & Wildlife Service, 300 Westgate Center Drive, Hadley, MA 01035; 413-253-8501; john_organ@fws.gov

Gary Potts, North Central Section Representative; Illinois Dept. of Natural Resources, 129 North Kennedy Blvd., Vandalia, IL 62471; 618-283-3070; gpotts@dnrmail.state.il.us

WILDLIFE SOCIETY
ALABAMA CHAPTER
Attn: President, 331 Funchess Hall, Auburn University
Auburn, AL 36830 United States

Founded: N/A

Scope: State

Contact(s):

James Armstrong, President; Auburn University 108 M. White Smith Hall, Auburn, AL 36830; 334-844-9233; Fax: 334-844-9234; jarmstro@acesag.auburn.edu

Tommy Counts, Past-President; P.O. Box 278, Double Springs, AL 35553; 205-489-5111; Fax: 205-489-3427; tom.counts@al.usda.gov

Jeff Makemson, Secretary-Treasurer; 11481 Colonial Dr., Duncanville, AL 35456; 205-345-3807; Fax: 205-333-2900

WILDLIFE SOCIETY
ALASKA CHAPTER
Attn: President, P.O. Box 1413
Homer, AK 99603 United States
Phone: 907-235-8191

Founded: N/A

Scope: State

Description: Professional Organization

Contact(s):

Gino Del Frate, President; AK Dept. of Fish and Game 3298 Douglas Place, Homer, AK 99603-8027; 907-235-8191; Fax: 907-235-2448; gino_delfrate@fishgame.state.ak.us

Jackie Kephart, Secretary-Treasurer

Doug Larsen, President-Elect; AK Dept. of Fish and Game 1910 Glacier Ave., Juneau, AK 99801-7802; 907-465-5277; Fax: 907-465-6142; doug_larsen@fishgame.state.ak.us

Roger Post, Past-President; P.O. Box 72962, Fairbanks, AK 99707; 907-455-6583; Fax: 907-455-6583; rpost@mosquitonet.com

Kevin White, Newsletter Editor

WILDLIFE SOCIETY
ALBERTA CHAPTER
Attn: President, Rural Route 4
Sherwood Park, T8A 3K4 Alberta Canada
Phone: 780-778-7116
Website: www.rr.ualberta.ca/wildlifesociety/

Founded: N/A

Scope: State

Contact(s):

Elston Dzus, President; AB Pacific Forest Ind. Inc. P.O. Box 8000, Boyle, Alberta T0A 0M0; 780-525-8393; Fax: 780-525-8097; dzusel@alpac.ca

Michael Dorrance, Past-President; RR4, Sherwood Park, Alberta T8A 3K4; 780-467-4396; Fax: 780-436-9540; mathdorr@telusplanet.net

Ronald Mumme, Secretary-Treasurer; Dept. Bio. Allegheny College, Meadville, PA 16335; 814-332-2382; rmumme@alleg.edu

Troy Sorensen, Newsletter Editor; Suite 203, 111-54 St., Edson, Alberta T7E 1T2; 780-723-8244; Fax: 780-723-8502; troy.sorensen@gov.ab.ca

Arlen Todd, President-Elect; 1263 Berkley Dr. NW, Calgary, Alberta T3K 1T1; 403-297-7349; Fax: 403-297-3362; arlen.todd@gov.ab.ca

WILDLIFE SOCIETY
ARIZONA CHAPTER
Attn: President
P.O. Box 41337
Phoenix, AZ 85080 United States
Phone: 928-523-8374
E-mail: hrs@u.arizona.edu
Website: aztws

Founded: 1964

Membership: 101–1,000

Scope: State

Description: Professional Wildlife Biologists

Keyword(s): Agriculture/Farming, Forests/Forestry, Land Issues, Wildlife & Species

Contact(s):

Tad Theimer, President

WILDLIFE SOCIETY
ARKANSAS CHAPTER
Attn: President, P.O. Box 279 - Arkansas Tech University
Altus, AR 72821-0279 United States

Founded: N/A

Scope: State

Contact(s):
Kendall Moles, President; P.O. Box 599, State University, , AR 72467; 870-972-3082

WILDLIFE SOCIETY
CALIFORNIA CENTRAL COAST CHAPTER
Attn: President, USDA Forest Service 6144 Calle Real
Goleta, CA 93117 United States
Website: www.wildlife.org

Founded: N/A

Scope: State

Contact(s):
Maeton Freel, President; 273 Santa Barbara Shore Dr., Goleta, CA 93117; 805-681-2764
Kevin Cooper, Vice-President; 452 Lawrence Dr., San Luis Obispo, CA 93401; 805-925-9538; Fax: 805-681-2781; lecoop@juno.com
Michael Hanson, Treasurer; 1203 Madonna, San Luis Obispo, CA 93405; 805-541-0272; Fax: 805-756-1419; mthanson@calpoly.edu
Justin Vreeland, Secretary; UCCE 425 Waupelani Dr. #508, State College, PA 16801; 814-237-8567; jkv104@psu.edu

WILDLIFE SOCIETY
CALIFORNIA NORTH COAST CHAPTER
Attn: President, Simpson Timber Co., P.O. Box 68
Korbel, CA 95550 United States
Website: www.wildlife.org

Founded: N/A

Scope: State

Contact(s):
Sandra Arb, President; P.O. Box 532, Scotia, CA 95565-0532; 707-764-4488; Fax: 707-764-4118; vonarb@scopac.com

WILDLIFE SOCIETY
COLORADO CHAPTER
CNHP
Colorado State University
254 General Services Building
Fort Collins, CO 80523 United States
E-mail: cws-fmp@cws.cnchost.com
Website: cws.cncehost.com

Founded: N/A

Scope: State

Contact(s):
Francie Pusateri, President; 317 Prospect Rd., Ft. Collins, CO 82526; 970-472-4336; franciep@concentric.net

WILDLIFE SOCIETY
FLORIDA CHAPTER
Paul Moler
4005 South Main St.
Gainesville, FL 32601 United States
Phone: 352-955-2230 Fax: 352-376-5359
E-mail: paul.moler@fwc.state.fl.us
Website: http://www.nettally.com/fltws/

Founded: 1968

Membership: 101–1,000

Scope: State

Keyword(s): Agriculture/Farming, Ecosystems (precious), Forests/Forestry, Land Issues, Oceans/Coasts/Beaches, Pollution (general), Population, Public Lands/Greenspace, Recreation/Ecotourism, Water Habitats & Quality, Wildlife & Species

Contact(s):
Paul Moler, President; 352-955-2230; Fax: 352-376-5359; molerp@fwc.state.fl.us

WILDLIFE SOCIETY
GEORGIA CHAPTER
Mr. Mark Whitney, President TWS-GA
Georgia Dept. Natural Resources
2109 U.S. Hwy. 278, SE
Social Circle, GA 30025 United States
Phone: 770-761-1697
E-mail: Mark_Whitney@mail.dnr.state.ga.us

Founded: N/A

Membership: 101–1,000

Scope: State

Description: An international, nonprofit, scientific and educational organization comprised of professionals serving the resource management fields, especially wildlife ecology and management. Founded in 1937 and based in Bethesda, Maryland, The Wildlife Society has more than 9,000 members from 40 countries. This chapter serves the needs of the state of Georgia.

Contact(s):
Sara Schweitzer, President; U. of Ga., D.B. Warnell Sch. Forest Res., Athens, GA 30602-2152; 706-542-1150; Fax: 706-542-8356; schweitz@smokey.forest.uga.edu
Douglass Hall, Past-President; 1161 Crooked Creek Rd., Watkinsville, GA 30677; 706-546-2020; Fax: 706-546-2004; douglas.i.hall@usda.gov
Douglas Hoffman, Secretary-Treasurer; 120 Diamond Dr., Athens, GA 30605; 706-546-2020; Fax: 706-546-2004; douglas.m.hoffman@usda.gov
Chuck Waters, Newsletter Editor; 2150 Dawsonville Highway, Gainesville, GA 30501; 770-535-5700; Fax: 770-535-5953; chuck_waters@mail.dnr.state.ga.us
Mark Whitney, President-Elect; 1057 Plantation Way SE, Conyers, GA 30094; 770-761-1697; Fax: 706-557-3042; mark_whitney@mail.dnr.state.ga.us

WILDLIFE SOCIETY
HAWAII CHAPTER
40 Kunihi Ln., #221
Kahului, HI 96732 United States

Founded: N/A

Scope: State

Contact(s):
Carrie Haurez, President; 40 Kunihi Ln. #221, Kahului, HI 96732; 808-877-1455
Fern Duvall, President-Elect; 211 Ulana St., Makawao, HI 96768-8034; 808-873-3502; Fax: 808-873-3505; mawildl@aloha.net
Cathleen Hodges, Newsletter Editor; 20 Kumano Dr., Pukalani, HI 96768; cathleen_hodges@nps.gov
Cathleen Hodges, Past-President; 20 Kumano Dr., Pukalani, HI 96768; cathleen_hodges@nps.gov
Dan McNulty-Huffman, Treasurer; 85 Haele Place, Makawao, HI 96768-8053; 808-572-4485; dmh@t-link.net
Joy Tamayose, Secretary; c/o Haleakala National Park P.O. Box 369, Makawao, HI 96822; 808-572-4492; Fax: 808-572-4498; ulukitty@aol.com

WILDLIFE SOCIETY
IDAHO CHAPTER
Attn: President
College of Forestry, Wildlife & Range Sciences
University of Idaho
Moscow, ID 83843-1136 United States
E-mail: tws@uidaho.edu
Website: uidaho.edu/student-orgs/wlfsoc

Founded: N/A

Scope: State

Contact(s):
Robyn Januszewski, President; Fax: 208-324-1160; mcommons@idfg.state.id.us

WILDLIFE SOCIETY
ILLINOIS CHAPTER
Attn: President, Max McGraw Wildlife Foundation, P.O. Box 9
Dundee, IL 60118 United States
Phone: Fax: 618-453-6944
Website: www.eiu.edu/~biology/ICTWS/

Founded: N/A

Scope: State

Contact(s):

Tim Van Deelen, President; 607 E. Peabody, Champaign, IL 61820; 217-333-6856; Fax: 618-453-2806; feldhamer@zoology.siu.edu

WILDLIFE SOCIETY
INDIANA CHAPTER
Department of Forestry and Wildlife Resources 1159 Forestry Building
West Lafayette, IN 47907-1159 United States
Phone: 765-494-3601 Fax: 765-496-2422
E-mail: gener@fnr.purdue.edu
Website: www.fnr.purdue.edu

Founded: N/A
Membership: 101–1,000
Scope: State
Description: Indiana Chapter of the Wildlife Society
Keyword(s): Agriculture/Farming, Ecosystems (precious), Executive/Legislative/Judicial Reform, Forests/Forestry, Land Issues, Pollution (general), Public Lands/Greenspace, Recreation/Ecotourism, Sprawl/Urban Planning, Water Habitats & Quality, Wildlife & Species

Contact(s):

Olin Rhodes, President; Department of Forestry and Natural Resources, 1159 Forestry, West Lafayette, IN 47907; 765-494-3601; Fax: 765-496-2422; gener@fnr.purdue.edu

Linda Byer, Newsletter Editor; 6615 S. 875 E., Monterey, IN 46960; 219-896-3522; Fax: 219-896-3038; byer@pwtc.com

Brian MacGowan, President-Elect; Courthouse Annex Bldg., 115 South Line Street, Columbia City, IN 46725; 219-248-4231; Fax: 219-244-6751; bmacgowan@fnr.purdue.edu

Patrick Mayer, Secretary-Treasurer; Huntington Reservoir, 517 N Warren Rd., Huntington, IN 46750; 219-468-2165; pmayer@dnr.state.in.us

Phil Seng, Past President; 1010 Yeardley Ln., Mishawaka, IN 46544-6766; 219-258-0100; Fax: 219-258-0189; phil@djcase.com

Jeff Thompson, Member at Large; Sugar Ridge FWA, 2310 E SR 364, Winslow, IN 47598; 812-789-2724; jthompson@dnr.state.in.us

WILDLIFE SOCIETY
IOWA CHAPTER
631 West Washington Boulevard
Washington, IA 52353 United States
Phone: 319-653-4912
E-mail: dpfeiffer@onlineia.com
Website: www.wildlife.org

Founded: N/A
Membership: 1–100
Scope: State
Description: Professional biologists and educators in the management of wildlife and their habitats.

Contact(s):

Donald Pfeiffer, President; 631 West Washington Blvd., Washington, IA 52353; 319-653-4912

Donald Sievers, Past-President; 109 W. Wilcoxway, Jefferson, IA 50129; 515-747-8383; Fax: 515-747-3951; dsiever@pionet.net

Chuck Steffen, President-Elect; USDA Service Center, 700 Farm Credit Drive, Ottumwa, IA 52501; 641-682-3552

Todd Bogenschutz, Secretary-Treasurer; Wildlife Res. Sta. 1436 255 St., Boone, IA 50036; 515-432-2823; Fax: 515-432-2835

Peter Fritzell, Newsletter Editor; Boone Research Station, 1436 255th St., Boone, IA 50036; 515-432-2823

WILDLIFE SOCIETY
KANSAS CHAPTER

Founded: N/A

Scope: State

Contact(s):

Elmer Finck, President; Emporia State U. Div. of Bio. Sci. Box 4050, Emporia, KS 66801; 620-341-5623; Fax: 620-341-5607; finckelm@emporia.edu

Charles Lee, Secretary-Treasurer; Kansas State University 127 Call Hall, Manhattan, KS 66505-1600; 758-532-5734; Fax: 785-532-5681; clee@oz.oznet.ksu.edu

M. McCord, President-Elect; 4413 Ponderosa Ln., Temple, TX 76502; 254-742-9812; Fax: 254-742-9848; brad.mccord@tx.usda.gov

M. McCord, Newsletter Editor; 4413 Ponderosa Ln., Temple, TX 76502; 254-742-9812; Fax: 254-742-9848; brad.mccord@tx.usda.gov

Michael McFadden, Past-President; 1110 North 900 Road, Lawrence, KS 66047; 785-295-2530; Fax: 785-295-7630; miketmks@aol.com

WILDLIFE SOCIETY
KENTUCKY CHAPTER
Attn: President, KY Dept. Fish & Wildlife, #1 Game Farm Rd.
Frankfort, KY 40601 United States

Founded: N/A

Scope: State

Contact(s):

Roy Grimes, President; #1 Game Farm Road, Frankfort, KY 40601; 502-564-4404; Fax: 502-564-6508; roy.grimes@mail.state.ky.us

Mark Cramer, Newsletter Editor; KY Dept. F & W Resources #1 Game Farm Road, Frankfort, KY 40601; 502-564-4404; Fax: 502-564-6508; roy.grimes@mail.state.ky.us

Charles Elliot, President-Elect; Dept. of Biology EKU 521 Lancaster Ave., Richmond, KY 40475-3102; 606-622-1538; Fax: 606-622-1020; bioelliott@acs.eku.edu

Dan Figert, Secretary-Treasurer; KY Dept. Fish & Wildlife #1 Game Farm Rd., Frankfort, KY 40601; 800-858-1549; Fax: 502-564-4859; dan.figert@mail.state.ky.us

Robert Morton, Past-President; 8407 U.S. 41 A, Henderson, KY 42420-9637; 502-827-2673; mmorton@apex.net

WILDLIFE SOCIETY
LOUISIANA CHAPTER
Attn: President, 5492 Grand Chenier Hwy
Grand Chenier, LA 70643 United States

Founded: N/A

Scope: State

Contact(s):

Martin Floyd, President; 2044 Bayou Road, Cheneyville, LA 71325; 318-473-7690; Fax: 318-473-7747; marty_floyd@la.usda.gov

Edmond Mouton, Past-President; LDWF 2415 Darnall Rd, New Iberia, LA 70560; 318-373-0032; Fax: 318-373-0181; mouton_ec@wlf.state.la.us

Mike Olinde, President-Elect; 2130 Terrace Ave., Baton Rouge, LA 70806; 225-765-2353; olinde_mw@wlf.state.la.us

John Pitre, Treasurer; 263 White Oak Blvd., Boyce, LA 71409; 318-473-7809; Fax: 318-473-7616; john.pitre@la.usda.gov

Virginia Rettig, Secretary; USFWS 1010 Gause Blvd. Bldg. 936, Slidell, LA 70458; 540-646-7555; Fax: 504-646-7588; virginia_rettig@fws.gov

Frank Rohwer, Newsletter Editor; Louisiana State U. Forestry, Wildlfe, & Fisheries, Baton Rouge, LA 70803; 504-388-4131; Fax: 504-388-4227; frohwer@lsu.edu

WILDLIFE SOCIETY
MAINE CHAPTER
Attn: Secretary, ME Dept. Inland Fish & Wildlife
P.O. Box 416
Ashland, ME 04732 United States

Founded: N/A

Scope: State

Contact(s):

James Ecker, President; 58 Canterbury Rd., Brewer, ME 04412; 207-827-6191; Fax: 207-827-8441; jestump@aol.com

Mitschka Hartley, Past-President; U of ME Natl. Audubon Soc. 230 E. Lake Rd., DeRuyter, NY 13052; 315-662-7900; mhartley@audubon.org

James Nelson, Executive Committee; 34 Cates Rd., Thorndike, ME 04986; 207-948-3131; Fax: 207-948-6277; jnelson@unity.unity.edu

Joseph Wiley, Secretary-Treasurer; Bureau of Parks and Lands 22 State House Station, Augusta, ME 04333; 207-287-4921; Fax: 207-287-8111; joe.wiley@state.me.us

WILDLIFE SOCIETY
MANITOBA CHAPTER
Attn: President, Dillion Consulting Ltd., 6 Donald St. S.
Winnipeg, R3L 0K6 Manitoba Canada
Website: twsmb.tripod.com

Founded: N/A

Scope: State

Contact(s):

Cory Lindgren, President; One Hammock Marsh Box 1160, Stonewall, Manitoba R0C 2Z0; 204-437-3000; c_lindgren@ducks.ca

Rhiannon Christie, Past-President; 3-395 River Ave., Winnipeg, Manitoba R3L 0C5; 204-632-2938; Fax: 204-693-9673; rchristie@mb.sympatico.ca

Neil Mochnacz, Student Representative; 468 Chelsea Avenue, Winnipeg, Manitoba R2K 1A1; 204-984-2425; Fax: 204-983-2403; mochnaczn@dfg-mpo.gc.ca

Marc Schuster, Newsletter Editor; 242 Hartford Ave., Winnipeg, Manitoba R2V 0W1; 204-269-2184; Fax: 204-983-5248; marc.schuster@ec.gc.ca

Tanys Uhmann, Secretary and Treasurer; 1017 Kilkenny Dr., Winnipeg, Manitoba R3T 4K5; 204-261-2184; Fax: 204-261-0038; umuhmann@cc.umanitoba.ca

WILDLIFE SOCIETY
MARYLAND-DELAWARE CHAPTER
Attn: President, 1053 Hampton Dr.
Crownsville, MD 21032-1315 United States

Founded: N/A

Scope: State

Contact(s):

Philip Norman, President; 723 Roland Ave., Bel Air, MD 21014; 410-313-1675; Fax: 410-313-4660; pnorman@co.ho.md.us

Brenda Belensky, Newsletter Editor; 25 Montrose Manor Ct. #H, Baltimore, MD 21228; 410-313-4724; Fax: 410-313-4660; bbelensky@co.ho.md.us

Carol Bernstein, Past-President; 1053 Hampton Drive, Crownsville, MD 21032-1315; 410-962-3208; Fax: 410-962-4698; carol.l.bernstein@usace.army.mil

Amy Deller-Jacobs, Secretary; P.O. Box 1455, Cambridge, MD 21613-5455; 410-330-3911

Edward Morgereth, President-Elect; Biohabitat, Inc. #602 15 W. Aylesbury Rd., Timonium, MD 21093; 410-337-3659; Fax: 410-583-5678; edward@biohabitat.com

Donald Rohrback, Treasurer; Reg. Wldlf. Manager Indian Springs WMA 14038 Blairs Valley Rd., Clear Spring, MD 21722; 301-842-3355

WILDLIFE SOCIETY
MICHIGAN CHAPTER
Attn: President, 5525 Hayes Tower Rd.
Gaylord, MI 49735 United States

Founded: N/A

Scope: State

Contact(s):

Craig Albright, President; Hwy. 2, 41, & M-35, Gladestone, MI 49837; 906-786-2351; Fax: 906-786-1300; albrighc@state.mi.us

Craig Albright, Newsletter Editor; Hwy. 2, 41, & M-35, Gladestone, MI 49837; 906-786-2351; Fax: 906-786-1300; albrighc@state.mi.us

Larry Caldwell, Past-President; Central MI Univ. Biology Dept., Mt. Pleasant, MI 48859; 517-774-3387; Fax: 517-774-3462; larry.caldwell@cmich.edu

Henry Campa, President-Elect; MI State University Dept. of Fish & Wldlfe., East Lansing, MI 48824; 517-353-2042; Fax: 517-432-1699; campa@pilot.msu.edu

Kelly Millenbah, Secretary-Treasurer; MI State U. 13 Natural Resources Bldg., East Lansing, MI 48824-1222; 517-353-4802; Fax: 517-432-1699; millenba@pilot.msu.edu

WILDLIFE SOCIETY
MINNESOTA CHAPTER
Attn: President
3651 SE 128th Street
Blooming Prairie, MN 55917 United States
Phone: 507-455-5841
Website: www.crk.umn.edu/tws/mn

Founded: 1944

Membership: 101–1,000

Scope: State

Description: Membership is open to all individuals interested in the perpetuation of Minnesota's wildlife resources. Our objectives are to manage wildlife resources on a sound biological basis that benefit ecosystems and people and to encourage the highest possible professional standards in those working with wildlife resources. We share knowledge and ideas through meetings and publications and recognize and commend outstanding work by professional and lay individuals and groups.

Keyword(s): Agriculture/Farming, Energy, Forests/Forestry, Land Issues, Transportation, Water Habitats & Quality, Wildlife & Species

Contact(s):

Gary Huschle, Past President; RR 1 Box 114, Thief River Falls, MN 56701-9739; 218-449-4115; Fax: 218-449-3241; honkerharmony@wiktel.com

Jeanine Vorland, President; 3651 SE 128th Street, Blooming Prairie, MN 55917; 507-455-5841; Fax: 507-446-2326; jvorland@citlink.net

Shelly Gorham, Newsletter Editor; 217 East River Street, Lake Bronson, MN 56734; 218-436-2427; rmgorham@wiktel.com

Brian Haroldson, Membership; RR 1 Box 181, Madelia, MN 56062; 507-642-8478, ext. 29; Fax: 507-642-3178; brian.haroldson@dnr.state.mn.us

Doug Wells, Secretary-Treasurer; 20274 250th Street, Fergus Falls, MN 56537; 218-736-0636; bdwells@prtel.com

WILDLIFE SOCIETY
MISSISSIPPI CHAPTER
Attn: President, P.O. Box 451
Jackson, MS 39205 United States
Website: www.cfr.msstate.edu/mstws

Founded: N/A

Scope: State

Contact(s):

Kristina Godwin, President; 610 Hospital Rd., Starkville, MS 39759; 662-325-3014; Fax: 662-325-3690; kris.godwin@usda.gov

K. Godwin, President-Elect; 610 Hospital Rd., Starkville, MS 39759; 662-325-5119; Fax: 662-325-8726; dgodwin@cfr.msstate.edu

Julie Marcy, Secretary-Treasurer; P.O. Box 820161, Vicksburg, MS 39182; 601-631-5302; Fax: 601-631-7133; julie.b.marcy@usace.army.mil

Darren Miller, Newsletter Editor; Weyerhaeuser Co. Southern Forestry Res., Box 2288, Columbus, MS 39704-2288; 662-245-5249; Fax: 662-245-5228; darren.miller@weyerhaeuser.com

Marcus Spencer, Past-President; 104 Jess Dean Dr., Brandon, MS 39047-9539; 601-364-2229; Fax: 601-364-2209; randys@mdwfp.state.ms.us

WILDLIFE SOCIETY
MISSOURI CHAPTER
Attn: President, 21999 Hwy. B
Maitland, MO 64466 United States

Founded: N/A

Scope: State

Contact(s):

Dave Murphy, President; 1709 Cliff Drive, Columbia, MO 65201; 573-443-2687; mgallopavo@aol.com

Dennis Browning, Secretary; 1811 Eastview Dr., Trenton, MO 64683; 816-675-2205; Fax: 816-675-2221; brownd@mail.conservation.state.mo.us

Donald Martin, Newsletter Editor; 2207 Oak Cliff Dr., Columbia, MO 65203; 573-751-4115; martind@mail.conservation.state.mo.us

Donald Martin, President-Elect; 5875 Van Horn Tvrn. Rd. W., Columbia, MO 65203; 573-751-4115; martind@mail.conservation.state.mo.us

Phil Rockers, Treasurer; P.O. Box 248, Sullivan, MO 63080; 573-468-3335; Fax: 573-468-5434; rockep@mail.conservation.state.mo.us

Dan Zekor, Past-President; P.O. Box 180, Jefferson City, MO 65102; 573-753-4115

WILDLIFE SOCIETY
MONTANA CHAPTER
Attn: President, 107 Mark Jensen Ln.
Polson, MT 59860 United States
Website: www.montanatws.org/

Founded: N/A

Scope: State

Contact(s):

Bev Dickerson, President-Elect; 3710 Fallon, Suite C, Bozeman, MT 59718; 406-522-2541; Fax: 406-522-2528; bdixon@fs.fed.us

Marion Cherry, Secretary-Treasurer; 518 Fieldstone Dr., Bozeman, MT 59715; 406-587-6257; mcherry@fs.fed.us

Frank Pickett, President; 45 Basin Creek Road, Butte, MT 59701; 406-533-3445; Fax: 406-533-6000; fjpickett@pplmt.com

Daniel Young, Newsletter Editor; Box 916, Eureka, MT 59917; 406-296-2536; Fax: 406-296-2588; lyoung@fs.fed.us

WILDLIFE SOCIETY
NATIONAL CAPITAL CHAPTER
United States

Founded: N/A

Scope: State

Contact(s):

Douglas Hobbs, President; 5807 Blaine Dr., Alexandria, VA 22303-1914; 703-960-4271; doug_hobbs@fws.gov

Douglas Hobbs, Newsletter Editor; 5807 Blaine Dr., Alexandria, VA 22303-1914; 703-960-4271; doug_hobbs@fws.gov

Stephanie Hussey, Newsletter Editor; 208 N. Trenton St. #4, Arlington, VA 22203; 703-526-0272; saoffice1@pipeline.com

Stephanie Hussey, Secretary-Treasurer; 208 N. Trenton St. #4, Arlington, VA 22203; 703-526-0272; saoffice1@pipeline.com

Kristen La Vine, Past-President; 1912 N. Rhodes Street, Arlington, VA 22201; 703-519-0013; Fax: 703-519-9565; kp_lavine@yahoo.com

WILDLIFE SOCIETY
NEBRASKA CHAPTER
Grand Island, NE 68801 United States
Website: www.wildlifeconsult.com/netws

Founded: N/A

Scope: State

Contact(s):

Garry Steinauer, President; Nebraska Game and Parks Commission, 1703 L Street, Aurora, NE 68818; 402-694-2498; Fax: 402-684-2816; gstein@hgpc.state.ne.us

Laurel Badura, Secretary; 306 E. 29th, Kearney, NE 68847; 308-865-5332; Fax: 308-865-5309; lbadura@ngpc.state.ne.us

Mark Czaplewski, Past-President; NE Game & Parks Commission1617 First Avenue, Kearney, NE 68847; 308-385-6282; Fax: 308-385-6285; czaplews@linux3.nrc.state.ne.us

Mark Humpert, Newsletter Editor; 45090 Elm Island Rd., Gibbon, NE 68840; 308-865-5308; Fax: 308-865-5309; mhumpert@ngpun.ngpc.state.ne.us

Mark Humpert, President-Elect; 45090 Elm Island Rd., Gibbon, NE 68840; 308-865-5308; Fax: 308-865-5309; mhumpert@ngpun.ngpc.state.ne.us

Jeanine Lackey, Treasurer; 18909 N. 84th St., Ceresco, NE 68017-4209; jlackey2@unl.edu

WILDLIFE SOCIETY
NEVADA CHAPTER
Attn: President, 4321 Jody Ave.
Las Vegas, NV 89120 United States

Founded: N/A

Scope: State

Contact(s):

James Jeffress, President; 2085 Skyland Blvd., Winnemucca, NV 89445; 702-623-4959

Alan Jenne, Secretary and Treasurer; 4080 Bluewing Ln., Carson City, NV 89704; 775-888-7689

David Pulliam, President-Elect; 8003 Moss Creek Dr., Reno, NV 89506; 775-688-1561; dpulliam@govmail.state.nv.us

WILDLIFE SOCIETY
NEW ENGLAND CHAPTER
United States

Founded: N/A

Scope: National

Contact(s):

John McDonald, President; MA Div. Fish and Wildlife Field HQ, Westborough, MA 01581; 508-792-7270; Fax: 508-792-7275; john.mcdonald@state.us

Jenny Dickson, President-Elect; 391 Jackson St., Thomaston, CT 06787-2016; 860-675-8130; Fax: 860-675-8141; jenny.dickson@po.state.ct.us

Robert Gilmore, Newsletter Editor; P.O. Box 121, West Simsbury, CT 06092; 860-424-3866; Fax: 860-424-4075

Susan Langlois, Secretary-Treasurer; MA Div. Fish and Wildlife Field Headquarters, Westboro, MA 01581; 508-792-7270; Fax: 508-792-7275; sue.langlois@state.ma.us

Paul Rego, Past-President; Sessions Woods WMA P.O. Box 1550, Burlington, CT 06013; 860-675-8130; Fax: 860-675-8141; paul.rego@po.state.ct.us

WILDLIFE SOCIETY

NEW JERSEY CHAPTER
Attn: Secretary
139 George Street
Lambertville, NJ 08530-1611 United States
Phone: 609-633-6755

Founded: N/A
Membership: 1–100
Scope: State
Description: Wildlife professionals from the government and private sector
Contact(s):

James Sciasca, Treasurer; 4667 McDermott Rd., Bangor, PA 18013; 908-735-8975
Laurance Torok, Secretary; 139 George St., Lambertville, NJ 08530-1611; 609-633-6755

WILDLIFE SOCIETY

NEW MEXICO CHAPTER
United States

Founded: N/A
Scope: State
Contact(s):

Eric Rominger, President-; 141 Sereno Dr., Santa Fe, NM 87501; 505-992-8651; e_rominger@gmfsh.state.nm.us
James Biggs, Past President; M887ESH-20, Albuquerque, NM 87545; 505-665-5714; Fax: 505-667-0731; biggsj@lanl.gov
Gail Tunberg, Past-President; 331 Camino de la Tierra, Corrales, NM 87048-8554; 505-842-3151; Fax: 505-842-3457; gtunberg@fs.fed.us

WILDLIFE SOCIETY

NEW YORK CHAPTER
NY United States
Website: cobleskill.edu/nychaptws

Founded: N/A
Scope: State
Contact(s):

George Mattfeld, President Elect
Michael Matthews, President; NYS DEC 108 Game Farm Road, Delmar, NY 12054; 518-457-3720; mjmatthe@gw.dec.state.ny.us
Chuck Dente, Vice-President; 14 Marvin Ave., Demar, NY 12054; 518-478-3009; Fax: 518-478-3004; cxdente@gw.dec.state.ny.us
Richard Chipman, Secretary; USDA/APHIS/WS, 1930 Route 9, Castleton, NY 12033-9653; 518-477-4837; Fax: 518-477-4899; richard.b.chipman@usda.gov
James Daley, Treasurer; 9 Dunbar Rd., Westerlo, NY 12193-2505; 518-783-5733; jgdaley@gw.dec.state.ny.us
Nancy Heaslip, Newsletter Editor; 3750 Skyline Dr., Schenectady, NY 12306; 518-357-2156; Fax: 518-357-2460; nxheasil@gw.dec.state.ny.us
Mark Lowery, Past-President; 325 Randall Road, Ridge, NY 11961; 516-444-0350; Fax: 516-444-0349; mdlowery@gw.dec.state.ny.us

WILDLIFE SOCIETY

NORTH CAROLINA CHAPTER
The Wildlife Society
P.O. Box 37742
Raleigh, NC 27627 United States
Phone: 910-695-3323
Website: main.nc.us/nctws/

Founded: N/A
Membership: 101–1,000
Scope: State
Description: State chapter of TWS composed of wildlife professionals from many different agencies and the private sector. Agencies represented include: USDA Wildlife Svcs., NCWildlife Resources Commission, USFWS, NRCS, etc.
Keyword(s): Agriculture/Farming, Ecosystems (precious), Forests/Forestry, Land Issues, Public Lands/Greenspace, Reduce/Reuse/Recycle, Sprawl/Urban Planning, Wildlife & Species
Contact(s):

Peter Campbell, President; 144 Pine Ridge Dr, Whispering Pines, NC; 910-695-3323; pete_campbell@fws.gov
Mike Carraway, President-Elect; 828-646-9913; carrawmb@brinet.com
Patrick Farrell, Treasurer; 1793 Old Cullowee Rd, Sylva, NC; 828-293-5231; pjf@dnet.net
Mark Johns, Secretary; P.O. Box 564, Cary, NC; 919-852-5124; johnsme@mindspring.com
Gary Marshall, Past President; Latta Plantation Nature Center, 6211 Sample Road, Huntersville, NC 28078; 704-875-1391; Fax: 704-875-1394; marshgd@co.mecklenburg.nc.us
Chris Moorman, Board Member; Box 8003, NC State University, Raleigh, NC; 919-515-5578; chris_moorman@ncsu.edu
Donald Seriff, Newsletter Editor; 9401 Plaza Rd. Ext, Charlotte, NC 28215; 704-432-1391; Fax: 704-432-1420; serifdw@co.mecklenburg.nc.us

WILDLIFE SOCIETY

NORTH DAKOTA CHAPTER
Attn: President, USFWS, 1500 E. Capital Ave.
Bismarck, ND 58501 United States
Website: ndctws.homestead.com/ndctws_home.html

Founded: N/A
Scope: State
Contact(s):

Greg Hiemenz, Secretary-Treasurer; 830 N. 34th Street, Bismarck, ND 58501; 701-250-4242; Fax: 701-250-4590; ghiemenz@gp.usbr.gov
Tim Phalen, President-Elect; 701-439-2007; phalen@rrt.net
John Schulz, President-Past; 7928 45th St. NE, Devil's Lake, ND 58301-8501; 701-662-3617; Fax: 701-662-3618; jwschulz@state.nd.us
Alicia Waters, Newsletter Editor; 6721 Valley Vista Lane, Bismarck, ND 58501; 701-250-4242; Fax: 701-250-4590

WILDLIFE SOCIETY

OHIO CHAPTER
OH United States

Founded: N/A
Scope: State
Contact(s):

Scott Butterworth, President; 952 Lima Ave., Findley, OH 45840; 419-424-5000
Tim Plageman, Treasurer; 7403 Twp. Rd. 32, Jenera, OH 45841; 419-424-5000; Fax: 419-422-4875; tim.plagman@dnr.state.oh.us
Edward Smith, Newsletter Editor; OSU Ext. E. District Ofc. 16714 SR 215, Caldwell, OH 43724; 740-732-2381; Fax: 740-732-5992; smith.25@osu.edu
Kendra Wecker, Secretary; 107 Glenmont Ave., Columbus, OH 43214; 614-265-7043; Fax: 614-262-1143; kendra.wecker@dnr.state.oh.us

WILDLIFE SOCIETY

OKLAHOMA CHAPTER
OK United States

Founded: N/A
Scope: State

Contact(s):
Michael Porter, President; Noble Foundation P.O. Box 2180, Ardmore, OK 73402-2180; 580-221-7272; Fax: 580-221-7320; mdporter@noble.org
Jerry Brabander, Treasurer; U.S. Fish and Wildlife Services 10960 S. 241st West Ave., Sapulpa, OK 74066; 918-581-7458; Fax: 918-581-7467; jerry_brabander@fws.gov
Eric Jorgensen, Newsletter Editor; Environmental Protection Agency, Robt. S. Kerr Env. Res. Center, 919 Kerr Research Drive, Ada, OK 74820; 580-436-8545; Fax: 580-436-8703; jorgensen.eric@epamail.epa.gov
James Shaw, Past-President; OK State U. Dept. of Zoology, Stillwater, OK 74078; 405-744-9668; Fax: 405-744-7824; shawjh@okstate.edu
John Skeen, President-Elect; OK Dept. Wldlf. Cons. HCR 75 Box 308-12, Broken Bow, OK 74728-9020; 580-241-7875; okwild@pine-net.com
Jullianne Whitaker-Hoagland, Secretary; OK Dept. of Wildlife. Cons.1801 N. Lincoln Blvd. P.O. Box 53465, Oklahoma City, OK 73152; 405-522-0189; Fax: 405-521-6235; jhoagland@odwc.state.ok.us

WILDLIFE SOCIETY
OREGON CHAPTER
P.O. Box 2214
Corvallis, OR 97339-2214 United States
Website: www.orst.edu/dept/fish_wild/tws

Founded: N/A

Scope: State

Publication(s): On Target

Contact(s):
Jim Thraikill, President; OR Coop. Wldlf. Res. Unit McKenzie Ecological 45304 Goodpasture Rd., Vida, OR 97488; 541-687-9076; Fax: 541-687-1065; jimt@pond.net
Edward Arnett, Treasurer; Weyerhaeuser Co. OR State U. 321 Richardson Hall, Corvallis, OR 97331; 541-737-8469; Fax: 541-737-1393; ed.arnett@orst.edu
Katherine Beal, Secretary; P.O. Box 429, Lowell, OR 97452; 541-937-2131; Fax: 541-937-3401; kat.beal@usace.army.mil
Cheryl Friesen, President-Elect; 45304 Goodpasture Road, Vida, OR 97488; 541-822-7232; Fax: 541-822-7254; cafriesen@msh.com
Laura Todd, Past-President; P.O. Box 50, Rhododendron, OR 97049; 503-231-6179; Fax: 503-231-6195; Laura_Todd@fws.gov

WILDLIFE SOCIETY
PENNSYLVANIA CHAPTER
Attn: President, 415 E. McCormick Ave.
State College, PA 16801 United States

Founded: N/A

Scope: State

Contact(s):
Shayne Hoachlander, President; RD 2 Box 140 Factory Rd., Corry, PA 16407; 814-664-8867; shoachlander@tbscc.com
J. Benner, Secretary; RD 1 Box 87, Liverpool, PA 17045; 717-787-3706; Fax: 717-783-5109; mbenner@dcnr.state.pa.us
Michelle Cohen, President-Elect; 3490 North Third Street, Harrisburg, PA 17110; 717-232-0593; Fax: 717-232-0593; mcohen@skellyloy.com
Michelle Cohen, Past-President; 3490 North Third Street, Harrisburg, PA 17110; 717-232-0593; Fax: 717-232-0593; mcohen@skellyloy.com
Thomas Hardisky, Treasurer; 2621 E. Winter Rd., Loganton, PA 17747; 570-725-2287; Fax: 570-725-2287; disky@cub.kcnet.org
Carolyn Mahan, Newsletter Editor; Penn State Altoona Dept. Bio. 205 Force Bldg., Altoona, PA 16601; 814-949-5530; Fax: 814-865-3725; cgm2@psu.edu

WILDLIFE SOCIETY
SACRAMENTO-SHASTA CHAPTER
Attn: President, W.M. Beaty & Associates
P.O. Box 990898
Redding, CA 96099-0898 United States
Website: www.tws-west.org/sac-shastal/index.html

Founded: N/A

Scope: State

Contact(s):
Robert Carey, President; W.M. Beaty & Associates P.O. Box 990898, Redding, CA 96099-0898; 530-243-2783; Fax: 530-243-2900; bobc@sunset.net
Craig Bailey, President-Elect; 1313 Shadowglen Rd., Sacramento, CA 95864-2723; 916-331-8810; Fax: 916-331-8755; craig_bailey73@hotmail.com
Thomas Boullion, Secretary-Treasurer; 18005 Willow Dr., Cottonwood, CA 96022; 530-244-8600; Fax: 530-244-7656; boullion@shasta.com
Michael Bradbury, Past-President; 3251 S Street, Sacramento, CA 95816; 916-227-7527; Fax: 916-227-7554; mbradbur@water.ca.gov
Debra Hawk, Newsletter Editor; P.O. Box 610, Mammoth Lakes, CA 93546-0610; 760-872-1134; dhawk@dfg.ca.gov

WILDLIFE SOCIETY
SAN FRANCISCO BAY AREA CHAPTER
CA United States
Website: www.tws-west.org/bayarea/index.html

Founded: N/A

Scope: State

Contact(s):
David Cook, President; Sonoma County Water Agency, Oakland, CA 94605-0381; 707-547-1944; dcook@scwa.ca.gov
John Baas, President-Elect; 210 MacCalvey Dr., Martinez, CA 94553; 510-335-9778; Fax: 510-335-9778; karthikl@value.net
Steven Bobzien, Past-President; 2950 Peralta Oaks Ct. P.O. Box 5381, Oakland, CA 94605-0381; 510-635-0138; Fax: 510-635-3478; sbobzien@ebparks.org
Jessica Martini-Lamb, Secretary-Treasurer; 2643 Diablo Street, Napa, CA 94558; 707-547-1903; Fax: 707-524-3782; jesmartini@hotmail.com

WILDLIFE SOCIETY
SAN JOAQUIN VALLEY CHAPTER
Attn: President, P.O. Box 9622
Bakersfield, CA 93389 United States

Founded: N/A

Scope: State

Contact(s):
Scott Frazer, President; 1017 Jefferson Avenue, Los Banos, CA 93635; 209-826-3508; Fax: 209-826-1445; scott_frazer@fws.gov
Brian Cypher, Past-President; Endangered Species Rec. Prog. P.O. Box 9622, Bakersfield, CA 93389-9622; 661-398-2201; Fax: 661-398-0549; bcypher@tcsn.net
Brian Cypher, Newsletter Editor; Endangered Species Rec. Prog. P.O. Box 9622, Bakersfield, CA 93389-9622; 661-398-2201; Fax: 661-398-0549; bcypher@tcsn.net
Christine Horn, Treasurer; 3517 Sedona Way, Bakersfield, CA 93309; 661-834-6781; cvanjob@aol.com
Michelle Selmon, Secretary; 628 W. Euclid Ave., Clovis, CA 93612; mselmon@esrp.org
Marcia Wolfe, President-Elect; P.O. Box 10254, Bakersfield, CA 93389; 661-837-1169; Fax: 661-837-8467; yakimapark@aol.com

WILDLIFE SOCIETY
SOUTH CAROLINA CHAPTER
SC United States
Website: www.tws-west.org/sjvc/

Founded: N/A

Scope: State

Contact(s):

Kevin O'Conner, President; koconner@dfg.ca.gov
William Baughman, President-Elect; P.O. Box 1950, Summerville, SC 29485; 843-851-4629; Fax: 843-873-2654; wmbaugh@westvaco.com
Karen Dulik, Newsletter Editor; kdulik@water.ca.gov
Paul Jones, Secretary-Treasurer; 2441 Williston Rd., Aiken, SC 29803; 803-725-5337; Fax: 803-725-3309; jones@srel.edu
Benjamin Miller, Past-President; Mulberry Plantation 1904 N. Mulberry Dr., Moncks Corner, SC 29461; 843-761-5220; Fax: 843-761-5292

WILDLIFE SOCIETY
SOUTH DAKOTA CHAPTER
200 South Tyler Ave
Pierre, SD 57501 United States
Phone: 605-773-4194
Website: www.wfs.sdstate.edu/sdtws.htm

Founded: N/A
Membership: 101–1,000
Scope: State
Description: Wildlife science and management

Contact(s):

Paul Coughlin, President; 523 East Capital, Pierre, SD 57501; 605-773-3658; paul.coughlin@state.sd.us
Daniel Hubbard, Past President; SDSUP.O. Box 2140B, Brookings, SD 57007; 605-688-6121; Fax: 605-688-4515; Daniel_Hubbard@sdstate.edu
Carl Madsen, Past President; 2205 North Shore Dr., Brookings, SD 57006; 605-697-2500; Fax: 605-697-2505; Carl_Madsen@fws.gov

WILDLIFE SOCIETY
SOUTHERN CALIFORNIA CHAPTER
CA United States

Founded: N/A

Scope: State

Contact(s):

Brad Blood, President; 12702 Cowley Ave., Downey, CA 90242; 626-683-3547; Fax: 626-683-3548; pizonyx@aol.com
Mari Schroeder, Vice President; 12551 Hinton Way, Santa Ana, CA 92705; 949-261-5414; Fax: 649-261-8950; mschroeder@chambersgroupinc.com
Kathleen Keane, Secretary; 5546 E. Parkcrest St., Long Beach, CA 90808; 310-425-6842
Mari Schroeder, President- Past; 12551 Hinton Way, Santa Ana, CA 92705; 949-261-5414; Fax: 649-261-8950; mschroeder@chambersgroupinc.com
John Stephenson, Treasurer; 199 Via Del Cerrito, Encinitas, CA 92024; 619-436-8340; jstephen/r5_cleveland@fs.fed.us

WILDLIFE SOCIETY
TENNESSEE CHAPTER
TN United States
Website: www.utm.edu/department/gr/agnatres/tn-tws/tn-tws.html

Founded: N/A

Scope: State

Contact(s):

Eric Pelren, President; Dept. Agri. & Nat. Res. 114 Brehm Hall, Martin, TN 38238; 901-587-7263; Fax: 901-587-7968; epelren@utm.edu
David Buehler, Past-President; U. of Tennessee Dept. For., Wldlf. & Fish P.O. Box 1071, Knoxville, TN 37901; 423-974-7992; Fax: 423-974-4714; dbuehler@utk.edu
Lisa Muller, Secretary-Treasurer; Dept. For., Wldlf., & Fish. P.O. Box 1071, Knoxville, TN 37901; 423-974-7981; Fax: 423-974-4714; lmuller@utk.edu
Edward Warr, Newsletter Editor; Tennessee Wldlf. Res. Agency Wildlife Division P.O. Box 40747, Nashville, TN 37204; 615-781-6613; Fax: 615-781-6654; ewarr@mail.state.tn

WILDLIFE SOCIETY
TEXAS CHAPTER
TX United States
Website: www.tctws.org

Founded: N/A

Scope: State

Contact(s):

Kirby Brown, President; Texas Wildlife Association, 401 Isom Road #237, San Antonio, TX 78216; 210-826-2904; Fax: 210-826-4933; k_brown@texas-wildlife.org
Terry Blankenship, President Elect; Welder Wildlife Foundation, P.O. Box 1400, Sinton, TX 78387; 361-364-2643; Fax: 361-364-2650; welderwf@aol.com
Neal Wilkins, Vice President; Dept. Wildlife and Fisheries Sciences, SFSC 2258, TAMU, College Station, TX 77843; 979-845-7471; Fax: 979-845-7103; nwilkins@tamu.edu
Donald Davis, Treasurer; TX A&M U. Dept. Vet. Pathology, College Station, TX 77843; 409-845-5174; Fax: 409-862-1088; ddavis@cvm.tamu.edu
Fidel Hernandez, Secretary; Dept. Wildlife Sciences, 700 University Blvd., MSC 218, TAMUK, Kingsville, TX 78363; 915-828-3926; Fax: 361-593-3924; fidel.hernandez@tamuk.edu

WILDLIFE SOCIETY
UTAH CHAPTER
Attn: President, Bureau of Land Management, 318 N. 100 E.
Kanab, UT 84741 United States

Founded: N/A

Scope: State

Contact(s):

Kathleen Paulin, President; Vernal Ranger District Ashley National Forest 355 North Vernal Avenue, Vernal, UT 84078; 435-781-5160; kpaulin@fs.fed.us
Harry Barber, Past-President; BLM 318 N. 100 E., Kanab, UT 84741; 435-644-4311; Fax: 435-644-2672; hbarber@ut.blm.gov
Stanley Beckstrom, Newsletter Editor; 4311 S. 4625 W., Salt Lake City, UT 84120-4931; 435-865-6112; nrdwr.sbeckstr@state.ut.us
Stanley Beckstrom, Secretary; 4311 S. 4625 W., Salt Lake City, UT 84120-4931; 435-865-6112; nrdwr.sbeckstr@state.ut.us
Lisa Church, President-Elect; 1381 S. Ford, Kanab, UT 84741; 435-644-4600; Fax: 435-644-4620; lchurch@ut.blm.gov
Randall Thacker, Treasurer; P.O. Box 337, Altamont, UT 84001; 435-454-3081; mrdwr/rtjacler@state.ut.us

WILDLIFE SOCIETY
VIRGINIA CHAPTER
VA United States

Founded: N/A

Scope: State

Contact(s):
Bruce Lemmert, President; 21 S. Church St., Lovettsville, VA 22080; 540-822-4219; blemmert@dgif.state.va.us
Jefferson Waldon, Vice-President; VPI & SU, Fish & Wildlife Info Exchange, 203 W. Roanoke St., Blacksburg, VA 24061; 540-231-7348; Fax: 540-231-7019; fwiexchg@vt.edu
Jack Gwynn, Newsletter Editor; 2503 Brunswick Rd., Charlottesville, VA 22903; 804-295-4681; Fax: 804-975-1005; jackgwynn@aol.com
Ralph Keel, Treasurer; 1232 Geranium Crescent, Virginia Beach, VA 23456; 757-986-3706; Fax: 757-986-2353; r5rw_gdsnwr@mail.fws.gov
Jesse Overcash, Past-President; 110 Southpark Dr., Blacksburg, VA 24060; 540-522-4641; Fax: 540-552-4376; jovercas@vt.edu
Lisa Sausville, Secretary; 966 Rt. 17 W., Addison, VT 05491

WILDLIFE SOCIETY
WASHINGTON CHAPTER
WA United States
Phone: 509-663-8121
Website:
www.washingtonwildlifesoc.org/ns/default_ns.htm

Founded: 1966
Membership: 101–1,000
Scope: State
Contact(s):
Paul Fielder, President; 1633 Concord Place, Wenatchee, WA 98801; 509-663-8121; Fax: 509-664-2338; paul@chelanpud.org
Don Utzinger, President Elect; 44691 Baker Lake Road, Concrete, WA 98237; 360-853-7806; Fax: 360-853-7806; utzinger@fidalgo.net
Kenneth Bevis, Newsletter Editor; Yakima Indian Nation Wildlife P.O. Box 151, Toppenish, WA 98948-0151; beviskrb@dfw.wa.gov
John Lehmkuhl, President-Past; 1133 N. Western Ave., Wenatchee, WA 98801; 509-662-4315; jlehmkhul/r6pnw_wenatchee@fs.fed.us
Catherine Raley, Treasurer; Forestry Sciences Lab 3625 93rd Ave. SW, Olympia, WA 98502; 360-753-7686; craley@fs.fed.us
Ann Sprague, Secretary; Box 188, Twisp, WA 98856; 509-997-2131; Fax: 509-997-9770; sprague@nethow.com

WILDLIFE SOCIETY
WEST VIRGINIA CHAPTER
WV United States

Founded: N/A
Scope: State
Contact(s):
Jim Fregonara, President; 210 Boundary Ave., Elkins, WV 26241; 304-637-0245; Fax: 304-637-0250
Christopher Ryan, Vice-President; P.O. Box 73, Shirley, WV 26434; 304-758-2681
James Anderson, Secretary-Treasurer; WV DNR-Wildlife 2006 Robert C. Byrd Drive, Beckley, WV 25801; 304-293-2941, ext. 2445; Fax: 304-293-2441; jander25@wvu.edu
Shawn Head, Past-President; WV DNR P.O. Box 67, Elkins, WV 26241; 304-637-0245

WILDLIFE SOCIETY
WISCONSIN CHAPTER
Rt. 3 Box 174D
Ashland, WI 54806 United States

Founded: N/A
Scope: State
Publication(s): Wisconsin Association for Environmental Education Bulletin
Contact(s):
Jonathan Gilbert, President; 25350 Fischer Rd., Ashland, WI 54806; 715-682-6619; Fax: 715-682-9294; jgilbert@glifwc.org
Gerald Bartelt, Past President; 6315 Clovernook Rd., Middletown, WI 53562-3824; 608-221-6344; Fax: 608-221-6353; barteg@dnr.state.wi.us
Alan Crossley, Newsletter Editor; 459 Sidney St., Madison, WI 53703; 608-275-3242; Fax: 608-275-3338; crossa@dnr.state.wi.us
Gary Zimmer, Secretary-Treasurer; P.O. Box 116, Laona, WI 54541; 715-674-4481; Fax: 715-276-3594; gzimmer@fs.fed.us

WILDLIFE SOCIETY
WYOMING CHAPTER
Attn: President, 260 Buena Vista
Lander, WY 82520 United States
Phone: 307-766-5415
Website: www.wyotws.org

Founded: N/A
Scope: State
Description: Professsional society
Contact(s):
Stan Anderson, President; Wyoming Cooperative Fish and Wildlife Research Unit, Dept. of Zoology & Physiology, Biology Sciences Bldg., Room 419, Laramie, WY 82071; 307-455-2466; anderson@uwyo.edu
Mark Hinschberger, Past President; U.S. Forest Service P.O. Box 186, Dubois, WY 82513; 307-455-2466; mhinschb/r2_shashone@fs.fed.us
Karli Allanson, Secretary; 307-548-6541; kallanson@fs.fed.us
Frank Bloomquist, Treasurer; 307-328-4207; frank_bloomquist@blm.gov
Tim Byer, Present Elect; 307-358-3670; tbyer@fs.fed.us
Christina Schmidt, Newsletter Editor; 307-733-2383, ext. 32; christina.schmidt@wgf.state.wy.us

WILDLIFE TRUST, INC
Lamont-Doherty Earth Observatory
The Nafe House #8
61 Route 9W
Palisades, NY 10964 United States
Phone: 845-365-8337 Fax: 845-365-8177
E-mail: homeoffice@wildlifetrust.org
Website: www.wildlifetrust.org

Founded: 1971
Membership: 1,001–10,000
Scope: Regional, National, International
Description: Wildlife Trust conserves threatened wild species and their habitats in partnership with local scientists and educators around the world.
Publication(s): On the Edge, Annual Report, Wild Times, The, Dodo Dispatch, Dodo, The
Keyword(s): Wildlife & Species
Contact(s):
Thomas McHenry, President
Virginia Mars, Vice President
Allen Model, Vice President
Joanne Gullifer, Director of Administration
Fred Koontz, Director of Conservation Program
Mary Pearl, Executive Director
Peter Wilmerding, Director of Development
A. Aguirre, International Field Veterinarian
Victoria Mars, Secretary
John Tuten, Treasurer

WILDLIFE WAYSTATION
14831 Little Tujunga Canyon Rd.
Angeles National Forest, CA 91342-5999 United States
Phone: 818-899-5201 Fax: 818-890-1107
Website: www.waystation.org

Founded: 1969

Scope: National

Description: A southern California nonprofit refuge providing medical care, refuge, rehabilitation, and placement services for over 4,000 wild and exotic animals annually. Public tours and educational programs available.

Publication(s): Wildlife Waystation (newsletter), Wild Proofing the Human Habitat (brochure).

Keyword(s): Wildlife & Species

Contact(s):
Martine Colette, Founder and President

WILSON ORNITHOLOGICAL SOCIETY

Wilson Ornithological Society
Museum of Zoology, Univ. of Michigan
1109 Geddes Ave.
Ann Arbor, MI 48109 United States
Phone: 508-543-8988 Fax: 508-286-8278
E-mail: wedavis@bu.edu
Website: www.ummz.lsa.umich.edu/birds/wos.html

Founded: 1888

Membership: 1,001–10,000

Scope: International

Description: To advance the science of ornithology and to secure cooperation in measures tending to this end.

Publication(s): Wilson Bulletin, The

Keyword(s): Wildlife & Species

Contact(s):
Charles Blem, First Vice President; Dept. of Biology, 816 Park Ave., P.O. Box 842012, Virginia Commonwealth University, Richmond, VA 23284-2012; 804-828-1562; Fax: 804-828-0503; cblem@saturn.vcu.edu
William Davis, President; College of General Studies, 871 Commonwealth Avenue, Boston University, Boston, MA 02215; 617-353-2886; Fax: 617-353-5868; wedavis@bu.edu
Doris Watt, Second Vice President; Dept. of Biology, Saint Mary's College, Notre Dame, IN 46556-5001; 219-284-4668; Fax: 219-284-4716; dwatt@jade.saintmarys.edu
Sara Morris, Secretary; Dept. of Biology, Canisius College, 2001 Main St., Buffalo, NY 14208; 716-888-2567; Fax: 716-888-3157; morriss@canisius.edu
John Smallwood, Editor; Dept. of Biology, Montclair State University, Upper Montclair, NJ 07043; 973-655-5345; Fax: 973-655-7047; smallwood@saturn.montclair.edu

WINCHESTER NILO FARMS

Olin Corporation, 427 N. Shamrock
E. Alton, IL 62024 United States
Phone: 618-258-3133 Fax: 618-258-2370
Website: NiloFarms.com

Founded: N/A

Membership: 1–100

Scope: National

Description: Wildlife Hunting Preserve

Contact(s):
Roger Jones, Manager; 618-466-0613

WINDSTAR FOUNDATION, THE

7 Avenida Vista Grande #304
Santa Fe, NM 87505 United States
Phone: Fax: 970-963-1463
E-mail: windstar@rof.net
Website: www.wstar.org

Founded: 1976

Scope: National

Description: A nonprofit organization co-founded by John Denver and Tom Crum. Windstar works to inspire individuals to make responsible choices and take direct action to achieve a peaceful and environmentally sustainable future.

Contact(s):
Cheryl Charles, Chairman of Board of Trustees
Beth Miller, Secretary and Treasurer
Jeanie Tomlinson, Liaison; 970-963-5534

WINDSTAR WILDLIFE INSTITUTE

10072 Vista Court
Myersville, MD 21773 United States
Phone: 301-293-3351 Fax: 301-293-3353
E-mail: wildlife@windstar.org
Website: www.windstar.org

Founded: 1986

Membership: 1,001–10,000

Scope: National

Description: WindStar Wildlife Institute is a national 501(c)(3) non-profit, conservation organization whose mission and solution to the loss of native plants and wildlife habitat focuses on effectively teaching wildlife habitat improvement practices through proven methods such as "neighbor helping neighbor" and "education through demonstration".

Publication(s): Wildlife Habitat Improvement Kit, Tips on Improving Wildlife Habitat, WindStar Wildlife Garden Weekly

Keyword(s): Agriculture/Farming, Forests/Forestry, Water Habitats & Quality

WISCONSIN ASSOCIATION FOR ENVIRONMENTAL EDUCATION, INC. (WAEE)

233 Nelson Hall, UWSP
Stevens Point, WI 54481 United States
Phone: 715-346-2796 Fax: 715-346-3835
E-mail: waee@uwsp.edu
Website: www.uwsp.edu/waee

Founded: 1974

Membership: 101–1,000

Scope: State

Description: Promotes environmental education in schools and other institutions and organizations in Wisconsin.

Publication(s): EE News

Keyword(s): Water Habitats & Quality

Contact(s):
Paul Denowski, Chair; 262-642-7466; pdenowski@yahoo.com
Jim McGinity, Co-Chair; 414-964-8505; irishmist@rocketmail.com
Christy Allar, Administrative Assistant; 715-346-2796; Fax: 715-346-3835; callar@uwsp.edu

WISCONSIN ASSOCIATION OF LAKES (WAL)

P.O. Box 126
Stevens Point, WI 54481-0126 United States
Phone: 608-662-0923 Fax: 715-346-3624
E-mail: info@wisconsinlakes.org
Website: www.wisconsinlakes.org

Founded: 1980

Scope: State

Description: WAL is a coalition of 287 lake management organizations, as well as hundreds of individual members. The organization is dedicated to the protection of lake ecosystems in Wisconsin. WAL works closely with the Wisconsin Department of Natural Resources and University Extension in the Wisconsin Lakes Partnership.

Publication(s): Lake Connection, The

Keyword(s): Land Issues, Pollution (general), Water Habitats & Quality

Contact(s):
Jim Burgess, President; 608-257-4443; jeburg@aol.com
Donna Sefton, Executive Director
Judy Jooss, Secretary; 414-877-9301; jjooss@techheadnet.com
Hal Krueger, Communications and Development Coordinator
John Seibel, Treasurer; 715-479-4714; jpsmis@nnex.net
Debra Sweeney, Membership Coordinator
Susan Tesarik, Water Classification Outreach Coordinator

WISCONSIN B.A.S.S. CHAPTER FEDERATION

Attn: President, 6503 Lani Ln.
McFarland, WI 53558 United States
Phone: 608-838-3040 Fax: 608-838-3040
Website: www.swiftsite.com/wsbf

Founded: N/A
Scope: State
Description: An organization of Bassmaster chapters, affiliated with the Bass Anglers Sportsman Society, organized to fight pollution, assist state and national conservation agencies in their efforts, and teach young people good conservation practices. Dedicated to the realistic conservation of our water resources.
Publication(s): Wisconsin Bass News
Contact(s):
Chuck Rolfsmeyer, President
Kevin Fassbind, Conservation Director; 12 Bel Aire, Madison, WI 53713; 608-224-0029; fassbind@hotmail.com

WISCONSIN DEPARTMENT OF NATURAL RESOURCES

101 S. Webster St. P.O. Box 7921
Madison, WI 53707-7921 United States
Phone: 608-266-2121 Fax: 267-938-9380
Website: www.dnr.state.wi.us

Founded: N/A
Scope: National
Contact(s):
Darrell Bazzell, Secretary

WISCONSIN LAND AND WATER CONSERVATION ASSOCIATION

One Point Place, Suite 101
Madison, WI 53719 United States
Phone: 608-833-1833 Fax: 608-833-7179
E-mail: wlwca@execpc.com
Website: www.execpc.com/~wlwca

Founded: 1952
Membership: 1–100
Scope: State
Description: Wisconsin Land and Water Conservation Association is a 501(c) (3) non-profit organization representing Wisconsin's 72 county land conservation committees and departments, assisting them with the protection, enhancement and sustainable use of Wisconsin's natural resources, and representing them through education and government interaction.
Publication(s): Thursday Note
Keyword(s): Agriculture/Farming, Pollution (general), Public Health, Public Lands/Greenspace, Reduce/Reuse/Recycle, Water Habitats & Quality, Wildlife & Species
Contact(s):
Marvin Fox, President; N2538 Cty Road, J, Kaukauna, WI 54130; 414-766-3242
Robert Washkuhn, Vice President; W8225 Sand Rd., Shell Lake, WI 54871; 715-468-7657
Rebecca Baumann, Executive Director; One Point Place, Ste. 101, Madison, WI 53719-2809; 608-833-1833; Fax: 608-833-7179; wlwca3@execpc.com
Roger Hahn, Board Member; 705 Pease St., Augusta, WI 54722; 715-286-5343

WISCONSIN PARK AND RECREATION ASSOCIATION

6601-C Northway
Greendale, WI 53129 United States
Phone: 414-423-1210 Fax: 414-423-1296
E-mail: wpra@execpc.com
Website: www.nrta.org/member/wpra/

Founded: N/A
Membership: 1,001–10,000
Scope: State
Description: A nonprofit organization, affiliated with the National Recreation and Park Association, working with other groups and organizations to achieve the best in park services and recreational opportunities.
Publication(s): Impact Magazine, P.R. Monthly Newsletter
Contact(s):
Roger Kist, President; Washington County,
Steve Thompson, Editor; 7000 Greenway, Suite 201, Greendale, WI 53129; 414-423-1210

WISCONSIN SOCIETY FOR ORNITHOLOGY, INC., THE

5188 Bittersweet Ln.
Oshkosh, WI 54901 United States
Phone: 920-233-1973
Website: www.uwgb.edu/birds/wso

Founded: 1939
Membership: 1,001–10,000
Scope: Regional
Description: To stimulate interest in and promote the study of birds in Wisconsin for a better understanding of their biology and basis for their preservation.
Publication(s): Passenger Pigeon, Badger Birder
Keyword(s): Water Habitats & Quality, Wildlife & Species
Contact(s):
William Brooks, President; Ripon College Dept. of Biology, Ripon, WI 54971
Daryl Christenson, Vice President
Jane Dennis, Secretary; 138 S. Franklin Ave., Madison, WI 53705-5248; 608-231-1741
Bettie Harriman, Publicity Chair; 5188 Bittersweet Ln., Oshkosh, WI 54901; 920-233-1973
R. Highsmith, Editor; 702 Schiller Ct., Madison, WI 53704; 608-242-1168
Alex Kailing, Treasurer; W330 N8275 W. Shore Dr., Hartland, WI 53029; 414-966-1072
Mary Uttech, Editor; 262-675-6482; muttech@asq.org

WISCONSIN WATERFOWL ASSOCIATION, INC.

78 Enterprise Rd. Ste. A
Delafield, WI 53018-0496 United States
Phone: 262-646-5926 Fax: 262-646-5949
E-mail: h2ofowl@powercom.net
Website: www.wisducks.org

Founded: 1983
Membership: 1,001–10,000
Scope: State
Description: A statewide nonprofit environmental/educational organization that establishes, promotes, assists, and contributes to conservation, restoration, and management of Wisconsin wetlands to perpetuate waterfowl and wildlife. Represents waterfowl enthusiasts via a unified statewide voice on Wisconsin migratory bird hunting regulations and conservation legislation benefiting the protection of wetlands. Educational programs and waterfowl hunting seminars.
Publication(s): Wisconsin Waterfowl
Keyword(s): Reduce/Reuse/Recycle, Water Habitats & Quality, Wildlife & Species
Contact(s):
Dennis Tetzlaff, President; 262-646-5926, ext. 10; Fax: 262-646-5949
Kelcy Boettcher, Director of Administrative Services; 262-646-5926, ext. 21; Fax: 262-646-5949; h2ofowl@powercom.net
Jeff Bord, Regional Director; 262-646-5926, ext. 24; Fax: 262-646-5949; jbord@powercom.net
Jeff Nania, Executive Director/Project Director; W11360 Hwy. 127, Portage, WI 53901; 608-742-6699; Fax: 608-742-1669
Tom Seibert, Regional Director; 262-646-5926, ext. 23; Fax: 262-646-5949

WISCONSIN WILDLIFE FEDERATION

2036 W. 9th Street
Oshkosh, WI 54904 United States
Phone: 920-235-9136 Fax: 920-235-6030
E-mail: wiwf@execpc.com
Website: www.execpc.com/-wiwf

Founded: N/A
Membership: 1,001–10,000
Scope: State
Description: A representative statewide organization, affiliated with the National Wildlife Federation, dedicated to the protection and enhancement of wildlife and its habitat through public education and government interaction.
Publication(s): Wisconservation
Keyword(s): Reduce/Reuse/Recycle, Water Habitats & Quality, Wildlife & Species
Contact(s):
James Weishan, President and Alternate Representative
Daniel Gries, Editor
Russell Hitz, Treasurer
Martha Kilishek, Representative
Ruth Lee, Education Programs Contact

WISCONSIN WOODLAND OWNERS ASSOCIATION

P.O. Box 285
Stevens Point, WI 54481-0285 United States
Phone: 715-346-4798 Fax: 715-346-4821
Website: www.wisconsinwoodlands.org

Founded: 1979
Membership: 1,001–10,000
Scope: Local, State
Description: A statewide, nonprofit, educational association for and by private woodland owners in Wisconsin who want to learn more about good forest stewardship. Publish a quarterly award-winning magazine, co-sponsor conference, workshops, and field days for woodland owners. Thirteen local chapters throughout Wisconsin offer field days for woodland owners. Affiliated with the National Woodland Owners Association.
Publication(s): WWOA Seedlings, Woodland Management
Keyword(s): Ecosystems (precious), Forests/Forestry, Land Issues
Contact(s):
Marvin Meier, President; 715-355-9034
Alvin Barden, Vice President; 715-479-8449
Nancy Bozek, Executive Director; 715-346-4798; Fax: 715-346-4821; nbozek@uwsp.edu
Evelyn Charlson, Secretary; 920-982-4076
Timothy Eisele, Editor; 608-233-2904
Dale Lightfuss, Treasurer; 920-244-7668

WOLF EDUCATION AND RESEARCH CENTER

P. O. Box 217
Winchester, ID 83555 United States
Phone: 208-924-6960 Fax: 208-924-6959
E-mail: werc@camasnet.com
Website: www.wolfcenter.org

Founded: 1992
Membership: 1,001–10,000
Scope: State, Regional
Description: The Wolf Education and Research Center is dedicated to providing public information, education, and research concerning endangered species, with an emphasis on the gray wolf, its habitat and ecosystem in the Northern Rocky Mountain region. Our efforts seek to improve public awareness of endangered and threatened species in the area and to develop, in concert with regional cultures and residents, ways to coexist with these species.
Publication(s): Sawtooth Pack Sponsorship Newsletter, Wolf Education and Research Center Membership Newsletter, Educational Track of Wolf - monthly publication, Wild Wolves Sponsorship Newsletter.
Keyword(s): Ethics/Environmental Justice, Public Lands/Greenspace, Recreation/Ecotourism, Wildlife & Species
Contact(s):
Douglass Christensen, President; Fax: 208-726-1982; 1dmc@sunvalley.net
Roy Farrar, Vice President; Fax: 208-384-0540; wolfsta@mce.net
Sally Farrar, Secretary; 208-336-6562; Fax: 208-384-0540

WOLF GROUP, THE

P.O. Box 303
Cherokee, TX 76832 United States
Phone: 915-622-4810
E-mail: sky@wolf.com
Website: www.wolf.com

Founded: 1996
Membership: 10,001–100,000
Scope: International
Description: Advocates for wolves and other endangered species and habitat
Keyword(s): Agriculture/Farming, Ecosystems (precious), Land Issues, Wildlife & Species

WOLF HAVEN INTERNATIONAL

3111 Offut Lake Rd.
Tenino, WA 98589 United States
Phone: 360-264-4695 Fax: 360-264-4639
E-mail: info@wolfhaven.org
Website: www.wolfhaven.org

Founded: 1982
Membership: 1,001–10,000
Scope: National, International
Description: The organization's mission is "Working for Wolf Conservation" done primarily through providing public education on the value of all wildlife; providing sanctuary for captive-born wolves; promoting wolf reestablishment in historic ranges; and protecting our remaining wild wolves. Wolf Haven is also one of three pre-release breeding facilities for the Mexican Wolf Recovery Program.
Publication(s): Wolf Tracks
Keyword(s): Wildlife & Species
Contact(s):
Rick Schaefer, President
Rick Castellano, Executive Director
Julie Palmquist, Communications Director; julie@wolfhaven.org
Dana Maher, Treasurer

WOMEN'S ENVIRONMENT AND DEVELOPMENT ORGANIZATION (WEDO)

355 Lexington Avenue, 3rd Floor
New York, NY 10017 United States
Phone: 212-973-0325 Fax: 212-973-0335
E-mail: wedo@iwedo.org
Website: www.wedo.org

Founded: 1990
Scope: National
Description: On January 27, 1995, Women USA Fund, Inc. changed its name to WEDO. The organization is an international advocacy network actively working to transform society to achieve social, political, economic, and environmental justice for all through the empowerment of women, in all their diversity, and through their equal participation with men in decision-making from grassroots to global arenas.
Publication(s): News and Views (contact WEDO for a comprehensive list)
Keyword(s): Population, Public Health, Reduce/Reuse/Recycle

Contact(s):
Jocelyn Dow, President; jocelyndow@hotmail.com
Thais Corral, Vice President
Bisi Ogunleye, Vice President
June Zeitlin, Executive Director
Elizabeth Calvin, Secretary
Brownie Ledbetter, Treasurer

WOMEN'S SHOOTING SPORTS FOUNDATION

4620 Edison Ave., Suite C
Colorado Springs, CO 80915 United States
Phone: 719-638-1299 Fax: 719-638-1271
E-mail: wssf@worldnet.att.net
Website: www.wssf.org/

Founded: 1993
Membership: 1,001–10,000
Scope: National
Description: The Women's Shooting Sports Foundation is a national, nonprofit membership organization offering an ongoing series of programs to expand shooting opportunities for women.
Publication(s): Outdoors for Women, Women's Resource List, The
Keyword(s): Ethics/Environmental Justice, Recreation/Ecotourism, Wildlife & Species
Contact(s):
Shari Legate, Executive Director

WORLD ASSOCIATION OF GIRL GUIDES AND GIRL SCOUTS (WAGGGS)

World Bureau Olave Centre; 12c Lyndhurst Rd.
London, NW3 5PQ United Kingdom
Website: www.waggsworld.org

Founded: 1928
Membership: 101–1,000
Scope: International
Description: WAGGGS is a voluntary worldwide movement open to all girls and young women. Based on spiritual values and dedicated to the education of girls and young women, WAGGGS provides them with opportunities of self-training in the development of character, responsible citizenship, and service in their own and world communities. WAGGGS works for peace by promoting increased understanding between individuals through community, environmental, and international projects.
Keyword(s): Development/Developing Countries, Ethics/Environmental Justice, Public Health
Contact(s):
Lesley Bulman, Director
Carol Brown, Treasurer
Larae Orvillian, World Board Vice Chairman
Ginny Radford, World Board Chairman

WORLD BIRD SANCTUARY (WBS)

125 Bald Eagle Ridge Road
Valley Park, MO 63088 United States
Phone: 636-938-6193 Fax: 636-938-9464
E-mail: info@worldbirdsanctuary.org
Website: www.worldbirdsanctuary.org

Founded: 1977
Membership: 1,001–10,000
Scope: International
Description: (formerly The Raptor Rehabilitation and Propagation Project Inc.) The WBS was established by Walter C. Crawford, Jr. near St. Louis, Missouri. It is a nonprofit, tax-exempt organization whose mission is to preserve the earth's biological diversity and to secure the future of threatened bird species in their natural environments. We work to fullfill that mission through education, propagation, and rehabilitation. We also have a hands-on internship program.
Publication(s): Education Department, Mews News, Stress in Captive Birds of Prey, Techniques for Artificial Incubation and Hand-rearing of Raptors, Methods of Feather Replacement in Birds of Prey.
Keyword(s): Wildlife & Species
Contact(s):
Walter Crawford, Jr., Executive Director; 636-861-3225, ext. 13; info@worldbirdsanctuary.org
Simon Davies, Director of Development; 636-861-3225; info@worldbirdsanctuary.org
Roger Holloway, Director of Interpretive Services; 636-225-4390; WBSEducation@aol.com
Jeffery Meshach, Director of Animal Management; 636-938-6175; info@worldbirdsanctuary.org

WORLD CONSERVATION UNION

Rue Mauverney 28
Gland, 1196 Switzerland
Phone: 41-22-999-0001
Website: www.iucn.org

Founded: N/A
Description: The IUCN mission is to influence, encourage and assist societies throughout the world to conserve the integrity and diversity of nature and to ensure that any use of natural resources is equitable and ecologically sustainable.
Contact(s):
Yolanda Kakabadse-Navarro, President; president@iucn.org
William Jackson, Director of Global Programme; 412-299-0276; Fax: 412-299-0025; bill.jackson@iucn.org
Achim Steiner, Director General; 412-299-0297; Fax: 412-299-0029; achim.steiner@iucn.org

WORLD FORESTRY CENTER

4033 SW Canyon Rd.
Portland, OR 97221 United States
Phone: 503-228-1367 Fax: 503-228-4608
Website: www.worldforrest.org

Founded: 1966
Scope: National
Description: The World Forestry Center is a nonprofit organization promoting a greater appreciation and understanding of the world's forests and related natural resources. The Center operates a forestry museum adjacent to the Hoyt Arboretum, conference facilities, an international institute, and an 80-acre demonstration forest and outdoor education site. Public tours and classes, school programs, exhibits and special events, conferences, curriculum materials, and publications are available.
Publication(s): Forest Education Program Guide, Branching Out Newsletter
Keyword(s): Forests/Forestry, Reduce/Reuse/Recycle
Contact(s):
Dennis Dykstra, President
Rick Zenn, Education Director

WORLD PAL (WORLD POPULATION ALLOCATION LIMITED INC.)

52 Stevens St., Suite 1100
White Plains, NY 10606 United States
Phone: 914-684-6539 Fax: 914-684-9607
Website: www.worldpal.org

Founded: N/A
Membership: 1–100
Scope: International
Description: World Pal is concerned with increasing the awareness that young people have for their environment. World Pal conducts educational awareness programs on the decks of a newly-built, four-masted barquentine. The programs are offered in many ports throughout Latin America, from the Rio Grande to Patagonia. While on board, passengers are encouraged to participate in the educational program.
Publication(s): Information available upon request

Keyword(s): Development/Developing Countries, Ecosystems (precious), Population

Contact(s):
D. Anderson, Executive Director

WORLD PARKS ENDOWMENT INC.
1616 P St., NW, #200
Washington, DC 20036 United States
Phone: 202-939-3808 Fax: 202-939-3868
E-mail: worldparks@worldparks.org
Website: www.worldparks.org

Founded: 1988
Membership: N/A
Scope: International
Description: World Parks Endowment, Inc. is a unique low-overhead organization that acquires land in the rain forest and other critical sites for biological diversity. It provides funds for park management of tropical rain forests and other ecosystems of great conservation importance, and has developed projects in over 12 countries, including the Sierra de las Minas Biosphere Reserve in Guatemala and the Bilsa Reserve in Ecuador.
Publication(s): Annual Report
Keyword(s): Forests/Forestry, Land Issues, Wildlife & Species
Contact(s):
Daniel Katz, Chairman and Board President
Byron Swift, President and Board Member
Roger Pasquier, Vice President and Treasurer
Cheri Sugal, Executive Director; 202-939-3255; cheri_sugal@yahoo.com

WORLD PHEASANT ASSOCIATION
P.O. Box 5 Lower Basildon
Reading, Berks, RG8 9PF United Kingdom
Phone: 1189845140 Fax: 1189843369
E-mail: wpa@gr.apc.org

Founded: 1975
Scope: National
Description: Aims are to develop, promote, and support conservation of all species of the order galliformes with initial emphasis on the family phasianidae.
Contact(s):
Keith Howman, President
Derek Bingham, Editor; c/o World Pheasant Association, P.O. Box 5, Lower Basildon, Reading, Berks RG8 9PF
Nicola Chalmers-Watson, Administrator
Richard Howard, Chairman

WORLD RESOURCES INSTITUTE
10 G St., NE, Suite 800
Washington, DC 20002 United States
Phone: 202-729-7600 Fax: 202-729-7610
E-mail: front@wri.org
Website: www.wri.org

Founded: 1982
Membership: 101–1,000
Scope: International
Description: A policy research center created with funding from the John D. and Catherine T. MacArthur Foundation and others, to help governments, international organizations, the private sector, and others address vital issues of environmental integrity, natural resource management, economic growth, and international security.
Publication(s): Policy Studies Series, World Resources Report, Research Report Series
Keyword(s): Air Quality/Atmosphere, Climate Change, Development/Developing Countries, Ecosystems (precious), Energy, Forests/Forestry, Oceans/Coasts/Beaches, Reduce/Reuse/Recycle, Transportation
Contact(s):
Jonathan Lash, President; jlash@wri.org
Marjorie Beane, V.P. for Administration and Cfo

WORLD SOCIETY FOR THE PROTECTION OF ANIMALS (WSPA)
34 Deloss Street
Framingham, MA 01702 United States
Phone: 508-879-8350 Fax: 508-620-0786
E-mail: wspa@wspausa.com
Website: www.wspa-usa.org

Founded: 1981
Scope: International
Description: The World Society for the Protection of Animals (WSPA) is a unique international organization dedicated to raising the standard of animal welfare throughout the world. We provide direct hands-on help to stop cruelty and relieve animal suffering. WSPA achieves long-term improvements for animals by lobbying for effective animal welfare laws and providing education to change attitudes towards animals.
Publication(s): Animals International, WSPA Campaign News, WSPA World, Annual Report.
Keyword(s): Wildlife & Species
Contact(s):
Andrew Dickson, Chief Executive
Laura Salter, USA Director
John Walsh, International Projects Director

WORLD WILDLIFE FUND
1250 24th St., NW
Washington, DC 20037 United States
Phone: 202-243-4800 Fax: 202-293-9211
E-mail: archer@wwfus.org
Website: www.worldwildlife.org

Founded: 1961
Scope: International
Description: WWF is the largest private U.S. organization working worldwide to protect wildlife and wildlands—especially in the tropical forests of Latin America, Asia, and Africa. WWF has helped create and protect more than 450 national parks and nature reserves; supports scientific investigations; monitors international trade in wildlife; promotes ecologically-sound development; assists local groups to take the lead in needed conservation projects; and seeks to influence public opinion and the policies
Publication(s): FOCUS
Keyword(s): Reduce/Reuse/Recycle, Wildlife & Species
Contact(s):
Kathryn Fuller, President
Bruce Bunting, Asia, Conservation Finance and Species Conservation Vice President
William Eichbaum, U.S. Conservation and Global Threats Vice President
David Evanich, Marketing, Membership and Communications Vice President
Deborah Hechinger, Managing Vice President for Operations
Twig Johnson, Latin America and Caribbean Vice President
James Leape, Senior Vice President
Diane Wood, Vice President of Research and Development
Margaret Ackerly, General Counsel
Edward Bass, Chairman of Executive Committee
Lou Ann Dietz, LAC Senior Program Officer; 202-778-9657; dietz@wwfus.org
Roger Sant, Chairman of Board

WORLD WILDLIFE FUND
GULF OF CALIFORNIA REGIONAL OFFICE
A.P. 423
Guaymas, Sonora, Mexico
Phone: 62211902
E-mail: nnwwfmex@campus.zym.itesm.mx

Founded: 1999

Description: Conservation of the Gulf of California ecoregion through land management enforce policy, partnerships, communications, conservation biologies, natural protected areas, etc.

Contact(s):
Juan Barrera, Office Coordinator; gce-wwfmex@campus.gym.itesm.mx
Norma Nvitez, Communications Officer; nnwwfmex@campus.gym.itesm.mx

WORLD WILDLIFE FUND

PERU PROGRAM OFFICE
Av. San Felipe 720
Jesus Maria
Lima, Peru
Phone: 5112615300 Fax: 5114634459
E-mail: fiorella@wwfperu.org.pe

Founded: N/A

Description: Conservation of biodiversity and ecological processes

Contact(s):
Fiorella Ceruti, Env. Ed. and Communication Officer; 511-261-5300; Fax: 511-463-4459

WORLDWATCH INSTITUTE

1776 Massachusetts Ave., NW
Washington, DC 20036-1904 United States
Phone: 202-452-1999 Fax: 202-296-7365
E-mail: worldwatch@worldwatch.org
Website: www.worldwatch.org

Founded: 1974

Membership: 10,001–100,000

Scope: International

Description: A nonprofit research organization designed to inform policymakers and the public about emerging global problems and trends and the complex links between the world economy and its environmental support systems. Recent studies have covered issues such as global warming, world water shortages, soil erosion, and the decline in food production compared to population growth, renewable energy, deforestation, transportation, oceans, fisheries, carrying capacity and environmental refugees.

Publication(s): Worldwatch papers, Environmental Book series, Vital Signs 2002, State of the World 2002, World Watch Magazine.

Keyword(s): Agriculture/Farming, Climate Change, Development/Developing Countries, Ecosystems (precious), Energy, Ethics/Environmental Justice, Finance/Banking/Trade, Forests/Forestry, Oceans/Coasts/Beaches, Pollution (general), Population, Public Health, Recreation/Ecotourism.

Contact(s):
Christopher Flavin, President; 202-452-1999; Fax: 202-296-7365; cflavin@worldwatch.org
Adrianne Greenlees, Vice President for Development; 202-452-1999; Fax: 202-296-7365; agreenlees@worldwatch.org
Leanne Mitchell, Director of Communications; 202-452-1999; Fax: 202-296-7365; lmitchell@worldwatch.org
Elizabeth Nolan, Vice President for Business Development; 202-452-1999; Fax: 202-296-7365; enolan@worldwatch.org
Gary Gardner, Director of Research; 202-452-1999; Fax: 202-296-7364; garygardner@worldwatch.org
Ed Ayres, Worldwatch Magazine Editor; 202-452-1999; Fax: 202-296-7365; edayres@worldwatch.org
Dick Bell, Senior Policy Advisor; 202-452-1999; Fax: 202-296-7365; dbell@worldwatch.org
Patrick Settle, Info Tech Manager and Web Master; 202-452-1999; Fax: 202-296-7365; psettle@worldwatch.org
Lori Brown, Research Librarian; 202-452-1999; Fax: 202-296-7365; lorib@worldwatch.org

WWF JAPAN (WORLD WIDE FUND FOR NATURE JAPAN)

Nihonseimei Akabanebashi Bldg., 3-1-14 Shiba
Minato-Ku, Tokyo, 1050-0014 Japan
Phone: 337691711 Fax: 337691717

Founded: 1971

Membership: 10,001–100,000

Scope: International

Description: WWF Japan is a national organization of WWF - World Wide Fund for Nature - which is one of the world's largest private international conservation organizations.

Contact(s):
Makoto Hoshino, Chief Executive Director
Prince Akishino, Honorary President
Hisako Hatakeyama, Chairperson
Mitsugu Kawamura, Vice Chairman
Tomio Yoshida, Vice Chairman

WYOMING ASSOCIATION OF CONSERVATION DISTRICTS

2304 E 13Th St.
Cheyenne, WY 82001 United States
Phone: 307-632-5716 Fax: 307-638-4099
E-mail: waocd@trib.com
Website: www.conservewy.com

Founded: N/A

Membership: 1–100

Scope: State

Contact(s):
Olin Sims, President; 307-632-5716; Fax: 307-632-5716
Veronica Canfield, Vice President; P.O. Box 952, Sundance, WY 82729; 307-283-2062; Fax: 307-283-2170
Bobbie Frank, Director
Tracy Renner, Board Member; P.O. Box 271, Meeteetse, WY 82433; 307-868-2355; Fax: 307-868-2470

WYOMING B.A.S.S. CHAPTER FEDERATION

Attn: President, 1008 Rosewood Dr.
Rock Springs, WY 82901 United States
Phone: 307-362-5863
E-mail: jweber@wyoming.com

Founded: N/A

Scope: State

Description: An organization of Bassmaster chapters, affiliated with the Bass Anglers Sportsman Society, organized to fight pollution, assist state and national conservation agencies in their efforts, and teach the young people of our country good conservation practices. Dedicated to the realistic conservation of our water resources.

Publication(s): Wyoming B.A.S.S. Frederation (Newsletter).

Contact(s):
John Weber, President
Leonard Nichols, Conservation Director; 421 Sage Avenue, Kemmer, WY 83101; 307-877-3629; nichols@hamsfork.net

WYOMING NATIVE PLANT SOCIETY

P.O. Box 3452
Laramie, WY 82071 United States
Phone: 307-766-3020
Website: www.uwadmnweb.uwyo.edu/wyndd/wnps/wnps_home.htm

Founded: 1981

Membership: 101–1,000

Scope: State

Description: The Wyoming Native Plant Society promotes the use and appreciation of the state's native flora through education and supporting research.

Publication(s): Landscaping with Wildflowers and Native Plants, Castilleja.

Keyword(s): Agriculture/Farming, Land Issues, Wildlife & Species

Contact(s):
Joy Handley, President
Nina Haas, Vice President
Walter Fertig, Secretary and Treasurer and Editor

WYOMING OUTDOOR COUNCIL

262 Lincoln St.
Lander, WY 82520 United States
Phone: 307-332-7031 Fax: 307-332-6899
E-mail: woc@wyomingoutdoorcouncil.org
Website: www.wyomingoutdoorcouncil.org

Founded: 1967
Membership: 1,001–10,000
Scope: State
Description: A statewide membership organization dedicated to the conservation of Wyoming's natural resources. Promotes sound environmental policy and education of the public for wise decisionmaking. Serves as an active citizen lobby for environmental policies, conducts research, and monitors state and federal agencies.
Publication(s): Various reports and alerts, Frontline Report (newsletter), State Legislative Analysis
Keyword(s): Air Quality/Atmosphere, Ecosystems (precious), Energy, Ethics/Environmental Justice, Forests/Forestry, Pollution (general), Public Lands/Greenspace, Reduce/Reuse/Recycle, Water Habitats & Quality

Contact(s):
Joyce Evans, President
Nancy Debevoise, Vice President
Dan Heilig, Executive Director
Barbara Oakleaf, Secretary
Lorna Wilkes, Treasurer

WYOMING WILDLIFE FEDERATION

P.O. Box 106
Cheyenne, WY 82003 United States
Phone: 307-637-5433 Fax: 307-637-6629
E-mail: admin@wyomingwildlife.org
Website: www.wyomingwildlife.org

Founded: 1937
Membership: 1,001–10,000
Scope: State
Description: A representative statewide organization, affiliated with the National Wildlife Federation, dedicated to the protection and enhancement of wildlife and its habitat through public education and government interaction.
Publication(s): The Pronghorn News

Contact(s):
Larry Durante, Treasurer
Jim Narva, Alternate Representative
Vicky Urbanek, Editor and Education Programs Contact
Mark Winland, Representative

X

XERCES SOCIETY, THE

4828 SE Hawthorne Blvd.
Portland, OR 97215 United States
Phone: 503-232-6639 Fax: 503-233-6794
E-mail: xerces@teleport.com
Website: www.xerces.org

Founded: 1971
Membership: 1,001–10,000
Scope: National
Description: An international nonprofit organization dedicated to invertebrates and the preservation of critical biosystems worldwide. The Society is committed to protecting invertebrates as major components of biological diversity. Emphasis: aquatic invertebrate monitoring to assist in conservation of Pacific Northwest watersheds, butterfly farming in NE Costa Rica, enhancing wild pollinator populations in out-of-play areas of selected Columbia Plateau golf courses, and education through publications.
Publication(s): Wings: Essays on Invertebrate Conservation (membership magazine), Common Names of North American Butterflies, The, Butterfly Gardening: Creating Summer Magic in Your Garden
Keyword(s): Wildlife & Species

Contact(s):
Thomas Eisner, President; Cornell University, Neurobiology and Behavior, W347 Mudd Hall, Ithaca, NY 14853-2702; 607-255-4464
Kathy Parker, Vice President
Scott Hoffman Black, Executive Director
Ed Grosswiler, Secretary, Treasurer
Katherine Janeway, Legal Advisor; 1932 First Avenue, Suite 510, Seattle, WA 98101; 206-583-8304
Matthew Shepherd, Editor

Y

YELL COUNTY WILDLIFE FEDERATION

Route 3 Box 223
Dardanelle, AR 72834 United States
Phone: 501-229-4692

Founded: 1946
Membership: 101–1,000
Scope: Local
Description: Local County affiliate of Arkansas Wildlife Federation consisting primarily of sportsmen, rod and gun enthusiasts, conservationists, nature-lovers and others recognizing basic responsibility to fish and wildlife conservation.
Keyword(s): Ecosystems (precious), Executive/Legislative/Judicial Reform, Forests/Forestry, Land Issues, Pollution (general), Public Lands/Greenspace, Recreation/Ecotourism, Water Habitats & Quality, Wildlife & Species

Contact(s):
Keith Blakemore, President; Route 3 Box 380, Dardanelle, AR 72834; 501-229-1133

YMCA NATURE AND COMMUNITY CENTER

1413 Highway 45
McClellanville, SC 29458 United States
Phone: 843-887-4195 Fax: 843-887-4256
E-mail: ymcawoodruff@aol.com
Website: hometown.aol.com/natureymca/go.html

Founded: 1999
Membership: N/A
Scope: Regional
Description: Provides creative nature education opportunities through various community programs. YMCA programs include a nature based summer camp for 7-12 year olds, Earth Leadership Institute camp for 13-17 year olds, a Teen YMCA Earth Service program, a Tree Ecology and Conservation program utilizing the YMCA's 71 acres and onsite nursery, and our discovery programs.
Keyword(s): Ecosystems (precious), Forests/Forestry, Pollution (general), Recreation/Ecotourism, Reduce/Reuse/Recycle, Water Habitats & Quality, Wildlife & Species

Contact(s):
Diane Moore Woodruff, Assistant Director; 843-887-4195; Fax: 843-887-4256; ymcawoodruff@aol.com
Lori Sheridan, Education Director; 843-887-4195; Fax: 843-887-4256; ymcals@hotmail.com

YOSEMITE RESTORATION TRUST

1212 Broadway, Suite 810
Oakland, CA 94612 United States
Phone: 510-763-1403 Fax: 510-208-4435
Website: www.yosemitetrust.org

Founded: 1990

Scope: National

Description: To ensure protection of the natural, scenic, and historic resources of Yosemite National Park and its ecosystems, and to ensure that visitors have the highest quality experience of the park's natural environment.

Publication(s): Yosemite Viewpoints (Newsletter), special reports on regional transportation, day-use reservations, and housing.

Keyword(s): Land Issues, Public Lands/Greenspace, Recreation/Ecotourism, Sprawl/Urban Planning, Transportation

Contact(s):
Janet Cobb, President
Hal Browder, Vice President
Walter Kieser, Vice President
Thomas Gwyn, Treasurer

YOUNG ENTOMOLOGISTS SOCIETY, INC.

6907 W. Grand River Ave.
Lansing, MI 48906-9131 United States
Phone: 517-886-0630 Fax: 517-886-0630
E-mail: yesbugs@aol.com

Founded: 1965

Membership: 101–1,000

Scope: National

Description: An international nonprofit organization educates and serves youth and amateur entomologists via publications, programs and the minibeast Zooseum and Education Center; assists in information, talent, scientific literature, and insect specimen exchanges (informational networks); distributes and develops resource materials; and promotes awareness of arthropod importance and the contributions youth and amateur entomologists make to the science of entomology. Founded as Teen International Entomology

Publication(s): Caring for Insect Livestock, Insect Indentification Guide, Project B.U.G.S., Insect World

Keyword(s): Recreation/Ecotourism, Wildlife & Species

Contact(s):
Dianna Dunn, Executive Director; 517-887-0499
Gary Dunn, Director of Education

YUKON FISH AND GAME ASSOCIATION

P.O. Box 4434
Whitehorse, Y1A 3T5 Yukon Canada
Phone: 403-667-2843

Founded: N/A

Scope: State

Description: Affiliated with the Canadian Wildlife Federation.

Z

ZERO

158 Fife Ave., Greenwood Park, P.O. Box 5338
Harare, Zimbabwe
Phone: 2634791333 Fax: 2634732858
E-mail: zero@harare.iafrica.com

Founded: 1987

Scope: International

Description: ZERO, a regional environmental organization, is an independent professional, not-for-profit institution dedicated to the development of the rural peoples of southern Africa, especially through the promotion of sustainable management of land resources. ZERO pursues this goal through applied research, policy analysis and influencing national, regional, and international environmental policy making.

Keyword(s): Development/Developing Countries, Land Issues

Contact(s):
Joseph Matowanyika, Director
Yemi Katerere, Chairperson to the Board
Sam Moyo, Secretary to the Board
J. Mutsigwa, Librarian and Information Officer

ZERO POPULATION GROWTH, INC.

1400 16th St., NW.
Washington, DC 20036 United States
Phone: 202-332-2200 Fax: 202-332-2302
E-mail: info@zpg.org
Website: www.zpg.org

Founded: 1968

Membership: 10,001–100,000

Scope: National

Description: ZPG is a national nonprofit membership organization that works to educate and motivate Americans to help meet the global population challenge. ZPG mobilizes grassroots support for the adoption of policies and programs necessary to stabilize global population growth.

Publication(s): ZPG Reporter, Action Alerts, Factsheets, Backgrounders, Teachers' PET Term Paper

Keyword(s): Development/Developing Countries, Population, Public Health, Reduce/Reuse/Recycle

Contact(s):
Elizabeth Borg, Director of Membership and Development; liz@zpg.org
Tim Cline, Director of Communications; tim@zpg.org
Brian Dixon, Director of Government Relations; brian@zpg.org
Jay Keller, Field Director; jay@zpg.org
John Seager, Executive Director; john@zpg.org
Pamela Wasserman, Director of Population Education; pam@zpg.org
Peter Kostmayer, Policy Counselor; peter@zpg.org

ZUNGARO COCHA RESEARCH CENTER

EXPLORATION EDUCATIONAL EXPEDITIONS
P.O. Box 696
Raton, NM 87740 United States
Website: www.nvo.com/zungarococha

Founded: 1997

Scope: International

Description: Working to promote both human and wildlife interests in the Peruvian Amazon and provide information to help resolve their conflicts with special attention to acculturation. A permanat facility in collaboration with U.S. and Peruvian institutions for long-term research and training in pure and applied environmental sciences and conservation.

Keyword(s): Forests/Forestry, Wildlife & Species

Contact(s):
Denise Bacca, President; P.O. Box 696, Raton, NM 87740; 505-445-3603; Fax: 505-445-4101; tsi@raton.com
Carlos Acosta, Manager; Prospero 652, Iquitos; 0115194232; Fax: 011-519-423-2131

NON-GOVERNMENTAL FOR-PROFIT ORGANIZATIONS

A

ABSEARCH, INC.
NATURAL RESOURCE DATABASES
ASHA
530 South Asbury Street
Suite 2C
Moscow, ID 83843 United States
Phone: 800-867-1877 Fax: 208-883-5554
E-mail: sales@absearch.com
Website: www.absearch.com

Founded: 1992

Scope: Local, State, Regional, National, International

Description: Produces ABSEARCH databases which include thousands of abstracts and citations from professional research journals in the area of natural resources. The databases are updated as new research becomes available. Format: CD-ROM and online subscription.

Contact(s):
Leah Lipar, Director of Operations; 208-883-5544; Fax: 208-883-5554; sales@absearch.com
Jennifer Bulson, Marketing Manager; 208-883-5594; Fax: 208-883-5554; marketing@absearch.com

AMERICAN AQUATICS, INC
103A Valley Court
Oak Ridge, TN 37830 United States
Phone: 865-483-0600 Fax: 865-483-0674
E-mail: jfredd@aol.com
Website: www.american-aquatics.com

Founded: 1996
Membership: 1–100
Scope: State, Regional
Description: Biological consulting firm that specializes in collecting fish, benthic organisms and wildlife particularly from contaminated sites.
Keyword(s): Water Habitats & Quality, Wildlife & Species
Contact(s):
J. Heitman, President; 865-483-0600; Fax: 865-483-0674; jfredd@aol.com

AMERICAN CHEMICAL SOCIETY
1155 16th St. NW
Washington, DC 20036 United States
Phone: 202-872-4582 Fax: 202-872-4403
E-mail: est@acs.org
Website: www.acs.org

Founded: N/A
Membership: 100,001–500,000
Scope: National
Publication(s): Environmental Science and Technology
Contact(s):
Sally Pecor, Key Contact

AMERICAN WILDERNESS CAMPAIGN
122 C Street, NW, suite 240
Washington, DC 20001 United States
Phone: 202-544-3691 Fax: 202-544-5197
Website: www.leaveitwild.org

Founded: N/A
Membership: 1–100
Scope: State
Description: The American Wilderness Campaign works with you to add public land to the National Wilderness Preservation System for the benefit of future generations.
Contact(s):
John Gilroy, Associate Director
Mike Matz, Executive Director
Sherry Lynn McLaughlin, Administrative Director; Administrative Office, 850 1/2 Main Avenue, Durango, CO 81301; 970-247-2888; Fax: 970-247-2774
Ken Rait, Policy Director
Jen Schmidt, Field Director
Doug Scott, Policy Director
Susan Whitmore, Communications Director
Jonathan Greenberg, Internet Organizer

ANIMALS AGENDA
P.O. Box 25881
Baltimore, MD 21224 United States
Phone: 410-675-4566 Fax: 410-675-0066
E-mail: office@animalsagenda.org
Website: www.animalsagenda.org

Founded: N/A

Scope: International

Publication(s): The Animals' Agenda

Contact(s):
Kim Stallwood, Editor In Chief

ARENA CONSULTORES
ADMINISTRACION DE RECURSOS NATURALES, S.A. DE C.V.
ARENA ENVIRONMENTAL CONSULTANTS
Boulevard Costero # 263-5
Zona Centro
Ensenada, 22800 Mexico
Phone: 646-178-3319 Fax: 646-178-3319
E-mail: ecoarena@telnor.net

Founded: 1991
Membership: 1–100
Scope: Local, State, Regional, National
Description: Arena provides services pertaining to environmental assessment, environmental risk, restoration, air quality monitoring and environmental analysis.
Keyword(s): Air Quality/Atmosphere, Energy
Contact(s):
Varinka Aguilar, Coordinadora Tecnica; 646-178-3319; Fax: 646-178-3319; ecoarena@telnor.net

AUSTRALIAN MINERAL FOUNDATION
63 Conyngham St.
Glenside, S.A., 5065 Australia
Phone: 61883790444
E-mail: amf@amf.com.au
Website: www.amf.com.au/amf

Founded: N/A

Description: Produces "Australian Earth Sciences Information System (AESIS)", a bibliographic database covering Australian-generated published and unpublished documented material over the full range of the geo sciences. AESIS also covers materials published on continental Australia by non-Australian sources.

B

B.A.S.S. DIVISION OF ESPN PRODUCTIONS INC
5845 Carmichael Rd.
Montgomery, AL 36117 United States
Phone: 334-272-9530 Fax: 334-270-8549
E-mail: conservation@bassmaster.com
Website: www.bassmaster.com

Founded: 1968
Membership: 500,001–1,000,000
Scope: Local, State, National, International
Description: Organized to fight pollution, assist state and national conservation agencies in their efforts, and teach the young people of our country good conservation practices. Dedicated to the realistic conservation of our water resources.

Publication(s): Guns & Gear, Television Show: The Bassmasters, Fishing Tackle Retailer, B.A.S.S. Times, Bassmaster Magazine

Keyword(s): Executive/Legislative/Judicial Reform, Land Issues, Oceans/Coasts/Beaches, Pollution (general), Recreation/ Ecotourism, Reduce/Reuse/Recycle, Water Habitats & Quality, Wildlife & Species

Contact(s):
Bruce Shupp, National Conservation Director; ext. 422; bruce.shupp@bassmaster.com
Al Smith, National Federation Director; ext. 406; al.smith@bassmaster.com

BERLET FILMS AND VIDEOS
1646 West Kimmel Rd
Jackson, MI 49201 United States
Phone: 517-784-6969 Fax: 517-796-2646
E-mail: mark@berletfilms-video.com
Website: www.berletfilms-video.com

Founded: N/A

Scope: International

Description: Produces environmental/nature audio-video resources. Free catalogues upon request.

Contact(s):
Mark Snedeker, General Manager

BRAUER PRODUCTIONS
530 S. Union St
Traverse City, MI 49684 United States
Phone: 231-941-0850 Fax: 231-941-0947
E-mail: brauer@brauer.com
Website: www.brauer.com

Founded: 1978

Scope: National

Description: Full Service film and video production company serving Traverse City and clients throughout Michigan and the N.W. since 1978.

Contact(s):
Richard Brauer, President
Susan McQuaid, Contact

BUILDINGGREEN, INC.
122 Birge St.
Suite 30
Brattleboro, VT 055301 United States
Phone: 802-257-7300 Fax: 802-257-7304
E-mail: ebn@buildinggreen.com
Website: www.buildinggreen.com

Founded: 1992

Membership: 1,001–10,000

Scope: International

Description: Publisher of Environmental Building News, the leading newsletter on environmentally responsible design and construction.

Publication(s): Environmental Building News and Green Spec Directory

Keyword(s): Energy, Reduce/Reuse/Recycle, Sprawl/Urban Planning

Contact(s):
Dan Woodbury, Publisher

BULLFROG FILMS
Olney, PA 19547 United States
Phone: 800-543-3764 Fax: 610-370-1978
E-mail: video@bullfrogfilms.com
Website: www.bullfrogfilms.com

Founded: N/A

Description: Films and videos rented and sold worldwide to educational institutions. Most programs come with study guide, with suggested activities, research topics, debate subjects, and bibliographies. Free catalogues available.

Contact(s):
Sieglinde Abromaitis

BUSINESS PUBLISHERS, INC.
8737 Colesville Rd.
Suite 1100
Silver Spring, MD 20910 United States
Phone: 301-589-5103 Fax: 301-587-4530
E-mail: bpinews@bpinews.com
Website: www.bpinews.com

Founded: N/A

Contact(s):
Beth Early

C

C.A.R.E (CITIZENS AGAINST RACCOON EXTERMINATION)
5125 Paso Venado
Carmel, CA 93923 United States
Phone: 831-647-8400 Fax: 831-373-8531
Website: www.drpasten.com

Founded: N/A

Scope: Local

Description: The goal of C.A.R.E is to save the raccoons on the Central Coast.

Contact(s):
Mari Fuentes-Jones, Administrator

CHESAPEAKE FARMS
7319 Remington Dr.
Chestertown, MD 21620 United States
Phone: 410-778-8400 Fax: 410-778-8405

Founded: 1956

Membership: N/A

Scope: Local, State, Regional

Description: Operated by DuPont Crop Protection to demonstrate, research, and promote sustainable farming and wildlife management practices. Provides a forum for exploring agricultural issues and interactions between environmental and economic sustainability. Agricultural project conducted by coalition of Dupont, universities, government and private organizations. Wildlife research conducted through graduate fellows.

Keyword(s): Agriculture/Farming

Contact(s):
Mark Conner, Manager; 410-778-8402; Fax: 410-778-8405; mark.c.conner@usa.dupont.com

CJE ASSOCIATES
237 Gretna Green Ct.
Alexandria, VA 22304 United States
Phone: 703-823-0662 Fax: 703-823-5923
E-mail: eeiserer@netscape.net

Founded: N/A

Scope: National

Publication(s): Ecology USA

Contact(s):
Elaine Eiserer, Editor

CONGRESSIONAL GREEN SHEETS, INC.
ENVIRONMENT AND ENERGY WEEKLY BULLETIN
GREEN SHEETS EXPRESS
NEWSROOM
406 E St., SE
Washington, DC 20003 United States
Phone: 202-546-2220 Fax: 202-546-7490
E-mail: wb@greensheets.com
Website: www.greensheets.com

Founded: 1975
Membership: 1,001–10,000
Scope: Local, State, Regional, National, International
Description: Newsletter
Publication(s): Environment and Energy Weekly Bulletin, Newsroom, Green Sheets Express
Keyword(s): Agriculture/Farming, Air Quality/Atmosphere, Climate Change, Development/Developing Countries, Ecosystems (precious), Energy, Ethics/Environmental Justice, Executive/Legislative/Judicial Reform, Finance/Banking/Trade, Forests/Forestry, Land Issues, Oceans
Contact(s):
John Dineen, Editor

CONNECTICUT CARIBOU CLAN

P.O. Box 9344
Bolton, CT 06043 United States
Phone: 860-643-2948
E-mail: captundra@aol.com
Website: hometown.aol.com/captundra/index.html

Founded: 1989
Scope: National
Description: Tundra Talk Newsletter focuses on energy, transportation, and the environment, with special emphasis on permanently preserving the Arctic Refuge.
Keyword(s): Ecosystems (precious), Energy, Transportation, Wildlife & Species
Contact(s):
Rodney Parlee, Editor/Publisher

CROWNPOINT INSTITUTE OF TECHNOLOGY

NATURAL RESOURCE DEPARTMENT
P.O. Box 849
Crownpoint, NM 87313 United States
Phone: 505-786-4100
E-mail: mattie@cit.cc.nm.us
Website: www.cit.cc.nm.us

Founded: N/A

CUTTER INFORMATION CORPORATION

37 Broadway
Arlington, MA 02474 United States
Phone: 781-641-9876
E-mail: cdoucette@cutter.com
Website: www.cutter.com

Founded: N/A
Membership: 1–100
Scope: International
Publication(s): Business & The Environment ISO 140 update, Air Quality Global Environmental Change Report, Environmental Design Update
Contact(s):
Christine Doucette

E

EAGLES 4 KIDS

258 Baker Street
Berea, OH 44017 United States
Phone: 440-239-0903
E-mail: dylags@aol.com
Website: www.eagles4kids.com

Founded: 2001
Membership: N/A
Scope: Local, State, National
Description: Educational materials and merchandise based on our mascot, Elmer the Eagle. Elmer travels the U.S. educating elementary students about Bald Eagles.
Keyword(s): Reduce/Reuse/Recycle, Wildlife & Species

EARTH SCHOOL

P.O. Box 337
Tuckasegee, NC 28783 United States
Phone: 828-293-5569 Fax: 828-293-0849
E-mail: richard@lovetheearth.com
Website: www.lovetheearth.com/

Founded: N/A
Membership: N/A
Scope: Local, State, Regional
Description: Earth School promotes nature awareness & self reliance through a dedication to reconnecting people to the natural world. Programs are available for all ages.

ENDANGERED SPECIES AND WETLANDS REPORT

P.O. Box 5393
Takoma Park, MD 20913 United States
Phone: 12 Fax: 301-891-3507
E-mail: poplar@crosslink.net
Website: www.eswr.com

Founded: 1995
Scope: National
Description: Independent monthly publication covering the ESA, wetlands and “takings” issues.

ENVIRONMENT AND ENERGY PUBLISHING, LLC

122 C St., NW
Washington, DC 20001 United States
Phone: 202-628-6500 Fax: 202-737-5299
E-mail: pubs@eenews.net
Website: www.eenews.net

Founded: N/A
Membership: 1–100
Scope: International
Publication(s): Land Letter (The Newsletter for Natural Resource Professionals), Greenwire and Environmental and Energy Daily.
Contact(s):
Drew Gagliano, Marketing Director
Kevin Braun, Managing Editor

ENVIRONMENTAL CAREER CENTER

100 Bridge Street
Building C
Hampton, VA 23669 United States
Phone: 757-727-7895 Fax: 757-727-7904
E-mail: eccinfo@environmentalcareer.com
Website: www.environmentalcareer.com

Founded: 1980
Membership: 1,001–10,000
Scope: National, International
Description: Helping people work for the environment since 1980 through: paid environmental internships, National Environmental Employment Report - monthly newspaper, EnvironmentalCAREER.com jobs and resume database, careers research, and career seminars/conferences.
Contact(s):
John Esson, President And Executive Director

ENVIRONMENTAL MEDIA CORPORATION

1008 Paris Ave.
Port Royal, SC 29935-2418 United States
Phone: 843-986-9034, ext. 10 Fax: 843-986-9093
E-mail: envmedia@hargray.com
Website: www.envmedia.com

Founded: 1989
Scope: International
Description: Environmental Media designs, produces, and distributes media to support environmental education.

Programs are curriculum-based and most are accompanied by teaching guides. Free catalogue available and other educational material.

Publication(s): See publications on website

Keyword(s): Ecosystems (precious), Oceans/Coasts/Beaches, Pollution (general), Reduce/Reuse/Recycle, Water Habitats & Quality, Wildlife & Species

Contact(s):
Eileen Newton, Reseller Manager
Bill Pendergraft, Owner

G

GECKO PRODUCTIONS, INC.

Attn: Director Nathalie Ward P.O. Box 573
Woods Hole, MA 02543 United States
Phone: 508-548-3317 Fax: 508-548-3317
E-mail: nward@mbl.edu

Founded: 1995

Description: Designs conservation education materials and workshops about marine endangered species and marine protected areas, with emphasis on bringing environmental awareness and cultural understanding to the Caribbean, United States and beyond.

Contact(s):
Nathalie Ward, Director

GRANT TECH CONSULTING AND CONSERVATION SERVICES

9564 Cheyenne Rd.
Meriden, KS 66512 United States
Phone: 785-876-0106 Fax: 785-876-0106
E-mail: kellyhiesberger@hotmail.com
Website: www.granttechconsulting.com

Founded: 1999

Scope: Local, State, Regional, National

Description: At Grant Tech Consulting and Conservation Services our goal is to bring nature and people together one habitat project at a time. We offer a broad range of services to private land owners, schools, community organizations, and non-profit organizations. We offer funding proposal development, trail design and construction services, design for outdoor education and recreation sites, interpretive nature programs, wetland development, teacher in-service training programs, and much more.

Keyword(s): Agriculture/Farming, Ecosystems (precious), Land Issues, Public Lands/Greenspace, Recreation/Ecotourism, Water Habitats & Quality, Wildlife & Species

GREEN MOUNTAIN POST FILMS

Turners Falls, MA 01376 United States
Phone: 413-863-4754 Fax: 413-863-8248
Website: www.gmpfilms.com

Founded: 1975

Membership: 1–100

Scope: International

Description: A film/video production and distribution company that specializes in media concerning environmental issues.

Contact(s):
Charles Light, Business Manager

GREENWIRE

ENVIRONMENT AND ENERGY PUBLISHING, LLC
122 C St., NW Suite 722
Washington, DC 20001 United States
Phone: 202-628-6500 Fax: 202-737-5299
E-mail: pubs@eenews.net
Website: www.eenews.net

Founded: N/A

Description: An online daily publication providing comprehensive coverage of environmental, energy and natural resources issues, politics, developments and policy action. Greenwire tracks and reports on the White House, federal agencies, states, court decisions and the stories being reported on by the media nationwide.

Publication(s): The Environment and Energy Daily, Greenwire, and Land Letter

Contact(s):
Drew Gagliano, Marketing Director

I

ILOVEPARKS.COM

913 Totonaca Lane
El Paso, TX 79912 United States
Phone: 915-587-6641
E-mail: info@iloveparks.com
Website: iloveparks.com

Founded: 2000

Membership: 101–1,000

Scope: International

Description: ILoveParks.com is helping people connect with parks around the world through information provision and education for a variety of related issues.

Keyword(s): Development/Developing Countries, Ecosystems (precious), Ethics/Environmental Justice, Executive/Legislative/Judicial Reform, Forests/Forestry, Land Issues, Oceans/Coasts/Beaches, Pollution (general), Population, Public Lands/Green–space, Recreation/Ecotourism

INSTITUTE FOR GLOBAL COMMUNICATIONS

P.O. Box 29904
San Francisco, CA 94129-0904 United States
Phone: 12 Fax: 415-561-6101
E-mail: econet@igc.apc.org
Website: www.igc.org

Founded: 1984

Scope: International

Description: Creates and manages “EcoNet”. Through the development of communication and information sharing systems, EcoNet seeks to increase collaboration and cooperation between organizations seeking environmental sustainability.

Contact(s):
Debra Farrell, Executive Director

INTERNATIONAL ACADEMY

ENVIRONMENTAL
Santa Barbara, CA 93140 United States
Phone: 12 Fax: 805-564-4634
E-mail: info@iasb.org
Website: www.iasb.org

Founded: N/A

Scope: International

Description: Produces “Environmental Bibliography”, bibliographic database covering more than 400 scientific and popular journals in social, political and philosophical issues, air, energy, land and water resources, nutrition and health. Author Abstracts, 1997 forward.

Publication(s): CD Rom Issued Quarterly Online, Environmental Knowledge Base By Subscription.

Contact(s):
Joann St. John, President
Steven Popps, Director of Sales and Customer Service
Eric Boehm, Chairman
Lauren Everett, Editor
Amy Rushing, Editor

INTERNATIONAL RESEARCH AND EVALUATION

21098 IRE Control Center
Eagan, MN 55121 United States
Phone: Fax: 952-888-9124

Founded: N/A

Description: Environmental library for the application of knowledge, methods and means.

Publication(s): Waste Management Information Database, World Environment Report, World Environment Directory

Contact(s):
R. Danford

J

JAGRATA JUBA SHANGHA (JJS)

96 South Central Rd.
Khulna, 9100 Bangladesh
Phone: 88041731013 Fax: 88041730146
E-mail: jjs@khulnanet.net

Founded: 1985

Description: JJS is working with the people living around the Sundarban (world's largest Mangroves) in Bangladesh for conservation of the resources of the Sundarban environment.

Publication(s): JJS News, Posters on Sundarbans, Jagrata Barta

Contact(s):
Atm Hossain, Executive Director; zakir@khulnanet.net
Khadiza Khatun, Manager Administration
Mesbahul Mokarebin, Manager Education
Saifuddin Ahmed, Finance Officer
Kaniz Fatima, Hopla
Khaza Mohiuddin, Head of Program

JERE MOSSIER PRODUCTIONS/ UNDERWATER IMAGES

P.O. Box 1415
Hayden, ID 83835 United States
Phone: 208-683-8112
Website: www.jeremossier.com

Founded: N/A

Scope: International

Description: Licensing of underwater and wildlife stock footage and professional video production of fisheries, underwater programs, wildlife, and natural history videos.

Publication(s): Videos, Underwater Exploration

Contact(s):
Jere Mossier

JONES AND STOKES

2600 V Street
Sacramento, CA 95818 United States
Phone: 916-737-3000 Fax: 916-737-3030
Website: www.jonesandstokes.com

Founded: 1970

Scope: Local, State, Regional, National

Description: Jones and Stokes provide their clients with scientifically accurate, innovative, and practical solutions to their environmental challenges. Their reputation for providing clients with incomparable quality and the broadest diversity of expertise in the industry is unsurpassed. Their unique teams of knowledgeable, experienced professionals embrace a multidisciplinary, problem-solving philosophy and approach that benefits both their clients and the environment.

Contact(s):
John Cowdery, President; 916-737-3000; Fax: 916-737-3030
Michael Stuhr, VP Business Development; 916-737-3000; Fax: 916-737-3030
Julie Jessen; julieb@jsanet.com

L

LAST WIZARDS, THE

3400 W. 111th St. #154
Chicago, IL 60655 United States
Phone: 708-507-4306 Fax: 708-974-4356
E-mail: info@lastwizards.com
Website: www.lastwizards.com/

Founded: 2002

Membership: N/A

Scope: Local, State, Regional, National, International

Description: When visiting The Last Wizards website you will find essays and discussions on the tools, techniques and forces that shift and alter perceptions in our world. The Last Wizards are concerned with philosophy, environmental politics, postmodernism, mass media, scholarly occult theory, culture and the legacies and prophecies of world war, globalization, and technology.

Publication(s): Book of Green Shadows

Keyword(s): Agriculture/Farming, Ecosystems (precious), Finance/Banking/Trade, Forests/Forestry, Pollution (general), Public Health, Wildlife & Species

Contact(s):
James Bell, Editor; 708-507-4306; james@lastwizards.com

LEXIS/NEXIS ACADEMIC AND LIBRARY SOLUTIONS

4520 East-West Hwy., Suite 800
Bethesda, MD 20814-3389 United States
Phone: 301-654-1550 Fax: 301-657-3203
E-mail: academicinfo@lexis-nexis.com
Website: www.lexisnexis.com/academic

Founded: N/A

Scope: International

Description: Publishes indexes, electronic databases and microform collections that provide access to information published by government, private and international sources.

Publication(s): Enviroline, Environment Abstracts

Contact(s):
Henry Stoever, Marketing Director
Marcy Taylor, Contact

LUMMI ISLAND HERITAGE TRUST

P.O. Box 158
Lummi Island, WA 98262-0158 United States
Phone: 360-758-7997 Fax: 360-758-7001
E-mail: heritagetrust@nas.com
Website: www.nas.com/heritagetrust

Founded: N/A

Scope: National

Contact(s):
Dave Kershner

N

NATIONAL GROUND WATER INFORMATION CENTER

601 Dempsey Rd.
Westerville, OH 43081 United States
Phone: 12 Fax: 614-898-7786
E-mail: smaste@ngwa.org
Website: www.ngwa.org

Founded: N/A

Description: Produces "Ground Water Network", a fee-based information service conducting literature searches and document delivery. Maintains six databases with over 82,000 abstracts related to ground water, water treatability, NGWA

Certified Ground Water Contractors and U.S. Census on housing and water source information.

Contact(s):
Sandy Masters, Director of the Information Center

NEAL COMMUNICATIONS

1220 Bald Eagle Rd.
Kingston Springs, TN 37082 United States
Phone: 615-952-5323 Fax: 615-952-4522
E-mail: cindy@nealcommunications.com

Founded: N/A
Membership: 1–100
Scope: International
Description: Produce outreach videos and communications consulting services supporting sustainable ecosystems and development, conservation of natural resources, wildlife, and cultural integrity. Specialists in translating complex issues into compelling, motivating communications.

NISC (NATIONAL INFORMATION SERVICES CORPORATION)

3100 St. Paul St.
Suite 806
Baltimore, MD 21218 United States
Phone: 410-243-0797 Fax: 410-243-0982
E-mail: sales@nisc.com
Website: www.nisc.com

Founded: N/A
Scope: Local, State, Regional, National, International
Description: National Information Services Corporation (NISC) publishes information products for access through BiblioLine, our Web search service, or on CD-ROM. NISC's bibliographic and full-text databases cover a wide range of topics in the natural sciences.
Keyword(s): Agriculture/Farming, Oceans/Coasts/Beaches, Public Health, Water Habitats & Quality, Wildlife & Species
Contact(s):
Debbie Durr, Sales & Marketing Manager

NOLTE ASSOCIATES, INC.

15090 Avenue of Science, Suite 101
San Diego, CA 92128 United States
Phone: 858-385-0500 Fax: 9858-385-0400
E-mail: info@nolte.com
Website: www.nolte.com

Founded: 1949
Membership: N/A
Scope: Local, State, Regional
Description: The value of a practice that spans more than a half century is a legacy of experience and knowledge. Nolte is a full-service civil engineering firm with the expertise to successfully complete a wide variety of projects. We are committed to using sustainable development practices whenever possible to reduce potable water consumption, protect storm water quality, create environmentally responsible land use patterns, preserve habitat, provide livable communities, and control development costs.
Keyword(s): Agriculture/Farming, Development/Developing Countries, Ecosystems (precious), Energy, Land Issues, Reduce/Reuse/Recycle, Transportation, Water Habitats & Quality

P

PARQUE NACIONAL SIERRA NEVADA

MUCUBAJF NATURE CENTER
Apartado Postal 63011
Chacaito Caracas, 1067-A Venezuela
Phone: 58-416-607-4585
E-mail: carivero@telcel.net.ve

Founded: 1994
Membership: N/A
Scope: Local, State, Regional, National, International
Description: A Nature Center in the high Venezuelan Andes, at 11.444 feet elevation. The exhibits feature the Paramo ecosystem, and its inhabitants, the Sierra Nevada National Park and the Venezuelan Park System. Carlos Rivero-Blanco Ph.D., and Machela Rivero designed the exhibits and hold the concession since 1994. The Nature Center is visited yearly by several thousand people. It serves students from the vicinity and tourists from abroad.
Keyword(s): Ecosystems (precious), Land Issues, Recreation/Ecotourism, Wildlife & Species
Contact(s):
Carlos Rivero-Blanco, Director
Machela Rivero, Directora
Carlos Rivero-Fuentes, Asistente

POINT TO POINT COMMUNICATIONS

39576 John Wolford Rd.
Waterford, VA 20197 United States
Phone: 540-882-9090 Fax: 540-882-9006
E-mail: skenyon@erols.com
Website: www.pt2ptcom.com

Founded: 1997
Scope: Local, State, Regional, National
Description: Point to Point Communications specializes in helping the conservation community communicate. We are a full service public relations firm dedicated to conservation issues.

PROPERTY CARETAKING OPPORTUNITIES WORLDWIDE

P.O. Box 540
River Falls, WI 54022 United States
Phone: 715-426-5500
E-mail: caretaker@caretaker.org
Website: www.caretaker.org

Founded: 1983
Membership: 10,001–100,000
Scope: International
Description: Helping landowners and property caretakers find one another since 1983
Publication(s): The Caretaker bi-monthly newsletter
Keyword(s): Agriculture/Farming, Land Issues, Public Lands/Greenspace, Recreation/Ecotourism
Contact(s):
Gary Dunn, Owner; 715-426-5500; caretaker@caretaker.org

PUBLIC LANDS INTERPRETIVE ASSOCIATION

SOUTHWEST NATURAL AND CULTURAL HERITAGE ASSN.
6501 Fourth NW Suite I
Albuquerque, NM 87107 United States
Phone: 505-345-9498 Fax: 505-344-1543
Website: www.publiclandsinfo.org

Founded: 1981
Scope: Regional
Description: Educational and interpretive not for profit operating bookstores in federal visitor centers as well as publisher of local interpretive booklets.
Publication(s): Wild & Scenic Rio Grande, Merrit Island National Wildlife Refuge, Pecos Wilderness Trail Guide, Bosque Del Apache Nation
Contact(s):
Lisa Madsen, CEO
Ted Peay, President
Stephen Maurer, Director of Publications

S

SHARING NATURE FOUNDATION

14618 Tyler Foote Road
Nevada City, CA 95959 United States
Phone: 530-478-7650 Fax: 530-478-7562
E-mail: joseph@sharingnature.com
Website: www.sharingnature.com

Founded: 1979
Membership: 1,001–10,000
Scope: International
Description: Established in 1979 by naturalist and author, Joseph Cornell, the Sharing Nature Foundation uses creative nature activities to give people joyful experiences of nature. We believe it's only by uplifting people's consciousness that we change their way of looking at, and relating to the world around them. To do this we use Flow Learning™, a playful and inspirational teaching strategy that works with people where they are and gently brings them to a deeper, more profound experience of nature.
Publication(s): Journey to the Heart of Nature, With Beauty Before Me, John Muir: My Life with Nature, Listening to Nature, Sharing Nature with Children I & II

SPORTSMANS NETWORK, INC., THE

501 S. Kentucky Ave
Corbin, KY 40702 United States
Phone: Fax: 606-528-2287
E-mail: sportsmen@sportsmansnetwork.org
Website: www.sportsmansnetwork.org

Founded: 1991
Scope: State
Description: The Sportsman's Network is an incorporated statewide nonprofit conservation organization dedicated to educating the public and raising awareness of wildlife conservation through programs which promote controlled hunting, fishing, and other related activities. Also produces "A Moment in Conservation" radio program.
Keyword(s): Land Issues, Public Lands/Greenspace, Recreation/Ecotourism, Water Habitats & Quality, Wildlife & Species
Contact(s):
Keith Fullwood, Vice President
Elmer Chavies, Jr., Regional Director
Ernie Samples, Executive Director
Paul Cookendorfer, Secretary
Ken Hale, Treasurer
Peter Samples, State Chairman

T

TURNER ENDANGERED SPECIES FUND

1123 Research Dr.
Bozeman, MT 59718 United States
Phone: 406-556-8500 Fax: 406-556-8501
E-mail: tesf@montana.net
Website: www.tesf.org

Founded: N/A
Contact(s):
Kyran Kunkel

U

UNASOLATIERRA.COM

AREAS NATURALES PROTEGIDAS DE VENEZUELA Y EL MUNDO
NATURAL PROTECTED AREAS OF VENEZUELA AND THE WORLD
Apartado 63011
Chacaito
Caracas, 1067-A Venezuela
Phone: 58-416-607-4585
E-mail: carivero@telcel.net.ve
Website: venezuelatuya.com/natura

Founded: 2001
Membership: N/A
Scope: Local, State, Regional, National, International
Description: Research and publication of information on natural protected areas in Venezuela and the rest of the World. Will soon be aired as a very colorful and informative web site.
Keyword(s): Development/Developing Countries, Ecosystems (precious), Land Issues, Recreation/Ecotourism, Wildlife & Species
Contact(s):
Carlos Rivero-Blanco, Director; 58-416-607-4585; carivero@telcel.net.ve

V

VIDEO PROJECT, THE

P.O. Box 77188
San Francisco, CA 94107 United States
Phone: 800-475-2638
E-mail: video@videoproject.net
Website: www.videoproject.net/

Founded: N/A
Description: Media for a safe and sustainable world. Affordable films and videos on environmental and related issues. The project now offers over 600 programs for sale.

W

WALKABOUT PRODUCTIONS, INC.

45 Old Solomons Island Rd.
Suite 201
Annapolis, MD 21401 United States
Phone: 410-573-1228 Fax: 410-573-9521
E-mail: info@walkaboutinc.com
Website: www.walkaboutinc.com

Founded: 1980
Membership: N/A
Scope: International
Description: Walkabout Productions, Inc., is an EMMY award winning production team that focuses on environment, wildlife, and science documentaries. Filmography is available.
Contact(s):
Allison Nichols, Producer

WELLSPRING INTERNATIONAL, INC.

830 Bear Tavern Rd
Suite 301
Ewing, NJ 08628 United States
Phone: 609-530-1990 Fax: 609-530-1991
E-mail: mschoen@wellspringwireless.com
Website: www.wellspringwireless.com

Founded: 1995

Scope: Local, State, Regional, National, International

Description: Wellspring is a water conservation and sub-metering company with offices nationwide. Water sub-metering (metering individual apartment units) promotes conservation by giving tenants direct control over their water bills; wasted water (e.g. long showers and leaky toilets) is money down the drain. As a result of this connection between tap and wallet, sub-meterd communities generally see a 20% reduction in water usage.

Keyword(s): Energy, Reduce/Reuse/Recycle, Water Habitats & Quality

Contact(s):

Michael Schoen, Environmental Affairs; 609-530-1990; Fax: 609-530-1991; mschoen@wellspringwireless.com

WYOMING NATURAL DIVERSITY DATABASE

P.O. Box 3381
Laramie, WY 82071-3381 United States
Phone: 307-766-3023 Fax: 307-766-3026
E-mail: wndd@uwyo.edu
Website: www.uwyo.edu/wyndd

Founded: N/A
Membership: 1–100
Scope: Regional

Contact(s):

Gary Beauvais

A

ACADIA UNIVERSITY

24 University Ave., Patterson Hall
Wolfville, B0P 1X0 Nova Scotia Canada
Phone: 902-542-2201 Fax: 902-585-1059
E-mail: biology@acadiau.ca
Website: www.acadiau.ca

Founded: 1838
Membership: 1–100
Scope: National, International
Description: Primarily an undergraduate university, emphasizing a liberal education in a balanced blend of arts, science, and professional studies. Masters degrees are offered in biology, chemistry, computer science, education, English, geology, political science, physiology, and sociology.
Publication(s): See publication web site
Contact(s):
Tom Herman, Head of Biology Department; 902-585-1469; tom.herman@acadiau.ca
Glyn Bissex, Recreation Management; glyn.bissex@acadiau.ca
Soren Bondrup-Nielsen, Wildlife, Fisheries, Aquatic Biology, Marine Ecology, Mammal; 902-585-1424; Fax: 902-585-1059; soren.bondrup-nielsen@acadiau.ca
Robert Raeside, Environmental Geology; 902-585-1323; robert.raeside@acadiau.ca
Don Stewart, Assistant Professor, Biology Department; 902-585-1391; Fax: 902-585-1059; don.stewart@acadiau.ca
David Stiles, Environmental Chemistry; 902-585-1325; Fax: 902-585-1114; david.stiles@acadiau.ca

ALFRED UNIVERSITY

DIVISION OF ENVIRONMENTAL STUDIES
Saxon Dr.
Alfred, NY 14802-1205 United States
Phone: 607-871-2634 Fax: 607-871-2697
E-mail: ens@alfred.edu
Website: www.alfred.edu

Founded: 1971
Scope: State
Description: The program offers an undergraduate degree in multidisciplinary environmental studies in a liberal arts setting. Students can focus on either natural or social sciences, and many take a second major in biology, geology, political science, economics, etc. The project-oriented program is supervised by fifteen faculty members from different disciplines.
Contact(s):
Michele Hluchy, Chair of Division Ens and Professor of Geology and Environme; 507-871-2634; ens@alfred.edu
Diana Sinton, Assistant Professor of Geography and Environmental Studies; ens@alfred.edu

ANTIOCH COLLEGE

795 Livermore St
Yellow Springs, OH 45387 United States
Phone: 937-767-7331 Fax: 937-767-7331
E-mail: admissions@anitoch-college.edu
Website: www.antioch-college.edu/

Founded: N/A
Membership: 101–1,000
Scope: National
Publication(s): Colleges that Changes Lives
Contact(s):
Charles Taylor, Physics and Solar Energy/Alternative Technology; ext. 5355; ctaylor@antioch-college.edu
Peter Townsend, Geology; ext. 6879; ptownsend@antioch-college.edu
Jill Yager, Biology; ext. 6878; jyager@antioch-college.edu

ANTIOCH NEW ENGLAND GRADUATE SCHOOL

40 Avon St.
Keene, NH 03431-3552 United States
Phone: 603-357-6265 Fax: 603-357-0718
E-mail: admissions@antiochne.edu
Website: www.antiochne.edu

Founded: 1964
Scope: Local, State, Regional, National
Description: Currently offers graduate programs in education, management, psychology, and environmental studies which are practitioner oriented and designed primarily for the professional advancement of the adult learner. It is dedicated to continual self examination and change. Also committed to diversity, our aim is to use creatively the tension between our diversity and our independence so as to enrich our vision of what is human.

ANTIOCH NEW ENGLAND GRADUATE SCHOOL, ENVIRONMENTAL STUDIES

40 Avon St.
Keene, NH 03431-3552 United States
Phone: 603-357-3122 Fax: 603-357-0718
E-mail: admissions@antiochne.edu
Website: www.antiochne.edu

Founded: 1964
Scope: Local, State, Regional, National
Description: Antioch New England Graduate School offers professional training for effective, reflective, environmental leadership. The M.S. Degree in Environmental Studies is a field-oriented program that stresses professional preparation in environmental biology, teaching, communication, administration, policy, and environmental education. Biology and general science teacher certifications are available.

ANTIOCH UNIVERSITY SEATTLE

ENVIRONMENT AND COMMUNITY PROGRAM
2326 Sixth Avenue
Seattle, WA 98121-1814 United States
Phone: 206-441-5352 Fax: 206-441-3307
E-mail: jjoichi@antiochsea.edu
Website: www.antiochsea.edu/ec

Founded: 1852
Scope: Local, State, Regional, National, International
Description: The E&C program approaches environmental challenges via social science perspectives and natural science literacy for professionals in environmental or community development fields. Students gain a clear understanding of the social, economic, political, and institutional dimensions of environmental issues. The program publishes "Sense of Place", the Environment and Community Newsletter.
Contact(s):
Jean Joichi, Admission Associate; 206-268-4208; jjoichi@antiochsea.edu
Jonathan Scherch, Program Chair; 206-268-4710; scherch@antiochsea.edu

APPALACHIAN STATE UNIVERSITY

426 Sanford Hall
Boone, NC 28608 United States
Phone: 828-262-2000 Fax: 828-262-6472
Website: www.appstate.edu

Founded: N/A
Membership: 1,001–10,000
Scope: State
Contact(s):
Jeff Boyer, Sustainable Development Minor, Director; 426 Sanford Hall, Boone, NC 28608; boyerjc@appstate.edu
Kim Siegenthaler, Recreation Management Program, Director; 828-262-2540; siiegenthalkl@appstate.edu
Francis Borkowski, Chancellor

ARIZONA STATE UNIVERSITY
CENTER FOR ENVIRONMENTAL STUDIES
Box 873211, Arizona State University
Tempe, AZ 85287-3211 United States
Phone: 480-965-2975 Fax: 480-965-8087
Website: www.asu.edu/ces or http://caplter.asu.edu

Founded: N/A

Scope: State

Description: The Center is involved in the Central Arizona-Phoenix Long Term Ecological Research (CAP LTER) project at Arizona State University, funded by the NSF and is one of the first urban sites in the LTER network. CAP LTER provides a unique addition to LTER research by focusing upon an arid-land ecosystem profoundly influenced, even defined by the presence and activities of humans.

Keyword(s): Air Quality/Atmosphere, Climate Change, Pollution (general), Population, Public Lands/Greenspace, Sprawl/Urban Planning, Transportation, Water Habitats & Quality, Wildlife & Species

Contact(s):
Nancy Grimm, Co-Project Director
Charles Redman, Co-Project Director
Shirley Stapleton, Administrative Assistant to the Director; 965-2975; Fax: 965-8087; shirley.stapleton@asu.edu

ARKANSAS STATE UNIVERSITY
DEPARTMENT OF BIOLOGICAL SCIENCE
P. O. Box 1030
State University, AR 72467 United States
Phone: 870-972-3082 Fax: 870-972-2638
Website: www.csm.astate.edu/~biology/biology.html

Founded: N/A

Scope: State

Contact(s):
Jerry Farris, Director of Environmental Sciences Program; 870-972-2007; Fax: 870-972-2638; envirsci@navajo.astate.edu

ARKANSAS TECH UNIVERSITY
DEPARTMENT OF PARKS, RECREATION, AND HOSPITALITY ADMINISTRATION
1205 North El Paso Avenue
Russellville, AR 72801 United States
Phone: 479-968-0852 Fax: 479-968-0600
E-mail: theresa.herrick@mail.atu.edu

Founded: 1909

Scope: State

Description: Recreation and Park Adminstration offers five areas of emphasis: Recreation Administration, Therapeutic Recreation, Park Administration, Turf Management and Interpretive Naturalist

Contact(s):
Theresa Herrick, Recreation and Park Administration, Director; Williamson Hall, Room 100, Russellville, AR 72081; 501-968-0378; theresa.herrick@mail.atu.edu
Joseph Stoeckel, Fisheries and Wildlife Biology, Director; 501-964-0852; joe.stoeckel@mail.atu.edu
Charlie Gagen, Head of Biological Sciences; 501-964-0814; charlie.gagen@mail.atu.edu

ARKANSAS TECH UNIVERSITY
FISHERIES AND WILDLIFE BIOLOGY PROGRAM
McEver Science Building
1701 North Boulder Avenue
Russellville, AR 72801 United States
Phone: 479-964-0852 Fax: 479-960-0837
E-mail: joe.stoeckel@mail.atu.edu
Website: pls.atu.edu/biology/fw

Founded: 1964

Membership: N/A

Scope: State

Description: Tech offers B.S. and M.S. degrees in Fisheries and Wildlife Biology. Our location, in the Arkansas River Valley between the Ouachita and Ozark mountains, is ideally suited to this program, because it encompasses an exeptionally wide range of fish and wildlife habitats. A trademark of our program is a field-oriented approach that provides numerous opportunities for hands-on learning through field laboratories, research projects, and solid working relationships with natural resource agencies.

Keyword(s): Ecosystems (precious), Forests/Forestry, Public Lands/Greenspace, Water Habitats & Quality, Wildlife & Species

AUBURN UNIVERSITY
COLLEGE OF AGRICULTURE
DEPARTMENT OF FISHERIES AND ALLIED AQUACULTURES
Swingle Hall
Auburn University, AL 36849 United States
Phone: 334-844-4786 Fax: 334-844-9208
Website: www.ag.auburn.edu/dept/faa/

Founded: N/A

Membership: 101–1,000

Scope: State

Description: The department sponsors the Southeastern Cooperative Fish Disease Project, providing a fish-kill diagnostic service, training in fish diseases and research on fish diseases to the cooperating member states.

Publication(s): Publications on website

Contact(s):
B. Duncan, Director, International Center for Aquaculture and Aquatic E; bduncan@acesag.auburn.edu
John Grizzle, Associate Project Director
John Jensen, Department Head; jjensen@acesag.auburn.edu

AUBURN UNIVERSITY
COLLEGE OF SCIENCES AND MATHEMATICS
DEPARTMENT OF BIOLOGICAL SCIENCES
59 Duggar Dr., Extension Cottage
Auburn University, AL 36849 United States
Phone: 334-844-4830 Fax: 334-844-5748
Website: www.auburn.edu/cosam

Founded: N/A

Scope: State

Description: Newly formed from merger of Zoology and Botany departments.

Contact(s):
Alfred Brown, Department Co-Head; 101 Life Science Bldg., Dept. of Biological Sciences, Auburn University, AL 36849; 334-844-1661; Fax: 334-844-1645

AUBURN UNIVERSITY
SCHOOL OF FORESTRY AND WILDLIFE SCIENCES
108 M. White Smith Hall
Auburn University, AL 36849-5418 United States
Phone: 334-844-1007 Fax: 334-844-1084
Website: www.forestry.auburn.edu/

Founded: N/A

Membership: 1–100

Scope: International

Contact(s):
Richard Brinker, Dean

B

BALL STATE UNIVERSITY
DEPARTMENT OF NATURAL RESOURCES AND ENVIRONMENTAL MANAGEMENT
NREM Dept.
Muncie, IN 47306 United States
Phone: 765-285-5780 Fax: 765-285-2606
E-mail: nrem@bsu.edu
Website: www.bsu.edu/nrem

Founded: N/A
Membership: 1–100
Scope: State
Contact(s):
Hugh Brown, Dept. Chair; Soil Resources; 765-285-5788; hbrown@bsu.edu
Paul Chandler, International Resource Management; 765-285-5788; pchandle@bsu.edu
James Eflin, Energy Resources and Environmental Policy; 765-285-2327; jeflin1@bsu.edu
Thad Godish, Occupational/Industrial Hygiene; Air Quality; 765-285-5782; 00tjgodish@bsu.edu
Timothy Lyon, Natural Resource Studies; 765-285-5783; tlyon@bsu.edu
John Pichtel, Waste Management; 765-285-2182; jpichtel@bsu.edu
Amy Sheaffer, Environmental Communication; Park and Recreation Mgt.; 765-285-5781; asheaffer@bsu.edu
Fred Siewert, Water Resources; 765-285-5790; fsiewert@bsu.edu

BARD COLLEGE
DEBARD CENTER FOR ENVIRONMENTAL POLICY
P.O. Box 5000
Annandale-on-Hudson, NY 12504-5000 United States
Phone: 845-758-7071 Fax: 845-758-7636
E-mail: cep@bard.edu
Website: www.bard.edu/cep

Founded: N/A
Membership: 1–100
Scope: State
Description: Bard College offers an intensive graduate degree program leading to a Master of Science in Environmental Studies. Students develop an understanding of key ecological and natural concepts and the ability to become effective environmental professionals. Coursework is offered during the summer in two four-week sessions. Students can complete degree requirements, including course and thesis, in three summers. In the year 2001, Bard is launching a master's degree program during the academic year.
Publication(s): Open Forum Report
Contact(s):
Joanne Fox-Przeworski, Director
Marie Beichert, Assistant Director; 845-758-7071
Kris Feder, Associate Director

BEMIDJI STATE UNIVERSITY
CENTER FOR ENVIRONMENTAL, EARTH AND SPACE STUDIES
P.O. Box 27, 1500 Birchmont Dr., NE
Bemidji, MN 56601 United States
Phone: 218-755-2910 Fax: 218-755-4107
Website: www.bemidji.msus.edu/

Founded: 1968
Scope: International
Description: The Center for Environmental Studies is a research and teaching unit directed towards understanding our physical, biological, and social environment, and preventing its deterioration. The center conducts laboratory and field studies, both internally and externally funded, and offers baccalaureate and master's degree programs.
Contact(s):
Patrick Welle, Director

BOSTON UNIVERSITY
SCHOOL FOR FIELD STUDIES
16 Broadway
Beverly, MA 01915-4499 United States
Phone: 800-989-4453 Fax: 978-927-5127
E-mail: admissions@fieldstudies.org
Website: www.fieldstudies.org

Founded: 1980
Description: The mission of The School for Field Studies is to provide highly motivated young people from the U.S. and abroad with an excellent practical education in environmental studies, in order that tomorrow's leaders may become more environmentally literate/aware as well as make immediate and future contributions toward the sustainable management of natural resources.
Contact(s):
Terry Andreas, President

BOWLING GREEN STATE UNIVERSITY
Center for Environmental Programs
153 College Park Office Building
Bowling Green, OH 43403 United States
Phone: 419-372-8207 Fax: 419-372-7243
E-mail: envs@bgnet.bgsu.edu
Website: www.bgsu.edu/department/envp

Founded: 1969
Membership: 101–1,000
Scope: State
Description: Offer undergraduate environmental degree programs in Environmental Policy and Analysis and Environmental Science through the College of Arts & Sciences and a degree in Environmental Health through the College of Health and Human Services.
Publication(s): Curriculum Resource Room for P-12 educators specializing in Early Childhood environmental education
Contact(s):
Holly Myers-Jones, Director

BRADLEY UNIVERSITY
ENVIRONMENTAL SCIENCE PROGRAM
1501 W. Bradley Ave.
Peoria, IL 61625 United States
Phone: 309-677-3020 Fax: 309-677-3558
Website: www.bradley.edu/academics/las/bio/

Founded: N/A
Membership: 1–100
Scope: Local, State, Regional, National, International
Description: Environmental Science program at Bradley University.
Contact(s):
Janet Gehring, Plant Biology; 309-677-3017; jgehring@bradley.edu
Kelly McConnaughay, Plant Ecology; 309-677-3018; kdm@bradley.edu

BROWN UNIVERSITY
CENTER FOR ENVIRONMENTAL STUDIES
Box 1943
Providence, RI 02912 United States
Phone: 401-863-3449 Fax: 401-863-3503
E-mail: envstu@brown.edu
Website: envstudies.brown.edu/Dept/

Founded: 1978
Membership: 1–100
Scope: Local, State, Regional, National, International
Description: The Center for Environmental Studies offers three interdisciplinary degrees (A.B., Sc.B., and M.A.) in environmental problem-solving; coordinates and facilitates environ-

mental efforts within the university community; and collaborates with both state government agencies and community-based groups on projects to improve environmental quality for all Rhode Island residents. All programs aim to integrate teaching, scholarship, and service.

Keyword(s): Air Quality/Atmosphere, Climate Change, Ethics/Environmental Justice, Forests/Forestry, Land Issues, Oceans/Coasts/Beaches, Public Health, Reduce/Reuse/Recycle, Sprawl/Urban Planning, Water Habitats & Quality

Contact(s):
Harold Ward, Director; harold_ward@brown.edu
Patti Caton, Administrative Manager; patti_caton@brown.edu
Kurt Teichert, Environmental Coordinator; Kurt_Teichert@brown.edu

C

CALIFORNIA POLYTECHNIC STATE UNIVERSITY
COLLEGE OF ARCHITECTURE AND ENVIRONMENTAL DESIGN
One Grand Ave.
San Luis Obispo, CA 93407 United States
Phone: 805-756-1321 Fax: 805-756-5986
E-mail: caed@polymail.calpoly.edu
Website: www.calpoly.edu/~caed/

Founded: N/A
Scope: State
Publication(s): Publications on website
Contact(s):
Walter Bremer, Department Head, Landscape Architecture; wbremer@calpoly.edu
William Siembieda, Department Head, City and Regional Planning; 805-756-1315; wsiembie@calpoly.edu

CALIFORNIA STATE UNIVERSITY AT CHICO
DEPARTMENT OF RECREATION AND PARKS MANAGEMENT
Dept. of Recreation and Parks Management
Chico, CA 95929-0560 United States
Phone: 530-898-6408 Fax: 530-898-6557
E-mail: recr@csuchico.edu
Website: www.csuchico.edu/recr

Founded: N/A
Membership: 1–100
Scope: National
Description: Areas of study include environmental education and interpretation, recreation and natural resource management, parks maintenance and operations, and planning and design.
Contact(s):
Jon Hooper, Coordinator, Parks and Natural Resources Management Option; 530-898-5811
Emilyn Sheffield, Department Chair; 530-898-4855; esheffield@csuchico.edu

CALIFORNIA STATE UNIVERSITY AT FULLERTON
SCHOOL OF HUMANITIES AND SOCIAL SCIENCES ENVIRONMENTAL STUDIES PROGRAM
Humanities H-420A
Fullerton, CA 92834 United States
Phone: 714-278-4373
E-mail: mhogarth@fullerton.edu
Website: hss.fullerton.edu/envstud/index.html

Founded: 1970
Scope: State
Description: Interdisciplinary graduate program leading to master's degree in environmental sciences, environmental policy and planning, or environmental education and communication.
Contact(s):
Robert Voeks, Program Director; 714-278-3361

CALIFORNIA STATE UNIVERSITY AT SACRAMENTO
ENVIRONMENTAL STUDIES DEPARTMENT
6000 J St.
Sacramento, CA 95819 United States
Phone: 916-278-6620 Fax: 916-278-7582
E-mail: infodesk@csus.edu
Website: www.csus.edu\index.stm

Founded: N/A
Membership: 1–100
Scope: State
Description: Biology department offers a concentration in Biological Conservation. Interdisciplinary Environmental Studies program offers a B.A. Recreation and Leisure Studies program offers a B.S. or B.A. in Park and Recreation Resource Management.
Contact(s):
Cary Goulard, Graduate Coordinator, Recreation and Leisure Studies; goulardc@hhsserver.hhs.csus.edu
Steven Gray, Chair, Recreation and Leisure Studies; graysw@csus.edu
Laurel Heffernan, Chair, Dept. of Biological Sciences; 916-278-6535; Fax: 916-278-6993
Tom Krabacher, Environmental Studies; 916-278-6620; Fax: 916-278-7582; wrighta@csus.edu
C. Vanicek, Advisor, Conservation Biology; 916-278-6569

CALIFORNIA UNIVERSITY OF PENNSYLVANIA
BIOLOGICAL AND ENVIRONMENTAL SCIENCES DEPARTMENT
250 University Ave.
California, PA 15419-1394 United States
Phone: 724-938-4200 Fax: 724-938-1514
Website: www.cup.edu

Founded: N/A
Scope: State
Description: University Biology Department
Keyword(s): Ethics/Environmental Justice, Forests/Forestry, Pollution (general), Wildlife & Species
Contact(s):
David Argent, Wildlife Biology, Option; 724-938-1529; argent@cup.edu
David Boehm, Biology, Chair; 724-938-4200
William Kimmel, Environmental Pollution Control, Option; 724-938-4213; kimmel@cup.edu
Allan Miller, Environmental Studies Program Coordinator; 724-938-4462; miller@cup.edu
Thomas Moon, Environmental Conservation; 724-938-4204; moon@cup.edu
Brian Paulson, Professor; 724-938-5978; paulson@cup.edu

CENTRAL MICHIGAN UNIVERSITY
Department of Biology, 184 Brooks Hall
Mt. Pleasant, MI 48859 United States
Phone: Fax: 987-774-4000
Website: www.cmich.edu/

Founded: N/A
Contact(s):
Michael Hamas, Conservation Biology, Contact; 517-774-3185
John Krull, Wildlife, Contact; 517-774-3412
Scott McNaught, Water Resources, Contact; 517-774-1335
Douglas Peterson, Fisheries, Contact; 517-774-3377

CITY UNIVERSITY OF NEW YORK
COLLEGE OF STATEN ISLAND
ENVIRONMENTAL SCIENCE MASTERS PROGRAM
6S-310, 2800 Victory Blvd.
Staten Island, NY 10314 United States
Phone: 718-982-2000 Fax: 718-982-3923
E-mail: gerstle@postbox.csi.cuny.edu
Website:
www.library.csi.cuny.edu/dept/as/ces/escpgm.htm

Founded: N/A

Scope: Local

Description: The interdisciplinary masters program in Environmental Science includes ecology, geology, chemistry, environmental engineering, and computer modeling. The objective of the masters program is to expose the students to the scientific principles underlying environmental problems. Research is carried out on wetlands, park planning, air, water and soil pollution, waste disposal, aquatic toxics, environmental epidemiology and risk analysis. Courses are offered in the evenings for full and part time setting.

Contact(s):
Alfred Levine, Director

CITY UNIVERSITY OF NEW YORK
HUNTER COLLEGE
695 Park Ave.
New York, NY 10021 United States
Phone: 212-772-4490
Website: www.hunter.cuny.edu

Founded: N/A

Contact(s):
Charles Heatwole, Department of Geography; 212-772-5265; Fax: 212-772-5268
Jeffery Osleeb, Energy and Environmental Policy Studies Program; 212-772-5413; Fax: 212-772-5268
Louise Sherby, Wexler Library Chief Librarian; 212-772-4146; Fax: 212-772-4142

CLARK UNIVERSITY
INTERNATIONAL DEVELOPMENT, COMMUNITY PLANNING AND ENVIRONMENT
950 Main St.
Worcester, MA 01610 United States
Phone: 508-793-7201 Fax: 508-793-8820
E-mail: idce@clark.edu
Website: www.clarku.edu

Founded: 1972

Membership: 1–100

Scope: Local, State, Regional, National, International

Description: The International Development Program uses a multidisciplinary approach in research and teaching to analyze issues of underdevelopment in Asia, Africa, and Latin America. It draws on faculty from the fields of geography (including GIS), environmental studies, management, anthropology, economics, politics, and history, and serves both U.S. and international students. (B.A. and M.A. degree offered)

Publication(s): Tools of Gender Analysis, A Manual for Socio-Economic and Gender Analysis, Implementing PRA, PRA Handbook, Introduction to PRA

Keyword(s): Agriculture/Farming, Air Quality/Atmosphere, Development/Developing Countries, Ethics/Environmental Justice, Forests/Forestry, Land Issues, Pollution (general), Population, Public Health, Recreation/Ecotourism, Reduce/Reuse/Recycle, Sprawl/Urban Planning

Contact(s):
Richard Ford, Center for Community-Based Development, Director; 508-793-7691; rford@clarku.edu
William Fisher, International Development Community Planning & Environment; 508-421-3765; wfisher@clarku.edu
Barbara Thomas-Slayter, International Development Program; 508-793-7454; bslayer@clarku.edu

CLEMSON UNIVERSITY
AQUACULTURE, FISHERIES AND WILDLIFE
G08 Lehotsky Hall
Clemson, SC 29634 United States
Phone: 864-656-3117 Fax: 864-656-5332
Website: www.virtual.clemson.edu/groups/AFW/

Founded: N/A

Membership: 101–1,000

Scope: State

Description: The curriculum leading to a B.S. degree provides a solid foundation in basic and applied science, social science, and communication skills. Emphasis areas permit students to broaden their technical knowledge in their chosen career path. Those interested in pursuing a graduate degree program in aquaculture, fisheries, or wildlife management should have sound undergraduate training in the biological or related sciences. Programs of study are designed to emphasize relationships between wild animals

Publication(s): See publication web site

Contact(s):
Robert Barkley, Director of Admissions; 864-656-2287; Fax: 864-656-2464
John Sweeney, Chair; 864-656-5333; jrswny@clemson.edu

CLEMSON UNIVERSITY
SCHOOL OF THE ENVIRONMENT
342 Computer Court Rich Lab, Research Park
Anderson, SC 29625 United States
Phone: 864-656-5568 Fax: 864-656-0672
Website: www.ces.clemson.edu/ees/

Founded: 1995

Membership: 1–100

Scope: Local, State, Regional, National, International

Description: Made up of the Environmental Engineering and Science Dept., the Environmental Toxicology Dept., and the Geological Sciences Dept. Administers university-wide Environmental Science and Policy Program.

Keyword(s): Air Quality/Atmosphere, Ecosystems (precious), Pollution (general), Reduce/Reuse/Recycle, Water Habitats & Quality, Wildlife & Species

Contact(s):
Alan Elzerman, Geological Science, Chair; 864-656-5568; awlzrmn@clemson.edu
Alan Elzerman, Chair of Env. Engineering and Science, Director; 864-656-5568; awlzrmn@clemson.edu
Pam Fjeld, Student Services Coordinator; 864-656-1010; hpamela@clemson.edu
John Rodgers, Environmental Toxicology, Chair; 864-646-2691

COASTAL RESOURCES CENTER
U.R.I. Narragansett Bay Campus, South Ferry Rd.
Narragansett, RI 02882 United States
Phone: 401-874-6224 Fax: 401-789-4670
E-mail: cyoung@gso.uri.edu
Website: www.crc.uri.edu

Founded: 1971

Membership: 1–100

Scope: Local, State, Regional, National, International

Description: CRC is active in the U.S. and world advancing coastal management through field projects, education and training, research and learning and sharing lessons learned throughout the coastal community.

Publication(s): Intercoast Network, a manual for assessing progress in coastal management, and Aquidneck Island: Our Shared Vision

Keyword(s): Oceans/Coasts/Beaches

Contact(s):
Chip Young, Community Liaison; 401-874-6630; Fax: 401-789-4670

COLLEGE OF THE ATLANTIC

HUMAN ECOLOGY
105 Eden St.
Bar Harbor, ME 04609 United States
Phone: 207-288-5015 Fax: 207-288-2328
E-mail: inquiry@ecology.coa.edu
Website: www.coa.edu

Founded: N/A
Membership: 1–100
Scope: National, International
Description: The College of the Atlantic is a fully accredited four-year residential college. Students are attracted to its excellent programs in marine biology, environmental studies and ecology, environmental design, public policy, education, and selected humanities. Over 250 students. Awards a B.A. and M. PH. In human ecology. Summer programs in field studies for teachers.
Contact(s):
Steven Katona, President

COLLEGE OF WILLIAM AND MARY

VIRGINIA INSTITUTE OF MARINE SCIENCE/SCHOOL OF MARINE SCIENCE
P.O. Box 1346
Gloucester Point, VA 23062 United States
Phone: 804-684-7000 Fax: 804-684-7097
Website: www.vims.edu/

Founded: 1940
Description: A state institution founded for providing research, advisory services, and education for the public and for state and federal agencies responsible for managing marine resources.
Contact(s):
E. Burreson, Director of Research and Advisory Services; 804-684-7108
L. Wright, Dean and Director; 804-684-7103
William Dupaul, Head of Marine Advisory Services; 804-684-7164
J. Graves, Fisheries Sciences, Chair; 804-684-7352
S. Kuehl, Physical Sciences, Chair; 804-684-7118
M. Roberts, Environmental Sciences, Chair; 804-684-7260
Gene Silberhorn, Coastal and Ocean Policy, Chair; 804-684-7382
Richard Wetzel, Biological Sciences, Chair; 804-684-7381

COLORADO MOUNTAIN COLLEGE

TIMBERLINE CAMPUS
901 S. Hwy. 24
Leadville, CO 80461 United States
Phone: 719-486-2015 Fax: 719-486-3212
Website: www.coloradomtn.edu

Founded: N/A
Membership: 1–100
Scope: Local, State, Regional, National
Description: CMC/Timberline offers two-year degrees (AS) in Natural Resource Mgmt., Natural Resource Recreation Mgmt., and Outdoor Recreation Leadership; one-year certificates in International Environmental Studies and Wilderness Studies; one semester certificate-Outdoor Semester in the Rockies. These programs combine on-campus academic classes/activities, as well as hands-on field components and/or work experience. CMC is a public 2-year community college with transfer options to 4-year schools.
Keyword(s): Air Quality/Atmosphere, Climate Change, Development/Developing Countries, Ecosystems (precious), Ethics/Environmental Justice, Land Issues, Oceans/Coasts/Beaches, Pollution (general), Population, Recreation/Ecotourism, Reduce/Reuse/Recycle, Water Habitats
Contact(s):
Virginia Espinoza, Admissions; 719-486-4291; tespinoza@coloradomtn.edu
Jerry Andrew, Associate Professor Outdoor Recreation Leadership; 719-486-4218; jandrew@coloradomtn.edu
Nancy Cain, Associate Professor of Biology; 719-486-4241; ncain@coloradomtn.edu
Jessica Clement, Division Director; 719-486-4209; jclement@coloradomtn.edu
Kent Clement, Professor of Outdoor Recreational Leadership; 719-486-4270; kclement@coloradomtn.edu
Karmen King, Associate Professor of Environmental Technology; 719-486-4230; kking@coloradomtn.edu
Rosemarie Russo, Assistant Campus Dean; 719-486-4215; rrusso@coloradomtn.edu

COLORADO STATE UNIVERSITY

COLLEGE OF NATURAL RESOURCES
101 Metro Resources Bldg
Fort Collins, CO 80523 United States
Phone: 970-491-6675 Fax: 970-491-0279
E-mail: webadmin@cnr.colstate.edu
Website: www.cnr.colostate.edu

Founded: N/A
Scope: State
Contact(s):
David Anderson, Cooperative Fish and Wildlife Research Unit, Leader; 970-491-1414
Joyce Berry, Assistant Dean; 970-491-5405; Fax: 970-491-0279; joyceb@cnr.colostate.edu
Dennis Child, Rangeland Ecosystem Science, Head; 970-491-4994; Fax: 970-491-2339; dennisc@cnr.colostate.edu
A. Dyer, Dean; 970-491-4997
Judith Hannah, Earth Resources, Head; 970-491-5662
Michael Manfredo, Natural Resources Recreation and Tourism, Head; 970-491-0474; Fax: 970-491-2255; manfredo.cnr.colostate.edu
Randall Robinette, Fishery and Wildlife Biology, Head; 970-491-5020
Susan Stafford, Forest Sciences, Head; 970-491-6911; Fax: 970-491-6754; stafford@cnr.colostate.edu
Diana Wall, Natural Resources Ecology Laboratory, Contact; 970-491-2504

COLORADO STATE UNIVERSITY

DEPARTMENT OF POLITICAL SCIENCE ENVIRONMENTAL POLITICS AND POLICY
Political Science Department
Clark Building C-346
Fort Collins, CO 80523-1782 United States
Phone: 970-491-5157 Fax: 970-491-2490
Website: www.colostate.edu/depts/polisci/grad.html

Founded: 1975
Scope: State
Description: All Ph.D. students in the program choose Environmental Politics and Policy as one of three subfields in political science offered in preparation for their degree. The program prepares doctoral students for university positions and a wide variety of private and public sector careers related to environmental politics and policy.
Contact(s):
Dimitris Stevis, Graduate Coordinator; sksmith@lamar.colostate.edu

CONNECTICUT COLLEGE

270 Mohegan Ave.
New London, CT 06320 United States
Phone: 860-439-5021 Fax: 860-439-2519
Website: www.conncoll.edu

Founded: 1911
Scope: International

Description: Environmental Studies has a long and successful history at Connecticut College beginning in 1931 with the establishment of the Connecticut College Arboretum. Since then, a common theme in the program has been to understand the structure and functioning of both natural and managed ecosystems.

Contact(s):

Glenn Dreyer, Center for Conservation Biology and Environmental Studies; 860-439-2144; Fax: 860-439-5482; gddre@conncoll.edu

Peter Siver, Director, Environmental Studies Program; 860-439-2160; Fax: 860-439-2519; pasiv@conncoll.edu

Phillip Barnes, Zoology Department, Chair; 860-439-2148; Fax: 860-439-2519; ptbar@conncoll.edu

T. Owen, Botany Department, Chair; 860-439-2147; tpowe@conncoll.edu

CONWAY SCHOOL OF LANDSCAPE DESIGN

46 Delabarre Ave.
Conway, MA 01341 United States
Phone: 413-369-4044 Fax: 413-369-4032
E-mail: info@csld.edu
Website: www.csld.edu

Founded: 1972
Membership: N/A
Scope: Local, State, Regional

Description: CSLD is a ten-month graduate program in environmentally sound site design and land use planning. The degree offered is a M.A. degree in Landscape Design. The curriculum is structured around professional level work for residential clients, municipal agencies, and non-profit organizations. Through these projects, students produce the drawings and reports characteristic of the designer/planner while learning technical skills and developing intellectual abilities.

Publication(s): Con Text (annual newsletter)

Keyword(s): Ecosystems (precious), Land Issues, Public Lands/Greenspace, Recreation/Ecotourism, Sprawl/Urban Planning

Contact(s):

Nancy Braxton, Administrative Director
Donald Walker, Director

CORNELL UNIVERSITY

COLLEGE OF AGRICULTURAL AND LIFE SCIENCES
DEPARTMENT OF NATURAL RESOURCES
118 Fernow Hall
Ithaca, NY 14853 United States
Phone: 607-255-2821 Fax: 607-255-0349
Website: www.dnr.cornell.edu

Founded: N/A
Membership: 1–100
Scope: International

Contact(s):

Richard Baer, Environmental Ethics; 607-255-7797; rab12@cornell.edu

Timothy Fahey, Forest Science; 607-255-5470; tjf5@cornell.edu

Marian Hovencamp, Undergraduate Program, Assistant; 607-255-2809; mth6@cornell.edu

Barbara Knuth, Co-Leader, Human Dimensions Research Unit; 607-255-2822; bak3@cornell.edu

James Lassoie, Chair; jpl4@cornell.edu

Edward Mills, Cornell Biological Field Station; 900 Shackelton Point Rd., Bridgeport, NY 13030-9750; 315-633-9243; Fax: 315-633-2358; elm5@cornell.edu

Charles Smith, Plant and Wildlife Inventory; 607-255-3219; crs6@cornell.edu

D

DALHOUSIE UNIVERSITY

SCHOOL FOR RESOURCE AND ENVIRONMENTAL STUDIES (SRES)
1312 Robie St.
Halifax, B3H 3E2 Nova Scotia Canada
Phone: 902-494-3632 Fax: 902-494-3728
E-mail: sres@is.dal.ca
Website: www.mgmt.dal.ca/sres/

Founded: 1975
Scope: Regional

Description: Graduate school within the Faculty of Management of Dalhousie University, offering a master of environmental studies (M.E.S.) degree, through a two year programme (thesis required). Emphasis of programme is on policy and management aspects.

Contact(s):

Peter Duinker, Director

DARTMOUTH COLLEGE

ENVIRONMENTAL STUDIES PROGRAM
6182 Steele Hall, Rm. 113
Hanover, NH 03755-3577 United States
Phone: 603-646-2838 Fax: 603-646-1682
Website: www.dartmouth.edu/

Founded: 1970
Scope: International

Description: Interdisciplinary academic program providing students with the opportunity to assess the seriousness and complexity of environmental problems and to understand how to search for solutions. Faculty research interests include biological conservation, ecosystem ecology, air pollution, economics, and international environmental governance.

Contact(s):

Andrew Friedland, Chairman

DELTA COLLEGE

SMALL SCALE CHEMISTRY
GREEN CHEMISTRY PROJECT
Green Chemistry Project
C-141 Chemistry Dept.
Delta College
Unversity Center, MI 48710 United States
Phone: 989-686-9272, ext. 9272 Fax: 989-686-8736
E-mail: slime@alpha.delta.edu
Website: www.delta.edu/slime/ssc.html

Founded: 1997
Membership: N/A
Scope: Local, State, Regional

Description: The Green Chemistry Project is a group of environmentally concerned instructors at Delta College, who promote source reduction, small-scale chemistry, micro-scale chemistry, and training. The goal is to spread the knowledge and use of positive green methods in education and training programs in Michigan.

Publication(s): Case Study-Small Scale Green Chemistry.

Keyword(s): Air Quality/Atmosphere, Oceans/Coasts/Beaches, Pollution (general), Reduce/Reuse/Recycle

Contact(s):

Michael Garlick, Laboratory Manager; 221 Victor Drive, Saginaw, MI 48609; 989-686-9272, ext. 9272; Fax: 989-686-8736; slime@alpha.delta.edu

DEPAUL UNIVERSITY

BIOLOGICAL SCIENCES
McGowan Center - Biology
2325 North Clifton Ave.
Chicago, IL 60614-3207 United States
Phone: 773-325-7595 Fax: 773-325-7596
Website: www.depaul.edu/~biology

Founded: N/A
Membership: 1–100
Scope: State, Regional
Description: Department of Biological Sciences
Contact(s):
Stan Cohn, Contact

DEPAUL UNIVERSITY

ENVIRONMENTAL SCIENCES
2325 N. Clifton Ave.
Chicago, IL 60614-3207 United States
Phone: 773-325-7422 Fax: 773-325-7448
Website: www.depaul.edu/~envirsci/

Founded: N/A
Contact(s):
Thomas Murphy, Chairman

DONALD BREN SCHOOL OF ENVIRONMENTAL SCIENCE AND MANAGEMENT

University of California
Santa Barbara, CA 93106-5131 United States
Phone: 805-893-7611 Fax: 805-893-7612
E-mail: gradasst@bren.ucsb.edu
Website: www.bren.ucsb.edu

Founded: 1991
Membership: 101–1,000
Scope: Local, State, Regional, National, International
Description: We are an environmental graduate program on the UC Santa Barbara campus where science, management, and law converge to shape the future. The Bren School offers a professional Master's and traditional Ph.D. in environmental science and management.
Contact(s):
Jill Richardson, Outreach Coordinator; 805-893-7980; jrichardson@bren.ucsb.edu

DREXEL UNIVERSITY

SCHOOL OF ENVIRONMENTAL SCIENCE, ENGINEERING, AND POLICY
32nd and Chestnut St.
Philadelphia, PA 19104 United States
Phone: 215-895-2266 Fax: 215-895-2267
E-mail: sesep@drexel.edu
Website: www.drexel.edu/sesep/

Founded: N/A
Scope: International
Description: Environmental Engineering and Science undergraduate and graduate study is offered by the School of Environmental Science, Engineering, and Policy at Drexel University. Over 25 faculty participate in SESEP programs. Degrees available with specializations in air pollution, environmental assessment, environmental biotechnology, environmental chemistry, environmental health, hazardous and solid waste, subsurface contaminant hydrology, water and wastewater treatment, water resources, and more.
Contact(s):
Claire Welty, Associate Director; 215-895-2281; weltyc@drexel.edu

DUKE UNIVERSITY

NICHOLAS SCHOOL OF THE ENVIRONMENT AND EARTH SCIENCES
Box 90328
Durham, NC 27708-0328 United States
Phone: 919-613-8000 Fax: 919-684-8741
E-mail: envadm@duke.edu
Website: www.env.duke.edu

Founded: 1991
Membership: N/A
Scope: Local, State, Regional, National, International
Description: The Nicholas School of the Environment and Earth Sciences is one of the world's premier graduate/professional schools for the interdisciplinary study of the environment, combining resources from the biological, physical and social sciences.
Contact(s):
William Schlesinger, Dean; 919-613-8004; Fax: 919-613-8007; schlesin@duke.edu
Ken Knoerr, Director of Graduate Studies, Environmental Sciences and Pol; gradadm@pinus.env.duke.edu
Michael Orbach, Director, Duke University Marine Laboratory; 252-504-7604; Fax: 252-504-7648; mko@duke.edu
Cindy Peters, Director of Enrollment Services; 919-613-8070; Fax: 919-684-8741; envadm@duke.edu
Lincoln Pratson, Director of Graduate Studies, Earth and Ocean Sciences; 919-681-8077; Fax: 919-684-5833; lincoln.pratson@duke.edu
Dan Rittschof, Director of Graduate Studies, Program in the Ocean Sciences; 252-504-7634; Fax: 252-504-7648; ritt@duke.edu
Norman Christensen, Professor of Ecology and Founding Dean; 919-613-8052; Fax: 919-684-8741; normc@duke.edu
Richard Di Giulio, Enviromental Toxicology and Chemistry; richd@duke.edu
Jeffrey Karson, Earth and Ocean Sciences; 919-684-2731; Fax: 919-684-5833; jkarson@duke.edu
Randall Kramer, Program Chair of Resource Economics and Policy; 919-613-8072; Fax: 919-684-8741
Kenneth Reckhow, Water & Air Resouces; reckhow@duke.edu
Curtis Richardson, Chair, Division of Environmental Sciences and Policy; 919-613-8009; Fax: 919-684-8741
Daniel Richter, Forest Resource Management and Resource Ecology; drichter@duke.edu

DUKE UNIVERSITY - ORGANIZATION FOR TROPICAL STUDIES

LA SELVA BIOLOGICAL STATION
LAS CRUCES BIOLOGICAL STATION AND WILSON BOTANICAL GARDEN
PALO VERDE BIOLOGICAL STATION
Box 90630
Durham, NC 27708-0630 United States
Phone: 919-684-5774 Fax: 919-684-5661
E-mail: nao@duke.edu
Website: www.ots.duke.edu/

Founded: 1963
Membership: 1–100
Scope: International
Description: OTS, a nonprofit consortium of universities and research institutions from the U.S., Costa Rica, Peru, Mexico, South Africa, Canada, and Australia, provides leadership in education, research, and the responsible use of natural resources in the tropics. OTS offers graduate, undergraduate, and professional training; facilitates research; participates in tropical forest conservation; and maintains three biological stations in Costa Rica.
Publication(s): Liana, see web site.

Keyword(s): Agriculture/Farming, Climate Change, Development/Developing Countries, Ecosystems (precious), Forests/Forestry, Oceans/Coasts/Beaches

Contact(s):

Gary Hartshorn, President and CEO; 919-684-5774; Fax: 919-684-5661; ghartsho@duke.edu
Luis Gomez, Director; 506-773-4004; Fax: 506773-3665; ldgomez@hortus.ots.ac.cr
Eugenio Gonzalez, Director; 506-384-6106; Fax: 506-240-6783; egonza@jabiru.ots.ac.cr
Jorge Jimenez, Director in Costa Rica; 506-240-6696; Fax: 506-240-6783; jjimenez@ots.ac.cr
Robert Matlock, Scientific Director; 506-766-6565; Fax: 506-766-6535; rmatlock@sloth.ots.ac.cr

E

EASTERN ILLINOIS UNIVERSITY
Department of Biological Sciences
600 Lincoln Avenue
Charleston, IL 61920 United States
Phone: 217-581-3126 Fax: 217-581-7141
E-mail: cfkck@eiu.edu
Website: www.eiu.edu/~biology/

Founded: 1972
Membership: 101–1,000
Scope: State
Description: Eastern Illinois University offers an undergraduate degree in Biology, with three options: Teacher Certification, Environmental Biology and Biological Sciences. Within the Biological Sciences, students choose from among 4 concentrations: Biology, Botanical Sciences, Ecology and Systematics, and Cell and Functional Biology. Emphasis is placed upon a fundamental understanding of biology and environmental concerns.

Contact(s):

Charles Costa, Biological Sciences, Contact; 217-581-2520; cfcjc@eiu.edu
Robert Fischer, Environmental Biology Option Coordinator; 217-581-2817; cfruf@eiu.edu
Kipp Kruse, Biology, Chair; 217-581-3126; cfkck@eiu.edu
James McGaughey, Biology Teacher Certificate Option Coordinator; 217-581-2928; cfjam@eiu.edu

EASTERN KENTUCKY UNIVERSITY
Biological Sciences Department, 521 Lancaster Ave.
Richmond, KY 40475-3102 United States
Phone: 859-622-1531 Fax: 859-622-1399
Website: www.eku.edu

Founded: N/A
Membership: 1–100
Scope: National
Publication(s): Newsletter

Contact(s):

Ross Clark, Biology—Botany Option; bioclark@acs.eku.edu
Charles Elliott, Environmental Studies, Contact; 859-622-1531; bioelliott@acs.eku.edu
Robert Frederick, Wildlife Management, Contact; 859-622-1531; biofred@acs.eku.edu
William Martin, Lillie Woods Research Natural Area; narmartin@acs.eku.edu
Barbara Ramey, Applied Ecology, Contact; 606-622-1531; bioramey@acs.eku.edu
Guenter Shuster, Biology—Aquatic Option; bioschus@acs.eku.edu

EASTERN MICHIGAN UNIVERSITY
316 Mark Jefferson
Ypsilanti, MI 48197 United States
Phone: 734-487-4242 Fax: 734-487-9235
Website: www.emich.edu

Founded: N/A
Scope: National, International

Contact(s):

Ben Czinski, Kresge Environmental Education Center, Director; 2816 Fish Lake Rd., Lapeer, MI 48446; 810-667-2350; bio_czinski@online.emich.edu
Catherine Bach, Conservation Resource Use, Contact; 734-487-0212; bio_bach@online.emich.edu
Michael Kasenow, Geography and Geology, Head; 203 Strong Hall, EMU, Ypsilanti, MI 48197; 734-487-0218; geo_kasenow@online.emich.edu
Robert Neely, Biology, Head; 316 Mark Jefferson, EMU, Ypsilanti, MI 48197; 734-487-4242; bio_neely@online.emich.edu

EMORY UNIVERSITY
BIOLOGY DEPARTMENT
Rollins Research Center Emory University
Atlanta, GA 30322 United States
Phone: 404-727-6048 Fax: 404-727-2880
Website: www.emory.edu/biology/

Founded: N/A
Membership: 1–100
Scope: State

Contact(s):

Chris Beck, Ecology and Evolution, Professor
John Lucchesi, Biology Department, Chair

EMPORIA STATE UNIVERSITY
BIOLOGICAL SCIENCES
Biological Sciences Campus Box 4050
Emporia, KS 66801 United States
Phone: 316-341-5311 Fax: 316-341-5607
E-mail: mooredwi@emporia.edu
Website: www.emporia.edu/biosci/biology

Founded: N/A
Scope: State
Publication(s): See publication web site

Contact(s):

Marshall Sundberg, Dept. of Biological Sciences, Ecology and Wildlife Biology

F

FAU PINE JOG ENVIRONMENTAL EDUCATION CENTER
6301 Summit Blvd.
West Palm Beach, FL 33415 United States
Phone: 561-686-6600 Fax: 561-687-4968
Website: www.pinejog.org

Founded: 1960
Membership: 1–100
Scope: Local, Regional
Description: Pine Jog is an environmental education center within the College of Education of Florida Atlantic University. The purpose of the Center is to provide environmental education programs which foster an awareness and appreciation of the natural world, promote an understanding of ecological concepts, and instill a sense of stewardship towards the earth and all of its inhabitants.

Contact(s):

Patricia Welch, Executive Director; 561-686-6600
Donald Mathis, Chair, Board of Directors; Sartory, Mathis, & Beedle, 5840 Corporate Way, West Palm Beach, FL 33407; 561-683-7500

FERRIS STATE UNIVERSITY
COLLEGE OF ALLIED HEALTH SCIENCES
200 Ferris Dr.
Big Rapids, MI 49307-2740 United States
Phone: 231-591-2313 Fax: 231-591-3788
Website: www.ferris.edu/htmls/colleges/alliedhe/

Founded: 1964
Membership: 1–100
Scope: State
Description: Educational institution offering B.S. in industrial and environmental health management with options in general environmental health, hazardous materials management, industrial hygiene, and industrial safety.
Contact(s):
Ellen Haneline, Health Management Department, Head; 231-591-2313; ellen_j_haneline@ferris.edu

FERRUM COLLEGE
DEPARTMENT OF FORESTRY AND WILDLIFE
P.O. Box 1000
Ferrum, VA 24088 United States
Phone: 540-365-2121
E-mail: webmaster@ferrum.edu
Website: www.ferrum.edu

Founded: N/A
Scope: Local, State, Regional, National
Description: An interdisciplinary program in the U.S.'s second oldest Environmental Science major. A living laboratory, including a 700 acre campus, abundant forestland, three ponds, streams, stands of white and loblolly pines, and wildlife, located on the eastern slope of the Blue Ridge Parkway, allows for exceptional field-oriented instruction and learning.
Publication(s): Ferrum Alumni Magazine, The Chrysalis, The Iron Blade
Keyword(s): Agriculture/Farming, Air Quality/Atmosphere, Climate Change, Ecosystems (precious), Energy, Forests/Forestry, Land Issues, Oceans/Coasts/Beaches, Pollution (general), Public Lands/Greenspace, Recreation/Ecotourism, Reduce/Reuse/Recycle, Water Habitats & Quality.
Contact(s):
Rathin Basu, Economics; 540-365-4204; rbasu@ferrum.edu
James Bier, Chemistry; 540-365-4362; jbier@ferrum.edu
George Byrd, Agriculture; 540-365-4378; gbyrd@ferrum.edu
David Johnson, Chemistry; 540-365-4364; djohnson@ferrum.edu
John Leffler, Biology/Zoology; 540-365-4361; jleffler@ferrum.edu
Kathy Mengak, Leisure Services and Recreation; 540-365-4387; kmengak@ferrum.edu
Daryl Nash, Agriculture; 540-365-4363; dnash@ferrum.edu
Bob Pohlad, Biology; 540-365-4367; bpohlad@ferrum.edu
Jason Powell, Chemistry/Physics; 540-365-4374; jpowell@ferrum.edu
Ron Stephens, Agriculture; 540-365-4360; rstephens@ferrum.edu
Joseph Stogner, Environmental Studies; 540-365-4369; jstogner@ferrum.edu
Carolyn Thomas, Environmental Science/Biology; 540-365-4368; cthomas@ferrum.edu
Linda Williams, Biology/Agriculture; 540-365-4372; lmwilliams@ferrum.edu

FLORIDA STATE UNIVERSITY
UNIVERSITY RELATIONS
216 Westcott Bldg
Tallahassee, FL 32306 United States
Phone: 850-644-2525 Fax: 850-644-3612
Website: www.fsu.edu

Founded: N/A
Membership: 1–100
Scope: Regional
Contact(s):
Bruce Grindal, Anthropology, Chairman; Bellamy G-24, Tallahassee, FL 32306-2150; 850-644-8147; Fax: 850-644-4283; bgrindal@mailer.fsu.edu
Patrick O'Sullivan, Geography, Political Geography and Environmental Studies; P.O. Box 2190, Tallahassee, FL 32306-2190; 850-644-7175; Fax: 850-644-5913; kmcclell@mailer.fsu.edu
Thomas Roberts, Biological Science, Chairman; P.O. Box 4340, Tallahassee, FL 32306-4340; 850-644-3700; Fax: 850-644-9829
David Stuart, Meteorology, Chairman; 404 Love Building, Tallahassee, FL 32306-4520; 850-644-6205; Fax: 850-644-9642; stuart@met.fsu.edu
Wilton Sturges, Oceanography, Chairman; 329 OSB, West Call Street, Tallahassee, FL 32306-4320; 850-644-6700; Fax: 850-644-2581; sturges@ocean.fsu.edu
J. Tull, Geology, Chairman; Carraway Bldg., Tallahassee, FL 32306-4100; 904-644-1448; Fax: 904-644-4214; tull@gly.fsu.edu

FROSTBURG STATE UNIVERSITY (UNIVERSITY OF MARYLAND)
DEPARTMENT OF BIOLOGY
101 Braddock Rd.
Frostburg, MD 21532 United States
Phone: 301-687-4166 Fax: 301-687-3034
Website: www.fsu.umd.edu

Founded: N/A
Scope: State
Description: Wildlife and Fisheries Program (B.A, M.A., Ph.D.), Wildlife/Fisheries Biology (M.S.), Applied Ecology; Conservation Biology (M.S.), Biology (B.S., Ph.D.)
Publication(s): See publication web site
Contact(s):
David Morton, Dept. Chair; 301-687-4355; dmorton@frostburg.edu.

G

GEORGE WASHINGTON UNIVERSITY
2121 I Street NW
Washington, DC 20052 United States
Phone: 202-994-1000
Website: www.gwu.edu/

Founded: N/A
Scope: State
Contact(s):
Henry Merchant, Environmental Studies, Director; 202-994-7118
Henry Merchant, Environmental and Resource Policy, Director; 202-994-7123; Fax: 202-994-6100
Theodore Toridis, Environmental Engineering, Acting Chair; 801 22nd St., Washington, DC 20052; 202-994-6749; Fax: 202-944-0238; toridis@seas.gwu.edu

GEORGE WASHINGTON UNIVERSITY
LAW SCHOOL
2000 H. St., NW
Washington, DC 20052 United States
Phone: 202-994-6260
Website: www.law.gwu.edu/

Founded: 1865
Scope: International
Description: Nation's largest graduate and undergraduate environmental law program. Twenty-two environmental courses for J.D. and LL.M. students in addition to land use and other related topics. Emphasizes a practical approach.
Contact(s):
Laurent Hourcle, Co-Director; 202-994-4823; lhourcle@main.nlc.gwu.edu

GEORGETOWN COLLEGE
ENVIRONMENTAL SCIENCE PROGRAM
400 E. College St.
Georgetown, KY 40324 United States
Phone: 502-863-8088 Fax: 502-868-7744
Website: www.georgetowncollege.edu

Founded: N/A

Scope: State

Description: Environmental Science Degree with tracks in Chemical Science, Biological Science, Chemical-Biological Science and Environmental Policy.

Contact(s):
Rick Kopp, Program Coordinator; Fax: 502-868-7744; rkopp@georgetowncollege.edu

GEORGETOWN UNIVERSITY
LAW CENTER
600 New Jersey Ave., NW
Washington, DC 20001 United States
Phone: 202-662-9000 Fax: 202-662-9444
E-mail: admis@law.georgetown.edu
Website: www.law.georgetown.edu/

Founded: N/A
Membership: 101–1,000
Scope: National

Contact(s):
Judith Areen, Dean

GEORGIA INSTITUTE OF TECHNOLOGY
GEORGIA WATER INSTITUTE
School of Civil & Environmental Engineering
Georgia Institute of Technology
Atlanta, GA 30332-0335 United States
Phone: 404-894-3776 Fax: 404-894-3828
Website: www.gatech.edu

Founded: N/A

Scope: State

Contact(s):
Aris Georgakokos, Director, Georgia Water Institute; 404-894-2240

H

HAMLINE UNIVERSITY
CENTER FOR GLOBAL ENVIRONMENTAL EDUCATION
1536 Hewitt Ave.
St. Paul, MN 55104-1284 United States
Phone: 651-523-2480 Fax: 651-523-3041
E-mail: cgee@hamline.edu
Website: cgee.hamline.edu

Founded: 1990

Scope: Local, State, Regional, National, International

Description: CGEE was founded to nurture greater understanding of the interconnectedness of local and global environments among educators, students, scientists, and citizens.

Publication(s): Publications on website

Keyword(s): Ecosystems (precious), Energy, Pollution (general), Reduce/Reuse/Recycle, Water Habitats & Quality

Contact(s):
Tracy Fredin, Director; 651-523-3105; Fax: 651-523-2987; tfredin@gw.hamline.edu
Renee Wonser, Coursework Director; 651-523-2419; Fax: 651-523-3041; rwonser@gw.hamline.edu

HOCKING COLLEGE
SCHOOL OF NATURAL RESOURCES
3301 Hocking Parkway
Nelsonville, OH 45764 United States
Phone: 740-753-3591 Fax: 740-753-2021
E-mail: admissions@hocking.edu
Website: www.hocking.edu

Founded: 1969

Scope: State

Description: The mission of our School of Natural Resources is to prepare individuals for careers as technicians in the natural resources profession. Emphasis is placed on basic theory, developing a sustained postive work ethic and the practical application of the development of the competencies required for entry-level positions in recreation, wildlife, forestry, timber harvesting/tree care and a wide variety of land management technology fields.

Contact(s):
Albert Lecount, Wildlife, Biologist, ext. 2919; lecount_a@hocking.edu
Russell Tippett, Dean; 740-753-3591, ext. 2317; tippet_r@hocking.edu
Lloyd Wright, Fisheries, Biologist, ext. 2919; wright_ll@hocking.edu

HUMBOLDT STATE UNIVERSITY
1 Harpst St.
Arcata, CA 95521-8299 United States
Phone: 707-826-3256 Fax: 707-826-3562
E-mail: cnrs@humboldt.edu
Website: www.humboldt.edu/~cnrs/

Founded: N/A

Scope: State

Description: College of Natural Resources and Sciences—one of the largest and most highly respected programs in the nation.

Contact(s):
James Howard, Dean, College of Natural Resources and Sciences; 707-826-3256
Mike Anderson, Chair, Environmental Resources Engineering; 707-826-3617
Russel Boham, Director, Indian Natural Resources, Sciences, and Engineering; 707-826-4994
Susan Bicknell, Chairman, Forestry and Watershed Management; 707-826-4243
Milton Boyd, Chairman, Biological Sciences; 707-826-3246
Steven Carlson, Chairman, Natural Resources Planning and Interpretation; 707-826-4147
Steven Carlson, Chairman, Rangeland Resources and Wildland Soils; 707-826-4147
Mark Colwell, Chairman, Wildlife; 707-826-3723
Marie Deanglis, Chairman, Oceanography; 707-826-4147
Walter Duffy, Leader, Cooperative Fishery Research Unit; 707-826-3268
David Hankin, Chairman, Fisheries; 707-825-5645
Robert Ziemer, Project Leader, Experiment Station, Pacific Southwest Forest; 707-825-2936

I

IDAHO STATE UNIVERSITY
DEPARTMENT OF BIOLOGICAL SCIENCES
Box 8007
Pocatello, ID 83209 United States
Phone: 208-282-3765 Fax: 208-236-4570
E-mail: bios@isu.edu
Website: www.isu.edu/departments/bios/

Founded: N/A

Description: The Department of Biological Sciences at Idaho State University has high quality degree programs in ecology. Strong basic coursework and original investigations are emphasized at the undergraduate and graduate levels.

Habitats available for study range from cold sagebrush deserts to heavily forested areas and includes streams and riparian areas in the Snake River Canyon to its headwaters in Yellowstone National Park.

Contact(s):
Rod Seeley, Ecology; 208- 28-2181; seelrodn@isu.edu
Mary Watwood, Associate Professor; 208- 23-3090; watwmari@isu.edu

ILLINOIS STATE UNIVERSITY
ENVIRONMENTAL HEALTH PROGRAM, DEPARTMENT OF HEALTH SCIENCES
Campus Box 5220
Normal, IL 61790-5220 United States
Phone: 309-438-8329 Fax: 309-438-2450
Website: www.ilstu.edu/

Founded: 1974
Membership: 1–100
Scope: State
Description: Undergraduate education for B.S. in environmental health. Five faculty persons and 165 enrolled students. Four-year undergraduate curriculum accredited by National Environmental Health Science and Protection Accreditation Council. Graduate Education for M.S. in Environmental Health and Safety.
Contact(s):
Marilyn Morrow, Program Director, Acting
Thomas Bierma, Masters Program Coordinator

INDIANA STATE UNIVERSITY
Science Bldg., Rm. 256
Terre Haute, IN 47809 United States
Phone: 812-237-2400 Fax: 812-237-4480
Website: www.biology.indstate.edu/dls/

Founded: N/A
Membership: 1–100
Scope: State
Publication(s): See publication web site
Contact(s):
Marion Jackson, Ecology and Wildlife; lsmjack@scifac.indstate.edu

INDIANA UNIVERSITY
SCHOOL OF PUBLIC AND ENVIRONMENTAL AFFAIRS
1315 E. 10th St.
Bloomington, IN 47405 United States
Phone: 812-855-2840 Fax: 812-855-7802
E-mail: speainfo@indiana.edu
Website: www.spea.indiana.edu

Founded: 1972
Membership: 101–1,000
Scope: Local, State, Regional, National, International
Description: The School of Public Environmental Affairs brings an interdisciplinary approach to the study of the environmental sciences. The focus of the academic programs is to teach techniques that will help graduates preserve and protect the quality of natural resources, identify environmental hazards, and significantly contribute to solutions to enhance quality of life in the world's communities.
Contact(s):
John Mikesell, Director of Graduate Programs; 812-855-9485; mikesell@indiana.edu
Roger Parks, Director of Ph.D. Programs In Public Policy/Public Affairs; 812-855-0563; parks@indiana.edu
J. Randolph, Director of Ph.D. Programs In Environmental Science; 812-855-4953; randolph@indiana.edu
Frank Vilardo, Director of Undergraduate Programs; 812-855-9485; vilardo@indiana.edu
Astrid Merget, Dean; 812-855-1432; merget@indiana.edu
Jeffrey White, Associate Dean; 812-855-5058; whitej@indiana.edu

IOWA STATE UNIVERSITY
COLLEGE OF AGRICULTURE
COMMUNICATIONS OFFICE
304 Curtis Hall
Ames, IA 50011-1050 United States
Phone: 515-294-5616 Fax: 515-294-8662
E-mail: edadcock@iastate.edu
Website: www.ag.iastate.edu/

Founded: N/A
Membership: 1–100
Scope: Regional
Description: Communications and information in Iowa State University agriculture, natural resources, food and nutrition, and other areas
Contact(s):
Jeff Iles, Horticulture, Head; Rm. 106B Horticulture Hall, 50011-1100; 515-294-5893; Fax: 515-294-0730; iles@ia.state.edu
J. Kelly, Forestry, Chairman; Dept. of Forestry, Ames, IA 50011-1021; 515-294-1166; jmkelly@iastate.edu
Bruce Menzel, Animal Ecology, Fisheries and Wildlife Biology, Chairman; 515-294-6148; bmenzel@iastate.edu

IOWA STATE UNIVERSITY
COLLEGE OF DESIGN
146 College of Design, Iowa State University
Ames, IA 50011 United States
Phone: 515-294-5676
E-mail: landarch@iastate.edu
Website: www.design.iastate.edu/

Founded: N/A
Scope: State
Publication(s): Design News
Contact(s):
J. Keller, Landscape Architecture, Chairman; 515-294-5676; tkeller@iastate.edu
Riad Mahayni, Community and Regional Planning, Chair; 515-294-8958; Fax: 515-294-4015; rmahayni@iastate.edu

J

JOHN GRAY HIGH SCHOOL, GRAND CAYMAN
JOHN GRAY RECYCLERS
P.O. Box 174 NS
North Side
Grand Cayman
North Side, B W I United Kingdom
Phone: 345-947, ext. 7649
E-mail: johngrayrecyclers@hotmail.com
Website: johngrayrecyclers.org

Founded: 1996
Membership: 1–100
Scope: Local, National, International
Description: We are an environmental/recycling club at the John Gray High School in Grand Cayman, Cayman Islands. Our major aim is to protect coral reefs worldwide. We would like other young people to join us with our conservation work. Our pledge is to increase the public's awareness of the importance of the protection of the ocean and the world's coral reefs. We believe that we must all take action to conserve the ocean to sustain the wonderful web of life on our planet Earth.
Keyword(s): Oceans/Coasts/Beaches

JOHNS HOPKINS UNIVERSITY
CENTER FOR A LIVABLE FUTURE
BLOOMBERG SCHOOL OF PUBLIC HEALTH
615 N. Wolfe Street, Suite 8503
Baltimore, MD 21205 United States
Phone: 410-502-7578 Fax: 410-502-7579
E-mail: clf@jhsph.edu
Website: www.jhsph.edu/environment/

Founded: 1996
Scope: International
Description: The mission of the Center for a Livable Future is to establish a global resource to develop and disseminate information and to promote policies for the protection of health, the global environment, and our ability to sustain life for future generations.
Contact(s):
David Brubaker, Program Director, Henry Spira/Grace Project; 410-502-7577; dbrubake@jhsph.edu
Robert Lawrence, Director; 410-614-4590; rlawrenc@jhsph.edu
Leo Horrigan, Project Coordinator, Urban Agriculture; 410-502-7575; lhorriga@jhsph.edu
George Jakab, Associate Director for Science; gjakab@jhsph.edu
Polly Walker, Associate Director; 410-502-7578; pwalker@jhsph.edu

JOHNS HOPKINS UNIVERSITY
DEPARTMENT OF GEOGRAPHY AND ENVIRONMENTAL ENGINEERING
313 Ames Hall
3400 North Charles St.
Baltimore, MD 21218 United States
Phone: 410-516-7092 Fax: 410-516-8996
E-mail: dogee@jhu.edu
Website: www.jhu.edu/~dogee
Founded: N/A
Membership: 1–100
Scope: State, Regional, National, International
Description: The Department of Geography and Ennvironmental Engineering is concerned with the improved understanding and description of environmental problems including questions of pollutant fate and transport, water resources engineering, environmental chemistry, geomorphology, drinking water and wastewater treatment, ecosystem dynamics, and technology, society, and environmental change. Drawing from a number of disciplines and approaches, elements within these systems are examined.
Contact(s):
Edward Bouwer, Environmental Engineering, Contact; 410-516-7437; bouwer@jhu.edu
Grace Brush, Ecology, Contact; 410-516-7107; gbrush@jhu.edu
Alan Stone, Environmental Chemistry, Contact; 410-516-8476; astone@jhu.edu
M. Wolman, Natural Resources, Contact; 410-516-7090; wolman@jhu.edu

JOHNS HOPKINS UNIVERSITY
SCHOOL OF PUBLIC HEALTH
PEW ENVIRONMENTAL HEALTH COMMISSION
111 Market Pl., Suite 850
Baltimore, MD 21202 United States
Phone: 410-659-2690 Fax: 410-659-2699
E-mail: cllee@jhsph.edu
Website: pewenvirohealth.jhsph.edu/
Founded: N/A
Scope: National
Description: The Pew Environmental Health Commission works to strengthen the country's public health system to protect against sickness and disease caused by environmental threats.
Publication(s): America's Environmental Health Gap, Attack Asthma, Healthy From the Start
Contact(s):
Shelley Hearn, Executive Director
Paul Locke, Deputy Director

JOHNSON STATE COLLEGE
DEPARTMENT OF ENVIRONMENTAL AND HEALTH SCIENCES
337 College Hill
Johnson, VT 05656-9464 United States
Phone: 800-635-2356 Fax: 802-635-1230
E-mail: jscapply@badger.jsc.vsc.edu
Website: http://ehs.academic.jsc.vsc.edu/
Founded: N/A
Scope: Local, State, Regional, National
Description: All academic programs (biology, environmental science, health science, and outdoor education) in the Dept. of Env. and Health Sciences aim to foster the development of content-rich curricula for students through active engagement in scientific inquiry and analysis. Across the disciplines in our department, emphasis is placed on development of critical thinking skills; laboratory and field-based problem solving skills; scientific and general writing; library and Internet research; and teamwork.
Keyword(s): Agriculture/Farming, Air Quality/Atmosphere, Climate Change, Ecosystems (precious), Energy, Ethics/Environmental Justice, Forests/Forestry, Land Issues, Oceans/Coasts/Beaches, Pollution (general), Population, Public Health, Public Lands/Greenspace, Recreation
Contact(s):
John Wrazen, Babcock Nature Preserve, Director
Tania Bacchus, Associate Professor
Robert Genter, Biology
Leslie Kanat, Associate Professor of Geology; 802-635-1327; Fax: 802-635-1461; kanatL@badger.jsc.vsc.edu
Brad Moskowitz, Outdoor Education
Karen Uhlendorf, Outdoor Education
John Wrazen, Ecology

K

KANSAS SCHOOL NATURALIST
Kansas School Naturalist
Department of Biology, Box 4050
Emporia State University
Emporia, KS 66801 United States
Phone: 620-341-5614 Fax: 620-341-5997
E-mail: ksnaturl@emporia.edu
Website: www.emporie.edu/ksn/
Founded: 1954
Membership: 10,001–100,000
Scope: State, International
Description: The Kansas School Naturalist is an accurate, high-interest natural history publication that serves science teachers, naturalists, Scout leaders, and others interested in all aspects of physical and biological sciences. From one to four issues are published each year. It is free upon request. Some issues have been translated into Spanish and Chinese. In-print back issues are available free upon request. Out-of-print issues are photocopied and sent for $1.00 each to cover costs.
Publication(s): Kansas School Naturalist

KANSAS STATE UNIVERSITY
COLLEGE OF AGRICULTURE
117 Waters Hall College of Agriculture
Manhattan, KS 66506-5506 United States
Phone: 785-532-6151 Fax: 785-532-6897
E-mail: jax1@ksu.edu
Website: www.ag.ksu.edu/
Founded: N/A
Membership: 1–100
Scope: International
Contact(s):
Ted Cable, Natural Resource Management; 785-532-1408; tcable@oznet.ksu.edu

David Mengel, Dept. of Agronomy, Head; 2004 Throckmorton Plant Science Center, Manhattan, KS 66506; 785-532-6101; Fax: 785-532-6094; dmengel@bear.agron.ksu.edu
Michel Ransom, Soil and Water Conservation; mdransom@ksu.edu
Thomas Warner, Horticulture, Forestry and Recreation Resources, Dept. Head; 2021 Throckmorton Plant Science Center, Manhattan, KS 66506; 785-532-6170; twarner@oznet.ksu.edu

KANSAS STATE UNIVERSITY
DEPARTMENT OF LANDSCAPE ARCHITECTURE / REGIONAL AND COMMUNITY PLANNING
302 Seaton Hall
Manhattan, KS 66506-2909 United States
Phone: 785-532-5961 Fax: 785-532-6722
E-mail: la-rcp@ksu.edu
Website: www.aalto.arch.ksu.edu/lar/

Founded: N/A

Scope: State, International

Contact(s):
C. Keithley, Regional and Community Planning, Director; 785-532-2440; cak@ksu.edu
Dan Donelin, Dept. Head; dandon@ksu.edu

KANSAS STATE UNIVERSITY
DIVISION OF BIOLOGY
232 Ackert Hall
Manhattan, KS 66506 United States
Phone: 785-532-6615 Fax: 785-532-6653
Website: www.ksu.edu/biology/

Founded: N/A

Scope: State

Contact(s):
David Hartnett, Director, Konza Prairie Research Natural Area; 785-532-5925; dchart@ksu.edu
Brian Spooner, Director of Biology; spoon1@ksu.edu

KEENE STATE COLLEGE
DEPARTMENT OF ENVIRONMENTAL STUDIES
229 Main St.
Keene, NH 03435 United States
Phone: 603-352-1909 Fax: 603-358-2897
Website: www.keene.edu/

Founded: 1909

Scope: State

Description: A multipurpose, predominantly undergraduate college with a central focus in the liberal arts and sciences. B.S. in Environmental Studies with options in Environmental Policy and Environmental Science and specializations in Environmental Biology, Environmental Chemistry and Environmental Geology

Contact(s):
Tim Allen, Program Coordinator; 603-358-2571; tallen@keene.edu

L

LAKE SUPERIOR STATE UNIVERSITY
SCHOOL OF NATURAL SCIENCES
650 W. Easterday Ave.
Sault Ste. Marie, MI 49783 United States
Phone: 906-635-2267 Fax: 906-635-2266
Website: www.lssu.edu

Founded: N/A

Scope: Local, State

Description: Degrees offered in Biological science, conservation law enforcement, environmental chemistry, environmental science, fisheries/wildlife management and natural resources technology (A.D.).

Contact(s):
Michael Donovan, Dean of the College of Natural and Health Sciences; 906-635-2267; Fax: 906-635-2266; mdonovan@lssu.edu
David Myton, Chemistry and Environmental Science, Chair; 906-635-2431; dmyton@gw.lssu.edu
Gregory Zimmerman, Biology, Chair; 906-635-2470

LAKEHEAD UNIVERSITY
FACULTY OF FORESTRY AND FOREST ENVIRONMENT
955 Oliver Rd.
Thunder Bay, P7B 5E1 Ontario Canada
Phone: 807-343-8507 Fax: 807-343-8116
E-mail: sandy.dunning@lakeheadu.ca
Website: www.lakeheadu.ca/~forwww/forestry.html

Founded: N/A

Scope: Local, State, Regional, National, International

Description: H.B.Sc. in Forestry, Bachelor of Environmental Studies, Honours Bachelor of Environmental Studies, M.Sc.F. and M.F. in Forestry

Contact(s):
Reino Pulkki, Dean; 807-343-8564; Fax: 807-343-8116; reino.pulkki@lakeheadu.ca
Sandy Dunning, Administrative Assistant; 807-343-8507; Fax: 807-343-8116; sandy.dunning@lakeheadu.ca
K. Brown, Chair, Graduate Forestry Programs; 807-343-8114; ken.brown@lakeheadu.ca
L. Meyer, Chair, Undergraduate Forestry Programs; 807-343-8445; leni.meyer@lakeheadu.ca
Yves Prevost, Chair, Environmental Studies Program; 807-343-8342; yves.prevost@lakeheadu.ca

LEWIS AND CLARK COLLEGE
COLLEGE OF ARTS AND SCIENCES
ENVIRONMENTAL STUDIES PROGRAM
0615 S.W. Palatine Hill Road
Portland, OR 97219 United States
Phone: 503-768-7699
E-mail: etw@lclark.edu
Website: www.lclark.edu

Founded: 1997

Membership: N/A

Scope: Local, State, Regional, National, International

Description: Undergraduate major in Environmental Studies. Interdisciplinary with participating faculty drawn from all divisions of the college.

Contact(s):
Evan Williams, Director of Environmental Studies; 503-768-7699; Fax: 503-768-7369; etw@lclark.edu

LEWIS AND CLARK COLLEGE
LAW SCHOOL
10015 S.W. Terwilliger Blvd .
Portland, OR 97219 United States
Phone: 503-768-6613 Fax: 503-768-6850
E-mail: lawadmss@lclark.edu
Website: law.lclark.edu

Founded: N/A

Scope: International

Description: Strong environmental law training program (Environmental Law Certificate at J.D. level and specialized LL.M. in Environmental and Natural Resources Law); publish journal of Environmental Law; research program in Natural Resources Law Institute (newsletter: NRLI News); conferences and workshops through continuing education program; internships in natural resources; and environmental clinical opportunities.

Publication(s): Brochures, 2002-2003 Catalog

Keyword(s): Ethics/Environmental Justice

LOUISIANA STATE UNIVERSITY SCHOOL OF FORESTRY, WILDLIFE AND FISHERIES

SCHOOL OF FORESTRY, WILDLIFE AND FISHERIES
Forestry Building, Rm. 124
Baton Rouge, LA 70803 United States
Phone: 225-388-4184 Fax: 578-388-4144
Website: www.coa.lsu.edu/fores/fores.html

Founded: N/A
Membership: 1–100
Scope: State
Contact(s):
Charles Bryan, Cooperative Fish and Wildlife Research Unit, Leader
Mary Ehrett, Secretary; mehrett@lsu.edu
Megan Lapayere, Assistant Leader - Fisheries

LOUISIANA TECH UNIVERSITY

SCHOOL OF FORESTRY
WILDLIFE CONSERVATION
FORESTRY
P.O. Box 10138
Ruston, LA 71272 United States
Phone: 318-257-4985 Fax: 318-257-5061
Website: www.ans.latech.edu/forestry-index.html

Founded: N/A
Membership: 1–100
Scope: Regional
Description: Located in Louisiana's major forest region, the School of Forestry offers Bachelor of Science degrees in Forestry and Wildlife Conservation. Highlights include a practical, field-oriented education, a GIS/Remote Sensing Laboratory, a highly trained and diverse faculty, and a successful placement record.
Publication(s): Wildlife of Southern Forests
Contact(s):
Mark Gibson, Interim Director; 318-257-4985; mgibson@latech.edu
James Dickson, Coordinator, Wildlife Program; 318-257-4020; jdickson@rans.latech.edu

M

MANCHESTER COLLEGE

KOINONIA ENVIRONMENTAL AND RETREAT CENTER
604 College Ave.
North Manchester, IN 46962 United States
Phone: 219-982-5010 Fax: 219-982-5043
Website: www.ares.manchester.edu/academic/koin.html

Founded: 1974
Scope: Regional
Description: The100-acre facility is used extensively to provide hands-on environmental science education for area students in grades, K-12. A two-story building houses the nature center with many educational displays. The retreat facility will accommodate 32 persons.
Contact(s):
Barbara Ehrhardt, Director

MCGILL UNIVERSITY

DEPARTMENT OF NATURAL RESOURCE SCIENCES
AVIAN SCIENCE AND CONSERVATION CENTRE (ASCC)
21,111 Lakeshore Road
Ste. Anne de Bellevue, H9X 3V9 Quebec Canada
Phone: 514-398-7760 Fax: 514-398-7990
Website: www.nrs.mcgill.ca/ascc

Founded: 1974
Membership: 1–100
Scope: Regional, National, International
Description: To promote the study of birds and their conservation, we conduct pure and applied research in the field and laboratory; breed, release and manage endangered species; and train students and interns from all over the world. The Centre publishes an annual newsletter, The Talon.
Publication(s): The Talon
Keyword(s): Agriculture/Farming, Development/Developing Countries, Ecosystems (precious), Energy, Forests/Forestry, Pollution (general), Public Lands/Greenspace, Recreation/Ecotourism, Water Habitats & Quality, Wildlife & Species
Contact(s):
David Bird, Director
Ian Ritchie, Curator; 514-398-7932; Fax: 514-398-7540; ritchie@nrs.mcgill.ca
Rodger Titman, Associate Director; 514-398-7933; Fax: 514-398-7990; titman@nrs.mcgill.ca

MCNEESE STATE UNIVERSITY

DEPARTMENT OF AGRICULTURE, WILDLIFE
Lake Charles, LA 70609 United States
Phone: 318-475-5690
Website: www.mcneese.edu/

Founded: N/A
Scope: State
Contact(s):
Billy Delany, Department of Agriculture, Wildlife Mangement Professor; 318-475-5690

MIAMI UNIVERSITY

INSTITUTE OF ENVIRONMENTAL SCIENCES
Boyd Hall
Oxford, OH 45056 United States
Phone: 513-529-5811 Fax: 513-529-5814
E-mail: havener@muohio.edu
Website: www.muohio.edu/ies

Founded: 1969
Membership: 1–100
Scope: Regional
Description: The Institute of Environmental Sciences has offered a professional Master of Environmental Science degree since 1969. This interdisciplinary program stresses problem solving and community service. The curriculum provides practical experience in an area of concentration, preparing students for a variety of practical careers in public and private sector jobs.
Keyword(s): Air Quality/Atmosphere, Ecosystems (precious), Energy, Pollution (general), Reduce/Reuse/Recycle, Water Habitats & Quality
Contact(s):
Gene Willeke, Institute of Environmental Sciences, Director; 513-529-5811; Fax: 513-529-5814; willekge@muohio.edu

MICHIGAN STATE UNIVERSITY

DEPARTMENT OF FISHERIES AND WILDLIFE
13 Natural Resources Building
East Lansing, MI 48824-1222 United States
Phone: 517-355-4478 Fax: 517-432-1699
E-mail: webmaster@perm3.sw.msu.edu
Website: www.fw.msu.edu

Founded: 1951
Scope: Local, State, Regional, National, International
Description: The Department of Fisheries and Wildlife focuses on the management of natural resources with particular reference to the management of ecosystems that support wild populations of birds, mammals, fish and other vertebrates. The Department's mission is to provide the education, research, and outreach needed by society for the conservation and rehabilitation of fish and wildlife resources and their ecosystems.
Contact(s):
Thomas Coon, Associate Chair; 517-355-4478; Fax: 517-432-1699; coontg@msu.edu

William Taylor, Chair; 517-355-4478; Fax: 517-432-1699; taylorw@msu.edu
Jim Schneider, Academic Specialist - Academic Adviser; 517-353-9091; Fax: 517-432-1699; schne181@msu.edu

MICHIGAN TECHNOLOGICAL UNIVERSITY SCHOOL OF FORESTRY AND WOOD PRODUCTS

SCHOOL OF FORESTRY AND WOOD PRODUCTS
1400 Townsend Dr.
Houghton, MI 49931 United States
Phone: 906-487-2454 Fax: 906-487-2915
E-mail: forestry@mtu.edu
Website: www.forestry.mtu.edu/

Founded: N/A

Scope: State

Description: Undergraduate concentrations and graduate programs in forest management science, forest biology and ecology, wildlife biology and ecology, and wood science and technology.

Publication(s): See publication web site

Contact(s):
Glenn Morz, Forestry, Dean; 906-487-6303

MIDDLE TENNESSEE STATE UNIVERSITY ENVIRONMENTAL EDUCATION CENTER

CENTER FOR ENVIRONMENT EDUCATION
BIOLOGY DEPARTMENT
Box 60
Murfreesboro, TN 37132 United States
Phone: 615-898-5449, ext. 2 Fax: 615-898-5920
E-mail: csmithwa@mtsu.edu
Website: www.mtsu.edu/%7Ecntr4ee/

Founded: 1970

Scope: Local, State, Regional

Description: The Center for Environment Education, an arm of the Middle Tennessee State University Biology Department, offers a wide variety of environmental programs on topics including but not limited to, waste reduction & recycling. We host after school workshops for teachers & youth leaders twice a semester, consult with teachers, youth leaders, & education organizations in environmental education, curriculum, teacher training, outdoor classrooms, & hands-on learning.

Publication(s): Consulting, Microscope loan program

Keyword(s): Agriculture/Farming, Air Quality/Atmosphere, Ecosystems (precious), Energy, Ethics/Environmental Justice, Forests/Forestry, Oceans/Coasts/Beaches, Pollution (general), Population, Reduce/Reuse/Recycle, Water Habitats & Quality, Wildlife & Species

Contact(s):
Padgett Kelly, Professor; 615-898-5615; Fax: 615-898-5920; jpkelly@mtsu.edu
Cindi Smith-Walters, Biology Professor; 615-898-5449, ext. 1; Fax: 615-898-5920; csmithwa@mtsu.edu
Karen Hargrove, Outreach Coordinator; 615-898-2660; Fax: 615-898-5920; khargrov@mtsu.edu
Kim Sadler, Assistant Professor; 615-904-8283; Fax: 615-898-5920; ksadler@mtsu.edu

MISSISSIPPI STATE UNIVERSITY

COLLEGE OF FOREST RESOURCES
Box 9820
Mississippi State, MS 39762 United States
Phone: 662-325-8530 Fax: 601-325-8726
Website: www.cfr.msstate.edu/

Founded: 1954

Scope: State

Description: The mission of the CFR is to promote the professional and intellectual development of its students, expand through research the fundamental knowledge upon which the natural resource disciplines are based, and help with the development and use of the forest, wildlife, and water resources of the state and nation through appropriate applied research, service, and technology transfer activities.

Contact(s):
Sam Foster, Dean; Box 9680, MS State, MS 39762; 662-325-2696; Fax: 662-325-8726; sfoster@cfr.msstate.edu
Steve Bullard, Forest Products, Interim Head; 601-325-2119; sbullard@cfr.msstate.edu
Bob Karr, Assiciate Dean; Box 9680, Mississippi State, MS 39762; 601-325-2793; bkarr@cfr.msstate.edu
Bruce Leopold, Wildlife and Fisheries, Head; 601-325-2619; bleopold@cfr.msstate.edu
Douglas Richards, Forestry, Head; Box 9681, Mississippi State, MS 39762; 601-325-2949; drichards@cfr.msstate.edu
Warren Thompson, Emeritus; Box 9680, Mississippi State, MS 39762; 601-325-2952; wthompson@cfr.msstate.edu

MISSISSIPPI STATE UNIVERSITY

FOREST AND WILDLIFE RESEARCH CENTER
Box 9680
MS State, MS 39762 United States
Phone: 662-325-8530 Fax: 662-325-8726
Website: www.cfr.msstate.edu/fwrc/fwrc.htm

Founded: 1994

Scope: State

Description: The mission of the FWRC is to conduct research and technical assistance programs relevant to the efficient management and utilization of the forest, wildlife, and fisheries of the state and region, and the protection and enhancement of these resources.

Contact(s):
Sam Foster, Director; Box 9680, MS State, MS 39762; 662-325-2696; Fax: 662-325-8726; sfoster@cfr.msstate.edu
Bob Karr, Associate Director; Box 9680, MS State, MS 39762; 662-325-2793; Fax: 662-325-8726; bkarr@cfr.msstate.edu
Steve Bullard, Interim Head; Box 9820, MS State, MS 39762; 662-325-2781; Fax: 662-325-8126; sbullard@cfr.msstate.edu
Bruce Leopold, Head; Box 9690, MS State, MS 39762; 662-325-2619; Fax: 662-325-8726; bleopold@cfr.msstate.edu
Doug Richards, Head; Box 9681, MS State, MS 39762; 662-325-2948; Fax: 662-325-8726; drichards@cfr.msstate.edu

MONTANA STATE UNIVERSITY

COLLEGE OF AGRICULTURE
202 Linfield Hall
P.O. Box 172860
Bozeman, MT 59717 United States
Phone: 406-994-5744 Fax: 406-994-6579
E-mail: agweb@montana.edu
Website: www.montana.edu/agriculture/College/

Founded: N/A

Scope: State

Contact(s):
Pete Burfemy, Animal & Range Sciences
D. Harmsen, Veterinary Molecular Biology
Jeffery Jacobson, Dept. of Land Resources and Environmental Sciences, Head; Leon Johnson Hall, P.O. Box 173120, Bozeman, MT 59717; 406-994-7060; Fax: 406-994-3933; jefj@montana.edu, general information: kathyj@montana.edu
Greg Johnson, Entomology
Myles Watts, Ag Economics & Economics
Norman Weeden, Dept. of Plant Sciences and Horticulture, Head; 119 AgBioScience Building, Bozeman, MT 59717-3150; 406-994-4832; Fax: 406-994-7600; nweeden@montana.edu, for general information: plantsciences@montana.edu

Educational Institutions

MONTANA STATE UNIVERSITY DEPT. OF ECOLOGY

DEPARTMENT OF ECOLOGY
Lewis Hall
Bozeman, MT 59717 United States
Phone: 406-994-4548 Fax: 406-994-3190
E-mail: ecology@montana.edu
Website: www.montana.edu/ecology/

Founded: N/A
Membership: 1–100
Scope: State
Description: Biology Dept. offers B.S. in Biology, Biology Teaching, Biomedical Sciences or Fish and Wildlife Management and M.S. and Ph.D. programs with a concentration in Ecology, Conservation Biology, Plant Biology or Neurobiology.
Contact(s):
Lynn Irby, Fish and Wildlife Management Program, Coordinator; 406-994-3252; ubili@montana.edu
Jay Rotella, Department Head; 406-994-5676; rotella@montana.edu

MONTCLAIR STATE UNIVERSITY

COLLEGE OF SCIENCE AND MATHEMATICS
One Normal Ave.
Upper Montclair, NJ 07043 United States
Phone: 973-655-4448
Website: csam.montclair.edu/

Founded: N/A
Contact(s):
Bonnie Lustigman, Biology, Chair; lustigman@saturn.montclair.edu
Robert Taylor, Earth and Environmental Science, Professor; taylorr@saturn.montclair.edu

MOREHEAD STATE UNIVERSITY

DEPARTMENT OF BIOLOGICAL AND ENVIRONMENTAL SCIENCES
123 Lappin Hall
Morehead, KY 40351 United States
Phone: 606-783-2944 Fax: 606-783-5002
Website: www.morehead-st.edu

Founded: N/A
Membership: 1–100
Scope: State
Publication(s): See publication website
Contact(s):
David Magrane, Biology; d.magrane@morehead-st.edu

MOUNT UNION COLLEGE

BRUMBAUGH CENTER FOR ENVIRONMENTAL SCIENCE
HUSTON-BRUMBAUGH NATURE CENTER
1972 Clark Avenue
Alliance, OH 44601 United States
Phone: 330-823-7487 Fax: 330-823-8531
E-mail: mucnature@igc.org

Founded: 1988
Membership: N/A
Scope: Local, State
Description: The Brumbaugh Center for Environmental Science offeres environmental education for college students, children and youth, and adults with an emphasis on outdoor activities.
Keyword(s): Forests/Forestry, Land Issues, Water Habitats & Quality
Contact(s):
Charles McClaugherty, Director; 330-823-3655; Fax: 330-823-8531; mcclauca@muc.edu
Patricia Rickard, Naturalist; 330-823-7487; Fax: 330-823-8531; rickarpa@muc.edu

MURRAY STATE UNIVERSITY

WILDLIFE
334 Blackburn Science
Murray, KY 42071-3346 United States
Phone: 270-762-2786 Fax: 270-762-2788
Website: www.murraystate.edu

Founded: N/A
Membership: 1–100
Scope: State
Description: Offering B.S. and M.S in Biology, and Wildlife and Conservation Biology
Publication(s): See publication web site
Contact(s):
Tom Timmons, Department of Biological Sciences, Fisheries, Chairman; 270-762-6754; tom.timmons@murraystate.edu
David White, Center for Reservoir Research, Contact; 270-474-2272; david.white@murraystate.edu
Stephen White, Wildlife, Contact; 270-762-6298; steve.white@murraystate.edu
Howard Whiteman, Conservation Amphibian Research; 270-762-6753; Fax: 270-762-2788; howard.whiteman@murraystate.edu

MUSASHI INSTITUTE OF TECHNOLOGY

3-3-1 Ushikubo-nishi, Tsuzuki-ku
Yokohama, 224-0015 Japan
Phone: 81452600 Fax: 81452626

Founded: 1938
Description: The University consists of two departments: Civil Engineering and Environmental and Information Studies. Publishes Conservation Biology and Issues on Environment.

N

NEW MEXICO STATE UNIVERSITY

COLLEGE OF AGRICULTURE AND HOME ECONOMICS
DEPARTMENT OF ANIMAL AND RANGE SCIENCES
Agriculture & Home Economics
Box 30003
Las Cruces, NM 88003 United States
Phone: 505-646-0111 Fax: 505-646-5975
Website: www.nmsu.edu/~dars

Founded: N/A
Scope: State
Description: In the Department of Animal and Range Sciences, students can major in animal or range science. The Department also offers pre-veterinary studies. In addition to undergraduate degrees, the Department offers graduate degrees at the Master of Science and Doctor of Philosophy levels. The M.S. or Ph.D. in Animal Science can emphasize nutrition or physiology, and the M.S. or Ph.D. in Range Science students have the option to study in areas including, but not exclusive to, range ecology and watershed
Contact(s):
Jerry Schickedanz, Dean

NEW MEXICO STATE UNIVERSITY

COLLEGE OF AGRICULTURE AND HOME ECONOMICS
DEPARTMENT OF FISHERY AND WILDLIFE SCIENCES
P.O. Box 30003, Dept. 4901
Las Cruces, NM 88003 United States
Phone: 505-646-7051 Fax: 505-646-1281
E-mail: natres@nmsu.edu
Website: leopold.nmsu.edu

Founded: N/A
Scope: State
Description: The Department offers training in Fishery & Wildlife Science at the undergraduate and graduate level. The curricula are designed to prepare students for work in the fields of research, teaching, extension and management. With a

diversified faculty working in a broad range of terrestrial and aquatic systems, students have excellent opportunities for study in a wide variety of sub-disciplines in the fishery and wildlife sciences.

Contact(s):
Donald Caccamise, Department Head

NORTH CAROLINA STATE UNIVERSITY
COLLEGE OF AGRICULTURE AND LIFE SCIENCES
Box 7642 115
Raleigh, NC 27695-7642 United States
Phone: 919-515-2614 Fax: 919-515-5266
Website: www.cals.ncsu.edu/

Founded: N/A
Scope: State
Contact(s):
William Grant, Director of Undergraduate Biology Programs; 919-515-3341
James Gilliam, Zoology, Head; 919-515-5978
John Havlin, Soil Science, Head; 919-515-2655; john_havlin@ncsu.edu
Gerald Leblanc, Environmental and Molecular Toxicology, Head; 919-515-7404; Fax: 919-515-7169; gal@unity.ncsu.edu
Samuel Mozley, Ecology, Environmental Sciences; 919-515-1981
Gerald Van Dyke, Botany, Head; 919-515-2222
James Young, Biological and Agricultural Engineering, Head; 919-515-2694; Fax: 919-515-6772; jim_young@ncsu.edu

NORTH DAKOTA STATE UNIVERSITY
DEPARTMENT OF BIOLOGICAL SCIENCES
Stevens Hall
Fargo, ND 58105 United States
Phone: 701-231-7087 Fax: 701-231-7149
Website: www.ndsu.nodak.edu/zoology/

Founded: 1890
Membership: 1–100
Scope: Local, State, Regional, National, International
Description: Wildlife and Fisheries Biology Option in Zoology
Keyword(s): Agriculture/Farming, Water Habitats & Quality
Contact(s):
Will Bleier, Department Chair; Vertebrate Pest Management; 701-231-8421; Fax: 701-231-7149; William.Bleier@ndsu.nodak.edu
Mac Butler, Professor, Aquatic Ecology; 701-231-7398; Fax: 701-231-7149; Malcolm.Butler@ndsu.nodak.edu
Gary Clambey, Associate Professor; Ecology; 701-231-8404; Fax: 701-231-7149; Gary.Clambey@ndsu.nodak.edu
Mark Clark, Assistant Professor; Population Biology; 701-231-8246; Fax: 701-231-7149; M.E.Clark@ndsu.nodak.edu
Gary Nuechterlein, Professor; Behavorial Ecology; 701-231-8436; Fax: 701-231-7149; Gary.Nuechterlein@ndsu.nodak.edu
Wendy Reed, Assistant Professor; Physiological Ecology of Coots; 701-231-7012; Fax: 701-231-7149; Wendy.Reed@ndsu.nodak.edu
Craig Stockwell, Assistant Professor; Conservation Biology; 701-231-8449; Fax: 701-231-7149; craig.stockwell@ndsu.nodak.edu

NORTHEASTERN UNIVERSITY
BIOLOGY DEPARTMENT
414 Mugar Life Sciences, 360 Huntington Ave.
Boston, MA 02115 United States
Phone: 617-373-2260 Fax: 617-373-3724
Website: www.dac.neu.edu/biology

Founded: N/A
Membership: 1–100
Scope: State
Contact(s):
Joseph Ayers, Marine Science Center/Marine Biology, Director; East Point, Nahant, MA 01908; 617-581-7370; lobster@neu.edu
Gwilym Jones, Vertebrate Systematics and Ecology; 617-373-2851; g.jones@nunet.neu.edu

NORTHERN ARIZONA UNIVERSITY
COLLEGE OF ARTS AND SCIENCES
NAU Box 5640
Flagstaff, AZ 86011-5621 United States
Phone: 520-523-2381 Fax: 520-523-7500
E-mail: biology@nau.edu
Website: www.nau.edu/

Founded: N/A
Scope: State
Description: Dept. of Biology offers an emphasis in the areas of: Applied Plant Science, Aquatic Biology, Ecology, Cellular and Molecular Biology and Fish and Wildlife Management. Available emphasis areas for Environmental Science are: Biology, Chemistry, Applied Geology, Applied Mathematics, Microbiology, Environmental Administration and Policy, Environmental Communications and Environmental Management.
Contact(s):
Lee Drickamer, Chair, Dept. of Biological Sciences; 520-523-7501; Fax: 520-523-7500; lee.drickamer@nau.edu

NORTHERN ARIZONA UNIVERSITY
COLLEGE OF ECOSYSTEM SCIENCE AND MANAGEMENT
Box 15018
Flagstaff, AZ 86011-5018 United States
Phone: 520-523-3031 Fax: 520-523-1080
E-mail: esm.info@nau.edu
Website: www.cesm.nau.edu

Founded: N/A
Scope: State
Description: Northern Arizona University is in an ideal location for the study of both forestry and recreation. Near Flagstaff are the largest ponderosa pine forest in America, five life zones within fifty miles, recreation and aesthetic areas, and extensive wildlife, grazing and watershed areas.
Contact(s):
Donald Arganbright, Interim Dean; donald.g.arganbright@nau.edu

NORTHERN ARIZONA UNIVERSITY
COLLEGE OF ECOSYSTEM SCIENCE AND MANAGEMENT
DEPARTMENT OF GEOGRAPHY AND PUBLIC PLANNING
Box 15016
Flagstaff, AZ 86011-5016 United States
Phone: 928-523-2650 Fax: 928-523-1080
Website: www.geog.nau.edu/

Founded: N/A
Scope: State
Description: for Public Planning, choice of emphasis in Land Use Planning or Environmental Planning
Contact(s):
Alan Lew, Chair, Department of Geography and Public Planning

NORTHERN ARIZONA UNIVERSITY

NORTHERN ARIZONA ENVIRONMENTAL EDUCATION RESOURCES CENTER
CENTER FOR ENVIRONMENTAL SCIENCES AND EDUCATION
S. San Francisco St. 860011
Flagstaff, AZ 86011 United States
Phone: 928-523-9011 Fax: 520-523-5441
E-mail: paul.rowland@nau.edu
Website: www.nau.edu/~envsci/naeerc/index.html

Founded: 1994

Contact(s):

Paul Rowland, Associate Director; 520-523-5853

NORTHERN MICHIGAN UNIVERSITY

1401 Presque Isle Ave.
Marquette, MI 49855 United States
Phone: 906-227-2700 Fax: 906-227-2703
E-mail: artssci@nmu.edu
Website: www.nmu.edu

Founded: N/A

Scope: State

Publication(s): Update (Newsletter)

Contact(s):

Michael Broadway, Department of Geography, Earth Science, Conservation, and Pl; Luther S. West Science Bldg., Rm. 213, Marquette, MI 49855; 906-227-2500; Fax: 906-227-1621; mbroadwa@nmu.edu

Neil Cumberlidge, Department of Biology, Head; Luther S. West Science Bldg., Rm. 277, Marquette, MI 49855; 906-227-2310; Fax: 906-227-1063; ncumberl@nmu.edu

NORTHLAND COLLEGE

SIGURD OLSON ENVIRONMENTAL INSTITUTE
1411 Ellis Ave
Ashland, WI 54806 United States
Phone: 715-682-1223 Fax: 715-682-1218
Website: www.northland.edu/soei

Founded: 1972
Membership: 1,001–10,000
Scope: Regional, National
Description: The Sigurd Olson Environmental Institute was founded at Northland College in 1972 to increase public understanding of the complex relationships between natural and cultural environments in the Lake Superior region and to assist in developing workable solutions to regional environmental problems. The institute seeks to carry out Sigurd Olson's vision by fostering environmental citizenship and educating citizens for a sustainable future.

Keyword(s): Air Quality/Atmosphere, Ecosystems (precious), Forests/Forestry, Land Issues, Water Habitats & Quality, Wildlife & Species

Contact(s):

Kenneth Bro, Executive Director
Carolyn Hanna, Officer Manager; 715-682-1392; Fax: 715-682-1218; channa@northland.edu
Paula Bonk, Assistant/Lake Superior Binational Forum
Mike Gardner, Assistant Director; 715-682-1481; Fax: 715-682-1218; mgardner@northland.edu
Jim Musso, Advisory Board Chair
Jerri Ridlon, Communications Specialist
Pam Troxell, Timber Wolf Alliance Coordinator

NORTHWESTERN STATE UNIVERSITY OF LOUISIANA

WILDLIFE PROGRAM
Biology Dept.
Natchitoches, LA 71497 United States
Phone: 318-357-5323 Fax: 318-357-4518
Website: www.nsula.edu

Founded: N/A
Membership: 1–100
Scope: Local
Description: To educate students in principles and science of wildlife management; to prepare students for management of natural resources at the professional entry levels; and to provide an emphasis on biodiversity and ecosystems; to orient students toward interpersonal communication

Contact(s):

Steven Gabrey, Biology/Wildlife Management, Advisor; 318-357-5375; steveng@alpha.nsula.edu
Dick Stalling, Biology Sciences, Head

O

OBERLIN COLLEGE

ADAM JOSEPH LEWIS CENTER
ENVIRONMENTAL STUDIES PROGRAM
122 Elm Street
Oberlin, OH 44074-1095 United States
Phone: 440-775-8747 Fax: 440-775-8946
E-mail: bev.burgess@oberlin.edu
Website: www.oberlin.edu/~envs/

Founded: N/A

Description: An interdisciplinary program which includes 30+ courses across ten departments. Students are required to do significant academic work that spans the sciences, social sciences, and the humanities. The program offers significant off-campus opportunities for students through a Watershed Education Program, a local initiative in sustainable agriculture, and work with the city on energy and development issues.

Contact(s):

David Orr, Program Chair

OHIO STATE UNIVERSITY

SCHOOL OF NATURAL RESOURCES
2021 Coffey Rd.
210 Kottman Hall
Columbus, OH 43210-1085 United States
Phone: 614-292-2265 Fax: 614-292-7432
Website: snr.osu.edu

Founded: N/A
Membership: N/A
Scope: Local, State, Regional, National, International
Description: We offer BS, MS and PhD programs in Natural Resources.

Contact(s):

Gary Mullins, Director of the School of Natural Resources; mullins.2@osu.edu

OKLAHOMA STATE UNIVERSITY

COOPERATIVE FISH AND WILDLIFE RESEARCH UNIT
Fishery & Wildlife
Stillwater, OK 74078 United States
Phone: 405-744-5000 Fax: 405-744-5006
E-mail: coopunit@okstate.edu
Website: www.okstate.edu

Founded: N/A

Scope: Local, State, Regional, National

Description: Research and education in resource conservation.

Contact(s):

David Engle, Range Management, Program Coordinator; 477 Ag Hall, Stillwater, OK 74078; 405-744-6410
Becky Johnson, Department of Botany, Head; 405-744-5559
Edward Knobbe, Environmental Science, Program Coordinator; 405-744-9229
David Leslie, Cooperative Fish and Wildlife Research Unit, Leader; 404 Life Sciences West; 405-744-6342
Craig McKinley, Department of Forestry, Head; 405-744-5437
James Shaw, Department of Wildlife/Fisheries/Ecology/Zoology, Head; 405-744-5555

OREGON STATE UNIVERSITY DEPT. OF FISHERIES AND WILDLIFE

DEPARTMENT OF FISHERIES AND WILDLIFE
104 Nash
Corvallis, OR 97331 United States
Phone: 541-737-4531 Fax: 541-737-3590
Website: fw.oregonstate.edu/

Founded: N/A
Membership: 101–1,000
Scope: State, Regional
Description: Education in Fisheries & Wildlife topics
Contact(s):
Michael Unsworth, Center for Analysis of Environmental Change, Director
Robert Anthony, Cooperative Fishery and Wildlife Research Unit, Leader
Daniel Edge, Fisheries and Wildlife, Head of Wildlife
Steven Radosevich, Sustainable Forestry Program, Leader of Forestry
Harold Salwasser, Forestry and Forest Recreation, Dean
Carl Schreck, Cooperative Fishery and Wildlife Research Unit, Leader
George Stankey, Consortium on Social Values of Natural Resources, Coordinator

P

PENNSYLVANIA STATE EXTENSION SERVICES

217 Agricultural Administration Bldg., Pennsylvania State University
University Park, PA 16802-2600 United States
Phone: 814-863-3438 Fax: 814-863-7905
Website: www.extension.psu.edu

Founded: N/A
Membership: N/A
Scope: State
Description: The mission of Penn State Cooperative Extension is to extend nonformal outreach educational opportunities to individuals, families, businesses, and communities throughout Pennsylvania. Cooperative Extension education programs enable the Commonwealth to maintain a competitive and environmentally sound food and fiber system and prepare Pennsylvania's youth, adults, and families to enhance the quality of their lives and participate more fully in community decisions.
Contact(s):
Theodore Alter, Director of Extension; 217 Agricultural Administration Building, Pennsylvania State University, University Park, PA 16802; 814-863-3438; Fax: 814-863-7905
Mary Jo Depp-Nestlerode, Interim Associate Director of Extension; 217 Agricultural Administration Bldg., Pennsylvania State University, University Park, PA 16802-2600; 814-863-3438; Fax: 814-863-7905; mjdepp@psu.edu
Jack Watson, Assistant Director of Extension, State Program Leader; 401 Agricultural Administration Bldg., Pennsylvania State University, University Park, PA 16802; 814-863-6114; Fax: 814-863-7776; jackwatson@psu.edu

PENNSYLVANIA STATE UNIVERSITY

SCHOOL OF FOREST RESOURCES
113 Ferguson Bldg. Schl. Forest Resources, University Park, PA 16802 United States
Phone: 814-863-7093 Fax: 814-865-3725
Website: www.sfr.cas.psu.edu

Founded: N/A
Membership: 101–1,000
Scope: State
Contact(s):
Charles Strauss, Director Interim
M. Brittingham, Wildlife and Fisheries, Contact; 320 Forest Resources Lab, University Park, PA 16802; 814-863-8442; Fax: 814-863-7193; mxb21@psu.edu
Robert Carline, Fisheries and Wildlife Cooperative Research Unit, Leader; 113A Merkle Bldg., Univeristy Park, PA 16802; 814-865-4511; Fax: 814-863-4710; f7u@psu.edu
John Janowiak, Wood Products, Professor; 307 Forest Resources Laboratory, University Park, PA 16802; 814-865-5722; Fax: 814-863-7193; jjj2@psu.edu

PINES ROWAN UNIVERSITY

120-13 Whitesbog Rd.
Browns Mills, NJ 08015 United States
Phone: 609-893-1765 Fax: 609-893-8297

Founded: N/A
Scope: State
Contact(s):
Gary Patterson, Director
Maria Peter, Program Coordinator

POLYTECHNIC UNIVERSITY OF NEW YORK

CIVIL AND ENVIRONMENTAL ENGINEERING DEPARTMENT
6 Metro Tech Center
Brookyn, NY 11201 United States
Phone: 718-260-3220 Fax: 718-260-3433
E-mail: cee@poly.edu
Website: www.poly.edu/cee

Founded: N/A
Membership: 1–100
Scope: International
Description: The Department is engaged in teaching and research in several areas of environmental science and engineering. Masters degrees with environmental focus are offered in civil engineering, environmental engineering, and environmental health science. The Ph.D. is also offered.
Contact(s):
David Chang, President
F. (Bud) Grisses, Dept. Chair of Civil Engineering

PORTLAND STATE UNIVERSITY

ENVIRONMENTAL SCIENCES AND RESOURCES
P.O. Box 751
Portland, OR 97207-0751 United States
Phone: 503-725-4980 Fax: 503-725-3888
E-mail: envir@pdx.edu
Website: www.esr.pdx.edu

Founded: N/A
Scope: State
Description: The focus of the program is research on the problems of the environment and resources. The program offers Ph.D. degrees in cooperation with the departments of biology, chemistry, civil engineering, economics, geography, geology, and physics. Master programs include M.S., M.E.M. (Master of Environmental Management), and M.S.T (Master of Science in Teaching). Bachelor's programs (B.A., B.S.) include tracks in environmental science and environmental policy and management.
Contact(s):
Roy Koch, Director; 503-725-8038; kochr@mail.pdx.edu

PRESCOTT COLLEGE, LIBERAL ARTS AND THE ENVIRONMENTAL STUDIES PROGRAM

ENVIRONMENTAL STUDIES PROGRAM
220 Grove Ave.
Prescott, AZ 86301 United States
Phone: 520-778-2090 Fax: 928-776-5137
Website: www.prescott.edu/rdp/rdp_es.html

Founded: N/A
Scope: Regional
Description: The Environmental Studies Program is one of four programs within Prescott College. The program emphasizes experiential and interdisciplinary learning, and focuses on the interrelationaships between the human and nonhuman worlds and the reciprocal influences each has on the other.
Publication(s): Wolfberry Sun, semi-annual newsletter, Alligator Juniper. Poems, stories and photographs, Transitions, brochure
Contact(s):
Lisa Floyd-Hanna, Program Coordinator

PURDUE UNIVERSITY
DEPARTMENT OF FORESTRY AND NATURAL RESOURCES
1159 Forestry Bldg.
West Lafayette, IN 47907-1159 United States
Phone: 765-494-3591 Fax: 765-496-2422
Website: www.fnr.purdue.edu/
Founded: N/A
Scope: State
Contact(s):
W. Mills, Undergraduate Programs, Director of Student Services; 765-494-3575; Fax: 765-496-2422
Robert Swihart, Graduate Program, Director of Graduate Studies; 765-494-3621; Fax: 765-496-2422
Dennis Lemaster, Department of Forestry and Natural Resources, Head; 765-494-3590; Fax: 765-496-2422

R

RAPTOR CENTER, THE
University of Minnesota
1920 Fitch Avenue
St. Paul, MN 55108 United States
Phone: 612-624-4745 Fax: 612-624-8740
E-mail: raptor@umn.edu
Website: www.raptor.cvm.umn.edu
Founded: 1974
Membership: 1,001–10,000
Scope: International
Description: The Raptor Center specializes in the medical care, rehabilitation, and conservation of birds of prey (eagles, hawks, owls, and falcons). In addition to treating approximately 800 raptors a year, the internationally known program provides specialized training in raptor medicine and surgery for veterinarians from around the world. The Raptor Center also reaches 250,000 people each year through public education programs and events.
Publication(s): Raptor Release, The, Care and Management of Captive Raptors
Keyword(s): Wildlife & Species
Contact(s):
Patrick Redig, Director; 612-624-4969; Fax: 612-624-8740; redig001@umn.edu
Lori Arent, Rehabilitation Coordinator; 612-624-0762; Fax: 612-624-8740; arent@umn.edu
Sue Kirchoff, Publications Editor; Fax: 612-624-8740; kirch004@umn.edu

RENSSELAER POLYTECHNIC INSTITUTE
DEPARTMENT OF EARTH AND ENVIRONMENTAL SCIENCES
Jonsson-Rowland Science Center, Rm. 1C25
Troy, NY 12180-3590 United States
Phone: 518-276-6474 Fax: 518-276-6680
E-mail: ees@rpi.edu
Website: www.rpi.edu/dept/geo/
Founded: N/A
Scope: International
Contact(s):
Frank Spear, Chair; spearf@rpi.edu

RENSSELAER POLYTECHNIC INSTITUTE
ENVIRONMENTAL MANAGEMENT AND POLICY PROGRAM
110 8th St., Pittsburgh Building
Troy, NY 12180-3590 United States
Phone: 518-276-6565 Fax: 518-276-2665
E-mail: emap@rpi.edu
Website: emat.mgmt.rip.edu/
Founded: N/A
Scope: International
Description: Rensselaer's EMP program educates students at the masters of science level to undertake a professional role in companies, governmental agencies, and other organizations dealing with environmental and energy matters from a base of technical and managerial knowledge and understanding.
Publication(s): Corporate Environmental Strategy
Contact(s):
Frank Mendelson, Director, Acting

RHODE ISLAND SCHOOL OF DESIGN
DEPARTMENT OF LANDSCAPE ARCHITECTURE
Two College St.
Providence, RI 02903 United States
Phone: 401-454-6282 Fax: 401-454-6299
E-mail: ldardept@risd.edu
Website: www.risd.edu
Founded: N/A
Membership: 1–100
Scope: State
Description: Graduates depart RISD with the necessary training to work from an informed position, with an environmental ethic, a personal philosophy, their interpretive abilities honed and with creative vision.
Contact(s):
Derek Bradford, Professor; 401-454-6292; dbradfor@risd.edu
Elizabeth Hermann, Associate Professor; edherman@risd.edu
Miekyoung Kim, Associate Professor; 401-454-6286; info@mikyoungkim.com
Leonard Newcomb, Associate Professor; 401-454-6282
Colgate Searle, Head Dept. of Landscape Architecture; csearle@risd.edu

RICE UNIVERSITY
Architecture MS 50, 6100 Main Street
Houston, TX 77005 United States
Phone: 713-348-4864 Fax: 713-348-5277
E-mail: arch@rice.edu
Website: www.arch.rice.edu/
Founded: N/A
Membership: 1–100
Scope: Regional
Description: Master of Architecture in Urban Design for individuals who already hold a professional degree qualifying them for registration as architects or landscape architects
Publication(s): See publication web site
Contact(s):
Lars Lerup, Dean; lars@rice.edu

RICE UNIVERSITY
6100 Main St.
Houston, TX 77251 United States
Phone: 713-527-8101
Website: www.rice.edu
Founded: 1912
Contact(s):
Frank Fisher, Director of Wetland Studies, Ecology Dept.; 713-527-5917; fisher@rice.edu

C. Ward, Energy and Environmental Systems Institute, Director; 6100 Main St., MS 316, Houston, TX 77005; eesi@rice.edu
Ronald Sass, Ecology and Evolutionary Biology Dept., Chair; 6100 Main St., MS 170, Houston, TX 77005; 713-527-4919; Fax: 713-285-5232; sass@ruf.rice.edu

RICHARD STOCKTON COLLEGE
DIVISION OF NATURAL SCIENCES AND MATHEMATICS
P.O. Box 195
Pomona, NJ 08240 United States
Phone: 609-652-1776 Fax: 609-748-5515
E-mail: dennis.weiss@stockton.edu
Website: www.stockton.edu/

Founded: 1969
Scope: State, Regional
Description: 4 year public liberal arts college
Publication(s): NANS Safety
Contact(s):
Gordan Grguric, Marine Science
Charlie Helands, Mathematics Coordinator
Edward Paul, Chemistry Coordinator
Peter Straub, Biology Coordinator
Dennis Weiss, Dean
George Zimmerman, Environmental Science & Geology

ROGER WILLIAMS UNIVERSITY
DEPARTMENT OF BIOLOGY, MARINE BIOLOGY, CHEMISTRY AND ENVIRONMENTAL SCIENCE
One Old Ferry Rd.
Bristol, RI 02809 United States
Phone: 401-254-3108 Fax: 401-254-3310
Website: www.rwuonline.cc/

Founded: 1969
Membership: 1–100
Scope: International
Contact(s):
Delia Anderson, Assistant Dean; danderson@rwu.edu

RUTGERS UNIVERSITY, COOK COLLEGE
DEPARTMENT ENVIRONMENTAL SCIENCE
14 College Farm Road
New Brunswick, NJ 08901-8551 United States
Phone: 732-932-9185
Website: www.envsci.rutgers.edu/

Founded: 1920
Membership: 101–1,000
Scope: Local, State, Regional, National, International
Description: We believe we are the oldest Department of Environmental Science in the world (1920). We focus on the science of pollution control, fate and effects of pollutants, atmospheric science, environmental toxicology, and pollution exposure assessment. We offer undergraduate, graduate, and professional programs.
Keyword(s): Air Quality/Atmosphere, Climate Change, Pollution (general), Public Health, Reduce/Reuse/Recycle, Water Habitats & Quality
Contact(s):
Maurice Hartley, Undergraduate Director; hartley@aesop.rutgers.edu
Peter Parks, Graduate Director; parks@aesop.rutgers.edu
Peter Strom, Graduate Program Director; 732-932-8078; strom@envsci.rutgers.edu
Adesoji Adelaja, Executive Dean, Cook College and the New Jersey Agricultural; Cook College, Martin Hall, Lipman Drive, New Brunswick, NJ 08901-8551; 732-932-9155; Fax: 732-932-8887; adelaja@aesop.rutgers.edu
Robert Tate, Undergraduate Program Coordinator; 732-932-9810; tate@envsci.rutgers.edu
Lily Young, Environmental Sciences Dept., Chair; 14 College Farm Road, New Brunswick, NJ 08901-8551; 732-932-9185; Fax: 732-932-8644; chair@envsci.rutgers.edu

S

SAN FRANCISCO STATE UNIVERSITY
WILDLANDS STUDIES PROGRAM
3 Mosswood Circle
Cazadero, CA 95421 United States
Phone: 707-632-5665 Fax: 707-632-5665
E-mail: wildlnds@sonic.net
Website: wildlandsstudies.com/ws

Founded: 1979
Scope: Regional, National, International
Description: Wildlands Studies offers a year-round series of field study programs in North American and international wilderness locations. Participants join backcountry research teams in a search for answers to important environmental problems concerning wildlife populations and/or wildlands habitats. Participants can earn 3-14 units of university credit.
Publication(s): Course Catalog
Contact(s):
Crandall Bay, Director; 707-632-5665

SAN JOSE STATE UNIVERSITY
DEPARTMENT OF ENVIRONMENTAL STUDIES
One Washington Sq.
San Jose, CA 95192-0115 United States
Phone: 408-924-5450 Fax: 408-924-5477
E-mail: envstdys@email.sjsu.edu
Website: www.sjsu.edu/depts/envstudies/

Founded: 1970
Scope: State
Description: Special interests of the faculty include habitat restoration, environmental impact assessment, energy, water, and forest resource management, human ecology, international development, coastal resource management, solid waste management, and environmental education for teachers. Credit is given for beyond-the-classroom experiences for appropriate Peace Corps Service, Internships programs, Center for Development of Recycling (CDR) and Environmental Resource Center (ERC).
Contact(s):
Lester Rowntree, Department Chairperson

SANTA CLARA COMMUNITY ACTION PROGRAM
ENVIRONMENTAL AWARENESS
500 El Camino Real
P.O. Box 2946
Santa Clara, CA 95053-2946 United States
Phone: 408-551-4182

Founded: 2001
Membership: 1–100
Scope: Local, State, National, International
Description: Based in Santa Clara University's Community Action Program, the Environmental Awareness network empowers students to plant native vegetation at a local habitat restoration site, reduce campus consumption, collaborate with local conservation groups, educate each other on issues of international importance, and explore overall the ways in which we as students can and do affect the living earth.
Keyword(s): Ecosystems (precious), Energy, Ethics/Environmental Justice, Land Issues, Pollution (general), Public Health, Reduce/Reuse/Recycle, Sprawl/Urban Planning, Transportation

SHAWNEE STATE UNIVERSITY
DEPARTMENT OF NATURAL SCIENCES
940 Second St.
Portsmouth, OH 45662 United States
Phone: 740-354-3205
Website: www.shawnee.edu

Founded: N/A
Membership: 1–100
Scope: State
Description: B.S. in Natural Science field with minor or certificate in Environmental Studies
Contact(s):
Jeffrey Bauer, Environmental Certificate Advisor; 740-351-3421; Fax: 740-351-3596; jbauer@shawnee.edu

SHEPHERD COLLEGE
INSTITUTE FOR ENVIRONMENTAL STUDIES
P.O. BOX 3210
Byrd Center
Shepherdstown, WV 25443 United States
Phone: 304-876-5227 Fax: 304-876-5028
Website: www.shepherd.wvnet.edu/iesweb/

Founded: N/A
Membership: 1–100
Scope: State
Description: B.S. in Environmental Studies with focus in physical and biological sciences or resource management.
Contact(s):
Ed Snyder, Director; 304-876-5227; Fax: 304-876-5028; iesweb@shepherd.edu

SILLMAN UNIVERSITY
CENTER OF EXCELLENCE—COASTAL RESOURCE MANAGEMENT
Dumaguete City, 6200 Philippines
Phone: 63 35 225 6711/225 6855 Fax: 63 35 225 4608
E-mail: admsucrm@mozcom.com
Website: su.edu.ph

Founded: 1901
Description: Sillman University, with USAID, created an environmental awareness program. Starting with a coastal resource management, it specifically works with the marine laboratory of the university and is currently working on environmental education and environmental communication within the university and in the community through extension programs.
Contact(s):
Hilconida Calumpong, Researcher; 633-522-5250; mlsucrm@mozcom.com
Janet Estacion, Researcher/Professor; 633-522-5250; mlsucrm@mozcom.com
Mikhail Maxino, Dean, College of Law/Researcher; 633-522-5671; admsucrm@mozcom.com
Roy Olsen de Leon, Researcher/Teacher; 633-522-5671; admsucrm@mozcom.com
Betsy Tan, Dean, College of Education; 633-522-5671; admsucrm@mozcom.com

SLIPPERY ROCK UNIVERSITY
101 Eisenberg Bldg. SRU
Slippery Rock, PA 16057 United States
Phone: 724-738-2068
E-mail: paulette.johnson@sru.edu
Website: www.sru.edu/

Founded: N/A
Scope: State, National, International
Description: Slippery Rock University provides five environmental degree programs. They include three undergraduate: environmental education, studies and science and two graduate programs: environmental education and sustainable systems
Contact(s):
Paulette Johnson, Pennsylvania Center for Environmental Education, Director; 724-738-4555
Bruce Boliver, Park and Resource Management, Chairman; 724-738-2068
Beverly Buchert, Environmental Studies, Coordinator; 724-738-2389
Dan Dziubek, Institute for the Environment Executive, Committee Chair; 724-738-2958
Dan Dziubek, Environmental Education, Coordinator; 724-738-2958
Michael Stapleton, Environmental Science, Program Coordinator; 724-738-2495

SONOMA STATE UNIVERSITY
DEPARTMENT OF ENVIRONMENTAL STUDIES AND PLANNING
1801 E. Cotati Ave.
Rohnert Park, CA 94928 United States
Phone: 707-664-2306 Fax: 707-664-4202
E-mail: ensp@sonoma.edu
Website: www.sonoma.edu/ensp/

Founded: N/A
Scope: National
Description: Interdisciplinary academic program with B.S. and B.A. degrees. Study tracks in environmental education, energy management and design, city and regional planning, water quality, hazardous materials management, and environmental conservation and restoration
Contact(s):
Steve Orlick, Department Chair; 707-664-2414; steve.orlick@sonoma.edu

SONOMA STATE UNIVERSITY
EARTH LAB
Earth Lab Environmental Studies and Planning
Sonoma State University
Rohnert Park, CA 94928 United States
Phone: 707-664-2577 Fax: 707-664-3920
E-mail: EarthLab@sonoma.edu
Website: www.sonoma.edu/ensp/earthlab.html

Founded: N/A
Description: The Earthlab is an on-campus demonstration, education, and research center which serves the campus and surrounding communities through programs in environmental education, professional training, teacher workshops, demonstration projects, and scientific research.

SOUTH DAKOTA STATE UNIVERSITY
DEPARTMENT OF WILDLIFE, FISHERIES SCIENCES
P.O. Box 2140B
Brookings, SD 57007-1696 United States
Phone: 605-688-6121 Fax: 605-688-4515
E-mail: charles_scalet@sdstate.edu
Website: wfs.sdstate.edu

Founded: 1963
Scope: Local, State, Regional, National
Description: Fish and wildlife research, education, and services with emphasis on fisheries management, wildlife management, fisheries and wildlife ecology, and wetland ecology and management.
Contact(s):
Charles Berry, Cooperative Fish and Wildlife Research Unit, Leader; charles_berry@sdstate.edu
Michael Brown, Associate Professor; michael_brown@sdstate.edu
Steven Chipps, Assistant Professor; steven_chipps@sdstate.edu
Lester Flake, Distinguished Professor; lester_flake@sdstate.edu

Kenneth Higgins, Professor; kenneth_higgins@sdstate.edu
Daniel Hubbard, Professor; daniel_hubbard@sdstate.edu
Jonathan Jenks, Professor; jonathan_jenks@sdstate.edu
Charles Scalet, Head; charles_scalet@sdstate.edu
David Willis, Professor; david_willis@sdstate.edu

SOUTHERN CONNECTICUT STATE UNIVERSITY

CENTER FOR THE ENVIRONMENT
501 Crescent St., Jennings Hall, Rm. 342
New Haven, CT 06515 United States
Phone: 203-392-6600 Fax: 203-392-6614
Website: www.scsu.ctstateu.edu

Founded: N/A
Membership: 1–100
Scope: International
Description: The Center for the Environment is an academic center granting graduate and undergraduate degrees in environmental areas, conducting research, and developing epistemological models. An active field study program includes experiences in Costa Rica, South Africa, Madagascar, Ecuador (including the Galapagos Islands) and various sites in the U.S.
Publication(s): SEED Newsletter
Contact(s):
Vincent Breslin, Professor of Environmental Studies
Susan Hageman, Chair of Science Education and Environmental Studies

SOUTHERN ILLINOIS UNIVERSITY CARBONDALE

DEPARTMENT OF FORESTRY
Southern Illinois University, Carbondale
Department of Foresty
1205 Lincoln Drv., Rm 184
Carbondale, IL 62901-4411 United States
Phone: 618-453-3341 Fax: 618-453-7475
E-mail: plc1@siu.edu
Website: www.siu.edu/~forestry.com

Founded: 1956
Membership: 1–100
Scope: Local, State, Regional, National, International
Description: The SIUC forestry program provides a comprehensive foundation in forestry. Our educational program leads to a bachelor of science degree in forestry and is accredited by the Society of American Foresters (SAF). Forestry students may choose to specialize in forest resource management or outdoor recreation resource management. In addition to the bachelor's degree, the department offers a master's degree in forestry and cooperative doctor's degrees in geography and plant biology.
Contact(s):
John Phelps, Professor and Department Chair; SIUC-Department of Forestry, 1205 Lincoln Dr., Rm 184, Mailcode 4411, Carbondale, IL 62901-4411; 618-453-3341; Fax: 618-453-7475; jphelps@siu.edu
Sara Baer, Researcher II; 618-453-3708
David Close, Researcher II; 618-453-7467; dclose@siu.edu
Patti Cludray, Office System Spec. I, Student Services - Web Master; 618-453-3341; plc1@siu.edu
Bonnie Middleton, Account Tech. III, Departmental Accountant; 618-453-3341
Cem Basman, Assistant Prof., Forest Recreation, Visitor Behavior, Social Psych.; 618-453-7476; cbasman@siu.edu
John Burde, Professor, Forest Recreation; 618-453-7463; jburde@siu.edu
Andrew Carver, Assistant Professor, Land Use and Resource Planning; 618-453-7461; acarver@siu.edu
John Groninger, Assistant Professor, Ecophysiology and Silviculture; 618-453-7462; jgroninge@siu.edu
Jean Mangun, Associate Professor, Human Dimensions of Natural Res. Mgmnt.; 618-453-3341; mangfor@siu.edu
Paul Roth, Professor, Forest Management and Protection; 618-453-7468
Charles Ruffner, Assistant Professor, Forest Measurements, Historical Ecology; 618-453-7469; ruffner@siu.edu
Karl Williard, Assistant Professor, Forest Hydrology, Watershed Mgmnt.; 618-453-7478; williard@siu.edu
James Zaczek, Assistant Professor, Forest Resources; 618-453-7465; zaczek@siu.edu

SOUTHERN OREGON UNIVERSITY

ENVIRONMENTAL EDUCATION PROGRAM
BIOLOGY DEPARTMENT
1250 Siskiyou Blvd .
Ashland, OR 97520 United States
Phone: 541-552-6797 Fax: 541-552-6415
Website: www.sou.edu/biology/enved/mainpage.htm

Founded: 1990
Membership: 1–100
Scope: State
Description: This graduate program grants a Master of Science degree, and provides hands-on learning experiences in conservation biology, interpretive practices, field interpretation, and field studies in southwestern Oregon and elsewhere in the state for students committed to careers in environmental education. Studies are also required in biology and related disciplines of choice to complete the program.
Contact(s):
Stewart Janes, Contact

SOUTHWEST CENTER FOR ENVIRONMENTAL RESEARCH AND POLICY (SCERP)

5250 Campanile Drive
San Diego, CA 92182-1913 United States
Phone: 619-594-0568 Fax: 619-594-0752
E-mail: scerp@mail.sdsu.edu
Website: www.scerp.org

Founded: 1989
Membership: N/A
Scope: Local, State, Regional, National, International
Description: Research and policy for environmental, ecological and human health issues in the U.S.-Mexican border region
Publication(s): Technical reports, Border Institute reports, Border Monograph
Keyword(s): Agriculture/Farming, Air Quality/Atmosphere, Climate Change, Development/Developing Countries, Ecosystems (precious), Energy, Ethics/Environmental Justice, Executive/Legislative/Judicial Reform, Finance/Banking/Trade, Forests/Forestry, Land Issues, Oceans
Contact(s):
D. Van Schoik, Director; 619-594-0568; Fax: 619-594-0752; scerp@mail.sdsu.edu

ST. CLOUD STATE UNIVERSITY

720 4th Ave., S
St. Cloud, MN 56301 United States
Phone: 320-255-3235 Fax: 320-654-5122
E-mail: ets@condor.stcloudstate.edu
Website: www.stcloudstate.edu

Founded: N/A
Scope: State
Description: Linking the human and natural world with programs designed to foster environmental and technological literacy and prepare students who can integrate the interconnections of science, technology, society and the environment through research and assessment.
Contact(s):
Charles Rose, Director of Environmental
Michael Karian, Associate Professor; 320-255-3966

ST. LAWRENCE UNIVERSITY

ENVIRONMENTAL STUDIES PROGRAM
Canton, NY 13617 United States
Phone: 315-229-5814 Fax: 315-229-5802
Website: web.stlawu.edu/envstudies

Founded: 1856

Scope: State

Description: St. Lawrence University is a liberal arts and sciences institution. The institution offers one of the oldest environmental studies programs in the nation. The university is committed to environmentally responsible management practices and comprehensive outdoor education programs.

Contact(s):
Glenn Harris, Director

ST. NORBERT COLLEGE

CENTER FOR INTERNATIONAL EDUCATION
100 Grant St.
De Pere, WI 54115-2099 United States
Phone: 920-403-3100 Fax: 920-403-4083
E-mail: mediarel@mail.snc.edu
Website: www.snc.edu/

Founded: 1990

Scope: State

Description: The Center conducts an Annual Global Ecology Series on themes such as the Great Lakes as an endangered resource of North America, Africa and women, population, and international policy-making. Instructional resources and in-service programs are provided for K-1

Contact(s):
Joseph Tullbane, Associate Dean for International Studies; 920-403-3378; Fax: 920-403-4083; tulljd@mail.snc.edu

STANFORD UNIVERSITY

DEPARTMENT OF BIOLOGICAL SCIENCES
CENTER FOR CONSERVATION BIOLOGY
Herrin Labs, 385 Sierra Mall
Stanford, CA 94305-5020 United States
Phone: 650-723-5924 Fax: 650-723-5920
E-mail: consbio@bing.stanford.edu
Website: www.stanford.edu/group/CCB/index.htm

Founded: 1984

Scope: National

Description: To develop the science of conservation biology, including its application to solutions for critical conservation problems. The Center conducts scientific and policy research that is building a sound basis for the conservation, management, and restoration of biotic diversity around the world. The overall goal is to develop ways and means for protecting Earth's life support systems and thus enhancing future human well-being.

Publication(s): See publication web site

Contact(s):
Paul Ehrlich, President

STANFORD UNIVERSITY

MORRISON INSTITUTE FOR POPULATION AND RESOURCE STUDIES
371 Sierra Mall, MC 5020
Stanford, CA 94305-5020 United States
Phone: 650-723-7518 Fax: 650-725-8244
E-mail: morrinst@stanford.edu
Website: www.stanford.edu/group/morrinst/

Founded: 1986

Scope: National, International

Description: To support research and education in the interconnected global issues of population growth, its effects on the environment, the pressure on natural resources, and the capacity of many nations to achieve sustainable socioeconomic development. Issues are approached through interdisciplinary perspectives of population biology, economics, and social and medical sciences.

Contact(s):
Marcus Feldman, Director; 650-725-1867

STATE UNIVERSITY OF NEW YORK AT CORTLAND

GEOLOGY DEPARTMENT
P.O. Box 2000
Cortland, NY 13045 United States
Phone: 607-753-2011 Fax: 607-753-2927
E-mail: stouts@cortland.edu
Website: www.cortland.edu/

Founded: N/A

Scope: State

Contact(s):
Christopher Cirmo, Environmental Geology and Environmental Sciences, Coordinator; 607-753-2924; cirmoc@cortland.edu
Jack Sheltmire, Environmental and Outdooor Education, Coordinator; 607-753-5488; sheltmirej@cortland.edu

STATE UNIVERSITY OF NEW YORK AT STONY BROOK

MARINE SCIENCES RESEARCH CENTER
Stony Brook, NY 11794 United States
Phone: 631-632-8700 Fax: 631-632-8820
Website: www.msrc.sunysb.edu/

Founded: N/A

Description: University-wide center to develop marine and atmospheric research, instructional programs and facilities for the State University of New York. Ongoing research projects are directed toward coastal oceanographic processes, marine environmental problems and management, atmospheric sciences and resources management. Among the Center's organized units are the Living Marine Resources Institute, the Waste Reduction and Management Institute, and the Coastal Ocean Action Strategies Institute.

Contact(s):
Marvin Geller, Dean and Director; 516-632-8701; mgeller@notes.cc.sunysb.edu
Nicholas Fisher, Associate Dean; 516-632-8649; nfisher@notes.cc.sunysb.edu
Glenn Lopez, Graduate Programs; 516-632-8660; glopez@notes.cc.sunysb.edu
W. Wise, Associate Director; 516-632-8656

STATE UNIVERSITY OF NEW YORK COLLEGE OF ENVIRONMENTAL SCIENCE AND FORESTRY

1 Forestry Dr.
Syracuse, NY 13210-2778 United States
Phone: 315-470-6500 Fax: 315-470-6953
E-mail: esfinfo@esf.edu
Website: www.esf.edu

Founded: 1911

Scope: State

Description: Research has been a hallmark of ESF since its inception. Recent wildlife studies have aimed toward reintroducing lynx and moose to the Adirondack Park; application of molecular biology techniques to identify migrant bird populations; restoration of muskellunge and sturgeon in the St. Lawrence River system; analysis of flamingo population dynamics in Mexico; tailoring black cherry clones for fast growth and straight limbs; and researching willow plantations as a source of biomass energy.

Contact(s):
Israel Cabasso, Polymer Research Institute, Director; 315-470-4767

Robert Hanna, N.C. Brown Laboratory for Ultrastructure Studies, Director; 315-470-6880
Hannu Makkonen, Empire State Paper Research Institute, Director; 315-470-6900
William Porter, Adirondack Ecological Center, Director; 315-470-6798
Neil Ringler, Roosevelt Wildlife Station, Director; 315-470-6770
Richard Smardon, Great Lakes Research Consortium, Co-Director; 315-470-6816
Richard Smardon, Environmental Institute, Randolf G. Pack, Director; 315-470-6636
H. Underwood, Cooperative Park Studies Unit, Director; 315-470-6820
Christopher Westbrook, Forest Technician Program, Director; 315-848-2566
William Winter, Cellulose Research Institute, Acting Director; 315-470-6855
Thomas Amidon, Faculty of Paper Science and Engineering, Chair; 315-470-6502
William Bentley, Faculty of Forestry, Chair; 315-470-6536
James Hassett, Faculty of Environmental Resources and Forest Engineering; 315-470-6633
John Hassett, Faculty of Chemistry, Chair; 315-470-6855
George Kyanka, Faculty of Construction Management and Wood Products Engineering; 315-470-6880
Neil Ringler, Faculty of Environmental and Forest Biology, Chair; 315-470-6743
Richard Smardon, Faculty of Environmental Studies, Chair; 315-470-6636
Wayne Zipperer, U.S. Forest Service Unit, Deputy Project Leader; 315-448-3201

STEPHEN F. AUSTIN STATE UNIVERSITY ARTHUR TEMPLE COLLEGE OF FORESTRY

ARTHUR TEMPLE COLLEGE OF FORESTRY
P.O. Box 6109
Nacogdoches, TX 75962-6109 United States
Phone: 936-468-3301 Fax: 936-468-2489
Website: www.sfasu.edu

Founded: N/A
Membership: 1–100
Scope: State
Contact(s):

R. Beasley, Water Quality/Forest Hydrology
R. Beasley, Dean; 936-468-2164; sbeasley@sfasu.edu
Mingteh Chang, Forest Hydrology; 936-468-2195; mchang@sfasu.edu
Edward Dougal, Forest Products; 936-468-2006; edougal@sfasu.edu
Jeffery Duguay, Forest Resources/Wildlife Management; 936-468-2196; jduguay@sfasu.edu
Kenneth Farrish, Soil Science; 936-468-2475; kfarrish@sfasu.edu
Michael Fountain, Silviculture/Forest Ecology; 936-468-2313; mfountain@sfasu.edu
James Kroll, Forest Wildlife Management; 936-468-1198; jkroll@sfasu.edu
Gary Kronrad, Forest Economics; 936-468-2473; gdkronrad@sfasu.edu
David Kulhavy, Landscape Ecology
David Kulhavy, Forest Entomology; 936-468-2141; dkulhavy@sfasu.edu
Michael Legg, Forest Recreation Management; 936-468-2246; mlegg@sfasu.edu
Shiyou Li, Medicinal Plants; 936-468-2071; lis@sfasu.edu
Brian Oswald, Fire Management and Silviculture; 936-468-2275; boswald@sfasu.edu
Paul Risk, Interpretation/Conflict Resolution; 936-468-2492; prisk@sfasu.edu
Peter Siska, GIS/Remote Sensing; 936-468-1347; siska@sfasu.edu
Daniel Unger, Remote Sensing/Mensuration; 936-468-2234; unger@sfasu.edu
R. Whiting, Forest Wildlife Management; 936-468-2125; mwhiting@sfasu.edu
Hans Williams, Urban Forestry
Hans Williams, Forest Eco-Physiology; 936-468-2127; hwilliams@sfasu.edu

STERLING COLLEGE

Attn: Director of Admissions, P.O. Box 72
Craftsbury Common, VT 05827-0072 United States
Phone: 802-586-7711 Fax: 802-586-2596
E-mail: admissions@sterlingcollege.edu
Website: www.sterlingcollegeedu

Founded: 1958
Scope: Regional
Description: Sterling College offers a Bachelor of Arts degree with concentrations in outdoor education and leadership, sustainable agriculture, and wildlands ecology, and management.
Publication(s): Common Voice
Contact(s):

John Williamson, President
John Zaber, Director of Admissions
Chris Monz, Dean; cmonz@sterlingcollege.edu

T

TANZANIA SCHOOL OF JOURNALISM

Box 4067
Dar-Es-Salaam, 4067 Tanzania
Phone: 255-51-700236 Fax: 255-51-700756
E-mail: info@tsjtz.com
Website: www.tsjtz.com

Founded: N/A
Scope: International
Description: The Tanzania School of Journalism is charged by law with journalism training. It annually enrollls about ninety university potential students, turning out the same number of journalists.
Keyword(s): Ethics/Environmental Justice
Contact(s):

Wilhelmina Balygatti
Robert Mfugale
Ernest Mrutu
Jerome Ng'itu
Ayub Rioba, Coordinator of Studies
Mwajabu Rossi, Principal Prof.

TEMPLE UNIVERSITY

ENVIRONMENTAL STUDIES PROGRAM
309 Gladfelter Hall
Philadelphia, PA 19122 United States
Phone: 215-204-5918 Fax: 215-204-7833
Website: www.temple.edu/env-stud

Founded: N/A
Scope: State
Description: Students majoring in Environmental Studies will be equipped with the scholarly background and intellectual skills to understand a wide range of pressing environmental issues, and they will come to appreciate the physical, economic, political, demographic, and ethical factors that define those issues. Among the many environmental problems central to our program are groundwater contamination, suburban sprawl, river basin management, and the greening of abandoned urban spaces.
Contact(s):

Robert Mason, Director

TENNESSEE TECHNOLOGICAL UNIVERSITY

DEPARTMENT OF BIOLOGY
Department of Biology Box 5063TTU
Cookeville, TN 38505 United States
Phone: 931-372-3134 Fax: 931-372-6257
E-mail: dlcombs@tntech.edu
Website: www.tntech.edu/www/acad/biol/

Founded: N/A

Contact(s):

Daniel Combs, Wildlife and Fisheries Science; dlcombs@tntech.edu

Dale Ensor, Environmental Science; P.O. Box 5055, Cookeville, TN 38505; 931-372-3493; densor@tntech.edu

TEXAS A AND M UNIVERSITY AT COLLEGE STATION

COLLEGE OF AGRICULTURE AND LIFE SCIENCES
113 Administration Bldg.
College Station, TX 77843-2142 United States
Phone: 979-845-4747 Fax: 979-845-9938
E-mail: agprogram@tamu.edu
Website: www.agprogram.tamu.edu

Founded: N/A
Membership: 101–1,000
Scope: State

Contact(s):

Bob Brown, Institute for Renewable Natural Resources, Director; 979-845-5777

Bob Brown, Wildlife and Fisheries Sciences, Head; 979-845-5777

Tat Smith, Forest Science, Head; 979-845-5000

Bob Whitson, Rangeland Ecology and Management, Head; 979-845-5579

Peter Witt, Recreation, Parks, and Tourism Sciences, Head; 979-845-7324

TEXAS A AND M UNIVERSITY AT COMMERCE

DEPARTMENT OF AGRICULTURAL SCIENCES
2600 S. Neal St.
Commerce, TX 75429-3011 United States
Phone: 903-886-5358 Fax: 903-886-5990
Website: www.tamu-commerce.edu

Founded: 1889
Membership: 1–100
Scope: State
Description: Educational institution offering B.S. and M.S. degrees in agricultural fields and pre-wildlife management programs.

Contact(s):

David Crenshaw, Pre-Wildlife Management, Advisor; 903-886-5329; david_crenshaw@tamu-commerce.edu

Robert Williams, Interim, Dept. Head

TEXAS A AND M UNIVERSITY AT KINGSVILLE

CAESAR KLEBERG WILDLIFE RESEARCH INSTITUTE
MSC 218
Kingsville, TX 78363 United States
Phone: 361-593-3922 Fax: 361-593-3924
Website: ckwri.tamuk.edu/

Founded: 1981
Membership: N/A
Scope: State, Regional, International
Description: A nonprofit institute that emphasizes research on wildlife and range management in Texas. Some work also done in Mexico and Canada. Research specialties include deer, quail, waterfowl, wild cats, wildlife diseases, semi-arid land ecology, animal nutrition, habitat requirements, GIS applications, and nongame wildlife.
Keyword(s): Ecosystems (precious), Land Issues, Wildlife & Species

Contact(s):

Fred Bryant, Director; 361-593-4025; Fax: 361-593-3924

TEXAS A AND M UNIVERSITY SYSTEM

TEXAS COOPERATIVE EXTENSION
DEPARTMENT OF WILDLIFE AND FISHERIES SCIENCES
111 Nagle Hall
2258 TAMU
Texas A&M
College Station, TX 77843-2258 United States
Phone: 979-845-7471 Fax: 979-845-7103
E-mail: nwilkins@tamu.edu
Website: wildlife.tamu.edu

Founded: N/A
Membership: N/A
Scope: Local, State, Regional, National, International
Description: Texas Cooperative Extension — Wildlife & Fisheries develops and delivers outreach, technology transfer and extension education programs to land managers, youth, and the citizens of Texas. We also participate in applied research projects, as well as provide liaison among public and private organizations on natural resource issues.
Keyword(s): Agriculture/Farming, Development/Developing Countries, Ecosystems (precious), Forests/Forestry, Land Issues, Oceans/Coasts/Beaches, Sprawl/Urban Planning, Water Habitats & Quality, Wildlife & Species

Contact(s):

Bob Brown, Director & Department Head; Institute of Renewable Natural Resources,

C. Hanselka, Associate Department Head and Extension Program Leader; Rangeland Ecology and Management, Rt. 2 Box 589, Corpus Christi, TX 78406-9704; 361-265-9203; Fax: 361-265-9434; c-hanselka@tamu.edu

Neal Wilkins, Associate Department Head and Extension Program Leader; Department of Wildlife and Fisheries Sciences, 2258 TAMU, 111 Nagle Hall, Texas A&M University, College Station, TX 77843-2258; 979-845-7471; Fax: 979-845-7103; nwilkins@tamu.edu

TEXAS CHRISTIAN UNIVERSITY

ENVIRONMENTAL SCIENCE PROGRAM
2800 South University Drive
Fort Worth, TX 76109 United States
Phone: 817-257-7000
Website: www.ensc.tcu.edu/

Founded: N/A

Contact(s):

Leo Newland, Director; L.Newland@tcu.edu

TEXAS TECH UNIVERSITY

DEPARTMENT OF RANGE WILDLIFE AND FISHERIES
P.O. Box 42125
Lubbock, TX 79409-2125 United States
Phone: 806-742-2841 Fax: 806-742-2280
Website: www.rw.ttu.edu/dept

Founded: N/A
Membership: 1–100
Scope: State
Description: University Department
Publication(s): See publication web site

Contact(s):

Ernest Fish, Wildlife Science and Fisheries Science, Chairman; fish@water.rw.ttu.edu

THE CENTRE FOR RESEARCH IN EDUCATION AND THE ENVIRONMENT

CREE, Department of Education, University of Bath
Bath, BA2 7AY United Kingdom
Phone: 4.4012258266e+012
Fax: 4.4012258261e+012
E-mail: cree@bath.ac.uk
Website: www.bath.ac.uk/education/cree

Founded: N/A

Scope: International

Description: The Centre for Research in Education and the Environment (CREE) is part of the Culture and Environment Research Group (CERG). Research focuses on the development of world views, and the implications of these for educational practice. A particular emphasis of the Centre is on environmental sustainability. The Centre incorporates those with interests in environment, language and culture in education.

Contact(s):

Stephen Gough, Lecturer. Director of Studies for Advanced Courses; S.R.Gough@bath.ac.uk

Elisabeth Barratt Hacking, Lecturer In Education; 44-122-6768; Fax: 44-122-6113; edsecbh@bath.ac.uk

Keith Bishop, Lecturer in Education; 01225 826826, ext. 5027; Fax: 01225 826113; K.N.Bishop@bath.ac.uk

John Fisher, Lecturer; 44 -122-6826, ext. 5330; Fax: 44 -122-6113; J.A.Fisher@bath.ac.uk

Alan Reid, Associate Lecturer; 44 -122-6294; Fax: 44 -122-6113; a.d.reid@bath.ac.uk

William Scott, Head of Department; 44 -1 2- 648; Fax: 44 -1 2- 113; w.a.h.scott@bath.ac.uk

Andrew Stables, Senior Lecturer; 44 -122-6826, ext. 5186; Fax: 44 -122-6113; A.W.G.Stables@bath.ac.uk

TREASURE VALLEY COMMUNITY COLLEGE

DEPARTMENT OF NATURAL RESOURCES
650 College Blvd.
Ontario, OR 97914 United States
Phone: 541-881-8822
Website: www.tvcc.cc.or.us/NatRes/

Founded: N/A

Description: Offers Associate of Applied Science focusing on forestry, range management or wildland fire management.

Contact(s):

John Russell, Professor; John_Russell@mailman.tvcc.cc.or.us

TUFTS UNIVERSITY CIVIL ENGINEERING

Anderson Hall
Medford, MA 02155 United States
Phone: 617-627-3211 Fax: 617-627-3994
Website: www.tufts.edu/

Founded: N/A

Scope: National, International

Contact(s):

Linfield Brown, Environmental Engineering, Contact; 617-627-2273; lbrown1@tufts.edu

John Durant, Hazardous Material Management, Contact; 617-627-5489; jdurant@emerald.tufts.edu

Christopher Swan, Environmental Geotechnology and Geotechnical Engineering; 617-627-2212; cswan@emerald.tufts.edu

Richard Vogel, Water Resources, Contact; 617-627-4260; rvogel@tufts.edu

TULANE ENVIRONMENTAL LAW CLINIC

ENVIRONMENTAL LAW CLINIC
6329 Freret St.
New Orleans, LA 70118-6231 United States
Phone: 504-865-5789 Fax: 504-862-8721
Website: www.tulane.edu/~telc

Founded: 1989

Membership: 1–100

Scope: State

Description: Provides free legal assistance through its student attorneys to community organizations and indigent persons seeking to protect public health and the environment.

Contact(s):

Adam Babich, Director

TULANE INSTITUTE FOR ENVIRONMENTAL LAW AND POLICY

TULANE ENVIRONMENTAL INSTITUTE
ENVIRONMENTAL INSTITUTE OF TULANE LAW SCHOOL
TULANE ENVIRONMENTAL LAW INSTITUTE
6329 Freret St.
New Orleans, LA 70118-6231 United States
Phone: 504-862-8827 Fax: 504-862-8760
E-mail: enlaw@law.tulane.edu
Website: www.law.tulane.edu/prog/specialty/environmental/envirolaw/institute.htm

Founded: N/A

Membership: N/A

Scope: Local, State, Regional, National, International

Description: The Institute is designed to enhance the intellectual contributions of the Tulane Law School as a leader in environmental law, to provide a center for discussion of critical issues, and to provide its law students with opportunities for involvement in environmental policy-making. It initiates and facilitates conferences, symposia and workshops that support the development of environmental policy.

Contact(s):

Eric Dannenmaier, Director; 504-862-8829; Fax: 504-862-8857; edan@law.tulane.edu

TULANE UNIVERSITY

DEPARTMENT OF ECOLOGY AND EVOLUTIONARY BIOLOGY
Dinwiddie Hall, Room 310
6823 Saint Charles Avenue
New Orleans, LA 70118 United States
Phone: 504-865-5191 Fax: 504-862-8706
Website: www.tulane.edu/~eeob

Founded: N/A

Membership: 1–100

Scope: State, Regional

Description: The faculty and students of the Department of Ecology and Evolutionary Biology (EEB) are actively engaged in the study of organisms, populations, communities, ecosystems, and global systems. We endeavor to create, communicate, and apply knowledge of these biological systems.

Keyword(s): Ecosystems (precious), Forests/Forestry, Land Issues, Oceans/Coasts/Beaches, Pollution (general), Population, Public Lands/Greenspace, Water Habitats & Quality, Wildlife & Species

Contact(s):

David Heins, Professor and Chair; 504-865-5563; heins@tulane.edu

TULANE UNIVERSITY, ENVIRONMENTAL LAW PROGRAMS, TULANE LAW SCHOOL

LAW SCHOOL
ENVIRONMENTAL LAW PROGRAM
Weinmann Hall, Suite 255
New Orleans, LA 70118 United States
Phone: 504-865-5946 Fax: 504-862-8855
Website: www.law.tulane.edu/

Founded: 1981

Scope: Local, State, Regional, National

Description: Environmental law education, research, and advocacy through faculty, staff, JD and graduate student body.
Publication(s): See publication web site
Contact(s):
Adam Babich, Director, Environmental Law Clinic
Eric Dannenmaier, Director, Institute of Environmental Law and Policy
Oliver Houck, Director; ohouck@law.tulane.edu
Gunther Handl, Chair, International Environmental Law

U

UNITY COLLEGE

90 Quacker Hill Rd
Unity, ME 04988 United States
Phone: 207-948-3131 Fax: 207-948-6277
Website: www.unity.edu/

Founded: 1966
Scope: National
Description: Unity College is a small, liberal arts college in rural Maine with degree programs specializing in natural resource management and wilderness-based recreation.
Contact(s):
Ed Beals, Botany and Ecology
A. Chacko, Aquaculture
Larry Farnsworth, Conservation Law Enforcement
Doug Fox, Arboriculture
Tom Mullins, Park Management,
Jim Nelson, Wildlife
David Oakes, Environmental Education
Dave Potter, Fisheries

UNIVERSIDADE FEDERAL DO PARANA

A.P. 19031 CENTRO
POLITECHNICO-CURITIBA, PARANA, 81531-970
Phone: 55-41-366-3144 Fax: 55-41-266-2042
E-mail: nimad@cce.ufpr.br

Founded: N/A
Contact(s):
Jose Andriguetto, Research Director
Edith Fanta, Adjunct Professor

UNIVERSIDADE FEDERAL DO PARANA

NIMAD-NUCLEOUS INTERDISCIPLINAR DE MELO AMBIENTE E DESENVOLVIMENTO
Centro Politechnico
Curitiba, Brazil
Phone: 5.5041366272e+011
Fax: 5.5041366272e+011
E-mail: nimad@cce.ufpr.br

Founded: 1989
Description: The objective of the NUCLEOUS e NIMAD is interdisciplinary research, teaching and extension directed to natural resource preservation, environmental education and sustainable development promotion.
Contact(s):
Jose Andriguetto, E. Research Coordinator and Research Director; 550-413-6627; nimad@cce.ufpr.br
Ziole Malhadas, E. Coordinator; 550-412-5244; ziolezm@cwb.matrix.com.br

UNIVERSITE LAVAL

Cite Universitaire
Quebec, G1K 7P4 Quebec Canada
Phone: 418-656-2131, ext. 2732 Fax: 418-656-7394
E-mail: sg@sg.ulaval.ca
Website: www.ulaval.ca/

Founded: 1852
Membership: 10,001–100,000
Scope: Local, State, Regional, National, International
Description: First francophone university in North America and firmly established as a leader among large research universities in Canada and in the francophone world, the Universite Laval has a highly enviable tradition and reputation with respect to teaching, research and creativity.
Keyword(s): Agriculture/Farming, Air Quality/Atmosphere, Climate Change, Development/Developing Countries, Ecosystems (precious), Energy, Ethics/Environmental Justice, Executive/Legislative/Judicial Reform, Finance/Banking/Trade, Forests/Forestry, Land Issues, Oceans
Contact(s):
Francois Tavenas, Rector; 1656, Pavillon des Sciences de l'education, Universite Laval, Quebec, Quebec G1K 7P4; 418-656-2131, ext. 2272; Fax: 418-656-7917; francois.tavenas@rec.ulaval.ca

UNIVERSITE LAVAL

CENTER FOR RESEARCH IN ECONOMICS OF AGRI-FOOD (CREA)
Pavillon Paul-Comtois
Universite Laval
Quebec, G1K 7P4 Quebec Canada
Phone: 418-656-2131, ext. 3254 Fax: 418-656-7821
E-mail: crea@eac.ulaval.ca
Website: www.fsaa.ulaval.ca/crea

Founded: N/A
Scope: Local, State, Regional, National, International
Description: Fields of expertise of the CREA are: agriculture; analysis of policies; comparative advantages; commerce; behavior of the consumer; durable development; agroalimentary economy; technical and allocative efficacy; world organization of trade (OMC); performance and strategy of enterprises; and food security.
Contact(s):
Robert Romain, Director; crea@eac.ulaval.ca

UNIVERSITE LAVAL

FACULTY OF AGRICULTURAL AND FOOD SCIENCES
1122, Pavillon Paul-Comtois
Universite Laval
Quebec, G1K 7P4 Quebec Canada
Phone: 418-656-2131, ext. 3145 Fax: 418-656-7806
E-mail: fsaa@fsaa.ulaval.ca
Website: www.fsaa.ulaval.ca

Founded: N/A
Scope: Local, State, Regional, National, International
Description: Programs in Agroeconomics, Agrobiology, Agronomy, Plant Biology, Integrated Rural Development, Agri-Food Economics and Management, Agricultural Economics, Environmental Studies, Agri-Food Engineering, Agri-Environmental Engineering, Horticulture and Landscape Management, Agricultural Microbiology, Plant Technology, Dairy and Beef Production, Soil and Environment Science.
Contact(s):
Jean-Claude Dufour, Dean; fsaa@fsaa.ulaval.ca

UNIVERSITE LAVAL

FACULTY OF ARCHITECTURE, PLANNING AND VISUAL ARTS
Edifice du Vieux-Seminaire de Quebec
1, Cote de la Fabrique
Universite Laval
Quebec, G1R 3V6 Quebec Canada
Phone: 418-656-2546 Fax: 418-656-3325
E-mail: faaav@faaav.ulaval.ca
Website: www.faaav.ulaval.ca

Founded: N/A
Scope: Local, State, Regional, National, International
Description: Program in Regional Planning and Development

Contact(s):
Claude Dube, Dean

UNIVERSITE LAVAL
FACULTY OF FORESTRY AND GEOMATICS
1151, Pavillon Abitibi-Price
Universite Laval
Quebec, G1K 7P4 Quebec Canada
Phone: 418-656-2131, ext. 2116 Fax: 418-656-3177
E-mail: ffg@ffg.ulaval.ca
Website: www.ffg.ulaval.ca

Founded: N/A

Scope: Local, State, Regional, National, International

Description: Programs in Agroforestry, Forest Ecosystem Management, Forestry, Geography, Forestry Management, Forest Operation, Wood Sciences, Forestry Sciences.

Contact(s):
Denis Briere, Dean; ffg@ffg.ulaval.ca

UNIVERSITE LAVAL
FACULTY OF LAW
2407, Pavillon Charles-DeKoninck
Universite Laval
Quebec, G1K 7P4 Quebec Canada
Phone: 418-656-2131, ext. 3036 Fax: 418-656-7230
E-mail: fd@fd.ulaval.ca
Website: www.ulaval.ca/fd

Founded: N/A

Scope: Local, State, Regional, National, International

Description: Program in International and Trans-national Law

Contact(s):
Pierre Lemieux, Dean

UNIVERSITE LAVAL
FACULTY OF MEDICINE
1236, Pavillon Ferdinand-Vandry
Universite Laval
Quebec, G1K 7P4 Quebec Canada
Phone: 418-656-2131, ext. 2331 Fax: 418-656-3442
E-mail: fmed@fmed.ulaval.ca
Website: www.fmed.ulaval.ca

Founded: N/A

Scope: Local, State, Regional, National, International

Description: Program in Community Health that analyzes environmental influences on social well-being.

Contact(s):
Marc Desmeules, Dean; 418-656-2131, ext. 2331; Fax: 418-656-3442; fmed@fmed.ulaval.ca

UNIVERSITE LAVAL
FACULTY OF PHILOSOPHY
644, Pavillon Felix-Antoine-Savard
Universite Laval
Quebec, G1K 7P4 Quebec Canada
Phone: 418-656-2131, ext. 2244 Fax: 418-656-7267
E-mail: fp@fp.ulaval.ca
Website: www.fp.ulaval.ca

Founded: N/A

Scope: Local, State, Regional, National, International

Description: Programs in Philosophy and Thought Critical Dialogue. Courses include discussion of environmental influences.

Contact(s):
Jean-Marc Narbonne, Dean; 418-656-2131, ext. 2244; Fax: 418-656-7267; fp@fp.ulaval.ca

UNIVERSITE LAVAL
FACULTY OF SCIENCES AND ENGINEERING
1033, Pavillon Alexandre-Vachon
Universite Laval
Quebec, G1K 7P4 Quebec Canada
Phone: 418-656-2131, ext. 2163 Fax: 418-656-5902
E-mail: fsg@fsg.ulaval.ca
Website: www.fsg.ulaval.ca

Founded: N/A

Scope: Local, State, Regional, National, International

Description: Programs in Biochemistry, Biotechnology, Chemistry, Earth Sciences and Oceanography.

Contact(s):
Pierre Moreau, Dean; 418-656-2131, ext. 2163; Fax: 418-656-5902; fsg@fsg.ulaval.ca

UNIVERSITE LAVAL
FACULTY OF SOCIAL SCIENCES
3456, Pavillon Charles-DeKoninck
Universite Laval
Quebec, G1K 7P4 Quebec Canada
Phone: 418-656-2131, ext. 2615 Fax: 481-656-2114
E-mail: fss@fss.ulaval.ca
Website: www.fss.ulaval.ca

Founded: N/A

Scope: Local, State, Regional, National, International

Description: Programs in Economics and Politics.

Contact(s):
Claude Beauchamp, Dean; 418-656-2131, ext. 2615; Fax: 418-656-2114; fss@fss.ulaval.ca

UNIVERSITE LAVAL
FOREST BIOLOGY RESEARCH CENTER (CRBF)
Pavillon Charles-Eugene-Marchand
Universite Laval
Quebec, G1K 7P4 Quebec Canada
Phone: 418-656-2131, ext. 3493 Fax: 418-656-7493
E-mail: crbf@crbf.ulaval.ca
Website: www.crbf.ulaval.ca

Founded: 1985

Scope: Local, State, Regional, National, International

Description: Fields of expertise of the CRBF are: biogeochemistry; in vitro culture; animal ecology; ecophysiology; entomology; genomics; hydrology; microbiology; pedology; pathology; physiology; and sylviculture.

Contact(s):
Louis Bernier, Director; crbf@crbf.ulaval.ca

UNIVERSITE LAVAL
GROUP FOR RESEARCH ON ENERGY, ENVIRONMENT AND NATURAL RESOURCE ECONOMICS (GREEN)
Pavillon J.-A.-DeSeve
Universite Laval
Quebec, G1K 7P4 Quebec Canada
Phone: 418-656-2131, ext. 2096 Fax: 418-656-7412
E-mail: green@ecn.ulaval.ca
Website: www.green.ecn.ulaval.ca

Founded: 1973

Scope: Local, State, Regional, National, International

Description: Fields of expertise of the GREEN are: theoretical and applied econometrics; theoretical and applied industrial engineering; renewable and not-renewable natural resources; regulation of the markets of energy; environmental regulation.

Contact(s):
Michel Roland, Director; 418-656-2131, ext. 2096; Fax: 418-656-7412; green@ecn.ulaval.ca

UNIVERSITE LAVAL
INTER-UNIVERSITY GROUP FOR OCEANOGRAPHIC RESEARCH IN QUEBEC (GIROQ)
Pavillon Alexandre-Vachon
Universite Laval
Quebec, G1K 7P4 Quebec Canada
Phone: 418-656-2131, ext. 5917 Fax: 418-656-2339
E-mail: giroq@giroq.ulaval.ca
Website: www.bio.ulaval.ca/giroq

Founded: 1970
Scope: Local, State, Regional, National, International
Description: Fields of the GIROQ are: littoral benthos; marine biochemistry; comportement of the marine invertebrates; marine ecology; carbon flux; genetics of the watery populations; macroalgaes; oceanography; plankton.
Contact(s):
Louis Fortier, Director; giroq@giroq.ulaval.ca

UNIVERSITE LAVAL
NORDIC STUDIES CENTRE (CEN)
Pavillon Abitibi-Price
Universite Laval
Quebec, G1K 7P4 Quebec Canada
Phone: 418-656-2131, ext. 3340 Fax: 418-656-2978
E-mail: cen@cen.ulaval.ca
Website: www.cen.ulaval.ca

Founded: 1961
Scope: Local, State, Regional, National, International
Description: Fields of expertise of the CEN are: climatic changes; ecology of the caribou; balances and stability of the Nordic ecosystems; geophysics of permafrost; Nordic hydrology and limnology; trees line; paleoecology; network of environmental telemetry.
Contact(s):
Yves Begin, Director; 418-656-2131, ext. 3340; Fax: 418-656-2978; cen@cen.ulaval.ca

UNIVERSITE LAVAL
RESEARCH CENTER FOR PLANNING AND REGIONAL DEVELOPMENT (CRAD)
Pavillon Felix-Antoine-Savard
Universite Laval
Quebec, G1K 7P4 Quebec Canada
Phone: 418-656-2131, ext. 5899 Fax: 418-656-2018
E-mail: marius.theriault@crad.ulaval.ca
Website: www.crad.ulaval.ca

Founded: 1972
Scope: Local, State, Regional, National, International
Description: Fields of expertise of the CRAD are: regional planning; regional development; studies of urban dynamics; social space analysis; spatiality of the ratios men and women; transports and behaviors of mobility; land market; economic effects; architecture; town planning; drinking water management; ecology of the disturbed environments; quantitative and qualitative methods; geographical information systems.
Contact(s):
Marius Theriault, Director; marius.theriault@crad.ulaval.ca

UNIVERSITY OF AKRON
CENTER FOR ENVIRONMENTAL STUDIES
215 Crouse Hall
Akron, OH 44325-4102 United States
Phone: 330-972-5389 Fax: 330-972-7611
Website: www.uakron.edu/envstudies/

Founded: 1970
Membership: 1–100
Scope: Local, State, Regional
Description: The Center is a cooperative effort of several departments; biology, chemistry, chemical engineering, civil engineering, economics, education, geography, geology, history, library, political science, and sociology. The Center has directed: an undergraduate and graduate certificate program of study; responses to local inquiries regarding environmental problems; workshops and seminars on environmental issues.
Contact(s):
Ira Sasowsky, Director

UNIVERSITY OF ALASKA AT FAIRBANKS
COLLEGE OF SCIENCE, ENGINEERING AND MATHEMATICS
DEPARTMENT OF BIOLOGY AND WILDLIFE
211 Irving
Fairbanks, AK 99775 United States
Phone: 907-474-7671 Fax: 907-474-5101
Website: www.uaf.edu/csem

Founded: N/A
Scope: State
Contact(s):
Brian Barnes, Institute of Arctic Biology, Interim Director; 907-474-7648
Joe Margraf, Alaska Cooperative Fish and Wildlife Research Unit, Leader; 209 Irving, UAF, Fairbanks, AK 99775-7020; 907-474-7661; Fax: 907-474-6716; ffjfm1@uaf.edu
David Woodall, Dean of College of Science, Engineering & Mathematics

UNIVERSITY OF ALASKA FAIRBANKS
SCHOOL OF FISHERIES AND OCEAN SCIENCES
245 O'Neill Building, P.O. Box 757220
Fairbanks, AK 99775-7220 United States
Phone: 907-474-7824 Fax: 907-474-7204
E-mail: fysfos@uaf.edu
Website: www.sfos.uaf.edu

Founded: N/A
Membership: 101–1,000
Scope: Regional, International
Publication(s): SFOS Today
Contact(s):
Vera Alexander, Dean

UNIVERSITY OF ALBERTA
FACULTY OF AGRICULTURE, FORESTRY, AND HOME ECONOMICS
2-14 Agriculture Forestry Centre
Edmonton, T6G 2PS Alberta Canada
Phone: 780-492-4933 Fax: 780-492-0097
Website: www.afhe.ualberta.ca/

Founded: N/A
Scope: National
Description: Undergraduate Degree Programs: B.Sc. in Agricultural and Food Business Management; Agriculture; Environmental and Conservation Sciences; Forest Business Management; Forestry; Human Ecology; Nutrition and Food Sciences; and Human Ecology/Bachelor of Education. Graduate Degree Programs: M.Sc., M. Ag., M.Eng., Ph.D. in Agricultural Food and Nutritional Science; M.A., MSc., and Ph.D. in Human Ecology; M.Sc., M. Ag., M.F., Ph. D., MBA/MF in Renewable Resources; MSc., MAg., Ph.D., MBA/MAg in Rural Ecology.
Contact(s):
Nancy Gibson, Human Ecology, Chair; 780-492-3883; Fax: 780-492-4821
John Kennelly, Agricultural, Food, and Nutritional Science, Chair; 780-492-3239; Fax: 780-492-4265
John Spence, Renewable Resources, Chair
Michele Veeman, Rural Economy, Chair; 780-492-4225; Fax: 780-492-0268

UNIVERSITY OF ARIZONA

DEPARTMENT OF HYDROLOGY AND WATER RESOURCES
P.O. Box 210011
Tucson, AZ 85721-0011 United States
Phone: 520-621-5082 Fax: 520-621-1422
E-mail: programs@hwr.arizona.edu
Website: www.hwr.arizona.edu

Founded: N/A
Membership: 101–1,000
Scope: State
Description: The mission of the department is to provide education, research, and service in the fields of hydrology and water resources and to engage in basic and applied research. The department offers comprehensive programs in all areas of surface and subsurface hydrology, water quality, and water resources systems (management, administration, engineering).
Publication(s): Publications website www.hwr.arizona.edu, Arizona HWR report.
Contact(s):
Victor Baker, Department Head; Dept. of Hydrology, ; 520-621-7120; Fax: 520-621-1422; baker@hwr.arizona.edu
Carla Stoffle, Main Library; P.O. Box 210055, ; 520-621-7440; Fax: 520-621-9733
Terrie Thompson, Academic Advising Coordinator; 520-621-3131; Fax: 520-621-1422; terrie@hwr.arizona.edu

UNIVERSITY OF ARIZONA

SCHOOL OF RENEWABLE NATURAL RESOURCES
325 Biological Sciences East
P.O. Box 210043
Tucson, AZ 85721-0043 United States
Phone: 520-621-7255 Fax: 520-621-8801
E-mail: llee@ag.arizona.edu
Website: www.ag.arizona.edu/srnr

Founded: N/A
Scope: Local, State, Regional, National, International
Description: The School of Renewable Natural Resources provides instruction, research, and extension in a range of disciplines. The specific academic programs of landscape resources, rangeland and forest resources, watershed resources, and wildlife and fisheries resources provide undergraduate and graduate education. Physical and biological sciences are integrated with socioeconomic and political factors necessary for the conservation, protection, and management of renewable natural resources.
Contact(s):
C.P. Reid, Director; 520-621-7257; Fax: 520-621-8801; cppr@ag.arizona.edu
Scott Bonar, Cooperative Fish and Wildlife Research Unit, Leader; 520-626-8535; Fax: 520-621-8801; sbonar@ag.arizona.edu
Carl Edminster, Forest Service Cooperative Research Unit, Leader; 520-556-2177
D. Guertin, Landscape Studies Program Chair; 520-621-1723; Fax: 520-621-8801; phil@srnr.arizona.edu
William Halvorson, Cooperative National Park Resources Studies Unit, Leader; 520-621-1174; Fax: 520-621-8801; halvor@srnr.arizona.edu
Michael Johnson, Cooperative Social Sciences Institute, USDA Natural Resource; 520-626-4685; Fax: 520-621-8801; mdjnrcs@ag.arizona.edu
Mitchel McClaren, RNR Studies Program Chair; 520-621-1673; Fax: 520-621-8801
C. P. Reid, Watershed Resources Acting Program Chair; 520-621-7257; Fax: 520-621-8801; cppr@ag.arizona.edu
George Ruyle, Rangeland and Forest Resources; 520-621-1384; Fax: 520-621-8801; gruyle@ag.arizona.edu
William Shaw, Wildlife and Fisheries Resources Program Chair; 520-621-7265; Fax: 520-621-8801; wshaw@ag.arizona.edu
Malcom Zwolinski, Associate Director; 520-621-1432; Fax: 520-621-8801; mjz@ag.arizona.edu

UNIVERSITY OF ARKANSAS AT LITTLE ROCK

DEPARTMENT OF BIOLOGY
AR United States
Website: www.ualr.edu/~biology/programs/wild/

Founded: N/A

UNIVERSITY OF ARKANSAS AT LITTLE ROCK

DEPARTMENT OF BIOLOGY
2801 S. University Ave.
Little Rock, AR 72204-1099 United States
Phone: 501-569-3270 Fax: 501-569-3271
E-mail: webmaster@valer.edu
Website: www.ualr.edu

Founded: N/A
Scope: Local, State, Regional
Description: The Environmental Health Sciences Program (www.ualr.edu/~ehsp/) curriculum consists of a common core and a choice from four areas of concentrated study: Environmental quality management; occupational safety and health; environmental planning; and environmental/public health sciences. Fish and Wildlife Management Program (www.ualr.edu/~biology/programs/wild/) prepares students for conservation biology research and management positions.
Contact(s):
Gary Heidt, Professor and Chair of Biology Dept.; 501-569-3511; gaheidt@ualr.edu
Carl Stapleton, Director, Environmental Health Sciences Program; 501-569-3501; crstapleton@ualr.edu

UNIVERSITY OF ARKANSAS AT MONTICELLO

SCHOOL OF FOREST RESOURCES/ARKANSAS FOREST RESOURCES CENTER
P.O. Box 3468, Forestry & Wildlife
Monticello, AR 71656 United States
Phone: 870-460-1052 Fax: 870-460-1092
Website: www.afrc.uamont.edu/sfr/index.htm

Founded: N/A
Membership: 1–100
Scope: State
Contact(s):
Richard Klunder, Dean

UNIVERSITY OF BATH

CENTRE FOR RESEARCH IN EDUCATION AND THE ENVIRONMENT (CREE)
Department of Education
University of Bath
Bath, BA14 6LP United Kingdom
Phone: 4.4122538665e+011
Fax: 4.4122538611e+011
E-mail: cree@bath.ac.uk
Website: www.bath.ac.uk/cree

Founded: 1995
Membership: N/A
Scope: Local, Regional, National, International
Description: The Centre, based at the University of Bath, carries out research and evaluation studies on environmental and sustainable education. The academic journals Environmental Education Research, and Assessment and Evaluation in Higher Education are edited from the Centre.
Contact(s):
William Scott, Director; cree@bath.ac.uk
Andrew Stables, Reader; a.w.g.stables@bath.ac.uk
Keith Bishop, Lecturer; k.n.bishop@bath.ac.uk
John Fisher, Lecturer; j.a.fisher@bath.ac.uk
Stephen Gough, Lecturer; s.r.gough@bath.ac.uk
Elisabeth Hacking, Lecturer; e.c.b.hacking@bath.ac.uk
Alan Reid, Lecturer; a.d.reid@bath.ac.uk

UNIVERSITY OF BRITISH COLUMBIA
ENVIRONMENTAL PROGRAMS
2075 Wesbrook Mall
Vancover, V6T 1Z1 British Columbia Canada
Phone: 604-822-8111 Fax: 604-822-1637
Website: www.hse.uvc.ca

Founded: N/A
Membership: 1–100
Scope: Local
Contact(s):

M. Healey, Westwater Research Centre, Director; 1933 W. Mall Annex, Rm. 200, Vancouver, British Columbia V6T 1Z2
L. Lavkulich, Institute for Resources and Environment, Director; Rm. 436E, 2206 E. Mall, Vancouver, British Columbia V6T 1Z3
J. Berger, Zoology Department, Head; 6270 University Blvd., Vancouver, British Columbia V6T 1Z4
M. Isaacson, Civil Engineering Department, Head; 2324 Main Mall, Vancouver, British Columbia V6T 1Z4
A. Lewis, Oceanography Department, Head; 6270 University Blvd., Vancouver, British Columbia V6T 1Z2
J. McLean, Forestry, Acting Dean; 2424 Main Mall, Vancouver, British Columbia V6T 1Z4
Moura Quayle, Agricultural Sciences, Dean; 248-2357 Main Mall University Campus, Vancouver, British Columbia V6T 1Z4
D. Shackleton, Animal Sciences Department, Contact; 248-2357 Main Mall University Campus, Vancouver, British Columbia V6T 1Z4
G. Wynn, Geography Department, Head; 1984 West Mall, Vancouver, British Columbia V6T 1Z5

UNIVERSITY OF CALIFORNIA AT DAVIS
COLLEGE OF AGRICULTURE AND ENVIRONMENTAL SCIENCE
One Shields Ave.
Davis, CA 95616-8571 United States
Phone: 530-752-6586 Fax: 530-752-4154
Website: www.wscb.ucdavis.edu

Founded: N/A
Membership: 1–100
Scope: State
Description: Agricultural research programs and 21 departments.
Contact(s):

Ruth Reck, Director, National Institute for Global Environmental Change; 530-757-3401; Fax: 530-756-6499; rareck@ucdavis.edu
Arnold Bloom, Chair, Vegetable Crops Program; 530-752-1743; Fax: 530-752-9659; ajbloom@ucdavis.edu
D. Burger, Chair, Environmental Horticulture; 530-752-0130; Fax: 530-752-1819; dwburger@ucdavis.edu
Colin Carter, Chair, Agricultural and Resource Economics; 530-752-1517; Fax: 530-752-5614; cacarter@ucdavis.edu
Deborah Elliot-Fisk, Chair, Wildlife, Fish, & Conservation Biology; 530-752-6586; Fax: 530-752-4514; dlelliottfisk@ucdavis.edu
Larry Harper, Chair, Human and Community Development; 530-752-3624; lharper@ucdavis.edu
Harry Kaya, Chair, Nematology; 530-752-1051; Fax: 530-752-5809; hkkaya@ucdavis.edu
Dean MacCannell, Chair, Landscape Architecture; 530-752-6437; edmaccannell@ucdavis.edu
Jim Macdonald, Chair, Plant Pathology; 530-752-6897; Fax: 530-752-5674; jdmacdonald@ucdavis.edu
Marion Miller, Chair, Environmental Toxicology; 530-752-4526; mgmiller@ucdavis.edu
Michael Parrella, Chair, Entomology; 530-752-0492; mpparrella@ucdavis.edu
Gary Polis, Chair, Environmental Science and Policy; 530-754-8994; Fax: 530-752-3350; gapolis@ucdavis.edu
Dennis Rolston, Chair, Land, Air and Water Resources; 530-752-2113; Fax: 530-752-1552; derolston@ucdavis.edu
Roger Shaw, Vice-Chair, Land, Air and Water Resources; 530-752-1822; Fax: 530-752-1552; rhshaw@ucdavis.edu
Jo Stabb, Chair, Environmental Design; 530-752-6809; jcstabb@ucdavis.edu

UNIVERSITY OF CALIFORNIA AT DAVIS
HERBARIUM
One Shields Ave.
Herbarium Plant Biology, University of California
Davis, CA 95616 United States
Phone: 530-752-1091 Fax: 530-752-5410
Website: www.herbarium.ucdavis.edu

Founded: 1923
Scope: State
Description: The UC Davis Herbarium is the center for research in plant systematics at the University of California, Davis. The Herbarium, of worldwide scope, includes 200,000 specimens. Holdings from California include documentation for many rare and endangered species.
Contact(s):

Ellen Dean, Director and Curator

UNIVERSITY OF CALIFORNIA AT LOS ANGELES
COLLEGE LETTERS AND SCIENCE
1312 Murphy Hall
Box 951438
Los Angeles, CA 90095-3801 United States
Phone: 310-825-9009 Fax: 310-825-9368
Website: www.college.ucla.edu/

Founded: N/A
Scope: National
Contact(s):

Roger Wakimoto, Chair, Department of Atmospheric Sciences; 310-825-1751

UNIVERSITY OF CALIFORNIA AT LOS ANGELES
SCHOOL OF ENGINEERING AND APPLIED SCIENCE
CIVIL AND ENVIRONMENTAL ENGINEERING DEPARTMENT
5731 Boelter Hall, P.O. Box 951593
Los Angeles, CA 90095-1593 United States
Phone: 310-825-1346 Fax: 310-206-2222
E-mail: deeona@ea.ucla.edu
Website: www.cee.ucla.edu/

Founded: N/A
Membership: 1–100
Scope: Local, International
Contact(s):

Jiann-Wen Ju Ju, Chair; 310-206-1751; Fax: 310-206-2222; juj@seas.ucla.edu

UNIVERSITY OF CALIFORNIA AT RIVERSIDE
GRADUATE SCHOOL OF ENVIRONMENTAL SCIENCE AND ENGINEERING
2217 Geology, University of California
Riverside, CA 92521 United States
E-mail: karenh@mail.ucr.edu
Website: ese.ucr.edu/

Founded: N/A

UNIVERSITY OF CALIFORNIA AT RIVERSIDE ENVIRONMENTAL DEPT
DEPARTMENT OF ENVIRONMENTAL SCIENCE
Riverside, CA 92521 United States
Phone: 909-787-1012
Website: envisci.ucr.edu/

Founded: 1971

Scope: State
Description: The Environmental Sciences Program offers four curriculum tracks: Natural Science, Social Science, Environmental Toxicology and Soil Science. Opportunities are available for students to conduct research and to engage in environmental internships. Graduate Degrees available in Soil and Water Science.
Contact(s):
Walt Farmer, Chair of Environmental Sciences; 909-787-5116; wfarm@citrus.ucr.edu

UNIVERSITY OF CALIFORNIA AT SAN DIEGO

SCRIPPS INSTITUTION OF OCEANOGRAPHY
9500 Gilman Dr.
La Jolla, CA 92037 United States
Phone: 858-534-3206 Fax: 858-534-7889
E-mail: siodept@sio.ucsd.edu
Website: www.sio.ucsd.edu/

Founded: 1903
Membership: 101–1,000
Scope: International
Description: A part of the University of California, San Diego, the Scripps Institution of Oceanography is one of the oldest, largest, and most important centers for marine science research and graduate training in the world. The Birch Aquarium serves as the public education center for the institution.
Publication(s): Explorations
Contact(s):
Charles Kennel, Director and Vice Chancellor for Marine Sciences; ckennel@ucsd.edu
Myrl Hendershott, Chair of the Graduate Department

UNIVERSITY OF CALIFORNIA AT SANTA BARBARA

ENVIRONMENTAL STUDIES PROGRAM
Environmental Studies Program @ University of California
Santa Barbara, CA 93106-4170 United States
Phone: 805-893-2968 Fax: 805-893-8686
E-mail: envst_info@envst.ucsb.edu
Website: www.es.ucsb.edu

Founded: N/A
Scope: State
Description: The Environmental Studies Program at UCSB remains one of the strongest in terms of student demand and national reputation. The Environmental Studies curriculum is designed to provide students with the scholarly background and intellectual skills necessary to understand complex environmental problems and formulate decsions that are environmentally sound. While the E.S. Program offers both a B.S. and B.A. degree.
Publication(s): See publication web site
Contact(s):
Jo-Ann Shelton, Program Chair, ext. 4505
Eric Zimmerman, Academic Advisor, ext. 3185

UNIVERSITY OF CALIFORNIA AT SANTA CRUZ

ENVIRONMENTAL STUDIES
Santa Cruz, CA 95064 United States
Phone: 831-459-2634
E-mail: studies@zzyx.ucsc.edu
Website: zzyx.ucsc.edu/ES/es.html

Founded: N/A
Contact(s):
David Goodman, Chairperson

UNIVERSITY OF CALIFORNIA, BERKELEY

DEPARTMENT OF ENVIRONMENTAL SCIENCE, POLICY AND MANAGEMENT
145 Mulford Hall
Berkeley, CA 94720-3114 United States
Phone: 510-642-6730 Fax: 510-642-4034
E-mail: undergraduate.espmug@nature.berkeley.edu
Website: www.cnr.berkeley.edu/departments/espm/

Founded: N/A
Scope: International
Description: The Department has a strong undergraduate program awarding the B.S. degree in Forestry, Resource Management, Molecular Environmental Biology and Conservation and Resource Studies. The graduate degree program (M.S., Ph.D.) integrates the biological, social and physical sciences to provide advanced education in basic and applied environmental sciences, develops critical analytical abilities and fosters the capacity to conduct research on the structure and function of ecosystems through ecosystem
Contact(s):
Sue Jennison, Director of Student Services; 510-642-6410; susan@nature.berkeley.edu

UNIVERSITY OF COLORADO

SCHOOL OF LAW
NATURAL RESOURCES LAW CENTER
Campus Box 401
Boulder, CO 80309-0401 United States
Phone: 303-492-1286 Fax: 303-492-1297
E-mail: nrlc@spot.colorado.edu
Website: www.colorado.edu/law/nrlc

Founded: N/A
Membership: 1–100
Scope: National, International
Description: Conducts research on environmental and natural resources law and policy, including water, public lands, minerals, Indian law, etc. Sponsors conferences and workshops and hosts visiting scholars. Publishes books, research papers, and Resource Law Notes newsletter.
Contact(s):
Gary Bryner, Director

UNIVERSITY OF COLORADO AT BOULDER

ENVIRONMENTAL CENTER
Campus Box 207
Boulder, CO 80309 United States
Phone: 303-492-8308 Fax: 303-492-1897
E-mail: ecenter@stripe.colorado.edu
Website: www.colorado.edu/ecenter

Founded: 1970
Membership: 101–1,000
Scope: Local
Description: The CU Environmental Center is the nation's largest student-run environmental resource center. With over 40 student staff and interns, five permanent staff and 100 volunteers, it is the focal point for efforts to make the Boulder campus more environmentally responsible. Besides giving students applied experience in interdisciplinary environmental problem solving, the center provides direct services to the University community, including award-winning recycling and student bus pass programs.
Publication(s): Blueprint for a Green Campus, Finding A New Way.
Contact(s):
Will Toor, Director; 303-492-8309; toor@spot.colorado.edu

UNIVERSITY OF CONNECTICUT

WBY, Room 308, 1376 Storrs Road, Unit 4087
Storrs, CT 06269-4087 United States
Phone: 860-486-2840 Fax: 860-486-5408
Website: www.canr.uconn.edu/nrme/

Founded: N/A

Scope: State

Description: The Dept. offers degrees in natural resources with emphasis in forestry, fisheries, wildlife, biometeorology, watershed hydrology, remote sensing, soil and water conservation and natural resources engineering.

Contact(s):

David Schroeder, Department Head; dschroed@canr.uconn.edu

UNIVERSITY OF DAR ES SALAAM

JOINT ENVIRONMENT AND DEVELOPMENT MANAGEMENT ACTION (JEMA)
MAIN CAMPUS
P.O. Box 35081
Dar es Salaam, Tanzania
Phone: 255-51-410500-8, ext. 2403 Fax: 255-51-410078
E-mail: jema@ucc.udsm.ac.tz
Website: udsm.ac.tz/jema.html

Founded: N/A

Description: JEMA aims at facilitating technical community outreach services which are environmentally sound to the rural society for sustainable utilization of available natural resources towards poverty alleviation.

Publication(s): Biodiversity conservation study on the slopes of Mt. Kilimanjaro, environmental learning programme in schools and communities in East and S. Africa, environmental assessment of institutional transformation programmes in East Africa.

Keyword(s): Agriculture/Farming, Development/Developing Countries, Forests/Forestry, Land Issues, Recreation/Ecotourism, Reduce/Reuse/Recycle, Sprawl/Urban Planning, Wildlife & Species

Contact(s):

Cosmas Bahali, Coordinator; Fax: 255-514-1007; jema ucc.udsm.ac.tz
Theodora Bali, Gender Advocacy; 255- 51- 410
Romuli John, Executive Secretary
Rogasian Massue, Treasurer
Filos Mayayi, Publicity Secretary

UNIVERSITY OF DELAWARE

COLLEGE OF AGRICULTURE AND NATURAL RESOURCES
531 S. College Ave., Townsend Hall
Newark, DE 19717 United States
Phone: 302-831-2501 Fax: 302-831-6758
Website: www.ag.udel.edu

Founded: N/A

Membership: 1–100

Scope: State, Regional

Description: B.S. in wildlife conservation; M.S. and Ph.D. in entomology and applied ecology

Contact(s):

Judith Hough-Stein, Department of Entomology and Applied Ecology, Chairperson; 302-831-8889; Fax: 302-831-3651; jhough@udel.edu
Roland Roth, Professor Entomology and Applied Ecology; rroth@udel.edu

UNIVERSITY OF FLORIDA

SCHOOL OF FOREST RESOURCES AND CONSERVATION
P.O. Box 110410
Gainesville, FL 32611-0410 United States
Phone: 352-846-0850 Fax: 352-392-1707
E-mail: sfrc@gnv.ifas.ufl.edu
Website: www.sfrc.ufl.edu

Founded: 1937

Membership: N/A

Scope: Local, State, Regional, National, International

Description: The School seeks to advance the understanding and management of natural resources, especially forests, and the interactions between the ecological, social, and economic demands placed on them. This is accomplished through established programs in undergraduate and graduate education, research, and extension.

Publication(s): Extension Information

Keyword(s): Agriculture/Farming, Air Quality/Atmosphere, Climate Change, Development/Developing Countries, Energy, Finance/Banking/Trade, Forests/Forestry, Land Issues, Public Lands/Greenspace, Recreation/Ecotourism, Sprawl/Urban Planning, Water Habitats & Quality, Wildlife & Species.

Contact(s):

Wayne Smith, Director; whsmith@ufl.edu
George Blakeslee, Assoc. Director of Academic Programs; 352-846-0845; Fax: 352-392-1707; gb4stree@ufl.edu
Alan Long, Assoc. Professor of Extension; 352-846-0891; Fax: 352-392-1707; ajl2@ufl.edu
Scott Sager, Student Services Coordinator; 352-846-0847; Fax: 352-392-1707; sasager@ufl.edu

UNIVERSITY OF FLORIDA

SOLAR ENERGY AND ENERGY CONVERSION LABORATORIES
237 MEB, Box 116300
Gainesville, FL 32611 United States
Phone: 352-392-0812 Fax: 352-392-1071
E-mail: solar@cimar.me.ufl.edu
Website: www.me.ufl.edu/SOLAR/

Founded: 1954

Scope: International

Publication(s): Principles of Solar Engineering (textbook), Advances in Solar Energy, Solar Touch Newsletter.

Contact(s):

D. Goswami, Director

UNIVERSITY OF FLORIDA INSTITUTE OF FOOD AND AGRICULTURAL SCIENCES

CENTER FOR NATURAL RESOURCES
1051 McCarthy Hall
P.O. Box 110230
University of Florida
Gainesville, FL 32611-0230 United States
Phone: 352-392-7622 Fax: 352-846-2856
E-mail: cnr_mail@mail.ifas.ufl.edu
Website: cnr.ifas.ufl.edu/

Founded: 1973

Membership: N/A

Scope: Local, State, Regional, National, International

Description: The Center for Natural Resources works to conserve, preserve and restore our nation's natural resources by facilitating interdisciplinary collaborations between University of Florida faculty members and external stakeholders. CNR sponsors and organizes various natural resource-related research, training workshops, conferences and seminars.

Publication(s): A series of fact sheets highlighting UF natural resources programs and issues along with pertinent contact information, Quarterly publication highlighting current natural resource issues and developments

Keyword(s): Agriculture/Farming, Air Quality/Atmosphere, Climate Change, Ecosystems (precious), Energy, Ethics/Environmental Justice, Forests/Forestry, Land Issues, Oceans/Coasts/Beaches, Pollution (general), Public Lands/Greenspace, Recreation/Ecotourism, Reduce/Reuse/Recycle.

Contact(s):
Randall Stocker, Director
Wendy Graham, Associate Director
Nancy Peterson, Program Coordinator
Aziz Shiralipour, Associate Director - Biomass Programs
Margie Owens, Office Manager

UNIVERSITY OF GEORGIA
DANIEL B. WARNELL SCHOOL OF FOREST RESOURCES
Daniel B. Warnell School of Forest Resources
Athens, GA 30602-2152 United States
Phone: 706-542-2686 Fax: 706-542-8356
Website: www.uga.edu/wsfr/

Founded: N/A
Membership: 101–1,000
Scope: State
Description: The undergraduate degree (B.S.F.R) offers majors in Forestry, Wildlife, Fisheries and Aquaculture and Forest Environmental Resources. Graduate programs (M.S.,M.F.R., Ph.D.) offer a focus in Wildlife Ecology and Management, Fisheries and Aquaculture and a variety of forest biology and management fields.

Contact(s):
Arnett Mace, Dean
Scott Merkle, Graduate Program Coordinator; 706-542-1183; Fax: 706-542-8356

UNIVERSITY OF GEORGIA
MARINE INSTITUTE
UGA Marine Institute
Sapelo Island, GA 31327 United States
Phone: 912-485-2221 Fax: 912-485-2133
Website: www.uga.edu/ugami/

Founded: 1953
Membership: 1–100
Scope: Regional
Description: Concerned with research into the system-ecology, biology, chemistry, and geology of the salt marshes, barrier islands, and nearshore zone of the Georgia coast.
Publication(s): University of Georgia Marine Institute Collected Reprints

Contact(s):
Jon Garbisch, Education Program Specialist; jgarbisch@peachnet.campuscwix.net

UNIVERSITY OF GEORGIA
SAVANNAH RIVER ECOLOGY LABORATORY
Aiken, SC 29802-1030 United States
Phone: 803-725-2472 Fax: 803-725-3309
E-mail: forrest@srel.edu
Website: www.uga.edu/srel/

Founded: N/A
Membership: 101–1,000
Scope: Regional, International
Description: Learning and communicating ecological processes and principles is the mission of the University of Georgia's Savannah River Ecology Laboratory. The Lab accomplishes its mission through research, outreach and education, and service. Research is conducted in wetlands ecology, wildlife ecology and toxicology, and biogeochemical ecology, including radioecology. Outreach and education activities reach more than 120,000 people annually in Georgia and South Carolina.
Publication(s): EcoLines, most publications on website

Contact(s):
Paul Bertsch, Director
Whit Gibbons, Outreach and Education Director
Rosemary Forrest, Public Relations
Carl Strojan, Associate Director; Savannah River Ecology Lab, Drawer E, Aiken, SC 29802; 803-725-8217; strojan@serl.edu

UNIVERSITY OF GUELPH
ONTARIO AGRICULTURAL COLLEGE
OAC Deans Office
Guelph, N1G 2W1 Ontario Canada
Phone: 519-824-4120 Fax: 519-766-1423
E-mail: oacinfo@oac.uoguelph.ca
Website: www.oac.uoguelph.ca

Founded: N/A
Scope: International

Contact(s):
John Fitzgibbon, Executive Director, College Faculty of Environmental Design, ext. 6784; jfitzgib@rpd.uoguelph.ca
Alan Watson, Arboretum Director; 519-824-4120, ext. 2356; awatson@uoguelph.ca
Stu Hilts, Chair of Land Resource Science
S. Marshall, University of Guelph Insect Collection, Curator, ext. 2720; smarshal@evbhort.uoguelph.ca
Nathan Perkins, Undergraduate Program Coordinator, ext. 8758; nperkins@la.uoguelph.ca
Mark Sears, Environmental Biology, Dept. Chair, ext. 3921; msears@evbhort.uoguelph.ca

UNIVERSITY OF HAWAII
COLLEGE OF TROPICAL AGRICULTURE AND HUMAN RESOURCES
3050 Maile Way
Honolulu, HI 96822 United States
Phone: 808-956-8131 Fax: 808-956-9105
E-mail: research@ctahr.hawaii.edu

Founded: 1901
Membership: 101–1,000
Scope: State
Description: Plan and implement research and extension in agriculture, natural resources, and human resources relevant to Hawaii and the tropics, with emphasis on the Pacific and Asia.
Publication(s): Various research and extension publications.
Keyword(s): Agriculture/Farming, Land Issues, Pollution (general), Public Health, Reduce/Reuse/Recycle, Wildlife & Species

Contact(s):
Catherine Chanhalbrandt, Associate Dean and Associate Director for Research

UNIVERSITY OF HAWAII AT MANOA
WATER RESOURCES RESEARCH CENTER
2540 Dole St.
Room 283
Honolulu, HI 96822 United States
Phone: 808-956-7847 Fax: 808-956-5044
E-mail: jmoncur@hawaii.edu
Website: www.hawaii.edu/wrrc/WRRC.html

Founded: 1964
Membership: N/A
Scope: State, Regional
Description: WRRC's mission is to coordinate and conduct research to identify, characterize and quantify water and environmental concerns of the state, the nation and other Pacific Islands and formulate methods for resolving these concerns. WRRC produces reports, national and international journal articles, books, newsletters and project bulletins and organizes seminars, workshops and conferences.

Publication(s): Technical Report, Project Reports and Special Publications, Publications List, Cooperative Report, Annual Report, Technical Memorandum Report
Keyword(s): Energy, Oceans/Coasts/Beaches, Pollution (general), Public Health, Water Habitats & Quality
Contact(s):
James Moncur, Director; 808-956-7847; Fax: 808-956-5044; jmoncur@hawaii.edu
Philip Moravcik, Communications Coordinator

UNIVERSITY OF HOUSTON

DEPARTMENT OF CIVIL AND ENVIRONMENTAL ENGINEERING
4800 Calhoun Rd.
Houston, TX 77204-4003 United States
Phone: 713-743-4250 Fax: 713-743-4260
Website: www.egr.uh.edu/cive/

Founded: N/A
Membership: 1–100
Scope: International
Contact(s):
Theodore Cleveland, Environmental Engineering Program, Director; 713-743-4250; cleveland@uh.edu

UNIVERSITY OF IDAHO

COLLEGE OF NATURAL RESOURCES
P.O. Box 441136
Moscow, ID 83844-1136 United States
Phone: 208-885-6434 Fax: 208-885-6226
Website: www.its.uidaho.edu/cnr

Founded: N/A
Scope: Local, State, Regional
Contact(s):
Kerry Reese, Professor of Wildlife Resources
J. Scott, Cooperative Fish and Wildlife Research Unit, Leader; 208-885-6336

UNIVERSITY OF IDAHO

WOMEN IN NATURAL RESOURCES
P. O. Box 441114
Moscow, ID 83844-1114 United States
Phone: 208-885-6754 Fax: 208-885-5878
Website: www.its.uidaho.edu\winr

Founded: 1968
Membership: 101–1,000
Scope: International
Publication(s): Jobs Flyer (Monthly), Women in Natural Resources (Quarterly)
Contact(s):
Sandra Martin, Editor; winr@uidaho.edu

UNIVERSITY OF IDAHO EXTENSION

P.O. Box 442338
Moscow, ID 83844-2338 United States
Phone: 208-885-6639 Fax: 208-885-6654
E-mail: extdir@uidaho.edu
Website: www.uidaho.edu/extension/

Founded: 1914
Membership: 101–1,000
Scope: State
Description: The University of Idaho Extension (UIExt) is a partnership with the Cooperative Extension System. Cooperating County, State, and Federal governments deliver knowledge and education to the people of the State to improve social, economic, and environmental conditions. UIExt is located across the State, in 11 research and extension centers and 42 county extension offices.
Contact(s):
Leroy Luft, Extension Director; extdir@uidaho.edu
Paul McCawley, Associate Extension Director, Interim; 208-885-5883; anauman@uidaho.edu
Ronald Mahoney, Extension Forester; Univ. of Idaho, College of Natural Resources, Moscow, ID 83844-1140; 208-885-6356; Fax: 208-885-6226
Lou Riesenberg, Agriculture and Extension Education; 1134 W. 6th Street, Moscow, ID 83844; 208-885-6358; lriesenb@uidaho.edu

UNIVERSITY OF ILLINOIS AT URBANA-CHAMPAIGN

205 N. Mathews Ave.
1114 Newmark Civil Engineering Laboratory
Urbana, IL 61801 United States
Phone: 217-333-1000
E-mail: consult@uiuc.edu
Website: www.uiuc.edu/

Founded: N/A
Contact(s):
Vincent Bellafiore, Landscape Architecture, Head
Patrick Brown, Natural History Survey Professor
David Daniel, Civil Engineering, Head
Scott Robinson, Animal Biology, Head
Gary Rolfe, Natural Resources and Environmental Sciences, Head
Christopher Silver, Urban and Regional Planning, Head
Colin Thorn, Geography, Head

UNIVERSITY OF ILLNOIS EXTENSION

214 Mumford Hall (MC-710), 1301 W. Gregory Dr.
Urbana, IL 61801 United States
Phone: 217-333-5900 Fax: 217-244-5403
E-mail: web_extension@aces.uiuc.edu
Website: www.extension.uiuc.edu/welcome.html

Founded: N/A
Scope: Local
Contact(s):
Patricia Buchanan, Assistant Dean, Extension Operations; buchananp@mail.aces.uiuc.edu
Dennis Campion, Associate Dean; dcampion@uiuc.edu
John Van Es, Assistant Dean, Extension Program Coordination; e-van1@uiuc.edu
Richard Warner, Assistant Dean Office of Resource; 211 Mumford Hall (MC-710) 1301 W. Gregory Dr., Urbana, IL 61801; 217-333-5199; Fax: 217-244-3219

UNIVERSITY OF IOWA

2700 Steinelder Bldg.
Iowa City, IA 52242 United States
Phone: 319-335-9627 Fax: 319-335-9200
Website: www.public-health.uiowa.edu

Founded: N/A
Scope: State
Contact(s):
James Merchant, Environmental Health Sciences Research Center, Director; 2707 Steindler Bldg., Iowa City, IA 52242; 319-335-9833; james-merchant@uiowa.edu
Robert Ettema, Civil and Environmental Engineering Program, Dept. Chair; Dept. Office: 2130 Seamans Center, Iowa City, IA 52242; 319-335-5647; Fax: 319-335-5660; cee@engineering.uiowa.edu

UNIVERSITY OF ITO PUNJAB

INSTITUTE OF EDUCATION AND RESEARCH
New Campus
Lahore, 54590 Pakistan
Phone: 92425864468 Fax: 92425864004

Founded: N/A
Description: Environmental Education for Masters students

Contact(s):
Hafiz Qzbal, Contact; hafizm@paknet4.ptc.pk

UNIVERSITY OF KANSAS
DEPARTMENT OF ENVIRONMENTAL STUDIES
517 W 14th St., Bldg. 138
Lawrence, KS 66045 United States
Phone: 785-842-2059 Fax: 785-842-4041
E-mail: env-studies@ku.edu
Website: www.ku.edu/~kuesp

Founded: N/A
Membership: 1–100
Scope: State
Description: Environmental Studies Program offers options in ecology and field biology, environmental policy, environmental impact analysis, environmental health, geology and meteorology, water resources, and environmental land-use analysis
Contact(s):
Stanford Loeb, Director; 785-842-2059
Deborah Snyder, Secretary

UNIVERSITY OF KANSAS FIELD STATION AND ECOLOGICAL RESERVES
Kansas Biological Survey
2335 Irving Hill Road
Lawrence, KS 66045-7612 United States
Phone: 785-864-7720 Fax: 785-864-5093
E-mail: martinko@ku.edu
Website: www.ksr.ku.edu

Founded: 1947
Membership: 1–100
Scope: Local, State, Regional, National
Description: The University of Kansas Field Station and Ecological Reserves (KSR) is the field station for the University of Kansas. Both terrestrial and aquatic research projects are ongoing at KSR, located 10 miles north of the KU campus.
Contact(s):
Edward Martinko, Director, Univ. Kansas Field Station and Ecological Reserves; 785-864-7720; Fax: 785-864-5093; martinko@ku.edu
W. Kettle, Assoc. Dir. Univ. Kansas Field Station & Ecological Reserves; 785-864-3241; Fax: 785-864-5093; kettle@ku.edu

UNIVERSITY OF KENTUCKY
COLLEGE OF AGRICULTURE
Lexington, KY 40546 United States
Phone: 606-257-7596
Website: www.ca.uky.edu

Founded: N/A
Contact(s):
Karen Goodlet, Landscape Architecture; 606-257-7295; kgoodlet@ca.uky.edu
Donald Graves, Forestry, Chairman
Dewayne Ingram, Horticulture, Chair; 606-257-1758; dingram@ca.uky.edu

UNIVERSITY OF LOUISVILLE
Belknap Campus
Louisville, KY 40292 United States
Phone: 502-852-6771 Fax: 502-852-0725
Website: www.louisville.edu/a-s/biology.edu

Founded: N/A
Membership: 1–100
Scope: Local, Regional
Description: The Large River Laboratory was established in 1992 to conduct research on river and freshwater systems in Kentucky and surrounding states. Community and population studies of rivers and smaller streams constitute the primary focus of the laboratory.
Contact(s):
Jeff Jack, Dept. of Biology; 502-852-5940; jdjack01@gwise.louisville.edu
William Pearson, Professor; 502-852-3727; wdpear01@gwise.louisville.edu

UNIVERSITY OF MAINE
COLLEGE OF NATURAL SCIENCES, FORESTRY AND AGRICULTURE
5782 Winslow Hall, Suite 105
Orono, ME 04469-5782 United States
Phone: 207-581-3202 Fax: 207-581-3207
Website: www.umaine.edu/

Founded: N/A
Scope: State
Contact(s):
Mark Anderson, Program Director
Dave Townsend, School of Marine Sciences, Director
Daniel Belknap, Department of Geological Sciences, Chair; 207-581-2152
Rodney Bushway, Department of Food Science and Human Nutrition; 207-581-1621
Christopher Campbell, Department of Biological Sciences, Chairman; 207-581-2551
George Criner, Department of Resource Economics and Policy, Chairman; 207-581-3150
Ivan Fernandez, Department of Plant, Soil, and Environmental Science, Chairman; 207-581-2932
David Field, Department of Forest Management, Chairman; 207-581-2856
Dan Harrison, Department of Wildlife Ecology
William Krohn, Cooperative Fish and Wildlife Research Unit, Leader; 207-581-2870
William Livingston, Department of Forest Ecosystem Science, Chairman; 207-581-2884
John Singer, Department of Biochemistry, Microbiology and Molecular Biology; 207-581-2810
Charles Wallace, Chairman for Animal & Horticultural Sciences; 207-581-2770
Bruce Wiersma, Dean; 207-581-3202

UNIVERSITY OF MAINE AT FORT KENT
25 Pleasant St.
Fort Kent, ME 04743 United States
Phone: 207-834-7617 Fax: 207-834-7503
E-mail: sselva@maine.main.edu
Website: www.umfk.maine.edu/

Founded: N/A
Scope: Regional
Description: Located in the heart of Maine's Acadian forest region. Our Bachelor of Science in Environmental Studies degree program provides a solid experiential and academic background to students preparing for careers in education, industry, and public service.
Publication(s): University Catalog and Brochures
Contact(s):
Don Zillman, President, Interim
Steven Selva, Professor of Biology and Environmental Studies; sselva@maine.main.edu

UNIVERSITY OF MAINE AT ORONO
SCHOOL OF MARINE SCIENCES
5741 Libby Hall
Orono, ME 04469 United States
Phone: 207-581-4381 Fax: 207-581-4388
E-mail: marine@maine.edu
Website: www.umaine.edu/

Founded: N/A
Scope: State
Contact(s):
Bruce Sidell, Chair; 207-581-4381

UNIVERSITY OF MAINE COOPERATIVE EXTENSION

FORESTRY AND WILDLIFE OFFICE
5755 Nutting Hall
Orono, ME 04469-5755 United States
Phone: 207-581-2892 Fax: 207-581-3466
Website: www.umext.maine.edu

Founded: N/A
Membership: N/A
Scope: State
Description: University of Maine Cooperative Extension is a major outreach education and applied research arm of the university. Our mission is "To help Maine people improve their lives through an educational process that uses research-based knowledge focused on issues and needs."
Contact(s):
Catherine Elliott, Program Administrator; 207-581-2902; Fax: 207-581-3325; celliott@umext.maine.edu
Les Hyde, Forestry Educator; 5755 Nutting Hall, UMaine, Orono, ME 04469-5755; 207-581-2818; Fax: 207-581-3466; lhyde@umext.maine.edu
James Philip, Forestry Specialist; 5755 Nutting Hall, UMaine, Orono, ME 04469-5755; 207-581-2885; Fax: 207-581-3466; jphilp@umext.maine.edu

UNIVERSITY OF MANITOBA

DEPARTMENT OF ZOOLOGY
320 Duff Roblin
Winnipeg, R3T 2N2 Manitoba Canada
Phone: 204-474-9245 Fax: 204-474-7588
Website: www.umanitoba.ca/faculties/science/

Founded: N/A
Scope: International
Publication(s): See publication web site
Contact(s):
Norman Hunter, Environmental Science Program, Director; 231C Machray Hall, Winnipeg, Manitoba R3T 2N2; 204-474-9897; Fax: 204-275-3147; hunter@ms.umanitoba.ca
Richard Baydack, Natural Resources Institute, Associate Director; 307 St. Pauls College, West Wing,
Erwing Huebner, Zoology, Head; Z320 Duff Roblin Bldg., Winnipeg, Manitoba R3T 2N2; 204-474-9245; Fax: 204-474-7588; ehuebner@ccumanitoba.ca
David Punter, Botany Dept., Head; 505 Buller Bldg., Winnipeg, Manitoba R3T 2N2; 204-474-9813; Fax: 204-474-7604; punterd@cc.umanitoba.ca

UNIVERSITY OF MARYLAND - AT COLLEGE PARK

COLLEGE OF AGRICULTURE AND NATURAL RESOURCES
0107 Symons Hall
College Park, MD 20742 United States
Phone: 301-405-7761 Fax: 301-405-8570
Website: www.agnr.umd.edu

Founded: N/A
Scope: State
Contact(s):
Mark Varner, Director of Graduate Program & Avian Sciences; Animal Sciences Center, College Park, MD 20742; 301-405-1396; varner@umd5.umd.edu
John Doerr, Dept. of Animal and Avian Sciences, Undergraduate Coordinator; Animal Sciences Center, College Park, MD 20742; 301-405-1373; Fax: 301-314-9059
Thomas Fretz, Dean
Richard Weismiller, Dept. of Natural Resource Sciences and Landscape Architecture; Room 2104, Plant Sciences Bldg., College Park, MD 20742; 301-405-1306; Fax: 301-314-9308; rw22@umail.umd.edu

UNIVERSITY OF MARYLAND AT EASTERN SHORE

DEPARTMENT OF NATURAL SCIENCES
Carver Hall
Princess Anne, MD 21853 United States
Phone: 301-651-2200
Website: hawk.umes.edu/sciences/index.html

Founded: N/A
Description: Environmental Sciences (B.S.), Marine Sciences (B.S., M.S.), Marine, Estuarine, and Environmental Sciences (M.S., Ph.D), Environmental Chemistry (B.S., M.S.)
Contact(s):
Gian Gupta, Environmental Science/Marine Science, Contact; 410-651-6030; GGUPTA@UMES_BIRD.UMD.EDU
Charles Hocutt, Coastal Ecology Research Center, Contact
Joseph Okoh, Dept. Chair, Acting
Steve Rebach, Marine, Estuarine, and Environmental Sciences, Contact; 410-651-6013

UNIVERSITY OF MARYLAND BALTIMORE COUNTY

DEPARTMENT OF BIOLOGICAL SCIENCES
1000 Hilltop Cir.
Baltimore, MD 21250 United States
Phone: 410-455-2261 Fax: 410-455-3875
E-mail: ellis@umbc.edu
Website: www.umbc.edu/biosci

Founded: N/A
Scope: State
Description: Ecology and Environmental Biology focus with a strong emphasis on research, scientific approach, faculty contact and extensive lab offerings
Contact(s):
Lasse Lindahl, Professor and Chair; lindahl@umbc.edu

UNIVERSITY OF MARYLAND CENTER FOR ENVIRONMENTAL SCIENCE

P.O. Box 775
Cambridge, MD 21613 United States
Phone: 410-228-9250 Fax: 410-228-3843
Website: www.umces.edu

Founded: 1925
Scope: International
Description: UMCES is an institution of the University System of Maryland, with a special mission in multidisciplinary environmental research on Chesapeake Bay, the mid-Atlantic region, and coastal systems around the world.
Contact(s):
Donald Boesch, President; P.O. Box 775, Cambridge, MD 21613-0775; 410-228-9250, ext. 601; boesch@ca.umces.edu
Louis Pitelka, Appalachian Laboratory, Director; 301 Braddock Rd., Frostburg, MD 21532; 301-689-7101; Fax: 301-689-7200; pitelka@al.umces.edu
Michael Roman, Horn Point Laboratory, Director and Professor; 410-221-8406; Fax: 410-221-8490; roman@hpl.umces.edu
Kenneth Tenore, Chesapeake Biological Laboratory, Director; P.O. Box 38, Solomons, MD 20688; 410-326-7241; Fax: 410-326-7263; tenore@cbl.umces.edu

UNIVERSITY OF MARYLAND, COLLEGE PARK

GRADUATE SCHOOL
2123 Lee Bldg.
College Park, MD 20742-5121 United States
Phone: 301-405-4198 Fax: 301-314-9305
E-mail: gradmit@deans.umd.edu
Website: www.inform.umd.edu/grad/

Founded: N/A
Membership: 1–100

Scope: State
Publication(s): Graduate applications available on website
Contact(s):
Trudy Lindsey, Director

UNIVERSITY OF MARYLAND EASTERN SHORE

MARYLAND COOPERATIVE FISH AND WILDLIFE RESEARCH UNIT
1120 Trigg Hall
Princess Anne, MD 21853 United States
Phone: 410-651-7663 Fax: 410-651-7662

Founded: 1994
Membership: 1–100
Scope: National
Description: The unit is sponsored by the Biological Resources Division, U.S. Geological Survey, Maryland Department of Natural Resources, U.S. Fish & Wildlife Service, University of Maryland Eastern Shore and the Wildlife Management Institute. Fish and Wildlife research, graduate education, and technical assistance are the unit's primary purposes.
Contact(s):
Dr. Dixie Bounds, Assistant Unit Leader of Wildlife; 410-651-6913; dlbounds@mail.umes.edu
Dr. Steven Hughes, Assistant Unit Leader of Fisheries; 410-651-7664; sghughes@mail.umes.edu
James Wiley, Unit Leader; 410-651-7654; jwwiley@mail.umes.edu

UNIVERSITY OF MASSACHUSETTS

DEPARTMENT OF NATURAL RESOURCES CONSERVATION
Holdsworth NRC
Amherst, MA 01003-9285 United States
Phone: 413-545-2665 Fax: 413-545-4358
Website: www.umass.edu/forwild/

Founded: N/A
Membership: 1–100
Scope: State
Contact(s):
Kevin Friedland, U.S. National Oceanic and Atmospheric Administration Cooperative; 413-545-2842
Guy Lanza, Environmental Sciences, Program Director; 413-545-3747
Richard Degraaf, U.S. Forest Service; 413-545-0357
Martha Mather, U.S. Geological Survey, Massachusetts Coop Fish and Wildlife; 413-545-4895
William McComb, Department of Natural Resources Conservation, Head

UNIVERSITY OF MASSACHUSETTS

URBAN HARBORS INSTITUTE
100 Morrissey Blvd.
Boston, MA 02125-3393 United States
Phone: 617-287-5570 Fax: 617-287-5575
E-mail: urbanurban.harbors@usb.edu
Website: www.uhi.umb.edu

Founded: 1989
Membership: 1–100
Scope: International
Description: The Urban Harbors Institute was founded as a center for the study of harbor, coastal and ocean issues. It conducts multidisciplinary research on the policy and management issues affecting the coastal area, with emphasis on the urban waterfront. It also promotes linkages between scientists, government, academic, and business communities to improve decision-making. The institute publishes research, sponsors seminars, conferences, and public forums to disseminate and exchange information.
Publication(s): The Coastlines
Contact(s):
Richard Delaney, Director; rich.delaney@umb.edu

UNIVERSITY OF MIAMI

ROSENSTIEL SCHOOL OF MARINE AND ATMOSPHERIC SCIENCE
4600 Rickenbacker Causeway
Miami, FL 33149 United States
Phone: 305-361-4000 Fax: 305-361-9306
E-mail: libcirc@rsmas.miami.edu
Website: www.rsmas.miami.edu/

Founded: N/A
Scope: State
Contact(s):
Otis Brown, Dean

UNIVERSITY OF MICHIGAN

SCHOOL OF NATURAL RESOURCES AND ENVIRONMENT
Dana Bldg., 430 East University
Ann Arbor, MI 48109-1115 United States
Phone: 734-764-6453 Fax: 734-615-1277
Website: www.snre.umich.edu/

Founded: N/A
Contact(s):
Bunyan Bryant, Resource Policy and Behavior, Concentration Chair
James Diana, Resource Ecology and Management, Concentration Chair
Donna Erickson, Landscape Architecture, Concentration Chair
Daniel Mazmanian, Dean

UNIVERSITY OF MINNESOTA AT CROOKSTON

NATURAL RESOURCES DEPARTMENT
2900 University Ave.
Crookston, MN 56716 United States
Phone: 218-281-8129 Fax: 218-282-8603
Website: www.crk.umn.edu

Founded: N/A
Membership: 1–100
Scope: Regional
Description: Offers a broadly-oriented natural resource program which prepares students for entry-level resource management positions. Practical and field instruction in integrated land management is emphasized leading to a B.S. degree in Natural Resource Management, Wildlife Management, Park Management, Water Resource Managment, or Natural Resources Law Enforcement.
Contact(s):
David Arscott, Riparian Ecology Professor; 218-281-8141; darscott@mail.crk.umn.edu
Philip Baird, Park & Recreation Professor; 218-281-8130; pbaird@mail.crk.umn.edu
Thomas Feiro, Environmental Health and Safety Specialist; 218-281-8131
Ross Hier, Wildlife Management Adjunct Professor; Minnesota Department of Natural Resources, 203 West Fletcher, Crookston, MN 56716; 218-281-6063
John Loegering, Wildlife Management Professor; 218-281-8132; jloegeri@mail.crk.umn.edu
Daniel Svedarsky, Program Leader and Wildlife Professor; Natural Resources Department, University of Minnesota, Crookston, MN 56716; 218-281-8129; dsvedars@mail.crk.umn.edu

UNIVERSITY OF MINNESOTA AT ST. PAUL

FISHERIES WILDLIFE CONSERVATION BIOLOGY
200 Hodson Hall, 1980 Falwell Ave
St. Paul, MN 55108 United States
Phone: 612-624-3400 Fax: 612-625-5299
E-mail: jperry@umn.edu
Website: www.fw.umn.edu/

Founded: 1903

Membership: N/A
Scope: Local, State, Regional, National, International
Description: The mission of the College of Natural Resources is to foster a quality environment by contributing to the management, protection, and sustainable use of our natural resources through teaching, research, and outreach.
Contact(s):
Patrick Brezonik, Water Resources Center, Director; 612-624-9282
Francesca Cuthbert, Conservation Biology Program, Director; 612-624-1756
Bill Ganzlin, Student Services Office, Director; 612-624-6768
David Smith, Conservation Biology Program, Director; 612-624-5369
Ira Adelman, Department of Fisheries and Wildlife; 612-624-3600
Jean Albrecht, Forestry Library, Librarian; B-50 Natural Resources Administration Bldg., 2003 Upper Buford Cir., St. Paul, MN 55108; 612-624-3222
David Andersen, Minnesota Cooperative Fish and Wildlife Research Unit, Leader; 612-624-3421
Dorothy Anderson, Center for Environmental Learning and Leadership; 612-624-2721
Barbara Coffin, Institute for Sustainable Natural Resource Management; 612-624-4986
Steven Daleylaursen, Outreach and Extension, Associate Dean; 612-624-9298
Alan Ek, Department of Forest Resources, Head; 612-624-3400
Anne Kapuscinski, Institute for Social Economic and Ecological Sustainability; 612-624-7719
Dave Lime, Cooperative Park Studies Unit, Senior Research Associate; 612-624-2250
Joseph Massey, Department of Wood and Paper Science, Head; 612-624-5200
Jim Perry, Department Head
Jim Perry, Center for Natural Resources Policy and Management, Head; 612-624-9796
Robert Sterner, Department of Ecology, Evolution and Behavior, Head; 1987 Upper Buford Cir., St. Paul, MN 55108; 612-625-6790
Alfred Sullivan, Dean of College of Natural Resources

UNIVERSITY OF MISSOURI

SCHOOL OF NATURAL RESOURCES
103 Anheuser-Busch Natural Resources Bldg.
Columbia, MO 65211-7220 United States
Phone: 573-882-6446 Fax: 573-884-2636
Website: www.snr.missouri.edu

Founded: N/A
Membership: 1–100
Scope: State
Contact(s):
Albert Vogt, Director
R. Hammer, Soil and Atmospheric Sciences Department, Chair; 302 Anheuser-Busch Natural Resources Bldg.; 573-882-6301
Jack Jones, Fisheries and Wildlife Dept., Chair; 302 Anheuser-Busch Natural Resources Bldg.; 573-882-3436
Charles Rabeni, Cooperative Fish and Wildlife Research Unit, Leader; 302 Anheuser-Busch Natural Resources Bldg.; 573-882-3524
Carl Settergren, Forestry Dept., M.S., Ph.D.; 302 Anheuser-Busch Natural Resources Bldg.; 573-882-2627

UNIVERSITY OF MONTANA SCHOOL OF FORESTRY

32 Campus Dr.
Missoula, MT 59812-0576 United States
Phone: 406-243-5521 Fax: 406-243-4845
E-mail: jilyon@forestry.umt.edu
Website: www.forestry.umt.edu

Founded: N/A
Membership: 1–100
Scope: State
Description: Educators and Researchers
Contact(s):
Perry Brown, Montana Forest and Conservation Experiment Station, Director; 406-243-5522
Daniel Pletscher, Wildlife Biology Program, Director; 406-243-5272
Perry Brown, School of Forestry Dean; 406-243-5522
James Burchfield, Bolle Center for People and Forests; 406-243-6650
Wayne Freimund, Wilderness Institute; 406-243-5184
Paul Hansen, Riparian/Wetland Research Program; 406-243-2050
Kelsey Milner, Inland Northwest Growth and Yield Cooperative; 406-243-6653
Norma Nickerson, Institute for Tourism and Recreation Research; 406-243-5686
Robert Pfister, Mission Oriented Research Program; 406-243-6582
Steven Running, Numerical Terradynamic Simulation Group; 406-243-6311
Jack Thomas, Boone and Crockett Wildlife Conservation Program; 406-243-5566
Hans Zuuring, Quantitative Services Group; 406-243-6465

UNIVERSITY OF MONTANA WILDLIFE

SCHOOL OF LAW
Building 32 Campus Drive
Missoula, MT 59812-6552 United States
Phone: 406-243-5272 Fax: 406-243-4557
Website: www.umt.edu/law/

Founded: N/A
Scope: International
Contact(s):
Edwin Eck, Dean

UNIVERSITY OF NEBRASKA

SCHOOL OF NATURAL RESOURCE SCIENCES
309 Biochemistry Hall, Box 830758
Lincoln, NE 68583-0759 United States
Phone: 402-472-9873 Fax: 402-472-3610
Website: www.snrs.unl.edu

Founded: N/A
Scope: State
Contact(s):
Marcy Tintera, Graduate Programs; 402-472-6622; fofw031@unlvm.unl.edu

UNIVERSITY OF NEVADA - AT RENO

DEPARTMENT OF ENVIRONMENTAL AND RESOURCES SCIENCES
1000 Valley Rd.
Reno, NV 89512 United States
Phone: 775-784-6763 Fax: 702-784-4583
Website: www.unr.edu/

Founded: N/A
Membership: 1–100
Scope: State, Regional, National, International
Description: The mission of the Department of Environmental and Resource Sciences is to provide and apply scientific knowledge and understanding of inter-relationships among people, living organisms and the environments of the Intermountain West, through outreach in teaching, research and service.
Publication(s): See publication web site
Contact(s):
Michael Collopy, Professor, Chair; 775-784-6763; Fax: 775-784-4583; mcollopy@cabnr.unr.edu

James Sedinger, Professor; 775-784-5665; Fax: 775-784-4583; JSedinger@cabnr.unr.edu
Dale Johnson, Natural Resource Management, ext. 4511
Glenn Miller, Environmental Science; 775-784-4108; Fax: 775-784-1142; gcmiller@scs.unr.edu
Watkins Miller, Department of Environmental and Resource Sciences, Chairman
James Sedinger, Associate Professor; jsedinger@cabnr.unr.e
Roger Walker, Natural Resource Management, ext. 4039; walker@unr.edu

UNIVERSITY OF NEVADA AT LAS VEGAS
ENVIRONMENTAL SCIENCE PROGRAM
4505 Maryland Parkway, Box 454030
Las Vegas, NV 89154-4030 United States
Phone: 702-895-3011 Fax: 702-895-3956
E-mail: biology@neveda.edu
Website: www.unlv.edu/Other_Programs/Environmental_Studies/

Founded: N/A
Membership: 1–100
Scope: Local
Contact(s):
Carl Reiber, Chairman; reiber@nevada.edu
Helen Neil, Environmental Studies Dept.; neil@nevada.edu

UNIVERSITY OF NEVADA AT LAS VEGAS
WATER RESOURCES PROGRAM
4505 Maryland Pkwy.
Las Vegas, NV 89154-4029 United States
Phone: 702-895-4006 Fax: 702-895-4064
E-mail: wrmunlv@hotmail.com
Website: www.unlv.depts/wrm

Founded: N/A
Scope: State
Description: The Water Resources Management Graduate Program at the University of Nevada is an interdisciplinary environmental program. The curriculum includes studies in water quality and quantity; surface water and groundwater; and water law, regulation, and management. Offers environmental programs at graduate level.
Contact(s):
David Kreamer, Director; kreamerd@nevada.edu

UNIVERSITY OF NEVADA COOPERATIVE EXTENSION
University of Nevada Cooperative Extension, 2345 Red Rock St.
Las Vegas, NV 89146 United States
Phone: 702-222-3130 Fax: 702-222-3100
Website: www.unce.unr.edu

Founded: N/A
Scope: Local, State, Regional
Description: Community-based education and research.
Keyword(s): Agriculture/Farming, Air Quality/Atmosphere, Climate Change, Development/Developing Countries, Ecosystems (precious), Energy, Ethics/Environmental Justice, Forests/Forestry, Land Issues, Oceans/Coasts/Beaches, Pollution (general), Population, Public Health
Contact(s):
Dixie Allsbrook, Area Director; 702-222-3130; Fax: 702-222-3100; allsbrookd@unce.unr.edu
Karen Hinton, Dean and Director
John Burton, Assistant Director; 702-784-7070
John Cobourn, Western Area Water Specialist; 702-832-4150
Jason Davidson, Central Area Agronomy and Range Specialist; 702-428-0212
Ed Smith, Western Area Natural Resources Specialist; 702-782-9960
Sherman Swanson, State Range Specialist and Riparian Scientist; 1000 Valley Rd., Reno, NV 89512; 702-784-4057; Fax: 702-784-4583
Mark Walker, State Water Specialist; 702-784-1938

UNIVERSITY OF NEW BRUNSWICK
FORESTRY AND ENVIRONMENTAL MANAGEMENT
P. O. Box 44555
Fredericton, E3B 6C2 New Brunswick Canada
Phone: 506-453-4501 Fax: 506-453-3538
E-mail: daug@unb.ca
Website: www.unb.ca/departs/forestry/

Founded: N/A
Scope: State
Description: B.S. in Forest Ecosystem Management or Forest Engineering; Minors include Environmental Science, Wildlife Conservation and Management and Parks and Wilderness.
Contact(s):
Tony Diamond, Director of Graduate Studies; diamond@unb.ca
David Daugharty, Assistant Dean and Undergraduate Information; daug@unb.ca
David Maclean, Dean; macleand@unb.ca

UNIVERSITY OF NEW HAMPSHIRE
215 James Hall Natural Resources 56 College Rd.
Durham, NH 03824 United States
Phone: 603-862-1234 Fax: 603-862-1234
Website: www.unh.edu

Founded: N/A
Scope: State
Description: Department of Natural Resources
Publication(s): New Hampshire, The, Campus Journal
Contact(s):
John Aber, Natural Resources, Program Coordinator
Russell Congalton, Natural Resources, Program Coordinator
Robert Eckert, Environmental Conservation, Program Coordinator
Theodore Howard, Department of Natural Resources, James Hall, Chair
William McDowell, Water Resources Management, Program Coordinator
Peter Pekins, Wildlife Ecology, Program Coordinator
Elizabeth Roschett, Soil Science, Program Coordinator; 603-862-0713; roschett@cisunix.unh.edu
Richard Weyrick, Forestry, Program Coordinator

UNIVERSITY OF NEW HAVEN DEPT. OF BIOLOGY AND ENVIRONMENTAL SCIENCES
GRADUATE AND UNDERGRADUATE PROGRAMS IN ENVIRONMENTAL SCIENCES
300 Orange Ave.
West Haven, CT 06516 United States
Phone: 203-932-7101 Fax: 203-931-6097
E-mail: rldavis@newhaven.edu
Website: www.newhaven.edu/

Founded: N/A
Scope: National
Description: We offer full and part-time undergraduate and graduate programs leading to a B.S. or M.S. in Environmental Science. Five-year combined program also available. Graduate concentrations include Env. Geoscience, Geographical Information Systems, Env. Ecology, Env. Health and Safety, and a "make-your-own" concentration. We are also implementing a new concentration in Environmental Education. The University of New Haven is affiliated with the Gerace Research Station on San Salvador Island, Bahamas.
Publication(s): Bahamian Field Station Affiliation, Geographical Information System Lab.

Keyword(s): Development/Developing Countries, Land Issues, Oceans/Coasts/Beaches, Public Lands/Greenspace, Water Habitats & Quality

Contact(s):

Carmela Cuomo, Coordinator of Program in Marine Biology; 203-932-7101; Fax: 203-931-6097; ccuomo@newhaven.edu

R. Laurence Davis, Coordinator of Programs in Environmental Science; 203-932-7108; Fax: 203-931-6097; rldavis@newhaven.edu

Michael Rossi, Chair of Biology and Environmental Science; 203-932-7101; Fax: 203-931-6097; mrossi@newhaven.edu

Roman Zajac, Professor of Biology and Environmental Science; 203-932-7101; Fax: 203-931-6097; rzajac@newhaven.edu

UNIVERSITY OF NEW ORLEANS

DEPARTMENT OF ENVIRONMENTAL ENGINEERING ORLEANS URBAN WASTE MANAGEMENT AND RESEARCH CENTER
Lakefront Campus
New Orleans, LA 70148 United States
Phone: 504-280-6189 Fax: 504-280-5586
E-mail: jsuthe9831@aol.com
Website: www.uno.edu

Founded: 1991
Membership: N/A
Scope: Local, State, Regional, National, International

Description: A University research organization working in the fields of solid waste management, storm water collection, urban air quality, brownfields and wastewater collection and treatment.

Publication(s): Projects Summaries

Keyword(s): Air Quality/Atmosphere, Development/Developing Countries, Ethics/Environmental Justice, Executive/Legislative/Judicial Reform, Public Health, Reduce/Reuse/Recycle, Sprawl/Urban Planning, Water Habitats & Quality

Contact(s):

Kenneth McManis, Director; 504-280-6668; Fax: 280-5586; kmcmanis@uno.edu

Rita Czek, Projects Manager; 504-280-6686; Fax: 280-5586; rlcce@uno.edu

Marty Tittlebaum, Associate Director; 504-280-6668; Fax: 280-5586; mtittleb@uno.edu

UNIVERSITY OF NORTH CAROLINA AT ASHEVILLE

ENVIRONMENTAL STUDIES DEPARTMENT
CPO 2330, One University Heights
Asheville, NC 28804-8511 United States
Phone: 828-251-6441 Fax: 828-251-6041
Website: www.unca.edu/envr_studies/

Founded: 1983
Membership: N/A
Scope: State

Description: UNCA offers a Bachelor of Science Degree in Environmental Studies, with degree concentrations in Earth Science, Ecology and Environmental Biology, Natural Resource Management, and Pollution Control, plus individualized courses of study. The Environmental Studies degree is enhanced with a required internship that provides real-world experience and potential employment opportunities from many public and private organizations located in the Asheville area, elsewhere in the U.S., and abroad.

Contact(s):

Richard Maas, Contact; 828-251-6366; maas@unca.edu

UNIVERSITY OF NORTH CAROLINA AT CHAPEL HILL

Campus Box 7400 Rosenau Hall
Chapel Hill, NC 27599-7431 United States
Phone: 919-966-1171 Fax: 919-966-7911
Website: www.unc.edu

Founded: N/A
Membership: 1–100
Scope: State

Contact(s):

Louise Ball, Environmental Health Sciences; Environmental Science and Engineering, 4114 E McGavran-Greenberg Hall, Chapel Hill, NC 27599; 919-966-7306; lmball@sph.unc.edu

Russell Christman, Aquatic and Atmospheric Sciences; Environmental Science and Engineering, 164 Rosenau Hall, Chapel Hill, NC 27599; 919-966-1683; russ_christman@unc.edu

William Glaze, Environmental Sciences and Engineering; Environmental Science and Engineering, 105 Miller Hall, Chapel Hill, NC 27599; 919-966-9917; bill_glaze@unc.edu

Richard Kamens, Air, Radiation, and Industrial Hygiene; Environmental Science and Engineering, 115 Rosenau Hall, Chapel Hill, NC 27599; 919-966-5452; kamens@unc.edu

Christopher Martens, Marine Sciences; 12-4A Venable Hall, Chapel Hill, NC 27599; 919-962-0152; martens@marine.unc.edu

Frederic Pfaender, Institute for Environmental Science & Engeneering; Environmental Science and Engineering, 157 Rosenau Hall, Chapel Hill, NC 27599; 919-966-3842; fred_pfaender@unc.edu

Seth Reice, Ecology, Chairman; 244 Wilson Hall, Chapel Hill, NC 27599; 919-962-1375; sreice@biomass.bio.unc.edu

Philip Singer, Water Resources Engineering; Environmental Science and Engineering,110 Rosenau Hall, Chapel Hill, NC 27599; 919-962-3865; phil_singer@unc.edu

UNIVERSITY OF NORTH CAROLINA AT CHAPEL HILL

ENVIRONMENTAL RESOURCE PROGRAM
CB# 1105 Miller Hall
Chapel Hill, NC 27599 United States
Phone: 919-966-7754 Fax: 919-966-9920
E-mail: erp@sph.unc.edu
Website: www.sph.unc.edu/erp

Founded: 1985
Scope: State

Description: The ERP was established to link the resources of the University with the citizens of North Carolina. Since its inception, the ERP has provided information, technical assistance, and training to citizen groups, local governments and school teachers, and has facilitated collaborative decision-making about environmental issues.

Publication(s): CEHS Sentinel, The Guide To North Carolina Environmental Groups, Working Together Community Based Approaches, The Superfund Scoop, The Link

Keyword(s): Public Health

Contact(s):

Frances Lynn, Director
Kathleen Gray, Associate Director

UNIVERSITY OF NORTH DAKOTA

BIOLOGY DEPARTMENT
Box 19019
Grand Forks, ND 58202-9019 United States
Phone: 701-777-2621 Fax: 701-777-2623
Website: www.und.nodak.edu/

Founded: 1883
Membership: 1–100
Scope: Local, State, Regional, National, International

Description: Wildlife - B.S., M.S., Ph.D. Dr. Richard D. Crawford, Dr. Richard S. Sweitzer. Fisheries - B.S., M.S., Ph.D. Dr. Steven Kelsch. Conservation Biology - Specialization within B.S.,M.S., and Ph.D. in Biology Dr. Issac Schlosser, Dr. Robert Newman.

Keyword(s): Agriculture/Farming, Climate Change, Ecosystems (precious), Energy, Land Issues, Population, Public Lands/ Greenspace, Water Habitats & Quality, Wildlife & Species

Contact(s):

Richard Crawford, Professor; richard.crawford@und.nodak.edu
Robert Newman, Associate Professor; robert.newman@und.nodak.edu
Issac Schlosser, Professor; issac.schlosser@und.nodak.edu
Richard Sweitzer, Assistant Professor; richard.sweitzer@und.nodak.edu
Steven Kelsch, Fishery Research Unit, Leader; steven.kelsch@und.nodak.edu

UNIVERSITY OF NORTH TEXAS

INSTITUTE OF APPLIED SCIENCES
NT Box 310559
Denton, TX 76203 United States
Phone: 940-565-2694 Fax: 940-565-4297
Website: www.ias.unt.edu/

Founded: 1976

Scope: State

Description: An interdisciplinary unit whose primary research activities are oriented towards land and water resources. Research includes aquatic toxicology, surface and groundwater quality, archaeology, remote sensing, geographic information systems and environmental modeling. In 1998, the institute took on an environmental outreach program which includes the Outdoor Environmental Learning Area (ODELA) and the Sky Theater.

Contact(s):

Miguel Acevedo, Environmental Modeling Laboratory, Director; 940-565-2091
Samuel Atkinson, Center for Remote Sensing, Director; 940-565-2694
Robert Doyle, Wetlands Research, Director; 940-565-2694
Reid Ferring, Center for Environmental Archaeology, Director; 940-565-2694
Eugene Hargrove, Faculty for Environmental Philosophy, Executive Director; 940-565-2266
Bruce Hunter, Environmental Visualization Laboratory, Director; 940-565-2694
James Kennedy, Water Research Field Station, Director; 940-565-2694
Thomas Lapoint, Director; 940-369-7776
Tom Lapoint, Experimental Stream Director; 940-565-2694
Chris Littler, Planetarium Director; 940-565-2694
Mike Nieswiadomy, Center for Environmental Economics, Director; 940-565-2573
Farida Saleh, Environmental Chemistry Laboratory, Director; 940-565-2694
Andy Schoolmaster, Center for Spatial Analysis, Director; 940-565-2901
William Waller, Aquatic Toxicology and Reservoir Limnology, Director; 940-565-2694
Samuel Atkinson, Graduate Program In Environmental Science, Coordinator; 940-565-2694
Kenneth Dickson, Professor
Jan Dickson, Faculty for Environmental Ethics, Coordinator; 940-565-2727
Eugene Hargrove, Graduate Program In Environmental Ethics, Coordinator; 940-565-2266
Steve Spurger, Elm Fork Education Center, Coordinator; 940-565-2694
Sandra Terrell, Interdisciplinary Graduate Studies, Dean
Rudi Thompson, Elm Fork Education Center, Coordinator; 940-565-2694

UNIVERSITY OF NORTHERN BRITISH COLUMBIA

3333 University Way
Prince George, V2N 4Z9 British Columbia Canada
Phone: 250-960-5555 Fax: 250-960-5538
Website: www.unbc.ca

Founded: 1990

Scope: State

Description: UNBC is a research intensive, small university founded in 1990 as "a university in the north, for the north." The faculty of Natural Resources and Environmental Studies develops managers and scientists to effectively meet the demands for natural resources products and services while maintaining a quality environment. Natural Resource Management offers majors in Wildlife and Fisheries, Forestry (accredited by the Canadian Forestry Accreditation Board) and Resource Recreation.

Contact(s):

Winifred Kessler, Natural Resources Management; 250-950-6664; winifred@unbc.ca
Jeff Zeiger, Resource Based Tourism, Environmental Studies; 250-960-5308; zeiger@unbc.ca

UNIVERSITY OF NORTHERN COLORADO

DEPARTMENT OF BIOLOGICAL SCIENCES
501 20th St.
Greeley, CO 80639 United States
Phone: 970-351-2921 Fax: 970-351-2335
Website: www.unco.edu/biology/

Founded: N/A

Membership: 1–100

Scope: State

Description: The UNC Dept. of Biological Sciences offers undergraduate and masters degrees in Biology and a Ph.D. in Biology Education, which may emphasize environmental education research.

Contact(s):

Curt Peterson, Dept. Chair, Biological Sciences; 970-351-2923; curt.peterson@unco.edu
Gerry Saunders, Associate Professor, Biological Sciences

UNIVERSITY OF OREGON

INSTITUTE FOR A SUSTAINABLE ENVIRONMENT
5247 University of Oregon
Eugene, OR 97403-5247 United States
Phone: 541-346-0675 Fax: 541-346-2040
E-mail: rribe@darkwing.uoregon.edu
Website: gladstone.uoregon.edu~evviro

Founded: 1994

Membership: 1–100

Scope: Regional

Description: Foster research and education at the University of Oregon with regard to environmental issues. The Institute's programs encompass environmental themes in the natural sciences, the social sciences, policy studies, humanities and professional fields.

Publication(s): Organization Brochure

Contact(s):

Robert Ribe, Director

UNIVERSITY OF OREGON

SCHOOL OF LAW
1221 UOFO School of Law
Eugene, OR 97403-1221 United States
Phone: 541-346-3852 Fax: 541-346-1564
Website: www.law.uoregon.edu/home.html

Founded: N/A

Scope: State

Contact(s):
Michael Axline, Western Natural Resource Law Clinic, Director; maxline@law.uoregon.edu
Rennard Strickland, Dean; mholland@law.uoregon.edu

UNIVERSITY OF PENNSYLVANIA
GRADUATE SCHOOL OF FINE ARTS
DEPARTMENT OF LANDSCAPE ARCHITECTURE
119 Meyerson Hall, 210 S. 34th St
Philadelphia, PA 19104-6311 United States
Phone: 215-898-6591 Fax: 215-573-3770
E-mail: larp@pobox.upenn.edu
Website: www.upenn.edu/gsfa/

Founded: N/A
Scope: National
Contact(s):
James Corner, Department of Landscape Architecture, Chairman; corner@pobox.upenn.edu

UNIVERSITY OF PITTSBURGH
BIOLOGY DEPARTMENT
Langley Hall
Fifth & Luskin Aves.
Pittsburgh, PA 15260 United States
Phone: 412-624-4266 Fax: 412-624-4759
Website: www.pitt.edu/~biolohome/main.html

Founded: N/A
Membership: 1–100
Scope: State
Description: The Biology Department offers a major in Ecology and Evolution, designed to provide the student with a selection of courses covering various aspects of these two fields of biology. The Department operates the Pymatuning Laboratory of Ecology with laboratories and teaching facilities in northwestern Pennsylvania, offering year-round research opportunites and summer courses.
Contact(s):
Gail Johnston, Ecology and Pymatuning Laboratory of Ecology, Director
James Pipas, Department of Biological Sciences, Chairman; 412-624-4350; Fax: 412-624-9311
Stephen Tonsor, Associate Professor

UNIVERSITY OF PITTSBURGH
DEPARTMENT OF GEOLOGY AND PLANETARY SCIENCE
200 Space Research Coordination Center
4107 O'Hara Street
University of Pittsburgh
Pittsburgh, PA 15260 United States
Phone: 412-624-8780 Fax: 412-624-3914
E-mail: geology@pitt.edu
Website: www.geology.pitt.edu

Founded: N/A
Membership: 1–100
Scope: National
Description: B.A. in Environmental Science based on a strong interdisciplinary framework of courses, co-requisites and a variety of electives in natural and social sciences. B.S. in Environmental Geology also offered.
Keyword(s): Air Quality/Atmosphere, Climate Change, Ecosystems (precious), Land Issues, Water Habitats & Quality
Contact(s):
Mark Collins, Undergraduate Coordinator; 412-624-6615; Fax: 412-624-3914; mookie@pitt.edu
James Maher, Advisory Board Chair
Harold Rollins, Chairman; 412-624-8783; snail@pitt.edu

UNIVERSITY OF PITTSBURGH
GRADUATE SCHOOL OF PUBLIC HEALTH
DEPARTMENT OF ENVIRONMENTAL AND OCCUPATIONAL HEALTH
260 Kappa Dr.
Pittsburgh, PA 15238 United States
Phone: 412-967-6500 Fax: 412-624-1020
Website: server.ceoh.pitt.edu/

Founded: N/A
Scope: International
Description: The mission of the Department of Environmental and Occupational Health is to reduce the health risks associated with exposure to chemical, physical, and biological agents found in industry and nature. Three degrees and a specialty certificate in risk assessment are offered.
Contact(s):
Herbert Rosenkranz, Chairperson

UNIVERSITY OF REGINA
DEPARTMENT OF BIOLOGY
3737 Wascana Parkway
Regina, S4S 0A2 Saskatchewan Canada
Phone: 306-585-4145 Fax: 306-585-4894
E-mail: william.chapco@uregina.ca
Website: www.uregina.ca/science/biology/index.htm

Founded: 1973
Membership: 1–100
Scope: Local, Regional, National, International
Description: An academic department in a university with 12 faculty members, 4 of whom currently do conservation oriented research.
Contact(s):
Mark Brigham; m.brigham@uregina.ca
William Chapco, Dept. Head; 306-585-4478; William.Chapco@uregina.ca
Peter Leavitt, Limnology Laboratory; 306-585-4253; Leavitt@uregina.ca
Mary Vetter; mary.vetter@uregina.ca
Rolf Vinebrooke
Scott Wilson, Plant Ecology Laboratory; 306-585-4287; scott.wilson@uregina.ca

UNIVERSITY OF RHODE ISLAND
DEPARTMENT OF NATURAL RESOURCES SCIENCE
105 Coastal Institute
Kingston, RI 02881 United States
Phone: 401-874-2495 Fax: 401-874-4561
E-mail: nrs@uri.edu
Website: www.edc.uri.edu/nrs/

Founded: 1983
Membership: 1–100
Scope: State, Regional, National, International
Description: The teaching mission of the Department of Natural Resources Science is to help students acquire the technical knowledge and practical skills needed to understand and wisely manage natural and disturbed ecosystems and their basic components: soil, water, air and biota. The research mission of the department is to use hypothesis-based methods of scientific inquiry toward development of applicable solutions to environmental problems.
Keyword(s): Climate Change, Ecosystems (precious), Oceans/ Coasts/Beaches, Public Health, Water Habitats & Quality, Wildlife & Species
Contact(s):
Thomas Husband, Professor and Chair; 401-874-2912; Fax: 401-874-4561; tom@uri.edu

UNIVERSITY OF RHODE ISLAND

GRADUATE SCHOOL OF OCEANOGRAPHY AND COASTAL RESOURCES CENTER
URI Bay Campus, South Ferry Rd.
Narragansett, RI 02882-1197 United States
Phone: 401-874-6246 Fax: 401-874-6889
E-mail: student_info@gso.uri.edu
Website: www.gso.uri.edu

Founded: 1972
Membership: 101–1,000
Scope: State
Description: Dedicated to advancing coastal ecosystem management, nationally and internationally.
Publication(s): Publications on website
Contact(s):
David Farmer, Director
Scott Nixon, Director, RI Sea Grant College Program
Chip Young, CRC Communications Director; 401-874-6630; cyoung@gso.uri.edu

UNIVERSITY OF SASKATCHEWAN

COLLEGE OF AGRICULTURE
2D30 - 51 Campus Dr.
Saskatoon, S7N 5A8 Saskatchewan Canada
Phone: 306-966-7881 Fax: 306-966-8894
Website: www.ag.usask.ca/

Founded: N/A
Scope: Regional
Contact(s):
M. E. Fulton, Head of Agricultural Economics
Jim Germida, Dept. of Soil Science, Head; 5E34.1, Agriculture Building, 51 Campus Dr., Saskatoon, Saskatchewan S7N 5A8; 306-966-6836; Fax: 306-966-6881; germida@sask.usask.ca
B. Laarveld, Head, Department of Animal Poultry Science
Graham Scoles, Dept. of Plant Sciences, Head; Rm. 4D36 Agriculture Bldg., 51 Campus Dr., Saskatoon, Saskatchewan S7N 5A8; 306-966-5855; Fax: 306-966-5015; graham.scoles@sask.usask.ca
R. Tyler, Head Dept. Applied Microbiology & Food Science

UNIVERSITY OF SOUTH CAROLINA

P.O. Box 1630
Georgetown, SC 29442 United States
Phone: 843-546-3623 Fax: 843-546-1632
Website: www.baruch.sc.edu

Founded: N/A
Membership: 1–100
Scope: Regional
Contact(s):
Dennis Allen, Resident Director; 843-546-3623; dallen@belle.baruch.sc.edu

UNIVERSITY OF SOUTH CAROLINA; MARINE SCIENCE PROGRAM

MARINE SCIENCE PROGRAM
Marine Science Program; University of South Carolina
Columbia, SC 29208 United States
Phone: 803-777-2692 Fax: 803-777-3935
E-mail: marisci@vm.sc.edu
Website: marine-science.sc.edu/

Founded: N/A
Scope: State
Description: The Marine Science Program, in the College of Science and Mathematics at the University of South Carolina, is an interdisciplinary educational program offering curricula which lead to the bachelor of science, master of science, and doctor of philosophy degrees.
Contact(s):
Bjorn Kjerfve, Marine Science Program Director; 803-777-2692

UNIVERSITY OF SOUTHERN CALIFORNIA

DEPARTMENT OF CIVIL AND ENVIRONMENTAL ENGINEERING
Los Angeles, CA 90089-2531 United States
Phone: 213-740-7832
E-mail: civileng@usc.edu
Website: www.usc.edu/dept/engineering/

Founded: N/A
Publication(s): Publications
Contact(s):
Donald Lewis, Environmental Social Sciences Program, Dean of the Division
L. Wellford, Chair, Civil and Environmental Engineering Department

UNIVERSITY OF SOUTHERN CALIFORNIA

ENVIRONMENTAL STUDIES PROGRAM
Allan Hancock Foundation Bldg. Rm. M232
Los Angeles, CA 90089-0373 United States
Phone: 213-740-7770 Fax: 213-740-8566
E-mail: environ@usc.edu
Website: www.usc.edu/dept/LAS/envir

Founded: N/A
Membership: 1–100
Scope: National
Description: B.A. combines basic science with the study of social aspects of environmental issues. B.S. combines a concentration in Geology, Biology or Chemistry with social science. The graduate program offers a choice of three concentrations: Global Environmental Issues and Development; Law, Policy and Management; and Environmental Planning and Analysis.
Contact(s):
Linda Duguay, Director; duguay@usc.edu

UNIVERSITY OF SOUTHERN MISSISSIPPI

DEPARTMENT OF BIOLOGICAL SCIENCES
USM, P.O. Box 5018
Hattiesburg, MS 39406 United States
Phone: 601-266-4748 Fax: 601-266-5797
Website: www.biology.usm.edu

Founded: N/A
Membership: 1–100
Scope: State
Publication(s): See publication web site
Contact(s):
David Beckett, Aquatic Biology, and Aquatic Ecology
Patricia Biesiot, Marine Biology, Contact
Glenn Matlack, Resource Mangement and Environmental Planning, Contact
Stephen Ross, Fisheries Biology and Aquatic Ecology

UNIVERSITY OF TENNESSEE - AT KNOXVILLE

DEPARTMENT OF FORESTRY, WILDLIFE AND FISHERIES
Plant Sciences Bldg
Knoxville, TN 37996 United States
Phone: 865-974-7126 Fax: 865-974-4714
E-mail: fwf@utk.edu
Website: fwf.ag.utk.edu

Founded: 1964
Membership: 1–100
Scope: State, Regional, National, International
Description: Offer B.S. degree in forestry, forest management concentration, wildland recreation concentration, M.S. in forestry, Thesis and Non-Thesis Option, and B.S. and M.S. degrees in wildlife and fisheries science. Ph.D in Natural Resources.
Keyword(s): Agriculture/Farming, Air Quality/Atmosphere, Ecosystems (precious), Forests/Forestry, Land Issues, Public

Lands/Greenspace, Recreation/Ecotourism, Water Habitats & Quality, Wildlife & Species

Contact(s):

Richard Evans, Superintendent, Forestry Experiment Station; revans@utk.edu

George Hopper, Professor and Department Head; ghopper@utk.edu

J. Wilson, Associate Dept. Head, Fisheries; jlwilson@utk.edu

UNIVERSITY OF TENNESSEE AT MARTIN

COLLEGE OF AGRICULTURE AND APPLIED SCIENCES
Martin, TN 38238 United States
Phone: 901-587-7250 Fax: 901-587-7968
Website: www.utm.edu/departments/agr/agr.html

Founded: N/A

Scope: National

Description: Offers a B.S. degree in natural resources management with concentrations in wildlife biology, environmental management, soil and water conservation, and park and recreation administration.

Contact(s):

Jim Byford, Dean

UNIVERSITY OF THE DISTRICT OF COLUMBIA

4200 Connecticut Avenue, NW
Washington, DC 20008 United States
Phone: 202-832-4888
Website: www.udc.edu/index-b.htm

Founded: N/A

Contact(s):

Freddie Dixon, Department of Biological and Environmental Sciences, Acting; Bldg. 44; 202-274-7401

UNIVERSITY OF THE SOUTH (SEWANEE)

DEPARTMENT OF FORESTRY AND GEOLOGY
735 University Ave.
Sewanee, TN 37383 United States
Website: www.sewanee.edu/Forestry_Geology/ForestryGeology.html

Founded: N/A

Description: B.S. in Forestry, B.S. or B.A. in Geology or Natural Resources

Contact(s):

Stephen Shaver, Chairman; 931-598-1116; sshaver@seraph1.sewanee.edu

UNIVERSITY OF THE VIRGIN ISLANDS

DIVISION OF SCIENCE AND MATHEMATICS
CENTER FOR MARINE AND ENVIRONMENTAL STUDIES
No. 2 John Brewers Bay
Charlotte Amalie, St. Thomas, VI 00802-9990 United States
Phone: 340-693-1230 Fax: 340-693-1245
Website: www.uvi.edu

Founded: 1962

Scope: State

Description: Historically Black University, with undergraduate degrees in the sciences, including Marine Biology and research activities in Marine Science through the Center for Marine and Environmental Studies

Publication(s): The Effect of Natural Variation in Substrate Architecture on the Survival of Juvenile Bi-color Dansel Fish by R.S. Nemeth, Monitoring the Effects of Land Development on Near Shore Reef Environment of St. Thomas, U.S. Virgin Islands written by R.S. Nemeth

Contact(s):

Richard Nemeth, Maclean Marine Science Center, Center for Marine and Environ; 340-693-1381; Fax: 340-693-1385; rnemeth@uvi.edu

Robert Stolz, Division of Science and Mathematics, Chair

UNIVERSITY OF TORONTO

FORESTRY DEPARTMENT
33 Willcocks St.
Toronto, M5S 3B3 Ontario Canada
Phone: 416-978-6152 Fax: 416-978-3834
E-mail: gradprog@forestry.utoronto.ca
Website: www.forestry.utoronto.ca

Founded: N/A

Scope: State

Description: Master of Forest Conservation Program (M.F.C.)

Contact(s):

D. Balsillie, M.F.C. Coordinator; 416-978-4638; david.balsillie@utoronto.ca

Rorke Bryan, Dean; r.bryan@utoronto.ca

UNIVERSITY OF TULSA

PETROLEUM ABSTRACTS
600 S. College
101 Harwell
Tulsa, OK 74104-3189 United States
Phone: 918-631-2295 Fax: 918-599-9361
E-mail: dbrown@utulsa.edu
Website: www.pa.utulsas.edu

Founded: N/A

Membership: 1–100

Scope: State

Description: Information on ecology and pollution related to petroleum exploration, production and transportation, plus environmental, health and safety topics. TULSA, includes 50,000 environmentally related entries updated weekly.

Contact(s):

David Brown, Marketing Manager

UNIVERSITY OF VERMONT, SCHOOL OF NATURAL RESOURCES

SCHOOL OF NATURAL RESOURCES
George D. Aiken Center, 81 Carrigan Dr.
Burlington, VT 05405 United States
Phone: 802-656-4280 Fax: 802-656-8683
Website: www.nature.snr.uvm.edu/

Founded: N/A

Membership: 1–100

Scope: State

Contact(s):

Alan McIntosh, Water Resources and Lake Studies Center, Director

Ian Worley, Environmental Studies Program, Interim Director

Donald Dehayes, Dean

Donald Dehayes, Natural Resources

David Hirth, Wildlife and Fisheries Biology Program

Robert Manning, Recreation Management,

Alan McIntosh, Environmental Sciences Program, Dir. of Water

Carlton Newton, Forestry

John Shane, Chair of Forestry Program; jshane@nature.fnr.uvn.edu

Patricia Stokowski, Graduate Program Coordinator; pstokows@nature.fnr.uvm.edu

Deane Wang, Natural Resources Planning; 802-656-2694; dwang@snr.uvm.edu

UNIVERSITY OF WEST FLORIDA

11000 University Parkway
Pensacola, FL 32514 United States
Phone: 850-474-2000
Website: www.uwf.edu

Founded: N/A
Membership: 1,001–10,000
Scope: International
Contact(s):

Joe Lepo, Institute for Coastal & Estuarine Research, Acting Director; 850-857-6098; jlepo@uwf.edu
George Stewart, Departmant of Biology, Chair; 850-474-2748

UNIVERSITY OF WISCONSIN AT EAU CLAIRE

Eau Claire, WI 54701 United States
Phone: 715-836-4166 Fax: 715-836-5089
Website: www.uwec.edu

Founded: N/A
Membership: 1–100
Scope: State
Contact(s):

Brady Foust, Geography, Chairman
Paula Kleintjes, Environmental Science; Minor
Michael Weil, Biology, Chairman

UNIVERSITY OF WISCONSIN AT GREEN BAY

NATURAL AND APPLIED SCIENCES DEPARTMENT
2420 Nicolet Dr.
Green Bay, WI 54311-7001 United States
Phone: 920-465-2000 Fax: 920-465-2558
Website: www.uwgb.edu

Founded: N/A
Membership: 1,001–10,000
Scope: State
Description: Natural and Applied Sciences Dept. offers a bachelor's degree in Environmental Studies. Areas of emphasis focus on Physical Systems and Ecology and Biological Resources. The Dept. of Public and Environmental Affairs offers a bachelor's degree in Environmental Studies and Planning with an emphasis in public policy or planning.
Contact(s):

Robert Howe, Cofrin Arboretum Center for Biodiversity, Director; 920-465-2272; hower@uwgb.edu
Hallett Harris, Environmental Science, Chair; 920-465-2369; Fax: 920-465-2376; harrish@uwgb.edu
Denise Scheberle, Interim Dean of Liberal Arts and Science; Theatre Hall 335; 920-465-2595; scheberd@gbms01.uwgb.edu
Ronald Stieglitz, Environmental Science and Policy Program, Associate Dean; 920-465-2123; Fax: 920-465-2718; gradstu@uwgb.edu.

UNIVERSITY OF WISCONSIN AT LA CROSSE

COLLEGE OF SCIENCE AND ALLIED HEALTH
1725 State St.
La Crosse, WI 54601 United States
Phone: 608-785-8218 Fax: 608-785-8221
Website: www.perth.uwlax.edu/sah/

Founded: N/A
Membership: 1,001–10,000
Scope: Local
Description: Biology, Chemistry and Geography offer B.S. degrees with a concentration in Environmental Science. Biology also offers a concentration in Aquatic Sciences for B.S. and M.S. degrees.
Contact(s):

Mark Sandheinrich, River Studies Center, Director; 608-785-8261; sandhein@mail.uwlax.edu
Roger Haro, Aquatic Science Advisor; 608-785-6970; haro_rj@mail.uwlax.edu
George Huppert, Geography and Earth Science, Chairman; 608-785-8333; Fax: 608-785-8332; huppert@mail.uwlax.edu
Bruce Osterby, Chemistry Dept., Chair; 608-785-8266; Fax: 608-785-8281; oster_br@mail.uwlax.edu
Robin Tyser, Biology Dept./Environmental Science, Contact; 608-785-8238; Fax: 608-785-6959; tyser@mail.uwlax.edu

UNIVERSITY OF WISCONSIN AT MADISON

SCHOOL OF NATURAL RESOURCES
1450 Linden Dr.
Madison, WI 53706-1562 United States
Phone: 608-262-4930 Fax: 608-262-4556
Website: www.cals.wisc.edu

Founded: N/A
Scope: State
Description: The School of Natural Resources is within the college of Agricultural and Life Sciences. The school offers 13 undergraduate options in natural resources. Graduate instruction is available in many specialized and interdisciplinary areas.
Contact(s):

Kevin McSweeney, Director, School of Natural Resources; 1450 Linden Dr., Rm. 146, Madison, WI 53706; 608-262-6968
Elton Aberle, College Dean

UNIVERSITY OF WISCONSIN AT STEVENS POINT

COLLEGE OF NATURAL RESOURCES
1900 Franklin Street
Stevens Point, WI 54481 United States
Phone: 715-346-2853 Fax: 715-346-3624
Website: www.uwsp.edu/acad/cnr

Founded: N/A
Scope: State
Description: Located in Central Wisconsin, the College of Natural Resources began in 1946 with the nation's first conservation education major. The College now has over 60 faculty and staff, 1,750 undergraduates and 80 graduate students. The college offers 16 majors and 13 minors.
Publication(s): Becoming an Outdoors Woman
Contact(s):

Eric Anderson, Wildlife Degrees
Michael Bozek, Cooperative Fishery Unit, Leader
Randy Champeau, Environmental Education,
Mike Dombeck, Professor of Global Environmental Management; 715-346-3946; Fax: 715-346-4554; mike.dombeck@uwsp.edu
Michael Gross, Resources Management,
Ronald Hensler, Soil Science
Robert Miller, Forestry
Victor Phillips, Dean
Stan Szczytko, Water Science,
Christine Thomas, Associate Dean, ext. 4185; Fax: 715-346-4554; cthomas@uwsp.edu

UNIVERSITY OF WISCONSIN-MADISON

INSTITUTE FOR ENVIRONMENTAL STUDIES (IES)
550 N. Park St., Science Hall
Madison, WI 53706 United States
Phone: 608-265-5296 Fax: 608-262-0014
Website: www.ies.wisc.edu/

Founded: 1970
Membership: N/A
Scope: Local, State, Regional, National, International
Description: IES promotes, develops and administers interdisciplinary environmental instruction, research, and public service programs at the University of Wisconsin-Madison. It offers graduate degrees in conservation biology and sustainable development, environmental monitoring, land resources, and water resources management; special graduate curricula in air

resources management and energy analysis and policy; and an undergraduate certificate program in environmental studies

Keyword(s): Air Quality/Atmosphere, Climate Change, Development/Developing Countries, Ecosystems (precious), Energy, Ethics/Environmental Justice, Land Issues, Pollution (general), Water Habitats & Quality, Wildlife & Species

Contact(s):
Thomas Yuill, Director; tmyuill@facstaff.wisc.edu

UNIVERSITY OF WYOMING

P.O. Box 3166
University Station
Laramie, WY 82071 United States
Phone: 307-766-5415 Fax: 307-766-5400
Website: www.uwyo.edu/

Founded: N/A

Scope: Regional

Description: Teaching and research in wildlife and fisheries biology

Publication(s): Newsletter

Contact(s):
Henry Harlow, National Park Service Research Center, Director; 307-766-4227; Fax: 307-766-5625
Joseph Meyer, Red Buttes Environmental Biology Laboratory, Director; 307-766-2017; Fax: 307-766-5625
Merav Ben-David, Asst. Professor; 307-766-5307; bendavid@uwyo.edu
Steve Buskirk, Prof; 307-766-5626; marten@uwyo.edu
Fred Lindzey, Assoc. Prof; 307-766-5415; flindzey@uwyo.edu
James Lovvorn, Professor; 307-766-6100; lovvorn@uwyo.edu
David McDonald, Asst. Prof.; 307-766-3012; dbmcd@uwyo.edu
Stanley Anderson, Wyoming Cooperative Fish and Wildlife Research Unit, Leader; 307-766-5415; Fax: 907-766-5400
Nancy Stanton, Department of Zoology and Physiology, Head; 307-766-4207; Fax: 307-766-5625

UNIVERSITY OF WYOMING

INSTITUTE AND SCHOOL FOR ENVIRONMENT AND NATURAL RESOURCES, (IENR AND SENR)
P.O. Box 3971
Laramie, WY 82071 United States
Phone: 307-766-5080 Fax: 307-766-5099
E-mail: ienr@uwyo.edu
Website: www.uwyo.edu/enr/

Founded: 1994

Membership: 1–100

Scope: Local, State, Regional, National, International

Description: Current projects include providing research and information on: preserving open space; the Endangered Species Act and private property; and collaborative natural resource management.

Publication(s): Private Property and the ESA, Reclaiming NEPA's Potential

Keyword(s): Land Issues, Public Lands/Greenspace, Sprawl/Urban Planning, Wildlife & Species

Contact(s):
Harold Bergman, Director; 307-766-5150; bergman@uwyo.edu
Diana Hulme, Assistant Director; 307-766-5354

UTAH STATE UNIVERSITY

BERRYMAN INSTITUTE FOR WILDLIFE DAMAGE MANAGEMENT
Logan, UT 84322-5270 United States
Phone: 435-797-2436 Fax: 435-797-1871
E-mail: conover@cc.usu.edu
Website: www.usu.edu/~cn r/fishwild/berry.htm

Founded: 1990

Scope: State

Description: The Jack H. Berryman Institute is a national non-profit organization which is centered at Utah State University. It engages in research, education, and extension activities aimed at resolving human and wildlife conflicts, enhancing the positive aspects of wildlife, and increasing human tolerance of wildlife problems.

Contact(s):
Michael Conover, Director; conover@cc.usu.edu

UTAH STATE UNIVERSITY

COLLEGE OF NATURAL RESOURCES
5200 Old Main Hill
Logan, UT 84322-5200 United States
Phone: 435-797-2445 Fax: 435-797-2443
Website: www.cnr.usu.edu/

Founded: N/A

Membership: 1–100

Scope: International

Description: The College of Natural Resources at Utah State University promotes, through undergraduate and graduate education, scholarship and creativity in discovery, synthesis and transfer of knowledge for the mutual sustainability of terrestrial and aquatic ecosystems and human communities.

Publication(s): See publication web site

Contact(s):
Martyn Caldwell, USU Ecology Center, Director; 435-797-2555; ecol@cc.usu.edu
Joanna Endter-Wada, Natural Resource Policy Institute, Director
Fee Busby, College of Natural Resources, Dean; 435-797-2452; Fax: 435-797-2443; feebusby@cnr.usu.edu
Raymond Dueser, College of Natural Resources, Assoc. Dean; 435-797-2445; Fax: 435-797-2443; dueser@cnr.usu.edu
Chris Luecke, Aquatic, Watershed, and Earth Resources Dept. Head; 435-797-2459; Fax: 435-797-1871; luecke@cc.usu.edu
David Roberts, Forest, Range, and Wildlife Sciences Acting Dept. Head; 435-797-3219; dvrbts@nr.usu.edu
Terry Sharik, Environment and Society Dept. Head; 435-797-1790; Fax: 435-797-4040; tlsharik@cnr.usu.edu
Derrick Thom, Geography Dept. M.S. Program, Contact; 435-797-1292; djthom@cc.usu.edu

UTAH STATE UNIVERSITY

COLLEGE OF NATURAL RESOURCES
DEPARTMENT OF FISHERIES AND WILDLIFE
5210 Old Main Hill
Natural Resources Room 206
Logan, UT 84322-5210 United States
Phone: 435-797-2459 Fax: 435-797-1871
E-mail: fishnwlf@cc.usu.edu
Website: www.usu.edu/fw

Founded: N/A

Scope: Local, State, Regional, National, International

Description: The Department of Fisheries and Wildlife at Utah State University offers comprehensive educational opportunities for students interested in the analysis and management of fish and wildlife populations, their habitats, and the related ecosystems.

Keyword(s): Climate Change, Ecosystems (precious), Land Issues, Oceans/Coasts/Beaches, Sprawl/Urban Planning, Water Habitats & Quality, Wildlife & Species

Contact(s):
Frank (Fee) Busby, Dean; 435-797-2452; Fax: 435-797-2443; feebusby@cnr.usu.edu
Chris Luecke, Interim Department Head; 435-797-2463; Fax: 435-797-1871; luecke@cnr.usu.edu

V

VANDERBILT CENTER FOR ENVIRONMENTAL MANAGEMENT (VCEMS)

1207 18th Avenue South
Nashville, TN 37212 United States
Phone: 615-322-8004 Fax: 615-322-8081
E-mail: vcems@vanderbilt.edu
Website: www.vanderbilt.edu/vcems

Founded: 1995
Membership: N/A
Scope: Local, State, Regional, National, International
Description: VCEMS is a Vanderbilt University system-wide initiative jointly led by the School of Engineering, the Graduate School, the Owen Graduate School of Management, the Law School, and the Institute for Public Policy Studies. VCEMS offers two different Master's degrees and a Ph.D. in Environmental Management Studies. Center activities are interdisciplinary and focus on environmental business, management and technology.
Publication(s): Annual Newsletter.
Keyword(s): Transportation
Contact(s):
Mark Abkowitz, Center Co-Director; 615-343-3436
Mark Cohen, Center Co-Director; 615-322-8004
Tricia Drake, Program Director; 615-322-8004; Fax: 615-322-8081; vcems@vanderbilt.edu

VANDERBILT UNIVERSITY

CIVIL AND ENVIRONMENTAL ENGINEERING
VU Station B 351831
Nashville, TN 37235 United States
Phone: 615-322-2697 Fax: 615-322-3365
Website: www.cee.vanderbilt.edu/

Founded: N/A
Membership: 1–100
Scope: Local, State, Regional, National, International
Description: We tackle tough problems with a major impact on individuals, communities, the nation, and the world.
Contact(s):
David Kosson, Professor and Chairman

VERMONT LAW SCHOOL

ENVIRONMENTAL LAW CENTER
P.O. Box 96
South Royalton, VT 05068 United States
Phone: 800-277-1395, ext. 2201 Fax: 802-763-2940
E-mail: elcinfo@vermontlaw.edu
Website: www.vermontlaw.edu/elc

Founded: 1973
Scope: International
Description: Administers three degrees in environmental law: the Master of Studies in Environmental Law (M.S.E.L.), the J.D./M.S.E.L. (joint degree), and the LL.M. in Environmental Law. The curriculum at VLS includes approx. fifty courses in environmental law, policy, science, and ethics. Its Summer Session offers over thirty courses for law students, attorneys, and non-lawyers interested in environmental policy and management and public interest advocacy.
Contact(s):
Anne Mansfield, Assistant Director; 803-763-8303; Fax: 803-763-2940

VIRGINIA POLYTECHNIC INSTITUTE

FISH AND WILDLIFE INFORMATION EXCHANGE
DEPARTMENT OF FISHERIES AND WILDLIFE
203 W. Roanoke St.
Blacksburg, VA 24060 United States
Phone: 540-231-7348 Fax: 540-231-7019
E-mail: fwiexchg@vt.edu
Website: fwie.fw.vt.edu

Founded: N/A
Description: Produces "The Master Species File", an archive of species accounts compiled by state and federal fish and wildlife agencies in North America.
Contact(s):
Sheila Ratcliff

VIRGINIA POLYTECHNIC INSTITUTE AND STATE UNIVERSITY

COLLEGE OF NATURAL RESOURCES
Attn: Peggy Quarterman, 324 Cheatham Hall
Blacksburg, VA 24061-0324 United States
Phone: 540-231-5481 Fax: 540-231-7664
E-mail: cfwr@vt.edu
Website: www.cnr.vt.edu

Founded: N/A
Membership: 101–1,000
Scope: State
Contact(s):
John Cairns, Center for Environmental and Hazardous Materials Studies; 540-231-7075
Gregory Brown, Dean; browngn@vt.edu
Harold Burkhart, Department of Forestry, Head; 540-231-5483; burkhart@vt.edu
C. Dolloff, U.S. Forest Service Coldwater and Trout Research Unit, Leader; 540-231-4864; adoll@vt.edu
Richard Neves, Cooperative Fish and Wildlife Unit, Leader; 540-231-5927; mussel@vt.edu
Donald Orth, Department of Fisheries and Wildlife Sciences, Head; 540-231-5573; dorth@vt.edu
Paul Winistorfer, Wood Science & Forest Product

VIRGINIA TECH UNIVERSITY

COLLEGE OF NATURAL RESOURCES
CONSERVATION MANAGEMENT INSTITUTE
203 W. Roanoke St.
Blacksburg, VA 24061 United States
Phone: 540-231-7348 Fax: 540-231-7019
E-mail: fwiexchg@vt.edu
Website: fwie.fw.vt.edu/

Founded: 2000
Membership: 1–100
Scope: State, Regional, National, International
Description: The Conservation Management Institute was established to address multidisciplinary research questions that affect conservation management effectiveness in Virginia, North America, and the world. Faculty from Virginia Tech and other research institutions work collaboratively to provide support to conservation and management agencies and organizations worldwide in their efforts to assess, monitor, protect, and manage the earth's renewable natural resources.
Keyword(s): Agriculture/Farming, Development/Developing Countries, Ecosystems (precious), Forests/Forestry, Land Issues, Oceans/Coasts/Beaches, Recreation/Ecotourism, Sprawl/Urban Planning, Transportation, Water Habitats & Quality, Wildlife & Species
Contact(s):
Jefferson Waldon, Asst. Director; 540-231-7348; Fax: 540-231-7019; fwiexchg@vt.edu

W

WASHINGTON STATE UNIVERSITY

Attn: William Budd, 305 Troy Hall
Pullman, WA 99164-4430 United States
Phone: 509-335-8536 Fax: 509-335-7636
Website: www.wsu.edu

Founded: N/A
Scope: State
Description: WSU has tripartite goals of providing higher education, research, and outreach/service programs relevant to

the needs of Washington's citizens. The Department of Natural Resource Sciences (NRS) (http://coopext.cahe.wsu.edu/~nrs/) and Program in Environmental Science and Regional Planning (ESRP) (http://www.sci.wsu.edu/envsci/) are the chief academic units at WSU.

Contact(s):

William Budd, Environmental Science and Regional Planning, Chair; Washington State University, P.O. Box 644430, Pullman, WA 99164-4430; 509-335-8536; Fax: 509-335-7636

Edward Deputit, Natural Resource Sciences, Chair; Washington State University, P.O. Box 646410, Pullman, WA 99164-6410; 509-335-6166; Fax: 509-335-7862

Charles Johnson, Horticulture and Landscape Architecture, Chair; Washington State University, P. O. Box 646414, 149 Johnson Hall, Pullman, WA 99164-6414; 509-335-9502; Fax: 509-335-8690

WASHINGTON UNIVERSITY, BIOLOGY DEPARTMENT

BIOLOGY DEPARTMENT
1 Brookings Dr., Campus Box 1137
St. Louis, MO 63110 United States
Phone: 314-935-6860 Fax: 314-935-4432
Website: www.biology.wustl.edu

Founded: N/A

Scope: State

Description: The laboratory is active in applying modern genetic techniques to problems in conservation biology such as conservation forensics (e.g., DNA fingerprinting of elephant tusks), systematics (identifying taxa that are significant evolutionary units), inter- and intraspefic hybridizataion, and genetic management of captive, translocated, and natural populations.

Contact(s):

Ralph Quatrano, Department of Biology, Head; 314-935-6868; rsq@wustl.edu

WAYNE STATE UNIVERSITY DEPARTMENT OF BIOLOGICAL SCIENCES

DEPARTMENT OF BIOLOGICAL SCIENCES
5047 Gullen Mall
Detroit, MI 48202-3917 United States
Phone: 313-577-2873 Fax: 313-577-6891
Website: biology.biosci.wayne.edu/biology/

Founded: N/A

Scope: National

Description: Courses offered in such subjects as limnology, ornithology, mammalogy, biogeography, natural history of vertebrates, animal behavior, population genetics, population ecology, microbial ecology, aquatic botany, ecology, advanced ecology, and evolutionary ecology.

Contact(s):

Allen Nicholson, Chairman; 313-577-2783

WEST VIRGINIA UNIVERSITY

COLLEGE OF AGRICULTURE, FORESTRY AND CONSUMER SCIENCES
P.O. Box 6125
Morgantown, WV 26506 United States
Phone: 304-293-2941 Fax: 304-293-2441
Website: www.caf.wvu.edu/

Founded: N/A

Scope: International

Contact(s):

Joseph McNeel, Division of Forestry, Director; P.O. Box 6125, Morgantown, WV 26506-6125; 304-293-2941; jmcneel@wvu.edu

James Armstrong, Wood Industries, Program Coordinator; 304-293-2941, ext. 2486; jarmstro@wvu.edu

Donald Armstrong, Landscape Architecture, Chair; 304-293-2142, ext. 4489; Fax: 304-293-3752; darmstro@wvu.edu

Alan Collins, Agricultural and Resource Economics, Undergraduate Coordinator; P.O. Box 6108, Morgantown, WV 26506; 304-293-4832; acollins@wvu.edu

Tim Phipps, Natural Resource Economics, Coordinator; P.O. Box 6108, Morgantown, WV 26506; 304-293-4832; tphipps@wvu.edu

Steve Selin, Recreation and Parks Management, Program Coordinator; 304-293-2941, ext. 2442; sselin@wvu.edu

Robert Whitmore, Wildlife and Fisheries Management, Program Coordinator; 304-293-2941, ext. 2491; u0eae@wvnvm.wvnet.edu

WESTERN ILLINOIS UNIVERSITY

DEPARTMENT OF BIOLOGY SCIENCES
372 Waggoner Hall
Macomb, IL 61455 United States
Phone: 309-298-2408 Fax: 309-298-2270
E-mail: mibiol@wiu.edu
Website: www.wiu.edu/users/mibiol/

Founded: N/A

Membership: 1–100

Scope: Regional

Description: Office of Aquatic Studies offers courses at the Shedd Aquarium in Chicago

Contact(s):

Sean Jenkins, Director; 309-298-2045

Thomas Dunstan, Wildlife; 309-298-1752; thomas_dunstan@ccmail.wiu.edu

Larry Jahn, Fisheries; 309-298-1266; la-jahn@wiu.edu

WESTERN MICHIGAN UNIVERSITY

ENVIRONMENTAL STUDIES PROGRAM
3930 Wood Hall
Kalamazoo, MI 49008-5419 United States
Phone: 616-387-2716 Fax: 616-387-2272
Website: www.wmich.edu/environmental-studies

Founded: N/A

Membership: 101–1,000

Scope: Local, State

Description: This undergraduate interdisciplinary program provides intellectual and practical experience that provokes thought about the complex interrelationships between humans, the social and technological systems they develop, and the natural environment. The program encourages students to develop an appreciation for the many elements of planetary health and to devise creative solutions to environmental problems.

Contact(s):

Kathy Mitchelll, Program Coordinator for Environmental Studies

WESTERN WASHINGTON UNIVERSITY

HUXLEY COLLEGE OF THE ENVIRONMENT
516 High Mail Stop 9079
Bellingham, WA 98225 United States
Phone: 360-650-3520 Fax: 360-650-2842
E-mail: huxley@cc.wwu.edu
Website: www.ac.wwu.edu/~huxley/

Founded: 1968

Membership: 101–1,000

Scope: State, Regional

Description: Principally a two-year, upper division and M.S. program; B.A., B.S. in environmental studies; M.S. in environmental science. Also cooperative programs, M.S. in marine and estuarine science and M.A. in political science and environmental studies.

Publication(s): Available on web

Contact(s):

John Hardy, Center for Environmental Science, Director; 360-650-6108; Fax: 360-650-7284; jhardy@cc.wwu.edu

Wayne Landis, Institute of Environmental Toxicology and Chemistry, Director; 360-650-6136; Fax: 360-650-6556; landis@cc.wwu.edu
Robin Matthews, Institute for Watershed Studies, Director; 360-650-3510; rmatthews@wwu.edu
John Miles, Center for Geography and Environmental Social Science, Director; 360-650-3284; Fax: 360-650-7702; jcmiles@cc.wwu.edu
Bradley Smith, Dean; bfs@admsec.wwu.edu

WIDENER UNIVERSITY

DEPARTMENT OF CIVIL ENGINEERING
One University Place
Chester, PA 19013-5792 United States
Phone: 610-499-4042 Fax: 610-499-4059
E-mail: solid.waste@widener.edu
Website: www.widener.edu/solid.waste

Founded: 1821
Membership: N/A
Scope: International
Description: The Department of Civil Engineering at Widener University offers undergraduate and graduate degrees which include courses in water resources, solid waste management, and environmental engineering. Continuing education seminars are taught in solid waste management and recycling. Research and development is performed in solid waste and recycling and water resources and water quality. The department publishes The Journal of Solid Waste Technology and Management.
Publication(s): Proceedings of International Conference on Solid Waste Technology and Management, The Journal of Solid Waste Technology and Management
Contact(s):
Vicki Brown, Chair of Civil Engineering; 610-499-4607; vicki.l.brown@widener.edu
Ronald Mersky, Waste Management Programs, Coordinator; 610-499-1146; Fax: 610-499-4059; solid.waste@widener.edu
Theresea Taborsky, Wolfgram Memorial Library; One University Pl., Chester, PA 19013-5792; 610-499-4087

WILKES UNIVERSITY DEPT. OF GEO-ENVIRONMENTAL SCIENCES AND ENGINEERING

GEO-ENVIRONMENTAL SCIENCES/ENGINEERING DEPARTMENT
Stark Learning Center 441
Wilkes Barre, PA 18766 United States
Phone: 570-408-4610 Fax: 570-408-7865
E-mail: gse@wilkes.edu
Website: www.wilkes.edu

Founded: N/A
Membership: 1–100
Scope: Local
Description: The department offers two degree programs. The Environmental Engineering curriculum highlights a balance among the basic areas of water and waste-water engineering, water quality measurement, air pollution measurement and control technology, as well as the more recent demands in the areas of hazardous and solid waste management. The Earth and Environmental Science curriculum requires a concentration of departmental electives that can be used to create an area of specialization.
Contact(s):
Dale Bruns, Co-Chairman; 717-408-4610; Fax: 570-408-7865; dbruns@wilkes.edu
Sid Halfor, Co-Chairman; 570-408-4611; Fax: 570-408-7865; shalfor@wilkes.edu

WILLIAMS COLLEGE

CENTER FOR ENVIRONMENTAL STUDIES PROGRAM
P.O. Box 632
Williamstown, MA 01267 United States
Phone: 413-597-2346 Fax: 413-597-3489
Website: www.williams.edu/

Founded: 1967
Scope: State
Description: The Center for Environmental Studies offers an integrated undergraduate program of studies to liberal arts students in combination with their major discipline. The Center also administers the 2,400 acre Hopkins Memorial Forest, a research and educational facility, as well as the Environmental Science Laboratory and the Matt Cole Memorial Library.
Publication(s): Field Notes-Newsletter
Contact(s):
Kai Lee, Director
Andrew Jones, Hopkins Memorial Forest Manager
Rachel Louis, Program Assistant

WILLOW MIXED MEDIA INC.

P.O. Box 194
Glenford, NY 12433-0194 United States
Phone: 845-657-2914
E-mail: willowmx@ulster.net
Website: www.hudsonvalley.com/willow

Founded: 1979
Scope: Local
Description: Willow Mixed Media is a not for profit organization, dealing with documentary video and arts projects on issues of social concern—health, environment, the arts, criminal justice, ect.
Publication(s): Building the Ashokan Reservoir, Cancer: Just a Word...Not a Sentence, The Hudson River PCB Story: A Toxic Heritage.
Contact(s):
Tobe Carey, President; willowmx@ulster.net

Y

YALE LAW SCHOOL

CAREER DEVELOPMENT OFFICE
127 Wall Street
New Haven, CT 06511 United States
Phone: 203-432-1676 Fax: 203-432-8423
E-mail: cdolaw@yale.edu
Website: www.law.yale.edu/cdo

Founded: N/A
Scope: National
Contact(s):
Cathy Woods, Contact

YALE UNIVERSITY

SCHOOL OF FORESTRY AND ENVIRONMENTAL STUDIES
205 Prospect St.
New Haven, CT 06511 United States
Phone: 203-432-5100 Fax: 203-432-5942
Website: www.yale.edu/environment

Founded: 1900
Scope: Local, State, Regional, National, International
Description: The mission of the school is to provide leadership in the science and management of natural resource and environmental systems. The school trains managers for governmental, non-governmental, and corporate institutions, and educates teachers and researchers
Publication(s): Bulletin of Yale University, Yale School of Forestry and Environmental Studies Bulletin Series

Contact(s):
Emly McDiarmid, Admissions Director; emly.mcdiarmid@yale.edu
Gordon Geballe, Associate Dean

YORK UNIVERSITY

ENVIRONMENTAL STUDIES DEPARTMENT
355 Lumbers Bldg., 4700 Keele St.
Toronto, M3J 1P3 Ontario Canada
Phone: 416-736-5252 Fax: 416-736-5679
E-mail: fesinfo@yorku.ca
Website: www.yorku.ca/faculty/fes

Founded: 1968
Membership: 1–100
Scope: National
Description: The faculty of Environmental Studies offers interdisciplinary, flexible, individualized programs at both the undergraduate and graduate levels. FES is committed to a broad definition of environment, offering the opportunity to study natural, built, organizational, and social environments.
Contact(s):
Mora Campbell, Graduate Program Director
Raymond Rogers, Undergraduate Program Director; rrogers@yorku.ca
Barbara Rahder, Graduate Planning Programs Coordinator; rahder@yorku.ca
Brent Rutherford, MES Program Coordinator; brentr@yorku.ca

ORGANIZATION NAME INDEX

A

B

C

D

E

H

I

M

N

Q

R

S

T

U

V

X

Y

Z

KEYWORD INDEX

AGRICULTURE/FARMING

AIR QUALITY/ATMOSPHERE

CLIMATE CHANGE

DEVELOPMENT/DEVELOPING COUNTRIES

ECOSYSTEMS (PRECIOUS)

ENERGY

ETHICS/ENVIRONMENTAL JUSTICE

EXECUTIVE/LEGISLATIVE/JUDICIAL REFORM

FINANCE/BANKING/TRADE

FORESTS/FORESTRY

LAND ISSUES

OCEANS/COASTS/BEACHES

POLLUTION (GENERAL)

Keyword Index

POPULATION

PUBLIC HEALTH

PUBLIC LANDS/GREENSPACE

RECREATION/ECOTOURISM

REDUCE/REUSE/RECYCLE

SPRAWL/URBAN PLANNING

TRANSPORTATION

WATER HABITATS & QUALITY

WILDLIFE & SPECIES

STAFF NAME INDEX

C

D

E

F

G

H

L

M

T

U

V

W

Staff Name Index

GEOGRAPHIC INDEX

COLOMBIA

COSTA RICA

CZECH REP

ECUADOR

EGYPT

FINLAND

Geographic Index

COLORADO

FLORIDA

GEORGIA

LOUISIANA

MAINE

Geographic Index

OKLAHOMA

OREGON

PENNSYLVANIA

PUERTO RICO

RHODE ISLAND

SOUTH CAROLINA

Geographic Index

UTAH

Geographic Index

WASHINGTON

WEST VIRGINIA

VENEZUELA

VIETNAM

YUGOSLAVIA

ZAMBIA

ZIMBABWE

UPDATE YOUR LISTING/CHANGE OF ADDRESS

Please help us keep the information in the directory up to date. Use this form to let us know of changes to your listing such as a new address or a new e-mail.

Please type or print clearly.

ORGANIZATION NAME ______________________________

ADDRESS: STREET ______________________________

CITY ______________ STATE ______________ ZIP ________ - ________

COUNTRY ______________ E-MAIL ______________

WEB SITE ______________________________

PHONE NUMBER ______________ FAX NUMBER ______________

PAGE NUMBER IN 2002 DIRECTORY ______________

CHANGES TO YOUR DESCRIPTION ______________

____

____

____

ADD CONTACT PERSON ______________________________

REMOVE CONTACT PERSON ______________________________

Please give us a contact name for the person we can obtain updates from.

NAME ______________________ PHONE ________ - ________ - ________

Further updating materials will be sent to all organizations listed in the ***2003 Conservation Directory*** when updating begins for the ***2004 Conservation Directory.***

Please mail form to:

NATIONAL WILDLIFE FEDERATION
ATTN: CONSERVATION DIRECTORY
11100 WILDLIFE CENTER DRIVE
RESTON, VA 20190-5362
PHONE: 703-438-6000
FAX: 703-438-6061

Information may be submitted on photocopies of this form.

Visit the *Conservation Directory* online at www.nwf.org to update your organization's information automatically at any time.

APPLICATION REQUEST

If you would like your organization to be listed in the *Conservation Directory* or you have a suggestion of an organization that should be listed in the directory, please let us know. An electronic version of this form is available at www.nwf.org/printandfilm/publications/consdir/infoform.html.

Please type or print clearly.

❑ Request for Listing ❑ Suggested New Organization

ORGANIZATION NAME ____

ADDRESS: STREET ____

CITY __________________ STATE ______________ ZIP _________ - _________

COUNTRY __________________ E-MAIL ____________________________

WEB SITE ____

PHONE NUMBER __________________ FAX NUMBER ______________________

CONTACT PERSON ____

Please mail form to:

NATIONAL WILDLIFE FEDERATION
ATTN: CONSERVATION DIRECTORY
11100 WILDLIFE CENTER DRIVE
RESTON, VA 20190-5362
PHONE: 703-438-6000
FAX: 703-438-6061

Information may be submitted on photocopies of this form.

Visit the *Conservation Directory* online at www.nwf.org to add a listing automatically at any time.